Employment Law Answer Book
Eighth Edition

by Mark R. Filipp and James Ottavio Castagnera

The last few years have witnessed extraordinary developments in many areas of employment law. U.S. Supreme Court rulings, legislation, and the increasing globalization of our economy have combined to alter the landscape. *Employment Law Answer Book* provides analysis of the latest judicial and legislative developments in employment law and provides "nuts and bolts" approaches to legal issues affecting the workplace. It is designed to provide quick, accurate, and up-to-date answers to employers, human resources managers, lawyers, and all professionals who need current information about employment law.

Highlights of the Eighth Edition

The *Employment Law Answer Book, Eighth Edition*, incorporates the latest cases, statutes, and developments, including:

- Recent cases involving the ADEA, including disparate impact cases (Chapter 4)

- Recent cases under the PDA and ADA, including the application of the "ministerial" exception to a teacher at a religious school, and whether side effects from medical treatment can constitute a disability (Chapter 4)

- Recent cases analyzing vesting issues for retiree health benefits and fiduciary obligations under ERISA (Chapter 8)

- Recent cases involving exceptions under the FLSA, including the "executive" exemption and the Supreme Court's recent decision upholding the use of the outside salesman exemption for pharmaceutical marketing employees that do not actually "sell" drugs (Chapter 8)

- Recent cases involving IRCA, including the Supreme Court's decision on a controversial Arizona statute involving unlawful aliens (Chapter 1)

- Recent cases under Title VII, including claims involving sexual stereotypes and transgender persons (Chapter 4)

- Recent cases involving WARN and the defense of "unforeseen business circumstances" (Chapter 13)

- Discussion of Dodd-Frank Wall Street Reform and Consumer Protection Act and recent cases involving retaliation under Dodd-Frank (Chapter 1)
- Challenges to recent NLRB decisions and actions (Chapter 11)
- Recent cases involving challenges to drug testing (Chapter 5)
- Recent cases concerning the enforceability of non-competition agreements (Chapter 6)
- Updated information concerning the Affordable Care Act (Chapters 1 & 8)
- A discussion of social media policies and challenges by the NLRA (Chapter 2)
- The application of the "qualified privilege" in defamation cases (Chapter 3)
- Discussion of HHS's omnibus final rules under HIPAA, effective March 26, 2013 (Chapter 5)
- Discussion of whether an employer's access of an employee's personal e-mail or social media site violates the employee's privacy (Chapter 5)
- Analysis of the Drug Free Workplace Act and the new medical marijuana laws (Chapter 7)
- The latest affirmative action developments affecting government contractors, notably disparate impact implications of criminal record checks (Chapter 9)
- Discussion of immigration reform proposals (Chapter 12)
- Updated discussion on organized labor in Europe, recent labor reforms in China, and changes in labor and employment laws in Australia (Chapter 15)

9/13

For questions concerning this shipment, billing, or other customer service matters, call our Customer Service Department at 1-800-234-1660.

For toll-free ordering, please call 1-800-638-8437.

Employment Law
Answer Book

Eighth Edition

Mark R. Filipp
James Ottavio Castagnera

Wolters Kluwer
Law & Business

Copyright © 2013 CCH Incorporated. All Rights Reserved.

No part of this publication may be reproduced or transmitted in any form or by any means, including electronic, mechanical, photocopying, recording, or utilized by any information storage or retrieval system, without written permission from the publisher. For information about permissions or to request permissions online, visit us at *www.aspenpublishers.com/licensing/default.aspx*, or a written request may be faxed to our permissions department at 212-771-0803.

Published by Wolters Kluwer Law & Business in New York.

Wolters Kluwer Law & Business serves customers worldwide with CCH, Aspen Publishers and Kluwer Law International products.

Printed in the United States of America

ISBN 978-1-4548-2550-0

1 2 3 4 5 6 7 8 9 0

SUSTAINABLE FORESTRY INITIATIVE

Certified Sourcing
www.sfiprogram.org
SFI-01234

SFI label applies to the text stock

About Wolters Kluwer Law & Business

Wolters Kluwer Law & Business is a leading global provider of intelligent information and digital solutions for legal and business professionals in key specialty areas, and respected educational resources for professors and law students. Wolters Kluwer Law & Business connects legal and business professionals as well as those in the education market with timely, specialized authoritative content and information-enabled solutions to support success through productivity, accuracy and mobility.

Serving customers worldwide, Wolters Kluwer Law & Business products include those under the Aspen Publishers, CCH, Kluwer Law International, Loislaw, Best Case, ftwilliam.com and MediRegs family of products.

CCH products have been a trusted resource since 1913, and are highly regarded resources for legal, securities, antitrust and trade regulation, government contracting, banking, pension, payroll, employment and labor, and healthcare reimbursement and compliance professionals.

Aspen Publishers products provide essential information to attorneys, business professionals and law students. Written by preeminent authorities, the product line offers analytical and practical information in a range of specialty practice areas from securities law and intellectual property to mergers and acquisitions and pension/benefits. Aspen's trusted legal education resources provide professors and students with high-quality, up-to-date and effective resources for successful instruction and study in all areas of the law.

Kluwer Law International products provide the global business community with reliable international legal information in English. Legal practitioners, corporate counsel and business executives around the world rely on Kluwer Law journals, looseleafs, books, and electronic products for comprehensive information in many areas of international legal practice.

Loislaw is a comprehensive online legal research product providing legal content to law firm practitioners of various specializations. Loislaw provides attorneys with the ability to quickly and efficiently find the necessary legal information they need, when and where they need it, by facilitating access to primary law as well as state-specific law, records, forms and treatises.

Best Case Solutions is the leading bankruptcy software product to the bankruptcy industry. It provides software and workflow tools to flawlessly streamline petition preparation and the electronic filing process, while timely incorporating ever-changing court requirements.

ftwilliam.com offers employee benefits professionals the highest quality plan documents (retirement, welfare and non-qualified) and government forms (5500/PBGC, 1099 and IRS) software at highly competitive prices.

MediRegs products provide integrated health care compliance content and software solutions for professionals in healthcare, higher education and life sciences, including professionals in accounting, law and consulting.

Wolters Kluwer Law & Business, a division of Wolters Kluwer, is headquartered in New York. Wolters Kluwer is a market-leading global information services company focused on professionals.

WOLTERS KLUWER LAW & BUSINESS
SUPPLEMENT NOTICE

This product is updated on a periodic basis with supplements to reflect important changes in the subject matter. If you have purchased this product directly from Wolters Kluwer Law & Business, we have already recorded your subscription for the update service.

If, however, you purchased this product from a bookstore and wish to receive future updates and revised or related volumes billed separately with a 30-day examination review, please contact our Customer Service Department at 1-800-234-1660 or send your name, company name (if applicable), address, and the title of the product to:

Wolters Kluwer Law & Business
Distribution Center
7201 McKinney Circle
Frederick, MD 21704

Important Contact Information

- To order any title, go to *www.aspenpublishers.com* or call 1-800-638-8437.

- To reinstate your manual update service, call 1-800-638-8437.

- To contact Customer Service, e-mail *customer.service@wolterskluwer.com*, call 1-800-234-1660, fax 1-800-901-9075, or mail correspondence to: Order Department—Aspen Publishers, Wolters Kluwer Law & Business, PO Box 990, Frederick, MD 21705.

- To review your account history or pay an invoice online, visit *www.aspenpublishers.com/payinvoices*.

Preface

Since the Seventh Edition was published, we have witnessed major developments in many areas of employment law. Numerous U.S. Supreme Court rulings, legislative enactments, and administrative regulations have combined to alter the landscape—and the liability of employers in the workplace. *Employment Law Answer Book, Eighth Edition*, analyzes these changes with a thorough discussion of the breadth of employment law. This edition provides "nuts and bolts" approaches to responding to the types of issues typically faced by employers. It is designed to provide quick, accurate, and up-to-date answers to employers, human resources managers, lawyers, and all professionals who need current information about employment law.

With its close scrutiny of judicial, administrative, and legislative changes and detailed coverage of developing issues in employment law, *Employment Law Answer Book, Eighth Edition,* works to ensure that employers and labor law professionals have the latest and most up-to-date information at their fingertips. That knowledge, together with sensible, practical suggestions for putting it to work, will open clearer paths through the ever-growing thicket of employment law.

Employment Law Answer Book, Eighth Edition, provides comprehensive current information on employment law in an easy-to-use question-and-answer format using simple, straightforward language and avoiding technical jargon wherever possible. Numerous examples illustrate how different laws have been applied in specific cases. Citations are provided in brackets as research aids to those who wish to pursue particular subjects in greater detail. For additional assistance in locating related topics, there is an extensive system of cross-referencing to relevant material in other sections of the text.

Format. The question-and-answer format breaks down complex subject areas into concise units. Introductory text provides an overview of the subject that is covered in detail in the questions and answers.

Numbering System. The questions are numbered consecutively within each chapter.

List of Questions. The detailed list of questions that follows the table of contents helps the reader locate areas of immediate interest. A series of subheadings organizes questions by topic within each chapter.

Tables. Reference tables keyed to question numbers are provided for U.S. Code, Code of Federal Regulations, and cases.

Index. A detailed topical index is provided as a further aid to locating specific information. All references are to question numbers rather than page numbers.

Mark R. Filipp, J.D.
James Ottavio Castagnera, J.D., Ph.D.
August 2013

About the Authors

Mark R. Filipp, J.D., is a shareholder and director of Kemp, Klein, Umphrey, Endelman and May, P.C. in Troy, Michigan. He practices primarily in the labor and employment area, primarily representing management. Mr. Filipp has defended a vast array of employment lawsuits, including defense of claims alleging wrongful discharge, discrimination, sexual harassment, retaliatory discharge, and hearings and appeals before various administrative bodies, including state agencies and the Equal Employment Opportunity Commission. In addition, Mr. Filipp provides regular counsel to employers concerning such matters as reductions in force and employee discipline. Mr. Filipp is a regular speaker on employment law, having conducted numerous seminars and in-house training sessions for employers on such matters as the Americans with Disabilities Act, the Family and Medical Leave Act, and sexual harassment. He has authored or co-authored many other publications, including *Covenants Not to Compete, Third Edition*, and *The Practical Guide to Employment Law*, both published by Wolters Kluwer Law and Business.

Mr. Filipp received his J.D. from the University of Detroit School of Law in 1981 and was the Editor-in-Chief of the Law Review and recipient of the Clarence M. Burton Scholar award. He received his B.A. degree with honors from Michigan State University. He is active in the State Bar of Michigan, having served as past Chairperson of the Law Practice Management Section and current Member of the Labor and Employment Section. He is also active in the Oakland County Bar Association.

James Ottavio Castagnera, J.D., Ph.D., is a freelance journalist, practicing attorney, and law professor. He has been a faculty member at several institutions and a communications specialist for the U.S. Coast Guard and at an R1 university. He is currently legal counsel at a regionally ranked teaching university. He also has been a labor lawyer with a major Philadelphia law firm and the general counsel/corporate secretary for a convenience store chain in New Jersey and for the nation's number one econometric forecasting organization. He has published 19 books, as well as more than 50 professional/scholarly articles and book chapters. He is a frequent commentator in newsletters, newspapers, and magazines, and on the Internet, where he writes the popular blog "Castagnera on Risk Management (and More)." His teaching has taken him to the University of Texas-

Austin, the Wharton School of the University of Pennsylvania, and the Widener University School of Law. He has recently completed his 17th year as Associate Provost and Associate Counsel for Academic Affairs at Rider University in Princeton/Lawrenceville (NJ), where he also holds the rank of Associate Professor of Legal Studies and has been the Acting Director of the Law & Justice Program. At Rider, his responsibilities include human resources, discrimination, labor relations, governance, regulatory matters, contracts and grants, risk management, and international programs, within the Academic Affairs and Student Affairs Divisions of the institution. Dr. Castagnera is also the managing director of a freelance writing and consulting company, K&C Human Resource Enterprises. His most recent book is *Counter Terrorism Issues* (Boca Raton: CRC Press 2013).

Acknowledgments

In the *Eighth Edition*, our primary goal was to provide practical and useful information in areas we have found to pose potential difficulty for management. This was a significant undertaking. However, with the invaluable assistance provided by many, including the wonderful editorial guidance from our publisher, we think you will find that our goal has been achieved.

Mark Filipp would like to thank and acknowledge Thomas L. Boyer, J.D., shareholder and director of Kemp, Klein, Umphrey, Endelman and May, P.C., Troy, Michigan, for his many past contributions to this work.

Jim Castagnera wishes to acknowledge the invaluable assistance of his daughter and editorial assistant, Claire Castagnera, a freelance writer, editor, and graphic artist based in Philadelphia (http://clairecastagnera.wordpress.com/).

Contents

Contents

Contents

Contents

Tables

List of Questions

Chapter 1 The Legal Framework

Chapter 2 The Employment Relationship

Chapter 3 Hiring and Evaluating Employees

Chapter 4 Employment Discrimination

Title VII

Sexual Harassment

Chapter 5 Personnel Files and Privacy Issues

Chapter 6 Security Issues

Employee Dishonesty and Theft

Safety and Violence in the Workplace

Computer Security

Copyright

Trade Secrets and Confidentiality Agreements

Non-Competition Agreements

Chapter 7 Job Safety

OSH Act

Emergency Planning and Right to Know Act

Smoking in the Workplace

AIDS

Chapter 8 Employee Compensation and Fringe Benefits

Fair Labor Standards Act

Wages

Minimum Wage

Hours Worked

Compensation and Withholding

Fringe Benefits

Employee Retirement Income Security Act

Chapter 9 Government Contractors

Wages and Benefits

Whistleblowers

Chapter 10 Public Employees

Collective Bargaining

Federal Employees

Constitutional and Civil Rights

Compensation

Ethical Issues

Occupational Health and Safety

Chapter 11 Labor Unions

Union Organizing

Picketing

Unfair Labor Practices

Chapter 12 Immigration and Naturalization

Basics

Discrimination Against Aliens

Immigration Act of 1990

Relationship of Other Laws to Aliens and Immigration

Chapter 13 Employment Termination

Termination Issues

Chapter 14 Managing Labor and Employment Litigation

Case Management

Alternative Dispute Resolution

Avoiding Employee Claims

Chapter 15 Employment Law in the Global Marketplace

International Labor Relations

Employment Law and Multinational Corporations

Employee Safety Concerns in the Global Marketplace

International Organizations

Chapter 1

The Legal Framework

Few areas in the law are as regulated and specialized as employment law. Its legal framework contains a vast array of federal legislation, executive orders, state legislation, and common law—all of which affect the employment relationship from hiring to termination and beyond. Virtually every employment decision that an employer makes has some bearing or relevance to federal or state law. As a result, compliance with regulatory statutes and avoidance of employment litigation is a challenging task. This chapter explores federal employment law and discusses its evolution, including sweeping changes to employee-sponsored health care plans under the Patient Protection and Affordable Care Act and the Health Care and Education Reconciliation Act of 2010, retaliation claims under the Dodd-Frank Wall Street Reform and Consumer Protection Act of 2010, and recent case law interpreting and applying federal law.

Federal Employment Law

Q 1:1 What are the significant federal laws affecting the employment relationship?

The federal government has passed many laws that affect the workplace. Each has its own requirements, provisions for applicability, penalties, and enforcement guidelines. Following are some significant federal laws that affect the workplace:

- The Fair Labor Standards Act
- The Davis-Bacon Act

- The Service Contract Act
- The Walsh-Healey Act
- The Employee Retirement Income Security Act
- The Consolidated Omnibus Budget Reconciliation Act of 1985
- The Health Insurance Portability and Accountability Act of 1996
- The Mental Health Parity Act of 1996, as amended by the Wellstone-Domenici Mental Health Parity and Addiction Act of 2008
- The Family and Medical Leave Act
- Title VII of the Civil Rights Act of 1964
- The Equal Pay Act
- Executive Order 11246
- The Age Discrimination in Employment Act
- The Americans with Disabilities Act
- The Occupational Safety and Health Act
- The Drug-Free Workplace Act
- The National Labor Relations Act
- The Employee Polygraph Protection Act
- The Immigration Reform and Control Act of 1986
- The Worker Adjustment and Retraining Notification Act
- The Whistleblower Protection Act
- Executive Order 13145
- Executive Order 11478
- The Uniformed Services Employment and Reemployment Rights Act
- The Genetic Information Non-Discrimination Act of 2008
- The Sarbanes-Oxley Act
- The ADA Amendments Act of 2008
- The Patient Protection and Affordable Care Act and the Health Care and Education Reconciliation Act of 2010
- The Dodd-Frank Wall Street Reform and Consumer Protection Act of 2010

Q 1:2   What is the *Fair Labor Standards Act*?

The *Fair Labor Standards Act (FLSA)* [28 U.S.C. §§ 201 *et seq.*] establishes the federal minimum wage, the payment of required overtime pay, and child-labor standards. The FLSA covers all employees of employers that are engaged in interstate commerce or the production of goods for interstate commerce and that meet a volume-of-business requirement. Businesses with fewer than two employees are not covered by the FLSA.

The federal minimum wage rose to $7.25 per hour beginning July 24, 2009. The overtime pay provisions of the FLSA require that employees who are not otherwise exempt under its regulations be paid no less the the federal minimum wage and be paid time and a half for hours worked in excess of 40 hours during a workweek. Employees who are exempt from the overtime pay requirements of the FLSA include those employed in a bona fide executive, administrative, or professional capacity or as an outside sales person. The regulations provide guidance and rules for determining whether an employee fits the criteria for an exempt classification. In addition, an employee who fits within a designated exempt category must be paid on a salary basis. [29 C.F.R. § 541.118] Subject to limited exceptions, this means that the employee must receive his or her full salary for any workweek in which he or she performs any work, regardless of the number of hours or days worked. However, just because an employee is paid a salary does not make him or her exempt from overtime pay. Rather, only exempt employees who are paid on a salary basis are exempt.

The Department of Labor (DOL) administers the FLSA, and, through the Secretary of Labor, it may bring an action for violations of the Act. Individuals can exercise a private right of action under the Act as well. Relief for violations are many, including the recovery of unpaid minimum wages, overtime compensation, liquidated damages, and penalties. Willful violation can subject an employer, or somebody acting on behalf of the employer, to criminal penalties as well. (See chapter 8 for a more detailed look at the FLSA.)

Q 1:3   Have there been any developments involving the FLSA?

Yes. DOL regulations, which took effect on August 23, 2004, provided new standards as they relate to the determination of whether an employee is exempt from the overtime requirements under the FLSA. Essentially, the new regulations provide for both clearer and generally more expansive standards for defining and delineating the exceptions for executive, administrative, professional, computer, and outside sales employees. Chapter 8 discusses these regulations in greater detail. In addition, the regulations provide more exceptions to the general rule that exempt employees must be paid their full salary for any workweek that they perform work.

Under the regulations, there are now seven exceptions to the "no pay-docking" rule for exempt employees. Under the new regulations, exempt employees do not have to be paid for the following:

- Absence from work for one or more full days for personal reasons, other than sickness or disability.
- Absence from work for one or more full days due to sickness or disability if the deductions are made under a bona fide plan, policy, or practice of providing wage replacement benefits for these types of absences.
- Reducing salary to offset any amounts received as pay for jury fees, witness fees, or military pay.
- Penalties imposed in good faith for violating safety rules of "major" significance.
- Unpaid disciplinary suspensions of one or more full days imposed in good faith for violations of workplace conduct rules.

- A proportionate part of an employee's full salary may be paid for time actually worked in the first and last weeks of employment.
- Unpaid leave taken pursuant to the Family and Medical Leave Act (FMLA).

Q 1:4   What is the *Davis-Bacon Act?*

The *Davis-Bacon Act* [40 U.S.C. §§ 276a *et seq.*] requires the payment of prevailing local wages and fringe benefits to laborers and mechanics employed by contractors and subcontractors on certain federal government contracts for construction, alteration, repair, painting, or decoration of public buildings or public works. The Act applies to public works and public buildings in excess of $2,000.

This Act, like the FLSA, is enforced through the DOL. Contractors and subcontractors who fail to abide by the Davis-Bacon Act, including its wage-reporting requirements, are subject to liabilities and penalties, including liability for the underpayment of wages and benefits, contract termination, and exclusion from federal contracts for a period of time. In addition, contractors and subcontractors may be subject to civil or criminal penalties for falsification of records that must be filed with the government under the Act.

Q 1:5   What is the *Service Contract Act?*

The *Service Contract Act* [41 U.S.C. §§ 351 *et seq.*] is analogous to the Davis-Bacon Act. It provides for the payment of prevailing local wages and fringe benefits and sets safety and health standards for employees of contractors and subcontractors providing services under federal contracts in excess of $2,500. The DOL enforces the Service Contract Act. When it finds violations, the Department may seek a wide range of relief, including withholding from contractors the amount of any wage underpayments, cancellation of the contracts, and debarring willful violators from federal service contracts for a period of time.

Q 1:6   What is the *Walsh-Healey Act?*

The *Walsh-Healey Act* [41 U.S.C. §§ 35 *et seq.*] provides wage, hour, and safety requirements and health standards for employees who manufacture or furnish materials, supplies, articles, or equipment in connection with federal contracts in excess of $10,000. Protections under the Act extend only to those employees actually engaged in or connected with the manufacturing and furnishing operations and does not apply to office workers, custodians, executives, administrators, professionals, or outside sales people.

The DOL enforces the Walsh-Healey Act. It investigates complaints and may seek redress against the violators through the assessment of monetary or liquidated damages, cancellation of contracts, or debarment from contracts for a period of time.

Q 1:7   What is the *Employee Retirement Income Security Act?*

The *Employee Retirement Income Security Act (ERISA)* [29 U.S.C. § 1001 *et seq.*] is a comprehensive statute that defines and establishes uniform standards for employee pension and welfare benefit plans (e.g., minimum participation requirements, accrual and vesting requirements, fiduciary responsibilities, standards of conduct, recordkeeping, and disclosure requirements). The recordkeeping and disclosure requirements of the Act are significant, including the preparation and filing of summary plan descriptions and annual financial reports (Form 5500) and the furnishing of a summary annual report to participants and beneficiaries. In addition, the Act creates numerous rights and obligations with regard to plan formation, plan termination, and the managing and investing of plan assets. It also prohibits discrimination against plan participants and beneficiaries.

The Act is comprehensive, preempting most state laws with regard to plans it covers. The DOL enforces the Act. It can assess civil penalties for failure to comply with recordkeeping and disclosure requirements and monetary penalties for engaging in prohibited transactions. Covered individuals also have a private right of action under the Act in federal court, and a participant or beneficiary can bring civil action for civil or equitable relief or to enforce provisions of the law.

Q 1:8   Why was ERISA enacted?

ERISA was enacted in response to numerous instances of pension fund mismanagement and abuse. In some cases, the pension benefits of retired employees had been reduced or terminated because the pension plans had not been adequately funded or had been depleted through mismanagement. In other instances, employees retiring after numerous years of service were ineligible for their pension benefits because of complex and strict eligibility requirements created by employers. ERISA was intended to prevent such abuses and to protect the interests of plan participants and their beneficiaries.

Q 1:9   What benefit plans are subject to ERISA?

ERISA applies to two general categories of benefit plans provided by employers to their employees: (1) employee welfare benefit plans; and (2) employee pension plans.

Employee welfare benefit plans are broadly defined to include plans, funds, or programs established or maintained by an employer for the purpose of providing medical, surgical, hospital care, sickness, accident, disability, death, unemployment or vacation benefits, apprenticeship or other training programs, day care centers, scholarship funds, pre-paid legal services, or severance benefits to participants or beneficiaries. [Donovan v. Dillingham, 688 F.2d 1367, 1371 (11th Cir. 1982)]

An *employee pension benefit plan* is any plan, fund, or program established or maintained by an employer that seeks to provide retirement income to employees or defers income by employees through defined contribution plans. Defined contribution plans generally include profit sharing plans, 401(k) plans, and stock bonus arrangements.

General payroll practices, like the payment for vacation, holidays and the like, are not generally considered employee welfare plans. Similarly, one-time discretionary severance payments or buy-outs that do not require an ongoing administrative scheme generally are not covered by ERISA. [*See* Velarde v. Pace Membership Warehouse, 105 F.3d 1313 (9th Cir. 1997).]

Q 1:10   What types of ERISA claims do participants and beneficiaries have?

Participants and beneficiaries have many types of ERISA claims, including: (1) breach of fiduciary duty; (2) claims for benefits; (3) claims for failure to abide by ERISA recording and disclosure requirements; and (4) discrimination claims.

ERISA requires that every plan identify a fiduciary. A *fiduciary* is one who exercises discretionary control or authority over the management or administration of a plan, or the description of its assets, or provides advice. Fiduciary obligations include acting solely in the interests of participants and beneficiaries for their exclusive benefit with the care, skill, and prudence a reasonable person would utilize in similar circumstances. In *Guididas v. Community National Bank Corp.* [No. 8:11-cv-2545-T-30TBM, 2012 WL 3025162 (M.D. Fla. July 24, 2012)], the court held that a fiduciary, who was aware of a bank's improper business and banking practices, breached its fiduciary duty when it continued to offer the bank's stock as an investment option despite this knowledge. As the court held in *Guyan International, Inc. v. Professional Benefits Administrators, Inc.* [689 F.3d 793 (6th Cir. 2012)], plan administrators who engage in self-dealing with fund assets, leaving hundreds of thousands of dollars of unpaid claims for plan participants, clearly breached their fiduciary duties.

ERISA provides limited remedies for those participants or beneficiaries who feel that they have been unjustly denied benefits from an ERISA benefit plan. A claim for benefits under an employee benefit plan is an ERISA claim that generally preempts any state law claims relating to the matter. Under ERISA Section 502(a)(1)(B), a participant or beneficiary can bring a civil cause of action to recover benefits due under a plan, or to enforce rights under a plan.

ERISA Section 503 requires that each plan contain reasonable claim procedures for assessing benefit claims by participants and beneficiaries. Section 503(2) of ERISA requires that each plan provide an appeals process for any benefit claim denial. With respect to claim procedures, the regulations require that a review on appeal be made within 60 days of the appeal, or, in special circumstances, within 120 days or at the next quarterly board meeting subsequent to the appeal. In addition, the plan administrator has an obligation to include specific reasons and specific references to the pertinent plan provisions upon which the appeal decision is based.

Prior to bringing litigation under ERISA to seek benefits under the plan at issue, aggrieved participants or beneficiaries are generally required to exhaust administrative remedies of appeal, unless it can be demonstrated that resort to administrative remedies would be futile. [Miller v. Metropolitan Life Ins. Co., 925 F.2d 979 (6th Cir. 1991)] If the administrative remedies provided by the plan are not exhausted first, the lawsuit brought to challenge the denial of benefits may be dismissed, or the case may be remanded to the plan administrator for further consideration. Assuming administrative remedies have been exhausted or are futile, the standard of review with respect to denial decisions is limited.

Assuming that the plan provides the plan administrator with discretion to determine the benefit decision under the plan, a de novo review of the denial is not provided under ERISA. Rather, the issue is whether the administrator abused its discretion based upon the information available to the administrator prior to arriving at a decision. With respect to the interpretation of plan documents, the issue is generally whether the plan administrator's interpretation of the plan was reasonable under the circumstances. In *Khoury v. Group Health Plan, Inc.* [615 F.3d 946 (8th Cir. 2010)], a plan administrator, having discretionary authority, did not abuse its discretion when, in determining "basic monthly earnings" from which long-term disability payments would be determined, did not take into consideration wages paid for on-call work performed by the physician during his employment. The court found that the on-call services were essentially extra work and akin to overtime which the plan did not provide to be taken into consideration for determining the "basic monthly earnings" from which long-term disability payments would be determined. In *Kovach v. Zurich American Insurance Co.* [587 F.3d 323 (6th Cir. 2009)], a beneficiary of an accidental death and dismemberment policy sued a plan administrator challenging the denial of benefits in connection with a motorcycle accident. The plan administrator denied the benefits on the basis that the beneficiary was intoxicated at the time of the motorcycle accident. Because of the intoxication, the plan administrator claimed that the incident was not "accidental" within the terms of the policy and, in any event, was a "self-inflicted" wound, an exception from coverage. Although the court acknowledged that the beneficiary intentionally drank in excess and then rode his motorcycle, the court found that he did not do so with the mind toward harming himself and therefore could not be considered "self-inflicted" and could not view the accident as "highly likely" to occur as the result of the drinking which would be necessary to find that the incident was not "accidental." As a result, the court found the plan administrator's decision to be arbitrary and capricious. In *Weitzenkamp v. Unum Life Insurance Company of America* [2011 WL 4375637 (7th Cir. Oct. 25, 2011)], the court held that a 24-month limitation in a disability policy for conditions primarily based on self-reported symptoms did not apply to a condition that was diagnosed and objectively verifiable, even though the primary symptom, pain, involved self-reporting. The court concluded that the plan administrator's interpretation and application of the limitation was arbitrary and capricious.

ERISA Section 510 prohibits an employer from discriminating against an employee for exercising any right to which he or she is entitled under an ERISA plan, or for the purpose of interfering with an employee's attainment of any right under an ERISA plan. ERISA Section 510 provides:

> *Interference with protected rights.* It shall be unlawful for any person to discharge, fine, suspend, expel, discipline or discriminate against a participant or beneficiary for exercising any right to which he is entitled under the provisions of an employee benefit plan, this subchapter (ERISA Title I), section 1201 of this title, or the Welfare and Pension Plans Disclosure Act, or for the purpose of interfering with the attainment of any rights to which such participant may become entitled under the plan, this subchapter, or the Welfare and Pension Plans Disclosure Act. It shall be unlawful for any person to discharge, fine, suspend, expel, or discriminate against any person because he has given information or has testified or is about to testify in any inquiry or proceeding relating to this chapter or the Welfare and Pension Plans Disclosure Act. The provisions of section 1132 [§ 502] of this title shall be applicable in the enforcement of this section.

However, protection from discrimination and retaliation does not extend to an employee's unsolicited internal complaints to management. Rather, the information or testimony that the individual has or is about to provide must be related to an inquiry or proceeding related to ERISA. [*See* Edwards v. A.H. Cornell & Son, Inc., 610 F.3d 217 (3d Cir. 2010).]

Q 1:11 What is the *Consolidated Omnibus Budget Reconciliation Act of 1985?*

The *Consolidated Omnibus Budget Reconciliation Act of 1985* (COBRA) requires employer-sponsored group health plans to allow qualified beneficiaries who would otherwise lose coverage as a result of certain qualified events to continue receiving coverage, at their own expense, for a period of time. Generally, COBRA applies to all group health plans, except those for which the employer employs fewer than 20 employees during the preceding calendar year. The qualifying events that trigger a loss of group health coverage and the application of COBRA are:

- The employee's death;
- Voluntary or involuntary termination of employment (other than by reason of the employee's gross misconduct), or a reduction of hours of employment;
- Divorce or legal separation;
- Medicare entitlement;
- Cessation of status as a dependent; and
- The employer's filing for bankruptcy.

Qualified beneficiaries include an employee, his or her spouse, and any dependent child. However, eligible employees that are terminated for "gross misconduct" are not entitled to COBRA coverage. [29 U.S.C. § 1163(2)] An employee who is terminated for knowingly misrepresenting his credentials to obtain a teaching position, and was convicted of student aid fraud in obtaining what qualifications he did possess for the position was found to have engaged in "gross misconduct" such that he was not required to be offered COBRA coverage by the employer. [Moore v. Williams Coll., 702 F. Supp. 2d 19 (D. Mass. 2010)]

Employers must notify qualified beneficiaries of their COBRA rights when the employee becomes covered by the group health care plan and must notify all qualified beneficiaries of their continuation rights when a qualifying event occurs. It is the employer's responsibility to notify all qualified beneficiaries. As a result, cautious employers will retain copies of the notice and ensure that notices are sent to all qualified beneficiaries through certified mail, return receipt requested, registered mail, or hand delivery, with acknowledgment of receipt. However, COBRA does not require that the beneficiary or dependents actually receive the required notice, but rather notice sent by the employer by first class mail to the covered employee or beneficiary's last known address is generally deemed to be sufficient under COBRA. As such, when an administrator mailed notice to the employee and beneficiary to the same address that appeared on the health insurance enrollment form filled out by the employee, such notice was deemed good faith compliance with COBRA despite the fact that it did not contain the employee and beneficiary's apartment number, such that the notice was not actually received. [Robinson-Reeder v. American Council on Educ., 626 F. Supp. 2d 11 (D.D.C. 2009)] Similarly, an affidavit from human resource personnel indicating that the COBRA notice was mailed in accordance with established company procedure to the last known address of the employee is sufficient to establish proper notice despite having only an unsigned copy of a form letter addressed to the former employee. [Polito v. Tri-Wire Eng'g Solutions, Inc., 699 F. Supp. 2d 480 (E.D.N.Y. 2010)] In *Burden v. City of Opa Locka* [2012 WL 4764592 (S.D. Fla. Oct. 7, 2012)], the employer sent the COBRA notice certified mail, return receipt requested but the employee did not pick up the mail from the post office after an attempted delivery. Although the employee did not receive the notice, the employer had sent it to the plaintiff in accordance with COBRA such that notice was deemed sufficient.

A qualified beneficiary notified of continuation rights has 60 days from the date of the notice to elect or not elect continuation coverage and has 45 days after electing coverage to pay the premium due for the notice and election beneficiary. The qualified beneficiary must pay premiums no later than 30 days after each premium payment is due thereafter.

In general, COBRA coverage continues for a maximum of 18 months after health benefits are lost through termination of employment or a reduction in work hours. Since the enactment of the Health Insurance Portability and Accountability Act of 1996 (HIPAA), coverage can be extended to 29 months for both employees and other qualified beneficiaries who become disabled during the first 60 days of coverage. In addition, regulations provide for additional coverage, for a maximum of 36 months for qualified beneficiaries of Medicare recipients. The new amendments also allow beneficiaries to add newborns and adopted children during the coverage period, without having to wait for the next open enrollment date, which was a criterion under prior law.

In addition, HIPAA limits exclusions for preexisting conditions within health insurance plans, prohibits discrimination against employees and their dependents based upon their health status, and guarantees the availability of health insurance for certain individuals. HIPAA limits the definition of *preexisting conditions* to include only those conditions for which medical advice, diagnosis, or treatment is recommended or received during the six-month period prior to an individual's enrollment date, and provides that the preexisting condition exclusion may not last more than 12 months after an employee's enrollment date or 18 months for late enrollees. Furthermore, the exclusion period must be reduced by the number of days of the individual's prior "creditable" health insurance coverage. Creditable coverage is credit for previous health insurance coverage that occurred without a break in coverage of 63 days or more, including COBRA coverage. Since June 1, 1997, group health plans or health insurance insurers are required to provide certificates of credible coverage to individuals who lose coverage or begin COBRA that specify the time periods of prior coverage to be utilized for purposes of determining creditable coverage in order to reduce any preexisting illness limitations.

The DOL enforces COBRA. Violations can result in an employer losing its income tax deductions for its group health insurance expenses. [*See* I.R.C. § 162(i)(2).] In addition, because a private right of action exists under the Act, individual participants or beneficiaries may sue to enforce their rights to continuation coverage. [*See* 29 U.S.C. § 1132(a).] In *Gomez v. St. Vincent Health, Inc.* [649 F.3d 583 (7th Cir. 2011)], the court held that when employees did not receive proper notice of their COBRA continuation rights after a qualifying event occurred, it was not error for the lower court to award damages equal to the employee's out-of-pocket costs expended for medical treatment that would have been covered by insurance had COBRA notices been properly sent to the employee, minus whatever premium cost the employee would have incurred for COBRA continuation of the medical insurance at issue.

Q 1:12   How did the American Recovery and Reinvestment Act affect COBRA?

Under the *American Recovery and Reinvestment Act (ARRA)* [Pub. L. No. 111-5], a covered employee who is "involuntarily terminated" between September 1, 2008 and December 31, 2009, may be considered an "assistance eligible individual" (AEI) and receive a 65 percent subsidy of the COBRA premium he or she pays. An AEI may receive such subsidy for a maximum of nine months. According to the ARRA, the employee's COBRA premiums will be deemed to be paid in full as long as the employee pays 35 percent of the premium.

In the case of an underwritten group plan, the employer must first advance 65 percent of the subsidy. Then the employer will be entitled to be repaid by the federal government in the form of an offset credit against the federal quarterly payroll taxes that are paid to the federal government. This can be offset against employee income-tax withholdings and both the employee's and the employer's FICA tax.

The ARRA was made effective as of February 17, 2009, but the premium subsidies begin as of the first premium period after the bill was signed. Thus, ARRA applies for a premium billing as of March 1, 2009 and an eligible employee may begin to receive a subsidy beginning March 1, 2009.

The bill is not retroactive. Therefore, even where an employee was terminated between September 1, 2008 and March 1, 2009, an employer need not pay any subsidies for premiums owed by the employee prior to March 1, 2009.

A one-time notice must be sent to all possible current and former COBRA beneficiaries who may qualify for a subsidy (not just the covered employee), regarding (a) the subsidy, (b) the one-time special extended election period, and (c) other information about ARRA rights. These notices must be provided by April 18, 2009.

Those already on COBRA then have 90 days after the notice to elect the subsidy. Those who rejected or were discontinued from COBRA but are now eligible for the premium subsidy have 60 days following the notice to elect COBRA with a the premium subsidy.

People newly eligible for COBRA coverage (i.e., terminated on or after February 17, 2009, when the ARRA was enacted) will be informed about the ARRA subsidy through the general COBRA notice that they receive within 45 days of being laid off.

Q 1:13 What is *HIPAA*?

HIPAA [Pub. L. No. 104-191] was signed into law on August 21, 1996. This law amended significant portions of ERISA and COBRA to offer protection for employees with preexisting medical conditions and prohibits discrimination in health coverage based upon factors relating to an employee's health. Essentially HIPAA includes changes that: (1) limit exclusions for preexisting conditions within health insurance plans; (2) prohibit discrimination against employees and their dependents based upon their health status; (3) allow special enrollment for employees and their dependents outside the regular enrollment periods specified in the plan document; and (4) guarantee availability of health coverage for certain individuals.

In addition, HIPAA required the Secretary of Health and Human Services (HHS) to promulgate regulations protecting the privacy of individually identifiable health information (hereafter "Protected Health Information") if Congress failed to enact privacy legislation by August 1999.

Effective September 23, 2009, the HHS issued its interim final regulations under the Health Information Technology for Economic and Clinical Health (HITECH) Act. [74 Fed. Reg. 56123 (Oct. 30, 2009)] Under the HITECH Act, business associates are required, among other things, to comply with security rule provisions directing the implementation of safeguards for electronically stored health information, and provide breach notifications in the event of disclosures of protected health information in violation of HIPAA. Business associate agreements, prepared prior to the HITECH Act should be modified to include all new rules for business associates with respect to security and breach notifications as required by the HITECH Act.

Q 1:14 How does HIPAA limit coverage denials because of preexisting illness limitations under a plan?

Prior to HIPAA, many plans contained significant exclusions with respect to preexisting illnesses of employees and their dependents. As a result, a participant changing from one plan to another, through a job change or the like, could lose the ability to be covered for an illness because of a preexisting illness limitation contained within the plan documents. HIPAA works to limit the use of the preexisting illness exclusion in a number of ways, first by defining *preexisting condition* specifically as a condition for which medical advice, diagnosis, or treatment is recommended or received during the six-month period prior to an individual's enrollment date. In addition, HIPAA provides that the preexisting condition exclusion may not last for more than 12 months after an individual's enrollment date or 18 months for late enrollees. Furthermore, the 12- or 18-month exclusion period must be reduced by the number of days of the individual's prior "creditable" health insurance coverage. *Credible coverage* is credit for previous health insurance coverage that occurred without a break in coverage of 63 days or more, including COBRA coverage. HIPAA also prohibits the utilization of preexisting exclusions in connection with pregnancy, newborns, and certain children adopted or placed for adoption, provided the child becomes covered under the health plan within 30 days of the birth or adoption.

Q 1:15 Who is responsible for notifying the employee or the employee's dependents of "creditable" coverage?

Creditable coverage under HIPAA works to reduce the 12- or 18-month preexisting condition exclusion period permitted under HIPAA. Group health plans and health insurance issuers are required to furnish a certificate of credible coverage to an individual to provide documentation of the individual's prior creditable coverage. Generally, the certificate is required to be provided automatically by the plan or the issuer when an individual either loses coverage under the plan or becomes entitled to elect COBRA coverage and when the individual's continuation coverage ceases. In general, by June 1, 1997, plans or issuers of insurance must have sent creditable certificates to individuals who lost coverage or became eligible for COBRA between October 1, 1996 and May 31, 1997. After June 1, 1997, plans or issuers of insurance must provide certificates to individuals who lose coverage or begin COBRA. The certificate specifies the time periods of prior coverage to be utilized for purposes of determining credible coverage to reduce any applicable preexisting illness limitations.

Q 1:16   Does HIPAA prohibit discrimination against employees and their dependents based upon their health status?

HIPAA prohibits plans and insurers from establishing rules for eligibility, including conditions of continued eligibility, based on "health status related factors." These factors are one's health status, physical condition, mental condition, claims experience, receipt of health care, medical history, genetic information, evidence of insurability, or disability. These prohibitions would prevent an insurer from dropping an employee or dependents from coverage if they were stricken by a particular illness; however, under HIPAA, it appears that plans may still establish limits or restrictions on benefits or coverage provided that such limits or restrictions are not a violation of any other federal law. [*See, e.g.,* the Americans with Disabilities Act (ADA) and/or the Mental Health Parity Act of 1996 (MHPA).] A plan that conditioned continued coverage upon passing a physical examination would likely be deemed impermissible under HIPAA.

Q 1:17   What are HIPAA's special enrollment provisions?

Group health plans and health insurance carriers usually provide for a regular annual enrollment date, and limited access to the benefit plans at all other times. HIPAA works to do away with these limitations by providing "special enrollment" if an individual with other health insurance coverage loses that coverage, or if a person becomes a dependent through marriage, birth, adoption, or placement for adoption. A special enrollee is not faced with the limitations typically accorded late enrollees in traditional plans. For example, under HIPAA, the maximum preexisting exclusion that applies to a special enrollee is the same (12 months) as that for someone who enrolls in accordance with the plan's regular enrollment date. The 18-month maximum for late enrollees would not be applicable to special enrollees under HIPAA.

Q 1:18   What are *domestic partner benefits*?

Traditionally, employees, their spouses, and their dependents have been eligible for employee benefits. *Eligible spouses* are traditionally defined as individuals recognized as being married under applicable state law. The national trend toward prohibiting sexual orientation discrimination in the workplace on a company-by-company, state-by-state, or local basis has been followed by a trend toward providing for domestic partner benefits in this country. However, much like sexual orientation discrimination, no federal law requires companies to provide for domestic partner benefits, but as this publication goes to press, a number of Fortune 500 companies had begun offering such benefits in connection with their employee welfare benefit plans. AT&T, Boeing, IBM, Walt Disney, and Coca-Cola Company are some of the prominent companies offering domestic partner benefits. [*See* "Gay Rights Advocate Cites Growth in Employer's Domestic Partner Benefits," 14 *Employment Discrimination Report (EDR)* (BNA) 913 (June 28, 2000).] The number of large companies offering domestic partner benefits has grown significantly over the years (a list of companies can be found at: http://www.salaryfor.com).

Following this national trend, it was reported that the State of Maine signed into law a requirement that health insurance providers and health maintenance organizations offer domestic partner benefits to their policyholders to the same extent and manner that benefits are offered to spouses of legally married individuals. [*See* "Maine Law Calls for Domestic Partner Coverage," 16 *Employment Discrimination Report (EDR)* (BNA) 803 (June 13, 2001).]

Q 1:19 What are the HIPAA Privacy Rules?

HIPAA, enacted in 1996, required the Secretary of HHS to promulgate regulations protecting the privacy of individually identifiable health information (hereafter "Protected Health Information"), upon Congress' failure to enact privacy legislation by August 1999. In December 2000, HHS Secretary, Donna Shalala, released the final regulations, and in August 2002, after extensive comment, revised final regulations were issued by current HHS Secretary, Tommy Thompson. Under the revised final regulations, compliance deadlines for the HIPAA Privacy Rules for covered entities was April 14, 2003, with the exception of small health plans (i.e., ones with annual receipts of $5 million or less), which had until April 14, 2004 to comply.

Q 1:20 What entities are covered by the HIPAA Privacy Rules?

The HIPAA Privacy Rules prohibit "covered entities" from using Protected Health Information except as authorized by the individual who is the subject of the information or as explicitly required or permitted by the regulations. The covered entities are limited to the following:

- Health care plans;
- Health care clearinghouses; and
- Any health care provider who transmits health information in electronic form in connection with transactions covered by HIPAA's administrative requirements.

Employers and health care plan sponsors are not covered entities. Under the regulations, covered entities must comply with the full range of HIPAA's privacy requirements to prevent the unauthorized disclosure or use of PHI including establishing policies and procedures for managing PHI uses and disclosures in accordance with the regulations. Employers are not included as covered entities and therefore are not subject to HIPAA generally. However, an employer may be indirectly covered by HIPAA Privacy Rules if it sponsors and administers a health plan. The final revised regulations specifically prohibit the disclosure of Protected Health Information by covered entities to non-covered entities, such as employer plan sponsors for employment-related decisions. [45 C.F.R. § 164. 504(f)(3)(iv)] In fact, one of the stated purposes of HIPAA's Privacy Rules is to prohibit employers from utilizing Protected Health Information in connection with personnel decisions.

Q 1:21 What are the compliance obligations for employees under the HIPAA Privacy Rules?

Although employers in the medical services industry will undoubtedly be covered as health care providers under the HIPAA Privacy Rules, other employers may or may not have to undertake implementation of HIPAA's rules depending upon whether they are merely sponsors of fully insured health plans, or if they are both sponsors and administrators of health plans that need or use Protected Health Information in connection with the administration of such plans.

If an employer is merely a sponsor of a fully insured health plan, and does not create or receive Protected Health Information, it will not have to modify its policies and procedures for purposes of meeting compliance with the HIPAA privacy regulations. Specifically, these employers can notify the administrators of the fully insured health plan that it does not seek Protected Health Information, but rather will accept what is referred to as "summary health information" concerning the participants, which is information that is stripped of all potentially identifying information such as names, Social Security numbers, etc. An employer plan sponsor of fully insured health plans does not need to comply with HIPAA's Privacy Rules if it is content with receipt of only de-identified information concerning its participants from the plan.

On the other hand, if an employer is not only a plan sponsor but also an administrator of a plan, it will fall within HIPAA and will be required to comply with HIPAA's regulatory compliance scheme. Although the compliance scheme is complicated, and every employer in this category is advised to seek counsel to create and implement a scheme that complies with the HIPAA Privacy Rules, generally, the regulations require the following:

- Employers must create a firewall between the employees who administer the plan and/or receive Protected Health Information and other employees to prevent the dissemination of that information from those who administer the plan and/or receive Protected Health Information to other employees.

- Plan documents need to be amended that describe the permitted or required uses of Protected Health Information, define those employees who will have access to that information, and provide a mechanism for resolving issues of suspected non-compliance.

- Employers must make written certification to the plan that they will comply with HIPAA privacy regulations.

- Employers must designate a privacy official who is responsible for implementing privacy policies, provide training to employees with respect to uses of Protected Health Information, and provide sanctions for employees who violate privacy policies.

Q 1:22   What is the *MHPA*?

The *MHPA* [Pub. L. No. 104-204 (1996)] was signed into law on September 26, 1996. The law, which is limited in its application, provides for parity in benefits for physical and mental health treatment. Under the MHPA, group health plans, insurance companies, and HMOs that offer mental health benefits will not be allowed to set annual or lifetime limits on such benefits that are less than those imposed for medical and surgical benefits. Historically, most plans provide significant limits in the amount of coverage available for mental health benefits versus benefits under physical, medical, and surgical coverage. The MHPA seeks to do away with this disparity by prohibiting such limitations in certain circumstances; however, plans may continue to require that benefits for mental health illnesses be subject to various terms and conditions, including cost sharing (so-called "co-pays") and limits on the number of visits or days of coverage. Significantly, the MHPA does not require plans actually to include mental health benefits; therefore, one possible negative consequence of MHPA may be the dropping of mental health care coverage from employer group health plans. Undoubtedly to avoid this consequence, the MHPA provides that it does not apply to employers who do not have more than 50 employees, or to any plan that would incur a cost increase of 1 percent or more because of the application of MHPA requirements. According to many commentators, this threshold for the application of the MHPA is high, and would exempt most plans from the MHPA. [91 *Employment Discrimination Reporter (EDR)* (BNA) 196 (Aug. 6, 1997)] The MHPA applies to group health plans for plan years beginning on or after January 1, 1998.

The *Wellstone-Domenici Mental Health Parity and Addiction Act of 2008* [Pub. L. No. 110-343], effective January 1, 2010, amends the MHPA, to further work to eliminate disparities between the treatment of mental health and substance abuse disorders and medical and surgical benefits. Financial treatment (i.e., co-pays, deductibles and the like) and limitations for mental health and substance abuse disorders must be in parity with the financial treatment and limitations for medical and surgical benefits. There is still a cost exemption from the amendment to requirements, but it only applies for one year if the cost for compliance exceeds 2 percent.

Q 1:23   What is the *FMLA*?

The *FMLA* [29 U.S.C. §§ 2601 *et seq.*] requires covered employers to allow eligible employees to take as many as 12 weeks of unpaid leave for the care of a child, spouse, or parent with a serious health condition, the birth or adoption of a child, or the employee's own serious health condition. In addition, employees must be reinstated to the same or equivalent position after a leave, and their health benefits must continue during a leave. The FMLA applies to all employers that have 50 or more employees for 20 or more calendar weeks in the current or preceding calendar year and that engage in a business that affects commerce.

In January 2008, the National Defense Authorization Act (NDAA) [Pub. L. No. 110-181] was enacted which, among other things, amended the FMLA to provide two new leave entitlements for military personnel and their families as follows:

Military care giver leave. Also known as Covered Service Member Leave, this new entitlement allows eligible employees who are family members of a covered service member to take up to 26 work weeks of leave in a single 12-month period to care for a covered service member with a serious illness or injury incurred in the line of duty. This provision also extends FMLA protection to additional family members (i.e., next of kin) beyond those who may take FMLA leave for other qualifying reasons.

Qualifying exigency leave. The second new leave entitlements enacted by the NDAA provides that the normal 12 weeks of FMLA job protected leave available to eligible employees with a covered military member serving in the National Guard or Reserves may use FMLA leave for "any qualifying exigency," which arises from the fact that the military member is on active duty or called to active duty status in support of military operations. "Qualifying exigency," according to the DOL's final rules effective January 16, 2009, refers to a broad number of activities including short-notice deployment, military events and related activities, child care and school activities, counseling, financial and legal arrangements, rest and recuperation, and post-deployment activities.

Employees who are denied rights under the FMLA may pursue their employer in a private action in state or federal court or file a claim with the DOL. Employers found to have violated the Act may be liable for damages equal to wages, salary, benefits, or other compensation lost or denied in violation of the Act. If no compensation has been lost, the employer may be liable for the actual monetary loss sustained by the employee, including the cost of providing care to family members and the like. In addition, employees may seek equitable relief by way of injunction, reinstatement, promotion, and additional monetary relief for reasonable attorneys' fees and costs attendant to such actions.

Q 1:24 Which employees are eligible for FMLA?

The FMLA only applies to *covered employers*, which means that the employer must have employed 50 or more employees for 20 or more calendar weeks in the current or preceding calendar year. The FMLA utilizes the expansive "FLSA" payroll test for determining if employers meet the 50-or-more-employee threshold. All employees on the payroll are counted, even if part-time, temporary, or on temporary leave. But even for covered employers, only eligible employees are entitled to benefits under the FMLA. It is not unusual for covered employers to have few employees eligible for FMLA leave. In order to be eligible, the employee must have:

- Worked for the employer at least 12 months;
- Provided at least 1,250 hours during the previous 12-month period before commencing the leave; and

- Worked at a worksite where the employer employs 50 or more employees within a 75-mile radius of the employee's worksite.

With respect to the 12-month requirement, the time period need not be contiguous. As a result, an employee with a cumulative 12 months of employment over an extended time period will meet this requirement.

The issue of whether an employee had the requisite number of hours worked was also at issue in *Maples v. Illinois Bell Telephone Co.* [594 F. Supp. 2d 937 (N.D. Ill. 2009)] The employee, a union steward, wanted credit for time spent on internal union business in addition to his other hours worked to satisfy the 1,250 hours of service required under the FMLA during the previous 12-month period. Although the FMLA does not define "hours of service," the statute specifies that the legal standards established under the FLSA shall apply to determine whether an employee meets the requisite hours of service. Under the FLSA, time spent adjusting grievances by union employees on the employer's premises is considered hours worked and in addition, the FLSA will count other union time as hours worked as provided in the relevant collective bargaining agreement or as treated as a matter of custom and practice between the union and employer. Although the time spent by the employee on internal union business far exceeded time spent in adjusting grievances on the employer's premises, historically, the employer had treated all internal union business time worked as hours worked for the union steward under the FMLA, and as such, time spent on internal union business for the employee was creditable toward FMLA eligibility. In *Bailey v. Pregis Innovative Packaging, Inc.* [600 F.3d 748 (7th Cir. 2010)], an employee claimed her employer had violated the FMLA when her employment was terminated. As to eligibility, however, the employee had not worked 1,250 hours in the prior 12 months, but claimed eligibility because her failure to work 1,250 hours was due to prior FMLA leave taken. The court, in rejecting the claim, said that the requirement that the employee work 1,250 hours in the prior 12 months cannot be "tolled" due to the fact that the employee was unable to achieve 1,250 hours due to previous FMLA leave.

As it relates to the 1,250-hour service requirement, an employer should review compensable hours of work as determined by the FLSA to determine if this requirement is met. [29 C.F.R. § 825.110] This would include all hours an employee worked for or has been in service for the employer. Under the FLSA, employers are not required to keep a record of hours worked for exempt employees (executive, administrative, and professional employees). According to the FMLA regulations, the employer has the burden of demonstrating that the requisite hours have not been worked if the employer does not have a record of the exempt employee's hours worked. [29 C.F.R. § 825.110]

As to the 75-mile-radius test, the distance between worksites is measured by surface miles, using available surface transportation over public streets, highways, or waterways by the shortest route, not as the "crow flies." [29 C.F.R. § 825.111]

Q 1:25   **Under what conditions is the FMLA applicable?**

The FMLA provides for job-protected leave, with a continuation of group health benefits, for an employee's absence from work attributable to the following:

- The birth and care of a newborn;
- Placement with the employee of a son or daughter for adoption or foster care.
- To care for the employee's spouse, son, daughter, or parent with a serious health condition; or
- A serious health condition that makes the employee unable to perform the function of his or her job.

Prior to the adoption of the DOL's final rules, a *serious health condition*, under the FMLA regulations, meant an illness, injury, impairment, or physical or mental condition that involves any one of the following:

- Inpatient care (i.e., an overnight stay) in a hospital, hospice, or residential medical facility, including any period of incapacity or subsequent treatment in connection with or consequent to such inpatient care;
- A period of incapacity of three consecutive calendar days (including any subsequent treatment or period of incapacity relating to the same condition) that also involves continuing treatment by a health care provider, such as either of the following:
  - Two or more times by a health care provider;
  - By a health care provider on at least one occasion that results in a regiment of continuing treatment (for example, a course of prescription medicine), under the supervision of the health care provider;
- Any period of incapacity for pregnancy or prenatal care;
- A chronic condition that requires periodic visits for treatment by a health care provider and that continues over an extended period of time and that may cause episodic rather than a continuing period of incapacity (e.g., asthma, diabetes, or epilepsy);
- A permanent or long-term condition that requires supervision by a health care provider; or
- Any period of absence to receive multiple treatments by a health care provider for non-chronic conditions (such as restorative surgery after an accident) or for a condition that would result in a period of incapacity of more than three consecutive calendar days in the absence of medical intervention or treatment. [See Appendix B, 29 C.F.R. Part 825, FMLA; final rule.]

The FMLA regulations also required an employer to notify an employee that the employee's absence is being attributed to the employee's FMLA entitlement, generally within two business days after the employer is aware that the absence qualifies under the FMLA. [29 C.F.R. § 825.208]

Q 1:26   Were the regulations adopted by the DOL when the FMLA was enacted upheld by the courts?

The regulations implementing the FMLA prepared by the DOL [29 C.F.R. §§ 825.100 *et seq.*] provide that employers who provided leave benefits (paid or unpaid) in addition to the FMLA can designate leaves of absence taken in connection with employer-provided leave benefits as FMLA leave, and it can be counted against FMLA leave time provided the leave qualifies as FMLA leave and the employer promptly notifies the employee of such designation, typically within two business days after acquiring knowledge of its applicability to the FMLA. [29 C.F.R. § 825.208] The regulations specifically provide that if the employer fails to make the appropriate designation, the leave does not count against the employee's FMLA entitlement. [29 C.F.R. § 825.700(a)]

The penalty for failure to designate leave time as FMLA leave was challenged by an employer who had provided an employee 30 weeks of leave under its own policies. The U.S. Supreme Court, in *Ragsdale v. Wolverine World Wide, Inc.* [535 U.S. 81 (2002)], held that the regulation, which forfeits an employer's right to allocate leave under its own policies to FMLA if it fails to designate the leave was a penalty, went beyond the authority of the DOL.

The *Ragsdale* decision was followed in *Thompson v. Diocese of Saginaw.* [2004 U.S. Dist. LEXIS 29480 (E.D. Mich. Jan. 6, 2004)] In that case, the employee had been unable to work from August 2000 until March 2001 due to her pregnancy and birth of her child. At no time during her absences was any time off designated by the company as qualifying for FMLA leave, as required by the FMLA regulations. Although the regulations provide that an employer may not designate leave as FMLA leave retroactively, following *Ragsdale*, the court concluded that an employer's violation of the notice regulations does not automatically entitle an employee to additional leave beyond 12 weeks. Rather, an employee must demonstrate that he or she has suffered prejudice by the employer's failure to properly notify him or her of the allocation of the time off to FMLA leave. Recognizing that the plaintiff could not have returned to work within 12 weeks after her leave commenced, regardless of the notice from the company, the court concluded that she could not avail herself of protections under the Act. Simply put, an employee who does not return to work within the 12-week period after a leave commences may not claim protections under the Act.

The *Ragsdale* ruling was also followed by the Third Circuit in *Fogleman v. Greater Hazelton Health Alliance.* [122 Fed. Appx. 581 (3d Cir. Pa. 2004)] In that case, an employee who had not been advised of her FMLA rights had been on a leave that extended beyond 12 weeks. Following *Ragsdale*, the court found that in order to show prejudice, the employee was required to demonstrate that had she been advised of her FMLA rights, she could have returned to work after the 12-week period. However, the testimony in the case indicated that the employee was not able to return to her position at the expiration of the 12-week period, and as such, there was no prejudice for the employer having failed to provide notice to the employee of her FMLA rights. However, if an employee can demonstrate prejudice by failure of an employer to provide notice of application of leave toward the FMLA, such failure may result in the time off not being counted toward FMLA leave. Such was the situation in *Downey v. Rodney J. Strain Jr.* [510 F.3d 534 (5th Cir. 2007)] In that case, the employee had time off for which the employer had never notified her that the time off would be attributable to FMLA leave. When time off for a subsequent surgery, when added to the prior leave, was determined by the company to exceed 12 weeks, it then transferred the claimant to a different job upon her return, claiming that she had exhausted her FMLA leave rights before the end of her leave in connection with her surgery. The issue was whether the prior time off could be counted toward her FMLA allotment, despite the fact that she had never received notice from the company in connection with her prior leave. Based upon the claimant's claims that had she been aware of the allocation to FMLA for her prior leave and that she could have rescheduled her surgery to a later time period to take advantage of additional FMLA accruals, the court held that the claimant was prejudiced by the company's failure to notify her of its allocation to FMLA leave for her prior leave, and as such, upheld the determination that the prior leave could not be counted against the claimant's FMLA allotment.

However, one of the more onerous aspects of the FMLA from management's perspective was upheld by the Sixth Circuit. The FMLA regulations provide that an employee need only provide verbal notice sufficient to make the employer aware that the employee needs time off for an FMLA-qualifying event. [29 C.F.R. § 825.302] The employee need not even mention the FMLA. In *Gerking v. Wabash Ford/Sterling Truck Sales, Inc.* [2002 U.S. Dist. LEXIS 17365 (S.D. Ind. Sept. 6, 2002)], the court upheld that verbal notice in and of itself was sufficient. In that case, Gerking had notified his boss of the need for time off for an FMLA-qualifying event but refused to fill out company-required paperwork in connection with the leave (paperwork not required by FMLA regulations). The company attempted to defeat Gerking's reinstatement by maintaining that Gerking was not on FMLA leave because of his failure to execute company-required paperwork. The court held that verbal notice was sufficient under the regulations. [*See* 19 *Employment Discrimination Report (EDR)* (BNA), 371 (Oct. 2, 2002).] Verbal communication may even be sufficient when the medical condition that requires absences from work is yet to be diagnosed. In *Lincoln v. Sears Home Improvement Products, Inc.* [2004 U.S. Dist. LEXIS 402 (D. Minn. Jan. 9, 2004)], an employee communicated to his supervisor a need for time off attributable to his parents' medical conditions. Although the company claimed the details surrounding the medical conditions were "sketchy" and/or "convoluted," the employee had communicated to the company that his father was undergoing surgery, that his mother was ill and depressed, and that he needed to be with them. The company sought to have the FMLA aspects of the case dismissed for lack of proper notification of a need for FMLA leave and the lack of any medical diagnosis as it related to the mother's depressed condition. The court refused to dismiss the FMLA claims, finding that the employee had provided adequate notice of a need for time off attributable to the employee's father and declined to award summary judgment to the company based on the mother's undiagnosed illness.

As to the issue of undiagnosed illnesses, *Helfrich v. Lehigh Valley Hospital* [2003 U.S. Dist. LEXIS 23708 (E.D. Pa. Dec. 19, 2003)] is particularly on point. In the case, an employee who was experiencing serious migraine headaches and blurred vision took time off from work to undergo medical evaluations for his condition. Although his condition did not incapacitate him from being able to work, his symptoms resulted in his doctor's request that he undergo further medical evaluations to determine the cause of his symptoms. Although the employee did not allege that he was incapable of performing his job, the court, in reading the FMLA, concluded that a serious health condition under the FMLA also includes situations where employees take time off for purposes of medical evaluation and diagnosis. As the court stated, "It seems unlikely that Congress intended to punish people who are unlucky enough to develop new diseases or suffer serious symptoms for some period of time before the medical profession is able to diagnose the cause of the problem."

In a challenge to the city's policy of denying annual leave bonuses to employees who used sick pay, in *Chubb v. City of Omaha, Nebraska* [424 F.3d 831 (8th Cir. 2005)], the Eighth Circuit held that the policy did not violate the FMLA discrimination provisions as applied to an employee who had taken sick leave during an FMLA leave because the employee elected to use sick pay, something not required under the FMLA.

As to damages under the FMLA, and considering that emotional damages are not contained within the damages expressly provided for under the statute and regulations, the court in *Brumbalough v. Camelot Care Center, Inc.* [427 F.3d 996 (6th Cir. 2005)] held that emotional damages are not recoverable under the FMLA.

Q 1:27 Have there been any developments involving military service members and the FMLA?

In January 2008, the NDAA [Pub. L. No. 110-181] was enacted which, among other things, amended the FMLA to provide two new leave entitlements for military personnel and their families as follows:

- *Military care giver leave.* Also known as covered service member leave, this new entitlement allows eligible employees who are family members of a covered service member to take up to 26 work weeks of leave in a single 12-month period to care for a covered service member with a serious illness or injury incurred in the line of duty. This provision also extends FMLA protection to additional family members (i.e., next of kin) beyond those who may take FMLA leave for other qualifying reasons.

- *Qualifying exigency leave.* The second new leave entitlement enacted by the NDAA provides that the normal 12 weeks of FMLA job protected leave available to eligible employees with a covered military member serving in the National Guard or Reserves may use FMLA leave for "any qualifying exigency" which arises from the fact that the military member is on active duty or called to active duty status in support of military operations. "Qualifying exigency" according to the DOL's final rules effective January

16, 2009 refers to a broad number of activities including short notice deployment, military events and related activities, child care and school activities, counseling, financial and legal arrangements, rest and recuperation, and post-deployment activities.

In November 2008, the DOL adopted its final FMLA rules, effective January 16, 2009, which provide guidance regarding some open-ended issues posed by its prior rules.

With respect to the definition of a serious health condition which involves more than three consecutive full days of incapacity plus two visits to a health care provider, the two visits must occur within 30 days of the beginning of the period of incapacity and the first visit must take place within seven days of the first day of incapacity. Under prior rules, a serious health condition was also determined to have occurred if the incapacity is more than three consecutive full calendar days plus a regimen of continuing treatment. The new rules clarify that the first visit to a health care provider in connection with this definition must take place within seven days of the first day of incapacity. With respect to the definition of serious health condition involving "periodic visits" for chronic health conditions, the final rules provide guidance by providing that "periodic visits" means that the employee must have at least two visits to a health care provider per year.

The final FMLA rules have been revised to reflect current law following the Supreme Court's decision in *Ragsdale*. Specifically, the final rules remove the categorical penalty provisions and clarify that when an employee suffers individualized harm because the employer failed to follow the notification rules, the employer may be liable.

The DOL's final rules clarify an employee's obligation with respect to providing notice to the employer for unforeseeable leave. Although prior rules allowed the employee up to two business days to provide notice after commencement of the leave, the final rules provide that the employee must follow the employer's usual and customary call-in procedures for reporting an absence (e.g., before the employee's shift starts), absent unusual circumstances. Many employers hope that this change will result in employees providing more timely notice of FMLA leave, which was noted by the DOL to have been stated to have been an issue with many employers.

The DOL's final rules added a requirement that when engaged in the medical certification process, any contact by the employer with the health care provider of the employee must be through the employer's health care provider, the employer's human resource professional, leave administrator or other management official, but in no case may the contact be made by the employee's direct supervisor. Moreover, employers may not ask the employee's health care provider for additional information beyond that required by the certification form itself. In addition, if the employer deems the medical certification to be incomplete or insufficient, the employer must specify in writing what information is lacking and give the employee seven calendar days to cure the deficiency.

Clarifying an open-ended issue under the prior regulations, the new rules provide that for illness of long duration, or intermittent reoccurring conditions, employers can request recertification of an ongoing condition every six months in conjunction with an absence.

Q 1:28   Is retaliation prohibited under the FMLA?

There are three provisions under the FMLA that courts look to establish retaliation claims. Section 2615(a) of the FMLA provides that, "It shall be unlawful for any employer to interfere with, restrain, or deny the exercise of or the attempt to exercise, any right provided under this subchapter" [29 U.S.C. § 2615(a)(1)] Subsection 2 from this provision provides, "It shall be unlawful for any employer to discharge or in any other manner discriminate against any individual for opposing any practice made unlawful by this subchapter." [29 U.S.C. § 2615(a)(2)] In addition, 29 C.F.R. § 825.220(c) prohibits employers from "discriminating against employees or prospective employees who had used FMLA leave." There are many recent cases demonstrating the employer's potential for liability when employees suffer adverse employment actions following the exercise or attempted exercise of their rights under the FMLA.

In *Erdman v. Nationwide Insurance Co.* [582 F.3d 500 (3d Cir. 2009)], an employee claimed that he had been terminated as a result of his request to take FMLA leave. The employer claimed that a retaliation claim could not be maintained because the employee had merely requested the right to take the leave, as opposed to having taking the leave itself. The court, reviewing both the statutory provisions of Section 2615(a) and its regulations concluded that retaliation claims extended not only to those that have taken leave, but those that requested as well. However, if a clear request for time off in connection with an FMLA qualifying event has not occurred, a retaliation claim cannot be maintained. In *Fischer v. NYC Department of Education* [666 F. Supp. 2d 309 (E.D.N.Y. 2009)], an employee had not requested time off for an FMLA qualifying condition, but had merely requested a medical leave form. The employee claimed that he had suffered adverse employment action as a result of having requested the leave form, but the court concluded that merely requesting the medical leave form, without more, was insufficient to show that he had exercised rights protected by the FMLA, such that a retaliation claim could not be maintained.In *Pellegrino v. Communication Workers of America, AFL-CIO, CLC* [Civil Action No. 10-0098 (W.D. Pa. May 19, 2011)], the court held that an employee terminated for violating company policy by engaging in unapproved travel during a time period that she was accepting sick leave pay served as a legitimate reason for termination and not retaliation under the FMLA.

As with most retaliation claims, timing is an issue, and the close proximity in time of the adverse employment action with the exercise of FMLA rights typically sets the stage for possible retaliation claims. Although courts generally hold that timing is usually insufficient, in and of itself, to support a claim, any additional relevant evidence together with close proximity in timing, will generally allow employees to maintain a retaliation claim. An employee who was demoted following maternity leave under the FMLA claimed retaliation, but the court affirmed the dismissal of the case because, although the plaintiff claimed that timing showed causation and retaliation, the court found that the professional deficiencies that the employer discovered in the employee's work while the employee was on leave provided legitimate reasons for the demotion. [Schaff v. Smithkline Beecham Corp., 602 F.3d 1236 (11th Cir. 2010)] Similarly, in *Estrada v. Cypress Semiconductor (Minnesota), Inc.* [616 F.3d 866 (8th Cir. 2010)], the court rejected a claim that termination was an interference with the former employee's rights under the FMLA, finding that the employer's termination of her employment for poor attendance was well documented and justified and that the employer would have made the same termination decision regardless of whether the employee had exercised her alleged FMLA rights. In *Krutzig v. Pulte Home Corp.* [602 F.3d 1231 (11th Cir. 2010)], the court held that the failure of the employer to have knowledge of an employee's request for FMLA leave precluded any claim for retaliation under the FMLA. In *Burkhart v. American Railcar Industries, Inc.* [603 F.3d 472 (8th Cir. 2010)], the court found that disciplinary action following a complaint for a violation of Title VII was insufficient to establish a causal connection because the employee had an extensive history of poor performance preceding the challenged employment action. Moreover, the employee's discharge, seven months after her complaint, was a gap in time between the protected activity and adverse employment action from which an inference of retaliatory motive could not be maintained. Similarly, in *Leonard v. Eastern Illinois University* [606 F.3d 428 (7th Cir. 2010)], the court held that a six-month time frame between the employee's civil rights complaint and unsuccessful interview for a promotion was insufficient, in and of itself, to establish a causal connection necessary to maintain a retaliation claim under Title VII.

In *Follis v. Memorial Medical Center* [No. 08-3056 (C.D. Ill. Sept. 11, 2009)], an employee who was terminated soon after requesting intermittent leave under the FMLA filed a retaliation claim against her employer. Although the court acknowledged that timing alone was insufficient to support the claim, the employee testified that her supervisor expressed opposition to the intermittent leave request when it was requested and the court held this information, together with the proximity in timing, was sufficient to survive the employer's motion for summary disposition.

Although employees must be "eligible" to obtain an FMLA leave, there may be circumstances when an ineligible employee can nonetheless maintain a retaliation claim under the FMLA.

In *Reynolds v. Inter-Industry Conference on Auto Collision Repair* [594 F. Supp. 2d 925 (N.D. Ill. 2009)], an employee who, at the time, was ineligible for FMLA, requested time off under the FMLA after the period that he would have been eligible under the FMLA. Even though the employee was terminated prior to becoming eligible under the FMLA, the court nonetheless concluded that this employee could maintain a retaliation claim because he would have been eligible by the time the requested time off occurred.

Q 1:29   What is *Title VII of the Civil Rights Act of 1964?*

Title VII [42 U.S.C. §§ 2000e, *et seq.*] prohibits discrimination by covered employers, employment agencies, and unions on the basis of race, color, religion, sex, or national origin and prohibits discrimination in employment against women affected by pregnancy, childbirth, or related medical conditions. Title VII applies to any employer engaged in an industry affecting commerce that has 15 or more employees for each working day in each of 20 or more calendar workweeks in the current or preceding calendar year. Title VII does not apply to independent contractors. In *Murray v. Principal Financial Group, Inc.* [613 F.3d 943 (9th Cir. 2010)], the court held that insurance agents that sued an insurance company for sex discrimination were independent contractors and as such, could not maintain claims under Title VII.

Although Title VII is one of many federal laws that prohibit job discrimination (other laws include the Equal Pay Act (EPA), the Age Discrimination in Employment Act, and the ADA), Title VII has the broadest coverage of all federal antidiscrimination laws. It applies to private and public industry and covers virtually all aspects of employment—including recruitment, hiring, job transfer, assignment, promotion, demotion, termination, compensation, layoff, working conditions, and selection for training.

The Equal Employment Opportunity Commission (EEOC) is responsible for enforcing Title VII. As amended by the Civil Rights Act of 1991, a wide range of damages are available for victims of Title VII discrimination—including compensatory damages (both back pay and future losses), emotional losses, and punitive damages for intentional discrimination. Punitive damages are available for discriminatory practices where malice or reckless indifference to a federally protected right can be demonstrated, subject to the following limitations:

The Number of Employees in Each of 20 or More Calendar Weeks in the Current or Preceding Calendar Year	Limitation
More than 14 and fewer than 101	$ 50,000
More than 100 and fewer than 201	$100,000
More than 200 and fewer than 501	$200,000
More than 500	$300,000

The Ninth Circuit, in *Lansdale v. Hi-Health Supermart Corp.* [314 F.3d 355 (9th Cir. 2002)], upheld a challenge to the statutory limitations, finding no basis for constitutional challenge when the court reduced a damage award from $1 million to $200,000 based on the limitations. How the federal caps for compensatory damages are to be applied in cases where both federal and state claims are brought was decided by the Eleventh Circuit in *Bradshaw v. School Board of Broward County Florida.* [486 F.3d 1205 (11th Cir. 2007)] In the case, a school board employee brought parallel state and federal civil rights claims against her employer on the basis of sexual harassment and was awarded $500,000 in compensatory damages by the jury after trial. Although the jury did not separate the award vis-à-vis federal and state law claims, the school board claimed that the federal cap of $300,000 effectively limited the plaintiff's total recovery to $300,000, whereas the employee maintained that she was entitled to $300,000 under the federal cap and an additional $100,000 under the $100,000 cap under her state law claims. Reviewing the statute and recognizing that the federal cap, by its terms, applied to "the amount of compensatory damages awarded under this section" [*Bradshaw*, at 1208], that being the Title VII claim, the court concluded that the employee was entitled to $300,000 under the federal cap and an additional $100,000 under the state law cap, for a total of $400,000.

Although there is a private right of action in federal court under Title VII to commence litigation, Title VII requires that the complaining party first file a charge with the EEOC within 180 days of the alleged discrimination or 300 days in a jurisdiction that maintains a qualifying state or local fair employment agency, which enforces state laws prohibiting unlawful practices based on race, color, religion, sex, national origin, or disability. Typically, charges are filed by the individual's verification by oath or affirmation of the written contents of a charge on EEOC Form 5, Charge of Discrimination. Although failure to file a charge within the requisite time period is typically viewed as a bar to further proceedings under federal law, the U.S. Supreme Court, in *Edelman v. Lynchburg College* [535 U.S. 106 (2002)], held that a formal charge that was filed after the requisite time period was valid because it related back to a letter the petitioner had faxed to the EEOC, detailing his claim, prior to the expiration of the requisite time period. If, after the charge is filed, the charge is not resolved at the agency level, the charging party is typically given a 90-day right to pursue the claim in federal court after termination of the EEOC's involvement, a so-called "right-to-sue" letter. Failure to allow the EEOC to complete its investigation by withdrawing the charge will cause any later lawsuit under Title VII dismissed for failure to exhaust the administrative EEOC process.

In *White v. Northern Michigan Regional Hospital* [659 F. Supp. 2d 858 (W.D. Mich. 2009)] a former employee of a hospital had filed charges with both the EEOC and the Michigan Department of Civil Rights alleging, among other things, Title VII discrimination. However, before the process was completed, the employee notified the Agency of her desire to withdraw the charge and pursue the matter in court. Although she had clearly filed charges with the EEOC, the EEOC process, which includes both investigation and attempts at conciliation, had not been exhausted and as such, the court found that she could not maintain her Title VII claim. The case was dismissed, albeit without prejudice to her later filing the claim, after the administrative process was exhausted.

The Supreme Court clarified to what extent acts of discrimination occurring before the 180- or 300-day requirement are actionable. In *National Railroad Passenger Corp. v. Morgan* [536 U.S. 101 (2002)], the Court held that, in a discrimination case, discrete acts of alleged discrimination that occurred more than 300 days before the charge was filed with the EEOC are not actionable. However, with respect to the claim of hostile work environment, to the extent that acts which occurred more than 300 days before the charge was filed with the EEOC were part of the same hostile work environment that occurred during the 300-day period, as alleged in the initial charge, those acts could be part of the claim. In *McIntire v. Tulsa County Sheriff* [121 Fed. Appx. 295 (10th Cir. 2005)], the court clarified the limits of the U.S. Supreme Court's *Morgan* decision. Although continuing violations may, in certain circumstances, allow conduct that occurs before the 300/180-day time period, nonetheless, if no allegations attendant to a claim occurred within the 300/180-day time period prior to the filing of an EEOC charge, the claim will be time barred. (See chapter 4 for a more detailed discussion of Title VII.)

Q 1:30　Is the 15-employee threshold for the application of Title VII jurisdictional?

The U.S. Supreme Court was asked to determine whether the 15 or more employee requirement of Title VII was jurisdictional or whether it is to be treated as an essential element of a plaintiff's Title VII claim. In *Arbaugh v. Y&H Corp.* [546 U.S. 500 (2006)], after exhaustively reviewing the statute, the court concluded that Congress did not intend to make the 15 or more employee requirement jurisdictional, but rather remain as an essential element of a Title VII case. As such, and although issues of jurisdiction are never waived, because the employer had not raised the lack of 15 or more employees as a defense to the claim in the court below, the court held that the defense was waived and could not form the basis of a dismissal of the case and the court held that the defense was remanded for further proceedings. The impact of *Arbaugh* is unclear, but it will be interesting to see how courts grapple with this ruling going forward. One point is certain, however, there will now be situations where employers with fewer than 15 employees are nonetheless held accountable for Title VII claims under the unique factual situations, such as the one found in Arbaugh. Expanding this concept to COBRA, the court in *Thomas v. Miller* [489 F.3d 293 (6th Cir. 2007)] concluded that likewise, under COBRA, the 20 or more employee threshold was not jurisdictional, such that an employer with less than 20 employees necessarily always fits within the small-employer exception. At issue was whether the employer, who had previously offered COBRA benefits to another employee despite the fact that the company had always maintained less than 20 employees, nonetheless was estopped from denying COBRA benefits to the former employee in the case at hand. The former employee based the estoppel claim on representations that she "overheard" between management and another former employee regarding the availability of COBRA benefits. Although recognizing that the doctrine of estoppel may, in certain circumstances, prevent an otherwise small employer from fitting within the small-employer exception under COBRA, the court nonetheless concluded that overhearing representations made to another employee was insufficient for purposes of maintaining an estoppel claim. As such, the employer could take full benefit of the small-employer exception under COBRA.

Q 1:31　Is Title VII applicable to religious institutions?

A number of courts have accepted what is commonly referred to as a ministerial exception to Title VII when the Constitution operates to bar a claim, the resolution of which would limit a religious institution's right to select or maintain those who perform spiritual functions. This doctrine was thoroughly explored in *Petruska v. Gannon University*. [462 F.3d 294 (3d Cir. 2006)] In *Petruska*, a former chaplain of a private Catholic college claimed her termination was, among other things, gender discrimination and retaliation in violation of Title VII. Recognizing other circuits that had adopted the ministerial exception, and recognizing that the plaintiff was the former chaplain for the private Catholic college, the court concluded that no Title VII claims could be pursued in this case.

Q 1:32   Is an adverse employment action required to maintain a Title VII claim?

Aside from Title VII claims predicated on harassment for hostile work environment, to maintain a prima facie case of discrimination under Title VII, the employee must demonstrate that he or she has suffered an adverse employment action as a result of the alleged discrimination. Courts have found adverse employment action in: (1) cases in which one of the employees' compensation, fringe benefits, or other financial terms of employment are diminished, including termination; (2) cases in which a nominally lateral transfer with no change in financial terms significantly reduces the employee's career prospects by preventing him or her from using his or her skills and experience, so that the skills are likely to atrophy and the career stunted as a result; and (3) cases in which the employee is not moved to a different job or the skill requirements of her present job altered, but the conditions in which he or she works are changed in a way that subjects him or her to a humiliating or degrading, unsafe, unhealthful or otherwise significantly negative alteration in his or her work environment. [*See* O'Neal v. City of Chicago, 393 F.3d 909 (7th Cir. 2004).] In *O'Neal*, a female police sergeant who was transferred from her position as administrative sergeant to beat sergeant brought an action against the City alleging gender and race discrimination in violation of Title VII, claiming the transfer to be an adverse employment action. After reviewing the differences between the two positions, the court concluded that it was a lateral job transfer; although it may result in de minimis changes to her job responsibilities and work conditions, it was not material enough to amount to an adverse employment action for which Title VII liability applies. However, if the changes to job responsibilities and work conditions are material, adverse employment action will be satisfied. In *Burlington Northern & Santa Fe Railroad Co. v. White* [126 S. Ct. 2405 (2006)], the U.S. Supreme Court concluded that adverse employment action had been demonstrated when the plaintiff's job duties were changed to less favorable duties, and when the plaintiff was suspended without pay for 37 days, despite the fact that she was thereafter reinstated with full back pay. As to the suspension, the court opined that having an employee on suspension without pay for a month, in and of itself, may be sufficiently material to satisfy the adverse employment action requirement for Title VII claims, even if the employee is thereafter reinstated with full back pay. In *Holland v. Gee* [No. 8:08-cv-2458-T-33AEP, 2011 WL 940291 (N.D. Fla. Mar. 17, 2011)], the court held that the reassignment of a pregnant employee to a more menial position because of concerns related to the pregnancy, no matter how well intentioned, cannot justify differential treatment. Although the reassignment from a technician position to the so-called "Help Desk" did not affect the pregnant employee's pay, nonetheless, because it was viewed as a "demotion," in that the position had significantly less responsibility and more menial tasks than the technician position, the reassignment could be viewed as an adverse action supporting a claim of discrimination under the PDA. However, in *Vance v. Ball State University* [646 F.3d 461 (7th Cir. 2011)], the court held that providing a verbal warning to a food-service employee based on complaints from co-workers was not sufficiently material to constitute an adverse employment action.

Oftentimes employers believe that if an employee quits his or her employment, there would be no adverse employment action and the employer cannot be held liable for the separation of employment under Title VII. Although this may be the case for a true voluntary quit situation, under the doctrine of constructive discharge, if the employee's decision to resign is due to working conditions that have become so intolerable that a reasonable person in the employee's position would have felt compelled to resign, the resignation will be treated as a formal discharge for Title VII purposes. As the U.S. Supreme Court stated in *Pennsylvania State Police v. Sueters* [124 S. Ct. 2342 (2004)], under the doctrine of constructive discharge, "an employee's reasonable decision to resign because of unendurable working conditions is assimilated to a formal discharge for remedial purposes." [124 S. Ct. at 2351] As such, in *Robinson v. Waste Management of Texas* [122 Fed. Appx. 756 (5th Cir. 2004)], when a former employee, claiming gender discrimination, quit her employment because she merely felt "frustrated" after being passed over for promotion, the court held that the constructive discharge claim could not stand.

Q 1:33   Is sexual harassment prohibited by Title VII?

Sexual harassment is sex discrimination in violation of Section 703 of Title VII. Section 1604.11(a) of the EEOC's "Guideline on Discrimination Because of Sex" defines *sexual harassment* as follows:

> Unwelcome sexual advances, request for sexual favors, and other verbal or physical conduct of a sexual nature constitutes sexual harassment when:
>
> - Submission to such conduct is made either explicitly or implicitly a term or condition of an individual's employment; or
>
> - Submission to or rejection of such conduct by an individual is used as the basis for employment decisions affecting such individual; or
>
> - Such conduct has the purpose or effect of unreasonably interfering with an individual's work performance or creating an intimidating, hostile, or offensive work environment.

Q 1:34   Have there been any developments in the area of sexual harassment law?

The area of sexual harassment continues to be subject to constant change and development. Although the EEOC has long maintained that a man as well as a woman may be a victim of sexual harassment and a woman, as well as a man, may be the harasser, so-called same-sex harassment cases have divided many courts. Some courts have maintained that because sexual harassment is a form of gender discrimination, same-sex harassment is not actionable under Title VII. Other courts have argued that there is no logical reason to deny relief to somebody who is harassed by somebody of the same gender, as opposed to someone of the opposite gender. In *Oncale v. Sundowner Offshore Services, Inc.* [523 U.S. 75 (1998)], the U.S. Supreme Court resolved this dispute by allowing claims of same-sex sexual harassment.

The U.S. Supreme Court, in the companion cases of *Burlington Industries, Inc. v. Ellerth* [524 U.S. 775 (1998)] and *Faragher v. City of Boca Raton* [542 U.S. 775 (1998)], provided further guidance on the issue of employer liability for a supervisor's harassment, holding that an employer is vicariously liable for sexual harassment by a supervisor, subject only to an affirmative defense if the employer can demonstrate that the victim failed to take reasonable advantage of the employer's policies and procedures aimed at preventing and correcting harassment, in the instances where no tangible job detriment has been suffered.

In *Cherry v. Menard Inc.* [101 F. Supp. 2d 1160 (N.D. Iowa, 2000)], a federal district court in Iowa held that a tangible job detriment can be maintained in situations where an employee quits his or her job, but the circumstances are so intolerable as to amount to a constructive discharge. [*See* "Constructive Discharge Is Tangible Action in Sexual Harassment Case, Court Decides," 15 *Employment Discrimination Report (EDR)* (BNA) 76 (July 19, 2000).] In *Suders v. Easton* [325 F.3d 432 (3d Cir. 2003)], the Third Circuit followed *Cherry*, holding that constructive discharge is tantamount to a discharge such that it is to be treated as a tangible adverse employment action.

Since the *Ellerth* and *Faragher* decisions, employers, mindful of the requirements enunciated in these cases, need to undertake efforts to prevent and correct harassment for purposes of maintaining the affirmative defense. Typically, such measures include publication of a sexual harassment policy with a complaint procedure, training supervisors and other employees regarding sexual harassment, encouraging the internal reporting of complaints where harassment is thought to occur, investigating complaints of harassment, and taking appropriate remedial measures. Now, more than ever, employers need to understand the necessity to educate, encourage, and investigate complaints of harassment, lest an employer's failure to take appropriate preventative and corrective action erodes the ability of the employer to take full advantage of the affirmative defense. (See chapter 4 for more recent decisions and other developments.)

In both the *Ellerth* and *Faragher* decisions, the Court reiterated language from earlier decisions that harassment is actionable only if it is so "severe or pervasive" as to "alter the conditions" of the employee's employment and create an "abusive working environment." [*See Faragher*, 524 U.S. at 786, and *Ellerth*, 524 U.S. at 752.] In a retaliation case, the U.S. Supreme Court ruled that a single isolated incident wherein a supervisor read aloud a comment made by an applicant in a report, "I hear making love to you is like making love to the Grand Canyon," was such that "no reasonable person could have believed that the single incident recounted above violated Title VII's Standard." [Clark Cnty. Sch. Dist. v. Breeden, 532 U.S. 268, 271 (2001)]

Similarly, in *Walpole v. City of Mesa* [162 Fed. Appx. 715 (9th Cir. 2006)], the court held that an employee's romantic interest in a co-employee after a nine-month friendship (culminating in hand holding, professed love, and a request for a kiss that was refused), coupled with staring, was not sufficiently severe or pervasive to amount to sexual harassment.

As to the issue of retaliation, although the court held that a hospital could not avoid liability for the alleged harassment of a nurse because the alleged harasser was a physician independent contractor, the physician's alleged conduct of making nasty and uncivil remarks to the nurse in an attempt to persuade the nurse to drop her complaint of harassment was not an adverse employment action necessary to maintain a retaliation claim against her employer. [Dunn v. Washington Cnty. Hosp., 429 F.3d 689 (7th Cir. 2003)]

Sometimes employers are reluctant to take claims of harassment seriously when the complaints involve the conduct and behavior of customers and clients. For example, in *Pickett v. Sheridan Health Care Center* [610 F.3d 434 (7th Cir. 2010)], a nursing home nurse complained that she was being subjected to harassment by nursing home residents. However, because it involved its clients, the employer was unwilling to take the claims seriously and did not take appropriate action. In the case, the jury verdict award of $15,000 in compensatory damages and $50,000 in punitive damages was upheld by the Seventh Circuit. In *EEOC v. Karenkim, Inc.* [698 F.3d 92 (2d Cir. 2012)], the court held that a grocery store manager that subjected teenage female-store employees to a continuous barrage of sexual comments and innuendos, and consistently touched, massaged, or engaged in other inappropriate personal contact with the females, which the employer did nothing to correct after notice, was sufficiently severe and pervasive to not only support a jury verdict in excess of $1 million dollars against the employer, but also the court held, the issuance of an injunction ensuring that the store manager would not be in a position to sexually harass the employees in the future.

Q 1:35 Are damages for lost future wages subject to statutory caps under the 1991 amendments to Title VII?

With respect to issues involving damages and the utilization of the caps under Title VII discussed in chapter 4, the U.S. Supreme Court was asked to determine in *Pollard v. E.I. du Pont de Nemours & Co.* [532 U.S. 843 (2001)] whether front pay compensation for future lost wages attributable to a termination was compensatory damages subject to the statutory cap for such damages under Section 1981(a) of 42 U.S.C., or whether it was relief that was otherwise available under Title VII before the 1991 Act's amendment and therefore not subject to the caps contained in Section 1981 in the 1991 Act's amendments. The Supreme Court, in an 8-0 decision, after reviewing relief awardable under Title VII before the 1991 amendments, and relief specifically added to Title VII with the 1991 amendments subject to the statutory caps, concluded that the front pay was in essence pay in lieu of reinstatement, which was authorized by Title VII before the 1991 amendments, and therefore was not subject to the statutory cap for the additional remedies provided in the Act's 1991 amendments. [42 U.S.C. § 1981 (a)]

Q 1:36   Does Title VII prevent retaliation?

Section 704 of Title VII [42 U.S.C. § 2000e-3(a)] makes it unlawful for an employer to discriminate against any employee for either of the following reasons:

- Opposition to any practice made an unlawful employment practice by this subchapter (Title VII); or
- A charge, testimony, assistance, or participation in any manner in an investigation, proceeding, or hearing under Title VII.

Title VII retaliation claims have been picking up steam over recent years, protecting individuals who have opposed unlawful activity or participated in Title VII claims, even though the individuals themselves were not the victims of the alleged unlawful conduct that resulted in opposition or participation. For example, an individual who complains to management about the sexual harassment of another employee would be protected from an adverse employment action resulting from that complaint about the alleged unlawful conduct. As employers adopt and disseminate policies encouraging employees to come forward and report claims of sexual harassment or other unlawful activity, the retaliation provisions of Title VII will come into play more frequently. As a result, the number of claims under Title VII retaliation provisions and comparable claims under analogous state civil rights law statutes are expected to increase. Responding to the increase of activity in this area, in May 1998, the EEOC issued its "Guidance on Investigating, Analyzing Retaliation" claims. [12 *Employment Discrimination Report (EDR)* (BNA) 317 (Mar. 3, 1999)] According to the EEOC's charge and litigation statistics through Fiscal Year 2000, retaliation claims under Title VII have risen steadily, comprising 24.7 percent of overall changes in Fiscal Year 2000, from just 14.4 percent of overall changes in Fiscal Year 1993. [16 *Employment Discrimination Report (EDR)* (BNA) 99 (Jan. 17, 2001)] Fiscal Year 2001 showed a leveling off of Title VII retaliation claims with the EEOC reporting a slight decrease from Fiscal Year 2000. [17 *Employment Discrimination Report (EDR)* (BNA) 677 (Dec. 12, 2001)] For Fiscal Year 2002, Title VII retaliation claims reportedly edged up to prior levels, comprising 24.6 percent of overall charges (20,814 retaliation claims and total charges of 84,442). [20 *Employment Discrimination Report (EDR)* (BNA) 106 (Jan. 15, 2003)] According to the EEOC's Web site [http://www.eeoc.gov], Title VII retaliation claims totaled 20,615 in Fiscal Year 2003 and 20,240 in Fiscal Year 2004, comprising about 25 percent of overall charges for both years. In Fiscal Years 2005 and 2006, Title VII retaliation claims increased slightly to 25.8 percent of total charges filed. In Fiscal Year 2007, Title VII retaliation claims totaled 23,371, comprising 28.3 percent of total charges filed. In Fiscal Year 2008, Title VII retaliation claims totaled 28,698, comprising 30.1 percent of total charges filed. In Fiscal Year 2009, Title VII retaliation claims totaled 28,948, comprising 31 percent of all charges filed, a 5 percent increase since 2004. In Fiscal Year 2011, retaliation claims totaled 99,947 charges, 37.4 percent of all charges filed.

There are limitations to retaliation claims, however. The U.S. Supreme Court held that employee complaints regarding a single isolated incident which was neither severe nor persuasive cannot form the basis of a retaliation claim when "no reasonable person could have believed that the single incident violated Title VII's standards." [Clark Cnty. Sch. Dist. v. Breeden, 532 U.S. 268, 271 (2001)]

Q 1:37   Is discrimination based on sexual orientation prohibited under civil rights employment law?

Laws protecting employees from discrimination based on sexual orientation, although increasing in number, are receiving mixed support. Currently, sexual orientation is not specifically protected under federal civil rights laws; however, in May 1998, President Clinton signed an executive order, amending Executive Order 11478, which prohibits discrimination in the federal government's civilian workforce on the basis of sexual orientation. A similar executive order was signed by Houston Mayor Lee Brown in 1998 that bans discrimination based on sexual orientation in municipal government. [See 10 Employment Discrimination Report (EDR) (BNA) 246 (Feb. 25, 1998).] On December 11, 2000, outgoing Delaware Governor, Tom Carper, signed an executive order banning sexual orientation discrimination within the executive branch of Delaware. [16 Employment Discrimination Report (EDR) (BNA) 16 (Jan. 3, 2001)] According to a study published by the Government Accountability Office (GAO), in 2001, 12 states (California, Connecticut, Hawaii, Maryland, Massachusetts, Minnesota, Nevada, New Hampshire, New Jersey, Rhode Island, Vermont, and Wisconsin) and the District of Columbia had passed laws prohibiting discrimination on the basis of sexual orientation. [See GAO-02-665R, Sexual-Orientation-Based Employment Discrimination.] Contrary to the concerns of some commentators, the GAO report analyzed data concerning sexual orientation discrimination charges filed with state agencies and did not find an explosion of claims in those states that have extended protection for sexual orientation. [16 Employment Discrimination Report (EDR) (BNA) 585 (Mar. 28, 2001)] The Employment Non-Discrimination Act, a federal bill first introduced some time ago, prohibits discrimination based on sexual orientation. It has been reintroduced many times since, but to date, has not been passed.

According to the National Gay and Lesbian Task Force (http://www.ngltf. org), 21 states (California, Colorado, Connecticut, Delaware, Hawaii, Illinois, Iowa, Maine, Maryland, Massachusetts, Minnesota, New Hampshire, New

Jersey, New Mexico, New York, Nevada, Oregon, Rhode Island, Vermont, Washington and Wisconsin) and the District of Columbia currently have state laws banning discrimination based on sexual orientation.

Although sexual orientation is not a protected category under Title VII, discrimination based on sexual stereotypes may lie if a company discriminates against a homosexual employee because he or she does not conform to gender stereotypes. In *Koren v. Ohio Bell Telephone Co.* [2012 WL 3484825 (N.D. Ohio Aug. 14, 2012)], a homosexual male claimed he was terminated for failing to conform to gender stereotypes because, contrary to gender norms, he had taken his spouse's surname. However, the court concluded that there were sufficient issues of fact precluding summary judgment on the issues. In *Hunter v. United Parcel Service, Inc.* [697 F.3d 697 (8th Cir. 2012)], a transgender applicant claimed that he was not hired because he was transgendered, but could not maintain a claim under Title VII when there was no evidence that the employer was aware of his transgendered status.

Q 1:38   What is the *Equal Pay Act?*

An amendment to the FLSA, the *EPA* [Pub. L. No. 88-38] requires that male and female employees who perform the same work for the same employer receive the same rate of pay.

Q 1:39   Are there any exceptions to the rule that male and female employees receive equal pay for equal work?

There are several exceptions. An employer may pay one employee more than another for the same work based on greater productivity or seniority. In addition, if a company has more than one facility and its operations are in different labor markets, wages may vary to reflect labor supply and demand.

Under the so-called "ministerial" exception, civil employment laws, including the EPA, do not apply to claims of ministers and other church employees who serve in a position that is important to the spiritual and pastoral mission of the church. [*See* 42 U.S.C. § 2000e and Rayburn v. Gen. Conference of Seventh-Day Adventists, 772 F.2d 1164, 1159 (4th Cir. 1985).] As such, the Tenth Circuit held that a minister's claim under the EPA was barred by the ministerial exception barring claims by a minister concerning the functions that accompanied her selection, which includes her claims under the EPA. [Skrzypczak v. Roman Catholic Dioceses of Tulsa, 611 F.3d 1238 (10th Cir. 2010)]

Q 1:40   How do you determine whether a violation of the EPA has occurred?

To determine whether a violation under the EPA has occurred, a court must analyze the job duties and responsibilities of the positions at issue to determine if they are the same thereby warranting the same pay. In *Brickey v. Employers Reassurance Corp.* [293 F. Supp. 2d 1227 (D. Kan. 2003)], a municipal bond portfolio manager claimed that her employer violated the EPA by paying a male municipal bond portfolio manager substantially more money for substantially equal work. The company claimed that although both the female claimant and her male counterpart were both municipal bond portfolio managers, the male employee had materially different job responsibilities warranting the difference in pay. Specifically, the company claimed that the male employee retained managerial and supervisory responsibilities that his female counterpart did not have, and that the male employee managed larger municipal bond portfolio bond assets and generated greater revenues than his female counterpart. In addition, the company pointed to other factors aside from sex to explain the disparity, including the male portfolio manager's prior salary at a previous company, his reputation, and his experience. Based on these factors, the company moved for summary disposition, but the court, in analyzing both the pay differential and duties and responsibilities of both employees, concluded that there remained genuine issues of fact to be resolved by a jury and denied the company's motion for summary judgment. Specifically, the court noted that, even prior to assuming supervisory responsibilities, the male counterpart received bonuses and compensation well in excess of the female manager, and during testimony, a company manager refused to state that there was any direct correlation between an employee's salary and the value of an employee's portfolio. In a similar case, the court in *Schimek v. MCI, Inc.* [3:05-CV-0045-P, 2006 U.S. Dist. LEXIS 54747 (N.D. Tex. Aug. 7, 2006)] held that two jobs having merely the same job titles with pay disparities is insufficient to maintain a claim for violation of the EPA. Rather, one must analyze the job and work itself to determine whether in fact the positions are comparable for purposes of EPA analysis. In *Westrich-James v. Dallas Morning News, Inc.* [2012 WL 4068982 (N.D. Tex. Sept. 17, 2012)], a manager of a news program claimed that her employer had violated the EPA by not paying her as much as two other managers for the news organization. However, finding that the male employees worked in different geographic zones involving substantially different responsibilities, the court held that the claim could not be maintained because plaintiff had not shown that the male employees' jobs were comparable to hers in accordance with the EPA.

A determination of whether the EPA has been violated necessarily requires a comparative analysis of at least two positions in the company. As demonstrated above, position titles are less important than the actual work that the individual and the individual's counterpart actually performed. This point was well made when a female employee sued her prior employer claiming violations of Kentucky's EPA, whose language is similar to the federal EPA. Although the female employee claimed that she performed work equal to that of male employees at the office—and was paid substantially less—the court concluded that the position she assumed, environmental specialist, was a new position at the company. No other employee performed the work she did, and as a result, she could not establish a prima facie claim for a violation of the EPA. As the court stated: "Admittedly, the circumstances [no comparables] make allegations of an equal pay violation difficult to sustain." [Wiseman v. Whayne Supply Co., 359 F. Supp. 2d 579 (W.D. Ky. 2004)] Similarly, in *Vasquez v. El Paso*

Community College District [177 Fed. Appx. 422 (5th Cir. Tex. 2006)], an employee who had a unique position in the library department was not able to establish a violation of the EPA due to a lack of comparables in the department. However, the determination of whether teachers with different certificates could be considered comparables in connection with the analysis of an EPA claim was determined by the court, in *Heller v. Elizabeth Forward School District* [182 Fed. Appx. 91 (3d Cir. 2006)], to be a factual issue that must be determined by the jury.

Following the termination of a male bank vice president, a female cashier was promoted to a position of vice president. However, she was not paid as much as the other male vice presidents at the company and filed a claim under the EPA. In comparing her job responsibilities, as opposed to job title, with other vice presidents, the court concluded that although she assumed various duties of the male vice president that she replaced, she did not have the responsibilities of the other vice presidents or her predecessor warranting equal pay. Although she claimed, "If someone is going to be promoted to the title of vice president, they should have sufficient duties and responsibilities to warrant a vice president's pay," the court concluded that job titles and job classifications are not dispositive and ultimately the actual responsibilities and work in the positions will be examined to determine whether there has been a violation of the EPA. Not surprisingly, the court affirmed summary judgment on this issue. [Tenkku v. Normandy Bank, 348 F.3d 737, 741 (8th Cir. 2003)]

The importance of analyzing the actual work and duties performed, as opposed to a position or even written job descriptions was highlighted in *Horn v. University of Minnesota*. [362 F.3d 1042 (8th Cir. 2004)] In that case, the University posted openings for an "Assistant Women's Ice Hockey" position, and two employees were hired for the positions—a man and a woman. The positions had identical job descriptions and titles in their contracts with the University. However, the male coach position paid $2,000 a month while the female coach received $3,000 a month. Despite the identical job descriptions in the posting and contracts, the court analyzed the two positions and concluded that the female assistant coach performed duties significantly in excess of those of the male assistant coach. The female coach, in addition to administrative duties the male coach performed, also performed significant public relations duties for which she had prior skill and experience and which the court concluded prevented the two positions from being "substantially equal" under the EPA. A top-level executive claimed that disparities in pay between her and other top-level executives was in violation of the EPA. However, the employer successfully argued that the pay differential was based on factors other than sex, in accordance with the company's top-level executive ranking system, which provided for differentials based on such factors as experience, training ability, and attainment of objectives. [Gaujacq v. EDF, Inc., 601 F.3d 565 (D.C. Cir. 2010)]

Although wage discrepancies can be based on differentials in pay between current employees and an employee and his or her predecessor, EPA claims can also be based upon wage discrepancies between an employee and his or her successor.

In *Dixon v. University of Toledo* [638 F. Supp. 2d 847 (N.D. Ohio 2009)], a former university employee claimed a violation of the EPA when her replacement was paid more than she was paid when she performed the job. Although not previously ruled on by the Sixth Circuit, the court concluded that the EPA does allow claims based on differentials in a successor's pay.

It is important to note that when wages are compared to determine whether there is in fact a wage disparity under the EPA, courts generally review all forms of remuneration received by the parties for purposes of making the comparison. For example, in *Ghirardo v. University of Southern California* [156 Fed. Appx. 914 (9th Cir. 2005)], the employee claimed that her annual raises were less than those of her male colleagues performing similar work. However, the court concluded that she failed to show that her total compensation was less than the average compensation earned by her male colleagues who performed substantially equal work, and entered summary judgment in favor of the University. [*See also* 29 C.F.R. § 1620.10, which defines wages to include "all payments" made to the employee as remuneration for employment, and all forms of compensation.]

Q 1:41   Do employers have affirmative defenses to EPA claims?

Even if a plaintiff can establish a prima facie case under the EPA, the employer can defeat the EPA claim if the employer can demonstrate that the pay differential is justified for one of the following reasons:

1. A seniority system;
2. A merit system;
3. A system based on quantity or quality of production; or
4. Any factor other than gender. [29 U.S.C. § 206 (d)(1)].

In *Harrison-Pepper v. Miami Univ.* [103 Fed. Appx. 596 (6th Cir. Ohio 2004)], a university professor claimed a violation of the EPA based on the pay differential between her and other male university professors, she being the lowest paid of the eight full professors in her department. Although the pay differential was clear, the court found that the university sufficiently explained the disparity based on its justification for pay differences based on its merit-based system of awarding raises. Although the system was somewhat subjective, the court concluded that the university's reliance on the university professor's extended absences in determining her raises was sufficient justification to legitimize the disparities between her salary and that of her male counterparts. Similarly, in *Reznick v. Associated Orthopedics & Sports Medicine, PA* [104 Fed. Appx. 387 (5th Cir. Tex. 2004)], the court was asked to determine whether or not the clinic had a legitimate reason for the pay discrepancy between two orthopedic surgeons—a male and female—working at a clinic. Even assuming that the jobs were substantially similar, the court noted that it was undisputed that the male orthopedic surgeon generated nearly twice the revenue as the female orthopedic surgeon, and as a result, the employer satisfied its affirmative defense demonstrating that the disparity in earnings was a reflection of the male surgeon's "quantity or quality" of production.

Use of the affirmative defense to justify pay differentials on factors other than sex requires more than merely articulating a legitimate non-discriminatory reason for the differential, but rather, the employer bears the burden of proving that the pay differential was based on a factor other than sex.

In *Drum v. Leeson Electric Corp.* [565 F.3d 1071 (8th Cir. 2009)], a female employee brought an action against her employer under the EPA alleging that her male replacement earned significantly more than she did when she performed the job. Although the company argued various "market force theories" to articulate why the replacement was paid more than the female employee, they could not point to any factor other than gender to substantiate a discrepancy, such that the employer's motion for summary disposition was denied. In *Mallison v. Haworth, Inc.* [488 Fed. Appx. 88 (6th Cir. Mich. 2012)], the court found that discrepancies in pay between a female employee and other male employees was due to differences in supervisory and manufacturing experience, and not illegal discrimination under the EPA as alleged. Similarly, a female professor at the University of Texas claimed violations of the EPA in connection with the discrepancies between her pay and other male professors at the university, but the court found that the discrepancy in pay was attributable to factors other than gender, including seniority. [*Suter v. University of Tex. at San Antonio*, 859 F. Supp. 2d 851 (W.D. Tex. 2012)]

Q 1:42 What is *Executive Order 11246?*

Executive Order 11246 prohibits discrimination against an employee or applicant for employment on the basis of race, color, religion, sex, or national origin by federal contractors and subcontractors, and it requires the contractors and subcontractors to take affirmative action to ensure that employees and applicants are treated without regard to race, color, religion, sex, or national origin. The order applies to any contractor or subcontractor that performs government contracts or federally assisted construction contracts that total at least $10,000 in any 12-month period. In addition, it requires non-construction federal contractors with 50 or more employees and contractors with federal contracts in excess of $50,000 to develop written affirmative action plans. Generally, an affirmative action plan under Executive Order 11246 must:

- Identify the employees of the workforce by race, national origin, and sex.
- Group the workforce by job title or job;
- Determine whether minorities or women are being underutilized in any group in relationship to their availability;
- Establish specific goals and timetables to correct a situation in which minorities or women are being under-utilized; and
- Compile and maintain data to log the contractor's progress with respect to achieving its goals.

Executive Order 11246 is enforced through the Office of Federal Contractor Compliance Programs (OFCCP), which requires covered employers to file the standard Form 100 (EEO-1) annually. In addition, covered contractors and subcontractors must report their compliance with Executive Order 11246 in the course of bidding for federal contracts. If violations are found that cannot be corrected according to the conciliation procedures, the OFCCP can impose such penalties and sanctions as injunctions against violations and compensatory damages (including back pay). In addition, the OFCCP can cancel or suspend a contractor's or subcontractor's contract or declare the contractor or subcontractor ineligible to receive future federal contracts for a period of time.

Q 1:43   What is the *Age Discrimination in Employment Act?*

The *Age Discrimination in Employment Act (ADEA)* [29 U.S.C. § 621] prohibits employers from discriminating against employees 40 years of age or older. Age is unique among the categories protected against discrimination under federal law in that it is the most universal. Consequently, Congress seems to have considered it inappropriate to include age under Title VII. Rather, the ADEA is closely tied, in its rights and remedies, to the FLSA. As the U.S. Supreme Court held in *Gross v. FBL Financial Services, Inc.* [129 S. Ct. 2343 (2009)], to maintain an ADEA claim, the employee must demonstrate that the employer took adverse action "because of age" and that "age" was the reason that the employer decided to act. As such, although stray comments may demonstrate that age may have been a motivating factor in an adverse employment decision, such stray comments will typically be insufficient for purposes of maintaining an ADEA claim. A 68-year-old attorney who applied for an in-house legal position with a company claimed that he was denied the position in violation of the ADEA. He claimed, among other things, that the employer indicated that she was searching for a lawyer at a "more junior level." The court found that this comment, in and of itself, was not evidence of age discrimination, but rather, was focused on the level of employee and experience that the company was looking for, and held that this comment was not probative of the employer's discriminatory intent. [Moss v. MBC Software, Inc., 610 F.3d 917 (5th Cir. 2010)] Likewise, a supervisor's reference to a candidate reinstated by a company as "this young man" did not raise an inference of discrimination against an older employee who was not reinstated. [Medlock v. United Parcel Serv., Inc., 608 F.3d 1185 (10th Cir. 2010)] An employee claimed that she was not promoted to a position with her employer due to age discrimination claiming, among other things, that one of the decision makers indicated the need to fill the position with "new blood." Finding that the person who was ultimately chosen for the position was more experienced than the plaintiff, and had performed better during the interview process, the court held that the phrase "new blood" was too ambiguous to demonstrate age animus. [Velazquez-Ortiz v. Vilsack, 657 F.3d 64 (1st Cir. 2011)] A supervisor's stray remark that he was eager for several older workers to retire and facts indicating only "bad blood" between the supervisor and the employee were not sufficient to maintain an ADEA claim alleging that a demotion was because of age. [*Vasbinder v. Secretary Dep't of Veterans Affairs*, 487 Fed. Appx. 746 (3d. Cir. 2012)]

Q 1:44   Does the ADEA protect younger workers ages 40 and older from reverse discrimination?

The U.S. Supreme Court, in a case of first impression, concluded that the ADEA does not protect younger workers, ages 40–49, from so-called reverse discrimination. Reviewing the ADEA's text, structure, purpose, history and relationships to other federal statutes, the Court concluded that the ADEA was enacted to protect older workers against younger workers, and not to protect younger workers against older workers, even though the younger workers are 40 or older, the threshold criterion for applicability of the ADEA. In the case before the Court, it was the younger workers, those between ages 40–49, who claimed discrimination on the basis of the older workers, ages 50 and older, receiving full retirement benefits which were being eliminated for the younger workers. This type of disparate treatment was not, the Supreme Court concluded, discrimination which the ADEA intended to prohibit. [General Dynamics Sys., Inc. v. Cline, 540 U.S. 581 (2004)]

Q 1:45   What are the differences in how Title VII and the ADEA are enforced?

Because the ADEA is related to the FLSA and is not directly derived from Title VII, it differs from Title VII in several important substantive and procedural ways. First, an individual filing a complaint with the EEOC under Title VII must obtain a 90-day "letter to sue" from the agency before taking a case to federal court. The ADEA complainant must wait only 60 days after filing a complaint with the EEOC before filing suit in federal court without the agency's permission. The discrimination victim filing under Title VII does not encounter a statute of limitations until the EEOC issues a letter to sue, which may be long after the complaint is filed. The statute of limitations for the ADEA complainant begins, however, on the date of the discriminatory act (e.g., termination of employment). The FLSA's procedures, including its statute of limitations, thus govern actions under the ADEA.

Q 1:46   Have there been amendments to the ADEA?

Yes. In 1990, Congress passed and the president signed the Older Workers Benefit Protection Act, in response to a Supreme Court decision that outraged many members of Congress and segments of their constituencies. In *Public Employees Retirement System of Ohio v. Betts* [492 U.S. 158 (1989)], the Supreme Court held that the ADEA did not forbid age discrimination in the area of employee benefits, except in unusual circumstances.

The Older Workers Benefit Protection Act amended the ADEA and expressly rejected the Supreme Court's controversial *Betz* decision by defining "compensation, terms, conditions or privileges of employment" in the ADEA as including all employee benefits, even those provided under a bona fide employee benefit plan. Consequently, Section (a)(1) of the ADEA now forbids discrimination in employee benefits as well as in every other aspect of employment not protected by some specific exemption.

In addition, the Older Workers Benefit Protection Act provides rules for determining whether a waiver of an age claim is enforceable. This issue arises frequently when an employer attempts to obtain a release or waiver in exchange for consideration in the event of a reduction or reorganization of a workforce. To be enforceable, a waiver must comply with the following:

- The individual must be given 21 days to consider the waiver agreement;
- The individual must be provided seven days to revoke the waiver agreement after signature;
- The agreement must be written in plain, understandable English;
- The individual must be advised, in writing, to consult legal counsel; and
- The release must specifically refer to a waiver of rights or claims under the ADEA.

In addition, if the waiver agreement is offered to a group or class of employees, the employer must provide at least 45 days for the group to consider the agreement, and comply with the informational requirements of the ADEA, which require the employer to provide written information to the individual as to:

- Any class, unit, or group of individuals covered by the program and eligibility factors and time limits applicable to the program; and
- The job titles and ages of all individuals eligible or selected for the program and the job titles and ages of all individuals in the same job classification or organizational unit who were not eligible or selected for the program.

Q 1:47   What federal antidiscrimination laws apply to handicapped individuals?

The Rehabilitation Act of 1973 [29 U.S.C. §§ 791 *et seq.*], prohibits employment discrimination based on a handicap against persons otherwise qualified to perform a job. It applies to all federal employees, federal contractors, and anyone receiving federal financial assistance. The ADA [42 U.S.C. §§ 12101 *et seq.*] expands the scope of the Rehabilitation Act to include most employers. The ADA became effective for employers with 25 or more employees on July 26, 1992, and applied to employers with 15 to 24 employees as of July 26, 1994. In addition, Title III of the ADA, which concerns access to public accommodations, became effective January 26, 1992, for older facilities and on January 26, 1993, for new construction.

Q 1:48   What is the *ADA*?

The *ADA* [42 U.S.C. §§ 12101 *et seq.*] prohibits discrimination against qualified individuals with disabilities in all aspects of the employment process. The ADA applies to employees with 15 or more employees, including part-time employees, for 20 or more weeks in the current or preceding year. The employment process includes, but is not limited to: job application procedures; hiring; advancement; discharge; compensation; job training; recruitment and advertising; job assignments; job classifications; organizational structures; position descriptions; lines of progression; seniority lists; leaves of absence; sick leave; fringe benefits available by virtue of employment (whether or not administered by the employer); employer-sponsored activities (including social or recreational programs); and other terms, conditions, and privileges of employment.

In addition, the ADA prohibits pre-employment inquiries into an applicant's medical condition, provides that an employer must not conduct medical examinations of applicants until after a bone fide offer of employment is made, and requires reasonable accommodation by the employer so that qualified employees with a disability can perform their essential job functions.

Q 1:49   How can a claim of discrimination be maintained under the ADA?

A prima facie case of discrimination under the ADA can be maintained if the employee can demonstrate that (1) the employee is disabled within the meaning of the ADA; (2) the employee is qualified and able to perform the essential functions of the job with or without reasonable accommodation; and (3) the employee was terminated or not hired because of the employee's disability. [White v. York Int'l Corp., 45 F.3d 357, 360–61 (10th Cir. 1995)] To be disabled under the ADA, the individual must have a physical or mental impairment that substantially limits one or more major life activities, a record of such an impairment, or been regarded as having such an impairment. [42 U.S.C. § 12102(2)]

Once a prima facie case can be maintained, the burden shifts to the employer to articulate a legitimate non-discriminatory reason for the adverse employment action at issue. [Castaneda v. East Otero Sch. Dist. R-1, 2005 U.S. Dist. LEXIS 40026 (D. Colo. Dec. 1, 2005)] Once a legitimate non-discriminatory reason is articulated, it is incumbent upon the plaintiff to demonstrate that the employer's proffered non-discriminatory reason for the adverse employment action is really a pretext for discrimination. As in *Castaneda,* if the employee is able to raise evidence that casts doubt or raises questions as to the legitimacy or validity of the employer's proffered reasons for the adverse employment action, the case will then typically survive summary disposition and proceed to trial. [*See also* Smith v. Dist. of Columbia, 430 F.3d 450 (D.C. Cir. 2005).]

Q 1:50   How do you determine whether somebody is "disabled" under the ADA?

The threshold issue in any ADA case is whether the individual is, has a history of, or is regarded as being disabled. To be disabled, an individual must have, have a history of, or be regarded as having a physical or mental impairment that substantially limits one or more major life activity. [42 U.S.C. § 12102(2)(A)] Even if an individual has a recognized "impairment," if it does not substantially limit one or more major life activities, it will not be sufficient to qualify as a disability under the ADA.

Q 1:51   Can side effects of medical treatment constitute a disability?

Subject to limitations, side effects from medical treatment may themselves constitute an impairment protectable under the ADA, even though the underlying condition is not itself a disability. As the court stated in *Sulima v. Tobyhanna Army Depot* [602 F.3d 177 (3d Cir. 2010)], side effects may constitute a disability if:

1. The treatment was required;

2. The treatment was not just an attractive option; and

3. The treatment was not required solely in anticipation of an impairment resulting from plaintiff's voluntary choices.

Q 1:52   How is the ADA enforced?

Title I of the ADA incorporates the powers, remedies, and procedures set forth in the Civil Rights Act of 1964. The EEOC enforces the Act. The ADA provides that the powers and procedures available to persons discriminated against because of disability be the same as, and parallel to, those available to persons discriminated against because of race, color, religion, gender, or national origin. In addition, the ADA contains broad obligations as it relates to an employer's duty to accommodate qualified individuals with disabilities. Successful plaintiffs suing under the ADA may receive compensatory or punitive damages in some circumstances.

Q 1:53   Has the interpretation of the ADA evolved since its passage?

Although the ADA was unchanged from its passage until the amendments in 2008 under the ADAAA, the ADA evolved through the years with respect to its interpretation and applicability. A growing trend, which began as early as 1993, was for federal courts to apply a so-called "medicated" standard to determine whether a person is a qualified individual with a disability, entitled to protection against discrimination under the ADA. By using a medicated, as opposed to non-medicated, standard, an individual with a medical condition who with medication can substantially perform major life functions is not protected from discrimination under the ADA. A growing number of courts appeared to be accepting the medicated standard approach. In the long-awaited companion decisions of *Sutton v. United Air Lines, Inc.* [527 U.S. 471 (1999)] and *Murphy v. United Parcel Services, Inc.* [527 U.S. 516 (1999)], the Supreme Court held that mitigating measures an employee takes, both positive and negative (such as drug therapy and other corrective measures), must be taken into consideration when analyzing whether an individual is disabled (whether the mental or physical impairment substantially limits a major life activity), and therefore entitled to protection under the ADA.

The Supreme Court also reaffirmed the EEOC's long-stated position that individuals who are not actually disabled may nonetheless be protected by the ADA if an employer takes action against an employee or applicant based on the mistaken notion that an employee is disabled, even if he or she actually is not.

Under *Sutton*, an individual is "regarded as" disabled if the employer mistakenly believes the employee has an impairment that substantially limits one or more major life activities. As to limitations involving the ability to perform a job, the mistaken perception of a restriction must apply to a class of jobs or broad range of jobs within a class, not just one particular job or specialized position. In January 2001, a federal court in Minnesota, citing *Sutton*, permitted a "regarded as" claim instituted by the EEOC to go to trial against a company that allegedly discriminated against an employee because of a mistaken perception of a disability after the employee suffered a heart attack. [16 *Employment Discrimination Report (EDR)* (BNA) 342 (Mar. 7, 2001)]

Another issue is whether an individual self-certified as "totally disabled" for Social Security purposes can still maintain an ADA claim, which requires that the individual be able to perform the essential functions of a job, with or without accommodation. This apparent contradiction in position had split the circuits, and in *Cleveland v. Policy Management Systems Corp.* [526 U.S. 795 (1999)], the Supreme Court ruled that self-certification of "total disability" for purposes of obtaining Social Security benefits was not a per se bar to the ability of an employee to file an ADA claim. The Court noted that to maintain the claim the employee would have to proffer sufficient explanation for the apparent contradiction. Similarly, the D.C. Circuit, in *Solomon v. Vilsack* [628 F.3d 555 (D.C. Cir. 2010)], held that an individual receiving Federal Employee's Retirement System's disability benefits was not per se barred from maintaining an ADA claim, and moreover, the court refused to provide a rebuttable presumption that the individual receiving disability benefits is not disabled under the ADA.

In March 1999, the EEOC issued its long-awaited "Policy Guidance on Reasonable Accommodation under the ADA" [12 *Employment Discrimination Report (EDR)* (BNA) 317 (Mar. 3, 1999)], providing further instructions on the measures companies must consider when analyzing and implementing accommodations for qualified persons with disabilities.

With respect to emerging issues involving genetic testing, in March 2000 EEOC Commissioner Paul Miller reiterated the EEOC's long-held position that discrimination based on genetic testing violates the "regarded as" prong under the ADA. [14 *Employment Discrimination Report (EDR)* (BNA) 432 (Mar. 29, 2000)] The Burlington Northern Santa Fe Railroad stated that it would stop the practice of genetically testing workers with carpal tunnel syndrome after the EEOC instituted litigation against the Railroad for violating the ADA. [16 *Employment Discrimination Report (EDR)* (BNA) 221 (Feb. 14, 2001)]

In *Board of Trustees of the University of Alabama v. Garrett* [531 U.S. 356 (2001)], the Court held that the ADA does not apply to states, finding that it was not Congress' intent to abrogate the States' Eleventh Amendment immunity when enacting the ADA. In *Toyota Motor Manufacturing Kentucky, Inc. v. Williams* [534 U.S. 184 (2002)], the Court held that for a carpal tunnel syndrome condition alleged to substantially impair the performance of manual tasks, to "substantially impair a major life activity" (a requirement of the ADA), the condition must prevent or restrict the individual from performing activities that are of central importance to most people's daily lives, not just impair the individual's ability to perform the manual tasks of his or her job only. In *US Airways, Inc. v. Barnett* [535 U.S. 391 (2002)], the Court held that a requested accommodation of a union worker that conflicts with seniority rules under a collective bargaining agreement (CBA) is ordinarily sufficient to show that the requested accommodation is unreasonable, absent special circumstances.

The U.S. Supreme Court has issued significant decisions involving the ADA. In *Chevron USA v. Echazabal* [536 U.S. 73 (2002)], the Court settled a dispute among various district courts as to whether an individual's posing a "direct threat" to himself, in connection with performing a job, is a defense to an ADA claim. Although it is well settled that posing a direct threat to others is a defense, courts were split as to whether this defense also included the so-called "threat-to-self" situation. In that case, the employee had a liver condition that would be aggravated by continued exposure to toxins at the employer's refinery, according to the company doctors. Although the statute contains an explicit provision for defense based on threat to others, the EEOC in its regulations has long provided that threat-to-self was also a legitimate defense to an ADA claim, and the Supreme Court agreed.

Although initially established as part of sexual harassment doctrine, a claim of hostile work environment under the ADA has been recognized by many federal circuits. To establish a prima facie claim, the employee must demonstrate that (1) he is a qualified individual with a disability; (2) he was subjected to unwelcome harassment; (3) the harassment was based on his disability; (4) the harassment was sufficiently severe or pervasive to alter a term, condition, or privilege of his employment; and (5) some factual basis exists to impute liability for the harassment to the employer. [*See* Rohan v. Networks Presentations, LLC, 375 F.3d 266 (4th Cir. 2004).]

The determination of whether or not the situation is sufficiently hostile to maintain a claim is viewed under both an objective and subjective analysis, similar to the analysis in sexual harassment cases. In *Edmunson v. Potter* [2004 118 Fed. Appx. 726 (4th Cir. 2004)], an employee with carpal tunnel syndrome claimed that she was subjected to a hostile work environment on account of her disability. In reviewing the alleged acts in support of her claim of hostile work environment, the court concluded that the acts were isolated and ordinary adversities in the workplace, and not sufficiently severe or pervasive when viewed objectively. In 2004, the Tenth Circuit joined other circuits that have recognized hostile work environment claims under the ADA. [*See* Lanman v. Johnson Cnty., Kan., 393 F.3d 1151 (10th Cir. 2004).]

One issue that courts have been struggling with is whether "interacting with others" is a major life activity under the ADA. In *Doebele v. Sprint Corp.* [168 F. Supp. 2d 1247, 1261 (D. Kan. 2001)], the Tenth Circuit noted that it had not yet held "interacting with others" to be a major life activity. This issue was addressed by the court in *Price v. Facility Management Group, Inc.* [403 F. Supp. 2d 1246 (N.D. Ga. 2005)] In *Price* the employee suffered from bipolar disorder, a clear mental impairment, and claimed that his condition substantially limited his ability to interact with others, which he claimed was a major life activity under the ADA. Recognizing that the Eleventh Circuit has yet to decide whether "interacting with others" is a major life activity, the court held that even assuming that it is a major life activity, the employee had not demonstrated that it is an activity in which he is substantially limited. The plaintiff pointed to his difficulties in dealing with others and various outbursts to maintain the claim, but the court held that the record indicated that he was not "unable" to interact with others—he just occasionally did so in an inappropriate manner. As such, and without having to decide whether "interacting with others" is a major life activity, the court held that the employee's claim failed in this regard.

Q 1:54 What is the *ADA Amendments Act* and how has it modified the ADA?

In 2008, the *ADA Amendments Act (ADAAA)* [Pub. L. No. 110-235] was signed into law. The ADAAA, effective January 1, 2009, repudiates a number of U.S. Supreme Court decisions that, over the years, limited the application of the ADA. The ADAAA reverses this trend by significantly expanding the definition of individuals with disabilities entitled to protection under the Act. Although the ADAAA applies to conduct on or after January 1, 2009, courts have consistently held that the ADAAA is not applied retroactively, and as a result, the ADA and U.S. Supreme Court decisions interpreting the ADA prior to January 1, 2009 will continue to apply to actions occurring prior to January 1, 2009. [*See* Kemp v. Holder, 610 F.3d 231 (5th Cir. 2010).]

Q 1:55 What is *major life activity* under the ADAAA?

The ADAAA expands the definition of "*major life activity*" by including a non-exclusive list of activities within its definition, including caring for oneself, performing manual tasks, seeing, hearing, eating, sleeping, walking, standing, lifting, bending, speaking, breathing, learning, reading, concentrating, thinking, communicating and working. Also, the ADAAA expands "major life activities" to include the operation of any number of significant bodily functions listed in the amendments. In addition, as a rule of construction, the ADAAA specifically provides that an impairment that substantially limits one major life activity need not limit other major life activities in order to be considered a disability under the ADA. The amendment also departs from prior precedent by specifically providing that periodic or episodic impairments are a disability if they would substantially limit a major life activity when they are active. All of these amendments will work to expand the number of individuals that will qualify as having a disability under the ADA. Although "working" has always been considered a major life activity, many of the prior court decisions narrowly construe the requirements to qualify as a major life activity. This is likely to change, as the ADAAA provides that the definition of a disability under the ADA must be construed broadly in favor of coverage of individuals under the Act, to the maximum extent permitted by the Act.

Q 1:56   Are mitigating measures like medication or devices to be considered when determining if someone is disabled under the ADAAA?

The ADAAA reflects a 180-degree change from prior law in that, the ADAAA specifically prohibits consideration of mitigating measures when determining whether an impairment is a disability under the ADA. Contrary to the U.S. Supreme Court decision in *Sutton v. United Airlines, Inc.* [527 U.S. 471 (1999)], mitigating measures that have ameliorative effects in controlling a condition, such as medication, medical supplies, equipment, prosthetics and the like, are specifically not to be considered when determining whether an impairment substantially limits a major life activity.

Q 1:57   What is *perceived disability* under the ADAAA?

Before January 1, 2009, to establish a claim under the "regarded as" language under the ADA, an individual had to establish that he or she was perceived by the employer as having a substantial impairment of one or more major life activities. Under the ADAAA, an individual qualifies as being "regarded as" disabled if he or she can establish that they were subjected to an action prohibited under the ADAAA because of actual or perceived physical or mental impairment, whether or not the impairment limits or is perceived to limit a major life activity. However, the ADAAA also provides that impairments that are transitory in nature are excluded from protection under the "regarded as" basis for recovery and defines a transitory impairment as one with an actual or expected duration of six months or less.

Q 1:58   Are episodic or periodic impairments disabilities under the ADAAA?

Effective January 1, 2009, an impairment may qualify as a substantial limitation of a major life activity even if it is episodic or periodic. The ADAAA specifically provides that an impairment which is episodic or in remission will still qualify as a disability if it could substantially limit a major life activity when active.

Q 1:59   What is *Executive Order 13145*?

Executive Order 13145, signed into law by President Clinton in February 2000, prohibits discrimination on the basis of protective genetic information in the executive branch of the government. In August 2000, the EEOC issued its policy guidance on genetic information in federal employment, providing further guidance on the application of the executive order to federal employees. Essentially, the order is intended to ensure that applicants and employees in the executive branch are not discriminated against based upon genetic testing that may indicate the possibility that they might, at some point in the future, develop some disease or medical condition. The executive order places stringent rules on the collection, use, and disclosure of protected genetic information. This order sowed the seeds for the passage of the Genetic Information Non-Discrimination Act of 2008, discussed later in this chapter.

Q 1:60   What is the *Occupational Safety and Health Act?*

The *Occupational Safety and Health Act (OSH Act)* [29 U.S.C. §§ 651 *et seq.*] requires employers to provide employees with a workplace free from certain recognized hazards that can lead to death or serious physical harm, and provides for the establishment of safety and health standards to which employers and employees must adhere. The OSH Act applies to all employment performed in a workplace in the United States, provided that the employer is engaged in a business affecting commerce.

The DOL, through the Secretary of Labor, inspects and investigates suspected violations of the Act. The OSH Act provides a wide range of relief for violations, including issuance of citations, abatement requirements in connection with a citation, and civil and criminal penalties for willful violations in certain circumstances.

Q 1:61   What is the *Drug-Free Workplace Act?*

The *Drug-Free Workplace Act* [41 U.S.C. §§ 701 *et seq.*] requires covered federal contractors and federal grantees to take action to maintain a drug-free workplace. The Act applies to all federal grantees and federal contractors with contract amounts of $25,000 or more. The Act requires each of them to publish a drug policy, offer a drug-free awareness program, and follow various notification requirements in the event of a violation of the company's drug policy or of criminal drug statutes.

Each federal contracting agency is empowered to enforce the Act. If a violation is found, a wide range of remedies and penalties exist, including suspension of payments, termination of the contract, or suspension from future federal contracts or grants.

Q 1:62   What is the *National Labor Relations Act?*

The *National Labor Relations Act (NLRA)* [29 U.S.C. §§ 151 *et seq.*] protects the rights of workers to organize, engage in certain concerted protected activities, and bargain collectively through representation of their own choice. The NLRA applies to all employers and employees whose activities affect commerce. Among other things, the NLRA governs an employee's right to join (or not to join) a labor union and defines the unfair labor practices of employers and unions with respect to unionization, economic pressure (e.g., strikes and lockouts), and collective bargaining. It also protects employees who are not represented by labor unions but who engage in certain protected concerted activities. It prohibits employers from interfering with the formation or administration of any labor organization, interfering with an employee's membership in a labor organization, discriminating against an employee engaged in protected activity, or retaliating against an employee who exercises his or her rights under the Act.

The National Labor Relations Board enforces the Act. The commission of any act prohibited under the NLRA constitutes an unfair labor practice and, upon the filing of a charge, will be investigated by the board. If an unfair labor practice is determined, the board can issue cease and desist orders and take other action warranted under the circumstances.

Q 1:63   Have there been any developments regarding the NLRA?

Yes. The U.S. Supreme Court, in *NLRB v. Kentucky River Community Care, Inc.* [582 U.S. 706 (2001)], decided that registered nurses at a mental health facility were "supervisors," such that they were not subject to representation under the NLRA. In a controversial decision, the Supreme Court held that illegal aliens had no right to obtain redress under the NLRA due to their illegal status. [Hoffman Plastic Compounds, Inc. v. NLRB, 535 U.S. 137 (2002)] In May 2012, the NLRB purportedly amended its procedures for determining whether the majority of employees wanted to be represented by a union—amendments that some viewed as favorable for union representation and unfavorable to employers. The rule was purportedly adopted by a vote of two NLRB board members, but without the attendance of the third board member. The purported rule was challenged and recently, a district court found that the required quorum of three members for rule making purposes was not met, and therefore, the two board members did not have authority to pass a rule amending the procedures for determining whether the employees wanted union representation. [*Chamber of Commerce v. NLRB*, 879 F. Supp. 2d (D.D.C. 2012)] In August 2011, the NLRB issued a final rule entitled "Notification of Employee Rights under the National Relations Act." The rule required (1) that the employer post notices informing employees of their rights under the NLRA, and (2) provided that failure to post such notice was an unfair labor practice for which the statute of limitations would be tolled against employers who failed to post. Not surprisingly, the rule was challenged and the first court to address the issue, the District Court of the District of Columbia, held that the broad rule-making authority of the NLRB under the NLRA provided authority to require employers to post the required notice, but held that that portion of the rule, which provides that failure to post was an unfair labor practice for which the statute of limitations would be tolled exceeded the authority of the NLRB. [*National Ass'n of Manufacturers v. NLRB*, 846 F. Supp. 2d 34 (D.D.C. 2012)] This decision was enjoined pending appeal. [*National Ass'n of Manufacturers v. NLRB*, 2012 WL 4328371 (D.C. Cir. Apr. 17, 2012)] While the appeal of the District of Columbia case was pending, a district court in South Carolina found the rule in its totality overstepped the authority of the NLRB. [*Chamber of Commerce v. NLRB*, 856 F. Supp. 2d 778 (D.S.C. 2012)] (NLRB lacked authority to require employers to post notices informing employees of their rights under the NLRA.)

Q 1:64   What is the *Employee Polygraph Protection Act*?

The *Employee Polygraph Protection Act* [29 U.S.C. §§ 2001 *et seq.*], subject to limited exception, prohibits the use of lie detectors in the workplace both in the application process and during the employment relationship. The Act applies to any employer engaged in or affecting commerce or producing goods for commerce. The Act requires employers to post a notice explaining the Act's prohibitions; the DOL enforces the Act. Violations can be remedied through a broad range of measures, including penalties of as much as $10,000 and relief for employees or prospective employees affected by a violation. These measures include, but are not limited to, reinstatement, promotion, employment, payment of lost wages, and payment of benefits.

Q 1:65   What is the *Immigration Reform and Control Act of 1986*?

The *Immigration Reform Control Act of 1986 (IRCA)* [8 U.S.C. § 1101] is an amendment to the employment provisions of the Immigration and Nationality Act. It prohibits the hiring of illegal aliens, imposes duties on prospective employees to verify their employment eligibility, prohibits employment discrimination against legal aliens, and authorizes the limited use of imported, temporary agriculture workers. The Act applies to all employers engaged in commerce. Under it, employers must verify the employment eligibility of new employees by requiring them to fill out Section 1 of Form I-9. Employers must also require new employees to confirm their identity and employment eligibility in connection with the I-9 process. Employers must physically examine the documentation they provide and must retain completed and verified I-9 Forms. The Immigration and Naturalization Service (INS), Department of Justice, has prepared a list of acceptable documents for employers to use in connection with the completion of Form I-9, and employers are cautioned to review this information carefully before completing and verifying the form.

Both the INS and the Secretary of Labor oversee and enforce the Immigration Reform Control Act. They both can seek penalties and sanctions for non-compliance.

Q 1:66   What are the purposes of the IRCA?

The Act has three main purposes: to help control illegal immigration to the United States by requiring employers to verify employment eligibility; to make limited changes in the system for legal immigration; and to provide a controlled legalization program for undocumented aliens who entered the United States before 1982.

Q 1:67   How does the IRCA control illegal immigration?

The IRCA changed prior federal laws that permitted employers to hire illegal aliens without penalty. It subjects employers to civil or criminal penalties if they hire undocumented aliens or continue the employment of undocumented aliens.

Congress believes that most undocumented aliens enter the country to find jobs; therefore, the Act creates a system whereby employers share responsibility for controlling illegal immigration. An employer that fails to carry out this responsibility, which primarily involves demanding and reviewing suitable identification (e.g., birth certificate, Social Security card, and driver's license) from all new employees, is penalized. The imposition of penalties for violating the Act will, presumably, deter employers from hiring illegal aliens. The employers' reluctance to hire will, in turn, deter aliens from illegally entering the United States.

Q 1:68　　Which employees are affected by the IRCA?

The Act applies only to unauthorized aliens hired after November 6, 1986. It does not apply to employees hired before that time.

Q 1:69　　Have there been any developments under the IRCA?

Yes. In a somewhat controversial 5-4 decision, the U.S. Supreme Court, in *Hoffman Plastic Compounds, Inc. v. NLRB* [535 U.S. 137 (2002)], held that an illegal alien who utilized false documentation in connection with the I-9 process under IRCA to secure employment could not be provided relief under the NLRA for being fired for union activities—a clear unfair labor practice under the Act.

However, post-*Hoffman* decisions indicate its limitations with many courts as it applies to the rights of illegal aliens working in this country. For example, in the decision in *Madeira v. Affordable Housing Foundation, Inc.* [315 F. Supp. 2d 504 (2004)], the court, although recognizing the *Hoffman* decision, held that it had no applicability to claims under state labor laws. Specifically, the court held that the employee's alien status did not prevent him from recovering compensatory damages for the company's violation of New York labor law. As the court stated:

> And the fact is, undocumented aliens do obtain work in the United States. Recognizing this incontrovertible fact, New York's public does not bar compensation in the form of back pay for undocumented workers who are injured in the manner of the instant plaintiff. [315 F. Supp. 2d at 507]

Not to be outdone, the Ninth Circuit went even further in what may appear to some to be a clear attempt to avoid the apparent mandate of *Hoffman*. In *Rivera v. Nibco, Inc.* [364 F.3d 1057 (9th Cir. 2004)], a number of female immigrants formerly employed by a factory brought an action against their employer alleging national origin discrimination in violation of Title VII. During discovery, the defendant corporation sought to determine the plaintiffs' immigration status, undoubtedly seeking to determine whether they would have a *Hoffman*-based defense to the claims. The plaintiffs refused to provide information regarding their immigration status, and the trial court entered a protective order precluding the employer from using discovery to inquire into the plaintiffs' immigration status. On appeal, the Ninth Circuit concluded that the harm caused by forcing the plaintiffs to disclose their immigration status outweighed any right of the employer to obtain this discovery in that, by revealing their immigration status, any plaintiffs found to be undocumented might face criminal prosecution or deportation. As to *Hoffman*, the court read the decision narrowly and seriously questioned whether it had any applicability to Title VII cases, and concluded it clearly did not speak as to discovery issues. In what only can be viewed as a direct affront to *Hoffman*, in *Agri Processor Co., Inc. v. NLRB* [514 F.3d 1 (9th Cir. 2008)], the Ninth Circuit held that illegal aliens were "employees" as the term is defined under the NLRA, and as such, are entitled to protection by the NLRA. The court distinguished *Hoffman* by saying that it only applied to the issue of what remedies could be awarded to undocumented workers upon a finding of an unfair labor practice by the NLRB. In *Zavala v. Wal-Mart Stores, Inc.* [393 F. Supp. 295 (D.N.J. 2005)], the court held, in accordance with a growing number of courts, that despite *Hoffman*, illegal aliens still have rights to be paid in accordance with the FLSA for work performed. In a similar situation, the Second Circuit held that IRCA did not preempt New York's scaffold law that allowed illegal aliens injured in construction accidents to recover lost earnings as a result of the injury. [Madeira v. Affordable Housing Found., Inc., 469 F.3d 219 (2d Cir. 2006)] In *Sandoval v. Rizzuti Farms, Ltd.* [2009 WL 959478 (E.D. Wash. Apr. 7, 2009)], the court was faced with the issue of whether to allow the employer to obtain information regarding the plaintiffs' immigration status in connection with a class action complaint alleging violation of several federal and state laws protecting workers. Citing *Rivera*, the court held that the potential harm in providing immigration information to the employer outweighed any benefit in connection with these proceedings and granted the issuance of a protective order to prevent the employer from obtaining such information. Similarly, in *Widjaja v. Kang Yue USA Corp.* [2010 WL 2132068 (E.D.N.Y. May 20, 2010)], the court denied the employer's motion to gain access to the plaintiffs' immigration status that sued their employer for wage claims under the FLSA.

IRCA contains an express preemption clause that states that IRCA "preempts any state or local law imposing civil or criminal sanctions (other than licensing and similar laws) upon those who employ, recruit or refer for a fee for employment, unauthorized aliens." [8 U.S.C. § 1324 a(h)(2)] As such, other than the savings clause which permits state "licensing" or similar laws, state laws providing for civil or criminal sanctions for the employment of illegal aliens are preempted. At issue in *Chicanos por la Causa, Inc., v. Napalitano* [544 F.3d 976 (9th Cir. 2008)] was an Arizona law that allowed the superior courts of Arizona to suspend or revoke the business licenses of employers who knowingly or intentionally hire unauthorized aliens. [Ariz. Rev. Stat. § 23-212] The law was challenged claiming that it was preempted by IRCA and Arizona countered that its law fell within the savings clause which permits state "licensing and similar laws." After reviewing the Arizona statute the court concluded that Arizona's statute was a "licensing" measure that falls within the savings clause of IRCA's preemption provision. In 2012, the Supreme Court reviewed an Arizona statute relating to unlawful aliens and although the court found much of the statute preempted by IRCA, it overturned, as premature, an injunction against provisions in the Arizona statute authorizing police officers to verify an individual's status if there was reasonable suspicion that the individual was in the state unlawfully. [*Arizona v. United States*, 132 S. Ct. 2492 (2012)] A similar result occurred in *United States v. Alabama* [691 F.3d 1269 (11th Cir. 2012)], where the court, although finding numerous provisions under Alabama's statute preempted by IRCA, nonetheless upheld a provision that permitted police officers to investigate the status of a lawfully detained individual provided that the officer had reasonable suspicion to believe that the individual was unlawfully in the state.

The Illegal Immigration Reform and Immigration Responsibility Act of 1996 has changed the numbers and types of identification forms employers are allowed to request to confirm that a person is eligible for employment in the United States. On November 7, 2007, the U.S. Citizenship and Immigration Service (USCIS) announced the availability of the revised version of Form I-9 and accompanying handbook, Handbook for Employers, Instructions for Completing Form I-9, M-274. The USCIS also announced that employers must transition to the revised Employment Eligibility Verification Form I-9 no later than December 26, 2007, and that employers who fail to use the revised form will be subject to applicable penalties.

Employers can receive information and new forms as follows:

Both the revised Form I-9 and the "Handbook for Employers, Instructions for Completing the Form I-9" are available online at http://www.uscis.gov. To order forms, call the USCIS toll-free at 1-800-870-3676. For forms and information on immigration laws, regulations, and procedures, call the National Customer Service Center at 1-800-375-5283.

Q 1:70 What are the changes on the new Form I-9 that were effective December 26, 2007?

The highlights of the new Form I-9 are as follows:

- Five documents have been removed from List A of the List of Acceptable Documents to establish identity and employment eligibility:
  — Certificate of U.S. Citizenship (Form N-560 or N-561)
  — Certificate of Naturalization (Form N-550 or N-570)
  — Alien Registration Receipt Card (I-151)
  — Unexpired Reentry Permit (Form I-327)
  — Unexpired Refugee Travel Document (Form I-571)
- One document was added to List A of the List of Acceptable Documents to establish identity and employment eligibility:
  — Unexpired Employment Authorization Document (I-766)
- All Employment Authorization Documents with photographs have been consolidated as one item on List A.

- Instructions regarding Section 1 of the Form I-9 now indicate that the employee is not obligated to provide his or her Social Security number in Section 1 of the Form I-9, unless he or she is employed by an employer who participates in E-Verify.

- Employers may now sign and retain Forms I-9 electronically.

- The Spanish version of Form I-9, available on line, may be filled out by employers and employees in Puerto Rico ONLY. Spanish-speaking employers and employees in the 50 states and other U.S. territories may only complete the form in English to meet employment eligibility verification requirements.

The following lists of acceptable documents and their uses are contained in the new Form I-9, revised June 5, 2007, and effective through June 30, 2008.

- List A: List of acceptable documents that establish both identity and employment eligibility:
  - U.S. passport (unexpired or expired)
  - Permanent Resident Card or Alien Registration Receipt Card (Form I-551)
  - An unexpired foreign passport with a temporary I-551 stamp
  - An unexpired Employment Authorization Document that contains a photograph (Form I-766, I-688, I-688A, I-688B)
  - An unexpired foreign passport with an unexpired Arrival-Departure Record, Form I-94, bearing the same name as the passport and containing an endorsement of the alien's non-immigrant status, if that status authorizes the alien to work for the employer
- List B: List of acceptable documents that establish identity:
  - Driver's license or ID card issued by a state or outlying possession of the United States, provided it contains a photograph or information such as name, date of birth, gender, height, eye color, and address
  - ID card issued by federal, state, or local governmental agencies or entities, provided it contains a photograph or information such as name, date of birth, gender, height, eye color, and address
  - School ID card with a photograph
  - Voter's registration card
  - U.S. Military card or draft record
  - Military dependent's ID card
  - U.S. Coast Guard Merchant Mariner Card
  - Native American tribal document
  - Driver's license issued by a Canadian government authority
  - For persons under age 18 who are unable to present a document listed above: School record or report card; clinic, doctor, or hospital record; or day-care or nursery school record
- List C: Documents that establish employment eligibility:

— U.S. Social Security card issued by the Social Security Administration (other than a card stating it is not valid for employment)

— Certification of Birth Abroad issued by the Department of State (Form FS-545 or Form DS-1350)

— Original or certified copy of a birth certificate issued by a state, county, municipal authority, or outlying possession of the United States bearing an official seal

— Native American tribal document

— U.S. Citizen ID Card (Form I-197)

— ID Card for use of Resident Citizen in the United States (Form I-179)

— Unexpired employment authorization document issued by DHS (other than those listed under List A)

Q 1:71   What problems can employers create if they are too zealous with workers they suspect are undocumented under IRCA?

Zamora v. Elite Logistics, Inc. [449 F.3d 1106 (10th Cir. 2006)] underscores the problems an employer can embroil itself in when they are too zealous with workers who may be undocumented. In *Zamora*, the employer had received a tip that the INS may soon conduct an investigation of its facility to determine compliance with IRCA. The employer perceived that it had problems and retained an outside company to check the Social Security numbers of all of its employees. The outside contractors reported that someone else had used the plaintiff's Social Security number in the past, and the defendant's personnel director told the plaintiff he had 10 days to provide Social Security documentation that he had the right to work in the United States. When he did not, he was terminated. Although the plaintiff produced INS documents at the time of hire, the company insisted that he provide Social Security documents. Based on this evidence, the court concluded that it raised a genuine issue of material fact as to whether a Title VII claim for discharge on the basis of race, nationality, or national origin existed and remanded the matter for trial.

Under IRCA, employers are subject to civil and criminal liability if they employ undocumented workers "knowing" their undocumented status; the term *knowing* includes "constructive" knowledge. [8 U.S.C. § 1324a (a)(1)(2)] As defined in the regulations, constructive knowledge is "knowledge that may fairly be inferred through notice of certain facts and circumstances that would lead a person, through the exercise of reasonable care, to know about a certain condition." [8 C.F.R. § 274a.1] As many employers may know, the Social Security Administration (SSA) periodically reviews employee's names and Social Security numbers and when they do not match, sends a letter to the employer advising them of the discrepancies. One might think that receipt of so-called no-match letters from SSA would provide the employer at least constructive knowledge that an employee is an undocumented alien. However, such is not necessarily the case. For example in *Aramark Facility Services v. Service Employees International Union, Local 1877, AFL-CIO* [530 F.3d 817 (9th Cir. 2008)], an employer received a no-match letter from SSA advising that 48 of its employees' names did not match the Social Security number. The employer then informed the employees and their union, that they had three days to reconcile this with SSA or their employment would be terminated. When matters were not reconciled, the employees were terminated and the union grieved and ultimately arbitrated the matter, claiming that the employer did not have good cause to terminate the employment of the employees as required by the CBA. The arbitrator concluded that the no-match letters were not knowledge or constructive knowledge and reinstated the employees and reinstated the employees and awarded back pay and other damages. After the company appealed, the U.S. District Court vacated the award, saying that implementation of the award would effectively violate public policy under IRCA and the union appealed. On appeal before the Ninth Circuit, and noting that for purposes of IRCA, constructive knowledge is narrowly construed, the court held that mere receipt of no-match letters in and of themselves cannot provide either knowledge or constructive knowledge that the employees are undocumented aliens and as such, reversed the district court.

Q 1:72 What is the *Workers Adjustment and Retraining Notification Act?*

The *Workers Adjustment and Retraining Notification (WARN) Act* [29 U.S.C. §§ 2101 *et seq.*] was enacted to provide certain employees advance notice of plant shutdowns and mass layoffs. The WARN Act requires employers with 100 or more employees to provide 60-day written notice. The regulations under the WARN Act define mass layoffs and plant closings subject to the Act. A plant closing is the permanent or temporary shutdown of a single employment site consisting of one or more facilities or operating units. The shutdown must result in an employment loss and must affect 50 or more full-time employees during any 30-day period. With reference to mass layoffs, the WARN Act requires, among other things, that the reduction in work force affect at least 50 full-time employees, who comprise at least 33 percent of full-time employees or at least 500 full-time employees.

An employer's failure to provide the required notice may subject it to litigation in federal court, with liability for the payment of back pay, lost benefits, civil penalties, and attorneys' fees. The WARN Act is enforced through private actions instituted by employees in federal court. Many states and municipalities have enacted similar legislation; these laws should also be considered in the event of plant closing or mass layoffs.

Q 1:73 What are whistleblower laws?

Both federal and state legislatures have restricted the traditional employment-at-will rule where public health, safety, or ethics in government is involved. The legislation is intended to provide protection for employees who report their employer's statutory violations to appropriate government agencies or authorities. Whistleblower protection is generally limited to good-faith reports of suspected violations.

Q 1:74 What are the provisions of federal whistleblower laws?

A number of federal statutes that protect civil service employees prohibit the government from taking any action against an employee who discloses information he or she reasonably believes reveals mismanagement, waste of funds, abuse of authority, a violation of the law, or a substantial and specific failure to protect public safety and health. In April 1989, the Whistleblower Protection Act of 1989 (WPA) was enacted. [5 U.S.C. §§ 7502, 7512 *et seq.*] It protects federal employees from reprisals from whistleblowing on waste, fraud and unnecessary government expenditures, and establishes a special counsel's office to act in the interests of these employees. Other federal laws provide whistleblower protection to employees in certain private sectors, such as the nuclear energy industry. The issue of what disclosure is necessary to maintain a claim under the WPA was addressed in *Bonds v. Leavitt*. [647 F. Supp. 2d 541 (D. MD. 2009)] The employee, a doctor at the National Institutes of Health, brought, among other things, a WPA claim on the basis of her disclosure, to her supervisors, that she felt one of her subordinates had obtained genetic information in connection with research in violation of the law without the subject's consent. Recognizing that it has been held that to maintain a WPA claim, disclosure must evidence an intent to raise the issue to a higher authority who is in a position to correct the wrongdoing, and that disclosure that would be part of an employee's normal duties are not actionable, the court held that the WPA claim could not be maintained because the doctor's disclosures were part of the ordinary course of her job as project manager and did not rise to the level of an actionable disclosure under WPA.

Q 1:75 Can a whistleblower win punitive damages in a lawsuit alleging employer retaliation?

Yes. Early in 1991, the Second Circuit Court of Appeals ruled that a plaintiff demoted by the New York State Department of Education after reporting alleged financial wrongdoing was entitled to keep the punitive damages awarded by a jury. [Vasbrinder v. Ambach, 926 F.2d 1333 (2d Cir. 1991)]

Punitive damages are awarded on top of compensatory (i.e., actual) damages when jurors feel a defendant must be punished for particularly egregious conduct. In *Vasbrinder*, the plaintiff claimed his supervisors demoted him after he contacted the FBI about his suspicions of wrongdoing in a federally funded program overseen by the Department's Office of Vocational Rehabilitation. According to the Second Circuit, the trial judge had correctly instructed the jury that they could award punitive damages if the defendant's conduct was shown to be "motivated by evil motive or intent, or when it involves reckless or callous indifference to the federally protected rights of others." [*See* 1991 *BNA Daily Labor Report* 51, Mar. 15, 1991, at A-5.]

Q 1:76 What must an employee show to prevail in a claim of wrongful discharge under the federal whistleblower laws?

The employee must generally establish that the following events occurred:

- The employee engaged in protected activity (i.e., reporting suspected violations of law to a public body);
- The accused official knew of the protected activity;
- An adverse employment action occurred; and
- A causal link was established (i.e., the adverse employment action was in retaliation for the employee engaging in protected activity).

It should be noted that to establish a causal connection between the protected activity and the alleged adverse employment action for which retaliation is based, courts will look to the proximity and timing of the events, and if too much time has passed, will conclude that the claim cannot be maintained because a jury could not reasonably find a causal relationship. Such was the case in *McGrath v. Clinton.* [674 F. Supp. 2d 131 (D.D.C. 2009)] In the case, a former foreign-service employee sued Hillary Rodham Clinton, claiming that his eventual separation from the foreign service was in retaliation for a prior EEOC complaint. However, the court noted that the eventual separation took place two years after the filing of the EEOC complaint and 16 months after the conclusion of the EEOC's investigation. The court held that this time frame places the adverse employment action outside of a time frame from which a jury could reasonably infer a causal connection.

Q 1:77   Do the federal whistleblower laws preempt state law claims?

In 1989, the U.S. Supreme Court unanimously held that Section 210 of the Energy Reorganization Act—the whistleblower provision—does not preempt a state law claim of intentional infliction of emotional distress by a worker in the nuclear power industry. [McMonagle v. Northeast Women's Ctr., 493 U.S. 901 (1989)] Two lower courts had previously dismissed the lawsuit of a former General Electric employee who claimed she had been transferred, harassed, and finally fired because of her complaint to the Nuclear Regulatory Commission about allegedly inadequate clean-up efforts at a nuclear fuel processing plant in Wilmington, North Carolina. In a unanimous decision, Justice Blackmun stated that Congress never intended to preempt all state law remedies when it enacted nuclear safety regulations. The court held that there was no irreconcilable conflict between Section 210 and a state-law tort claim for harassment.

Q 1:78   What is the *Uniformed Services Employment and Reemployment Rights Act?*

The *Uniformed Services Employment and Reemployment Rights Act of 1994 (USERRA)* [Pub. L. No. 103-353] was signed into law on October 13, 1994. USERRA applies to all individuals who are serving or who have served in the uniform services and applies to all employers in the public and private sectors, including federal employers. The law seeks to minimize disadvantages associated with being absent from civilian employment to serve in the country's uniform services by insuring that those who serve their country can retain their civilian employment and benefits and can seek employment free from discrimination due to their service for the country. Generally, to be eligible:

- The employee must provide advance notice of military service, when possible.
- The employee must have left his or her civilian job for purposes of service in the uniform services. The position must not have been temporary (i.e., the employee must have had some reasonable expectation that it would last for a significant period of time).
- The length of the employee's military leave must not, in most instances, exceed five years.

Eligible employees on military leave are entitled to the same rights and benefits that the civilian employer would provide for any other leave of absence and are entitled to accrue seniority and other rights or benefits based on seniority that they would have attained if they had remained continuously employed. In addition, the individual may elect to continue health plan coverage for up to 18 months after leave commenced. Employees returning from military leave are generally entitled to reinstatement to the same or equivalent position. The law requires individuals returning from military leaves of absence to apply for reinstatement within a specific period of time.

Q 1:79   What is the *Genetic Information Non-Discrimination Act of 2008*?

The *Genetic Information Non-Discrimination Act of 2008 (GINA)* [Pub. L. No. 110-233], applicable to all employees covered under Title VII, prohibits an employer from discriminating against employees on the basis of genetic information and limits an employer's acquisition or monitoring of genetic information except as expressly provided in the Act. For example, GINA allows genetic monitoring of the biological effects of toxic substances in the workplace, provided that the employee voluntarily authorizes such monitoring after written notice by the employer or if such monitoring is required by law and the employee is informed of the individual monitoring results. In addition, the law provides that any genetic information obtained by the employer must be kept in a separate file and treated as confidential. The law took effect on May 21, 2008 and procedures for enforcement and remedies are the same as those provided for under Title VII.

Q 1:80   What is the *Sarbanes-Oxley Act*?

The *Sarbanes-Oxley Act*, protects employees that report or assist in the investigation of conduct that violates federal law or regulations relating to fraud against a company's shareholders. [18 U.S.C. § 1514A(a)(1)] To maintain a claim, the plaintiff must prove that (1) plaintiff engaged in protective activity; (2) defendant knew of the protected activity; (3) plaintiff suffered an unfavorable employment action; and (4) circumstances exist that the protected activity contributed to the unfavorable action. [Collins v. Beazer Homes USA, Inc., 334

F. Supp. 2d 1365, 1375 (N.D. Ga. 2004)] It is not necessary that an employee demonstrate an actual violation of SOX to maintain a whistleblower claim under SOX, but the employee must have a good faith and reasonable belief that the company had engaged in fraudulent activities in violation of SOX. [Sharkey v. J.P. Morgan Chase & Co. [805 F. Supp. 2d 45 (S.D.N.Y. 2011)] However, plaintiffs are not engaged in protected activity if they report fraudulent activities to the media, as opposed to the specific regulatory or supervisory individuals referenced in the statute. [Tides v. The Boeing Co., 644 F.3d 809 (9th Cir. 2011)]

Q 1:81 What are the Patient Protection and Affordable Care Act and the Health Care and Education Reconciliation Act and how do they effect employers?

On March 23, 2010, President Barack Obama signed the Patient Protection and Affordable Care Act (H.R. 3590) [Pub. L. No. 111-148] into law. Then on March 30, 2010, the President signed the related Health Care and Education Reconciliation Act (H.R. 4872) [Pub. L. No. 111-152] into law. Below is a summary of provisions of these health care reform Acts which affect employers. Most of the requirements are expected to take effect in 2014.

Amendments to the FLSA

The Acts amend the FLSA to require certain employers to automatically enroll new full-time employees and continue the enrollment of current employees in one of the health benefits plans offered through the employer. [H.R. 3590, § 1511] Employers subject to this requirement are those that (1) employ more than 200 full-time employees and (2) offer employees enrollment in one or more health benefit plans. The automatic enrollment program must include adequate notice and the opportunity for an employee to opt out of any such coverage.

Employers also have the duty to inform employees of their coverage options, including any options which may be available through an "Exchange" established by each state to help individuals and small businesses to obtain coverage. [H.R. 3590, § 1512] The notice must inform the employees of the existence of the Exchange and potential tax credits that may be available through the Exchange.

In addition, employers with 50 or more employees must provide employees who are nursing mothers with a reasonable break time during the child's first year to express milk. [H.R. 3590, § 4207] Such employers must also provide a private place, other than a bathroom, where the mother may express milk shielded from view and free from intrusion from coworkers and the public. The employer will not be required to compensate an employee receiving the break time. Employers with less than 50 employees are not subject to this requirement if the requirements would pose an undue hardship.

Amendments to the Code

The Acts make several amendments to the Code generally in order to incentivize employers to provide healthcare to employees.

Large Employers

Large employers (generally those with 50 or more employees) must pay an assessment of $2,000 per full-time employee (not including the first 30 employees) if the employer (1) does not offer coverage, and (2) has at least one full-time employee who receives a premium assistance tax credit through the Exchange or cost-sharing reduction under the Acts. [H.R. 3590, § 1513; H.R. 4872, § 1003] In addition, employers that offer coverage that is not affordable or coverage that does not cover at least 60 percent of allowable costs must pay $3,000 for any employee that receives a tax credit through the Exchange up to a cap of $2,000 for every full-time employee. The requirements for employers to furnish coverage to their employees is effective January 1, 2014. However, the extent of employee coverage depends upon the number of employees in 2013 and the number of hours worked by those employees in 2013. Therefore, to avoid an unpleasant surprise on New Year's Day, 2014, employers must review their employee demographics in detail to determine whether adjustments in the workforce are needed to predict the employer's health care coverage obligations in 2014.

The Act requires large employers to either offer health insurance to their full-time employees or pay a penalty through the IRS. A *full-time employee* is defined as an employee who averages 30 or more hours per week. A large employer is one that averages 50 or more full-time employees and full-time equivalent employees (FTEs).

To determine if an employer is a large employer necessitates finding out the number of employees who average at least 30 hours a week in 2013 and adding to that figure the number of FTEs. The number of FTEs an employer has is based upon taking the aggregate monthly hours worked by part-time employees (those who work fewer than 30 hours per week) counted on a monthly basis during calendar year 2013, divided by 120. Consequently, whether an employer has 50 or more employees triggering compliance in 2014 not only includes employees who work more than 30 hours per week but an equivalency based on hours worked by part-time employees during 2013.

Small Businesses

The Acts provide tax credits for small businesses that contribute at least 50 percent of an employee's health insurance premium costs. [H.R. 3590, § 1421] The small business must employ no more than 25 full-time employees and the average annual wage of such employees must not exceed a given threshold. For the years 2011 through 2013, an eligible employer may receive a credit in the amount of 35 percent of the employer's contributions; in 2014, the credit increases to 50 percent of such contributions.

All Employers

Employers must disclose the value of the benefit provided by the employer for each employee's health insurance coverage on the employee's annual Form W-2. [H.R. 3590, § 9002]

Q: 1:82   What is the *Dodd-Frank Wall Street Reform and Consumer Protection Act of 2010*?

The *Dodd-Frank Wall Street Reform and Consumer Protection Act of 2010* (Dodd-Frank) enacted in the wake of the 2008 financial crisis, contains incentives and protections for whistleblowers and creates a private cause of action for whistleblowers who are subject to retaliatory discharge. [15 U.S.C. § 78 u-6(h)1(B)(i)] In *Asadi v. GE Energy (USA), LLC* [2012 WL 2522599 (S.D. Tex. June 28, 2012)], the court held that Dodd-Frank's retaliation provision does not apply extraterritorially, such that a claim of retaliation due to disclosure of alleged corrupt conduct by his employer in Iraq, and for which the SEC would have no jurisdiction, did not provide a basis for relief under Dodd-Frank. In *Nollner v. Southern Baptist Convention, Inc.* [852 F. Supp. 2d 986 (M.D. Tenn. 2012)], the court held that the anti-retaliation provisions in Dodd-Frank protect disclosures that are required or protected by laws, rules, or regulations within the SEC's jurisdiction, such that disclosure of violations of other laws, like the Foreign Corrupt Practices Act, cannot form the basis of a Dodd-Frank retaliation claim.

Federal Enforcement and Penalties

Q 1:83   What are the major agencies charged with the enforcement of federal labor laws?

The EEOC and the DOL are the two principal agencies involved in enforcement of federal employment laws. The DOL principally covers the compliance-oriented wage and benefits statutes (e.g., the FLSA, The Davis-Bacon Act, the Service Contract Act, the Walsh-Healey Act, the Employment Retirement Income Security Act, and the FMLA), whereas the EEOC principally covers the federal civil rights statutes (e.g., Title VII; the EPA; the Age Discrimination in Employment Act; the ADA; and its companion statute, the Rehabilitation Act of 1973).

Q 1:84   What is the *EEOC*?

The *EEOC* is an independent federal agency charged by Congress with enforcing Title VII, the EPA, Title I of the ADA, the Rehabilitation Act of 1973, the Civil Rights Act of 1991, and the ADEA. It operates out of regional offices in major cities across the country where intake officers assist employees in filing charges of discrimination. EEOC investigators conduct fact-finding conferences, subpoena business records, and interview witnesses to ascertain whether probable cause exists that an employer violated federal law. When discrimination is found to have occurred, attempts are made to remedy the illegal behavior through conciliation meetings. When these attempts fail, a suit may be brought by the EEOC in federal court on behalf of the employee. However, the likelihood of an EEOC lawsuit is slight. According to the EEOC's statistics posted on their Web site (http://www.eeoc.gov), in Fiscal Year 2008, 325 lawsuits were filed; in

Fiscal Year 2006, 403 lawsuits were filed. In Fiscal Year 2005, 416 lawsuits were filed; in Fiscal Years 2004, 421 lawsuits were filed; and in Fiscal Year 2003, 370 lawsuits were filed. Because the average number of charges filed in each fiscal year during this time period was approximately 78,000, this means the chances of a charge evolving into EEOC litigation was about one-half of 1 percent. In Fiscal Year 2012, only 155 lawsuits were filed, with over 99,000 charges filed.

Q 1:85   Is the EEOC's investigation file admissible in court?

A Texas appeals court was asked to determine whether the EEOC's investigation file, which included a determination of age discrimination under the ADEA, could be introduced as evidence in a subsequent jury trial. Recognizing that the determination and factual findings of the EEOC fell within the exception to the hearsay exclusion rule under the federal rules of evidence, the court nonetheless concluded that the evidence was properly excluded by the court at the trial level, because its admission spoke directly to an ultimate issue in the case and would be more prejudicial than probative. [Guerra v. N. E. Indep. Sch. Dist., 496 F.3d 415 (5th Cir. 1997)]

Q 1:86   Have there been any developments in the processing of charges by the EEOC?

In 1995, EEOC Vice-Chairman, Paul Igasaki, announced that the EEOC was an agency in crisis. The volume of charges had ballooned during the previous years, and the backlog of claims exceeded the agency's ability to handle charges. Because of this, a vice-chairman was appointed to reform the charge-processing procedures. The revised procedures (the so-called National Enforcement Plan), which took effect in June 1995, provide that all new charges be classified as follows:

- Category A charges are high-priority charges involving pattern or practice discrimination and high-profile targets in which probable cause is likely.
- Category B charges have merit but will require additional investigation.
- Category C charges are susceptible to dismissal by the EEOC.

Before these reforms, EEOC investigators had to work the charges on their dockets in the order they were received, fully investigating each charge. Investigators can now dismiss charges that do not warrant full investigations so they can concentrate on large-scale and egregious cases that fall within the agency's National Enforcement Plan. The EEOC, like the IRS, is attempting to concentrate its resources against targeted defendants in an effort to gain publicity and thereby encourage voluntary compliance. The class action litigation brought by the EEOC against Mitsubishi Motor Manufacturing of America, Inc., possibly the largest single case of sexual harassment brought under Title VII, is an example of this new policy of selecting high-profile targets. [EEOC v. Mitsubishi Motor Mfg. of Am., Inc., 102 F.3d 869 (7th Cir. Ill. 1996)] EEOC Vice-Chairman Igasaki said, "The action the EEOC is taking today (against

Mitsubishi) will have significant impact on the lives of working women throughout the country, especially those attempting to earn a living in jobs long dominated by men." [6 *Employment Discrimination Report (EDR)* (BNA) 507 (Apr. 17, 1996)]

In combination with its National Enforcement Plan, the EEOC instituted alternative dispute resolution (ADR) programs throughout various districts in an attempt to infuse ADR principles within the initial stages of the investigation process. By 1996, district offices that established ADR programs utilized mediators, often through the Federal Mediation and Conciliation Service, for purposes of providing the charging party and the respondent an opportunity to mediate a charge voluntarily prior to investigation by the EEOC. In 1999, as part of the Clinton administration's civil rights initiative, the EEOC began implementation of its National Mediation Program, a program that offers the opportunity to mediate charges nationwide.

Although *mediation* is the term used in connection with this process, it is a strictly voluntary process and there is no binding mediation or arbitration agreement. Rather, the parties are offered an opportunity to meet with a selected mediator whose job it is to facilitate resolution discussion, and determine whether or not the parties can agree upon a mutually acceptable basis to resolve and settle the charge.

Typically, after the charge is filed, the district office of the EEOC sends letters to the charging party and the respondent asking each party whether they will agree to ADR with a federal mediator. If either party refuses, the matter is referred to the EEOC investigator for further proceedings. On the other hand, if both parties agree, the matter is assigned to a mediator who contacts both parties for purposes of arranging a date and time for the mediation. If the mediation results in resolution, the parties sign a settlement agreement that is ultimately reviewed and subject to the approval of the EEOC. If the matter is not resolved, the federal mediator refers the matter back to the EEOC investigator for further proceedings.

This program, begun as a pilot program in 1993, has been successful in terminating the need for investigation of many charges that can be resolved early in the EEOC process.

Q 1:87 Does an enforceable arbitration agreement signed by an employee preclude the EEOC from an enforcement action?

In *EEOC v. Waffle House, Inc.* [534 U.S. 279 (2002)], the U.S. Supreme Court held that an arbitration agreement would not prevent the EEOC from pursuing an enforcement action and seeking victim-specific judicial relief on behalf of the employee.

Q 1:88 What are the advantages of using the EEOC's ADR program?

There are many advantages to the ADR process. First, it allows the parties and/or their representatives to meet face to face and discuss the nature and basis of their respective claims and defenses. Both sides have the opportunity to analyze their positions and possibly rethink them. In addition, through the ADR process, an agreement might be reached, which from either party's point of view is advantageous, given the time, effort, and expense needed in connection with the investigation process. Furthermore, the process affords each party with the opportunity to have an objective neutral observer, the federal mediator, analyze and assess the strengths or weaknesses of each party's position. This can be helpful. Most charging parties believe they have legitimate claims and most companies believe they have done nothing wrong. Analysis and input by the federal mediator can be extremely helpful to the parties, and often facilitates a realistic appraisal of the claim. Lastly, according to the EEOC, mediation works.

Q 1:89 Should a party be represented by counsel at the EEOC mediation?

Although it is not technically necessary, it is always helpful to be represented by counsel throughout this process. Certainly, if one party intends to be represented by counsel during the proceeding, the other party is well advised to have counsel present as well; however, even if the other party does not intend to have counsel present, the party should consider counsel, for it would afford their attorneys an opportunity to listen to the other party's position and gauge the strength or weaknesses of their case and/or defense. Quite frankly, the information obtainable by an attorney during these informal meetings can be invaluable, and the opportunity should not be missed.

Q 1:90 Are there any disadvantages to the EEOC and ADR process?

Not really, other than the expense and time expended in connection with the conciliation process. The process, in its current form, is strictly voluntary, and a party who is not satisfied can always terminate the process. Although some might argue that just agreeing to sit through the process, in and of itself, is a tacit admission of liability, those notions are now somewhat antiquated. The concepts of ADR, conciliation, and mediation have grown continuously through recent years, and appear to be well received by attorneys and clients alike. Because even the most principled of clients usually compromise their position and settle employment disputes ultimately, utilization of the EEOC ADR program provides the parties an opportunity to address the situation sooner rather than later and avoid the time and expense of further proceedings.

Q 1:91 Are all charges mediated through the ADR program?

In its current form, the opportunity to participate in the EEOC's ADR program is by invitation only, and only exists for those charges selected for ADR by the EEOC. After a charge is filed, the EEOC reviews it to determine its suitability for ADR. If so, invitations are sent to the respective parties to participate in the process. Either party has the option to refuse ADR. If ADR does not occur the matter is sent for further processing by the investigator. Although many states have adopted obligatory mediation of lawsuits, this is not the current format being utilized by the EEOC and obligatory mediation of EEOC charges would appear not to be on the immediate horizon.

Q 1:92 Upon resolution of an EEOC charge, what settlement documentation is utilized by the EEOC?

The EEOC utilizes a wide range of settlement documents in connection with the resolution of the EEOC charges; however, most EEOC settlement agreements, in addition to outlining the terms and conditions of the settlement itself, contain provisions that:

- Acknowledge that the settlement is not an admission of wrongdoing by the respondent of a violation of Title VII, the ADEA, or the ADA;

- Require the respondent to agree that there will be no discrimination or retaliation of any kind against any person because of the opposition to any activity declared illegal under applicable law, or as a result of filing a change, giving testimony, assisting, or participating in any matter in the investigation, proceeding, or hearing;

- Declare that the settlement agreement is a final and complete statement of the entire agreement between the parties; and

- Provide an agreement between the parties that the EEOC is authorized to investigate and monitor compliance with the settlement agreement which may be specifically enforced in court by the EEOC or the parties, and which may be used as evidence in a subsequent proceeding where a breach of the settlement agreement is alleged.

The settlement agreement is typically signed by the charging party and the respondent and it is thereafter sent to the EEOC for signature and approval. All settlement agreements are subject to the approval of the EEOC; for example, if the settlement agreement is signed during the conciliation process, the matter is not concluded until the EEOC receives and approves the settlement document, signs the settlement agreement, and submits copies to the respective parties. In addition, the EEOC typically contains language in the settlement agreement that provides, despite the settlement, that the EEOC does not waive or in any manner limit its right to investigate or seek relief in any other charge, including, but not limited to, a charge filed by a member of the commission against the respondent.

It is important to recognize that the settlement of an EEOC charge utilizing EEOC settlement documents is typically just a settlement of the charge itself. EEOC settlement agreements are generally drafted so as to envision a complete and final resolution of the EEOC charge with the request that the EEOC accept the settlement by signing the settlement agreement, and terminating its investigation with respect to the charge. This is a far more limited resolution than most management attorneys recommend to their clients when settling employment disputes. Generally, respondents attempt to provide for a release of all claims, which includes not only claims arising from a charge but any other claims that may exist when the settlement agreement is reached. This type of settlement is not condoned or sanctioned by the EEOC, and if it is to be undertaken, it generally requires an additional document in the EEOC settlement agreement. The EEOC itself will not typically approve a settlement of all claims, and the documentation usually needs to be drafted separately and signed between the respondent and the charging party at the same time the EEOC settlement documentation is signed. Although the EEOC documentation will result in a dismissal of the charge, utilization of a comprehensive "addendum" to the settlement agreement offers the employer far more protection in connection with the settlement of EEOC charges and employers should be aware of the opportunity of a comprehensive settlement agreement in connection with an EEOC charge.

Q 1:93 What types of provisions are contained within a standard settlement agreement that are not contained within the EEOC's typical settlement format?

There are many standard provisions contained within settlement agreements that are not contained within the standard documentation offered by the EEOC. Specifically, they include the following.

Complete release. Most settlement agreements contain a release of all claims, alleged or not alleged, pled or not pled, up through the date of the settlement. These provisions are generally fairly lengthy, and refer specifically to the federal and state statutes that are the subject of the release. If the claimant is 40 years of age or older, under the Older Workers Benefit Protection Act, the ADEA of 1967 must be specifically listed in the release, along with language clearly stating that the release includes any and all claims in any way related to the ADEA.

No future lawsuits or claims. Most settlement agreements contain provisions that the claimant withdraw any and all charges or litigation filed that have been released in the complete release of all claims, and include provisions that if any future lawsuit or claim is filed that is the subject of the complete release, the claimant must pay any and all costs or charges suffered by the respondent as a result thereof, including attorneys' fees and costs.

Confidentiality. Most settlement agreements contain a confidentiality agreement requiring that the claimant keep the terms of the settlement agreement confidential, and not disclose or discuss the terms with any other party, except necessary disclosure to his or her immediate family and professional advisors on a strict need-to-know basis. In addition, many confidentiality provisions require these other parties to agree to keep the terms and conditions of the settlement confidential, as a condition of that disclosure. Confidentiality provisions also typically provide that the claimant agrees that irreparable harm would result if the settlement agreement was disclosed and permit the respondent to institute a claim for injunctive relief to stop a continuing or threatened violation of this provision, with the additional provision that the claimant pay all costs, including attorneys' fees, suffered by the respondent as a result. In addition, confidentiality agreements often contain liquidated damage provisions that include a specific amount of monetary relief to which the respondent is entitled in the event that the claimant breaches the confidentiality provision. The enforceability of the liquidated damages penalty if unreasonable is questionable: Courts are generally not disposed to enforce liquidated damage provisions that are viewed as a penalty as opposed to a reasonable sum of money based upon the facts and circumstances in each particular situation.

Tax considerations. Although it is now clear that most monetary consideration provided in connection with employment disputes is taxable, the issue of whether the consideration paid is attributable to wages, so the employer will withhold taxes and issue a Form W-2 to the respondent, or whether the sum or portions of the sum are attributable to non-wage loss matters, in which case a Form 1099 will issue and there will be no withholding, still needs to be analyzed and resolved. If the amounts are all attributable to wages, the agreement should specify that the consideration will be paid by payroll check, minus normal payroll deductions. If any sums are being allocated to non-wage loss issues, the agreement should specify the amount, and indicate that a Form 1099 will issue and that the respondent agrees to pay any and all taxes owed with respect thereto. Many of these provisions also contain an indemnification by the employee agreeing to hold the company harmless from any and all claims that may be made against the company as a result of the employee's failure to pay any taxes with respect to these sums. From the company's standpoint, the safest route is to pay by payroll check, but in many instances, a portion of consideration is properly allocable to non-wage loss issues for which withholding is not required and a Form 1099 is appropriate. See chapter 14 for a more complete discussion of the tax ramifications involved in settling employment disputes.

Acknowledgment for employees age 40 or older. If the substance of the EEOC charge is an ADEA claim, the settlement documentation contained within the EEOC settlement agreement will undoubtedly contain the required time for consideration of the settlement agreement before signing (usually 21 days) and the seven-day revocation period after the respondent's signature, in accordance with the Older Workers Benefit Protection Act. If the charge is something other than an age claim, the EEOC settlement documentation usually does not include this language. Parties seeking an addendum to the settlement agreement that contains a release of all claims, including those under the ADEA, must ensure that the settlement documentation complies with the Older Workers Benefit Protection Act in order to be effective against a potential age claim. As a result, the addendum to the settlement agreement should contain both a 21-day period for the respondent to consider the agreement before signing and a seven-day revocation period after signature. Companies are generally unwilling to pay the consideration until after the time periods have expired under the Older Workers Benefit Protection Act; as a result, it is recommended that the mechanics of the settlement be worked such that the consideration is not paid until the expiration of the time periods provided for both consideration and revocation under the Older Workers Benefit Protection Act.

State Law and Its Relationship to Federal Law

Q 1:94   What does the DOL oversee?

Under the direction of the Secretary of Labor, the DOL enforces labor and employment laws, including the FLSA, the Occupational Health and Safety Act, the FMLA, and the Labor-Management Reporting and Disclosure Act. It also regulates federal contract programs and investigates labor racketeering. In addition, it performs various other functions, including research under the auspices of the Bureau of Labor Statistics and the Women's Bureau.

Q 1:95   What are the penalties for non-compliance with federal employment and labor laws, and what remedies are available to employees?

Penalties and remedies vary from statute to statute. A common thread running through a number of these federal laws (e.g., the National Labor Relations Act, Title VII, and the Age Discrimination in Employment Act) is the "make whole" remedy. The successful employee-claimant, or plaintiff, is made whole by an award of lost wages and fringe benefits, plus reinstatement if he or she is wrongfully discharged. An applicant who is denied a job on a discriminatory basis may be awarded the position in the company for which he or she applied, or perhaps a comparable position. Under these laws, compensatory damages for pain and suffering (or humiliation) are not available. The Civil Rights Act of 1991 does, however, make compensatory and punitive damages available to victims of discrimination under certain circumstances, up to set statutory caps. In *Pollard v. E.I. du Pont de Nemours & Co.* [533 U.S. 843 (2001)], the U.S. Supreme Court held that front pay (future lost wages) does not constitute compensatory or punitive damages under the 1991 amendments, and therefore is not subject to the Act's statutory caps.

Some of the older federal civil rights acts [42 U.S.C. §§ 1981–1985], which apply to race discrimination in employment, allow juries to award compensation for humiliation; in some cases, substantial (six-figure and, occasionally, seven-figure) damages have been awarded under these laws. Punitive damages (i.e., damages for particularly egregious wrongdoing) are seldom permitted under federal law, but there are significant exceptions. For instance, violations of the FLSA and the ADEA can be punished by doubling the back pay to which the successful claimant is entitled when the employer had no good-faith reason, such as advice of counsel, for its violation of the law. More important, under the Civil Rights Act of 1991, which amends, among other things, Title VII, punitive damages can be awarded for intentional discriminatory practices, subject to limits based on the size of the employer.

Rather than award damages to successful claimants, some laws, such as the Occupational Safety and Health Act, assess fines against offending employers. This Act allows substantial fines for willful violations. By leveling a separate statutory maximum fine for each instance in which its regulations were violated (for instance, for each day or each individual machine), the Occupational Safety and Health Administration has hit large corporate offenders (such as foundries accused of repeated lead- or mercury-poisoning violations) with extremely large fines, sometimes totaling millions of dollars.

Q 1:96   Are state laws part of the legal framework of employment law?

Yes. Most states and such territories as Puerto Rico and the Virgin Islands maintain comprehensive statutes prohibiting discrimination in employment on specified bases. Federal antidiscrimination statutes, such as Title VII, do not supersede state or local laws except to the extent that state laws encroach on federal rights or obligations. A state law that provides greater rights and obligations is permitted. As a result, in any given situation, any number of federal, state, or even local laws may apply. In addition, many states maintain laws that provide greater protection than that contained in federal statutes. For example, Michigan's Elliott-Larsen Civil Rights Act also prohibits discrimination on the basis of height and weight. These are not categories afforded protection under Title VII. Similarly, the Massachusetts Fair Employment Practices Act prohibits, among other things, discrimination on the basis of sexual orientation, which is also not a protected category under Title VII. Some municipalities have also enacted ordinances prohibiting discrimination on the basis of sexual orientation. As a result, federal, state, and potentially applicable local law should be considered in making employment decisions.

Q 1:97   What is the legal framework of state laws affecting the workplace?

State law affecting the workplace is generally of two types—statutory and common law. State statutes comprise of legislation that affects many facets of the employment relationship (e.g., civil rights, unemployment compensation, workers' compensation, personnel files, wages, and fringe benefits). Common law is not found in statutory compilations. It is based on principles and rules that have been developed through judicial precedent and, in many cases, derive from general principles developed in England and the American colonies. Generally, common law is built on two types of principles, one founded in tort and the other in contract. In the employment context, developments in both tort and contract law apply to the employment relationship.

Q 1:98   What types of state statutes apply to the employment relationship?

Throughout the country, state statutes applicable to the employment relationship are many and varied. Most states have adopted civil rights laws analogous to such federal civil rights laws as Title VII. Many of these state statutes provide greater civil rights protection than that provided under the civil statutes. For example, Michigan's Elliott-Larsen Civil Rights Act extends civil rights protection to individuals discriminated against in an employment relationship as a result of their height or weight. These are not protected categories under Title VII. In addition, Michigan's Persons with Disabilities Civil Rights Act, although analogous to the ADA, applies to employers with more than one employee, as opposed to the 15-employee requirement of the federal act.

In addition, many states have statutes with no federal counterpart, for instance, laws regulating the maintenance and disclosure of personnel files. Michigan's Bullard-Plawecki Employee Right to Know Act [MCLA §§ 423.501 *et seq.*], for example, regulates the disclosure of personnel records to both employees and third parties. Although Title VII has not been extended to offer protection from discrimination on the basis of sexual orientation, a growing number of states, such as Massachusetts and various local municipalities, have enacted legislation and ordinances protecting discrimination on this basis.

A number of states have enacted versions of the Uniform Trade Secrets Act, which protects an employer's trade secrets from misappropriation. A trade secret is generally defined under the Act as information that is not generally known which the employer attempts to keep secret and which enhances the employer's ability to compete with its competitors. Remedies for violations vary from state to state but generally include injunctive relief, actual damages, and attorneys' fees. [*See, e.g.*, Maryland's Uniform Trade Secret Act, Md. Code Ann. Com. Law §§ 11-1201–1209.]

Q 1:99 What are examples of state common law that apply to the workplace?

Common law can essentially be divided into two categories—tort and contract. With respect to contract, many states maintain that the employment relationship, absent any comments or statements to the contrary, is an at-will relationship that can be terminated by either party without redress or liability; however, most states permit employees to bring an action against an employer on contractual common law principles when they are discharged in violation of promises that the employer made to them. These "implied contracts" usually spring from representations of job security and the like that an employer allegedly made to induce employees to work for it. Once these representations have been made, the employer must, under implied contract theory, honor them, and if the employer breaches its promise, employees may pursue the employer for breach of implied contract under common law principles.

Numerous torts developed under common law can also apply to the workplace. Invasion of privacy, defamation, intentional infliction of emotional distress, negligent hiring, and negligent retention have been developed in various jurisdictions and may provide redress for employees under certain circumstances.

Chapter 2

The Employment Relationship

Chapter 1 discusses the statutory structure upon which employment law rests. This chapter explores the employment relationship and the legal ramifications associated with its creation, including discussion of employment contracts (oral and written) and company policies commonly contained within employee handbooks. In addition, this chapter discusses the subjects of leased employees and independent contractors.

The Employer-Employee Relationship

Q 2:1   What constitutes an employer-employee relationship?

No single definition of the employer-employee relationship is recognized. Rather, the existence of such a relationship is determined by the circumstances and the economic realities that apply. Generally, an employer-employee relationship is created by the terms of an agreement (i.e., contract), either oral or written, or the courts find it to be implied because of the parties' conduct. The traditional concept of master and servant is generally recognized as creating an employment relationship under federal and state labor laws. Under those laws, however, the concept of employment has been greatly expanded. Specifically, the Fair Labor Standards Act (FLSA) applies the term *employee* to situations in which an employer suffers or permits another to perform work for it. Permitting or suffering work suggests much less action than is required by the common law; mere knowledge by an employer of work done for it by another is usually sufficient to create the employment relationship under most federal and state labor laws. With respect to claims of discrimination, federal civil rights statutes generally apply to employees, as opposed to independent contractors, partners, or other non-employees. The question of whether an employer-employee relationship exists under federal civil rights statutes is answered by specific analysis of whether the employer controls the manner and means of the employee's work performance. A number of factors are considered, including the employer's right of control. [*See* Nationwide Mut. Ins. Co. v. Darden, 503 U.S. 318, 323–24 (1992); EEOC Compliance Manual § 2-III A.1.] At issue in *Thibault v. Bellsouth Telecommunications, Inc.* [612 F.3d 843 (5th Cir. 2010)], was whether a splicer hired by a telecommunications company to repair telecommunication grids after a hurricane was an employee or independent contractor of the telephone company. Utilizing the "economic realities test," the court concluded that the splicer was in fact an independent contractor because, among other things, the telecommunication company did not control how the splicer did his work, the splicer supplied much of his own tools and equipment, and did not work exclusively for the telecommunications company.

The EEOC lists the following factors to be considered as to whether an employer-employee relationship exists:

- The employer has the right to control when, where, and how the worker performs the job;
- The work does not require a high level of skill or expertise;
- The employer furnishes the tools, materials, and equipment;
- The work is performed on the employer's premises;
- There is a continuing relationship between the worker and the employer;
- The employer has the right to assign additional projects to the worker;
- The employer sets the hours of work and the duration of the job;
- The worker is paid by the hour, week, or month rather than the agreed cost of performing a particular job;
- The worker does not hire and pay assistants;
- The work performed by the worker is part of the regular business of the employer;
- The employer is in business;
- The worker is not engaged in his/her own distinct occupation or business;
- The employer provides the worker with benefits such as insurance, leave, or workers' compensation;
- The worker is considered an employee of the employer for tax purposes (i.e., the employer withholds federal, state, and Social Security taxes);
- The employer can discharge the worker; and
- The worker and the employer believe that they are creating an employer-employee relationship.

[EEOC Compliance Manual § 2-III A.1]

For FLSA purposes, the DOL does not follow the common law "economic realities test," but rather, considers the following factors to determine whether an employment relationship exists, or whether the relationship is that of an independent contractor:

- The extent to which the services rendered are an integral part of the principal's business;
- The permanency of the relationship;
- The amount of the alleged contactor's investment in facilities and equipment;
- The nature and degree of control by the principal;
- The alleged contractor's opportunities for profit and loss;
- The amount of initiative, judgment, or foresight in open market competition with others required for the success of the claimed independent contractor; and
- The degree of independent business organization and operation.

[See DOL Fact Sheet #13, http://www.dol.gov.]

Q 2:2 Can multiple entities be determined to be the employer of an employee under federal civil rights laws?

Yes, under two general theories. In the event that multiple entities are intertwined with respect to their operations, management, labor and/or ownership, the entities may be viewed as one employer both for purposes of having a sufficient number of employees to which Title VII is applicable (20 employees) and for purposes of liability. The factors to be considered are as follows:

1. The degree of interrelation between the operations
   - Sharing of management services such as check writing, preparation of mutual policy manuals, contract negotiations, and completion of business licenses
   - Sharing of payroll and insurance programs
   - Sharing of services of managers and personnel
   - Sharing use of office space, equipment, and storage
   - Operating the entities as a single unit
2. The degree to which the entities share common management
   - Whether the same individuals manage or supervise the different entities
   - Whether the entities have common officers and boards of directors
3. Centralized control of labor relations
   - Whether there is a centralized source of authority for development of personnel policy
   - Whether one entity maintains personnel records and screens and tests applicants for employment

- Whether the entities share a personnel (human resources) department and whether inter-company transfers and promotions of personnel are common

- Whether the same persons make the employment decisions for both entities

4. The degree of common ownership or financial control over the entities

- Whether the same person or persons own or control the different entities

- Whether the same persons serve as officers and/or directors of the different entities

- Whether one company owns the majority or all of the shares of the other company

In addition, when two or more employers are not integrated but exercise sufficient control of an employee to qualify the entity as an employer, the Equal Employment Opportunity Commission (EEOC) classifies them as joint employers—both for purposes of coverage and liability. [EEOC Compl. Man. § 2-III (B) (1) (iii) (b)] This is most likely to occur in the employee-leasing or temporary staffing situation where one employer, the leasing or staffing agency, leases or contracts the employee to another entity.

Q 2:3   Can multiple entities be determined to be the employer of an employee under the FLSA?

Yes. Under the FLSA, which provides, among other things, for payment of minimum wages and overtime, two or more employers, although presenting themselves as separate employers, may be sufficiently connected such that a joint employment relationship will be determined to exist. In a joint employment situation, hours worked in a workweek for both these employers will be counted for purposes of determining whether overtime compensation is owed for hours worked in excess of 40 during a workweek for non-exempt employees. [See 29 C.F.R. § 791.2.] Under the regulations, joint employment is generally considered to exist in the following situations:

- Where there is an arrangement between the employers to share the employee's services, as, for example, to interchange employees; or

- Where one employer is acting directly or indirectly in the interest of the other employer (or employers) in relation to the employee; or

- Where the employers are not completely disassociated with respect to the employment of a particular employee and may be deemed to share control of the employee, directly or indirectly, by reason that one employer controls, is controlled by, or is under common control of the other employee. [29 C.F.R. § 791.2]

The determination of whether an employer-employee relationship exists for the purposes of the FLSA is grounded in the "economic realities" as opposed to technical concepts and relationships. Analyzing the economic realities of the circumstances as a whole, as opposed to isolated factors, four factors have been identified as helpful in determining whether a putative employer-employee relationship exist: whether the employer (1) had the right to hire and fire the employees, (2) supervised and controlled work schedules or conditions of employment, (3) determined the method and rate of payment, and (4) maintained employment records. [Herman v. RSR Sec. Servs. LTD, 172 F.3d 132, 139 (2d Cir. 1999)]

In *Barfield v. New York City Health and Hospitals Corporation* [537 F.3d 132 (2d Cir. 2008)], one of the issues was whether a hospital was liable for overtime pay due a nurse who was employed by an independent nursing referral agency and assigned to the hospital to perform services. Reviewing the economic realities of the situation, the court concluded that the hospital, although not formally the nurse's employer, exercised sufficient functional and formal control over the nurse to qualify the hospital as her joint employer.

Under the Family and Medical Leave Act of 1993 (FMLA), integrated employers and joint employers can create employment relationships recognized by the Act. Likewise, the EEOC provides specific rules for determining whether multiple entities constitute a single employer as part of an "integrated enterprise" or joint employer relations. [EEOC Compl. Man. § 2-III (B)(1)(a.3)]

Q 2:4   Is the employment relationship a contractual relationship?

In one sense, employment relationships all have certain aspects of a traditional commercial contract relationship. If an employer verbally agrees to hire an employee at a specific rate and then refuses to pay him or her the agreed-upon amount after the employee finishes the work, the employee can pursue the employer under various contract or equitable theories of recovery. A commercial contract, which is agreed upon by both parties, can be modified only by mutual consent. If employment agreements were treated as commercial contractual relationships, employers would be bound to obtain the consent of the employee before any changes in the relationship could occur.

This is not necessarily always the case. In fact, under the presumption of at-will employment prevalent in most jurisdictions, employers can unilaterally terminate employment and change the terms and conditions of the working relationship on a prospective basis—including wages, benefits, and compensation—without liability for breach of contract. However, retroactive modifications typically would be considered a breach of contract, and in violation of state wage and hour laws.

Q 2:5   Can the employment relationship be modified?

Both written and oral employment agreements can be modified by the mutual consent of the parties. When an agreement is embodied in a written contract, the contract often contains a clause requiring that every modification to the contract take the form of an amendment to be signed by both parties. Oral contracts, on the other hand, generally take two forms—those that, by virtue of negotiation, rise to a level of express oral contract and those that are implied by law based on unilateral representations of the employer. For express oral agreements, mutual consent is usually required to alter the terms of the mutual understanding. Implied agreements typically result from unilateral representations and promises made by an employer to the employee or applicant concerning such issues as job security, which, when relied on by the employee or applicant, must be honored; however, in many implied situations based on unilateral statements by the employer, the employer may change the terms of the employment relationship through unilateral action. As such, an employer's unilateral pronouncement of an at-will policy (as discussed in Qs 2:6 through 2:16) is typically sufficient and applicable for all employees except those who have express contracts, either oral or written that require mutual consent for modification.

At-Will Employment

Q 2:6   What is *employment at will*?

In its simplest form, employment at will is an employer-employee relationship in which workers are free to sell their skills and labor to the highest bidder and move freely from job to job and employers are free to hire and fire employees without notice and without cause. Employment at will is the opposite of employment for a fixed term and termination for cause.

If an employer is an at-will employer, it does not have to demonstrate good cause when discharging an employee. If an employer is not an at-will employer, either through express written contracts or verbal express or implied contracts, a discharged employee has a right to challenge any discharge decision on the grounds that employment can only be terminated for just cause. Although most employers do not arbitrarily fire employees and usually believe that they have legitimate reasons for terminating particular employees, an employer may nonetheless not always be able to convince a jury (typically a jury of employees) that it had sufficient cause for terminating an employee. In light of the amount of time and resources necessary to litigate, employers find it advantageous to establish a clear at-will employment policy to prevent such wrongful-discharge litigation.

Q 2:7   What are the legal limits on the at-will relationship?

The at-will concept is limited by employment contracts (express or implied), federal and state statutes (i.e., civil rights laws), and such common-law doctrine as public policy and the implied duty of good faith and fair dealing, which are recognized by some states.

Q 2:8   Are there any advantages in employment at will to employers?

Although statutes and courts have narrowed employers' unfettered rights to discharge employees, employment at will is still a concept of value. Most employees are still hired with no guarantee of any fixed term of employment. The extensive use of this approach suggests that most employers still value the right to discharge workers when they deem it appropriate. The more practical advantage of employment at will is as a defense to wrongful discharge claims brought under contract theory. Although it has no effect against discrimination claims, public policy or other law, it nonetheless reduces an employer's exposure to employment litigation.

Q 2:9   How does an employer know if employment at will is the right choice?

Whether or not the at-will form of employment relationship is right for an employer depends on such business considerations as:

- The relevant laws of the state(s) in which the business operates;
- The bargaining power of the employees that the employer needs to attract and keep;
- The employer's business philosophy; or
- The business cycles of the employer's industry and the fluctuations in personal needs those cycles dictate.

In addition, employers should consider the more practical aspects of having their termination and discharge decisions reviewed by juries. If an employer is not an at-will employer, nearly all employer discharge decisions are subject to litigation. Few discharged employees agree with the employer's decision. Any dismissed employee, particularly one who has a difficult time finding subsequent employment, will be able to commence litigation against the employer by alleging the following:

- The employer, through its policies, statements or communications, represented that the employee would be terminated only for cause;
- The employee relied on these policies, statements, and representations;
- The employer, so the employee believes, did not have good cause to terminate the relationship; and
- The employee has been damaged as a result of the termination.

Juries, by and large, have been sympathetic to discharged employees. In addition, even if an employer prevails at trial, it will nonetheless have expended significant resources in defense of its actions. Discharge cases are time-consuming and costly. Attorneys' fees for pretrial activity alone often exceed $40,000. Trial fees almost always are greater than $20,000 for any type of discharge case. As a result, employers, although they do not intend to arbitrarily fire discharged employees at will, see value in adopting at-will policies to prevent litigation from discharged employees under contractual theories.

Q 2:10 Does employment at will vitiate the need for written acknowledgments and agreements?

Although many (perhaps most) employees work without written contracts, employment at will can be, and sometimes should be, combined with the written terms of employment. For instance, because the courts in a growing number of states have taken over the role that labor unions used to play in protecting workers' job security, many companies have job applicants and current employees acknowledge their at-will status in writing. This can be done on the employment application or by having a new employee sign a receipt for a handbook that includes a notice that the employee is employed at will. Although these documents are not written employment contracts per se, they help prevent an employee from later claiming that the employer made promises that made their relationship other than an at-will one.

Q 2:11 How can an employer make it clear that the employment relationship is at will?

An employer can, in a written statement in an employment application, employment contract, or employee handbook, state the at-will status of the employment relationship. The following is a typical acknowledgment:

> I understand and agree that my employment is for no definite period and may, regardless of the date of payment of my wages and salary, be terminated at any time, with or without cause.

Although such acknowledgments are typical, they are usually insufficient. Courts have routinely held, as a matter of common law, that acknowledgments and agreements can be amended in writing or orally at a later time. Consequently, a standard acknowledgment does not necessarily define the employer-employee relationship. For example, if an employee who signs a standard acknowledgment claims a supervisor later represented that he or she would not be terminated except for good cause, some courts will allow the case to move forward, reasoning that an acknowledgment could have been amended orally or in writing at a later time.

To skirt this loophole in at-will acknowledgments, an employer should understand how implied contract claims arise. People generally intuitively believe that they will not be fired as long as they do a good job; however, this belief is not, in and of itself, sufficient to alter an at-will arrangement. Only when an employee legitimately relies on statements and representations by someone in authority that his or her job will be terminated only for good cause does an at-will situation change. The employee must be relying on legitimate assurances of job security and of the terms and conditions under which his or her employment will be terminated. To forestall such a situation, employers should also include a provision in their contracts, applications, and handbooks that says:

No person, supervisor, or manager of the company has authority to alter the at-will status of your employment or to enter into any contract for a definite period of time, except the president of the company, in writing.

This provision limits the person by whom and methods under which any alteration to the at-will nature of the relationship can be made and thus prevents a fired employee from claiming he or she was legitimately promised job security by others.

Q 2:12   Can a written document alter the at-will relationship?

Yes. The at-will relationship can be changed by written language and oral representations to the contrary. Agreements for employment for a specific term, agreements providing job security, and written policies specifying that discipline can be exercised only for just cause can, for example, alter the presumption of an at-will relationship.

In addition, an employer's statement that promises job security and informs the employee that his or her employment will be terminated only for good cause is usually sufficient to overcome a common-law presumption of at-will employment. Once the employer communicates that the employment relationship is something other than at will (i.e., the presumption under law), the employer is bound by its representations, particularly if there is written evidence of the communication.

The more difficult issue arises when an employer on the one hand represents the employer-employee relationship as employment at will (e.g., in the employment application) but on the other hand promises job security (e.g., in its letter offering employment to the prospective employee). Under such circumstances, courts generally rule in favor of the employee regarding the nature of the employment relationship.

Q 2:13   Can a written disciplinary policy alter an at-will relationship?

An employer's written disciplinary policy has been held to have created an implied contract that employees will be fired only for good cause; therefore, an employee may have the right to expect that, in light of his or her satisfactory performance evaluations and the absence of any rule violations, he or she will not be fired. [Mitchell v. Jewel Food Stores, 586 N.E.2d 827 (Ill. 1990)] This case typically arises where an employer adopts a discipline policy with a graduating level of discipline based on both the number and severity of an employee's infractions. (For instance, the first violation of policy results in a verbal warning; the second, a written warning; the third, a suspension; and the fourth, termination.) Because such a written policy essentially provides that employment will be terminated only for good cause, it overrules any presumption under state law of employment at will. If the written policy provides for discipline only for what the employer defines as good cause, it also probably can be used to defeat acknowledgments of at-will employment that the employees have signed during the application process.

In some jurisdictions, it is still possible to impose some degree of progressive discipline without destroying an employment at-will relationship. The written description of this progressive disciplinary policy is usually phrased as a guideline that the employer states it is not required to follow and that declares that nothing contained within it alters the at-will nature of the employer-employee relationship or the employer's right to terminate the employee's relationship, with or without cause. Thus, a watered-down policy, carefully written so as to not be directly inconsistent with the at-will language in an employment handbook or policy, is not likely to alter the at-will nature of the employer-employee relationship.

Q 2:14   Can an employer be liable for terminating an at-will employee?

The essence of the at-will doctrine is that both the employer and the employee reserve the right to terminate the relationship, with or without cause. This means that an employer does not need to demonstrate "good cause" to support dismissal, and the employee cannot challenge the employer's decision in court claiming that it did not have sufficient cause to terminate employment. Although an at-will employer is free from a contractual standpoint to terminate employment, it cannot do so if the termination is a violation of other federal or state laws.

Potential bases for litigation are numerous, and although varying from jurisdiction to jurisdiction, they generally comprise the following:

Discrimination. An employer cannot discharge any employee, at will or not, if to do so is discrimination under federal or state civil rights statutes. Employers cannot utilize the at-will doctrine as a defense against discrimination under Title VII, the Americans with Disabilities Act (ADA), the Age Discrimination in Employment Act (ADEA), and other federal civil rights statutes. Put another way, the fact that employees are at-will employees who can be terminated with or without cause, does not mean their employers can discriminate against them in violation of state and federal civil rights laws. A federal judge ruled that the prohibitions against racial discrimination in terminating contracts in the post-Civil War Reconstruction Civil Rights Statutes [42 U.S.C. § 1981] were applicable to a racially-based termination of at-will employment. Although termination of the at-will employee did not breach the employment contract, it may nonetheless violate Section 1981 prohibitions against terminating a contract if it was based on race. [12 *Employment Discrimination Report (EDR)* (BNA) 205 (Feb. 10, 1999)] This conclusion has not been adopted by other federal courts. [*See* "District Courts Disagree on Whether the 1866 CRA Can Apply to an At-Will Employment Contract," 11 *Employment Discrimination Report* (EDR) (BNA) 348 (Sept. 2, 1998).]

Retaliation. Title VII specifically protects employees from discharge and discrimination for opposing unlawful acts under Title VII or participating in Title VII proceedings. Other civil rights statutes contain similar prohibitions against retaliation. As a result, an employer is not free to terminate its at-will employees if to do so would result in retaliation under Title VII or other similar statutes.

Violations of public policy. Even at-will employees are protected from discharge that violates so-called public policy exceptions to the at-will doctrine. The public policy exceptions generally apply when the employer discharges an employee in order to contravene the public policy of a state. For example, the discharge of an employee: (1) in violation of an explicit legislative statement prohibiting discharge of the employee who acts in accordance with the statutory right or duty, (2) for failure or refusal to violate the law in the course of employment, or (3) for exercising a right conferred by a well-established legislative enactment have all been held to be sufficient reasons to invoke the public policy exceptions to the at-will doctrine. [Dolan v. Continental Airlines, 208 Mich. App. 316 (Mich. Ct. App. 1995)]

Violation of whistleblower protection acts. Federal law and most jurisdictions maintain statutes that prohibit employers from terminating or discriminating against employees for reporting or being about to report a suspected violation of law to a governmental body. For example, Michigan's Whistleblowers Protection Act provides:

> An employer shall not discharge, threaten or otherwise discriminate against an employee regarding an employee's compensation, terms, conditions, locations or privileges of employment because the employee, or a person acting on behalf of the employee, reports or is about to report, verbally or in writing, a violation or a suspected violation of a law or regulation or rule promulgated pursuant to law of this state, a political subdivision of this state, or the United States to a public body unless the employee knows that the report is false, or because an employee is requested by a public body to participate in an investigation, hearing, or inquiry, held by that public body, or a court action. [Mich. Comp. Laws An. § 15.362]

Federal Whistleblowers Protection Act. The Federal Whistleblowers Protection Act [5 U.S.C. §§ 7502, 7512] protects federal employees from reprisals from whistleblowing on waste, fraud, and unnecessary governmental expenditures.

Violation of the implied covenant of good faith and fair dealing. A limited number of jurisdictions—most notably Alaska, California, Connecticut, Massachusetts, Montana, and New Hampshire—imply a covenant of good faith and fair dealing in the employment relationship. Improper motive (e.g., terminating an employee to avoid paying a commission) is the usual basis for liability.

Q 2:15 Does at-will employment survive today?

The concept of employment at will is alive and well in most jurisdictions today; through common or statutory law, most jurisdictions have a presumption of employment at will. Over the years, employees have sought to attack the traditional notion of employment at will by holding employers responsible for promises and representations they have made employees that their employment is not at will and will be terminated only for good and sufficient cause. Where the representations and promises rise above a certain threshold, courts have held that the relationship can be terminated by the employer only for good cause. When the representations and promises were not significant, however, courts have generally held that the presumption has not been rebutted.

In response, employers have begun publishing and disseminating at-will disclaimers and statements to ensure their at-will status and prevent the presumption of employment at will from being rebutted. Courts generally have held these disclaimers and statements sufficient to defeat claims founded upon the employer-employee relationship being anything other than one of employment at will, provided the policy is crafted carefully and is not inconsistent with other published policies and procedures.

The Pennsylvania Supreme Court issued a ringing reaffirmation of employment at will in *Paul v. Lankenau Hospital.* [569 A.2d 346 (Pa. 1990)] The court reversed a jury's award of more than $400,000 to Dr. Paul, who claimed he was fired for taking property from the hospital after having been given permission to do so. The plaintiff had successfully argued at trial that after allegedly giving him permission to remove some equipment, the defendant-hospital was estopped from firing him because he had relied on the responsible employee's word that he could have the equipment. The Pennsylvania high court reasoned that, as an at-will employee, Dr. Paul could just as easily have been fired the day before he took the machinery home for no reason whatsoever. "The doctrine of equitable estoppel is not an exception to the employment-at-will doctrine. An employee may be discharged with or without cause, and our law does not prohibit firing an employee for relying on an employer's promise." [*Paul*, 569 A.2d at 348]

This reasoning is consistent with the position that Michigan courts have taken concerning the relationship of the promissory estoppel doctrine to the employment at-will doctrine. In *Cunningham v. 4-D Tool Co.* [182 Mich. App. 99 (1989)], the plaintiff claimed that he resigned from his position in reliance upon a promise of employment by the defendant, a promise that was repudiated before the new employment was scheduled to begin. Although the defendant was an at-will employer, the plaintiff argued that the at-will doctrine should not apply, but rather, the doctrine of promissory estoppel should apply and provide him relief. The court disagreed. Despite the fact that the defendant repudiated the offer before the plaintiff was allowed to commence job duties, no cause of action was maintainable:

> We cannot distinguish the instant situation where the employee is fired after one day of employment. Plaintiff concedes that, had defendant employed him for one day and then fired him, he would have no cause of action. Arguably, then, plaintiff would have no cause of action had defendant fired him after one hour, or even one minute on the job. [*Cunningham 182 Mich App.* at 105]

The *Cunningham* decision has been cited with approval. [*See* Meerman v. Murco, Inc., 205 Mich. App. 610 (1994); Marrero v. McDonnell Douglas Corp., 200 Mich. App. 438 (1993); Barnell v. Taubman Co., Inc., 203 Mich. App. 110 (1993).]

Q 2:16   Are there any drawbacks to employment at will?

Many employers have questioned whether employment at-will disclaimers in their applications and employee handbooks affect employee morale. The answer is yes. An employment at-will statement makes it crystal clear that the employer has the right to terminate the employment relationship at any time, with or without cause. Most employment at-will statements also declare that there is no job security or a contract of employment for any definite duration and that the policy can be modified only in writing by the head of the organization.

Most employees assume that as long as they do their jobs they will not be fired. When employees are told that the company may terminate their employment without cause, at any time, they naturally become upset and feel that an employment at-will disclaimer in and of itself is unfair. Clearly, companies need to consider the impact of an at-will statement on their workforces. If employees are told by management in an at-will disclaimer that they have no job security, some may seek other means to get job security, such as union organization. In fact, this has happened. Although employers could not say for certain that the union organization campaigns are direct results of the employment at-will statements, they certainly have some impact; therefore, although an employment at-will statement is effective for purposes of defending and defeating wrongful discharge cases, it is not without its drawbacks.

Some employers have decided voluntarily to limit their right to discharge at will, whether formally through written policy or informally by corporate tradition. They do so because:

- Few employees are available with the training or talent needed;
- They wish to avoid problems with employee morale; and
- They wish to avoid union intervention.

Public Policy

Q 2:17   What is *public policy*?

Public policy is a standard of law applied throughout a particular state to such matters as public health, safety, and welfare. Most state courts hold that a particular activity or type of behavior is sanctioned (or forbidden) by public policy only if some state or federal law deals with the subject on which they are ruling. For instance, the courts in almost all states recognize that jury duty is a significant civic responsibility; therefore, a company that discharged an employee for missing work to serve as a juror is held to have violated a clear mandate of public policy. Generally, if an employee exercises rights conferred by a well-established legislative enactment, it is generally determined to be a violation of public policy to discharge him or her for exercising those rights. In the classic example, exercising rights under workers' compensation has generally been found to be a matter of public policy, and retaliation against an employee for exercising those rights is deemed a violation of public policy.

Jurisdictions usually restrict public policy to well-established legislative enactments; therefore, if an employee claims a right that is not supported by applicable state or federal law, the courts are unlikely to find that right a matter of public policy by the courts.

Q 2:18 How do courts use public policy to restrict or provide redress for firing an at-will employee?

Essentially there are two situations in which the public-policy exception to the at-will doctrine applies. The first occurs when an employee is discharged in violation of an explicit legislative statement prohibiting the discharge of employees who act in accordance with a statutory right or duty. The most common example is employees exercising their rights under a workers' compensation statute. The second occurs when an employee is discharged for failure or for refusal to violate the law in the course of his or her employment.

Federal law, for example, prohibits the use of lie detectors by employers in the workplace in most circumstances, and the law in some states makes it a misdemeanor to require an employee or job applicant to take a polygraph examination as a condition of employment. If an employer that suspects its supervisor is stealing tells that manager to take a lie detector test under circumstances that violate federal or state laws and if the manager refuses to take the test and is consequently fired, the discharged employee can sue the employer, asserting that he or she was wrongfully terminated. This is so even for at-will employees. The court hearing the manager's case is likely to rule that, because the employer's demand violated the law, the employer cannot be allowed to fire the manager for refusing the demand. Even though, under the common law of employment at will, the employer could dismiss the manager for any reason or no reason, it could not fire the manager because he or she refused to take the polygraph test.

Would it make any difference if the employer had published a written at-will policy that the manager signed? The public-policy exception to the at-will doctrine applies to both employers that have the presumption of employment at will and those that actually publish and disseminate clear at-will policies. Although the employer-employee relationship is at will and the employer reserves in writing the right to terminate its employees for any reason at any time, an employer cannot fire an employee if doing so would violate public policy.

This exception is analogous to that exercised in discrimination claims: Even though an employer reserves the right to terminate with or without cause, it still must abide by federal and state laws that prohibit it from discriminating against its employees in making employment decisions. The public-policy exception to the at-will doctrine, like the exception at work in discrimination cases, does not permit an otherwise at-will employer to violate the law or violate someone's legitimate exercise of rights conferred by law.

Many at-will employers that analyze a particular discharge in light of federal and state civil rights laws feel only those laws expose them to liability. This is not true. Managers should question supervisors about conduct that might result in a public-policy claim before sanctioning a termination. Under Missouri common law, if an employer discharged an at-will employee because that employee refused to violate a law or any well-established and clear mandate of public policy as expressed by the constitution or statute, or because the employee reports to his superiors or public authorities serious misconduct that constitutes violations of the law, the employee may maintain an action for wrongful discharge. [Fleshner v. Pepose Vision Inst., PC, 304 S.W.3d 81, 91 (Mo. 2010)] However, if an employee attempts to maintain a claim based upon reporting serious misconduct that constitutes a violation of law, failure to allege serious misconduct of a specific legal provision which is either established law or clearly mandated public policy will fail. In the case, the employee merely cited two violations of company policy as opposed to statutory law or clear mandates of public policy, and as a result, could not maintain a claim of public policy exception to the at-will doctrine. [Frevert v. Ford Motor Co., 614 F.3d 466 (8th Cir. 2010)]

However, the employee may not use the public policy exception to the at-will doctrine to maintain a claim for wrongful discharge if the statute, upon which the employee relied to maintain that the employer's actions were in violation of public policy, provides its own remedy for the employee.

In *Kassem v. Washington Hospital Center* [513 F.3d 251 (D.C. Cir. 2008)], an employee claimed that he was discharged as a result of his refusal to participate in a violation of law. The plaintiff was a nuclear medical technologist, and claimed that he was asked to participate in an investigation involving a radioactive incident that he claimed was being taken for the purpose of covering up the incident from the nuclear regulatory agency that should have obtained notice of the incident. Because, however, the federal law at issue that plaintiff claimed the employer violated contains its own remedies for parties aggrieved for violations, the court held that the public policy exception to the at-will doctrine wrongful discharge claim could not be maintained.

Q 2:19 What are some of the most common public-policy grounds that employees use to challenge their terminations?

Most wrongful discharge cases were ruled illegal because they were acts of retaliation by employers for the following employee actions:

- Absence from work to serve on a jury or as a witness in response to a subpoena [Shea v. Rockland, 810 F.2d 27 (2d Cir. 1987); Wiskotoni v.Michigan Nat'l Bank, 716 F.2d 378 (6th Cir. 1983); United States v. Adamita, 3 BNA IER Cases No. 1770 (S.D.N.Y. 1988)];

- Filing a claim for workers' compensation [Ford v. Blue Cross & Blue Shield of Conn., 216 Conn. 40, 578 A.2d 1054 (1990); Twilley v. Daubert Coated Prods. Inc., 536 So. 2d 1364 (Ala. 1988); Ryherd v. General Cable Co., 504 N.E.2d 745 (Ill. 1986)];

- Refusing to violate a law (e.g., "doctoring" the company's books or neglecting to report an accident or health-code violation to the proper government agency) or whistle-blowing. [Schlear v. Fiber Materials Co., 574 A.2d 876 (Maine 1990); Wagner v. Globe, 722 P.2d 250 (Ariz. 1986); Armstrong v. American Colloid Co., 721 P.2d 1069 (Wyo. 1986)]

Wrongful discharge can also occur in other instances. In an extreme example of the public-policy doctrine, a plaintiff successfully argued that she was fired for refusing to participate in an activity that was tantamount to indecent exposure. [Wagenseller v. Scottsdale Mem'l Hosp., 710 P.2d 1025 (Ariz. 1985)]

The following example illustrates one of the limitations to the application of the public-policy doctrine.

Example. An employee receiving a job offer is asked by the employer to report to a medical clinic for a medical examination and drug testing. At the facility, the employee is asked to provide his Social Security number to identify his drug sample. The employee refuses, claiming that under the law he is not obligated to provide his Social Security number and that the sample could be otherwise identified, perhaps with a driver's license number. After discussing the situation with the clinic, the employer revokes its job offer. The employee maintains that the revocation is a violation of public policy because he has the right to withhold his Social Security number from the medical facility.

Because it is a violation of public policy for an employer to discharge an individual for exercising rights under law or refusing to violate the law, the employee cites the Privacy Act of 1974 [5 U.S.C. § 552A(b)] and general procedure manuals of the Social Security Administration and other authorities, all of which restrict the dissemination of Social Security numbers by government officials and give individuals the right not to disclose Social Security numbers to government officials unless otherwise specifically sanctioned under law; however, no law sanctions the disclosure of a Social Security number to a private clinic, and the employer is not a federal, state, or local government body. Although many legislative enactments address Social Security numbers and their use for government officials, there is no such specific statutory basis to claim this argument applies to a private corporation. As a result, the argument for the public-policy exception to the at-will doctrine in this example should fail.

Q 2:20   What are the general principles behind the public-policy exception to employment at will?

Most states have embraced public policy as an exception to the employment at-will doctrine. The general principles behind this development in common law were well stated by a Michigan court in *Sventko v. The Kroger Co.*:

It is apparently true that the employment relationship in this case was an employment at will. And, while it is generally true that either party may terminate an employment at will for any reason or no reason, that rule is not absolute. It is too well-settled to require citation that an employer at will may not suddenly terminate the employment of persons because of their sex, race or religion. Likewise, the better view is that the employer at will is not free to discharge an employee when the reason for the discharge is an intention on the part of Employer to contravene the public policy of this state. [59 Mich. App. 644, 646–647 (1976)]

The general guidelines under which the public-policy exception to the doctrine of employment at will is understood were reaffirmed in *Dolan v. Continental Airlines*:

> The Supreme Court in *Suchodolski v. Michigan Consolidated Gas Co.*, 412 Mich. 692 (1982), has recognized three situations in which the grounds for discharge are so contrary to public policy to be actionable even when the employee is at will. First, when the employee is discharged in violation of an explicit legislative statement prohibiting discharge of the employee who acts in accordance with the statutory right or duty. Second, when the employee is discharged for failure or refusal to violate the law in the course of employment. Third, when the employee is discharged for exercising a right conferred by a well-established legislative enactment. [208 Mich. App. 316, 322 (1995)]

Moreover, the employee must be able to articulate a causal connection between the exercise of public policy right and the adverse employment action at issue. For example, in *Yon v. Principal Life Insurance Company* [605 F.3d 505 (8th Cir. 2010)], there was no question but that the employee had filed complaints with the DOL concerning the employer's alleged violations of the FLSA, FMLA, and state wage payment laws. However, because it was undisputed that the employee had not met the employer's sales expectations for some time prior to his complaint, and that by the time he informed his supervisors about his complaints to the DOL his sales had already declined and he had already received warnings, no causal connection could be established between the complaints to the DOL and his eventual discharge.

Q 2:21   How can an employer defend a public-policy lawsuit?

In suits brought under the public-policy exception to the employment at-will doctrine, there are essentially two separate defenses—the public-policy exception is not applicable or public policy was not violated. An employer and counsel should first determine whether the alleged violation of public policy falls within the public-policy exceptions recognized in the jurisdiction in which the case is brought. Public-policy exceptions are limited and typically require that there be some violation of state law or retaliation for an employee's refusal to violate state law or for an employee's exercise of rights under the law. If the allegations fit within a recognized public-policy exception to the at-will doctrine, an employer's defense should consist of demonstrating that the employment action was not the result of any violation of a legislative enactment or an act of retaliation but rather was done for legitimate business reasons. If, for example, an employer could prove that it fired an employee not because he or she refused to take an illegal polygraph test but because the security department's investigation concluded that the employee stole company property, the public-policy limitation would not apply.

Q 2:22   What is the *covenant of good faith and fair dealing* implied by some courts in the employment relationship?

Some states—including Alaska, California, Connecticut, Massachusetts, Montana, and New Hampshire—imply a covenant of good faith and fair dealing in the employment relationship, regardless of whether these terms are contained in any writings or representations by the employer. The covenant usually comes into play when an employee's discharge is improperly motivated (e.g., when the employer terminates a salesperson to prevent him or her from collecting commissions). Improper motive and bad faith in making employment decisions is usually the basis for liability.

This covenant gives rise to much litigation. Good faith and fair dealing, like beauty, is often in the eye of the beholder. Even employees discharged for heinous performance often maintain that they were not treated fairly by their employers. Not surprisingly, many states and the District of Columbia have simply refused to imply the covenant of good faith and fair dealing in the employment relationship—Arizona, Arkansas, Hawaii, Kansas, Maryland, Michigan, New York, Pennsylvania, South Carolina, Tennessee and Wisconsin, just to name a few.

Employment Contracts and Agreements

Q 2:23   What constitutes an employment agreement?

One party must make an offer, and the other party must accept it. Both parties must intend to make a contract. To be enforceable, a contract must be supported by consideration. This simply means that each party to the agreement must give the other something tangible (e.g., money) or intangible (e.g., a promise to give something in the future). In the case of an employment contract, the employer's consideration is a wage or salary plus fringe benefits. The employee's consideration is performance of the job that the employer needs done.

When a company places an employment advertisement in a newspaper or other publication, that advertisement is not a job offer. It is an invitation to qualified, interested persons to submit applications. Those applications are not offers either. Only after the applicant has been interviewed, and his or her job references have been checked, does an employer finally make a job offer that the applicant accepts or rejects. Typically, the offer of employment is considered a unilateral offer by the employer, which in most cases can be accepted only by commencement of performance. Whether an offer is oral or written, once it is made and the employee commences work, an employment contract exists. The nature and terms of the contract depend on the nature of the offer and its acceptance. Employment relationships are presumed to be relationships at will, which can be terminated by either party, with or without cause. Likewise, terms and conditions contained within the employment relationship (e.g., wages, salary, and benefits) are typically accorded similar treatment. Employers are generally free to change compensation and benefits prospectively at will, with no resulting liability. Retroactive changes will, however, usually result in a breach of contract or violation of state wage and hour laws.

The only exception to this rule occurs when an employer undertakes, in writing, to promise an employee that the compensation package will continue for a certain time, usually to be paid over a number of months or years. Generally, per diem statements of salaries and benefits are not sufficient to create a contractual commitment to maintain the compensation and benefits for any time period, unless clearly intended otherwise. Declaring in a job offer letter, for example, that the employee will be paid at a rate of $25,000 per year is not sufficient to create a contractual obligation to pay the employee that salary for one year. Rather, courts generally state that the per diem rate is merely a method of computing salary, which may be changed by the employer unilaterally and prospectively at its discretion.

Q 2:24   Is an offer letter a contract of employment?

In one sense, all employment relationships resemble traditional contracts. If an employer hires an employee for a specified rate of compensation, and the employee performs a service in reliance upon the employer's representations regarding compensation, the employer will be contractually bound to pay the employee the agreed-upon compensation. In this sense, even a simple offer letter that specifies salary can be viewed as a contract.

Most commercial contracts, once agreed upon, cannot be unilaterally changed by one party; rather, they can be modified only by mutual consent. In the employment context, in most jurisdictions, employment relationships are deemed to be at will, which means that the employer can terminate the relationship or alter the terms and conditions of employment (including salary and benefits) at its will, with or without cause. This changes the nature of the employment relationship, although such changes will only be typically permitted if they are prospective—retroactive modifications are generally impermissible.

As a result, an offer letter can be viewed as a contract, in the sense that it describes the terms and conditions under which an employee is employed by the employer. On the other hand, if the employer is an at-will employer, the offer letter will not work to prevent the employer from unilaterally changing the terms and conditions of employment prospectively. Whether an employer is an at-will employer or not is, in and of itself, an issue that bears discussion.

Most employers in most jurisdictions operate under a presumption that they are at-will employers, able to terminate the employment relationship and alter its terms and conditions with or without cause, at any time. In most jurisdictions, this presumption may be overcome by statements of policy or written or oral representations that alter the at-will presumption. One such method would be an agreement to retain somebody for a specific period of time, in writing. If an offer letter states specifically that somebody is being hired for a specific period of time, such as two years, courts will generally imply that the employer is bound to honor its two-year commitment and may only terminate the employment relationship prior to the expiration of that period for good cause. Another way to alter the at-will presumption would be language in the offer letter that promises that, although it is employment for an unspecified duration, the employer will only terminate the relationship upon good cause. Other language would include information contained within the offer letter promising job security, such that the relationship would not be terminated by the employer arbitrarily or without good reason, but would only sever the employment relationship for serious misconduct. If this type of language is contained within the offer letter, the employer will be contractually bound in most jurisdictions to honor its promise, and it would necessarily alter the ability of the employer to sever the employment relationship at will.

As a result, employers should take great care in the preparation of offer letters, and avoid any promises or representations that may be utilized by the employee to override the at-will presumption that is effective in most jurisdictions.

Q 2:25 What are the elements of an effective offer letter?

An effective offer letter is important not only in what it says, but what it does not say. Offer letters should not contain promises of job security, length of employment, or the promise not to terminate except for "good cause," unless the employer intends to honor its commitments and be vulnerable to litigation if the employee believes that the employer has broken its promises. Offer letters should generally address the following:

Job description. Most offer letters identify the position that the person has been hired to assume and describe generally the duties and responsibilities associated with the position. Often, the offer letter will refer to a job description, if one has been prepared for the position, which can be attached to the offer letter. In addition, the offer letter should contain language indicating that the employee is required to perform not only those duties described in the offer letter or the attached job description, but also such other duties as may be assigned to the employee by management. It is important that the offer letter provide some flexibility as to job duties, in the event that the job description or the explanation of the job duties contained within the offer letter is not complete.

Full-time efforts. If an employee is hired on a full-time basis, the offer letter should contain language to the effect that the employee is required to devote full-time business efforts to the performance of duties with the employer. If, on the other hand, the position is part-time, this should be specified within the offer letter.

Salary and compensation. The offer letter should indicate the initial salary, computed on a per diem rate or hourly basis, minus normal payroll deductions, payable on whatever periodic basis the employer maintains for its payroll. Typical language would provide: "You will receive an initial salary computed at the rate of $ per year, minus normal payroll deductions, currently payable on a bi-weekly basis." Typically, courts do not view such references to salary rates on a per diem basis as constituting a promise to retain an employee for a year. Rather, it is merely a reference to how salary will be determined, as opposed to a promise to either retain the employee for a year or pay them a specified rate during the year.

Benefits. Offer letters typically contain some description of the benefits for which the employee may be eligible. These include group insurance benefits, such as medical and prescription coverage, dental coverage, life insurance and accidental death and dismemberment coverage, vision coverage, short-term disability coverage, and long-term disability coverage. Many companies offer additional benefits such as sick pay, holiday pay, vacations, and tuition reimbursement programs. Many employers also maintain pension plans, 401(k) plans, retirement plans, and the like. With respect to insurance and retirement plans, employers are required, under Employee Retirement Income Security Act, to maintain summary plan descriptions (SPDs) for employee welfare plans and pension plans, and the offer letter can merely state that the employee may be eligible to participate in such plans, pursuant to the terms and conditions of such plans in accordance with the SPDs. It is important in an offer letter that the employer not make independent representations concerning the terms and conditions of these plans lest the employer be susceptible to contract and/or misrepresentation claims. With respect to other company-provided benefits, such as sick pay, holiday pay or vacations, the employer typically maintains an employee handbook that describes these benefits in greater detail. The offer letter should merely refer to the employee handbook and advise the employee of his or her eligibility, according to the terms and conditions of such policies.

Within the terms of the offer letter, the employer should, however, make it clear that it disclaims any obligation to maintain any such benefits during the term of the employee's employment relationship. This can be accomplished through language that specifically provides that all benefit plans referenced in the offer letter are subject to change, as determined by the employer, in its sole discretion from time to time. In addition, it is always advisable that the employer clearly state, whenever it provides information to employees concerning benefits, that all benefit programs are subject to the terms and conditions of the benefit programs themselves, and that the employer never promises or guarantees any insurance coverage or benefits; all benefits are to be provided pursuant to the terms and conditions of the insurance contract or benefit plan.

Commissions. If the employee is to be paid a commission, employers are strongly encouraged to state specifically how the commission will be calculated, how and when it is to be paid, and any terms and conditions of payment. Commission disputes are prevalent in employment law, and most disputes revolve around the eligibility, calculation or payment of commissions, either during employment or subsequent to employment (so-called post-termination commissions). A number of issues should be covered within any commission program, including:

- *How commissions are earned.* Commissions can be earned based on a number of different factors, including all sales to certain accounts or specified territories, or be limited to sales that are "procured" by the employee. Any use of procurement as a basis for earning a commission should define what procurement means (i.e., typically, sales generated by the efforts of the employee). Exactly when commissions are earned should also be specified (e.g., when purchase orders are received, when purchase orders are accepted, when shipments are made, or when purchase orders are paid after shipment).

- *How commissions are calculated.* Although usually referred as a percentage of the sales price, employers need to specify whether ancillary charges such as freight, setup fees, or tooling interest are included.

- *How commissions are paid.* Commissions are not usually paid until earned, unless a draw against commissions is utilized, and the employer should specify when they will be paid (e.g., on or before the 15th day of each month for commissions earned the prior month).

- *Whether commissions are paid after separation of employment.* In some jurisdictions, when there is no agreement to the contrary, employees can obtain post-separation commissions for orders they procured during the employment relationship. Orders can last for years, so employers should address this issue in writing at the outset of the relationship.

- *Allowance for deductions or repayment of commissions for returns and discounts.*

At-will employment. It is important in the offer letter to address whether the employment relationship is for a specific period of time, such that the employer can only terminate the employment relationship "for cause," or, if the employment relationship is "at-will," such that it is of indefinite duration and either party can terminate the relationship, with or without cause, at any time at the discretion of either party. If the employer intends to maintain the at-will presumption, and to defeat potential disputes for breach of contract upon termination of employment, it is important that the employer include suitable at-will language within its offer letter. Such language should provide that the parties understand that the employment with the employer is at-will, which means that it is terminable by either party, at any time, for any reason, with or without cause. Just having suitable at-will language contained within an offer letter is not, however, sufficient in itself, and the employer needs to ensure that it does not contradict its at-will policy contained in its offer letter with other information that may be provided to the employee during the hiring process or thereafter.

Conditions of employment. There may be many conditions to employment that must be satisfied before the commencement of duties, both as a matter of law and as a matter of company policy. For example, when hiring employees, it is incumbent upon the employer to satisfy the requirements contained under the Immigration Reform and Control Act of 1986 (IRCA), which requires employers to verify the employment eligibility of new employees by filling out Section 1 of Form I-9 at the time of hire. Under IRCA, employees are obligated to provide sufficient evidence of proof of employment authorization and proof of identity within a specific time period upon hiring. [See chapter 12 for more information regarding IRCA.] In addition, many employers condition commencement of employment upon physical examinations, which include drug screens. The ADA does not permit medical examinations, as opposed to drug screens, prior to a bona fide offer of employment. Once an offer has been made, it is permissible under the ADA for an employer to ask the employee to submit to a medical examination, and the employer may condition commencement of duties upon satisfactory completion of the medical examination. (Satisfactory completion typically means that the employee must be able to perform the essential job functions with or without reasonable accommodation.) If an employer conditions employment upon such medical testing and medical examinations, the offer letter should contain this requirement, specifying that commencement of job duties is conditioned upon satisfactory completion of medical examinations and drug testing. Under the ADA, however, if an employer wants to rescind the offer based upon the results of a medical examination, the employer must provide the information to the individual, and determine with the employee, whether the essential functions of the job can be performed through reasonable accommodation.

Agreement to abide by company policies and procedures. The offer letter should also indicate that the employee is required to abide by the employer's company policies and procedures as are usually contained within an employee handbook. Provided that the employer has an employee handbook, it is not necessary that the offer letter itself reiterate the terms and conditions. It is sufficient merely to express that the employee acknowledges and agrees that it must abide by these rules, terms, and conditions of employment in connection with the employment relationship. Handbooks should be carefully worded documents, and employers are strongly discouraged from attempting to summarize the terms and conditions within an offer letter.

Supplemental agreements. For many reasons, employers may consider using supplemental agreements such as confidentiality agreements, and non-competition agreements, and invention, patent, and trademark agreements in connection with the employment relationship. To the extent the employer maintains such agreements, the offer letter should refer to these agreements and provide that the employment relationship is conditioned upon the employee's execution of these supplemental documents.

Q 2:26 Can employers be liable under common law to employees for post-termination commissions?

As a matter of common law, some jurisdictions employ the so-called "procuring cause" doctrine for outside independent sales representatives and brokers retained on a commission basis to market and sell products. Under the procuring cause doctrine, as long as the sales representative is the procuring cause of a sale, once the sale has occurred, the sales representative will receive all commissions flowing from the sale, even if the sales representative's relationship is terminated by the employer. [*See, e.g.*, Reed v. Kurdziel, 352 Mich. 287 (1958).] The procuring cause doctrine is a common law doctrine that typically only comes into play when there is no other agreement between the employer and the outside sales representative. The parties are free to contract as they wish with respect to post-termination commissions. If no agreement is provided, the court, utilizing agency and equity principles, will generally provide the sales agent with the "fruits" of his or her efforts, regardless of whether the employer has terminated the relationship before the "fruits" have been realized.

After a sales representative has been hired to procure sales, the employer will not be able to avoid its obligations to the sales agent by arbitrarily terminating the sales representative. In essence, this doctrine is founded on agency and equitable principles—having received the benefit from the sales representative's services, the employer cannot terminate the relationship in order to avoid the obligations owed to the sales representative for the services. The sales representative is still entitled to commissions resulting from the sale.

In some jurisdictions, commentators have argued that the procuring cause doctrine historically applied to independent sales representatives should also be applicable to the employee sales agent. [*See, e.g.*, Bird, " 'Procuring Cause' and the Employee Sales Agent," *Michigan Bar Journal*, Jan. 1995 at 46.] Various cases have recognized the applicability of this doctrine to the employee sales agent. [*See, e.g.*, Harris v. Specialties Distribution Co., 305 Mich. 373 (1943); Fortune v. National Cash Register Co., 373 Mass. 96 (1977).] This could potentially expose an employer to costs it had not envisioned when terminating an employee; however, it is usually rather simple to eliminate the procuring cause doctrine as it applies to sales agents and to the employee sales agent as well. Providing within the written commission policy language that post-termination commissions are not paid, or are only paid under limited circumstances for a limited period of time, will usually do away with imposition of the procuring cause under common law principles. For employers employing sales agents paid, at least in part, on commission, it is important to address these issues in a written agreement to avoid unintended liability for post-separation commissions.

Q 2:27　What are the issues to be considered when developing a commission payment plan?

Commission arrangements should be prepared in writing to avoid dispute and litigation. Issues that should be addressed include the following:

1. *How is the commission earned?* The commission policy should state specifically how the employee earns commissions. Many different earnings criteria can be contained within a commission policy; often, the commission program contains a combination of various criteria. One common criterion is an exclusive arrangement whereby the employee will obtain commissions for all sales within an exclusive territory. This exclusive territory approach is relatively straightforward and does away with potential disputes involving procuring cause or issues that tend to complicate other approaches. When utilizing a territory approach, take care to ensure that the language covers situations in which a product is

sold within one territory but delivered to another. Similarly, the territory involved should be specified as exactly as possible. For example, phrases like "Western Michigan and Southern Ohio" should be avoided, and specific reference to city, county, or state boundaries is recommended. Boundaries for territorial exclusivity also can be established by reference to highways or rivers. In other situations, earnings criteria are based upon specific customers or accounts. This is similar to the territory approach, and often provides earnings for all sales to particular customers or accounts. Again, care should be taken to ensure that accounts or customers are sufficiently identified, and to the extent a customer maintains affiliates, divisions and the like, this should be addressed within the commission plan. Although utilizing exclusive territory and customers is a relatively straightforward approach for purposes of commission earnings, employers are often reluctant to provide commissions to an employee who expends little or no effort in actually obtaining a sale. If an exclusive territory is utilized, presumably all sales within the territory are subject to commissions, including direct sales and sales from existing accounts within the territory before the employee commenced employment. As a result, when using an exclusive territory approach, employers often carve out from earnings eligibility existing customers or exclude orders for which the employee was not the procuring cause of the sale. If an employer wishes to utilize a procuring cause arrangement for earnings of commission as the basis for all commissions or as a limitation to territorial or customer earnings formulas, the definition of *procuring cause* should be specifically contained within the commission plan. The employee generally has procured a sale because he or she has solicited that sale directly. In some circumstances, it may be sufficient to express that *procured orders* mean those orders submitted by the employee to the employer that result directly from the employee's solicitation of the customer or potential customer.

Even if an order is submitted that satisfies whatever criteria the employer wishes to utilize in connection with its commission plan, generally all orders are subject to the approval of the employer; therefore, the commission plan should specifically state that the employer reserves the right to accept or reject, in its sole discretion, any and all orders received from the employee. Most employers agree that there should be no earning of commissions until this additional condition has been met.

Even if an order has been accepted by an employer, many employers are generally reluctant to pay commissions or have the employee earn commissions until the transaction has occurred and the employer has received payment for it. As a result, with respect to earnings, most employers desire an earnings formula that provides that the employee does not earn commissions until the employer has been paid for the order by the customer for which the commission is to be paid. This prevents the employer from having to pay a commission on a sale that results in an account receivable on rejected or returned goods.

2. *Calculation of commissions.* Most commission arrangements are based upon a percentage of the sale; however, commission plans should specify, with as much detail as possible, the formula or method by which the total sales commission should be calculated. Often commission arrangements are conditioned on payments of money by customers or clients, but the term *payments received* is generally insufficient to define the sum against which the employer establishes the commission. The employer must define what sum of money will be utilized for determining the percentage. Sums received from customers may include costs, such as sales tax and freight charges, for which commissions are not usually afforded. In addition, in many industries, such as the tool machine industry, commissions are generally not paid for amounts received for tooling, set-up, and the like. Employers often exclude from commission formulas any returns, discounts, or other special allowances. To alleviate these problems and to specify more clearly how commissions will be calculated, many employers provide that the commission amount is applied against net receipts, which is specifically defined within the commission plan. An acceptable definition might state:

Net receipts means actual receipts received by the employer from the customer, minus all tooling, freight, sales tax, or returns.

Some commission plans vary the percentage based upon the amount of sums received through sales during any particular period of time. This sliding scale approach to commissions is utilized in many industries, and may include a sliding scale downward or a sliding scale upward. The sliding scale approach is common, but again, care should be taken to ensure that commission policy specifically provides a clear method of computing the commissions to avoid ambiguity and disputes.

3. *Payment of commissions.* Commissions are generally not owed by the employer until they are earned by the employee; however, even if earned, the commission schedule should provide specifically how and when the commission is to be paid by the employer to the employee. Many employers provide that commissions earned during any given month are paid at the end of the month following the month in which they are earned. Although any time period can be provided, it is important that it be clearly specified in the commission program.

4. *Commissions after termination or separation of employment.* The commission plan or program should specifically identify whether the employee is entitled to any commissions after termination or separation of employment. If the commission plan provides that commissions are only earned after receipt of payment by a customer, the commission plan could provide that the employee is only entitled to commissions earned up to the effective date of termination, thereby disallowing commissions after the effective date of separation or termination of employment. Provided the concept of earnings is specifically and clearly stated in the commission policy, such language would be effective in preventing employees from claiming commissions after separation of employment. On the other hand, many employers provide that an employee may receive

commissions on sums received attributable to approved orders received prior to the termination; however, any time an employer agrees to provide for the payment of commissions post-separation, there is always a danger that there will be a dispute as to the amount owed. For example, in many industries, customers submit so-called blanket orders, followed by smaller volume "release" orders, which may occur over a great period of time. In such circumstances, there could be disagreement as to whether the employee is entitled to a commission for the partial release or for all releases attributable to a blanket order previously submitted by the employee. To limit the risk of disagreement in these circumstances, if there is any commission to be paid subsequent to any separation of employment, the commission plan could provide, notwithstanding anything to the contrary, that no commissions will be owed for any money received by the employer for any customer or order within a set time following separation or termination of employment—for example, 90 days.

Many employers want to do away with their obligation to provide for post-termination commissions in the event the employee is terminated "for cause." Although this provision seems reasonable, disagreement is always expected as to whether the termination was for cause. If the time period during which post-termination commissions apply is rather limited, the burden of this approach is probably far greater than any benefit. On the other hand, if the employer still wishes to utilize a "for-cause" termination approach for purposes of stopping commission payments at the point of termination, the agreement should attempt to define *for-cause* termination. Generally, a for-cause provision for termination would include intentional or willful misconduct, failure to abide by a material policy or procedure of the company, material injury to the employer, or a conviction for a serious crime.

Q 2:28   Do any states have laws that penalize an employer for non-payment of commissions due and owing to its sales personnel?

Under Michigan's Sales Representative Statute, sales representatives are provided unique protection and remedies in the event that after termination of the relationship they do not receive commissions due and owing to them in accordance with the agreement between the parties. [Mich. Comp. Laws Ann. § 600.2961] The application of the statute is broad and applies to any principal that either manufactures, produces, imports, sells, or distributes a product in the state of Michigan, or contracts with a sales representative to solicit orders or sell products in the state of Michigan. [Mich. Comp. Laws Ann. § 600.2961(d)] Similarly, the definition of *sales representatives* is broad, applying to any person who contracts with or is employed by a principal for the solicitation of orders or sale of goods when they are paid, in whole or in part, by commission. [Mich. Comp. Laws Ann. § 600.2961(e)] In essence, the statute requires that all commissions due at the termination of a contract between a sales representative and a principal must be paid within 45 days after the date of termination. Any determination of whether or not commissions are due is based upon the agreement between the parties. If there is no agreement between the parties, past practices between the parties are considered. If there are no past practices, the custom and usage prevalent for the business in Michigan are considered. If a principal fails to pay commissions within 45 days after the date on which they become due, after termination of the relationship, a principal becomes liable for the following:

- Actual damages (i.e., the commission due);
- If the principal intentionally failed to pay the commissions, an amount equal to two times the amount of the commission due or $100,000, whichever is less; and
- Attorneys' fees and court costs awarded to the prevailing party. [Mich. Comp. Laws Ann. § 600.2965]

This statute, together with the imposition of the procuring cause doctrine (discussed in Q 2:26), which allows sales representatives in certain instances to procure commissions after termination of the relationship, allows sales representatives to recover significant sums attributable to post-termination sales.

Q 2:29   Can an employer create an employment contract without intending to do so?

In a sense, all employment relationships are employment contracts; the act of hiring an employee is obviously an intention to create an employment relationship. The issue really is what are the nature, terms, and conditions of the employment relationship. Terms of employment may be embodied in a written contract or they may be found in the personnel manual or employee handbook. In the absence of these sources, the words and actions of the employer and employee are evidence of the terms of employment.

Q 2:30   Can an employer's oral promises be enforced?

A promise that is clear and definite and intended to be relied upon and which is, in fact, relied upon by the employee to his or her detriment, may be enforceable under the doctrine of promissory estoppel. [*See* Barber v. SMH (US), Inc., 202 Mich. App. 366 (1993).] However, promises that are not definite and clear will not be enforced. For example, a statement by the employer that an employee would have a job "as long as he was profitable and doing the job" was held not to be sufficiently definite and clear to support a claim under the promissory estoppel doctrine. [Barber v. SMH (US), Inc., 202 Mich. App. 366, 376 (1993)]

Handbooks

Q 2:31   What is an *employee handbook*?

An *employee handbook* is nothing more than a codification of the policies and procedures of an employer. Almost all employers, regardless of size, have various policies and procedures that they must follow under state and federal law, as well as company-created policies and procedures. For example, state law requires that non-exempt employees be paid time and one-half for all hours worked over 40 hours in a workweek. Most employers with hourly, non-exempt personnel have policies on and procedures for working overtime and recording those work hours so the employers can comply with this law. Likewise, employers typically have sick leave, holiday, and vacation policies that they follow, formally or informally. Numerous employers, particularly manufacturing operations, also have numerous safety rules by which they require their employees to abide.

Many employers are taken aback by the very notion of creating an employee handbook; however, the truth is that an employee handbook simply reflects what an employer is already doing or what an employer should be doing to comply with state and federal law.

Q 2:32   What are the benefits of an employee handbook?

For those employers that have never assembled an employee handbook, doing so is an educational experience. Employers have general policies for vacations, holiday pay, work rules, discipline, and the like. Putting those policies into writing leads to the creation of better policies and removes any ambiguities and inconsistencies. It also encourages an employer to think ahead to formulate policies for situations that have not yet occurred.

In addition, the employer can use a well-drafted handbook as a defense in litigation. For example, most federal civil rights claims begin when similarly situated employees are not treated in the same way. Discrepancies in vacations and payment for holidays, for instance, provide a source for discrimination claims. One way to prevent those claims is to publish a written policy on accumulating and taking vacation time that the employer will apply consistently for similarly situated employees.

In addition, an employer can use an employee handbook proactively to reduce its risk to exposure and litigation. Proactive policies typically found in employee handbooks include those on sexual harassment, non-discrimination, medical examinations, drug and alcohol, e-mail, confidential information, conflict of interest, and employment at will. Employers that want to reduce their risk and exposure to litigation should strongly consider creating and publishing employee handbooks.

Employers that do not have handbooks generally create policies and procedures on an ad hoc basis when circumstances arise. As a practical matter, employee handbooks can also reduce the potential for legal exposure and the anxiety of dealing with situations as they occur. For example, an employer does not have a drug policy but suspects that one of its employees is using illegal drugs on the job. Having no policy to look to, the employer must decide how to deal with the situation. Should the employee be driven home? Should the employee be tested? What rights do the employee and employer each have? A drug and alcohol policy would provide a road map for dealing effectively with the situation. Without a handbook, the employer must create policy at a moment's notice, a haphazard and ill-advised method of operation.

Q 2:33   What are the disadvantages of an employee handbook?

Anything of value takes time and effort. One of the possible downsides is that the employer will produce a hastily written handbook that is poorly drafted and inconsistent with the practical day-to-day operations of the company.

Drafting employee handbooks is difficult. The process is technical and the language used must be unambiguous, consistent, well-written, and clearly understandable. To the extent that the employee handbook does not meet these criteria, it becomes a problem itself. Second, each policy an employer creates in its employee handbook must be practical and workable for that employer. For example, policies for alcohol and drug testing vary greatly, depending on the employer and its needs. For instance, most employers provide for mandatory testing upon reasonable suspicion that an employee is under the influence during work hours. Some employers merely provide for testing upon reasonable suspicion; others provide a format to determine the legitimate basis for this suspicion. Policies like the latter commonly include written field tests that the supervisor must fill out as to the condition of the employee and the basis for the supervisor's reasonable suspicion. Although having such a written field test may be wise for some employers, it may not be so for others. Adopting a field-test approach when the employer knows, as a matter of course, it will never be followed is not advisable. Great care must be taken to ensure that the policies and procedures that the company adopts in the handbook are realistic and practical under the circumstances in which they will be used.

The most obvious disadvantage of an employee handbook is that employee policies and procedures change. If a handbook created in 1990 has not been modified to reflect changes in the workplace, obsolete features can be used against an employer. A handbook is, in a sense, a living document that must be continuously amended whenever changes in policy and procedure occur.

Q 2:34   What is the goal of an employee handbook from a legal perspective?

From a legal perspective, an employee handbook has many goals:

1. *To reduce the risk of employee litigation for such claims as discrimination, breach of implied contract, and harassment.* Discrimination litigation often arises when similarly situated people are not treated similarly or when policies and procedures have an adverse impact on a protected class. Written policies that address the many discrimination issues

inherent in an employment context ensure that employees are treated similarly when similar situations arise. Thus, these policies reduce the risk of discrimination claims. In addition, by reviewing and analyzing previously accepted policies before reducing them to writing, an employer can spot any policy that appears to have an adverse impact on a particular class or group of people and refine it to prevent claims of discrimination by disparate impact.

An employment at-will policy helps prevent claims for wrongful discharge based on implied contract. These claims are substantiated by assertions by employees that they were promised job security and that they would be discharged only for good cause. An employment at-will disclaimer ensures that an employer maintains its at-will status and the right to terminate, with or without cause. In addition, every employee handbook ought to have a harassment policy to reduce risk and exposure to litigation. This is particularly important today, in light of the U.S. Supreme Court decisions *Burlington Industries v. Ellerth* [524 U.S. 742 (1998)] and *Faragher v. City of Boca Raton* [524 U.S. 775 (1998)] (discussed in chapter 4) that require an employer to undertake preventative and corrective measures in the area of sexual harassment in order to affirmatively defend claims involving harassment by supervisors. The policy should define sexual harassment claims, demonstrate the company's intolerance toward it, encourage employees to come forward to report any incidents of it, and prohibit retaliation for coming forward.

Moreover, even if a company is not large enough to be covered by the FMLA, companies should consider developing medical leave policies to provide a framework to deal with employees that are unable to work due to medical conditions or disability for an extended period of time. This allows a company to put in place a uniform policy applicable to all employees and determine such things as how long the leave can last, whether the leave is paid or unpaid, whether benefits will continue, and whether reinstatement is guaranteed.

2. *To ensure compliance with all applicable laws.* Numerous state and federal laws are applicable to employers. Under federal law, for example, exempt employees do not have to be paid overtime; however, if an employer follows a policy of docking a salaried exempt employee for tardiness, that employer risks losing that employee's exempt status, which entitles the employee to overtime pay for all hours worked in excess of 40 hours. An employer can prevent unintended violations of law by reviewing company policies and procedures while drafting an employee handbook. There are other ways of disciplining a tardy, exempt employee. As another example, the FMLA requires that employers notify employees of their rights under the FMLA through posting, and, in various provisions, provide that various policies the employer has adopted relating to the FMLA be contained within any handbook maintained by the employer. [*See, e.g.*, 29 C.F.R. § 825.311(c) regarding required fitness-for-duty certifications upon return to work.] Given the technical nature of the

employment relationship under federal and state laws, an attorney should review the employee handbook to spot potential problems.

Q 2:35   What are some general guidelines for effectively drafting an employee handbook?

Although no two employee handbooks are alike, some general rules should always be followed.

1. *The employee handbook should be clear, concise, and consistent.* It should be read many times and revised repeatedly until the language is distilled to its essence and clearly states what is intended.

    If a policy is not practical and will not be followed, the handbook should not include it. The best policy in the world becomes the worst if it is not followed. Inconsistencies between written policies and day-to-day practice will undoubtedly be used against the employer. As a result, all the policies should be analyzed from a practical standpoint to determine whether they will be followed. If they will not, the employer should revise them.

2. *All policies should be consistent with one another.* All policies, even if established separately, interrelate. They must be consistent in order to work together. For example, family and medical leave is a federally mandated requirement for an employer with 50 or more employees; however, most employers, particularly those with 50 or more employees, already have company-created medical leave policies. Those policies, although separate, need to be woven together with legislative policies to ensure that they work together in a legal, practical, and consistent manner.

3. *The employer should avoid fluff.* If it does not need to say something, it should not. When companies draft employee handbooks, they oftentimes feel compelled to include feel-good language vaguely praising the organization and its employees. Typical fluff is contained in such sections as "Company History." Not only does fluff serve no purpose, it often is used against an employer in litigation. An aggrieved employee's attorney, when considering employment litigation, carefully reads the employee handbook and studies every clause to determine if there is anything he or she can use to advance the employee's claim. Not surprisingly, such assistance is often contained in off-handed comments found in the fluff sections.

4. *The employer should subject the employee handbook to a thorough and critical review.* Undoubtedly, inconsistencies and ambiguities will be uncovered, as well as issues that are not addressed. If, for example, a company has created a vacation policy whereby an employee earns vacation time every year at his or her anniversary date and the number of vacation days rises with the employee's years of seniority, the company may have mentioned nothing about whether earned but unused vacation can be carried over from year to year. Does the policy provide for payment

in lieu of taking a vacation? What if an employee voluntarily resigns, is he or she entitled to payment for earned but unused vacation? What about discharge for willful misconduct? A critical review would necessarily reveal these issues and offer the employer an opportunity to deal with them before the employee handbook is distributed.

Many policies (e.g., at-will policies, FMLA policies, non-discrimination policies, harassment policies, medical examination policies, drug and alcohol policies, and FLSA policies) are created to either reduce risk and exposure to employee litigation or promote compliance with law. The employer should review these policies carefully with its employment attorney, and should be cautious against modifying or deleting these policies, except on the advice of counsel.

Q 2:36 Generally, what types of policies and procedures are contained within an employee handbook?

Employee handbooks can be broken down into a number of categories:

1. *General employment policies.* This category contains the general employment policies that the employer has adopted for its workplace. Employment at will, sexual harassment, discrimination, medical examinations, confidentiality, nepotism, and smoking policies are typically included.

2. *Compensation policies.* Within this category are typically included policies about the classifications of employment (e.g., exempt, non-exempt, full-time, part-time, and temporary), work hours, recording work hours, breaks, pay procedures, overtime, and overtime pay.

3. *Time-off benefits.* This category typically includes policies that address vacation time, holidays, personal days, sick days, medical leaves of absence, personal leaves of absence, leaves under the FMLA, bereavement leaves of absence, jury and witness duty leaves, and military leaves of absence.

4. *Work rules and employee conduct.* This category details the employer's policies on attendance, punctuality, work rules, personal appearance, demeanor, e-mail, telephone use, confidentiality, and the like.

5. *Insurance and retirement benefits.* Company policies with respect to group insurance benefits (e.g., health and dental benefits), Consolidated Omnibus Budget Reconciliation Act (COBRA) benefits, workers' compensation, and any pension plan or welfare benefit that the employer maintains can be found in this category.

Q 2:37 What are the elements of an effective employment at-will policy?

The purpose of an employment at-will policy is to preserve the presumption of employment at will that most jurisdictions provide either through common or statutory law. The policy attempts to ensure that employees have no objective or legitimate expectation that their employment is terminable only for just cause.

Although not exactly alike, most effective employment at-will policies provide the following, in language that is clear and consistent with other policy statements:

- Employment is for no definite period.
- The employment relationship can be terminated by the employer at any time, with or without cause.
- The policy can be amended only by the employer's president or some senior officer and then only in writing.
- The employee handbook is not a contract of employment.
- The policy should be disseminated in such a fashion to evidence the employee's receipt of the policy (i.e., included within a handbook, the receipt of which the employee acknowledges by signature).

Q 2:38   What is an example of an at-will policy?

Generally, an at-will policy will contain language like the following:

AT-WILL EMPLOYMENT

This Employee Handbook is intended as a general reference guide to the benefits, conditions, rules, and procedures governing your employment with the Company. This Handbook is not a contract of employment. THE COMPANY IS AN AT-WILL EMPLOYER, WHICH MEANS THAT YOUR EMPLOYMENT RELATIONSHIP WITH THE COMPANY IS FOR NO DEFINITE PERIOD AND MAY BE TERMINATED AT ANY TIME, WITH OR WITHOUT CAUSE AND WITH OR WITHOUT NOTICE, AT THE WILL OF EITHER THE COMPANY OR YOU. Just as you may terminate your employment with the Company at any time, for any reason, or no reason, so may the Company terminate its employment relationship with you, at any time, for any reason or no reason. The direction and control of all work for all employees is the sole discretion of the Company and includes, by way of illustration and not limitation, the right to hire, lay off, transfer, reassign, demote, or discharge.

No manager or representative of the Company, other than the President, has authority to enter into an agreement for employment for any specific period of time or make any agreement contrary to the foregoing. Further, any such agreement by the President is not enforceable unless it is in writing.

Q 2:39   What are the elements of an effective policy on discrimination and sexual harassment?

A policy on discrimination and sexual harassment should proclaim an employer's commitment to equal opportunity and its refusal to tolerate discrimination and harassment in the workplace. By having such a policy, an employer hopes to reduce the risk of such evils and provide a mechanism, through an internal complaint procedure, to deal effectively with a potentially explosive situation before an administrative charge or litigation is filed. To accomplish these goals, an employer should adopt the following format:

- Policies should begin with a strict definition of discrimination and sexual harassment under applicable state and federal law. Because of the nuances of state law, these definitions can change from jurisdiction to jurisdiction. In Michigan, for example, a non-discrimination policy would include prohibitions against discrimination on the basis of height, weight, and marital status under the state's Elliot-Larsen Civil Rights Act. Such prohibitions do not necessarily exist in other jurisdictions. Likewise, some states' definitions of sexual harassment may be more expansive than those provided by federal law. The definitions used in employers' policies should strictly follow prohibitions established by applicable law. Employers should not define sexual harassment and discrimination in such a way that provides more protection than is legally required. Otherwise, an employer risks being held responsible for conduct that is not otherwise a violation of the law. Most employers do not want to do this.

- Because courts now recognize harassment claims involving protected categories beyond sex (i.e., racial harassment, national origin harassment, or disability harassment), the policies need to reference the inclusion of such conduct within the harassment policy.

- All policies should provide for an internal procedure that encourages complaints by making them easy to register. The purpose of the policy is to avoid litigation and provide a mechanism to deal with troublesome situations promptly and effectively. A cumbersome procedure may reduce the number of complaints registered, but failure to complain through a cumbersome company procedure is usually not considered a bar to litigation. As a result, a user-friendly procedure should be established that allows employees to register even verbal complaints to anybody in management. Although it is extremely important to reduce the claim to writing before it is investigated, initial claims need not be in writing. Requiring that individuals speak first with their supervisor is not recommended either; often, it is the supervisor whose conduct is at issue.

- The employer should not promise confidentiality but should endeavor to keep internal complaints as confidential as practical under the circumstances. Once an employer receives a complaint, it cannot determine whether a violation of policy has occurred until after an investigation. Details of the complaint must be mentioned to the alleged wrongdoers to determine whether or not a violation of the policy has occurred. As a result, complete confidentiality cannot be maintained and should never be promised.

- A policy should provide that if an investigation reveals that a violation of policy has occurred, the wrongdoer will be subject to disciplinary action up to and including discharge. It is wise to at least maintain some degree of flexibility in discipline; use of the phrase "up to and including discharge" provides that flexibility.

- The policy needs to have clear language advising employees that the company prohibits retaliation against an employee who, in good faith, brings a complaint forward.

In addition, the policy should specify that if employees believe they are being retaliated against, they should utilize the same complaint procedure for claims of harassment.

Q 2:40 What is an example of a policy on discrimination and sexual harassment?

The policies vary, particularly from state to state, to take into account state law protections that may not exist under federal law. The following was prepared for Michigan clients and references protections under Michigan's civil rights law.

SEXUAL HARASSMENT

The Company prohibits sexual harassment of any kind by any person. *Sexual harassment* includes unwelcome sexual advances, unwelcome requests for sexual favors, and other unwelcome verbal or physical conduct or communication of a sexual nature when:

- Submission to such conduct or communication is made either explicitly or implicitly a term or condition of the individual's employment;

- Submission to or rejection of such conduct or communication by an individual is used as the basis for employment decisions affecting such individual; or

- Such conduct or communication has the purpose or effect of substantially interfering with an individual's employment or creates an intimidating, hostile, or offensive work environment.

Conduct in violation of this policy may result in disciplinary action, up to and including discharge.

COMPLAINT PROCEDURE

If you believe that you or another employee has been the subject of discrimination or harassment, you should report the situation to your supervisor promptly or, if you feel that your supervisor has failed to address the situation adequately or would rather not approach your supervisor, you should speak directly with the President or any other manager or officer of the Company.

A prompt investigation of all complaints will be undertaken. To the extent practicable under the circumstances, efforts will be made to maintain the confidences and privacy of the complaining party and other involved parties during the investigation. Any employee who, after investigation, is determined to have participated in or engaged in discrimination or harassment may be subject to discipline, up to and including discharge.

The Company prohibits any retaliation against an employee who, in good faith, has made a complaint under this procedure. Any employee of the Company who, after reasonable investigation, has been determined to have retaliated against an employee for making a good faith complaint under the complaint procedure may be subject to discipline, up to and including discharge. If an employee believes he or she has been the subject of retaliation, the employee should use the complaint procedure described above.

Q 2:41   What are the elements of a good policy on substance abuse?

Alcohol and drug policies take many forms, but any policy should:

- Prohibit the use or possession of alcoholic beverages on the employer's property or during the course of business. This is a general prohibition common to many alcohol and drug policies. To the extent that employees entertain at lunch, however, and otherwise engage in employer-sponsored events that include the consumption of alcohol, an exception to this prohibition should include such limited authorized use, albeit in moderation.

- Prohibit the illegal use of drugs and the sale, transfer, use, or possession of illegal drugs on the employer's property or during the course of business. A policy on only use is insufficient. Most employers also consider it equally reprehensible to sell or possess illegal drugs on company property or in the course of its business.

- Establish parameters for the use of legal drugs. Use of a legally prescribed drug, even a controlled substance, should not violate an employer's substance-abuse policy. Among other reasons, this policy might be unenforceable under the ADA as it relates to disabled employees (see chapter 4). Even legal use of drugs can affect employees, however, by making it difficult or dangerous for them to operate machinery or fulfill their other duties. As a result, an employer's alcohol and drug policy should instruct employees to advise their supervisors of any legally prescribed drugs they use if those drugs could be a source of danger in the workplace.

- Create a mechanism for alcohol and drug testing. No drug policy is complete without a mechanism for alcohol and drug testing. Many employers oppose random drug testing and test only when they have a reason to believe that an employee is under the influence of an illegal drug or alcohol in violation of policy. The policy should also provide that when the employer has such a suspicion, the employee must submit to an alcohol and drug test reasonably requested by the employer. Failure to consent to testing typically results in discharge.

- Advise employees of the employer's right to search and seizure. If an employer believes that an employee possesses illegal drugs or alcohol in violation of its policies, it will need a procedure for searching for and seizing this contraband. Many problems are associated with any search and seizure, the most obvious being a possible claim of invasion of privacy by the employee. Employers should therefore advise employees in their policies that they reserve the right to search employees' lockers, lunch pails, and the like. This way, an employee will not expect privacy as it relates to such searches.

• Take into consideration assistance programs. Although it is not required to do so, an employer may, as part of its substance-abuse policy, encourage employees with substance-abuse problems to seek treatment. An employer that does so should nonetheless state in its policy that an employee voluntarily seeking such treatment for dependency will not, by virtue of seeking treatment, avoid disciplinary action.

Q 2:42   Do medical marijuana laws affect an employer's right to enforce its substance abuse policies?

Many states have adopted medical marijuana laws to permit limited consumption of marijuana for medicinal purposes. Many employers, on the other hand, have drug and alcohol policies that provide for, among other things, random drug testing and termination for positive marijuana results. In *Casias v. Wal-Mart Stores, Inc.* [695 F.3d 428 (6th Cir. 2012)], an employee, who was terminated for testing positive for marijuana claimed that the employer had violated Michigan's Medical Marijuana Act, which permitted limited use of marijuana for medicinal reasons. However, the court, in reviewing the statute, found that the statute did not apply to private employers such that the claim could not be maintained.

Q 2:43   What is an example of a substance abuse policy?

Below is a sample of a "reasonable suspicion" policy. These policies vary greatly depending upon the company's business and its concerns in this regard.

DRUG AND ALCOHOL POLICY

The Company regards substance abuse, including both illegal drug and alcohol abuse, as a serious, medical, business, social, and economic problem. It is the intent of this policy to provide a workplace free from the adverse impact of alcohol and illegal drug use and to take reasonable measures to ensure that their use does not jeopardize the success of the Company or otherwise affect our employees or customers.

Alcohol

The use or possession of alcoholic beverages on Company property or on Company business (except in moderation at Company authorized functions or events) is prohibited. Reporting to work while under the influence of alcohol is also prohibited. An employee will be considered to be "under the influence" of alcohol if the employee tests positive for alcohol or when its consumption has impaired or is likely to impair the employee's job performance in the sole judgment of the Company.

Illegal Use of Drugs

The sale, purchase, transfer, use, or possession of any illegal drug while on Company property or on Company business is prohibited. An employee will be considered "under the influence" of a drug if the employee tests positive for illegal drugs or when its use has impaired or is likely to impair job performance in the sole judgment of the Company.

Legal Use of Prescription Drugs and Over-the-Counter Medication

Prescription drugs and over-the-counter medication are only a cause for concern to the Company if they affect the ability of an employee to work safely. It is the responsibility of the employee to review any work restriction that should be observed while taking the drug. If there is a work restriction, it is also the responsibility of the employee to review that restriction with his/her supervisor before the commencement of job duties.

Alcohol and Drug Testing

Any employee who is involved in a job-related accident or whose on-the-job behavior indicates that he or she may be under the influence of drugs or alcohol in violation of this policy, in the sole judgment of the Company, may be required to submit to alcohol and drug testing conducted by medical personnel designated by the Company. An employee's refusal to submit to drug and alcohol testing is considered insubordination and may subject the employee to disciplinary action, up to and including termination. If the results of testing indicate evidence of alcohol or drug usage in violation of this policy, the employee may be subjected to disciplinary action, up to and including discharge. The Company will endeavor to keep the results of any alcohol and drug test confidential and disclosed only on a need-to-know basis.

Alcohol and Drug Dependency

An employee suffering from alcoholism or drug dependency is encouraged to seek proper medical treatment. An employee's decision to seek treatment will not be used as a basis for disciplinary action against the employee. However, satisfactory job performance and adherence to Company policy are still mandatory, and an employee seeking treatment will not avoid disciplinary action if he/she does not otherwise meet satisfactory job performance standards and other Company policies.

Q 2:44   What is commonly found in compensation policies contained in employee handbooks?

Compensation policies address employee pay. These include classifications of employment, wherein an employer distinguishes among full-time, part-time, exempt, non-exempt, and (possibly) temporary employees. The benefits of making such distinctions are many. Exempt employees are salaried, whereas non-exempt employees, who are typically paid an hourly wage, are eligible for overtime pay in accordance with state and federal law. When distinguishing between exempt and non-exempt employees in the employee handbook, employers often come to appreciate the differences between these two classifications. Many employers believe that if they pay an employee a salary, they do not have to pay overtime. This is not necessarily the case. Although to maintain their exempt status, exempt employees must be paid a salary, otherwise non-exempt employees do not become exempt by being paid a salary.

The distinction between full-time and part-time employment is equally important; it often affects insurance and benefits such as time off. Many employers require an employee to be full-time and hold certain tenure with the company to qualify for vacations, sick days, health insurance, and the like. Contrary to popular belief, there is no federal law or regulation that equates full-time employment with a 40-hour workweek. In fact, many employees, particularly in the service sector, actually work less than 40 hours per week even though they are considered full-time. When defining what is full-time employment (typically for benefit purposes), ensure that actual hours worked are counted accurately to properly reflect hours regularly worked in a workweek for your full-time employees. Simply put, if your full-time employees work 9:00 to 5:00, with an unpaid hour for lunch, full-time employment would be 35 hours as opposed to 40.

Typically hired for a specific duration or hired for the completion of a particular job, temporary employees are usually not eligible for employer benefits. By establishing an employee classification of temporary employees, an employer can make it clear that those employees are treated similarly to others within that classification.

In addition to employee classifications, compensation policies also typically define regular work hours for employees and the requirement that employees work beyond them when asked by the employer. Even salaried employees may be required to work beyond their regular hours. Most work-hour provisions describe the circumstances under which an employee is authorized to work overtime and provide for overtime pay for non-exempt employees only in accordance with federal and state statutes and regulations. One of the most important aspects of a work-hour policy is to provide the flexibility that allows an employer to alter work hours when necessary; therefore, whatever hours are specified in the employee handbook should always be followed with such language as "or other work hours as may be determined by your supervisor, at his or her sole discretion." This enables an employer to set a general framework that still provides flexibility.

Employers should also include any requirements they impose on their hourly and salaried employees for recording their time. Typically, non-exempt employees "on the clock" must follow a rigorous procedure for recording time, in part because of the requirements of the Federal Labor Standards Act. Policies should specify that it is the employee's responsibility to ensure that an accurate record of his or her hours is kept and should provide for discipline if an employee falsifies or otherwise does not keep accurate hours on whatever time-recording system the employer uses. Many employers see the benefit of salaried employees also keeping such records. Although compensation for exempt employees is not measured by the hour, most employers want some time sheet or written record of hours worked. This may be of some assistance in resolving workers' compensation claims when a salaried employee claims on-the-job injuries.

Most compensation policies also outline when employees will be paid and the procedure for claiming exemptions under federal law. Most employers include in their policies a direction to employees to review their paychecks and report any discrepancies immediately.

Q 2:45   What is an example of a classifications of employment policy?

The specifics of a company's policy may vary depending upon how the company defines full-time employment and who is eligible for benefits. Below is a sample classifications employment policy.

CLASSIFICATIONS OF EMPLOYMENT

For purposes of salary administration and eligibility for overtime payments and employee benefits, the Company classifies its employees as follows:

1. *Full-Time Employees.* Employees hired to work at least 40 hours per week on a regular and consistent basis. Such employees may be "exempt" or "non-exempt" as defined below.

2. *Part-Time Employees.* Employees hired to work less than 40 hours per week on a regular and consistent basis. Part-time employees receive benefits required under law, but are ineligible for most Company provided benefits, (see Benefit Section for more detail). Such employees may be "exempt" or "non-exempt" as defined below.

3. *Temporary Employees.* Employees engaged to work for a limited period on the Company's payroll with the understanding that their employment will be terminated no later than upon completion of a specific assignment. Such employees may be "exempt" or "non-exempt" as defined below. Temporary employees receive no benefits, except those required under law.

4. *Non-Exempt Employees.* Employees who are required to be paid overtime at the rate of one and one-half times their regular rate of pay for all hours worked beyond 40 hours in a workweek, in accordance with applicable wage and hour laws.

5. *Exempt Employees.* Salaried employees who are not required to be paid overtime under applicable wage and hour laws, for work performed beyond 40 hours in a workweek. Executives, professional employees, outside sales representatives, and certain employees in administrative positions are typically exempt.

You will be informed of your initial employment classification and of your status as an exempt or non-exempt employee upon your hire. If you change positions during your employment as a result of a promotion, transfer, or otherwise, you will be informed by a member of the management of any change in your classification and exemption status.

Q 2:46   What is an example of a work hours policy?

These policies vary greatly, depending upon the business and industry. The policy below was prepared for a business with ever-fluctuating work hours, with schedules varying from week to week. For this reason, great care was taken to ensure the flexibility of the company to establish work hours as needed and responsibility on behalf of the employee to meet these needs.

WORK HOURS

Regular working hours for employees of the Company vary depending upon their job, workload, and customer service needs. Regular work hours may be scheduled on any day, Sunday through Saturday, and at any time during the 24 hours of any day. Generally, normal business hours are from 9:00 a.m. through 5:00 p.m., Monday through Friday.

Your Supervisor will provide you with your regular work schedule. Daily and weekly regular working schedules may be changed, at any time, at the sole discretion of the Company, as it deems necessary to meet the varying conditions of its business. Changes in work schedules will be announced as far in advance as practicable.

Lunches

A paid lunch break of 60 minutes is provided to employees. Lunches are to be taken at times approved by your supervisor.

Overtime

Employees are expected to work beyond their scheduled hours (overtime) when requested to do so, oftentimes with little advance notice. On occasion, overtime may be required, if deemed necessary by the Company. The Company will try to give advance notice as soon as practicable. An employee's supervisor shall assign overtime and no employee is permitted to work overtime without the prior approval of his/her supervisor. Overtime for non-exempt employees is paid in accordance with state and federal law at 1½ times your regular rate of pay for hours worked in excess of 40 hours in a workweek. Paid holidays, paid lunches, and paid vacations are not hours worked and are not used for purposes of determining overtime.

Q 2:47   What is an example of time recording procedures policy?

Although the manner in which time worked is tracked varies greatly from industry to industry, everything from punch clocks to computer terminal software programs, most policies can be created through use of some or all of the following.

TIME RECORDING PROCEDURES

Hourly Employees. To ensure that an accurate record is kept of hours actually worked, hourly employees are required to record their time worked by punching their timecard in and out on the Company's time clock according to their work schedule. Any time you leave Company premises, except in connection with Company business, you must punch out and punch in when you return. You must also punch out during lunch and punch in upon promptly returning to work. Any alterations to your timecard must be initialed and approved by your supervisor.

Salaried Employees. Salaried employees are required to maintain an accurate record of their time worked by filling out their time sheet on a daily basis. Any time you are away from the Company's premises, except in connection with Company business, you must note such time on your time sheet.

All employees are responsible for their own timecard or time sheet. Falsification of any time sheet or timecard, unauthorized alteration of a timecard or time sheet, punching another employee's timecard, or allowing another employee to punch your timecard is prohibited and may result in discipline, up to and including discharge.

Q 2:48 What are typical employer policies on vacation pay, personal days, sick days, and the like?

All of these benefits are voluntarily provided by an employer in most jurisdictions and vary greatly, but certain issues should be addressed in policies that provide for time off.

The first issue is accrual. How are the vacation, personal, and sick days earned? Typically, accrual is a progressive process that increases as the number of years the employee has worked with the company increases. Some employers use anniversary years, some use calendar years, some use benefit years to measure time off earned; it makes no real difference. However, care must be taken to ensure that the policy is clear and unambiguous. This schedule illustrates a common error:

Length of Service	Vacation Days Earned
0–2 years	5 days
2–3 years	10 days

There are several problems with this schedule. Arguably, it suggests that upon commencing job duties, the employee earns five days of vacation. This is probably not intended by the employer. At two years of employment, is the employee entitled to five or ten vacation days? Both possibilities exist under this schedule. The employer should take care that no such ambiguities exist in its policy.

In addition, the policy should stipulate whether the time-off benefit is paid or unpaid. If benefits are paid, the policy should address whether payment will be made for earned but unused benefits if employment is terminated. Many employers provide that earned but unused vacation time will be paid upon termination. If nothing further is stated, this policy applies even to employees terminated for willful misconduct. Many employers provide an exception for such employees. To protect themselves further, employers should define *willful misconduct* in their policies. Many employers use the definition in their state's unemployment compensation laws.

If paid vacation is provided, can employees receive payment in lieu of taking vacation? Employers are free to choose what they want to do, but they must address this issue. A vacation policy should also address scheduling of vacations. Scheduling or approval procedures should be described in the policy.

Time-off benefits also raise the issue of carryover. Whatever policy an employer applies should be clearly stipulated in the section on time-off benefits. For instance, an employer may say "use it or lose it," or it may allow carryovers from year to year but set a maximum number of days or period of carryover time to ensure that it does not face the prospect of numerous employees taking large blocks of time in the future.

Q 2:49   What are the elements of an effective policy on leaves of absence?

The FMLA requires employers with 50 or more employees to provide as many as 12 weeks of unpaid leave during any 12-month period for a variety of circumstances, including the serious health condition of the employee, the employee's spouse, parent, or child. However, many employers do not meet the threshold criterion of the FMLA, and even those that do meet the threshold provide paid leave in addition to the unpaid leave provided by the FMLA. Thus, many employers have a policy for medical leaves of absence. These policies should be reviewed in light of FMLA requirements. All policies on medical leaves of absence should address:

Eligibility. Employers typically require full-time employment and a certain tenure with the company. The FMLA, on the other hand, has specific criteria for eligibility.

Medical certification. All such policies should specify the criteria under which the employer may seek medical certification of the condition for which the leave is sought. Requiring the employee to provide medical certification and stipulating that the employer may seek recertification should it question the initial medical certification are wise strategies and are sanctioned under the FMLA. Most employers demand recertification at designated intervals to prevent abuses.

Notice. Most policies demand notice of a request for a medical leave of absence; however, the notice requirements under the FMLA are rather minimal. Oral notice of the need for time off for a condition or situation that falls within the FMLA is sufficient.

Paid or unpaid. Although nothing under federal law requires that any medical leaves be paid, many employers pay for certain portions of a medical leave. Again, the employer must be specific about its procedures for payment and include that information in the employee policy.

Accrual and continuation of benefits during a medical leave. The FMLA requires that health benefits continue during an FMLA leave to the same nature and extent as if the employee had continued working. Co-pay requirements therefore continue as if the employee were still actively working for the company. In non-FMLA situations, the employer may decide the nature and extent to which benefits continue during a leave and, if so, at whose expense. All of these issues should be addressed within the policy and consistently applied to all employees who take medical leaves of absence. As for accrual of other benefits, some employers do not allow employees on medical leaves of absence to earn additional vacation time, sick time or the like, but often they restore the benefits upon the employee's reinstatement. This is consistent with the FMLA.

Job reinstatement. Unless otherwise required under FMLA, the employer should consider establishing a policy that does not guarantee reinstatement after leave. Stating that the employer endeavors but does not promise to reinstate provides flexibility often needed by the employer.

In addition, the policy should specify that if an employee believes he or she is being retaliated against, that employee should utilize the same complaint procedure for claims of harassment.

Q 2:50   What is an example of a general medical leave policy?

Below is a general medical leave policy that is not an FMLA policy but an employer-provided policy.

MEDICAL LEAVE POLICY

An employee may request unpaid medical leaves of absence for absences due to an employee's illness or disability (including a condition relating to pregnancy). Although medical leave is unpaid, any earned vacation days or other paid time-off benefits may be taken in connection with an approved medical leave. All medical leave requests must be accompanied by appropriate medical certification from your physician indicating the condition necessitating your leave request and your projected date of return to work.

Leaves of absence are at the sole discretion of the Company, and after approval, are subject to further review and approval on a periodic basis. If your medical leave is granted, you are required to provide the Company with additional physician's statements as may be requested by the Company, attesting to your continued disability and inability to work. You may also be required to provide the Company access to your medical records or to submit to a medical examination at any time by a medical facility designated by the Company, at its sole discretion.

Before being permitted to return from a medical leave, you are required to present the Company with a note from your physician indicating that you are able to return to work. The Company may require you to submit to a medical examination by a medical professional designated by the Company, before commencement of job duties.

Subject to state and federal law, reinstatement cannot be guaranteed to employees returning from medical leaves of absence under this policy. However, the Company endeavors to place employees returning from approved medical leaves in their former position or in a comparable position, subject to, including but not limited to, budgetary restrictions, the Company's need to fill vacancies, and the ability of the Company to find qualified temporary replacements.

Subject to federal and state law, the Company currently continues regular Company contributions for premium payments for group insurance health benefits during an approved medical leave of absence, up to three calendar months following the calendar month of the commencement of the leave.

An approved medical leave does not affect anniversary dates. However, vacation days are not earned during a medical leave but will be treated as if earned upon an employee's return to work.

Q 2:51   What is an example of an FMLA policy?

Below is an example of an FMLA policy. This policy is general and does not attempt to delve into the intricacies of the regulations. However, it has been this author's experience that FMLA policies, which attempt to provide more detailed information, are typically flawed because they do not accurately reflect the rules contained in the regulations. Moreover, regulations or various rules determined by a court to be enforceable may change over time. This policy is provided for informational purposes only; consult your labor attorney before implementing any policy.

FMLA

In accordance with the Family and Medical Leave Act (FMLA), if the leave is foreseeable, eligible employees (as defined under the FMLA) may be granted up to 12 weeks of unpaid FMLA leave in any 12-month period for the following reasons:

- For the birth of the employee's child and to care for the newborn child;
- For the placement with the employee of a child for adoption or foster care;
- To care for the employee's spouse, child, or parent with a serious health condition; or
- Because of a serious health condition that makes the employee unable to perform the functions of the job.

In accordance with the FMLA, if the leave is foreseeable, the employees must provide the Company at least 30 day's advance notice before an FMLA is to begin. If not foreseeable, notice must be given as soon as practicable. The 12-month period used for purposes of establishing the 12-week entitlement for FMLA leave is a "rolling" 12-month period measured backward from the date an employee uses any FMLA leave. Under the FMLA, employees may be required to provide medical certification and recertification to substantiate leave requests.

Group health plan benefits, as defined under the FMLA, shall continue during any authorized FMLA leave, provided the employee continues to pay any normally required employee contribution. Any employee contributions are due at the same time as it would be made if by payroll deduction. Although FMLA leave is unpaid, earned vacation and sick days may be used at the commencement of any FMLA leave and will be paid to the employee during the authorized FMLA leave. Such paid time will be counted toward the 12-week limitation for FMLA leave. An FMLA leave will not affect seniority or anniversary dates. Vacation days and sick days will not be earned during a FMLA leave but will be treated as if earned upon an employee's return to work.

Subject to certain exceptions under the FMLA, employees on FMLA leave will be returned to the same position held when the FMLA leave commenced, or to an equivalent position as defined under the FMLA. All employees who take FMLA leave due to their own serious health condition are required to provide medical certification that they are able to resume their work before being reinstated.

This section is intended to provide you general information concerning your rights under the FMLA. Due to the complexity of the issues involved in the FMLA, employees who have any questions regarding their rights under the Act or who wish to take an FMLA leave of absence should contact Human Resources for additional information.

Q 2:52   What is an example of a medical exam and testing policy?

Oftentimes, companies may include a separate medical examination policy to give clear notice to its employees the company's ability to require medical examinations in conjunction with any number of its policies. Although it is written broadly, medical examinations should never be undertaken except in strict conjunction with its other written policies (i.e., medical leave policy and business necessity).

MEDICAL EXAMINATIONS AND TESTING

Employees may be required to undergo periodic medical examinations (including alcohol and drug screenings) at times determined by the Company, in its sole discretion. In connection with these examinations, employees are required to provide the Company with access to their medical records, if requested. The Company pays for all Company-required medical examinations. Situations that may require a medical examination include, but are not limited to, medical examinations conducted under the Company's Drug and Alcohol Policy, Sick Day Policy, Medical Leave Policy, and applicable laws and regulations.

Any refusal of an employee to consent to a medical examination reasonably requested by the Company may result in discipline, up to and including discharge.

Q 2:53   What kinds of policies concerning employee conduct are addressed in an employee handbook?

Generally, employers cover such items as attendance, punctuality, work rules, personal appearance, and demeanor. If the employer is an at-will employer, it should not use language in this section that detracts from or is inconsistent with its at-will employment policy. A progressive discipline system that provides that termination will occur only for good cause or following a sequence of graduated discipline is inconsistent with employment at will. Nonetheless, an at-will employer can establish various, carefully drafted rules about expected conduct at the workplace without affecting its at-will status.

Policies on personal appearance and demeanor differ greatly, depending on the business. Professional organizations typically have more stringent guidelines for personal appearance and demeanor, whereas manufacturing operations are more concerned with safety when setting standards for personal appearance and demeanor. Employers should consider civil rights issues when drafting these policies. For example, a particular skin condition prevalent among African-American males can be ameliorated only by growing a beard. An outright ban on beards might be unlawful because it would have a disparate impact on African-American males. On the other hand, requiring beards to be cropped short for legitimate business reasons may be permissible under the law.

Q 2:54   What is an example of an attendance and punctuality policy?

Although policies vary depending on the company's needs, below is a sample policy.

ATTENDANCE AND PUNCTUALITY POLICY

Attendance and promptness are very important to the Company and to you. Violations of this policy cause problems and place a hardship on your fellow workers and the Company.

The Company requires you to be at work and ready to work on the days and times when you are scheduled to work. If you are unable to work, you must directly notify your supervisor prior to your scheduled starting time on each day of your absence unless you are on an authorized leave, in which case different policies and procedures apply. (*See* the Leave of Absence policies discussed below).

All absences or tardiness will be recorded and retained as part of your personnel file. You may examine these records by making a request to your supervisor.

Absenteeism or tardiness that is excessive in the sole discretion and judgment of the Company may result in discipline, up to and including discharge. This policy does not apply to any time off in connection with authorized leaves of absence or other authorized time off for vacations.

IF AN EMPLOYEE FAILS TO REPORT TO WORK AND NOTIFY HIS/HER SUPERVISOR FOR THREE CONSECUTIVE SCHEDULED WORK DAYS, THE EMPLOYEE WILL BE CONSIDERED AS HAVING VOLUNTARILY QUIT HIS/HER EMPLOYMENT.

Q 2:55   What is an example of a personal appearance and demeanor policy?

These policies vary greatly depending upon the company's business. Below is a sample policy.

PERSONAL APPEARANCE AND DEMEANOR

Discretion in style of dress and behavior are essential to the safe and efficient operation of this Company. Although the Company maintains no formal dress code, employees are, nonetheless, required to dress for work in appropriate attire consistent with their position and frequency of contact with visitors and customers, and to behave in a professional, businesslike manner. Inappropriate casual clothing may not be worn by employees at any time while engaged in Company business. In addition, employees are expected to adhere to acceptable grooming standards. Plant employees are required to adhere to additional policies regarding dress for safety reasons. (*See* Workplace Safety Policy.)

Q 2:56   What is an example of an automobile policy?

This policy applies to both use of company vehicles and employees that use their own vehicles on company business.

AUTOMOBILE POLICY

The Company has established the following policy governing the use of Company vehicles and use of your own vehicle on Company business.

- Employees who drive a personal vehicle for business reasons or who operate a Company vehicle must have a valid driver's license, and must drive safely and obey all applicable traffic laws and regulations, including wearing seat belts.

- Employees are not permitted, under any circumstances, to operate a personal vehicle for Company business or a Company vehicle when any impairment causes the employee to be unable to drive safely. This includes, but is not limited to, circumstances in which the employee is temporarily unable to operate a vehicle safely or legally because of illness, medication, or intoxication.

- Employees must immediately report to their supervisor any accident, theft, or damage involving a Company vehicle or personal vehicle while on Company business, and, in the event of an accident, must immediately contact their supervisor, remain on the scene, and cooperate fully with authorities.

Q 2:57   What is an example of a work rules policy?

Below is a sample work rules policy.

EXAMPLES OF INAPPROPRIATE CONDUCT

The policies contained in this section are meant to illustrate particular types of conduct which the Company considers inappropriate. This list is not meant to include all types of inappropriate conduct. The Company retains the right to determine, in its sole discretion, whether particular employee conduct is unacceptable. This policy does not alter your at-will status, and the Company's right to terminate your employment at any time, with or without cause.

Types of behavior and conduct that the Company considers inappropriate include, but are not limited to, the following:

1. Theft or misappropriation of property of the Company, employees, vendors, suppliers, or customers.
2. Abuse, destruction, damage, or reckless operation of Company property or equipment.
3. Possession of any type of weapon or firearm on Company property or on Company business.
4. Falsifying or omitting information when applying for a job or when completing Company personnel documents.
5. Falsification or tampering with Company documents or records.
6. Falsification of any time sheet.
7. Insubordination.
8. Leaving the Company premises during your working hours without authorization from your supervisor.
9. Fighting, rough housing, or disorderly conduct.
10. Use of lewd, abusive, or threatening language.
11. Loitering, loafing, or horseplay.
12. Failure to be at your work area dressed and ready for work at your scheduled starting time.
13. Conviction of a criminal felony.
14. Dishonesty.
15. Excessive tardiness or absenteeism.
16. Violation of safety policies and procedures.
17. Violation of the Alcohol and Drug Policy.
18. Violation of the Non-Discrimination Policy.
19. Deliberately restricting output, or inducing others to do so.
20. Posting, defacing, or removal of signs or writings on Company property or equipment.
21. Failure to use safety equipment or devices.

22. Violation of any Company policy reflected in this Employee Manual or other Company policies communicated to you from time to time.

Behavior or conduct in violation of the above policies, or other behavior or work which the Company determines to be unacceptable or unsatisfactory, regardless of when discovered, may result in discipline, up to and including discharge.

Q 2:58   Should employers prepare policies concerning the use of computer networks and the Internet?

As the workplace becomes more technically advanced, e-mail and other electronic encoded transmissions are becoming commonplace. Equally common in today's world are internal investigations of suspected unlawful activity (e.g., sexual harassment) and searches for evidence of wrongful activity (e.g., an employee's violation of a non-compete agreement). E-mail and other electronically encoded information are a virtual cornucopia of possible evidence. As most people are now aware, even deleted information can oftentimes be recovered by forensic computer investigators. Uncovering racial slurs, sexual jokes, and other material can assist employees in prosecuting claims. Likewise, in an attempt to reduce risk and exposure to sexual harassment claims, and to demonstrate the company's sincere efforts to take preventative and corrective measures to deal with harassment, some companies have hired computer forensic investigators. These investigators typically monitor e-mail and Internet use to determine if there are any violations of company policy as it relates to use of the systems (e.g., accessing pornographic material). To reduce risk and exposure, employers need to promulgate a written policy that clearly prohibits the use of electronic transmissions except for legitimate business reasons and does away with any expectation of privacy in connection with the system's use.

The following is a sample policy involving e-mail and the Internet that addresses these issues:

COMPUTER NETWORK AND THE INTERNET

The Company's e-mail system is the property of the Company and is intended solely for conducting company business. All messages transmitted via e-mail will be treated as business messages. Any employee who sends a personal message on the system should be aware that it will not be considered a personal, confidential message of the employee.

Please be advised that the Company has the right to enter the e-mail system at any time, to review, copy, or delete any messages, and disclose such messages to others. The use of passwords to gain access to e-mail is for the protection of the firm, not the employee. By using the firm's computers for e-mail, all employees waive any right to privacy in the use of e-mail and consent to the access and disclosure of e-mail messages by the firm.

Use of the Internet is strictly intended for business purposes and must not be used for personal reasons or entertainment. Use of the Internet for personal business may result in the loss of that privilege, or discipline. Further, the firm will not tolerate individual abuse through the accessing of chat rooms, or pornographic or other inappropriate materials. Such action may result in discipline up to and including termination of employment. Employees should be aware that Internet use is not private, and may be monitored or retrieved by the company, and employees waive any right to privacy in connection therewith.

Below is another sample policy that allows for some personal use of company computers and property.

USE OF COMPANY PROPERTY FOR PERSONAL REASONS

Company property, including telephones, computers, copiers, software, facsimile machines and the like are available during working hours for Company business and should not be used for personal business. In accordance with this policy, the following guidelines will be followed:

- Use of Company telephones should largely be confined to business calls. Personal telephone calls are limited to those which are absolutely necessary, and they should be brief. This restriction on the use of telephones applies to personal calls to fellow employees as well. Incoming personal calls are discouraged and should be taken only when absolutely necessary. Additionally, long distance personal calls are prohibited on Company phones.

- Use of any Company facsimile machines, copiers, or mail facilities for personal reasons is strongly discouraged, and should not be used unless absolutely necessary. Use of Company stationery for personal reasons is prohibited.

- Use of computers and voice or electronic message systems are strictly limited, (including the Internet, e-mail and voice mail), and are provided for business purposes. Personal use is only permitted to the extent its use is occasional, brief, within reasonable limits, and otherwise consistent with Company policy (see also Internet Policy below). Utilization of Company computers and other property for the creation of non-business related websites or programming is strictly prohibited. In addition, employees may not use the Company's computers to download games or other entertainment software or play games over the Internet or otherwise.

- To ensure that the use of business equipment is consistent with the Company's legitimate business interests, the Company may monitor the use of such equipment (including downloading and reviewing information stored in computers) from time to time, and employees waive any right to privacy in connection therewith.

- No Company property can be removed from Company premises without the prior signed authorization from your supervisor.

Violations of this policy may result in discipline up to and including termination.

INTERNET POLICY

Internet access to global electronic information resources on the World Wide Web is provided by the Company to assist certain employees in their work. The following additional guidelines have been established to help ensure reasonable and productive Internet usage.

- No employee can access the Internet without prior Company authorization.

- While Internet usage is intended for certain employees for job-related activities, incidental and occasional brief personal use is permitted within reasonable limits.

- All Internet data that is composed, transmitted, or received via our computer communications system is considered part of the records of the Company. Consequently, employees should always ensure that the business information contained in Internet, e-mail, and other transmissions is accurate, appropriate, ethical, and lawful.

- Data that is composed, transmitted, accessed, or received via the Internet must not contain content that could be considered discriminatory, offensive, obscene, threatening, harassing, intimidating, or disruptive to any staff member or other person. Examples of unacceptable content may include, but are not limited to, pornographic materials, sexual comments or images, racial slurs, gender-specific comments or any other comments or images that could reasonably offend someone on the basis of race, weight, age, sex, height, religious beliefs, national origin, disability or any other characteristic protected by law.

- The unauthorized use, installation, copying, or distribution of copyrighted, trademarked, or patented materials on the Internet is expressly prohibited. Generally, if a staff member did not create material, does not own the rights to it, or has not received authorization for its use, it should not be reproduced, used inappropriately, or put on the Internet. Staff members are also responsible for ensuring that the person sending any materials over the Internet has the appropriate distribution rights.

Q 2:59   What should an employer consider when formulating the policies involving group benefits?

Most employers maintain group insurance and pension and welfare benefit plans for their employees and refer to these benefits in their handbooks. They must ensure that the descriptions of these benefits in the employee handbook accurately describe the benefit policies themselves. Insurance benefits, group insurance benefits employee benefit plans, and pension plans are provided in accordance with written plans that are specific and detailed as to eligibility, benefits, and coverage. Unless an employer wants to be potentially responsible for affirmative representations as to the terms and conditions of coverage, benefits and eligibility, it should merely give a brief and accurate description of the types of benefits provided and refer employees to the SPDs or insurance policies for more information. The employee should be alerted that eligibility, benefits, and coverage are determined by the plan documents, notwithstanding anything contained within the employee handbook or otherwise represented by the employer. This caveat prevents the employee from legitimately relying on employer representations concerning eligibility, benefits, or coverage that may turn out to be untrue. Otherwise, an employer that makes such a misrepresentation may face an action and have to make good on its careless language.

Above all, the employer must, in this section, reserve the right to amend or discontinue at its sole discretion any benefits mentioned. Similar language should be contained in any SPDs for the employee welfare benefit or pension plan. Doing so prevents contractual claims, should the employer choose to modify the terms of the plan after its creation.

The group benefits section of the employee handbook should also contain a brief statement about COBRA (if applicable), workers' compensation, and 401(k) or any other pension plan maintained by the employer. Again, when referencing any plan, the handbook should direct the employee to the plan documents themselves, and no representation other than general descriptions should be made in the handbook itself. The employer should reserve the right to amend, discontinue, or otherwise modify any plan permitted under applicable law.

Q 2:60   What are social media policies?

Social media policies are created by employers to provide rules and limitations concerning its employees' use of social media in ways that may have impact on the employer and the workplace. Although social media policies take many different forms, many social media policies address the following:

- Prohibit the posting of confidential and/or proprietary information of the employer and its clients or customers.
- Require employees to be respectful and prohibit derogatory posts concerning the employer, management, and employees. Require employees to state that any opinions are solely that of the employees, and not the opinions of the employer or its management.

Prohibit the use of the employer's logo or images on sites.

Q 2:61   Can social media policies violate the National Labor Relations Act, even for non-union employees?

Yes. All employees, both union and non-union, have Section 7 rights under the National Labor Relations Act (NLRA) to engage in concerted activity with other employees regarding the terms and conditions of employment. Typically, this involves conversations and meetings between employees and management. However, with the advent of social media, those protections may now extend to postings on social media sites. Some social media policies may be overbroad, and include prohibitions against engaging in conduct that may be protected under Section 7. For example, broad prohibitions against "disrespectful conduct" could reasonably be construed by employees to preclude Section 7 activity, and as such, be in violation of the NLRA. (See chapter 11 for more information regarding social media policies and the NLRA.)

Q 2:62   How can an employee handbook create an implied contract?

Enforceable implied contracts are based on the representations an employer made in writing or orally upon which an employee legitimately relied. Representations contained in an employee handbook may be construed as statements that an employee reasonably relied upon in accepting or continuing employment with a given employer. If an employer makes promises in an employee handbook about the terms and conditions under which the employment relationship will be terminated, those promises may be legally enforceable; therefore, the employer is advised to consult a professional to determine whether the language contained in its employee handbook creates such a contract. If it does, measures should be taken to revise it.

Q 2:63   What guidelines can an employer follow to avoid liability stemming from language in an employee handbook?

To protect itself from litigation, an employer should use the following guidelines in preparing an employee handbook:

- Do not make promises about career opportunities, compensation, or expected job duties.
- Avoid such terms as *job security* and *just cause.*
- Use disclaimers to condition assertions (e.g., "unless our plans change," "if we continue to do as well as we have in the past").
- Note the impermanence of benefits by using such qualifications as "currently," "at present" or "now," and note that plans are subject to change at the company's sole discretion.
- Include a statement that employment is at will, such as:
    The employee or employer may terminate the employment at any time, with or without cause, and no oral or written promises regarding any terms or conditions of employment can be made, or should be relied upon, except for those made in writing by a designated officer of the organization.
- State clearly that the handbook is not a contract of employment.

Q 2:64   Do courts recognize and enforce an employer's disclaimer that a handbook is not a contract?

A disclaimer must be explicit and prominently communicated, preferably in the same document it seeks to disclaim. Courts have shown a clear tendency to respect employers' disclaimers and reservations of the right to revise their employee handbooks unilaterally. [Hamilton v. Air Jamaica Ltd., 945 F.2d 74

(3d Cir. 1991); Doe v. First Nat'l Bank, 865 F.2d 864 (7th Cir. 1989); Pratt v. Brown Mach. Co., 855 F.2d 1225 (6th Cir. 1988); Dell v. Montgomery Ward & Co., 811 F.2d 970 (6th Cir. 1987)]

Not all disclaimers can defeat an employee's claim. One reason that some disclaimers are deliberately written in ambiguous language is that the employer does not want to undermine the value of its handbook—or employee morale—by publishing too blatant a disclaimer or reservation of the right to amend the handbook unilaterally without notice to employees. Thus, where a company's handbook gave as one of its purposes the provision of a clear explanation of the corporation's employment policies, a court ruled that whether or not the handbook was an employment contract should be left to the jury to decide. [McDonald v. Mobil Coal Producing Inc., 820 P.2d 986 (Wyo. 1991)]

This illustrates an unresolvable dilemma for employers. On one hand, they like the loyalty and positive morale inspired by promises of fairness, job security, career advancement, and the like. On the other hand, they want strong disclaimers embedded in their handbook to ensure that their feel-good representations are not legally binding. This cannot be done. Use of an employment at-will disclaimer, the antithesis of job security, negatively affects employee morale. An employer cannot sugarcoat the harsh reality of an at-will policy, but it can take some solace in knowing that many employees do not take time to read their handbooks.

If an employment at-will disclaimer is not prominently and clearly communicated, a court may refuse to enforce it against an employee. In a case decided in 1991, the following disclaimer was placed near the middle of a welcome letter from the company's general manager to all new employees. It was not underlined, capitalized, or otherwise made to stand out from the rest of the text:

> [This handbook] is not meant to cover everything and is not intended to be a contract between the company and its employees. Rather, the handbook is intended to explain most procedures and policies that we try to operate by.

The court held that the company could not use the handbook to demand employee loyalty and performance levels, as well as to discourage unionism, and then subtly reserve the firm's right to alter or back off from handbook terms favorable to those employees. [Arellano v. AMAX Coal Co., 6 BNA IER Case 1399 (D. Wyo. 1991); *accord*, Jiminez v. Colorado Interstate Gas Co., 690 F. Supp. 977 (D. Wyo. 1988)]

An issue that remains controversial is the effect of a disclaimer inserted into a subsequent version of a handbook, months or even years after the employee has commenced work. In *Robinson v. Ada S. McKinley Community Services Inc.* [19 F.3d 359 (7th Cir. 1994)], the plaintiff commenced her employment in 1978, having received an offer letter and a manual that together provided her protections against the at-will termination of her employment. In 1986, the employer amended the manual by adding a disclaimer of any contractual obligation to follow that handbook's provisions. When the plaintiff, having been terminated, sued to enforce her rights under the original letter and manual received in 1978, the company defended itself on the theory that the plaintiff's decision to continue working after the new manual was released amounted to acceptance of its revisions. The court rejected this contention, saying:

> [Such acceptance] cannot be inferred from Robinson's continued work. By continuing to work, Robinson was merely performing her duties under the original contract. According to McKinley's logic, the only way Robinson could preserve her rights under their original employment contract would be to quit working after McKinley unilaterally issued the disclaimer. [That] is ridiculous. [*Robinson*, 19 F.3d at 359]

Other courts have rejected disclaimers for more traditional reasons. Where a health care provider's handbook did not contain an express disclaimer of contractual effect, the Supreme Court of North Dakota refused to infer such a disclaimer from language in the handbook's termination policy that said: "[E]mployment in the hospital is based upon mutual consent. Either the employee or the hospital may find it necessary to sever the employment relationship." Rejecting the employer's reliance on this provision, the court concluded:

> The language does not rise to the level of a conspicuous and explicit disclaimer. The statements can as easily be construed as consistent with the existence of enforceable contract rights as being inconsistent with their existence. The policies in this case are silent on whether the terms and benefits set out affected or modified the defendants' right to terminate the employment relationship at will. [Osterman-Levitt v.MedQuest Inc., 513 N.W.2d 70 (1994)]

Similarly, where the disclaimer in the employee policy manual was "untitled, in fine print, and on a signature page allegedly unsigned by the plaintiff," it was ineffectual in defeating the contractual rights created by that manual. [Dicker v. Middlesex Mem'l Hosp., 1994 Conn. Super. LEXIS 790 (Conn. Super. Ct. Mar. 25, 1994)] In addition, a jury in a wrongful discharge action found that a disclaimer in a handbook applied to some of the handbook's provisions yet did not apply to its disciplinary policy protections, under which the plaintiff had been fired for allegedly committing "an immediately terminable offense." [Nicosia v. Wakefern Food Corp., 136 N.J. 401, 643 A.2d 554 (1994)]

A disclaimer in a handbook that the handbook is not a contract can have some unintended consequences for the employer. At issue before a Michigan Court of Appeals in *Heurtebise v. Reliable Business Computers, Inc.* [207 Mich. App. 308 (1994)], was whether an arbitration provision contained within a handbook was enforceable against a state law discrimination claim under the Elliott-Larsen Civil Rights Act. [Mich. Comp. Laws Ann. §§ 37.2101 *et seq.*] Although there was still disagreement among jurisdiction as to the enforceability of pre-dispute arbitration agreements at the time of the decision, the Court of Appeals held that the clause was enforceable, citing the U.S. Supreme Court decision in *Gilmer v. Interstate/Johnson Lane Corp.* [500 U.S. 20 (1991)] The Michigan Supreme Court [452 Mich. 405 (1996)], on the other hand, reversed the Court of Appeals, stating that if the arbitration was to be enforceable, it must at a minimum meet the requirements of *Gilmer*, which requires that there be an express contract for arbitration of pre-dispute arbitration agreements. Reviewing the handbook, the Supreme Court relied upon the disclaimer in the handbook that specifically provided that it was not a contract of employment to defeat the claim that the parties had contractually agreed to arbitration.

Q 2:65   Can disciplinary rules published in an employee handbook support the denial of unemployment compensation benefits on the basis of willful misconduct?

To be eligible for unemployment compensation in many jurisdictions, an employee must not have been dismissed for willful misconduct. The burden of proving willful misconduct for purposes of denying benefits falls on the employer, and unemployment referees typically make this a very heavy burden. Almost uniformly, they require an employer to present documentation of the work rules it alleges the employee willfully violated. When the employer cannot prove that the employee was aware of the relevant disciplinary rule in the employee handbook (i.e., that the rule was clearly written and clearly communicated), willful misconduct is not found and unemployment benefits are not denied.

Having an incomplete list of written work rules can also defeat an employer's claim that an employee was terminated for willful misconduct. To provide objective support for defeating claims for unemployment, an employer's work rules should state, in generic fashion, the most common forms of employee misconduct.

Q 2:66   What happens if an employer's published employment policies are inconsistent?

The general rule of contract interpretation is that where contract language is ambiguous, the court interprets it against the party that drafted the language. This rule has been applied in cases of ambiguous or inconsistent language in employee handbooks and other employment documents.

Where a company placed a disclaimer on the back of its employment application but placed a "termination for just cause only" statement in its handbook, and the employee testified he had not read the disclaimer before signing the job application, the court enforced the just-cause policy in the handbook against the employer. [McLain v. Great Am., Ins. Cos., 208 Cal. App. 3d 1476 (1989); *accord*, Dicker v. Middlesex Mem'l Hosp., 1994 Conn. Super. LEXIS 790 (Conn. Super. Ct. Mar. 25, 1994) (untitled disclaimer, published in fine print on a page the employee was supposed to sign, but never did, was to no effect)] The court refused to enforce an employment at-will clause in a preprinted employment application that it found was nothing more than a solicitation of employment—not a contract of employment—that was not integrated into the employment relationship by reference in any of the employer's other documents. [Harden v. Maybelline Sales Corp., 230 Cal. App. 3d 1550 (1991)]

The most common situation in which handbooks are materially inconsistent occurs when an employer attempts to maintain an at-will disclaimer and a policy of progressive discipline that provides for termination only for just cause. Although an employer can give its supervisors some guidelines for determining appropriate levels of discipline, a strictly progressive disciplinary policy that allows termination only for just cause is blatantly inconsistent with an employment at-will policy, which reserves the right to terminate without cause. When such blatant inconsistencies occur, courts apply general principles of contract interpretation, rule against the drafter of the contract, and enforce the policy about progressive discipline.

Q 2:67   Is an employment at-will disclaimer in a handbook enforceable against existing employees?

Employment at will is a rebuttable presumption in most states. To the extent that this presumption was rebutted by representations and promises sufficient to create an implied contract, a newly effected at-will disclaimer is effective—generally, for new employees and existing ones as well. This conclusion is based upon the fundamental axiom, consistent with most jurisdictions that maintain an at-will presumption that an employer is free to set unilaterally whatever policies and procedures it determines (within the confines of state or federal legislative enactments). Having the right to make unilateral policy also allows the employer to change, unilaterally, its policy. As a result, although there may have been representations or promises in the past that, if tested, may have amounted to an implied contract, the employer can do away with those claims by unilaterally adopting an employment at-will disclaimer.

Nevertheless, most courts maintain that a certain amount of time must pass after the publication of the at-will disclaimer before it is effective for existing employees. An employer cannot publish an at-will policy on Thursday and terminate on Friday an employee who has been with the company for 20 years and received enough promises and representations to create an implied contract. A reasonable amount of time must pass first; 90 days can be used as a rule of thumb.

Of course, unilateral at-will disclaimers cannot defeat claims arising from express contracts. If an employer and an employee negotiate an employment contract that includes job security, a unilateral proclamation by the employer of its at-will status will not defeat claims arising from this agreement. Most employment contracts that rise to the level of express agreement are ultimately reduced to writing and require mutual consent to be amended. If the employee consents, obviously, a contract can be modified to provide for employment at will. One cautionary note: It is not absolutely essential in most jurisdictions that the express contract be reduced to writing. Courts look to the nature and extent of negotiations and discussions of job security before the acceptance of employment to determine whether an implied contract exists, or one that rises to the level of an express oral agreement.

Q 2:68   After an employee handbook has been created, how should it be disseminated?

Even when employers publish employee handbooks, issues often arise as to whether a particular employee received a handbook or whether the handbook was applicable to that particular employee. It can be difficult to determine whether a handbook is applicable to an employer's entire workforce. For example, an employee handbook is created and distributed to hourly employees, with copies to the salaried supervisors. Is the handbook applicable to salaried personnel, or is it merely provided to them in connection with their supervision of hourly employees? Supervisors frequently maintain that the employee handbook, if it is not favorable to their cases, does not apply to them. Likewise, when employers attempt to use an employee handbook against employees in litigation, the employees often claim that they never received a copy of the handbook and therefore it does not apply to them.

The employer should have each employee sign a receipt that is removed from the employee handbook and placed in that employee's personnel file. The signed receipt acknowledges that the employee received a copy of the employee handbook that it is applicable to him or her.

Q 2:69   Is publishing an employee handbook online sufficient?

Although the answer may vary from state to state, cases suggest that online publishing may be sufficient.

In *Highstone v. Westin Engineering, Inc.* [187 F.3d 548 (6th Cir. 1999)], the employer made revisions to its policy manual to state that all employees are at will. The revisions were complete in late 1994 and were published online in March of 1995. At the time that the revisions were published online, two e-mails were also sent to all employees advising them of the changes. Notice was also given during staff meetings. The employee/plaintiff was fired one month after the revised manual was published online. The court held that the employer "satisfied its burden by reasonably notifying affected employees of the changes to the manual." [*Highstone*, at 553.]

In *Mannix v. Monroe* [348 F.3d 526 (6th Cir. 2003)], the court held that "[d]istribution of a new employee handbook constitutes reasonable notice, regardless of whether the affected employee actually reads it." In this case, the employer revised its handbook and published it online. The online publication occurred four months before the employee/plaintiff was fired. The revised handbook was posted on an internal database available to employees, and the employer held meetings between department heads and employees. The policies were also placed on the employer's e-mail system in order to give notice. Thus, the court held that the employer had provided its employees with reasonable notice of the handbook. The employee/plaintiff at issue argued that he never read the revised handbook. The court held that actual notice to the employee was not required, only reasonable notice to the workforce in general. Further, the court noted that "[c]onsidering the advancement and ubiquity of electronic corporate communications, we will not induce a return to older practices by imposing a paper receipt requirement." [*Mannix*, at 536.]

Q 2:70   What if, when receiving an employee handbook, an employee refuses to sign the acknowledgment of receipt form?

By signing an acknowledgment form, an employee acknowledges receipt of the handbook. Many employees are reluctant to sign acknowledgment forms. Yet, in most situations, it is not the purpose of the form for employees to agree to company policies. Rather, its purpose is to provide evidence that the employee received the employee handbook, which contains company policies. If an employee refuses to sign the form, an employer should simply ask the employee to acknowledge that he or she received the employee handbook but refused to sign the acknowledgment form. Most employees will write this out, and writing this document provides the same evidentiary value as the acknowledgment form itself. These written refusals to sign the acknowledgment form should be kept in employees' personnel files for later use.

For even more recalcitrant individuals who refuse to acknowledge their refusal to sign the acknowledgment form, an employer still has alternatives. It should send a letter to the employee acknowledging the employee's receipt of the employee handbook, acknowledging the employee's refusal to sign the acknowledgment, and asking the employee to acknowledge receipt of the letter by initialing it at the bottom of the page. It may be necessary to go to great lengths, in writing, to assure the holdouts that by initialing the letters they do not agree with anything but merely acknowledge receipt of the letter. With enough perseverance, employers usually obtain the evidence they need.

As a practical matter, when employee handbooks are distributed, one person should ensure that acknowledgments are received by each employee who receives a manual. This practice helps ensure that the implementation is successfully accomplished.

Q 2:71   If an employer runs the risk of having a handbook used against it, is it better off without one?

Although an employer can forego issuing a handbook, most experts advise employers to adopt written employment policies, whether in a handbook or another form. Employee handbooks are now being used by businesses of all sizes. They are effective tools for providing employees information on policies, wages, employee benefits, and other relevant subjects. Many managers find they must curtail the time they can spend resolving employee problems on a case-by-case basis; an employee handbook can be used to establish policies and improve communication. This helps a business run efficiently, because employees who are informed tend to be secure and therefore loyal and productive.

Other reasons often cited as justification for having a handbook are to avoid the forming of a union and to avoid litigation. Employees with concerns about job security sometimes turn to a labor union to provide the sense of security that an employer has denied them. Many employers, through employee handbooks and policy manuals, willingly give up a measure of the discretion available under the at-will employment doctrine because they want their employees to feel secure.

Nonetheless, most employment law professionals maintain that an employer is better off not having a handbook than having a bad one; however, most handbooks are not inherently bad, they just need work. Employers should have their handbooks reviewed by an attorney and, if there are problems, fix them. The benefit of an employee handbook is clear. In addition to the advantages just discussed, employee handbooks work proactively to reduce the risk and exposure to litigation, provide direction in dealing with situations the employer has not yet faced, and help the employer avoid violating state and federal law. All of these goals and objectives are well worth the trouble and expense of reviewing and modifying an employee handbook.

Oral Contracts

Q 2:72   What elements create an enforceable oral contract?

If all the basic components of a valid contract are present (i.e., offer, acceptance, intention, and consideration), an oral contract is usually enforceable in a court of law; however, in many states, a statute of frauds requires that certain types of contracts or contracts that will be in effect for longer than one year be put in writing. In these states, an employer and employees who orally agree to an employment contract that will run more than one year must put their agreement in writing. Even in states that have no statute of frauds (e.g., Pennsylvania), oral contracts create problems of proof that make them inadvisable. Complex employment contracts sealed with only a handshake frequently result in costly litigation.

The reason for this is that evidence of the oral discussions can be distorted by any of the parties, either through faulty memory or dishonesty. Disgruntled employees who feel they have been wronged are fertile sources for so-called oral-contract litigation. If oral contracts can be enforced in some circumstances, an employer should take great pains to ensure that it has no oral contracts. Fees associated with the preparation of a written employment contract are minuscule compared to those incurred in defending employee litigation.

Q 2:73   Are written contracts of employment preferable to oral ones?

Some employers think they are better off if employment agreements are not in writing. Apparently, they think they are not locked into a contract if it is oral; however, as noted above, courts often enforce oral employment contracts. The danger in not putting the agreement in writing is that if the employment relationship goes sour, the employer and employee may not agree about the exact terms of the oral understanding. In such a situation, a judge may leave it up to a jury to hear both views and decide which version it believes.

This is not to say that all employees should have written contracts. Lower-level clerical and blue-collar workers are usually at-will employees; therefore, written contracts are not necessary for them, employee handbooks are usually sufficient. Higher-level employees (i.e., managers, administrators, and professionals) often demand express agreements. Legal disputes can often be anticipated and avoided by spelling out the terms of their employment in a written document, even if this is no more than a letter from the employer, with the employer's file copy signed by the new employee.

Q 2:74 Can an employer's gratuitous promises become binding terms of an employment relationship?

Oral promises can create legal difficulties for unwary employers. Promises can sometimes create contractual obligations, even when the employer does not intend them to do so. For instance, an applicant for the job of vice-president of finance is told that if she takes the job, she can look forward to a long and exciting career with the company. There is no written contract and no fixed period of employment, but, based at least in part on the representations about a bright future, she sells her townhouse in an expensive neighborhood, quits a good job, and moves to San Diego, where the corporate headquarters is located.

Three months later, a severe economic downturn forces the company president to cut costs. He asks the company treasurer to take over the duties of vice-president of finance so he can eliminate this position. Soon the company receives a letter from an attorney, retained by the terminated vice-president, stating that his client moved, gave up her home and job, and relocated because she was promised a bright future with the firm.

Courts do not like to enforce promises that are not intended to become contracts, and this employer never intended to create a contract with this employee for a term of years. Besides, no specific time was ever discussed. Was the employee entitled to employment at least for a reasonable length of time? Some of the factors that a judge would look at in resolving this dispute include:

- Were the representations actually promises or just predictions?
- If the representations were promises, did the employer expect or intend them to cause the employee to take actions to her detriment (i.e., selling her home, quitting her job, relocating)?
- Did the employee in fact change her position, fully or partly, in reliance on such representations?
- Was the employee behaving as a reasonable person when she changed jobs in full or partial reliance on such representations?

If the answers to these questions are yes, and the employer is not an at-will employer, it may be liable.

Written Employment Contracts

Q 2:75   What purposes do written employment contracts serve?

In addition to specifying the expectations of both the employer and employee about tasks and compensation, written employment contracts also provide for termination policies, buy-out provisions, covenants not to compete, confidentiality agreements, choice-of-law provisions, and other concerns that are particular to specific employers' practices or professions.

Q 2:76   What are the components of a written contract of employment?

A written contract can be as simple or complex as the parties want it to be. Regardless of the form the contract takes, the following items should be covered in the agreement:

Nature of the employment. This is a description, usually general in nature and limited to one or two paragraphs, of what the employee is expected to do during the course of employment. The following is an example:

> Employee will be the vice-president and general manager of Employer's Blackacre facility, with responsibility for the management and supervision of all departments and activities of that facility, as well as for the coordination of the activities of Employer's Blackacre facility with the activities of the Employer's enterprise as a whole.

Compensation. This section should deal (at a minimum) with the salary or wages the employee will receive: how much, how often, and any special components (e.g., commissions or bonuses).

Fringe benefits. Although perks are part of an employee's compensation, they should be addressed separately from salary. It is rarely necessary or wise to spell out every benefit in great detail. For instance, it is usually sufficient to state that the new employee will receive pension, health, and other benefits equivalent to those enjoyed by others of similar stature in the organization. The details will be spelled out in the company's employee benefit plans and summary plan descriptions.

Term and termination. This section should focus on the length of employment, if all goes well, and how employment will be terminated if the relationship goes sour. An employer must balance its desire to provide for a certain degree of certainty about the length of the employment relationship but still retain flexibility in case the employee does not do his or her job or circumstances change and the employee is no longer needed. Employers often establish an initial period, say one year, during which the employer can terminate only for cause—that being defined as the employee's material breach of the duties and obligations described in the employment agreement. After the passing of the initial time period, the relationship can be terminated by either party, with or without cause on reasonable notice—say, 30 or 60 days.

Written employment contracts might also include the following clauses:

Protection of trade secrets and unfair competition. These provisions usually prohibit the employee from using or disclosing confidential, proprietary information during or after the relationship. They also restrict the employee from competing with the employer, in a certain geographic area or market for a period of time after the relationship has ended.

Choice of law. Employers usually specify that the law of the state in which they are located will apply in interpreting the contract. If the employee will be working at a facility in another state, it may be wise for legal counsel to check contract law in that state for more favorable provisions.

Consolidation clause. The contract should state that it contains all the terms agreed to by the two parties and that no other oral or written negotiations or promises (before or contemporaneous with the provisions in the contract) apply.

Amendments. The contract should specify that all changes and extensions must be made in writing and signed by the parties.

Non-assignment. The contract should state that the employee cannot assign the employment contract to another person (i.e., he or she should not be allowed to hire someone to serve in his or her place).

Q 2:77   How can a written contract be terminated?

Although the parties can make any termination provisions they want, the employer usually wants the option to terminate the contract at its discretion, and if severance pay is involved, to terminate at a price the company can afford; however, the employer should be advised that the law may consider the contract unenforceable if the terms allow the employer to cancel the agreement at any time while denying the employee the same privilege.

Q 2:78   What is a typical termination provision?

A typical provision is as follows:

> Employer may terminate this agreement upon written notice to Employee, with or without cause, 90 days before the desired date of termination. In lieu of said notice, Employer may pay employee three months' severance pay at his (her) regular monthly salary.

Q 2:79   What if a key employee demands more employment security than that provided by at-will employment?

Key employees who are not satisfied to work at will may demand some employment security. Some employment contracts specify a duration of employment (rarely more than five years). As an alternative, or in tandem with a term of years, a company may promise not to fire the employee except for certain specified reasons, such as for just cause or malfeasance amounting to criminal conduct. The problem with the first of these reasons is that employer and employee rarely agree after the fact on what constituted just cause. The trouble with the latter is that it nearly eliminates the employer's right to terminate the agreement prematurely.

Many companies combine two means of termination. They terminate at the employer's discretion with notice or severance pay, or without them when the employee has committed some mutually agreed-upon level of misconduct. The termination clause may also require the employee to pay a price for early termination. For instance, it might include the following provision:

> Employee may terminate this agreement on 90 days' written notice. Failure to furnish such notice to the Employer shall result in Employee's forfeiture of his (her) entitlement to a pro rata share of his (her) annual bonus.

Q 2:80   What is an example of a written employment agreement?

Although these agreements take many forms, below is a general employment agreement.

EMPLOYMENT AGREEMENT

THIS IS AN EMPLOYMENT AGREEMENT (the "Agreement") between ABC Company ("Company"), and John Doe ("Employee"). The parties agree as follows:

1. *Effective Date and Term.* This Agreement is effective as of March 1, 2003 and will remain in effect during the Employee's Employment, and thereafter, as to those provisions which expressly state that they will remain in effect after termination of the Employment.

2. *Employment.* The Employee will serve as an Operations Manager of the Company, or such other positions as may be assigned by the Company, (the "Employment"). The Employee's initial duties will be to engage in management training throughout the Company's departments on a rotating basis, and perform such other duties as may be assigned by the Company, from time to time, consistent with the Employee's position. The Employment will be full time, and the Employee's entire business time and efforts will be devoted to the performance of Employee's duties for the Company during the term of the Employment.

3. *Term of Employment.* The term of the Employment will be indefinite and will continue until terminated pursuant to Paragraph 5.

4. *Compensation.* The Employee will be compensated during the Employment as follows:

   (a) *Salary.* The Employee's salary will be at a rate of $65,000 per year, subject to normal payroll deductions, payable on regular paydays for other employees as established by the Company, from time to time.

(b) *Bonus*. The Employee will be eligible to participate in any bonus program(s) established by the Company for the position in which Employee serves. Unless otherwise provided in writing by the Company, all bonuses are discretionary, the Employee must be employed on the date bonuses are paid to be eligible to receive the bonus, and all bonus programs are subject to change in the Company's sole discretion.

(c) *Benefits*. The Employee will be eligible during the Employment to participate in fringe benefit programs covering the Company's salaried employees as a group, subject to the terms of those programs.

(d) *Plan Terms and Changes*. The terms of applicable insurance policies and benefit plans in effect from time to time will govern with regard to specific issues of coverage and benefit eligibility. It is understood that all benefit programs are subject to change in the discretion of the Company.

5. *Termination of Employment*. During the term of this Agreement, Employee's Employment may be terminated in the following circumstances:

(a) *Death*. The Employment will terminate automatically in the event of Employee's death.

(b) *Disability*. If Employee is unable to perform Employee's duties under this Agreement due to physical or mental disability for a continuous period of 90 days or longer, the Company may elect to terminate Employee's Employment due to such disability.

(c) *Termination by Company for Cause*. The Company may terminate the Employment immediately for Cause, defined as Employee's material breach of this Agreement, neglect, continued failure or inability to perform, poor performance of duties, consistent failure to attain assigned objectives, misappropriation of Company property, intentional damage to Company property, activities in aid of a competitor, insubordination, dishonesty, conviction of a felony, violation of Company policy, or performance of any act (including any dishonest or fraudulent act) detrimental to the interests of the Company.

(d) *Discretionary Termination by Employee*. Employee may terminate the Employment at will, without cause, with at least 60 days advance written notice, and Employee agrees not to prepare to leave the Employment with Company without giving such notice.

(e) *Discretionary Termination by Company*. Company may terminate the Employee's Employment at will, without cause, with at least 60 days advance written notice.

Upon termination of Employee's Employment, Employee shall not be entitled to any further compensation from Company, except: (i) unpaid salary through the effective date of termination; and (ii) any vested benefits accrued prior to the date the Employment terminates under the terms of any written benefit program.

6. *Access to Trade Secrets and Confidential Information*. The Employee recognizes that during the course of the Employee's Employment, the Employee may receive, develop, otherwise acquire, have access to or become acquainted with trade secrets or other confidential information relating to the business of the Company. The Employee further recognizes that the knowledge and information acquired by the Employee concerning the Company's customers, fee arrangements for customers, employees, customer contacts, pricing schedules, advertising, business systems and marketing techniques and procedures represent a vital part of the Company's business and constitute, by their very nature, trade secrets and confidential information of the Company, (hereafter "Trade Secrets and Confidential Information")

7. *Non-Disclosure*. Except in connection with the performance of Employee's duties in connection with Employee's employment with the Company, Employee agrees that the Employee will not, either directly or indirectly, for competitive or other purposes, disclose or cause to be disclosed, use or cause to be used any Trade Secret or Confidential Information of the Company, either during the Employee's employment or at any such time thereafter. The Employee also agrees that all such Trade Secret or Confidential Information, and any copy, extract or summary thereof, whether originated or prepared by or for the Employee or otherwise coming into the Employee's knowledge, possession or control, shall be and remain the exclusive property of the Company.

8. *Employee's Return of Information*. In the event of termination of Employment with the Company, the Employee shall immediately deliver to the Company all equipment, keys, materials, notebooks, documents, memoranda, reports, supplies, equipment, manuals, files, books, correspondence, customer lists, software, hardware, computer programs or other written or electronically encoded records or property of or relating to the Company or its business, including information containing Trade Secret or Confidential Information, and any copies, transcripts from or extracts of any of the foregoing, that are in the Employee's possession or under the Employee's control.

9. *Non-Solicitation*. Except in connection with the performance of Employee's duties in connection with Employee's Employment with the Company, Employee agrees that during the term of the Employee's Employment by the Company, and for a period of 1 year thereafter, the Employee shall not, either directly or indirectly, solicit or contact or assist others in soliciting or contacting any of the Customers of the Company for the purpose of engaging in business similar to or in competition with the Company for the Employee's own benefit, or for the benefit of

any other person, corporation, or business enterprise. For purposes of this Agreement, a Customer is any person, entity, or business that has purchased goods or services from the Company within 2 years prior to the termination of this Agreement.

10. *Non-Interference.* During the period of the Employee's Employment and for a period of 1 year following the termination, the Employee shall not disrupt, damage, impair or interfere with the business of the Company in any manner, including, without limitation, inducing any employee to leave the employ of the Company or inducing any Customer to sever its relationship with the Company.

11. *Non-Competition.* In consideration for the terms and conditions of this Agreement and for other good and valuable consideration, including, but not limited to, the provision of training, facilities, customer contacts and experience by the Company, the receipt of which is hereby acknowledged, the Company and Employee freely choose to include this non-competition clause as part of this Agreement. The Company and Employee agree and recognize that this non-competition clause is necessary to protect the business and goodwill of the Company. Employee covenants and agrees that during the term of this Agreement, and for a period of 1 year following the termination of Employee's Employment, Employee will not, either directly or indirectly, engage in, or acquire an interest in (as an individual, partner, stockholder, director, officer, principal, agent, employee, lender of money, or in any relation or capacity whatsoever) any business that is competitive with the business of Company. A business shall be deemed competitive for purposes of this provision if it performs services or conducts business similar to the services and business of the Company and is conducted within 75 miles of the city limits of Detroit, Michigan (the "Covenant Area"). The Company and Employee recognize, acknowledge and agree that the territorial limitation barring Employee from competing with the Company within the Covenant Area is reasonable because the Company provides the majority of its services to customers residing within the Covenant Area and that this geographical restriction is necessary to protect the Company's business and goodwill. The Company and Employee recognize, acknowledge, and agree that the durational limitation provided above is reasonable because of the time it will take to train an employee to perform the same services as are being performed by Employee on the Company's behalf and that this durational restriction is necessary to protect the Company's business and goodwill. Employee acknowledges and agrees that Employee will still be able to earn a livelihood after termination of employment, despite this restriction.

The Company and Employee recognize and acknowledge that reasonable people may differ on the scope of any covenant not to compete. Accordingly, if any court of competent jurisdiction determines that the scope described above exceeds the maximum permitted by applicable law, then such court shall reform such provision to the maximum extent permitted by applicable law.

12. *Ideas, Concepts, and Inventions Relating to Company's Business.* All business ideas and concepts and all inventions, improvements, and developments made or conceived by the Employee, either solely or in collaboration with others, during the Employment, whether or not during working hours, and relating to the Company's business or any aspect thereof, or to any business or product the Company is considering entering or developing, shall become and remain the exclusive property of the Company, its successors, and assigns. The Employee shall disclose promptly in writing to the Company all such inventions, improvements and developments, and will cooperate in confirming, protecting, and obtaining legal protection of the Company's ownership rights. This provision shall continue in effect after termination of the Employment.

13. *Injunctive Relief.* The Employee understands and acknowledges that any violation of Paragraph(s) 6, 7, 8, 9, 10, 11, or 12 of this Agreement by Employee would result in irreparable injury to the Company, the loss of which cannot be reasonably compensated in damages in an action at law. The Employee understands and acknowledges that in addition to any other rights or remedies that the Company may possess, including recovery of damages, the Company shall also be entitled to injunctive and other equitable relief to prevent a threatened or continuing breach by the Employee.

14. *Entire Agreement.* This Agreement supersedes any preexisting employment agreements and any other agreements on the subjects covered by this Agreement, and is the entire Agreement between the Parties concerning the subject matter of this Agreement.

15. *Amendment and Waiver.* No provisions of this Agreement may be amended, modified, waived, or discharged unless such waiver, modification, or discharge is agreed to in writing and signed by the Employee and by a duly authorized officer of the Company. No waiver by either party at any time of any breach or non-performance of this Agreement by the other party shall be deemed a waiver of any prior or subsequent breach or non-performance.

16. *Severability.* The invalidity or unenforceability of any provision of this Agreement will not affect the validity or enforceability of any other provision of this Agreement, which will remain in full force and effect.

17. *Assignability.* This Agreement contemplates personal services by the Employee, and Employee may not transfer or assign Employee's rights or obligations under this Agreement. However, this Agreement may be assigned by the Company.

18. *The Company Policies.* The Company's policies, as contained within its Employee Handbook or otherwise, shall apply to Employee's Employment, except to the extent any such policy is

inconsistent with the terms of this Agreement, in which event, this Agreement shall control.

19. *Notices.* Notices to a party under this Agreement must be personally delivered or sent by certified mail (return receipt requested) and will be deemed given upon post office delivery or attempted delivery to the recipient's last known address. Notices to the Company must be sent to the attention of the Company's Chief Executive Officer.

20. *Governing Law.* The validity, interpretation, and construction of this Agreement are to be governed by the laws of the State of Michigan without regard to principles of conflicts of law.

IN WITNESS WHEREOF, the parties have signed this Agreement as of the date and year first above written.

Witnesses   *"Company"*

_____   **By:**_____

Date:_____   **Its:**_____

                                         "Employee"

_____   _____

                                         Employee Name

                                         Street Address

                                         City, State Zip Code

Date:_____   Social Security No.

Q 2:81   How can an employer protect its confidential information from misuse, or prevent unfair competition by ex-employees?

Although various legislation protects employees in this area (for example, the Economic Espionage Act of 1996 is federal law that provides severe criminal penalties for people who take and use trade secrets that belong to someone else and many states have enacted laws similar to the Uniform Trade Secrets Act which protects employers from the unauthorized use and disclosure of trade secrets), most of these laws are insufficient to provide the level of protection many employers desire. Employers themselves have the ability to create policies and agreements that further protect against the misuse of confidential information and unfair competition by employees, even after their termination. Usually, these take the form of written agreements signed by the employee as a condition of employment, or continued employment that may prohibit one or more of the following:

- Use or disclosure of confidential information or trade secrets during or after employment;
- Competition with the employer during employment and a time period after employment ceases, limited to a reasonable scope and duration;

- Solicitation of the employer's employees and customers after termination of employment, limited to a reasonable scope and duration;
- Ownership claims by employees regarding inventions, acknowledging instead the employer's ownership of all inventions made by the employee in connection with the employment relationship; and
- Interference with the employer's business, including inducing its customers to sever their relationship with the employer, limited to a reasonable scope and duration.

The subject of confidentiality and non-compete agreements are discussed in more detail in chapter 6.

Q 2:82   What is *arbitration*?

Arbitration is a means of resolving disputes other than by traditional civil litigation. Although some similarities exist, the differences between arbitration and traditional court litigation are significant.

In arbitration, the dispute is resolved through a hearing conducted before one or more arbitrators. Arbitrators are typically selected either by the mutual consent of the parties or through a selection procedure adopted by the alternative dispute resolution (ADR) agency.

The arbitration hearing somewhat resembles a trial. The parties (with or without counsel) present testimony, exhibits, and other evidence, and when the hearing is concluded, the arbitrator makes a decision; however, unlike a traditional court case, prehearing discovery (e.g., depositions, interrogatories, and requests for the production of documents) is not typically available unless the parties agree to it. The procedures of the American Arbitration Association (AAA), for example, do not provide for prehearing discovery, except by mutual consent of the parties. As a result, the delay and costs of the discovery phase are avoided.

No juries are present in arbitration. Decisions are made by arbitrators who are typically professionals with knowledge about the subjects and can therefore make informed decisions. Jury members often have little or no such knowledge. During arbitration, procedural rules for documentary evidence, testimony, and the like are not as rigidly followed as they are in a typical court action. Through the application of evidentiary rules in courts of law, judges take great pains to ensure that juries are not persuaded by irrelevant, prejudicial, or unreliable information; however, seasoned arbitrators are not likely to be influenced by such evidence and thus typically have wide discretion in bending traditional evidentiary rules to make hearings efficient and cost-effective. For example, the AAA Rules provide: "The arbitrator will be the judge of the relevance and materiality of the evidence offered, and conformity to legal rules of evidence shall not be necessary." [Rule 30, AAA Employment Arbitration Rules and Mediation Procedures (June 1, 2009)]

Another difference between arbitration and court litigation lies in motion practice. In courts of law, procedural rules allow judges to dispose of lawsuits summarily. For example, under federal rules and in state jurisdictions, parties can bring motions for summary disposition, judgment notwithstanding the verdict, and directed verdict. Because these procedural motions have been typically unavailable in arbitration, strategies for the prosecution and defense of arbitration claims used to differ significantly from those for typical court cases. However, because dispositive motions play such an important role in the defense of employment cases, the new rules adopted by the AAA in July 2006 provide: "The arbitrator may allow the filing of a dispositive motion if the arbitrator determines that the moving party has shown substantial cause that the motion is likely to succeed and dispose of or narrow the issues in the case." [Rule 27, AAA Employment Arbitration Rules and Mediation Procedures (June 1, 2009)]

Q 2:83   Are arbitration clauses in individual employments contracts enforceable?

Under the Federal Arbitration Act (FAA) [9 U.S.C. § 1–15] and many analogous state arbitration statutes, arbitration clauses are fully enforceable. Thus, a party to an employment contract with a dispute concerning breach of the contract that contains an arbitration clause can get a court order to compel the other party to submit to arbitration, and the victorious party can sue to enforce the arbitrator's award against a recalcitrant opponent.

The more interesting issue is whether arbitration agreements that employees must sign as a condition of employment can divest employees of the right to proceed under the federal discrimination laws. The EEOC has long maintained that mandatory, as opposed to voluntary, arbitration of employment discrimination claims violates federal civil rights laws. The EEOC believed that mandatory arbitration is a relinquishment of statutory rights, including the federal EEOC process, which in and of itself violates the federal civil rights laws. The EEOC issued guidance on the subject. [*See* EEOC Notice No. 915.002, Apr. 10, 1997.] Nevertheless, arbitration clauses are standard in the securities industry, covering approximately 6,000 companies and their 400,000 employees. In 1991, the U.S. Supreme Court in *Gilmer v. Interstate/Johnson Lane Corp.* [500 U.S. 20 (1991)], ruled that the plaintiff securities broker who signed a standard arbitration clause had to arbitrate an age discrimination claim.

The U.S. Supreme Court settled the issue in its decision in *Circuit City Stores, Inc. v. Adams* [532 U.S. 105 (2001)]. At issue in *Circuit City Stores* is whether a pre-dispute arbitration agreement contained within an employment application mandated that a discrimination claim, filed two years later, must be determined in arbitration as opposed to state court. The clause in the employment application provided:

> I agree that I will settle any and all previously unasserted claims, disputes or controversies arising out of or relating to my application or candidacy for employment, employment and/or cessation of

employment with Circuit City, exclusively by final and binding arbitration by a neutral arbitrator. By way of example only, such claims include claims under federal, state and local statutory common law, such as the Age Discrimination in Employment Act, Title VII of the Civil Rights Act of 1964, as amended, including the amendments of the Civil Rights Act of 1991, the Americans with Disabilities Act, the law of contract and the law of tort.

After reviewing the FAA and related case law, including its prior decision in *Gilmer*, the Court concluded that the FAA applied to employment contracts, touting the pro-arbitration purposes of the FAA, and the Court's refusal to accept the historical EEOC position that arbitration necessarily involves a participant to forego substantive legislative rights. As the Court quoted from *Gilmer*:

> By agreeing to arbitrate a statutory claim, a party does not forego the substantive rights afforded by the statute; it only submits to the resolution in an arbitral, rather than a judicial form. [532 U.S. at 124, *citing Gilmer*, 500 U.S. at 26]

However, because arbitration agreements are contracts, they are still susceptible to challenge under doctrines generally available under contract law. For example, in a case, it was reported that a federal judge in New York refused to compel arbitration under an arbitration agreement because the court found it to be unconscionable. [*See* "Court Finds Unconscionable Contract to Arbitrate Bias Claims Unenforceable," 18 *Employment Discrimination Report (EDR)* (BNA) 114 (Jan. 23, 2002).] The arbitration clause was reported to have been contained within a 16-page, single-spaced, fine print agreement. Also, the employees were given virtually no time to read it and were pressured to sign it. [*See* "Court Finds Unconscionable Contract to Arbitrate Bias Claims Unenforceable," 18 *Employment Discrimination Report (EDR)* (BNA) 114 (Jan. 23, 2002).] Although pre-dispute arbitration agreements have long been held to apply to Title VII and other employment statutes requiring that cases be brought in arbitration rather than courts, under the Employee Polygraph Protection Act (EPPA), the statute specifically provides that "the rights and procedures provided by [the EPPA] may not be waived by contract or otherwise. . . . " [29 U.S.C. § 2005(d)], and as such, will not require an employee who claims violations of the EPPA to arbitrate those claims under a contract signed with the employer. [Harmon v. CB Squared Servs. Inc., 2009 WL 234982 (E.D. Va. Jan. 30, 2009)]

The subject of arbitration agreements in the employment context is discussed in more detail in chapter 14.

Other Employment Relationships

Q 2:84   What is the difference between an employee and an independent contractor?

Essentially, an independent contractor differs from an employee in that an employer cannot control the work activity of an independent contractor. The employer and independent contractor typically negotiate a fee for an agreed-upon product or service to be delivered at a certain time.

Determining whether someone is an employee or independent contractor is a complicated analysis that depends on the facts of each case. The outcome of that analysis determines how, or if, the federal tax code and civil rights laws, as well as state tax codes and civil rights statutes, will be applied. For example, Title VII does not apply to independent contractors. In *Murray v. Principal Financial Group, Inc.* [613 F.3d 943 (9th Cir. 2010)], the court held that insurance agents that sued an insurance company for sex discrimination were independent contractors and as such, could not maintain claims under Title VII.

Although who controls work activity is critical to the analysis, many factors must be considered to determine whether someone is a true independent contractor. Not surprisingly, the issue comes up most often in connection with the tax code, and the IRS has promulgated a 20-factor control test for determining the question. Although this test is not dispositive outside of the tax code, it is based on common-law principles; thus, it is helpful to consider these factors when characterizing a particular relationship.

The 20 factors established by the IRS [Rev. Rul. 87-41, 1987-1] follow:

1. *Instructions.* A worker who must comply with other persons' instructions about when, where, and how he or she works is ordinarily an employee. This control factor is present when the person or persons for whom the worker performs services can require compliance with their instructions.

2. *Training.* Training a worker by requiring an experienced employee to work with him or her, corresponding with him or her, requiring the worker to attend meetings, or using other methods indicates that the person or persons for whom the services are performed want them performed in a particular method or manner.

3. *Integration.* Integration of the worker's services into the business operations generally shows that the worker is subject to direction and control. When the success or continuation of a business depends to an appreciable degree on the performance of certain services, the workers who perform those services must necessarily be subject to a certain amount of control by the owner of the business.

4. *Services rendered personally.* If the services must be rendered personally, presumably the person or persons for whom the services are performed are interested in the methods used to accomplish the work, as well as in the results.

5. *Hiring, supervising, and paying assistants.* If the person or persons for whom the services are performed hire, supervise and pay assistants that factor generally shows control over the workers on the job; however, if one worker hires, supervises, and pays the other assistants pursuant to a contract under which the worker agrees to provide materials and labor and under which the worker is responsible only for the attainment of a result, this factor indicates that the worker is an independent contractor.

6. *Continuing relationship.* A continuing relationship between the worker and the person or persons for whom the services are performed indicates that an employer-employee relationship exists. A continuing relationship may exist when work is performed at frequently recurring though irregular intervals.

7. *Set hours of work.* The establishment of set hours of work by the person or persons for whom the services are performed is a factor indicating control.

8. *Full time required.* If the worker must devote substantially full time to the business of the person or persons for whom the services are performed, such person or persons have control over the amount of time the worker spends working and by implication restrict the worker from doing other gainful work. An independent contractor, on the other hand, is free to work when and for whom he or she chooses.

9. *Doing work on the employer's premises.* If the work is performed on the premises of the person or persons for whom the services are performed, that factor suggests control over the worker, especially if the work could be done elsewhere. Work done off the premises of the person or persons receiving the services indicates some freedom from control; however, this fact by itself does not mean that the worker is not an employee. The importance of this factor depends on the nature of the service involved and the extent to which an employer generally would require that employees perform such services on the employer's premises. Control over the place of work is indicated when the person or persons for whom the services are performed can compel the worker to travel a designated route, to canvass a territory within a certain time, or to work at specific places.

10. *Order or sequence set.* If a worker must perform services in the order or sequence set by the person or persons for whom the services are performed that factor shows that the worker is not free to follow the worker's own pattern of work. Often, because of the nature of an occupation, the person or persons for whom the services are performed do not set the order of the services or set the order infrequently. Control is showing, however, when such person or persons retain the right to do so.

11. *Oral or written reports.* A business requirement that a worker submit regular oral or written reports indicates a degree of control over the worker.

12. *Payment by hour, week, or month.* Payment by the hour, week, or month generally points to an employer-employee relationship, provided that this method of payment is not just a convenient way of paying a lump sum agreed on as the cost of a job. Payment made by the job or on a straight commission generally indicates that the worker is an independent contractor.

13. *Payment of business or traveling expenses.* If the person or persons for whom the services are performed ordinarily pay the worker's business or traveling expenses, the worker is ordinarily an employee. An

employer, to control expenses, generally retains the right to regulate and direct the worker's business activity.

14. *Furnishing of tools and materials.* The fact that the person or persons for whom the services are performed furnish significant tools, materials, and other equipment tends to indicate an employer-employee relationship.

15. *Significant investment.* If the worker invests in facilities that he or she uses in performing services and that are not typically maintained by employees (e.g., the maintenance of an office rented at fair value from an unrelated party) that factor tends to indicate that the worker is an independent contractor. On the other hand, lack of investment in facilities indicates dependence on the person or persons for whom the services are performed for such facilities and, accordingly, the existence of an employer-employee relationship. Special scrutiny is required with respect to such facilities as home offices.

16. *Realization of profit or loss.* A worker who can realize a profit or suffer a loss as a result of his or her services is generally an independent contractor, but the worker who cannot is an employee. For example, if a worker is subject to a real risk of economic loss because of significant investments or a bona fide liability for expenses (e.g., salary payments to unrelated employees) that factor indicates that the worker is an independent contractor. The risk that a worker will not receive payment for his or her services is common to both independent contractors and employees and thus does not constitute a sufficient economic risk to support treatment as an independent contractor.

17. *Working for more than one firm at a time.* If a worker performs more than de minimis services for a multiple of unrelated persons or firms at the same time that factor generally indicates that the worker is an independent contractor. A worker who performs services for more than one person may, however, be an employee of each of the persons, especially where such persons are part of the same service arrangement.

18. *Making services available to the general public.* The fact that a worker makes his or her services available to the general public on a regular and consistent basis indicates he or she is an independent contractor.

19. *Right to discharge.* The right to discharge a worker is a factor indicating that he or she is an employee and the person possessing the right is an employer. An employer exercises control through the threat of dismissal, which causes the worker to obey the employer's instructions. An independent contractor, on the other hand, cannot be fired so long as he or she produces a result that meets contract specifications.

20. *Right to terminate.* If the worker has the right to end his or her relationship with the person for whom the services are performed at any time he or she wishes without incurring liability factor indicates an employer-employee relationship.

For FLSA purposes, the DOL does not follow the common law "economic realities test," but rather, considers the following factors to determine whether an employment relationship exists, or whether the relationship is that of an independent contractor:

- The extent to which the services rendered are an integral part of the principal's business;
- The permanency of the relationship;
- The amount of the alleged contactor's investment in facilities and equipment;
- The nature and degree of control by the principal;
- The alleged contractor's opportunities for profit and loss;
- The amount of initiative, judgment, or foresight in open market competition with others required for the success of the claimed independent contractor; and
- The degree of independent business organization and operation.

[See DOL Fact Sheet #13, http://www.dol.gov.]

Q 2:85   What does *right to control* mean?

The phrase *right to control* means the authority to direct a worker's activities on the job. This is a concept with sweeping impact. Determining the right of control can be difficult, and each situation should be addressed individually.

Example 1. A firm's office manager hires a temporary worker employed by an employee-leasing company. She receives a paycheck and benefits from the leasing company. The firm pays a fee to the company that is large enough to cover wages plus overhead (providing a profit for the leasing company). Because the firm's office manager will supervise the temporary worker while she substitutes for the regular secretary, the firm has the right to control her activities, and she is, therefore, its employee for many legal purposes. If the leasing company fails to comply with state and federal minimum wage and overtime laws, for example, or to make proper payments to the federal and state taxing authorities, the firm may be secondarily liable for those amounts.

Example 2. XYZ Company, wanting to trim its labor force, convinces its security guard to continue to provide security services for XYZ but as an independent contractor. The guard signs an agreement that designates her as an independent contractor and not an employee of XYZ. The security guard performs only services for XYZ, and XYZ continues to require the security guard to follow the rules and procedures adopted by XYZ in performing security work. The security officer's work is monitored by XYZ, and she is reprimanded if she does not follow XYZ's directives in terms of how to conduct her job. Clearly, despite language in the agreement to the contrary, XYZ has the right to control the activities of the security guard, and she is most likely an employee of XYZ.

Example 3. The same security guard referred to in the previous example approaches XYZ and tells the company that she is planning to open up her own business for providing security services to XYZ and others. XYZ agrees, verbally, to retain her company's services. The woman forms her own company, ABC; hires employees; and assigns employees to work sites, including XYZ. The parameters of services being performed are discussed with XYZ, but the head of ABC herself supervises the security guards at the various locations and directs how the jobs are to be performed. Although XYZ has the right to terminate the services being offered by ABC, it retains no right to reprimand, hire, or fire ABC employees. Under these facts, XYZ does not have the right to control the security guards on its premises, and, despite the absence of a written agreement, the security guards would most likely be determined to be independent contractors, not employees of XYZ.

Q 2:86   What is a *joint-employer relationship?*

In a *joint-employer relationship*, two unrelated companies together employ a single worker or group of workers. The most important aspects of this relationship are the shared management of the employees and participation in creating employment policies. The two most common joint-employer situations involve leased employees and borrowed servants.

When two corporations that make use of and direct the services of a single group of employees are under common ownership, they may be considered a single employer for the purposes of labor law. When unionized construction companies set up non-union counterparts, with or without common ownership, to avoid their union obligations in an attempt to increase their competitiveness, the joint-employer structure is called a double-breasted operation.

Rules and regulations issued by the DOL under the FMLA [29 C.F.R. Part 825] provide specific guidance in determining joint employment for purposes of the Act. These guidelines should also be considered in other situations in which the issue of joint employment arises. Under Section 825.106, the DOL provides that: "Where two or more businesses exercise some control over the working conditions of the employee, the businesses may be joint employers" under the FMLA. As specifically noted in the regulations of the FMLA, joint employment is ordinarily found to exist when temporary or leasing agencies supply employees to another employer. When joint employment is determined to exist, both employers have responsibilities and obligations to the employee under the Act and other labor laws.

The joint-employment relationship can be found to exist despite the fact that the employers are legally separate and distinct entities, with separate owners, separate managers, and separate facilities.

Under the FLSA, when the employee performs work that simultaneously benefits two or more employers or works for two or more employers at different times during the work week, a joint employment relationship generally will be considered to exist where:

- There is an arrangement between employers to share an employee's services or to interchange employees;

- One employer acts directly or indirectly in the interest of the other employer in relation to the employee; and

- The employers are not completely disassociated with respect to the employee's employment and may be deemed to share control of the employee, directly or indirectly, because one employer controls, is controlled by, or is under common control of the other employer.

[29 C.F.R. § 825.106]

Joint employment principals can also be used to demonstrate sufficient "control" needed to establish an employment relationship, as opposed to an independent contractor relationship. For example, a security firm that had assigned security personnel to provide security for a Saudi prince claimed that the assigned security personnel were independent contractors because the security firm did not have the requisite control over the security personnel such that the FLSA did not apply and the district court agreed. However, the court of appeals in *Schultz v. Capital International Security, Inc.* [466 F.3d 298 (4th Cir. 2006)] concluded that the Saudi prince and the security firm were joint employers under the FLSA, such that the degree of control exerted by the Saudi prince was sufficient to make the security personnel employees and not independent contractors under the FLSA.

The determination of whether an employer-employee relationship exists for the purposes of the FLSA are grounded in the "economic realities" as opposed to technical concepts and relationships. Analyzing the economic realities of the circumstances as a whole, as opposed to isolated factors, four factors have been identified as helpful in determining whether a putative employer-employee relationship exist: whether the employer (1) had the right to hire and fire the employees, (2) supervised and controlled work schedules or conditions of employment, (3) determined the method and rate of payment, and (4) maintained employment records. [Herman v. RSR Sec. Servs. LTD, 172 F.3d 132, 139 (2d Cir. 1999)]

In *Barfield v. New York City Health and Hospitals Corporation* [537 F.3d 132 (2d Cir. 2008)], one of the issues was whether a hospital was liable for overtime pay due a nurse who was employed by an independent nursing referral agency and assigned to the hospital to perform services. Reviewing the economic realities of the situation, the court concluded that the hospital, although not formally the nurse's employer, exercised sufficient functional and formal control over the nurse to qualify the hospital as her joint employer.

Q 2:87　What are leased employees?

Leased employees work for a leasing or temporary employment service that pays them their wages and benefits. They report for work at the client company, where their activities are directed by the client's managers. In the case of a temporary service, the employment relationship is usually short-term (e.g., while a regular employee is on vacation or temporary leave or short-term disability). With leasing companies, the client-employee relationship is more likely to be long-term. The client company is often a small firm that turns to a leasing company for its employees because the leasing firm, with hundreds or even thousands of employees, can use economies of scale to maximize compensation packages, provide improved group benefits, and minimize paperwork costs.

The use of leased or contracted employees has risen over the last few years. Although traditionally an option for large employers, small and medium-sized companies are now leasing employees and even moving their entire workforce to leasing companies or forming their own leasing companies that lease the employees to the employer. Employers that lease their employees are often surprised to find that a leased workforce does not shield them from civil rights charges and related litigation. The company that leases its employees is still held accountable and liable for violations of federal employment laws. If the company can exercise control over the method and operation of the work being performed, an employment relationship may exist for the purposes of federal civil rights laws. Although use of leased employees has many advantages, removing exposure to federal or state civil rights claims is not one of them.

Q 2:88   What are the advantages of becoming a joint employer through employee leasing?

Employee leasing has caught on in recent years with some smaller enterprises, such as medical partnerships. For one thing, subscribers save administrative costs in the human resources area and benefits costs. Awkward discharge problems can also be avoided because the leasing company can transfer an undesired employee to another of its subscribers.

Leasing some or all of its workforce does not, however, shield an employer from liability under federal or state civil rights laws. Under most civil rights laws, the liability of an employer using leased workers does not depend on the leasing agreements, but rather a review of the arrangement and economic realities of the employer's relationship to its workers. To the extent that the employer leases its employees but nonetheless maintains control over their work and working conditions, the company will be deemed to be an employer of the leased employees. Thus, the leasing relationship does not protect the employer from claims for discrimination, harassment, and the like. Newer statutes, such as the Family and Medical Leave Act, specifically provide that leasing arrangements are joint-employment operations for which the leasing company and the company leasing the employees owe various duties and obligations under the Act.

Q 2:89   What are an employer's legal responsibilities in a leased employee situation?

Generally, because the firm with the right to control its leased employees is a joint employer with the leasing company, its managers must comply with all the applicable job discrimination laws as if it had directly hired the employees.

The firm's contract is with the leasing company, but its legal duty extends to the workers as well.

In addition, various federal statutes specifically impose obligations on joint employers. Under the FMLA, joint employers are divided into two categories—primary and secondary employers. Each has different duties and responsibilities. The primary employer, typically the leasing company, must provide certain notices to its employees concerning entitlements and the maintenance of health benefits under the Act. Job restoration, in accordance with the Act, is mostly the responsibility of the primary employer; however, the secondary employer must accept an employee returning from leave under the Act if the employer continued to use an employee from the leasing agency for the position at issue. A secondary employer must also comply with federal provisions prohibiting certain actions with respect to temporary or leased employees.

Q 2:90 When may joint-employer status give rise to legal liability?

If joint employment is determined to exist, both employers may find themselves liable for any number of violations of federal and state labor laws, including Title VII, the Americans with Disabilities Act, the Age Discrimination in Employment Act, and the Family and Medical Leave Act. Particular statutes (e.g., the FMLA) detail the secondary employer's obligations in connection with its leased employees.

Example. An employee who is leased from Agency A complains of being sexually harassed by an employee leased from Agency B. Employer X decides to have the respective agencies remove the employees from its workforce, thereby "solving" the problem; however, this is no solution because the employer faces potential liability in connection with the claim of sexual harassment. Employer X should still undertake an investigation and reach conclusions about the harassment charge, much as it would with any other employee.

Liability also can arise in a double-breasted operation if the union challenges the arrangement and the National Labor Relations Board finds a joint-employer situation. The board's remedy is to extend the union contract to cover the non-union branch of the double-breasted operation. Usually, the interchange of workers, equipment, and bids leads to this overlapping result.

Q 2:91 Does the company gain any legal protection by leasing its employees?

The one great advantage joint employers have over non-joint employers is in the area of on-the-job injury. The employer's obligation is limited to insurance under the state workers' compensation statute; whereas third parties, such as the manufacturer of a machine that injures a worker, can face unlimited liability. To receive this protection in an employee-leasing or other joint-employer relationship, the employer must ensure that relevant contract requires workers' compensation coverage.

Employers that lease employees are often surprised that they do not gain protection from claims of discrimination and violations of federal and state civil rights laws as they relate to the leased employees. Under either a joint-employer analysis or "right of control analysis," leased employees can be determined to be either leased employees or true employees of the company leasing them, and as a result, the employer gains no protections.

In the case of the FMLA, a company that leases its employees has specific obligations to them. Such obligations can exist even when the secondary employer is not an employer under the Act. For example, even if the secondary employer does not have 50 or more employees (even counting its leased employees), it may not discriminate against the leased employees because they are availing themselves of rights under the Act if the leased employees are covered by the Act through their employment agency. For example, a secondary employer may not release a leased employee back to his or her agency merely because the leased employee intended to exercise rights under the Act. This is true even though the secondary employer is not covered by the Act because it has fewer than 50 employees.

Chapter 3

Hiring and Evaluating Employees

This chapter describes the legal aspects of the application process and the evaluation of employee performance. It discusses job advertising, information that can be gathered from the application or interview process, methods of evaluating employee performance, work rules, and employee discipline. Just as chapter 1 demonstrated how federal and state laws have diminished the historic freedom of employers, similarly, these various laws specifically restrain what employers can and cannot do and say in hiring and evaluating the performance of their employees.

Advertising and Recruiting

Q 3:1 What are the legal restrictions on how a company advertises for new employees?

Under federal civil rights laws (such as Title VII, the Americans with Disabilities Act [ADA], and the Age Discrimination in Employment Act [ADEA]), it is illegal for advertising to reflect an intention to discriminate on the basis of gender, race, religion, national origin, age, or disabilities. The only narrow exception would be a bona fide occupational qualification (BFOQ) as it applies to gender, religion, or national origin.

Advertisements that read "help wanted-male" are improper. Gender-specific job descriptions, such as "waitresses," "waiters," "busboys," "foremen," or "maids," are also inappropriate. A more subtle example of discriminatory advertising considered suspicious by the Equal Employment Opportunity Commission (EEOC) is the phrase, "college students wanted," because it discourages older workers from applying, from which discriminatory motive might be inferred.

With respect to BFOQs, Section 703(e)(1) of Title VII permits discrimination on the basis of gender, religion, and/or national origin when gender, religion, or national origin is a BFOQ for the particular job. Importantly, the statute provides no BFOQ for race or color, as it is inappropriate for any such criteria to be a BFOQ in the manner in which the concept of BFOQ is construed under Title VII. The application of a BFOQ is extremely narrow, and exists where only an individual of one particular gender, religion, or national origin can perform the "duties and functions" of the job in question. The criteria of gender, religion, or national origin must be an actual qualification to perform the job itself. It is important to note that customer preferences, business necessity, or stereotypical notions of physical strength or mental capabilities are not sufficient to invoke the BFOQ doctrine. In fact, any BFOQ related to gender is highly unlikely to withstand Title VII scrutiny. Although an employer may believe that the physical requirements of a particular job are not well suited to many women, undoubtedly, the employer will not be able to demonstrate that gender is a BFOQ for the position. It is also important to note that the employer, if it wishes to maintain gender, religion or national origin as a BFOQ, has the burden of establishing that only individuals of one particular gender, national origin, or religion can perform the duties of the job involved. In essence, the employer must show that "the business operation would be undermined by not hiring members of one gender (or national origin or religion) exclusively." [Diaz v. Pan-American Airlines, 442 F.2d 385, 388 (5th Cir. 1971)]

Although application of the BFOQ is extremely narrow, it may be viable in unique circumstances. In *Robino v. Iranon* [145 F.3d 1109 (9th Cir. 1998)], the court held the female gender was a BFOQ for correctional officers in a woman's correctional facility, noting that the all-female positions were reasonably necessary to protect the privacy interests of the inmates and reduce sexual conduct between the inmates and officers. [*See* 10 *Employment Discrimination Report (EDR)* (BNA) 734 (June 10, 1998).] Similarly, the Sixth Circuit in *Everson v. Michigan Dep't of Corrections* [391 F.3d 737 (6th Cir. 2004)], held that female gender was a BFOQ for correction officers in a female prison housing unit. In *EEOC v. Mike Fink Corp.* [No. 3-96-0790 (M.D. Tenn. 2000)], the EEOC challenged a purported BFOQ of a chain of "Cock of the Walk" restaurants, which only permitted male servers. Apparently "Cock of the Walk" is slang that referred to "the toughest man" in the riverboat era, the historical theme adopted by the restaurants. Although the restaurant's suit claimed the male-only requirement was necessary as a BFOQ to perpetuate its historical theme, the jury disagreed, concluding that it was illegal gender discrimination. [14 *Employment Discrimination Report (EDR)* (BNA) 419 (Mar. 29, 2000)]

Advertisements can have legal ramifications even when intentional discrimination is avoided. For example, under the ADA, employers must accommodate qualified individuals with disabilities. That obligation relates to the essential functions of a particular position. If an employer undertakes in an advertisement to describe the duties of a position, the employer should ensure that all essential job functions are included. If an employer fails to mention duties in the advertisement, it will have a difficult time later arguing that they are essential functions for the position.

Even if an advertisement is well-drafted, its placement may support a charge of discrimination. For an employer located in a diverse community, advertising only in publications circulated to individuals of a particular group or gender may be construed as discriminatory. Advertising to a select group or gender may violate Title VII under the disparate impact theory, even if discriminatory motive is absent. Advertising in a trade publication for skilled positions may, however, be defensible on the theory of business necessity and job-relatedness, even though the publication has limited circulation.

Q 3:2 Given the legal problems that may result from advertising, is it wise for an employer not to advertise, and to obtain applicant referrals only by word of mouth?

It is not uncommon for employers that want to avoid dealing with potential legal issues involving legal advertising to "throw the baby out with the bath water" and decide not to do any advertising at all, but rather rely upon word-of-mouth references from existing employees as a general hiring practice. The difficulty with this approach, from a legal perspective, is that if the shop suffers from the past effects of prior discrimination, intentional or unintentional, relying exclusively on referrals from existing employees to fill vacancies may, in and of itself, be perceived as a perpetuation of prior discrimination and thereby a violation of federal or state civil rights laws. An employer with a non-diverse workforce, in relationship to the surrounding communities, may fall prey to this type of liability, even if there is no conscious intention to discriminate. If, for example, an employer maintains a largely white male workforce and does not advertise for vacancies, but rather relies upon its existing all-white-male workforce for referrals for possible employment, the method of hiring chosen by the employer may have a disparate impact on minorities and women, even if there is no intention to discriminate. Liability under federal and state civil rights laws includes both disparate impact and disparate treatment theories. Disparate treatment is intentional discrimination. Disparate impact, on the other hand, is actionable when the employer, innocently and without intentional discriminatory motives, undertakes policies and procedures that result in discrimination. Although disparate impact has long been recognized under Title VII, in 2005, the U.S. Supreme Court held that disparate impact claims can be maintained under the ADEA. [Smith v. City of Jackson, Miss. [125 S. Ct. 1536 (2005)] In addition, for companies seeking to build a more diverse workforce, word-of-mouth is usually inadequate. Such companies should begin by reviewing their advertising procedures, taking steps to insure that qualified minorities and women receive a notice of job vacancies. This can be accomplished in many ways, including through minority publications and schools, job placement organizations, and the like. There are many resources available. For example, the American Bankers Association, working with the office of Federal Contracting Compliance Programs, published a guidebook to assist federal contractors in the implementation of required affirmative action programs, entitled "Equal Hiring Opportunity, Helping Banks Take Affirmative Action." [*See* 10 *Employment Discrimination Report EDR* (BNA) 153 (July 29, 1998).] The guidebook provides, among other things, information on how to notify minority applicants of job openings.

Q 3:3   Should help-wanted advertising include an equal employment opportunity policy?

Yes. The words "equal-opportunity employer" should be included to evidence the employer's lack of discriminatory motive, policies, or procedures.

Q 3:4   Are oral promises of employment enforceable between employers and new hires?

Assume an employer makes a verbal offer of employment to an individual, but prior to the start date changes its mind and decides not to hire the individual, revoking the offer. The individual, on the other hand, in reliance on the employer's verbal offer, quits his or her existing employment, only to find that the new job does not exist. What type of liability exists in this situation?

If the employer is an at-will employer, arguably the employer would be within its rights to terminate the employee soon after the individual commences work, assuming that the termination is not otherwise illegal, in violation of discrimination laws, retaliation laws, public policy, whistleblowers statutes, and the like. Given this, how can the employer face liability if it terminates the prospective employment relationship before the employee commences job duties? Although equitable principles and/or estoppel principles would appear to argue in favor of the employee, if the employer is truly an at-will employer, many courts would hold that the employer faces no exposure in the preceding example, regardless of whether the employee quits his or her prior job to commence work for the employer, based on the employer's promise of a position. [*See, e.g.*, Cunningham v. 4-D Tool Co., 182 Mich. App. 99 (1989).]

This position finds support in traditional notions of contract law, where an offer of employment is generally a unilateral contract with the employer making an offer or promise the employee can only accept by performing the act upon which the promise is expressly or impliedly based. Commencement of job duties is generally deemed "acceptance" of the offer; therefore, if the offer is revoked prior to the employee's acceptance through the performance of duties, there can be no breach of contract under general principles of contract law. [*See Cunningham*, 182 Mich. App. at 106.]

Certainly, if the situation at issue is other than an oral promise by an at-will employer, a different result can occur. Furthermore, if the decision to revoke the offer is based upon discrimination, violation of public policy, or the like (for example, if the employer has learned, after the offer is made, that the individual suffers from a disability), the revocation of the offer will be deemed discrimination for which the employer will be held liable.

Q 3:5 Can an employer be liable to an employee for a misrepresentation made by the employer during the interview process?

Common law fraud, as is enunciated in many jurisdictions, involves a material misrepresentation of fact made by one individual to another with the intent it be relied upon, where reliance upon that fact results in injury to the other party. Although common law fraud is rarely used in the employment context, a Michigan Court of Appeals decision indicates that it may be applicable in the interview process.

In *Clement-Rowe v. Michigan Health Care Corp.* [212 Mich. App. 503 (1995)], the employee accepted an offer to become an employee health nurse with the defendant health care company. In order to work, the employee relocated from Saginaw to Detroit. About one month after she was hired, Michigan Health Care Corporation terminated her employment along with that of 150 of its other employees in response to a severe financial crisis. The plaintiff claimed, among other things, fraud in the interview process. According to the decision, the elements of fraud existed in that:

- A material representation;
- That is false;
- That the defendant made knowing it to be false, or that it made recklessly without any knowledge of its truth and as a positive assertion;
- With the intent it should be acted upon by the plaintiff;
- That it was acted upon by the plaintiff;
- Resulting in the plaintiff's injury.

According to the plaintiff, the defendant's representatives indicated to the plaintiff during the interview that "money for her position had been allocated," indicating that the company had the funds for the position. Given the severe financial crisis the company was in, the court concluded that the plaintiff could maintain a claim for fraud against the employer based on either theories of traditional fraud or silent fraud, which is a failure to divulge a fact or facts that the defendant had a duty to disclose. As the court stated:

> Today's employment market is both tenuous and difficult. Nearly all employment is at-will. The economic well-being and financial stability of a potential employer is an important factor in accepting a job offer. Consequently, an employer who succeeds in asserting its economic health to attract qualified employees, knowing the assertions are untrue, may not later hide behind an at-will employment contract. Neither

may it be permitted to avoid liability after omitting to disclose, when asked, known economic instability which later leads to economically-based layoffs. [*Clement-Rowe*, 212 Mich. App. at 508–509]

Although a somewhat novel theory, the *Clement-Rowe* decision has been cited with approval in a number of subsequent decisions. [*See* Garrity v. Mac Valves, Inc., 2003 Mich. App. LEXIS 1098 (Mich. Ct. App. May 8, 2003); Forest Beach Joint Venture v. Laketown Twp., 2002 WL 31058329 (Mich. App. Aug. 13, 2002); McCrerry v. Seacor, 921 F. Supp 489, 492 (W.D. Mich. 1996); Hord v. Environmental Research Inst. of Mich., 228 Mich. App. 638, 642 (1998); *see also* "Truth-In-Hiring Claims and the At-Will Rule: Should an Employer Have a License to Lie," 1997 *Colum. Bus. L. Rev.* 105, 131 (1997).]

Q 3:6   Are oral promises by employers to new hires regarding the terms and conditions of employment enforceable?

Many employers believe that they cannot be held to a promise unless it is made in writing. Although it is true that under the statute of frauds, promises which by their terms cannot be performed within one year are deemed unenforceable if not in writing and signed by the party to be charged, there are equitable doctrines that exist to enforce oral promises. If an employer makes a clear and unequivocal promise of job security to the applicant, which the applicant relies upon in making his or her decision to accept the position, courts in many jurisdictions will hold the employer liable if it later breaches its promise. Courts typically utilize precedent under implied contract and/or promissory estoppel doctrines to establish these causes of action. See the landmark case of *Toussaint v. Blue Cross & Blue Shield* [408 Mich. 579 (1980)], for a discussion of these principles.

Applicant Evaluation

Q 3:7   What types of inquiries should be avoided on application forms?

With respect to particular inquiries, questions concerning disability or race are clearly prohibited under law, with no exception. On the other hand, some inquiries (e.g., regarding English language skills), may or may not be unlawful, depending upon the skills required to perform the job function at issue. In addition, even if a particular inquiry may not violate federal law, innumerable additional protections afforded individuals under state and local law may be applicable. For example, Michigan's Elliott-Larsen Civil Rights Act prohibits discrimination on the basis of height or weight. [Mich. Comp. Laws Ann. § 37.2202] An inquiry regarding height or weight, absent a demonstration that the information relates to a bona fide occupational qualification, may expose the employer to liability under state law. Except in a few situations, the inquiry on applications is not in and of itself actionable. Rather, if there is not a legitimate reason for the inquiry, the applicant will use the inquiry as evidence of discrimination. In other words, if there is no good reason to ask a question, one possible explanation for the employer's desire to obtain this information would be unlawful discrimination against the applicant. One important exception is the ADA, which by statute prohibits pre-employment inquiries concerning medical conditions. If a question on an application violates the ADA, the mere asking of the question itself is actionable under the ADA.

Care should be taken with regard to the following types of inquiries in connection with applications of employment:

Race or color. There is no permissible basis under federal law to make inquiries regarding race or color. In addition, inquiries that may lead to information regarding race or color should also be scrupulously avoided. For example, many applications ask applicants to list all clubs, societies, or organizations to which they belong. This type of inquiry may lead to the applicant's disclosure of organizations that are particularly tied to race (e.g., the Wolverine Bar Association, NAACP), which could be identified by the applicant as evidence of the employer's intent to obtain improper disclosure of race in order to discriminate on the basis of race. In addition, any requirement that a photograph be provided with an application, absent business necessity, could be utilized by the applicant to demonstrate that the employer attempted to obtain information about the applicant's race or color in violation of Title VII or similar state civil rights laws.

Religion. It is generally considered impermissible under federal and most state laws to inquire as to the applicant's religious denomination, religious affiliations, church, parish, pastor, or indication of religious holidays observed. Unless the employer is permitted under applicable law to discriminate on the basis of religion (e.g., religion as a BFOQ or exceptions to religious discrimination for religious educational institutions under Section 703(e)(2) of Title VII), there is no legitimate basis for this type of inquiry and it should be avoided.

National origin/citizenship. It is unlawful under federal law to discriminate against an applicant on the basis of national origin or citizenship, if the person is a lawfully immigrated alien, legally eligible to work in the United States, except in the interest of national security or as otherwise determined by U.S. statute or Presidential Executive Order. As a result, making a specific inquiry as to an applicant's lineage, ancestry, national origin, descent, parentage, or national origin should be avoided in an application. Similarly, questions regarding the nationality or national origin of an applicant's parents or spouse, and questions regarding foreign languages, if not job-related, should also be avoided.

With respect to citizenship, the Immigration Reform and Control Act requires that the employer, at the time of hire, require the employee to provide evidence of his or her ability to work lawfully in the United States. If not asked as part of the federal I-9 process, specific questions regarding citizenship should be avoided, other than to state on the application that as a condition of employment the employee will be required to provide evidence that he or she can legally work in the United States, in accordance with the federal I-9 process.

Language. Closely tied to the issue of national origin is the issue of language. Because language is often an essential national-origin characteristic, questions regarding language on applications can help form the basis of national origin discrimination claims. Two common types of questions on an application could be problematic. The first is a question as to whether the applicant speaks fluent English. The EEOC has determined that fluency requirements may form the basis of national-origin discrimination, unless the employer can demonstrate a legitimate business necessity for this requirement. [*See* 29 C.F.R. § 1606. 6(b)(1).] The second situation would be questions that inquire as to languages other than English that the applicant speaks. Unless there is a legitimate, nondiscriminatory reason to elicit the information, these questions may be viewed as a red flag to identify persons of foreign ancestry and should be avoided much like questions that lead to identifying an individual's age or race.

Gender. Any inquiry regarding gender should be avoided. The only possible basis for such an inquiry is if gender is a BFOQ of a particular position. The scrutiny imposed regarding BFOQs is strict, and the ability to maintain a BFOQ defense to gender discrimination is extremely limited; therefore, an employer will be hard pressed to demonstrate a legitimate basis for any such inquiry.

Age. Inquiries regarding an applicant's date of birth or age should be avoided. The ADEA prohibits discrimination on the basis of age with respect to individuals age 40 or older. A 68-year-old attorney who applied for an in-house legal position with a company claimed that he was denied the position in violation of the ADEA. He claimed, among other things, that the employer indicated that she was searching for a lawyer at a "more junior level." The court found that this comment, in and of itself, was not evidence of age discrimination, but rather, was focused on the level of employee and experience that the company was looking for, and held that this comment was not probative of the employer's discriminatory intent. [Moss v. MBC Software, Inc., 610 F.3d 917 (5th Cir. 2010)] Likewise, a supervisor's reference to a candidate reinstated by a company as "this young man" did not raise an inference of discrimination against an older employee who was not reinstated. [Medlock v. United Parcel Serv., Inc., 608 F.3d 1185 (10th Cir. 2010)] The only permissible purpose for requesting an applicant to state his or her age is limited to when an age requirement would be a BFOQ for the particular position; however, employers will likely be unable to provide a sufficient basis to invoke a BFOQ defense with respect to age, and, as a result, there is generally no basis to request this information.

Conviction records. With respect to convictions, it may be permissible for an employer to consider the relationship between a conviction and the applicant's fitness for a particular job. As a result, it is not unusual for employers to ask whether or not an applicant has been convicted of a crime; generally, this will not violate Title VII or applicable state statutes. However, to avoid potential liability, the inquiry should be accompanied by a statement that a conviction will not necessarily be a bar to employment. If it is, it could be held to be unlawful under disparate impact doctrines if it can be determined that such a policy has a disproportionate impact on protected categories. On April 25, 2012, the EEOC issued its Guidance on an employer's use of arrest and conviction records, "Consideration of Arrest and Conviction Records in Employment Decisions under Title VII of the Civil Rights Act of 1964." [EEOC Enforcement Guidance No. 915.002] This Guidance codifies the EEOC's position that an employer's neutral policy excluding applicants on the basis of criminal convictions may disproportionately impact individuals protected under Title VII and may violate the law if not job related and consistent with business necessity. The Guidance can be found at http://www.eeoc.gov.

Handicap or disability. The ADA specifically prohibits inquiries with regard to the medical condition of an applicant. Questions in an application that separate those needing accommodation under the ADA from those that do not are also troublesome. If there is to be any inquiry whatsoever, an employer may, under the ADA, ask if the individual can perform the job, with or without reasonable accommodation. A yes/no answer is all that is necessary, and any follow-up questions that ask the applicant to describe the nature and extent of the accommodation open the employer up to possible ADA claims.

Economic status. In the absence of business necessity, inquiries as to an employee's financial condition, such as bankruptcy, ownership of a house, car ownership and past garnishment of wages, may violate Title VII. Rejection of applicants because of poor credit ratings has been found to have a disparate impact on minority groups, absent business necessity. In fact, discrimination against an applicant who has filed for protection under federal bankruptcy statutes is, in and of itself, a violation of federal bankruptcy law. [11 U.S.C. § 525 (b)]

Q 3:8   May the company inquire into an applicant's health?

The ADA and many similar state laws prohibit employers from asking about an applicant's medical condition before offering a job. Although the company may ask whether an applicant can perform the essential functions of the job, with or without reasonable accommodation, such inquiries into past disabilities as "Have you ever missed work because of back problems?" are forbidden. Likewise, general inquiries concerning health (i.e., "Rate your health") should be scrupulously avoided. In *EEOC v. Wal-Mart Corp.* [No. Civ. 5-99-0414 (E.D. Cal. Dec. 17, 2001)], Wal-Mart reportedly agreed to pay over $6 million to resolve allegations that a pre-offer test administered between 1994 through 1998 impermissibly sought disclosures of applicants' disabilities in violation of the ADA. [18 *Employment Discrimination Report (EDR)* (BNA) 17 (Jan. 2, 2002)]

Q 3:9   May an employer test for AIDS?

Under the ADA and many state laws, applicants may not be subject to medical examinations until after they receive a bona fide offer of employment. A medical examination (which may include testing for AIDS) is permissible once an offer is made, provided it is required of all entering employees in the same job category.

Even then, unless the test is related to the job in question, an employer may have nothing to gain and much to lose by testing for AIDS. Under the ADA, it is illegal to refuse to employ people because they have AIDS if they are healthy enough to do the job, with reasonable accommodation, and do not pose a direct threat to employees or others. The threshold of establishing a direct threat is high (requiring a significant risk of substantial injury that cannot be reduced or eliminated through a reasonable accommodation) and should always be determined by a competent medical professional. Lay opinions in this area are notoriously wrong. Damages for violations in this area can be great. In what is reported to be the "highest" pain and suffering award granted by the EEOC, in *Mack v. West* [EEOC No. 01983217 (June 23, 2000)], the EEOC reinstated a pain and suffering award for an HIV individual who had been fired by the VA after he disclosed his HIV status. [15 *Employment Discrimination Report (EDR)* (BNA) 21 (July 5, 2000)] As a result of the discharge, the ex-employee lost his possessions, lost custody of his child, and became homeless. Although the case was brought under the Rehabilitation Act (the ADA counterpart for government employees), the EEOC's decision underscores the potential cost to employers that take adverse employment actions based upon unfounded fears or prejudice involving AIDS/HIV. However, if the nature of the employee's work is such that the worker does pose a direct threat to others that cannot be reduced or eliminated through accommodation, a violation of the ADA may not occur. [*See* "Dental Practice Established Direct Threat in Firing HIV Positive Hygienist, Court Says," 18 *Employment Discrimination Report (EDR)* (BNA) 35 (Jan. 9, 2002), where the court determined that a dental hygienist works in an environment with sharp objects, patients that routinely bleed, and the risk of blood-to-blood transmission.]

Q 3:10 Does the ADA forbid any medically related questions on a job application?

Employers may not conduct a medical examination or make an inquiry regarding medical conditions before making a bona fide offer of employment. As a result, job applicants may not be required to identify diseases or medical conditions from which they suffer or have suffered in the past. The ADA does, however, permit an employer to explain the essential functions of the job and ask the applicant whether he or she can perform those functions with or without a reasonable accommodation. For example, an employer may state that the job involves extensive lifting of heavy objects and ask whether the applicant can meet this job requirement, with or without reasonable accommodation. The employer may not ask whether the applicant has a congenital back problem that may prevent him or her from lifting heavy objects.

The EEOC has stated that the following application or interview questions are forbidden:

- "Is there any health-related reason why you may not be able to perform the job for which you are applying?"
- "How many days were you absent from work because of illness last year?"

- Any questions related to an applicant's workers' compensation history.

Employers who have adopted various per se physical requirements for positions should be particularly cautious in this area for two main reasons. Most important, per se rules, by their very nature, do not take into account assessment of the individual applicant's ability to perform the job, with accommodations, and are therefore susceptible to attack. [See 16 *Employment Discrimination Report (EDR)* (BNA) 8–9 (Jan. 3, 2001) for a discussion of the EEOC's successful challenge of a UPS rule banning applicants with monocular vision from truck driver positions.] Second, even with a per se rule that is supported by business necessity, the employer cannot make a medical inquiry or examination until after a bona fide offer is made.

It is important to note that the manner in which the inquiry is made with respect to the performance of essential job functions, with or without accommodation, can lead to impermissible inquiries if not carefully drafted in the application. Merely asking in an application: "Can you perform the essential job functions, with or without reasonable accommodation?" will not violate the ADA. But if follow-up questions segregate those who need accommodation from those who do not, it could be argued that the employer is attempting to segregate those people with disabilities from those without, in violation of the ADA. Similarly, although an employer who is aware of the applicant's disability (but not as a result of an impermissible pre-employment inquiry) may ask the applicant to describe or demonstrate how he or she would perform the job, with reasonable accommodation, engaging in this type of inquiry in the application should be scrupulously avoided. As the absolute prohibition against medically related inquiries only extends through the pre-offer state, employers should train their interviewers to avoid any impulses to seek medically related information. Analysis should be left until the post-offer medical exam.

Q 3:11   May the applicant be asked what languages he or she speaks?

Yes, but only if the job necessarily requires skills in a particular language. The question should be deleted if it is merely part of a stock printed form or is used to assess achievement. An inquiry into foreign languages could be used to argue that the employer intended to discriminate on the basis of national origin. For this reason, employers should never ask an applicant's primary language because this too might be seen as evidence of an intent to discriminate. In addition, asking if an applicant is fluent in English could be problematic unless fluency in English is a requirement of the job, based on business necessity. It has been reported that the EEOC has increased its focus and attention on national origin discrimination, and English-only rules in particular, that are not legitimately based on business necessity, resulting in an increase in claims and EEOC litigation. [15 *Employment Discrimination Report (EDR)* (BNA) 609 (Nov. 1, 2000)] Maintaining English-only policies in the workplace that are not a business necessity can be costly. In *EEOC v. Regis Corp.* [2001 U.S. Dist. LEXIS 11351 (N.D. Ill. Jan. 17, 2001)], the EEOC pursued a hair salon that maintained an English-only policy that allegedly discriminated against Hispanic stylists. Although the salon denied the charges, it reportedly entered into a consent decree that, among other things, paid six employees $240,000 to resolve the charges. [19 *Employment Discrimination Report (EDR)* (BNA) 163 (Aug. 7, 2002)]

Q 3:12   May the employer ask the applicant's age or date of birth?

No, except in compliance with federal or state child labor laws. That question may provide evidence of age discrimination. The fact that the company needs this information to provide benefits is no excuse. This information can be obtained on a separate benefits form after the applicant has been hired.

Q 3:13   May an employer inquire about an applicant's marital status?

Any questions concerning an employee's marital status, children, and child-rearing plans should be carefully avoided. Even innocent discussion of the subject in interviews may result in future litigation if an applicant believes she was rejected because the employer believed her present or future family responsibilities might interfere with job performance. Moreover, some states, like Michigan, include marital status as a protected category in its civil rights statutes. Michigan's Elliott Larsen Civil Rights Act prohibits discrimination in employment or housing on the basis of marital status. [Mich. Comp. Laws Ann. § 37.2202]

Q 3:14   May an employer ask about pregnancy or plans to become pregnant?

No. Even innocent discussions during interviews regarding pregnancy and child-rearing plans can lead to problems. The Pregnancy Discrimination Act prohibits discrimination on the basis of pregnancy, and requires employees to accord pregnant employees the same treatment as other employees facing similar temporary medical conditions; however, an employer is entitled or even duty-bound to alert female applicants if the job involves exposure to radiation or chemicals that could damage a fetus.

There may be circumstances when a particular job requires a commitment regarding work that, when posed to the applicant, may elicit information regarding pregnancy or similar medical conditions. The inquiry is not unlawful if handled properly and is legitimately based upon business necessity. For example, if an employer is attempting to fill a position that will require immediate training to fill an urgent need in the near future, the employer could describe the training and work required and ask the applicant if he or she is aware of anything that might prevent him or her from undergoing training and performing the job. If the applicant at this point volunteers that she is pregnant and that her projected leave date would force her to be absent from work soon following training, and assuming the employer's decision regarding this applicant would be consistent with any other applicant with a similar temporary medical condition, it would not appear to violate the Pregnancy Discrimination Act for the employer to pass on this applicant.

Nonetheless, any specific inquiry regarding pregnancy should be avoided. In *EEOC v. Wal-Mart Stores, Inc.* [156 F.3d 989 (9th Cir. 1998)], an applicant who claimed she was denied employment because of her pregnancy was permitted to have the jury address the issue of punitive damages based on pregnancy discrimination. [*See* 11 *Employment Discrimination Report (EDR)* (BNA) 444 (Sept. 30, 1998).] In *EEOC v. Downey Communication* [No. S 97-1726 (D. Md.), 12 *Employment Discrimination Report (EDR)* (BNA) 131 (Jan. 27, 1999)], the defendant company paid almost $100,000 in settlement of litigation brought by the EEOC to a job applicant who claimed she was discriminated against because of her pregnancy. In *Wagner v. Dillard Dep't Stores* [17 Fed. Appx. 141 (4th Cir. 2001)], the U.S. Court of Appeals affirmed a jury determination of pregnancy discrimination, finding that a six-months pregnant applicant was rejected due to the employer's concerns about absences attributable to pregnancy and childbirth. [17 *Employment Discrimination Report (EDR)* (BNA) 308 (Sept. 12, 2001)]

Q 3:15   Are questions concerning criminal arrest records acceptable?

The EEOC has historically taken the position that, because members of certain minority groups are more likely to be arrested, this inquiry can have an illegally adverse impact on such groups. In addition, in its 2012 Guidance, the EEOC stated that, because an arrest does not establish that criminal conduct has occurred, the arrest, in and of itself, cannot be "job related" or "consistent with business necessity," defenses to claims of Title VII discrimination. [See EEOC Enforcement Guidance No. 915.002 (Apr. 25, 2012).] In some states (e.g., Michigan), it is a violation of an applicant's civil rights to inquire as to his or her arrest record, except for information related to felony charges. [Mich. Comp. Laws Ann. § 32.2205a]

Q 3:16   May the applicant be asked about criminal convictions?

The EEOC feels that inquiries regarding criminal convictions can have an adverse impact on members of certain minority groups; however, the EEOC and the courts recognize that employers have a legitimate right to know whether an applicant has ever been convicted of crimes. This concern is particularly significant when cash, drugs, valuable property, or one-on-one customer, patient, or client contacts are involved. In these cases, the question may be asked. If the question is included on the application, it should, however, be accompanied by the statement, "Criminal convictions are not an absolute bar to employment but will be considered only with respect to the specific require-ments of the job for which you are applying." This will help in avoiding discrimination claims. On April 25, 2012, the EEOC issued its Guidance on an employer's use of arrest and conviction records, "Consideration of Arrest and Conviction Records in Employment Decisions under Title VII of the Civil Rights Act of 1964." [EEOC Enforcement Guidance No. 915.002] This Guidance codifies the EEOC's position that an employer's neutral policy excluding applicants on the basis of criminal convictions may disproportionately impact individuals protected under Title VII and may violate the law if not job related and consistent with business necessity. The Guidance can be found at http://www. eeoc.gov.

Q 3:17   May applicants be asked about their military records?

This inquiry, if made, should be limited to the relevant skills and training the applicant may have acquired as a consequence of military service. Employers should not inquire into military service in another country, as it could be construed to be an attempt to discriminate on the basis of national origin. Nor should applicants be asked about the type of discharges they received; if this inquiry is made, it should be accompanied by a statement that a less-than-honorable discharge is not an absolute bar to employment. Care also should be taken when inquiring about reservist and National Guard responsibilities. If employment is denied, the applicant's military time may appear to be the reason, and this would be illegal.

Q 3:18   May an applicant be asked to provide references?

It is permissible to request personal and professional references. As increasing numbers of former employers are limiting reference information to a mere confirmation of the applicant's dates and position of employment, other character and professional references are assuming increased significance. Two caveats are in order. First, the employer should not ask any questions that would be illegal if they were asked of the applicant (e.g., inquiries into disabilities or workers' compensation claims). Second, the employer must not insist that a character reference come from a member of the clergy; such a reference could be viewed by the EEOC as an oblique way of ascertaining the applicant's religion.

Q 3:19   Are prior employment reference checks and background investigations permitted?

An employer has the legal right to ask about an applicant's prior employment and to follow up with written or oral inquiries to the previous employers. The problem is that many companies, concerned about lawsuits, only verify the former employee's dates of employment, position, and salary. This is a prudent policy for the prior employer but not very helpful to the potential employer. One solution is to build a relationship of trust with human resources managers at companies in the same line of business, companies that are likely to turn up as prior employers on job applications. Sometimes trade associations or professional organizations can help in establishing these contacts on a social level. A more expensive solution, but often highly effective, is to hire a firm that specializes in background investigations. Because of the cost, these firms should probably be used only when filling key positions. Furthermore, companies retained to obtain background checks are generally subject to the same limitations that apply to employers when they are making inquiries concerning disabilities, workers' compensation claims, and the like. Moreover, any time an outside firm is used to check background or references, the employer is required by amendments to the Fair Credit Reporting Act to obtain a stand-alone written notice and authorization form signed by the applicant. (See Q 3:28 for more detail.)

Q 3:20 How hard is it to get adequate references from former employers?

Many companies, concerned about defamation lawsuits by former employees, have adopted a policy of responding to reference checks with only the former employee's dates of employment and position held. (The authors recommend to their clients that they provide only this factual data.) According to some attorneys, this practice has become so pervasive that it is nearly impossible for companies to get adequate referrals on job applicants. A firm's reference policy depends on many factors, including the applicable state's law of defamation (e.g., whether a qualified business privilege is applied to reference checks), the need for quid pro quo referrals from frequently contacted companies, and the reliability of the company's personnel who respond to such calls.

In response to growing concerns of employers concerning references, some states have enacted specific laws to protect employers that provide references. Michigan has enacted legislation that provides employers immunity from civil liability if they, in good faith, disclose information to an employee's prospective employer relating to the employee's job performance that is documented in the employee's personnel file. However, immunity is not extended to situations where:

- The employer knew the information was false or misleading;
- The information was disclosed with reckless disregard of the truth; or
- The disclosure is prohibited under law.

[Mich. Comp. Laws Ann. § 423.452]

Q 3:21 May an applicant be asked if friends or relatives work at the company?

Yes, but not without risk. A preference for applicants who are connected can adversely affect a particular race that is under-represented at the company. A hiring policy that favors friends and relatives may be viewed as a perpetuation of prior discriminatory practices.

Q 3:22 May an applicant be asked if friends or relatives work for a competitor?

An employer concerned about its trade secrets may make this inquiry. If, for example, the applicant indicates that his or her spouse is employed at a competing company, the potential employer may legitimately withhold an offer of employment.

Q 3:23   Should an applicant be asked whether he/she has signed an agreement with a prior employer that might affect his or her job duties?

Yes. The use of non-competitive agreements, non-solicitation agreements, and confidentiality agreements has risen through the years, particularly in certain industries, including professional firms, placement firms, and sales positions in almost every industry. In many jurisdictions, an employee who has signed an enforceable restrictive covenant with a prior employer may be enjoined from working with the new employer, provided the restriction is reasonable as to scope and duration, and serves to protect the legitimate interest of the prior employer. For these reasons, it is wise to ask whether the applicant has signed any agreements that might interfere with or affect his or her job duties.

Preferably, the inquiry should be in writing, with the applicant acknowledging in writing that he or she has not entered into any agreements that in any way restrict or affect his or her ability to perform work for the company and that if he or she is selected for the position, the performance of job duties would not be in breach of any contract or agreement into which he or she has entered. These acknowledgments should include a provision that allows the applicant to designate any agreements that may be contrary to the acknowledgment with the following language: "except as to those Agreements designated below." Companies should examine any such agreements designated to determine their enforceability or impact on the applicant's ability to perform the job.

Q 3:24   Can an employer be liable for an employee's breach of a restrictive covenant with a prior employer?

Although agreements are only enforceable between the parties, if an employer solicits and encourages an employee to violate an agreement with another employer, the employer might be exposing itself to liability under any number of theories, including the common-law claim of tortious interference with contract relations. However, to be held accountable for the breach, the employer must be aware of the existence of the contract and induce the employee to violate his or her restrictive covenants. If, after inquiry, an employer finds out that its employee has an agreement with a prior employer that may impact on the employee's ability to perform his or her job, the authors favor the following approach:

- Have the agreement reviewed by an employment attorney as to its enforceability;
- If it is enforceable, in whole or in part, consider whether the employee's duties can be performed and/or modified such that he or she will not violate enforceable restrictions; and
- If his or her duties cannot be modified or performed in a manner other than violating enforceable restrictions, consider approaching the prior employer to negotiate a resolution of the issue. It has been the author's experience that dealing with the issue up front is oftentimes far more

successful than reacting to the issue after the prior employer learns that the covenants have been violated behind his or her back.

Q 3:25   May an employer ask an applicant about clubs and other voluntary associations?

This question should not be included on the application form. It is very likely to reveal the applicant's race, religion or national origin, while having only a remote relationship to job duties and qualifications. An application may, however, ask about memberships in professional societies pertinent to the open position. Questions concerning political affiliations are unlawful in some states. [*See, e.g.,* Hutchcraft Van Serv., Inc. v. City of Urbana Human Relations Comm'n, 433 N.E.2d 329 (Ill. App. Ct. 1982); Blackhawk Teachers' Fed'n v. Wisconsin Emp't Relations Comm'n, 326 N.W.2d 247 (Wis. App. 1982); *see also* Rutan v. Republican Party of Illinois, 497 U.S. 62 (1990) (rejection of job application on basis of party affiliation violated First Amendment).]

Q 3:26   May an applicant be asked about personal finances?

Not without potential exposure. Questions concerning the financial status of the applicant (e.g., credit history, wage garnishment, home and automobile ownership, bank and charge accounts) may negatively affect certain minority groups and single women. In addition, the relationship of personal finances to job requirements is often only tangential. On the other hand, an employer frequently does have a legitimate interest in whether an applicant is a stable resident of the community or has the use of an automobile. Inquiries as to how long the individual has lived in the area and whether the applicant has access to reliable transportation can elicit the desired information without running a risk of inadvertently violating equal employment opportunity laws. Treating applicants differently on the basis of personal finances may, depending on the circumstances, violate federal or state law (see Q 3:27).

Q 3:27   May an applicant be asked about his or her credit rating?

In most circumstances, employers should avoid questions concerning credit ratings. Such questions usually do not bear on the performance of job duties and may put some protected groups in the applicant pool at a disadvantage, opening the employer to charges of disparate impact discrimination. For example, the EEOC has taken the position that poor credit ratings may be more prevalent in certain areas among minority groups, and questions regarding credit ratings may segregate these groups from other applicants, thereby resulting in disparate treatment whether or not discrimination is intended. In addition, there may be protection under federal or state law for employees with bad credit ratings. Under the Federal Bankruptcy Code [11 U.S.C. § 525(b)], it is unlawful for an employer to discriminate against an applicant or an employee who has filed for protection under federal bankruptcy laws. As a result, questions regarding credit ratings can lead to liability for employers.

On the other hand, there may be legitimate reasons, security or otherwise, for employers to obtain information regarding the applicant's creditworthiness. This would be more prevalent in industries where the jobs involve handling cash, or in the banking industry, where the employee has access to cash and customers' accounts. Provided there is a legitimate reason for the inquiry, such inquiries should not lead to exposure.

Q 3:28 What steps must an employer follow if it uses a third party to conduct credit or background checks for applicants?

Employers often utilize outside agencies, so-called consumer reporting agencies, to provide them with credit reports and background checks regarding the applicant. The Fair Credit Reporting Act, among other things, regulates the use of credit reports and investigative reports that employers can obtain from a consumer reporting agency. A *consumer reporting agency* is generally defined as an organization that, among other things, regularly sells consumer reports (including credit reports) to others for a variety of purposes, including employment purposes, in order to evaluate a "consumer for employment, promotion, reassignment or retention as an employee." [15 U.S.C. § 1681a]

If an employer uses a consumer reporting agency to obtain a consumer report regarding applicants, it is incumbent upon that employer to meet the disclosure requirements contained within the amendments of the Fair Credit Reporting Act. [15 U.S.C. § 1681b] As a condition for the furnishing and use of a consumer report for employment purposes, before the report is procured the employer must provide a clear and conspicuous disclosure to the applicant that a consumer report may be obtained on the applicant for employment purposes, and the applicant must specifically authorize the procurement of the report by the employer in writing. Subsection (2) of that U.S. Code section provides:

> A person may not procure a consumer report, or cause a consumer report to be procured, for employment purposes with respect to any consumer, unless:
>
> (A) A clear and conspicuous disclosure has been made in writing at any time before the report is procured or caused to be procured, in a document that consists solely of the disclosure, that a consumer report may be obtained for employment purposes; and
>
> (B) The consumer has authorized in writing the procurement of the report by that person.

The disclosure must be contained in a stand-alone document, and it is not sufficient to include this within boilerplate language contained on an application. This is different from the requirements found elsewhere in the Fair Credit Reporting Act that merely require pre-notification with respect to an employer's ability to obtain investigative reports concerning the applicant or employee. The investigative report section of the Act continues to require notification that an investigative report may be made consisting of information obtained through personal interviews with third parties, including inquiries regarding character, reputation, and the like. Whatever notification employers historically have been using with respect to investigative reports is not modified by amendments to the Fair Credit Reporting Act; however, for purposes of obtaining credit reports from the consumer reporting agencies, the previous form of notification is not sufficient, and now the employer must first have a separate authorization signed by the applicant that contains required disclosure before the credit report can be obtained from a consumer reporting agency.

Furthermore, if the employer is going to take adverse action based upon information obtained within a credit report, a copy of the report must be provided to the applicant prior to taking any adverse action and a summary of the applicant's rights under the Fair Credit Reporting Act must be given to the applicant. The summary of rights can be obtained from the consumer reporting agency from which the report was obtained.

Q 3:29 May a company deny employment on the basis of a credit report?

An employer should have a legitimate reason before it takes action on the basis of a poor credit report. As discussed previously, adverse action may have a disparate impact on minorities or other protected categories and, as a result, acting on the basis of this information can be a violation of Title VII or other state statutes. The only exception is when the employer can demonstrate it has a legitimate business reason for the adverse employment decision at issue. Unless the employer can articulate the specific risk or danger with respect to employees with poor credit ratings in the performance of their job, the criteria will not be determined to be job-related and required by business necessity and the basis for the adverse job decision will not sustain judicial review.

In addition to Title VII issues, employers must consider the Fair Credit Reporting Act. Although this law is better known for its impact on retail sales and credit cards, some of its sections deal with background investigations of employment applicants. For example, if an employer denies employment to an applicant on the basis of a report prepared by a consumer reporting agency, the employer must advise the applicant of the report's existence and that it was the reason for denying employment. In addition (as discussed in Q 3:28), the Fair Credit Reporting Act was modified to require a specific stand-alone agreement to be signed by the applicant prior to obtaining the credit report from a consumer reporting agency, which discloses that the employer intends to obtain a credit report from a consumer reporting agency in connection with the employment process, and the applicant must specifically sign the disclosure form, authorizing utilization of the consumer reporting agency. Additional laws protect individuals with poor credit histories. For example, under the federal bankruptcy code, an employer may not discriminate against an applicant or employee who has filed for bankruptcy. [11 U.S.C. § 525(b)]

Q 3:30   How can a company validate necessary job requirements against claims of disparate impact?

This question is addressed in the Uniform Guidelines on Employee Selection Procedures developed by the EEOC. Perhaps most significantly, the guidelines outline a procedure known as the four-fifths rule:

> The illegal disparate impact of a job test or requirement is demonstrated when the proportion of applicants from the protected group (e.g., African-Americans or women) with the lowest selection (or pass) rate is less than 80 percent of the selection (or pass) rate of the group (e.g., whites or males) with the highest selection rate.

For example, a company gives an aptitude test to all applicants and requires a minimum score to be considered for employment. If 25 percent of all Hispanic applicants achieve this score and 75 percent of all white applicants score at least the minimum, the four-fifths rule is violated because 36 percent is less than 80 percent. The aptitude test is presumably illegal because it has a disparate impact on a protected group.

One of the exemptions from liability for disparate impact claims under the ADEA is if the employer can demonstrate that its actions were based on "reasonable factors other than age" (RFOA). In the U.S. Supreme Court case of *Meacham v. Knolls Atomic Power Laboratory* [128 S. Ct. 2395 (June 19, 2008)], the Court was asked to determine who bears the burden of proof as it relates to an alleged RFOA. Recognizing that an RFOA is essentially an affirmative defense which an employer must raise, the Court determined that the employer bears both the burden of production and burden of persuasion to demonstrate an RFOA.

Q 3:31   May a company specify height and weight requirements for employees?

Minimum height and weight requirements for a job may be discriminatory under federal law. Many such requirements have been stricken down through the years in such occupations as police work and firefighting, as being illegal gender discrimination under disparate-impact analysis. In addition, some state laws (e.g., Michigan's Elliott-Larsen Civil Rights Act) specifically prohibit height and weight discrimination, absent a bona fide occupational qualification defense. Therefore, such requirements must be proved a job-related necessity, in accordance with BFOQ (bona fide occupational qualification) analysis to be permissible. (See chapter 4 for a discussion of BFOQ.)

Q 3:32   What sort of validation might satisfy height and weight requirements against an attack under federal law?

Statistical evidence correlating height and weight requirements with job performance or safety is potentially acceptable according to the EEOC's Uniform Guidelines on Employee Selection Procedures. The evidence must show that an applicant who does not meet these requirements cannot perform the job adequately and safely.

Q 3:33   May applicants and employees be tested for drugs?

Although the ADA prohibits applicant medical examinations, it does allow pre-employment testing for the use of illegal drugs, which may include a urine or blood test; however, to the extent the testing seeks information that is beyond the scope of limited testing for the use of illegal drugs, it may be an impermissible medical examination under ADA. A pre-offer drug test and related inquiries were held to be a violation of the ADA as an impermissible medical examination and impermissible medical-related inquiries in the pre-offer stage. [Harrison v. Benchmark Elec. Huntsville, Inc., 593 F.3d 1206 (11th Cir. 2010)] It may also be appropriate to request that an employee be tested if his or her behavior at work suggests the use of drugs or alcohol. To reduce risk and exposure to liability, employers should have a written policy, consistently applied, as to the circumstances under which a test may be requested. Refusal can be characterized as insubordination, resulting in termination of employment. Random testing of public employees without any reason to suspect drug abuse has been ruled a constitutional violation by a number of courts and, absent particular need or justification, may be a legally risky policy in the private sector.

However, if the determination of who is subject to testing is not consistent, and if it can be demonstrated that only employees or applicants of a particular race, national origin, or other protected category are subject to testing, there is a potential that the practice will result in a discrimination charge or claim, particularly if adverse employment actions are taken on the basis of such testing.

The U.S. Department of Transportation regulations require both periodic and reasonable-cause testing of truck drivers. [49 C.F.R. Part 40 (Oct. 1, 1989)] These regulations, which took effect for big trucking companies in December 1989 and for smaller outfits in December 1990, detail the requisite methods of specimen collection, laboratory analysis, and reporting and disclosure requirements.

Q 3:34   How should the interviewer respond to applicants' questions regarding job security or the like?

It is not uncommon for applicants to ask interviewers questions regarding job security, particularly if the applicant is currently employed and attempting to decide whether it is within his or her best interest to quit his or her current job and move to another employer. Interviewers should be aware that in these circumstances if they make promises regarding job security they expose the employer to liability if these promises are not kept, even if the promises are only made verbally. If an interviewer tells an applicant, after inquiry, that the employer does not fire people arbitrarily, but only for good cause, or that the applicant will have a job as long as he or she does a good job, or explains to the applicant that the employer does not fire anybody until after they have been warned of the deficiencies in their performance, the employer may be susceptible to breach of contract claims if it should, in the eyes of the employee, fail to honor these promises. From a legal perspective, the best response to any inquiry regarding job security is advising the applicant that the employer is an at-will employer and reserves the right to terminate the employment relationship at any time, with or without cause. Although this is the best response from a legal perspective, it is hardly the type of response that any interviewer is likely to provide. A better response, from a practical perspective, may be to inform the applicant that the employer always hopes for a long and mutually beneficial arrangement, but the interviewer can make no guarantees or promises with regard to either length of employment or termination matters. Emphasizing to the applicant that the interviewer can make no promises or guarantees will assist in maintaining the employer's at-will status, which is generally a presumption in most jurisdictions. Such language will be tolerable to most applicants and will not work to destroy the at-will presumption in most jurisdictions.

Q 3:35 May an applicant be required to acknowledge that, if hired, the employment will be "at will"?

Yes. In fact, employers commonly require applicants to sign a form saying something like: "I understand that, if hired, I will be an employee at will; that is, my employment will be for no definite period of time but rather will be subject to termination by myself or the company at any time for any reasons, with or without cause."

Q 3:36 How should applications be drafted to protect an employer's interests?

Applications should avoid questions that touch on protected classifications under Title VII or inquiries that could be inferred to provide a basis for discrimination in the hiring process. As such, applications should not seek information relating to a person's age, race, national origin, religion, gender, or any other protected category under applicable law. Unnecessary questions regarding affiliation with clubs or organizations can elicit information concerning an individual that can match up with a protected category, and therefore, should be avoided. Although many employers ask whether the applicant has been convicted of a crime, a per se policy that rules out all individuals who have been convicted of a crime may run afoul of discrimination laws. In the seminal case *Green v. Missouri Pacific Railroad* [523 F.2d 1290 (8th Cir. 1975)], the court held such a per se rule to constitute discrimination on the basis of race under a disparate impact theory when it was found that the policy disproportionately impacted on African Americans and was not justified by business necessity. Applications should, however, do more than avoid areas of possible discrimination; they should provide an employer a basis to defend against or limit employment litigation. The following paragraphs describe ways in which an application can be drafted to protect an employer's interests:

After-acquired evidence. In defending wrongful discharge and discrimination claims, employers often review applications to determine whether they contain any false or misleading information that can be used to limit lost wage claims. To employ this defense effectively, an employer must have carefully drafted the application to ensure that after-acquired evidence rules can be used. Specifically, applicants should be required to provide a complete educational background: names and addresses of schools attended; courses of study; years completed; whether the applicant graduated; and the diploma(s) or degree(s) received. In addition, an applicant must be required to provide his or her entire work history, including: dates of employment; names, addresses, and telephone numbers of employers; rates of pay from start to finish; supervisors' names and titles; and reasons for leaving. A statement should be included above the applicant's signature that provides a certification by the applicant that: all of the information provided in the application is true and complete; there are no misrepresentations, misleading information, or omissions; and if there are any misrepresentations, misleading information or omissions, the applicant accepts that his or her employment will be terminated, regardless of when such misinformation is discovered, even after commencement of employment.

Release of liability. Above the applicant's signature on the application should be a sentence authorizing the employer to investigate and check all information provided in the application and expressly releasing both the employer and the organizations contacted from any liability or damages in connection with such an investigation. However, if the employer intends to hire an outside business to perform the investigation, the Fair Credit Reporting Act requires the applicant to sign an agreement authorizing the investigation. Most companies that perform these services will have forms available for this purpose. These forms should be reviewed by labor counsel to ensure they meet the requirements of the Fair Credit Reporting Act.

At-will employment. The application of an at-will employer should contain a clear at-will employment statement prominently above the applicant's signature and preferably in bold print.

Arbitration. Employers often find arbitration an attractive way to solve employment disputes, so they should consider including an arbitration agreement in the hiring process. As of the last publication, the enforceability of arbitration agreements in civil rights claims was an open issue. The EEOC claims that requiring the agreement was itself a violation of federal civil rights laws. In *Circuit City Stores, Inc. v. Adams* [532 U.S. 105 (2001)], the U.S. Supreme Court upheld the use of a pre-dispute arbitration agreement to compel arbitration of a civil rights claim. Typically, employers will use separate agreements to compel arbitration, as opposed to including the provision in an application. However, recent case law suggests that stand-alone agreements may not be required in all instances. In *In re Halliburton Co.* [2001 WL 1873035 (Tex. May 30, 2002)], the Texas Supreme Court upheld binding arbitration of an employment dispute when the employer notified all of its employees of the adoption of the program requiring binding arbitration of all employment disputes, and that by working after its implementation would mean acceptance of the program, and the employee, mindful of its adoption, continued working at the facility. The court found that the employee's continuation of employment after adoption of the policy was tantamount to "acceptance" of the policy.

Drug testing and post-offer medical exams. Applicants may be tested for current illegal use of drugs under the ADA. If testing applicants for drug use is part of an employer's procedures, the application should state that undergoing and successfully passing a screening for the illegal use of drugs is a condition for employment. In addition, the application should state that any offer of employment is contingent on the results of a medical examination that the employee must undergo before commencing work. This procedure does not violate the ADA.

Consider reducing the statutes of limitation for claims. Some states will enforce contractually agreed upon limitation periods that are significantly less than statutes of limitations contained in federal or state statutes. For example, in Michigan, courts have held that six-month time limitations are enforceable, despite the allowance of longer time frames under state discrimination laws (i.e., three years). [*See, e.g.,* Wells v. ABC Warehouse, 2004 Mich. App. LEXIS 250 (Mich. Ct. App. Jan. 27, 2004); Krusinski v. DaimlerChrylser Co., 2004 WL 315171 (Mich. App. Feb. 19, 2004); Wright v. DaimlerChrysler Co., 220 F. Supp. 2d 832 (E.D. Mich. 2002).]

Negligent Hiring

Q 3:37   What is *negligent hiring*?

It is the hiring or retaining of employees with a history of violent or aberrant behavior when a reasonable background investigation would have revealed this history. However, if the prospective employer had no knowledge of facts that would lead a reasonably prudent person to investigate the prospective employee, claims of negligent hiring will be difficult to maintain. In *Bouchard v. New York Archdiocese* [719 F. Supp. 2d 255 (S.D.N.Y. 2010)], a parishioner who was allegedly sexually abused by a visiting priest, brought a claim for negligent hiring against the Archdiocese for hiring a visiting priest that allegedly had a propensity to commit sexual abuse. However, because the plaintiff could provide no evidence that the church had any knowledge of facts that would lead the church to investigate the background of the visiting priest, the court dismissed the claim.

Q 3:38   How can employers best avoid negligent-hiring suits?

The goal is to avoid hiring the wrong employees in the first place. An employer should examine its screening procedure to see whether it thoroughly assesses an applicant's suitability for employment. Although the EEOC believes otherwise, inquiry into felony criminal convictions may be a useful way of obtaining information in this area. However, caution needs to be taken. The EEOC, in its Guidance issued in April 2012 stated that prohibitions excluding applicants based on criminal conduct may violate Title VII if not job related and consistent with business necessity. [See EEOC Enforcement Guidance No. 915.002, which can be found at: http://www.eeoc.gov.]

Q 3:39   What tests do courts use to determine whether an employer has acted negligently in a hiring decision?

The employer must satisfy the court that it sufficiently investigated the employee's background for the job for which he or she was hired. Employers should evaluate the information this investigation provides with regard to the risk of harm or injury to coworkers or third parties that could result from the conduct of an unfit employee.

In *Nigg v. Patterson* [806 P.2d 841 (Cal. 1991)], a laundromat that hired troubled juveniles through a state-run rehabilitation program was held not to be insulated from a negligent hiring lawsuit by public policy favoring such programs. The employee was a resident of a San Diego treatment center known as Stepping Stones. The plaintiff claimed that while she was in the laundromat, the young man attacked her with his fists and a hammer. She sued the employer for failing to exercise ordinary care by investigating her attacker's background and discovering his vicious disposition. The complainant in the case alleged that residents of Stepping Stones were juvenile criminal offenders, and the particular employee had a history of, and propensity for, heavy drug use, extreme violence, and bizarre sexual attacks. The court held that except for a single, unannounced visit to the laundromat by a Stepping Stones counselor, employees there were unsupervised. "It is foreseeable," said the court, "that a business invitee might be injured by an unsupervised employee with vicious propensities, especially where the business is open late at night and the potential for one-on-one encounters is likely." In *Woods v. Town of Danville, West Virginia* [712 F. Supp. 2d 502 (S.D.W.Va. 2010)], the court refused to dismiss a negligent retention claim against a town involving the actions of a police officer when it was demonstrated that the police officer who had only been on the job for eight days and was given minimal training, had a history of a propensity towards anger, a spotty employment history, and an other than honorable discharge from the Navy.

If an employer establishes a policy of conducting criminal background checks in situations that warrant it, and failed to do so, it leaves itself vulnerable to liability for negligent hiring if an employee turns out to have propensities for violence that would have been uncovered through a background check. For example, in *Blair v. Defender Services, Inc.* [386 F.3d 623 (4th Cir. 2004)], a college student sued a janitorial staffing company for injuries sustained as a result of a violent attack upon her by a janitor of the staffing company. As to her claim for negligent hiring, the college student claimed that despite its contract with the college, the janitorial service had failed on three prior occasions to do a criminal background check of the janitor that attacked her, which would have disclosed a prior protective order entered in a neighboring county resulting from an alleged attack of a female patron of a restaurant. Although the janitor in question had no criminal convictions per se, the court concluded that there was ample evidence that if a background criminal check had been done, as required by the janitorial service's contract with the college, that the protective order in the neighboring county would have been discovered. The janitorial service acknowledged that had it been aware of the protective order, it would not have assigned the janitor to the college. As such, the court concluded that the case could proceed to trial. In *Hobirn, Inc. v. Aerotek, Inc.* [787 F. Supp. 2d 1298 (S. D. Fla. 2011)], a company hired an employee from a provider of contract employees and sued the provider for negligent hiring for losses suffered due to theft by the employee referred to the company. The company that provided contract employees to the plaintiff employer acted pursuant to a service agreement that required background checks of referred employees which the provider company did not perform. Had the provider conducted a background criminal search, it would have found that the referred employee had an extensive criminal background, including convictions for theft; the court concluded that the plaintiff properly stated a claim for negligent hiring.

In *Shaw v. Pizza Hut of America, Inc.* [8:08-cv-27-T-24-EAJ, 2009 WL 591182 (M.D. Fla. Mar. 6, 2009)], the plaintiff who was in an automobile accident with a pizza delivery driver, sued Pizza Hut alleging, among other things, negligent hiring of its pizza delivery driver. The plaintiff claimed that if Pizza Hut conducted a background check of his driving record, it would have found that he had a DWI and multiple speeding violations. As such, the plaintiff alleged that Pizza Hut knew or should have known of his lack of fitness to be a driver and that it was therefore unreasonable and negligent for Pizza Hut to have hired this employee in light of the information it knew or should have known. Although Pizza Hut claimed it had no obligation to conduct a background check and that it hired this driver consistent with its internal policies applicable to all of its drivers, the court held that because all employers have a duty to exercise reasonable care in hiring, and because the job of pizza delivery involves driving on public roads for almost the employee's entire shift, Pizza Hut had a duty to use reasonable care in hiring safe drivers who would not pose a danger to the public in carrying out their duties, including inquiry into the driver's fitness to drive which the jury could find would involve a review of the driver's driving record. However, in *Keen v. Miller Environmental Group, Inc.* [702 F.3d 239 (5th Cir. 2012)], in a case of first impression, the Fifth Circuit held that there was no generalized duty under Mississippi law to conduct a background check on applicants, despite an internal corporate policy to do so, such that there could be no claim of negligent hiring against an employer for hiring a manual laborer that allegedly raped a co-worker.

However, just because an employee engages in a wrongful or criminal behavior during his employment does not make the employer liable for negligent hiring. Rather, there must be some evidence that the employer knew or should have known of the employee's propensity to engage in such behavior and should not have hired him. The key to negligent hiring is the foreseeability of the wrongful or criminal behavior by the employer. In *Cole v. American Community Services, Inc.* [2:04-cv-738, 2006 U.S. Dist. LEXIS 75431 (S.D. Ohio Oct. 17, 2006)], the magazine salesman assaulted a homeowner when the homeowner declined to purchase magazine subscriptions from him. According to the facts, the salesman stuck his foot in the door to prevent the homeowner from closing it, pushed the door open, shouted at the customer, walked into the customer's house, and shoved him into the wall. Although unquestionably wrongful, the plaintiffs proffered no evidence that the aggressive salesman had ever been previously arrested or even had a prior customer complaint filed against him prior to the incident at hand. The plaintiffs, having no evidence that the salesman had a propensity to engage in this type of conduct, previous to the incident in question, the salesman's dangerous propensities could not have been foreseeable by the company, and the claim for negligent hiring was dismissed.

Provided that employers make a good-faith effort to check references and receive no unfavorable information suggesting a dangerous propensity for damage or harm, a claim for negligent hiring will be difficult to maintain even if a more thorough search may have demonstrated otherwise. In *Doe v. Fulton-Dekalb Hospital Authority* [1:05-CV-2277-TWT, 2007 U.S. Dist. LEXIS 76247 (N.D. Ga. Oct. 5, 2007)], former patients of a drug dependence unit at a hospital, who were alleged victims of sexual harassment by a counselor, contended that the hospital negligently hired the counselor who, at previous jobs, had engaged in sexual misconduct. The employer, on the other hand, maintained that it had contacted the prior employers, that two did not respond, and the one that did provided no negative information about the counselor. Moreover, a criminal background check was conducted, and it was negative. Although the employee had engaged in sexual misconduct prior to being hired, the fact that the hospital conducted a good-faith background check and received no information suggesting the candidate's dangerous propensities persuaded the court that the claim could not be maintained. As the court stated, "Mere mistakes and incomplete and inaccurate information in an employment application are not sufficient to impose liability upon an employer. Whether a more thorough background investigation would have revealed that [the candidate] was an unsuitable employee requires entry into the realm of speculation and conjecture." [*Fulton-Dekalb*, at 3.] As such, the negligent hiring claims were dismissed. In *Beyene v. Hilton Hotels Corp.* [815 F. Supp. 2d 235 (D.D.C. 2011)], the court refused to dismiss a claim of negligent retention when the plaintiff asserted that the defendant employer conducted an inadequate investigation of his complaints of harassment, and had it conducted a proper investigation by interviewing all witnesses, it would have determined that the employee had dangerous propensities.

In *Khan v. Houston NFL Holdings LP* [277 Fed. Appx. 503 (5th Cir. 2008)], a number of football stadium patrons sued the stadium's owner for negligent hiring, arising from an altercation with security guards at the stadium. The security guards were hired by the stadium to provide security and all were off-duty police officers. Although plaintiffs claimed that had the employer obtained copies of the personnel records of the police officers, there would have been indications of overly aggressive behavior, in order to show a predisposition towards violent behavior. The court found that all were officers in good standing with the police department, there was no confirmed evidence of excessive force in the personnel files of any of the officers, and no evidence of an industry practice to obtain personnel files in connection with the hiring of these off-duty officers. As such, the court concluded that there was insufficient evidence to maintain the claim for negligence in hiring.

Q 3:40   What is *negligent retention*?

Generally, *negligent retention* is based on a duty flowing from the employer to the public to protect those the employer might reasonably anticipate would be injured as a result of the retention of an employee. Negligent retention generally does not require the employer actually know of the employee's lack of fitness, but depends on whether the employer knew or should have known that the employee posed a risk of harm to the public. Liability based on a theory of negligent retention requires a duty on the part of the employer toward the public and negligent retention must generally be considered to be the proximate cause of the plaintiff's injuries and the injury must be foreseeable. [*See* Spencer v. Health Force, Inc., 135 N.M. 554 (N.M. App. 2004).]

Q 3:41   How do courts determine whether an employer has acted negligently in retaining an employee?

The issue of whether or not negligent retention can be maintained depends upon the facts of each case. In *Mills v. Deehr* [2004 Ohio 2338 (Ohio Ct. App. 2004)], a parishioner claimed that a church employee had molested and sexually assaulted him, and that the church and church management were liable under the doctrine of negligent retention. Although the case was dismissed by the trial court, on appeal the court pointed to allegations involving the church employee's close contact with the parishioner at odd hours on multiple occasions that should have alerted church officials of alleged criminal, tortious, or dangerous conduct. Based on these facts, the court concluded that sufficient alleged facts existed to withstand a motion to dismiss and remanded the matter to the trial court for further proceedings.

In *McClements v. Ford Motor Co.* [2004 Mich. App. LEXIS 1043 (Mich. Ct. App. Apr. 22, 2004)], an unpublished decision, the plaintiff, an employee for an independent food service company, claimed that Ford Motor Company was negligent in retaining a superintendent who allegedly sexually assaulted her. Although the case was dismissed by the trial court, on appeal the court pointed to numerous prior allegations of sexual harassment regarding the superintendent, as well as a prior conviction of indecent exposure, that should have alerted Ford Motor Company to the superintendent's dangerous propensities. Due to these facts, the court concluded that there were sufficient allegations to allege that Ford Motor Company knew or should have known of the superintendent's propensities, such that it could be liable for negligent retention.

However, to state a claim for negligent retention, the allegations of harm must be proximately caused by the negligent retention. In *Spencer et al. v. Health Force, Inc.* [135 N.M. 554 (N.M. App. 2004)], an employee hired by caregiver Health Force was alleged to have caused the death of the plaintiff's decedent by injecting her with heroin. Apparently, prior to the alleged incident involving the death, evidence existed that the caregiver may have taken the decedent's narcotic prescription pills while on duty. Noting that the negligent retention must be the proximate cause of the plaintiff's injury and injury must be foreseeable, the court concluded that a jury could not reasonably find that the defendant's retention of the caregiver after he allegedly stole three narcotic pills could be considered the proximate cause of the decedent's death more than three weeks later. However, to establish negligent retention, a single prior isolated instance of misconduct may be insufficient to maintain a negligent retention claim.

The issue of whether a single prior incident of misconduct is sufficient for purposes of maintaining a negligent retention claim based on additional misconduct was addressed by the court in *Doe v. ATC, Inc.* [624 S.E.2d 447 (S.C. App. 2005)] In that case, the mother of a disabled adult brought an action against a transportation company based on the bus driver's having allegedly touched her disabled adult daughter inappropriately while she was being "transported" to physical therapy sessions. Several months prior to this bus incident, the bus driver had allegedly made inappropriate sexual advances toward a co-employee, and the incident was reported to a supervisor. The trial court directed a verdict in favor of the transportation company, and, on appeal, the court considered whether, as a matter of law, a single prior incident of misconduct was sufficient for purposes of maintaining a negligent retention case. Although allowing that other states had found that negligent retention requires that the plaintiff demonstrate some propensity, proclivity, or course of conduct sufficient to put the employer on notice of possible dangers to third parties such that a single prior incident of misconduct fails to state a claim for negligent retention as a matter of law, the court held that a single incident of prior misconduct may support a negligent retention claim, provided the prior misconduct has a sufficient nexus to the ultimate harm. However, in this case, the court concluded that the misconduct directed to the co-employee lacked sufficient nexus to the conduct involving the disabled rider and affirmed the dismissal of the case. The court seemed to suggest that had there been a similar prior act of misconduct by the bus driver involving bus riders, it may have held otherwise. In the similar tort of negligent supervision, liability arises when "an employer knew or should have known its employee behaved in a dangerous or otherwise incompetent manner and that the employer, armed with that actual or constructive knowledge, fails to adequately supervise the employee." [Brown v. Argenbright Sec. Inc., 782 A.2d 752, 760 (D.C. 2001)]

In *Godfrey v. Iverson* [559 F.3d 569 (D.D.C. Cir. 2009)], a nightclub patron sued Allen Iverson for negligent supervision of his bodyguard stemming from a fight between the nightclub patron and Iverson's bodyguard. Although Iverson claimed that the case should be dismissed due to the plaintiff's failure to provide expert testimony as to any duty Iverson owed, in this case, given that Iverson was present during the altercation, the court said expert testimony was unnecessary and that a jury could determine the standard of care that Iverson owed to the nightclub patron for supervision of his bodyguard without need of the assistance of expert testimony.

In *Alleman v. YRC* [787 F. Supp. 2d 679 (N.D. Ohio 2011)], the court held that no claim for negligent supervision could be maintained against a trucking company whose employee truck driver was involved in an accident where there was no evidence that the truck driver was incompetent, in that the truck driver had been involved in driving tractor-trailers for over 20 years without having caused an accident, regularly attended safety meetings and was properly licensed, trained, and certified.

Q 3:42 What damages are recoverable for negligent hiring?

Unlike "respondeat superior" liability, which generally results in the employer being responsible for its employee's conduct in the scope of the employee's employment, the tort of negligent hiring is independent of respondeat superior theory, and if found, the employer becomes liable for all foreseeable harm, even if outside the scope of employment. In *Prymak v. Contemporary Financial Solutions, Inc.* [2007 U.S. Dist. LEXIS 87734 (D. Colo. Nov. 29, 2007)], a securities firm that hired a broker, knowing that the broker had defrauded customers in the past, was liable for damages caused to its clients, even though the fraud at issue occurred after the broker left employment with the firm. The court reasoned that based on its knowledge of the broker's past fraudulent conduct, it was foreseeable that the broker would engage in his propensity to defraud clients, both during and after he left the firm's employment, such that the matter was allowed to proceed to trial.

Q 3:43 What are some ways to recognize and avoid hiring unfit workers?

Employers should:

- Inspect the information an applicant provides to determine whether there are gaps in employment and other suspicious or unusual entries or omissions;
- Obtain the applicant's consent to get information from past employers, personal references and other sources, as well as a waiver and release from liability in connection with the reference checks;
- Document efforts to obtain information from each previous source, especially if pertinent information was not obtainable from these sources;
- Decide whether any information provided by the applicant or learned from previous employers or personal references calls for a criminal record search; and
- Advise applicants that employment is contingent on a satisfactory reference check.

Assessing Honesty in Applicants and Employees

Q 3:44   What is a *polygraph* and how does it work?

A *polygraph* is a device that continuously, visually, permanently, and simultaneously records changes in cardiovascular, respiratory, and electrodermal (relating to electric charges on the skin) patterns. The results of the test are used for rendering a diagnostic opinion regarding a person's truthfulness in answering a particular set of questions.

Q 3:45   Is polygraph testing legal?

In 1988, Congress passed a polygraph law, the Employee Polygraph Protection Act (EPPA), which virtually eliminates most employers' use of polygraph testing in the employment context. In addition, many states have passed laws banning the use of lie detectors in the workplace.

Q 3:46   What is the *Employee Polygraph Protection Act*?

The *EPPA* includes the following:

- The law permits private security firms and drug companies to continue administering lie detector tests to job applicants and employees.
- Federal, state, and local government employers are exempt from the ban, and the federal government is allowed to test private consultants or experts under a national security exemption.
- Employers are prohibited from disciplining, discharging, discriminating against, or denying employment or promotions to prospective or current workers solely on the basis of lie detector test results. Employers may request that an employee submit to a lie detector exam during an investigation of a workplace theft or other incident that causes economic loss or injury to the employer if the employee had access to the property under investigation, the employer has a reasonable suspicion the employee was involved, and the employer provides the employee with a written statement giving its reasons for testing particular employees.
- The Secretary of Labor, as well as employees and job applicants, are authorized to bring civil suits under the Act, and federal courts are given the power to award legal and equitable relief.
- The Department of Labor may seek civil fines of up to $10,000 against employers that violate the law.
- The law prescribes detailed procedures that employers must follow during any permitted lie detector tests.
- No state or local laws or collective bargaining agreements that prohibit lie detector tests or are more restrictive with respect to lie detector tests than the federal law are pre-empted by the federal law.

Q 3:47   Can a contractor of the government use the national security exemption under the EPPA?

In *Polkey v. Transtecs Corp.* [404 F.3d 1264 (11th Cir. 2005)], a contractor of the Department of Defense (DOD) whose employees must meet a "secret clearance level" from the government, maintained that it was exempted from the EPPA under the national security exception in connection with its administration of a polygraph examination to employees as a result of a "mailroom incident" violating federal law. The court, in reviewing the statute and regulations, held that the national security exemption exists to allow the federal government to take lie detector tests of employees of a contractor of the DOD, but does not allow contractors to conduct the test themselves. As the court held, the national defense exemption applies to the federal government only, and a private contractor's attempt to rely on the national security exemption is misplaced. [*Polkey*, at 1269]

Q 3:48   What is the investigation exception under the EPPA?

Under the EPPA, employers investigating theft or other similar occurrences may request that an employee submit to a lie detector test provided that the tested employee had access to the subject of the investigation and the employer had reasonable suspicion that the employee was involved. In *Cummings v. Washington Mutual* [650 F.3d 1386 (11th Cir. 2011)], the court held that the employer-bank had satisfied the criteria for the investigative-use exception in administering a polygraph to its bank manager, one of four employees that had access to the missing funds. In addition to access, the court also found that the bank manager repeatedly violated the employer's "dual control policy" which required that more than one person be present when cash is handled. Although the court noted that "access" alone could not satisfy the reasonable suspicion test, in this case, access together with violations of the dual control policy were sufficient to demonstrate reasonable suspicion. In *Polkey v. Transtecs Corp.* [404 F.3d 1264 (11th Cir. 2005)], a contractor for the federal government claimed, among other things, that its administration of lie detector tests fit within the exemption of an ongoing investigation, in that it had reasonable suspicion for the individuals who were asked to take polygraphs and could demonstrate that the employees had access to the subject of the investigation. The case centered on a "mailroom incident," where an employee discovered someone, in violation of federal law, had accessed mail that the contractor was processing. The employer requested a number of employees who had access to the mail to submit to polygraph examinations, which they refused. The employer argued that these employees fell within the investigation exception based on reasonable suspicion and access to the subject matter of the investigation. However, the court concluded that the employer provided no basis for reasonable suspicion. The court held that to maintain a "reasonable suspicion," it must be based upon an "observable articulable basis in fact which indicates that a particular employee was involved and responsible for an economic loss," citing 29 C.F.R. § 801.12(f)(1). [*Polkey*, at 1270] The employer provided no basis for reasonable suspicion other than access to the mail that was the subject of the mailroom incident, and the court concluded that fact, standing alone, did not constitute reasonable suspicion.

Even in cases where the investigative use exception does not apply, an employer may still be able to terminate an employee who failed a lie detector test if the employer can demonstrate that irrespective of the test results, the employee's employment would have been terminated in any event.

In *Worden v. Suntrust Banks, Inc.* [549 F.3d 334 (4th Cir. S.C. 2008)], an employee of a bank, who failed two lie detector tests following a bank robbery, claimed that the employer did not fall within the investigative-use exception, and as a result, his employment which was terminated following the second failed test was in violation of the EPPA. Although the court noted that the investigative-use exception did not apply and that it was not necessary for the employee to demonstrate that the failed lie detector tests were the "sole" basis for his termination to maintain a claim, but rather needed to only show that it was a factor in the decision to terminate him from his employment, the court concluded that the plaintiff could not maintain a claim in this case because there was sufficient uncontested evidence that the plaintiff's employment would have been terminated in any event, irrespective of the failed tests. Specifically, the decision makers that terminated plaintiff's employment claimed that plaintiff's employment was terminated because they had lost trust in him due to his probable involvement in the attempted bank robbery, based on information that was provided to them by law enforcement officials, irrespective of the tests at issue. Concluding that the record plainly showed that the employer would have terminated the plaintiff's employment in any event, the court held that a claim under the EPPA could not be maintained.

Q 3:49 Can an employer assist police who want to take a polygraph of an employee in connection with a criminal investigation without violating the EPPA?

The regulations under the EPPA specifically provide that employers who merely cooperate with police during an investigation are not deemed to have engaged in prohibitive conduct under the EPPA, provided that such conduct is "passive" in nature. [29 C.F.R. § 801.4(b)] The regulation specifically provides that an employer is allowed to "release an employee during working hours to take a polygraph test at police headquarters." [29 C.F.R. § 801.4(b)] However, if the employer is more than passively involved, a violation of the EPPA may occur. In *Watson v. Weekends Only, Inc.* [2007 U.S. Dist. LEXIS 37522 (E.D. Mo. May 23, 2007)], an employee who was instructed by his supervisor to have a polygraph test at the local police station, and was fired for insubordination when he refused to do so, could possibly maintain a claim for violation of the EPPA, in that the court determined that a jury might reasonably conclude that the employer was more than passively involved.

Q 3:50 What types of legal claims can arise from lie detector testing?

Employees have relied on a number of successful theories to bring lawsuits relating to lie detector testing:

Public policy tort theory. Some states have recognized a cause of action when a statute prohibits submitting an employee to a lie detector as a term or condition of employment.

Breach of contract. If the employment relationship is governed by an implied contract not to discharge except for just cause, the employee may argue that discharge in reliance on the results of a lie detector examination cannot establish cause.

Invasion of privacy. The constitutions of several states deal with privacy and may apply to the private sector. [*See, e.g.,* Alaska Const., art. I, § 22 (1972); Cal. Const., art. I, § 1 (1972); Hawaii Const., art. I, § 6 (1978).]

Defamation. A discharge shortly after a lie detector exam could lead co-workers to infer that the employee was terminated because he or she lied, and could result in the publication of a defamatory statement in the workplace. Under the doctrine of compelled self-publication, an employer's liability may extend to instances in which a former employee seeking employment was compelled to reveal that he or she had been fired for failing a lie detector test.

Negligence. If an employee can prove that an exam was not up to industry standards, the examiner's negligence could be imputed back to the employer.

Intentional infliction of emotional distress. The issue in this type of litigation is whether the employer's conduct was outside the bounds of "civilized society."

Discrimination. Employees have made claims that lie detector tests disproportionately fail African-Americans because of physiological particularities. Other potential claims include sexual discrimination or sexual harassment based on the polygraph examiner's conduct or offensive questions about sexual preferences and practices.

Q 3:51 What must be demonstrated by an employee to maintain a claim for violation of the EPPA?

The EPPA prohibits an employer from engaging in any adverse employment action (employees and applicants) that is based on the results of a polygraph. In *Bass v. Wendy's of Downtown, Inc.* [2012 WL 1552264 (N.D. Ohio May 1, 2012)], an employee, who submitted to a polygraph exam following a missing bank deposit, claimed that the negative results were later used against him to deny his promotion to general manager or assistant manager. Although the employer acknowledged that it had a "trust" issue with the plaintiff stemming from his failed polygraph test, nonetheless presented abundant evidence demonstrating that it would not have promoted the plaintiff to the position of general manager and/or assistant manager even if it was unaware of the plaintiff's failed polygraph test, such that no claim under the EPPA could be maintained.

Whether an adverse employment action resulted from a polygraph exam is determined on a case-by-case basis. For example, in *Worden v. Suntrust Banks, Inc.* [2007 U.S. Dist. LEXIS 20678 (D.S.C. Mar. 22, 2007), a bank employee, who was suspected by the police of being involved in a robbery at the bank at which he was employed, agreed to voluntarily take a polygraph examination in connection with the police investigation and failed. The bank terminated the employee's employment after the polygraph, but claimed it based its decision on the bank's conclusions that the employee was involved in the crime and not on any polygraph administered by the police. Given that no evidence existed to suggest that the employer requested that the polygraph examination take place, no evidence existed to suggest that the bank was apprised by the police department of the results of the polygraph examination, and abundant evidence existed that the bank terminated the employee's employment due to a reasonable and good-faith belief that he was involved in the attempted bank robbery, the court concluded that no violation of the EPPA occurred.

Q 3:52   Has the federal EPPA produced litigation?

One of the DOL's most significant actions under the Act thus far is a $305,000 fine, assessed against the operator of a chain of Wendy's Restaurants in Kansas City, Missouri, which allegedly required its employees to take illegal lie detector tests. The fine, which was announced by the department's Wage and Hour Division in April 1991, consisted of individual penalties of $2,000 each for a total of 152 allegedly illegal polygraph tests purportedly administered between December 1988 and June 1990. An additional $1,000 penalty was assessed for alleged recordkeeping violations. The company exercised its right to request a hearing before an administrative law judge to contest the penalty. The company claimed that the penalty was based upon improper wording in the notice that was provided to employees before administration of the test, and that if the wording was indeed legally incorrect, it was the fault of the firm that administered the tests. Although pre-dispute arbitration agreements have long been held to apply to Title VII and other employment statutes requiring that cases be brought in arbitration rather than courts, under the EPPA, the statute specifically provides that "the rights and procedures provided by [the EPPA] may not be waived by contract or otherwise . . . " [29 U.S.C. § 2005(d)], and as such, will not require an employee who claims violations of the EPPA to arbitrate those claims under a contract signed with the employer. [Harmon v. CB Squared Servs. Inc., 2009 WL 234982 (E.D. Va. Jan. 30, 2009)]

Q 3:53   Can a polygraph examiner be liable to an employee for the negligent administration of the exam?

This issue was considered by the Fifth Circuit. In the case, a former employee of an automobile dealership who had been terminated after he had been given a polygraph examination in connection with an ongoing investigation of theft sued the dealership and the examiner hired to perform the examination, asserting claims of negligence in connection with the administration of the examination and violations of the EPPA. As to the claims under the EPPA, the court concluded that the polygraph examiner must be an "employer" within the meaning of the EPPA to be held liable for violations. The court concluded that whether a polygraph examiner is an employer under the EPPA requires consideration of whether the examiner went beyond the role of an independent examiner and asserted control over the employer's compliance with EPPA. In determining the degree of control necessary, the court considered whether the examiner was involved in making the decision that the polygraph examination should be administered and who should be examined, and whether the examiner decided disciplinary action or merely reported results of the polygraph examination to the employer. On the basis of the economic reality test, the court concluded that the polygraph examiner was not an employer under the EPPA. As to the claim of negligence, the court concluded that, under Texas state law, the polygraph examiner owed no legal duty of reasonable care in administering the polygraph examination. [Calbillo v. Cavender Oldsmobile, Inc., 288 F.3d 721 (5th Cir. 2002)] In *Maybury v. Slaton* [2010 WL 518041 (S.D. Ohio Feb. 2, 2010)], at issue was whether the company's attorney that became involved in the investigation of an incident during which the attorney requested a polygraph examination of one of the company's employees was an "employer" under the EPPA, such that the attorney could be individually liable for an EPPA violation. Although the attorney was certainly involved in the investigation, the plaintiff proffered insufficient evidence to establish, under the "economic realities" test, that the attorney acted "directly or indirectly in the interest of an employer in relation to an employee," as required by 29 U.S.C. § 2001(2).

Q 3:54   Are former employees protected by the EPPA?

In *Fritz v. John Monnich & Holahan* [2003 Mich. App. LEXIS 1170 (Mich. Ct. App. May 20, 2003)], a former employee claimed violations of both federal and state polygraph statutes based upon his refusal to take the polygraph test after he was no longer employed. Having found that the grievant was no longer an employee at the time the test was administered, the court concluded that no liability could arise under state or federal polygraph statutes.

Q 3:55   Can polygraph test results be used in grievance actions involving public employees?

In a Louisiana case, a former patrolman claimed that the use of the results of a polygraph examination in connection with an administrative hearing concerning his discharge was a violation of the EPPA and inadmissible. Recognizing that the Act specifically exempts federal, state, and local government employees from its general prohibitions from use in the workplace, the court, although recognizing that the results of the polygraph examination would not be admissible in criminal matters, nonetheless held that the polygraph test results were "competent evidence," such that they would be admissible at the administrative hearing concerning the civil servant's discharge. [Evans v. DeRidder Mun. Fire and Police Civil Serv. Bd., 815 So. 2d 61 (La. 2002)]

Q 3:56   Are there other types of honesty tests?

Some pencil-and-paper honesty tests are well respected. Although numerous states now forbid or severely restrict the use of polygraphs, few have similar restraints on pencil-and-paper tests; however, to avoid invasion of privacy and defamation actions, an employer should ensure that the job for which an individual is applying warrants such a test and should keep the test results strictly confidential.

There are basically three types of honesty tests:

- The overt integrity test, which asks about an individual's attitudes toward theft and other illegal activities;
- The personality test, which is intended to predict workplace behavior with respect to dependability, job performance and drug use, as well as honesty; and
- The combination test, which combines both types of questions to measure honesty.

Q 3:57   What are the pros and cons of honesty tests?

These tests are criticized for their unreliability at measuring a person's propensity for honest behavior. On the other hand, paper-and-pencil integrity tests generally are not prohibited by federal or state law, and they have not aroused the same vociferous animosity and distrust from labor unions and civil liberties groups as have polygraphs. Some well-established testing companies claim a high correlation between test results and later employment experience, but it is important to track hiring patterns in relation to test results. If honesty testing leads, for example, to an above-average rejection rate of minority applicants, the test could be held to have an illegal adverse impact on that minority group under federal or state discrimination laws. A second caveat: Pencil-and-paper tests may well be the next target of lawyers and organizations that oppose any intrusion into employees' privacy. Some polygraph statutes (e.g., in Massachusetts) may already be broad enough to cover pencil-and-paper tests. Employers should keep abreast of new legal challenges in this area.

Medical Examinations

Q 3:58   After an applicant is hired, may an employer demand a post-hire physical examination under the provisions of the ADA?

Once an employer has offered a job to an applicant, it may conduct any medical inquiry or examination as long as it requires the same inquiry and examination of all successful applicants in the same job category. In fact, an offer of employment may be contingent on the result of the medical examination. At this point, questions may also be asked about previous injuries and workers' compensation claims. If the medical inquiry or exam reveals a disability for which no reasonable accommodation exists to enable the employee to perform essential job functions, the employer may rescind the employment offer. In addition, if the examination reveals a disability that poses a significant direct threat to the health or safety of the individual or to others that cannot be eliminated or reduced by a reasonable accommodation, the employer may refuse to hire this person; however, it is incumbent upon the employer, under the ADA, that if it wishes to withdraw an offer based on a disability it explain the basis for that decision to the employee. The employer may often be able to offer accommodation alternatives to allow the employee to perform his or her job duties. Quite frankly, if the employer revokes the job offer with no explanation to the employee, based upon a physical examination, one might conclude that the employer acted improperly as if it had something to hide. A better approach is for the employer to express candidly the information it received from the medical professional about the employee's ability to perform the essential job functions with reasonable accommodation, and offer the employee an opportunity to rebut this conclusion with other information at his or her disposal, including information from another medical professional.

Q 3:59   Does the ADA permit medical examinations of current employees?

Employees who are injured on or off the job and become disabled within the meaning of the ADA may be required to undergo a job-related medical examination. Similarly, employers may require job-related medical examinations of employees returning from workers' compensation or disability leave, as long as the requirement extends to all employees within that job classification rather than only to those who, for example, had previously lodged insurance claims.

Employers may continue to conduct voluntary medical examinations of their employees as part of an employee health program. Any information learned as a result of a voluntary or involuntary medical examination must be kept confidential and must not be used to discriminate against any employee.

Congress carved out two very important exceptions to the ADA's restrictions on medical examinations—drug tests and fitness for duty exams. Any practices currently in place regarding drug screening or exams assessing fitness for duty may remain despite the restrictions on other types of medical exams and inquiries.

The ADA also limits medical exams of current employees to those that are job-related and consistent with business necessity. The examination may be triggered by some evidence of problems related to job performance or safety. However, the scope of the examination must, be related to the functions of the job in question.

Q 3:60   If there is a pandemic, like H1N1, is there any guidance on how employers balance the health risks in the workplace with the protections for employees under the ADA?

The EEOC provided technical assistance during 2009's H1N1 threat by providing guidance to employees in what actions they could and could not take in the face of the workplace health threat and protections afforded to employees under the ADA. The document, entitled "Pandemic Preparedness in the Workplace and the Americans with Disabilities Act" can be found at the following EEOC link: http://www.eeoc.gov/facts/pandemic_flu.html. The document covers responses to frequently asked questions both before a pandemic is reached and after. Not surprisingly, the guidance defers to objectively determined information from health organizations to balance the competing interests. For example, if the CDC determines there to be an H1N1 pandemic and advises that employees should not work if they suffer influenza symptoms, it would not be a violation of the ADA according to the EEOC's guidance to send employees with influenza symptoms home, because, due to the CDC's findings, they would pose a direct threat.

Performance Evaluations

Q 3:61   What are *performance evaluations*?

Performance evaluations vary almost as much as the corporations, partnerships, and other business organizations that use them. Some are objective and quantitative, measuring and assessing the number of sales calls, orders, key strokes, or billable hours the employee has recorded over the evaluation period. Others are subjective and qualitative, requiring the manager or supervisor to judge the subordinate's knowledge, attitude, initiative, cooperativeness, and the like. One popular evaluation method, managing by objectives, involves the supervisor and subordinate setting specific goals for the subordinate to achieve, and subsequently evaluating together whether the employee attained these objectives.

Corporations usually have concluded that the more complex and qualitative the job, the more important are periodic performance evaluations. When most Americans filled slots on assembly lines, managers had little difficulty measuring quantity and quality of performance by such factors as number of parts assembled per hour or day, number of rejects, and days absent. Today, even where number of keystrokes or sales calls is a relevant measure, more subtle indicators of an employee's contribution also should be identified and tracked over time.

Q 3:62   Should companies use performance evaluations?

Yes. Performance reviews, if done well, serve many purposes. They can:

- Establish a formal communication system between managers and subordinates;
- Provide an opportunity to commend employees for good service;
- Provide a powerful source of documentary evidence to defend wrongful-discharge and discrimination suits; and
- Identify inadequacies and inefficiencies in a company's training and production methods.

To benefit fully from performance evaluations, an employer must design a review procedure and then implement and maintain it properly. A slipshod or irrelevant evaluation system is far worse than none at all, because it harms employee morale and creates unwarranted disparities in the evaluation and testing of employees, perhaps resulting in claims of illegal discriminatory motivation.

Q 3:63   What are the elements of an appropriate employee evaluation program?

No one evaluation program is right for all organizations, but all employee evaluation programs should have at least the following in common. They should:

- Evaluate employee behavior and attributes that actually relate to the particular job and the needs of the specific business;
- Force supervisors to focus on meaningful issues and to provide useful information;
- Facilitate constructive dialogue between supervisors and subordinates;
- Inform the employee of behavior and performance deficiencies in a way that allows him or her to rebut unfair or inaccurate criticism; and
- Provide enough selection options (e.g. numbers, grades, phrases) on an evaluation form to allow accurate evaluations.

Q 3:64   Should objective or subjective criteria be used in the evaluation process?

Objective measurements of employee performance have the advantage of being readily verifiable (e.g., the number of drawings a drafter produced or the number of programs a computer programmer created or analyzed). Even with highly sophisticated jobs, some objective measurements are available, such as the number of hours a lawyer bills to clients of the firm or the number of patients seen by a dentist in a clinic. By contrast, subjective measurements are difficult to verify and apply uniformly throughout a company, and this can breed favoritism and prejudice among supervisors. To avoid litigation, employers should use objective, quantifiable criteria as much as possible; however, employers also should remember that the relationship between the criteria and the job must be validated. Just because something can be measured does not mean it is relevant. For example, an evaluation procedure limited to the number of drawings produced by a drafter, but unmindful of the complexity or novelty of each person's work, would be objective but not accurate.

Q 3:65   How can subjective evaluations be limited or avoided?

All evaluations involve some subjective evaluation of performance. One way to limit subjectivity is to set goals and then see if they have been met. Another way is to emphasize performance and behavior, not personal characteristics.

Q 3:66   Can employee attitudes be evaluated?

Although many employers believe that, of all traits, employee attitude is the most important, employers should avoid concentrating on general and oblique references to an employee's attitude in evaluations. Far too often, an employee termination or disciplinary problem is explained by saying, "He had a bad attitude," or "She and her supervisor had a personality conflict." This sounds pretty tenuous to an EEOC investigator when the supervisor and employee are of different genders or races. The supervisor should focus on job performance in order to help keep illegal bias out of the evaluation process. If attitude is a problem, the employer should refer to specific examples.

Q 3:67   How complex should the evaluation form be?

The evaluation form should cover all relevant performance criteria. In general, the more sophisticated the job, the more complex the evaluation. Regardless of length, it should be comprehensible to both evaluator and employee. If the evaluator does not understand the form, he or she cannot administer it properly or make an effective witness if the company must defend a personnel action based in whole or in part on the evaluation. The less the employee comprehends the evaluation, the more likely he or she is to challenge it.

Q 3:68   What are the goals of an evaluation?

Written evaluations are a useful tool in personnel management. They provide supervisors with an opportunity to assess employees and tell them what they are doing right and what they are doing wrong. Evaluations are not only helpful in managing a workforce, they also provide written evidence of problems associated with an employee's performance, in the event that an employee later claims discrimination or wrongful discharge. As with every other written document contained in a personnel file, an evaluation that is not prepared carefully and is thus inaccurate can prove disastrous for the employer. If the employer's evaluation does not reflect the employee's actual performance, it may be difficult for an employer to argue otherwise against a claim of discrimination or wrongful discharge. To avoid such a possibility, supervisors should keep the following goals in mind when evaluating employees:

- The evaluation should be an honest and accurate evaluation of the employee;
- The evaluation should be consistent with the evaluations of similar employees for similar conduct; and
- Each employee should be evaluated according to the requirements for the position.

Q 3:69 Why is it important for evaluations to be honest and accurate?

Written performance evaluations are often the only written evidence that an employer has bearing on the employee's performance. If employment litigation occurs, chances are it will result from a discharge, and it will be incumbent upon the employer to defend the discharge claiming either that it had cause to terminate the employee (to defeat claims of breach of contract) or that its decision was based on legitimate business reasons and not the result of discrimination under federal or state statutes. If an evaluation is inaccurate, in that it does not properly describe the deficiencies and problems associated with the employee's performance, the employer, from an evidentiary standpoint, is going to be "stuck" with its written evaluations and it will be difficult to convince a judge or jury otherwise. For this reason, of all goals, job one is for supervisors to prepare written evaluations that accurately and honestly assess an employee's performance. It is often difficult for supervisors to provide frank, honest, and accurate evaluations. Sometimes the truth hurts, and supervisors are afraid of hurting morale and working with a disgruntled employee as a result of a bad evaluation. Supervisors need to know that an inaccurate or dishonest evaluation of an employee hurts the employer. In addition, failure to point out deficiencies to an employee hurts the employee as well, and undermines the very purpose of an evaluation. Honest and accurate information in a performance evaluation, even if it hurts, is good for both the employee and the employer.

Q 3:70 Why is it important that evaluations of similar employees with similar conduct be consistent?

If similar employees are not treated similarly for similar infractions, and if the distinction breaks along racial, gender or other protected category grounds, the employer faces the prospect of a discrimination claim under federal or state civil rights statutes. Disparity of treatment alone can suffice, in certain circumstances, to maintain a prima facie claim of discrimination. To avoid these claims, supervisors need to be apprised of the importance of treating similar employees similarly for similar infractions. This does not mean that everybody needs to be treated identically. There often can be good reasons for treating situations differently; however, the reasons for the exceptions should be articulated in a way that will evidence that this dissimilar treatment is not the result of unlawful discrimination.

Q 3:71   Why is it important that an employee be evaluated according to the requirements of the position?

Most evaluation forms that a company uses are generic forms utilized for all jobs within the company. But because job descriptions within a company vary widely, supervisors should analyze the employee based upon the requirements of each particular job. This avoids undue emphasis on minor or relatively unimportant criteria by a supervisor when evaluating employees. If a supervisor does stray outside the job functions, an inaccurate or imbalanced performance evaluation may result, which may be difficult thereafter to defend.

Q 3:72   What are common problems to avoid when preparing evaluations?

Preparing evaluations is difficult and time-consuming. Supervisors often do not devote the time necessary to prepare an accurate evaluation and are often reluctant to evaluate poor performance honestly for fear that doing so might lower morale. Employers should advise their supervisors to avoid the following common problems when preparing evaluations:

- Not budgeting enough time to prepare evaluations;
- Failing to measure the skills for the particular position;
- Preparing an evaluation that fails to measure the entire time period being evaluated and that puts emphasis on recent performance;
- Choosing to ignore conflicts and problems;
- Being reluctant to identify poor performance for fear of not being liked by subordinates; or
- Preparing an evaluation that is inaccurate.

Evaluations are not only helpful in managing a workforce, they also provide written evidence of problems associated with an employee's performance in the event that an employee later claims discrimination or wrongful discharge. As with every other written document contained in a personnel file, an evaluation that is not prepared carefully and is thus inaccurate can prove disastrous for the employer. If the employer's evaluation does not reflect the employee's actual performance, it may be difficult for an employer to argue otherwise against a claim of discrimination or wrongful discharge.

Q 3:73   How can the company use employee evaluations?

Besides determining the adequacy of employee performance and identifying inadequate performers, evaluations can be used to:

- Teach employees how to improve their performance;
- Give formal recognition to outstanding performers;
- Identify weak departments and programs in the organization;
- Promote and demote employees;

- Provide a basis for merit pay increases; and
- Provide a basis for future/further discipline and/or discharge.

Q 3:74   Based on a performance evaluation, may one employee be paid more than another for doing the same job?

Employees may be paid on the basis of merit, and in many instances this is a key incentive; however, the employer must be able to provide objective evidence of the merit that justifies the pay disparity. Without it, an employer risks being accused of:

- Violating the Equal Pay Act by paying an employee of one gender more than a co-worker of the opposite gender, simply because one is male and the other female; or
- Setting salaries in a discriminatory manner on the basis of race, age, or another forbidden factor.

In the case of unionized employees, an employer may need to bargain with the union not only about giving merit raises but also about using evaluation forms in the first place.

Q 3:75   What is a *graphic rating scale*?

Various relevant characteristics (e.g., quantity of work; quality of work; knowledge of the job; ability to communicate with superiors, subordinates, or peers; dependability) are listed, usually vertically, along the left side of the form. Across is some sort of scale, usually numerical. For example, the form's instructions may state that a "1" is outstanding or superior and a "5" unsatisfactory. Often, each of the various criteria is accompanied by a short definition. Appraisers also may be asked to add the various ratings for a total score. The form may provide space for the appraiser's more subjective or summation-type comments, as well as for the employee's reaction to the appraisal.

Q 3:76   What are the advantages and disadvantages of graphic rating scales?

They are fairly easy to develop and can be adapted to many types of jobs; however, broad general characteristics (e.g., leadership or problem solving) may prove hard to relate to the actual requirements of specific jobs. In addition, the human resource specialist must watch out for common errors and quirks in making appraisals. For instance, if "1" signifies the best, some supervisors will only award it if the employee walks on water, whereas the head of another department may award a "1" more generously. Yet a third manager may feel unfamiliar with a certain employee's work or be reluctant either to flatter or criticize too strongly; such a supervisor may give everyone a "2" or "3."

Q 3:77   Can legal problems arise when appraisers give inaccurate or inconsistent ratings?

Yes. First and foremost, a rating system that presents criteria having no genuine relationship to actual job requirements may have a discriminatory impact on a protected group, such as women, and have no defensible business justification. Second, appraisers who group subordinates around the middle of the rating scale are creating future difficulties for themselves and the human resource department, because when it comes time to terminate a problem employee, the record of poor performance and appropriate counseling simply will not be there to justify the termination. Third, the basis for most discrimination lies in not treating similar people similarly for similar conduct and infractions. Consistency in evaluations is a fundamental way to avoid discrimination claims.

Q 3:78   How does a behavioral anchored rating scale work?

When using the behavioral anchored rating scale, the employer first identifies the most important duties of a job. These aspects of the job are described in the performance appraisal form. The appraiser chooses from a set of sentences on the form that describe the employee's behavior with respect to these aspects, ranging from the least desirable to the most worthwhile characterization of an employee's performance in relation to each job characteristic. The appraiser picks the sentence that most closely conforms to that employee's performance.

This method of assessing performance has been demonstrated to provide accurate appraisals of performance in almost any job, when properly applied. Although graphic rating scales are easily developed and used by even relatively unsophisticated managers, substantial expertise is necessary to administer the behavioral anchored rating scale properly. Thus, not only does this appraisal method severely strain the human resources of a small corporation, but even in a larger organization the exhaustive job analyses demanded to make this system may frequently become obsolete in high-technology sectors of the economy.

Q 3:79   What is *essay rating*?

In essay-type appraisals, the appraisers are free to say what they will about their subordinates' strengths and weaknesses. Appraisers who are not well-trained can create ammunition for plaintiff-employees in discrimination lawsuits. Even offhanded and seemingly innocent observations, such as: "She brings a welcome 'woman's touch' to her classroom," or "I'm afraid you just can't teach an old dog new tricks" can come back to haunt the organization, becoming the centerpiece of a charge of gender or age discrimination. [*See, e.g.,* Price Waterhouse v. Hopkins, 490 U.S. 228 (1989) (partners' comments on plaintiff's manners and dress helped form the basis of a successful gender discrimination suit).]

Q 3:80   What is *critical incident rating*?

A variation of essay rating is critical incident rating, in which the appraiser keeps a sort of running narrative or log of significant (at least in the appraiser's view) performance events throughout each appraisal period. This approach also requires proper training and orientation. Its advantage over essay rating is that it forces the appraiser to focus on job-related occurrences, rather than allowing the appraiser to ramble down tangential paths.

Q 3:81   What kinds of ranking methods are available?

Several methods of ranking employees within a department, section, or job classification have been developed by human resource professionals and industrial psychologists.

In *paired comparison ranking*, each employee in a group is compared one-on-one to every other employee in the group. This exercise may be performed for as many criteria as are desired and practical. If the job group is big, and must be judged on several significant criteria, the task can be time-consuming; however, the result can be a fairly solid, quantitative measurement of the strongest, average, and weakest members of the group. On the other hand, deciding how the group compares to the ideal group for doing the particular job is elusive.

In *alternation ranking*, the appraiser picks one member of the job group as most effective, another as least effective in a given criterion, and so forth, moving toward the middle or average point on the spectrum of group members. This method overcomes the danger, presented by more common graphic rating scales, of clustering employees around the median. It is also less time-consuming than paired comparison ranking. Like the paired comparison method, it tells the company only how group members compare to one another, not how they stack up against the competition.

An even easier method is *forced distribution ranking*. It usually requires the appraiser to put a percentage of the group on each rung of the hierarchy (e.g., 10 percent of the group on the highest rung, 20 percent on the next rung, 40 percent in the mid-range, 20 percent below, and 10 percent on the bottom plateau).

Attendance

Q 3:82   Should a company have a written attendance policy?

Yes. Clearly stated attendance policies and uniform enforcement works to both enhance good attendance and provide objective legitimate reasons for discharge/discipline for those that violate the policy. Many companies, especially small ones, believe that an attendance policy is unnecessary. Such an approach is seldom advisable. In the absence of specific attendance requirements, supervisors apply personal standards and do so unevenly, depending on each supervisor's attitude toward each subordinate. Employees who are good producers, who are difficult to replace, or whom the supervisor likes, are treated more leniently than those less favorably regarded. The consequence for the company may be charges of illegal discrimination, morale problems, and the possibility of a union-organized effort to correct the inconsistent treatment.

Q 3:83   What aspects of attendance should a policy address?

An attendance policy should address absenteeism, late arrivals, and early departures. An absence occurs when the employee does not report to work at all. Tardiness can occur at the start of the shift, at the completion of the lunch hour, or at some other break. An early departure involves leaving the job before the end of the employee's normal workday or shift. In addition, many companies' attendance policies address the failure of the employee to call before to the start of the workday or shift, if the employee is going to be late or absent.

Q 3:84   What types of attendance policies exist?

Just as disciplinary policies can be broadly divided into punitive and positive programs, attendance policies can be divided into fault and no-fault policies.

Q 3:85   What is meant by a fault attendance policy?

A fault policy is the traditional attendance policy that distinguishes between excused and unexcused absences. Typically, excused absences include sicknesses for which the employee can produce a doctor's certificate and bona fide emergencies and justifiable absences or tardiness. Unexcused absences are those that the employer (from the company's subjective perspective) does not deem justifiable. Usually, only unexcused absences are counted against the employee with respect to disciplinary action.

Q 3:86   What is a *no-fault attendance policy*?

Under a typical no-fault system, employees are permitted to have a specified number of absences over a given period of time (e.g., 12 absences per calendar year). Every absence from work is counted against the employee's allotment, regardless of the reason for the absence. A philosophical basis is that "good" employees will expend their allotment of absences only in bona fide circumstances, and enough absences are allowed that good employees will not get themselves terminated for excessive absenteeism.

Q 3:87   How are late arrivals and early departures handled under an attendance policy?

Whether the attendance policy is fault or no-fault, tardiness and early departures are usually counted as partial absences, such as one-half or one-third of an absence.

Q 3:88   What are the advantages and disadvantages of a no-fault attendance policy?

The primary advantage of a no-fault policy is the ease of administration. The employer need not inquire into the reason for an absence. The company need only record the event and keep a running total for each employee. The disadvantage of such a mechanical policy is that employees may feel the policy is too rigid to accommodate special circumstances, and this may be disturbing to employees. The irony is that "good" employees, without attendance problems, seem to experience this anxiety at least as fully as "bad" employees who have a history of attendance problems.

Q 3:89   Are there any legal pitfalls to a no-fault attendance policy?

A no-fault attendance policy typically assigns points to absences and tardiness, and provides for progressive, graduated discipline upon the accumulation of points, irrespective of the reason for the absence or tardiness. Under the typical system, there is no safe harbor for excused time off, and all time off is treated similarly. From an administrative point of view, the system is appealing, providing an objective basis to address attendance and punctuality issues; however, it is not without its own pitfalls.

Under the Family and Medical Leave Act (FMLA), employers are not permitted to penalize an employee for time off allowed under the Act (i.e., for the birth, adoption, or foster care of a child, the serious health condition of the employee, or to care for the employee's spouse, child, or parent with a serious health condition). Employees need not specify that they desire an FMLA leave to invoke FMLA protections, but need merely to notify the employer that they require time off from work because of a condition that falls within the FMLA. In *Lichtenstein v. University of Pittsburgh Medical Center* [691 F.3d 294 (3d Cir. 2012)], the court held that an employee that called her supervisor stating that she was in the emergency room with her mother who had been taken there via ambulance and that she would not be able to work that day, provided sufficient notice to the employer that her absence may be covered under the FMLA. Any time off that falls within the FMLA cannot be used to support discipline and, as a result, an employer's no-fault attendance policies must ensure that no disciplinary action is being taken against employees for use of FMLA time. This can be a significant administrative burden. For example, under the FMLA, any absence by an employee for a pregnancy-related condition is a serious health condition, and is authorized FMLA time. If an eligible employee reports to work late because of a pregnancy-related condition, that time may be FMLA-sanctioned. If it is, the employer may not count it in connection with a no-fault attendance policy. Diligence in this area can be very helpful in reducing risk and exposure. A former casino worker obtained a $500,000 verdict against a casino that fired the worker for excessive absences. [16 *Employment Discrimination Report (EDR)* (BNA) 23 (Jan. 3, 2001)] The court determined that, in making its decision to dismiss the employee, the casino relied on some absences that were protected under the FMLA. [16 *Employment Discrimination Report (EDR)* (BNA) 23 (Jan. 3, 2001)]

It is not unusual for employers that utilize a no-fault approach and are covered by the FMLA to treat FMLA leave as different and separate from other absences or tardiness. Unless supervisors are aware of and communicate time off attributable to FMLA to the company administrators, there is always a danger that a no-fault policy, even with stated FMLA exceptions, will violate the FMLA in practice. Again, it is not necessary under the FMLA for the employee to state specifically that he or she wants FMLA leave. Under federal regulations, all that is required is that the employee notifies the employer of the need for time off for a condition that qualifies under the FMLA. Merely stating, "I cannot come in until noon because I am having morning sickness," even if FMLA is never mentioned specifically, is usually sufficient to invoke protection under the FMLA. In this circumstance, it would be incumbent upon the supervisor or the individual who receives the call to ensure that the time off attributable to morning sickness is not utilized against the employee in a no-fault attendance policy. Obviously, a no-fault policy that admonishes that it does not concern itself with the reasons an employee is absent is doomed from its inception. Under the FMLA, an employer must always be cognizant that it may not discipline an employee on the basis of time off that is protected under the FMLA. This is true even if the employee never formally requests FMLA protection or utilizes the term FMLA in connection with the absence.

Q 3:90   Can a violation of an attendance policy be a good defense for claims of discrimination?

Discipline and/or discharge in connection with an attendance policy that is applied uniformly, with similar situations treated similarly, can provide a good defense against claims that the adverse employment action was motivated for illegal reasons.

Work Rules

Q 3:91   What are *work rules*?

A company's *work rules* are the dos and don'ts that its employees are expected to obey in the day-to-day performance of their jobs. They may be promulgated to the employees in an employee handbook, posted on a company bulletin board, or distributed in memoranda. Depending on the size and culture of the corporation, these rules may be numerous and detailed or may consist of only a few general guidelines as to what is expected.

Q 3:92   Should a company have written work rules?

Yes. In today's litigious society, even small organizations of professional employees may have employment disputes. Most often, these disputes become lawsuits when the organization terminates or attempts to terminate a professional's employment. When this happens, the employer almost always finds it helpful to refer to specific rules of performance or conduct against which the discharged employee transgressed. In the absence of such written rules, the employer risks accusations of discriminatory treatment, inconsistent discipline, and *ex post facto* justice, along with the morale problems and legal exposure that these accusations create.

Q 3:93   What work rules should a company have?

If the company is small, close-knit, informal, and consists primarily of professional employees, work rules can be limited to a general statement of the company's expectations, perhaps supplemented by a few specific guidelines. For instance, a medical clinic—composed of doctors, nurses, and therapists or technicians—might adopt a general statement about good professional practice and appropriate patient relations, as well as a few specific rules, such as: "Patient records must be kept in absolute confidence. Breach of a patient's right of confidentiality and HIPAA Privacy Rules is an extremely serious offense and will result in immediate termination." The larger the organization, and the more blue-collar and lower-level clerical workers employed, the more likely it is that a fairly extensive and detailed set of work rules are needed.

Q 3:94   What is an example of a work rules policy contained in a handbook?

Work rules vary depending upon the employer and the industry. Below is an example of a work rule policy that was prepared for a manufacturing client.

EXAMPLES OF INAPPROPRIATE CONDUCT

The policies contained in this section are meant to illustrate particular types of conduct which the Company considers inappropriate. This list is not meant to be exhaustive. The Company retains the right to determine, in its sole discretion, whether particular employee conduct is unacceptable and retains the right to terminate employment with or without cause in accordance with the Company's "At-Will" policy.

Types of behavior and conduct that the Company considers inappropriate include, but are not limited to, the following:

Sleeping on duty;

Falsification of Company records (including improper use of time records and equipment);

Reporting for work under the influence of drugs/alcohol;

Possession of intoxicants/illegal drugs on Company property;

Possession of firearms or weapons (including illegal weapons) on Company property;

Theft;

Insubordination toward any supervisor;

Fighting on Company property;

Failure to cooperate in the use of any guards or other safety devices, including personal protective equipment, such as safety glasses;

Leaving building/work without supervisor's permission;

Gambling on Company property;

Any intentional act which destroys or defaces Company property (such as graffiti);

Restricting output, wasting time, or loitering;

Making scrap, failure to report scrap-making, or careless workmanship;

Coercing, insulting, intimidating, or threatening employees or visitors, or interfering with the work of any Company employee;

Misuse or removal of Company records, blueprints, or other documents from the premises without proper authorization;

Making or publishing false or malicious statements concerning any employee, supervisor, the Company, or its products;

Unauthorized distribution or posting of communication material (not applicable to union bulletin board);

Smoking in no-smoking areas;

Littering Company property;

Soliciting, vending, panhandling, or circulating petitions, or taking up collections on Company time (lunch time is excluded);

Misuse, abuse, or unauthorized use of vending machines, uniforms, telephones, Company tools, vehicles, equipment, and property;

Violation of any Company policy reflected in this employee manual or other policy communicated to you from time to time.

Behavior or conduct in violation of the above policies, regardless of when determined, or other behavior or work which the Company determines to be unacceptable or unsatisfactory, may result in discipline, up to and including discharge.

Q 3:95 What are *major disciplinary offenses*?

Major disciplinary offenses are those that, on the first violation, typically result in immediate termination of employment. Generally, these offenses are so serious that even without a written rule an employee would expect to be fired for committing them. Some examples are striking a supervisor, being intoxicated on the job, stealing from the company, or committing a blatant safety violation that endangers the employee or co-workers.

Q 3:96 What are *minor disciplinary offenses*?

Minor disciplinary offenses involve undesirable conduct that typically is not serious enough to require discharge of the employee, at least not for the first time that the behavior occurs. In addition, some rules related to undesirable conduct are particular to a company or industry, and therefore, an employee might not realize that a behavior is prohibited in the absence of a written guideline. Some examples of rules covering minor disciplinary offenses are those that prohibit wasting time on the job, personal use of the telephone during working time, and smoking in locations other than the employee lounge.

Q 3:97 What are *safety rules*?

Safety rules generally tend to fall into two categories. First, are general, common-sense rules of safe behavior, such as those that prohibit horseplay on the job, throwing paper or other debris on the floors, or driving at excessive speeds in the company parking lots. Second, are safety rules that are particular to the company's business activities. For example, a factory or warehouse may have rules regarding the operation of forklifts and other mobile equipment.

Disciplinary Programs and Procedures

Q 3:98 Are violations of safety rules subject to disciplinary action?

As a general rule, violations of safety rules are covered under major and minor disciplinary rules. Under the heading of major disciplinary rules, companies typically include as a reason for immediate termination the violation of any safety rule that endangers the physical safety of an employee or his or her co-workers or which results in damage to company property. Under the minor disciplinary rules (which are usually subject to progressive, step discipline), companies define violations that do not endanger the employee or co-workers.

Q 3:99 What disciplinary programs exist?

There are two broad types of disciplinary programs: (1) punitive discipline; and (2) affirmative, or positive, discipline.

Q 3:100 What is *punitive discipline*?

A typical punitive disciplinary program covers two types of offenses—major offenses that lead to immediate termination and minor offenses that are usually subject to a progressive or step discipline. The first minor disciplinary violation usually results in an oral reprimand; the second, in a written reprimand; the third, in a suspension of one or more days without pay; and the fourth, in termination of employment. The system is called punitive because its objective is to change the employee's behavior by punishing the employee each time an offense occurs. This is the most common system used in both union and nonunion companies in the United States.

Q 3:101 What is *affirmative* (or positive) *discipline*?

The philosophy of affirmative or positive discipline is that an employee, if given the opportunity to alter undesirable behavior (and assisted by the supervisor), will generally choose to do so. Sometimes, there is little or no difference between the way punitive and positive disciplinary codes treat the breaking of rules. When an employee commits a serious violation, discharge from employment is the appropriate result under both systems. The real distinction is how minor infractions are treated. Whereas the progression under a punitive system results in oral and written warnings, suspension without pay and termination, positive or affirmative discipline takes the employee through a series of steps from a dramatically different perspective. Usually, instead of being given a warning, the employee is asked to verbalize the reasons for the inappropriate behavior and then is asked to sign a written proposal or agreement embodying mutually agreed-on behavioral modifications. Generally, the most dramatic difference between the positive and punitive systems is that under an affirmative system, the employee will be given a "decision day" off with pay, instead of an unpaid suspension. The employee is asked to consider during that day whether continued employment is in the employee's best interest. On returning to work, he or she is asked to state a desire to continue employment and to make the behavior modifications necessary to facilitate the continuation of the working relationship. Positive or affirmative discipline has proved more attractive and more successful in white-collar (as opposed to blue-collar) work environments and in non-union (as opposed to union) workplaces.

Q 3:102   Are there any legal pitfalls to a mandatory progressive discipline system?

Yes, for at-will employers. As discussed in chapter 2, a written progressive discipline policy, if not carefully drafted, may vitiate the employer's at-will status, making it susceptible to claims of wrongful discharge.

Q 3:103   Can an employer be held liable for defamation in connection with employee reviews and/or discipline?

Under common law, to claim actionable defamation, the employee must prove that the alleged defamatory statement was untrue, that it was published to a third party, and that the employer acted with malice. Malice is necessary to overcome the qualified privilege that employers possess in the employment context under common law. In *Lecours v. Mobile Corp.* [2005 WL 3500802 (N.J. Super. A.D. unpublished opinion)], an employee brought a defamation action against his employer based on statements made by his supervisor in e-mail messages about the plaintiff's work performance. In reviewing the e-mail messages, the court concluded that they were "opinions" as opposed to "facts" and that they were similar to employee evaluations, which do not historically qualify as defamation. Moreover, the court concluded, even if the statements were statements of fact, such statements are subject to a qualified privilege in the employment context that can be overcome only if the employee establishes that the publisher knew the statement to be false or acted in reckless disregard of its truth or falsity. With no such evidence in this case, the court confirmed dismissal of the defamation count. In *Kia v. Imaging Sciences International, Inc.* [735 F. Supp. 2d 256 (E.D. Pa. 2010)], the court held that a critical performance review of an employee's work by his supervisor was not defamation. Similarly, in *Birch v. JP Morgan Chase & Co.* [685 F. Supp. 2d 350 (E.D.N.Y. 2010)], an employer's alleged defamatory statements during an evaluation that the employee created a hostile work environment was subject to a qualified privilege made in connection with the evaluation of an employee's performance, and without evidence of malice, could not sustain a claim of defamation. An employee who was terminated for allegedly lying during the course of an internal investigation of the employee's behavior could not maintain a defamation claim for statements made by the investigator during the course of the investigation, as such statements were subject to a qualified privilege and there was no evidence of malice. [Sherman v. Rinchem Co., Inc., 687 F.3d 996 (8th Cir. 2012)] In *Moriarity v. Dyson, Inc.* [2012 WL 5389684 (N.D. Ill. Oct. 30, 2012)], a former employee could not maintain a defamation action based on statements made during an investigation of her complaints of sexual harassment arising from her sexual relationship with the former president, because such statements were protected by a qualified privilege and there was no evidence of malice.

Even if an employee can maintain that the reasons provided in a termination report distributed to employees is false, if the distribution of the report was only to those employees whose duties include handling such reports, no "publication" exists, and the defamation claim cannot be maintained at all. In *Smith v. Boyd Bros. Transportation, Inc.* [406 F. Supp. 2d 1238 (M.D. Ala. 2005)], a terminated employee claimed that the statements concerning the reasons for his termination were false, and sued the company for publication of the material within the company. The company countered by, among other things, demonstrating that the only people who had access to the report were those whose duties included handling such reports. Citing previous precedent, the court found that this type of internal distribution is insufficient to meet the "publication" requirement for defamation as a matter of law, and dismissed the claim. In *Taylor v. CAN Corp.* [2010 WL 3430911 (E.D. Va. Aug. 27, 2010)], the court held that an employer's investigation report regarding an employee's sexual harassment was subject to a qualified privilege, and in the absence of malice, could not sustain a claim of defamation. Similarly, in *Lee v. Eden Medical Center* [690 F. Supp. 2d 1011 (N.D. Cal. 2010)], the court held that a human resource director's statements about a nurse's mental health to the hospital's management and counsel were subject to a qualified privilege and not actionable without evidence of malice under California defamation law.

However, the qualified privilege has its limitations, as was demonstrated in *Rachal v. State of Louisiana Department of Wildlife & Fisheries*. [918 So. 2d 570 (La. App. 3d Cir. 2005)] In that case, employees sued for defamation arising out of a report prepared and disseminated by a supervisor that outlined the details of an alleged telephone call the supervisor received, in which the caller reported that he observed the plaintiff employees engaging in sex during working hours. On appeal, the court concluded that, based on the inconsistent testimony of the supervisor and the testimony of the witnesses for the employees, it was questionable whether the supervisor did in fact receive the so-called anonymous call regarding the plaintiffs, but that even if he did receive the anonymous call, it was not error for the jury to conclude that it was not reasonable for the supervisor to believe that it was true. As such, the qualified privilege was overcome in this instance. Although statements made to co-workers that plaintiff was terminated for stealing were subject to a qualified privilege under Minnesota law, issues of fact existed as to whether a supervisor had malice based on evidence of having used racial slurs toward plaintiff, such that summary disposition for the employer was inappropriate. [Walker v. Wanner Eng'g, Inc., 867 F. Supp. 2d 1050 (D. Minn. 2012)]

In *Soto-Lebron v. Federal Express Corporation* [538 F.3d 45 (1st Cir. 2008)], a terminated employee sued his employer alleging defamation based on rumors among co-workers concerning serious misconduct which purportedly caused his discharge. Apparently, very soon after the employee's initial suspension by management, he received inquiries from his co-workers asking whether it was true that he had been suspended because his wife had given him a package containing drugs, in violation of company policy. Although the employee, because of its timing, believed that the rumors must have been started by management, the court concluded that there was insufficient circumstantial evidence to substantiate the claim.

In *Mangan v. Corporate Synergies Group, Inc.* [10-5829, 2011 WL 3328785 (D.N.J. Aug. 1, 2011)], the court held that statements made regarding the reasons for the plaintiff's termination to the effect that the company had lost faith in the plaintiff's leadership ability and management skills were statements of opinion that could not form the basis of a defamation claim. However, insinuations that the plaintiff had engaged in financial improprieties and "cooked the books" of the company were statements of fact such that if untrue, could form the basis of a defamation claim.

Chapter 4

Employment Discrimination

Discrimination law is among the most dynamic areas of labor and employment law in the United States. Since this book was first published in 1988, substantive changes in the statutory law as well as developments in the federal common (court-made) law of employment discrimination have been dramatic. For example, the Americans with Disabilities Act of 1990 (ADA), signed into law by President George Bush, sought to significantly change how employees with disabilities may be treated in the workplace and whether disability-related inquiries can be made in the application process. However, over time, U.S. Supreme Court decisions significantly restricted application of the ADA. These decisions, however, were recently overturned with the passage of amendments to the ADA that will dramatically expand the application of the ADA. Over the years, sexual harassment law has grown significantly both in its definition of sexual harassment and in how the employer should respond to internal claims of sexual harassment. This chapter updates federal discrimination law by discussing recent developments in this constantly evolving area.

Title VII

Q 4:1   What is *Title VII?*

Title VII of the Civil Rights Act of 1964 (Title VII) prohibits employment discrimination. It expands the protection extended originally by the post-Civil War antidiscrimination laws [41 U.S.C. §§ 1981–1986] beyond race to sex, national origin, color, and religion. Title VII is enforced by the Equal Employment Opportunity Commission (EEOC), which affords victims of discrimination a relatively quick, inexpensive means of seeking redress, often without the assistance of an attorney.

Q 4:2   What rights are outlined in Title VII?

Title VII makes it illegal for companies to discriminate in employment decisions (including those related to hiring, promoting, paying, terminating, and disciplining employees) on the basis of race, religion, national origin, and gender. Title VII established the EEOC to help enforce its prohibition against discriminatory employment decisions and allows individuals access to federal courts for private litigation after termination of the EEOC process.

Q 4:3   Can Title VII claims be assigned?

This issue of first impression was confronted by the Eleventh Circuit in *Evans v. Boyd Restaurant Group, LLC.* [240 Fed. Appx. 393 (11th Cir. 2007)] At issue was whether a Title VII claim could be assigned as a matter of law. The court, likening Title VII claims to personal injury claims, concluded that a purported assignment of a Title VII claim to another party was invalid under both the applicable state law and federal law.

Q 4:4   Are foreign companies doing business in the United States subject to the antidiscrimination provisions of Title VII?

Yes. U.S. district courts have held that foreign employers doing business in the United States must do so according to federal laws prohibiting discrimination. [*See, e.g.,* Ward v. W&H Voortman Ltd., 685 F. Supp. 231 (MD Ala. 1988).]

Q 4:5   Are U.S. companies operating overseas subject to the antidiscrimination provisions of Title VII?

Yes. Section 109 of the Civil Rights Act of 1991 extends protection of Title VII, as well as the ADA, to U.S. citizens employed by U.S. companies abroad.

Enforcement of Title VII by the EEOC

Q 4:6   What is the *EEOC?*

The *EEOC* is the federal agency that enforces Title VII. It has offices in most major U.S. cities. In these offices, investigators accept discrimination charges and determine, through investigation, whether there is probable cause to believe that the law has been broken, and if so, they attempt to resolve meritorious claims. In certain instances, particularly egregious cases, attorneys for the EEOC may institute federal suits on behalf of charging parties.

Q 4:7   What reporting and recordkeeping requirements does the EEOC impose under Title VII?

Employers with 100 or more employees must annually file Standard Form 100 (Employer Information Report EEO-1) and must retain a copy of the most recent report filed by each reporting unit at the company or division headquarters. The EEOC has not adopted any generally applicable requirement that employers make or keep other employee records, although it can do so. It can also impose recordkeeping requirements on individual employers or groups of employers whenever it determines that such records are necessary for the operation of the EEO-1 reporting system or to further the purposes of Title VII.

To the extent an employer does generate employee records (e.g., application forms and records of hiring, promotion, and demotion), it must retain them for six months after the personnel action or making of the record, whichever is later. An employer must keep a record of termination for six months from the date of termination. When a charge of discrimination has been filed or an action brought by the EEOC or Attorney General under Title VII, the employer must retain all relevant personnel records until final disposition of the matter.

Q 4:8   When can an employee initiate a discrimination charge with the EEOC?

Usually, the employee must file a charge with the EEOC within 180 days of the event (e.g., termination of employment) claimed to be discriminatory.

Q 4:9   Must an employee always file a discrimination charge with the EEOC within 180 days?

To eradicate discrimination effectively, Congress has permitted the states to establish their own antidiscrimination agencies, similar to the EEOC, to enforce state civil rights laws similar to Title VII. Most states have done so; they are called deferral states. In a deferral state, an employee who chooses to file a discrimination charge with the EEOC has 300 days to do so, rather than 180 days.

Q 4:10   Can a claim contain allegations of wrongful conduct prior to the 180/300-day period?

In *National Railroad Passenger Corp. v. Morgan* [536 U.S. 101 (2003)], the Supreme Court was asked to determine under what circumstances wrongful conduct, which occurred prior to the 180/300-day period, can be included within a claim. In the race discrimination/retaliation claim under Title VII, the Court held that discrete acts of alleged discrimination, which occurred prior to the time period for filing, could not be included within the claim. However, with respect to the hostile work environment claim, to the extent that conduct that occurred prior to the requisite time period was part of the same hostile work period as that which occurred during the relevant time period, such conduct could be included within the claim. In *McIntire v. Tulsa County Sheriff* [121 Fed. Appx. 295 (10th Cir. 2005)], the court clarified the limits of the U.S. Supreme Court's *Morgan* decision. Although continuing violations may, in certain circumstances, allow conduct that occurs before the 180/300-day time period, nonetheless, if no allegations attendant to a claim occurred within the 180/300-day time period prior to the filing of an EEOC charge, the claim will be time-barred.

In *Greer v. Paulson* [505 F.3d 1306 (D.C. Cir. 2007)], the court used the rationale in the U.S. Supreme Court *Morgan* decision to conclude that incidents relating to the employee's hostile work environment claim could be used in support of her claim, even though she was not physically present at the workplace when such incidents occurred. Specifically, the incidents occurred while she was absent from the workplace on another assignment. However, because the incidents formed a part of her whole claim in accordance with *Morgan*, they could be considered in connection with her claim.

The decision of *Ledbetter v. Goodyear Tire & Rubber Co.* [550 U.S. 618 (2007)] has provided further insight into *Morgan* and the continuing violation doctrine. In this Title VII case, a female retiree claimed that, on the basis of past evaluations, she was discriminated against because of her sex in connection with her pay. The decisions that were made, which resulted in the pay discrepancy, were all made prior to 180 days before she filed her claims with the EEOC; however, the lingering effects of the discrimination continued throughout the 180-day time period. Recognizing that Title VII requires that charges must be filed within the specific time period, either 180 or 300 days (depending on the state) after the alleged unlawful employment practice occurred, the court held that the charge must have been brought, in this case, within the 180 days after the employee received the poor performance evaluation that resulted in the discrepancy of pay. The court held that because the charge was filed after the applicable 180-day time period, the case was untimely.

In early 2009, the Lilly Ledbetter Fair Pay Act of 2009 [Pub. L. No. 111-2] was signed into law by President Barack Obama. The Act amends the Civil Rights Act of 1964, and resets the 180-day statute of limitations for filing an equal-pay lawsuit for pay discrimination with each new discriminatory paycheck. The law was a direct rebuff of *Ledbetter v. Goodyear Tire & Rubber Co.* [550 U.S. 618 (2007)], which held that the statute of limitations for presenting an equal-pay lawsuit begins at the date the pay was agreed upon, not at the date of the most recent paycheck.

Q 4:11   Does an invalid release signed by an employee toll the 180/300-day EEOC filing requirements?

Invalid waivers do not necessarily toll the 180/300-day EEOC filing requirement. In *Ruehl v. Viacom, Inc.* [500 F.3d 375 (3d Cir. 2007)], an employee executed a release in connection with his separation of employment, which did not comport with the requirements of the Older Workers Benefit Protection Act, and therefore was not effective to release claims under the Age Discrimination in Employment Act (ADEA). After having signed the release, but after the 300-day time period for the employee to file an age discrimination charge with the EEOC ran, the employee commenced litigation against his former employer under the ADEA. Although the employee claimed that the 300-day time period should be tolled after he signed his release, the court found that the employee failed to demonstrate any misleading conduct by the employer to cause delay in filing his charge with the EEOC, and the mere fact that he may have been misled based on an invalid release in believing he had no ADEA claim is insufficient for equitable tolling. As such, the court found that the invalid release did not toll the 300-day time period requirement, and upheld the trial court's decision that the employee's claim was time-barred.

Q 4:12   What does the EEOC do with a discrimination charge after it has been filed?

First, a copy of the charge is sent to the employer, which then must file a response. Once the employer has answered the charge, the investigator usually holds a fact-finding conference to acquire further information about the case.

Q 4:13   Must a charge be filed with the EEOC before instituting a federal lawsuit under Title VII?

Title VII contains a specific administrative scheme for the EEOC's investigation, conciliation, and disposition of discrimination claims filed under Title VII before redress to federal court. [42 U.S.C. § 2000e-5] Title VII provides for redress in federal court by aggrieved individuals within 90 days after a notice of a "right to sue" has been given by the EEOC under various circumstances. [42 U.S.C. § 20005e-5(f)(1)] In those jurisdictions where states have anti-discrimination laws comparable to Title VII, Title VII requires that "no charge may be filed . . . by the person aggrieved before the expiration of 60 days after proceedings have been commenced under state . . . law, unless such proceedings have been earlier terminated." [42 U.S.C. § 2000e-5(c)] With respect to the 60-day requirement concerning charges commenced with a state administrative agency, the court in *Whitfield v. City of Knoxville* [756 F.2d 455, 460 (6th Cir. 1985)] stated:

Where a state agency exists that may grant or seek relief from discriminatory practices, a private plaintiff may not commence a . . . discrimination action until 60 days after state administrative proceedings have commenced. Although a plaintiff need not wait longer than 60 days for a state agency to act, the plaintiff must commence state proceedings and wait 60 days before filing an action.

With respect to charges filed with the EEOC, the receipt of a right to sue has been held to be a conditional prerequisite to instituting litigation in federal court. [*See* Shannon v. Ford Motor Co., 72 F.3d 678, 684 (8th Cir. 1996).] As the court stated in *Shannon*:

Exhaustion of administrative remedies is central to Title VII's statutory scheme because it provides the EEOC the first opportunity to investigate discriminatory practices and enables it to perform its roles of obtaining voluntary compliance and promote conciliatory efforts.

Many courts review this requirement strictly and, even if charges had previously been filed with the EEOC, if the charges did not include other claims of discrimination currently pled in a federal lawsuit, the other claims are subject to dismissal. In *Spain v. Colonial Penn Insurance Co.* [97-4010, 1997 U.S. Dist. LEXIS 19788 (E.D. Pa. Dec. 12, 1997)], the plaintiff filed a count of sex discrimination in her federal lawsuit after having filed charges with the administrative agency. Because the administrative charges did not include a charge of sex discrimination, however, the court dismissed the sex discrimination count on the basis that the plaintiff had failed to comply with the prerequisite administrative filing as to this claim. [10 *Employment Discrimination Report (EDR)* (BNA) 48 (Jan. 14, 1998)] In *Zawacki v. Realogy Corp.* [628 F. Supp. 2d 274 (D. Conn. 2009)], an employee filed an ADEA claim with the EEOC alleging disparate treatment discrimination under the ADEA. When the employee later sued for the additional claims of disparate impact and retaliation under the ADEA, the court dismissed the claims because the employee had failed to exhaust administrative remedies by failing to allege such claims in the EEOC charge. The claim filed in court must have a reasonable relationship to the charges included in the EEOC charge, and if not, will be dismissed. [*See* Jones v. Res-Care, Inc., 613 F.3d 665 (7th Cir. 2010).]

Q 4:14   Does failure to exhaust administrative remedies bar a federal suit?

Some courts have held that the failure to exhaust administrative remedies in accordance with Title VII is a jurisdictional bar to bringing a suit in federal court. [*See* Montoya v. Valencia Cnty., 872 F. Supp. 904, 906 (D.N.M. 1994).] In other circuits, the courts have not treated the exhaustion of remedies as a complete jurisdictional bar, but rather as a condition precedent to commencing a federal district court action that may be considered by the court's discretion. [*See, e.g.,* the decision in Wixson v. Dowagiac Nursing Home, 866 F. Supp. 1047, 1056 (W.D. Mich. 1994).] The Supreme Court, in *Love v. Pullman Co.* [404 U.S. 522, 523 (1972)], stated the requirement as follows:

A person claiming to be aggrieved by a violation of Title VII may not maintain a suit for redress in federal district court until he has first unsuccessfully pursued certain avenues of administrative relief.

The requirement to resort to administrative remedies prior to bringing federal suit in accordance with the preceding cases is central to the statutory scheme developed under Title VII and may not be disregarded by plaintiffs. In situations where plaintiffs do not resort to and exhaust administrative remedies in connection with Title VII, employers should be successful in dismissing federal lawsuits prematurely filed, albeit without prejudice. In *White v. Northern Michigan Regional Hospital*, [659 F. Supp. 2d 858 (W.D. Mich. 2009)] a former employee of a hospital had filed charges with both the EEOC and the Michigan Department of Civil Rights alleging, among other things, Title VII discrimination. However, before the process was completed, the employee notified the Agency of her desire to withdraw the charge and pursue the matter in court. Although she had clearly filed charges with the EEOC, the EEOC process, which includes both investigation and attempts at conciliation, had not been exhausted and as such, the court found that she could not maintain her Title VII claim. The case was dismissed, albeit without prejudice to her later filing the claim, after the administrative process was exhausted.

Q 4:15   How does the EEOC process charges of discrimination?

In late April 1995, the Charge Processing Task Force, under the direction of Vice Chairman Paul Igasaki, made its recommendations for wide-ranging changes in the way charges are processed.

First among the changes is that all new charges must be triaged to one of three categories. Category A charges have high priority because they involve patterns of discrimination and high-profile targets, and their probable cause is likely. Category B charges have merit but require additional investigation. Category C charges are susceptible to dismissal by the EEOC. Before these reforms took effect, EEOC investigators had to work their dockets on a first-come, first-served basis and investigate each charge fully. These reforms allow them to dismiss charges that do not warrant complete investigations and to concentrate their efforts in accordance with the EEOC's National Enforcement Plan, discussed later.

Second, the task force recommendations emphasized settling discrimination claims. Taking its lead from Congress, which in the 1991 Civil Rights Act encourages the use of alternative dispute resolution (ADR) techniques, the EEOC indicated that it will use mediation to settle claims through a non-binding mediation process using volunteer employment law mediators.

Third, the EEOC announced its intent to allow its attorneys in its 10 regional offices to exercise increased discretion in deciding which cases to take into federal court. This change will free commissioners to deal with broad policy issues.

The National Enforcement Plan (NEP), developed in 1995, attempts to focus the EEOC's resources on large-scale and egregious cases of employment discrimination. *EEOC v. Mitsubishi Motor Manufacturing of America, Inc.* [No. 96-CV-1192 (D.C. Ill. 1996)] is a good example of a high-profile, allegedly egregious case of sex discrimination that is consistent with the plan.

The triage system, together with efforts to mediate disputes, was instituted for several reasons. One reason was to dispose of those cases that do not merit the use of scarce resources to investigate. The second reason was to focus the EEOC's energies in accordance with its NEP, in order to pursue more serious and significant charges of discrimination. Recent information indicates that, statistically, the 1995 recommendations may have obtained some measure of result. According to information supplied by the EEOC in Spring 1998, and despite the fact that the number of charges nationwide continued to increase from approximately 78,000 in Fiscal Year 1996 to approximately 81,000 in Fiscal Year 1997, the EEOC's backlog of pending matters continued to drop during Fiscal Year 1997 and litigation activity and money recovered for claimants increased during Fiscal Year 1997. [*See* Commission Reaped Record Benefits, Culled Backlog of Charges Last Year, 10 *Employment Discrimination Report (EDR)* (BNA) 372 (Mar. 25, 1998).] For Fiscal Year 1998, the EEOC reported its backlog of charges continued to decrease, from 65,000 in Fiscal Year 1997 to 52,000 by the end of Fiscal Year 1998, with new charges decreasing slightly from Fiscal Year 1997 (81,000) to Fiscal Year 1998 (79,000). [12 *Employment Discrimination Report (EDR)* (BNA) 183 (Feb. 10, 1999)] For Fiscal Year 1999, the EEOC reported its backlog of unresolved charges to be approximately 40,000, a significant decrease with new charges decreasing slightly to 77,444. [14 *Employment Discrimination Report (EDR)* (BNA) 153 (Feb. 2, 2000)] For Fiscal Year 2000, the EEOC reported its backlog of unresolved charges to be reduced to about 34,300, a record low, with the new charges increasing slightly to 79,900. [16 *Employment Discrimination Report (EDR)* (BNA) 75 (Jan. 17, 2001)] It was reported that Fiscal Year 2001 showed a modest decrease of unresolved charges (32,500), with a slight increase of new charges during the year (80,000). [18 *Employment Discrimination Report (EDR)* (BNA) 259 (Feb. 27, 2002)] Fiscal Year 2002 closed with a pending inventory of just less than 30,000 charges, with an overall increase of total charges filed (84,442). [20 *Employment Discrimination Report (EDR)* (BNA) 106 (Jan. 15, 2003)] In Fiscal Year 2009, the EEOC received 93,207 charges, up considerably from the 75,768 charges in Fiscal Year 2006. In Fiscal Year 2005, the EEOC received 75,428 total charges, less than the 79,432 received in Fiscal Year 2004, and resolved 77,352 charges, leaving the EEOC with a pending inventory of 33,562 in Fiscal Year 2005, a slight increase from 29,966 for Fiscal Year 2004. In Fiscal Year 2010, the agency received the highest number of charges in its 45-year history (99,922) but resolved almost 105,000 current and pending charges leaving Fiscal Year 2010 with a pending inventory of 86,338 charges. In Fiscal Year 2011, 99,947 charges were filed, and the agency reported a total of 112,499 resolutions of pending claims. According to the EEOC's Performance and Accountability Report for Fiscal Year 2012, 99,412 charges were filed and a total of 111,139 charges were resolved, with a reduction of pending inventory by 7,824 charges.

No doubt, because of the results of the 1995 recommendations by the Task Force, the EEOC has implemented charge-processing and litigation recommendations. One such recommendation directed the Office of General Counsel and the Office of Field Programs in conjunction with the district offices to develop local enforcement plans (LEP) in order to establish goals unique to the particular community that the district office serves, and that are consistent and developed in accordance with the NEP. The development of the LEP in conjunction with the NEP signaled the EEOC's continuing effort to focus its energies on those issues of discrimination it deems particularly significant to this society.

The EEOC's current strategic plan, covering a four-year period from Fiscal Year 2012 through Fiscal Year 2016 is committed to pursuing the following objectives and outcome goals: (1) combat employment discrimination through strategic law enforcement; (2) prevent employment discrimination through education and outreach; and (3) deliver excellent and consistent service through a skilled and diverse work force and effective systems. [http://www.eeoc.gov]

Q 4:16   How does the EEOC ADR mediation program work?

Another growing development in how the EEOC processes charges is the use of ADR mediation programs to attempt to facilitate and mediate charges after they are filed. Although conciliation has always been part of the investigative process, the EEOC has not traditionally processed claims by using a separate ADR process. The ADR project, which started in 1993–1994 as a pilot voluntary project in Washington, D.C., Houston, New Orleans, and Philadelphia, was expanded to various districts throughout the country. In October 1998, Congress designated $13 million of the EEOC's budget for further expansion of ADR. Currently, the EEOC Mediation Program is being implemented nationwide, as an alternative to the traditional investigative process.

In accordance with the program, local district EEOC offices review charges of discrimination and determine whether they would be suitable for ADR. If so, the district office invites the parties to participate in a voluntary non-binding ADR process, used to assist in voluntary settlement of the EEOC charges. Either party can deny the invitation, without recourse, at which point the matter is forwarded to the assigned investigator for traditional charge processing, including investigation. If both parties agree to take advantage of the ADR program, the parties are assigned a federal mediator—an outside individual who is not involved in the investigation of the charge for the EEOC—who will meet with the parties and attempt to assist them in determining whether any mutually agreeable basis exists for resolution of the charge. The information discussed during the mediation is confidential and not shared with the EEOC investigator, should the matter not be resolved. The program appears to be successful in relieving the EEOC of the responsibility of investigating charges that can be resolved early on in the proceedings, and the use of ADR in connection with EEOC charges can be expected to become more prevalent in years to come. ADR is clearly viewed by many as an attractive supplement to the traditional administrative and judicial process. [*See* published text of the EEOC's Mediation Program Fact Sheet, 12 *Employment Discrimination Report (EDR)* (BNA) 244 (Feb. 17, 1999).] Despite the budgetary pressures, the EEOC gave the mediation program high marks for Fiscal Year 2000, claiming to have mediated about 8,000 cases during the year. [*See* 16 *Employment Discrimination Report (EDR)* (BNA) 76 (Jan. 17, 2001).] Similarly, in Fiscal Year 2001, despite continuing budgetary pressures, Cari Dominguez, chair of the EEOC, stated that more than 7,000 charges were resolved through the mediation program. [*See* 17 *Employment Discrimination Report (EDR)* (BNA) 641 (Dec. 15, 2001).] In Fiscal Year 2002, the EEOC reportedly resolved almost 8,000 charges through mediation. Dominguez proclaimed that "Mediation will continue to be on center stage during 2003." [20 *Employment Discrimination Report (EDR)* (BNA) 75 (Jan. 15, 2003)] In Fiscal Year 2003, according to the EEOC's Web site (http://www .eeoc.gov), the EEOC resolved approximately 70 percent of charges that went through the mediation process, resolving 7,990 charges in total. In Fiscal Year 2008, 72.1 percent of all charges were resolved at mediation. For Fiscal Year 2010, the EEOC reported that its mediation program resulted in a total of 9,362 resolutions, 10 percent more than Fiscal Year 2009. In Fiscal Year 2012, the EEOC reported that it successfully mediated 8,714 charges to resolution out of 11,380 mediations, resulting in a success rate of 76 percent.

The EEOC has posted a number of materials regarding mediation on its Web site, including a description of the process, common questions and answers, the EEOC's ADR Policy Statement, and a detailed history of the mediation program. [*See* http://www.eeoc.gov/employees/mediation.cfm.]

Q 4:17　What is a *position statement?*

Typically, after a charge is received by the EEOC, the written charge is provided to the employer and a written response, referred to as a *position statement*, is requested. This request may be accompanied with interrogatories and document requests. This is the employer's opportunity to provide the EEOC with information to refute the charge and possibly result in the dismissal of meritless claims. Given the current triage procedures, and the EEOC's willingness to dismiss meritless claims, employers should make every effort to provide a thorough, accurate and complete response, usually with the assistance of legal counsel.

Q 4:18　What is a *fact-finding conference?*

It is a formal meeting at which the EEOC reviews a discrimination charge and the employer's response to it in the presence of both parties. Both the employee and the employer have ample opportunity to reply to the other's positions and, using the investigator as an intermediary, to solicit additional information from one another. Although no transcript of the proceedings is taken, the investigator or an assistant often takes copious notes. If appropriate, the fact-finding conference is used as a forum for discussing a settlement of the charge.

Q 4:19   What happens after the fact-finding conference?

Frequently, the EEOC requests additional documents or other information from the employer and charging party. Then, after reviewing the file, the investigator determines whether, based on the investigation, there is probable cause to believe that the law has been broken.

Q 4:20   What happens if the EEOC investigator finds probable cause to believe that the employer has committed illegal employment discrimination?

His or her next duty is to try to conciliate the charge. Conciliation is an attempt to persuade the employer to remedy the illegal discrimination by such actions as providing back pay or reinstatement.

Q 4:21   What if the employer refuses to conciliate the charge?

If the employer refuses to resolve the dispute by giving the employee an appropriate remedy, the investigator can either turn the case over to the EEOC's litigation department or merely issue the employee a letter to sue, which gives the complainant 90 days in which to locate an attorney and initiate a lawsuit in federal court.

Q 4:22   Does the EEOC initiate litigation on the basis of charges filed with the Commission?

According to EEOC litigation statistics, found on the EEOC's Web site (http://www.eeoc.gov), the EEOC initiated a total of 403 lawsuits in Fiscal Year 2006 on the basis of charges filed with the Commission. This compares to 416 in Fiscal Year 2005, 421 in Fiscal Year 2004, and 400 in Fiscal Year 2003. Although not a precise calculation, because total charges filed between Fiscal Year 2003 through Fiscal Year 2006 averaged about 78,000 charges per year, this approximates one-half of 1 percent of charges filed resulting in EEOC litigation. In Fiscal Year 2007, the EEOC initiated 362 lawsuits; this is the first time the total number of lawsuits fell below 400 since Fiscal Year 2002. In Fiscal Year 2008, the EEOC initiated 325 lawsuits. In Fiscal Year 2009, the EEOC initiated 314 lawsuits, almost 25 percent less than in Fiscal Year 2005. In Fiscal Year 2010, the EEOC initiated a total of 271 lawsuits; 14 percent less than Fiscal Year 2009. In Fiscal Year 2011, the EEOC filed 300 lawsuits. In Fiscal Year 2012, the EEOC filed 155 lawsuits.

Q 4:23   What if the investigator finds no probable cause to believe that discrimination has occurred?

If the investigator concludes that the employer did not violate the law, the investigation by the EEOC is terminated and the charge is dismissed.

Q 4:24   Does termination of the EEOC or state investigation resolve the employee's discrimination claim?

A finding of no probable cause and termination of the investigation by the EEOC does not bar the employee from further action. The employee is still issued a letter to sue, which affords the employee (typically) 90 days in which to find a lawyer and file suit in federal court; however, as a practical matter, an unfavorable finding usually puts an end to the matter, either because the employee becomes discouraged or because it is difficult to find an attorney who will take such a case on a contingent-fee basis. Employers and their legal counsel should therefore make a strong attempt to prevail before the EEOC.

Q 4:25   Can the EEOC force an employer to cooperate in its investigation?

Yes. The EEOC can subpoena employer records if the employer refuses to respond to the agency's request for documents and other information pertaining to the discrimination charge. It is not unusual, if an employer refuses to cooperate in informal discovery, for the investigator unilaterally to schedule an onsite investigation, during which the investigator reviews documents and interviews personnel. These types of investigations can prove to be a disastrous fishing expedition for the unprepared and uninformed employer, and full cooperation with informal discovery methods is greatly recommended.

General Principles of Discrimination Law

Q 4:26   What constitutes a *prima facie case of discrimination*?

The Supreme Court has held that a *prima facie case of discrimination* exists if the following are proved:

- The plaintiff is in a protected class;
- The plaintiff was qualified for the job or promotion;
- The qualified plaintiff did not get the job or promotion; and
- The employer hired or promoted someone less qualified or at least continued to look for qualified people after rejecting the plaintiff.

With minor variations, this formula can be applied to any employment decision, including discipline, termination, and wage increases. [*See, e.g.,* McDonnell Douglas v. Green, 411 U.S. 782 (1973); Texas Dep't of Cmty. Affairs v. Burdine, 450 U.S. 248 (1981).]

Q 4:27   Does an employer have to intend to break the law to be guilty of illegal discrimination?

No. The most widely recognized type of discrimination is *disparate treatment*, which means intentional discriminatory treatment based on a person's race, sex, national origin, color, religion, age, or disability; however, the law also recognizes another form of illegal discrimination based on disparate impact. Illegal disparate impact occurs when an apparently neutral employment policy has a discriminatory (and perhaps inadvertent and unintended) impact on one of the protected classes of employees. However, in accordance with exceptions under Title VII, if a company maintains a facially neutral compensation policy keyed to production, to maintain a Title VII claim of discrimination, a plaintiff must present evidence that the policy disparately impacts a protected group and must show intent on behalf of the employer to discriminate. [*McReynolds v. Merrill Lynch & Co.,Inc.*, 694 F.3d 876 (7th Cir. 2012). *See also* Wood v. City of San Diego, 678 F.3d 1075 (9th Cir. 2012) (facially neutral survivor benefit policy provided by a city, which disparately impacted single women, could not form the basis of a Title VII complaint absent showing an intent by the city to discriminate).]

Q 4:28   What is an example of disparate impact?

In a classic case involving disparate impact that was decided by the U.S. Supreme Court, a company had a rule stating that, except for the maintenance department, all department employees must have at least a high school diploma. [Griggs v. Duke Power Co., 401 U.S. 424 (1971)] When the case was initiated, many more white people had high school diplomas than did black people. Consequently, almost all of the positions outside the maintenance department (the lowest department in pay and status in the company) were filled by white people. The court declared that, although the requirement of a high school diploma was neutral on the surface, it had a discriminatory disparate impact on black workers; therefore, the policy was a violation of Title VII. However, the U.S. Supreme Court has held that a city violated Title VII when it refused to certify the results of a promotional examination, based on the city's belief that its use would have a disparate impact on minority firefighters. In *Ricci v. DeStefano* [129 S. Ct. 2658 (2009)], a promotion exam was distributed to New Haven firefighters, and the city, when reviewing the results, concluded that it dispro-portionately excluded minorities and refused to certify the results of the promotional examination. However, as the Supreme Court held, it is a violation of Title VII to make such a race-conscious decision absent some valid defense, such as a strong basis in evidence to believe it will be subject to disparate impact liability if it fails to make the race-conscious decision and a strong basis in evidence to believe that the examinations were not job-related and consistent with business necessity.

Q 4:29   What is a *protected group*?

A *protected group*, also referred to as a suspect class, is a class or substrata of the population that historically has been subjected to discriminatory treatment (e.g., blacks, women, or handicapped individuals). The term has been some-what broadened in recent years to include so-called reverse discrimination, to describe, for example, the discriminatory treatment of white males; however, reverse discrimination cases usually are not as closely scrutinized by courts and federal agencies as are cases involving the traditional targets of discrimination, in which discrimination is more strongly suspected.

Q 4:30   Can a policy that has a disparate impact on a protected group ever be legal?

Yes. If a job requirement is a bona fide occupational qualification (BFOQ), it may fulfill legal guidelines even though it has a disparate impact on a certain class of employees. For instance, in an airline or a police force, a mandatory retirement at a given age may be required for the effective and safe operation of certain kinds of equipment or the maintenance of the public safety, even if it has a disparate impact on older employees. Similarly, educational requirements and test scores may be permissible if they are directly related to the requirements of the job. The courts have held, however, that a BFOQ with respect to race cannot exist.

Q 4:31   Has the difficulty of proving disparate impact changed over the years?

Yes. In the years following *Griggs v. Duke Power Company Co.* [401 U.S. 424 (1971)], the judicial climate for enforcing Title VII in the federal courts cooled. In *Wards Cove Packing Company Co. v. Atonio* [490 U.S. 642 (1989)], the Supreme Court modified *Griggs* by increasing the burden of proof on an employee charging disparate impact. *Wards Cove* involved Alaskan salmon canneries where unskilled jobs were filled predominantly by non-white employees and skilled jobs were filled predominantly by white employees. The employees based their claim of discriminatory hiring practices on this disparity.

The Court held, however, that merely showing different racial proportions in various jobs was insufficient to support a claim of discrimination by disparate impact. Instead, the workers had to show that the percentage of non-whites in skilled jobs was out of balance with the percentage of non-whites who applied and were qualified for the jobs. The workers had not shown this imbalance. The court said that the workers had to point to specific employment practices that had demonstrably caused the disparity; they could not just state that overall practices caused it. Finally, even if the workers had proved that specific employment practices had a discriminatory impact (still assuming the employer had no intention to discriminate), the employer could defend its actions by providing a reasonable business justification for them; the workers would have to show that the company's explanation was inadequate.

In response to the *Wards Cove* decision, the Civil Rights Act of 1991 was enacted. It overruled *Wards Cove* and reinstated statistical evidence as a powerful evidentiary weapon for plaintiffs in disparate-impact cases.

The U.S. Supreme Court has ruled that disparate impact claims, claims historically recognized under Title VII, also applied to the ADEA. [Smith v. City of Jackson, Miss., 125 S. Ct. 1536 (2005)]

Q 4:32   How can the employer defend against a prima facie case of discrimination?

If the employer demonstrates a legitimate, bona fide business reason for the allegedly discriminatory decision or action, the plaintiff must prove that the employer's explanation is only a pretext for illegal discrimination. Typically, a plaintiff attempts to prove this by some combination of direct and indirect evidence. This is commonly referred to as the McDonnell Douglas burden shifting analysis developed in the seminal decision *McDonnell Douglas v. Green* [411 U.S. 782 (1973)].

Circumstantial evidence may be sufficient to show that the employer's business justification is not reasonably believable, suggesting that the employer had a discriminatory (and therefore, illegal) motive. Sometimes the employer's motive is mixed—that is, it has both a legitimate business reason and a discriminatory motive behind an employment decision. If the plaintiff cannot prove that the legitimate business reason offered by the employer is a mere pretext, most courts require the plaintiff to present some additional evidence that discrimination was also a substantial motivating factor. [*See, e.g.*, Price Waterhouse v. Hopkins, 490 U.S. 228 (1989).] This additional evidence can be direct and/or circumstantial evidence, which the U.S. Supreme Court ruled was appropriate even in so-called mixed-motive cases. [Desert Palace, Inc. v. Costa, 539 U.S. 90 (2003)]

Q 4:33   Is an adverse employment action by the employer generally required as a condition to maintaining a discrimination claim?

Aside from Title VII claims predicated on harassment for hostile work environment, to maintain a prima facie case of discrimination under Title VII, the employee must demonstrate that he or she has suffered an adverse employment action as a result of the alleged discrimination. Courts have found adverse employment action in: (1) cases in which the employee's compensation, fringe benefits or other financial terms of employment are diminished, including termination; (2) cases in which a nominally lateral transfer with no change in financial terms significantly reduces the employee's career prospects by preventing him from using his skills and experience, so that the skills are likely to atrophy and the career becomes stunted as a result; and (3) cases in which the employee is not moved to a different job or the skill requirements of her present job altered, but the conditions in which she works are changed in a way that subjects her to a humiliating or degrading, unsafe, unhealthful, or otherwise significantly negative alteration in his or her work environment. [*See* O'Neal v. City of Chicago, 392 F.3d 909 (7th Cir. 2004).] In *O'Neal*, a female police sergeant who was transferred from her position as administrative sergeant to beat sergeant brought an action against the City alleging gender and race discrimination in violation of Title VII, and claimed that the transfer was an adverse employment action. After reviewing the differences between the two positions, the court concluded that it was a lateral job transfer that although may result in diminimus changes to her job responsibilities and work conditions, was not material enough to amount to an adverse employment action for which Title

VII liability applies. Likewise, the court in *Fercello v. County of Ramsey* [612 F.3d 1069 (8th Cir. 2010)], held that changing an employee's parking space location and relocating the employee to an office without a window were not adverse employment actions. In *Vance v. Ball State University* [646 F.3d 461 (7th Cir. 2011)], the court held that providing a verbal warning to a food service employee based on complaints from co-workers was not sufficiently material to constitute an adverse employment action.

Q 4:34   Can there be an adverse employment action by the employer if an employee quits?

Oftentimes employers believe that if an employee quits his or her employment, there would be no adverse employment action and the employer cannot be held liable for the separation of employment under Title VII. Although this may be the case for a true voluntary quit situation, under the doctrine of constructive discharge, if the employee's decision to resign is due to working conditions that have become so intolerable that a reasonable person in the employee's position would have felt compelled to resign, the resignation will be treated as a formal discharge for Title VII purposes. As the U.S. Supreme Court stated in *Pennsylvania State Police v. Sueters,* under the doctrine of constructive discharge "an employee's reasonable decision to resign because of unendurable working conditions is assimilated to a formal discharge for remedial purposes." [124 S. Ct. 2342, 2351 (2004)] As such, in *Robinson v. Waste Management of Texas,* [122 Fed. Appx. 756 (5th Cir. 2004)], when a former employee, claiming gender discrimination, quit her employment because she merely felt "frustrated" after being passed over for promotion, the court held that the constructive discharge claim could not stand.

Racial Discrimination

Q 4:35   What employment decisions and actions constitute racial discrimination?

Almost any decision an employer makes that is based on race or any policy that is not job-related and is inconsistent with business necessity and adversely affects employees or applicants because of their race is actionable race discrimination under Title VII. Specifically, Title VII provides that it is unlawful for an employer:

> To fail or refuse to hire or to discharge any individual, or otherwise discriminate against any individual with respect to his compensation, terms, conditions or privileges of employment because of such individual's race . . . or to limit, segregate, or classify his employees or applicants for employment in any way which would deprive or tend to deprive any individual of employment opportunities or otherwise adversely affect his status as an employee because of such individual's race . . . [2 U.S.C. § 2000e-2]

Employer actions that may result in racial discrimination prohibited by Title VII fall within many categories, including but not limited to hiring, promotions, demotions, discipline, discharge, and denial of privileges of employment. In addition, racial harassment is a form of race discrimination much like sexual harassment is a form of sex discrimination. An employer may be found liable to aggrieved employees for tolerating or engaging in the creation of a hostile work environment on the basis of race. The so-called "quid pro quo" theory of harassment is unique to sexual harassment, and is generally not considered a basis for race discrimination, even if the victim alleges that his or her race was a motivating factor for the harassment.

Q 4:36   Does racial discrimination have to be intentional to be actionable under Title VII?

No. Discrimination can be maintained under the theories of disparate treatment or disparate impact. Under disparate treatment, an employer is found to have intentionally used race as a basis for an employment decision. Under disparate-impact theory, an employer can be liable for the unintended results of a racially neutral employment policy or procedure that has a disparate impact on the employment of members of a particular race. [Griggs v. Duke Power Co., 401 U.S. 424 (1971)] Once an adverse impact is established to have resulted from a racially neutral policy or procedure, the employer must justify its continued use as a business necessity to avoid liability.

In addition, employers must beware of policies that perpetuate past discrimination. A good example is a company with a history of avoiding hiring individuals of a particular race now hiring only by word-of-mouth or only the friends of existing employees. In *Chaney v. Plainfield Healthcare Center* [612 F.3d 908 (7th Cir. 2010)], the court held that a nursing home, which included a written policy of not allowing black nursing assistants to provide care for residents who did not want care from black assistants, was hostile and abusive in violation of Title VII.

Q 4:37   Are members of racial minorities the only class protected against racial discrimination under Title VII?

Although the purpose and effect of Title VII was clearly to prohibit discrimination in the workplace against minorities and women, so-called reverse discrimination is potentially actionable under Title VII. Such claims have risen over the years and are gaining acceptance. In *Mullis v. Houston Community College System* [6 *Employment Discrimination Report (EDR)* (BNA) 212 (Feb.21, 1996)], a white staff member obtained a jury verdict of $500,000 for the college's predisposition to select a minority candidate for the position of assistant dean. With increasing frequency, municipal employees (e.g., police officers and firefighters) are challenging selection criteria for hiring and promotion as having a disparate impact on white employees. In *Albright v. City of New Orleans* [DCE La. No. 96-679 (Feb. 23, 1996)], a group of white police officers asked a federal judge to enjoin the City of New Orleans from enforcing residency requirements on the grounds that this policy discriminates against white police officers. In *Richardson v. Hampton*, a federal court jury awarded $200,000 to a white male firefighter who claimed he was denied a promotion because of illegal preference being given to minorities and women. [7 *Employment Discrimination Report (EDR)* (BNA) 73 (July 17, 1996)] In *Lambert v. Fulton County, Georgia* [253 F.3d 588 (11th Cir. 2001)], the Eleventh Circuit upheld jury verdicts in excess of $2.5 million in favor of three white supervisors who were found by the jury to have been disciplined more harshly than black supervisors in connection with a hostile work environment investigation. [*See* 16 *Employment Discrimination Report (EDR)* (BNA) 836 (June 20, 2001).] In *Albright v. City of New Orleans* [208 F. Supp. 2d 634 (E.D. La. 2002)], a federal judge awarded almost $500,000 to white police officers who claimed they were passed over for promotion due to their race, in violation of Title VII. [*See* 18 *Employment Discrimination Report (EDR)* (BNA) 190 (Feb. 13, 2002).] In *Gagnon v. Sprint Corp.*, the court held that direct evidence of reverse discrimination, "I'm not going to pay him. He's just a white guy," was sufficient to allow the jury to determine whether the failure of Gagnon to receive a recommended increase in salary was based on racial discrimination. [284 F.3d 839, 848 (8th Cir. 2002)] In another case, the U.S. Supreme Court held that a city violated Title VII when it refused to certify the results of a promotional examination, based on the city's belief that its use would have a disparate impact on minority firefighters. In *Ricci v. DeStefano* [129 S. Ct. 2658 (2009)], a promotion exam was distributed to New Haven firefighters and the city, when reviewing the results, concluded that it disproportionately excluded minorities and refused to certify the results of the promotional examination. However, as the U.S. Supreme Court held, it is a violation of Title VII to make such a race-conscious decision absent some valid defense, such as a strong basis in evidence to believe it will be subject to disparate impact liability if it fails to make the race-conscious decision and a strong basis in evidence to believe that the examinations were not job-related and consistent with business necessity. In *Stockwell v. City of Harvey* [597 F.3d 895 (7th Cir. 2010)], the court held that a white firefighter who claimed reverse discrimination against the city could not maintain the claim because the city had produced a legitimate non-discriminatory reason for failing to promote the white firefighter. In essence, the evidence provided by the city demonstrated that the fire chief, who made the decision, believed that the white firefighter would not support him and that he was among those who the fire chief believed would resist change in the department.

Q 4:38 Under what circumstances can an employer provide preferences for minorities in hiring and promotion decisions?

Employers can defend against claims of reverse discrimination when the complained-of actions were taken pursuant to a protected affirmative action plan. Protected affirmative action plans are maintained pursuant to Section 713(b)(1) of Title VII, Executive Order 11246, and consent decrees and court judgments pursuant to Section 108 of the Civil Rights Act of 1991. All three are discussed below.

Title VII Section 713(b)(1). The EEOC, as enabled by Section 713(b)(1) of Title VII, issued specific affirmative action guidelines to protect employers who take reasonable actions under legitimate affirmative action plans. It is not sufficient, however, for an employer to declare, without any other action that it prefers a minority or female to seek affirmative action. Rather, the guidelines as contained in 29 C.F.R. Sections 1608 *et seq.* provide specific measures that affirmative action plans must contain to gain protection:

- *Self-analysis.* The purpose of Title VII is to "improve the economic and social conditions of minorities and women by providing a quality of opportunity in the workplace." [29 C.F.R. § 1608.1(b)] To qualify as a protected plan, the employer must determine through self-analysis whether its employment practices do or tend to exclude, disadvantage, restrict, or result in adverse impact or disparate treatment of a protected group or leave uncorrected the effects of prior discrimination. It is not necessary that the self-analysis establish a violation of Title VII. If, through self-analysis, the employer determines that its employment practices have had or tended to have an adverse effect on the employment opportunities of members of previously excluded groups, or that they leave uncorrected the effects of prior discrimination or result in disparate treatment, the employer can then, and only then, proceed to develop an affirmative action plan.

- *Reasonable action to correct prohibited behavior.* After identifying prohibited behavior, an employer must ascertain what reasonable action it can take to remedy it. In so doing, the employer must follow various guidelines to ensure that the affirmative action plan is protected.

Generally, the EEOC considers the following standards:

- The plan should be sufficiently tailored to solve the problems identified by the self-analysis;
- Goals and timetables should be specified; and
- The self-analysis and plan must be written and dated.

There has been some disagreement as to whether, as a result of the Civil Rights Act of 1991, only those affirmative action plans that are mandatory (i.e., required as a result of court-ordered remedies, conciliation agreements, or the like) are subject to protection under Title VII. The EEOC, in its Revised Enforcement Guidance on Recent Developments in Disparate Treatment Theory [EEOC Notice No. N-915.002 (July 14, 1992)], maintained that voluntary affirmative action plans, provided they meet EEOC guidelines, also provide protection for employers from charges of reverse discrimination.

Executive Order 11246. Administered by the Office of Federal Contract Compliance Programs, this order requires certain federal contractors, as a condition of obtaining and maintaining federal work, to maintain written affirmative action programs.

Section 108 of the Civil Rights Act of 1991. Affirmative action plans that are part of consent decrees or litigated judgments are specifically protected under

Section 108 of the Civil Rights Act of 1991 from challenge by persons who had actual notice and a reasonable opportunity to object to them or whose interests were adequately represented by another party who challenged the decree or judgment on the same legal grounds. Likewise, affirmative action plans entered into by consent decrees or as ordered by a court of law in a state or local matter are also accorded protection under Title VII from challenge of racial discrimination.

Increasingly, affirmative action plans that have become obsolete are being challenged. The theory supporting such a challenge is that, although the plan was once legitimate, its objectives have been met and now it is no longer entitled to protection. That is, the fundamental basis for allowing preferences to minorities and women no longer exists. This theory has been gaining acceptance over the years. In *Middleton v. Flint, Michigan* [92 F.3d 396 (6th Cir. 1996)], the Sixth Circuit struck down an affirmative action plan requiring 50 percent of all promotions to police sergeant be minorities, declaring the plan in violation of the Fourteenth Amendment. Any employer who seeks to take action on the basis of an affirmative action plan should therefore conduct periodic self-analysis and monitor the attainment of the plan's goals to ensure that the plan is still worthy of protection under Title VII.

Q 4:39   How have U.S. Supreme Court decisions affected affirmative action programs?

In *Adarand Constructors, Inc. v. Pena* [515 U.S. 200 (1995)], the U.S. Supreme Court set significant limitations on affirmative action programs for federal contractors. In the case, a contracting company challenged a clause within federal agency contracts that provided monetary incentives for hiring subcontractors certified as small businesses owned and controlled by "socially and economic disadvantaged individuals." Diverting from the course of prior decisions, the Supreme Court concluded that to withstand constitutional challenges under the Fifth and Fourteenth Amendments, affirmative action plans must be analyzed under strict scrutiny and are constitutional only if they contain narrowly tailored measures that serve compelling governmental interests. In other words, the plan itself must be specifically designed to remedy the practice and lingering effects of racial discrimination against minorities and women.

The *Adarand* decision sparked numerous challenges to affirmative action and minority set-aside programs. In December 1995, the University of California released a plan to end its affirmative action mandates in hiring and contracting by January 1, 1996, and affirmative action-based admissions criteria for students by January 1997. [6 *Employment Discrimination Report (EDR)* (BNA) 14 (Jan. 3, 1996)] Also in California, a 1996 initiative (The California Civil Rights Initiative, also referred to as Proposition 209) proposed legislation that would prohibit the government or any government instrumentality from giving preferential treatment to minorities and women under affirmative action plans. The initiative passed by election in November 1996, effectively barring affirmative action in state and local employment, contracting, and education decisions. Following its passage, the Coalition of Economic Equity instituted litigation against Proposition 209, claiming it to be unconstitutional. Initial claims were defeated, and a federal judge issued a "final judgment" upholding the constitutionality of the California Civil Rights Initiative. It now appears that nothing stands in the way of implementation of the law. [See "Judge Upholds Constitutionality of Proposition 209 Initiative," 10 *Employment Discrimination Report (EDR)* (BNA) 212–13 (Feb. 18, 1998).]

In Minnesota, two contractors sued the Minnesota Department of Transportation, claiming that minority set-aside programs for contractors are unconstitutional. [See "Contractors Challenge Legality of Transportation Set-Aside Program," 6 *Employment Discrimination Report (EDR)* (BNA) 256 (Feb.28, 1996).]

In *Middleton v. Flint, Michigan* [92 F.3d 396 (6th Cir. 1996)], the Sixth Circuit struck down an affirmative action plan requiring 50 percent of all promotions to police sergeant be minorities. The court declared the plan unconstitutional, in violation of the Fourteenth Amendment, when analyzed under the "strict scrutiny" standard.

Governor Mike Foster of Louisiana issued an executive order on January 11, 1996, banning affirmative action and minority set-aside programs in government. He later amended that executive order on February 14, 1996, providing that race and gender may still be considered in awarding contracts as long as they are not the decisive and predominant factors. [6 *Employment Discrimination Report (EDR)* (BNA) 245 (Feb. 28, 1996)]

In an attempt to follow the strict scrutiny standard, the Justice Department in 1996 issued guidelines for federal agencies to follow regarding use of their affirmative action programs. The guidelines seek to ensure that the preferences for minorities and women are sufficiently tailored to remedy the effects of existing or lingering discrimination. [See "Justice Department Issues Guidance of Affirmative Action after *Adarand*," 6 *Employment Discrimination Report (EDR)* (BNA) 272 (Mar. 6, 1996).]

In 1998, the U.S. Supreme Court refused to review a decision by the Eleventh Circuit that held that a minority- and gender-based set-aside ordinance is unconstitutional. In the case, various contracts or organizations attacked various minority business and gender-based programs dating back to the 1980s. Maintaining these minority and gender-based programs did not pass a strict scrutiny standard, rendering them susceptible to being stricken down after careful judicial scrutiny. [For more discussion, *see* "Justices Decline Review of Ruling Striking Down Preferences," 10 *Employment Discrimination Report (EDR)* (BNA) 331 (Mar. 11, 1998).]

Similarly, in 1999, the U.S. Supreme Court declined review of a Fifth Circuit Appeals Court decision that held that the city of Dallas' affirmative action plan, which resulted in preference in promotions in the fire department for blacks, Hispanics and women, was an unconstitutional violation of the Equal Protection Clause. [See 12 *Employment Discrimination Report (EDR)* (BNA) 483 (Mar. 31, 1999).] In *Lee General Contracting, Inc. v. City of Atlanta* [N.D. Ga. No.

1:99-CV-2194 (June 21, 2001)], a federal judge upheld an arbitration award of over $500,000 to a contractor who claimed that the City's set-aside program for minority contractors was unconstitutional. [*See* 16 *Employment Discrimination Report (EDR)* (BNA) 863 (June 27, 2001).] In *Berkley v. United States* [287 F.3d 1076 (Fed. Cir. 2002)], the court held that an Air Force memorandum that instructed those conducting a reduction in force (RIF) to be particularly sensitive to women and minorities in light of past attitudes and required a report specifying women and minority selection as compared to all others considered was facially discriminatory against white males deserving of strict scrutiny by the court. [18 *Employment Discrimination Report (EDR)* (BNA) 555 (May 8, 2002)] As the court held in *Humphries v. Pulaski County Special School District* [580 F.3d 688 (8th Cir. 2009)], if a school district failed to promote a white school district employee because of her race on the basis of an affirmative action plan, it would constitute evidence of unlawful discrimination and the affirmative action plan at issue would be examined to determine if it was a valid plan under Title VII.

Q 4:40 What types of evidence are used to prove racial discrimination under disparate-treatment theories?

Racial discrimination through disparate treatment occurs when an employer, because of an employee's race, treats an employee less favorably than others similarly situated. To succeed under a disparate-treatment theory, the aggrieved individual must prove that the employer acted from a discriminatory motive. This does not mean that the respondent must prove the employer intended to discriminate illegally; discriminatory motives may be inferred solely from the difference in treatment. Direct evidence of discriminatory motive is not necessary; it is difficult, if not impossible, to obtain. Rather, proof of disparate treatment can be established by an inference through the use of the following:

Comparative evidence. Because direct evidence of motive is often difficult to obtain, comparative evidence is commonly used to establish racial discrimination through disparate treatment. Comparative evidence establishes whether similarly situated individuals are treated differently based on race. It necessarily requires an analysis of who the similarly situated individuals are, to what extent their treatment differs, and (if it does) whether it differs along racial lines. Individuals may be similarly situated for one employment decision but not for another. In hiring and promotion decisions, the EEOC takes the approach that all qualified applicants or employees seeking a job or promotion are similarly situated. In a discharge case, the EEOC looks at how the employer treated other employees who engaged in similar misconduct. The term *similar situation* does not necessarily mean identically situated, and the EEOC uses an expansive approach to determine whether disparate treatment has occurred from which a discriminatory motive can be inferred.

Statistical evidence. If a member of a minority group who is not hired for a position, but is qualified for it, provides statistical evidence that no minorities have been hired by the employer, despite their presence in the surrounding geographic area, this evidence can suggest discriminatory treatment and motive;

however, if after analysis it is determined that the employer advertised in its geographic area but no other qualified minorities applied for a position with it, the inference of discrimination would weaken dramatically. Clearly, in race discrimination claims where assertions of pattern and practice discrimination are made, it is likely that an employer will have to provide information detailing its personnel actions regarding employees and applicants for many years prior to the alleged offense to negate those assertions. Small employers with few employees and thereby few applicants are not likely subjects for successful statistical analysis; their numbers are so small it is nearly impossible to draw conclusions. Generally, for statistical evidence to be probative, a large employer with large pools of applicants is necessary.

Direct evidence of a discriminatory motive. Although direct evidence of discriminatory motive is often difficult, if not impossible, to obtain, evidence of racial slurs, stereotyping, and the like are all examples of direct evidence of discriminatory motive that can be used to maintain an inference of disparate treatment. In *Ash v. Tyson Foods, Inc.* [126 S. Ct. 1195 (2006)], the U.S. Supreme Court held that evidence that a supervisor had sometimes referred to two African American employees as "boy" was in and of itself potentially probative of discriminatory animus in connection with their Title VII claim.

Assuming the evidence obtained indicates that a prima face case of disparate treatment can be made, the employer must demonstrate that it had a legitimate, non-discriminatory reason to take the action complained of. If the employer meets this burden, the burden shifts back to the complainant to demonstrate that the employer's proffered reason is nothing more than a pretext to conceal illegal discrimination.

Q 4:41 What types of evidence are used to prove disparate-impact racial discrimination?

Disparate impact, unlike disparate treatment, does not require that a discriminatory motive be established. Rather, the issue is whether an employment policy has a demonstrable affect on employees because of their race. Statistical evidence is generally used to determine whether the selection criteria for hiring employees disproportionately adversely affect individuals of a particular race. An analysis is generally made of the applicant pool, the demographic makeup of the employer's workforce, and the demographic composition of the surrounding geographic area. To the extent that the statistical data demonstrates a sufficiently adverse impact, discrimination can be inferred.

Another way that an inference of discrimination through disparate impact can be demonstrated is through hiring policies and procedures that perpetuate past discrimination. For example, the EEOC has taken the position that an employer that historically has hired only white workers and today accepts applicants only through recommendations from its all-white workforce has adopted a policy that has the foreseeable effect of perpetuating the effect of the company's past discriminatory hiring practices. [Comm'n Decision No. 72-0978, CCH EEOC Decisions (1973) 6345] Whenever proof of disparate impact exists, the employer must rebut this evidence by proving that its selection, promotion, or other employment decisions are job-related and supported by business necessity. Unless business necessity can be demonstrated, it is likely that such racially neutral policies and procedures will be held to violate Title VII race discrimination.

Q 4:42   Have significant monetary awards been made in cases of race discrimination?

The following cases illustrate that race discrimination continues to subject employers to major costs and tenacious litigation. Some 13 years after he was fired for admittedly conspiring to falsify an alcohol breath test and physically abusing a girlfriend, an African-American state trooper won a $211,000 jury verdict in a Boston courthouse in January 1994. The ex-trooper's attorney convinced the jurors that, although his client had done the things of which his superiors accused him, the discipline they imposed was far harsher than that received by white troopers for similar offenses. The trooper had worked sporadically as a truck and bus driver following his termination, thereby mitigating the damages; however, the Massachusetts State Police will also have to pay some $70,000 in interest on top of the award if the verdict withstands appeal, according to the plaintiff's attorney. [*See* "Federal Jury Awards $211,000 to Black Trooper Fired in 1981," 19 *BNA Daily Labor Report* 10, Jan. 31, 1994.]

The U.S. Court of Appeals for the Seventh Circuit, sitting in Chicago, affirmed in January 1994 a $102,000 award of back pay to an African-American salesman from Milwaukee who claimed a constructive discharge based on racial slurs. Writing for the court, Circuit Judge Joel M. Flaum observed, "Title VII does not guarantee stress-free employment, but it does protect employees from toiling in a hostile working environment created by their employer's use of racial slurs and epithets." In the case, the plaintiff had compiled an outstanding record as a member of the defendant's sales force over some seven years before being promoted to a management post. Thereafter, his district manager reportedly subjected him to racist comments. The plaintiff testified that he took it as long as he could, then quit; the courts concluded that he was entitled to do so under the circumstances. [*See* "Supervisors' Racial Slurs Warrant $102,000 Award to Milwaukee Salesman," 5 *BNA Daily Labor Report* 5, Jan. 7, 1994.]

In New Jersey, a federal judge allowed a plaintiff of Indian ancestry to proceed with his race discrimination claim under the post–Civil War civil rights acts, despite the fact that the defendant's supervisor had never met the litigant. The plaintiff, pointing out that he speaks English with the pronounced accent characteristic of the Indian subcontinent, says he was contacted by Anheuser-Busch after responding to an advertisement for a brewery job. An assistant manager reportedly called the plaintiff to inquire about a six-year gap in his resume. The plaintiff claims he explained that his brewing experience had been in India and that for the last half dozen years he had owned and operated a delicatessen that he had recently sold. The manager later sent him a letter that said the plaintiff would not be hired "at this time." Denying the brewing company's motion for summary judgment, the trial judge said that a jury might well find that the plaintiff's accent gave away his race, thus entitling him to try to prove at trial that racial bias was the basis for his unsuccessful job application. [See "Race, National Origin Bias Claims by Indian Job Applicant Can Proceed," 209 BNA Daily Labor Report 14, Feb. 14, 1994.]

The largest verdict in 1994 was awarded by a California jury to a plaintiff in a case involving race discrimination and breach of contract. The jurors handed down a verdict of $1.1 million for the plaintiff's economic losses and a like sum for non-economic damages. [Cobb v. University of Southern California, 30 Cal. App. 4th 1663, 36 Cal. Rptr. 2d 440 (1994)] Reported verdicts since 1994 continue to demonstrate significant monetary awards for race discrimination.

A Washington jury awarded an African-American salesman $1.5 million in compensatory damages for J.C. Penney's maintenance of a hostile work environment and infliction of emotional distress. [Lucas v. JC Penney Co., Inc., No. C93-1804 C (D. Wash. Jan. 26, 1996)] The employee claimed that he was frequently subjected to racial slurs and that the company, although aware of the racially hostile work environment, did nothing to improve working conditions. Indeed, when the plaintiff complained of the actions, his employer not only did nothing but told him that he would be fired if he continued to complain. The plaintiff went out on disability and it was determined that he was constructively discharged from employment. [See "J.C. Penney to Appeal $1.5 Million Award for Former Employee's Emotional Distress," 6 Employment Discrimination Report (EDR) (BNA) 158 (Feb. 7, 1986).]

In 1996, a California jury awarded $1.88 million to a plaintiff who claimed he was denied promotion because of his race. [Douthered v. Coca-Cola Bottling Co. of Sacramento, Cal. Sup. Ct. No. 544495 (Feb. 21, 1996)] The plaintiff claimed he was repeatedly passed over for promotion, despite his former district manager's repeated suggestions that he be promoted. In Mungin v. Katten Muchin & Zavis [941 F. Supp. 153 (D.D.C. 1996)], a federal jury awarded $2.5 million to a black attorney who claimed that his law firm discriminated against him because of his race. The essence of Mungin's complaint was that he was treated differently from other white associates at the office in terms of salary, work assignments, consideration for partnership, and other terms and conditions of employment, leading up to his constructive discharge. [See "Jury Awards Black, Ex-Law Firm Associate $2.5 Million for Alleged Race Discrimination," 6 Employment Discrimination Report (EDR) (BNA) 439 (Apr. 3, 1996).]

A California state jury awarded $7.6 million in damages to a waste management company manager who claimed discharge because he was an African-American. [Hudson v. Brand Servs. Inc., Cal. Sup. Ct. Nos. 726837-7, 734935-1 (Apr. 24, 1996)] Of the award, $6.8 million were for punitive damages, representing the clear outrage of the jury. [See "California Jury Awards $7.6 Million to Manager Discharged Because of Race," 6(17) Employment Discrimination Report (EDR) (BNA) 54 (Apr. 24, 1996).]

In one of the most notorious race discrimination cases in recent history, Texaco Corporation, in late 1996, agreed to settle a race discrimination lawsuit costing the company $176 million for damages, pay increases, and costs associated with programs designed to enhance equal opportunity at the company. [*See* 7 *Employment Discrimination Report (EDR)* (BNA) 618 (Nov. 20, 1996).]

In *Gilford v. Detroit Edison Co.* [Mich. Cir. Ct., No. 93-333296-NO (Feb. 9, 1998)], Detroit Edison agreed to pay up to $65 million to former employees to settle a race and age discrimination class action claim, which makes it "one of the most sweeping agreements to settle class-wide race discrimination in recent years," according to the plaintiffs' attorneys. [*See* "Detroit Utilities to Pay Up to $65 Million to Settle Class Claims of Race/Age Bias," 10 *Employment Discrimination Report (EDR)* (BNA) 220 (Feb. 18, 1998).] The more than 100-page settlement agreement provides that Detroit Edison will pay at least $17.5 million, up to a maximum of $65 million, to affected employees who demonstrate injury, to be decided through arbitration. Up to 3,500 employees may be eligible for payments.

A 1999 settlement of a class-action lawsuit by African-American employees against CSX Transportation, a large railroad company, was reported to have amounted to $25 million. [*See* 12 *Employment Discrimination Report (EDR)* (BNA) 164 (Feb. 3, 1999).]

In the highly publicized race discrimination class action claim against Coca-Cola, it was reported that a federal judge had approved a $192.5 million settlement agreement for the approximately 2,000 current and former African-American employees. [Abdallah v. Coca-Cola Co, N.D. Ga., No. 1:98-CV-3679 (May 27, 2001); *see* 16 *Employment Discrimination Report (EDR)* (BNA) 770 (June 6, 2001).]

It was reported that Toshiba has agreed to settle race discrimination claims brought by a class of African-Americans alleging discrimination in hiring and employment practices at its Lebanon and Nashville, Tennessee locations for $1.4 million. [18 *Employment Discrimination Report (EDR)* (BNA) 309 (Mar. 13, 2002)]

Also, a construction contractor from Steamboat Springs, Colorado reportedly agreed to settle a class action race suit by the EEOC on behalf of minority applicants denied employment for $2.5 million. [20 *Employment Discrimination Report (EDR)* (BNA) 521 (Apr. 16, 2003)]

Q 4:43 Can an employer be held accountable for racially motivated harassment in the workplace?

Yes. Under Title VII, an action for racial harassment can be brought against an employer when the employee claims that the employer subjected the employee to a racially hostile work environment.

Hudson v. Brand Services, Inc. [Cal. Sup. Ct. Nos. 726837-7, 734935-1 (Apr. 17, 1996)] exemplifies the seriousness of racial harassment. The plaintiff, a project manager who worked for an industrial waste firm, was subjected to racial harassment and fired. Although he had presumably performed well (as evidenced by his receipt of a large bonus prior to his termination), the plaintiff was subjected to racial slurs and his supervisor reportedly stated that the plaintiff was the "wrong color" for the market and that a lesser qualified, white employee would do better. The jury awarded $7.6 million in compensatory and punitive damages—punitive damages comprising $6.89 million of the overall verdict. [*See* "California Jury Awards $7.6 Million to Manager Discharged Because of Race," 6(17) *Employment Discrimination Report (EDR)* (BNA) 541 (Apr. 24, 1996).]

The theory of harassment in the racial context is analogous to the basis for establishing hostile work environment claims in the more developed area of sexual harassment law. If it can be demonstrated that the environment is sufficiently offensive and abusive, and the employer knew or should have known of the hostile environment and did not take action to remedy the situation, it is likely that an actionable race harassment claim can be maintained. Even the use of one particularly inflammatory racist epithet may be sufficient, depending upon the facts, to support a claim of racial harassment. In *Taylor v. Metzger* [N.J. Sup. Ct. No. A-9-97 (Feb. 18, 1998)], the State Supreme Court reinstated a claim by an officer that she had been subjected to a hostile work environment actionable under New Jersey state law, when the county sheriff called her a particularly inflammatory racial slur. According to the court in *Taylor*, not unlike the test for hostile work environment in a federal setting, if the harassment is offensive and so severe or pervasive that it alters the working environment, a case of hostile work environment on the basis of race can be maintained. The court rejected a regular and pervasive test that would have doomed any claim based upon any single incident, regardless of how offensive it might be.

The 1998 U.S. Supreme Court decisions in *Burlington Industries, Inc. v. Ellerth* [524 U.S. 742 (1998)] and *Faragher v. City of Boca Raton* [524 U.S. 775 (1998)], adopted specific standards for sexual harassment as it relates to an employer's liability for a supervisor's creation of a hostile work environment. In situations involving supervisors, *Ellerth* and *Faragher* held that employers are vicariously liable for a supervisor's conduct, subject to an affirmative defense if an employer adopts and implements suitable preventative and corrective measures. Federal courts are expanding the *Ellerth* and *Faragher* principles to race harassment cases involving supervisors. As a result of these U.S. Supreme Court decisions, in *Allen v. Michigan Department of Corrections* [165 F.3d 405 (6th Cir. 1999)], the Sixth Circuit reinstated a case of race harassment involving severe and pervasive racial insults by department of corrections supervisors directed to a African-American subordinate. Although the case was previously dismissed by the district court, finding no evidence that the employer condoned or tolerated the conduct, the Sixth Circuit found that the employer could nonetheless be vicariously liable for the supervisors' conduct under *Ellerth* and *Faragher*. [*See* 12 *Employment Discrimination Report (EDR)* (BNA) 76 (Jan. 20, 1999).] In *Gibson v. Bell Helicopter Textron* [Tex. Dist. Ct. No. 236165928-96], a jury awarded an African-American employee $4 million resulting from damages incurred by a racially hostile work environment. [*See* 16 *Employment Discrimination Report (EDR)* (BNA) 18 (Jan. 3, 2001).]

In *EEOC v. Ford Motor Co.* [No. 01-73705 (E.D. Mich. 2001)], Ford agreed to pay a class of African-American employees a reported $300,000 for allegations of racial harassment at their suburban Detroit plant. The employees are reported to have complained of insulting racial remarks and hangman's nooses at the plant. [18 *Employment Discrimination Report (EDR)* (BNA) 45 (Jan. 9, 2002)]

Q 4:44   **Is it a violation of Title VII to discriminate against an employee because of the employee's association with someone of a different race?**

Title VII of the Civil Rights Act of 1964, in relevant part, provides that it is "an unlawful employment practice for an employer . . . to discharge any individual . . . because of *such* individual's race." [42 U.S.C. § 2000e-2(a)(1) (emphasis added)] In light of this, can a Title VII claim be maintained if the discrimination is allegedly the result of an individual's association with somebody of another race? At first blush, it would appear not since the statute makes clear that Title VII discrimination is because of "such" individual's race, the employee at issue. This issue was addressed in *Holcomb v. Iona College.* [521 F.3d 130 (2d Cir. 2008)] In the case, a white head-coach of a college's men's basketball team claimed that he was fired because of his marriage to an African-American woman. Although the opinion acknowledged that courts from other jurisdictions have held otherwise, the court rejected the notion that the white coach's claim that he was discharged for marrying an African-American woman was because of his wife's race, but rather, because of the employee's own race, in that, if an employer disapproves of an interracial association, the employee suffers discrimination because of the employee's own race. As such, the court held that, in this matter of first impression, a claim of adverse action based on an employee's association with a person of another race is cognizable under Title VII.

National Origin Discrimination

Q 4:45   **What is *national origin discrimination*?**

National origin discrimination occurs when an employment event (e.g., hiring) is based on the employee's ethnic origins. The EEOC, in its Guidelines on Discrimination Because of National Origin, defines *national origin discrimination* broadly as including:

> Denial of equal opportunity because of an individual's ancestors or national origin; or because an individual has the physical, cultural or linguistic characteristics of a national origin group. [29 C.F.R. Chapter XIV, § 1606.1]

In addition, national origin discrimination is deemed to have occurred if an individual is denied equal opportunity as a result of: the individual's marriage or association with persons of a particular national origin group; membership in or association with an organization identified with or seeking to promote the interest of a national origin group; attendance or participation in schools, churches, or other places of worship by persons of a national origin group; or because an individual's name or spouse's name is associated with a national origin group. [29 C.F.R. Chapter XIV, § 1606.1 (July 1, 1991)]

National origin should be distinguished from citizenship discrimination, wherein an alien is treated less favorably than a U.S. citizen. Under the Immigration Reform and Control Act of 1986 (IRCA), legal aliens who are entitled to work cannot be discriminated against with respect to most jobs.

Q 4:46   To maintain a claim for national origin discrimination must the employee allege a particular country of origin to maintain the claim?

Although typically, claimants alleging national origin discrimination will claim discrimination based upon a particular country from which they came, a specific designation of any particular sovereign nation is not necessary.

This point was emphasized in *Kanaji v. Children's Hospital of Philadelphia* [276 F. Supp. 2d 399 (E.D. Pa. 2003)]. An employee at Children's Hospital in Philadelphia alleged national origin discrimination against his employer based on his "direct African descent," without identifying a particular country. The employee pointed to numerous actions of the hospital to demonstrate the hospital's animus toward Afrocentric arts, speech, dress, and the like. The hospital claimed that the national origin discrimination claim must be dismissed because the plaintiff had not specified any country or nation of origin and that being of "African" descent is not sufficient to maintain a claim. In reviewing case law and legislative history as to the basis and grounds for national origin discrimination, the court concluded that national origin discrimination was meant to be interpreted broadly as a place of origin and not a particular sovereign nation. As such, the court allowed the case to proceed and refused the hospital's request for dismissal.

Q 4:47   Is a requirement that employees speak "English-only" at a workplace considered discrimination on the basis of national origin?

Because language is an essential characteristic of national origin, the EEOC presumes that a rule that all employees must speak only English at all times in the workplace violates Title VII as illegal discrimination on the basis of national origin. Such a blanket rule, although arguably facially neutral, has a disproportionate impact on persons whose native tongue is other than English. If an employer adopts such a rule, the EEOC will conclude that the policy is discriminatory, unless the employer can demonstrate that the requirement is justified through business necessity. There may be limitations to a speak-English-only rule or other circumstances that sufficiently rebut the presumption of illegal discrimination. If, for example, the rule permits workers to communicate with one another in a language other than English, but requires workers to communicate in English with customers who generally speak English, it may pass strict scrutiny because of its limited application and business necessity. Even a speak-English-only rule that is not so limited in scope may rebut the presumption in extreme circumstances of business necessity.

In 1995, the U.S. Court of Appeals for the Ninth Circuit held that Arizona's English-only rules for state employees were overly broad and in violation of the Fifth Amendment. The Arizona amendment requires all state employees to use English in performing their duties. The Ninth Circuit, in its ruling, found that language is an essential characteristic of national origin and that the amendment may mask discrimination against Hispanics. On appeal, the U.S. Supreme Court avoided the issue altogether, declaring the issue moot on technical grounds and dismissing the appeal. [*See* Arizonans for Official English v. Arizona, 520 U.S. 43 (1997).]

Deciding an appeal from yet another lawsuit filed to prevent the implementation of the English-only amendment in Arizona, on April 28, 1998, the Arizona Supreme Court held that the English-only amendment was unconstitutional under the Fourteenth and First Amendments of the U.S. Constitution. [*See* Ruiz v. Hull, 191 Ariz. 441 (Ariz. 1998).] In its decision, the court noted that although English-only provisions had been adopted by 21 other states and 40 municipalities, Arizona's amendment was "a sweeping injunction against speech in any language other than English." As such, given the breath of the prohibition, the amendment could not withstand constitutional scrutiny under the Fourteenth and First Amendments. As the court stated, the English-only amendment "unconstitutionally inhibits the free discussion of government affairs" by depriving non-English-speaking people access to the government and its services and also deprives officials of the ability to communicate with non-English-speaking constituents. [*See* "State's Top Court Strikes Down Amendment That Placed English-Only Rule on Government," 10 *Employment Discrimination Report (EDR)* (BNA) 566 (May 6, 1998).]

In 1999, the U.S. Supreme Court denied review of a petition filed by the Arizonans for Official English seeking to overturn the Arizona Supreme Court decision in April 1998, finally ending the 11-year battle to implement a voter-approved measure to make English the "official" language in Arizona. [12 *Employment Discrimination Report (EDR)* (BNA) 58 (Jan. 13, 1999)]

In a class-action case filed by the EEOC, a Texas university reportedly agreed to a settlement of $2.4 million to resolve charges that it subjected Hispanic housekeepers to abuse if caught speaking Spanish on the job by their supervisor. [*See* EEOC v. University of the Incarnate Word, W.D. Tex., No. SA-99-CV-10900G, 16 *Employment Discrimination Report (EDR)* (BNA) 593 (Apr. 25, 2001).]

However, if speaking English is justified by business necessity, English-only rules at certain necessary times may be permissible. In *Gonzales v. All Island Transportation* [2007 WL 642959 (E.D.N.Y. Feb. 26, 2007)], a taxi-cab company instituted a limited English-only policy at its main office. No Spanish was to be spoken unless a customer did not speak English. An employee claimed that this policy was tantamount to Title VII discrimination based on national origin, and the company maintained it was necessary to avoid miscommunication, especially between taxi-drivers and dispatchers. Recognizing that employers may have English-only policies at certain times when justified by business necessity, the court concluded that the taxi-cab company met its burden and dismissed the case.

Q 4:48   Is a requirement that employees speak a language in addition to English considered discrimination on the basis of national origin?

The issue of whether a worker was required to speak a language in addition to English as a condition of employment was addressed recently by the Fifth Circuit in *Church v. Kare Distribution, Inc.* [211 Fed. Appx. 278 (5th Cir. 2006)] In the case, a company, whose customers primarily spoke Spanish, implemented a policy requiring that its sales representatives be bilingual in English and Spanish. The terminated employee, a Caucasian who did not speak Spanish, claimed that his termination was tantamount to discrimination on the basis of national origin. The court, recognizing that the bilingual policy was implemented for a legitimate business reason and applied across the board to all affected employees and to whom the company provided company-sponsored courses in Spanish, held that the policy was not discriminatory based on national origin and affirmed the dismissal of the terminated employee's complaint.

Q 4:49   Have charges of discrimination based on national origin by individuals of Arab descent increased after 9/11?

The EEOC is reported to have received an "unprecedented" increase (threefold) of claims involving workers of Middle Eastern, Muslim, and South Asian descent since September 11, 2001, prompting the EEOC to step-up outreach efforts to educate employers and more precisely track the volume of these type of clams by specific internal designation in the future. [18 *Employment Discrimination Report (EDR)* (BNA) 268 (Mar. 6, 2002)] The EEOC reported that in the eight months following 9/11, it received 497 complaints of discrimination against Muslims, as opposed to 193 during the same time period in the prior year. [18 *Employment Discrimination Report (EDR)* (BNA) 605 (May 22, 2002)] The National Asian Pacific American Legal Consortium Rights group is reported to have received over 70 reports of harassment and discrimination against workers of predominately Indian and Pakistani descent in the six months following 9/11. [18 *Employment Discrimination Report (EDR)* (BNA) 298 (Mar. 13, 2002)] Since Fiscal Year 2001, charge statistics maintained by the EEOC show that national origin charges of discrimination have increased from 8,025 in Fiscal Year 2001, to 11,134 in Fiscal Year 2009. In Fiscal Year 2011, the agency reported a total of 11,833 charges of national origin discrimination filed. In Fiscal year 2012, the EEOC reported that 10,883 national origin discrimination charges were filed. [http://www.eeoc.gov]

Q 4:50   Do illegal aliens enjoy the same benefits under U.S. labor laws as documented aliens who are authorized to work in the United States?

In a controversial decision, the U.S. Supreme Court ruled that the National Labor Relations Board (NLRB) could not order a company to give back pay to an illegal alien as a penalty for committing an unfair labor practice (discharging the illegal alien for union activities in violation of the National Labor Relations Act). [Hoffman Plastic Compounds, Inc. v. NLRB, 535 U.S. 137 (2002)] However, post-*Hoffman* decisions indicate its limitations with many courts as it applies to the rights of illegal aliens working in this country. For example, in *Madeira v. Affordable Housing Foundation, Inc.* [315 F. Supp. 2d 504 (2004)], the court, although recognizing the *Hoffman* decision, held that it had no applicability to claims under state labor laws. Specifically, the court held that the employee's alien status as an illegal alien did not prevent him from recovering compensatory damages for the company's violation of New York labor law. As the court stated:

> And the fact is, undocumented aliens do obtain work in the United States. Recognizing this incontrovertible fact, New York's public does not bar compensation in the form of back pay for undocumented workers who are injured in the manner of the instant plaintiff. [315 F. Supp. 2d 504, 507]

Not to be outdone, the Ninth Circuit went even further in what may appear to some to be a clear attempt to avoid the apparent mandate of *Hoffman*. In *Rivera v. Nibco, Inc.* [364 F.3d 1057 (9th Cir. 2004)], a number of female immigrants formerly employed by a factory brought an action against their employer alleging national origin discrimination in violation of Title VII. During discovery, the defendant corporation sought to determine the plaintiffs' immigration status, undoubtedly seeking to determine whether they would have a *Hoffman*-based defense to the claims. The plaintiffs refused to provide information regarding their immigration status, and the trial court entered a protective order precluding the employer from using discovery to inquire into the plaintiffs' immigration status. On appeal, the Ninth Circuit concluded that the harm caused by forcing the plaintiffs to disclose their immigration status outweighed any right of the employer to obtain this discovery in that, by revealing their immigration status, any plaintiffs found to be undocumented might face criminal prosecution or deportation. As to *Hoffman*, the court read the decision narrowly and seriously questioned whether it had any applicability to Title VII cases, and concluded it clearly did not speak as to discovery issues. In *Zavala v. Wal-Mart Stores, Inc.* [393 F. Supp. 295 (D. Ct. N.J. 2005)], the court joined a growing number of courts and held that illegal aliens are covered by the Fair Labor Standards Act (FLSA). In *Sandoval v. Rizzuti Farms, Ltd.* [2009 WL 959478 (E.D. Wash. Apr. 7, 2009)], the court was faced with the issue of whether to allow the employer to obtain information regarding the plaintiffs' immigration status in connection with a class action complaint alleging violation of several federal and state laws protecting workers. Citing *Rivera*, the court held that the potential harm in providing immigration information to the employer outweighed any benefit in connection with these proceedings and granted the issuance of a protective order to prevent the employer from obtaining such information. Similarly, in *Widjaja v. Kang Yue USA Corp.* [2010 WL 2132068 (E.D.N.Y. May 20, 2010)], the court denied the employer's motion to gain access to the plaintiffs' immigration status that sued their employer for wage claims under the FLSA. In *Bollinger Shipyards, Inc. v. Director, Office of Workers' Compensation Programs* [604 F.3d 864 (5th Cir. 2010)], the court held that the fact that an employee had provided a false Social Security number to obtain employment in violation of IRCA did not preclude him from receiving workers' compensation benefits. In *Villareal v. El Chile, Inc.* [266 F.R.D., 207 (N.D. Ill. Mar. 1, 2010)], the court held that an employee's immigration status is not relevant to an FLSA claim for unpaid wages for work previously performed. In a Texas wrongful death action of an undocumented worker, a federal district court held that IRCA did not preempt state law permitting the award of lost future wages attributable to undocumented workers death. [*Vargas v. Kiewit La. Co.*, 2012 WL 2952171 (S.D. Tex. July 18, 2012)] The issue of future lost wages being awarded as damages to an undocumented worker who, under IRCA, may be deported such that future wages may not be obtained was squarely addressed by the court in *Wielgus v. Ryobi Technologies, Inc.* [2012 WL 2367883 (N.D. Ill. June 21, 2012)] The employee had sued the manufacturer of a table saw in a products-liability action and was seeking future lost wages from the manufacturer. Although the employee was undocumented, and therefore future lost wages at his current employer were uncertain due to his undocumented status, the court held that IRCA did not preempt state law allowing the recovery of future lost wages by the undocumented worker, albeit, at the rate that he would receive at the undocumented worker's residence country as opposed to his current employer.

Q 4:51   Can an employer that discharges an employee for failure to provide sufficient information to document that the employee can legally work in the United States be liable for national origin discrimination?

Due to the employer's IRCA obligations and the provision of civil and criminal penalties for knowingly employing illegal aliens, an employer that terminates an employee for failure to provide documentary evidence of his or her right to work within the United States should provide a sufficient defense to claims of national origin discrimination. In *Zamora v. Elite Logistics, Inc.* [316 F. Supp. 2d 1107 (D. Kan. 2004)], a Hispanic employee brought an action against his employer claiming, among other things, national origin discrimination in violation Title VII as a result of his layoff. Although the employee presented suitable documentation required by the IRCA when he was hired, subsequently, the employer, in preparation for possible inspection by the Immigration and Naturalization Service, received credible information indicating that the former employee's documentation was not genuine. The employer confronted the employee and offered him 10 days to produce documentation of his right to work within the United States. When he did not do so, the company informed him that he was being taken off work indefinitely. The court reasoned that, in light of the penalties, both criminal and civil, under the IRCA against employers for knowingly employing illegal aliens, the company had a legitimate non-discriminatory reason for both requiring the employee to produce documents that adequately evidenced his right to work in this country, and to lay him off indefinitely when he failed to do so after 10-days notice.

Q 4:52   If an employer treats an employee differently because of an accent, is such action national origin discrimination?

Individuals from different ethnic backgrounds may speak English with distinct accents and in distinct manners. For this reason, the EEOC will find national origin discrimination if an employer takes action against an employee because of an accent or manner of speaking connected with national origin, unless the employer can articulate a legitimate, non-discriminatory reason or business necessity for doing so. An individual who speaks severely broken English may not be qualified to fill a receptionist position, for example, as a matter of business necessity.

In *Rivera v. Baccarat* [S.D.N.Y. No. 95-9478 (Feb. 6, 1998)], a federal jury awarded $500,000 to a saleswoman for insults and ridicule attributable to her Spanish accent followed by a dismissal for speaking Spanish on the job. [*See* 10 *Employment Discrimination Report (EDR)* (BNA) 216-217 (Feb. 18, 1998).] This verdict was reduced by the court to $100,000, after finding that front pay was not awardable because of the plaintiff's failure to mitigate her damages. [12 *Employment Discrimination Report (EDR)* (BNA) 138 (Jan. 27, 1999)]

Q 4:53   How is national origin discrimination proved?

As with other discrimination prohibitions under Title VII, national origin discrimination can be proved through either evidence of disparate treatment or disparate impact. Under the theory of disparate treatment, discriminatory motive must be proved; it can be inferred through comparative or statistical evidence that demonstrates that people of one national origin are treated differently than other people under similar circumstances. Certainly, direct evidence of illegal motive through evidence of slurs and stereotypes provides a basis to infer disparate-treatment discrimination. Under the disparate-impact theory, general rules that are facially neutral but adversely affect individuals within specific national origins will also be treated as illegal discrimination, unless the facially neutral policy or procedure can be supported because it is job-related or a matter of business necessity.

Discrimination Based on Religion

Q 4:54   What is *religious discrimination*?

If employment decisions are based on an employee's religious affiliation or convictions, or if an employer refuses reasonably to accommodate an individual's religious convictions or obligations, religious discrimination has occurred.

Section 703 of Title VII provides that it is unlawful for an employer:

> (1) To fail or refuse to hire or [to] discharge any individual, or otherwise to discriminate against any individual with respect to his compensation, conditions or privileges of employment because of such individual's . . . religion . . . ; or
>
> (2) to limit, segregate or classify his employees or applicants for employment in any way which would deprive or tend to deprive any individual of any employment opportunities or otherwise adversely affect his status as an employee because of an individual's . . . religion. . . . [42 U.S.C. § 2000e-2]

In addition to these prohibitions, which are consistent with other forms of discrimination, there is an additional obligation for employers to accommodate an individual's religious beliefs. This obligation is found within the definition of *religion* under Title VII and provides:

> The term "religion" includes all aspects of religious observance and practice as well as belief, unless an employer demonstrates that he is unable to reasonably accommodate an employee's religious observance or practice without undue hardship on the conduct of the employer's business. [42 U.S.C. § 2000e(j)]

Q 4:55 What religious practices or beliefs are subject to protection under Title VII?

The EEOC interprets religious practices broadly to include "moral or ethical beliefs as to what is right or wrong, which are sincerely held with the strength of traditional religious views." [29 C.F.R. § 1605.1] Although traditional organized religion certainly falls within the standard for protection under Title VII, sincere beliefs that are not attached to traditional beliefs are also likely afforded protection under Title VII. The EEOC's standard for determining protected religious beliefs is taken from cases defining the scope of conscientious-objector status in the military. [Welsh v. United States, 398 U.S. 333 (1970); United States v. Seeger, 380 U.S. 163 (1965)]

In *Seeger* and *Welsh*, the Court was asked to determine whether an individual not affiliated with any traditional denomination can claim conscientious-objector status in the military. Although both Seeger and Welsh claimed to have been brought up in religious environments and to have attended church in their childhoods, neither continued their ties with their native churches into adulthood and neither belonged to or was affiliated with any religious group or adhered to any teaching of an organized religious group as adults. In addition, the organized religion that they observed as children did not teach their members not to engage in war at any time for any reason. Nonetheless, both insisted that they held deep conscientious beliefs against taking part in a war in which people were killed, and both believed that killing in war was wrong, unethical, and immoral. Seeger did not attach any specific belief in relation to any supreme being, but nevertheless decried the "spiritual price" man must pay to engage in killing people in war. Likewise, Welsh neither affirmed nor denied his belief in a supreme being, but left the question open.

Although neither plaintiff ascribed his conscientious-objector status to any organized or traditional religion or belief in a supreme being, the Court was satisfied that their beliefs were entitled to as much protection as those derived from traditional religious convictions. As the Court stated in *Welsh*:

> Because his beliefs function as a religion in his life, such an individual is as much entitled to a religious conscientious objector exemption under 6(j) as is someone who derives his conscientious objection to war from traditional religious convictions. [398 U.S. 33 at 335]

Following *Welsh* and *Seeger*, the EEOC accords religious protection to sincerely held views of right and wrong that fall outside traditional religious teachings and practices.

Dress and personal grooming habits related to religious beliefs may be subject to protection under religious discrimination law as well. For example, an arbitrator had held that a company did not have good cause to terminate a Muslim employee who refused for religious reasons to tuck in his shirt in accordance with a company dress code policy. [*See* 10 *Employment Discrimination Report (EDR)* (BNA) 42 (Jan. 14, 1998).] Similarly, a U.S. District Court granted an injunction against the suspension of a police officer who refused to cut his dreadlocks, claiming that his dreadlocks were based upon religious beliefs and his African-American culture. [*See* Robinson v. District of Columbia Gov't, D.C. No. 97-787 (July 17, 1997); 9 *Employment Discrimination Report (EDR)* (BNA) 150.] The Fourth Circuit reinstated a correctional officer's claims of religious discrimination based on discipline he received for dreadlocks that he wore based on his Rastafarian religious beliefs. [*See* Booth v. Maryland, No. 02-1657 (4th Cir. Apr. 30, 2003), discussed in 20 *Employment Discrimination Report (EDR)* (BNA) 646 (May 14, 2003).] In *Fraternal Order of Police Newark Lodge No. 12 v. Newark* [3d Cir. No. 97-5342 (Mar. 3, 1999)], the U.S. Court of Appeals for the Third Circuit held that a no-beard policy, subject only to exceptions for medical reasons, unlawfully discriminated against Muslim officers who grew beards for religious reasons. [*See* 12 *Employment Discrimination Report (EDR)* (BNA) 390 (Mar. 17, 1999).] As a result of a lawsuit instituted by the EEOC [EEOC v. Federal Express Corp., S.D. Ga. No. CV 100-50, consent decree filed May 24, 2001], Federal Express is reported to have agreed to modify its "no beard" policy by permitting employees who wear beards for religious reasons to seek an exception to the policy. [*See* 16 *Employment Discrimination Report (EDR)* (BNA) 868 (June 29, 2001).]

Although it seems that courts are deferential to professed religious beliefs when analyzing claims of religious discrimination, there are limits. For example, in *EEOC v. Allendale Nursing Home Center* [996 F. Supp. 712 (W.D. Mich. 1998)], the employee was fired for refusing to provide a Social Security number, claiming that the Social Security Administration was "unbiblical" and that her deeply held religious beliefs did not allow her to obtain a Social Security number. Despite her claim, the court ultimately concluded that the employee's discharge as a result of her refusal to provide a Social Security number was not religious discrimination under Title VII. The Seventh Circuit rejected a similar claim by an applicant who claimed that the Social Security number was the "mark of the beast" and refused to provide it to the employer. The court reasoned that it was not necessary for an employer to violate the Internal Revenue Code in order to accommodate the applicant's professed religious beliefs. [14 *Employment Discrimination Report (EDR)* (BNA) 321 (Mar. 8, 2000)] In 2002, a California court of appeals court held that veganism was not a religious belief, providing no basis for religious discrimination by an employee who was denied work for refusal to take a vaccine grown in chicken embryos. [*See* "California Appeal Court Decides Veganism Not Protected Religious Creed Under FEHA," 19 *Employment Discrimination Report (EDR)* (BNA) 335 (Sept. 25, 2002).]

Similarly, in *Baltgalvis v. Newport News Shipbuilding, Inc.* [132 F. Supp. 2d 414 (E.D. Va. 2001)], a newly hired employee refused to give her employer her Social Security number for religious reasons. She contended that use of the Social Security number represented the "mark of the beast" as described in the Bible's Book of Revelation. In order to accommodate her religious convictions, she asked that another number be used to identify her in the company records. After she was terminated for refusing to provide her Social Security number, she sued, claiming violation of Title VII for the company's refusal to accommodate her religious beliefs. Recognizing as the court did that the Internal Revenue Service (IRS), and not the company, requires employers to provide the Social Security numbers of their employees, and provides penalties for failure to comply, the court found that the plaintiff failed to establish a case of religious discrimination under Title VII. In addition, the request for accommodation, the court concluded, would pose an undue hardship for the company, in that failure to comply with the IRS is a violation of federal law.

In *Mohamed-Sheik v. Golden Foods/Golden Brands LLC* [3:03CV-737-H, 2006 U.S. Dist. LEXIS 11248 (W.D. Ky. Mar. 16, 2006)], the court, finding numerous precedents for the proposition that employers are not obligated to accommodate a religious concern when doing so would potentially create a safety risk, remanded the case to the trial court to determine whether such a risk was present in connection with a claimed policy that required employees to tuck in their shirts, which the discharged employee contended was against her religious beliefs If the employer can demonstrate that the requested accommodation concerning dress is a safety or security hazard, the employer will typically not be required to accommodate the request under Title VII. For example in *EEOC v. GEO Group, Inc.* [616 F.3d 265 (3d Cir. 2010)], the EEOC sued a private employer that was contracted to run a prison for a violation of Title VII for not allowing Muslim women employees to wear headdress, which the employees claimed was required by their religious beliefs. However, the court found that the banning of headdress was legitimate for safety and security reasons, and as such, the prison was not required to accommodate these employees under Title VII.

Q 4:56   How can religious discrimination be proved under Title VII?

As with other forms of discrimination, religious discrimination can be proved under either disparate-treatment or disparate-impact theories. To prove disparate treatment, the plaintiff must demonstrate that he or she was treated differently because of his or her religion. Under disparate-treatment theory, motive must be proved. Derogatory language and slurs based on religious beliefs are direct evidence of a discriminatory motive for religious discrimination. Because direct evidence of discriminatory motive is often difficult, if not impossible, to prove, as in other claims of discrimination, courts and administrative agencies look to circumstantial evidence to infer a discriminatory motive. This can be done by examining comparable situations and statistical evidence.

In addition, religious discrimination may be proved if a facially neutral policy or procedure has a disparate impact on an individual because of his or her religion. Even if adverse impact can be demonstrated, the procedure or practice is not illegal religious discrimination if the facially neutral policy or procedure is job-related or supported by business necessity. To avoid religious discrimination, employers must also accommodate applicants' or employees' religious practices and beliefs. The affirmative "reasonable accommodation" requirement is distinct for religious discrimination under Title VII and different from the reasonable accommodation obligations under the ADA.

Employees may also bring claims for hostile work environment—so-called religious harassment claims—under Title VII as well. The developed law covering hostile work environment claims in sexual harassment actions is typically utilized in assessing whether or not religious harassment can be maintained as a matter of law or effect.

Q 4:57   Can religious institutions discriminate on the basis of religion?

Title VII provides both exceptions and exemptions from religious discrimination claims for religious corporations, associations, and educational in situations under certain circumstances. By allowing these exceptions and exemptions, the law recognizes that it is legitimate for religious entities to rely on religion in making certain employment decisions. Specifically, Section 702 of Title VII contains an exemption for religious institutions that provides:

> (a) This subchapter [Title VII] shall not apply to an employer with respect to . . . a religious corporation, association, educational institution, or a society with respect to individuals of a particular religion to perform work connected with a carrying on by such corporation, association, educational institution or society of its activities. [42 U.S.C. § 2000e-1]

Similarly, Title VII provides a specific exception for religious educational institutions:

> It will not be an unlawful employment practice for a school, college, university or other educational institution or institution of learning to hire employees of a particular religion if such school, college, university

or other educational institution of learning is, in whole or in substantial part, owned, supported, controlled or managed by a particular religion or a particular religious corporation, association, society, or if the curriculum of such school, college or university or institution of learning is directed toward the propagation of a particular religion. [42 U.S.C. § 2000e-2(e)(2)]

In *Kennedy v. St. Joseph's Ministries, Inc.* [657 F.3d 189 (4th Cir. 2011)], the court held that a tax-exempt religious organization that operates a nursing care facility and conducts itself under the direction of a religious order within the Catholic church and maintains its facility in accordance with church principals was exempt from Title VII claims of religious discrimination by an employee under the religious organization exemption. However, religious institutions may have liability for other types of discrimination under Title VII subject to the so-called "ministerial exception" to civil rights laws recognized by many courts.

Claims of pregnancy discrimination periodically occur in connection with religious employers who, on the basis of church doctrine, terminate pregnant employees. In *Redhead v. Conference of Seventh-Day Adventists* [440 F. Supp. 2d 211 (E.D.N.Y. 2006)], a former teacher sued a religious school claiming that the school violated the Pregnancy Discrimination Act (PDA) and Title VII by terminating her for being pregnant and unmarried. The religious school maintained it had a right to terminate the teacher due to her employment agreement and school policy that provide for termination in the event of immoral or unsatisfactory personal conduct inconsistent with the principles of the church. Moreover, the religious school maintained that plaintiff could not maintain her claim either under the constitutional "ministerial exception" to civil rights laws or under the Religious Freedom Restoration Act (RFRA) which restricts governmental intrusion into the exercise of religion. Noting that there were allegations of male employees at the religious institution that may have engaged in sexual relations outside of marriage and who were not terminated, the court concluded that because the plaintiff's teaching duties were mainly secular, that neither the ministerial exception or the RFRA was applicable to their analysis of the case, and remanded the case for further proceeding as to whether, among other things, non-pregnant employees were treated differently than others as it relates to sex outside of marriage.

On the other hand, courts may provide protection to a religious institution for terminating employees who engage in conduct clearly contrary to established church doctrine. Such was the case in *Curay-Cramer v. Ursuline Academy of Wilmington, Delaware, Inc.* [450 F.3d 130 (3d Cir. 2006)] In *Curay-Cramer*, a former teacher claimed the Catholic school violated the PDA when she was terminated from the school as a result of her public endorsement in an advertisement supporting pro-choice and the U.S. Supreme Court decision of *Roe v. Wade.* [410 U.S. 1123 (1973)] Utilizing the analysis of the U.S. Supreme Court decision in *NLRB v. Catholic Bishop of Chicago* [440 U.S. 490 (1979)], which sets forth a framework to determine whether federal statute as applied in a particular factual situation violated the constitution, the court concluded that the circumstances in this case were such that to apply federal statute would impermissibly delve into inquiry into the religious employer's religious mission and religious justification for the employment decision, such that it raises serious constitutional questions and was therefore impermissible in the case at hand.

Q 4:58   What is reasonable accommodation of an employee's religious beliefs?

Section 701(j) of Title VII requires that, absent undue hardship, an employer must reasonably accommodate the religious needs of its employees. An employer may have to allow an employee to wear a costume, headpiece, or emblem peculiar to a particular religion or to allow the employee to work out a schedule that permits absence on religious holidays. Dismissing an employee who refuses to work on his or her Sabbath may leave an employer open to a charge of religious discrimination. Before an employer can fire such an employee, it must be sure that no reasonable accommodation of the employee's religious belief is possible without undue harm to the business. The emphasis is on "reasonable." For instance, an employer is not required to force some employees to work every Saturday so that a Seventh Day Adventist can consistently observe the Saturday Sabbath. Nor must an employer allow a Muslim to wear a turban in lieu of a hard hat if job safety requires the hard hat. In addition, increased costs to the employer, if significant, may constitute undue hardship under Title VII.

Probably the most significant case establishing the obligations and limitations of reasonable accommodation of religious beliefs is *Trans World Airlines, Inc. v. Hardison* [432 U.S. 63 (1977)]. Hardison was discharged when he refused to work on Saturdays, his Sabbath. Hardison's position with TWA was determined in accordance with a collective bargaining agreement between his union and TWA. At a prior position, Hardison had sufficient seniority under the collective bargaining agreement to avoid working on Saturday; however, Hardison then sought and received a transfer to a different position. In accordance with the collective bargaining agreement, Hardison was placed near the bottom of his new seniority list. With his seniority affected, Hardison was scheduled for Saturday work. When Hardison refused to work Saturdays, he was fired. Before he was terminated, TWA made some attempt to accommodate Hardison's religion by asking the union to seek a change of work assignment; the union refused to do so because it would have violated the seniority system. The union proposed that TWA permit Hardison to work only four days per week, but TWA refused on the basis that it would impair critical functions of the airlines operations.

The Supreme Court, in reviewing the case, concluded that TWA had reasonably accommodated Hardison and that it was not required to implement any of the accommodations proffered by the court of appeals because all would have imposed an undue hardship on the company. In determining reasonable accommodation, the Court enunciated two basic principles. First, absent evidence of discriminatory motive, a seniority system that is part of a collectively bargained agreement cannot be an unlawful employment practice, even if the system is discriminatory in its effect. In other words, TWA was not required to ignore a collectively bargained seniority system to accommodate Hardison's religious beliefs. Second, to require TWA to bear more than a de minimis cost to give Hardison Saturdays off would be an undue hardship. The facts of the case demonstrated that to allow Hardison to work only four days per week would pose an additional financial burden on TWA. Because the cost of overtime would be above the de minimis threshold, the Court concluded that TWA was not required to allow Hardison to work only four days a week to accommodate his religious beliefs.

In *Tiano v. Dillard Department Stores* [139 F.3d 679 (9th Cir. Ariz. 1998)], at issue was whether a department store engaged in religious discrimination by failing to accommodate an employee's request for a leave for purposes of traveling to Yugoslavia on a pilgrimage in response to a "calling from God" when the department store had a "no leave" policy during its busy season. Although the department store apparently offered the employee alternate leave periods after its busy season, the employee felt compelled to leave during the busy season and, as the company warned, was fired as a result. The court, in analyzing the case under Title VII religious discrimination law, held that the desire to embark on the pilgrimage, which involved viewing religious images in Yugoslavia at a particular time in October 1997, was not religious calling, there being no sufficient explanation as to why her religious beliefs required that she not delay her trip. [*See* 10 *Employment Discrimination Report (EDR)* (BNA) 377-78 (Mar. 25, 1998).] Similarly, in *Swartzentruber v. Gunite Corp.* [99 F. Supp. 2d 976 (N.D. Ind. 2000)], a federal judge held that a company's refusal to allow a self-professed KKK member to display an offensive tattoo openly was not religious discrimination, in that the employee failed to show how covering his tattoo while at work conflicted with his alleged religious beliefs. [*See* 15 *Employment Discrimination Report (EDR)* (BNA) 14 (July 5, 2000).] In *Anderson v. U.S.F. Logistics (IMC), Inc.* [274 F.3d 470 (7th Cir. Ind. 2001)], it was reported that the Seventh Circuit refused to issue an injunction against an employer that prohibited its employee from the salutation, "Have a blessed day," when ending communications with its customers that object to the phrase. It found that the salutation was not a religious practice per se and in any event, was reasonably accommodated by allowing the employee to selectively use the phrase with customers who do not object. [18 *Employment Discrimination Report (EDR)* (BNA) 7 (Jan. 2, 2002)]

In issues involving safety, courts are reluctant to impose obligations to accommodate when to do so would expose the worker to increased risk of injury. In *Kalsi v. New York City Transit Authority* [62 F. Supp. 2d 745 (E.D.N.Y. 1998)], a federal judge dismissed a religious discrimination claim based on the plaintiff's discharge for failure to wear a hard hat on the job. The plaintiff, a Sikh, claimed exemption for religious reasons. The court found the policy a legitimate safety-based requirement for the job, and refused to impose an obligation to transfer the plaintiff to a non-hard-hat-wearing position in violation of a bona fide seniority system under the collective bargaining agreement, determining such a transfer an undue hardship under *TWA v. Hardison*. [432 U.S. 63 (1977); *see* 12 *Employment Discrimination Report (EDR)* (BNA) 8 (Jan. 16, 1999).] In *EEOC v. GEO Group, Inc.* [616 F.3d 265 (3d Cir. 2010)], the EEOC sued a private employer that was contracted to run a prison for a violation of

Title VII for not allowing Muslim women employees to wear headdress, which the employees claimed was required by their religious beliefs. However, the court found that the banning of headdress was legitimate for safety and security reasons, and as such, the prison was not required to accommodate these employees under Title VII.

In addition, courts oftentimes determine that the accommodation offered by the employer is sufficient under the law. For example, in a First Circuit case, an employee of Costco Wholesale Corporation sued her employer claiming that it failed to offer her a reasonable religious accommodation after she alerted them of a conflict of the company's "no facial jewelry" policy in its dress code and her religious practice as a member of the Church of Body Modification. She claimed the failure of Costco to accommodate her religious beliefs was religious discrimination in violation of Title VII. In reviewing the prior court's decision, the First Circuit concluded that Costco had reasonably accommodated the employee by offering to reinstate her if she either covered her facial piercing with a band-aid or replaced it with a clear retainer. The court held that any further accommodations were not required under Title VII because to do so would impose an undue hardship on Costco. [Cloutier v. Costco Wholesale Corp., 390 F.3d 126 (1st Cir. 2004)] As the court held in *Porter v. City of Chicago* [700 F.3d 944 (7th Cir. 2012)], even though an employee was not interested in the employer's offer, the employer's suggestion that an employee change shifts to Sunday afternoon to accommodate her professed need to attend religious services on Sunday morning was an appropriate offer of an accommodation for her religious beliefs under Title VII, such that a violation of Title VII could not be maintained.

Q 4:59 Is reasonable accommodation in religious cases analogous to reasonable accommodation under the ADA?

Both the ADA and Title VII contain similar language for certain obligations of reasonable accommodation. Title VII imposes the obligation to accommodate an individual's religious beliefs, and the ADA requires reasonable accommodation for qualified individuals with disabilities. Both statutes provide that no accommodation is required that would impose an undue hardship on the employer. Nonetheless, the tests for determining what is and what is not a reasonable accommodation, and what is and what is not an undue hardship, are materially different under the two acts. In *TWA v. Hardison* [432 U.S. 63 (1977)], the Supreme Court held that any cost that exceeded a de minimis amount is an undue hardship for religious accommodation. On the other hand, under the ADA, an undue hardship is not determined until the cost of the accommodation, compared to the overall financial resources of the company, becomes excessively costly, excessively substantial, disruptive, or an accommodation that would substantially alter the nature or operation of the business.

Gender-Based Discrimination

Q 4:60   What is *sex discrimination*?

Sex discrimination exists under a variety of theories. Like other forms of discrimination, sex discrimination claims can be maintained under both disparate-treatment and disparate-impact theories. Generally, under disparate treatment, any employment decision based on a person's gender is actionable sex discrimination, unless there is a BFOQ for the gender-based distinction. Under disparate-impact theory, if a facially neutral policy disproportionately affects certain employees because of their gender, a claim for sex discrimination can be maintained unless the policy can be defended through its relationship to the job and business necessity. As Title VII provides:

(a) It shall be an unlawful employment practice for an employer—

(1) to fail or refuse to hire or to discharge any individual, or otherwise to discriminate against any individual with respect to his compensation, terms, conditions or privileges of employment because of such individual's sex; or

(2) to limit, segregate or classify his employees or applicants for employment in any way which would deprive to tend to deprive any individual of employment opportunities or otherwise adversely affect his status as employee because of such individual's . . . sex . . . [42 U.S.C. § 703(a)]

Sexual harassment is another form of sex discrimination prohibited under Title VII. Actions for sexual harassment can be maintained under theories of quid pro quo harassment, hostile work environment harassment, or gender-based harassment that is non-sexual in nature.

In 1978, Congress enacted the PDA, an amendment to Title VII that makes pregnancy discrimination unlawful sex discrimination [42 U.S.C. § 2000e(k)]

The terms "because of sex" or "on the basis of sex" [under Title VII] include, but are not limited to, because of or on the basis of pregnancy, child birth, or related medical conditions, and women affected by pregnancy, child birth or related medical conditions shall be treated the same for all employment-related purposes, including the receipt of benefits under fringe benefit programs, as other persons not so effected but similar in their ability or inability to work, and nothing in 703(h) of this Title shall be interpreted to permit otherwise. [42 U.S.C. § 2000(e)]

According to the EEOC's charge statistics, sex discrimination charges comprise about 30 percent of all charges filed each year since Fiscal Year 1997. [http://www.eeoc.gov]

Q 4:61   How is sex discrimination proved under Title VII?

Under the disparate-treatment theory of sex discrimination, a court looks to various evidence from which discriminatory motive may be inferred. Discriminatory motive must be found to maintain a claim based on disparate treatment. Direct evidence of discriminatory motive may exist in the form of slurs and gender-based stereotyping in sex discrimination cases, and such evidence is often difficult if not impossible to obtain; courts consequently look to the surrounding circumstances to determine whether a discriminatory motive can be inferred. Generally, this analysis employs comparables to determine whether similarly situated employees were treated differently on the basis of sex. In *Herron v. Chisolm* [2012 WL 4863128 (S.D. Ga. Oct. 4, 2012)], the court held that a claim that a male supervisor hired a male applicant because he was attracted to the male applicant does not state a gender discrimination claim because it suggests discrimination against both men and women who the supervisor is not sexually attracted to. [*See also* Herron v. Chisolm, 2012 WL 4753394 (S.D. Ga. Oct. 3, 2012).] In addition, particularly in cases of hiring, statistical evidence may be used to determine whether the practice of illegal sex discrimination can be inferred.

Assuming that an employee can show disparate treatment through direct, comparative or statistical evidence, the burden shifts to the employer to demonstrate that it had legitimate business reasons for its conduct. One possible defense to a charge of disparate treatment sex discrimination is that sex is a BFOQ for the position. Maintaining gender to be a BFOQ is extremely difficult and, more often than not, such a position is based upon sex stereotyping that is tantamount to illegal sex discrimination.

Another method of proving illegal sex discrimination is disparate-impact analysis. Under this analysis, sex discrimination can be inferred if a company's policies or procedures, even though facially neutral, have an adverse impact on an employee or prospective employee because of his or her gender. The employer must then demonstrate that, although disparate impact exists, the employer nonetheless has a legitimate non-discriminatory reason for its policy that is based on job-relatedness and business necessity.

Q 4:62   Can gender be a BFOQ for a position?

Historically, society often viewed certain jobs as either men's or women's work. Although many have attempted to demonstrate gender-based qualifications for various positions as BFOQs, those attempts have failed. Pursuant to the EEOC's guidelines on discrimination because of sex [29 C.F.R. § 1604.2], the commission specifies that a gender-based BFOQ should be interpreted narrowly and that a BFOQ defense does not provide a defense for illegal sex discrimination based on sexual stereotypes. The regulations specifically provide that a BFOQ may not be supported by the following:

- Assumptions that the turnover rate among women is higher than among men;
- Stereotyped characteristics of the sexes, such as men being less capable of assembling intricate equipment and women being less capable of aggressive salesmanship; or
- Refusal to hire an individual because of the preferences of co-workers, the employer, or clients and customers.

Some employers still believe that women, particularly married women, may be less dependable or have a higher turnover rate than men. This thinking is a good example of sex discrimination based on assumptions of comparative employment characteristics that the EEOC has determined are not sufficient to support a BFOQ. Antiquated notions of physical ability, agility, and suitability for a position based on gender are almost always founded on sexual stereotyping and, as a result, do not meet the burden of a BFOQ. If there is one lingering form of sex discrimination that some employers continue to condone, it occurs when an employer determines that its customer or client may have difficulty with a woman in a certain position and therefore restricts a woman's ability to enter into that position. Successful businesses know that the customer is always right, and employers often feel compelled to make gender-based decisions to propitiate a client or customer. Although many employers may feel such gender-based decisions are justified, the EEOC regulations make it clear that employment decisions based on the prejudices of clients, customers, or co-workers do not justify the BFOQ exception to gender-based decision.

Even the EEOC recognizes, however, that there may be some positions for which the BFOQ exception still survives. For instance, the regulations acknowledge that in the selection of actors, for purposes of authenticity, gender-based criteria may be used.

Q 4:63 Are only women protected under Title VII from illegal sex discrimination?

No. A man as well as a woman can be a victim of sex discrimination that is actionable under Title VII.

The issue of same-sex harassment was in contention in recent years. On the one hand, common sense would seem to dictate that Title VII should prohibit sexual harassment, regardless of whether the parties involved are of the same or opposite sex. If a victim is exposed to quid pro quo harassment or a hostile working environment, why should it make a difference under federal law whether the harasser is of the same or opposite sex? On the other hand, some argue that same-sex harassment was not an issue sought to be addressed by Title VII sex discrimination claims.

The Supreme Court, in *Oncale v. Sundowner Offshore Services* [523 U.S. 75 (1998)], settled this issue once and for all, holding that same-sex harassment is actionable under Title VII. Although, as the Court observed, male-on-male harassment was not the "principal evil" that was envisioned by Congress when it promulgated Title VII, it held that "sexual harassment must extend to sexual harassment of any kind that meets the statutory requirements." Joseph Oncale was employed as roustabout on an eight-man oil platform in the Gulf of Mexico. Oncale alleged that while working on the platform in an all-male environment, he was repeatedly subjected to sex-related, humiliating actions by co-workers and his supervisor, physically assaulted in a sexual manner, and threatened with rape. Oncale's complaints to supervisory personnel produced no remedial action. Although cautioning that its decision was not to be construed as a "general civility code" for workplaces, nonetheless, the Court held that objectively offensive sexual harassment that is sufficiently severe or pervasive to create a hostile and abusive work environment is actionable, even in an all-male/same-sex situation.

A critical criterion of any same-sex harassment claim, according to *Oncale*, is a showing that the conduct or behavior is "because of sex." Many courts, post-*Oncale*, have struggled with this requirement. Some courts have held that "because of sex" means that the conduct or communication is: (1) a sexual solicitation; (2) that the conduct or communications demonstrates a hostility of the gender in the workplace; or (3) that comparatively, the other gender was not exposed to the same conduct or communication. [*See* English v. Pohanka of Chantilly, 190 F. Supp. 2d 833 (E.D. Va. 2002), discussed in 19 *Employment Discrimination Report (EDR)* (BNA) 370 (Mar. 27, 2002).] The Sixth Circuit, following the "colorful" opinion of Judge Ralph Guy, criticized use of comparative gender analysis in same-sex situations and held that "because of sex" should not include situations where one does not expose the opposite sex to conduct which it exposes to its own sex, lest the "equal-opportunity" harasser evades liability. [EEOC v. Harbert-Yeargin, Inc., 266 F.3d 498 (6th Cir. 2001)] As Judge Guy wrote:

> Georgie Porgie pudding and pie
> Goosed the men and made them cry
> Upon the women he laid no hand
> So it cost his employer 300 grand.

Q 4:64   Is it reverse discrimination to treat biological mothers and fathers differently in disability leave policies?

Although one typically views Title VII sex discrimination claims as claims of illegal discrimination mounted by women, so-called reverse discrimination claims are cognizable under Title VII. In *Johnson v. University of Iowa* [431 F.3d 325 (8th Cir. 2005)], a biological father brought a class action challenging a public university's parental leave policy that allowed biological mothers to use accumulated sick leave upon the arrival of a new child but did not extend the same benefit to biological fathers. Although it would appear that the policy on its face was discriminatory, the court, in analyzing the policy, concluded that the sick leave was more akin to disability leave, as opposed to leave to care for the newborn, which could be used by both the biological mother and the biological father. However, having found the leave more akin to disability leave, and the fact that the biological father obviously did not go through the physical trauma of labor, this was a distinguishing characteristic between the biological mother and the biological father, which prevented the biological father from establishing a prima facie case under Title VII. Simply put, he could not argue that he was "similarly situated" to the mother for purposes of Title VII analysis.

Q 4:65 Are employment decisions that are gender-based stereotypes actionable under Title VII?

Use of stereotypical notions of the relative characteristics of males and females in making employment decisions is usually tantamount to illegal discrimination. In *Price Waterhouse v. Hopkins* [490 U.S. 228 (1989)], the Supreme Court held that an employer's use of sexual stereotypes in deciding whether to make a female employee a partner in an accounting firm was illegal discrimination under Title VII. The plaintiff in this case was evaluated for partnership and turned down. Her job performance apparently was outstanding in most ways; notably, she had brought a $25 million government account into the company's Washington office. Some partners commented, however, that she projected the wrong image of a female partner; those comments included suggestions that she wear more makeup and change her hairstyle, even that she enroll in "charm school." Consequently, *Hopkins* is an important case because it recognizes decisions based on stereotypes as illegal discrimination under Title VII.

Interestingly, however, there are limitations as to how far courts are willing to go on this subject. For example, in *Harper v. Blockbuster Entertainment Corp.* [139 F.3d 1385 (11th Cir. Fla. 1998)], four male employees who had been fired for violation of the company's hair length policy for males instituted discrimination claims for gender bias under Title VII. Although women were permitted to have long hair, men were not—clearly an embodiment of a stereotypical notion of male versus female grooming. The court dismissed the claim, noting that federal courts have uniformly rejected claims against company policies prohibiting males, as opposed to females, from having long hair. It has been reported that the EEOC has concluded that "court challenges to workplace grooming rules that differentiate between the length of male and female employees' hair are virtually impossible to win." [*See* 10(20) *Employment Discrimination Report (EDR)* (BNA) 636 (May 20, 1998).] As such, when men and women are treated similarly with respect to grooming standards, even if the grooming standards are different based on grooming standards for each sex, gender discrimination claims should fail. For example, in *Jesperson v. Harrah's Operating Co., Inc.* [392 F.3d 1076 (9th Cir. 2004)], a female bartender at the casino who was terminated for refusing to wear make-up and keep her hair in a "teased, curled or styled" manner, claimed sex discrimination under Title VII because men bartenders were not required to groom accordingly. However, under the casino's standards, men also had grooming standards that, although did not involve make-up and teased hair, nonetheless had requirements that burdened men only, such as the requirement that men maintain short haircuts and neatly trimmed nails. Although noting the Supreme Court decision of *Price Waterhouse v. Hopkins* [490 U.S. 228 (1989)], which held that failure to conform to commonly accepted gender stereotypes is sex discrimination in violation of Title VII, after canvassing relevant case law, the court concluded that *Price Waterhouse* has not been extended to address the specific question of whether an employer can impose different grooming standards on its male and female employees. Given that both sexes were required to conform to dress and grooming standards, although different, the court concluded the claim could not be maintained.

However, the issue of whether sex stereotyping in and of itself is sufficient to maintain a Title VII claim was recently addressed in *Lewis v. Heartland Inns of America, LLC.* [585 F. Supp. 2d 1046 (S.D. Iowa 2008)] In the case, the plaintiff claimed that she was terminated because she did not conform to traditional feminine stereotypes. The plaintiff testified that she was told prior to her termination that she lacked the "Midwestern girl look." Although the U.S. Supreme Court has long maintained that sex stereotyping may be a component to a discrimination claim under *Price Waterhouse v. Hopkins* [490 U.S. 228 (1989)], the plaintiff, must show that the treatment to which plaintiff was subjected to is such that it puts one person's sex at a disadvantage compared to a person of the opposite sex. As such, the court concluded that the mere existence of sex stereotyping is not, in and of itself, sufficient to support an actionable claim under Title VII. Although sexual orientation is not a protected category under Title VII, discrimination based on sexual stereotypes may lie if a company discriminates against a homosexual because he or she does not conform to gender stereotypes. In *Koren v. Ohio Bell Telephone Co.* [2012 WL 3484825 (N.D. Ohio Aug. 14, 2012)], a homosexual male claimed he was terminated for failing to conform to gender stereotypes because, contrary to gender norms, he had taken his spouse's surname. However, the court concluded that there were sufficient issues of fact precluding summary judgment on the issues. In *Hunter v. United Parcel Service, Inc.* [697 F.3d 697 (8th Cir. 2012)], a transgender applicant claimed that he was not hired because he was transgendered, but could not maintain a claim under Title VII when there was no evidence that the employer was aware of his transgendered status.

Q 4:66   May an employer discharge an employee because of pregnancy?

Private employers with 15 or more employees are subject to the PDA (see Q 4:60), which prohibits discriminatory treatment of pregnant women. Consequently, employers may not discharge an employee because of pregnancy or treat pregnancy-related disabilities differently from any other temporary disability. Employers should develop a neutral disability and sick-leave policy and make certain that the policy is administered so that it does not discriminate against pregnant women.

General guidelines include the following:

- A pregnant woman may not be denied any job solely because she is pregnant, if she is physically able to perform the necessary functions of the job.
- A pregnant employee may not be required to take a leave of absence if she is able to perform her job duties.

- A pregnant employee who requests leave is entitled to it on the same basis that leaves are granted for other temporary disabilities.

- If an employee cannot perform some of the functions of her job because of pregnancy or a related condition, her employer must allow her to perform modified tasks or an alternative assignment if it provides such opportunities to employees who are temporarily disabled for other reasons.

- An employer may not take adverse action against a pregnant employee because of the employer's preference for non-pregnant workers or the similar preferences of co-workers, customers, or clients.

- An employee on leave for a pregnancy-related condition must have the same right to return to her job or work as other employees on sick or disability leaves.

Q 4:67   How important is timing in a pregnancy discrimination case?

Adverse actions taken by an employer soon after it learns of its employee's pregnancy are always suspect, and absent sufficient evidence to the contrary, may result in the implication of pregnancy discrimination. In *Holland v. Gee* [803 F. Supp. 2d 1339 (M.D. Fla. 2011)], the court held that the reassignment of a pregnant employee to a more menial position because of concerns related to the pregnancy, no matter how well intentioned, cannot justify differential treatment. Although the reassignment from a technician position to the so-called "Help Desk" did not affect the pregnant employee's pay, nonetheless, because it was viewed as a "demotion," in that the position had significantly less responsibility and more menial tasks than the technician position, the reassignment could be viewed as an adverse action supporting a claim of discrimination under the PDA. However, although timing is important in pregnancy discrimination cases, even in situations of poor timing, employers can defeat claims, provided they can credibly articulate legitimate business reasons for the adverse action at issue. Such was in *McLaughlin v. W & T Offshore, Inc.* [78 Fed. Appx. 334 (5th Cir 2003)] An accounting clerk employed for three years went on maternity leave from July 2000 through September 2000. Upon her return to work, the company terminated her employment and told her that her position had been eliminated. Not surprisingly, the employee sued claiming discrimination in violation of the PDA. Although the timing was extremely suspicious, the company nonetheless demonstrated that while the employee was on pregnancy leave, it discovered that other employees could perform both their duties and the plaintiff's duties better and with fewer errors than she could alone. For this reason, the decision was made to eliminate her position. Although the plaintiff maintained a prima facie claim of pregnancy discrimination, the company articulated a legitimate non-discriminatory reason for the actions it took in terminating her employment, and she was incapable of demonstrating that the reasons proffered were not credible or a pretext for illegal discrimination. As a result, the court upheld dismissal of the claim. As the court held in *Riddick v. Maic, Inc.* [JKS 09-33, 2010 WL 4904681 (D. Md. Nov. 24, 2010)], timing alone, absent other direct or circumstantial evidence, is not sufficient to establish a prima facia case of pregnancy discrimination under the PDA. Moreover, if the employer has well-documented evidence justifying termination and no pretext can be demonstrated, the employer should succeed. Such was in *Arigbon v. Multnomah County.* [09-311-PK, 2010 WL 2038839 (D. Or. May 20, 2010)] Although the employee claimed pregnancy discrimination for her termination, the employer was able to demonstrate evidence of poor work performance justifying termination of the pregnant employee at issue. In *Bernett v. University of Tennessee-Knoxville* [2010 WL 1687062 (E.D. Tenn. Apr. 26, 2010)], an animal clinic employee, whose physician imposed restrictions preventing her from having contact with contagious animals, could not maintain a claim for pregnancy discrimination because of her termination, because contact with contagious animals was an unavoidable requirement of her job.

However, if, on the other hand, it can be demonstrated that the company's proffered reasons are not credible, the plaintiff will more than likely have her day in court. [Lyons v. Premium Armored Servs., Inc., 02 C 3779, 2003 U.S. Dist. LEXIS 19823 (N.D. Ill. Sept. 4, 2003)] In defense of a PDA claim arising from the termination of plaintiff's employment, the company claimed that the employee's employment was terminated for three reasons: excessive absenteeism; poor work performance; and unauthorized use of a UPS account. However, during the deposition of the supervisors who made the decision, they only testified that it was the plaintiff's unauthorized use of the UPS account that resulted in her termination. In response to the plaintiff's claim for unemployment, the company only mentioned excessive absenteeism and poor work performance as the reasons for the termination, making no mention of the unauthorized use of the UPS account. Based on the inconsistent reasons provided for the plaintiff's termination, the court agreed that there were reasonable inferences that the plaintiff may have been terminated, at least in part, because of her pregnancy, justifying a trial of plaintiff's case.

Nonetheless, timing remains one of the more essential issues as it relates to potential liability in pregnancy discrimination cases. As in *Hill v. Dale Electronics Corp.* [03 Civ. 5907 (MBM), 2004 WL 2937832 (S.D.N.Y. Dec. 19, 2004)], the court held that an employee, who acknowledged that there had been several customer complaints lodged against her, held that the employee had stated a cause of action under the PDA due to the fact that she was reprimanded and terminated a short time after she announced her pregnancy, finding that the temporal proximity between the plaintiff's announcement of her pregnancy and her firing was sufficient to raise an inference of discrimination. Timing was also important in *Meyer v. Maxim Healthcare Services, Inc.* [1:06-CV-00453, 2007 WL 3005947 (S.D. Ohio Oct. 12, 2007)] In the case, a pregnant employee had submitted her application for leave under the defendant's Family and Medical Leave Act (FMLA) leave policy in connection with her anticipated delivery and need for leave. In response to the request, the company sent the employee a letter informing her that she was not eligible for leave, was not working the required hours to maintain her group insurance benefits, and notified her that her employment would be terminated effective upon the date of her anticipated last day worked. Although the company claimed that the termination letter had been sent in error, the court reasoned that there was sufficient evidence to withstand a motion for summary disposition and allowed the case to proceed to trial.

However, when alleged comments and remarks are not made within a time period sufficient to establish a nexus between the comments and the adverse employment decision, such comments will be insufficient for purposes of evidencing direct evidence to support a claim under the PDA. In *Suits v. The Heil Co.* [192 Fed. Appx. 399 (6th Cir. 2006)], at issue were two statements by the plaintiff's supervisor that the plaintiff tried to use to establish direct evidence of discriminatory animus toward pregnant employees. He allegedly said to her that she was not the type of person to leave her child, and stated, "How are you going to come back to work and work here and leave that baby, you know you are not going to be able to do that." Because the plaintiff was unable to specify when the remarks were made, and the timeline the court was able to discern, suggested that they were made up to three months before the plaintiff's termination, the court concluded that there was not a sufficient nexus between the comments made and the adverse employment action to support a claim of pregnancy discrimination in connection with plaintiff's termination in conjunction with a company-wide reduction in force. Similarly, in *Jeffrey v. Met Logistics, Inc.* [No. 07-CV-3301, 2009 WL 674349 (N.D. Ill. Mar. 13, 2009)], the plaintiff attempted to maintain a pregnancy discrimination claim on the basis of allegedly negative stray comments to attempt to show discriminatory animus which was neither temporal to her discharge nor made by the decision makers. Because of this lack of direct evidence, and the fact that the company produced evidence that a prior female employee had taken leave attributable to a pregnancy and upon her return was given various accommodations and accolades, the court concluded that the pregnancy discrimination claim could not be maintained.

In *Jordan v. Radiology Imaging Associates* [577 F. Supp. 2d 771 (D. Md. 2008)], the plaintiff claimed that her termination, while pregnant, was a violation of the PDA and attempted to use direct evidence to substantiate her claim. The direct evidence proffered was that, when she was initially hired, her supervisor offered her part-time employment when he learned that she was a working mother stating words to the effect that many working parents prefer to work part-time. In addition, the deposition testimony revealed that when her supervisor learned that she was pregnant, he delayed informing her of the elimination of position due to her pregnancy. With respect to the comments made during the interview, the court held that they were not direct evidence of sex discrimination because they were gender neutral, and not limited to her gender. In addition, the delay in informing her of the elimination of her position because of her pregnancy was not information from which anyone could reasonably infer discrimination based on pregnancy. As such, the court concluded that the proffered direct evidence was not sufficient to maintain a prima facie case of pregnancy discrimination under the PDA. A supervisor's stray reference to a bank employee as a "pregnant girl teller" and the supervisor's proposal to allow the employee to report to work late after her morning sickness subsided were not direct evidence of pregnancy discrimination in violation of the PDA. As the court held, use of the word *pregnant* and offers to accommodate morning sickness do not reflect discriminatory animus. [Elam v. Regions Fin. Corp., 601 F.3d 873 (8th Cir. 2010)] Similarly, an employer's isolated remark in asking if an employee would be returning to work following her leave in connection with a pregnancy leave did not, in and of itself, prove discriminatory intent. [Payne v. Goodman Mfg., LP, 726 F. Supp. 2d 891 (E.D. Tenn. 2010)]

Q 4:68   Under the PDA, are employers required to give preferential treatment to pregnant workers and pregnant applicants, as compared to other temporarily disabled employees?

It is important to point out that the PDA does not require employers to do more for a pregnant employee than they would for other employees similarly situated with similar temporary health conditions. For example, in *Guarino v. Potter* [102 Fed. Appx. 865 (5th Cir. 2004)], an employee claimed that she was being discriminated against in violation of the PDA because the employer failed to provide her a limited duty position during her pregnancy. The court, in reviewing the company's limited duty policies found that limited duty assignments were only available to employees as a result of an on-the-job injury. As the court stated, the PDA "does not require employers to give pregnant women benefits that other, similarly situated employees do not get." [*Guarino*, 102 Fed. Appx. at 868] Similarly, in *Reeves v. Swift Transportation Co., Inc.* [446 F.3d 637 (6th Cir. 2006)], a former employee, who was pregnant and was restricted by her physician to light duty work only, brought a claim of pregnancy discrimination against her employer which maintained a policy of providing light duty work only to employees on workers compensation leaves (i.e., employees who had sustained on-the-job injuries). Reviewing the district court's grant of summary judgment de novo, the court disagreed with the plaintiff's characterization of the policy as a "per se" violation of the Pregnancy Discrimination Act, rather, the court concluded that the plaintiff was treated the same as any other worker—male, female, pregnant or not—who suffered an injury off duty. As such, like the *Guarino* case, the court concluded that the claim was not a request for relief from discrimination, but rather a demand for preferential treatment which is not required by the PDA. As the court stated in *Elam v. Regions Financial Corp.,* [606 F. Supp. 2d 999 (S.D. Iowa 2009)] "the PDA does not create substantive rights to preferential treatment. On the contrary, the PDA allows employers to treat pregnant women as badly as they treat similarly affected but non-pregnant employees; the opposite, however, is also true—employers must treat pregnant women as well as they treat similarly affected employees." [*Elam*, 606 F. Supp. 2d at 1008, citing Deneen v. NW Airlines, Inc., 132 F.3d 431, 436–37 (8th Cir. 1998)] In *Nelson v. Chattahoochee Valley Hospital Society* [731 F. Supp. 2d 1217 (M.D. Ala. 2010)], the court held that the PDA did not require the employer to provide specific accommodations for pregnant employees but rather, required that pregnant employees be treated similar to non-pregnant employees in the same position. Similarly, in *Serednyj v. Beverly Healthcare, LLC* [656 F.3d 540 (7th Cir. 2011)], the court held that a light duty policy for employees in need of accommodations under the ADA and workers injured on the job did not violate the PDA, because it treated pregnant and non-pregnant employees alike; neither could avail themselves of the light duty policy unless they were entitled to accommodations under the ADA or were injured on the job. However, in Chapter 7 *Trustee v. Gate Gourmet, Inc.* [683 F.3d 1249 (11th Cir. 2012)], the court held that a food service worker that was terminated by her supervisor because of medical restrictions attributable to pregnancy presented sufficient evidence of pregnancy discrimination when the supervisor did not attempt to determine if there were any light duty jobs available to accommodate the pregnant employee's work restrictions, such that summary disposition in favor of the employer was inappropriate.

With respect to hiring, sick-leave benefits, medical benefits, disability benefits, alternative work assignments, right to work, and reinstatement, the PDA requires only that the pregnant employee be treated similarly to other employees that are temporarily disabled. Arguably, to the extent that an employer adopts a policy giving preferential treatment to women who are pregnant, those policies may be challenged as illegal discrimination against males under Title VII.

To avoid violations of the PDA, employer policies should not make specific references to leaves related to pregnancy (i.e., maternity leaves), but rather should use uniform language to treat all temporary disabilities in the same way. Different policies for maternity leaves and pregnancy-related conditions versus other temporary disability leaves form the foundation of illegal discrimination under the Act. Employers should review their policies and procedures to ensure uniform treatment with respect to these issues.

Q 4:69   Under the PDA, can an employer require a pregnant woman to return to work within a specified period after delivery or after a physician has certified that the woman can return to work?

Any policy with respect to work for women on pregnancy leave should be the same as that for other employees with temporary disabilities. To the extent that the employer requires them to return to work after a physician certifies that they are able, an employer may require an employee on leave for pregnancy to return to work upon receipt of such certification. Any policy that requires employees to return to work after a certain time should be followed by an employee on leave because of pregnancy or related conditions in the same manner as it is by employees with other temporary disabilities.

Since the passage of the FMLA, certain eligible employees of covered employers now have a right to 12 weeks of unpaid leave during any 12-month period for conditions related to pregnancy and can take time off to care for a newborn.

Q 4:70   Must an employer guarantee to reinstate a pregnant worker in the same position she held before maternity leave?

Under the PDA, an employer need not return an employee to the position she occupied prior to leave (or to any job for that matter) unless the employer's policy promises to do so. If the employer guarantees reinstatement in the same job to persons who return to work from disability leave for other non-occupational illness or injuries, however, refusing reinstatement following leave associated with pregnancy is considered discriminatory. Consequently, an employer that extends reinstatement to employees after medical leaves of absence must pursue the same policy for pregnant women. Under the FMLA, which covers employers with 50 or more employees, employers are required to provide as many as 12 weeks unpaid leave during any 12-month period to eligible employees for conditions related to pregnancy, the birth of a child, and care for the child. Although not required under the PDA, the FMLA requires that employees be reinstated on expiration of leave to the same or equivalent position.

Some states have passed laws requiring covered employers in those states to guarantee reinstatement following pregnancy leave, and the Supreme Court has held that those state laws are constitutional. In recent years, parental leave bills that afford such a right to both male and female employees—not only for maternity and paternity purposes but also to care for an ill child, spouse, or parent—have been introduced repeatedly in both houses of Congress, thus far without success. The following states, the District of Columbia, and Puerto Rico have adopted some form of family, parental, or maternity leave law or regulation: California, Colorado, Connecticut, Hawaii, Iowa, Kansas, Maine, Maryland, Massachusetts, Minnesota, Montana, Nevada, New Jersey, North Dakota, Oklahoma, Oregon, Rhode Island, South Carolina, Tennessee, Utah, Washington, and Wisconsin.

Q 4:71   When a woman returns to her job after a pregnancy leave, may her seniority or benefits be affected?

An employer's seniority policy must be the same for employees absent for pregnancy or related reasons as for employees who are absent for other temporary disabilities. Treatment of benefits must also be the same for pregnancy and related conditions as that for other temporary disabilities; however, under the FMLA, covered employers must restore benefits to eligible employees upon return from an FMLA-related leave.

Q 4:72   May a company lay off a pregnant employee as part of a fetal protection program?

No. *United Auto Workers v. Johnson Controls, Inc.* [499 U.S. 187 (1991)], appears to be a powerful statement by the Supreme Court in favor of a woman's right to decide for herself what reproductive risks she will run on the job. The decision turns not only on the Court's reading of Title VII; Justice Blackmun's opinion also makes a statement about workplace safety. A company cannot substitute a discriminatory fetal protection policy for its obligation under the Occupational Safety and Health Act to police its premises and keep them free from hazards. Following *Johnson Controls*, any employer desiring to implement or maintain a fetal-protection policy must be prepared to prove that such a policy qualifies as a BFOQ.

Q 4:73   Is an employer's failure to accommodate a female employee for breastfeeding a violation of the PDA?

Although breastfeeding, like pregnancy, is a uniquely female attribute, courts have consistently held that failure to accommodate female employees for breastfeeding or related pumping procedures does not violate the Act. See, for example, *Vachon v. R. M. Davis, Inc.* [03-234-P-H, 2004 WL 1146630 (D. Me. Apr. 23, 2004)], wherein, after an exhausted review of relevant case law, the court concluded that the failure to "accommodate" an employee's need to breastfeed and pump was not an adverse employment action, such that a claim under the PDA could not be maintained. Similarly, in *Derungs v. Wal-Mart Stores, Inc.*, a public accommodation case alleging PDA violations under analogous state accommodation statute arising from Wal-Mart's refusal to accommodate shoppers for breastfeeding, the court, reviewing comparable analyses of breastfeeding cases in the employment context concluded that no cases to date have expanded the PDA in the employment context to include breastfeeding. [374 F.3d 428, 438–40 (6th Cir. 2004)] In *Falk v. City of Glendale* [2012 WL 2390556 (D. Colo. June 25, 2012)], the court held, after reviewing decisions in other courts that have addressed the issue, that failure to accommodate an employee who requested breaks to pump breast milk does not violate the PDA. In 2012, the EEOC instituted litigation against a Texas company claiming that the company had terminated an employee because the employee wanted to pump breast milk at work, which, according to the EEOC, was pregnancy discrimination. However, the court found no support for the EEOC's position, holding that "the law does not punish lactation discrimination." [*EEOC v. Houston Funding II, Ltd.*, 2012 WL 739494 (S.D. Tex. Feb. 2, 2012)] However, under the new health care reform law, the Patient Protection and Affordable Care Act, signed into law by President Barack Obama on March 30, 2010, employers with 50 or more employees will be required to provide nursing mothers with both breaks and a private location other than a bathroom to express milk. Smaller employers (less than 50 employees) may be exempt from these requirements if an undue hardship can be demonstrated. [Pub. L. No. 111-148]

Q 4:74   Does an employee have to be pregnant to maintain a claim under the PDA?

Although it would seem logical to presume that an employee must be pregnant to be able to make claims under the PDA, such is not necessarily the case. The U.S. Supreme Court, some time ago, held that the PDA prohibits an employer from discriminating against a woman "because of her capacity to become pregnant." [International Union v. Johnson Controls, Inc., 499 U.S. 206 (1991)] In *Kocak v. Community Health Partners of Ohio* [400 F.3d 466 (6th Cir. 2005)], a former employee claimed that her employer failed to rehire her due to a prior pregnancy that resulted in her resignation from employment. It was undisputed that the former employee was not pregnant at the time of her application for rehire, she did not bear any children during the period of her application, and no medical conditions related to pregnancy manifested themselves during the time of her application. Nonetheless, citing the Supreme Court's decision in *Johnson Controls*, the court held that if the former employee could produce sufficient evidence that the company refused to rehire her based on her "potential pregnancy," a case under the PDA would stand. However, the court in reviewing the evidence found that the former employee provided no such direct or circumstantial evidence to withstand a motion for summary disposition.

Q 4:75   Is harassment a recognized claim under the PDA?

As with other protected categories under evolving harassment law under both federal and most state statutes, a prima facie case of hostile work environment, harassment under the PDA, can be maintained if: (1) the employee belongs to a protected group (i.e., is pregnant); (2) the employee was subjected to unwelcome harassment; (3) the harassment comprising the complaint was based on her pregnancy; (4) the harassment was sufficiently severe or pervasive to alter the terms and conditions of employment and create a discriminatorily abusive working environment; and (5) there is a basis for holding the employer liable. [Walker v. Golden Pantry Food Stores, Inc., 3:04-CV-91 (CDL), 2005 WL 3179988 (M.D. Ga. Nov. 29, 2005), citing Mendoza v. Borden, Inc., 195 F.3d 1238, 1245 (11th Cir. 1999)] In that case, the employee claimed that she had endured the alleged harassment for approximately one month and that the harassment included the following: (1) statements that pregnant people are "sorry" and "lazy"; (2) statements that she would not have been hired had the company known she was pregnant; (3) comments about the pregnant woman's uniform not fitting properly; (4) questions as to what the employee would do if she were to become sick; (5) company statements that the employee "wouldn't be here long"; and (6) "nit picking" the employee's performance. Recognizing that the Eleventh Circuit had created a relatively high bar for the assertion of hostile work environment claims, the court held that although the allegations indicated insensitivity and obnoxious behavior on behalf of the employer, the conduct was not sufficiently severe and pervasive to alter the terms and conditions of the employee's employment. In *Dollman v. Mast Indus., Inc.* [2010 WL 3239067 (S.D.N.Y. Aug. 17, 2010)], two occurrences in which the pregnant employee was hugged and congratulated by her supervisor's mother and not being given time off for one of her many medical appointments did not establish a hostile work environment under the PDA.

Q 4:76   Can a church that terminates a pregnant employee based on church doctrine be held liable under the PDA?

Claims of pregnancy discrimination periodically occur in connection with religious employers who, on the basis of church doctrine, terminate pregnant employees. In *Redhead v. Conference of Seventh-Day Adventists* [440 F. Supp. 2d 211 (E.D.N.Y. 2006)], a former teacher sued a religious school claiming that the school violated the PDA and Title VII by terminating her for being pregnant and unmarried. The religious school maintained it had a right to terminate the teacher due to her employment agreement and school policy that provide for termination in the event of immoral or unsatisfactory personal conduct inconsistent with the principles of the church. Moreover, the religious school maintained that plaintiff could not maintain her claim either under the constitutional "ministerial exception" to civil rights laws or under the RFRA, which restricts governmental intrusion into the exercise of religion. Noting that there were allegations of male employees at the religious institution who may have engaged in sexual relations outside of marriage and who were not terminated, the court concluded that because the plaintiff's teaching duties were mainly secular, that neither the ministerial exception or the RFRA was applicable to their analysis of the case, and remanded the case for further proceeding as to whether, among other things, non-pregnant employees were treated differently than others as it relates to sex outside of marriage. In *Hamilton v. Southland Christian School, Inc.* [680 F.3d 1316 (11th Cir. 2012)], although a Christian school claimed it terminated a teacher who was pregnant for pre-marital sex as opposed to her pregnancy, the teacher provided sufficient evidence to demonstrate that the termination was due to her request for maternity leave, such that summary disposition in favor of the employer was inappropriate. On the other hand, courts may provide protection to a religious institution for terminating employees who engage in conduct clearly contrary to established church doctrine. Such was the case in *Curay-Cramer v. Ursuline Academy of Wilmington, Delaware, Inc.* [450 F.3d 130 (3d Cir. 2006)] In *Curay-Cramer*, a former teacher claimed the Catholic school violated the PDA when she was terminated from the school as a result of her public endorsement in an advertisement supporting pro-choice and the U.S. Supreme Court decision of *Roe v. Wade.* [410 U.S. 1123 (1973)] Utilizing the analysis of the U.S. Supreme Court decision in *NLRB v. Catholic Bishop of Chicago* [440 U.S. 490 (1979)], which sets forth a framework to determine whether federal statute as applied in a particular factual situation violated the constitution, the court concluded that the circumstances in this case were such that to apply federal statute would impermissibly delve into inquiry into the religious employer's religious mission and religious justification for the employment decision, such that it raises serious constitutional questions and was therefore impermissible in the case at hand.

Q 4:77   Is abortion protected by the PDA?

The Third Circuit in *Jane Doe v. CARS Protection Plus, Inc.* [527 F.3d 358 (3d Cir. 2008)], and as a matter of first impression, held that it is a violation of the PDA for an employer to discriminate against an employee because she has exercised her right to have an abortion.

Q 4:78   Does a woman being treated for infertility fall under the PDA?

A district court held that it is not a violation of the PDA for discrimination on the basis of a woman's infertility or fertility treatments. Specifically, in *Panizzi v. City of Chicago Board of Education* [2007 WL 4233755 (N.D. Ill. Nov. 19, 2007)], the court held that the PDA was an amendment to Title VII, and as such, the underlying requirement of Title VII that the discrimination must be on the "basis of sex" was required. Because infertility is not gender specific and a condition that affects both women and men, it would not be a violation of the PDA for an employer to discrimination against a woman on that basis.

However, the Seventh Circuit came to the opposite conclusion. In the case, the specific IVF treatments that the employee underwent involved reproductive technologies that involved surgical impregnation procedures, and as such, only involved women. Therefore, when this woman claimed that she was terminated for taking time off to undergo these procedures, the court held she stated a claim under the PDA. [Hall v. Nalco Co., 534 F.3d 644 (7th Cir. 2008)]

Sexual Harassment

Q 4:79   What is *sexual harassment*?

Sexual harassment is either establishing terms and conditions of employment with reference to sexual favors (called quid pro quo sexual harassment) or creating, maintaining, or tolerating a sexually hostile work environment. A hostile, abusive, or offensive work environment as the foundation for a claim of sexual harassment was recognized by the U.S. Supreme Court in *Meritor Savings Bank v. Vinson*. [477 U.S. 57 (1986)] Just how hostile, offensive, or abusive the environment must be to support such a cause of action remains a matter of legal dispute and judicial controversy.

In *Harris*, a unanimous Supreme Court ruled that for conduct to be actionable under Title VII for creating an "abusive work environment" it need not be so severe as to have caused the plaintiff-employee to suffer psychological injury. In so holding, the majority opinion stated:

> This standard . . . takes a middle path between making actionable any conduct that is merely offensive and requiring the conduct to cause a tangible psychological injury. As we pointed out in *Meritor*, "mere utterance of an . . . epithet which engenders offensive feeling in a [sic] employee," . . . does not sufficiently affect the conditions of employment to implicate Title VII. Conduct that is not severe or pervasive enough to create an objectively hostile or abusive work environment, an environment that a reasonable person would find hostile or abusive, is beyond Title VII's purview. Likewise, if the victim does not subjectively perceive the environment to be abusive, the conduct has not actually altered the conditions of the victim's employment, and there is no Title VII violation. But Title VII comes into play before the harassing conduct leads to a nervous breakdown. A discriminatorily abusive work environment, even one that does not seriously affect employees' psychological well-being, can and often will detract from employees' job performance, discourage employees from remaining in the job, or keep them from advancing in their careers. [Harris v. Forklift Sys. Inc., 510 U.S. 17, 21 (1993)]

Q 4:80   What types of conduct are considered sexual harassment under Title VII?

Title VII states:

> It shall be an unlawful employment practice for an Employer . . . to fail or refuse to hire or to discharge any individual, or otherwise to discriminate against any individual with respect to his compensation, terms, conditions or privileges of employment, because of such individual's race, color, religion, sex or national origin. [Title VII § 703(a)(1), 42 U.S.C. § 2000e-2(a)]

In *Meritor Savings Bank v. Vinson* [477 U.S. 57 (1986)], the Supreme Court affirmed the EEOC's guidelines, which establish sexual harassment as a form of sex discrimination. The EEOC Guidelines on Discrimination Because of Sex, published in 1980, defines *actionable sexual harassment* under Title VII as follows:

> Unwelcome sexual advances, requests for sexual favors, and other verbal or physical conduct of a sexual nature constitute sexual harassment when:
>
> (1) Submission to such conduct is made either explicitly or implicitly a term or condition of an individual's employment;
>
> (2) Submission to or rejection of such conduct is used as the basis for employment decisions affecting such individual; or
>
> (3) Such conduct has the purpose or effect of unreasonably interfering with an individual's work performance or creating an intimidating, hostile or offensive working environment. [29 C.F.R. § 1604.11]

The behavior described in the first two sections is generally referred to as quid pro quo sexual harassment. Conduct referred to in the third is generally known as hostile work environment sexual harassment. These two types of sexual harassment differ both in theory and in potential liability. Employers need to understand the two theories and their differences to properly assess their liability and exposure to sexual harassment claims.

Q 4:81   What is *quid pro quo sexual harassment*?

A literal translation of *quid pro quo* is "something for something." Under the EEOC's guidelines, unwelcome sexual conduct constitutes quid pro quo sexual harassment when submission to such conduct is made, either explicitly or implicitly, a term or condition of an individual's employment. Quid pro quo harassment also occurs when submission to or rejection of such unwelcome conduct is used as the basis for employment decisions affecting an employee.

The core of quid pro quo harassment is abuse of power—that is, a supervisor or manager uses his or her authority over a subordinate to engage or attempt to engage in prohibited unwelcome conduct. Although the classic case of quid pro quo sexual harassment is that of a supervisor demanding sexual favors in return for a subordinate retaining his or her job or position, it is not necessary that the conduct be this blatant to qualify. Indeed, the sexual conduct need only be implicitly a term or condition of employment to support a claim. As a result, even if no express demand is made for sexual favors, a court might find that the verbal or physical conduct of a sexual nature was implicitly a term or condition of employment.

To support a claim, the complainant must generally offer proof of some tangible adverse employment action that resulted from the rejection of sexual advances. Alternatively, the complainant must show that adverse employment action was avoided through unwelcome submission to the sexual advances. This requirement need not be met under a hostile work environment claim.

Q 4:82   Can quid pro quo sexual harassment occur between two co-employees?

No. The critical element of quid pro quo sexual harassment is that a person who occupies a position of authority over another uses that authority to attempt to coerce the subordinate to engage in unwelcome sexual conduct. If an employee is not a manager or supervisor and has no authority to affect the employment relationship, quid pro quo sexual harassment cannot occur.

Q 4:83   How does an employer determine whether an employee is a supervisor for quid pro quo sexual harassment under Title VII?

Generally, the courts and the EEOC use a reality-based approach. The fact that an employee's title does not include the words "manager" or "supervisor" is not determinative. Generally, the total circumstances of the employment relationship are examined and the job functions performed by an individual are considered in determining whether that person acts in a supervisory capacity. To the extent that the facts reveal that an individual has been given authority by the company to make decisions affecting the employment status of others (e.g., hiring, firing, or promotion) that person is determined to be a supervisor.

Q 4:84   Is the employer responsible for the quid pro quo sexual harassment of its supervisors?

Generally, yes. The EEOC takes the position in its guidelines that employers will always be responsible for acts of quid pro quo sexual harassment by their supervisors. This position was noted with approval by the Supreme Court in *Meritor Savings Bank v. Vinson*, which stated:

> Where a supervisor exercises the authority actually delegated to him by his Employer, by making or threatening to make decisions affecting the employment status of his subordinates, such actions are properly imputed to the Employer whose delegation of authority empowered the supervisor to undertake them. [477 U.S. 57, 70–73 (1986)]

Although most employers have promulgated policies prohibiting sexual harassment and would never authorize a supervisor to engage in quid pro quo sexual harassment, employers are nonetheless generally held responsible for quid pro quo sexual harassment committed by supervisors. The justification for this imposition of what is often referred to as strict liability relies on general agency principles. Because an employer undertook to provide the person with authority, use of authority for purposes of engaging in quid pro quo sexual harassment must necessarily be imputed to that employer, which will be held responsible for the illegal conduct.

Q 4:85   Is it quid pro quo sexual harassment if the sexual advance is welcome?

No. As in all instances of sexual harassment, the conduct complained of must be unwelcome to be actionable. Welcome advances do not form the basis of quid pro quo sexual harassment claims. Whether the advance is welcome or unwelcome is usually far from clear. Not surprisingly, this issue is often the main contention between the parties in quid pro quo sexual harassment litigation.

In defending quid pro quo sexual harassment cases, it is usually the position of the supervisor that, although admittedly sexual advances were made, the sexual advances were welcome and, therefore, no sexual harassment occurred. Often, the supervisor points to the subordinate's voluntary acquiescence to sexual activity in an attempt to show that the activity was welcome; however, just because the complainant voluntarily engaged in sexual activity does not necessarily mean that the activity was welcome. Although a subordinate voluntarily has sexual relations with his or her supervisor, if the subordinate did not want to have sexual relations, but only agreed to the conduct because of the supervisor's threats of termination if he or she did not acquiesce, the activity will be determined to have been unwelcome.

Generally, the courts use an objective analysis in determining whether the alleged conduct was welcome or unwelcome. The complainant's subjective feelings generally do not control, and courts look objectively to the complainant's conduct and communications to determine whether the alleged conduct was welcome or unwelcome.

As such, terminating an employee because of a prior consensual relationship may not, under certain circumstances, state a Title VII claim. A female employee who was terminated claimed that she was terminated by her boss, to whom she had made sexual overtures, because of her sex. In the case, the former employee admitted that she had initiated in sexual banter, touching, and other activity with her supervisor in the presence of others. The supervisor maintained that when his wife found out about it, she made him choose between his subordinate or her and their children. For this, the plaintiff was terminated. The court held that under these circumstances, it was not a sex discrimination claim on the basis of the employee's status as a man or a woman, but rather based on plaintiff's own actions in engaging her boss in a sexual way. Simply put, being terminated for engaging in conduct that caused jealousy with the boss's wife is not a Title VII discrimination claim. [Tenge v. Phillips Modern AG Co., 446 F.3d 903 (8th Cir. 2006)]

Q 4:86 What types of evidence are considered in determining whether or not a sexual advance is welcome or unwelcome under quid pro quo claims?

Welcome conduct is a complete defense to all sexual harassment claims, including quid pro quo claims. The question of admissibility of evidence is therefore of great importance, and each issue of admissibility depends on the facts and circumstances of each particular case.

Generally, defense lawyers seek to have admitted as much information as they can with respect to a complainant's sexual history, sexual conduct, and other lifestyle information for purposes of demonstrating that the sexual advance was welcome. On the other hand, plaintiff attorneys attempt to keep out any evidence of a plaintiff's sexual conduct, sexual history, or other behavior that they feel might unduly prejudice the court in deciding whether the advance at issue was welcome. Plaintiff lawyers fear that the court will be swayed by a plaintiff's off-the-job sexual conduct and ignore the particular facts and circumstances surrounding the sexual advance at issue.

Although each issue of admissibility must necessarily be determined on a case-by-case basis, two principles are generally followed. To the extent that the conduct or communication that the defendant seeks to admit occurred when the complainant was acting in the capacity of an employee, that information generally will be admissible to the extent that it is relevant for purposes of determining whether the conduct was welcome or unwelcome (e.g., evidence of a complainant's sexually provocative speech or dress). On the other hand, conduct or communication by the complainant outside his or her role as an employee generally will not be held admissible for purposes of determining whether particular conduct was welcome or unwelcome (e.g., the fact that the complainant is sexually active outside of the workplace).

Q 4:87 Can sexual advances that are initially welcome ever become unwelcome at a later time?

Yes. The fact that sexual conduct at one time is welcome does not necessarily mean that all future similar sexual conduct is also welcome. This situation often arises when a supervisor and a subordinate engage in a consensual affair that ends. Although the complainant's prior consent to the sexual conduct is obviously relevant for purposes of determining whether all of the conduct was welcome or unwelcome, it does not necessarily bar a claim of later harassment, provided the conduct became unwelcome and there is sufficient evidence to support such a finding.

Because the conduct was welcome at one point, courts require a more stringent notification by the alleged victim that the continuation of the conduct is, in fact, unwelcome. If the complainant says nothing and does nothing to indicate that the initially welcome conduct has become unwelcome, the complainant will not be able to maintain a claim. If, however, the subordinate clearly notifies the supervisor that the conduct is no longer welcome, future conduct will be unwelcome for the purposes of analyzing the sexual harassment complaint.

The potential liability employers face in instances where supervisors and subordinates are engaged in consensual sexual activity is clear. Office romances that come to an end can easily lead to sexual harassment litigation, and employers should do what they can to discourage such liaisons. When an adverse employment action is taken with respect to anyone who has engaged in sexual conduct with a supervisor, the potential exists that employee may now claim that the activity was unwelcome, and the adverse employment action was a result of his or her ultimate rejection of the continued advance. Supervisors should be educated about the danger in which they place their company when they engage in sexual affairs with subordinates.

Q 4:88   What is *hostile work environment sexual harassment?*

Under the EEOC guidelines, unwelcome sexual conduct, requests for sexual favors, or other verbal or physical conduct of a sexual nature that "unreasonably interferes with an individual's job performance" or creates an "intimidating, hostile, or offensive working environment" will support a claim of hostile work environment sexual harassment. It is not necessary in a hostile work environment claim, as it is with a quid pro quo claim, that the conduct be a term or condition of employment, express or implied, or that submission to or rejection of such conduct be the basis of any employment decision affecting the complaint. Rather, the hostile environment itself is sufficient for purposes of maintaining the claim.

Furthermore, it is not necessary that the complainant suffer severe psychological injury as a result of the complained conduct. The threshold of personal injury is relatively low, and as long as sufficient evidence is introduced to support a finding of an "abusive" environment, any measurable effect on the complainant will be sufficient to support the claim. However, not all bawdy language and comments by co-workers will rise to the level of creating a sufficiently severe and pervasive environment from which a hostile work claim can be maintained under Title VII. For example, in *McGullam v. Cedar Graphics, Inc.* [609 F.3d 70 (2d Cir. 2010)], a co-worker's reference to women as "chickies" and remark to the plaintiff that a woman friend of his was not worth the trip to her house unless they could have sexual relations, although demeaning, were not sufficiently severe or pervasive to maintain a claim of hostile work environment under Title VII. Similarly, in *Overly v. Keybank National Association* [662 F.3d 856 (7th Cir. 2011)], the court held that a supervisor's occasional condescending gender-based remarks referring to a female employee as "cutie" and having a "pretty face" are not sufficiently severe or pervasive to rise to the level of a hostile work environment. In *O'Leary v. Accretive Health, Inc.* [657 F.3d 625 (7th Cir. 2011)], the court held that a female co-worker's boast of sexual exploits with co-workers at a dinner party could not reasonably be considered harassment, such that a male co-worker's complaints regarding the comments was not protected activity to support a claim of Title VII retaliation.

Q 4:89 Does a hostile work environment claim have to be unwelcome conduct?

Yes. As with all instances of sexual harassment, the fundamental element of any claim is that the conduct be unwelcome. As with quid pro quo harassment claims, courts will look to the relevant facts to determine whether the conduct was welcome or unwelcome. In a hostile work environment claim, the complainant's reaction to the alleged offensive conduct is crucial. What may be offensive to some may not be offensive to others. If, upon reviewing the facts, it is determined that the complainant participated in the conduct complained of—used vulgar language or told offensive jokes, for instance—without any negative response, the conduct generally will not be found to be unwelcome.

The complainant must subjectively believe that the conduct was so offensive that it created a hostile and offensive work environment. An environment may objectively support a claim for hostile work environment harassment, but if, subjectively, the environment is not found to be abusive by the complainant, a hostile work environment complaint cannot be maintained. For this reason, the analysis of hostile work environment claims involves both subjective and objective components for purposes of determining whether or not the alleged offensive conduct is actionable.

Q 4:90 If the complainant initially engaged in provocative language or the telling of offensive jokes, is he or she forever barred from being able to maintain a hostile work environment claim?

No. Initial participation does not forever bar the complainant from maintaining that later conduct was, in fact, unwelcome. Further, occasional participation in an activity does not in and of itself mean that all of the offensive conduct alleged was necessarily welcome. As with quid pro quo sexual harassment claims, the complainant's initial participation in the offensive conduct (even if limited) will, however, be relevant for purposes of determining whether the conduct was welcome or unwelcome. And as with a quid pro quo complaint, if the conduct is initially welcome, the courts require the complainant to give notice that the continued conduct is unwelcome in order to maintain a claim. Simply ceasing to further participate in the conduct is usually not sufficient.

Q 4:91 Can employees maintain a claim for hostile work environment if they knowingly place themselves in a so-called rough working environment?

Yes. Employers would like to think that assumption of risk is a complete defense to a hostile work environment claims brought by a women employed in traditionally male-dominated workplaces with reputations for vulgarity, but it is not. A woman's decision knowingly to place herself in an all-male workplace where pin-ups, lewd posters, and vulgar remarks are common will undoubtedly be considered by an employer's defense team to be relevant for purposes of determining whether the conduct was welcome. Nevertheless, if the complainant can demonstrate that the conduct was unwelcome through complaints to the management and the like, a claim of hostile work environment can be maintained. If there is evidence to support the assertion that the conduct was unwelcome, the fact that the employee knowingly sought a position in a sexually charged atmosphere will not be sufficient to dispose of the claim in most instances.

To pose an extreme example, does this mean that a strip tease dancer could maintain a claim for hostile work environment sexual harassment based on the banter exchanged between patrons and dancers at such establishments? To the extent that the conduct rises beyond a tolerable level under both a combined subjective and objective analysis, it is theoretically possible that a stripper would be able to maintain a claim for hostile work environment discrimination.

The Supreme Court decision in *Oncale v. Sundowner Offshore Services, Inc.* [523 U.S. 75 (1998)] provides further support for this position. In the case, Oncale, a male, was employed as a roustabout on an eight-man oil platform crew in the Gulf of Mexico. Oncale claimed that he was forcibly subjected to sex-related humiliating actions against him by the crew of supervisory personnel. Although clearly most would anticipate a raw and rowdy environment, the Court reversed the Fifth Circuit Court of Appeals and allowed the case to proceed to trial. As the Court noted:

> Common sense and an appropriate sensitivity to social context will enable courts and juries to distinguish between simple teasing or rough housing among members of the same-sex, and conduct which a reasonable person in plaintiff's position would find severely hostile or abusive. [*Oncale*, 525 U.S. at 82]

In *Briseno v. Diamond Video World, Inc.* [2002 Cal. App. Unpub. LEXIS 1123 (Cal. App. 2d Dist. May 15, 2002)], in an unpublished opinion, the court affirmed a jury award for an adult video store employee who claimed his boss harassed him. The harassment reportedly included his female boss's insistence that he try out some of the adult sex merchandise. [*See* 18 *Employment Discrimination Report (EDR)* (BNA) 642 (May 29, 2002).]

Q 4:92 Does the conduct complained of in a hostile work environment claim have to be sexual in nature?

No. Although hostile work environment claims typically involve offensive conduct of a sexual nature, it is also possible to have a hostile work environment claim if the conduct is gender-specific and gender-based—for instance, offensive conduct or language such as derogatory, gender-based slurs directed at subordinates. The requirement that the conduct be gender-based or because of gender is fundamental to stating a claim for sexual harassment, which is a form of sex discrimination.

Q 4:93 What remedies are available to a complainant under either a hostile work environment or quid pro quo sexual harassment claim under Title VII?

The remedies available to a complainant alleging sexual harassment prohibited by Title VII include monetary relief and a wide range of injunctive and affirmative relief. Monetary relief is available to compensate victims of sexual harassment for redress of economic losses resulting from the sexual harassment, particularly loss of income and the value of any fringe benefits lost as a result of the harassment. Typically, loss of income has two components—back-pay for lost income and fringe benefits to the date of the verdict and front pay for future lost income and fringe benefits resulting from the harassment.

The Civil Rights Act of 1991, which amended Title VII, makes monetary relief available to compensate victims of intentional harassment for mental anguish as well as pecuniary losses. In addition, in the event of employer malice or reckless indifference, punitive damages may be imposed under the Act. All compensation for non-pecuniary losses is subject to caps established by the Act. For example, the cap for employers with more than 500 employees is $300,000. This cap has no application to back- or front-pay awards.

In addition to monetary relief, victims of sexual harassment also have a wide range of injunctive and affirmative relief available. Injunctions can take many forms, such as reinstatement of the victim to the position he or she would have occupied but for the sexual harassment. In addition, a prevailing plaintiff is entitled to recover from the employer his or her attorneys' fees, together with all costs properly taxable in the litigation.

Q 4:94 Does a hostile work environment claim require that the harasser be a supervisor?

No. Unlike quid pro quo sexual harassment claims, hostile work environment claims may be maintained on the basis of conduct engaged in by co-employees, vendors, customers, or other non-employees. Employers have an affirmative duty to take steps to prevent harassment and, if it can be determined that an employer knew or should have known of the conduct, failure to take prompt remedial action will expose the employer to liability under a hostile work environment claim.

Knowledge by the employer can be actual or ascribed constructively. Actual knowledge will be deemed to have existed, generally, if any supervisors were aware of the evidence upon which the hostile work environment claim is based. In addition to actual knowledge, the courts will impute constructive knowledge if it is ultimately determined that the harassment was so pervasive that the employer should have known of the conduct. Employers who hide their heads in the sand or turn a blind eye to what may appear to be sexual conduct or communication of an unwelcome nature do so at their own peril. Because employers may be held to have constructive knowledge of harassment even if they were in fact unaware of it, it is good practice for employers to ensure that all supervisory and management personnel understand they must report all instances of possible sexual harassment.

Q 4:95   If an employee tells a fellow employee a dirty joke, is it sexual harassment under a hostile work environment claim?

Probably not. In the first instance, as with all sexual harassment, the conduct complained of must be unwelcome. Therefore, to the extent that the other employee participated in the joke telling or did not express any displeasure with the conduct at the time, the evidence would appear to show that such conduct was not unwelcome. Second, the employer will only be held liable for hostile work environment claims to the extent it knew or should have known of the alleged conduct. If no actual or constructive knowledge of the event can be established, liability will not be imposed.

It is not the purpose of Title VII to eliminate or prohibit all conduct of a sexual nature in the workplace. Hostile work environment claims are a matter of degree. A solitary instance of vulgarity will not constitute sexual harassment because it is isolated. An infrequent joke, sporadic vulgarity, or occasional teasing is generally not sufficient to maintain a claim for hostile work environment. Although there is no precise formula, in analyzing the totality of the circumstances, the issue is whether the conduct complained of is sufficiently severe or pervasive to create a hostile working environment.

Q 4:96   When does a particular conduct complained of rise to the level of a hostile work environment claim?

When evaluating hostile work environment claims, the alleged conduct should be analyzed both for its severity and its pervasiveness. To the extent that the alleged conduct is trivial (i.e., an incident of staring) and not pervasive (e.g., two such incidents over a four-year period) it will not be sufficient to form the basis for a hostile work environment claim. The more severe the conduct, the less need to show the pervasive nature of the conduct. On the other hand, conduct that if sporadic would not amount to sexual harassment may rise to the level of a hostile work environment claim if it is pervasive enough.

The Supreme Court in *Harris v. Fork Lift Systems, Inc.* [510 U.S. 17 (1993)] addressed the issue of the level of conduct necessary to create an abusive and hostile work environment actionable under Title VII. In *Harris*, Theresa Harris was found to have been subjected to gender-based insults and unwanted sexual innuendoes throughout her tenure, ultimately quitting her employment as a result of this activity. Specifically, her supervisor was found to have said to her on several occasions, in the presence of other employees, words to the effect of "You're a woman, what do you know?" and "We need a man as the rental manager," and at least once told her she was a " dumb ass" woman. Also in front of others, her supervisor was found to have said that the two of them should go to the Holiday Inn to negotiate her raise, asked Harris and other female employees to get coins from his front pants pockets, and threw objects on the ground in front of Harris and other women and asked them to pick up the objects. When Harris complained, her supervisor expressed surprise that she was offended and said he was only joking and apologized. Although he promised that the conduct would stop, apparently he asked her on a later occasion, in front of customers, "What did you do, promise the guy . . . some [sex] Saturday night?" Thereafter, Harris quit and commenced litigation for hostile work environment sexual harassment under Title VII.

The Court, in addressing the law, held that when the workplace is permeated with discriminatory intimidation, ridicule, and insult that is sufficiently severe or pervasive to alter the conditions of the victim's employment and create an abusive working environment, Title VII is violated. [*Harris*, 510 U.S. at 22] The standard of review, according to *Harris*, is both objective and subjective—The conduct must be sufficiently severe or pervasive enough, from an objective sense in the mind of a reasonable person, to create a hostile or abusive working environment. In addition, the victim also must subjectively perceive the environment to be abusive and hostile.

In terms of the level of offensive behavior, the court in *Harris* took "a middle path" between any type of conduct that is merely offensive and requiring the conduct to cause tangible psychological injury. As the Court stated, "Title VII comes into play before the harassing conduct leads to a nervous breakdown." [*Harris*, 510 U.S. at 22]

On the other hand, tasteless, rude, and so-called "boorish" behavior, under certain circumstances, may not be sufficient to maintain a claim. In *Derrico v. Pinkerton's, Inc.* [1999 U.S. Dist. LEXIS 7220 (N.D. Ill. May 10, 1999)], a federal judge dismissed a hostile work environment claim based on the behavior of the plaintiff's supervisor. The supervisor was rude, made various sexual comments, and would grab his crotch, apparently to make a point during company meetings. Citing that the plaintiff was apparently no "blushing violet," the court found the behavior insufficiently sexual, severe, or pervasive to maintain the claim, when viewed both objectively and subjectively. [*See* 12 *Employment Discrimination Report (EDR)* (BNA) 786 (June 2, 1999).] In *Passananti v. Cook County* [689 F.3d 655 (7th Cir. 2012)], an investigator for the sheriff's department sued claiming sexual harassment based on her supervisor's repeated use of the word "bitch" when talking or referring to her. Although the district court vacated a jury verdict in favor of the employee, stating that the word "bitch" was not sufficient as a matter of law to maintain a claim for sexual harassment, the Seventh Circuit, on appeal, found that there was ample evidence in the record to support the jury's verdict that the repeated reference to the employee as a "bitch" was sufficient to maintain the harassment claim and reinstated the jury verdict.

Single incidents of harassing behavior are typically not sufficient to support a claim of hostile work environment unless they are particularly severe. In *Brooks v. City of San Mateo* [229 F.3d 917 (9th Cir. 2000)], the U.S. Court of Appeals for the Ninth Circuit affirmed a dismissal of a hostile work environment claim based on a single incident of fondling by a co-worker. The court reasoned that because the incident, although unsavory, was brief and isolated, it was not sufficient to meet the Harris standard; and this factor, together with the employer's quick remedial response, was sufficient reason to uphold a dismissal of the claim. [14 *Employment Discrimination Report (EDR)* (BNA) 855 (June 21, 2000)] However, if the harassment is severe and pervasive, such conduct may result in significant awards and relief. A grocery store manager that subjected teenage female store employees to a continuous barrage of sexual comments and innuendo, and consistently touched, massaged, or engaged in other inappropriate personal contact with the females, which the employer did nothing to correct after notice, was sufficiently severe and pervasive to not only support a jury verdict in excess of $1 million against the employer, but, the court held, the issuance of an injunction ensuring that the store manager would not be in a position to sexually harass the employees in the future. [*EEOC v. Karenkim, Inc.,* 698 F.3d 92 (2d Cir. 2012)]

Q 4:97   Are employers liable for the hostile work environment discrimination of their supervisors?

It has long been recognized that if a supervisor utilizes his or her authority to engage in what is commonly referred to as quid pro quo harassment, the employer is liable. Quid pro quo harassment requires adverse employment action by the supervisor, and because the adverse action is taken by virtue of the supervisor's power as provided by the company, employers are generally held responsible. In true hostile work environment situations, where there is no adverse employment action, the issue has been, until relatively recently, unclear. The U.S. Supreme Court decision in *Meritor Savings Bank, FSB v. Vinson* [477 U.S. 57 (1986)], established that principles of agency law should be utilized in determining the liability of companies for supervisory conduct, but *Meritor* also admonished that liability is not absolute in all circumstances. [*See Meritor,* 477 U.S. at 72.] Federal courts have struggled with determining the proper analysis for establishing employer liability for supervisor hostile environment claims, and the U.S. Supreme Court in two companion decisions issued on June 26, 1998, attempted to resolve and clarify this issue.

The companion cases are *Burlington Industries, Inc. v. Ellerth* [524 U.S. 742 (1998)] and *Faragher v. City of Boca Raton* [524 U.S. 775 (1998)]. In *Faragher,* a lifeguard claimed that she had been subjected to hostile work environment discrimination by her supervisor and it was found that the City had not, for all intents and purposes, promulgated and disseminated a harassment policy and Faragher had never complained to the City about her supervisor's conduct. In *Burlington,* Ellerth claimed that she was subjected to hostile environment discrimination by her supervisor, but acknowledged that she never complained about the behavior, despite a sexual harassment policy promulgated and disseminated by Burlington Industries. In both instances, neither victim suffered any adverse employment action by their supervisor as a result of the harassment. These were not situations where threats were fulfilled, but rather involved situations of unfulfilled threats. For example, in *Burlington,* Ellerth testified that her boss expressed the reservation during a promotion interview that she was not "loose enough," although she did in fact receive the promotion.

The Court, in *Burlington* and *Faragher*, reasoned through a myriad of agency principles followed by various circuits grappling with the liability issue, but ultimately adopted the following standard for liability:

> An employer is subject to vicarious liability to a victimized employee for an actionable hostile environment created by a supervisor with an immediate (or successively higher) authority over the employee. [*Faragher*, 524 U.S. at 807]

This standard for hostile work environment claims is consistent with the results reached in quid pro quo claims; however, with respect to hostile work environment cases, and mindful of *Meritor*, prior decisions have repeatedly admonished that a per se liability rule in hostile work environment claims involving supervisors is not appropriate. Prior federal courts have utilized theories of "constructive knowledge" where hostile work environments are severe, "scope of employment" analysis, and various analyses under agency principles to try to define a line between those situations where employers would be responsible for a supervisor's hostile work environment discrimination and those that would not impose liability. Recognizing both the interest in having an employer accountable for the actions of its supervisors, and the need not to have per se liability under these circumstances, the Court adopted an affirmative defense to vicarious liability of companies composed of two essential elements:

- The employer exercised reasonable care to prevent and correct promptly any sexually harassing behavior.
- The plaintiff/employee unreasonably failed to take advantage of any preventive or corrective opportunities provided by the employer.

Note that this affirmative defense is not applicable in the quid pro quo case, where a tangible adverse employment action occurs. It is only available in the so-called hostile work environment situation where the employee suffered no tangible adverse employment action. By providing an affirmative defense, the Supreme Court has attempted to hold employers accountable for the actions of their supervisors, while providing a safe harbor for an employer who does the right thing by attempting to prevent and correct harassment.

To some, these decisions impose strict liability on companies for supervisory conduct in hostile environment cases. If a supervisor engages in hostile work environment discrimination, which by definition must be severe or pervasive to be actionable, it would seem axiomatic that the employer had not taken sufficient preventive or corrective measures to prevent harassment as required under the first element of the affirmative defense. On the other hand, these decisions do provide better guidance to employers in terms of the steps they must undertake to lessen liability in this most difficult area.

Evolving case law underscores how reasonable preventative and corrective measures can shield an employer from liability. In *Coates v. Sundor Brands, Inc.* [160 F.3d 688 (11th Cir. Ga. 1998)], an employee alleged to have been subjected to severe and pervasive harassment by a co-worker (i.e., offering her money for sex). The company had instituted reasonable preventative and corrective measures of which the plaintiff failed to avail herself for some period of time. When ultimately notified, the employer took prompt and remedial action, suspending the co-worker, who ultimately resigned. Citing *Ellerth* and *Faragher*, the court found no liability and dismissed the lawsuit. [11 *Employment Discrimination Report (EDR)* (BNA) 721 (Dec. 2, 1998)] Similarly, in *Barrett v. Applied Radiant Energy Corp.* [240 F.3d 262 (4th Cir. Va. 2001)], the U.S. Court of Appeals for the Fourth Circuit found that an employee who claimed that she was subjected to sexual harassment by a supervisor could not maintain her claim because she had not utilized the company's complaint procedure and provided the company with an opportunity to correct the matter. [16 *Employment Discrimination Report (EDR)* (BNA) 273 (Feb. 28, 2001)]

Q 4:98 In cases where the employee claims constructive discharge, can the employer avail itself of the affirmative defenses described in *Ellerth* and *Faragher*?

The *Ellerth* and *Faragher* affirmative defenses to liability for a supervisor's conduct are available if the employer can demonstrate it utilized reasonable preventative and corrective measures to eliminate sexual harassment, which the employee failed to avail him or herself of, and which if they did, would have prevented or corrected the situation. In cases involving constructive discharge, a resignation by the employee is essentially treated as a discharge if the employee can demonstrate that the workplace became so intolerable that a reasonable person would have resigned under the circumstances. Many have questioned, in a constructive discharge situation, whether the employer can, nonetheless, maintain the affirmative defenses under *Ellerth* and *Faragher*.

In the June 14, 2004, decision *Pennsylvania State Police v. Suders* [542 U.S. 129 (2004)], the Supreme Court concluded that if an employee's decision to quit was a reasonable response to an adverse action officially changing her employment status or situation (e.g., a humiliating demotion, extreme cut in pay, or transfer to a position in which he or she would face unbearable working conditions) that the *Ellerth* and *Faragher* affirmative defense would not be available. On the other hand, if the decision to resign was not in response to such official action, the affirmative defenses under *Ellerth* and *Faragher* may be available. The Supreme Court specifically stated that the lower court's ruling that the affirmative defenses described in *Ellerth* and *Faragher* were never available in constructive discharge cases is not the case.

Q 4:99 Can a single incident of sexual harassment support a hostile work environment claim?

The infamous case *Jones v. Clinton* [99 F. Supp. 657 (E.D. Ark. 1998)], challenged some people's notion of hostile work environment harassment. Jones alleged that she was escorted to a hotel room occupied by then-Governor Clinton, who reportedly:

took her hand and pulled her toward him, according to Jones. She removed her hand and stepped back several feet, but he moved closer, made comments about her appearance, put her hand on his leg, and attempted to kiss her on the neck, according to [Jones'] statement of material facts. Jones said she objected, moved away from him, and sat down on the couch. Clinton allegedly lowered his trousers and underwear and exposed his [genitals], sat down on the couch next to her, and asked her to engage in sexual activity. When Jones said she had to leave, Clinton indicated that he did not want to make her do anything she did not want to do, and pulled up his pants. [*See* 10 *Employment Discrimination Report (EDR)* (BNA) 443 (Apr. 3, 1996).]

The court, in reviewing whether these allegations were sufficient for purposes of creating a hostile work environment, held that the conduct, "does not in any way constitute the kind of pervasive, intimidating, abusive conduct that courts require to establish a hostile work environment claim." Although the court acknowledged that a single incident of sexual harassment, if severe enough, may support a claim for hostile work environment, the court concluded that the conduct attributed to Clinton "is not one of those exceptional cases in which a single incident of sexual harassment, such as an assault, was deemed sufficient to state a claim of hostile work environment harassment." [*See* "Court Dismisses Claims Against President, Finding Lack of Evidence of Harm to Jones," 10 *Employment Discrimination Report (EDR)* (BNA) 443–44 (Apr. 3, 1996).]

Some commentators have argued that if the conduct attributed to Clinton, if true, is not sufficient to support a single-incident hostile work environment claim, what is? Some cynically view the decision as condoning a "first bite" rule with respect to hostile work environment claims. It should be noted, as it relates to quid pro quo analysis, that the court found no adverse employment decision as a result of the incident, which if a necessary component to quid pro quo harassment.

In 1993, the Supreme Court of Michigan had an opportunity to address the single-incident issue as it relates to hostile work environment claims. In *Radke v. Everett*, a veterinary technician, Ms. Radke, was alone with her boss when her boss sat next to her on a couch. According to the plaintiff's allegations:

She attempted to leave the couch the minute Dr. Everett sat next to her, but he physically restrained her by firmly placing his arm around her neck and holding her down. . . . "I tried to pull my head up three times and on the third time, I realized he was not going to let me go. Finally, when his arm relaxed, I sprung forward and I told him "you don't want to do this." Although plaintiff forcibly escaped his grip, Everett began to flatter her. Plaintiff rebuffed his new advances by stating, "You don't want to do this . . . I don't want to do this, you're married, I'm married." Everett responded by caressing plaintiff's neck and again she protested, but he simply ignored her pleas. Indeed, he then attempted to kiss her by grabbing her neck and pushing his face toward her. Plaintiff successfully pushed his face away, left the couch and walked across the room. The working day was finished without incident. [442 Mich. 367, 375–76 (1993)]

In assessing this incident, which lasted a total of approximately five minutes, the court concluded that the incident, although a single incident, was sufficiently offensive to permit the plaintiff to maintain a claim of hostile work environment.

In situations not involving supervisors, courts are consistent in their lack of support for claims involving isolated or single instances of alleged harassment. For example, in *Porta v. Dukes* [1998 U.S. Dist. LEXIS 12325 (E.D. Pa. Aug. 11, 1998)], a series of rude, and at least partially sexually offensive, statements made by a co-worker to a recently married woman on one occasion were found insufficient to support a claim. [11 *Employment Discrimination Report (EDR)* (BNA) 333 (Sept. 2, 1998); *see also* Brooks v. City of San Mateo (discussed in Q 4:96) where a single incident of fondling by a co-worker was insufficient to support a hostile work environment case.]

Q 4:100   Is the employer ever liable for sexual harassment conducted by a third party not employed by the employer?

The legal foundation for an employer's liability for sexual harassment in the workplace is that the harassing and discriminatory conduct affects the victim's terms and conditions of employment. Obviously, harassment by a supervisor or co-worker can create a hostile work environment; however, such an environment can also be caused by a third party. If an employer tolerates or encourages harassment by outsiders on the employer's premises, then the hostile work environment that results will be the employer's legal responsibility, even though the harassers are not employed by that company. For instance, if a law firm required a female associate attorney to deal with a valued client who sexually harassed the attorney and refused to act upon her subsequent complaints because the firm did not want to jeopardize the client relationship, that law firm could be liable for the damages resulting from the harassment. For example, in *Pickett v. Sheridan Health Care Center* [610 F.3d 434 (7th Cir. 2010)], a nursing home nurse complained that she was being subjected to harassment by nursing home residents. However, because it involved its clients, the employer was unwilling to take the claims seriously and did not take appropriate action. In the case the jury verdict award of $15,000 in compensatory damages and $50,000 in punitive damages was upheld by the Seventh Circuit.

Q 4:101   What steps should an employer take to limit its exposure and liability to sexual harassment claims?

In any workplace, the danger that an employer will be held responsible for a sexual harassment claim is real. Moreover, even marginal claims cost the company dearly in legal fees and resources. It is naive to assume that any employer can completely do away with potential exposure and liability. Nonetheless, there are general guidelines an employer can follow to reduce the risk and liability of sexual harassment claims:

- Create and disseminate a written sexual harassment policy, which provides a "user-friendly" mechanism to report known or suspected harassment situations;

- Educate all employees about the company's sexual harassment policy and train supervisors and management to spot and report potentially risky situations;

- Genuinely encourage employees to report instances of known or suspected harassment;

- Investigate promptly and thoroughly all internal complaints alleging sexual harassment; and

- Act promptly to remedy any sexual harassment found to have occurred, including disciplining the harasser (typically, discharge).

Q 4:102   What action should management take in response to a sexual harassment complaint?

Most employers have adopted a written company policy addressing sexual harassment; this policy should include an internal complaint procedure for known or suspected violations of its provisions. Yet merely adopting an official policy is not sufficient. Equally important is prompt and proper response. Management should immediately conduct an investigation in response to a complaint of sexual harassment or suspected violation of its policy.

Policies are critical, but actions speak louder than words. Two U.S. Court of Appeals decisions underscore this axiom. In *Carmon v. Lubrizol Corp.* [17 F.3d 791 (5th Cir. 1994)] and *Reed v. Delta Air Lines, Inc.* [1994 U.S. App. LEXIS 7440 (6th Cir. Tenn. Apr. 13, 1994)], claims against the employers were rejected because they responded promptly and properly to internal complaints of sexual harassment. Both *Reed* and *Carmon* emphasized the promptness nature of the company's response. In *Carmon*, the court found it significant that the company "sprang into action" when confronted with a complaint. Immediate response to a complaint emphasizes an employer's commitment to its policies and the importance that the company gives complaints made under its policy.

Q 4:103   Should an employer encourage its employee to come forward with internal complaints of sexual harassment?

Yes. Liability in some instances may be imputed to the employer by virtue of either supervisory conduct or evidence that the employer should have known of the offensive conduct even if it, in fact, did not. Moreover, defending sexual harassment litigation is extremely time-consuming and costly, with a significant potential for ultimate exposure and liability. Therefore, under basic benefit/risk analysis, employers should have procedures in place that encourage employees to come forward and internally report instances of known or suspected sexual harassment. This gives the employer an opportunity to remedy the situation before it escalates to litigation.

In addition, a prompt and thorough investigation of hostile work environment claims, assuming the employer had no actual or constructive knowledge of the offensive conduct, can be an effective defense to claims of sexual harassment. As a result of Supreme Court decisions, prompt and thorough investigations are integral to maintaining affirmation defenses to hostile work environment claims. Although an employer cannot always prevent individuals from engaging in behavior that may support a claim of sexual harassment, it can encourage employees to come forward with known or suspected violations to allow the employer to take action and possibly avoid liability.

As a result, it is generally recommended that a "user-friendly" procedure be adopted for reporting instances of harassment. This would include allowing complaints to be made verbally (at least initially) and permitting employees to bypass their immediate supervisors to other designated individuals (i.e., higher-ups and human resource personnel). Although ultimately, in the investigation, great pains should be taken to reduce all discussions to writing (e.g., signed statements, signed notes, and the like) to preserve the integrity of the investigation from an evidentiary standpoint, at least initially, the procedure to lodge a complaint should be "user-friendly" so as to encourage and not discourage people from coming forward.

Q 4:104   What is an internal investigation of sexual harassment complaints and who should conduct it?

A prompt and thorough investigation of internal complaints of sexual harassment is integral for any employer interested in reducing the risk and exposure to sexual harassment litigation. In co-worker sexual harassment claims, the company is only liable for sexual harassment that it either condones or tolerates. Companies are generally held responsible for situations they know about or should know about but do nothing to attempt to stop. Although liability is more strictly held in cases involving supervisors, there is still a potential that the liability of the company could be avoided if it promptly and thoroughly responds to the harassing conduct when it learns of the behavior. The U.S. Supreme Court decisions in *Faragher v. City of Boca Raton* [524 U.S. 775 (1998)] and *Burlington Industries v. Ellerth* [524 U.S. 775 (1998)], provide an affirmative defense to an employee's liability for hostile environments caused by a supervisor if the employer takes steps to correct sexually harassing behavior. As a result, internal investigations by a company are critical to the employer and are usually used as a basis to defend sexual harassment claims. The employer should do everything possible to document properly the investigation, the facts uncovered during the investigation, and the conclusions it reaches based on the facts, in a nature and manner that will hold up after careful review during litigation. The need for documentation cannot be overstated.

Usually, companies can utilize personnel within their ranks (usually two individuals) to conduct the investigation. Utilization of outside assistance is usually only called for in instances where the alleged harasser is the owner or highly placed official in the company. Companies should beware of using their own attorneys to conduct such investigations. Although attorneys can be very useful in coordinating and assisting the investigation behind the scenes, if the attorneys actually conduct the investigation themselves, they may become witnesses if the investigation is used as a defense to a later claim, and the attorney-client privilege would therefore be eroded. Moreover, the Federal Trade Commission issued an opinion that lawyers who conduct investigations for a fee are "consumer reporting agencies" to which the broad requirements of the Fair Credit and Reporting Act apply.

Q 4:105   What is the first step an employer should take when investigating a sexual harassment complaint?

Although investigations of sexual harassment claims vary depending upon the circumstances, there are general guidelines an employer should follow when investigating a sexual harassment complaint. First, investigators should be selected. As a rule of thumb, it is wise to have more than one investigator, but more than two can be cumbersome. Employers generally have managers or supervisory personnel who can adequately conduct the investigation; independent investigators are necessary only in unusual situations. Obviously, the alleged harasser should not be one of the investigators. In addition, it is recommended that the same investigators be involved in the entire investigation process.

After their selection, the investigators should review the employer's sexual harassment policy as well as applicable state and federal law on the subject. The investigators should then create a confidential investigation file within which all notes, statements, and other evidence is to be kept pending ultimate disposition of the claim. An employer should consult with its legal advisors, who can assist in monitoring and directing the investigation process.

The investigation is a fact-finding mission that involves interviews of the complainant, the alleged harasser, and other witnesses of the alleged conduct. Because sexual harassment complaints are fuel for office gossip and rumor, safeguards to ensure the confidentiality of the investigation should be implemented. Interviews should be conducted at a site that provides the highest level of confidentiality practicable under the circumstances.

Q 4:106   Once investigators have been selected, what is the first thing they should do in response to a claim of sexual harassment?

The place to begin the investigation is with the complainant. The investigators should interview the complainant and, in doing so, accomplish the following:

- Explain the process of the investigation to the complainant but make no promises about any conclusions that might be reached;
- Explain that the employer will endeavor to keep the investigation confidential but that, in order to investigate properly, the employer cannot promise complete confidentiality;
- Ascertain the facts of the incidents;

- Find out the names of any witnesses;
- Obtain and review any documentary or other physical evidence;
- Determine the effect of the alleged harassment on the complainant; and
- Ask the complainant what he or she would like the company to do.

When conducting the interview, the investigators should be objective and stick to the facts. Extensive notes should be made and, if possible, a written statement should be taken from the complainant. If he or she does not want to write out a complaint, the complainant should be asked to sign the notes taken during the interview affirming that they accurately state the complaint. During the interview, the complainant will undoubtedly ask the investigators what they are going to do to the alleged perpetrator. Investigators should simply reply that no conclusions will be reached until the investigation is concluded and that the results of the investigation will be discussed with the complainant at that time. Although all complaints of sexual harassment should be taken seriously, no decision should be made on the basis of the complaint itself. In addition, investigators should advise the complainant that any retaliation as a result of the complaint is illegal and that the complainant should come forward immediately if he or she believes that any retaliation has been threatened.

Q 4:107 After interviewing the complainant, what are the next steps in the investigation of a sexual harassment complaint?

After the complainant has been questioned, the person being accused should be interviewed. At the beginning of the interview, the investigator should explain its purpose and emphasize that no decision has been made regarding the truthfulness of the allegations. It is important to identify the specific basis for the sexual harassment complaint and ask the alleged perpetrator to respond to the charge. It is important to get specifics—to get the names of any witnesses, obtain documentary or other physical evidence and, if possible, a statement from the accused person. If it is not possible to obtain a statement, the employer should make sure that the alleged perpetrator reviews and signs the interview notes acknowledging that they are an accurate statement of his or her response to the charge. The employer should tell the accused person that the company will endeavor to keep the investigation confidential to the extent practicable under the circumstances, but it cannot promise complete confidentiality.

Next, assuming the investigators have no reason to re-interview the complainant, they may interview witnesses. The interviews should take place in the same manner and in the same form as those conducted with the complainant and the alleged perpetrator.

It is not at all uncommon for interviews to continue between the complainant, the alleged perpetrator, witnesses, and other parties. There is no rigid format once the alleged victim and the alleged perpetrator have been interviewed. The focus of the investigation is to determine the facts and evaluate the credibility of the complaint; therefore, as the investigation unfolds and more and more information is elicited, further interviews typically became necessary.

Q 4:108   After the interviews are over, how should an employer conclude its investigation of a sexual harassment complaint?

When an investigation is completed, a thorough and evenhanded report should be prepared by the investigators. This report should have a chronological format indicating when the complaint was first made, the details of the complaint, interviews conducted, the dates and times of all interviews, the substance of the interviews, and documents reviewed, if any. The investigators should conclude in the report whether or not the facts substantiate the claim of sexual harassment and provide specific justification. Although not absolutely necessary, it is recommended that a senior supervisor review the report to determine if further investigation is necessary.

If a violation is determined as a result of the investigation, the employer should take prompt remedial action to eliminate the violation and to ensure that it does not occur again. Typically, such remedial action will include, at a minimum, disciplinary action against the harasser.

On the other hand, if no determination is possible, the employer should inform the complainant and the alleged harasser of its finding. The employer should then reiterate to the complainant and the alleged harasser that the company is committed to the enforcement of its policy and will not tolerate sexual harassment or retaliation of any sort. Also, the complainant should be advised to provide additional information relating to any policy violations in the future or any actual or threatened retaliation for coming forward.

Q 4:109   How can employers avoid mistakes when faced with sexual harassment complaints?

The biggest mistake employers tend to make when faced with internal complaints of sexual harassment is that they rush to judgment even before the investigation is initiated. Information concerning sexual harassment is brought to light, and the employer, supplied with the accusation alone, immediately concludes that the allegations are correct and moves to discipline the alleged harasser. This is particularly common in situations where the allegations are detailed and outrageous. It almost seems that the wilder the story, the more compelled the employer is to believe the claim and to take action against the alleged harasser. This is a mistake.

It is not at all uncommon today that, if action is taken against an alleged harasser without careful investigation, the employer faces litigation from the accused for wrongful discharge, defamation, or similar claims. Recognizing that there are many potential sources of liability when somebody comes forward with an internal sexual harassment complaint, employers should not rush to judgment against the alleged harasser, but should reserve decision until after a full and complete investigation has been concluded. Even if the internal complaint, when first discovered, appears credible, no action should be taken until after the investigation. Experience shows that there are two sides to every story. Until an investigation is concluded, no decisions should be made about the resolution of the claim.

Another common mistake employers make is not taking the internal complaint seriously and rushing to a judgment that the complaint is not worthy of investigation. This often occurs when the allegations of harassment are somewhat ambiguous and non-alarming in nature, leading the employer to conclude that the allegations are not serious or worthy of further investigation. Any time an employee complains of sexual harassment, the complaint should be taken seriously, not because the employer believes the sexual harassment has occurred, but because the company is concerned with reducing its exposure to sexual harassment claims.

Q 4:110   What are the main points to keep in mind before undertaking an investigation of an internal sexual harassment complaint?

Before beginning an investigation it is well to remember that patience is essential. Beyond that it is wise to:

- Take all complaints seriously;
- Remember that the process of conducting the investigation is as important as the outcome in terms of reducing exposure to litigation;
- Make no decision until the investigation is concluded;
- Keep complete records of all interviews—what was said, when it was said, how long the interviews lasted;
- Have the persons interviewed sign statements or copies of the notes taken in order to preserve the integrity of the investigation and support its conclusion; and
- Make a meticulous effort to uncover the facts of any allegation, which is more likely to be viewed by others (e.g., a court) as thorough and objective.

Q 4:111   As long as a correct conclusion is reached, how important is it that an employer conduct a thorough investigation?

No employer can be certain that it has come to the right conclusion until after a thorough investigation has been conducted. Whether or not sexual harassment took place is an issue of fact; until an investigation is completed to determine the facts, an employer cannot conclude it has come to the right conclusion.

The only right conclusion is one that is based upon the facts learned during an investigation. Employers often focus immediately upon conclusions and worry about what actions they must take as a result of the internal sexual harassment complaint. The better approach is to focus upon the investigation. Once this has been completed, the conclusions usually are much easier to reach and flow directly from the information uncovered through the investigation.

Q 4:112   If, after an investigation, an employer cannot determine whether sexual harassment has occurred, should the employer take the side of the complainant to avoid liability?

No. If there is no factual basis for concluding that sexual harassment has occurred, and if both parties are equally credible, it would be unwise, from a liability standpoint, to disregard the investigation and discipline the alleged harasser anyway. There are two potential sources of liability when a sexual harassment complaint is made—one from the alleged victim and one from the alleged harasser. Taking action against an alleged harasser, without proper foundation, may expose the company to actions for wrongful discharge, defamation, or similar causes.

The better course of action is to meet with the complainant to explain the investigation process and the finding of insufficient evidence to support a claim of sexual harassment. The complainant should then be urged to come forward in the event that he or she becomes aware of further evidence of sexual harassment or experiences retaliation as a result of coming forward. The alleged harasser should also be informed of the employer's conclusions at which time the employer should reiterate its strong intolerance of sexual harassment or any retaliation as a result of the internal sexual harassment complaint.

Q 4:113   Are there any remedial steps an employer must take before it concludes its investigation of an internal complaint of sexual harassment?

In addition to undertaking a thorough and prompt investigation of an internal complaint, employers are required to take remedial action to prevent foreseeable sexual harassment. Most often, remedial action is taken after the conclusion of the investigation, by way of discipline of the person found to have engaged in sexual harassment. Nonetheless, in certain instances employers may want to take interim remedial measures if it appears that immediate measures are necessary to prevent foreseeable violations of a sexual harassment policy. Taking some measure of temporary remedial action at the outset may assist in reducing the risk of liability for an employer. If, for instance, a complainant says that he or she will resign if forced to return to his or her position, the employer might consider, rather than open itself to a claim of constructive discharge, a temporary transfer, a vacation, or a leave of absence for the complainant. Whatever measures are taken temporarily to relieve the situation, pending conclusion of the investigation, should be with the consent of the complainant, and care should be taken to ensure that the measures cannot be construed as an adverse action against the complainant. On the other hand, in extreme situations measures may be undertaken, at least temporarily, to remove the alleged harasser from his or her assignment, making it clear that no conclusion will be reached until after the investigation is concluded.

Q 4:114   What are the elements of a sexual harassment policy?

Sexual harassment policies vary greatly in wording and length; however, any good sexual harassment policy should contain certain elements.

The first element of a sexual harassment policy should be a clear and succinct definition of sexual harassment, preferably taken directly from the definition of sexual harassment provided in Title VII, as may be modified by state law. Whatever definition of sexual harassment is used should be succinct and limited to conduct that is illegal under applicable federal and state law. To the extent that an employer includes within its definition language more expansive than that provided under federal or state law, it runs a significant risk. Specifically, an employer might receive complaints about conduct that is not actionable under applicable federal or state law, but nonetheless is a violation of its sexual harassment policy, which provides a more expansive definition of sexual harassment. Courts have allowed such claims to go forward.

The policy should encourage individuals to report instances of threatened or actual violations of the policy. Some employers have a strict policy requiring that the initial report be in writing. Others do not impose such stringent requirements; they allow verbal reporting. The problem with a stringent written requirement is that it may discourage people from coming forward. The purpose of a sexual harassment policy is to avoid sexual harassment litigation, and requiring reporting to be done in writing, for what little value it may have in litigation at a later time, seems to work against that goal. Rather, a user-friendly approach should be taken. Although, once the situation has been reported, a written statement by the complainant is always advisable, a written statement should not be necessary merely to report a situation.

The policy also should identify to whom the complaint is to be directed. A reporting requirement that directs the complainant to report the situation to his or her supervisor is not advisable—particularly in quid pro quo sexual harassment claims, when it is the supervisor whom the complainant wishes to report; therefore, the policy should contain alternatives to reporting to a direct supervisor, such as the human resources department or some other manager or officer of the company.

In addition, the policy should provide that the employer will undertake a prompt and thorough investigation of the complaint. This is nothing more than what the courts require for the employer to avoid liability for a sexual harassment claim, particularly hostile work environment claims arising from coworker conduct of which the employer was not and should not have been aware.

The issue of confidentiality should be addressed in the sexual harassment policy. It is unwise to promise complete confidentiality. Clearly, whatever information is brought forward must necessarily be discussed with others in connection with the investigation. As a result, complete confidentiality or anonymity of the alleged victim cannot be maintained. The policy should state that the employer will endeavor to keep the complaint as confidential as is practicable in light of its need to disclose information, as necessary, during its investigation. For liability purposes, the employer should take steps to do what it can to keep the investigation confidential and discuss or disclose information only on a need-to-know basis.

Retaliation as a result of an internal sexual harassment complaint is a violation of Title VII; therefore, the policy should advise that no retaliation will be tolerated for reporting known or suspected violations of the employer's sexual harassment policy. Someone who believes retaliation has occurred or has been threatened should use the same procedure for reporting sexual harassment complaints.

The policy should make it clear that individuals found to have violated the employer's sexual harassment policy will be subject to discipline, up to and including discharge. Although discharge is typically the result, the employer should establish appropriate responses to circumstances that may not warrant discharge.

Q 4:115   What is an example of an anti-harassment policy?

Harassment policies can change from state to state based on unique rights in one state that may not be available in others. In addition, complaint procedures, although they should be user-friendly, can take a variety of forms. However, below is a sexual harassment complaint and complaint procedure contained within a non-discrimination policy, which includes protections unique under Michigan law.

NONDISCRIMINATION POLICY

The Company is an equal opportunity employer and prohibits discrimination on the basis of race, color, sex, age, religion, height, weight, national origin, marital status, handicap, or disability. This policy applies to all circumstances of employment, including but not limited to hiring, placement, promotion, termination, layoff, recall, transfer, leaves of absence, compensation, and discharge. As a part of this policy, the Company prohibits comments, communications, or other conduct in the workplace disparaging or unlawfully harassing any person on the basis of race, color, sex, age, religion, height, weight, national origin, marital status, handicap, or disability. Conduct in violation of this policy may result in disciplinary action, up to and including discharge.

Persons With Disabilities Act (PWDA)

In accordance with PWDA, an employee with a handicap must notify the Company, in writing, of any need for accommodation within 182 days after the date the employee knew or reasonably should have known that an accommodation was needed.

Sexual Harassment

The Company prohibits sexual harassment of any kind by any person. Sexual harassment includes unwelcome sexual advances, unwelcome requests for sexual favors, and other unwelcome verbal or physical conduct or communication of a sexual nature when:

- Submission to such conduct or communication is made either explicitly or implicitly a term or condition of the individual's employment;

- Submission to or rejection of such conduct or communication by an individual is used as the basis for employment decisions affecting such individual; or

- Such conduct or communication has the purpose or effect of substantially interfering with an individual's employment or creates an intimidating, hostile, or offensive work environment.

Conduct in violation of this policy may result in disciplinary action, up to and including discharge.

Complaint Procedure

If you believe that you or another employee has been the subject of discrimination or harassment, you should report the situation to your supervisor promptly or, if you feel that your supervisor has failed to address the situation adequately or would rather not approach your supervisor, you should speak directly with the President or any other manager or officer of the Company.

A prompt investigation of all complaints will be undertaken. To the extent practicable under the circumstances, efforts will be made to maintain the confidences and privacy of the complaining party and other involved parties during the investigation. Any employee who, after investigation, is determined to have participated in or engaged in discrimination or harassment may be subject to discipline, up to and including discharge.

The Company prohibits any retaliation against an employee who, in good faith, has made a complaint under this procedure. Any employee of the Company who, after reasonable investigation, has been determined to have retaliated against an employee for making a good faith complaint under the complaint procedure may be subject to discipline, up to and including discharge. If an employee believes he or she has been the subject of retaliation, the employee should use the complaint procedure described above.

Q 4:116   Should employers train all employees, including supervisors, to recognize sexual harassment?

Yes. Training is a critical element for any employer concerned with reducing its risk and exposure to sexual harassment claims. A policy alone will not protect an employer from liability. Violations need to be reported. Without proper training, employees and supervisors will not always recognize violations and may be unable to make informed decisions regarding reporting. In addition, education emphasizes an employer's intolerance for sexual harassment and the seriousness with which the employer treats the subject. If a company takes the time to educate employees, employees will more likely believe that the company is serious about its policy and will feel more inclined to come forward in situations of known or suspected violations of company policy.

Supervisors in particular need to understand their unique responsibilities when it comes to sexual harassment. As the eyes and ears of the employer, they must report such situations when they become aware of them, even if it does not involve one of their own subordinates. Failure to do so should be considered a failure of a supervisor properly to perform his or her job.

Q 4:117   Once training sessions in sexual harassment policies have been held, must there be additional training?

Yes. Sexual harassment training should be perceived as a continuing process. Personnel changes and the mere passage of time usually make it necessary for an employer to retrain on a year-to-year basis in order to obtain the desired impact.

The Americans with Disabilities Act

Q 4:118   What is the *Americans with Disabilities Act*?

The ADA is comprehensive federal legislation protecting disabled individuals. It affects private employers, public employers, public transportation, public accommodations, and the telecommunications industries. The ADA comprises five titles. Title I prohibits certain types of discrimination by covered employers. Title II covers public services and prohibits discrimination against persons with disabilities in public transportation. Title III addresses public accommodations and services operated by private entities that are open to the public; it provides for statutorily mandated construction of and alterations to public accommodations and facilities for disabled patrons. Title IV details specific rules applicable to the telecommunications industry. Title V contains miscellaneous provisions regarding limitations and enforcement mechanisms of the ADA.

Q 4:119   Generally, what does the ADA provide with respect to private employers?

Title I of the ADA applies to the employment practices of private employers with 15 or more employees. Title I protects a qualified person with a disability from discrimination in job application procedures, hiring, advancement, discharge, compensation, job training, and other terms, conditions, and privileges of employment. In addition, Title I establishes prohibitions with respect to medical inquiries of applicants before they receive a bona fide offer of employment. Generally, to obtain protection under the ADA, the individual must be both "qualified" and " disabled" within the meaning of the ADA. If both cannot be demonstrated, no protection from discrimination will be afforded under the ADA.

Q 4:120   What private employers are covered by Title I of the ADA?

Private employers with 15 or more employees are covered by the ADA. It is not necessary, however, that the employer have 15 or more employees throughout any given year. Rather, much like the FMLA, the ADA requires only that the employer have 15 or more employees for each working day in each of 20 or more calendar weeks in the current or preceding calendar year. Thus, seasonal employers whose payrolls fluctuate may find themselves covered by the ADA even though, through most of the year, they employ less than 15 employees. As with other civil rights statutes, under the "ministerial" exception, grounded in the religion clauses of the First Amendment, ministers cannot maintain employment claims under the ADA against their employer. As the Supreme Court held in *Hosanna-Tabor Evangelical Lutheran Church and School v. EEOC* [132 S. Ct. 694 (2012)], a teacher who filed suit against a Lutheran Church for violation of the ADA arising from her termination could not maintain the claim because as a teacher, she was a commissioned "minister" of her religion who had undergone significant religious training following a formal process and as such, was a minister within the ministerial exception grounded in the religion clauses of the First Amendment.

Q 4:121   Have there been amendments to the ADA?

In 2008, the ADA Amendments Act (ADAAA) [Pub. L. No. 110-325] was signed into law. The ADAAA, effective January 1, 2009, repudiates a number of U.S. Supreme Court decisions that, over the years, limited the application of the ADA. The ADAAA reverses this trend by significantly expanding the definition of individuals with disabilities entitled to protection under the Act. The specifics of the ADAAA are discussed throughout this section. Since the effective date of the ADAAA, two circuit courts have held that the amendments are not to be applied retroactively. [Milholland v. Summer Cnty. Bd. of Ed., 569 F.3d 562 (6th Cir. 2009); Lytes v. D.C. Water & Sewer Auth., 572 F.3d 936 (D.C. Cir. 2009)] As such, the old ADA standards will continue to apply to claims arising from conduct prior to January 1, 2009. [*See also* Kemp v. Holder, 610 F.3d 231 (5th Cir. 2010).]

Q 4:122   Who is a *person with a disability* under the ADA?

A *person with a disability* is defined under the ADA as one who:

- Has a physical or mental impairment that substantially limits one or more major life activities;
- Has a history of a physical or mental impairment; or
- Is regarded as having a physical or mental impairment.

A *physical impairment* is defined as any physiological disorder or condition, cosmetic disfigurement, or anatomical loss that affects any biological system, including neurological, musculoskeletal, respiratory, cardiovascular, reproductive, and digestive systems, as well as special sense and speech organs. The key to understanding the ADA's definition of physical impairment is that there must be some discernible disorder or abnormality. Being left-handed would not qualify as a physical impairment. A normal pregnancy, although a condition related to the reproductive system, is not considered an abnormal condition or disorder, and therefore does not qualify as a physical impairment under the ADA. Similarly, the following generally are not considered physical elements: environmental, cultural, and economic disadvantages; physical characteristics; and normal deviations in height, weight, or strength. A disorder related to a pregnancy that is not considered normal may qualify as a physical impairment, depending on the circumstances.

Mental impairment is generally defined as any mental or psychological disorder such as mental retardation, organic brain syndrome, emotional or mental illness, and special learning disabilities. Mental impairment does not include personality traits such as poor judgment or a quick temper. Rather, the condition must rise to the level of a discernible disorder in order to be recognized as a mental impairment under the ADA.

Even if an individual suffers from a physical or mental impairment, no protection will be afforded under the ADA unless this impairment substantially limits the individual's ability to perform one or more major life activities. Impairments of a short duration (e.g., a slight sprain or a minor fracture) would not meet this test. To determine whether the limitation is substantial, the severity of the impairment and its expected duration will be considered when judging its impact on the individual's ability to perform a major life activity.

Q 4:123   Can side effects of medical treatment constitute a disability?

Subject to limitations, side effects from medical treatment may themselves constitute an impairment protectable under the ADA, even though the underlying condition is not itself a disability. As the court stated in *Sulima v. Tobyhanna Army Depot* [602 F.3d 177 (3d Cir. 2010)], side effects may constitute a disability if:

1. The treatment was required;
2. The treatment is not just an attractive option; and
3. The treatment is not required solely in anticipation of an impairment resulting from plaintiff's voluntary choices.

Q 4:124   Can the ADA apply to people who are not disabled?

The ADA, in certain circumstances, clearly protects people who are not currently disabled. An individual who does not currently have a physical or mental impairment but has a history of such an impairment will qualify for protection by the ADA. For example, an individual with a history of heart problems, digestive problems, or the like would be protected. Further, the EEOC has continuously maintained that the ADA protects those individuals who are mistakenly regarded by an employer as having a physical or mental impairment. Even though the individual does not medically qualify as having a disability, if the employer regards the employee as having a disability, the employee would seem to be protected under the ADA. Prior to the adoption of the ADAAA, to establish a claim under the "regarded as" language under the ADA, an individual had to establish that he or she was perceived by the employer as having a substantial impairment of one or more major life activities. Under the ADAAA, an individual qualifies as being "regarded as" disabled if he or she can establish that they were subjected to an action prohibited under the ADAAA because of actual or perceived physical or mental impairment, whether or not the impairment limits or is perceived to limit a major life activity. However, the ADAAA also provides that impairments that are transitory in nature are excluded from protection under the "regarded as" basis for recovery and defines a transitory impairment as one with an actual or expected duration of six months or less.

In the mid-1990s, various courts began requiring individuals who currently alleged that they are suffering from a disability to show that the disability substantially limits one or more major life activities, even if the condition is controlled through medication or treatment. Considering a condition in its medicated state as opposed to a non-medicated state, some commentators argued, would render the ADA inapplicable to those cases of chronic medical conditions that, as a result of treatment, do not substantially limit one or more major life activities. [*See, e.g.,* J. Frierson, "Medical Treatments Should Not Be Considered When Courts Determine 'Disability' under the ADA," 10 *Employment Discrimination Report (EDR)* (BNA) 166–70 (Feb. 4, 1998); Kocsis v. Multi-Care Mgmt., 97 F.3d 876 (6th Cir. 1996); and Matczak v. Frankfort Candy & Chocolate Co., 950 F. Supp. 693 (E.D. Pa. 1997).] Carried to its extreme, does this mean that an individual suffering from a serious disease, such as cancer or an immune deficiency syndrome, who as a result of successful medical treatment is not substantially limited from performing one or more major life activities could be discriminated against by an employer with impunity?

The U.S. Supreme Court, in the much publicized decision *Sutton, et al. v. United Air Lines, Inc.* [527 U.S. 471 (1999)], ruled that individuals are to be examined in the medicated as opposed to non-medicated state for purposes of determining whether they are disabled under the ADA. As such, any determination of disability must be made with reference to measures that mitigate the individual's impairment, such as, in the case of *Sutton*, eyeglasses and contact lenses. Nonetheless, the Court noted that even if an individual does not qualify as disabled because of mitigating measures, the individual is still protected from discrimination under the ADA if the employer regards the individual, mistakenly, as having a physical or mental impairment that substantially limits one or more major life activities. The Court affirmed the viability of a "regarded as" claim, which would offer protection in situations of discrimination founded on fear and prejudice as to the effects of various medical conditions.

The ADAAA reflects a 180 degree change from prior law in that the ADAAA specifically prohibits consideration of mitigating measures when determining whether an impairment is a disability under the ADA. Contrary to the U.S. Supreme Court decision in *Sutton v. United Airlines, Inc.* [527 U.S. 471 (1999)], mitigating measures that have ameliorative effects in controlling a condition, such as medication, medical supplies, equipment, prosthetics, and the like, are specifically not to be considered when determining whether an impairment substantially limits a major life activity.

Q 4:125   Are owners and/or shareholders counted as employees for purposes of meeting the 15 or more employee threshold under the ADA?

A medical clinic claimed that its four physicians who owned the clinic were not employees under the ADA, and therefore should not be counted toward meeting the 15 employee threshold, in defense of an ADA claim brought by one of its employees. Although the ADA has no clear definition of an employee, the U.S. Supreme Court, in *Clackamas Gastroenterology Associates, P.C. v. Wells* [538 U.S. 440 (2003)], held that the common law "realities based" definition of an employee was sufficient to determine whether or not the physicians should be counted as employees for purposes of the ADA. Of central focus is whether the individual acts independently and manages the organization, or whether the individual is subject to the organization's control. To the extent that control can be demonstrated, a determination that the individual is an employee is likely in most instances. The Court utilized the following issues to determine whether control can be established:

- Whether the organization can hire or fire the individual or set the rules and regulations of the individual's work;
- Whether and if so to what extent the organization supervises the individual's work;
- Whether the individual reports to someone higher in the organization;
- Whether and if so the extent the individual is able to influence the organization;
- Whether the parties intended the individual to be an employee as expressed in written agreements or contracts; and
- Whether the individual shares in profits, losses, and liabilities of the organization. [*Clackamas*, 538 U.S. at 1680]

Although not any one of these considerations is dispositive, the Court indicated that all of these items should be examined to determine whether the individual is an employee for purposes of meeting the 15 employee threshold under the ADA.

Q 4:126   What is a *qualified person* with a disability under the ADA?

To obtain protection under the ADA, an individual must not only have a disability but must be qualified. To be qualified under the ADA, an individual must satisfy the prerequisites of the employment sought (e.g., appropriate education, experience, and skills) and must be able to perform the essential functions of the position with or without reasonable accommodation. The *essential functions of a job* are defined as the "fundamental job duties that are intrinsic to the position." Ascertaining what is and what is not an essential job function for a position is critical for purposes of the ADA; without such information, an employer cannot effectively comply with its obligations under the ADA. Yet this determination is difficult. Not everything within a generic job description is going to be an essential job function. Many of the tasks associated with most jobs are ancillary to those jobs, while other tasks will be intrinsic to the position itself. Each specific job needs to be reviewed and analyzed to discover those duties but for the performance of which there would be no position.

Example 1. XYZ Company has two vacant positions—a receptionist and a secretary. An individual who cannot speak applies for both positions. After an analysis of the positions, it is clear that it is essential for the receptionist to be able to answer the telephones, and therefore communicate verbally; thus, the ability to communicate verbally is an essential job function for the receptionist position. Review of the secretarial position demonstrates that it is essentially a typing position, and although communication is important, the need for spoken communication is not essential and there are alternative ways, such as writing and typing, for the secretary to communicate with his or her supervisors. As a result, verbal communication would not be an essential job function of the secretarial position.

Example 2. XYZ Company has an opening for a foreman. The position involves supervising employees who operate machinery. As needed, the foreman fills in for an absent machinery worker. An applicant applies for the position who has the qualifications and skills necessary to supervise machinists. However, the applicant is, disabled and, because of his disabilities, cannot under any circumstances physically perform the job of a machinist. Is it an essential job function that the foreman be able to perform a machinist's work when necessary? The answer depends on how frequently fill-ins are necessary and to what extent other workers are available to perform such a task. If it happens infrequently, it is probably not an essential job function of the foreman's position. On the other hand, if it is a critical and necessary ingredient to the foreman's job, because it happens regularly and no others are available to perform this task, it may be an essential job function.

Employers covered by the ADA should prepare job descriptions for positions so that when an ADA issue arises, they have a place to begin analyzing their obligations and liabilities under the ADA. Accuracy of job descriptions is critical for purposes of the ADA. Jobs change regularly, and job descriptions should change with them. Internal measures should be adopted to ensure that the job descriptions are regularly updated as responsibilities and duties change. Employers that undertake to prepare job descriptions should ensure that they accurately reflect both the essential and non-essential functions of the position.

Q 4:127   How are the courts using the "qualified" requirement to limit ADA protection?

The courts appear to be limiting protection under the ADA by requiring that the individual also be qualified. As discussed previously, an individual must be both qualified and disabled within the meaning of the ADA to receive protection from discrimination. Some courts have held that an otherwise disabled individual is not qualified to perform the job, despite the fact that the lack of qualification stems from the disability.

In *Tyndall v. National Education Centers* [31 F.3d 209 (4th Cir. 1994)], the U.S. Court of Appeals for the Fourth Circuit was asked to determine whether a teacher suffering from an autoimmune system disorder was discriminated against when she was terminated for excessive absenteeism caused by her disorder. It was undisputed that the teacher's disorder was severe and resulted in frequent absenteeism. For almost three years, the school attempted to accommodate her condition by allowing frequent breaks, sick leave, and flexible work hours. It was only when the situation grew worse that the school made its decision to terminate the teacher's employment.

Armed with these facts, the court concluded that the frequent and prolonged absences effectively rendered the employee unable to perform effectively as a teacher and, consequently, she could not perform her essential job functions with reasonable accommodation and was not "qualified." The court stated that a "regular and reliable" level of attendance is a necessary element of most jobs and specifically found it to be an essential function of the plaintiff's position, upholding a dismissal of the suit by the trial court.

A similar result was reached in a Michigan Court of Appeals decision concerning the interpretation of the Michigan Handicappers Civil Rights Act (MHCRA), an act similar to the ADA. In *Damoth v. Edward C. Levy Co.* [448 Mich. 900 (1995)], a truck driver suffering from severe seizures claimed he had been terminated in violation of MHCRA. The facts demonstrated that the seizure disorder was so severe that the truck driver could not even legally hold a license to drive an automobile. Under these severe circumstances, the employer refused to reinstate the employee in his truck driving position after expiration of his medical leave. In its decision, the court agreed with the employer and upheld dismissal of the claim, stating that the disability effectively precluded the employee from performing the essential duties of his position as a truck driver. The Court specifically determined that no accommodation existed that would have allowed the employee to perform his essential job junctions and, as a result, the individual was not "qualified."

The Michigan Court of Appeals held that an employee suffering from a mental impairment who divulges to her psychiatrist that she harbored homicidal thoughts against a supervisor can be fired, without liability under the ADA, despite the fact that the homicidal thoughts are a direct result of the employee's disability. [*See* "Employee May Be Fired for Homicidal Thoughts," 12 Mich. LW 716 (Mar. 23, 1998).] The case was brought up through appeal of an arbitrator's decision that held that the worker was protected from discharge under the ADA and MHCRA. Although the grounds for seeking review were narrow, requiring a demonstration that the arbitrator committed an error of law, the court determined that an employee who expresses frighteningly specific and detailed homicidal thoughts regarding a co-employee to a psychiatrist does not qualify for protection under the ADA. In essence, the court reasoned that the homicidal thoughts made the employee "unqualified" despite the fact that the basis for the disqualification was the disability at issue. [Collins v. Blue Cross Blue Shield of Mich., 228 Mich. App. 560, 543–74 (1998)]

As opposed to requiring an employer to demonstrate that the employee posed a direct threat as an affirmative defense, it appears that the evolving position adopted by many circuit courts is that employees that threaten the safety of others in the workplace are simply not "qualified"—a "qualified" person with a "disability" being a prerequisite to maintaining a prima facie ADA claim. In *Calef Jr. v. The Gillette Co.* [322 F.3d 75 (1st Cir. 2003)], an employee terminated for making threats on numerous occasions, despite prior warnings, claimed that his violent behavior was a result of his medical condition and, therefore, his discharge was in violation of the ADA. Canvassing decisions from other circuit courts, the court concluded that if an employee engages in threatening behavior, the individual is simply not "qualified" for the position, such that the individual has no claim under the ADA. As the court stated succinctly:

> Put simply, the ADA does not require that an employee whose unacceptable behavior threatens the safety of others be retained, even if the behavior stems from a mental disability. Such an employee is not qualified. That was the point of our decision in *EEOC v. Amigo, Inc.*, 110 F.3d 135 (1st Cir. 1997), it is also the view of every other circuit case that has addressed a similar situation under the ADA or the Rehabilitation Act. [Citing decisions from the Seventh, Second, Tenth, Eighth, and D.C. Circuits.]

As such, in the ADA case of *Rose v. Laskey* [110 Fed. Appx. 136 (1st Cir. 2004)], once the court concluded that it was undisputed that the former employee had threatened violence, the court concluded that it was appropriate for the employer to take the threat at "face value" and discharge the employee, and thereby dismissed the employee's ADA claim despite the fact that the employee claimed that his unacceptable behavior resulted from his mental impairment.

Q 4:128 What is *reasonable accommodation* under the ADA?

Understanding the "reasonable accommodation" obligations under the ADA is essential in understanding an employer's obligations and liabilities. Once a person is determined to be a qualified individual with a disability and once the essential job functions of the position are ascertained, an employer must next determine whether the individual can perform his or her essential job functions with reasonable accommodation. The accommodation obligations of employers are the means by which the ADA seeks to accomplish one of its primary goals—keeping disabled employees in the workplace. Throughout the legislative history of the ADA, great concern was expressed over the number of disabled individuals who were either not working or having difficulties remaining employed. By requiring employers to accommodate disabled individuals, the ADA provides a framework to ensure that disabled individuals obtain and keep gainful employment for which they are qualified. Accommodations can take many forms, including job restructuring, modified work schedules, flexible leave policies, equipment and devices, and the provision of readers or interpreters. The only limitation is that the accommodation not pose an "undue" hardship on the employer, a relatively high threshold.

In a U.S. Supreme Court decision, the Court held that reasonable accommodations under the ADA do not require employers to violate the employer's seniority system. In *US Airways, Inc. v. Barnett*, a disabled employee, recently transferred to a physically undemanding position in the mailroom, was bumped from the position by a more senior employee under the employer's seniority system. The disabled employee claimed he couldn't be bumped under the ADA; the employer was required to allow him to keep the mailroom position as a reasonable accommodation. The Supreme Court disagreed, holding that absent special circumstances, violating an employee's seniority system is not a "reasonable accommodation." [535 U.S. 391, 403 (2002)]

Q 4:129   Under what circumstances does an employer have an obligation to accommodate qualified individuals with disabilities?

An employer is required to provide reasonable accommodations to qualified individuals with disabilities in order to:

1. Ensure equal opportunity in the application process;
2. Enable a qualified individual with a disability to perform his or her essential job functions; and
3. Enable an individual with a disability to enjoy equal benefits and privileges of employment.

With respect to the first item, one of the principal goals of the ADA was to move unemployed qualified individuals with disabilities into the workforce. To this end, qualified individuals with disabilities must be accommodated to ensure that they have an equal opportunity to take whatever steps are necessary to complete the application process. If an applicant appears who is disabled but otherwise qualified for a position, an employer may need to provide whatever equipment or devices are necessary for this applicant to perform whatever tests are required in the application process. For example, supplying a hand rest for an applicant for a secretarial position who has carpel tunnel syndrome may be necessary to allow the applicant to have an equal opportunity to perform the secretarial test.

The second item is the most common form of accommodation that employers face—accommodations that allow an employee to perform essential job functions. Note, however, that an employer is not obligated to accommodate an employee so that he or she may perform what are considered non-essential job functions. As long as an employee is able to perform essential job functions, an employer cannot take action against that employee for failure to perform ancillary job-related tasks.

In addition, however, an employer may be obligated to accommodate individuals under the catch-all rule in the third item—"to enjoy equal benefits and privileges of employment." This phrase is largely undefined and comes into play whenever a disabled individual claims that failure to accommodate him or her under a certain set of circumstances would be detrimental to that individual's employment or advancement. For example, if attendance at a particular event is recognized as necessary for advancement in the company, an employer may be required to accommodate a disabled employee to attend that event if his or her disability would otherwise prevent the employee from attending.

Q 4:130   How is *reasonable accommodation* defined under the ADA?

Although there is no per se definition of *reasonable accommodation* and the issue is determined on a case-by-case basis, the ADA has listed the ways accommodations can be made. For example, accommodations can include job restructuring, part-time or modified work schedules (such as flextime), flexible or modified leave policies, modification or acquisition of equipment or devices, adjustment or modification of examinations and training materials, and the provision of readers or interpreters. In addition, demotion to a vacant position may be an accommodation; however, this should always be viewed as the accommodation of last resort. If an employer imposes a demotion accommodation on a disabled employee only to later find out that the employee could have been accommodated in his or her current position, the employer will be held accountable under the ADA.

Q 4:131   Are there any limitations to accommodation under the ADA?

Yes. Although accommodation can take many forms, it is clear under EEOC regulations that an employer does not have to create a position in order to accommodate a disabled employee. Although job restructuring to eliminate or reassign non-essential job functions is permissible as an accommodation under the ADA, an employer is not obligated to restructure essential job functions in order to create a new position for a disabled employee. Instead, the employer can transfer the employee to any vacant position that better accommodates the disabled employee. An employee, who had aggravated her back condition, requested an accommodation that would essentially have her working at home all but one day per week. The court, in analyzing the proposed accommodation, determined that the employee had failed to demonstrate that working at home for all but one day of the work week was "reasonable" and as such, rejected her claim that the employer had violated the ADA by failing to accommodate her requests. [Gomez-Gonzalez v. Rural Opportunities, Inc., 626 F.3d 654 (1st Cir. 2010)]

Nor is an employer obligated to accommodate a disabled employee if to do so would pose an undue hardship on the employer; however, an undue hardship is more than a mere hardship. The fact that an accommodation will create an expense for an employer is not considered an undue hardship.

Q 4:132　Do the ADA accommodation obligations give the disabled employee a preference in assignment to a vacant position when other applicants are more qualified than the disabled employee?

In *Huber v. Wal-Mart Stores, Inc.* [486 F.3d 480 (8th Cir. 2007)], a disabled employee claimed a violation of the ADA when her employer did not choose her for a vacant position that would have accommodated her disability, but rather, transferred her to another position that accommodated her disability, albeit at less pay. The employer, on the other hand, claimed that although it acknowledged that she was disabled and that the position for which she had applied would accommodate her disability, nonetheless, concluded that there were other more qualified candidates for the position and for which the selection of a more qualified candidate was not a violation of the ADA. At issue was whether the ADA required the employer to provide the disabled employee a preference for this vacant position over other, more qualified candidates. Reviewing the ADA and its regulations, the court concluded that the reassignment obligation was not one that required the employer to provide a preference to the disabled employee, and as such, found no violation under the ADA. In *Colwell v. Rite Aid Corp.* [602 F.3d 495 (3d Cir. 2010)], an employee, who was blind in one eye and admittedly disabled under the ADA, sought accommodation to work as a cashier on the day shift only, due to her inability to drive at night due to her disability. Although Rite Aid maintained it had no obligation to accommodate the employee to allow her to commute to and from work, the employer held that modification of work schedules to allow this employee to perform her job was consistent with its obligations under the ADA, such that summary disposition in favor of Rite Aid was inappropriate.

Q 4:133　How is an undue hardship determined under the ADA?

The determination of undue hardship is made on a case-by-case basis; the burden is on the employer. Factors to be considered when determining whether a reasonable accommodation would impose an undue hardship on an employer include the overall size of the business, the site involved, and the nature and cost of the accommodation needed. Additionally, the number of employees or applicants potentially benefiting from an accommodation may be a relevant consideration. Another factor is the availability of outside funding (from state vocational rehabilitation agencies or from federal, state, or local tax deductions or credits) to pay for accommodations.

The type of business operation is also a factor in determining whether an accommodation imposes an undue hardship. For example, to implement or maintain physical accessibility for a job applicant or employee who uses a wheelchair might fundamentally alter the nature of a construction site or be unduly costly if the site's terrain and building structure change daily as construction progresses.

Even if the requested accommodation imposes an undue hardship on the employer, that is not the end of the inquiry under the ADA. Rather, the employer must provide the disabled employee with an opportunity to pay as much as is necessary to make the accommodation not an undue hardship. For example, if an employer determined that a potential accommodation would cost X and the employer believes it can meet its burden to show that this cost would be an undue hardship, the employer must offer the disabled employee an opportunity to pay as much as is necessary not to make the accommodation an undue hardship. If Y is not an undue hardship, the employer must offer the disabled employee the opportunity to pay the difference. Only then is the employer relieved of its obligation to provide a reasonable accommodation.

The flexible definition of undue hardship is intended to discourage an employer that would, for example, elect to close a store that is only marginally profitable rather than undertake significant investments to make reasonable accommodations for employees with disabilities. The requirements of the ADA should not result in the closure of a business or in the loss of jobs. By providing a number of factors to take into consideration in each case, the ADA establishes a flexible approach in determining undue hardship.

Q 4:134   What can an employer do to avoid legal action for failure to accommodate under the ADA?

When a disability prevents someone from performing his or her essential job functions, common sense would seem to indicate that employers can take action without legal repercussions. It should be emphasized, however, that in these cases, the courts need to determine specifically that there were no reasonable accommodations that employers could undertake that would permit the employees to perform their essential job functions.

No employer should make any decisions based upon the nature of the disability itself without first examining what accommodation might be available with the employee that would permit the person to perform his or her essential job functions. Even in what appear to be open-and-shut cases, failure to exhaust the process of analyzing potential accommodations that may be required under state or federal law is a mistake. If after analysis it is determined that no accommodation exists to enable an employee to perform his or her essential job function, demonstrate that there is a point at which the employer's obligation and exposure to liability cease. An assistant manager with a shoulder condition sued his former employer claiming a violation of the ADA for his former employer's failure to accommodate his disability. At issue was whether manual tasks routinely performed by assistant managers were an essential function of the job. Factual analysis of the position's job duties demonstrated that the manual tasks were an important and integral function of the assistant manager's job and as such, were an essential function that the employee could not perform with or without reasonable accommodation. [Richardson v. Friendly Ice Cream Corp., 594 F.3d 69 (1st Cir. 2010)]

Q 4:135   In what areas of employment does the ADA prohibit discrimination?

Discrimination against a qualified individual with a disability is prohibited in every part of the employment process. The employment process specifically includes, but is not limited to, job application procedures, testing, hiring, advancement, discharge, compensation, training, recruitment and advertising, job assignments, job classifications, organizational structures, position descriptions, lines of progression, seniority lists, leaves of absence, sick leave, fringe benefits available by virtue of employment (whether or not administered by the employer), and employer-sponsored activities (including social or recreational programs).

Q 4:136   What actions by an employer may constitute discrimination under the ADA?

The ADA specifies particular types of actions that may constitute discrimination. Section 102(b)(1) of the ADA prohibits an employer from limiting, segregating, or classifying a job applicant or an employee in a way that adversely affects the opportunities or status of the applicant or employee based on that person's disability. Therefore, an employer cannot adopt different pay scales, benefits programs, promotion opportunities, or working areas for employees with disabilities.

Section 102(b)(2) of Title I provides that a covered entity (i.e., a business subject to the ADA) may not participate in a contractual relationship that has the effect of discriminating against its qualified applicants or employees.

Example. ABC Corporation is seeking to contract with XYZ Company to provide training for ABC's employees. The same responsibilities of accommodation that would apply to ABC Corporation if it provided the training itself also apply in the contractual relationship. Thus, if XYZ Company planned to hold its training program in a location inaccessible to ABC's employees with disabilities, ABC Corporation would have a duty to consider various reasonable accommodations, including asking the training company to identify other sites for the program that would be accessible to those employees, identifying other training companies that use accessible sites, paying to have the training company train disabled employees elsewhere (either on a one-to-one basis or with other employees who may have missed the training for other reasons), or providing any other accommodation that might result in making the training program available to those employees with disabilities.

Furthermore, the employer has an affirmative duty to investigate the accessibility of an off-site location that it plans to use for its employees. An employer can protect itself by simply ensuring that the contract with the host facility specifies that the rooms that are to be used for the function (e.g., meeting rooms, exhibit halls, sleeping rooms, and dining facilities) are accessible in accordance with applicable standards. If the facility breaches this accessibility provision, it will be liable to the employer for the cost of any accommodation needed to provide access to disabled individuals during the off-site function.

Other employer actions that may constitute discrimination include:

- Denying employment opportunities to a qualified individual with a disability because he or she has a relationship or association with a person with a disability;
- Refusing to make reasonable accommodation to a disabled and qualified applicant or employee unless and to the extent that the accommodation imposes an undue hardship on the employer;
- Using employment tests, qualification standards, or other criteria that screen out or tend to screen out individuals with disabilities unless those criteria are job-related; or
- Discriminating against an individual because he or she has opposed an employment practice that violates the ADA or filed a complaint, testified, assisted, or participated in an investigation, proceeding, or hearing to enforce the ADA.

Q 4:137 Does an employer have the obligation under the ADA to ensure that the behavior of third parties toward the employer's disabled employees is non-discriminatory?

When the covered employer enters into an arrangement, contract, or relationship with another that has the effect of discriminating against a qualified person with a disability, the employer may be held legally responsible under the ADA for the discrimination. For example, an employer cannot enter into a contract for liability insurance with an insurance company that refuses to cover accidents or injuries of persons with disabilities. Nor can the employer refuse to hire a person with a disability because its liability policy does not cover persons with disabilities.

In addition, an employer may not do anything through a contractual relationship that it cannot do directly because it would violate the ADA. An employer cannot, for example, contract with an employment agency or other agency to make medical inquiries during background checks of its applicants that it could not do directly. Similarly, an employer cannot take action through a collective bargaining agreement that it could not take directly. A union contract that impermissibly screens out people with disabilities who are qualified to perform the job with reasonable accommodation would be a violation of the ADA. Collective bargaining agreements often identify various functions of a particular job; however, just because the function is listed in such an agreement does not mean it is an essential function under the ADA. The same review of appropriateness of job-related criteria and essential job functions needs to be done when hiring union employees as is done for any other employee.

Q 4:138   Does the ADA prohibit discrimination against persons related to or living with a handicapped individual?

Under Section 102(b)(4) of the ADA, an employer cannot discriminate against an employee or an applicant because of an association with a person with a disability. This includes family and friends of disabled persons and those who provide care for persons with disabilities.

When employers become aware of an individual's relationship with a person with a disability, many assume that the employee will be unreliable or often away from work to care for the person with the disability. Action by an employer based on this assumption is specifically prohibited by the ADA. It is also impermissible for an employer to refuse employment or dismiss an individual because of the employer's fear of increased health cost associated with the disabled relation. An employer does not, however, have an obligation under the ADA to accommodate an employee so as to enable him or her to care for a disabled relative. The reasonable-accommodation obligations extend only to qualified individuals with disabilities.

In addition, an employer would violate the ADA if it discriminated against a qualified employee who did volunteer work with persons with AIDS, if the employer knew of the employee's association with the volunteer organization and if the employment action was motivated by association.

Section 102(b)(4) applies only when the employer knows of the association with the disabled person. The burden of proof is on the individual who is claiming discrimination; he or she must prove that the discrimination was motivated by his or her relationship or association with a person with a disability.

Although so-called associational discrimination claims under the ADA are relatively rare, various circuits that have addressed these claims have outlined three general theories into which "association discrimination" claims generally fall. The so-called "expense theory" involves situations where employers discriminate against an employee because of their association with a disabled individual covered under the employer's health plan, which is costly to the employer. Another theory involves situations where the employer fears that the employee may contract the disability of the person they are associated with (i.e., HIV), and another theory, so-called "distraction theory" is based on an employer discriminating against an employee who is associated with somebody with a disability because of the employer's unfounded fears that the employee will become distracted or inattentive to work due to their association with somebody with a disability. [See Larimer v. International Bus. Mach. Corp., 370 F.3d 698, 700 (7th Cir. 2004).] However, unless an employee can proffer evidence from which jurors can infer that an adverse action was taken against the employee because of the person's association with an individual with a disability, the case will be difficult to maintain. Although, in a another case, a terminated airport director's wife had a flair up of her chronic illness at the time he was fired by his employer airline corporation, the court found that there could be no inference of associational disability discrimination where the employer had known of the supervisor's wife's illness for years, the supervisor was not performing to the satisfaction of the airline, and there was no evidence that the decision to terminate was based on any fears that the wife's illness may cause the supervisor to be inattentive at work. [Stransberry v. Air Wisconsin Airlines Corp., 651 F.3d 482 (6th Cir. 2001)]

Q 4:139 What is the ADA's position regarding job qualification standards of disabled persons?

Section 102(b)(6) of the ADA prohibits the use of qualification standards, employment tests, or other selection criteria that screen out or tend to screen out persons with disabilities, unless the criteria are shown to be job-related and consistent with business necessity. Thus, it would be discriminatory to administer speaking and listening skills tests to a person with a disability that impairs speech and hearing if the essential functions of the job do not require those skills.

Q 4:140 What are the ADA's requirements regarding pre-employment medical examinations?

Employers may no longer conduct physical examinations or ask any medically related questions before offering employment. Application forms that list diseases or medical conditions and require the applicant to check any that pertain must be modified to remove those questions. The ADA does, however, permit an employer to explain the essential functions of the job for which the person is applying and ask whether the person can perform those functions with or without a reasonable accommodation. For example, an employer may state that the job involves extensive heavy lifting and ask if the applicant could meet this job requirement, with or without reasonable accommodation, but the employer may not ask if the applicant has a back problem. An employer may also ask the applicant to demonstrate an ability to perform the job. If the applicant indicates that he or she can perform with an accommodation, an employer may ask how the applicant would perform the job and with what accommodation.

In explaining the prohibition against pre-offer medical inquiries, the EEOC has stated that the following application or interview questions are impermissible: "Is there any health-related reason why you may not be able to perform the job for which you are applying?" and "How many days were you absent from work because of illness last year?" Any question about an applicant's workers' compensation history is prohibited. Many employers have routinely asked these types of questions and should be aware that such practices prior to making an offer of employment are illegal.

Once an employer has made a bona fide offer of employment to an applicant, it may conduct a medical inquiry or examination as long as it requires the same inquiry or examination of all employees in the same job category and the information is kept confidential. In fact, an offer of employment may be contingent on the results of the medical examination. At this point, questions may also be asked about previous injuries and workers' compensation claims, current illnesses, diseases, and other medical matters. If the post-offer medical inquiry or examination reveals a disability for which no reasonable accommodation exists, the employer can rescind the employment offer. The employer must be able to demonstrate, however, that the employee could not have performed the essential job functions with reasonable accommodation. A disability that has no effect on essential job functions would not be a permissible basis to rescind the employment offer. If the examination reveals a disability that is a direct threat to the health or safety of the individual or others that cannot be eliminated or reduced by a reasonable accommodation, the employer may also rescind the offer of employment.

Q 4:141   Is pre-employment testing permissible under the ADA?

Pre-employment testing for job qualifications is not per se illegal under the ADA, although testing is limited to ensure that it does not have an adverse impact on disabled individuals. The most common sort of testing is for competency in typing and computer skills.

To qualify as a permissible pre-employment test, it is important that the test be job-related and consistent with a business necessity. The test should relate to abilities to perform essential job functions; to the extent it does not, it may not qualify as permissible pre-employment testing. For example, requiring spoken communication in connection with a pre-employment test may be impermissible if spoken communication is not an essential job function. In addition, even if it is, the employer may be obligated to accommodate the applicant to perform the test and give the applicant a chance to enjoy equal opportunities in connection with the application process.

If a pre-employment test is determined to have an adverse impact on disabled applicants, the test will be scrutinized to determine whether the test is clearly job-related and consistent with a business necessity. Testing that routinely adversely affects disabled employees should be reviewed to ensure that the testing does not violate the ADA.

Q 4:142   Are there circumstances that permit an employer to inquire about the nature or severity of an applicant's disability?

Under the ADA, there are limited circumstances in which an employer may inquire about an applicant's disability prior to making an offer of employment. Such circumstances include an employer taking voluntary action to overcome the effects or conditions that could limit long-term opportunities for persons with disabilities, an employer taking remedial action to correct the effects of past discrimination, and an employer taking affirmative action required by Section 503 of the Rehabilitation Act. In any of these situations, the employer must make it clear that the information requested is intended for use solely in connection with its remedial actions and obligations or its voluntary or affirmative action efforts and that the information is to be furnished on a purely voluntary basis. The applicant should be clearly advised, in writing, of the reasons for the invitation to designate disability status and that the information is not required and no action will be taken for failure to provide it.

Q 4:143   What are the ADA's provisions regarding illegal drug use?

Section 104(a) of the ADA provides that a qualified individual with a disability does not include an employee or applicant who is a current user of illegal drugs. Section 104(b) of the ADA provides, however, that rehabilitated individuals and those in treatment who no longer use illegal drugs and individuals who are erroneously regarded as illegal drug users are not excluded from the category of individuals with disabilities. As in all other disability cases, the employee must prove that he or she has a history of a disability or is regarded as having a disability in order to be protected by the ADA.

Q 4:144   Are alcoholics protected under the ADA?

Although the ADA specifically excludes from its provisions protection for an employee or applicant who is currently engaged in the illegal use of drugs, it does afford protection to individuals who have the disease of alcoholism; however, the protections afforded the alcoholic are very limited. Indeed, employers are permitted to create, maintain, and enforce policies that prohibit the use or possession of alcohol in the workplace. In addition, EEOC regulations allow employers to hold the alcoholic accountable for his or her conduct at the workplace, despite the fact that violation of work rules and policies may be a result of alcoholism. Employers are permitted to impose their work rules with respect to absenteeism, tardiness, and drinking on the job on an alcoholic, just as it would any other employee. For example, a police chief who violated work rules prohibiting officers from public drunkenness when he was involved in a drunk driving accident was not qualified for the position under the ADA and could not perform the essential job functions because he was unable to operate a motor vehicle due to his suspended drivers license. [Budde v. Kane Cnty. Forest Preserve, 597 F.3d 860 (7th Cir. 2010)]

Q 4:145   If an employer establishes a policy to never re-hire former employees terminated for violations of its rules, and if an employee was fired for testing positive for illegal drug use, is the employer's policy a violation of the ADA for refusing to hire prior employees with a record of past illegal drug use?

Although the ADA does not protect employees currently using illegal drugs, nonetheless it does protect employees who have a past record of drug addiction, or who are perceived incorrectly as suffering from a drug addiction. In *Raytheon Co. v. Hernandez* [540 U.S. 44 (2003)], the company had established a policy not to re-hire any employee who violated any of its misconduct rules. In the case, the employee was terminated for testing positive for illegal drug use. When the employee attempted to seek re-hire, he was not considered in light of the

company's blanket prohibition against re-hiring employees previously terminated for violation of company rules. The employee claimed that the employer's
policy discriminated against him in violation of the ADA, for refusing to hire him
due to his record of past drug use and/or perceived drug addiction. The U.S.
Supreme Court concluded that the employer's unwritten policy against rehiring
former employees who are terminated for any violation of its misconduct rules
was a legitimate, non-disability based reason which did not violate the ADA.
The Court remanded the case to the trial court to determine whether, despite the
legitimate proffered reason for refusing to rehire, if nonetheless, the employee
could proffer sufficient evidence from which a jury could conclude that the
employer made its decision in this case based upon the employee's status as
disabled under the ADA.

Q 4:146   If an otherwise qualified individual with a disability poses a direct threat to employees or others, can the employer take action?

Yes. An employer can protect its employees from unsafe working conditions.
In fact, failure to do so may result in liability for the employer under the
Occupational Safety and Health Act or applicable state common law. Therefore,
an employer can require that all employees, including those who fall within the
definition of a qualified individual with a disability under the ADA, do not pose
a direct threat to the health or safety of others.

Under the ADA, the term *direct threat* is narrowly defined as a situation that
poses "a significant risk to the health or safety of others which cannot be
eliminated by reasonable accommodation." Typically, direct threats arise in
connection with contagious diseases and infections. The more interesting issue
is whether someone who poses a direct threat only to himself or herself, but not
to others, fits within the "direct threat" defense. In *Chevron USA Inc. v.
Echazabal* [536 U.S. 73 (2002)], the employee reportedly suffered from chronic
hepatitis C and posed a direct threat to himself, but apparently not others.
Although the employee was successful in the lower court, the U.S. Supreme
Court held that in accordance with EEOC regulations, "direct threat" includes a
situation where someone poses a substantial risk of harm to themselves.

When an employer becomes aware of a situation that may pose a direct
threat, it should not make the final determination. An employer may want to
discharge an employee immediately because the employer fears that the medical
condition of an employee poses a direct threat to the workplace. As is often the
case, an employer seeking professional advice would find, however, that its
belief is based on fear, not on any medically supportable opinion. If an employer
is not cautious and acts solely upon its own uninformed lay opinions, it may
violate the ADA. In *Bates v. United Parcel Service, Inc.* [465 F.3d 1069 (9th Cir.
2006)], the Ninth Circuit found that UPS's blanket policy of not hiring or
maintaining drivers that cannot pass Department of Transportation (DOT)
standards for hearing do not, in and of itself, shield the employer from violations
under the ADA. Although UPS maintained that business necessity required that
it not hire drivers that cannot pass DOT hearing tests, the Ninth Circuit agreed

with the district court that UPS did not provide evidence to show that deaf drivers posed a greater risk than other drivers hired by the company, and failed to demonstrate that it could not modify its existing program to determine which deaf drivers were safe or unsafe on a case-by-case basis.

In *EEOC v. E.I. Du Pont De Nemours & Co.* [480 F.3d 724 (5th Cir. 2007)], the employer, through repeated physician's examinations, concluded that an employee's walking impairment effectively barred her from performing work at a plant due to her inability to safely evacuate from the plant in case of an emergency. Although the company based its decision on functional capacity evaluations conducted by physicians, because the employee claimed that she had previously safely ambulated the evacuation route without assistance, and testified that she could safely evacuate without threatening the safety of others, the court concluded that the company had violated the ADA in making its determination.

Q 4:147   What does it mean to be substantially limited in performing a major life activity, such that the individual is disabled under the ADA?

The U.S. Supreme Court, in what many view as further limiting the ADA's reach, held that if the alleged substantial limitation of a major life activity involves performing manual tasks, merely being limited in a particular job is insufficient. Rather, the impairment must prevent or severely restrict the individual from performing activities of central importance to most people's daily lives. [Toyota Motor Mfg., Kentucky, Inc. v. Williams, 534 U.S. 184 (2002)] The former employee's carpal tunnel condition was insufficient to establish a disability under the ADA. In *Turner v. The Saloon, Ltd.* [595 F.3d 679 (7th Cir. 2010)], the court held that the condition of psoriasis, which periodically causes severe pain making the employee walk in a limp-like fashion, was not a substantial impairment of one or more major life activities, such that the employee was not disabled under the ADA. Similarly, the court held that certain adjustment to diet caused by diabetes was not a substantial impairment under the ADA. [Carreras v. Sajo, Garcia & Partners, 596 F.3d 25 (1st Cir. 2010)] Likewise, monocular vision (blind in one eye), was held not sufficiently substantially limiting of a major life activity such that the ADA would apply. [Kirkeberg v. Canadian Pac. Ry., 619 F.3d 898 (8th Cir. 2010)]. The court in *Griffin v. UPS* [661 F.3d 216 (5th Cir. 2011)], held that an employee suffering from insulin-dependent Type 2 diabetes, whose condition could be managed through modest dietary restrictions and lifestyle changes, was not disabled under the ADA because the condition was not a substantial impairment of one or more major life activities. In *Serednyj v. Beverly Healthcare, LLC* [656 F.3d 540 (7th Cir. 2011)], the court held that complications associated with pregnancy were not a "substantial" impairment of a major life activity, such that the pregnant employee was not disabled and no ADA claim could be maintained.

It is important to note that these cases were decided under the ADA, and not the amendments effective January 1, 2009 under the ADAAA.

When an employee testified that his depression and anxiety prevented him from performing his duties as a flight attendant, but did not prevent him from performing other jobs for the airline (i.e., gate agent, ticket agent, etc.), the employee was only limited to a narrow range of jobs and not a broad range of jobs available at the airline, such that the employee was not disabled under the ADA. [Pittari v. American Eagle Airlines, Inc., 468 F.3d 1056 (8th Cir. 2006)]

Although "working" has always been considered a major life activity, many of the above decisions narrowly construe the requirements to qualify as a major life activity. This is likely to change, as the ADAAA provides that the definition of a disability under the ADA must be construed broadly in favor of coverage of individuals under the Act, to the maximum extent permitted by the Act. The rules of construction also provide that an impairment that substantially limits one major life activity need not limit other major life activities in order to be considered a disability. With the enactment of the ADAAA, the definition of individuals who have or are regarded as having a physical or mental impairment that substantially limits one or more major life activity has been greatly expanded. Specifically, major life activities are now defined to include a non-exclusive list of major life activities, including caring for one's self, performing manual tasks, seeing, hearing, eating, sleeping, walking, standing, lifting, bending, speaking, breathing, learning, reading, concentrating, thinking, communicating, and working. Moreover, a major life activity is also defined as including the operation of any number of major bodily functions as defined under the Act. In addition, the Act specifically provides that the determination of whether somebody is disabled is to be assessed without reference to the ameliorative effects of mitigating measures such as medication, equipment, appliances or the like. Moreover, episodic conditions, which may not have historically qualified as being substantially limiting, are now included under the definition if the condition could substantially limit one major life activity when the condition is active.

Q 4:148   Is "interacting with others" a major life activity under the ADA?

One issue with which the courts have been struggling is whether "interacting with others" is a major life activity under the ADA. [See, e.g., Doebele v. Sprint Corp., 168 F. Supp. 2d 1247, 1261 (D. Kan. 2001), which noted that the Tenth Circuit had not as of yet held "interacting with others" to be a major life activity.] This issue was recently addressed by the court in Price v. Facility Management Group, Inc. [403 F. Supp. 2d 1246 (N.D. Ga. 2005)] In Price, the employee suffered from bipolar disorder, a clear mental impairment, and claimed that his condition substantially limited his ability to interact with others, which he claimed was a major life activity under the ADA. Recognizing that the Eleventh Circuit has yet to decide whether "interacting with others" is a major life activity, the court held that even assuming that it is a major life activity, the employee had not demonstrated that it is an activity in which he is substantially limited. The plaintiff pointed to his difficulties in dealing with others and various outbursts to maintain the claim, but the court held that the record indicated that he was not "unable" to interact with others—he just occasionally did so in an inappropriate manner. As such, and without having to decide whether "interacting with others" is a major life activity, the court held that the employee's claim failed in this regard.

Q 4:149 What does the ADA say about drug testing?

Under the ADA, employers can test their employees for the use of illegal drugs. An employer can terminate or refuse to hire someone whose test indicates the presence of an illegal substance. It would, however, be a violation of the ADA to discriminate on the basis of prescription drugs taken by individuals with disabilities who are under the care and supervision of a licensed health care professional. Although the ADA does not limit an employer's ability to test for drugs, in that drug testing for illegal use of drugs by applicants or employees or the making of employment decisions based on results of the tests is not encouraged, authorized or prohibited by the ADA, drug testing may, nonetheless, expose an employer to litigation if not done carefully.

Although the ADA does not permit pre-offer medical examinations, drug tests are wholly outside this prohibition. As a result, an employer may, consistent with the ADA, test applicants for illegal use of drugs; however, to avoid potential exposure, an employer should avoid common mistakes in applicant drug testing. First, an employer should adopt a written policy explaining that all applicants, or all applicants within certain classifications, will be tested for illegal use of drugs. If an employer singles out a particular applicant for drug testing and does not consistently test others, the tested applicant may claim that his or her selection for drug testing was discriminatorily motivated and, as a result, violates the federal civil rights laws. For example, testing one Hispanic applicant and no non-Hispanic applicants would implicitly suggest discriminatory motives.

Because other pre-offer medical inquiries are in violation of the ADA, although drug testing is permissible, the testing procedure should be examined to ensure that no impermissible inquiries are made in connection with the test until after the results are obtained. Typically, such forbidden inquiries occur when the testing facility asks broad questions about applicants' use of prescription drugs, or the like, prior to the taking of the test. This, according to the ADA, is not permissible. It is only after a positive finding that the medical facility is permitted to ask follow-up questions relative to legal use of drugs that may have affected the results of the examination.

For current employees, most employers adopt a reasonable-suspicion test rather than randomly testing for drugs. This policy typically requires that an employer have reasonable suspicion that the employee is under the influence of drugs or alcohol before he or she is asked to submit to a drug test. Such policy is not a violation of the ADA, but its enforcement could result in charges of discrimination. For example, singling out the only African-American who had an accident on the job for testing when no other employees involved in accidents are tested could lend itself to a federal civil rights charge. Employers should make certain that the reasonable-suspicion test and policies for testing employees in the case of accidents are followed consistently to avoid charges of discrimination.

Q 4:150   Do episodic or periodic impairments qualify as a disability?

Signaling a significant departure from prior law, under the ADAAA an impairment may qualify as a substantial limitation of a major life activity even if it is episodic or periodic. The ADAAA specifically provides that an impairment which is episodic or in remission will still qualify as a disability if it could substantially limit a major life activity when active.

Q 4:151   How is the ADA enforced?

Title I of the ADA incorporates the powers, remedies, and procedures in the Civil Rights Act of 1964. The EEOC has been designated as the enforcement agency for the ADA. The ADA provides that the powers and procedures available to persons discriminated against based on disability be the same as and parallel to those available to persons discriminated against based on race, color, religion, sex, or national origin. For employers that have 25 or more employees, Title I became effective in 1992; for employers with 15 to 24 employees, the ADA became effective in 1994. Additionally, the Civil Rights Act of 1991 provides that successful plaintiffs suing under the ADA may receive compensatory or punitive damages in some circumstances.

Q 4:152   Have juries awarded substantial damage amounts in ADA cases?

Although awards under the ADA are subject to caps, cases highlight the clear message being sent by juries to employers that violate the ADA. A federal jury in Dallas awarded $7.1 million to a former Coca-Cola Company executive who was fired one day before he was released from an outpatient program for alcoholism. Although the company maintained that the executive's employment was terminated for performance issues and violent and threatening behavior, the jury found for the executive, awarding $109,000 in back pay, $700,000 in front pay, $300,000 in compensatory damages, and $6 million in punitive damages. [Burch v. Coca Cola Co., 3:94 CV 1894-DB (N.D. Tex. June 28, 1995)] The combined compensatory and punitive damages exceeded the $300,000 cap under the Civil Rights Act of 1991, which governs remedies under the ADA; clearly the jury sent a message that it was upset with Coca-Cola's handling of the situation.

In *Wessel v. AIC Security Investigations Limited Ltd.* [No. 92-C-7330 (N.D. Ill. Mar. 1993)], the first reported jury verdict awarded under the employment provisions of the ADA resulted in $572,000 in damages to a plaintiff who claimed he had been fired because he had brain cancer. In addition to substantial size of the award, employers should note several other aspects of this case.

Historically, the EEOC has preferred to use its limited legal staff to pursue class actions, yet *Wessel* was brought on the employee's behalf by the EEOC. Such action appears to indicate the agency's keen interest in enforcing the ADA. The time line for *Wessel* was also extraordinary—it was filed in November 1992 and came to trial a mere four months later, in mid-March 1993.

The structure of the damage award in *Wessel* also deserves close analysis. It illustrates how a court and a jury, intent upon punishing what they perceive to be a guilty employer, can creatively collaborate to increase the bottom-line verdict beyond what the Act itself, in conjunction with the damages provisions of the Civil Rights Act of 1991, appears to contemplate. In the words of one commentator:

> The $500,000 in punitive damages included in the March 18 award nearly doubles the top amount of $300,000 generally available under the ADA and the Civil Rights Act of 1991, because the jury assessed separate awards of $250,000 against the owner and the [company]. The jury also awarded $22,000 in back pay and $50,000 in compensatory damages. [*BNA Daily Labor Report* 52, Mar. 19, 1993]

In *Wessel*, the EEOC charged the defendants with firing their executive director when he was diagnosed as having an inoperable brain tumor. According to the EEOC, the plaintiff was fired "not because of his inability to do his job, but because of predictions about his future health problems and because of stereotypical fears about disability." As for the verdict, the agency's general counsel observed: "The EEOC's primary goal is to educate businesses regarding their responsibility under the Americans with Disabilities Act. This verdict should distinctly accomplish that goal."

In January 1997, a federal jury in Michigan awarded a truck driver with epilepsy $5.5 million for his employer's refusal to reassign him to a yard-working position, citing safety concerns. However, this verdict was reduced by the judge to $491,000 based on the caps established by the Civil Rights Act of 1991. [8 *Employment Discrimination Report (EDR)* (BNA) 75 (Jan. 15, 1997)]

Even so-called technical violations of the ADA are resulting in substantial verdicts against employers. In *EEOC v. Community Coffee Co.* [No H-94-1061 (S.D. Tex. June 28, 1995)], a federal jury awarded a job applicant $30,000 in punitive damages and $15,000 in compensatory damages for an employer's illegal pre-offer inquiries regarding the nature and severity of the applicant's ability. Although the jury rejected the EEOC's claim that the company had discriminated against the plaintiff by refusing to hire him because of his disability, it nonetheless compensated the plaintiff for the illegal pre-offer interview questions regarding the nature and severity of his facial disfigurement. Impermissible inquiries alone, even though not relied upon, in this case resulted in a substantial judgment against the employer.

In what was claimed to have been the largest verdict to date for illegal pre-employment inquiries, a federal jury in New Mexico awarded an applicant $157,500. The applicant had lost his arm in a prior accident and was asked during an interview by a representative of Wal-Mart Stores, Inc., "What current or post-medical problems might limit your ability to do a job?" Although Wal-Mart maintained that the violation was innocent (the interviewer used an old form), and the inquiry had nothing to do with the reason the applicant was not hired, the jury apparently disagreed; $150,000 of the award was for punitive damages. [8 *Employment Discrimination Report (EDR)* (BNA) 319 (Mar. 5, 1997)] In *Eshelman v. Agere Systems, Inc.* [554 F.3d 426 (3d Cir. 2009)], the court held that the damage award may also include sums for increased tax burdens associated with a lump-sum back pay award.

In *EEOC v. Hill Country Farms, Inc.* [2012 WL 4747265 (S.D. Iowa Sept. 18, 2012)], the EEOC brought action against an employer that contracted intellectually disabled employees to an owner of a turkey processing plant to work on the plant's turkey processing line. The employer provided food and housing for the disabled men and paid them, according to tax records, a paltry $65 per month, well below minimum wage. Finding no basis under the FLSA or any other federal or state law to not pay these disabled employees what is required under state and federal law, the court found that the practice violated the ADA and awarded the plaintiffs damages in excess of $1 million.

Q 4:153 Does the ADA allow individual owners and managers to be named as defendants and held personally liable?

Historically, individual managers and owners have been named as defendants and assessed damages individually in employment discrimination cases. This was possible because federal antidiscrimination laws generally defined the term *employer* broadly. For example, the ADA states:

> The term "employer" means a person in an industry affecting commerce who has 15 or more employees for each working day in each of 20 or more calendar weeks in the current or preceding calendar year, and any agent of such person. [42 U.S.C. § 12111(5)(A)]

This definition is virtually identical to that in the 1964 Civil Rights Act [42 U.S.C. § 2000e(b)], the FLSA [29 U.S.C. § 203(d)], the Equal Pay Act (EPA), and the ADEA.

District court decisions involving the ADA and other federal civil rights laws signaled an evolving trend toward non-liability for individuals. A federal judge in Virginia, in *Stephens v. Kay Management Co.* [907 F. Supp. 169 (E.D. Va. 1995)], held that no individual liability for supervisors can be maintained under the ADA unless the individual independently meets the definition of an employer. In 1998, a California appeals court held that there is no personal liability under the ADA. [12 *Employment Discrimination Report (EDR)* (BNA) 14 (Jan. 6, 1999)] There is a growing consensus among the circuits that there is no personal liability under the ADEA, Title VII, or the ADA for individual supervisors.

Q 4:154   Does a policy barring light duty violate the ADA?

In some instances, light duty may be an acceptable form of accommodation under the ADA; however, if the employee is otherwise capable of performing essential job functions, with reasonable accommodation, a demotion to light duty with a consequent pay and benefit reduction could be a violation of the ADA. As a result, when the issue of light duty arises, employers need to analyze whether such duty is an acceptable non-discriminatory form of accommodation under the ADA. A policy barring light duty altogether may run afoul of the ADA to the extent that the specific light duty at issue is an acceptable accommodation under the ADA that an employer is obligated to implement. Although the ADA does not require employers to create jobs where none exists, if the light duty position is available and does not require the creation of a new position and there are no other means of accommodation, a light duty approach may be required.

Q 4:155   If an employer reserves light duty positions for employees who sustained occupational injuries under workers' compensation laws, does the ADA require the employer to consider the light duty position as a reasonable accommodation under the ADA?

To control workers' compensation costs and provide work to allow individuals on workers' compensation to return to work, many employers have began "reserving" light duty positions within their shops for employees with occupational injuries. Although the tour on light duty for these individuals is typically temporary, the employer permanently assigns or reserves various jobs throughout its facility for these employees. In such circumstances, the EEOC, in its Guidance on Workers' Compensation and the ADA, No. 915.003 issued in September 1996, states that these employers must also consider reassignments to these reserve positions in order to accommodate qualified individuals with disabilities under the ADA. Although the ADA does not require an employer to "create" a new position to accommodate the individual, the employer may not exclude consideration of these light duty positions when analyzing its ADA obligations for reasonable accommodation. On the other hand, forcing an individual to accept a light duty position as a reasonable accommodation under the ADA would run afoul of the ADA if the individual could otherwise be accommodated in his or her current position. But, assuming this cannot be done, a light duty position, even if historically reserved for occupational injuries, may be an acceptable form of accommodation under the ADA.

Q 4:156   If an employer has only temporary light duty positions, must the employer provide a permanent light duty position for an employee under the ADA?

In the EEOC's Guidance on Workers' Compensation and Americans with Disabilities Act, the EEOC acknowledges that an employer does not, under the ADA, have an obligation to turn a temporary light duty position into a permanent light duty position as an accommodation under the ADA; however, the obligation to provide temporary light duty for the qualified employee with a disability would still be consistent with the obligations of the employer to provide an accommodation under the ADA.

Q 4:157   What are the rules governing pre-employment inquiries under the ADA?

In 1994, the EEOC issued Enforcement Guidance on pre-employment disability-related inquiries and medical examinations aimed at assisting its own investigators in their legal analyses of such inquiries and exams. The guidance presents a lengthy list of questions labeled "disability-related inquiries that are illegal if asked before a conditional offer of employment is made." According to labor lawyer Robert F. Conte, "The ADA's prohibition against pre-offer inquiries and medical exams is designed to prevent discrimination against those with 'Disability' disabilities like cancer, mental illness, heart disease, and AIDS. Disability-related questions which are prohibited . . . include asking an applicant whether he or she has a particular impairment which constitutes a disability under the Act." [Robert F. Conte, "EEOC Issues Guidance on Pre-Employment Inquiries Under the ADA," Saul, Ewing, Remick & Saul, *Employment Law Update* (J.O. Castagnera, ed.), July 1994]

The following questions are examples of impermissible pre-offer inquiries:

- How many days were you sick last year?
- Have you ever filed for workers' compensation?
- How much alcohol do you drink each week?
- Have you ever been treated for alcohol-related problems?
- Have you ever been treated for mental health problems?
- What prescription drugs are you currently taking?

Beyond identifying specific questions that are prohibited, the EEOC guidance provides the general criterion that, if an employer might reasonably expect a pre-employment question to reveal the existence of a disability, that question is prohibited until a tentative offer of employment is made. Of course, the tentative offer may be conditioned upon the applicant's ability to perform the job. If, at the pre-offer stage, the applicant requests a reasonable accommodation in order to be able to perform the job, then an employer may ask that applicant to document the disability involved.

With respect to absenteeism and tardiness, an employer may state its attendance requirements and inquire whether or not the applicant will be able to meet them.

The EEOC guidance also addresses employers' obligations with regard to medical exams under the ADA. The agency defines *medical exams* as procedures or tests that "seek information about the existence, nature, or severity of an individual's physical or mental impairment" or that seek information regarding an individual's physical or psychological health. Factors for EEOC investigators to consider under the new guidance include whether:

- The test is administered or interpreted by a healthcare professional.
- The test is invasive.
- The test measures psychological or physiological response rather than the applicant's performance of a job task.
- The test normally is administered in a medical setting.
- Medical equipment or devices are used to give the test.

Many employers administer psychological tests, often including an I.Q. component. The EEOC apparently does not attack I.Q. testing, but psychological examinations are considered medical examinations if they are designed to determine if an applicant has a mental disorder or impairment.

The EEOC guidance does not forbid pre-offer testing for illegal drug use. If the same test should inadvertently and unintentionally reveal the use of legal drugs, the ADA has not been violated. Pre-offer testing for alcohol use probably is not legal for two reasons. First, the tests—requiring the analysis of blood, urine, or breath—are all deemed to be invasive. Second, alcohol, while frequently abused, is a legal drug. Consequently, companies are well advised not to conduct pre-offer alcohol tests.

Post-offer physicals and medical tests are legal under the ADA, according to the EEOC guidance, if the offers are in fact genuine and not ruses to conduct what are, in effect, pre-offer examinations. All relevant non-medical information on the candidate must have been evaluated before the offer was made. Post-offer medical information can be shared only with corporate decision makers who need that information, and it must be kept strictly confidential.

The following is a list of pre-employment inquiries that are permissible under current guidelines:

- Can you perform any or all job functions? (Acceptable also to ask whether they can be performed with or without reasonable accommodation.)
- Describe or demonstrate how you would perform the job, including any needed reasonable accommodations.
- (If an applicant has a known disability) How would you perform the job? (Describe or demonstrate.)
- Will you need reasonable accommodation in the hiring process?
- If you request reasonable accommodation in the hiring process, please document your disability.
- Can you meet our attendance requirements?
- Do you have any certifications or licenses? If so, please describe them.
- Do you have any criminal convictions? If so, what for?
- Do you currently use illegal drugs? (If the answer is "yes," testing is permissible.)
- Limited questions concerning the use of alcohol, but no responses should be elicited about how much alcohol an applicant drinks.

- (Voluntary information only) Do you have a disability? (Answer solicited only for purposes of a bona fide affirmative action program.)
- Provide medical certification that you can safely perform a job-related physical agility or fitness test.
- Psychological examinations may be given, provided they are not medical tests designed to identify a mental disorder or impairment.

Q 4:158   How should an employer confront the issue of AIDS under the ADA?

One of the purposes of the ADA was to eliminate employer decisions regarding disabilities based on lay perception, prejudice, and misinformation. For this reason, employers are not permitted to make pre-offer inquiries regarding medical conditions, and in the event that an individual is disabled, the Act imposes upon the employer an obligation to accommodate the qualified person with a disability to perform the essential functions of the job. The subject of AIDS should be approached on the same basis as any other similar medical condition that an employer might face. Employers should not make decisions out of fears and speculation. The individual with AIDS should be placed under no greater scrutiny than individuals with any other similar condition, and irrational fears of the employer or co-workers should not be allowed to dictate responses. If the employee with AIDS can be reasonably accommodated such that he or she can perform the essential job functions, without posing a "direct threat" to himself or herself or to other employees, the accommodation should be undertaken.

Q 4:159   Can an employer, under the ADA, shield itself from liability by relying solely on whatever information it receives from a medical professional?

Although it is true that employers are advised to rely on medical professionals, and not to allow lay opinions and prejudice to dictate responses to individuals with disabilities or perceived disabilities, blind reliance on a physician's judgment is not a blanket defense to an ADA claim. An employer has obligations reasonably to accommodate qualified individuals with disabilities, and if, in its conclusions, the employer relies on mistaken or incomplete information from a medical professional, the fact that the physician was in error does not alleviate the employer from obligation and liability. In *EEOC v. Texas Bus Lines* [5 AD Cases 878 (S.D. Tex. 1996)], an employer refused to hire an applicant who was extremely overweight based on an examining physician's conclusion that she was not qualified to drive a van because of her obesity. The opinion of the physician, according to the court, was not supportable by reasonable medical judgment and, as a result, when relied upon by the employer, equated to a violation of the ADA by the employer.

Although it is recommended that employers continue to use information from medical professionals as it relates to whether or not employees can be accommodated to perform their essential job functions or whether or not they pose a "direct threat" in the workplace, nonetheless, the *Texas Bus Lines* case indicates that blind reliance on a medical opinion that, in fact, is not based on reasonable medical judgment may result in a liability to the employer.

Q 4:160 Can an employer be sued for a claim of harassment under the ADA?

Although initially established as part of sexual harassment doctrine, a claim of hostile work environment under the ADA has been recognized by many federal circuits. To establish a prima facie claim, the employee must demonstrate that:

(1) he is a qualified individual with a disability;

(2) he was subjected to unwelcome harassment;

(3) the harassment was based on his disability;

(4) the harassment was sufficiently severe or pervasive to alter a term, condition, or privilege of his employment; and

(5) some factual bases exists to impute liability for the harassment to the employer. [*See* Rohan v. Networks Presentations, LLC, 375 F.3d 266 (4th Cir. 2004).]

The determination of whether or not the situation is sufficiently hostile to maintain a claim is viewed under both an objective and subjective analysis, similar to the analysis in sexual harassment cases. In *Edmonson v. Potter* [118 Fed. Appx. 726 (4th Cir. 2004)], an employee with carpal tunnel syndrome claimed that she was subjected her to a hostile work environment on account of her disability. In reviewing the alleged acts in support of her claim of hostile work environment, the court concluded that the acts were isolated and ordinary adversities in the workplace, and not sufficiently severe or pervasive when viewed objectively. The Tenth Circuit joined other circuits that have recognized hostile work environment claims under the ADA. [*See* Lanman v. Johnson Cnty., Kansas, 393 F.3d 1151 (10th Cir. 2004).]

Q 4:161 Can an employer be sued for retaliation under the ADA?

The ADA prevents employers from retaliating against employees who file administrative charges alleging disability discrimination with the EEOC. [42 U.S.C. § 12203(a)] To maintain a claim of retaliation, an employee must demonstrate: (1) that he engaged in protected opposition to discrimination, (2) that a reasonable employee would have found the challenged action materially adverse, and (3) that a causal connection existed between the protected activity and the materially adverse action. [Burlington N. & Santa Fe Ry. Co. v. White, 126 S. Ct. 2405 (2006)] Even in circumstances where a disabled employee filed a charge of discrimination and is thereafter terminated, a retaliation claim cannot be maintained unless the employee can demonstrate a causal connection between the administrative charge and the termination.

In *Proctor v. United Parcel Service* [502 F.3d 1200 (10th Cir. 2007)], a disabled employee was terminated four months after he had filed a charge of discrimination with the EEOC. Noting that the four-month time gap, in and of itself, was insufficient as a matter of law to support a presumption of causation, as well as the individual's lack of any other evidence to support a link between the administrative charge filing and termination, the court concluded that the retaliation claim was properly dismissed.

Age Discrimination

Q 4:162   What is the *ADEA*?

The *ADEA* was enacted in 1967 to prohibit arbitrary age discrimination against older workers and to promote employment of older workers based on their ability rather than their age. Congress, in enacting the statute, found that older workers were disadvantaged in their efforts to retain and regain employment, arbitrary age limits regardless of performance had become a common practice, and the incidence of unemployment was high among older workers. Specially, the ADEA provides that it is unlawful for an employer to:

- Fail or refuse to hire or to discharge any individual or otherwise discriminate against any individual with respect to his or her compensation, terms, conditions, or privileges of employment, because of that individual's age;

- Limit, segregate, or classify employees in any way that would deprive or tend to deprive any individual of employment opportunities or otherwise adversely affect his or her status as an employee, because of that individual's age; or

- Maintain a seniority system that requires or permits the involuntary retirement of any individual because of the age of that individual.

[29 U.S.C. § 623]

The ADEA exempts individuals elected to public office in any state or political subdivision of any state, their personal staff, appointees on a policy-making level, and immediate advisors with respect to the exercise of constitutional or legal powers of the office. [29 U.S.C. § 630(f)] In *Opp v. Office of the State's Attorney of Cook County* [630 F.3d 616 (7th Cir. 2010)], the court held that assistant state's attorneys, responsible for carrying out policy on behalf of the government, had sufficient input regarding governmental decisions, such that they were included within the exception to the ADEA for governmental appointees.

Q 4:163   Who is protected by the ADEA?

The purpose of the ADEA is to protect older workers from arbitrary age classification and arbitrary decisions based on age, rather than ability. For this reason, the ADEA specifically applies only to workers 40 years of age or older.

This age threshold for the ADEA is different from that of other civil rights statutes. For example, although Title VII was enacted to do away with long-standing discrimination against women and minorities, race claims can be maintained by a member of any race, and sex discrimination can be maintained by men and women alike. Some commentators have suggested that the ADEA's age threshold is itself tantamount to age discrimination. If a 39-year-old employee is fired because of an employer's desire to replace that employee with a younger employee, is that any less reprehensible than if the replaced employee had been 42 years old? Some would argue that discrimination based on age should be actionable regardless of the victim's age. A number of states have adopted civil rights laws that do not contain arbitrary age thresholds for protection from age discrimination. [MCLA §§ 37.2202 *et seq.*]

Q 4:164   Are involuntary retirement plans illegal under the ADEA?

With limited exception, it is illegal under the ADEA to establish or maintain a seniority system that requires or permits the involuntary retirement of any individual upon the attainment of a specific age. The ADEA provides:

> No such seniority system or employee benefit plan shall require or permit the involuntary retirement of any individual specified by Section 12(a) of this Act because of the age of such individual . . .

The ADEA does, however, permit the involuntary retirement of bona fide executives or high policy-making employees. As the act provides:

> Nothing in this Act shall be construed to prohibit compulsive retirement of any employee who has attained 65 years of age and who, for the 2-year period immediately before retirement, is employed in a bona fide executive or higher policy making position, if such employee is entitled to an immediate non-forfeitable annual retirement benefit from a pension, profit sharing, savings or deferred compensation, or any combination of such plans, of the employer of such employee which equals, in the aggregate, at least $44,000.00.

Q 4:165   Can acceptance of a voluntary early retirement plan be considered a "constructive" discharge in violation of the ADEA?

In *Embrico v. U.S. Steel Corp.* [404 F. Supp. 2d 802 (E.D. Pa. 2005)], the plaintiffs, former employees of the defendant, claimed that the Voluntary Early Retirement Program (VERP), which they accepted in Fall 2001 was not, in fact, a voluntary decision, but rather was coerced from them, such that the VERP violated the ADEA. In essence, all the plaintiffs claimed that they believed they had no choice but to resign and accept the VERP, and if they did not accept the VERP, that they would be terminated. As such, they felt they were compelled to resign and as a result, their resignation amounted to "constructive discharge." The court found that to demonstrate that the early retirement was involuntary, the court would apply an objective standard to determine whether a reasonable jury would conclude the employer permitted conditions so unpleasant or difficult such that a reasonable person would have felt compelled to resign. [Connors v. Chrysler Fin. Corp., 160 F.3d 971, 974 (3d Cir. 1998)] The court reasoned that the situation must be so intolerable that a reasonable person would have felt he had no choice but to resign. Although all the former employees believed that they would be fired if they did not accept the VERP, this conclusion was based upon the plaintiffs' subjective beliefs rather than on any clear information provided by the employer. The court found that the plaintiffs' general uncertainties to future prospects with the employer were not sufficient, and they must show that termination was objectively so certain that the plaintiffs had no choice but to retire.

Q 4:166   Can retirement plans that provide different levels of benefits based on age violate age discrimination status?

Kentucky established a disability retirement benefits plan for state and county employees that, among other things, disqualified employees from receiving disability retirement benefits upon reaching normal retirement benefit age, and also calculated benefits in such a way that younger employees received greater benefits than older employees when age was the only distinguishing characteristic between the employees. The Sixth Circuit held that the plan was facially discriminatory, establishing a prima facie claim of age discrimination and that as such, it was not necessary for the plaintiffs to provide additional proof of discriminatory animus for the case to proceed. [EEOC v. Jefferson Cnty. Sheriff's Dep't, 467 F.3d 571 (6th Cir. 2006)] On appeal, the U.S. Supreme Court reversed the Sixth Circuit's decision. The court referred to *Hazen Paper Co. v. Biggins* [113 S. Ct. 1701 (1993)], which states that in order for a plaintiff to maintain an age-related "disparate treatment" claim under the ADEA, the plaintiff must prove that age "actually motivated the employer's decision." Reviewing the plan at issue, the court concluded that although the plan rules may permit younger disabled workers to be treated more generously than older disabled workers with respect to the "timing" of their eligibility for normal retirement benefits, the amount of the retirement benefits were not disparate. The court held that the government failed to make the requisite showing that the differential treatment was motivated because of age. [Kentucky Ret. Sys. v. EEOC, 128 S. Ct. 2361 (June 19, 2008)]

Q 4:167   How are age discrimination claims proved under the ADEA?

As with other forms of discrimination, age claims can be based upon disparate-treatment or disparate-impact theories. As to disparate treatment, evidence can be obtained through direct evidence, comparative evidence, or statistical evidence. With disparate treatment, discriminatory employer motive must be inferred. Slurs and stereotypical remarks may be used as direct evidence of discriminatory motive. A good example that words matter is *Mora v. Jackson Memorial Foundation, Inc.* [597 F.3d 1201 (11th Cir. 2010)] In the case, an employee brought an ADEA claim against her former employer claiming her termination was because of age. Although the employer maintained that the employee was terminated for poor performance, the former employee testified that she was told when she was terminated that she was "too old." This testimony, which was supported by other witnesses, was sufficient to deny the employer's motion to dismiss. Comparative evidence, treating similarly situated employees differently on the basis of age, may also provide a basis upon which discriminatory motive may be inferred. Statistical evidence can be used to demonstrate a pattern and practice of treating older employees differently than younger employees from which discriminatory motive can also be inferred. However, in *Cameron v. Idearc Media Corp.* [685 F.3d 44 (1st Cir. 2012)], the court held that the termination of older sales representatives for poor performance because they failed to achieve levels of production under a minimum standards plan (MSP) provided a legitimate non-discriminatorial basis for termination, and the plaintiffs' presented no evidence to show that the MSP was merely a mask for illegal age discrimination. When a buyer of a Boeing division retained 87.5 percent of Boeing's workforce, and the resulting average age of the workforce was only 5 months younger than Boeing's after the purchase, the statistical evidence was not sufficient to demonstrate a "pattern or practice" of discrimination to support an ADEA class action lawsuit. [*Apsley v. Boeing Co.*, 691 F.3d 1184 (10th Cir. 2012)]

Under disparate-impact analysis, facially neutral policies and procedures that have a disproportionate impact upon individuals on the basis of their age may provide a basis to maintain a prima facie case of age discrimination. Once a prima facie case of age discrimination has been maintained, under either disparate treatment or disparate impact, the burden then shifts to the employer to demonstrate a legitimate business reason for its actions, policies, or procedures in question. Assuming the employer meets this burden, the burden shifts back to the complainant to demonstrate that the proffered business reason of the company is merely a pretext for illegal age discrimination. As the U.S. Supreme Court held in *Gross v. FBL Financial Services, Inc.* [129 S. Ct. 2343 (2009)] to maintain an ADEA claim, the employee must demonstrate that the employer took adverse action "because of age" and that "age" was the reason that the employer decided to act. As such, although stray comments may demonstrate that age may have been a motivating factor in an adverse employment decision, such stray comments will typically be insufficient for purposes of maintaining an ADEA claim. In a First Circuit case, an employee claimed that she was not promoted to a position with her employer due to age discrimination, claiming, among other things, that one of the decision makers indicated the need to fill the position with "new blood." Finding that the person who was ultimately chosen for the position was more experienced than the plaintiff, and had performed better during the interview process, the court held that the phrase "new blood" was too ambiguous to demonstrate age animus. [*Velazquez-Ortiz v. Vilsack*, 657 F.3d 64 (1st Cir. 2011)] A supervisor's stray remark that he was eager for several older workers to retire and facts indicating only "bad blood" between the supervisor and the employee were not sufficient to maintain an ADEA claim alleging that a demotion was because of age. [*Vasbinder v. Secretary Dep't of Veterans Affairs*, 487 Fed. Appx. 746 (3d Cir. 2012)] Statements by a supervisor in August and December of 2006 that the main problem at the plant was workers that had been at the plant for a long time that were not performing provided sufficient evidence for a jury to infer that age discrimination was the cause of a February 2007 discharge, such that summary judgment for the employer was reversed. [*Acevedo-Parrilla v. Novartis Ex-Lax, Inc.*, 696 F.3d 128 (1st Cir. 2012)].

In some cases, courts may also allow the introduction of testimony from other employees, even if they are not "similarly situated," who believe they were also discriminated against to show the employer's "general propensity" to discriminate based on age. A former 51-year-old employee whose employment was terminated in conjunction with a RIF claimed she was selected due to her age in violation of the ADEA, but lost at trial. On appeal, the former employee claimed that the court had committed error by excluding the testimony of other individuals who similarly felt that they were included within the RIF due to their age. The trial court had excluded the testimony due to the fact that the other employees were not supervised by the same supervisor of the former employee who brought the claim. However, the court, on appeal, held that evidence of the employer's general discriminatory propensity may be relevant and concluded that it was a reversible error for the circuit court not to admit the testimony of other individuals affected by the RIF who felt they were selected due to their age, even though they were not supervised by the same supervisor. [*Mendelsohn v. Sprint/United Mgmt. Co.*, 466 F.3d 1223 (10th Cir. 2006)]

The determination as to whether sufficient evidence has been presented to permit a case to be heard by the jury, as opposed to being dismissed by the court, depends on the facts of each case. In *Blair v. Henry Filters, Inc.* [505 F.3d 517 (6th Cir. 2007)], at issue was whether the employee had provided sufficient direct evidence of age discrimination, such that his claim under the ADEA could survive summary judgment and move forward to trial. Although the trial court felt otherwise, the court of appeals concluded that when the 57-year-old employee's supervisor "taunted" him as the "old man on the sales force," transferred him from a profitable account because he was "too old," and told another employee he "needs to set up a younger sales force," the employee has provided sufficient evidence to survive summary judgment and have the case determined by a jury. [*Blair*, at 520] A former university employee sued, claiming that the university violated the ADEA when it failed to promote her to the director of admissions. Comments by the university supervisor that he was not sure he wanted a "grandpa" working with college kids and that another candidate might be a better long-term choice, together with the superior qualifications of the plaintiff versus the younger candidate that was selected for the position, provided sufficient evidence of pretext for the trial court to deny the university's motion for summary disposition. [Jones v. National Am. Univ., 608 F.3d 1039 (8th Cir. 2010)]

However, comments about someone's age that are not negative per se, and where no context to link the comment to the adverse employment action exists, the comment will be insufficient for purposes of establishing direct evidence to infer age discrimination under the ADEA. A terminated airline employee claimed that she was terminated due to her age in violation of the ADEA, and claimed that she had produced sufficient direct evidence of age discrimination to survive a motion for summary judgment. Specifically, the employee claimed that her supervisor had noted on one occasion that she was as "old as her mother," told her at least once that she was "too old to be moving heavy luggage," and had admittedly tried to assign the employee to a less demanding gate. This evidence, although related to the plaintiff's age, was not necessarily derogatory, did not demonstrate any dissatisfaction with the employee's work, and no link between these comments and the termination decision existed. As such, the court concluded it was insufficient direct evidence from which an inference of age discrimination can be made, and the court affirmed the dismissal of the employee's ADEA claim. [Riggs v. Airtran Airways, Inc., 497 F.3d 1108 (10th Cir. 2007)] In *Matranga v. Catholic Charities of the Dioceses of Peoria*, [07-cv-1350, 2009 WL 2871183 (C.D. Ill. Sept. 2, 2009)] an employee alleged her discharge was in violation of the ADEA based on evidence that the employer characterized her discharge as a "retirement" to co-workers. However, the evidence revealed that this characterization was something done after the decision for discharge had been made, and as such, standing alone did not provide evidence of age discrimination. A 68-year-old attorney who applied for an in-house legal position with a company claimed that he was denied the position in violation of the ADEA. He claimed, among other things, that the employer indicated that she was searching for a lawyer at a "more junior level." The court found that this comment, in and of itself, was not evidence of age discrimination, but rather, was focused on the level of employee and experience that the company was looking for, and held that this comment was not probative of the employer's discriminatory intent. [Moss v. MBC Software, Inc., 610 F.3d 917 (5th Cir. 2010)] Likewise, a supervisor's reference to a candidate reinstated by a company as "this young man" did not raise an inference of discrimination against an older employee who was not reinstated. [Medlock v. United Parcel Serv., Inc., 608 F.3d 1185 (10th Cir. 2010)]

At issue before the U.S. Supreme Court in *Sprint/United Management Co. v. Mendelsohn* [128 S. Ct. 1140 (2008)] was whether a district court erred by allegedly applying a "per se" rule against the admissibility of allegedly discriminatory conduct by other supervisors. As the court noted, the question of admissibility of evidence of discrimination by other supervisors is a fact-based determination depending upon many factors, including the relationship of the evidence to plaintiff's circumstances and theory of the case. Although the district court's ruling on the issue did not delve into the basis for its determination, the court concluded that it was not clear that the incorrect per se rule was followed and the matter was remanded back to the district court to have the district court clarify the basis for its evidentiary ruling.

Q 4:168   If an employee is unsuccessful in demonstrating age discrimination in connection with a discharge, can the employee still maintain a hostile work environment claim under the ADEA?

In *Watcher v. Pottsville Area Emergency Medical Services, Inc.* [248 Fed. Appx. 272 (3d Cir. 2007)], a terminated employee had filed various claims of discrimination, including hostile work environment under the ADEA and termination in violation of the ADEA. The jury returned a verdict for the plaintiff under her harassment claim under the ADEA, but found that the evidence was insufficient to rule against the company for age discrimination under the ADEA in connection with the employee's termination from employment. On appeal, the company argued that because the jury concluded that age was not a motivating factor in her termination, the jury's finding of hostile work environment because of her age must be reversed. The appeals court, however, concluded that it was entirely consistent with the law and the evidence that a hostile work environment under the ADEA could be tenable, while at the same time concluding that the evidence was insufficient to demonstrate that age was a motivating factor in the employee's discharge. As such, the court upheld the jury's determination. In *Dediol v. Best Chevrolet, Inc.* [655 F.3d 435 (5th Cir. 2011)], addressing an issue of first impression, the Fifth Circuit held that a hostile work environment claim can be maintained under the ADEA. Although the employer sought to have the hostile work environment claims dismissed, the court held that the repeated profane references by the employee's supervisor to the 65-year-old employee, age-related comments on an almost daily basis, and other threatening behavior were sufficient to create an issue of fact, such that dismissal was inappropriate.

Q 4:169   Can disparate impact cases be maintained under the ADEA?

In *Smith v. City of Jackson, Mississippi* [125 S. Ct. 1536 (2005)], the U.S. Supreme Court held that disparate impact cases (i.e., cases where illegal motive is not an issue) may be maintained under the ADEA, contrary to the decision of many circuits that previously held that disparate impact theory was not cognizable under the ADEA. Disparate impact, as opposed to disparate treatment theory, has been recognized under Title VII since the U.S. Supreme Court decision of *Griggs v. Duke Power Co.* [91 S. Ct. 849 (1971)] In a case of first impression, the U.S. Supreme Court held in *Smith* that although the textual differences between the ADEA and Title VII make it clear that the disparate impact theory scope is narrower under the ADEA, it nonetheless exists as a theory of recovery under the ADEA. Specifically, unlike Title VII, if policies or procedures have a disparate impact in violation of the ADEA, it would nonetheless be acceptable, provided that the differentiation is based on reasonable factors other than age. In *Smith*, a number of police officers brought suit against the City of Jackson, claiming that a pay plan that provided substantially greater increases of salaries for younger officers violated the ADEA. Although the Court concluded that the pay plan did, in fact, differentiate between the younger and older officers in terms of pay raises, the city defended its actions based upon its need to increase the starting salaries for junior officers to allow the city to compete with other similarly situated municipalities. This, the Court concluded, was sufficient for purposes of demonstrating reasonable factors other than age, and thus the city's pay plan was not in violation of the ADEA.

One of the exemptions from liability for disparate impact claims under the ADEA is if the employer can demonstrate that its actions were based on "reasonable factors other than age" (RFOA). In the U.S. Supreme Court case of *Meacham v. Knolls Atomic Power Laboratory* [128 S. Ct. 2395 (2008)] the Court was asked to determine who bears the burden of proof as it relates to an alleged RFOA. Recognizing that an RFOA is essentially an affirmative defense, which an employer must raise, the Court determined that the employer bears both the burden of production and burden of persuasion to demonstrate an RFOA.

Q 4:170 What is necessary to establish a prima facie age discrimination claim?

Generally, courts have utilized the framework enunciated by the Supreme Court in *McDonnell Douglas Corp. v. Green* [411 U.S. 792 (1973)], which provides that:

- He or she was in the ADEA protected age group (PAG);
- He or she was discharged or demoted;
- At the time of discharge or demotion, he or she was performing the job at a level that met his or her employer's legitimate expectations; and
- Following his or her discharge or demotion, he or she was replaced by someone of comparable qualifications outside the PAG.

What if the person who replaced the individual within the PAG is within the PAG, but nonetheless significantly younger than the fired or demoted worker? This issue was addressed by the Supreme Court in *O'Connor v. Consolidated Coin Caterers Corp.* [517 U.S. 308 (1996)] Recognizing that no greater inference of age discrimination could be drawn when a 40 year old is replaced by a 39 year old (someone outside the PAG) than when a 56 year old is replaced by a 40 year old (someone within the PAG), the court concluded that replacement by somebody outside the PAG is not a proper element of the McDonnell Douglas prima facie case when applied to age discrimination claims. Rather, the fact that the replacement is "substantially younger" is a far more reliable indicator of age discrimination than the fact that someone may have been replaced by somebody outside the PAG.

Conner v. Hoechst Celanese Chemical Co. Inc. [2006 WL 3431518 (5th Cir. 2006)] demonstrates the establishment of a prima facie age discrimination claim for failure to promote. In *Conner*, the employer, as a result of having a vacant chemist position open because of the chemist's acceptance of a voluntary separation package in connection with a reduction in force, promoted a young employee to the position who was not nearly as qualified as a long-time employee over 50 years of age who also applied for the position. Although the employer articulated a legitimate reason for its decision, the court found that because the older employee's qualifications for the chemist position were so far superior to that of the younger employee, this information created a genuine issue of material fact, reversing summary judgment for the employer and remanding the case to trial.

Q 4:171   What is a sufficient age discrepancy between a former employee and his/her replacement to maintain an age claim under the ADEA?

In *Oglesby v. Hy-Vee, Inc.* [402 F. Supp. 2d 1296 (D. Ct. Kan. 2005)], the employer sought summary judgment based upon, among other things, the plaintiff's failure to maintain a prima facie case of age discrimination under the ADEA when the plaintiff was replaced by someone who was just five years and seven months younger. The court in *Oglesby* noted the U.S. Supreme Court decision of *O'Connor v. Consolidated Coin Caterers Corp.* [116 S. Ct. 1307 (1996)], which required that the plaintiff must show a "significant" age difference between him and the worker who replaced him to maintain a claim under the ADEA. The court then reviewed a number of circuit court decisions that came to a number of inconsistent results. [*See, e.g.*, Benjamin v. E.I. DuPont De Nemours & Co., 75 Fed. Appx. 65 (3d Cir. 2003) (seven-year gap sufficient); Damon v. Fleming Supermarkets of Fla., Inc., 196 F.3d 1354 (11th Cir. 1999) (five-year gap sufficient); Carter v. Decision One Corp., 122 F.3d 997 (11th Cir. 1997) (three-year gap sufficient); Schlitz v. Burlington NRR, 115 F.3d 1407 (8th Cir. 1997) (five-year gap insufficient); Kitchen v. Burlington N. & Santa Fe R.R. Co., 298 F. Supp. 2d 1193 (D. Kan. 2004) (six-year gap insufficient); Housely v. Boeing Co., 177 F. Supp. 2d 1209 (D. Kan. 2001) (four-year gap insufficient).] After reviewing these conflicting decisions and recognizing the standard with which the courts treat motions for summary disposition, the court assumed, without deciding, that a sufficient age difference existed between the plaintiff and the worker who replaced him—five years and seven months—such that a prima facie case under the ADEA could be maintained.

Similarly, in *Whittington v. Nordam Group, Inc.* [429 F.3d 986 (10th Cir. 2005)], the Tenth Circuit was asked by the employer to reverse a jury verdict in favor of a former employee under the ADEA because the employer claimed that the five-year age difference between the plaintiff and the employee who replaced the plaintiff was not sufficiently "significant" under the U.S. Supreme Court decision of *O'Connor*, such that an ADEA claim could not be maintained. The court, after having reviewed relevant decisions and based upon its appellate standard of review, concluded that the five-year age difference was not sufficiently insignificant as a matter of law such that the age discrimination claim could not be maintained and affirmed the verdict.

Q 4:172   Does the ADEA protect younger employees within the protected group from discrimination?

Although state courts under state civil rights laws have come to different conclusions, the U.S. Supreme Court in *General Dynamics Land Systems, Inc. v. Cline* [540 U.S. 581 (2004)], concluded that the ADEA did not protect allegations of impermissible discrimination against younger workers. In the case, present and former employees between the ages of 40 and 49 sued their employer under the ADEA alleging that the collective bargaining agreement's elimination of employer's retiree health insurance benefits program for workers then under 50 discriminated against younger workers. The court, in reviewing the legislative history behind the ADEA and subsequent case law, concluded that discrimination against the relatively young is outside of the ADEA's protection and therefore the employer did not violate the ADEA by eliminating health insurance benefits for workers under 50, while retaining such benefits for workers over 50.

Q 4:173 Can age be a BFOQ, exempt from illegal age discrimination under ADEA?

The BFOQ defense is available as a defense to illegal age discrimination under the ADEA; however, as with Title VII, the BFOQ defense is interpreted narrowly and is available only when it is determined to be bona fide to a specific job and reasonably necessary to the normal operations of the particular business. The employer has the burden of demonstrating in any age-based BFOQ that the age limit is reasonably necessary to the essence of the business, and either all or substantially all individuals excluded from the job involved are in fact disqualified. Some of the individuals so excluded possess a disqualifying trait that cannot be ascertained except by reference to age.

Q 4:174 Is there any protection against discrimination based on age for employees under 40 years old?

A few states have passed age discrimination acts that forbid disparate treatment on the basis of age for all employees. The courts have held that these laws are not preempted by federal law.

Q 4:175 Is the ADEA part of Title VII?

No. The ADEA was passed as a separate law several years after Title VII was enacted and is more closely related to the FLSA. Initially, the ADEA was enforced by the Department of Labor, whereas Title VII has always been enforced by the EEOC. When the ADEA was later amended, responsibility shifted to the EEOC. The EEOC investigates age discrimination complaints in much the same way that it investigates other accusations of discrimination. The time limitation for filing the complaint and other details are essentially the same as those under Title VII (see Qs 4:1–4:9).

Q 4:176 Are there any differences between enforcement of Title VII and enforcement of ADEA?

Because the ADEA is related to the FLSA and not directly derived from Title VII of the 1964 Civil Rights Act, there are several important substantive and procedural differences between them. First, an individual filing a complaint with the EEOC under Title VII must obtain a 90-day letter to sue from the agency before taking the case into federal court; the ADEA complainant, however, must wait only 60 days after filing an age complaint with the EEOC before filing a suit in federal court without the agency's permission. The discrimination victim filing under Title VII does not have a statute of limitations until the 90-day letter to sue is issued by the EEOC, which may be years after the initial filing of the complaint. The ADEA complainant should, however, be aware of the statute of limitations contained in the FLSA, which runs from the date of the discriminatory act (e.g., termination of employment), not from when the EEOC complaint was filed.

The ADEA derives its limitation of actions from the FLSA. Litigants can sue under the FLSA for willful violations of the law within three years of the illegal action. Non-willful violations must be pursued within two years of their occurrence. The same is true under the ADEA. These time periods run from the date of the last illegal action, despite timely filing of a complaint with the EEOC.

Q 4:177　What is the *Older Workers Benefits Protection Act*?

In 1990, Congress passed the Older Workers Benefits Protection Act (OWBPA). As has frequently happened in the history of labor and employment law, this legislation was passed in response to a Supreme Court decision, the outcome of which outraged many congressmen and important segments of their constituencies. In *Public Employees Retirement System of Ohio v. Betts* [492 U.S. 158 (1989)], the Court held that the ADEA did not forbid age discrimination in the area of employee benefits except in unusual circumstances. On September 24, 1990, the Senate approved OWBPA by an overwhelming 94 to 1 majority. The House of Representatives approved the measure by a margin of 406 to 17. OWBPA was subsequently signed into law by President George Bush, thus overturning *Betts*.

OWBPA expressly rejects the Supreme Court's controversial decision by defining "compensation, terms, conditions or privileges of employment" as including all employee benefits, even those provided under a bona fide employee benefit plan. Consequently, Section 4(a)(1) of the ADEA now forbids discrimination in employee benefits as well as in every other aspect of employment that is not protected by some specific exemption from coverage of the Act.

The law also codifies the concept of "equal benefit or equal cost," as part of the federal regulatory scheme for employee benefits. This concept was rejected by the Supreme Court in 1989 in *Betts*. Previously espoused in Department of Labor and EEOC interpretive letters, the principle of equal benefit or equal cost holds that a company must provide to its older workers benefits that are at least equal to those provided to younger workers, unless the company can prove that the cost of providing an equal benefit is higher for an older worker than for a younger one. The only exception to this equal benefit or equal cost rule is a voluntary early retirement incentive plan.

Q 4:178 What are OWBPA requirements with regard to early retirement incentive plans?

OWBPA sets out the following rules for voluntary early retirement incentive plans:

- The company may set a minimum age as a condition of eligibility for either a normal or an early retirement benefit.
- The company may provide pension subsidies to subsidize regular pension benefits. For example, it may make bridge payments until the early retiree becomes eligible for Social Security benefits.
- No discrimination based on age is permitted with respect to severance pay when employees are terminated; however, a company may offset severance payments, including up to 52 weeks of supplemental unemployment compensation benefits paid until the employee is eligible for a pension, by the value of any retiree health benefits that the pensioner is entitled to as well as any immediate and unreduced pension benefits that the terminated employee can get. OWBPA provides specific rules for determining the value of retiree health benefits under this deduction. Furthermore, if immediately available pension benefits are actuarially reduced, a pro rata reduction in the authorized deduction is also required.
- The company may reduce long-term disability benefits by a like amount of pension benefits that the retiree elects to receive or that he or she is eligible to receive after attaining the latter of age 62 or normal retirement age.
- The company may implement a new disability plan that reflects OWBPA's requirements and then give employees the option of being covered under either the old or the new plan. Old plans are thus grandfathered in for employees who elect the old plans or who fail to make an election.

When such a plan is challenged in court, the burden is on the employer to prove that its conduct does not violate OWBPA. This is a very different burden of proof than that set out under Title VII and the other discrimination acts discussed in this chapter.

Chapter 13 discusses the OWBPA and its requirements to release an ADEA claim in releases and severance agreements.

Tax Issues

Q 4:179 Are the damages a plaintiff receives in discrimination claims or settlements subject to income taxation?

In *United States v. Burke* [504 U.S. 229 (1992)], the U.S. Supreme Court, in ruling that amounts received in settlement of a Title VII sex discrimination case were taxable, suggested that if damages traditionally available in tort cases (i.e., compensation for pain and suffering) were recovered, the damages would not be taxable. Since *Burke* and the expansion of damages in civil rights to include emotional damages, most practitioners generally believed that damages attributable to pain and suffering under the ADEA were non-taxable. However, the Supreme Court, in *Commissioner v. Schleier* [515 U.S. 323 (1995)], held, that damages recovered under the ADEA are not excludable from gross income and are taxable. Specifically, the Court held that unless the damages received were "on account of personal injuries or sickness," the amounts received were taxable. With respect to personal injuries, the Court likened the situation to an automobile accident where the complainant receives damages for medical expenses, pain, suffering, emotional distress, and lost wages. All of these damages would be excludable from income because they were on account of personal injuries or sickness. On the other hand, in *Schleier*, the Court held that neither Schleier's age, nor discharge, could fairly be described as a "personal injury" or "sickness," and therefore, damages recovered were not excludable from gross income within the meaning of Section 104(a)(2) of the Internal Revenue Code. As a result of *Schleier*, it was widely believed that most damages recoverable in ADEA cases are taxable and that the *Schleier* decision would impact the tax treatment of damages attributable to other federal civil rights claims under Title VII.

The Small Business Job Protection Act of 1996, signed into law by President Clinton in August 1996, adopted the reasoning of *Schleier* and amended Code Section 104(a)(2) to make it clear that the exemption does not apply to emotional injuries and the like, but only physical injuries or physical sickness. In addition, the amendments are not limited to age claims, but apply to all discrimination and employment claims as well. On December 30, 1996, the IRS published Revenue Ruling 1996-53 adopting *Schleier*. As a result, absent recovery attributable to personal injury torts, a settlement or award in the typical discrimination case will be fully taxable, the only issue being whether sums are attributable to wage loss, such that employer withholding is required or whether sums are legitimately attributable to other losses, for which there may be no withholding obligation, but for which a Form 1099 must be filed with the IRS. It is highly advisable that if sums in a settlement of a discrimination claim are allocated to anything other than wages, that the settlement agreement identify the allocation, specify the non-wage matters to which the sums have been allocated, and that the allocation be reasonable in light of damages alleged and recovery permitted under the relevant statute(s).

Q 4:180   If taxable, are the payments made to an employee in a Title VII claim subject to withholding taxes?

Certainly monies attributable to back pay and lost wages would be subject to withholding taxes. However, to the extent that the sums are attributable to something other than lost wages (i.e., emotional pain and suffering, costs, and the like), they would not be subject to withholding tax, although the sums would nevertheless be taxable. However, if the sums are not allocated in the award or settlement agreement, courts will typically find the sums allocable to lost wages for which withholding will be required from the award and/or settlement amount. Such was the case in *Rivera v. Baker West, Inc.* [430 F.3d

1253 (9th Cir. 2005)] At issue was the settlement of a Title VII claim alleging discrimination and wrongful termination. The parties entered into a settlement agreement that did not specify how the funds were to be allocated, but merely had the settlement amount, $40,000, to be paid less "required withholdings." Because the settlement agreement did not allocate the settlement to items that would not be considered wages, but referenced "less required withholdings" in the settlement agreement, the court concluded that the sums were for lost wages subject to full withholding.

Q 4:181   Do ADEA claims survive the death of the employee?

A U.S. District Court in Minnesota was faced with the issue of whether ADEA claims survive the death of the employee. The trustee for the deceased employee's estate maintained that both the compensatory remedies under the ADEA and the liquidated damages provisions should survive the death of the employee. The court, although allowing that the remedial aspects of the ADEA claim that provide for compensation for back pay and the like clearly survived the death of the employee, the liquidated damages provisions contained under the ADEA are more akin to a penalty and, as such, did not survive the death of the employee. [Kettner v. Compass Group USA, 570 F. Supp. 2d 1121 (D. Ct. Minn. 2008)]

The Equal Pay Act

Q 4:182   What is the *EPA*?

The *EPA* is an amendment to the FLSA. It states that male and female employees who perform the same work for the same employer must receive the same rate of pay. The importance of analyzing the actual work and duties performed, as opposed to a position or even written job descriptions was highlighted in *Horn v. University of Minnesota.* [362 F.3d 1042 (8th Cir. 2004)] In the case, the University posted openings for an "Assistant Women's Ice Hockey" position and two employees were hired for the positions—a man and a woman. The positions had identical job descriptions and titles in their contracts with the University. However, the male coach position paid $2,000 a month and the female coach received $3,000 a month. Despite the identical job descriptions in the posting and contracts, the court analyzed the two positions and concluded that the female assistant coach performed duties significantly in excess to those of the male assistant coach. The female coach, in addition to the administrative duties the male coach performed, also performed significant public relations duties for which she had prior skill and experience and which the court concluded prevented the two positions from being "substantially equal" under the EPA. In *Musgrove v. Government of the District of Columbia* [775 F. Supp. 2d 158 (D.D.C. 2011)], the court found that a principal of a high school within the district, who complained that she was paid less than other male principals in other district high schools, did not provide any evidence to support her claims that in fact, the principals at these other high schools were similarly situated to her, other than self-serving assertions of comparable job duties. In fact, the plaintiff conceded that salary for high schools principals can be based on a variety of matters such as length of service, student body size, education and the like. In *Puchakjian v. Township of Winslow* [804 F. Supp. 2d 288 (D.N.J. 2011)], the court held that a municipal clerk, who was a department head, was not able to demonstrate that her position was substantially similar to the other department heads in the township. Similarly, in *Daniels v. UPS* [797 F. Supp. 2d 1163 (D. Kan. 2011)], the court found that a female dispatch specialist who was not responsible for supervising employees was not substantially equal to male supervisors with supervisory responsibilities.

Q 4:183   How long do employees have to file claims under the EPA?

Claims under the EPA must be filed within two years after the cause of action accrued or three years if the violation was willful. [29 U.S.C. § 255(a)] In claims involving the EPA, generally, each paycheck for which there is a claimed EPA violation is considered a separate and distinct act of discrimination, such that the claim must be filed within two years of that paycheck or three years in the event of willful violation. [*See* Collins v. Landmark Military Newspapers, Inc., 2007 WL 2301549, *9 (E.D. Va. Aug. 6, 2007).] However, under certain circumstances, the doctrine of equitable tolling may be applied to EPA statutes of limitation, such that the court will look beyond the two- to three-year statutory provision. [*See* Lange v. United States, 2007 WL 2198225, *4 (Fed. Cl. July 19, 2007).] Equitable tolling may be permitted in situations where the claimant, although actively pursuing his or her judicial remedies, filed a defective pleading during the statutory period or in circumstances where the complainant has been induced by the employer's misconduct into allowing the deadline to pass. [*Lange,* at *4]

Q 4:184   Are there any exceptions to the rule that male and female employees receive equal pay for equal work?

Even if a plaintiff can establish a prima facie case under the EPA, the employer can defeat the EPA claim if the employer can demonstrate that the pay differential is justified for one of the following reasons:

1. A seniority system;
2. A merit system;
3. A system based on quantity or quality of production; or
4. Any factor other than gender.

[29 U.S.C. § 206(d)(1)]

In *Harrison-Pepper v. Miami University* [103 Fed. Appx. 596 (6th Cir. Ohio 2004)], a university professor claimed a violation of the EPA based on the pay differential between her and other male university professors, she being the lowest paid of the eight full professors in her department. Although the pay differential was clear, the court found that the university sufficiently explained the disparity because of its justification for pay differences based on its merit-based system of awarding raises. Although the system was somewhat subjective, the court concluded that the university's reliance on the university professor's extended absences in determining her raises was sufficient justification to legitimize the disparities between her salary and that of her male counterparts. Similarly, in *Reznick v. Associated Orthopedics & Sports Medicine, PA* [104 Fed. Appx. 387 (5th Cir. 2004)], the court was asked to determine whether the clinic had a legitimate reason for the pay discrepancy between two orthopedic surgeons—a male and a female—working at a clinic. Even assuming that the jobs were substantially similar, the court noted that it was undisputed that the male orthopedic surgeon generated nearly twice the revenue as the female orthopedic surgeon, and as a result, the employer satisfied its affirmative defense by demonstrating that the disparity in earnings was a reflection of the male surgeon's "quantity or quality" of production.

In *Sims-Fingers v. City of Indianapolis* [493 F.3d 768 (7th Cir. 2007)], a female manager of one of the City's parks claimed a violation of the EPA because some of her male counterparts, who held the same title as the claimant, made significantly more money. However, the court noted that the male counterparts had advanced relevant education degrees and worked at parks far larger than the claimant's, which included many amenities that were not included in the claimant's park. Moreover, the court noted that many male park managers at smaller parks were paid less than the claimant. As such, the court held that the disparities in pay were not violations of the EPA. However, just because a male counterpart may have greater education, qualifications, and experience will not always justify disparities in pay under the EPA. In *Osborn v. Home Depot USA, Inc.* [518 F. Supp. 2d 377 (D. Conn. 2007)], a female kitchen designer for Home Depot claimed a violation of the EPA due to the fact that other male kitchen designers were paid significantly more. Although the company defended the pay disparity based upon the education, experience, and qualifications of her male counterparts, the court noted that the educational background, qualifications, and experience were not necessarily related to the position at issue and, as a result, may not be sufficient to justify the pay differential, such that the matter was remanded to the trial court for further proceedings.

In *Byra-Grzegorczyk v. Bristol-Myers Squibb Company* [572 F. Supp. 2d 233 (D. Ct. Conn. 2008)], a female employee claimed a violation of the EPA because she was allegedly paid less than her immediate predecessor, a male, performing allegedly the exact same job. However, the court found that plaintiff's predecessor had over 10 years seniority prior to the time that plaintiff was newly hired, that the two did not perform equal work in that the prior male employee worked in areas that plaintiff did not and had many direct reports which plaintiff did not have, and as such, granted a dismissal of plaintiff's claims against mere general allegations concerning violations of the EPA. In *Mallison v. Haworth, Inc.* [488 Fed. Appx. 88 (6th Cir. Mich. 2012)], the court found that discrepancies in pay between a female employee and other male employees was due to differences in supervisory and manufacturing experience, and not illegal discrimination under the EPA as alleged. Similarly, a female professor at the

University of Texas claimed violations of the EPA in connection with the discrepancies between her pay and other male professors at the University, but the court found that the discrepancy in pay was attributable to factors other than gender, including seniority. [*Suter v. University of Tex. at San Antonio*, 859 F. Supp. 2d 851 (W.D. Tex. 2012)]

Use of the affirmative defense to justify pay differentials on factors other than sex requires more than merely articulating a legitimate non-discriminatory reason for the differential, but rather, the employer bears the burden of proving that the pay differential was based on a factor other than sex. For example, in *Drum v. Leeson Electric Corp.*, [565 F.3d 1071 (8th Cir. 2009)] a female employee brought an action against her employer under the EPA alleging that her male replacement earned significantly more than she did when she performed the job. Although the company argued various "market force theories" to articulate why the replacement was paid more than the female employee, they could not point to any factor other than gender to substantiate a discrepancy, such that the employer's motion for summary disposition was denied.

Q 4:185   How do courts determine whether there is a violation of the EPA?

In *Kaplan v. Multimedia Entertainment, Inc.* [02-CV-00447C(F), 2005 WL 2837561 (W.D.N.Y. Oct. 27, 2005)], a television news reporter/anchor claimed that her employer had violated the EPA by paying her significantly less than a male television news reporter/anchor who performed substantially the same work. Although the court noted an annualized discrepancy of approximately $18,000, it nonetheless held that the media company was justified in the pay differential because of the additional 16 years of service that her male counter-part had with the company, noting that seniority is a legitimate factor to justify higher compensation under the EPA. However, in order to be justified, expla-nations of wage disparity must fit within the affirmative defenses under the EPA. In *Lewis v. Sheridan Broadcasting Network, Inc.* [2:04-cv-1015, 2005 WL 2977799 (W.D. Pa. Nov. 7, 2005)], the broadcasting company attempted to explain the disparity between a female anchor's pay and a male anchor's pay based on market factors, but the court concluded that the company must produce evidence that the wage disparity in fact was created by a legitimate non-discriminatory reason in order to obtain summary judgment. The company failed to do so, and the motion for summary judgment to the EPA claim was denied. In contrast, if the company can demonstrate that market pressures did in fact result in wage disparity, an EPA claim can be beaten. For example, in *Wernsing v. Department of Human Services, State of Illinois* [427 F.3d 466 (7th Cir. 2005)], the court held that in the agency's practice of paying transferees an initial salary equal to what they were earning in their old job plus a raise if that was possible under the pay scale for the new job, discrepancies resulting in female employees doing substantially the same job and receiving less pay is not a violation of the EPA. As the court held, the Act does not require the agency to ignore market pressures in setting salaries for new hires.

Although wage discrepancies can be based on differentials in pay between current employees and an employee and his or her predecessor, EPA claims can also be based upon wage discrepancies between an employee and his or her successor. For example, in *Dixon v. University of Toledo*, [638 F. Supp. 2d 847 (N.D. Ohio 2009)] a former university employee claimed a violation of the EPA when her replacement was paid more than she was paid when she performed the job. Although not previously ruled on by the Sixth Circuit, the court concluded that the EPA does allow claims based on differentials in a successor's pay. Employers with multiple locations may be determined to be separate establishments for analysis of EPA claims. In *Renstrom v. Nash Finch Company* [787 F. Supp. 2d 961 (D. Minn. 2001)], the court held that distribution centers maintained by a wholesaler in different geographical locations were separate establishments for purposes of the EPA. In *Collins v. Dollar Tree Stores, Inc.* [788 F. Supp. 2d 1328 (N.D. Ala. 2011)], the plaintiffs sought to have all Dollar Tree Stores in the United States treated as one establishment for this EPA claim filed by store managers throughout the country. However, there was little centralized control of personnel activity and pay practices to support use of "establishment" at the national or regional level, but the court did find there was sufficient centralized control of pay practices and personnel issues at the district level, such that all stores contained within one district would be an "establishment" under the EPA. In *Westrich-James v. Dallas Morning News, Inc.* [2012 WL 4068982 (N.D. Tex. Sept. 17, 2012)], a manager of a news program claimed that her employer had violated the EPA by not paying her as much as two other managers for the news organization. However, finding that the male employees worked in different geographic zones involving substantially different responsibilities, the court held that the claim could not be maintained because plaintiff had not shown that the male employees' jobs were comparable to hers in accordance with the EPA.

Q 4:186 Does the EPA apply to members of the military?

The EPA does not apply to military employees. However, many members of the military have dual civilian/military status such that, in certain circumstances, the EPA may apply. In a case of first impression, *Jentoft v. United States* [450 F.3d 1342 (Fed. Cir. 2006)], at issue was whether a national guard technician with dual civilian/military status was a civilian employee, such that the EPA would apply, or a military employee, such that she would be unable to maintain claims under the EPA. Recognizing her dual status and rights as a federal civilian employee under the National Guard Technician Act, the court held that the technician could pursue claims under the EPA.

Retaliation Claims

Q 4:187　Can an employer be held liable for retaliating against an employee who engages in protected activity under federal civil rights laws?

Section 704 of Title VII provides in relevant part:

> It shall be an unlawful employment practice for an employer to discriminate against any of his employees or applicants for employment . . . because he has opposed any practice made an unlawful employment practice by this subchapter, or because he has made a charge, testified, assisted, or participated in any manner in an investigation, proceeding or hearing under this subchapter.

[*See* 42 U.S.C. § 2000e-3, similar provisions are contained within the ADA; *see* 42 U.S.C. § 12203(a).]

In essence, these statutory provisions protect two different types of activities—opposition to unlawful activities and participation in a protected activity. Generally, in order to establish a prima facie case of unlawful retaliation, a plaintiff must establish that: (1) he or she opposed violations of the Act or participated in activities protected by the Act; and (2) the opposition or participation resulted in an adverse employment decision.

With respect to participation, courts generally require that the language of the statutes be read literally and that the institution of the proceedings leading to the filing of a charge or complaint is a prerequisite to protection under the participation clause.

With respect to opposition, the issue is more complex. In *Booker v. Brown & Williamson Tobacco Co.* [879 F.2d 1304 (6th Cir. 1989)], discussing analogous retaliatory language under Michigan's Elliott-Larsen Civil Rights Act, the court held that a vague charge of discrimination is, in and of itself, insufficient to constitute opposition to an alleged unlawful practice. The court in *Livingston v. Wyeth, Inc.* [520 F.3d 334 (4th Cir. 2008)] held that opposition must be against conduct that could reasonably be thought to violate the law in order for a retaliation claim to be maintained. With respect to ambiguous comments, the court in *Garcia-Paz v. Swift Textiles, Inc.* [873 F. Supp. 547, 560 (D. Kan. 1995)], discussing opposition under the ADEA, stated:

> At the same time, however, employers should not approach every employee's comment as a riddle puzzling over the possibility that it contains a cloaked claim of discrimination thus liability shall not attach unless the activity in question advances beyond advocacy and into recognizable opposition to an unlawful practice that the claimant reasonably believes to be unlawful. [873 F. Supp. 547, 559–60 (D. Kan. 1995)]

In *Evans v. Kansas City* [65 F.3d 98, 100 (8th Cir 1995)], the plaintiff criticized her supervisor as disregarding the needs of minority students and accused her supervisor of making a racially insensitive remark. Despite evidence of negative treatment following these remarks, the court held that the plaintiff's comments did not rise to the level of opposition in order to make a claim under the opposition clause. [*See also* Johnson v. Honeywell Info. Sys., Inc., 955 F.2d 409, 415 (6th Cir. 1992).] However, in *Truckenmiller v. Burgess Health Center* [814 F. Supp. 2d 894 (N.D. Iowa 2011)], the court refused to dismiss a retaliation claim filed under the EPA when it found that informal oral statements allegedly made by the HR director complaining of unequal pay based on gender were sufficient to find that there was an assertion of rights protected by the statute such that the case could not be dismissed, but decided by the jury. In 2009, the U.S. Supreme Court determined whether an employee who alleges retaliation under the opposition clause, can maintain the claim when the employee, herself, did not bring forth the opposition on her own, but rather, stated opposition in answer to questions during an employer's investigation of a co-worker's complaints of unlawful activity. Reviewing recognized definitions of the term to *oppose*, the court held that the statements made by the employee when she was interviewed indicated her disapproval of the sexually obnoxious behavior by a fellow employee and as such, was sufficient opposition upon which to base a claim. [Crawford v. Metropolitan Gov't of Nashville and Davison Cnty., Tenn., 129 S. Ct. 846 (2009)] Moreover, even if opposition or participation can be satisfied, there must be some causal connection between the alleged protected or opposition activity and the determination at issue. For example, in *Vaughan v. Harvard Industries, Inc.* [926 F. Supp. 1340, 1345 (W.D. Tenn. 1996)], the court held that evidence of proximity in time between an employee's workers' compensation claim and an adverse employment action is not sufficient to overcome a summary judgment motion in a retaliatory discharge case. Similarly, the Sixth Circuit, in *Cooper v. City of North Olmstead* [795 F.2d 1265, 1272 (6th Cir. 1986)], held that the mere fact that the employee was discharged four months after filing a discrimination claim is insufficient in and of itself to support an inference of retaliation. [*See also* Amrhein v. Health Care Serv. Corp., 546 F.3d 854 (7th Cir. 2008).] In *Slagle v. County of Clarion* [435 F.3d 262 (3d Cir. 2006)], a former corrections officer claimed that his termination was in retaliation for an EEOC charge he had filed approximately four months before he was fired. The court, however, found that the charge that was filed was facially invalid and summarily dismissed by the EEOC and, as a result, could not be used to form a basis of protected activity to support a claim of retaliation. Similarly, in *Velez v. Janssen Ortho, LLC* [467 F.3d 802 (1st Cir. 2006)], the court held that although the former employee had previously filed a sexual harassment claim against the employer and claimed that she was later refused a position due to this previous sexual harassment complaint, the letters that she had sent the employer expressing an interest in a variety of positions was insufficient to establish an application for a specific vacant position, a requirement in so-called failure-to-hire cases.

To establish a causal connection between the protected activity and the alleged adverse employment action for which retaliation is based, courts will look to the proximity and timing of the events, and if too much time has passed, will conclude that the claim cannot be maintained because a jury could not reasonably find a causal relationship. Such was the case in *McGrath v. Clinton.*

[674 F. Supp. 2d 131 (D.D.C. 2009)] In the case, a former foreign service employee sued Hillary Rodham Clinton, claiming that his eventual separation from the foreign service was in retaliation for a prior EEOC complaint. However, the court noted that the eventual separation took place two years after the filing of the EEOC complaint and 16 months after the conclusion of the EEOC's investigation. The court held that this timeframe places the adverse employment action outside of a timeframe from which a jury could reasonably infer a causal connection. In *Burkhart v. American Railcar Industries, Inc.* [603 F.3d 472 (8th Cir. 2010)], the court found that disciplinary action following a complaint for a violation of Title VII was insufficient to establish a causal connection because the employee had an extensive history of poor performance preceding the challenged employment action. Moreover, the employee's discharge, seven months after her complaint, was a gap in time between the protected activity and adverse employment action from which an inference of retaliatory motive could not be maintained. Similarly, in *Leonard v. Eastern Illinois University* [606 F.3d 428 (7th Cir. 2010)], the court held that a six-month time frame between the employee's civil rights complaint and unsuccessful interview for a promotion was insufficient, in and of itself, to establish a causal connection necessary to maintain a retaliation claim under Title VII.

In *Burlington Northern & Santa Fe Railway Co. v. White* [126 S. Ct. 2405 (2006)], the U.S. Supreme Court held that, to maintain a prima facie case of Title VII retaliation, a plaintiff must show that (1) he engaged in protective conduct; (2) reasonable employees would have found the challenged retaliatory materially adverse; and (3) the materially adverse action was causally linked to the protected conduct. [*Burlington*, at 2415] The issue of whether conduct was materially adverse under *Burlington* was addressed by the Eighth Circuit.

In *Weger v. City of Ladue* [500 F.3d 710 (8th Cir. 2007)], female communications officers, who had complained of sexual harassment by male officers in the department, claimed retaliation by these male officers for having come forward after the conclusion of the investigation. Among other things, the officers claimed that the chief issued directives after the investigation effectively isolating them from their co-workers, that their supervisor began "papering" their personnel files, and that, in general, they felt ostracized. In reviewing the directives, although the chief had adopted a number of policies that would work to prevent non-business-related communication with the communication officers, the court found that the procedures and policies only resulted in minor workplace changes, did not single out the plaintiffs, and as such, were not materially adverse. Although the plaintiffs claimed a materially adverse action in connection with the so called "papering" of the plaintiffs' files, the court found that the increased note taking with respect to the plaintiffs' work did not satisfy the materially adverse requirement when the notes were largely positive, neutral, and had no negative impact on their employment. Similarly, plaintiffs' claims that they felt ostracized by the chief and other officers were not materially adverse for lack of significant harm. As such, the plaintiffs could not maintain a prima facie case of retaliation under Title VII.

In *Niswander v. The Cincinnati Insurance Co.* [529 F.3d 714 (6th Cir. 2008)], an employee, who was embroiled in a class action sex discrimination with her employer, surreptitiously obtained confidential company documents, in violation of company privacy policies and gave them to her lawyer representing her in the sex discrimination case. When the company found out, it fired the employee in violation of its privacy policy and the employee sued for retaliation. However, because the court determined that the disclosure of the confidential documents to her attorneys did not constitute opposition under Title VII or participation as the term is defined under Title VII, the retaliation claim could not be obtained.

Employers should be uniquely sensitive to situations where employees complain to management concerning harassment or discrimination by others. Even if these individuals are not victims or subject to the alleged discriminatory or harassment conduct, once they make a claim, any adverse employment action that results from the complaint is in and of itself actionable. The characterization of these employees as "troublemakers" or "meddlers" in such circumstances provides strong ammunition for liability in the event of an adverse employment decision. Employers should recognize that victims are not the only group of people protected under federal civil rights laws. Protections from discrimination and retaliation also extend to those who may oppose violations of the law and those that participate in any formal proceedings instituted pursuant to the federal civil rights laws.

Q 4:188 Can an employer be held liable for retaliating against an employee because a family member of the employee engaged in protected activity under the federal civil rights laws?

In *Thompson v. North American Stainless, LP* [131 S. Ct. 863 (2011)], the U.S. Supreme Court held that an employer violates Title VII by discharging an employee in retaliation for his fiancé having filed an EEOC charge. Although the Court permitted this so-called third-party retaliation claim to be maintained, it did not describe or identify the class of relationships to be protected, other than to state that retaliation against employees whose close family members engage in protected activity will most likely constitute retaliation in violation of Title VII.

Q 4:189 Can offering a severance package conditioned upon signing a release be considered retaliation?

A rather novel issue was addressed by the Sixth Circuit concerning whether a so-called "preemptive retaliatory policy" can form the basis of a retaliation claim under Title VII. In *EEOC v. Sundance Rehabilitation Corp.* [466 F.3d 490 (6th Cir. 2006)], an employer, in connection with a reduction in force, provided employees with a severance agreement that included a general release. As part of the release, the agreement provided that in the future the individual would not institute any charge before the EEOC, language that has been held to be illegal and unenforceable. The EEOC took the position that by having this illegal language in the release amounted to a "preemptive retaliatory policy" in violation of Title VII. The court, however, disagreed with the EEOC, holding that the mere offer of a separation agreement cannot amount to retaliation.

Q 4:190 Must the plaintiff have suffered an adverse employment action to maintain a Title VII retaliation claim?

In *Waters v. Home Depot USA, Inc.* [159 Fed. Appx. 943 (11th Cir. 2005)], the plaintiff filed a complaint alleging that her former employer, Home Depot, retaliated against her in violation of Title VII. After she was discharged from Home Depot, the plaintiff filed an EEOC complaint against Home Depot alleging discrimination. The plaintiff also purchased an interest in a cleaning services company that had a cleaning service contract with Home Depot. After the EEOC claim was filed, Home Depot terminated the contract with the cleaning services company. The plaintiff alleged in the complaint that Home Depot's termination of the cleaning services contract was done to retaliate against her for her pending discrimination charge. Although the court acknowledged that former employees may file charges of retaliation against former employers for retaliation attributable to post-termination conduct, in order for the charges to be actionable under Title VII's anti-retaliation provisions, the former employee must show he or she suffered an adverse employment action. Because the actions of Home Depot did not affect her employment, but merely her investment interests, the court held that the claim could not be maintained.

Q 4:191 Have the number of retaliation claims continued to rise?

Retaliation claims have increased over the years. According to the EEOC, retaliation charges have risen steadily from Fiscal Year 1992 (15.3 percent of all charges) to Fiscal Year 1999 (25.4 percent of all charges). [14 *Employment Discrimination Report (EDR)* (BNA) 177 (Feb. 2, 2000)] From Fiscal Year 2000 to 2005, retaliation claims rose to approximately 29.5 percent of all charges, according to the EEOC's Web site (http://www.eeoc.gov). In Fiscal Year 2006, retaliation claims filed with the EEOC rose to 29.8 percent of all claims. In Fiscal Year 2007, retaliation claims continued to rise, with a total of 26,167 claims filed with the EEOC (32.3 percent of total charges filed). In Fiscal Year 2008, retaliation charges rose to 32,690, representing 34.3 percent of all charges filed. In Fiscal Year 2009, 33,613 retaliation charges were filed, representing an increase to 35 percent for all charges filed. The numbers continued to rise in Fiscal Year 2011, with the EEOC receiving 37,334 retaliation charges, representing 37.4 percent of all charges filed.

Q 4:192 Can retaliation claims be maintained under EPA?

The EPA, which is part of the FLSA, incorporates FLSA's enforcement scheme which prohibits an employer from discriminating against an employee who has "filed any complaint or instituted or caused to be instituted any proceeding under or related to this Chapter." [29 U.S.C. § 215(a)(3)] To establish a prima facie case of retaliation under the EPA, the Sixth Circuit has held that a plaintiff must show: (1) that the plaintiff engaged in protected activity; (2) that the defendant knew the plaintiff exercised protected rights; (3) that as a result of the exercise of protected rights the defendant took employment action adverse to the plaintiff; and (4) there is a causal connection between the protected activity and the adverse employment action. [EEOC v. Avery Dennison Corp., 104 F.3d 858, 860 (6th Cir. 1997)] One issue that appears unresolved among jurisdictions is what is necessary to show protected activity under the EPA. For example, at issue in *Bell-Holcombe v. KI, LLC* [2008 WL 4616858 (ED Va. 2008)] was whether an internal written complaint by an employee to her superiors alleging violations of the EPA was protected activity, such that her later termination could establish a basis for a retaliation claim if there was a causal connection. Noting that the Fourth Circuit had consistently held that the FLSA protection does not apply to an employee's internal complaint to the employer, *Ball v. Memphis Bar-B-Q Co, Inc.* [228 F.3d 360, 364 (4th Cir. 2000)], the court stated that even though, in this instance, the complaint was more formal in that it was written, it was still an internal complaint which did not rise to the level of protected activity required to maintain a claim for retaliation under the EPA. On the other hand, in *Denman v. Youngstown University* [545 F. Supp. 2d 671 (N.D. Ohio 2008)], the court held that an internal complaint that alleged violations of the EPA was protected activity consistent with Sixth Circuit authority cited for the proposition that EPA protected activity applies to the unofficial assertion of rights through complaints at work, citing *EEOC v. Romeo Community Schools* [976 F.2d 985, 989 (6th Cir. 1992)] However, there is no question but that filing charges with the EEOC alleging sex discrimination based on pay disparity is clearly protected activity such that adverse employment actions allegedly undertaken as a result are sufficient to state a prima facie case of EPA retaliation. Such was the case in *Tamayo v. Blagojevich* [526 F.3d 1074 (7th Cir. 2008)] In the case, the plaintiff alleged that she had been subjected to adverse employment action by Governor Blagojevich and the other defendants, in retaliation for her complaints alleging sex discrimination and pay discrepancy with the EEOC. Having alleged specific instances of retaliatory conduct and adverse employment actions that followed the filing of the charges, the court concluded that the plaintiff had maintained a prima facie case such that dismissal was not warranted at this time.

Chapter 5

Personnel Files and Privacy Issues

This chapter explores the competing interests of the employer's right to compile and maintain information concerning its employees and the employees' expectations of privacy. The understandable desire of employees to protect their privacy and the equally understandable need of employers to protect their companies has created tension in the workplace. This chapter examines recent cases concerning these conflicting objectives and other developments, like the Health Insurance Portability and Accountability Act (HIPAA) Privacy Rules that require employers that sponsor health care plans to safeguard an employee's protected health information from unauthorized disclosure or use.

Personnel Files

Q 5:1 Are employers required to keep and maintain personnel records?

Federal law requires that particular records regarding employees be kept and maintained for specific periods of time. The Fair Labor Standards Act (FLSA) requires that employers maintain and preserve payroll records for covered employees for two or three years, depending on the record. Payroll records include the names and addresses of employees, hours worked during a workweek, and total wages for each pay period. Similarly, the federal contracting statutes—the Davis-Bacon Act, the Service Contract Act, the Walsh-Healey Act, and the Contract Work Hours and Safety Standards Act—mandate that required wage and payroll information be maintained and preserved for three years from completion of the federal contract. The Equal Employment Opportunity Commission (EEOC), in connection with Title VII, requires that personnel records created or relied upon in making employment decisions be preserved for at least six months. The Americans with Disabilities Act (ADA) requires personnel records to be maintained for one to three years, depending on the record involved. The Employee Retirement Income Security Act (ERISA) requires plan administrators, and any other person subject to reporting and disclosure requirements, to maintain sufficient records regarding the implementation and operation of an employee benefit plan for six years. Under the Family and Medical Leave Act (FMLA), employers are required to make, keep, and preserve records pertaining to the employer's obligations under the FMLA for at least three years. [39 C.F.R. § 825.500] Such records include:

- Payroll records for eligible employees;
- Records reflecting FMLA-designated leave;
- Copies of FMLA notices; and
- Employer policies regarding the taking of paid or unpaid leave.

Moreover, in order to defend against employee litigation, including claims for breach of contract or federal or state civil rights claims, it is necessarily incumbent upon the employer to demonstrate in a credible and convincing manner the basis for its employment decision being challenged. Under federal civil rights statutes, once the plaintiff articulates a prima facie discrimination case, under disparate treatment analysis, the burden shifts to the employer to articulate a legitimate business reason for its employment decision. A well-maintained personnel file, which includes a written record of the employee's performance, discipline, and attendance records, is invaluable in articulating a legitimate business reason for the employer's actions. Without written records, the employer is significantly hampered in its ability to defend itself in employee litigation.

As a result, all employers should maintain personnel records for every employee that include not only those particular items required by federal or state law, but also all performance evaluations, written discipline, and other written records regarding the employee's performance that can be utilized in defense of employment litigation.

Q 5:2   Should employers maintain personnel files?

Yes. Some employers, particularly those smaller in size, do not make or keep a personnel file for their employees other than a repository for tax forms, benefit forms, and the like. Usually smaller companies do not keep written employee performance evaluations or written disciplinary records. This is a mistake. An employer's best way of reducing risk and exposure to employee claims is to be able to articulate a legitimate business reason for the action at issue and be able to evidence the reason through use of a written record, typically records maintained in the personnel file. An employer that does not actively maintain its personnel files is unnecessarily exposing itself to employee litigation and claims.

Q 5:3   How should an employer keep and maintain personnel files?

There is no single best way to keep and maintain personnel files, but there are a number of considerations that need to be examined to determine whether records are being properly kept:

Confidentiality. The information within a personnel file is confidential between the employee and the employer, and the employer should take reasonable steps to ensure that the documents are kept confidential by restricting access to the files (e.g., placing them in a locked file cabinet with keys given only to those responsible for maintaining the files). In large organizations, where many supervisors may have a need to access files, rather than provide keys to all supervisors, the employer should limit keys to the personnel director or human resources department.

Critical evidentiary value. In the event of an employee claim, the personnel records kept by the employer are of great evidentiary value. Employers defend discrimination claims by articulating a legitimate non-discriminatory reason for their actions. The personnel file is critical to demonstrating the credibility of the employer's position when it contains written evaluations and prior discipline records consistent with the employer's position. Without a written record, the employer's defense is hollow and may be perceived as a pretext to hide illegal discrimination. It is not unusual for records to be tampered with, supplemented, or mysteriously lost in the event of litigation. Employers need to take care to ensure personnel records are safely kept in a manner that will preserve their integrity and prevent mischief.

Q 5:4   Do employees have the right to review their personnel files?

Just as there is no federal law requiring the maintenance of personnel files, no federal law gives employees the right to review such files per se; however, many states have enacted laws to allow employees reasonable access to their personnel files for review or copying. For example, under Michigan's Bullard-Plawecki Employee Right-to-Know Act [Mich. Comp. Laws Ann. §§ 423.501 *et seq.*], employees have the right to review and receive copies of their personnel records as defined under the Act, at reasonable intervals. In addition, some states allow employees to submit explanatory or corrective statements that must be made part of the personnel file.

Under the Michigan Act, an employee is permitted, upon reasonable request, to review his or her personnel file at reasonable intervals, generally not more than twice a calendar year. The Act specifically provides that the review will take place at a location reasonably near the employee's place of employment during normal business hours and, if such a review would require an employee to take time off from work to review the file, the employer shall make other reasonable arrangements. The Act also provides that if, after review, the employee wishes to obtain a copy of the information, the employee can do so, provided the employee pays the actual "incremental cost" of duplicating the information if requested by the employee. [*See* Mich. Comp. Laws Ann. §§ 423.503–423.504.]

Even if a jurisdiction has no statutory mandate for employers to allow employees to review their personnel files, there is no reason not to allow the review, and some benefit to the procedure as well.

The issue in most discrimination cases is whether an employment decision is based on a legitimate non-discriminatory reason, or whether the proffered reason is a pretext to hide illegal discrimination. A personnel file containing a written record of discipline and evaluations supporting the employer's decision will go a long way toward deterring litigation—this reason alone should prompt disclosure. Attorneys analyzing whether to take a potential case for an employee typically ask their prospective client to provide copies of his/her personnel file for review before taking the case. Plaintiff attorneys typically charge on a contingency-fee basis (usually one-third of the sums recovered) and will be reluctant to invest time and energy on a case when the personnel file credibly demonstrates and supports a legitimate reason for the employer's conduct.

Before permitting an employee to review his or her personnel file, the employer should review the file to ensure that it includes all relevant personnel records (e.g., evaluations and written discipline) and take steps to preserve the integrity of the file during the review process (i.e., only permit the review under close supervision to ensure the records are not tampered with or removed).

Q 5:5 What steps should an employer take if an employee wishes to review his or her personnel file?

Every employer should know that if an employee wishes to review his or her personnel file, the prospect of litigation is looming. Before an attorney will agree to represent an employee in employment litigation, the attorney will generally want to review the employee's personnel file. Typically, the attorney is looking for indications of performance problems, discipline, or other information that may impact on the prospective client's case. As a result, care should be taken to ensure that the record provided is a complete record of all personnel information. For example, many supervisors maintain individual discipline files, separate and distinct from the employee's personnel file. The supervisor(s) of the employee at issue should be contacted to determine if there is any other disciplinary record concerning the individual to be included within the personnel file. If a personnel file is initially provided without these records but the records are produced later, during litigation, the credibility of the information produced later will be at issue. The employee may argue that the employer created these disciplinary documents after litigation.

It is generally better to be over-inclusive than under-inclusive. Documents that appear only after litigation commences are suspect. Plaintiff attorneys are keenly aware of the importance of credibility in employment cases, and any indication that personnel records have been papered after the fact greatly assists the plaintiff's lawyers in making their case. As a result, the question is not, "What documents do we include?" but rather, "Is there any justifiable reason not to produce any of these documents?" Always err on the side of disclosure.

In producing a personnel file, employers need to guard against another danger. Supervisors alerted that the employee has requested an opportunity to review his or her file may treat the request as an invitation to create documents. This is a huge mistake. The documents of the employer are the baseline defense to a litigation claim involving an employee. There is nothing worse in defending employment litigation than to find out that disciplinary records that appear, on their face, to have been prepared contemporaneously to the event are later determined to have been prepared in anticipation of litigation, well after the disciplinary event took place. Quite literally, the employer has taken a situation that may be entirely defensible and rendered it indefensible based upon the after-the-fact tampering of the file. An employer caught in a lie regarding its documents will have a hard time recovering its credibility. This activity alone may be sufficient to demonstrate pretext as to the employer's legitimate reason for the employment decision at issue.

All personnel files should be reviewed carefully prior to submission and the employer should consult with its employment attorney regarding this procedure before documents are provided. The company's attorney will be able to analyze the documents and spot any potential problems, including incomplete or questionable submissions. Undated disciplinary records that are not signed by the employee are particularly suspect as documents created after the fact. These documents should be analyzed with the supervisor closely to ensure that they are appropriate personnel records.

In addition, an employee should never be left alone with an original personnel file. The review should be monitored by the employer to ensure no tampering occurs.

Lastly, to ensure the employer maintains an accurate record of what has been produced to the employee, consider numbering the copies submitted. Retaining a copy with each page suitably marked will provide good evidence of what was produced and guard against attempts to later alter the file.

Q 5:6   Should internal investigation records of unlawful activity be produced with a personnel file?

Many states have laws that regulate the production of personnel files. With respect to employer investigations of possible criminal conduct by an employee, Michigan's Bullard-Plawecki Employee Right-to-Know Act [Mich. Comp. Laws Ann. §§ 423.501 *et seq.*], permits employers to keep a separate investigation file during the investigation, and not disclose its contents to an employee. [Mich. Comp. Laws Ann. § 423.509] After the investigation is concluded, the Act requires that the file be destroyed if no disciplinary action is taken. Although the Act does not specifically address the issue, presumably the file would become part of the employee's personnel file and suitable for disclosure if disciplinary action is taken.

Suppose the investigation file contains information concerning other employees that is personal in nature and would constitute a clearly unwarranted invasion of another employee's privacy. Under Michigan law, this information can be withheld from disclosure. [Mich. Comp. Laws Ann. § 423.501(2)(c)(v)] Even in those states that have no statutory guidance, the employer should consider withholding or redacting this information, but keeping a note in the file explaining the incomplete nature of the submission.

Suppose the internal investigation involves not criminal activity, but possible unlawful activity, like an internal investigation of a sexual harassment complaint. Generally, investigation files contain notes, statements, a summary of the investigation, and an assessment of whether the evidence indicates that a violation has occurred, together with the determination of any remedial relief if a violation is found (i.e., discipline). During the course of the investigation, and to enable the investigator to do the investigation, the alleged victim and alleged harasser will be exposed to the information obtained from the other parties and witnesses for purposes of rebuttal and obtaining further information. Once the investigation is concluded, it is recommended that a summary be prepared that includes the information obtained, an analysis of the evidence, and a determination of whether or not a policy has been violated, together with remedial action if a violation is found. Once a determination is made, the summary should be shared with both the alleged victim and the alleged harasser. In instances where discipline resulted, the employer should at least include a copy of the summary of the investigation in the personnel file of the party disciplined, and note the existence of the investigation records generally kept in a separate investigation file. Ultimately, if the integrity of the investigation is at issue, there is no reason not to allow the employee to review the remaining investigation file; however, steps need to be taken to ensure that the file is not tampered with and nothing is removed from the file.

Q 5:7   Who owns an employee's personnel file?

As is the case with virtually all company documents, a personnel file is the property of the company; however, because the materials in the file are personal, employees often feel that such files belong to them. Thus, even in the absence of a state law mandating employee access, reasonable access is perhaps a desirable policy for the sake of employee morale.

Q 5:8   Should a company that buys the assets of another and hires its employees take the selling company's personnel files?

An asset sale is very different from a stock transaction. In a stock transaction, the company never changes, just its owners do, and whatever employment relationships exist between the employees and the company, continue unaffected by the stock transaction.

In an asset sale, on the other hand, a company buys the assets, as opposed to the stock of the selling company. Even after the sale, the selling company's existence would continue as an entity, separate and distinct from the buyer. As such, the hiring of employees by the buyer would be the start of a new employment relationship. Usually, in these transactions, the buyer takes great pains to prevent it from being considered a successor corporation, responsible for the misdeeds of the seller. As such, many buyers would not want possession of the prior employee's personnel records, since they have no real relevance to the new employment relationship, and possession would be inconsistent with the nature of the transaction.

Q 5:9   Are there any employee records that are not treated as part of a personnel file?

Pennsylvania's Inspection of Personnel Files Act is a representative example of most other state acts regarding personnel files. The Act denies employees access to certain information that employers may retain about them by simply defining *personnel files* so as to not encompass such information:

> The term "personnel file" shall not include records of any employee relating to the investigation of a possible criminal offense, letters of reference, documents which are being developed or prepared for use in civil, criminal or grievance procedures, medical records or materials which are used by the employer to plan for future operations or information available to the employee under the Fair Credit Reporting Act. [43 Pa. Cons. Stat. Ann. § 1321 (1978)]

Michigan's Bullard-Plawecki Employee Right-to-Know Act defines a *personnel* file as:

> A record kept by the employer that identifies the employee, to the extent that the record is used or has been used, or may affect or be used relative to that employee's qualification for employment, promotion, additional compensation or disciplinary action.

The Act specifically provides that a personnel record does not include, among other things, medical reports and records available to the employee from his or her doctor or medical facility, and records involving investigations of criminal activity, together with information of the "personal nature" that, if disclosed to somebody other than the employee, would constitute a "clearly unwarranted invasion of the other person's privacy." [*See* Mich. Comp. Laws Ann. § 423.501(2)(c).]

Even in states that allow access to personnel files, the right to access is not absolute. Employers should therefore know precisely what is and what is not included in the definition of personnel file in each state where they have employees.

Federal law, through the ADA, specifically provides that medical records are not to be kept in a personnel file, but instead kept separately and in a secured fashion.

Q 5:10   What is a protective order, as it relates to the production of personnel records of co-employees during litigation?

Federal and state rules of civil procedure governing the conduct of lawsuits almost uniformly say that courts can fashion an order to protect both parties and non-parties. A protective order is one common way for a court to do this. A typical protective order involving employee files requested as part of employee litigation includes the following restrictions:

- Contents that are clearly irrelevant to the lawsuit will be identified but not turned over to the requesting party.

- Only the requesting party and his or her attorneys will review the files that are produced.

- The information will be held in confidence. It will only be used or disseminated in connection with the litigation.

- All files and copies will be returned to the producing employer upon the resolution of the lawsuit.

Access to Personnel Files by Third Parties

Q 5:11   When should the company make personnel records available to third parties?

Personnel records should be treated as confidential information between the employer and the employee, and third parties should not be provided personnel records unless authorized by the employee, in writing, or as may be required by law or court order.

Although employees are ordinarily allowed by law or company policy to view and even copy their own personnel files, they should not be accorded automatic access to the personnel files of co-workers, even when they sue the company. To the contrary, a corporate defendant should make every effort to protect and preserve the privacy of its employees who are not parties to the lawsuit. In this regard, the employer should not voluntarily release the contents of these files but should await service of a proper subpoena or request for production of documents. Corporate counsel may still wish to move for entry of a protective order before releasing copies of these files, requiring that the information be kept confidential and only used in connection with the litigation. Although many different types of protective orders can be entered, most address the following issues:

- Describe the information subject to the protective order;
- Identify the individuals permitted to review the information;
- Restrict the individuals from using or disclosing the information, except in connection with the litigation; and
- Provide for a return of the information, and any copies or summaries thereof, upon conclusion of the litigation.

For particularly sensitive information, orders may contain provisions for the information to be sealed by the court clerk if filed with the court.

As for other third parties, any requests for information should be in writing and, unless the employee consents to release of the information (e.g., salary verification for mortgage application), should only be released as required by law or court order.

Many states regulate the exchange of personnel information with third parties. Under Michigan's Bullard-Plawecki Employee Right-to-Know Act, if a request is made by a third party, and unless as may be otherwise ordered in an action, the employer has an affirmative obligation to review the personnel file and expunge any disciplinary records that are more than four years old. In addition, the employer is required to furnish written notice to the employee of the release of any disciplinary reports to any third party, the notice to be provided contemporaneously with the third-party disclosure. [Mich. Comp. Laws Ann. §§ 423.506, 423.507]

Q 5:12   Is there any potential danger in providing personnel information, as opposed to the records themselves, to third parties?

Absent a release from the employee, a release of information required by court order or as otherwise provided by law, there is always a potential danger of liability when sharing confidential personnel information with third parties. This information can be requested in a variety of scenarios. The most common would be one in which a prospective employer seeks a reference on a prior employee. In this situation, releasing negative information can have a detrimental impact on an ex-employee's ability to find work, and may subject the employer to claims of defamation. So-called "blackballing" is a common component of many employment litigation cases. A policy of only releasing positive information when someone calls for a reference, by implication, may work to the detriment of ex-employees whose prospective employer obtains no information. Although some states have enacted laws to attempt to shield employers from liability upon the release of information gleaned from personnel files in reference situations, even those statutes typically exempt from protection information that is untrue, information provided in reckless disregard of the truth, or information that is not contained within the personnel records themselves. For example, Michigan's Disclosure of Employee Information Act [Mich. Comp. Laws Ann. §§ 423.451 *et seq.*] provides in relevant part as follows:

> An employer may disclose to an employee or that individual's prospective employer information relating to the individual's job performance that is documented in the individual's personnel file upon the request of the individual or his or her prospective employer. An employer who discloses information under this section in good faith is immune from civil liability for the disclosure. An employer is presumed to be acting in good faith at the time of a disclosure under this section unless a preponderance of the evidence establishes one or more of the following: (a) That the employer knew the information was false or misleading. (b) That the employer disclosed the information with a reckless disregard for the truth. (c) That the disclosure was specifically prohibited by a state or federal statute.

Even situations where companies are required to release information concerning a former employee in order to maintain private licensing, the potential for liability exists. In accordance with the National Association of Securities Dealers (NASD) rules, whenever a registered employee is discharged by a member of the NASD, the member must fill out and submit to the association a form providing the reasons for termination. In *Rosenberg v. Metlife, Inc.* [453 F.3d 122 (2d Cir. 2006)], the security dealer had terminated the plaintiff, and in the required form, stated that the plaintiff was terminated for speculative insurance sales and possible accessory to money laundering. This resulted in a defamation claim and the court was asked to determine whether the employer would be accorded an absolute privilege, as Metlife maintained, or just a qualified privilege that could be defeated by demonstrating malice. Recognizing that public policy would suggest that employers be accorded an absolute privilege to ensure that honest and candid statements as to termination are provided by employers, the court also recognized that providing absolute privilege could result in abuse by employers and permit employers, acting with malice, to effectively "blackball" a broker from the industry. Unable to resolve the issue, the court certified the question to the New York Court of Appeals, which held that an absolute privilege should apply to statements made by an employer on a NASD termination notice to ensure full and frank disclosure. [8 N.Y.3d 359 (2007)]

Q 5:13 What is the safest policy for an employer to adopt as it relates to references to prospective employers of prior employees?

There are any number of claims that can be raised in connection with providing references in virtually every jurisdiction. Claims range from defamation for providing false negative information to retaliation, if the employee previously complained of discrimination or objected to illegal activity. To avoid potential liability issues, many employers establish written policies that they will not provide any information other than that confirming dates of employment and positions held. Although this type of policy, if adopted by all employers, would make reference checks a worthless exercise, it is nonetheless adopted by many companies that want to avoid liability in these situations. Many employers will not respond to requests for references unless the former employee requests the information to be provided to the potential employer in writing and formally releases the employer from any liability associated with furnishing the requested information to the potential employer. In such cases, defamation claims will be difficult to maintain because of the release of claims and because the statements from the former employer to the potential employer would be subject to a qualified privilege. [*See* Taylor v. Amcor Flexibles, Inc., 669 F. Supp. 2d 501 (D.N.J. 2009).]

Q 5:14 Do unions have a right of access to members' personnel files?

Under appropriate circumstances, it may be an unfair labor practice for an employer to deny a union's request for certain information in one or more members' personnel files. For example, a union representing an employee challenging discipline or discharge under the grievance/arbitration provision of the collective bargaining agreement usually has the right to review the grievant's disciplinary records. If that union is negotiating wages, benefits or working conditions, access to pertinent personnel records may be required of the company under its duty to bargain in good faith. Records involving health and safety concerns may also be subject to union review on the union's appropriate request.

Q 5:15   Are medical records part of a personnel file?

Under the ADA, medical records must be kept confidential and may not be included in an employee's personnel file. One theory behind this requirement is that when employers review personnel files to make employment decisions, they should not be swayed by medical information. All medical information concerning an employee should be kept in a separate file cabinet under lock and key, with keys distributed only to select managerial employees on a need-to-know basis.

Likewise, for example, under Michigan's Bullard-Plawecki Employee Right-to-Know Act, *personnel records* are defined as specifically excluding medical reports and records. As a result of both state and federal law, any employer that produces a personnel record in response to a request that contains medical information would essentially be admitting its violation of federal and possibly state law, as it relates to the maintenance of medical records. Specifically requested, medical records should be provided separately from personnel records.

Moreover, the HIPAA Privacy Rules, discussed later in this chapter (see Qs 5:30–5:37) create a comprehensive regulatory scheme that regulates covered entities' use or disclosure of protected health information (PHI as it is commonly referred to under the regulations). Although most entities in the medical profession are covered under the regulations, employers that receive PHI in connection with the administration of health benefits are also covered under HIPAA Privacy Rules. As a covered entity, companies are required to adopt privacy policies and implement procedures to prevent unauthorized uses or disclosures of PHI. Keeping this information safeguarded and separate from a personnel file is just one of the necessary steps that should be undertaken to comply with HIPAA Privacy Rules.

Retention of Personnel Files

Q 5:16   How long should personnel records and other information concerning an employee or applicant be retained?

Federal law requires certain wage and hour information to be kept for at least three years (see Q 5:1). Even if not specifically required, personnel records are the foundation for an employer's defense of employment litigation. In essence, a properly maintained file works both to provide support basis for an employer's adverse employment decision and, because it is in writing, to demonstrate the credibility of the discipline at issue. As a result, keeping personnel records in a safe and secure location is instrumental to defending employee claims. Generally, employment records should be kept in a locked cabinet, with limited access, and should be stored for as long as necessary to defend potential employment claims. All litigation is subject to limitation periods that provide if an action is not commenced within a specified period of time it will be waived forever; therefore at a minimum, records should be maintained as long as required by federal or state law and as long as the possibility of employment litigation remains.

Many claims are moot if not filed within a reasonably short time period. Title VII requires EEOC claims within 180 or 300 days, depending on whether the jurisdiction maintains civil rights statutes similar to Title VII; however, all relevant statutes of limitations for all claims that employees can maintain should be reviewed. Employers should retain all personnel records and other information concerning the employee for the longest statutes of limitations for any possible employment claim as evidence in case an employee institutes litigation. This time period (i.e., six years in many jurisdictions for claims filed under ERISA and for breach of express or implied contract) is much longer than limitations under many state discrimination laws (usually three years), and the longest applicable limitation period should be used as a benchmark for retention. Usually, this will mean up to six years in some jurisdictions.

Employee Privacy

Q 5:17 What is *invasion of privacy*?

Four common law torts of invasion of privacy have emerged over the years:

- Intrusion on the plaintiff's seclusion or solitude or into his or her private affairs;
- Public disclosure of embarrassing private facts about the plaintiff;
- Publicity, the effect of which is to place the plaintiff in a false light in public; and
- Appropriation of the plaintiff's name or likeness without his or her permission, to the pecuniary advantage of the defendant.

For employees in the public sector, additional protection is afforded under the federal Constitution, such as in the Fourth Amendment, which protects against unreasonable searches and seizures, and in the Fifth Amendment privilege against self-incrimination; however, the invocation of constitutional protection requires state or government action. As a result, these constitutional protections are not afforded to employees in the private sector.

Q 5:18   Can inadvertent and/or innocuous intrusions be actionable as an invasion of privacy?

In *Anderson v. City of Columbus, Georgia* [374 F. Supp. 2d 1240 (M.D. Ga. 2005)], the city operated a call center and notified operators at the call center that it would be monitoring calls. Call center personnel working the phones were provided headsets to use in the performance of their duties. After the recording system was installed, the call center operators discovered the system continued to record anything said into the headset while the telephone headset was off the receiver, even after a call was disconnected. In the case, after a call was disconnected, an operator complained about her boss, and the complaints were picked up by the recording and listened to by her boss, who then fired her for the disparaging comments. As to the claims of invasion of privacy under common law, the court concluded that in order to state a claim against the individual defendants, the plaintiff must be able to demonstrate that the recordings were an intentional intrusion upon the plaintiff's seclusion or solitude or into her personal affairs. To the extent that the intrusion was inadvertent and not intentional, a claim could not be maintained against the individual defendants.

Similarly, when an intrusion into a restroom is rather innocuous, under certain circumstances a claim for invasion of privacy will not stand. In *Williams v. City of Tulsa, Oklahoma* [393 F. Supp. 2d 1124 (N.D. Okla. 2005)], the city had equipped its underground collections department responsible for operating and maintaining the city's underground sewer system with an elaborate array of monitoring and surveillance devices and posted numerous signs warning persons in or about the facilities that the "premises [are] videotaped 24 hours a day." Although there were many issues in the case, the issue of invasion of privacy boiled down to alleged illegal surveillance in or about an office restroom. The camera at issue was not actually in the restroom, but pointed in the direction of the restroom door and could partially show the inside of the restroom only if the restroom door was propped wide open. Based on the limited nature of the intrusion, the court held that a tort for invasion of privacy could not be maintained as a matter of law. However, in *Jones v. Houston Community College System* [816 F. Supp. 2d 418 (S.D. Tex. 2011)], the court held that security officers had a reasonable expectation of privacy in a room where they changed clothes, such that the covert installation of cameras in the room stated a claim for violation of the Fourth Amendment against a public college.

In *Quon v. Arch Wireless Operating Co., Inc.* [445 F. Supp. 2d 1116 (D. Ct. Cal. 2006)], at issue was an audit of various city police department employees' use of their pager systems for among other things, text messages that resulted in the review of private text messages, oftentimes created when the employees were off duty. The city employees were required to keep the pagers with them at all times and the city allowed personal use, provided that the employees pay back the department for personal use beyond a certain amount. Because, under these circumstances, personal use was allowed by the city, the court concluded that the employees had a reasonable expectation of privacy in the text messages sent to and from a city-owned pager.

In *National Association of Letter Carriers, AFL-CIO v. United States Postal Service* [604 F. Supp. 2d 665 (S.D.N.Y. 2009)], the court, in addressing various claims brought by labor unions representing postal employees regarding the Postal Services policy of obtaining employees' personal medical information from health care providers without the employee's consent or knowledge, stated, among other things, that employees, as a matter of common law, have a reasonable expectation of privacy as it relates to the employee's medical records.

Q 5:19   Has invasion of privacy become a significant issue in employment law today?

The advent of drug testing in the workplace and technological advances enabling employers to conduct discreet surveillance of employees has led to a rash of litigation based on common law and constitutional law theories of privacy rights. [*See, e.g.,* Luedtke v. Nabors Alaska Drilling, Inc, 768 P.2d 1123 (Alaska 1989) (based upon Alaska Constitution Art. I, 22, which reads in pertinent part, "Right of Privacy. The right of the people to privacy is recognized and shall not be infringed"); Hennessey v. Coastal Eagle Point Oil Co., 589 A.2d 170 (N.J. Super. 1991) (plaintiff argued that random drug testing violated employees' rights of privacy under state common law).] As a general rule, private employers will not run afoul of common-law theories of invasion of privacy, provided that their activities do not violate an employee's reasonable expectations of privacy, arise from a legitimate business reason, and are limited to the employer's legitimate business interests. Certainly, for example, drug testing based on a reasonable suspicion that drugs are being used at the workplace would not typically constitute a common-law invasion of privacy in most states. Likewise, limited examination of e-mail information stored in company-owned computers on company premises to investigate a suspected violation of company policy does not typically run afoul of common-law privacy doctrine.

Q 5:20   Can random drug testing be a violation of the Constitution for public employees?

For government and public employees, to whom the Constitution applies suspicionless or random drug testing poses unique problems. Although no general Fourth Amendment prohibition against random drug testing exists, generally "individualized suspicion" is required before performing a drug test to meet constitutional muster. However, when "special needs" concerns other than crime detection arise, in which the privacy interests implicated by the search are minimal, and where an important governmental interest is furthered by the intrusion, "individualized suspicion" may not be necessary. Special needs usually can be demonstrated when the job being tested is "safety sensitive," such that the performance of duties in the position is fraught with the risk of injury to others. In *Crager v. Board of Education of Knott County, Kentucky* [313 F. Supp. 2d 690 (E.D. Ky. 2004)], a teacher challenged a random drug testing policy promulgated by the Board of Education of Knott County, claiming, among other things, a violation of the Fourth Amendment. The policy itself was not applicable to all employees, but rather random drug testing was limited to those in safety-sensitive positions, with all other teachers being tested under reasonable suspicion guidelines. Although no evidence of a pronounced drug or alcohol problem among Knott County teachers was found, the court noted that evidence of a significant drug problem was found in the area and in the school system on a more limited basis. Moreover, the court found that the policy had instituted adequate safeguards to ensure the reliability, privacy, and confidentiality of the testing results. The court also noted that the county's policy did not provide for the forwarding of any positive tests to law enforcement officials, but rather provided that positive results would only be released to Board members. Balancing the nature of the intrusion against what appeared to be a well-constructed policy, the court concluded that the random drug testing policy was not a violation of the Fourth Amendment, noting that it worked to further the interests of the school district in meeting its requirements under the Drug-Free Workplace Act. In *National Federation of Federal Employees-IAM v. Vilsack* [681 F.3d 483 (D.C. Cir. 2012)], a union challenged the adoption of a random drug testing policy for Department of Agriculture and Forest Service federal employees who worked with at-risk youth in the Job Corp. Although the government argued that it had "special" needs, the court disagreed finding, among other things, there were no staff drug problems necessitating the random test and insufficient evidence involving safety concerns to undermine a reasonable expectation of privacy held by the employees. In *Krieg v. Seybold* [481 F.3d 512 (7th Cir. 2007)], a former city street sanitation department employee claimed that a random drug test, which resulted in his termination, violated his Fourth Amendment rights, among other things. Recognizing that employee, when working for the City, was required to regularly operate a one-ton dump truck, a dump truck with a plow, and a front-end loader and backhoe near other vehicles and pedestrians, the position was a "safety-sensitive position," such that random drug testing was allowable. The court distinguished the former city employee's job with those involving public employees who drive cars and vans as posing less danger than the position at issue. In *Mollo v. Passaic Valley Sewerage Commissioners* [406 Fed. Appx. 664 (3d Cir. 2011)], a landscaper that worked at a publicly owned waste water treatment plant claimed that the suspicionless random drug test administered by the public employer, and which resulted in his termination when he tested positive, violated his Fourth Amendment rights. Noting that the position was a "safety sensitive" position, the court, in balancing the degree to which the search intruded upon the employee's privacy versus the degree to which the search is needed for the promotion of a legitimate government interest, the court held that the random drug test, administered in accordance with a random drug testing policy, did not violate the Fourth Amendment. In *Palmer v. Cacioppo* [429 Fed. Appx. 491 (6th Cir. 2011)], the court held that a requirement that an employee, in accordance with a last chance agreement, submit to a random drug test did not violate the Fourth Amendment. The employee had previously been convicted of illegal drug use and had voluntarily entered into the last chance agreement which required random drug testing for one year. The court held that the school's requirement that this teacher submit to a one-year random drug testing requirement was reasonable, and that it worked to promote the school district's drug-free work place policy.

To ensure that random programs will meet constitutional requirements, it is usually recommended that an outside third party be utilized for the purpose of selecting drug testing candidates. In a situation where a governmental employee allegedly tampered with the random drug testing selection procedure, to ensure the testing of certain individuals for purposes of gaining evidence to be used in a criminal matter, the court held that such manipulation would be a clear violation of the Fourth Amendment. [*See* Freeman v. Fallin, 310 F. Supp. 2d 11 (D.D.C. 2004).] Although private employers do not have to concern themselves with constitutional challenges, random drug testing can pose problems in situations where the employer does not discipline employees similarly for violations. If an employer does not treat similar situations similarly, and the differences break along gender, race, or another protected category, the employer exposes itself to discrimination claims under federal or state law.

Q 5:21 Can observed drug testing collection procedures violate the privacy of private employees?

Although Department of Transportation (DOT) regulations require observed collection procedures for certain commercial transportation workers, whether such a procedure violates the privacy of other private employees is not a settled issue. For example, in *Lockhart v. Examone World Wide, Inc.* [2012 WL 4955241 (S.D. Ind. Oct. 17, 2012)], a number of plaintiffs sued under a variety of common law tort theories for having to undergo observed urine collection, including negligent infliction of emotional distress and invasion of privacy. Finding that there were no cases in Indiana confronting the issue of the viability of these torts in such circumstances, the court certified the issue to the Supreme Court for guidance.

Q 5:22 Do private employees have a right to privacy?

The most common way employers invade their employees' privacy is to intrude on their seclusion, solitude, or private affairs. There is a delicate balance between the employer's legitimate need for the intrusion versus the employees' legitimate expectations of privacy regarding the intrusion. If the employer has a legitimate reason for the intrusion (e.g., to investigate theft or suspected illegal conduct), an intrusion that is reasonably limited to serve these legitimate interests will probably pass muster, provided the intrusion is reasonable. With regard to workplace investigation, surveillance and drug testing, an employee may have a difficult time maintaining a privacy claim if he or she could not have a legitimate expectation of privacy concerning the particular intrusion at issue. Consequently, a company considering action that may be considered an intrusion by some should notify the employees in advance of the intended intrusion, thereby working to eliminate the employees' expectations of privacy in the matter.

With respect to these issues, many employers include general policies within their employee handbooks that reserve the right of the employer to conduct reasonable monitoring, surveillance, or searches under a variety of circumstances, even though they have no immediate intention to do so, to attempt to do away with an employee's expectation of privacy concerning such conduct. As it relates to searches of an employee's desk or locker, some employers may wish to consider a policy similar to the following:

> The company reserves the right to conduct a search on demand, of an employee's locker, desk, packages, automobile and/or other personal belongings, if the company believes, in its sole discretion, that such a search is warranted to investigate a suspected violation of its policies, including its drug and alcohol policy, and to seize and test any item the company believes may evidence a violation of its policies.

Although no employer should attempt to conduct such a search without first contacting its employment attorneys, the preceding policy will assist in defending the search against any claimed invasion of privacy.

Even notices cannot shield an employer whose intrusions are not supported by legitimate business justifications or go beyond that which is justified. For example, in *Deal v. Spears* [980 F.2d 1153 (8th Cir 1992)], an employer who engaged in clearly unnecessary and abusive monitoring and recording of personal phone calls was held liable for over $40,000 in damages, despite giving notice to its employees.

Moreover, some employers unwittingly clothe employees with reasonable expectations of privacy when such an expectation may not otherwise exist. This occurs most frequently with lockers and desks. Some employers, in attempting to prevent employees from rummaging through co-workers' desks and lockers, post notices or policies prohibiting employees from such conduct, likening the locker or desk as the personal and private space of each employee. Although such policies may curtail employees from invading someone else's personal space, if these policies are not drafted carefully they could be used to create a legitimate expectation of privacy, and the foundation for a breach of privacy claim.

Q 5:23   What are examples of situations that typically raise privacy issues for private employers?

Although this list is not exhaustive, the following are situations that most often raise privacy issues:

- Employee surveillance;
- Monitoring and/or reviewing material stored in computer systems (i.e., voicemail, e-mail, and Internet usage/sites accessed);
- Requests for personnel information by third parties;
- Requests for medical information, particularly as a result of the new HIPAA Privacy Rules concerning PHI and the ADA;

- Eavesdropping (there are federal and state laws in a variety of states prohibiting certain conduct in this area); and
- Internal investigations of alleged illegal activity.

Q 5:24 Do employers need to be concerned about privacy and/or defamation claims when conducting an internal investigation of alleged harassment?

Since the *Ellerth* [524 U.S. 742 (1998)] and *Faragher* [524 U.S. 775 (1998)] decisions by the U.S. Supreme Court, it is the employer's obligation to engage in reasonable preventative and corrective measures towards combating sexual harassment in the workplace. These procedures include preparing and disseminating a sexual harassment policy, providing the procedure for lodging complaints, and a prompt and thorough investigation of all complaints that may be made to the company regarding sexual harassment. Once someone comes forward and complains of sexual harassment, the company has an obligation to diligently and promptly investigate the matter, which will necessarily include asking the alleged harasser and other witnesses what they know regarding the specific allegations upon which the claim for sexual harassment are based.

This investigation will certainly delve into matters of a highly and sometimes humiliating and embarrassing situation. Does the employer face exposure if its investigators discuss these sometimes very graphic situations with other employees in the course of the investigation? The answer is probably no, provided that the employer can demonstrate the nature and extent of its investigation was reasonably necessary to investigate the matter. For example, in *Cole v. Knoll, Inc.* [984 F. Supp. 1117 (W.D. Mich. 1997)], the court held that vague allegations of defamation by an alleged harasser based on statements made during the course of an investigation does not state a claim. In *Taylor v. CAN Corp.* [2010 WL 3430911 (E.D. Va. Aug. 27, 2010)], the court held that an employer's investigation report regarding an employee's sexual harassment was subject to a qualified privilege, and in the absence of malice, could not sustain a claim of defamation. Similarly, in *Lee v. Eden Medical Center* [690 F. Supp. 2d 1011 (N.D. Cal. 2010)], the court held that a human resource director's statements about a nurse's mental health to the hospital's management and counsel were subject to a qualified privilege and not actionable without evidence of malice under California defamation law. In *Knox v. Neaton Auto Products Manufacturing, Inc.*, a former employee sued her employer alleging, among other things, defamation. The defamation allegedly arose out of a written statement prepared by the former employee's supervisor in connection with an investigation by the employer's human resource department involving an altercation that had occurred at the employer's plant. In connection with the investigation, the supervisor attributed to the plaintiff statements that the plaintiff claimed were false and defamatory including allegations that the plaintiff said, "You are becoming more of a devil's advocate every day." [375 F.3d 451, 461(6th Cir. 2004)] The court concluded that because the statements were made in the course of business regarding matters of common interest between the plaintiff's supervisor and the human resource department concerning the plaintiff's performance on the job, the statements were subject to a qualified privilege, and no claim for defamation could be maintained. In *Moriarity v. Dyson, Inc.* [2012 WL 5389684 (N.D. Ill. Oct. 30, 2012)], a former employee could not maintain a defamation action based on statements made during an investigation of her complaints of sexual harassment arising from her sexual relationship with the former president, because such statements were protected by a qualified privilege and there was no evidence of malice. On the other hand, if the investigation goes beyond what is necessary to fully investigate the matter and the matter is discussed with individuals who have no reason to know of the content of the investigation, the potential for liability under common law theory exists.

Q 5:25   How can a company guard against privacy and defamation suits involving personnel files?

Corporations should consider adopting and enforcing a personnel file policy, published in the firm's employee handbook or policy manual. Of course, before adopting any such policy, the company must confirm with legal counsel that the appropriate laws of each state in which the firm does business do not accord employees greater access or privacy rights than are reflected in the policy. The following paragraphs provide an example of such a policy.

Collecting and retaining personal information. The company will follow the requirements of equal employment opportunity laws and other state or federal laws regarding the collection and retention of information from job applicants and employees. Appropriate information will include the following:

- Application forms, references checklists and forms, interviewers' reports, and test results;
- Letters of commendation;
- Written performance evaluations;
- Notices of suspension, disciplinary action, or termination; and
- Attendance records.

Review of records. The human resources department will maintain and review each employee's file annually. Managers and supervisors will review each employee's file before each performance evaluation.

Company access to employee records. Access to employee records is restricted to the following:

- Human resources employees with a business need to know;
- An individual employee's direct supervisor or departmental manager with a business need to know; and
- Company executives with a business need to know.

Employee access. An employee may examine his or her personnel records in the presence of a human resources representative. Records exempt from this inspection include potential job assignments or predictions of future salary and personnel planning information. Regarding any item in the file, an employee may write a statement of disagreement and ask that it be included within his or her file; however, the employee may not actually remove any item from the file.

Disclosure of employee information. All requests for information about a current, retired, or terminated employee must be referred to the human resources department for processing. The human resources manager may disclose to prospective employers dates of employment, final title or position, job location, and (with the employee's written permission) a five-year employment and salary history.

Information will also be given in response to duly authorized requests from law-enforcement agencies, including investigations, summonses, subpoenas, and judicial orders. Except as otherwise required under applicable law, the company need not inform an employee that personal information has been disclosed to law-enforcement agencies if the information is related to an investigation into the employee's on-the-job conduct, especially when the employee's actions may endanger other employees or company security and property. However, care should be taken not to provide employee information to those who have no need to know. Following the termination of a substitute teacher, the school personnel director told a reporter of a local paper that the substitute teacher was terminated for obscenity. In fact, the school personnel director knew that the termination was for "poor judgment" for showing "The Simpsons Movie" to the class which contained obscenities. Under these circumstances, a qualified privilege would not protect the school and school personnel director from potential liability and summary judgment was inappropriate. [Abdul-Salaam v. Lobo-Wadley, 2009 WL 3305913 (D. Conn. Oct. 14, 2009)] Although statements made to co-workers that plaintiff was terminated for stealing were subject to a qualified privilege under Minnesota law, issues of fact existed as to whether a supervisor had malice based on evidence of having used racial slurs toward plaintiff, such that summary disposition for the employer was inappropriate. [*Walker v. Wanner Eng'g, Inc.*, 867 F. Supp. 2d 1050 (D. Minn. 2012)]

Q 5:26 What policies should employers consider regarding employee use of e-mail and other encoded transmissions, such as on the Internet?

As the workplace becomes more technically advanced, e-mail and other electronic encoded transmissions are becoming commonplace. Equally common in today's world are internal investigations of suspected unlawful activity (e.g., sexual harassment) and searches for evidence of wrongful activity (e.g., an employee's violation of a non-compete agreement). E-mail and other electronically encoded information are a virtual cornucopia of possible evidence. As most people are now aware, even deleted information can oftentimes be recovered by forensic computer investigators. Uncovering racial slurs, sexual jokes, and other material can assist employees in prosecuting claims. Likewise, in an attempt to reduce risk and exposure to sexual harassment claims, and to demonstrate the company's sincere efforts to take preventative and corrective measures to deal with harassment, some companies have hired computer forensic investigators. These investigators typically monitor e-mail and Internet use to determine if any violations of company policy have occurred, as they relate to use of the systems (e.g., accessing pornographic material). To reduce risk and exposure, employers need to promulgate a written policy that clearly prohibits the use of electronic transmissions except for legitimate business reasons, and does away with any expectation of privacy in connection with the system's use.

The following is a sample policy involving e-mail and the Internet that addresses these issues:

USE OF E-MAIL AND INTERNET

The Company's e-mail system is the property of the Company and is intended solely for conducting company business. All messages transmitted via e-mail will be treated as business messages. Any employee who sends a personal message on the system should be aware that it will not be considered a personal, confidential message of the employee.

Please be advised that the Company has the right to enter the e-mail system at any time, to review, copy or delete any messages, and disclose such messages to others. The use of passwords to gain access to e-mail is for the protection of the firm, not the employee. By using the firm's computers for e-mail, all employees waive any right to privacy in the use of e-mail and consent to the access and disclosure of e-mail messages by the firm.

Use of the Internet is strictly intended for business purposes and must not be used for personal reasons or entertainment. Use of the Internet for personal business may result in the loss of that privilege, or discipline. Further, the firm will not tolerate individual abuse through the accessing of chat rooms, or pornographic or other inappropriate materials. Such action may result in discipline up to and including termination of employment. Employees should be aware that Internet use is not private, and may be monitored or retrieved by the company, and employees waive any right to privacy in connection therewith.

In the workplace, the issue of privacy typically relates to an employee's use of the employer's computer system. However, the issue of privacy becomes more complex if the employee is using his or her own computer in connection with work.

In *United States v. Barrows* [481 F.3d 1246 (10th Cir. 2007)], at issue was whether a public employee had a reasonable expectation of privacy with reference to a computer that he owned, took to work, and used for work-related purposes. The undisputed evidence indicated that he installed the computer in a public place and took no reasonable measures to prevent it from being accessed by others. As such, the court held that the employee did not have a reasonable expectation of privacy with respect to the computer and denied the employee's claim that the seizure and search of his computer, which disclosed child pornography, was in violation of the Fourth Amendment.

Q 5:27   Should employers consider Internet policies that allow for limited personal use, or is a complete prohibition against personal use a better approach?

From a purely legal standpoint, a complete prohibition against Internet use for any reasons other than business is typically advised. There are many potential problems associated with personal use, including employee distraction, utilization of company time for shopping, and the like. However, the most serious of these would involve accessing pornographic information and/or utilizing the Internet for personal communications that may be all too candid and may render the company culpable for any number of claims. When employees realize that the Internet is to be utilized for business use only and that the company monitors all use of its Internet, this type of policy goes a long way toward reducing the company's risk of exposure in a number of areas.

However, the greatest strength of this approach, a prohibition of all personal use, is also its greatest weakness. Policies become dangerous when they are not followed, and it is becoming an increasingly rare situation when even a model employee will not, on occasion, use the Internet for personal reasons (i.e., responding to an e-mail from a spouse, checking the weather, or accessing an Internet news web page when significant newsworthy events occur during working hours). In fact, it is not unusual for employees to use their sites to sign up for "breaking news" at various news services. If your employees will utilize the Internet for personal reasons on occasion and you do not intend to discipline or fire them as a result, a complete ban on personal use is not practical for your workplace and the policy should be reconfigured to allow for limited personal use. However, the policy should attempt to be clear in terms of what limited personal use means (i.e., how much time per day, what types of personal use are considered acceptable, emergencies, significant news events, or weather). However, the policy should completely forbid utilization of the Internet to access pornographic materials. Even if limited personal use is allowed, the policy should nonetheless contain a very clear provision that the company will monitor all Internet usage and that the employee waives any right to privacy in connection therewith.

The following is a sample policy that allows for limited personal use.

INTERNET POLICY

Internet access to global electronic information resources on the World Wide Web is provided by the Company to assist certain employees in their work. The following additional guidelines have been established to help ensure reasonable and productive Internet usage.

- No employee can access the Internet without prior Company authorization.

- While Internet usage is intended for certain employees for job-related activities, incidental and occasional brief personal use is permitted within reasonable limits.

- All Internet data that is composed, transmitted, or received via our computer communications system is considered part of the records of the Company. Consequently, employees should always ensure that the business information contained in Internet E-mail and other transmissions is accurate, appropriate, ethical, and lawful.

- Data that is composed, transmitted, accessed or received via the Internet must not contain content that could be considered discriminatory, offensive, obscene, threatening, harassing, intimidating or disruptive to any staff member or other person. Examples of unacceptable content may include, but are not limited to pornographic materials, sexual comments or images, racial slurs, gender-specific comments or any other comments or images that could reasonably offend someone on the basis of race, weight, age, sex, height, religious beliefs, national origin, disability or any other characteristic protected by law.

- The unauthorized use, installation, copying, or distribution of copyrighted, trademarked or patented materials on the Internet is expressly prohibited. Generally, if a staff member did not create material, does not own the rights to it, or has not received authorization for its use, it should not be reproduced, used inappropriately or put on the Internet. Staff members are also responsible for ensuring that the person sending any materials over the Internet has the appropriate distribution rights.

- Internet users should take the necessary anti-virus precautions before downloading or copying any file from the Internet.

- To .ensure that the use of business equipment is consistent with the Company's legitimate business interests, the Company may monitor the use of such equipment, (including down-loading and reviewing information stored in computers) from time to time, and employees waive any right to privacy in connection therewith.

Q 5:28   Should employers monitor Internet usage by employees?

Employers may obtain programs that allow them to obtain printouts of sites accessed by their employees. Monitoring in this fashion allows the employer to review employee usage to determine whether it is consistent with its rules. The authors believe that both advising employees that the company will monitor, and monitoring in this fashion, is helpful both in terms of policing the policy and as a deterrent against use beyond that permitted by the policy. If an employee knows that by visiting a particular site, the employer will know about it later, he or she will be less likely to visit it.

Q 5:29   Can an employer's access of an employee's personal e-mail account or social media site violate the employee's privacy?

If employees provide or permit the employer to have access to their personal account or site, the employee would likely have no reasonable expectation of privacy and hence, no viable invasion of privacy claims. However, if access is obtained illegitimately or expands beyond what was permitted, liability may result. In *Mintz v. Mark Bartelstein and Associates, Inc.* [2012 WL 5391779 (C.D. Cal. Nov. 1, 2012)], a sports agency hacked into the personal e-mail account of one of its agents that was leaving to work for a competitor and located and reviewed his compensation agreement with his new employer. Although the employer claimed that the intrusion was diminimis, the sports agency could provide no legitimate business reason for the intrusion and the court found the intrusion to be a serious violation of privacy, for which the employee's motion for summary disposition was granted. Some states have passed laws to protect employees' privacy as it relates to their personal e-mail account and use of social media. For example, Illinois's "Right to Privacy in the Workplace Act" [820 IlCS 55] prohibits, with limited exceptions, employers from requiring employees or applicants to provide passwords or other related personal account information to gain access to the employee's or applicant's account or profile on a social networking Web site.

Q 5:30   What are the HIPAA Privacy Rules?

HIPAA Privacy Rules, enacted in 1998 and effective, with limited exception, April 14, 2003, provide federally mandated policies and procedures to prevent the unauthorized use or disclosure of PHI. Generally, the Privacy Rules apply to those in the health and health insurance industry. Covered entities are limited to health care plans, health care clearing houses, and health care providers who utilize electronic means to transmit health information in connection with their practice. As covered entities, with the exception of small health care plans (i.e., those with annual receipt of $5 million or less, which have an additional year to comply), covered entities must implement procedures and policies provided for under the regulations to be in compliance with the Act. All of these regulations are geared toward restricting access to PHI, tracking instances of use or disclosure of health information, and undertaking procedures to ensure that PHI is not used or disclosed, except as specifically provided for under the regulations.

The Health Information Technology for Economic and Clinical Health (HITECH) Act, effective February 2009, expanded HIPAA's privacy and security regulations. Two of the most important changes under HITECH are the requirements that business associates of HIPAA-covered entities (1) comply directly with Security Rule provisions directing implementation of administrative, physical, and technical safeguards for electronic PHI; and (2) expanded breach notification rules for both covered entities and their business associates. Business associate agreements and other covered entity policies should be amended to include these additional requirements under the HITECH Act.

Q 5:31   Do HIPAA Privacy Rules apply to employers?

The Health and Human Services (HHS) Office of Civil Rights stated in its January 2002 Guidelines issued after publication of the final regulations, "The law does not give HHS the authority to regulate other types of private business or public agencies through this regulation. For example, HHS does not have the authority to regulate employers, life insurance companies or public agencies that deliver social security or welfare benefits." However, health care plans are covered by HIPAA, and as a result, employers that sponsor such plans will be impacted by HIPAA. The final regulations specifically prohibit the disclosure of PHI by covered entities to non-covered entities, such as disclosures to employers that sponsor health care plans. [45 C.F.R. § 164.504(f)(3)(iv)] In fact, one of the stated purposes of HIPAA Privacy Rules is to prevent employers from utilizing PHI in connection with personnel decisions.

Q 5:32   What are the compliance obligations for employers under the HIPAA Privacy Rules?

Although employers in the health care industry are covered if they are health care providers or clearinghouses under the HIPAA Privacy Rules, other employers are only impacted by HIPAA to the extent that they sponsor a health care plan. Those with health care plans may or may not have to undertake full implementation of HIPAA's regulatory scheme depending upon whether they are merely sponsors of fully insured health plans, or if they are both sponsors and administrators of health plans that need or use PHI in connection with the administration of such plans.

If an employer is merely a sponsor of a fully insured health plan, and does not need or receive PHI, the employer can notify the administrator of the fully insured health plan that they do not seek PHI, but rather will accept what is referred to as "summary health information" concerning the participants, which is information that is stripped of all potentially identifying information such as names, Social Security numbers, etc. On the other hand, if an employer is not only a plan sponsor but also an administrator of a plan using PHI, it will be required to comply with HIPAA's broad regulatory compliance scheme. Although the compliance scheme is complicated, and every employer in this category is advised to seek counsel to create and implement a scheme that complies with the HIPAA, generally, the privacy regulations require the following:

- Employers must create a firewall between the employees who administer the plan and/or receive PHI and other employees to prevent the dissemination of PHI from those who administer the plan and/or receive PHI to other employees.

- Plan documents need to be amended that describe the permitted or required uses of PHI, define those employees who will have access to PHI, and provide a mechanism for resolving issues of suspected non-compliance.

- Employers must make written certification to the plan that the employer will comply with HIPAA privacy rules.

- Employers must designate a privacy official who is responsible for implementing privacy policies, provide training to employees with respect to uses of PHI, and provide sanctions for employees who violate privacy policies.

- Privacy notices need to be sent to plan participants describing the company's privacy policy regarding use and disclosure of PHI, as mandated by HIPAA.

In addition to its privacy rules, HIPAA also contains security rules, enforcement rules, and breach notification rules if HIPAA is violated.

Q 5:33 Can an employer that is a sponsor of a health care plan reduce its obligations under the HIPAA Privacy Rules?

If the employer utilizes a third-party administrator to administer the plan, and if the employer does not otherwise need to receive PHI in connection with the administration of the plan benefits, the employer may be able to reduce its compliance obligations by entering into a suitable business associate agreement with its third-party administrator that, among other things, eliminates the ability of the employer to receive PHI from the third-party administrator. In such cases, the employer's burden in connection with HIPAA compliance, such as establishing firewalls, conducting training, and the like, would be significantly lessened.

Q 5:34 What is an example of a business associate agreement?

Under the HIPAA regulations, business associate agreements are required to contain specific information and agreements relative to the use and disclosure of PHI. The Department of Health and Human Services (HHS) at its Web site at http://www.hhs.gov, posted a standard business associate agreement that complies with the regulations and can be utilized for this purpose. Effective September 23, 2009, the HHS issued its interim final regulations under the HITECH Act. Under the HITECH Act, business associates are required, among other things, to comply with security rule provisions directing the implementation of safeguards for electronically stored health information, and provide breach notifications in the event of disclosures of protected health information in violation of HIPAA. Business associate agreements, prepared prior to the HITECH Act should be modified to include all new rules for business associates with respect to security and breach notifications as required by the HITECH Act. In January 2013, HHS issued its omnibus final rules regarding HIPAA that contains additional requirements relating to business associates and their subcontractors. [45 C.F.R. Pts. 160, 164] As such, business associate agreements may need to be modified to incorporate these requirements. The omnibus final rules are effective March 26, 2013 and compliance by covered entities is required by September 23, 2013.

Q 5:35 Are employers required to obtain written authorization to use and disclose PHI under the HIPAA Privacy Rules?

An employer that is a covered entity and has fully complied with the HIPAA Privacy Rules, will have the ability to use and disclose PHI in accordance with the regulations. However, there may be numerous instances where an employer may be asked to use or disclose PHI beyond that provided for in the regulations. For example, if an employer with a fully insured health plan that elects not to receive PHI (such that it does not have to comply with the HIPAA regulations) is nonetheless asked by the employee to assist in claims disputes that require the use or disclosure of PHI, the employer would need to obtain written authorization from the employee to assist in resolving the claims dispute. The regulations specifically provide for the utilization of authorizations for this purpose. To be sufficient, the written authorization must comply with a number of core requirements, including:

- A description of the information to be used or disclosed that identifies the information in a specific and meaningful fashion;
- The name or other specific identification of the person or class of persons authorized to make the requested use or disclosure;
- The name or other specific identification of the person or class of persons to whom the covered entity may make the requested use or disclosure;
- A description of each purpose of the requested use or disclosure;
- An expiration date or an expiration event that relates to the individual or the purpose of the use or disclosure; and
- Signature of the individual and date.

Q 5:36   What is an example of an authorization that complies with the HIPAA Privacy Rules?

AUTHORIZATION FORM

FOR RELEASE, USE OR DISCLOSURE OF PROTECTED HEALTH INFORMATION

Name of Group Health Plan: ABC, Inc. Health and Welfare Benefit Plan.

I, [Employee, Spouse, or Dependent] hereby authorize the release, use, or disclosure of my individually identifiable health information as described in this authorization.

Persons/organizations authorized to provide the information:

_____

Persons/organizations authorized to receive the information:

_____

Specific description of information to be used or disclosed (including dates):_____

_____

Specific purpose of the disclosure [e.g., to resolve claim with the insurance carrier or third-party administrator]:

_____

_____

I understand that I may refuse to sign this authorization and that my refusal to sign will not affect my ability to obtain payments from the Plan, my enrollment in the Plan, or my eligibility for benefits under the Plan.

This authorization expires [list the expiration date or expiration event (e.g., claim is resolved with the insurance company)]:

I also understand that:

- I may revoke this authorization at any time before its expiration date by notifying the Privacy Officer in writing, but the revocation will not have any affect on any actions taken before revocation is received.
- I may see and copy this authorization upon request.
- The information that is released, used, or disclosed pursuant to this authorization may be re-disclosed by the receiving persons or organizations and the information will no longer be protected by the federal privacy regulations.

Participant's Signature

_____

Signature of Employee, Spouse, or Dependent Date:_____

Name of Employee, Spouse, or Dependent (Print)

Personal Representative's Signature (if applicable)

By signing as the participant's personal representative, I represent that I have legal authority to sign and act on behalf of the participant for purposes of executing this authorization.

_____

Signature of Personal Representative Date:_____

Name of Personal Representative and relationship to participant (Print)

Q 5:37 Have there been any recent developments under HIPAA?

In January 2013, HHS issued its omnibus final rules under HIPAA, which affect, among other things, HIPAA's Privacy Rules, Security Rules, Enforcement Rules, and Breach Notification Rules. The final rules were effective March 26, 2013, and covered entities have 90 days to comply. In the final rules, which can be found at 45 CFR Parts 160 and 164, HHS summarizes its final rules as follows:

Summary of Major Provisions

This omnibus final rule is comprised of the following four final rules:

1. Final modifications to the HIPAA Privacy, Security, and Enforcement Rules mandated by the Health Information Technology for Economic and Clinical Health (HITECH) Act, and certain other modifications to improve the Rules, which were issued as a proposed rule on July 14, 2010.

These modifications:

- Make business associates of covered entities directly liable for compliance with certain of the HIPAA Privacy and Security Rules' requirements.

- Strengthen the limitations on the use and disclosure of protected health information for marketing and fundraising purposes, and prohibit the sale of protected health information without individual authorization.

- Expand individuals' rights to receive electronic copies of their health information and to restrict disclosures to a health plan concerning treatment for which the individual has paid out of pocket in full.

- Require modifications to, and redistribution of, a covered entity's notice of privacy practices.

- Modify the individual authorization and other requirements to facilitate research and disclosure of child immunization proof to schools, and to enable access to decedent information by family members or others.

- Adopt the additional HITECH Act enhancements to the Enforcement Rule not previously adopted in October 30, 2009, interim final rule (referenced immediately below), such as the provisions addressing enforcement of noncompliance with the HIPAA Rules due to willful neglect.

2. Final rule adopting changes to the HIPAA Enforcement Rule to incorporate the increased and tiered civil money penalty structure provided by the HITECH Act, originally published as an interim final rule on October 30, 2009.

3. Final rule on Breach Notification for Unsecured Protected Health Information under the HITECH Act, which replaces the breach notification rule's "harm" threshold with a more objective standard and supplants an interim final rule published on August 24, 2009.

4. Final rule modifying the HIPAA Privacy Rule as required by the Genetic Information Nondiscrimination Act (GINA) to prohibit most health plans from using or disclosing genetic information for underwriting purposes, which was published as a proposed rule on October 7, 2009.

Q 5:38 Can an employer perform background checks on applicants without violating their privacy?

Employers often perform extensive background checks, especially on applicants for high-level or highly sensitive positions. Although a release, usually included on the job application, is not necessary in many circumstances, it is recommended for many types of background checks. The most common kinds include checking references, prior employers, credit, consumer reports, and public records. Obtaining consent and releases from the applicant for background checks is a good way for companies to avoid liability in the application process.

Employers should take into consideration the Fair Credit Reporting Act (FCRA) when conducting a credit check. Although this law is better known for its impact on retail sales and credit cards, it also deals with background investigations of employment applicants. If employment is denied to an applicant because of a credit report that was prepared by a consumer reporting agency, the prospective employer must advise the applicant of the report's existence and that it was the reason for denying employment.

In addition, the FCRA amendments contain additional requirements for employers as it relates to background investigations. The FCRA regulates the use of both credit reports and investigative reports that employers can obtain from a consumer reporting agency. [15 U.S.C. § 1681(a)] Under new FCRA disclosure reporting requirements, if an employer utilizes a consumer reporting agency for purposes of obtaining a consumer report form for employment purposes, the employer must provide a clear and conspicuous disclosure to the applicant before the report is procured, indicating that the report may be obtained for the applicant for employment purposes, and the applicant must specifically authorize the procurement of the report by the employer in writing. [15 U.S.C. § 1681(b)(2)] The disclosure and consent must be contained within a "stand-alone" document; it is not sufficient to include this within boilerplate language contained in the application. This is a new requirement under the FCRA that must be followed. The prior requirements under the FCRA of notification only, as it relates to investigative reports, is still sufficient; however, for purposes of obtaining a credit report, notification alone is not sufficient, and there must be express authorization by the applicant in a stand-alone agreement.

Federal laws prohibit certain inquiries in the application state. The ADA prohibits pre-employment medical inquiries and undertaking background checks to obtain information otherwise impermissible under the law. For example, it is impermissible for an employer to question an applicant with regard to his or her workers' compensation history. Likewise, it would be inappropriate and a clear violation of the ADA for an employer to obtain background information from other sources regarding the applicant's workers' compensation history. (Chapter 3 discusses issues involving applicants in more detail.)

Surveillance

Q 5:39   Can a retail company "shop" its own stores without invading its clerks' rights of privacy?

Yes, most (if not all) retail corporations regularly conduct "shops" of their own stores to test the honesty of store managers and clerks. Employee privacy rights are typically not invaded by this activity.

Q 5:40   Can a company conduct videotaped surveillance of its employees?

As a general rule, reasonable videotaping of employees at the job site for legitimate business reasons does not usually violate their privacy rights; however, there are some exceptions to this general statement. Videotaping employees engaged in union activity is an unfair labor practice if the purpose is to intimidate or retaliate against them. Videotaping illegal strike activity to obtain an injunction or to sue for damages may be legal, albeit such filming often inflames an already volatile situation. Videotaping employees giving urine samples during drug testing (though intended to guard against cheating) would most likely violate the employees' privacy rights. Similarly, surveillance of locker rooms and bathrooms should be avoided.

It is becoming increasingly common for videotape surveillance to be conducted of employees who are on medical leave, or workers' compensation leave, and who are believed to be fraudulently obtaining benefits (i.e., the employee who is supposedly unable to lift over a nominal weight but is said to have been lifting canoes and climbing trees during a camping trip). Because of the possibility of claims in this area (i.e., retaliation claims in workers' compensation and potential FMLA or ADA claims), the employer should turn the matter over to its workers' compensation insurer or employment attorney for consideration.

Q 5:41   Generally, what is the best way for a private employer to avoid liability when conducting employee surveillance?

Although the answer may vary depending upon state statutes, generally, surveillance conducted by a private employer, which is reasonable and necessary for legitimate business reasons and is conducted in an area in which the employee has no reasonable expectation of privacy, is most likely to pass muster. A critical element in reducing privacy claims is to provide notice to employees of the surveillance so that, by the notice, the employee would lose any reasonable expectation of privacy in connection with the surveillance. This is particularly suitable in situations where an employer will place ongoing surveillance in parking lots, work areas, and the like. However, if notice would defeat the purpose of the surveillance, the surveillance may nonetheless pass muster, provided the surveillance chosen is reasonable and necessary for a legitimate business reason (i.e., catching an inside thief), and the surveillance is conducted in a manner so as not to unreasonably intrude in areas where an employee would clearly have an expectation of privacy (i.e., a bathroom or locker room).

Q 5:42   May a company eavesdrop on or record an employee's telephone calls?

Many states have enacted wiretap laws that may make it illegal to eavesdrop on employee telephone calls; however, these laws usually involve only the surreptitious monitoring of calls. In some companies, where telephone solicitation or taking orders is a substantial part of the business, such laws (if arguably applicable) may be satisfied by advising employees that their telephone performance will be randomly monitored.

A federal judge in Salt Lake City dismissed the invasion-of-privacy claim of a police dispatcher whose personal telephone calls were surreptitiously recorded, resulting in his being disciplined for violating a work rule against using the communications systems for personal purposes. Holding that the officer had no reasonable expectation of privacy, the judge said, "The Constitution does not prevent a public employer from making reasonable demands of its employees during business hours in an attempt to perform its work in an efficient, effective manner." The plaintiff had discussed a co-worker's marital problems. When that co-worker reported for her shift and reviewed the tapes, she complained to the supervisor. Facing discipline, the offending dispatcher resigned and sued, but the court rejected her claim. ["Monitoring Phone Calls Held No Breach of Privacy," 1993 *BNA Daily Labor Report* 57, Mar. 26, 1993, at 1]

Q 5:43 What is the *Electronic Communications Privacy Act,* and how might it apply to employee privacy rights?

The *Electronic Communications Privacy Act of 1986* comprehensively amended Title III of the Omnibus Crime Control and Safe Streets Act of 1968. [18 U.S.C. §§ 2510–2520] In the words of one commentator, the Act:

> added a new chapter to the federal wiretap statutes to govern access to electronically stored data. The impetus for the legislation derived, in large part, from a 1985 congressional agency study that used compelling language to describe the threat to civil liberties presented by unregulated intrusions into electronically transmitted communications. . . .
> The statute needed broadening if it clearly was to bring E-mail and other electronic communications within its purview. [Baumhart, "The Employer's Right to Read Employee E-mail: Protecting Property or Personal Prying?" 8 *The Labor Lawyer* 924, Fall 1992]

The Act defines *electronic communication* to include "any transfer of signs, signals, writing, images, sounds, data, or intelligence of any nature transmitted in whole or in part by a wire, radio, electromagnetic, photo-electronic or photo-optical system that affects interstate or foreign commerce." Clearly included in this definition is e-mail, which the federal government has described as a data processing system employing communications technology to transmit mail in electronic form. "If desired, the electronic output can be printed out in hard copy and delivered by the [U.S. Postal Service] or private carrier. But electronic mail also permits terminal-to-terminal communication where the message is never in paper form." [Office of Technology Assessment, *Federal Government Information Technology: Electronic Surveillance and Civil Liberties*, 45 (1985)]

Employers may have many motives to monitor or peruse their employees' use of e-mail. For instance, companies have an interest in ensuring that expensive equipment and services, as well as their employees' time, are being used for company business and not personal activities. Nonetheless, some legal commentators have contended that the Electronic Communications Privacy Act or some state wiretap acts may render such monitoring or eavesdropping illegal:

> [T]o blindly adopt the view that the statute imposes no access limitations on employers who possess their own systems ignores Congress' stated intent to procure parity in the protection of personal communications, regardless of the medium of transmission. [Baumhart, at 926]

Others contend that employers are free under federal law to monitor employees' e-mail at will. [*See* Hernandez, "ECPA and Online Computer Privacy," 41 *Fed Communications L. J.* 17, 39 (1988).] In fact, there is little federal court case law to guide employers with regard to the Act's impact upon employee privacy rights; however, the Act and most analogous state statutes recognize consent as a means of overcoming their prohibitions on electronic eavesdropping. Consequently, where corporations advise employees in advance of their intent to monitor e-mail, telephone calls and the like, these statutory prohibitions may not apply. Such a notice might be contained in the employee handbook and acknowledged by the employee signing an appropriate form following review of the document. The following is a sample e-mail policy:

> The e-mail and voicemail systems are the property of XYZ Company. These systems are to be used for business purposes only and should not be used to send messages of a personal nature. E-mail and voicemail messages are to be transmitted only to those individuals who have a business need to receive them.
>
> XYZ Company has the right to review all e-mail and voicemail messages at any time, and the use of the system's security features such as passwords and access codes does not in any way diminish this right of the company. All employees waive any right to privacy in the use of e-mail and voicemail and consent to the access, retrieval, and disclosure of e-mail and voicemail messages by the company.

Q 5:44   What is the *Stored Communications Act*?

The *Stored Communications Act* (SCA) prohibits intentional access without authorization of a facility through which electronic communication service is provided, or intentionally exceeding any authorization to access that facility. Essentially, any access of stored electronic communications, such as e-mails, without authorization is prohibited. If an employee is using a company-owned computer and the employee is advised that the company will monitor its use (see sample policies above) there would typically be no issue with the SCA for the employer's access to electronically stored information on the employee's computer.

Employers may, for purposes of investigating possible misconduct of an employee, desire to seek access and review electronically stored information through use of an employee's personal e-mail account. Under the SCA any unauthorized access of stored electronic information, including e-mails, is prohibited. [18 U.S.C. § 2701]

In *Pure Power Boot Camp v. Warrior Fitness Boot Camp* [587 F. Supp. 2d 548 (S.D.N.Y. 2008)], an employer sued its former employee for stealing customers trademarks, and other confidential information. As part of its evidence, the employer wanted to introduce various e-mails it obtained from the employee's personal Hotmail account. Apparently, the employer had obtained the employee's password for the account in the past for an unrelated reason, and when the employee's misconduct came to light, the employer utilized the password, without authorization, for purposes of searching the employee's personal Hotmail account to investigate, and found damaging evidence of the employee's misconduct. The court held that the employer's access of the account was without authorization and therefore a violation of the SCA. As a remedy, the court, among other things, would not allow the introduction of the e-mails by the employer in support of its claims, but allowed that such evidence could be used for impeachment purposes, should the employee open the door to such evidence during testimony. In *Bailey v. Bailey* [07-11672, 2008 WL 324156 (E.D. Mich. Feb. 6, 2008)], the court held that a husband in a divorce action, who surreptitiously accessed his wife's personal e-mails on a family owned computer, had violated the SCA. Similarly, in *Wyatt Technology Corp. v. Smithson* [2006 WL 5668246 (C.D. Cal. Aug. 14, 2006)], the court held that accessing and monitoring another's personal e-mail account without authorization is a violation of the SCA.

Q 5:45 Do state constitutions protect employee privacy rights?

The Bill of Rights of the U.S. Constitution applies only to actions by the federal government. The Due Process and Equal Protection clauses of the Fourteenth Amendment apply only to actions by state and local governments. Therefore, although public employees enjoy these constitutional rights with respect to their federal, state, and municipal employers (including public schools, colleges, and universities), the old saying in labor law has always been that "the Constitution stops at the private employer's front door."

Many states have granted their citizens a constitutional right of privacy (i.e., Alaska, Arizona, California, Florida, Hawaii, Illinois, Louisiana, Montana, South Carolina, and Washington). At least one state, Alaska, has extended this privacy right into the private workplace.

Chapter 6

Security Issues

Protecting company assets is a significant concern for most employers. Employee theft is considered by many to be a significant problem generating a large percentage of business losses. But protecting assets involves more than just guarding against employee theft. As companies continue to expand their use of computer systems in connection with their business operations, information technology security issues are becoming increasingly important to businesses attempting to protect their information and information systems from theft or sabotage. An employer's assets are more than just money and property; they also include intellectual assets (e.g., trade secrets and confidential information) and the company's workforce. This chapter explores non-competition agreements and issues concerning their enforceability.

Employee Dishonesty and Theft

Q 6:1   What are the types of employee theft?

Methods of employee theft vary according to the types of businesses involved. Each business seems to have a pattern of conduct that dishonest employees tend to follow. If cash is readily available to employees, for example, some will look for ways to divert it. If employees work at loading terminals, some may hide and remove merchandise there. So-called computer theft is becoming an increasingly common method. It can involve such acts as:

invoicing goods below established prices and getting cash kickbacks from customers; pilfering merchandise covered by doctored inventory lists; placing orders for side business; stealing computers; and using company time and facilities for personal projects.

Types of employee theft include:

1. *Theft of money.* This type needs no explanation.

2. *Sweethearting, another name for collusion.* One of the conspirators is the employee, the other a friend or relative. The employee, usually working a cash register, under-rings the friend's purchases or permits the relative to go out of the store with items not properly purchased. Variants of this phenomenon occur at warehouses and other non-retail facilities.

3. *Merchandise theft.* In a convenience store or supermarket, the theft may be as seemingly innocent as eating a candy bar every day, but a one-dollar candy bar per day times 1,000 employees equals $365,000 in sales lost to a retail chain.

4. *Time theft.* Often overlooked because of its lack of visibility, theft of time includes arriving late and leaving early, fraudulent filling out of time sheets, and goofing off during working hours.

5. *Theft of trade secrets.* Corporate espionage and the theft of trade secrets has been gaining increasing attention, as reflected by the passing of the Economic Espionage Act (18 U.S.C. § 1831), which proscribes criminal penalties for the theft of trade secrets, and the utilization of the Computer Fraud and Abuse Act (18 U.S.C. § 1030) to maintain a claim against an employee who utilized a computer to release his company's trade secrets to a competitor. [Shurgard Storage Ctrs., Inc. v. Safeguard Self Storage, Inc., 119 F. Supp. 2d 1121 (W.D. Wash. 2000)] In addition, over the last few years, a growing number of states have enacted forms of the Uniform Trade Secrets Act. The Act provides various remedies for both injunctive relief and money damages for the misappropriation of a company's trade secrets.

Q 6:2   Are companies that delegate their banking and check writing duties to one person susceptible to theft?

It is not unusual, particularly in smaller companies, to hire one person, typically a controller, who is responsible for all day-to-day financial matters, including collection and posting of account receivables, account payables, and reviewing bank statements. Concentrating these responsibilities within one position at a company can be dangerous. There are simply no checks and balances in the system to ensure that theft or fraud does not take place.

Theft under these circumstances can occur in a variety of ways. The controller can write himself a check and reference it as payment toward bogus invoices. If this person is the same one who reviews bank statements, there is no way in the normal course of business that another individual would have the opportunity to spot the theft. Even if this individual does not have check signing authority, with access to checks he or she has the opportunity to forge an otherwise unauthorized signature that would not be noticed if this forger is the same person who reviews bank statements. This problem is heightened by the fact that banks, even if they pay on a forged signature, will have an argument against liability if they can demonstrate that the forged document could have been determined by the company if it reviewed its bank statements. The fact that the company had the forger review the bank statements provides no defense to the company in this scenario. Therefore, companies should separate functions of financial matters among a number of employees to provide for checks and balances and not create a situation where one person has too much control over various functions, allowing the opportunity for theft and fraud.

Q 6:3   What telltale signs indicate employee dishonesty and theft?

Many signs can be found in irregularities in the workplace or in unusual employee behavior. For example, employers in retail or distribution organizations should suspect their employees if they observe some of the irregularities described in the following paragraphs.

Because money's fungible character makes it impossible to identify its owner, it is a prime target for theft. In most retail operations, cash, to be stolen, has to be removed from a register; the employer's inquiry, then, is how would the money be removed from the register without the employer knowing about it? After money has been diverted, the only way to reconcile the figure that the register displays with the amount of money left in the drawer is artificially to reduce the amount from sales actually made. To do this, the employee usually must fail to ring sales in an amount equaling the value of the money diverted. The following are some of the signs that an employee has failed to ring up sales:

Shortages or overages of cash. A cash overage is as much a red flag as a cash shortage. The only difference between the two is the timing by which the stealing scheme is carried out. In a cash shortage, the cash is first removed from the drawer; the employee later makes up for the discrepancy by under-ringing subsequent sales. If the register audit shows an overage, this may be evidence that the employee has already reduced the amount from sales rung, intending to remove the money later. Unannounced register checks can reveal shortages or overages before the employee has finished manipulating the cash and sales.

Early or late checkouts. To conceal their strategies, dishonest employees check out earlier or later than their co-workers in order to "fix" the registers.

Unusual register readings. This may involve either the frequency of certain register receipt readings (e.g., an unusual number of refunds) or the types of readings (e.g., no sales, cross-readings, returns, and voids).

Statistics point out that losses resulting from employee theft tend to be higher in the distribution and supply sectors than in the service and transport sectors. If the targeted items are supplies and merchandise, the following should be viewed as warning signals:

Out-of-place personal belongings. The presence in work areas of employees' belongings that are not usually kept there can be a signal that merchandise is being concealed and removed within these belongings.

Odd parking habits. A vehicle is usually necessary to remove a considerable amount of merchandise or a single large item. An employee's car that is not parked in its regular parking space (which should be located so that stolen merchandise cannot be carried to it) could signal that the owner of the car intends to perform an unlawful act. Even if the employee justifies this habit on the basis of health-related factors (e.g., difficulty in walking long distances), any irregular parking arrangement should be carefully scrutinized.

Unusual placement of trash cans or other large containers. This may indicate that such containers are being used for concealing and transporting merchandise.

Irregular visits to controlled areas. Records of visitors to restricted areas may show an unusual pattern. Further examination may indicate that certain visits occur only at specific hours. Unless the pattern is justified by a sound reason (e.g., the need to check on certain items delivered at a certain hour), this pattern may indicate a conspiracy between the visiting employee and the employee on the shift at that hour, or a pattern of conduct aimed at evading security controls.

Early or late checkouts or checking. As with cash thefts, dishonest employees may check out early or late to avoid other employees who might see them stealing merchandise and supplies.

Q 6:4   How can a company be proactive in preventing loss from employee dishonesty?

Although there are undoubtedly many actions an employer can take to reduce loss attributable to employee dishonesty, one of the best ways would be to ensure that dishonest employees are not employed. In other words, weeding out dishonest people from your applicant pool can go a long way in reducing your risk and exposure to loss. Background checks can be an effective way to spot a dishonest applicant. If using this approach, applications should be very carefully written so that dishonesty can be detected and effectively used to deny employment. Applications should require the applicant to provide complete and accurate information regarding the applicant's work history and educational background. Although, in most situations, criminal convictions may not be an absolute bar to employment (a recommended approach by the Equal Employment Opportunity Commission (EEOC) to avoid potential discrimination claims), nonetheless, applicants should be asked to describe any and all convictions. In addition, the application should specifically provide for the applicant's authorization for the employer to check and verify the information provided, provide for a release of all parties from any liability in connection therewith, and notify the applicant that if false or misleading information is provided, or if there are material omissions, the application and/or employment, regardless of when determined, will be terminated. If an outside agency is used for the background check, a stand-alone agreement is required by the Fair

Credit Reporting Act (FCRA) to provide authorization, as more specifically described in chapter 3.

Q 6:5 What techniques can prevent or detect employee theft?

Loss prevention and security experts have suggested that setting the following corporate policies can prevent and detect employee theft:

- View the security department as a potential profit center. In the words of one loss control specialist, "A dollar in new sales may yield a nickel to the bottom line after deductions for cost of goods, labor, rent, utilities and other expenses. But a dollar not lost to (inventory) shrink or robbery falls directly to the bottom line." [Castagnera & Szvetitz, "Survival of the Safest," *Convenience Store Decisions*, Jan. 1992, at 24]
- Consider security a bona fide career path, and seek out experts with appropriate education and sophistication, not just ex-police officers and retired military personnel.
- Involve the security department in all forms and sources of loss, rather than relegating it to supervising security guards and monitoring alarms and TV cameras.
- Integrate the security function with purchasing, accounting, human resources, and the general counsel's office.

Q 6:6 What guidelines exist for preventing employee theft?

Loss control experts suggest the following checklist to prevent employee theft:

- Conduct regular audits on the performance of the company.
- Keep complete and up-to-date records of all the company's transactions, goods, routes, and inventories.
- Implement a uniform system for reporting matters handled by employees.
- Limit access to supply and storage areas.
- Set established procedures to handle routine operations performed by employees.
- Stress the importance of observing company procedures.
- Set up a decentralized operating system for each of the company's units (e.g., have one person handle accounting and another perform the billing; have one group handle deliveries and a different group take care of shipping).
- Use electronic security systems and undercover investigators.

Q 6:7 How does an employer spot dishonest employees?

Employers can use such electronic devices as pinhole video cameras, closed-circuit TVs, and CB radios. They can also monitor all manner of functions and activities on the employees' PCs. An employer must, however, be mindful of the potential for violating an employee's privacy rights. Employees may have privacy rights in certain instances, provided they have a legitimate expectation of privacy in connection with the venue at issue. Employers can typically remove any legitimate expectation of privacy by adopting a policy limiting use of the PC for business purposes, and advising the employee that the employer may monitor its use. The use of the polygraph, or lie detector, is subject to federal (and often state) statutory restrictions. Searches and surveillance of employees can give rise to legal liability, if inappropriately performed.

Under proper professional and legal supervision, the employer can use an amazing array of devices and techniques for spotting dishonest employees, including:

- Arrest and conviction records;
- Attitude and honesty tests;
- Blood and urine tests to detect drug abuse;
- Computer monitoring of everything from the productivity of typists to employees' e-mail activities;
- Credit reports; and
- Telephone monitoring.

This list of employer devices and techniques is far from exhaustive. The employer should carefully scrutinize federal and state statutory and common law for limitations or outright prohibitions before using any of them.

In addition, employers can adopt various procedures, so-called checks and balances, to enable it to spot fraudulent activities. For example, do not consolidate both the check preparation and check signing functions within one person, but rather, two different persons. In addition, have someone other than the ones involved in check preparation and check signature review and reconcile bank statements and potentially spot irregularities. By utilizing these types of checks and balances, the company does not leave too much control within one person relative to matters that could be the subject of fraud and theft. It allows for individuals other than those involved in check writing and check signature to review bank statements, and possibly copies of checks, to spot irregularities or potential issues.

Q 6:8 Can an employer require employees to submit to polygraph tests?

Under the Employee Polygraph Protection Act (EPPA), employers, with few exceptions (i.e., public employers, driving companies, private security firms, and contractors of national security and defense agencies) cannot compel employees to take a polygraph, and even if they can under limited exceptions to the EPPA, the employer cannot take any adverse employment action against the employee based on the refusal of the employee to take the test or on the basis of the results of the test. One of the exceptions is the "investigative use" exception that allows covered employers to require polygraph tests to investigate such matters as theft and industrial espionage. To do so, the employer must have "reasonable suspicion" that the employee was involved, and be able to demonstrate that the employee had access to the missing or taken property. In *Cummings v. Washington Mutual* [650 F.3d 1386 (11th Cir. 2011)], the court held that the employer-bank had satisfied the criteria for the investigative-use exception in administering a polygraph to its bank manager, one of four employees that had access to the missing funds. In addition to access, the court also found that the bank manager repeatedly violated the employer's "dual control policy" which required that more than one person be present when cash is handled. Although the court noted that "access" alone could not satisfy the reasonable suspicion test, in this case, access together with violations of the dual control policy were sufficient to demonstrate reasonable suspicion.

Even then, the employer cannot take action against the employee based on a refusal to take the test or its results. For example, an employer, in *Dilworth v. LaSalle-Chicago 24-Hour Currency Exchange, Inc.* [2004 U.S. Dist. LEXIS 3992 (N.D. Ill. Mar. 11, 2004)], was held to have violated the EPPA when it fired an employee after an investigation into an apparent theft of $2,000 of the company's funds. The employee who was fired was asked to take a lie detector test, and was discharged after she refused. Although the employer claimed that it fit within the exemption under the EPPA to ask for the test because it had a reasonable suspicion that the employee was involved in the theft under investigation, since other employees claimed that they had seen her with the missing money, the employee continually denied having taken the money in dispute. On appeal for a judgment in favor of the discharged employee against the employer for a violation of the EPPA, the court concluded that it was not an error for the jury to conclude that the employer did not have reasonable suspicion that the employee had stolen the money, and that it was not error for the jury to conclude that the employment was terminated because she refused to take a lie detector test. The fact alone that other employees testified that they saw the plaintiff with the money was not sufficient to explain her termination. As such, the violation of the EPPA was upheld. To fit within the investigative use exception, the exception must be satisfied at the time the request to take a polygraph is made. In *Campbell v. Woodard Photographic, Inc.* [433 F. Supp. 2d 857 (N.D. Ohio (2006)], an employer, following a series of thefts at their shop, told all the employees at a meeting that everyone would have to take a polygraph test. Although later in the inquiry the investigation centered on a particular employee who fit within the investigative use exception, the initial demand was over-broad, did not involve "reasonable suspicion" and "access" for any particular employee, and as such, was a technical violation of the EPPA.

Even in cases where the investigative use exception does not apply, an employer may still be able to terminate an employee who failed a lie-detector test if the employer can demonstrate that irrespective of the test results, the employee's termination would have occurred in any event.

In *Worden v. Suntrust Banks, Inc.* [549 F.3d 334 (4th Cir. 2008)], an employee of a bank, who failed two lie-detector tests following a bank robbery, claimed that the employer did not fall within the investigative use exception, and as a result, his employment which was terminated following the second failed test was in violation of the EPPA. Although the court noted that the investigative use exception did not apply and that it was not necessary for the employee to demonstrate that the failed lie-detector tests were the "sole" basis for his termination to maintain a claim, but rather needed to only show that it was a factor in the decision to terminate him from his employment, the court concluded that the plaintiff could not maintain a claim in this case because there was sufficient uncontested evidence that the plaintiff's employment would have been terminated in any event, irrespective of the failed tests. Specifically, the decision makers that terminated plaintiff's employment claimed that plaintiff's employment was terminated because they had lost trust in him due to his probable involvement in the attempted bank robbery, based on information that was provided to them by law enforcement officials, irrespective of the tests at issue. Concluding that the record plainly showed that the employer would have terminated the plaintiff's employment in any event, the court held that a claim under the EPPA could not be maintained. In *Bass v. Wendy's of Downtown, Inc.* [2012 WL 1552264 (N.D. Ohio May 1, 2012)], an employee, who submitted to a polygraph exam following a missing bank deposit, claimed that the negative results were later used against him to deny his promotion to general manager or assistant manager. Although the employer acknowledged that it had a "trust" issue with the plaintiff stemming from his failed polygraph test, nonetheless presented abundant evidence demonstrating that it would not have promoted the plaintiff to the position of general manager and/or assistant manager even if it was unaware of the plaintiff's failed polygraph test, such that no claim under the EPPA could be maintained.

Q 6:9   Can a polygraph examiner be liable under the EPPA?

In *Fernandez v. MoraSan Miguel Elec. Coop., Inc.* [462 F.3d 1244 (10th Cir. 2006)], the court held that an independent polygraph examiner could not be held liable under the EPPA unless the examiner could be considered an "employer" under the Act. Applying the "economic realities" test, the question is whether the examiner exerts some degree of control over the employer's compliance with the EPPA. As the regulations provide, "[A] polygraph examiner either employed for or whose services are retained for the sole purpose of administering polygraph tests ordinarily would not be deemed an employer with respect to the examinees." [29 C.F.R. § 801.2(c)] In a somewhat related case, the court in *Watson v. Drummond Co.* [436 F.3d 1310 (11th Cir. 2006)] held that a union that offered former employees an opportunity to take a polygraph test in order to get their jobs back was not an employer under the EPPA and therefore would not have violated the EPPA as a result of the request. In *Maybury v. Slaton* [2010 WL 518041 (S.D. Ohio Feb. 2, 2010)], at issue was whether the company's attorney that became involved in the investigation of an incident during which the attorney requested a polygraph examination of one of the company's employees was an "employer" under the EPPA, such that the attorney could be individually liable for an EPPA violation. Although the attorney was certainly involved in the investigation, the plaintiff proffered insufficient evidence to establish, under the "economic realities" test, that the attorney acted "directly or indirectly in the interest of an employer in relation to an employee," as required by 29 U.S.C. § 2001(2).

Q 6:10   May a company electronically monitor employees?

The answer depends on the kind of monitoring being conducted, why it is being done, and how it is handled.

Concerning the kind of monitoring, many states have wiretap and eavesdrop laws that expressly forbid the secret monitoring of telephone conversations. With respect to why the employer is monitoring employees, there should be a demonstrable business purpose. For example, personal computers might be monitored to check efficiency, or telephones might be monitored to ensure that proper sales techniques are being used. Many transportation companies have installed devices that, with the utilization of global positioning satellites, allow the employer to pinpoint the location of company vehicles at all times. However, accessing an employee's personal e-mail account without authorization may result in liability. In *Mintz v. Mark Bartelstein and Associates, Inc.* [2012 WL 5391779 (C.D. Cal. Nov. 1, 2012)], a sports agency hacked into the personal e-mail account of one of its agents that was leaving to work for a competitor and located and reviewed his compensation agreement with his new employer. Although the employer claimed that the intrusion was de minimis, the sports agency could provide no legitimate business reason for the intrusion and the court found the intrusion to be a serious violation of privacy, for which the employee's motion for summary disposition was granted. Some states have passed laws to protect employees' privacy as it relates to their personal e-mail account and use of social media. For example, Illinois's "Right to Privacy in the Workplace Act" [820 IlCS 55], prohibits, with limited exceptions, employers from requiring employees or applicants to provide passwords or other related personal account information to gain access to the employee's or applicant's account or profile on a social networking Web site.

Finally, there is the issue of how the employer handles the monitoring. Advance notice to employees may circumvent a wiretap or eavesdrop statute by eliminating the element of secrecy. Notice may also diminish the employee's expectation of privacy, a necessary element in some states' common-law definition of the invasion of privacy tort, as well as in some Fourth Amendment search-and-seizure situations. Although employees may not like being monitored, a thoughtful employee communication program can help workers see the need for it, thus minimizing employee hostility and resentment. In addition, monitoring should always be conducted with as much consideration as possible. For instance, telephone monitoring should not intrude on permissible personal phone calls.

Q 6:11   May a company photograph or film its employees on the job?

A common method of catching thieves in the act is to place a time-lapse video camera with a pinhole lens behind a wall or partition in the vicinity of the suspected employee's cash register, desk, or workbench. There appear to be no reported cases holding this sort of surveillance to be illegal in a private workplace. If the suspected activity occurs, this evidence can be powerful in any subsequent court action. However, patience and a deep pocket are necessary when a company contracts this work to a private detective agency. Although time-lapse cameras can show the time and date of an incident on the videotape, many security professionals feel strongly that an operator should always be present at the taping so he or she can later testify to the authenticity of the pictures. Time-lapse cameras raise another problem. Hours of their film can be edited out so that a judge or jury sees only critical events or transactions. In short, videotape surveillance can be highly effective, but not in the hands of amateurs.

Q 6:12   How should an employer proceed if it suspects that an employee has engaged in theft or other dishonest behavior?

Terminating an employee under suspicion of theft or other dishonest behavior can be dangerous. An employer that lacks evidence may expose itself to claims of defamation, depending on how it proceeds, or it may be unable to defend itself against claims of discrimination or wrongful discharge. Nonetheless, when it suspects theft, an employer can undertake the following steps to minimize its risk and exposure to claims.

Investigate the allegations. When theft or other dishonest behavior is suspected, an investigation should be undertaken to accumulate evidence. Records should be reviewed, employees should be interviewed, and other reasonable measures should be undertaken to investigate the allegations. Notes should be taken, statements should be obtained, and generally the investigation should be conducted in the same way as an investigation of other alleged unlawful activity, such as sexual harassment (see chapter 4). Employers should keep a separate investigation file for the investigation, and keep a written record of all evidence uncovered. The investigation record should be limited to factual information, no conclusion should be drawn until the investigation is concluded, and no accusations or insinuations of theft or other dishonest behavior should be made. If the matter is serious, the police may be notified. They may undertake their own investigation of the matter. If the suspected theft involves utilization of the employer's computers (i.e., downloading or releasing trade secrets to a competitor), the employer should consider utilizing an investigator trained in computer forensic investigations to determine whether there is information in the computer that would evidence wrongdoing. A forensic examination can uncover information that might otherwise appear deleted. Provided the computer is owned by the company and its use is restricted to business purposes, if reasonable suspicion exists, then such an exam should not subject the employer to privacy claims. Note: Consultation with an employment lawyer is highly recommended before undertaking such an examination.

Confront the suspected thief. In almost all circumstances, an individual suspected of theft or other dishonest behavior should be confronted with the evidence obtained by the employer. The employee should be advised he or she is not being accused of any wrongdoing, but that the employer has obtained evidence and is asking the employee to respond to it. The employee should be shown the evidence and, preferably, should write out his or her explanation of the evidence the employer has gathered. Confronting someone who is suspected of theft or other dishonest behavior is almost always advisable. He or she may be able to explain the evidence or show that the evidence the employer has obtained is in error.

Draw conclusions. After the investigation is finished, an employer should determine whether any conclusions could be drawn. The evidence may show that the employee has committed theft or other dishonest behavior. Often the evidence only suggests wrongdoing, and the employee will continue to deny any wrongdoing. In such circumstances, an employer may not be able to conclude that the employee engaged in theft but may nonetheless determine that the employee otherwise violated company policy (e.g., cash-handling procedures). This violation may provide a basis to discipline the employee.

Discipline as facts warrant. Discipline should be exercised in accordance with the company's policies and procedures. If the investigation shows that the employee engaged not in dishonesty but rather in a minor infraction of company policy, then that employee should be disciplined consistently with other employees who engaged in similar infractions. Providing more serious discipline because the employer believes, but cannot prove that the employee engaged in theft, is unwise.

Do not threaten criminal prosecution. Unless the employee agrees to various conditions, many employers want to threaten the employee with criminal prosecution when faced with what may appear to be criminal activity. The conditions to which an employee may agree include the execution of a resignation and release, and the repayment of allegedly embezzled money. This approach can be dangerous. By boldly accusing the employee of criminal activity, the employer is firmly set in its position as to the reasons for separation; undoubtedly, an employee accused of criminal conduct will be fired even if the employer's stated conditions are not agreed to by the employee. If the accusation is not supported by credible evidence, the employer may face claims of defamation or, in circumstances where the employer is leaping to conclusions, claims of prejudice or discrimination. In addition, any resignation or release signed could be challenged as obtained under duress or coercion, possibly rendering the separation tantamount to a constructive discharge. Note as well that it is a federal crime for a person, having knowledge of the actual commission of a federal felony, actively to conceal and fail to report a commission of the crime to the authorities. [Misprision of Felony, 18 U.S.C. § 4]

Maintain confidentiality. In all aspects of the investigation, the employer should ensure confidentiality and limit the dissemination of information to a need-to-know basis. The possibility of litigation for defamation is great; the employer must not accuse the employee of a crime that ultimately cannot be proved.

Q 6:13 Should an employer prosecute an employee who steals?

If evidence indicates that guilt is nearly certain, prosecution is usually advisable. Failing to prosecute may suggest to other employees that the company is not serious about theft.

Q 6:14 How can an employer guard against allegations of defamation when terminating an employee for theft or other dishonest behavior?

The following actions should be considered when firing an employee for theft or dishonesty:

- Conduct as careful and thorough an investigation as possible.
- Be sure of the facts and confront the suspect-employee before making a decision.
- When making a record of the investigation and confronting the alleged culprit, stick closely to the facts and stay away from accusations, innuendo, and suppositions. It is unnecessary and risky actually to accuse the employee of illegal conduct. Show the employee the evidence and ask for an explanation.
- Only those managers and co-workers with an absolute need to know should be informed of the details of the termination.
- Do not try to make an example of the employee, except by referral to appropriate authorities. When terminating the employee, avoid using words like "theft" or "stealing," both in the separation meeting and company documents. Rather, refer to or describe the incident, sticking closely to the facts uncovered during the investigation (i.e., unauthorized removal of company property from the premises as opposed to stealing computer).

If an announcement to the employees must be made, word it carefully, have it reviewed by legal counsel, and limit distribution as much as possible without defeating its purpose. Although many states extend a limited privilege regarding these types of communications to other employees when necessary, the possibility of defamation looms, and innocuous references to the circumstances surrounding separation are preferable. Trying to make an example of the employee is almost always ill-advised. Off-handed remarks are ill-advised and can lead to problems. Following the termination of a substitute teacher, the school personnel director told a reporter of a local paper that the substitute teacher was terminated for obscenity. In fact, the school personnel director knew that the termination was for "poor judgment" for showing "The Simpsons Movie," which contained obscenities to the class. Under these circumstances, a qualified privilege would not protect the school and school personnel director from potential liability and summary judgment was inappropriate. [Abdul-Salaam v. Lobo-Wadley, 2009 WL 3305913 (D. Conn. Oct. 14, 2009)] Although statements made to co-workers that plaintiff was terminated for stealing were subject to a qualified privilege under Minnesota law, issues of fact existed as to whether a supervisor had malice based on evidence of having used racial slurs toward plaintiff, such that summary disposition for the employer was inappropriate. [Walker v. Wanner Eng'g, Inc., 867 F. Supp. 2d 1050 (D. Minn. 2012)]

Q 6:15   Is truth a defense to defamation?

Truth is a defense to defamation. The determination of whether truth has been demonstrated as an affirmative defense to a claim of defamation is based specifically on content of the alleged defamatory communication itself. For example, in *Grennan v. Nassau County* [2007 U.S. Dist. LEXIS 23087 (E.D.N.Y. Mar. 29, 2007)], a teacher claimed that she was falsely accused of falsifying various documents. However, at issue was the statement that "there is a DA investigation of a speech teacher for malicious intent to falsify legal documents." [*Grennan*, at 21] Although the teacher denied that she had falsified documents, the court noted that the statement at issue did not state that the teacher had in fact falsified documents, but rather that there was an investigation of a teacher for same. The court found that it could not be disputed that, in fact, the investigation described in the statement at issue was ongoing, such that the statement was substantially true and for which no claim for defamation could thereupon be maintained.

Safety and Violence in the Workplace

Q 6:16   Does an employer have a duty to maintain a safe workplace?

Yes. The common law and Occupational Safety and Health Act (OSH Act), as well as a growing number of analogous state statutes, require employers to maintain safe workplaces.

Q 6:17   Can an employer be liable to employees or third parties for violence in the workplace?

Injuries suffered in the course of employment, whether from personal negligence or that of a co-worker, are generally covered by workers' compensation insurance. Virtually all state workers' compensation laws limit the employer's liability to the benefits permitted under those laws, thus providing employers with immunity from liability for various torts. Some state workers' compensation laws do not provide this immunity when the injury is the result not of an accident, but of some intentional act of the employer. In some jurisdictions, this intentional-tort exception to workers' compensation coverage has been extended to situations in which the company has intentionally exposed its employees to a known and virtually certain hazard. For states that recognize the intentional-tort exception, if the employer knows that violence will occur, and nonetheless allows its employees to be exposed to violence, a cause of action may be outside workers' compensation; however, if the violence is not certain, but rather occurs suddenly and without warning, exposure to an intentional tort is unlikely.

Legal exposure to customers, vendors, and other business invitees is not covered under workers' compensation laws, and there are a host of theories for liability against an employer for violence in the workplace committed against nonemployees. Generally, an employer is required to use reasonable care to provide a safe environment to individuals invited to its premises. Failure to protect invitees from foreseeable danger, like adequate security in a crime-ridden area, may provide a basis for liability, although in many jurisdictions, criminal activity by its very nature is not considered foreseeable in most cases. In addition, if an employer knows, or should have known, of the dangerous propensities of an employee (e.g., as a result of threats or criminal conviction history), the employer may be liable under theories of negligent hiring or negligent retention of the employee, theories that are recognized as a matter of common law in some jurisdictions. If an employer establishes a policy of conducting criminal background checks in situations that warrant it, and failed to do so, it leaves itself vulnerable to liability for negligent hiring if an employee turns out to have propensities for violence that would have been uncovered through a background check. For example, in *Blair v. Defender Services, Inc.* [386 F.3d 623 (4th Cir. 2004)], a college student sued a janitorial staffing company for injuries sustained as a result of a violent attack upon her by a janitor of the staffing company. As to her claim for negligent hiring, the college student claimed that despite its contract with the college, requiring it to do so, the janitorial service had, on three prior occasions, failed to do a criminal background check of the janitor who attacked her. She claimed that such a check would have disclosed a prior protective order entered in a neighboring county resulting from an alleged attack of a female patron of a restaurant. Although the janitor in question had no criminal convictions per se, the court concluded that there was ample evidence that if a background criminal check had been done, as required by the janitorial service's contract with the college, the protective order in the neighboring county would have been discovered. The janitorial service acknowledged that had it been aware of the protective order, it would not have assigned the janitor to the college. As such, the court concluded that the case could proceed to trial. However, if the prospective employer had no knowledge of facts that would lead a reasonably prudent person to investigate the prospective employee, claims of negligent hiring will be difficult to maintain. In *Bouchard v. New York Archdiocese* [719 F. Supp. 2d 255 (S.D.N.Y. 2010)], a parishioner who was allegedly sexually abused by a visiting priest, brought a claim for negligent hiring against the Archdiocese for hiring a visiting priest that allegedly had a propensity to commit sexual abuse. However, because the plaintiff could provide no evidence that the church had any knowledge of facts that would lead the church to investigate the background of the visiting priest, the court dismissed the claim. In *Gargano v. Wyndham Skyline Tower Resorts* [2012 WL 5388949 (D. N.J. Nov. 2, 2012)], an employee who worked for a company that contracted to perform cleaning services at a hotel was sexually assaulted by a hotel employee and sued the hotel for negligent hiring. Although, prior to hiring, plaintiff had exhibited aggressive behavior, the court held that the two prior isolated outbursts of anger and aggression that did not result in physical injury could not have put the hotel on notice that the employee was a sexual threat such that no claim for negligent hiring could be maintained against the hotel.

In *Beyene v. Hilton Hotels Corp.* [815 F. Supp. 2d 235 (D.D.C. 2011)], the court refused to dismiss a claim of negligent retention when the plaintiff asserted that the defendant employer conducted an inadequate investigation of his complaints of harassment, and had it conducted a proper investigation by interviewing all witnesses, it would have determined that the employee had dangerous propensities.

In *Shaw v. Pizza Hut of America, Inc.* [2009 WL 591182 (M.D. Fla. Mar. 6, 2009)], the plaintiff who was in an automobile accident with a pizza delivery driver, sued Pizza Hut alleging, among other things, negligent hiring of its pizza delivery driver. The plaintiff claimed that if Pizza Hut conducted a background check of his driving record, it would have found that he had a DWI and multiple speeding violations. As such, the plaintiff alleged that Pizza Hut knew or should have known of his lack of fitness to be a driver and that it was therefore unreasonable and negligent for Pizza Hut to have hired this employee in light of the information it knew or should have known. Although Pizza Hut claimed it had no obligation to conduct a background check and that it hired this driver consistent with its internal policies applicable to all of its drivers, the court held that because all employers have a duty to exercise reasonable care in hiring, and because the job of pizza delivery involves driving on public roads for almost the employee's entire shift, Pizza Hut had a duty to use reasonable care in hiring safe drivers who would not pose a danger to the public in carrying out their duties, including inquiry into the driver's fitness to drive which the jury could find would involve a review of the driver's driving record. However, in *Keen v. Miller Environmental Group, Inc.* [702 F.3d 239 (5th Cir. Miss. 2012)], in a case of first impression, the Fifth Circuit held that there was no generalized duty under Mississippi law to conduct a background check on applicants, despite an internal corporate policy to do so, such that there could be no claim of negligent hiring against an employer for hiring a manual laborer that allegedly raped a co-worker.

The Second Circuit Court of Appeals held that if an employer is on notice of an employee's propensity for violent sexual misconduct due to pre-employment behavior in the past, the employer may be required to take reasonable steps to protect co-employees from becoming victims or face liability for sexual harassment. In the case, the employee, an airline employee, was an alleged serial rapist that raped a co-worker. [*See* 18 *Employment Discrimination Report (EDR)* (BNA) 33 (Jan. 9, 2002).]

Q 6:18   What can an employer do to reduce exposure to and liability for violence in the workplace?

Although this list is not exhaustive, the following are reasonable steps an employer should consider:

- Adopt an aggressive approach toward preventing violence in the workplace. This includes publishing work rules prohibiting violent behavior, including prohibitions against fighting, threatening behavior, and bringing weapons or firearms to work. In addition, many consultants recommend the preparation of plans and procedures to be followed in the event of a violent situation, much in the same way companies have various procedures to be followed in the event of a fire, tornado, or other disaster. Because many different factors are involved in the development of such a plan, such as location or building configuration, utilization of an expert in the field is recommended.

- In the event of a threat of workplace violence, take immediate steps to reduce the risk of violence. This includes calling security or local law enforcement agencies, evacuating the premises in circumstances of a bomb threat, and securing all entrances or exits in the event of a threat from someone outside the premises.

- Take threats seriously. If we have learned anything from the recent series of tragedies involving school bombings and shootings, it is that threats of violence should not be ignored, even if they come from unlikely sources such as school children.

- Conduct criminal conviction background checks of applicants. Although, absent unique circumstances, employers should not adopt an absolute bar to the hiring of any employee with a felony record (such an absolute bar, according to the EEOC, may be illegal disparate-impact discrimination against certain minorities), nonetheless, conviction records should be reviewed to avoid hiring individuals whose conviction records evidence dangerous propensities.

- If an employee is being harassed or stalked by an outsider, and there is reason to believe that the situation may spill over into the workplace, advise the employee to consider obtaining a personal protection order, enjoining the stalker from harassing the victim. Many states now maintain stalking statutes and although the employer usually cannot obtain the relief on its own accord, the employer can help the employee obtain relief, such as through legal counsel. This type of intervention into a potentially dangerous situation might avert escalation of the behavior into violence in the workplace.

Q 6:19   In light of recent events, should employers consider developing action plans to respond to workplace violence?

Until recent events, most discussions of workplace violence considered responding to disgruntled employees, angry spouses, spurned lovers, and the like. However, we now know that workplace violence can be caused by outsiders that have no relationship to your company whatsoever, utilizing means of destruction that are unthinkable. Not surprisingly, many companies have begun to develop action plans to attempt to provide some sense of order in what might turn out to be a very chaotic and unfathomable circumstance. These action plans cover a variety of issues, including: establishing some level of authority involving decision making when circumstances occur such that "somebody" will be in charge to deal with whatever issues may arise; establish evacuation plans if circumstances warrant; establishing protocols for handling certain types of situations (i.e., suspicious letters and packages); and providing for backup of sensitive and important information at an off-site or remote or secure location. There are many security firms that specialize in the creation of these types of action plans, and we strongly suggest you consider retaining them for this purpose.

Q 6:20   How can security experts and consultants be used in this area?

Qualified consultants in the security industry can provide an array of useful information and assistance to employers seeking to prevent or reduce loss attributable to workplace violence. Security consultants can be used to undertake a site review. Generally, during a site review the security consultant reviews the physical premises and makes recommendations to enhance physical security. Security consultants can also provide valuable assistance in connection with threat assessment. Although all threats must be taken seriously, assessing just how dangerous the threat is can be difficult, and utilization of outside professionals can be particularly helpful in providing recommendations on how to respond to threats. All threats need to be investigated, but the assistance of a professional can be helpful in directing the investigation and making recommendations on how to deal with the threat. Lastly, security experts can be helpful in assisting to prepare a plan to respond to situations. Specific protocols can be established for situations involving suspicious packages and the like. A crisis management team can be created that is empowered to take charge of responding to any particular act. Protocols regarding evacuations and/or contacting police can be established.

Q 6:21   Should employers be wary of the potential for violence in connection with an employee's discharge?

Assessing the potential for violence in connection with a discharge can help to reduce violence in the workplace. Generally, experts in this field will point to any number of characteristics to look for in assessing the level of risk in these types of situations, including whether the individual has a history of violence, made threats, demonstrated a fascination for weapons, or exhibited other disturbing or unusual behavior. If you are concerned, it is recommended that you consider retaining a qualified security consultant who can review the situation with you to determine whether or not concern is warranted. If so, then any number of actions can be taken to reduce the risk of violence in connection with the termination. Security guards can be used/retained for purposes of sitting through the discharge meeting, the individual can be escorted out of the company's premises by security guards immediately following the discharge, and security guards can be posted for some reasonable period of time following termination.

Q 6:22   Does the Americans with Disabilities Act (ADA) affect how an employer can treat an employee whose violent propensities or behavior is a manifestation of a disability?

Employers are obligated under various federal and state laws to provide a safe working environment for employees and to warn or take remedial action to avoid known or suspected dangers. On the other hand, employers are obligated under the ADA to accommodate qualified individuals with disabilities, which include both physical and mental impairment. These two divergent responsibilities collide when an employee's violent behavior is attributed to an impairment that rises to a level of a disability under the ADA.

Under the ADA, an employer is not obligated to accommodate a qualified individual with a disability if the individual poses a *direct threat* that is defined as a "significant risk to the health and safety of others that cannot be eliminated by reasonable accommodation." [§ 1630.2 of the Commission's ADA regulations] A person who poses a direct threat is not qualified and therefore is not afforded protection under the ADA. The determination of whether an individual poses a direct threat is based upon an assessment of an individual's present ability to safely perform the essential functions of the position. The regulations provide that this decision is not to be based on fears or stereotypes, but rather on reasonable medical judgment. Factors to be considered under the regulations include:

- The duration of the risk;
- The nature and severity of the potential harm;
- The likelihood that the potential harm will occur; and
- The imminence of the potential harm.

Q 6:23   How is potential workplace violence, attributed to an ADA-protected disability, handled under current case law?

Developing case law suggests that deference is given to employers who take reasonable action against an employee to avoid violence in the workplace, even if the violence is attributed to an ADA disability. In *Collins v. Blue Cross/Blue Shield of Michigan* [228 Mich. App. 560 (1998)], an employee who was ADA-disabled because of a mental impairment underwent an independent medical examination with a psychiatrist and expressed "homicidal thoughts" that were "frighteningly specific and detailed" concerning her supervisor. Although the employee never threatened the supervisor at work, and never directly made these homicidal thoughts known to others in the workplace, the court ruled that the thoughts expressed to the psychiatrist were sufficient to pose a direct threat to the health and safety of other individuals in the workplace. Although the employer fired the employee as a result of expression of homicidal thoughts to the psychiatrist, the court concluded that the termination did not violate the ADA. The court found that the employee, Ms. Collins, failed to satisfy the requirement that she be "qualified" under the ADA because she posed a direct threat, and the court reversed an arbitration ruling in her favor. [*See*

"Employee May Be Fired for Homicidal Thoughts," 12 *Mich. L.W.* 715–16.] As the court stated:

> We believe it is clear that employers must be afforded wide latitude to ensure a safe workplace for their employees. Where an employee's homicidal thoughts about a co-worker are either expressed in the workplace, or otherwise made known to others in the workplace, the law does not require the employer to establish that the employee would affirmatively act on her homicidal thoughts before discharging her. [*Collins*, 228 Mich. App. 560 at 573]

Although these homicidal thoughts became known to others in the workplace only through communication by the psychiatrist, and the employer could not affirmatively establish that Ms. Collins would act on her threat, the court nonetheless found a direct threat sufficient to disqualify Ms. Collins from protection under the ADA. The *Collins* case demonstrates the deference some courts are willing to provide employers who make reasonable decisions to prevent violence in the workplace.

Similarly, in *Palmer v. Cook County Circuit Court*, the Seventh Circuit held that an employee who threatens to kill another employee could be discharged for the threat, even if the threat is caused by a mental disability covered by the ADA. As the court stated:

> There is no evidence that Palmer was fired because of her mental illness. She was fired because she threatened to kill another employee. The cause of the threat was, we may assume, her mental illness . . . But if an employer fires an employee because of the employee's unacceptable behavior, the fact that behavior was precipitated by a mental illness does not present an issue under the Americans with Disabilities Act. The Act does not require an employer to retain a potentially violent employee. Such a requirement would place the employer on a razor's edge, in jeopardy of violating the Act if it fired such an employee, yet in jeopardy of being deemed negligent if it retained him and he hurt someone. The Act protects only qualified employees, that is employees qualified to do the job for which they were hired; and threatening other employees disqualifies one. [117 F.3d 351, 352 (7th Cir. 1997)]

As to accommodation obligations, the ADA only applies to qualified individuals with disabilities. If the individual who makes the threat is not qualified, as concluded by the court in *Palmer*, no accommodation obligation under the ADA exists. [*See Collins*, 228 Mich. App. 560 at 573–74 and *Palmer*, 117 F.3d 351 at 352.]

Similarly, in *Borgialli v. Thunder Basin Coal Co.* [235 F.3d 1284 (10th Cir. 2000)], the U.S. Court of Appeals for the Tenth Circuit upheld a discharge of a mine blaster who, as a result of mental and physical problems, was determined to have posed a direct threat to the safety of others in the workplace. [16 *Employment Discrimination Report (EDR)* (BNA) 44 (Jan. 10, 2001)] However, as opposed to requiring an employer to demonstrate that the employee posed a direct threat as an affirmative defense, it appears that the evolving position adopted by most circuit courts that have addressed the issue is that employees who threaten the safety of others in the workplace are simply not "qualified," a "qualified" person with a "disability" being a prerequisite to maintaining a prima facie ADA claim. In *Calef Jr. v. The Gillette Co.* [322 F.3d 75 (1st Cir. 2003)], an employee terminated for making threats on numerous occasions despite prior warnings claimed that his violent behavior was a result of his medical condition and, therefore, his discharge was in violation of the ADA. Canvassing decisions from other circuit courts, the court concluded that if an employee engages in threatening behavior, the individual is simply not "qualified" for the position, such that the individual has no claim under the ADA. As the court stated succinctly:

> Put simply, the ADA does not require that an employee whose unacceptable behavior threatens the safety of others be retained, even if the behavior stems from a mental disability. Such an employee is not qualified. That was the point of our decision in *EEOC v. Amigo, Inc.*, 110 F.3d 135 (1st Cir. 1997), it is also the view of every other circuit case that has addressed a similar situation under the ADA or the Rehabilitation Act. (Citing decisions from the Second, Seventh, Eighth, Tenth, and D.C. Circuits.)

As such, in the ADA case *Rose v. Laskey* [110 Fed. Appx. 136 (1st Cir. 2004)], once the court decided that it was undisputed that the former employee had threatened violence, the court concluded that it was appropriate for the employer to take the threat at "face value" and discharge the employee. The court thereby dismissed the employee's ADA claim despite the fact that the employee claimed that his unacceptable behavior resulted from his mental impairment.

Recent precedent demonstrates the continued deference to employers that terminate potentially violent employees, even when the violence stems from mental disabilities. In *Sista v. CDC Ixis North America, Inc.* [445 F.3d 161 (2d Cir. 2006)], at issue was whether an employee, who was terminated and who had repeatedly verbally threatened physical violence against co-workers and supervisors in the workplace, could maintain an ADA claim based upon his mental condition which he claimed caused his outbursts. The court, in analyzing the claim, held that it was not necessary to show the employee posed a "direct threat" to others, but rather, only demonstrate that its reasons for termination were legitimate and consistent with action taken against non-disabled employees for a similar infraction. As the court stated, quoting the *Palmer* decision, "The ADA does not require an employer to retain a potentially violent employee." [*Sista*, 445 F.3d at 172, quoting from Palmer v. Circuit Ct. of Cook Cnty., 117 F.3d 351 (7th Cir. 1997)]

Q 6:24   What is *criminal endangerment of employees*?

The stated purpose of Occupational Safety and Health Administration, OSHA is to ensure safe and healthful working conditions to workers and to preserve the nation's human resources. It is a comprehensive and complex regulatory body of law, designed primarily to prevent injuries in the workplace. OSHA authorizes and encourages the promulgation of safety standards and the issuance of citations, in order to prevent deaths or injuries from occurring.

OSHA has several levels of penalties, depending on the type of violation. Violations are categorized as serious, repeated, willful, criminally willful, and "other." Violations designated as "other" are essentially inconsequential. Serious violations bring a $1,000 fine per occurrence. Repeated and willful violations are on a par with one another and can bring a fine as high as $10,000 per occurrence. Criminally willful violations involve the death of an employee and can result in prison terms for managers, as well as substantial fines.

Q 6:25   Do employers risk liability for negligent hiring?

An employer's concern with crime and safety does not stop with protecting the employer's own property and proprietary information. An employer must protect its employees, business visitors, and anyone with whom its workers come into contact on its behalf. Under some circumstances, an employee's crime can become a company's crime.

The following is an example of an employer who was liable for negligent hiring. The owners of an apartment building hired a maintenance man who had recently been released from a state mental hospital, where he had been treated for about a month. Shortly after he was hired, the maintenance man sexually assaulted a female tenant. She sued the owners, arguing that they "knew, or should have known, that the employee possessed dangerous, immoral and perverted propensities." The jury awarded the tenant $175,000 against the landlord-owners. [Heifetz v. Philadelphia State Hosp., 482 Pa. 386, 393 A.2d 1160 (1978)] This case illustrates that the law expects an employer to maintain a safe workplace not only for its employees, but also for all who may come on the premises. In *Woods v. Town of Danville, West Virginia* [712 F. Supp. 2d 502 (S.D. W.Va. 2010)], the court refused to dismiss a negligent retention claim against a town involving the actions of a police officer when it was demonstrated that the police officer who had only been on the job for eight days and was given minimal training, had a history of a propensity towards anger, a spotty employment history, and an other than honorable discharge from the Navy.

In *Hobirn, Inc. v. Aerotek, Inc.* [787 F. Supp. 2d 1298 (S.D. Fla. 2011)], a company hired an employee from a provider of contract employees and sued the provider for negligent hiring for losses suffered due to theft by the employee referred to the company. The company that provided contract employees to the plaintiff employer acted pursuant to a service agreement that required background checks of referred employees, which the provider company did not perform. Since, had the provider conducted a background criminal search, it would have found that the referred employee had an extensive criminal background, including convictions for theft, the court concluded that the plaintiff properly stated a claim for negligent hiring.

Q 6:26   Can an employer be held liable for the crime of a third party against an employee?

Typically, employers are required to carry workers' compensation insurance, which, in return for the ease with which injured employees can obtain benefits, provides the employer immunity from suit. For example, if a retail clerk is the victim of a violent robbery and later sues the robber, the employer-retailer cannot be joined as a defendant either by the employee or the thief.

Q 6:27   What are some widely recognized techniques for preventing robberies?

Corporations have developed many techniques for guarding against robbery as a source of resource loss and endangerment of employees.

Discouraging robberies and minimizing losses:

- The employer should keep the cash on hand (in registers, cash drawers, and the like) to a minimum—$50 during daylight hours and even less if the establishment is open after dark (frequent bank deposits or cash-control safes are the preferred methods of accomplishing this goal).
- If there is a safe on the business premises, it should be locked at all times, even though this can entail some minor inconvenience and inefficiency.
- Employees should acknowledge every customer of the business, as well as vendors, as they enter the establishment. They should make eye contact to let the person know that the employee is alert and could identify the visitor to police later on.
- The employer should keep its establishment well lit after dusk, keep back rooms and warehouse areas well-illuminated at all times, and keep the front windows and sales counters of retail establishments unobstructed from outside view, such as that of passing police cruisers.
- In retail establishments, clerks should not stay behind their counters but should circulate around the store, cleaning and straightening up inventory and appearing active and alert.
- Employees should be instructed to watch for and report suspicious activities.
- The company should advertise its security procedures (e.g., decals on doors and signs in parking areas notifying visitors that security systems are in place and public relations efforts to tell the general public through the news media that the company cares about and invests in employee safety and security).
- The employer should train employees, and retrain them regularly, on security procedures.

Reacting to a robbery:

- The employee should cooperate and try to remain calm.
- The employee should make no sudden moves or unusual hand gestures.

- Any movements the employee must make should be explained to the robber in a calm voice (e.g., "I'm getting a bag in which to put the money").

- If more than one employee is on the premises but only one is visible at the time, that employee should advise the robber of the presence of the other employee.

- The employee should activate an alarm only if that can be done safely. Usually it is preferable to press the alarm button or dial 911 after the robber has left (if only a pay phone is available, a quarter should be kept taped to the bottom of the phone for this purpose).

- The employee should try to get a good look at the robber without staring.

- The employee should also try to recall the type, color, and license number of the criminal's vehicle, if the robber used a car.

- As the car departs from the premises, the employee should note the direction of travel away from the scene.

- If the robber shows a weapon, the employee should note, at least in general, the type of weapon.

Procedure after a robbery:

- The employee should lock the door of the store, warehouse, or other facility having been robbed.

- The employee should call the police. Even if there is an alarm, if it has not been activated yet and a phone is available, it is preferable to call the police and give some details over the telephone.

- The employee should call an appropriate company manager. If that person is unavailable, the employee should keep calling until a corporate official is reached.

- The employee or corporate officials on hand should keep people from disturbing areas where the criminal may have left fingerprints or other clues that may help the police to apprehend the robber.

- The company should cooperate fully with the police.

- The company should not disclose the amount of money or what other property was stolen except to the police and company management.

Computer Security

Q 6:28   Is computer crime perpetrated by employees a major problem for businesses?

Like all significant technological advances, the computer has created new opportunities for criminals, vandals, and unethical employees. Piracy of computer software, use of computers for embezzlement, malicious insertion of a computer virus, and theft of trade secrets stored in computer memories are a few of these crimes. Some crimes, like the illegal use of unlicensed software, are catching a growing number of employers whose employees, often innocently, copy the unlicensed software onto company computers. [*See* 30 Bottom Line Business, Vol. 2 at 6 (*Boardroom, Inc.*, Feb. 2001).]

Q 6:29   What are some ways to prevent computer crime?

Computer security experts recommend the following steps to prevent computer crime:

Formulate a written policy for responsible computer use. Some companies allow personal use; most do not. Employees need to know what they may and may not do on their office computers. Discipline for misuse should be addressed, so that the consequences of computer misuse are clear (e.g., "violations may result in discipline, up to and including discharge").

Notify employees that the company reserves the right to retrieve, monitor, or review any and all information contained in their computers, e-mail, or other forms of electronic communication. This notification helps to protect against privacy claims of intrusion into private and personal matters.

Train employees and, as far as possible, provide them with user-friendly software programs. Some employee sabotage stems from frustration.

Institute a clean desk policy. Employees should not leave disks and tapes lying around on their desks or elsewhere in the office.

Test the computer system regularly. It is too late when a large loss shows up.

Restrict access, distribution, and off-site use of hard copy. If, for instance, hard copies of customer lists are allowed to float freely around the office, an employee who walks out with one in his or her briefcase may later maintain that this information was not treated with the confidentiality expected of a trade secret.

Copyright

Q 6:30   Are there information technology experts who can assist employers in developing security measures to prevent computer crimes?

Businesses are increasingly dependent upon their information systems, subjecting them to potentially devastating loss if those systems are compromised or sabotaged. To help establish suitable protections, informational technology experts/consultants can assist companies in establishing security procedures with their informational technology systems to reduce the risk of compromise and reduce loss if the systems are compromised. Generally, a review begins with an audit of the information systems, the availability for access to the systems, and current security procedures to ascertain what can be done to enhance security.

Q 6:31   What are copyright laws?

Copyright is governed by federal statute. [17 U.S.C. §§ 101 *et seq.*] Trade secrets are protected by state law—frequently common law, rather than statutory. [*See, e.g.*, Uniform Trade Secrets Act; for discussions of common law protection of trade secrets and the difference between a trade secret and common law copyrights, *see* Brignoli v. Balch Hardy & Scheinman, Inc., 645 F. Supp. 1201 (S.D.N.Y. 1986); Warrington Assocs., Inc. v. Real-Time Eng'g Sys., Inc., 522 F. Supp. 367 (N.D. Ill. 1981); Data Mgmt. v. Greene, 757 P.2d 62 (Alaska 1988).] Because software companies make a tremendous investment in developing a software package, they want all the protection they can get from both federal and state sources. Their problem lies in the fact that federal law usually pre-empts or supersedes state law. Thus, it is questionable whether a software company can copyright a package and then get the additional protection that might be available under the common law of trade secrets.

At least one aspect of this concern has been put to rest. In *Warrington Associates, Inc. v. Real-Time Engineering Systems, Inc.* [522 F. Supp. 367 (N.D. Ill. 1981)], the court differentiated what federal copyright law protects from what state trade secret law shields from disclosure, noting that an analysis of the interests secured by copyright and trade secret law made it clear that the two claims are not equivalent.

Copyright protection extends to the way an author expresses an idea. In contrast, the protection provided by the common law of trade secret misappropriation extends to the very ideas of the author, subject to the requirement that the ideas have some originality and are as yet undisclosed or disclosed only on the basis of confidentiality.

Q 6:32   What is a *work for hire*?

Ordinarily, whenever an author expresses an idea, the expression, but not the underlying idea, is automatically and immediately accorded copyright protection. The author can enhance this protection by registering the work with the U.S. Copyright Office. Virtually any sort of written work or computer program can be copyrighted, including sales brochures, employee handbooks, and instruction manuals for a company's products. Obviously, when a company's employees produce these works in the normal course of their employment, neither employer nor employee intends for the copyright protection to descend upon the employee, albeit that employee is the author. Similarly, when companies turn to outsourcing (e.g., hiring consultants, computer programmers, systems analysts, and other independent contractors to author software works), the intent of the parties is usually that the copyright on the finished product will belong to the company that is paying the contractor to perform the work.

Both of these situations are provided for under the federal Copyright Act. [17 U.S.C. § 101] Under this law, a *work made for hire* is defined as either a work created by an employee within the scope of employment or a work ordered or commissioned under the terms of a written agreement that expressly identifies the project as a work for hire. Whether or not an employee has created a work within the scope of employment is determined within the parameters of the common law definition of that term.

The term *course of employment* comes up in many contexts. For example, it has been defined as "[a] requirement that to be eligible for worker's compensation benefits, an employee must have been injured while serving the employer's business." [Cihon & Castagnera, *Labor and Employment Law* 626 (1992)] What the employer's business is and when the employee ceases to serve it are additional concerns. For instance, a computer programmer hacks around at home and develops a software program that would be of value to his or her employer. If it had been developed between 9:00 a.m. and 5:00 p.m., it would clearly constitute work for hire, but if the programmer is paid a salary and sometimes works overtime hours without additional compensation, should the program developed at home belong to the company? Obviously the employee will argue that it was done during free time and may even assert that the PC belongs to him or her and that copyright resides with him or her as well. The corporation is therefore well-advised to deal with such eventualities with express terms contained in an employment contract or a handbook, the terms of which are acknowledged by each employee receiving a copy.

Q 6:33   What is the statutory definition of a *work made for hire*?

Section 101 of the federal Copyright Act [17 U.S.C. § 101] defines a *work made for hire* as:

> (1) a work prepared by an employee within the scope of his or her employment; or (2) a work especially ordered or commissioned for use as a contribution to a collective work, as part of a motion picture or other audiovisual work, as a translation, as a supplementary work, as a compilation, as an instructional text, as a test, as answer material for a test, or as an atlas, if the parties expressly agree in a written instrument signed by them that the work shall be considered a work made for hire.

Q 6:34   Can an independent contractor be treated as an employee with respect to a work made for hire under the auspices of the federal Copyright Act?

Cases interpreting Section 101 of the Copyright Act have tended to blur the distinction between employer and independent contractor with regard to works made for hire. In fact, a leading federal case has held that an independent contractor is an employee for purposes of the employer's ownership of the copyright, when the independent contractor's work has been supervised by the commissioning party (i.e., the purported employer). [Aldon Accessories Ltd. v. Spiegel Inc., 738 F.2d 548 (2d Cir.), *cert. denied*, 469 U.S. 982 (1984)]

Trade Secrets and Confidentiality Agreements

Q 6:35 What is a *trade secret*?

The term *trade secret* has been given a broad meaning in common law. As defined by the case law and sometimes the statutory law of most jurisdictions, a *trade secret* is almost any piece of unique proprietary information possessed by a company that is useful in competing against other firms in the same industry or business. Section 1(4) of the Uniform Trade Secrets Act, adopted by a number of states, gives this definition:

> "Trade Secret" shall mean information including a formula, pattern, compilation, program, device, method, technique or process, that: (i) derives independent economic value, actual or potential, from not being generally known to, and not being readily ascertainable by proper means, by other persons who can obtain economic value from its disclosure or use; and (ii) is the subject of efforts that are reasonable under the circumstances to maintain its secrecy.

The Michigan Supreme Court, in *Hayes-Albion Corp. v. Kuberski*, defined a *trade secret* as:

> A secret formula or process not patented but known only to certain individuals using it in compounding some article of trade having a commercial value [but the term] does not denote the mere privacy with which an ordinary commercial business is carried on. [421 Mich. 170, 181 (1984)]

Quoting from the Restatement of Torts, Section 757, *Hayes* adopted the following definition of a *trade secret*:

> A trade secret may consist of any formula, pattern, device or compilation of information that is used in one's business and which gives [him] an opportunity to obtain an advantage over competitors who do not know it or use it. It may be a formula for a chemical compound, a process of manufacturing, treating or preserving materials, a pattern for a machine or device, or a list of customers. [421 Mich. 170 at 181]

Various factors are considered in determining whether particular information is a trade secret, including the following:

- The extent to which the information is known outside of the employer's business;
- The extent to which the information it is known by employees and others involved in the employer's business;
- The extent of measures taken by the employer to guard the secrecy of the information;
- The value of the information to the employer and the employer's competitors;
- The amount of effort or money expended in developing the information; and

- The ease or difficulty with which the information could be properly acquired or duplicated by others. [421 Mich. 170 at 182]

A trade secret does not have to be so unique that it can be patented. On the contrary, trade secrets usually are not patentable but are sufficiently unique to the processor that even reverse engineering or other types of careful investigation cannot reveal the secret process or procedure to competitors. Some patentable trade secrets, such as certain soft drink formulas, were never patented by the holders because they did not want the process or formula to become a part of the public domain when the patent expired.

Clearly, in order for a court to provide trade secret protection, the product, process, formula, or information must be secret and treated as such by the employer. Each of the factors listed, when carefully considered, bear on whether something is really secret and whether it is considered by the employer as such. For example, if it is truly secret, the employer will not share the product, process, formula, list, etc. with anyone even within his or her own company except those who absolutely need to know in order for the business to function. Even then, it will likely only be shared in strict confidence or pursuant to a confidentiality or non-disclosure agreement.

Under the Federal Economic Espionage Act (18 U.S.C. § 1831), which makes it a federal crime to steal trade secrets, a *trade secret* is defined as follows:

> The term "trade secret" means all forms and types of financial, business, scientific, technical, economic, or engineering information, including patterns, plans, compilations, program devices, formulas, designs, prototypes, methods, techniques, processes, procedures, programs, or codes, whether tangible or intangible, and whether or how stored, compiled, or memorialized, physically, electronically, graphically, photographically, or in writing if: The owner thereof has taken reasonable measures to keep such information secret; and the information derives independent economic value, actual or potential, from not being generally known to, and not being readily ascertainable through proper means by, the public. [18 U.S.C. § 1839]

Q 6:36   How do courts determine whether information is a protectable trade secret?

The determination of whether information constitutes a trade secret is a fact-intensive analysis made by courts on a case-by-case basis. For example, in *American Home Shield of California, Inc. v. Fidelity Home Warranty Co.* [2003 Cal. App. Unpub. LEXIS 4743 (4th Dist. 2003)], a company in the home warranty business sued a competitor and former employees for violation of non-compete agreements and unfair competition in using various customer lists the former employees allegedly took from their prior employer. After concluding that the non-competition agreements were unenforceable under California law by prohibiting the former employees from soliciting business from their prior employer's customers after leaving its employment, the court focused on whether the customer lists the former employees took from their former employer constituted trade secrets and confidential information for which they can be liable for misappropriation and unfair competition. In analyzing the lists, the court concluded that all the information was obtained from public sources, was equally available to competitors, and was not a preferred or specially created list maintained or prepared by the prior employer and, as such, did not constitute protectable trade secrets under California law.

In *Storage Technology Corp. v. Cisco Systems, Inc.* [2003 U.S. Dist. LEXIS 174347 (D. Minn. Sept. 25, 2003)], various employees had left Storage Technology to form a competing company that was ultimately acquired by Cisco Systems. Storage Technologies alleged, among other things, that the employees had stolen various trade secrets from the company to be utilized in connection with their current employment. Both companies are technology companies involved in storage networking. Reviewing the alleged trade secret at issue, the court concluded that because the information was generally known or generally ascertainable, and Storage Technology did not derive any independent economic value from its secrecy in that it was never brought to market, the company could not maintain any claim for trade secrets violation under Minnesota's Uniform Trade Secret Laws.

Q 6:37   Is a customer list a trade secret?

A customer list can constitute a trade secret. In fact, the confidentiality of customer lists is at the heart of most trade secret lawsuits brought when an employee moves from one firm to a competitor. To be a trade secret, a customer list must contain information (e.g., renewal dates of insurance policies, customer requirements, and unusual pricing arrangements) that could not be ascertained from public records, such as telephone books or Dun & Bradstreet reports. The possessor of these trade secrets must also take reasonable steps to maintain secrecy, for example, making computer printouts available to employees on a need-to-know basis, with no access provided to salespeople, brokers, or to customers or clients not serviced by those employees. In *Lighthouse Worldwide Solutions, Inc. v. Giandomencio* [2008 WL 256974 (Cal. App. Jan. 31, 2008)], the court held that a customer list was a trade secret even though the ex-employee claimed that it was common knowledge, which companies might need particular types of the company's product and the company had listed some of its customers on its Web site. The trial court found that the company had taken steps to keep the list secret and it had independent economic value because it would take some effort to compile. In *Majestic Marketing, Inc. v. Nay* [2010 WL 338966 (Cal. Super. Ct. Jan. 29, 2010)], the court held that customer lists containing the names of customers that did business with the company over a period of two years was a trade secret and a covenant not to compete was enforceable to enjoin the former employee's use of such trade secret information. Similarly, in *Airport Commuter Limousine and Sedan Service, Inc. v. Albazian* [2009 WL 1588210 (Cal. Super. Ct. June 8, 2009)], the court held that airport commuter customer information maintained by a limousine service company was a protectable trade secret supporting an adverse verdict against former employees and an injunction pursuant to a non-compete agreement contained within the former employees' employment agreements. However, if the customer information is readily obtainable from other sources, the information may not be a trade secret. In *System Development Systems, Inc. v. Haarmann* [907 N.E.2d 63 (Ill. App. Ct. 2009)], the court held that customer lists maintained by an employer in a rural county were not trade secrets where the information was readily available from other sources in this close-knit rural community. In *Alpha School Bus Co., Inc. v. Wagner* [910 N.E.2d 1134 (Ill. App. Ct. 2009)], the court held that information regarding a school bus contract and bid dates were publicly available and as such, not trade secrets. In *Andreini & Co. v. MacCorkle Insurance Services, Inc.* [2011 WL 140194 (Cal. App. 1st Dist. Jan. 14, 2011)], the court held that client lists that an insurance broker brought to his new employer did not constitute trade secrets when the clients were brought by the insurance broker to his former employer and non-competition agreements which the insurance broker entered into with his former employer specifically carved out such clients. As such, no claims could be maintained for misappropriation of trade secrets against the insurance broker or the insurance broker's new employer.

Q 6:38 How can a company protect its trade secrets?

A company that wants the law to protect its proprietary information must undertake steps to preserve the confidentiality of its trade secrets. With the proliferation of personal computers, many companies permit their employees wide access to programs or data stored in corporate systems. The wiser course is to limit some employees' access to certain programs (e.g., customer lists) or to bar their access altogether. Similarly, if the trade secret is a formula or process, only a limited number of employees should have access to it. Some companies have even gone so far as to give individual employees only a piece of the total puzzle.

Confidentiality agreements, which prevent the use or disclosure of trade secrets except in connection with the company's business, are critical for any business concerned with protecting trade secrets. Failure to have such agreements can undermine an employer's claims that the information under dispute is a legally protected trade secret.

As discussed above, one method used by many courts to determine whether trade secret protection exists is to analyze the measures used by the employer to guard the secrecy of the information. A trade secret can be lost if the company does not treat the information as confidential, as it relates to its employees, visitors, and outside parties. As a result, companies that utilize trade secrets in order to compete successfully with their competitors are strongly advised to require that employees that become aware of such information sign confidentiality agreements as a condition of continued employment.

Q 6:39   What are the elements of a confidentiality agreement?

Confidentiality agreements vary greatly depending upon the particular needs of the client and the nature of the business at issue. Such agreements generally seek to preserve the company's proprietary information and prevent an employee from using it in unfair competition with the employer, either during or after employment. There are general categories of issues to be considered in the development of confidentiality agreements, including the following:

Access to trade secrets. Confidentiality agreements generally underscore the existence of trade secrets by stating that the company has developed and created trade secrets that, by virtue of the employee's employment, will be exposed to the employee in the performance of his or her duties. In essence, these provisions lay the foundation for trade secret protection to legitimize the agreement and assist in its future enforcement in court.

Definition of trade secrets. The agreement should contain a specific definition of trade secrets, listing those items the company deems to be trade secrets and confidential. Although fairly generic definitions have been utilized, companies should ensure that the list contains any particular items of great sensitivity, such as specific computer programs, formulas, or production matter. A common definition for *confidential information* follows:

> Information not generally known about the company or any of the its customers or potential customers that is disclosed or becomes known to the employee as a consequence of or through his or her employment activities including, but not limited to, matters of a technical nature, know-how, inventions, innovations, discoveries, production methods; matters of a business nature, such as information about costs, profits, markets, sales, business processes, computer programs, accounting methods, accounting systems, and business and financial plans and reports; and information concerning customers, including customer lists, customer information, and customer needs; and any other information that the company considers or treats as a trade secret, confidential or proprietary information.

Non-disclosure and non-use. Confidentiality agreements prohibit the employee from directly or indirectly disclosing or using any of the employer's trade secrets or confidential information, either during the employee's employment or at any time thereafter, except in connection with the company's business. Both use and disclosure must be covered to protect confidential information adequately.

Exclusive property of the employer/assignment of patents and inventions. Most confidentiality agreements provide that ideas, inventions, or discoveries an employee makes, either while working for the employer or developed after hours to the extent that the information was derived from any information obtained during the employment, are the sole and exclusive property of the employer, and that the employee waives any rights or claims in connection therewith. For companies involved in research and development, confidentiality agreements often contain specific and detailed assignments of patents and trademarks with respect to any and all inventions, discoveries, or ideas made by the employee under similar circumstances. These provisions also typically require that an employee notify the employer of any such inventions, discoveries or ideas when made, to prevent an employee from making discoveries or inventions on company time and (rather than disclosing the information to the employer) quitting employment and using this information in competition with the employer.

Return of confidential information upon termination. Most confidentiality agreements provide that employees are obligated to return all confidential information to the employer when terminating employment. In addition, the return obligation should extend to any and all copies, transcripts, or extracts of any of the confidential information.

Injunctive relief. Generally, most agreements provide for the imposition of injunctive relief upon a breach or threatened breach by the employee. To obtain injunctive relief, the employer must demonstrate irreparable injury; therefore, these provisions often provide language stating that the employee understands and acknowledges that a violation of the agreement would cause irreparable injury to the employer, setting up a foundation to obtain injunctive relief in court. In addition, these provisions typically provide that the employee is responsible for any and all attorneys' fees incurred by employer in connection with obtaining injunctive relief.

Q 6:40   How has the developing case law dealt with employers trying to protect their trade secrets?

Developing common law indicates that what courts protect as legitimate trade secrets depends not only upon how carefully the company strives to guard against misappropriation, but also (particularly in cases concerning employees who cannot help being exposed to proprietary information in their day-to-day employment activities) the culpability of the defendant accused of stealing information. When the confidential information can be developed from independent sources (albeit only through an investment of time and energy) and when the departing employee cannot help remembering information, a judge is less likely to prevent the defendant from using that knowledge for his or her own or a new employer's benefit. For example, in *Professional Staffing Group v. Champigny* [2004 Mass. Super. LEXIS 597 (Mass. Super. Ct. Nov. 17, 2004)], a professional staffing company alleged that a former employee had violated a non-disclosure clause that permanently and indefinitely required the employee to not disclose any of the identities of the former employer's customers at any time. Under its literal terms, the court concluded, no former employee could ever contact any known customer of the professional staffing company. In the case, drew upon her memory of old customers of the former employer to compete with her former employer after the one-year non-competition clause expired. Under Massachusetts law, the court reasoned, employees may be permitted to take their memory, but not a tangible record of confidential customer identities acquired in the course of employment. Furthermore, the court reasoned, the former employee's memory of the professional staffing company's customers is unlikely to be proprietary information entitled to perpetual protection. As such, the court concluded that the former employee's lawsuit was of doubtful merit and the defendant's counter-claim that the professional staffing company's lawsuit was instituted for the sole motive of tortiously interfering with the new company's contractual relationships with its customers could proceed. In *Rapid Temps, Inc. v. Lamon* [144 NM 804 (Ct. App. 2008)], the court held that an employer provided sufficient evidence to establish that the client database maintained by its former employee while employed was a trade secret such that a valid claim of misappropriation could be maintained based upon sufficient evidence demonstrating that the employee took the information for use in competition with her former employer.

Non-Competition Agreements

Q 6:41   What is a *non-compete agreement*?

Non-compete or *non-competition agreements* usually contained within employment agreements contain provisions that prevent the employee from competing with the employer during the term of the relationship and for a reasonable time thereafter. Non-compete agreements should be written in a manner most likely to be enforceable in accordance with state law. States vary on their rules to determine the enforceability of non-competition covenants, many contain express statutory requirements for enforceability and state law should be examined to draft the agreement in accordance with the state's requirements. [*See* Filipp, *Covenants Not To Compete*, 3d edition (Aspen Publishers, Inc. 2005).] Although variations exist from state to state, such agreements are generally enforceable, provided they are ancillary to another agreement (such as an employment agreement), are reasonably calculated to prevent unfair competition, are reasonably limited both as to duration and scope, and supported by valid consideration. If the clause is unreasonable, the non-compete provision will typically not be enforced as written. Instead, in some jurisdictions, the non-compete provision is read down by the court to reasonable limits as to duration and scope. In others, so-called blue-pencil jurisdictions, courts strike unreasonable provisions and determine if the remaining portions can be enforced. Generally, the non-compete clause should not be so expansive as to prevent an employee from earning a livelihood after termination of employment. Typically, non-compete clauses include a preamble highlighting the basis and reason for them, and provide that throughout the restrictive term, the employee will not, directly or indirectly, on his or her own behalf or on behalf of any other business enterprise, conduct business in competition with the employer. The provision will usually define *competition* as the performance of services or business similar to the services or business of the employer for a specific period of time within a designated territory surrounding the employer's business.

Following is a sample non-compete covenant contained within an employment agreement:

Non-Competition: In consideration of the terms and conditions of this Employment Agreement and other good and valuable consideration, including, but not limited to, the provision of training, facilities, client contracts, and experience by Employer, the receipt of which is hereby acknowledged, Employer and Employee freely choose to include this non-compete clause as part of this Agreement. Employer and Employee agree and recognize that this clause is necessary to protect the business and goodwill of Employer. Employee covenants and agrees that during the term of this Agreement and for a period of six (6) months following the termination of Employee's employment, Employee will not, either directly or indirectly, engage in, or acquire an interest in (as an individual, partner, stockholder, director, officer, principal, agent, employee, lender of money, or in any relation or capacity whatsoever) any business that is competitive with the business of Employer. A business shall be deemed competitive for purposes of this provision if it performs services or conducts business similar to the services and business of the Employer and is conducted within thirty (30) miles of Employer's business (the "Covenant Area"). Employer and Employee recognize, acknowledge, and agree that the territorial limitation barring Employee from competing with Employer within the Covenant Area is reasonable because Employer provides the majority of its services to clients residing in the Covenant Area and this geographical restriction is necessary to protect Employer's business and goodwill. Employer and Employee recognize, acknowledge, and agree that the duration limitation provided herein is reasonable because of the time it will take to train an Employee to perform the same services as are being performed by Employee on Employer's behalf and that this duration restriction is necessary to protect Employer's business and goodwill. Employee acknowledges and agrees that Employee will still be able to earn a livelihood after termination of employment, despite this restriction.

Employee acknowledges and agrees that a violation of this provision will cause irreparable injury to Employer, and, in addition to any other remedies under applicable law, Employer may seek injunctive relief to prevent a threatened or continuing breach of this Agreement, and Employee shall pay all costs and attorneys' fees incurred by Employer in connection therewith.

If any court of competent jurisdiction determines that the scope described is unenforceable as to scope or duration, then such court shall reform such provision to the maximum extent permitted by applicable law.

This sample non-compete clause prohibits the employee from engaging in a competitive business, limited geographically to the covenant area. Another type of limitation, although not limited by a geographic area, focuses on prohibiting the employee from doing business with clients of the employer for a reasonable duration after separation of the employment relationship.

Q 6:42   Are non-competition agreements enforceable?

Subject to variations from state to state (see Q 6:41), non-competition agreements are generally enforceable provided they are ancillary to another agreement (like an employment agreement) and if they are sufficiently limited as to scope and duration to prevent unfair competition. However, the determination of what is and what isn't reasonable in any situation depends upon the facts of each particular case. For example, in *Frontier Corp. v. Telco Communications Group, Inc.* [965 F. Supp. 1200, 1209 (S.D. Ind. 1977)], the court stated that "a customer limitation applied to customers to whom a former employee had no contact does not protect an employer's reasonable competitive interests." The *Frontier* court specifically concluded that where a former employee is competing through cold-calling and having no way of knowing if a potential customer belongs to her former employer, she would be permitted to sell to that customer "without using either the goodwill or confidential information of her former employer." In *Gordon Document Productions, Inc. v. Service Technologies, Inc.* [308 Ga. App. 445 (2011)], territorial restrictions contained within a covenant not to compete that included counties that the employees did not perform services was overbroad and unenforceable. In addition, general knowledge and skill that an employee acquires or develops through his employment may not be subject to the restraining covenant. As the court stated in *Kelsey-Hayes Co. v. Maleki* [765 F. Supp. 402, 406–07 (E.D. Mich. 1991)]:

> It has been uniformly held that general knowledge, skill or facility acquired through training or experience while working for an employer can pertain exclusively to the employee. The fact that they were acquired or developed during the employment does not, by itself, give the employer sufficient interest to support a restraining covenant, even though on-the-job training has been extensive and costly.

Furthermore, courts are not inclined to construe restrictive non-competition covenants liberally. As the court stated in *RAM Products Co. v. Chauncey* [967 F. Supp. 1071, 1091 (N.D. Ind. 1997)], it is well-settled that the language of contracts must be strictly construed against the interest of the drafter. As a result, in considering narrow construction rules, great care needs to be taken in drafting restrictive covenants and interpreting them as to their enforceability. In *Zupnik v. All Florida Paper, Inc.* [997 So. 2d 1234 (Fla. Dist. Ct. App. 3d 2009)], at issue was whether a covenant not to compete contained within a two-year employment contract commenced when the employment contract, by its terms, expired or when the employee's employment terminated two years after the expiration of the written agreement. The non-competition language included a 12-month restriction after termination of the employment agreement's term. Construing the restriction strictly, the court concluded that the restrictions ended after three years of employment (12 months after the expiration of the contract) and could not be used to prevent the former employee from competing roughly four years after the initial two-year contract term.

Q 6:43   If a restrictive non-competition covenant is enforceable, how is the court likely to enforce it?

If the covenant is enforceable, there are a number of different ways the court may be asked to enforce the terms of it—the most important is injunctive relief. Injunctive relief is contained within an order that essentially mirrors the restrictive provisions of the covenant and states that any violation would be contempt of court. Injunctive relief would typically come after a trial which, in a typical case, would be about one year after the case has started. This is not adequate for many employers and they seek to obtain what is called preliminary injunctive relief, which is injunctive relief during the pendency of the litigation. However, preliminary injunctive relief, before a trial on its merits, is difficult to obtain and generally the employer has to demonstrate the following:

- A likelihood of success and merits;
- That the failure to award preliminary injunctive relief would result in irreparable harm—harm that cannot be remedied through compensatory damages;
- The harm to the employer if a preliminary injunction is not entered far exceeds any possible harm to the employee if the injunction is issued; and
- Public interest should be served with the issuance of the injunction.

In addition to preliminary injunctive relief and so-called permanent injunctive relief, after trial, the court will also entertain claims for monetary damages, which would be lost business attributable to activities in violation of the non-competition provision.

Q 6:44　　How do courts determine whether a restriction is reasonable?

The determination of whether a non-competition restriction is reasonable is a factually intensive analysis made on a case-by-case basis under state law. In *Singh v. Batta Environmental Associates, Inc.* [2003 Del. Ch. LEXIS 59 (Del. Ch. Ct. May 21, 2003)], the court found that a two-year non-competition provision that prevented the former employee from competing within a 200-mile restriction was reasonable and enforceable: The time period was reasonable because it tracked the normal life cycle of the projects in which the employer was involved, and the 200-mile restriction was reasonable because it was tailored to include the area in which most of the employer's clients were located. In *Webster Bank v. Ludwin* [2011 WL 522050 (Conn. Super. Ct. Jan. 6, 2011)], the court held that a non-competition provision contained within the employment contract with a previous employer that prevented the employee from engaging in competition within a 25-mile radius of the employer or soliciting customers, was reasonable and supported the imposition of a temporary restraining order. In *Timber Lake Foods, Inc. v. Estess* [72 So. 3d 521 (Miss. Ct. App. 2011)], although the court noted that the geographic restriction of 250 miles was arbitrarily set by the employer, it was not unreasonable because the employer's market was large enough to support an even greater geographic territory subject to the restriction.

In *Pathfinder Communications Corp. v. Macey* [795 N.E.2d 1103 (Ind. App. 2003)], a disk jockey's prior employer sought enforcement of a non-competition agreement that, if read literally, would prevent the former employee from engaging in any work at various competing radio stations listed in the covenant. Although the court agreed that this restriction was overly broad, extending beyond the radio station's legitimate interests in preventing unfair competition, nonetheless, if the overly broad language contained within the restrictive covenant prohibiting the former employee from "engaging in activities" was deleted, the resulting language was sufficiently limited to render the covenant enforceable.

In *Bruce D. Graham, M.D., PA v. Cirocco, M.D.* [31 Kan. App. 2d 563, 69 P.2d 194 (2003)], a former physician of the employer had signed a non-competition agreement that provided that for a period of two years after the separation of employment, the physician would not solicit business within 150 miles of each of the employer's offices where the physician practiced and that the physician would not open an office for practice within a 25-mile radius of various hospitals, essentially prohibiting him from practicing in the entire metropolitan area. Reviewing the covenants at issue, the court found that the 150-mile non-solicitation provision was reasonable, but that the restrictions essentially barring him from practicing in the entire metropolitan area were excessive and unreasonable. However, in *Mercy Health System of Northwest Arkansas, Inc. v. Bicak, M.D.* [2011 Ark. App. 341 (2011)], the court held that a covenant contained within a covenant not to compete that restricted a physician from engaging in the practice of medicine within 18 miles of a hospital was unreasonably broad and greater than was necessary to protect the hospital from unfair competition and, as such, was unenforceable.

In *Comtech International Design Group v. Price* [2003 Mich. App. LEXIS 1275 (Mich. Ct. App. May 27, 2003)], an employee was subject to a preliminary injunction preventing her from violating a non-competition clause that prohibited her from working with any competitor within a 50-mile radius of the office or areas she was assigned to while working at the employer's office. Although she initially worked in competition with her prior employer at offices of a company located within the 50-mile range, she was later transferred by her subsequent employer to Florida, well outside the 50-mile radius. The trial court held that because her subsequent employer had an office within the 50-mile radius, she could not work for any other office of her employer, even outside the 50-mile range. On appeal, however, the court held that such an interpretation was too broad and would effectively bar the employee from working with her new company at any location in the world, clearly outside of what would be reasonable to protect her prior employer from unfair competition. [Quality Liquid Feeds, Inc. v. Plunkett, 89 Ark. App. 16 (Ark. Ct. App. 2004)] In *Team 1A, Inc., v. Lucas* [395 S.C. 237 (Ct. App. 2011)], the Supreme Court of South Carolina held that a nationwide territorial restriction is overly broad on its face under South Carolina law.

In *Quality Liquid Feeds, Inc. v. Plunkett* [89 Ark. App. 16 (2004)], a feed supplier to the cattle and dairy industries sought to enforce a two-year non-competition agreement with one of its former district sales managers. In the case, the court reiterated Arkansas' general principle that for a covenant to be enforced under Arkansas law, three requirements must be met: (1) the covenantee must have a valid interest to protect; (2) the geographical restriction must not be overly broad; and (3) a reasonable time limit must be imposed.

Recognizing that under Arkansas law the restraints imposed by the covenant must not be broader than necessary to protect the covenantee's interests, the court upheld the lower court's determination that the above restriction was overly broad and unreasonable. Specifically, the court found that although protecting a principal's desire that a former employee not appropriate its customers is a protectable interest, the court found that the former employee had done nothing other than sell liquid feed since he graduated high school, that much of the customer information was either known by the former employee before he worked for the employer or could otherwise be compiled from general information, and the restriction would have a severe impact on the former employee's ability to earn a living.

In *Mowery Clinic, LLC v. Hofer, M.D.* [122 P.3d 838 (Kan. App. 2005)], the court held that a restriction that prevented a physician from engaging in any medical services within a defined area was unenforceable as written as there was no evidence the physician was in actual competition with his former employer. Similarly, in *Sharvelle, M.D. P.C. v. Magnante, M.D.* [2836 N.E. 432 (Ct. App. Ind. 2005)], the court held that a covenant restricting an ophthalmologist from practicing "health care of every kind and nature" for a two-year period following termination of employment was unreasonably broad and unenforceable. As it relates to non-competition agreements involving doctors, in *Intermountain Eye and Laser Centers, PLLC v. Miller, M.D.* [127 P.3d 121 (S. Ct. Ind. 2005)], the court acknowledged that restrictive covenants involving the doctor/patient relationship required greater scrutiny than restrictions contained in other types of agreements. In a departure from other jurisdictions, the Tennessee Supreme Court held, in *Murfreesboro Medical Clinic, PA v. Udom* [166 S.W.3d 674 (2005)], that covenants not to compete entered into by a private medical firm and a doctor violated Tennessee public policy and are unenforceable.

The issue of enforceability of covenants not to compete against physicians was addressed by the Illinois Supreme Court in *Mohanty v. St. John Heart Clinic, S.C.* [225 Ill. 2d 52 (Ill. 2006)] Although the court noted that some jurisdictions prohibit restrictive covenants in physician contracts on public policy grounds, the court determined that the majority of jurisdictions had adopted the "modern view" that generally restrictive covenants are enforceable, provided they are supported by consideration, ancillary to a lawful contract, and reasonable, and finding that the Illinois legislature had not spoken on the issue, refused to declare such restrictions a violation of Illinois public policy.

In *Weichert Co. of Pennsylvania v. Young* [2007 Del. Ch. LEXIS 170 (Del. Ch. Dec. 7, 2007)], the court held that a covenant that provided that a former real estate sales employee would not, for a period of two years and within a 25-mile radius of his former employer's business, solicit, hire, or retain employees of the former employer was reasonable and enforceable under Delaware law. [Cambridge Eng'g, Inc. v. Mercury Partners 90 BI, Inc., 378 Ill. App. 3d 437 (Ill. App. Ct. 1st Dist. 2007)]

In *Cambridge Engineering, Inc. v. Mercury Partners 90 BI, Inc.* [378 Ill. App. 3d 437 (Ill. App. Ct. 1st Dist. 2007)], the court held that a restrictive covenant contained within a covenant not to compete in the employment context was overly broad in that it contained all of Canada despite the fact that the former employee did not conduct business on behalf of the former employer in all of Canada's provinces. Moreover, the scope of activities prohibited was overly broad in that it restricted the former employee from obtaining any job with a competitor, and as such, was not reasonable with respect to post-employment activities prohibited by the covenant.

In *Glenn v. Dow Agrosciences, LLC* [861 N.E.2d 1 (Ind. Ct. App. 2007)], a restrictive covenant contained within a non-competition agreement executed in the employment context, which did not contain geographical limitations, was found to be unenforceable because it did not adequately limit the restrictive covenant in scope and application. In *Bunker Hill International, LTD v. Nations-builder Insurance Services, Inc.* [309 Ga. App. 503 (2011)], a Georgia court refused to enforce a restrictive covenant under Illinois law when the covenant, which contained no territorial limit, was void under Georgia law.

In *Coates v. Bastian Brothers, Inc.* [276 Mich. App. 498 (2007)], a one-year restriction preventing a former employee from engaging in a competing business within 100 miles under the terms of a non-competition clause in an employment contract was reasonable and enforceable.

In *Charles Penzone, Inc. v. Koster* [2008 Ohio 327 (Ohio Ct. App. Jan. 31, 2008)], a hairstylist's covenant not to compete with her former employer, which prohibited her from soliciting or rendering services to customers she serviced with her prior employer within a nine-mile radius of the salon, was reasonable.

In *Advanced Environmental Recycling Technologies, Inc. v. Advanced Control Solutions, Inc.* [372 Ark. 286 (2008)], the court held that a geographical restriction in a covenant not to compete covering the entire state of Arkansas was not overbroad when testimony revealed that although the employee's former company did not do business in the majority of Arkansas communities, it did do work throughout the state.

In *Webster Financial Corp. v. McDonald* [2009 WL 416059 (Conn. Super. Jan. 27, 2009)], the court denied defendant's motion to strike on grounds that the covenant was unreasonable because it contained a provision that allowed the restriction to continue against employee for as long as the employee continued to receive benefits under a deferred compensation plan. The court held that the covenant in this instance is not per se unreasonable simply because it could last for an unlimited duration. Covenant was also not overbroad in requiring ex-employee not to solicit from "potential clients" of his former firm, where that clause only referred to potential clients in the last 12 months of his employ.

In *Trujillo v. Great Southern Equipment Sales, LLC* [289 Ga. App. 474 (Ct. App. 2008)], the court held that a non-solicitation covenant restricting solicitation beyond those customers that the former employee had business dealings with during his employment which did not contain a geographic restriction is over broad, rendering the non-competition clause invalid.

In *Jorgensen v. Coppedge* [145 Idaho 534 (2008)], the court held that a covenant not to compete between a pharmacist and a pharmacy that applied as long as the pharmacy was involved in the business, was indefinite and therefore void and unenforceable because it contained no time limitation.

In *Mercho-Roushdi-Shoemaker-Dilly Thoraco–Vascular Corp. v. Blatchford* [900 N.E.2d 786 (Ind. Ct. App. 2009)], at issue was whether a non-competition agreement involving physicians were enforceable. Although, the Indiana Supreme Court in *Central Indiana Podiatry, P.C. v. Krueger* [882 N.E.2d 723 (Ind. 2008)], held that non-competition agreements between physicians and their employers are not per se illegal, the court nonetheless held that they must be construed strictly to ascertain, among other things, the effect of the agreements upon the public. In light of the evidence provided by the physicians in this case demonstrating that if the non-competition agreement was enforced, that it would have a negative impact on the ability of the residents in the surrounding community to have an adequate choice for cardiovascular surgeons, the court determined that the non-competition agreement at issue was unenforceable under Indiana law.

In *Wichita Clinic, PA v. Louis, DO* [39 Kan. App. 2d, 848 (Ct. App. 2008)], the court held that a three-year non-competition provision prohibiting a physician from practicing in the county of his former employer was valid and enforceable.

In *Fairfield County Bariatrics and Surgical Associates, P.C. v. Ehrlich* [2010 WL 1375397 (Conn. Super. Ct. Mar. 8, 2010)], the court held that a two-year non-competition agreement contained within a partnership agreement preventing a surgeon from engaging in his surgical specialty within a 15-mile radius of the partnership's office was reasonable and enforceable. However, in *Global Link Logistics, Inc. v. Briles* [674 S.E.2d 52 (Ga. Ct. App. 2009)], the court held that restrictive covenants, with no time limitations, which prevented an employee from using his own "observations," and provisions barring the employee from engaging in any capacity, "directly or indirectly," in any competing business were overbroad and unenforceable.

In *Azzouz v. Prime Pediatrics, P.C.* [675 S.E.2d 314 (Ga. Ct. App. 2009)], the court held that a physician's non-compete agreement executed with his prior employer that prevented him from performing pediatric services for two years within a five-county area was reasonable as to scope and duration.

In *Reliance Wholesale, Inc. v. Godfrey* [51 So. 3d. 561 (Fla. Dist. Ct. App. 2010)], an employee that had access to the employer's database containing sales and client information and, at company's expense, worked to establish relationships with customers provided a legitimate basis for the enforcement of a non-compete, both for the protection of trade secrets and relationships with customers. The employer's alleged breach of payment of commissions under the employment agreement which contained the non-compete was no defense to the enforcement of the non-compete when the agreement expressly provided that its covenants were independent of each other and that any claim by the employee against the employer could not constitute a defense to the enforcement of the non-compete.

In *Peachtree Fayette Women's Specialists, LLC v. Turner* [305 Ga. App. 60 (2010)], a restrictive covenant that prohibited a former physician from practicing medicine at a hospital that the former employer no longer conducted business was overly broad and unenforceable.

In *Steam Sales Corp. v. Summers* [405 Ill. App. 3d 442 (2010)], an employers' long-standing relationship with customers provided a legitimate basis for the enforcement of a non-compete agreement prohibiting a former sales employee from soliciting or conducting business with customers he sold within two years prior to his termination of employment.

In *Reliable Fire Equipment Company v. Arredondo* [405 Ill. App. 3d 708 (2010)], an employer that sells fire suppression and related equipment sought to enforce a non-compete contained within an employment agreement against a former employee. Because in this highly competitive and sales-driven industry, the customers were widely known and pricing information was not confidential, the court found that there was no permanency of relationships with customers or confidential information to support the enforcement of a non-compete. On appeal, the state supreme court in *Reliable Fire Equipment Co. v. Arredondo* [965 N.E.2d 393 (Ill. 2012)], held that to determine the reasonableness of non-competition restrictions, the restriction must also work to promote a legitimate business interest of the employer, overruling *Sunbelt Rentals, Inc. v. Ehlers*. [394 Ill. App. 3d 421, 915 N.E.2d 862 (2009)]

Q 6:45   How do courts determine whether injunctive relief is appropriate?

Generally speaking, absent a showing of irreparable injury, injunctive relief will almost never be granted. The determination of whether or not irreparable injury may occur depends on the facts of each case.

In *Ormco Corp. v. Johns* [869 So. 2d 1109 (Ala. 2003)], the Alabama Supreme Court held that, in determining whether an employer has demonstrated irreparable injury such that a preliminary injunction should be entered during the pendency of the litigation enjoining a former employee from competing in accordance with a non-competition agreement, a rebuttable inference of irreparable injury exists in cases where a former employee salesperson is actively competing with his or her former employer in the same geographic area in violation of a non-competition agreement. However, the employee can then rebut this inference by producing sufficient evidence that the competition of the employee will not irreparably injure the employer.

In *Supinski, M.D. v. Omni Healthcare PA* [853 So. 2d 526 (Fla. Dist. Ct. App. 2003)], the Florida District Court of Appeals upheld a preliminary injunction prohibiting a former physician from practicing within 10 miles of any of the employer's facilities and from soliciting the former employer's patients in accordance with a non-competition agreement. Although the physician argued, among other things, that he should be restricted only from practicing within 10 miles of the facility where he worked, the court found that the company's facilities were not widespread but were localized in one geographic area and that the restrictions seemed reasonably tailored to protect the employer from unfair competition. As such, the court found that the employer had established, among other things, a likelihood of success on the merits and affirmed the issuance of the preliminary injunction, enforcing the restrictive covenants according to their terms during the pendency of the litigation.

In *Montville v. Mobile Medical Industries, Inc.* [855 So. 2d 212 (Fla. App. 2003)], in the lower court, the employer succeeded in obtaining a temporary injunction during the pendency of litigation arising out of its prior employees' alleged violation of a non-competition agreement, conditioned on the employer's posting a $50,000 bond. The former employees appealed, alleging that the bond should be significantly higher as they stood to lose over $400,000 if the employer was not successful at trial. Reviewing the facts, and noting that it appears likely that the court properly took into consideration the unlikelihood of the former employees overturning the temporary injunction, the court concluded that no clear abuse of discretion by the trial court occurred.

In *Merrill, Lynch, Pierce, Fenner & Smith, Inc. v. McClafferty* [287 F. Supp. 2d 1244 (D. Haw. 2003)], a securities brokerage firm demonstrated that it would be irreparably harmed absent a temporary restraining order during the pendency of the litigation, keeping a former financial advisor who had gone to work for a competitor from violating the covenants not to compete contained within an employment agreement.

In *D & W Diesel, Inc. v. McIntosh* [307 A.D.2d. 750 (N.Y. Sup. Ct. 2003)], the court held that a restrictive covenant that covered a regional sales manager for a company in the business of selling hydraulic hoses was likely unenforceable because the manager did not possess any trade secrets or unique talents. In addition, the court concluded that any loss of sales occasioned as a result of a violation of the non-competition agreement could be adequately remedied in the form of monetary damages. Therefore, the prior employer failed to demonstrate the likelihood of success on the merits or that its damages were irreparable, such that the preliminary injunction entered by the trial court was vacated.

In *Downeast Mortgage Corp. v. Balzano* [2004 WL 1925525 (Me. Super. June 29, 2004)], a mortgage company sought a temporary restraining order during the pendency of the litigation to enjoin the former employees from breaching their respective non-competition agreements. The defendants were all former employees of the mortgage companies, had signed non-competition agreements, and all resigned and went to work in similar positions at a competitor. The mortgage company claimed that, absent injunctive relief, it would lose its good will and client base. Recognizing that injunctive relief requires irreparable injury, as opposed to injury for which monetary relief is available, the court concluded that any loss of good will or future economic injury arising from the former employees' work for a competitor can be calculated by evidence of past earnings on accounts and expert testimony, such that damages can be awarded in terms of monetary relief, and that the allegations of irreparable injury are speculative. As such, the court refused to enter a temporary restraining order.

Under Illinois law, to obtain preliminary injunctive relief, the employer must show a protectable business interest in one of two ways: (1) by showing the former employee's use of confidential information, or (2) by demonstrating near-permanent relations with its customers, to whom the former employee would not have had access but for his or her employment with the employer. [Applebaum v. Applebaum, 823 N.E.2d 1074 (Ill. App. Ct. 2005)]

In *Access America LLC v. Mazzotta* [2005 Conn. Super. LEXIS 2597 (Conn. Super. Ct. Sept. 14, 2005)], the court upheld a temporary restraining order against a real estate agent who joined a competing firm within a 15-mile radius of his prior agency's office, in direct violation of the terms of the non-competition agreement.

In *Gundermann & Gundermann Insurance v. Brassill* [2007 N.Y. Slip Op. 9725 (App. Div. 2d 2007)], the court issued a preliminary injunction to enforce a non-compete clause in an insurance agent's contract with his prior employer, because the same was found necessary to protect both the employer's confidential information and the good will of its customers, which were generated at the employer's expense.

In *W.R. Grace & Co. v. Posey* [2007 WL 2462003 (Tex. App. Aug. 30, 2007)], the court found that denial of a temporary injunction was appropriate where no showing of probable, imminent, and irreparable injury occurred as a result of the alleged violations of the non-compete clause.

In *Aetna v. M. Fluegel* [2008 WL 544504 (Conn. Super. Mar. 5, 2008)] the court held that an injunction is not appropriate where employer claimed former employee would inevitably disclose trade secrets in breach of a confidential agreement when the employee claimed that he would be faithful to the confidentiality agreement, even to the detriment of his new employer.

In *Opticare, P.C. v. Zimmerman, MD* [2008 WL 1734933 (Conn. Super Mar. 27, 2008)], the court held that an injunction was not appropriate, and suit for damages the right course, despite the admission by doctor that he had violated the terms of a restrictive covenant and was seeing patients of previous employer because the former employer could not show irreparable harm in that they were quickly able to hire a replacement and damages would be easy to calculate.

In *Addison v. Torres* [2008 WL 1971028 (Conn. Super. Apr. 18, 2008)], the court held that injunctive relief was not appropriate because bail bondsman employer could not show that he would suffer irreparable harm, in that his company was still considered the highest volume bail bondsman in the city 19 months after the defendants left his employ, and there was no allegation that the defendants took any proprietary information or trade secrets.

In *Salamon, M.D. v. Anesthesia Pain Care Consultants, Inc.* [10 So. 3d 1112 (Fla. Dist. Ct. App. 2009)], the court held that temporary injunctions enforcing a non-compete provision contained within an employment agreement executed by a physician in connection with his prior employment was reasonable to protect a legitimate business interest of the employer where the physician had no patient contacts or referring physicians within the area other than as an employee of his former employer.

In *Retirement Group v. Galante* [98 Cal. Rptr. 3d 585 (Cal. App. 2009)], the court held that a preliminary injunction enjoining former employees from "directly or indirectly" soliciting the former employer's customers was overbroad and unenforceable because it was not narrowly crafted to prevent the use of trade secret information.

In *Spinks v. Automation Personnel Services, Inc.* [49 So. 3d 186 (Ala. 2010)], the state supreme court found that an employer can obtain preliminary injunctive relief from a trial court for an employee's breach of a non-compete and non-solicitation clause in an employment contract, even though the employment contract contains an arbitration provision requiring all disputes to be settled through arbitration.

In *Citadel Investment Group, LLC v. Teza Technologies, LLC* [398 Ill. App. 3d 724 (2010)], a non-competition provision which, by its terms, commences upon termination of employment will not support the issuance of a preliminary injunction for nine months because the language of the restriction clearly provides that the nine-month restriction begins upon termination of employment and there was no language contained within the restriction that would allow its extension in the event of a breach.

In *Zimmer, Inc. v. Davis* [922 N.E.2d 68 (Ind. Ct. App. 2010)], where there is no evidence that the former employee took or used confidential information and the former employer had no evidence that it lost any sales or customers as a result of the former employee's employment with a competitor in violation of a covenant not to compete, the court held that the harm attendant to the former employee that needed to work to earn a living outweighed the harm to the former employer for the non-issuance of a preliminary injunction, such that it was not an abuse of its discretion for the trial court to have denied preliminary injunctive relief.

In *Armacell, LLC v. Bostic* [698 S.E.2d 200 (N.C. App. 2010)], evidence showing that the defendant had access to trade secrets that were essentially the "DNA" of plaintiff's proprietary products and that defendant had downloaded sensitive data which, in the hands of third parties, would allow them to duplicate plaintiff's proprietary products was sufficient evidence to uphold the issuance of a preliminary injunction in this misappropriation of trade secrets case.

Q 6:46   Can a company that acquires the assets and retains employees of another company enforce a non-competition agreement executed between the retained employee and the other company?

Generally, non-competition restrictions contained within employment agreements are considered personal service contracts that typically cannot be assigned by a company absent the consent of the employee. In *Wolf, D.V.M. v.*

James G. Barrie, PA [858 So. 2d 1083 (Fla. Dist. Ct. App. 2003)], the District Court of Appeals of Florida, Second Circuit, held that a company that acquires the assets of another does not acquire the ability to enforce a covenant not to compete signed by an employee in connection with the employment by selling company without the employee's consent. Moreover, the court held, the enforceability of the covenant not to compete could not be resuscitated if, after the sale of assets, the sale is later rescinded.

In *Securitas Security Services USA, Inc. v. Jenkins* [16 Mass. L. Rptr. 486 (Mass. Super. July 18, 2003)], a Swedish security company commonly referred to Securitas acquired the assets and liabilities of Pinkerton in 2000. The employee at issue had signed a covenant not to compete with Pinkerton, and although he continued working for Securitas after its acquisition of Pinkerton, he never signed a non-competition agreement with Securitas or consented to the assignment of the non-compete to Securitas. Based on these facts, the court held that absent any consent by the employee to the assignment of the covenant not to compete from Pinkerton to Securitas, Securitas could not enforce the non-competition agreement against the employee.

However, a different result was reached in *RJS Security, Inc. v. Command Security Services, Inc.* [101 S.W.3d 1 (Miss. App. 2003)] RJS Security acquired the assets of Command Security Services, including all intangible assets which RJS claimed included covenant not to compete agreements signed by various employees of the seller. After the sale, the seller released various employees from their non-compete agreements and the buyer sued the seller for tortious interference with the employment contracts. Although none of the employees had consented to the assignment of the employment contracts which contained covenants not to compete, nonetheless, the court found that because the employment contracts were discussed during the negotiations, and because the contracts were a critical element in the buyer's decision to acquire the assets of the seller, the contracts constituted intangible assets that passed to the buyer in the transaction. As such, the seller's conduct in "releasing employees" from the non-compete agreements following the sale, such that they could compete with the buyer, was tantamount to tortious interference with contract relations.

In *Missett v. Hub International Pennsylvania, LLC* [6 A.3d 530 (Pa. Super. Ct. 2010)], the court held that although Pennsylvania law requires a specific assignment provision in an asset purchase agreement for a buyer to enforce a non-compete, such is not the case when stock of a corporation is acquired, and as such, is also not the case when an entity purchases member interests in a limited liability company (LLC).

Q 6:47   What is a *non-solicitation agreement*?

Although analogous to non-compete provisions, *non-solicitation agreements* are somewhat narrower, and only seek to prevent an employee from soliciting the employer's customers and employees after separation. General bars to solicitation are often further limited by referring only to customers that conducted business within a specific time frame prior to the separation, and refer only to employees who worked with, or were supervised by, the ex-employee.

Generally a non-solicitation agreement provides as follows:

Non-Solicitation. For a period of six (6) months following separation of employment, employee shall not, either for himself or herself, or on behalf of any other person or entity, directly or indirectly:

A. Solicit or call on any customer with whom the company conducts business in an effort to divert business from the employer.

B. Solicit or contact any employee of the company for the purpose of inducing the employee to leave his/her employment with the company.

These agreements also contain provisions such as those discussed in Q 6:45 for injunctive relief, and provisions providing for enforcement to the full extent permitted under applicable law should any provision contained within be determined to be too broad as written.

In *Bell v. Rimkus Consulting Group, Inc. of Louisiana* [8 So. 3d 64 (La. App. 2009)], the court held that a non-solicitation provision which prohibited a former employee from hiring his former employer's employees or ex-employees for a period of 18 months after the employees end their employment with the employer is unreasonable and unenforceable. Although the court noted that non-solicitation of employee clauses are not specifically covered by the non-competition statute in Louisiana, such clauses must, in any event, be reasonable to be enforceable as a matter of public policy, and without a reasonable time limitation, are unenforceable. However, in *Webster Financial Corp. v. Levine* [2009 WL 1056564 (Conn. Super. Ct. Mar. 24, 2009)], the court held that a non-solicitation provision that prevented a former employee from soliciting his former employer's clients for two years was reasonable and enforceable despite the fact that it contained no geographic limitation. In *Environmental Services, Inc. v. Carter* [9 So. 3d 1258 (Fla. Dist. Ct. App. 2009)], the court held that restrictive covenants contained within an employment agreement that prevented a former employee from soliciting services from any current, former, or prospective customer of the company with whom the employee had contact during his employment with the company for a period of one year was reasonable and enforceable. In *Fine v. Communication Trends, Inc.* [305 Ga. App. 298 (2011)], the court held that the non-solicitation provision that also prohibited a former employee from "accepting" business, without solicitation, was not reasonably limited in its scope of activity prohibited and as such, was unenforceable under Georgia law. In *Hamilton-Ryker Group, L.L.C. v. Keymon* [W2008-00936-COA-R3-CV, 2010 WL 323057 (Tenn. Ct. App. Jan. 28, 2010)], the court held that although the non-solicitation restrictive covenant at issue contained no geographic limitation, it was nonetheless reasonable because it was limited to the solicitation of the employer's customers. In *Murphree v. Yancey Brothers Co.* [311 Ga. App. 744, 716 S.E.2d 824 (2011)], a non-solicitation agreement that prevented employees from affirmatively seeking business with employers' customers was reasonable and enforceable under Georgia law.

Q 6:48   Can a company seeking to protect its trade secrets from employee misappropriation resort to criminal prosecution?

The federal Economic Espionage Act of 1996 prescribes severe criminal penalties for people who take and use trade secrets that belong to someone else. Someone who knowingly receives a stolen trade secret also risks the same penalties.

The Act provides that a person who "with the intent to convert a trade secret to the economic benefit of anyone other than the owner" takes, copies, downloads, receives, steals, or performs almost any other act involving the trade secret can get a substantial fine, be imprisoned for up to 10 years, or both. The fine for organizations may be as high as $5 million. It remains to be seen, however, whether prosecutors will make wide use of this new statute to protect trade secrets owned by private companies.

Chapter 7

Job Safety

Employees have the right to a safe workplace free from recognized hazards. The Occupational Safety and Health Act of 1970 (OSH Act) is the primary federal law governing workers' safety and health in the private sector and federal government. The Occupational Safety and Health Administration (OSHA) is responsible for enforcing the OSH Act. Employees are also protected from retaliation and discrimination by their employers as a result of exercising any rights that are granted under the OSH Act and have the right to refuse to work under a dangerous condition. This chapter covers these topics as well as smoking in the workplace, AIDS, drug abuse in the workplace, workplace violence, ergonomics, pandemic diseases, and green jobs hazards.

OSH Act

Q 7:1   Which law governs job safety?

The primary law governing on-the-job safety is the OSH Act, which was passed by Congress in 1970.

Q 7:2   What was Congress's intent in enacting the OSH Act?

During the late 1960s, approximately 14,500 workers were killed each year as a result of occupational or industrial accidents. Many others were exposed to hazardous substances and contracted diseases related to their working conditions. Congress passed the Act to limit workers' exposure to occupational hazards.

Q 7:3   To whom does the OSH Act apply?

The Act applies to all employees of companies that engage in business affecting interstate commerce. This coverage is extremely broad and reaches almost all employers and employees in the United States and its territories, with few exceptions. The Act does not apply to federal and state governments in their capacities as employers, to domestic servants, or to the self-employed.

Q 7:4   What are the goals of the OSH Act?

The Act has two broad goals: (1) to assure safe and healthful working conditions for working men and women; and (2) to provide a framework for research, education, training, and information in the field of occupational safety and health.

Q 7:5   Has the OSH Act achieved its goals?

Annual workplace deaths have stabilized, and according to the Bureau of Labor Statistics, 4,609 workers were killed on the job in 2011 (3.5 per 100,000 full-time equivalent workers, almost 90 a week or nearly 13 deaths every day). Although this is a slight increase from the 4,551 fatal work injuries in 2009, it is the third lowest annual total since the fatal injury census was first conducted in 1992. [http://www.osha.gov/oshstats/commonstats.html]

Q 7:6   What does the OSH Act generally require of employers?

The Act requires employers to furnish their workers with a workplace that is free from recognized hazards that cause, or are likely to cause, death or serious injury.

Q 7:7   What is a *recognized hazard* under the OSH Act?

A *recognized hazard* under the Act is a condition that is known to be dangerous, taking into account the standard of knowledge of that particular industry. The condition does not necessarily have to be hazardous to every employee on the job to meet this definition. Another important point is that it is not necessary that the employer have actual knowledge of the existence of the hazardous condition for that employer to violate the Act. Rather, it is sufficient to show that through the exercise of reasonable diligence the employer could have discovered the hazard.

Q 7:8   Is OSHA identifying and tracking workplaces with high injury and illness rates?

In early 2010, as the economic situation in the United States began to slowly improve, OSHA issued letters to the nation's top 15,000 employers with higher than average workplace injury and illness rates. These establishments had higher DART rates than other workplaces in similar industries. Employers receiving the letters were provided copies of their injury and illness data, along with a list of the most frequently cited OSHA standards for their specific industry. The letter offered assistance in helping to reduce workplace injuries and illnesses by suggesting, among other things, the use of OSHA's free safety and health consultation services for small businesses provided through the states. OSHA identified businesses with the nation's highest rates of workplace injuries and illnesses through employer-reported data from a 2009 survey of about 100,000 worksites. (This survey collected injury and illness data for calendar year 2008.) Workplaces receiving notifications had DART rates more than twice the national average among all U.S. workplaces.

The letters added that OSHA's consultation program is available to assist in addressing safety and health in the workplace for employers with 250 or fewer workers. This program is administered by a state agency and operated separately from OSHA's enforcement program. The service is free and confidential, and there are no fines even if problems are found. Designed for small employers, the consultation program can help an employer identify hazards while finding effective and economical solutions for repairing them. In addition, the OSHA state consultant can assist in developing and implementing a safety and health management system for the workplace. (See Q 7:24.)

According to an alert issued shortly after this OSHA announcement by the Philadelphia-based international law firm, Morgan Lewis, "The receipt of such a letter is a good indication that an OSHA inspection may occur under the Site Specific Targeting (SST) Program. In past years, SST inspections—which are based on high injury and illness rates—led to the inspections of a large number of worksites nationwide. This year, OSHA anticipates up to 4,500 inspections of employers identified in the SST Program."

The Morgan Lewis labor lawyers offered the following advice for those companies who received letters from OSHA:

1. Review injury and illness records for conformity to OSHA regulations (see Qs 7:77–7:83).
2. Review overall compliance status (see Q 7:39, explaining voluntary self-audits).
3. Be prepared to deal with a likely inspection; in particular, make sure managers understand what an employer's rights are with regard to such an incursion into the workplace (see Qs 7:99–7:104).

So what were the results for Fiscal Year 2011? The consulting firm of J.J. Keller and Associates, Inc. reported on March 17, 2011:

> From OSHA's perspective, enforcement remains vital to workplace safety and health. To accomplish its mission in reducing workplace injuries, illnesses, and fatalities, the agency has been targeting the most hazardous workplaces and employers with the highest injury and illness rates using innovative enforcement approaches. Programs such as the Severe Violator Enforcement Program (SVEP) that were introduced in 2010, as well as penalty structure changes and increased inspection activity have enabled the agency to effectively use its resources to identify serious hazards and employers who intentionally violate OSHA standards.
>
> As a result, there has been an increase in the number of violations that the agency has issued over the past five years—22.1% more serious violations, 217.1% more willful violations, and 8.1% more repeat violations have been issued. In FY 2010, OSHA found 96,742 violations of OSHA's standards and regulations in the nation's workplaces, a 15.3% increase since FY 2006.
>
> OSHA continues to maintain its high level of annual inspection activity. In FY 2010, OSHA conducted 40,993 total inspections; 24,759 programmed inspections; and 16,234 unprogrammed inspections including employee complaints, accidents, and referrals. The number of fatality investigations significantly decreased over the past five fiscal years.

[http://www.jjkeller.com/webapp/wcs/stores/servlet/content_home__
article_2011Mar17OSHAsummarizesenforcementeffortsfor2010-032011_
10151_-1_10551]

Q 7:9   How can hazards be prevented or controlled?

To prevent or control current or potential hazards identified by the employer, OSHA guidelines recommend establishing procedures using engineering techniques, safe work training, provision of personal protective equipment (PPE), and administrative controls. Other than procedural safeguards, the guidelines suggest that employers maintain facilities and equipment, plan and prepare for emergencies and establish a medical program, including on-site first aid and nearby emergency medical care.

Q 7:10   What should safety and health training encompass?

OSHA guidelines suggest that information employees need will vary, but that each employee should at least be informed about the general hazards and safety rules of the worksite; specific hazards, safety rules, and practices related to particular work assignments; and actions the employee should take in the event of an emergency.

Safety and health training of supervisors should include the information employees need, as well as information about safety and health management responsibilities.

A wide range of training materials is available on-line or upon request from OSHA. These materials can be identified at http://www.osha.gov/pls/publications/publication.html.

The OSHA Training Institute (OTI) provides training and education in occupational safety and health for federal and state compliance officers, state consultants, other federal agency personnel, and the private sector. The OTI Course Catalog is available at: https://learninglink.dol.gov/dol/user/site/browse Catalog.do.

OSHA offers the following certifications and professional development:

- Continuing Education Units (CEUs). CEUs are available to participants in OTI courses in accordance with the administrative and program criteria guidelines established by the International Association for Continuing Education and Training. These CEUs also meet the criteria of the American Board for Occupational Health Nurses, Inc. (ABOHN) for certification or recertification. Some states also accept these CEUs for licensure of nurses. The number of CEUs for courses offered by the OTI is listed with each course description. CEUs for abbreviated sessions offered at locations other than the OTI are available. The number of CEUs available for these abbreviated sessions can be obtained from the Registrar.

- American Board of Industrial Hygiene (ABIH) Certification Maintenance (CM) Points.

- CM points are available to certified industrial hygienists who complete courses awarded points under the ABIH maintenance of certification program. Board of Certified Safety Professionals (BCSP) Continuance of Certification (COC) Points.

- Continuation of Certification (COC) Points are available to certified safety professionals who complete courses in which at least half of the content is devoted to safety, health, or environmental topics. All OTI courses meet the BCSP criteria. The number of COC points available from the BCSP is the same as the number of CEUs listed in the course description.

Q 7:11   In addition to the employer's general duty under the OSH Act, does the employer have any specific responsibilities?

Besides the general duty to furnish a workplace free from hazards, the Act requires employers to meet various health and safety standards established for particular industries and situations and also to keep records of injuries, deaths, accidents, illnesses, and special hazards in their workplaces.

Q 7:12   Does OSHA have any regulations involving shutdown of equipment while under repair?

Yes. OSHA has rules on lockout/tagout procedures to safeguard employees from the unexpected energizing or startup of machinery and equipment, or the release of hazardous energy during service or maintenance activities.

According to the agency, approximately three million workers service equipment and face the greatest risk of injury if lockout/tagout is not properly implemented. Compliance with the lockout/tagout standard [29 C.F.R. § 1910.147] allegedly prevents an estimated 120 fatalities and 50,000 injuries each year. Workers injured on the job from exposure to hazardous energy lose an average of 24 workdays for recuperation.

Lockout/tagout (LOTO) interactive training is available on OSHA's Web site at: http://www.osha.gov/dts/osta/lototraining/index.html.

This site offers:

- A tutorial. It explains the standard in a question/answer format.
- Hot topics. It contains the five major issues under lockout/tagout standard with a detailed discussion of each major issue.
- Interactive case studies. It contains seven simulated LOTO inspections. The user will be making decisions on the application of the LOTO standard, based on information presented on the screen.

Q 7:13   What are the main components of an effective lockout/tagout policy?

The following are the main components of an effective lockout/tagout policy.

Supervisor's Responsibilities:

1. Maintains awareness of all aspects of the policy;
2. Ensures that all subordinates understand how the policy works and are issued appropriate locks and tags;
3. Conducts periodic inspections;
4. Certifies that the inspections have been performed.

Employee's Responsibilities:

1. Maintains awareness of all aspects of the policy and complies.

Safety & Security Department Responsibilities:

1. Provides training;
2. Conducts inspections;
3. Provides guidance;
4. Approves or disapproves exceptions.

General Considerations:

1. Implementation of the policy should be performed only by authorized, qualified personnel;
2. Before any employee performs any maintenance or repair of a machine or equipment, where unexpected start-up or release of stored energy could occur and cause injury, the machine or equipment must be isolated and rendered inoperative;
3. If an energy-isolating device is capable of being locked out, then a lockout and tagout procedure must be utilized;
4. If an energy-isolating device is incapable of being locked out, then a tagout must be utilized;
5. Whenever major replacement, repair, renovation, or modification of machines or equipment is performed, and whenever new machines or equipment are installed, energy-isolating devices for such machines and equipment must be designed to accept a lockout device.

(For additional information and resources, see http://www.osha.gov/SLTC/controlhazardousenergy/index.html.)

Q 7:14   In a lockout/tagout policy, what is meant by an *energy isolating device*?

A mechanical device that physically prevents the release of energy, including any of the following:

- Manually operated electrical circuit breaker
- Disconnect switch
- Manually operated switch
- Slide gate
- Slip blind
- Spectacle flange
- Line valve
- Blocks

Q 7:15   In a lockout/tagout policy, what is meant by an *energy source*?

An *energy source* is any electrical, mechanical, hydraulic, pneumatic, chemical, thermal, or other energy source that could potentially cause injury to personnel.

Q 7:16   In a lockout/tagout policy, what is meant by a *lockout device*?

A *lockout device* utilizes a lock and key to hold an energy-isolating device in the safe position and prevents a machine or equipment from being energized.

Q 7:17   In a lockout/tagout policy, what is meant by a *tagout device*?

A *tagout device* is a prominent warning device, such as a tag, that can be securely attached to equipment or machinery for the purpose of warning personnel not to operate an energy isolating device and identifying the authority who controls the procedure.

Q 7:18   What are the major elements of an effective occupational safety and health program?

According to OSHA guidelines, an effective occupational safety and health program has four elements:

1. Management commitment and employee involvement;
2. Worksite analysis;
3. Hazard prevention and control; and
4. Safety and health training.

For novices, OSHA offers its "Quick Start" compliance program at: http://www.osha.gov/dcsp/compliance_assistance/quickstarts/index.html.

At this site, OSHA introduced "Quick Start" as follows:

> Are you ready to learn more about how to prevent workplace injuries and illnesses and comply with the Occupational Safety and Health Act, but aren't sure where to start? By following this step-by-step guide, you can identify many of the major OSHA requirements and guidance materials that may apply to your workplace. Small and new businesses may find Quick Start helpful as an introduction to the compliance assistance resources on OSHA's Web site.
>
> This Quick Start feature is not comprehensive—there may be additional OSHA standards and guidance materials that also apply to your business. If you are in a state with an OSHA-approved state program, you are subject to state occupational safety and health regulations that may have more stringent or supplemental requirements. These state programs also provide compliance assistance services. Please contact your state program for additional information. In addition, you can request a free, confidential on-site consultation from the OSHA On-site Consultation Program.

While we offer this information for our readers' consideration, we do so with this cautionary note: Although OSHA, like the IRS and a number of other federal agencies, have presented a friendlier face in recent years than was historically the case, if your organization is in violation of the law, you should not leap into any such programs without competent counsel at your side.

Q 7:19   What measures can an employer take to ensure management commitment and employee involvement?

To ensure management commitment and employee involvement, OSHA guidelines recommend that employers:

1. Articulate a work site policy on safety and health.
2. Establish a clear goal for the program and identify objectives to meet the goal.
3. Make visible the involvement of top management in implementing the program.
4. Encourage employee involvement in the structure and operation of the program and in decisions that affect employee safety and health.
5. Divide all program responsibilities among management, supervisors, and employees.
6. Provide adequate authority and resources to individuals with program responsibilities.
7. Make individuals with program responsibilities accountable.
8. Review program operations annually.

Q 7:20   Does OSHA provide any voluntary guidelines for employers seeking to improve their employees' working conditions?

Yes. OSHA offers five major voluntary-compliance programs:

- The Alliance Program
- The Safety and Health Achievement Recognition Program
- The Challenge Program
- The Strategic Partnership Program
- The Voluntary Protection Programs (VPPs)

[*See* http://www.osha.gov/dcsp/compliance_assistance/index_programs. html.]

Q 7:21   What are OSHA's VPPs?

OSHA's VPPs are intended to recognize and promote improved management of health and safety concerns. VPPs are OSHA's premier recognition programs for employers and employees who have implemented exemplary workplace safety and health management systems. A hallmark of VPP is the principle that management, labor, and OSHA work together in pursuit of a safe and healthy workplace. To attain VPP status, employers must demonstrate management commitment to the safety and health of their employees and employees must be actively involved in activities that support the safety and health management system. Under these programs, labor, management, and the administration attempt to establish a cooperative three-way relationship in the relevant workplace under a powerful program that must include the following elements:

- Management promises to institute and operate an effective safety program incorporating an established set of health and safety criteria;
- Employees agree to cooperate with management in the implementation of the program criteria;
- OSHA, after initial verification that VPP criteria are being met, provides public recognition of the worksite's program as exemplary and removes that site from its list of routine inspection targets. However, the administration retains the right to investigate major incidents such as spills, accidents, deaths, and specific employee complaints;
- The administration also periodically reconfirms site compliance, under some programs annually, under others every three years.

[*See* http://www.osha.gov/dcsp/vpp/index.html.]

In practice, VPP sets performance-based criteria for a managed safety and health system, invites sites to apply, and then assesses applicants against these criteria. OSHA's verification includes an application review and a rigorous on-site evaluation by a team of OSHA safety and health experts.

OSHA approves qualified sites to one of three programs:

- Star
- Merit
- Star Demonstration: Recognition for worksites that address unique safety and health issues. Sites that make the grade must submit annual self-evaluations and undergo periodic on-site reevaluations to remain in the programs.

An example of a successful VPP participant is Fred Weber, Inc., an asphalt manufacturer in St. Louis, Missouri, which was honored by OSHA in February 2010 for achievement in the company's employee safety and health program at two St. Louis-area locations. The firm's South Asphalt Plant in St. Louis and the O'Fallon Asphalt Plant in O'Fallon, Missouri, have both been recognized as "star" sites, the highest level of recognition that OSHA's VPP offer, during a ceremony earlier this month. The asphalt producer earned VPP star recognition following comprehensive on-site evaluations by a team of OSHA safety and health experts. The complete news release is available at: http://www.osha. gov/ pls/ oshaweb/ owadisp. show_ document? p_table = NEWS_RELEASES &p_id = 17178.

Employers and employees should reach out to HR or in-house lawyers at firms, such as Fred Weber, before partnering with a regulatory agency.

Q 7:22 What is the Special Government Employee (SGE) Program?

The SGE program was established to allow industry employees to work alongside OSHA during VPP's on-site evaluations. Not only does this innovative program benefit OSHA by supplementing its on-site evaluation teams, but it also gives industry and government an opportunity to work together and share views and ideas. Qualified volunteers from VPP sites are eligible to participate in the SGE program. These volunteers must be approved by OSHA and funded by their companies to participate. After submitting an application and completing the required training, these volunteers are sworn in as SGEs and are approved to assist as VPP on-site evaluation team members.

[See http://www.osha.gov/dcsp/vpp/sge.html.]

Q 7:23   What are the alleged advantages of VPP participation?

According to OSHA, VPP participants report the following advantages:

- Improvement in employee morale and motivation, which in turn has improved work product quality and productivity;
- Lowered workers' compensation costs;
- Community recognition and public relations pluses; and
- 60 to 80 percent fewer lost workdays.

Q 7:24   What is OSHA's Consultation Service?

This is a free consultation service for employers who are interested in spotting hazards in their workplaces and improving their health and safety systems. Participation in this program can result in a one-year exemption from routinely scheduled inspections. Furthermore, the voluntary consultations come with immunity from citations and penalties. The confidential consultations are usually delivered by state, rather than federal, OSHA experts, typically on-site. Small and medium-sized businesses, particularly those in high-hazard industries or involved in hazardous operations, can use this free and confidential service to help improve their safety and health performance. Consultants from state agencies or universities work with employers to identify workplace hazards, provide advice on compliance with OSHA standards, and assist in establishing safety and health management systems. On-site Consultation services are totally separate from enforcement and do not result in penalties or citations.

In some cases, the consultant may identify an "imminent danger," requiring the host employer to take immediate corrective action to abate the threat. In the case of identified "serious violations," the employer will be required to cooperate with the consultant in creating a corrective-action plan. Either of these circumstances can include considerable costs to the employer.

[See http://www.osha.gov/dcsp/smallbusiness/consult.html.]

The consultation process is comprised of four steps:

1. Opening Conference. When the consultant arrives at your worksite for the scheduled visit, he or she will first meet with you in an opening conference to briefly review the consultant's role and the obligation you incur as an employer.

2. Walk Through. Together, you and the consultant will examine conditions in your workplace. OSHA strongly encourages maximum employee participation in the walk-through. Better informed and more alert employees can more easily work with you to identify and correct potential injury and illness hazards in your workplace. Talking with employees during the walk-through helps the consultant identify and judge the nature and extent of specific hazards. The consultant will study your entire workplace or the specific operations you designate and discuss the applicable OSHA standards. Consultants also will point out other safety or health risks that might not be cited under OSHA standards, but nevertheless may pose safety or health risks to your employees. They may suggest and even provide other measures such as self-inspection and safety and health training you and your employees can use to prevent future hazardous situations. A comprehensive consultation also includes (1) appraisal of all mechanical and environmental hazards and physical work practices, (2) appraisal of the present job safety and health program or establishment of one, (3) a conference with management on findings, (4) a written report of recommendations and agreements, and (5) training and assistance with implementing recommendations.

3. Closing Conference. The consultant will then review detailed findings with you in a closing conference. You will learn not only what you need to improve, but also what you are doing right. At that time you can discuss problems, possible solutions, and abatement periods to eliminate or control any serious hazards identified during the walk-through. In rare instances, the consultant may find an "imminent danger" situation during the walk-through. If so, you must take immediate action to protect all employees. In certain other situations that would be judged a "serious violation" under OSHA criteria, you and the consultant are required to develop and agree to a reasonable plan and schedule to eliminate or control that hazard. The consultants will offer general approaches and options to you. They may also suggest other sources for technical help.

4. Abatement and Follow Through. Following the closing conference, the consultant will send you a detailed written report explaining the findings and confirming any abatement periods agreed upon. Consultants may also contact you from time to time to check your progress. You, of course, may always contact them for assistance. Ultimately, OSHA requires hazard abatement so that each consultation visit achieves its objective—effective employee protection. If you fail to eliminate or control identified serious hazards (or an imminent danger) according to the plan and within the limits agreed upon or an agreed-upon extension, the situation must be referred from consultation to an OSHA enforcement office for appropriate action. This has rarely occurred in the past. (See Caution notes in Qs 7:18 and 7:21.)

Q 7:25   What will an OSHA on-site consultant do and not do?

The on-site consultant will:

- Help you recognize hazards in your workplace
- Suggest general approaches or options for solving a safety or health problem
- Identify kinds of help available if you need further assistance
- Provide you a written report summarizing findings
- Assist you to develop or maintain an effective safety and health program
- Provide training and education for you and your employees
- Recommend you for a one-year exclusion from OSHA programmed inspections, once program criteria are met

The on-site consultants will not:

- Issue citations or propose penalties for violations of OSHA standards
- Report possible violations to OSHA enforcement staff
- Guarantee that your workplace will "pass" an OSHA inspection (See Caution notes in Qs 7:18 and 7:21.)

[*See* http://www.osha.gov/dcsp/smallbusiness/consult_gettingstarted.html.]

Q 7:26   What is OSHA's Strategic Partnership Program (OSPP)?

The OSPP provides opportunities for OSHA to partner with employers, employees, professional or trade associations, labor organizations, State On-site Consultation projects, and other interested stakeholders. These voluntary partnerships are designed to encourage, assist, and recognize efforts to eliminate serious hazards and achieve model workplace safety and health practices. Each partnership develops its own unique, formal agreement that establishes specific goals, strategies, and performance measures. Partnerships are available to all private sector industries and government agencies where OSHA has jurisdiction.

[*See* http://www.osha.gov/dcsp/partnerships/index.html.]

Q 7:27   Can OSHA offer focused inspections as incentives to Strategic Partnerships?

Yes, so long as the partner has carefully identified the most serious hazards prevailing at the partnering work sites.

Q 7:28   Can OSHA offer enhanced penalty reductions as an inducement for employers to partner with it?

No. Current procedures already provide for substantial good-faith reductions for employers who implement effective safety and health programs. No enhanced reductions are provided under the partnership program.

Q 7:29   What is the role of workers in a Comprehensive OSHA Strategic Partnership?

All partnerships must have a high level of employee involvement from the outset. At non-union work sites, OSHA does not expect that employees will sign onto the partnership agreement, but evidence of their involvement and commitment is deemed highly desirable. OSHA expects workers to be involved in the development and operation of the partnership as well as the individual sites' safety and health programs.

Q 7:30   Do OSHA Strategic Partnership programs have to be written agreements among OSHA, the employees or their representative, and the employer?

Partnerships must be based upon a written agreement. The written agreement should spell out the goals and objectives and address other core elements of the partnership, so that all parties understand what is expected.

Q 7:31   Must the employer already have an effective health and safety program in place before it can join an OSHA Strategic Partnership?

No. OSHA can enter into a partnership when it has reasonable assurances that the participating employer will develop and implement effective safety and health programs in the near future. A partnership may have as a primary goal the timely development and implementation of workplace safety and health programs. Agency goals sometimes extend beyond individual employers as well Current partnerships include national, regional, and industry-wide pacts.

[*See* http://www.osha.gov/dcsp/partnerships/current_list.html#National.]

Q 7:32   In partnerships that require the employer to implement effective safety and health programs, is there an implementation time limit?

No. It is left to the judgment of the originating OSHA regional office to set a time limit.

An illustrative success story offered by OSHA involves the Kauffman Stadium renovation project in Kansas City, Missouri. The Kansas City Area Office of OSHA, Walton Construction, Hunt Construction Group, and the Builders' Association, as well as subcontractors working on the project recognized the need for a safe and healthy worksite. The main goal of this OSHA Strategic Partnership (OSP) was to ensure a safe working environment for all employees involved in the Kauffman Stadium renovation project. The project encompassed the renovation of the Kauffman Stadium ballpark for the Kansas City Royals.

The project consisted of approximately seven phases of construction including: outfield construction, a new three-story administration building in front of the stadium, a diamond club, broadcast booths, renovation of older suites, writing press and dining, expanded concourses, and other internal renovations. The project was successfully completed in July 2009.

During the 18 months that the Kauffman Stadium was renovated, a total of 148 employers and 2,956 employees participated in the OSP. All 2,956 employees went through two hours of mandatory site-specific safety training for a total of 5,912 training hours. Topics covered during the training included: hazard communication and the importance of reading material safety data sheets; lockout tagout procedures; fall protection; excavations; scaffolding; and crane safety. In addition to the training that the employees received, all 148 supervisors were also required to attend the following training sessions: 10-hour construction outreach training, first-aid/cardiopulmonary resuscitation (CPR), and a one-hour session on supervisors' safety responsibilities while performing work at the stadium.

The total workers' compensation cost on the project was approximately $0.41 per man hour worked. The actual injury and illness costs incurred were $565,619, which was nearly $1 million under the anticipated cost of $1,439,080. This dollar amount is reflected in the project's total Days Away from Work (DAFW) rate of 1.01, which is 47 percent below the 2007 Bureau of Labor Statistics' national average DAFW rate of 1.90 for the construction industry. [*See* http://www.osha.gov/dcsp/success_stories/partnerships/region7/625_kaufman_success.html.]

As this case study suggests, in situations such as a multi-stage construction project of major proportions, implementation of OSH programs may require concomitant stages, redundancies and the like.

Q 7:33   How does OSHA define an *effective* safety and health program?

As a general rule, an effective safety and health program should conform to OSHA's Safety and Health Program Management Guidelines. [http://www.osha.gov/pls/oshaweb/owadisp.show_document?p_table = FEDERAL_REGISTER&p_id = 12909] OSHA recognizes, however, that there may be situations where a safety and health program that is not based upon the guidelines might be appropriate under a particular Comprehensive OSHA Strategic Partnership program. Such an alternative program must be fully described in the partnership proposal and, at a minimum, must include the four main elements addressed in the guidelines and common to all comprehensive, effective safety and health programs. These are:

- Management leadership and employee involvement;
- Work site analysis;
- Hazard prevention and control; and
- Safety and health training.

Q 7:34   Why is OSHA willing—on a case-by-case basis—to establish strategic partnership programs with employers that have serious health and safety hazards and violations?

OSHA states that it does not want to close the door to any employer who wants to make a commitment to the health and safety of its employees. However, OSHA's guidelines state that these situations are expected to be the exception and not the rule under the partnership program. Such partners must still meet all program requirements. Furthermore, all partnership work sites remain subject to programmed and unprogrammed inspections.

Q 7:35   Can OSHA offer an exemption from programmed inspections as an incentive for an employer to enter the partnership program?

No. Such exemptions are reserved for more sophisticated voluntary compliance programs—e.g., the SHARP and VPP programs.

Q 7:36   Can OSHA still conduct unprogrammed inspections of partnership participants?

Yes. OSHA can, and states that it will, conduct unprogrammed inspections in response to complaints and accidents in accord with its established policies.

Q 7:37   How does the partnership policy affect OSHA's programmed inspection plans?

If a partnership employer appears on a special emphasis program or other list for programmed inspections, the inspection will likely still occur, despite the partnership. The inspection will be focused on hazards identified in the special emphasis program plan, as well as hazards identified in the partnership agreement. OSHA anticipates that the hazards identified in the special emphasis inspection plan will closely parallel the hazards identified in the partnership plan. If the programmed inspection is intended under its plan to be comprehensive, the existence of a partnership agreement will not narrow the scope of the inspection.

Q 7:38   How much inspecting does OSHA actually do, overall?

In Fiscal Year 2012, OSHA conducted 40,961 total inspections. In addition, OSHA conducted 51,133 18(b) state plan inspections. The following were the top 10 most frequently cited standards by Federal OSHA in fiscal year 2012 (October 1, 2011 through September 30, 2012):

- Fall protection, construction (29 C.F.R. § 1926.501)
- Hazard communication standard, general industry (29 C.F.R. § 1910.1200)

- Scaffolding, general requirements, construction (29 C.F.R. § 1926.451)
- Respiratory protection, general industry (29 C.F.R. § 1910.134)
- Control of hazardous energy (lockout/tagout), general industry (29 C.F.R. § 1910.147)
- Powered industrial trucks, general industry (29 C.F.R. § 1910.178)
- Electrical, wiring methods, components and equipment, general industry (29 CFR 1910.305)
- Ladders, construction (29 C.F.R. § 1926.1053)
- Machines, general requirements, general industry (29 C.F.R. § 1910.212)
- Electrical systems design, general requirements, general industry (29 C.F.R. § 1910.303)

[http://www.osha.gov/oshstats/commonstats.html]

New inspection initiatives in 2013 include:

- Re-establishment of the Maritime Advisory Committee on Health and Safety (MACOSH). The Department of Labor established MACOSH in 1995 to advise the secretary of labor, through the assistant secretary of labor for occupational safety and health, on various issues related to safe and healthful working conditions in the maritime industry, including safety and health standards, injury and illness prevention, training and outreach initiatives, and enforcement initiatives to improve the safety and health of maritime workers.

   Re-establishing MACOSH will allow the committee to continue its important work protecting the safety and health of workers in the maritime industry. Since receiving its first charter in 1995, MACOSH has made more than 100 recommendations to OSHA. The agency used these recommendations to develop guidance products and standards. MACOSH meetings are open to the public.

   [http://www.osha.gov/pls/oshaweb/owadisp.show_document?p_table = NEWS_RELEASES&p_id = 23913]

- A menu of new compliance-assistance products, including new web-based resources [https://www.osha.gov/dcsp/compliance_assistance/new_ca_products.html#web_resources] New OSHA publications for 2013-14 are available at: http://www.osha.gov/pls/publications/publication.AthruZ?pType = Types.

- The OSHA/American Wind Energy Alliance will continue to work together to provide AWEA's members and others with guidance and access to information and training resources that will focus on reducing and preventing exposures to fall, electrical, and crane hazards. The OSHA and AWEA Alliance Implementation Team members will finalize and implement several training programs on wind energy, including the "Wind

Energy Awareness–Climb Safety" training, and develop fact sheets on electrical equipment and cranes used in the industry. AWEA will post these resources on its Web site. OSHA will then add links to the resources on the OSHA and AWEA Web page, the Alliance Program Participants Developed Products Web page, and other appropriate locations on the Agency Web site. [https://www.osha.gov/dcsp/alliances/awea/awea_annualreport2011-2012.html]

Q 7:39   What are Voluntary Self-Audits under the OSH Act?

The OSHA Audit Policy developed in reaction to growing congressional criticism of OSHA's enforcement procedures and four components:

- OSHA does not routinely request to see voluntary audit reports when it conducts work site inspections;
- Where a voluntary audit identifies and corrects a hazard prior to a work site inspection, no citation is issued as long as the employer's corrective measures include steps to prevent the recurrence of the condition;
- Where the audit identifies an actual violation, OSHA does not use the audit reports as the basis for a willful violation;
- The audit can be used for good faith reductions in penalties later assessed.

Q 7:40   Are there any risks to conducting a self-audit?

The employer who undertakes a self-audit also undertakes the obligation of correcting the hazardous conditions that are discovered. Failure to do so creates at a minimum employer knowledge of the uncorrected condition, which in turn will be strong evidence later on of willful violations of the OSH Act.

In addition to the foregoing financial exposure, ambiguity in OSHA regulations leaves some significant uncertainties with regard to the actual extent of immunity from citations and penalties afforded employers by the audit policy.

An employer must make corrections to hazardous conditions in a "reasonable, timely, and diligent" manner in order to avoid citations and penalties. By not defining these three terms, they are left for case-by-case interpretation with considerable ambiguity allowing for wide variation from region to region.

OSHA reserves the right to request audit reports during inspections where there exists "an independent basis to believe that a specific safety or health hazard warranting investigation exists." In an unscheduled inspection, the compliance officer is on-site because of an employee complaint or other reason to believe a hazard exists. In all such cases, the compliance officer can request a copy of the self-audit under this regulation.

Q 7:41 What are the advantages and disadvantages of participating in an OSHA Compliance Assistance Program?

Advantages:

- A good working relationship with OSHA (but no guarantee of immunity from inspections, citations, and penalties);
- Decreased injury and illness rates;
- Potential for improved employee and/or labor relations.

Disadvantages:

- Potentially high abatement costs;
- Provision of damaging information to OSHA that might not be readily available to it otherwise;
- Possible issues under the National Labor Relations Act (NLRA) when employees and employee committees are given a degree of control over health and safety issues.

Q 7:42 Which have been OSHA's recent target industries?

- Logging
- Grain handling
- Overhead power lines
- Bridge and tunnel construction
- Residential construction
- Meat packing
- Powered industrial trucks
- Auto body shops
- Commercial diving
- Electroplating

[*See* http://www.osha.gov/dep/enforcement/enforcement_results_07.html.]

Q 7:43 What level of violations did OSHA encounter?

In Fiscal Year 2007, 88,846 violations of OSHA's standards and regulations were found in the nation's workplaces, a 6.4 percent increase since Fiscal Year 2003. The number of willful violations, while a decrease from the previous year, still represents an increase of 2.7 percent over the past five fiscal years. The number of both serious and repeat violations issued increased significantly over the previous fiscal year, as well as over the past five fiscal years.

Up-to-date data on citations by employer size (i.e., numbers of employees) and SICs is accessible at: http://www.osha.gov/pls/imis/citedstandard.html.

Q 7:44   Do the states have their own health and safety programs?

Section 18 of the OSH Act encourages the states to develop and operate their own job safety and health programs. OSHA is charged with approving and monitoring state plans. The State Plan Policy and Procedure Manual is accessible at: http://www.osha.gov/pls/oshaweb/owadisp.show_document? p_table = DIRECTIVES&p_id = 2430.

Q 7:45   What is the state's role in the OSH Act's enforcement scheme?

The Act requires OSHA to encourage the states to develop and operate their own workplace safety and health programs, as noted earlier. If the state decides to do so, its program must be at least as effective as the federal plan. When a state plan is accepted by OSHA, it is monitored shortly after its approval to determine that it is in compliance, and OSHA retains discretionary enforcement authority for three years. The state safety agency must file quarterly and semi-annual reports with OSHA. It will determine whether the state program is sufficiently effective to be delegated full authority or whether federal enforcement should be reinstituted, in that state. Once the state is fully certified, it is still required to change its standards to conform to any changes made in the federal standards, unless there is some compelling local reason against making the change. The state agency then can conduct inspections and issue citations as effectively as does the federal parent.

Q 7:46   Which states and territories have OSHA-approved health and safety programs?

The following 27 jurisdictions have OSHA-approved job safety and health programs:

- Alaska
- Arizona
- California
- Connecticut
- Hawaii
- Illinois
- Indiana
- Iowa
- Kentucky
- Maryland
- Michigan
- Minnesota
- Nevada
- New Jersey
- New Mexico

- New York
- North Carolina
- Oregon
- Puerto Rico
- South Carolina
- Tennessee
- Utah
- Vermont
- Virgin Islands
- Virginia
- Washington
- Wyoming

Note that the Connecticut, New Jersey, New York, and Virgin Islands OSH Acts cover only public sector (state and municipal) employees. Also worth noting is that some states have supplemented their basic OSH Acts with emergency preparedness and homeland security initiatives. [*See* http://www.osha.gov/dcsp/osp/innovations.html#emergency (particularly the beginning of the "Examples of State Plan Guidance Materials" section).]

Additional resources on state plans can be found on OSHA's Web site http://www.osha.gov/dcsp/osp/index.html.

Q 7:47 What is a state OSHA program?

If OSHA approves a state health and safety plan, the federal agency will pay up to 50 percent of the state's cost in implementing and operating the plan. According to Section 18 of the OSH Act, such a plan must adopt standards that are "at least as effective as" the comparable federal standards. Most of the 27 approved jurisdictions have adopted standards more or less identical to the federal standards. Three jurisdictions—Connecticut, New Jersey, and New York—apply their programs only to their public employees.

Q 7:48 What must a state with an approved OSHA program do to maintain OSHA approval and financial support?

The state must:

- Conduct inspections to enforce its program
- At a minimum, cover its public employees
- Operate training and education programs
- Provide free, on-site consultation for covered employers

Q 7:49   How does a state establish its own program?

To gain OSHA approval for a so-called "developmental plan," a state must assure OSHA that within three years it will have in place all the structural elements necessary for an effective program. These elements are:

- Appropriate legislation
- Regulations and procedures
- Sufficient qualified personnel

Q 7:50   What happens after the state has completed its developmental plan?

Completion of step one, above, leads to certification. Once the state appears capable of independently enforcing its standards, OSHA will enter into an Operational Status Agreement, committing the federal agency to the suspension of discretionary federal enforcement activities in that state.

Q 7:51   What is the ultimate step in establishing a state health and safety program?

The ultimate OSHA accreditation is termed *final approval*. A state must meet 100 percent of OSHA benchmarked staffing levels and participate in OSHA's computerized inspection data system. At this stage, OSHA relinquishes all jurisdiction over health and safety matters in that state.

Q 7:52   How does enforcement proceed after a state has received final approval of its program?

Complaints may then be filed with either the state or OSHA. Complaints about the adequacy of the performance of the state program may be filed with OSHA's Complaint About State Program Administration (CASPA) office in any regional office of the federal agency.

Q 7:53   Have states been innovative in implementing their plans?

The OSHSPA in its 2008 annual report [http://www.orosha.org/grassroots/pdf/2008-oshspa-report.pdf] lists the following noteworthy innovations:

- *Electronic access to information.* Many state plan states are following federal OSHA's lead in providing electronic access to occupational safety and health information via the Internet. These Web sites provide a wealth of program and reference information day and night, from any location with computerized access. Users retrieve standards, policy manuals, information on appeal rights, public hearing notices, and material safety data sheets (MSDSs) from terminals in their workplaces, homes, schools and libraries. In some states, the public can read proposed rule changes on the Internet, and comment by e-mail. Web resources are expanding beyond static information to include interactive on-line training (Oregon), and safety training videos that can be played directly over the Internet (Washington).

- *Partnerships.* The Oregon construction industry and OR-OSHA are working together to reduce construction injuries and fatalities. The Joint Emphasis Program (JEP) is a cooperative effort between management, labor and government to design and implement focused joint training sessions. The goals of JEP are to focus on hazards, design a curriculum, provide training to safety personnel, foremen, supervisors and OR-OSHA staff, and to communicate the problems and solutions to the industry and public through outreach efforts. Initial training will target fall hazards in roofing, scaffolding, elevated areas, and excavations.

  The MIOSHA program, a number of labor organizations, and the Michigan Department of Transportation (DOT) worked together to develop contract specifications to enhance worker health and safety on a very large international bridge refurbishing project. The project, which entails closing the bridge for 18 months, will include safety and health requirements that go beyond current rules. If proven successful at minimizing accidents, injuries and exposures, the specifications may serve as a model for future projects in Michigan.

  Minnesota initiated a pilot partnership program with an electrical utility and its union. An agreement was signed to exempt this utility from general scheduled inspections for one year after it passed a thorough evaluation by the MNOSHA Electrical Utilities Team.

  Virginia's Safety Network programs were designed to link large businesses with small businesses to promote workplace safety through shared expertise and resources. Begun in 1993 as the Blue Ridge Safety Network, this program has grown to include eight local chapters covering nearly half of Virginia. Two hundred thirty employers participate in the networks, which provided 39 training seminars in 1998. Kentucky organized a private, non-profit Safety and Health Network with participants representing business, labor, government and academia. Their mission is to increase awareness of safety and health in the workplace through educational programs, scholarships and endowments, as well as through statewide symposia.

  Tennessee uses an approach that has yielded tremendous benefits: Industry-TOSHA discussion groups when new standards and requirements are proposed, such as Blood-borne Pathogens, Hazard Communication, and Electrical Power Generation, Transmission and Distribution standards.

- *Plain language standards.* Rules written in plain language, not cumbersome bureaucratic language, are easier to understand and follow. Washington has been using clear rule writing principles for several years, and has published several standards in the new format. A two day class is available to agency staff who work with rules. Clearly written rules eliminate repetitive language, reduce cross-referencing and bureaucratic wording, simplify the overall outline structure, refer to the employer as "you," use questions for titles, and reduce large sections into smaller single topics. WISHA requested funds from the 1999 Washington State Legislature to redesign the WISHA standards, including a user's guide, table of contents, core rules, general rules, industry rules, index, and compliance guides for small businesses. If funding is approved, the innovative format will promote consistent application and greater levels of voluntary compliance.

- *Financial incentives.* Since 1993, Wyoming has given employers a 75 percent penalty reduction if they successfully reduce their workers' compensation claims by 25 percent over a 12 month period. About 60 percent of employers have met their 25 percent reduction goal, with another 20 percent making some reduction. Wyoming also offers employers a 50 percent penalty reduction if they fix hazards the same day. Many employers have taken advantage of this, working well into the night to fix problems. A recent innovative option is to waive all penalties if the employer agrees to a consultation visit and a follow-up enforcement inspection 12 months later. Any repeat violations found during the follow-up will cost at least two to five times more than the original penalty.

  Wyoming funds a loss control consultant through workers' compensation to help employers reduce job related accidents and to lower premiums. Upon request, a briefing is given to a specific employer or group of employers. Highlights include analysis of the workplace injuries, how much money can be saved by reducing the frequency and severity of injuries, and behavioral modification concepts. The loss control consultant may work in tandem with safety and health consultation personnel.

  Puerto Rico implemented the Quick Fix program in 1996, providing a 15 percent additional reduction in penalties for safety and health violations that are abated during the inspection.

  In Hawaii, a five percent workers' compensation premium discount is offered for workplace safety and health programs certified by state-certified professionals as effective, leveraging the state's consultation resources. Only poor safety performers can be placed into the assigned risk pool, and employers can "bet" on their future safety performance by negotiating for higher deductibles for workers' compensation.

- *Strategic and performance planning.* In 1995, OSHA encouraged state programs to develop an alternative to OSHA's traditional state plan monitoring and evaluation process. Between 1995 to 1997, several states developed unique performance agreements with OSHA, including Oregon, Wyoming, Michigan, Washington, and North Carolina. Washington's agreement featured streamlined targeting based on statewide safety and health priorities developed in partnership with business and labor, and enhanced coordination between the WISHA enforcement, consultation, and risk management programs (RMPs). OR-OSHA's performance agreement with federal OSHA, the first in the nation, was recognized in November, 1998, with Vice President Al Gore's "Hammer Award." The award recognizes outstanding efforts to make government more efficient and less expensive.

Q 7:54   What is the *Occupational Safety & Health State Plan Association*?

The *OSHSPA* is the organization of officials from the 27 states that operate OSHA-approved state plans. OSHSPA also serves as the link from the state plans to federal agencies that have occupational safety and health jurisdiction and to Congress. The group holds three meetings a year with Federal OSHA, giving state programs the opportunity to address common problems and share information. It also provides information to states or territories that are considering application for state plan status. OSHSPA representatives have appeared before congressional committees and other bodies to report on job safety and health issues. [*See* http://oshspa.org/.]

Q 7:55   Are there any exemptions from the OSH Act?

The Act contains no specific, industry-wide exemptions; however, if some other federal agency exercises authority to prescribe or enforce standards or regulations on job safety and health, the Act is preempted by that law. For this exemption to apply, the alternative law must have the safety of workers as one of its intentions, and the agency responsible for that law must have set regulations or standards applying to specific working conditions that might otherwise be covered by the Act. For example, workers on off-shore oil platforms are covered by health and safety regulations enacted and enforced by the U.S. Coast Guard and the U.S. Geological Survey.

Q 7:56   How does OSHA relate to the Environmental Protection Agency (EPA)?

OSHA requirements were once entirely separate from EPA regulatory programs; however, in recent years, many significant OSHA standards have become interwoven with EPA regulatory requirements. Thus, it is no longer possible to talk about one set of standards while ignoring and remaining ignorant of the existence of the other. This is particularly true with regard to:

- OSHA's hazard communication standards
- The preparation of MSDSs
- OSHA's process safety management and hazardous waste operations (HAZWOPER) standards
- The EPA's Risk Management Plan
- OSHA's standards for exposure to a wide range of chemicals
- Overlapping reporting requirements

Q 7:57   What is the *EPA*?

The *EPA* is the federal agency charged by Congress to enforce the following federal laws:

- Clean Air Act [42 U.S.C. §§ 7401–7671q; 40 C.F.R. Parts 50–88];

- Resource Conservation and Recovery Act [42 U.S.C. §§ 6901–6992; 40 C.F.R. Part 240–282];

- Clean Water Act [33 U.S.C. §§ 1251–1387; 33 C.F.R. Parts 320–330, 335–338; 40 C.F.R. Parts 104–140, 230–233, 401–471];

- Oil Pollution Act of 1990 [33 U.S.C. §§ 2701–2761; 15 C.F.R. Part 990; 33 C.F.R Parts 135–137; 40 C.F.R. Parts 112 and 300];

- Safe Drinking Water Act [42 U.S.C. §§ 300f–300j-26; 40 C.F.R. Parts 141–149];

- Federal Insecticide, Fungicide, and Rodenticide Act [7 U.S.C. §§ 136–136y; 40 C.F.R. Parts 152–186];

- Emergency Planning and Community Right to Know Act [42 U.S.C. §§ 11001–11050; 40 C.F.R. Parts 350, 355, 370, and 372];

- National Environmental Policy Act [42 U.S.C. §§ 4321–4347; 40 C.F.R. Parts 1500–1508];

- Endangered Species Act [16 U.S.C. §§ 1531–1544; 50 C.F.R. Parts 17, 401–424, and 450–453];

- Atomic Energy Act [42 U.S.C. §§ 2011–2297g-2; 10 C.F.R. Parts 0–171, 760–766, 810–962].

Q 7:58   What other initiatives has OSHA undertaken in recent years?

OSHA has taken the following initiatives:

- In late March 2009, OSHA released its revised Field Operations Manual to provide OSHA compliance officers with a single comprehensive resource of updated guidance in implementing the agency's mission and to more effectively protect employees from occupational injuries, illnesses and fatalities. "The manual will be a resource for workers and employers, giving them a consolidated reference on how OSHA expects workplaces to be safe and healthful," said OSHA Deputy Assistant Secretary of Labor Donald G. Shalhoub. "This document is part of OSHA's continuing commitment to make its standards and enforcement activities transparent and understandable to all parties." The Field Operations Manual, formerly called the Field Inspection Reference Manual, constitutes OSHA's general enforcement policy and procedures for use by the agency's field offices in conducting inspections, issuing citations and proposing penalties. The manual assists compliance officers in scheduling and conducting inspections, enforcing regulations, and encouraging continual improvement in workplace safety and health. It also offers guidance on how to inform employers about OSHA's free On-Site Consultation Service and compliance assistance. The most recent (2011) manual is available online at: http://www.osha.gov/OshDoc/Directive_pdf/CPL_02-00-150.pdf.

- OSHA has launched a new web feature dealing with disaster-response safety issues. The feature includes "activity sheets." The activity sheets are grouped into six categories. Each activity sheet contains a brief overview of the activity; a list of safety and health hazards and recommended engineering controls, work practices, administrative controls, and PPE; additional applicable training needs; and references to other potentially applicable activity sheets and reference materials. [http://www.osha.gov /SLTC/etools/hurricane/sheets.html]

- The agency is actively considering how the 2008–2009 stimulus programs, enacted by Congress, will impact safety considerations, as well as health and safety opportunities. [http://www.osha.gov/pls/oshaweb/owadisp. show_document?p_table = NEWS_RELEASES&p_id = 17696]

- In 2012, OSHA launched a nationwide outreach campaign and created a Web site [www.osha.gov/SLTC/heatillness], in order to raise awareness among workers and employers devoted exclusively to work-related heat illness and the hazards of working outdoors in hot weather. OSHA does not have a standard that deals directly with heat stress, but it could utilize the General Duty Clause of the Occupational Safety and Health Act of 1970 to cite employers for failing to take adequate steps to protect employees from heat illness. Therefore, employers should review their policies and practices to ensure they have procedures in place to deal with heat stress at their worksites.

- Similarly, OSHA launched a nationwide campaign to prevent falls in the construction industry. The OSHA Web site provides educational materials on how to prevent falls, train employees and plan jobs safely. Fall hazards are also a major focus of enforcement in the construction industry. It is important for construction employers to ensure full compliance with OSHA's standards related to fall protection.

In addition to these initiative, workers should also expect the following OSHA developments:

- *Injury and Illness Prevention Program (IIPP).*OSHA's IIPP rule is a regulatory priority that has been under development for almost three years. During the last several months, OSHA hinted it is ready to begin the Small Business Regulatory Enforcement Fairness Act process for the rule, whereby the agency would solicit input on the rule from affected small business entities. (However, OSHA has not officially started the process.) It is still unclear what an IIPP rule will look like because OSHA faces the challenge of creating mandatory requirements that can be applied to employers of all sizes and in all industries.

- *Crystalline silica.*The comprehensive regulation of crystalline silica is perhaps the most significant rulemaking for the construction industry given how ubiquitous crystalline silica is on job sites. OSHA's draft proposed regulatory text for the rule, which was published in 2002, considered lowering the permissible exposure limit for the substance; implementing extensive "housekeeping" requirements, including prohibiting dry sweeping; requiring exposure monitoring and the establishment of regulated areas; and imposing medical surveillance obligations. The proposed regulation is still under review by the Office of Management and Budget (OMB), where it was first submitted in February 2011. Despite the delay, this initiative should be watched closely.

- *Stricter injury and illness reporting obligations.* OSHA has proposed requiring employers to report workplace amputations to the agency within 24 hours, as well as all in-patient hospitalizations within eight hours. Existing recordkeeping rules require employers to report in-patient hospitalizations of three or more employees to OSHA within eight hours. Any workplace fatality would continue to be reportable as well. With this proposal, OSHA is following the actions of many states that have adopted more stringent reporting requirements for amputations and in-patient hospitalizations.

- *Confined spaces in construction and electric power transmission and distribution.* OSHA's Confined Spaces in Construction standard, proposed in 2007, is designed to bring the construction industry the same level of protection from confined space hazards that exists in general industry, but in a way that is more tailored to construction work. Similarly, the agency has been updating its standards for electric power transmission and distribution work to bring them in line with the regulatory framework of the general industry standard for electric power, transmission and distribution (contained in 29 C.F.R. § 1910.269). This rule has been under development for years and the final rule was submitted to OMB for review in early 2013.

[http://www.constructionexec.com/Issues/October_2012/Special_Section2.aspx]

Q 7:59   How is the OSH Act administered?

OSHA is the principal agency created to enforce the Act. It is an independent agency within the DOL, and it has the authority to promulgate standards, conduct workplace inspections, issue citations when violations occur, and recommend penalties. Additionally, the National Institute of Occupational Safety and Health (NIOSH) is an agency created by the Act to conduct research and promote the application of that research to ensure that no worker will suffer diminished health, reduced functional capacity, or decreased life expectancy as a result of the work experience. NIOSH provides technical assistance to OSHA through investigations and recommends standards for adoption by that agency. Finally, the Occupational Safety and Health Review Commission (OSHRC) is a quasi-judicial agency created by Congress to adjudicate contested enforcement actions by OSHA. While OSHA may issue citations and recommend penalties, only OSHRC can assess and enforce the penalties. OSHRC has three members who are appointed by the president for overlapping six-year terms, plus a number of administrative law judges (ALJs) who have lifetime tenure. OSHRC decisions can be appealed to appeals courts throughout the United States. Under 29 U.S.C. §§ 660(a), an appeal may be taken to the circuit court of appeals with jurisdiction over the territory in which the violation allegedly occurred or where the employer maintains its principal place of business, or the U.S. Court of Appeals for the District of Columbia Circuit.

Q 7:60   What standards are set by OSHA?

To provide hazard-free workplaces for all workers, the OSH Act requires the Secretary of Labor, through agency administration, to create and disseminate interim, permanent, and emergency standards.

An extensive set of links to a wide variety of OSHA standards is available at: http://www.osha.gov/pls/oshaweb/owasrch.search_form?p_doc_type = STANDARDS&p_toc_level = 0&p_keyvalue = .

Q 7:61   What are interim standards under the OSH Act?

During the first two years after the passage of the Act, the Secretary of Labor had power to issue interim standards. They generally were drawn from or modeled after preexisting industry consensus standards. The Secretary of Labor was not required to hold public hearings or other formal proceedings in adopting these consensus standards. Many of them remain in effect today, while others have been revoked or modified.

Q 7:62   What are permanent standards under the OSH Act?

Permanent standards can be either newly created or revised interim standards. In either case, they are developed by OSHA and NIOSH and are often based on suggestions made by interested parties such as companies, employees, states and cities, and labor unions. Once OSHA has developed a rule that it has proposed for a permanent standard, the Secretary of Labor publishes a notice in the Federal Register. This notice includes the reasons for adopting, changing, or revoking the standard. Interested parties are then allowed 30 days to submit written objections, comments, and data relating to the proposed standard. An interested party may also request a public hearing, and the Secretary of Labor has to publish a time and date for that hearing in the Federal Register. After this process has been completed, the rule (often in modified form) may become a permanent standard.

Q 7:63   What are emergency standards under the OSH Act?

Under special circumstances, the Secretary of Labor may avoid the procedures described above and issue temporary emergency standards. This may occur when the Secretary believes that employees are exposed to grave dangers from toxic substances. Actual injury does not have to occur before a temporary emergency standard may be promulgated. Emergency standards take effect immediately upon publication in the Federal Register. After publication, the Secretary of Labor must follow the procedures for formal adoption to convert an emergency standard to a permanent standard. This must be done within six months after publication of the emergency standard.

Q 7:64 How does a person or company appeal an OSHA standard?

Once a standard has been promulgated (i.e., officially announced) by the Secretary of Labor, any persons adversely affected by it can file a challenge to the validity of the standard. Such a challenge must be filed with an appropriate federal appeals court before the 60th day after the issuance of the standard. The appeals court reviews the standard and will uphold it if substantial evidence supports it. The Secretary of Labor has the burden of demonstrating that the standard was set in response to a significant risk of material health impairment. The Secretary must show that a finding was made before the standard was adopted, indicating that the standard was appropriate or reasonably necessary to protect workers from a significant risk.

Q 7:65 How are the concepts of technological and economic "feasibility" used by OSHA?

The OSH Act gives the Secretary of Labor the power to issue standards regarding the amount of toxic material or harmful physical agent that an employer can allow to come in contact with its employees. The standard the Secretary chooses must adequately assure, to the extent feasible, that no employee will suffer material impairment of health or functional capacity as a result of exposure to the hazard, even if the employee is regularly exposed. Feasibility must be examined from two perspectives—technological feasibility and economic feasibility.

At least one federal appellate court has held that technological feasibility under the Act is a "technology forcing" concept. [United Steelworkers of Am. v. Marshall, 647 F.2d 1189 (D.C. Cir.), *cert. denied*, 453 U.S. 913 (1980)] This means that OSHA may impose a standard that only the most technologically advanced plants in an industry have been able to achieve. Furthermore, OSHA may force an industry to develop and diffuse new technology to satisfy precise permissible exposure limits to toxic materials or harmful physical agents, if it can present substantial evidence to show that companies that act vigorously and in good faith can develop that technology.

Economic feasibility means that the cost of meeting a standard set by OSHA bears a reasonable relationship to the standard's benefits, despite the fact that the survival of some companies within an industry may be threatened. The standard does not have to be drafted by the Secretary of Labor in such a way that it guarantees the continued operation of any individual employer.

Q 7:66 Does the OSH Act require the Secretary of Labor to engage in cost-benefit analysis with respect to its standards?

No. Although the Secretary of Labor has the burden of proving both technological and economic feasibility, the DOL is not required to provide a cost-benefit analysis.

Q 7:67   Is it possible for a company to get a variance from an OSHA standard?

If a company or a class of employers believes that an OSHA standard is inappropriate to a particular situation, an exemption or variance may be sought. This variance can be either temporary or permanent.

Q 7:68   Under what circumstances will OSHA grant a temporary variance?

A temporary variance may be granted if the company is unable to comply with the standard by its effective date because of unavailability of professional or technological personnel or the materials or equipment necessary to comply with the standard. The company must show that all possible actions have been taken to protect employees and that all remaining actions necessary for compliance are being undertaken. Such a temporary variance can be granted only after the affected employees have been notified of the request and given an opportunity to be heard. A temporary variance can be granted for a one-year period and can be renewed for two subsequent six-month periods.

Q 7:69   Under what circumstances will OSHA grant a permanent variance?

A permanent variance is granted if a company establishes that its procedures provide as safe and healthful a workplace as the OSHA standard would provide. As with an application for a temporary variance, the affected employees must be informed of the request and given a chance to be heard.

Q 7:70   Is there any other kind of variance permitted under the OSH Act?

The Secretary of Labor has the authority to issue experimental variances that involve new or improved techniques to ensure workers' safety and health.

Q 7:71   What are OSHA's respirator standards?

All workplace respirator programs should have the following components:

1) A written plan with workplace-specific procedures tailored to the specific job site;
2) Hazard evaluation to identify and characterize respiratory dangers in order to assist in the selection of appropriate respirators;
3) Medical evaluation of workers' ability to wear and use the selected respirators;
4) Fit testing to insure tight-fitting face-seals and to guard against leakage;
5) Worker training; and
6) Periodic program evaluations.

On April 1, 2009, OSHA published new guidelines to be added to existing respiratory protection standards. The Assigned Protection Factors (APFs) provides employers with vital information for selecting respirators for employees exposed to contaminants in the air. [http://www.osha.gov/Publications/3352-APF-respirators.pdf.]

In January 2010, OSHA announced the availability of new videos to assist employers striving to comply with the new guidelines. OSHA's "Respirator Safety" video demonstrates how to correctly put on and take off common types of respirators, such as N95s. "The Difference between Respirators and Surgical Masks" video explains how they prevent exposure to infectious diseases. The videos also explain how workers can perform a user seal check to test whether a respirator is worn properly and will provide the expected level of protection. English and Spanish versions of the video are available at OSHA's Respiratory Protection page or the DOL's YouTube site. According to OSHA's respiratory protection standard, 29 C.F.R. § 1910.134, respirators must be used as part of a comprehensive respiratory protection plan. [http://www.osha.gov/pls/osha web/owadisp.show_document? p_table = NEWS_RELEASES& p_ id = 17031]

Q 7:72 How does OSHA go about creating its standards?

Public hearings and, sometimes, informal meetings with stakeholders—i.e., employers, workers, unions, manufacturers, and other potentially-affected parties—enable OSHA to fulfill its constitutional and statutory due process obligations and to ascertain how key audiences feel about new rules in the making.

Whistleblower Statutes

Q 7:73 Are whistleblowers protected under the OSH Act?

The Act was enacted to achieve safer and more healthful workplaces throughout the nation. It provides for a wide range of substantive and procedural rights for employees and representatives of employees.

To help ensure that employees are, in fact, free to participate in safety and health activities, Section 11(c) of the OSH Act prohibits any person from discharging or in any manner discriminating against any employee because the employee has exercised rights under the Act. These rights include complaining to OSHA and seeking an OSHA inspection, participating in an OSHA inspection, and participating or testifying in any proceeding related to an OSHA inspection.

Discrimination can include the following actions:

- Firing or laying off
- Assigning to undesirable shifts
- Blacklisting
- Demoting

- Denying overtime or promotion
- Disciplining
- Denial of benefits
- Failure to hire or rehire
- Intimidation
- Transferring
- Reassigning work
- Reducing pay or hours

OSHA enforces the whistleblower provisions of the OSH Act and 21 other statutes protecting employees who report reasonably perceived violations of various workplace, commercial motor vehicle, airline, nuclear, pipeline, environmental, railroad, public transportation, maritime, consumer product, motor vehicle safety, health care reform, corporate securities, food safety, and consumer financial reform laws and regulations. Additional information is available at: http://www.whistleblowers.gov.

The 14 statutes enforced by OSHA and the regulations governing their administration are listed below. Consult any statute to review the text of the whistleblower protection provisions.

- Section 11(c) of the Occupational Safety and Health Act of 1970 (OSHA)
- The Surface Transportation Assistance Act of 1982
- The Asbestos Hazard Emergency Response Act of 1986
- The International Safety Container Act of 1977
- The Safe Drinking Water Act of 1974
- The Federal Water Pollution Control Act of 1972
- TSCA
- The Solid Waste Disposal Act of 1976
- The Clean Air Act of 1977
- The Comprehensive Environmental Response, Compensation and Liability Act of 1980
- The Energy Reorganization Act of 1978
- The Wendell H. Ford Aviation Investment and Reform Act for the 21st Century
- Section 806 of the Corporate and Criminal Fraud Accountability Act of 2002 (Sarbanes-Oxley Act)
- Section 6 of the Pipeline Safety Improvement Act of 2002

The following are whistleblower regulations:

- 29 C.F.R. Part 1977—Discrimination Against Employees Exercising Rights under the Williams-Steiger Occupational Safety and Health Act of 1970
- 29 C.F.R. Part 1978—Rules for Implementing Section 405 of the Surface Transportation Assistance Act of 1982

- 29 C.F.R. Part 1979—Procedures for the Handling of Discrimination Complaints under Section 519 of the Wendell H. Ford Aviation Investment and Reform Act for the 21st Century
- 29 C.F.R. Part 1980—Procedures for the Handling of Discrimination Complaints under Section 806 of the Corporate and Criminal Fraud Accountability Act of 2002
- 29 C.F.R. Part 1981—Procedures for the Handling of Discrimination Complaints under Section 6 of the Pipeline Safety Improvement Act of 2002
- 29 C.F.R. Part 24—Procedures for the Handling of Discrimination Complaints under Federal Employee Protection Statutes

[http://www.whistleblowers.gov/regulations_page.html]

Q 7:74 What workplace policies are deemed to illegally discourage employees from reporting hazards and injuries?

In March 2012, OSHA identified the following workplace scenarios that the agency deems to illegally discourage workers from exercising their OSH Act reporting rights:

- OSHA says it has received reports of employers who have a policy of taking disciplinary action against employees who are injured on the job, regardless of the circumstances surrounding the injury. Reporting an injury is always a protected activity. OSHA views discipline imposed under such a policy against an employee who reports an injury as a direct violation of section 11(c) of the OSH Act and the Federal Railroad Safety Act (FRSA). In other words, an employer's policy to discipline all employees who are injured, regardless of fault, is not a legitimate non-discriminatory reason that an employer may advance to justify adverse action against an employee who reports an injury. In addition, such a policy is inconsistent with the employer's obligation to establish a way for employees to report injuries under 29 C.F.R. Part 1904.35(b), and where it is encountered, a referral for a recordkeeping investigation should be made. Note: Where OSHA encounters such conduct by a railroad carrier, or a contractor or subcontractor of a railroad carrier, a referral to the Federal Railroad Administration (FRA), which may conduct a recordkeeping investigation, may also be appropriate.
- In another situation, an employee who reports an injury or illness is disciplined, and the stated reason is that the employee has violated an employer rule about the time or manner for reporting injuries and illnesses. Such cases deserve careful scrutiny. Because the act of reporting the injury directly results in discipline, there is a clear potential for violating section 11(c) of the OSH Act and FRSA. OSHA recognizes that employers have a legitimate interest in establishing procedures for receiving and responding to reports of injuries. To be consistent with the statute, however, such procedures must be reasonable and may not unduly burden the employee's right and ability to report. For example, the rules cannot

penalize workers who do not realize immediately that their injuries are serious enough to report, or even that they are injured at all. Nor may enforcement of such rules be used as a pretext for discrimination. In investigating such cases, these factors may be considered: whether the employee's deviation from the procedure was minor or extensive, inadvertent or deliberate; whether the employee had a reasonable basis for acting as he or she did; whether the employer can show a substantial interest in the rule and its enforcement; and whether the discipline imposed appears disproportionate to the asserted interest. Again, where the employer's reporting requirements are unreasonable, unduly burdensome, or enforced with unjustifiably harsh sanctions, they may result in inaccurate injury records, and a referral for a recordkeeping investigation should be made.

- In a third situation targeted by OSHA, an employee reports an injury, and the employer imposes discipline on the ground that the injury resulted from the violation of a safety rule by the employee. OSHA encourages employers to maintain and enforce legitimate workplace safety rules in order to eliminate or reduce workplace hazards and prevent injuries from occurring in the first place. In some cases, however, an employer may attempt to use a work rule as a pretext for discrimination against a worker who reports an injury. A careful investigation is needed. Several circumstances are relevant. Does the employer monitor for compliance with the work rule in the absence of an injury? Does the employer consistently impose equivalent discipline against employees who violate the work rule in the absence of an injury? The nature of the rule cited by the employer should also be considered. Vague rules, such as a requirement that employees "maintain situational awareness" or "work carefully" may be manipulated and used as a pretext for unlawful discrimination. Therefore, where such general rules are involved, the investigation must include an especially careful examination of whether and how the employer applies the rule in situations that do not involve an employee injury. Enforcing a rule more stringently against injured employees than non-injured employees may suggest that the rule is a pretext for discrimination against an injured employee in violation of section 11(c) of the OSH Act and FRSA.

- Finally, some employers establish programs that unintentionally or intentionally provide employees an incentive to not report injuries. For example, an employer might enter all employees who have not been injured in the previous year in a drawing to win a prize, or a team of employees might be awarded a bonus if no one from the team is injured over some period of time. Such programs might be well-intentioned efforts by employers to encourage their workers to use safe practices. However, there are better ways to encourage safe work practices, such as incentives that promote worker participation in safety-related activities, such as identifying hazards or participating in investigations of injuries, incidents, or "near misses."

OSHA discourages all of these scenarios as either per se or potentially illegal.

Q 7:75   Where does the whistleblower protection program reside?

In 2012, the program was moved under the agency's Office of the Assistance Secretary. OSHA first announced that it would restructure its whistleblower program on August 1, 2011, as part of the agency's multifaceted plan for strengthening the enforcement of 21 whistleblower laws under its jurisdiction. Implementation of this plan began with the fiscal year 2012 budget as OSHA established a separate budgetary line item for the whistleblower program to better track and hold accountable its activities and accomplishments.

In 2012, OSHA also launched pilot projects in 10 of its regional offices to test structural changes that might strengthen the program.

Q 7:76   What are the whistleblower enforcement actions available under the Affordable Care Act?

OSHA has published an interim final rule in the Federal Register that governs whistleblower complaints filed under Section 1558 of the Affordable Care Act (ACA). The ACA contains various provisions to make health insurance more affordable and accountable to consumers. Among the policies to achieve its goals, the Affordable Care Act's Section 1558 provides protection to employees against retaliation by an employer for reporting alleged violations of Title I of the ACA or for receiving a tax credit or cost-sharing reduction as a result of participating in a health insurance exchange or marketplace. [78 Fed. Reg. 13222 (Feb. 27, 2013)]

Title I includes a range of insurance company accountability policies, such as the prohibition of lifetime limits on coverage and exclusions due to pre-existing conditions. If an employee reports a violation of one of these policies or requirements, the act's whistleblower provision prohibits employers from retaliating against the employee. If an employee is retaliated against in violation of the whistleblower provision, he or she may file a complaint with, and ultimately receive relief from, OSHA or the courts.

The ACA authorizes the secretary of labor to conduct investigations into complaints and issue determinations, which are functions delegated to OSHA. OSHA's interim final rule establishes the procedures and time frames for the filing and handling of such complaints, including investigations by OSHA, appeals of OSHA determinations to an administrative law judge for a hearing, review of such decisions by the Administrative Review Board and judicial review of the secretary's final decision.

A fact sheet about filing whistleblower complaints under the Affordable Care Act is available at: http://www.osha.gov/Publications/whistleblower/OSHAFS-3641.pdf.

[http://www.osha.gov/pls/oshaweb/owadisp.show_document?p_table = NEWS_RELEASES&p_id = 23673]

Enforcement

Q 7:77   Are there any recordkeeping requirements under the OSH Act?

Employers with eight or more employees must keep records of occupational injuries and illnesses and file periodic reports on these with OSHA. Occupational injuries must be recorded if they result in death, loss of consciousness, medical treatment other than minor first aid, one or more lost work days, the restriction of work or motion, or transfer to another job. A covered employer must maintain accurate records of employee exposure to potentially toxic materials. Any employee or representative of the employees may request an OSHA inspection if he or she believes that a violation of an OSHA standard exists and threatens physical harm or imminent danger. The latest recordkeeping requirements took effect October 2003 and can be found at: http://www.osha.gov/recordkeeping/index.html.

Q 7:78   Are any training materials available to assist with record-keeping requirements?

Training materials are available from OSHA at: http://www.osha.gov/record keeping/RKpresentations.html.

Q 7:79   What do the recordkeeping regulations include?

Notable are regulations involving needlesticks, enacted in compliance with the Needlestick Safety and Prevention Act, passed unanimously by Congress in November 2000.

The regulations also simplify the manner in which employers record MSDSs, replacing the current, cumbersome system, and conforming the regulations to the new ergonomics laws passed during the first days of the Bush administration in January 2001.

Additionally, the new regulations include:

1. Rules on restricted work and light duty assignments;
2. Promotion of greater employee awareness and involvement in the record-keeping process;
3. Enhanced worker and union access to recordkeeping forms;
4. A plain-language requirement;
5. Enhanced privacy protection for employees; and
6. Greater employer flexibility in using computers and telecommunications equipment in creating, maintaining, and transmitting records to OSHA.

Q 7:80 Which OSHA forms are relevant to recordkeeping regulations?

The forms employers should have on hand or know how to obtain are:

- Form 300 (Log of Work-Related Injuries and Illnesses)
- Form 301 (Injury and Illness Incident Report)
- Form 300A (Summary of Work-Related Injuries and Illnesses)

They are available at: http://www.osha.gov/recordkeeping/RKforms.html.

Q 7:81 What guidance has OSHA made available with regard to record keeping?

Guidance available on the Internet includes:

- Frequently Asked Questions: http://www.osha.gov/recordkeeping/entry faq.html
- Comprehensive Fact Sheet: http://www.osha.gov/OshDoc/data_Record keepingFacts/RKfactsheet1.pdf
- Interpretation Letters: http://www.osha.gov/recordkeeping/RK interpretations.html

Among the most recent of these are:

- 2/9/2009—Determining work-relatedness for recordkeeping of injury resulting from horseplay.
- 01/29/2009—Permissibility of using electronic signature to satisfy the Annual Summary certification for OSHA Form 300-A.
- 08/26/2008—Clarification of several recordkeeping scenarios regarding days away from work, restricted work activity, and work-relatedness.
- 07/14/2008—Whether to record two cases of employee injuries sustained in company parking lot during employees commute to work.

Q 7:82 What are the privacy requirements under the recordkeeping regulations?

The regulations:

1. Prohibit an employer from entering an employee's name on the Form 300 for certain types of injuries and illnesses (e.g., sexual assaults, HIV infections, mental illnesses);
2. Give the employer the right not to describe the nature of sensitive injuries where the employee's identity would be revealed;
3. Give employee representatives access to only that portion of the Form 301 that contains no personal identifiers;
4. Require the employer to remove employees' names before providing data to persons not enjoying access rights under the new rules.

Q 7:83   Have the recordkeeping and reporting regulations resulted in any litigation?

On August 2, 2004, the U.S. District Court for the Southern District of New York, which sits in Manhattan, released its decision in a case in which the *New York Times* sued OSHA under the Freedom of Information Act. The newspaper demanded "Lost Workday Injury and Illness" rates that OSHA was withholding. The court held that the rates were non-confidential commercial information that was not protected from disclosure, even though they might enable readers to extrapolate the numbers of hours worked by employees—data which could be confidential.

In the words of the international law firm of Morgan Lewis & Bockius, headquartered in Philadelphia, "This decision reiterates the importance of injury and illness recordkeeping for employers. Not only must this information be kept and verified by a company officer but it is also utilized by OSHA for establishment of a comprehensive inspection list under the Site-Specific Targeting (SST) Program."

Q 7:84   Does OSHA have any data requirements with regard to Hispanic workers or immigrants?

Yes, OSHA collects data on countries of origin and language capabilities of all workers involved in serious accidents and fatalities. OSHA also collects site-specific data on construction sites on the theory that many immigrants are among those who die on these sites annually.

OSHA also is a part of the Justice and Equality in the Workplace Program, based in Houston, Texas. The Labor Department's Wage & Hour Administration is also a participant and claims to have recovered some $700,000 in back wages on behalf of Hispanic workers since it began to focus on their needs under the program's umbrella. Other partners in the program are: the consulates of Colombia, El Salvador, Guatemala, and Mexico; the Equal Employment Opportunity Commission (EEOC); and the Mexican American Legal Defense and Education Fund. With fatal injuries on the rise among Hispanic workers in the United States, OSHA sees a clear role for itself in the program. [http://www.osha.gov/dcsp/compliance_assistance/index_hispanic.html]

Q 7:85   What rights do employees have under the OSH Act?

Employees have the right to a workplace free from recognized hazards. Additionally, employees are protected from retaliation or discrimination by their employers as a result of exercising any rights that are granted under the Act. Employees have the right to refuse to work under a dangerous condition.

Q 7:86   Must employees comply with certain procedures before they refuse to work under a dangerous condition?

Before an employee can exercise the right to refuse to work under a dangerous condition, the employee must attempt to have the company correct the hazardous condition. Furthermore, the dangerous condition triggering this employee's right must be such that a reasonable person, under the same circumstances, would conclude that there is a real danger of death or serious injury.

Q 7:87   Are there posting requirements with regard to workplace injuries?

Yes, effective February 1, 2008, employers must post injury/illness summaries. The summary must include the total number of job-related injuries and illnesses that occurred the previous year and were logged on the OSHA Form 300. To assist in calculating incidence rates, information about the annual average number of employees and total hours worked during the calendar year is also required. If a company recorded no injuries or illnesses, the employer must enter "zero" on the total line. The form must be signed and certified by a company executive. Form 300A should be displayed in a common area where notices to employees are usually posted.

Employers with 10 or fewer employees and employers in certain industries are normally exempt from federal OSHA injury and illness recordkeeping and posting requirements. A complete list of exempt industries in the retail, services, finance, insurance, and real estate sectors is posted on the OSHA Web site.

The DOL's BLS may still select exempted employers to participate in an annual statistical survey. All employers covered by OSHA need to comply with safety and health standards. All accidents that result in one or more fatalities or in the hospitalization of three or more employees must be reported verbally within eight hours to the nearest OSHA office.

[http://www.osha.gov/pls/oshaweb/owadisp.show_document?p_table = NEWS _RELEASES&p_id = 23637]

Q 7:88   What is OSHA's anti-retaliation standard?

The OSH Act proscribes retaliation if an employee does any of the following:

1. Institutes any proceeding under or related to the Act;
2. Testifies or is about to testify in an OSHA-related proceeding; or
3. Exercises any right on behalf of that employee or on behalf of any other employee under the Act.

If a worker believes his/her employer has discriminated against him/her because she/he exercised safety and health rights or other protected activity, she/he is advised to contact the local OSHA office as soon as possible. Most health and safety discrimination complaints fall under the OSH Act, which gives the worker only 30 days to report discrimination. Some of the other laws have complaint-filing deadlines that differ from OSHA's. (See Qs 4:8–4:11.)

In addition, depending on the statute, the complaining employee may need to file the complaint in writing. However, they can telephone, fax, or mail an OSHA 11(c) complaint. The complaint should be filed with the OSHA office responsible for enforcement activities in the geographical area where the employee resides or was employed, but may in fact be filed with any OSHA officer or employee.

OSHA regional offices and numbers are:

- Boston (617) 565-9860
- New York (212) 337-2378
- Philadelphia (215) 596-1201
- Atlanta (678) 237-0447
- Chicago (312) 353-2220
- Dallas (972) 850-4145
- Kansas City (816) 283-8745
- Denver (720) 264-6550
- San Francisco (415) 625-2547
- Seattle (206) 553-5930

Written complaints may be filed by mail (the agency recommends certified mail), fax, or hand delivery during business hours. The date postmarked, faxed, or hand-delivered will be considered the date filed.

OSHA claims to conduct an in-depth interview with each complainant to determine the need for an investigation. If evidence supports the worker's claim of discrimination, OSHA typically will ask the employer to restore the worker's job, earnings, and benefits. If the employer objects, OSHA may take the employer to court to seek relief for the worker.

[For additional information, including access to relevant manuals and guidelines, *see* http://www.whistleblowers.gov/regulations_page.html]

Q 7:89   Does OSHA's retaliation standard apply to other federal safety statutes?

No. In *Seymore v. Lake Tahoe Cruises, Inc.* [888 F. Supp. 1029 (E.D. Cal. 1995)], the court ruled that OSHA's anti-retaliation standard could not be stretched to protect a tour ship captain from a job termination for refusing to operate a leaky vessel, where the U.S. Coast Guard—and not OSHA—had jurisdiction.

Q 7:90   Are employers obliged to apprise their employees of their OSH Act rights?

Yes. Employers covered by the OSH Act are required to display the "Job Safety and the OSH Act Health Protection" poster (OSHA Doc. 2203), available upon request from the DOL Additionally, employers in the ground transportation industry, such as trucking companies and bus lines, must display the "Employee Information Poster-Motor Vehicle Operators" (OSHA Doc. 3113), also available upon request.

Q 7:91   What will employees learn about OSHA when they read OSHA's "Job Safety and Health Protection" poster?

The poster reflects the Act's major provisions regarding:

- Employers
- Employees
- Inspections
- Complaints
- Citations
- Proposed penalties
- Voluntary activities
- Consultations

Q 7:92   When may an employee file a complaint with OSHA?

One or more employees or their representative (e.g., a labor organization or an attorney) may file a complaint with OSHA's nearest local office, requesting an inspection of their employer's premises, if they have a good faith belief that unsafe or unhealthful conditions exist in their workplace.

Q 7:93   Will OSHA protect the identities of employees who file a complaint?

Yes. Upon request, OSHA will keep the complainants' identities confidential.

Q 7:94   What can employees, who believe they are victims of retaliation for having filed an OSHA complaint, do about it?

Such employees are entitled to file a second complaint, charging retaliation, with the same OSHA office. Employers should note that in some cases OSHA or a federal court has found that, while the underlying safety complaint lacked merit, the retaliation claim was meritorious and therefore the complainants were entitled to a remedy. Lack of merit of the initial, underlying safety complaint does not prevent such an outcome, so long as that underlying complaint was filed in good faith.

Q 7:95   What remedies can be accorded employees found to have been victims of retaliation for exercising their rights under the OSH Act?

Victims of retaliation can be entitled to:

• Reinstatement

• Back pay

• Front pay

Q 7:96   Does the OSH Act provide employees with a private right of action?

Employees must pursue their claims for employer violations of OSHA's safety regulations exclusively with OSHA; however, employees may file a federal lawsuit for alleged violation of OSHA's anti-retaliation provisions. State courts in general have been reluctant to recognize wrongful discharge actions grounded in public policy violations, where the underlying public policy is the OSH Act. [*See, e.g.*, Geary v. U.S. Steel Corp., 456 Pa. 171, 319 A.2d 174 (1974).]

Q 7:97   What rights do operators of motor vehicles have under the OSH Act with regard to unsafe working conditions?

Motor vehicle operators have the right to do the following if related unsafe working conditions exist:

1. Refuse to operate a commercial motor vehicle that fails to meet federal safety requirements;

2. Refuse to violate a DOT regulation;

3. Report violations of vehicle safety requirements; and

4. Refuse to drive under conditions that the driver reasonably believes might cause serious personal injury or injure members of the public.

Q 7:98   What is OSHA's Severe Violator Enforcement Program?

OSHA's Severe Violator Enforcement Program (SVEP) directive became effective on June 18, 2010, cancelling the Enhanced Enforcement Program. Under the SVEP, the criteria were changed to better focus enforcement efforts on significant hazards by concentrating inspection resources on employers who have demonstrated recalcitrance or indifference to their OSH Act obligations by committing willful, repeated, or failure-to-abate violations in one or more of the following circumstances: (1) a fatality or catastrophe situation; (2) in industry operations or processes that expose employees to the most severe occupational hazards and those identified as "high-emphasis hazards"; (3) exposing employees to hazards related to the potential release of a highly hazardous chemical; or (4) all egregious enforcement actions. The SVEP also created a nationwide referral procedure in which OSHA may inspect related worksites/workplaces of a SVEP employer if OSHA identifies a broader pattern of non-compliance. The high-emphasis hazards include fall hazards and specific hazards identified from the following selected national emphasis programs:

- Amputations
- Combustible dust
- Crystalline silica
- Excavation and trenching
- Lead poisoning
- Shipbreaking

[http://www.osha.gov/dep/2010_enforcement_summary.html]

Workplace Inspections

Q 7:99   Does OSHA provide for workplace inspections?

OSHA standards are enforced by means of physical inspections of workplaces. Practical realities of large numbers of workplaces and limited budgetary appropriations have forced OSHA to prioritize the inspection process. The following is a list of types of investigations, in order of priority:

1. Claims of imminent danger;
2. Fatal and catastrophic accidents;
3. Complaints filed by employees who allege hazardous working conditions;
4. Inspection of high-hazard industries; and
5. Random general investigations.

Q 7:100   What safety rules ought an employer have in place voluntarily?

Employers should observe the following rules:

1. Everything in and about the plant must be kept clean and in good order.
2. Each employee is held responsible for the condition of the plant and equipment under her/his control.
3. Running, shouting, throwing objects, and other horseplay are strictly forbidden.
4. Employees must wear clothing suitable to their jobs; gloves, goggles, and other protective gear are provided as needed.
5. Employees must pay attention to their supervisor's instructions and have them clearly in mind before commencing their work.
6. Anyone who does not know how to do a job safely must ask his or her supervisor immediately.
7. Always use all safeguards and safety equipment provided.
8. Keep materials out of walkways—especially boards with nails in them.

9. Any employee working above or below a co-worker must warn that co-worker of her/his presence.

10. Good teamwork promotes safety: When working with another employee, warn the co-worker before dropping a load, starting up a machine, or doing anything else that might cause injury.

11. Keep both hands free when climbing or descending a ladder.

12. Make sure all rungs of any ladder are solid, and, if wooden, securely nailed.

13. Report any unsafe condition to an immediate supervisor immediately.

14. Get help for lifting heavy objects and learn the correct way to lift an object before attempting it.

15. Report all injuries promptly.

16. If injured but mobile, seek first aid immediately.

17. Keep focused on the job: Alertness prevents injuries.

18. Never attempt to oil, clean, or adjust a machine while it is running.

19. Never drop or throw anything from a height until certain no one is below.

20. Do not look directly at welders or cutters while they are in operation.

21. Do not wear ragged sleeves, loose clothing, or flopping ties while operating machinery.

22. Do not try to use improper or broken tools to do a job.

23. Do not hitch a ride on a load being lifted by a crane.

24. Do not stand or walk under loads being lifted by cranes.

25. Do not hoist a load until it is securely made up and balanced.

26. Never start a machine, turn a valve, or pull a switch until personally making sure it is safe to do so.

27. Do not try to fix electrical equipment of any kind unless properly trained and responsible for that job.

28. Never aim compressed air at anyone.

Q 7:101 If the employer has a safety rule in place, will that alone insulate the employer from OSH Act liability?

Not necessarily. If employees regularly flaunt the rule, so that the employer knows or should know (by exercising reasonable diligence), then liability for these safety violations will be imputed to the employer. [See, e.g., D.A. Collins Constr. Co., Inc. v. Secretary of Labor, 117 F.3d 691 (2d Cir. 1997).]

Q 7:102 Can an employee fired for complaining about unsafe conditions win punitive damages?

Yes. [See Reich v. Cambridge Air Sys., Inc., 26 F.3d 1187 (1st Cir. 1994).]

On March 9, 2010, OSHA announced the imposition of punitive damages in a whistleblower case. The investigation found that the Port Authority Trans-Hudson Corp. of New York and New Jersey violated the rights of an employee when it imposed discipline on her for exercising her rights under the Federal Railroad Safety Act. The employee was injured when a chair she sat on broke, causing her to fall. When she reported the injury, the railroad charged her with having caused the accident herself. The employee then filed a whistleblower complaint with OSHA alleging that the railroad had disciplined her for reporting her injury. OSHA's investigation, conducted under the whistleblower provisions of the Federal Railroad Safety Act, found merit to the complaint. "Railroad employees have the legal right to report work-related injuries," said Robert Kulick, OSHA's regional administrator in New York. "Railroads that retaliate against employees for exercising their rights will be held accountable." As a result of its findings, OSHA has ordered The Port Authority to pay $1,000 in punitive damages and to take corrective actions, including expunging disciplinary actions and references to them from various records as well as compensating the worker for attorneys' fees. The railroad also was required to post and provide its employees with information on their FRSA whistleblower rights. PATH and the complainant had 30 days from receipt of the findings to file an appeal with the Labor Department's Office of Administrative Law Judges. Under FRSA, employees of a railroad carrier and its contractors and subcontractors are protected against retaliation for reporting on-the-job injuries as well as reporting certain safety and security violations and cooperating with investigations by OSHA and other regulatory agencies.

[http://www.osha.gov/pls/oshaweb/owadisp.show_document?p_table = NEWS_RELEASES&p_id = 17244]

Q 7:103   Is an OSHA inspector required to present a search warrant before entering a workplace?

The compliance officer conducting the inspection may enter without delay and at reasonable times any factory, business establishment, construction site, or workplace covered by the Act. This inspection may include all pertinent conditions, structures, machines, apparatus, devices, equipment, and materials on the inspection site. The office is also given authority to question privately any employer, owner, operator, agent, or employee.

The Act allows the employer and a representative authorized by the employees to accompany the inspector during the physical inspection of the work site.

In *Marshall v. Barlow's Inc.* [436 U.S. 307 (1973)], the Supreme Court held that an employer subject to an OSHA inspection may insist upon a search warrant. As a result of the Marshall decision, the compliance officer now must request permission to enter the workplace or other area that is to be the subject of the search. If the employer refuses entry or forbids the continuation of an inspection, the compliance officer must terminate the inspection or confine it to those areas where no objection has been raised. Following such a refusal, an ex parte application for an inspection warrant may be filed by the officer with a U.S. district judge or federal magistrate.

Q 7:104   If an OSHA inspector appears at a workplace, what rights does the employer have regarding the inspection?

An employer has the right to accompany the inspector during the physical inspection of the work site. A representative authorized by the employees may also accompany the inspector. At least one federal appellate court has ruled that having an employee representative accompany the OSHA inspector is an absolute right and is not within the discretion of the compliance officer. [Chicago Bridge Co. v. OSHRC, 535 F.2d 371 (7th Cir. 1976)] Alternatively, the employer may decline to allow entry, in which case the inspector must obtain a warrant. (See Q 7:103.)

Penalties

Q 7:105   What penalties and remedies does the OSH Act provide?

OSHA's new penalty structure, effective October 1, 2010, is as follows:

OSHA is implementing several changes to its administrative penalty calculation system. Many of the agency's current penalty adjustment factors have been in place since the early 1970s, resulting in penalties which are often too low to have an adequate deterrent effect. Administrative penalty adjustments will therefore be made to several factors which impact the final penalty issued to employers. These factors include:

- History Reduction
- History Increase
- Repeat Violations
- Severe Violator Enforcement Program
- Gravity-Based Penalty
- Size Reduction
- Good Faith
- Minimum Penalties
- Additional Administrative Modifications to the Penalty Calculation Policy

A brief description of each penalty adjustment factor and planned changes are provided below:

History Reduction. The time frame for considering an employer's history of violations will expand from three years to five. An employer who has been inspected by OSHA within the previous five years and has not been issued any serious, willful, repeat, or failure-to-abate citations will receive a 10 percent reduction for history.

History Increase. An employer that has been cited by OSHA for any high gravity serious, willful, repeat, or failure-to-abate violation within the previous five years will receive a 10 percent increase in their penalty, up to the statutory maximum. Employers who have not been inspected and those who have received citations for serious violations that were not high gravity will receive neither a reduction nor an increase for history.

Repeat Violations. The time period for considering the classification of repeated violations will be increased from three to five years.

Severe Violator Enforcement Program. Where circumstances warrant, at the discretion of the Area Director, high gravity serious violations related to standards and hazards identified in the SVEP will not normally be grouped or combined, and may be cited as separate violations, with individual proposed penalties.

Gravity-Based Penalty (GBP). The gravity of a violation is the primary consideration in calculating penalties and is established by assessing the severity of the injury/illness, which could result from a hazard and the probability that an injury or illness could occur. OSHA is adopting a gravity-based penalty structure for serious citations, which will range from $3,000 to $7,000.

Size Reduction. OSHA will be amending its penalty reduction structure based on the size of employers, allowing for a penalty reduction between 10 and 40 percent for those with less than 250 employees. No size reduction will be applied for employers with 251 or more employees.

Good Faith. The current good faith procedures in the Field Operations Manual will be retained. A penalty reduction is permitted in recognition of an employer's effort to implement an effective workplace safety and health program. Employers must have a safety and health program in place to get any good faith reduction. Good faith reductions are not allowed in the cases of high gravity serious, willful, repeat, or failure-to-abate violations. The 15% Quick-Fix reduction, which is currently allowed as an abatement incentive program to encourage employers to immediately abate hazards identified during inspections, remains unchanged. However, the 10% reduction for employers with a strategic partnership agreement will be eliminated.

Minimum Penalties. The minimum proposed penalty for a serious violation will be increased to $500. When the proposed penalty for a serious violation would amount to less than $500, a $500 penalty will be proposed for that violation. The proposed minimum penalty for a posting violation will increase to $250 if the company was previously provided a poster by OSHA.

Additional Administrative Modifications to the Penalty Calculation Policy. Final penalties will be calculated serially, unlike the current practice where all penalty reductions are added and the total percentage of reductions is then multiplied by the gravity-based penalty to arrive at the proposed penalty. All penalty adjustment factors will be applied serially.

[http://www.osha.gov/dep/administrative-penalty.html]

The firm's Washington Labor & Employment Wire continued, "Additionally, the new penalty structure expands the time period OSHA will consider when determining whether an employer's past compliance history justifies a penalty adjustment. Under the old regime, OSHA looked at the employer's history of violations over the previous three years, but will now consider the previous five years. An employer that has been cited for any high gravity serious, willful, repeat, or failure-to-abate violation during that period will receive a 10 percent increase in their penalty. Conversely, an employer who has been inspected in the previous five years and failed to receive any high gravity serious, willful, repeat, or failure-to-abate violation will receive a 10 percent reduction."

The bulletin added that the "good faith" procedures in the agency's Field Operations Manual mostly were retained, but the 10 percent penalty reduction for employers with an OSHA strategic partnership was stricken. Also blue-penciled out were good-faith reductions, where the high-gravity serious, willful, and repeat violations are at issue, as well as where OSHA asserts a failure to abate the hazard.

The Wire concludes, "Finally, the new policy provides for additional discretionary adjustments under OSHA's new Severe Violator Enforcement Policy (SVEP)." (See Q 7:98, above.)

[http://washlaborwire.com/2010/10/17/osha's-new-penalty-structure-effective-october-1-2010/]

Q 7:106   What is the Protecting America's Workers Act and how might it affect OSHA penalties if enacted?

The proposed Protecting America's Workers Act (PAWA) [H.R. 2067, accessible at http://www.opencongress.org/bill/111-h2067/show] includes critical provisions that deal with significant weaknesses in the OSH Act. The proposed statute's major provisions:

1. Expands its coverage to federal, state, and local government employees.

2. Authorizes the Secretary of Labor, under specified conditions, to cede OSHA jurisdiction to another federal agency with respect to certain occupational standards or regulations for such agency's employees.

3. Declares OSHA inapplicable to working conditions covered by the Federal Mine Safety and Health Act of 1977. Sets forth increased protections for whistleblowers under OSHA.

4. Sets forth strengthened provisions relating to:

   (a) the posting of employee rights;

   (b) a prohibition against the adoption or implementation of policies or practices by employers that discourage the reporting of work-related injuries or illnesses or that discriminate or provide for adverse action against any employee for reporting such injury or illness;

   (c) a prohibition against the loss of wages or employee benefits as a result of an employee participating in or aiding workplace inspections;

   (d) investigations of incidents in a place of employment resulting in a death or the hospitalization of two or more employees;

(e) a prohibition against designating a citation for an occupational health and safety standard violation as an unclassified citation;

(f) the rights of an employee who has sustained a work-related injury or illness that is the subject of an investigation;

(g) an employer's right to contest citations and penalties;

(h) the Secretary's assertion of an employer's failure to correct a serious hazard during an employer's contest to a citation; and

(i) employee objections to modifications of citations.

The provisions increase civil and criminal penalties for certain OSHA violators, and require a state that has an approved plan for the development and enforcement of occupational safety and health standards to amend its plan to conform to the requirements of the PAWA within 12 months after enactment of the Act.

The prospect for the PAWA, like those of other labor legislation aimed at reforming the National Labor Relations Act (see chapter 11), and beefing up regulation of the financial sector to prevent a repeat of the Great Recession, improved significantly in the spring of 2010, as the Democrats rallied their forces for their successful push to pass healthcare legislation, freeing them up to attempt other legislative initiatives prior to the November national elections. The Democrat-controlled Congress in fact did enact significant legislation including:

- The Patient Protection and Affordable Care Act (PPACA) [Pub. L. No. 111-148];

- The Dodd-Frank Wall Street Reform and Consumer Protection Act (H.R. 4173) [Pub. L. No. 111-203].

Unfortunately for those who hoped for a strengthening of workplace health and safety, the House of Representatives went to the Republican Party, including Tea Party freshmen, in November 2010. Although purely symbolic, since the Democrat-controlled Senate refused to go along, the GOP Congressmen flexed their muscles by voting repeal of the PPACA. The PAWA was not passed in 2012, but it was reintroduced by Senator Patty Murray on March 22, 2013.

Q 7:107   How is a company notified of a citation under the OSH Act?

If a citation is issued by OSHA following an inspection, the employer must be notified by certified mail within a reasonable time, not later than six months after the violation was identified.

Q 7:108   Can a company contest an OSHA citation?

A company has 15 working days from receipt of an OSHA citation to notify OSHA of its intention to contest either the citation or the proposed penalty.

Q 7:109   What happens if a company does not contest an OSHA citation?

If the employer does not contest an OSHA citation, the citation becomes final and is not subject to any other appeal or review in any other court or agency.

Q 7:110   How much time does an OSHA citation allow an employer to abate a hazard?

The citation must provide for a reasonable time to achieve abatement—usually not more than 30 days. The company is required to post the citation (or a copy of it) in a prominent place at or near the area at which the violation exists or occurred. The employees, or their representative, can then file a notice challenging the abatement period set in the citation if they believe it to be too long.

Q 7:111   Must an employer challenge both the citation and the penalty?

Yes, although the company may challenge the penalty and citation separately. If the company chooses to contest only the penalty, the violation itself is not subject to later review, even within the context of that penalty challenge.

Q 7:112   What happens if an employer challenges an OSHA citation?

If a company challenges an OSHA citation or the assessed penalty or abatement period in the citation, a hearing will be held in front of an adminis-trative law judge who will make findings of fact and conclusions of law that either affirm, modify, or vacate the citation. The judge's order becomes final within 30 days after it is filed with OSHA unless, within that time, a member of OSHRC exercises the statutory right to have the decision reviewed by the full Commission. Also, any party to the proceeding can file a petition requesting discretionary review. The final order of the Commission can be appealed to a U.S. appeals court.

Q 7:113   Can an employer defend itself against an OSHA citation by showing that it is impossible to comply with a standard?

A company has an absolute defense to a citation if it can prove that compliance with the standard is impossible; however, that a standard is merely impractical or difficult to meet will not excuse a company from compliance with that standard.

Q 7:114 What happens if a cited employer fails to abate the hazard in the time allowed by the OSHA citation?

If the violation is not corrected in the time allowed by the citation, the company is notified by certified mail of its failure to abate and of the proposed penalty. This notice and proposed penalty are final unless the company files a notice of contest within 15 working days. If the order is not contested, it is deemed final and is not subject to any subsequent judicial review.

Q 7:115 What if an employer has made a good-faith effort to comply with the abatement requirement in the citation?

If an employer has made a good-faith effort to comply with the citation's abatement requirements, but the abatement has not occurred because of factors beyond the reasonable control of the employer, a petition for modification should be filed. If OSHA or an employee objects to the extension or modification, a hearing must be held in front of OSHRC.

Q 7:116 What should a company's petition for modification of an abatement requirement state?

The petition must state in detail the steps that have already been taken by the employer to abate the hazard, the additional time necessary to abate, the reasons that additional time is necessary (including unavailability of technical or professional personnel or equipment), and the interim steps that are being taken to protect the employees.

Q 7:117 What happens if an employer fails to correct a citation violation after, the citation has become final?

In this situation, a fine of up to $1,000 per day can be imposed on that company. If it is later found that the violation was willful and it caused the death of any employee, a fine of up to $10,000 a day plus six months' imprisonment of the employer may be assessed.

Q 7:118 May an employer whose conduct does not meet OSHA requirements be subject to penalties other than those provided by the OSH Act?

In February 1989, the Illinois Supreme Court—the highest court yet to consider the question—ruled that the OSH Act does not prevent the state from prosecuting an employer under state criminal laws for conduct that was also regulated by OSHA and federal law. The court based its decision in *Illinois v. Chicago Magnet Wire Co.* [534 N.E.2d 962 (Ill. 1989)] on the fact that OSHA encourages the states to develop their own occupational safety and health plans. The court noted that criminal charges do not impose new responsibilities on employers, but instead impose additional sanctions for improper conduct that "threatens or results in serious physical injury or death to workers." According to the court, state penal sanctions would serve as retribution, as well as a deterrent, keeping employers from violating safety standards. [*Chicago Magnet Wire*, at 966] The Illinois Supreme Court's decision has spurred prosecutors in other states to plan criminal prosecutions of OSHA violators. The Illinois Supreme Court's decision was in agreement with the Department of Justice's position on the issue; however, in April 1991, following an eight-month, non-jury trial, Chicago Magnetic Wire Co. and five company executives were acquitted by a Cook County circuit judge. In rendering his verdict, the judge said that the State's Attorney proved only that the company's Elk Grove Village plant was "noisy, dirty, hot and noxious." But the prosecutors, he ruled, had failed to prove that these conditions had made employees sick. This case was the second setback for Illinois prosecutors seeking to establish that workplace safety violations can sustain criminal charges. In January 1991, a state appeals court overturned the convictions of three business executives for the death of an employee, Stefan Golab, from cyanide poisoning at Film Recovery Systems, Inc., a suburban Chicago company. [Illinois v. O'Neil, 550 N.E.2d 1090 (Ill. App. Ct. 1990)]

In a 2008 case, the California Supreme Court considered whether violation of a criminal statute, making it a misdemeanor for a contractor to move tools to within six feet of a live wire, could impose liability on homeowners as "employers." In this case, the parents of a worker for an unlicensed contractor, who was electrocuted while trimming trees when his pole saw came into contact with an overhead high voltage line, brought a wrongful death action against the homeowners. The plaintiffs' complaint further alleged there were in effect at the time of the decedent's death, regulations enacted pursuant to the California Occupational Safety and Health Act of 1973 (Cal-OSHA) [Cal. Code Regs., tit. 8, §§ 2940.2, 2941, 2946, 2950, 2951, 3247] governing operating procedures for work on or in proximity to overhead high voltage lines; that the homeowners were statutory employers of the decedent within the meaning of the workers' compensation laws; and that in that legal capacity they became liable for violations of the Cal-OSHA regulations, proximately causing the worker's death, as well as for failing to secure the payment of workers' compensation benefits for their "employee." [Lab. Code § 3706] Rejecting this legal theory, the high court held:

> The Court of Appeal's contrary holding effectively made these home-
> owners vicariously liable in tort to the deceased worker, whose own
> misdemeanor conduct violated section 385(b) and proximately caused
> his fatal injuries, without regard to the fact that the homeowners had no
> control over the manner in which either the hired contractor or his
> workers performed their job. As tragic as this accident was, we find the
> homeowners breached no special duty of care owed to unlicensed
> contractor Rodriguez or his workers under section 385(b), and that the
> trial court therefore properly refused to instruct on plaintiffs' negligence
> per se theory of liability under that section in conjunction with Evidence
> Code section 669. In light of that conclusion, we have no occasion to
> reach or address plaintiffs' further claim that the decedent was the
> homeowners' employee at law under Labor Code section 2750.5, which
> question, given our holding, is moot.

[Ramirez v. Nelson, 44 Cal.4th 908, 188 P.3d 659 (Cal. 2008)]

Q 7:119   What is the future of workplace safety criminal actions?

In light of the acquittals in *Chicago Magnet Wire* and the overturned convictions in *O'Neil* (see Q 7:118), prosecutors have been discouraged from pursuing many such criminal actions. The *Chicago Magnet Wire* trial was years in the making and lasted some eight months when it finally occurred in 1991. State attorneys and prosecutors in other jurisdictions generally have seen the Cook County experience as a legal experiment in which substantial human and tax resources were expended on a losing cause. With rare exceptions this has remained the general rule down to the present. For example, the April 2013 fertilizer plant explosion in West, Texas, killed and injured almost 200 and leveled nearby homes. Nevertheless, as this publication goes to press, the *International Business Times* reported, "It's too early to tell whether the explosion of the fertilizer plant in West, Texas, was the result of criminal negligence, state Attorney General Greg Abbott told a news conference Thursday afternoon (April 18)." [http://www.ibtimes.com/possibility-criminal-negligence-premature-texasplant-explosion-attorney-general-greg-abbott-1202753#] However, individual state developments should be consulted, depending upon where your organization operates.

Q 7:120   What is OSHA's policy regarding criminal penalties for workplace fatalities?

In 2005, OSHA issued procedures for the investigation of workplace fatalities. These procedures include the following guidance on criminal penalties:

A. Section 17(e) of the OSH Act provides criminal penalties for an employer who is convicted of having willfully violated an OSHA standard, rule or order when the violation results in the death of an employee. However, Section 17(e) does not apply to violations of the general duty clause. When there are violations of an OSHA standard, rule or order, or a violation of the general duty clause, criminal provisions relating to false statements and obstruction of justice may also be relevant.

B. The circumstances surrounding all occupationally related fatalities will be evaluated to determine whether the fatality was caused by a willful violation of a standard, thus creating the basis for a possible criminal referral. The evidence obtained during a fatality investigation is of paramount importance and must be carefully gathered and considered.

C. Early in the investigation, the Area Director, in consultation with the investigator, should make an initial determination as to whether there is potential for a criminal violation. Refer to Chapter III.C.2.e, Criminal/ Willful Violations, for additional information. The decision will be based on consideration of the following:

    (I) A fatality has occurred.

    (II) There is evidence that an OSHA standard has been violated and that the violation contributed to the death.

    (III) There is reason to believe that the employer was aware of the requirements of the standard and knew that he was in violation of the standard, or that the employer was plainly indifferent to employee safety.

If the Regional Administrator agrees with the Area Director's assessment of the case, the Regional Administrator will notify the Regional Solicitor.

  A. At the discretion of the Regional Administrator and the Area Director, and dependent upon Regional procedures in place, a Regional team or trained criminal investigator may assist in or perform portions of an investigation, as appropriate.

  B. In addition to criminal prosecution under Section 17(e) of the OSH Act, employers may potentially face prosecution under a number of other sections of the United States Code, including, but not limited to:

    (I) Crimes and Criminal Procedures, for actions such as conspiracy, making false statements, fraud, obstruction of justice, and destruction, alteration or falsification of records during a federal investigation

    (II) The Clean Water Act

    (III) The Clean Air Act

    (IV) The Resource Conservation and Recovery Act (RCRA)

    (V) The Comprehensive Environmental Response, Compensation, and Liability Act (CERCLA)

[http://www.osha.gov/pls/oshaweb/owadisp.show_document?p_table = DIRECTIVES&p_id = 3245]

Q 7:121 Who has the burden of proof when an employer challenges an OSHA citation?

The Secretary of Labor must prove by "substantial evidence on the record considered as a whole" that the cited employer violated the OSH Act. The employer may raise affirmative defenses in refutation of OSHA's prima facie case. The burden of proving these is on the employer.

Q 7:122 Are there preventative steps employers can take to try to forestall OSHA citations?

OSHA operates a free safety and health consultation service, which is voluntary and confidential, and is entirely separate from OSHA's regular inspection program. OSHA also operates a VPP aimed at recognizing exemplary work sites. Most insurance carriers or brokers offer free or inexpensive health and safety inspections and consultations.

Hazardous Materials

Q 7:123   What does *right to know* mean?

Both OSHA and many states have taken action to ensure that information about chemical hazards is conveyed to the employees who must handle these chemicals. This type of legislation is commonly called *right-to-know*. The primary source of right-to-know requirements is OSHA, which enforces them by requiring employers to provide comprehensive hazard communication programs involving the labeling of containers that hold hazardous chemicals, employee training on the handling of such chemicals, and to create and disseminate MSDSs with exhaustive information on the particular chemical. This latter approach may be the more prudent route to take, since OSHA does not usually award immunity to voluntary participants in its programs. At the very least, prompt abatement of all discovered hazards must be undertaken, whether or not the corporation has budgeted for them.

Q 7:124   Who must comply with OSHA's hazard communication program?

Initially, OSHA issued regulations that applied only to chemical manufacturers and importers and manufacturers that handled hazardous chemicals in their manufacturing processes. This limitation on the coverage of federal right-to-know regulations had two important results. First, many states and cities were lobbied intensively by unions and other interested parties, and in response to that political pressure adopted their own standards to cover the service and construction industries. Second, a federal court of appeals held that, while the state and local regulations were not preempted to the extent that they dealt with areas of the economy not covered by the federal regulations, OSHA should promulgate regulations for these other parts of the economy. [New Jersey Chamber of Commerce v. Hughey, 774 F.2d 587 (3d Cir. 1985)]

Q 7:125   Has OSHA's hazard communication standard been extended beyond the manufacturing sector?

In 2012, OSHA revised its hazard communication standard (HCS), aligning it with the United Nations' global chemical labeling system. In doing so, the agency estimated that 43 deaths would be avoided in the United States annually and that productivity would be enhanced to the tune of $475.2 million.

The HCS, being revised to align with the United Nations' Globally Harmonized System of Classification and Labeling of Chemicals, will be fully implemented in 2016 and is expected to benefit workers by reducing confusion about chemical hazards in the workplace, facilitating safety training, and improving understanding of hazards, especially for low literacy workers. OSHA's standard will classify chemicals according to their health and physical hazards, and establish consistent labels and safety data sheets for all chemicals made in the United States and imported from abroad.

The standard extends beyond manufacturing into all workplaces where hazardous chemicals are in use.

Q 7:126   What are a company's obligations under the federal right-to-know regulations?

Obligations can vary drastically depending on whether a company is a chemical manufacturer, importer or distributor, or is merely a user of hazardous chemicals. The greatest burden under the federal right-to-know regulations is placed on chemical manufacturers, importers, and distributors. Chemical manufacturers and importers must assess the hazards of the chemicals they sell. A chemical manufacturer is any company with a workplace in some other country in which chemicals are produced with the intention to supply these chemicals to distributors or purchasers inside this country. The distributor's obligation is more limited than that of a manufacturer or importer; it must simply transfer required information to purchasers.

Q 7:127   What obligations do the users of hazardous chemicals have under the federal right-to-know regulations?

Companies that are not chemical manufacturers, importers, or distributors have a more limited obligation under the federal regulations. These employers must ensure that labels on incoming containers of chemicals are not removed or defaced, that MSDSs are obtained and maintained in a readily accessible location in the workplace, and that the company's employees receive the information and training needed for their protection should a spill or leak occur.

Q 7:128   What chemicals are regulated by federal right-to-know regulations?

OSHA's hazard communication rules apply to every chemical known to be present in a workplace, as well as those chemicals that employees may be exposed to either under normal conditions or in a possible emergency. A chemical is considered to be any element, chemical compound, or mixture of elements and/or compounds.

Q 7:129   Has OSHA made any changes in chemical exposure limits?

In 1989, in what some observers describe as OSHA's most significant rulemaking to date, OSHA lowered the permissible exposure limits for about 400 chemicals. The exposure limits were reduced based on recommendations by the American Conference of Governmental Industrial Hygienists and the NIOSH. The recommendations reflect newly available medical and health information.

Many larger manufacturing and chemical companies have reported little impact, because they claim to be complying already with analogous standards of the American Conference of Governmental Industrial Hygienists. In contrast, smaller companies, such as family-owned firms, may be having some trouble meeting the more stringent limits. The new rules cover many of the most common workplace chemicals, including chloroform, carbon monoxide, hydrogen cyanide, and wood dust. Employers were permitted to comply with the new limits by using a combination of controls, including engineering, workplace practices, and respiratory protection.

Currently, OSHA lacks an automatic review mechanism that would allow the limits to reflect scientific data as they become available. Without such a mechanism, periodic reviews are required. One problem with a system requiring periodic reviews is that, until the reviews are made and revisions implemented, OSHA regulations can contain some standards that are outdated and unsafe.

In June 2012, OSHA passed the Hazard Communication Standard (HCS), a rule with significant impact and affecting over five million businesses that use or store chemicals, and 90,000 chemical manufacturers, importers, and distributors. HCS introduced a new set of criteria for classifying human health and physical hazards, as well as identifying OSHA-defined hazards. As of the new rule, companies must classify substances and/or products to ensure that the appropriate classifications are assigned. In many instances, safety data sheets and labels must be revised to conform to HCS requirements. (See Q 7:159 for a discussion of HCS and its requirements.)

[http://www.osha.gov/dsg/hazcom/]

Q 7:130   Have OSHA employees themselves suffered from chemical exposures of which they were not informed?

Yes . . . at least once, according to a March 25, 2005, AFL-CIO press release that reads as follows:

> Ten OSHA employees out of 271 tested have confirmed positive results for beryllium sensitization according to an internal memo sent to OSHA staff by Acting Assistant Secretary of Labor for OSHA, Jonathan Snare. In January, Chicago Tribune reporter Sam Roe revealed that three OSHA employees had tested positive. Beryllium is an extremely toxic metal that carries a high risk of causing chronic beryllium disease, a fast-progressing and potentially fatal lung disease.
>
> Snare opens the memo stating that "OSHA is committed to protecting the health and safety of its employees." You would hardly suspect from these statements that in April of 2002, former OSHA Assistant Secretary, John Henshaw, had pulled the plug on a 2000 plan to test OSHA inspectors for exposure to beryllium. OSHA Regional Administrator, Adam Finkel, disclosed OSHA's reversal to the press and in return for his service, was removed from his position as Regional Administrator. Finkel then filed a whistleblower complaint against OSHA. After several articles in the national press, Henshaw announced last April—four and a half years after the original screening was to go into effect—that OSHA would offer testing for beryllium disease to inspectors who may be been exposed to the toxic dust in the course of inspections.
>
> Although his fears have been vindicated, Finkel is still concerned. It's not clear whether those that tested positive had high exposures or

low exposures to beryllium. If those tested happen to have had low exposures, it would mean that those with higher exposures are at even more risk.

Furthermore, Finkel notes that Snare's memo said nothing about screening retirees, staff that left OSHA or state plan inspectors.

But fear not. Snare concludes the memo stating that "We value the health of all OSHA employees." We're sure he means former employees, retired employees and state plan employees as well. I mean, have they ever given us a reason to doubt their sincerity?

[http://spewingforth.blogspot.com/2005/03/ten- osha- staff- test- positive-for. html]

Of particular concern to organized labor was the fate of workers exposed to dangerous substances in the aftermath of the September 11, 2001, terrorist attacks. According to one such advocate, testifying before a Congressional committee:

> Nearly seven years ago, the September 11, 2001, terrorist attacks claimed the lives of 3,000 individuals, injured thousands more and brought unparalleled grief and anguish to the nation. But soon after the 9/11 attacks it became clear that those who died and were injured on that day were not the only victims. Tens of thousands rescue and recovery workers—including firefighters, police, emergency medical technicians, workers in the building and construction trades, transit workers and others—and hundreds of thousands of other workers and residents near Ground Zero were exposed to a toxic mix of dust and fumes from the collapse of the World Trade Center. The scale and scope of these exposures was massive and extraordinary, with tons of glass, pulverized concrete, asbestos, lead and burning jet fuel forming a dust and smoke cloud that engulfed the WTC site and lower Manhattan and spread throughout the area. The exposures continued for months as the fires at the WTC burned, rescue, recovery and clean-up operations ensued and toxic dust contaminated the area. The exposures were made much worse by EPA's pronouncements that the environment was safe and OSHA's failure to enforce workplace safety and health requirements during the entire 10-month period of rescue, recovery and clean-up operations at the WTC site. [Testimony of Margaret Seminario, Safety and Health Director, AFL-CIO before the House of Representatives, Committee on Energy and Commerce, Subcommittee on Health on the James Zadroga 9/11 Health and Compensation Act of 2008 (H.R. 6594), July 31, 2008; available at: http://www.aflcio.org/mediacenter/prsptm /tm07312008.cfm]

Q 7:131   Are there chemicals that federal right-to-know regulations do not cover?

The federal right-to-know regulations do not apply to hazardous wastes under the Solid Waste Disposal Act, which is administered under regulations of the EPA. The regulations also do not apply to: tobacco and tobacco products; wood and wood products; food, drugs, cosmetics, and beverages in retail establishments that are packaged for sale to customers; food, drugs, and cosmetics that are brought into the workplace by employees for their own use and consumption; substances that are really consumer products and are used in the workplace in the same way that they are used in the home; drugs in final form for administration to a patient in a health care facility; and articles that may have been created with hazardous chemicals but that, in final form, are not dangerous (e.g., plastic parts that contain chemicals that in their free form are dangerous).

Q 7:132 How are hazard determinations evaluated under the federal right-to-know regulations?

Chemical manufacturers and importers are responsible for evaluating the chemicals they produce or bring into the country to determine whether these chemicals are hazardous. The companies that use the chemicals are not required to perform independent evaluations unless they voluntarily choose not to rely on the manufacturer's or importer's assessment. Chemical manufacturers and importers must identify and consider available scientific evidence. As far as health hazards are concerned, evidence that is statistically significant and based on at least one positive study conducted in accordance with established scientific principles is enough to establish hazardous effect. Additionally, chemical manufacturers and importers must defer to two sources on hazardous chemicals, whether or not they agree with them. The first is a list of toxic and hazardous substances in OSHA's General Industry Safety and Health Standards. The second source is the American Conference of Governmental Industrial Hygienists' publication, "Threshold Limit Values for Chemical Substances and Physical Agents in the Work Environment." Finally, the National Toxicology Program's annual report on carcinogens, the International Agency for Research on Cancer's monographs, and the Toxic and Hazardous Substance Regulations in OSHA's general industry standards identify chemicals as carcinogens (cancer-causing chemicals); manufacturers and importers must then treat such chemicals accordingly.

Q 7:133 Do employees have the right to see the results of studies by chemical manufacturers?

Yes. Employees have the right to see this information, including written descriptions of the way in which the manufacturer conducted the evaluation.

An interesting, closely related question is whether employees injured by chemicals can sue a third party provider of the compounds. One case that addresses this issue is *Irrer v. Milacron, Inc.* [484 F. Supp. 2d 677 (E.D. Mich. 2007)] In this case, the plaintiffs allege that industrial lubricants called "metal-working fluids" (MWFs) caused their various injuries, including occupational asthma, chronic bronchitis, and hypersensitivity pneumonitis, cancer, dermatitis, and skin rashes. The plaintiffs were current or former GM employees who worked at the Buick plants in Flint, Michigan at various times between 1970 and 2007. Milacron, the defendant, manufactured and supplied MWFs to some of the

GM plants that the plaintiffs worked at. The plaintiffs sued the defendant on a "failure to warn" theory closely analogous to right-to-know principles.

The question before the court was whether the state of Michigan's "sophisticated user" rule insulated the defendant from liability. The federal judge ruled on the defendant's motion for summary judgment that the plaintiffs' employer, General Motors, was a "sophisticated user" of the defendant's products. The court further found that GM had an obligation under federal and state statutes, as well as under its collective bargaining agreement with the UAW, to advise its employees of the hazards involved with defendant's chemicals. Consequently, Michigan's 1995 tort reform statute governs the liability of a product manufacturer like Milacron who sells to sophisticated users like GM. The relevant statutory provision provides that:

Except to the extent a state or federal statute or regulation requires a manufacturer to warn, a manufacturer or seller is not liable in a product liability action for failure to provide an adequate warning if the product is provided for use by a sophisticated user. [Mich. Comp. Laws § 600.2947(4)]

The court concluded that the plaintiffs did not present any evidence that Milacron's Material Safety Data Sheets (MSDSs) provided to their employer (GM) failed to satisfy the requirements of the relevant federal regulations, cited by the judge above, and triggered the "except" clause in Michigan's sophisticated user defense statute. The plaintiffs' response didn't identify any specific MSDS for any specific Milacron MWF product sold to GM in a specific year that failed to satisfy Milacron's regulatory duty to warn GM under 29 C.F.R. § 1910.1200. In fact, the plaintiffs' own expert, Dr. Daniel Teitelbaum, admitted that he wasn't even qualified to say Milacron's MSDSs were not in compliance. Rather, the plaintiffs broadly argued that Milacron's MSDSs were inadequate to warn GM's employees about the health hazards created by GM's use of Milacron's MWFs in its metal machining plants. This was, in essence, an argument that Milacron's warnings to GM, a sophisticated user, were inadequate. As such, these claims fit comfortably within Michigan's statutory sophisticated-user doctrine. The "except" clause in Michigan's statutory sophisticated user defense didn't apply here. Milacron had no duty to warn that was any broader than the requirements set forth in the regulations. Accordingly, Milacron was entitled to rely on Michigan's 'sophisticated user' defense to avoid liability on Plaintiffs' product liability claims.

Note that in effect this ruling dumps responsibility squarely in GM's lap, because as the sophisticated user it presumably was obliged under OSHA, as well as common law considerations, to let its employees know of any dangers that the corporation knew or should know about.

Q 7:134   What is a *written hazard communication program*?

OSHA requires employers to develop and institute a *written hazard communication program* in the workplace. This written program must describe the way in which the employer plans to implement right-to-know regulations with respect to labels and other kinds of warnings, MSDSs, and employee training.

The written program must also include a list of all the hazardous chemicals known to be present in the workplace, with a cross-reference to the relevant MSDSs. The program must state how the employer will inform its employees of hazards associated with performing non-routine tasks, as well as chemicals that are carried in unlabeled pipes in their work areas. This written program must be available on request to employees and their designated representatives, as well as to OSHA and the director of NIOSH.

Q 7:135　How must chemicals be labeled under the right-to-know regulations?

Manufacturers, importers, and distributors of chemicals must make sure that each vessel containing a hazardous chemical is labeled, tagged, or marked with the identity of the hazardous chemical and the name and address of the manufacturer, importer, or other responsible party.

Q 7:136　Are companies other than chemical manufacturers and importers obligated to label hazardous chemicals?

All employers must ensure that containers of hazardous chemicals that come into their workplaces are labeled, tagged, or marked with the identity of chemicals in the container and the appropriate hazard warnings.

Q 7:137　What must be contained on an MSDS?

Each MSDS must be in English and contain the following information:

1. The identity of the chemical (which is equivalent to that on the label affixed to the container);
2. The chemical and common names of the substance (within the limits of trade-secret law);
3. A listing of the ingredients in the chemical if it is a mixture;
4. An indication of the ingredients that have been identified as carcinogens or that present other specific hazards; and
5. The specific hazards of the ingredients in a chemical mixture.

Q 7:138　What are the main components of an MSDS?

The main components of an MSDS are:

- Manufacturer's identifying information;
- Hazardous ingredients information;
- Physical and chemical characteristics; and
- Fire and explosive hazard data.

Q 7:139   Is any of the information from completed MSDSs, emergency and hazardous chemical inventory forms, or toxic release forms available to the public?

Yes. Information from MSDSs is available to the public upon request to the local emergency planning committee. Information from emergency and hazardous chemical inventory forms is available to the public upon written request to the local emergency planning committee or state emergency response commission. Information from toxic chemical release forms is available to the public from the administrator of the EPA, who is responsible for maintaining a national toxic chemical inventory computer database.

Q 7:140   Do the states have a role in right-to-know legislation?

Although OSHA regulations intersect almost all sectors of the economy and preempt to a large extent the states' role in this area, many states and localities have their own right-to-know laws and ordinances. Typically, these provisions require that information on hazardous chemicals be available to local safety forces and health care providers. Because these provisions are directed to a different group of people from those targeted by the OSHA regulations (which target a company's workers), these state laws and ordinances are not preempted by federal law at the present time. An employer must be aware of the existence of such laws in the state or community in which the business operates.

Emergency Planning and Right to Know Act

Q 7:141   What is the purpose of the Emergency Planning and Community Right to Know Act?

The Emergency Planning and Community Right to Know Act [42 U.S.C. §§ 11001–11050 (1986)] is designed to avert catastrophe if unacceptable levels of hazardous substances are released into the environment. The Act mandates decentralized emergency planning and institutes reporting requirements.

Q 7:142   What emergency planning measures are mandated by the Emergency Planning and Community Right to Know Act?

The Act calls for states to establish state emergency response commissions, emergency planning districts, and local emergency planning committees. It requires states to prepare comprehensive emergency response plans and emergency planning notification. Additionally, it includes provisions for emergency training and emergency system review.

Q 7:143   How are state emergency response commissions, emergency planning districts, and local emergency planning committees established?

The governor of each state appoints members to a state emergency response commission. Appointees should have technical expertise in the emergency response field, if practicable. The state emergency response commission designates emergency planning districts and appoints members to emergency planning committees.

Q 7:144   What are the responsibilities of the state emergency response commissions?

State emergency response commissions must designate emergency planning districts, appoint local emergency planning committees, supervise and coordinate the activities of the local emergency planning committees, establish procedures for receiving and processing public requests for information, and designate an information coordinator.

Q 7:145   Who must be included in local emergency planning committees?

Local emergency planning committees must include: representatives from the fields of law enforcement, civil defense, fire-fighting, first aid, and health; local environmental, hospital, and transportation personnel; members of the broadcast and print media and community groups; representatives of state and local officials; and owners and operators of facilities that use extremely hazardous substances.

Q 7:146   How many local emergency planning committees must be established?

One local emergency planning committee must be established for each emergency planning district.

Q 7:147   What are the responsibilities of the local emergency planning committees?

Local emergency planning committees must prepare comprehensive emergency response plans, review the plans annually or as required by changed circumstances, establish procedures for receiving and processing public requests for information, and designate an information coordinator.

Q 7:148   What emergency planning notification is required by the Emergency Planning and Community Right to Know Act?

The Act requires owners or operators of facilities that have extremely hazardous substances in excess of the established threshold to notify the facility's state emergency response commission that the facility is subject to the requirements of the Act.

Q 7:149 What provisions must be included in emergency response plans?

Emergency response plans must include provisions that identify facilities subject to the requirements of the Act within the emergency planning district, routes used for the transportation of extremely hazardous substances, and at-risk facilities near facilities subject to the requirements of the Act. Plans must also include:

1. Response procedures to be followed in the event of a release of extremely hazardous substances;
2. Provisions for designating community and facility emergency coordinators;
3. Notification procedures that coordinators must follow to inform a designated individual and the public that a release has occurred;
4. Methods for determining that a release has occurred and those who will be affected by it;
5. Descriptions of emergency equipment subject to the requirements of the Act; and
6. Methods for identifying those responsible for the equipment and facilities, evacuation plans, training programs, and methods and schedules for exercising the plan.

Emergency response plans must be made available to the public.

Q 7:150 When must emergency notification be provided?

Emergency notification must be provided immediately after the release of an extremely hazardous substance occurs. Facilities that use, produce, or store a hazardous chemical must provide emergency notification when:

1. The Comprehensive Environmental Response, Cooperation, and Liability Act of 1980 (CERCLA) [42 U.S.C. §§ 9601–9675 (1986)] requires notification of the national response center;
2. The release is not permitted by CERCLA; or
3. The administrator of the EPA determines that notification is required. Notification must also be provided when designated amounts of substances not requiring CERCLA notice are released.

Q 7:151 Are there any exceptions to the notification requirement?

Yes. Notification is not required when a release results in exposure only to people within the facility's site.

Q 7:152   What is a *release* within the meaning of the Emergency Planning and Community Right to Know Act?

A *release* occurs when any hazardous chemical, extremely hazardous substance, or toxic chemical is spilled, pumped, poured, emitted, emptied, discharged, injected, leached, dumped, or disposed or leaks or escapes into the environment. Disposal of materials that have first been enclosed in containers is included in the definition.

Q 7:153   To whom must emergency notification be provided?

Emergency notification must be provided to the community emergency coordinator for the local emergency planning committee of any area likely to be affected by the release and to the state emergency planning commission of any state likely to be affected by the release.

Q 7:154   What information must emergency notification provide?

Emergency notification must provide information about the nature of the release and the released substance; health risks, medical advice, and precautionary measures relevant to the release; and the name and telephone number of a person to contact for additional information.

Q 7:155   What reporting requirements are imposed on owners or operators of facilities subject to the requirements of the Emergency Planning and Community Right to Know Act?

The owners or operators of facilities subject to the requirements of the Emergency Planning and Community Right to Know Act must provide MSDSs and emergency and hazardous chemical inventory forms to the appropriate local planning committee, the state emergency response commission, and the fire departments with jurisdiction over the facilities. Toxic chemical release forms must be provided to the administrator of the EPA and the state official designated by the governor.

MSDSs and emergency and hazardous chemical inventory forms provide information about the types, quantities, and location of hazardous chemicals present at the facility. Toxic chemical release forms provide information about the manufacturing, processing, or use of toxic chemicals in excess of the statutorily established threshold amount. Additionally, toxic chemical release forms must provide information about the facility's principal business activities, waste treatment or disposal methods, and the amount of the toxic chemical entering the environment.

Q 7:156   Does the Emergency Planning and Community Right to Know Act require owners or operators of facilities subject to the requirements of the Act to provide any information directly to members of the public?

Yes. Owners or operators of facilities subject to the requirements of the Act are required to provide the specific chemical identity, if known, of any hazardous or toxic chemical or extremely hazardous substance to any health professional who requests such information in writing, provides a written statement of need (for diagnostic or treatment purposes), and provides a written confidentiality agreement.

Q 7:157   How may the owner or operator of a facility subject to the requirements of the Act comply with the mandated reporting requirements without disclosing trade secrets?

The specific chemical identity of a hazardous or toxic chemical or an extremely hazardous substance may be withheld if it is established to be a trade secret. In place of the withheld specific chemical identity, the owner or operator must provide the generic class or category of the hazardous or toxic chemical or extremely hazardous substance.

Q 7:158   Is OSHA enforcing the Emergency Planning and Community Right to Know Act?

Yes. OSHA is enforcing this Act, and is requiring covered companies to have plans in place in accord with the Act until the implementing regulations are promulgated. Where OSHA inspectors find employers lacking in this regard, OSHA is not only requiring future compliance but is also issuing citations and leveling fines.

OSHA also provides a guide for employers to plan for workplace emergencies and evacuations. The information can be accessed at http://www.osha.gov/Publications/osha3088.html. It includes information for employers on how to protect their employees and their business in a workplace emergency, how to establish evacuation routes and exits, and how to plan for rescue operations.

Q 7:159   What is OSHA's new hazard communication standard?

The hazard communication standard (HCS) is now aligned with the Globally Harmonized System of Classification and Labeling of Chemicals (GHS). This update to the HCS will provide a common and coherent approach to classifying chemicals and communicating hazard information on labels and safety data sheets. Once implemented, the revised standard will improve the quality and consistency of hazard information in the workplace, making it safer for workers by providing easily understandable information on appropriate handling and safe use of hazardous chemicals. This update will also help reduce trade barriers and result in productivity improvements for American businesses that regularly handle, store, and use hazardous chemicals while providing cost savings for American businesses that periodically update safety data sheets and labels for chemicals covered under the hazard communication standard.

The GHS is an international approach to hazard communication, providing agreed criteria for classification of chemical hazards, and a standardized approach to label elements and safety data sheets. The GHS was negotiated in a multi-year process by hazard communication experts from many different countries, international organizations, and stakeholder groups. It is based on major existing systems around the world, including OSHA's HCS and the chemical classification and labeling systems of other U.S. agencies.

The result of this negotiation process is the United Nations' document entitled "Globally Harmonized System of Classification and Labeling of Chemicals," commonly referred to as The Purple Book. This document provides harmonized classification criteria for health, physical, and environmental hazards of chemicals. It also includes standardized label elements that are assigned to these hazard classes and categories, and provide the appropriate signal words, pictograms, and hazard and precautionary statements to convey the hazards to users. A standardized order of information for safety data sheets is also provided. These recommendations can be used by regulatory authorities such as OSHA to establish mandatory requirements for hazard communication, but do not constitute a model regulation.

[http://www.osha.gov/dsg/hazcom/hazcom-faq.html#1]

The major changes to the HCS include:

- Hazard classification: Provides specific criteria for classification of health and physical hazards, as well as classification of mixtures.
- Labels: Chemical manufacturers and importers will be required to provide a label that includes a harmonized signal word, pictogram, and hazard statement for each hazard class and category. Precautionary statements must also be provided.
- Safety Data Sheets: Will now have a specified 16-section format.
- Information and training: Employers are required to train workers by December 1, 2013 on the new labels elements and safety data sheets format to facilitate recognition and understanding.

Q 7:160   Why did OSHA modify its hazard communication standard to adopt the GHS?

OSHA modified the HCS to adopt the GHS to improve safety and health of workers through more effective communications on chemical hazards. Since it was first promulgated in 1983, the HCS has provided employers and employees extensive information about the chemicals in their workplaces. The original standard is performance-oriented, allowing chemical manufacturers and importers to convey information on labels and material safety data sheets in whatever format they choose. While the available information has been helpful in improving employee safety and health, a more standardized approach to classifying the hazards and conveying the information will be more effective, and provide further improvements in American workplaces. The GHS provides such a standardized approach, including detailed criteria for determining what hazardous effects a chemical poses, as well as standardized label elements assigned by hazard class and category. This will enhance both employer and worker comprehension of the hazards, which will help to ensure appropriate handling and safe use of workplace chemicals. In addition, the safety data sheet requirements establish an order of information that is standardized. The harmonized format of the safety data sheets will enable employers, workers, health professionals, and emergency responders to access the information more efficiently and effectively, thus increasing their utility.

Adoption of the GHS in the United States and around the world will also help to improve information received from other countries—since the United States is both a major importer and exporter of chemicals, American workers often see labels and safety data sheets from other countries. The diverse and sometimes conflicting national and international requirements can create confusion among those who seek to use hazard information effectively. For example, labels and safety data sheets may include symbols and hazard statements that are unfamiliar to readers or not well understood. Containers may be labeled with such a large volume of information that important statements are not easily recognized. Given the differences in hazard classification criteria, labels may also be incorrect when used in other countries. If countries around the world adopt the GHS, these problems will be minimized, and chemicals crossing borders will have consistent information, thus improving communication globally. [http://www.osha.gov/dsg/hazcom/hazcom-faq.html#1]

Smoking in the Workplace

Q 7:161   Is smoking in the workplace regulated by law?

In recent years an increasing number of states and municipalities have passed laws and ordinances governing at least some aspects of workplace smoking. These laws may be divided into several categories:

1. Laws that are primarily intended to protect customers, clients and patients, such as those mandating non-smoking areas in restaurants, which have become quite common in this country. Obviously, these acts and ordinances affect where employees, as well as customers, of eating establishments may light up.

2. Laws limiting or forbidding smoking in publicly owned or operated facilities.

3. Most common of all, fire codes and safety standards that forbid smoking not for health, but rather for safety (e.g., fire prevention) reasons.

4. Far less common, but of increasing importance, statutes and ordinances requiring employers to maintain smoke-free areas in their workplaces or

to establish smoking lounges to which use of tobacco products must be limited.

A complete state-by-state compilation is available from the American Lung Association on its main web page: http://www.lungusa2.org/slati/states.php.

Q 7:162   Does the common law affect the rights of smokers and non-smokers?

Workplace smoking has been generating litigation for many years. Some noteworthy, early cases include:

1. *Barbosa v. Secretary of Health and Human Services* [923 F.2d 840 (1st Cir. 1990)]

2. *Millison v. E.I. DuPont* [545 A.2d 213 (N.J. 1988)]

3. *Lyons v. Heritage House Restaurants* [432 N.E.2d 270 (Ill. 1982)]

The battle to ban tobacco in offices and on the shop floor has pitted smokers against non-smokers. For example:

- Michigan's Smoke Free Air Law went into effect on May 1, 2010. The Dr. Ron Davis Smoke Free Air Act (Act No.188, Public Acts of 2009) prohibits smoking in work areas and food service establishments. A work area is defined as "a place of employment at which one or more employees perform services for an employer."

- In June 2008, Pennsylvania enacted a Clean Indoor Air Act that covers workplaces. While acknowledged to be an important step forward for the Keystone State, critics complain that (1) the statute deals only with the indoor portions of a worksite, permitting outdoor smoking, unless the employer itself enacts a prohibition into company policy; (2) the law contains a long list of exceptions, including rooms within lodging establishments, tobacco sellers and manufacturers, long-term care facilities, private clubs, and drinking establishments. [See http://www.palaborandemploy mentblog.com/2008/06/articles/workplace-trends/pennsylvania- enacts-clean-indoor-air-act-prohibiting-smoking-in-most-public-places-including-workplaces/.]

Q 7:163   Can discrimination law be involved in the workplace smoking controversy?

Both smokers and non-smokers have potentially valid arguments in the area of discrimination law. With respect to smokers, the argument may be made that smokers are addicted to tobacco and therefore are entitled to reasonable accommodation as handicapped individuals. With respect to non-smokers, the discrimination argument would seem to be limited to those individuals who are so seriously affected by tobacco smoke in the air that they can be classified as disabled workers. Again, reasonable accommodation may be required. In fact, in one federal case, it was held that a government employee was entitled to disability income benefits after he quit working because of his intolerance of secondary tobacco smoke in the work area. [Parodi v. Merit Sys. Prot. Bd., 690 F.2d 731 (9th Cir. 1982)]

Kansas constitutes a rare jurisdiction that actually protects the smoker from employment discrimination by statute:

> It is an unlawful practice for an employer:
>
> (1) To fail or refuse to hire, or to discharge any individual, or otherwise to discriminate against an individual with respect to compensation, terms, conditions, or privileges of employment, because of the individual's race, color, religion, national origin, sex, age forty (40) and over, because the person is a qualified individual with a disability, or because the individual is a smoker or nonsmoker, as long as the person complies with any workplace policy concerning smoking. [Kan. Rev. Stat. § 344.040]

Some other states have enacted so-called "life style" statutes, which at least arguably protect smokers from discriminatory treatment. [*See, e.g.*, Watson v. Public Serv. Co. of Colo., 207 P.3d 860 (Colo. Ct. App. 2008) (statute was originally proposed by the tobacco lobby to protect smokers and coverage of "all lawful activities" was intended to make bill more appealing to the legislature as a whole).]

Q 7:164   Does OSHA require elimination of smoking in the workplace?

OSHA does not in general regulate smoking in the workplace. The agency however does:

- Ban smoking in elevators [http://www.quizlaw.com/hremployment_law/what_does_osha_say_about_smoki.php];
- Ban smoking with regard to asbestos-related work [http://www.osha.gov/pls/oshaweb/owadisp.show_document?p_table = INTERPRETATIONS&p_id = 27328];
- Ban smoking around open flames and volatile gases and other chemicals, and recommends appropriate signage. [http://www.mavericklabel.com/osha-labels.html]

Q 7:165   Can an employee who voluntarily leaves the job because of tobacco smoke collect unemployment?

The Pennsylvania Commonwealth Court, in what appears to have been the only case of its kind for many years, held in 1981 that an employee who left his job because of the presence of tobacco smoke in the workplace had not "involuntarily" been separated from his employment. [Ruckstuhl v. Pennsylvania Compensation Bd. of Review, 57 Pa. Commw. Ct. 302, 426 A.2d 719 (1981)] The court therefore sustained the decision of the Unemployment Compensation Board of Review denying the employee benefits.

In 2002, the District of Columbia Court of Appeals remanded to the Department of Employment Services a case in which the claimant voluntarily quit her employment in a law office because the lawyer she worked for refused to quit smoking in her presence. The court ruled that the agency had failed to give the claimant's position proper consideration. [Branson v. D.C. Department of Emp't Servs., 801 A.2d 975 (D.C. 2002)]

With more and more states and municipalities banning workplace smoking, such cases are uncommon. The general rule of the American common law, which has emerged from the available, reported decisions seems to be that the employee must first complain to her/his employer before the unemployment agencies and appeals courts will recognize a claim based upon a voluntary quit characterized as a constructive discharge.

Q 7:166   Is there a constitutional right to a smoke-free workplace?

No. The Bill of Rights of the U.S. Constitution applies only to actions taken by federal, state, and local governmental agencies—not the private workplace. Even in the case of public employees, various lawsuits attempted under the First, Ninth, and Fourteenth Amendments have met with negative reactions in the federal courts, which uniformly appear to have held that a public employer's refusal to prohibit smoking in the workplace does not violate any constitutional provisions.

A January 2010 decision of U.S. District Court for Western Kentucky concerns an action by the federal government that does potentially implicate the First Amendment of the Constitution, since the federal courts have long held that even commercial advertising enjoys free-speech rights, albeit not at the same level of protection as political speech. [Commonwealth Brands, Inc. v. United States, 2010 WL 65013 (W.D. Ky. Jan. 5, 2010)]

On June 22, 2009, President Obama signed the Family Smoking Prevention and Tobacco Control Act into law. [Pub. L. No. 111-31, 123 Stat. 1776 (2009)] The Act aims "to curb tobacco use by adolescents," while "continu[ing] to permit the sale of tobacco products to adults." To that end, it significantly curtails the ability of tobacco manufacturers to market their products. The Act provides that "each manufacturer, distributor, and retailer advertising or causing to be advertised, disseminating or causing to be disseminated, any labeling or advertising for cigarettes or smokeless tobacco shall use only black text on a white background." [*See* Pub. L. No. 111-31, § 102(a)(2) (adopting 21 C.F.R. § 897.32(a)).] It requires tobacco companies to print new government "warnings" on the top 50 percent of both sides of all cigarette packaging for messages like "Cigarettes cause cancer," which must be in 17-point font and include "color graphics depicting the negative health consequences of smoking." [Pub. L. No. 111-31, § 201(a) (amending 15 U.S.C. § 1333 to add subsections (a)(2) and (d))] The Act's Modified Risk Tobacco Products (MRTP) provision prohibits (1) "the label, labeling, or advertising" of a tobacco product from "explicitly or implicitly" suggesting that the product is less harmful than other tobacco products, and (2) a "tobacco product manufacturer" from taking "any action directed to consumers through the media or otherwise . . . respecting the product that would be reasonably expected to result in consumers believing that the tobacco product or its smoke may" be less harmful than other tobacco products, without prior FDA approval of the product as "modified risk." [Pub. L. No. 111-31, § 101(b) (amending the FDCA to add § 911(b)(2)(A))] The Act also bans, subject to the Secretary's modification of the provision "in light of governing First Amendment case law," i.e., the Supreme Court's decision in *Lorillard Tobacco Co. v. Reilly* [533 U.S. 525 (2001)], all "outdoor advertising for cigarettes or smokeless tobacco, including billboards, posters, or placards, . . . within 1,000 feet of the perimeter of any public playground or playground area in a public park . . . , elementary school, or secondary school." [Pub. L. No. 111-31, §§ 102(a)(2)(E), 102(a)(2) (adopting 21 C.F.R. § 897.30(b))] Additionally, the Act bars tobacco manufacturers from promoting their brands through sponsorship of "athletic, musical, artistic, or other social or cultural event[s]"; from distributing any non-tobacco good in exchange for purchase of a tobacco product; from distributing any brand-name promotional items; from making any "express or implied" statement "through the media or advertising" that "conveys" that the product is "less harmful" because it is regulated by the FDA or complies with the FDA's prescribed standards; from distributing free samples of their cigarettes; from distributing free smokeless tobacco samples except in very limited circumstances; and from jointly marketing tobacco with any other product regulated by the FDA. [Pub. L. No. 111-31, §§ 101(a), 102(a)(2)(G), 103(b)(13)] Finally, the Act authorizes federal agencies, state and local governments, and Indian tribes to enact more stringent regulations pertaining to the marketing and sale of tobacco products. [Pub. L. No. 111-31, §§ 101(b) (amending the FDCA to add 21 U.S.C. § 916), and 203 (amending the Federal Cigarette Labeling and Advertising Act ("FCLAA") to add 15 U.S.C. § 1334(c))]

The district judge ruled that:

1. The ban on use of images of product packages, brand symbols and some uses of color on advertising and labels violated commercial free speech;

2. The prohibition on sponsorship was narrowly tailored;

3. The failure to limit authority of other agencies and state governments was not unconstitutional delegation of power;

4. The mandated use of updated "warnings" on packages was sufficiently tailored;

5. The Modified Risk Tobacco Products (MRTP) provision was not viewpoint-based restriction;

6. The ban on mentioning FDA regulation was facially violative of free speech;

7. The ban on free samples and rewards did not violate free speech; and

8. The district court lacked jurisdiction over takings claims.

Q 7:167   Can the prohibition of smoking in the workplace violate a collective bargaining agreement with the union?

Two issues are involved: (1) whether banning smoking in the workplace is a mandatory subject for bargaining under a collective bargaining agreement; and (2) whether an employee fired for violating a smoking ban in the workplace can be considered terminated for just cause under typical labor contracts. It might be possible for a union or an employee to file an unfair labor practice charge if the employer put a smoking ban into effect with respect to the unionized members of the workforce, although the National Labor Relations Board has not ruled on this issue.

Arbitrators who review the termination of employees who violate a smoking ban typically consider: whether the rule is reasonably related to the safe and efficient functioning of the workplace; whether the rule has been properly promulgated and the employee was given enough time to become familiar with it; whether it has been made clear that discipline, including discharge, is a consequence of breaking the rule; whether the rule has been applied in an evenhanded manner to all employees; and whether the discipline that was applied by the employer in the particular case was too severe for circumstances.

Q 7:168   Can an employer legally institute a smoking ban?

Yes. Currently, it appears that employers have the legal right to mandate smoke-free workplaces. The number of employers that ban or limit cigarette smoking on the job has increased steadily in recent years.

In addition, as outlined above, public laws banning smoking have supplemented policies of private businesses and have made it more difficult for cigarette smokers to indulge their habit in public.

Q 7:169   Is it advisable for a company to mandate a smoke-free workplace?

An outright ban on smoking may appear to be the simplest solution, but it raises some problems. For example, if an employer refuses to hire a smoker, the applicant may claim that he or she is being discriminated against on the basis of a disability (i.e., dependence on tobacco). Employers should consult with legal counsel before firing or refusing to hire a smoker. (See Q 7:163.)

Negligence in employment lawsuits have been brought by non-smoking employees who assert that an employer has a duty to provide a smoke-free workplace. The success of such claims depends in large part on individual city or county smoking ordinances. Some ordinances, such as the one enacted by New York City, have a $500 maximum penalty per violation.

Q 7:170   May a company refuse to hire smokers?

Some companies have concluded that, while they will "grandfather" current smoking employees (i.e., permit them to continue smoking in the workplace), the company will not hire new employees unless they agree not to smoke in the workplace. While this approach solves the morale problem of current employees who smoke, it still presents the risk of a discrimination action by an unsuccessful applicant who claims to be addicted to cigarette smoking. (See Q 7:163.)

Q 7:171   How can a company accommodate both smokers and non-smokers?

A variety of policies have been adopted by companies that have decided not to ban smoking in the workplace, but nevertheless intend to respect the rights of non-smokers. One approach is to restrict smoking to certain areas. Areas involving customer contact are often declared smoke free, as are employee common areas (e.g., employee cafeterias, washrooms, corridors, and stairwells). Some companies restrict smoking to the employee's immediate work area and then provide the employee with an air cleaner for the smoker's individual office or work space. Some companies take another approach, allowing non-smokers to post a sign (uniformly provided by the personnel department) on their office doors or in their work areas banning smoking from that particular work station.

Q 7:172   Do new medical marijuana laws require employers to accommodate an employee's medical marijuana smoking?

Most likely, no. The new laws specifically state that companies can still have certain drug use policies for their employees, and federal law still prohibits any possession of marijuana. The highest courts in California, Montana, Oregon, and Washington have ruled that employers do not have to accommodate medical marijuana use. In 2008, the California Supreme Court held that the state's Fair Employment and Housing Act does not require an employer to accommodate an employee's medical marijuana use. Nor did the Compassionate Use Act provide a clear mandate of public policy, preventing an employee's termination for failing to pass a drug test. The court concluded, that the Compassionate Use Act provides a defense in state criminal prosecutions, but was not intended to eliminate employer's legitimate interest in whether employees used drugs banned by federal law or to otherwise extend to employment law. [Ross v. RagingWire Telecomms., Inc., 42 Cal. 4th 920, 174 P.3d 200 (2008)] In 2012, the Ninth Circuit held that physician-supervised marijuana use was, in fact, federally prohibited drug use and, as such, was not protected by the Americans with Disabilities Act (ADA). [James v. City of Costa Mesa, 684 F.3d 825 (9th Cir. 2012), *amended*, 700 F.3d 394 (9th Cir. 2012)]

However, the federal government has yet to provide a dispositive policy pronouncement. An executive order could clear up the apparent conflict between the Drug-Free Workplace Act and the ADA and state marijuana statutes, at least as government contractors' drug-testing obligations are concerned. But until that happens, terminations of employment grounded upon marijuana use by disabled employees who are under their doctors' care pursuant to state medical marijuana laws will continue to be challenged in court.

In any case, employers absolutely should not allow employees to smoke medical marijuana while on the job.

(For more information on medical marijuana laws in relation to the Drug-Free Workplace Act, see Q 7:227.)

AIDS

Q 7:173   Does OSHA have any special rules regarding health care workers who may be exposed to the AIDS virus?

In February 1990, the DOL Office of Health Compliance Assistance issued extensive "Enforcement Procedures for Occupational Exposure to Hepatitis B Virus (HBV) and Human Immunodeficiency Virus (HIV)." These procedures apply to OSHA workplace inspections and citations for safety violations. These procedures stem from September 1986, when OSHA received a petition from various labor unions that represented health care employees to develop standards that would help protect their members from blood-borne diseases. Such standards are still in the development stage; according to the DOL, "the Agency has concluded that the risk of contracting hepatitis B and AIDS among members of various occupations within the health care system requires an immediate response through a variety of existing mechanisms."

In a 2007 opinion letter, OSHA explained how in particular the agency intended the exposure/testing regulations to be applied:

> As you may know, the bloodborne pathogens standard provides that "the source individual's blood shall be tested as soon as feasible" after an exposure incident and after consent is obtained. [29 C.F.R. § 1910.1030(f)(3)(ii)(A)] At the current time there are at least four FDA-approved tests available for "rapid HIV antibody testing," which usually can confirm negative HIV status in less than an hour after blood is drawn from a source individual. They are widely available, easy to use, and inexpensive. Standard enzyme immunoassay (EIA) testing can take a much longer time, especially if facilities to perform the tests are not available locally. Therefore, an employer's failure to use rapid HIV antibody testing when testing as required by paragraph 1910.1030(f)(3)(ii)(A) would usually be considered a violation of that provision. The use of rapid HIV antibody testing is supported by the current CDC recommendations for HIV post-exposure prophylaxis (PEP) in the *Updated U.S. Public Health Service Guidelines for the Management of Occupational Exposures to HIV and Recommendations for Postexposure Prophylaxis*, published on September 30, 2005. [Standard Interpretation 01/08/2007—Use of Rapid HIV antibody testing on a source individual after an exposure incident, http://www.osha.gov/

pls/oshaweb/owadisp.show_document?p_table = INTERPRETATIONS
&p_id = 25619]

Q 7:174   Is AIDS still a significant health and safety issue?

To date, neither a cure nor a vaccine has been developed for AIDS, albeit certain expensive drug "cocktails" have proven to be highly effective in controlling the virus and extending the victim's life and productivity. As far as the scientific community knows, contraction of AIDS is ultimately fatal in the absence of such intensive drug regimes in all instances, although an HIV-infected person may carry the virus in a dormant state for a decade or more before it moves into its more virulent and eventually fatal forms. However, in a study released in June 2013, researchers reported that a daily dose of a powerful anti-HIV medication successfully prevented contraction of the disease in 49 percent of those tested. [Julie Steenhuysen, "AIDS drugs halve HIV risk for intrarvenous drug users in study," Reuters, June 12, 2013, accessed at http://www.reuters.com/article/2013/06/12/us-hiv-drugs-prevention-idUSBRE95B0TO20130612]

[http://aids.gov/federal-resources/national-hiv-aids-strategy/overview/]

Current HIV/AIDS statistics are available at: http://kff.org/hivaids/fact-sheet/the-hivaids-epidemic-in-the-united-states/. According to this source, 1.1 million Americans currently (as of early 2013) are living with AIDS. There were 47,500 new HIV infections in 2010. However, only a small percentage of these infections originate in the workplace.

The Centers for Disease Control offer a comprehensive workplace program for prevention of HIV/AIDS. [http://www.cdc.gov/hiv/risk/other/workPlace/index.html] OSHA for its part, continues to emphasize needlestick injuries as a major concern related to the workplace transmission of HIV and other infections. [*See* http://www.osha.gov/dep/leps/RegionIV/reg4_2013_10.pdf.] Dentistry workers are also a special OSHA concern. [http://www.osha.gov/SLTC/dentistry/index.html]

Q 7:175   What are HIV, ARC, and AIDS?

In a very real sense AIDS is not so much a disease in its own right as the catalyst for a syndrome or combination of opportunistic diseases, which invade and eventually destroy the victim's body, because the body's protective immune system has been destroyed by the AIDS virus. This typically occurs in three distinct stages.

Initially, the victim's body is invaded by the human immunodeficiency virus. This initial HIV infection can have a long latency period, perhaps as long as a decade. The victim may suffer an initial illness and then appear to recover completely, or may exhibit no early signs of illness at all. While at this stage the individual is not considered to have AIDS, that person will test HIV-positive, is a carrier of the virus, and can transmit it to others.

The second stage of AIDS is labeled AIDS-related complex, or ARC. ARC is a somewhat poorly defined, intermediate stage of the fatal cycle, during which some of the characteristics of the final AIDS syndrome are apparent. Generally, however, the illnesses that beset the patient at this stage of the cycle are not life-threatening.

In the final stage of the AIDS cycle, the diseases that attack the victim are of the life-threatening variety, including Kaposi's sarcoma, virulent forms of pneumonia, chronic diarrhea, and a dramatically decreased ability to fight off even the mildest infections. This is the stage of the disease characterized by dramatic weight loss and ultimately death.

[*See generally* Greenhill, "AIDS: The Biological Mechanisms," *Trauma*, Apr. 1991, at 59; Langone, *AIDS: The Facts* (NY: Little, Brown 1991); Frumkin & Leonard, *Questions & Answers on AIDS* (NY: Medical Economics Books 1987); Johnston & Hopkins, *The Catastrophe Ahead* (NY: Praeger 1990); Haseltin & Wong-Staal, "The Molecular Biology of the AIDS Virus," *The Science of AIDS*, Piel ed., (NY: WH Freeman & Co. 1989).]

Q 7:176   How is HIV transmitted?

There are three recognized methods of transmitting HIV:

1. Sexual contact, which includes the transmittal of body fluids (although saliva is not included in the list of transmitting fluids);
2. Infected blood, transmitted to the victim such as via blood transfusion, special blood-derived products used by hemophiliacs, or needles shared by intravenous drug users; or
3. By an infected mother to her baby during the perinatal period.

HIV cannot be transmitted by:

- Casual contact, such as a handshake or a friendly kiss;
- Food prepared by the HIV-infected person;
- Saliva or perspiration;
- Clothing or other objects worn or handled by the HIV carrier; or
- The infected person's breath, cough, or sneeze.

In fact, HIV is an extremely fragile virus. Even in blood and other bodily fluids that are known to transmit the virus in quantities sufficient to cause infection, brief exposure to the open air will result in the destruction of most of the virus before infection of a new victim can occur.

Q 7:177   Is an HIV-infected employee capable of working?

The nationally publicized saga of Magic Johnson, the professional basketball player who announced he had tested HIV-positive, is the perfect illustration of the fact that a victim of HIV can lead a near-normal life for an indefinite period, potentially a decade or more. Just as Johnson was able to participate in the 1992

Olympics, HIV carriers can perform their jobs without any diminution in the quality or quantity of their output. As the federal CDC and other medical experts have found, there is no risk to co-workers or customers of the company (except in the health care industry). Courts have held that to deny HIV-infected persons employment constitutes illegal disability discrimination. [*See, e.g.*, Cain v. Hyatt, 734 F. Supp 671 (E.D. Pa. 1990).] During recent years, this principle has become firmly established in the American common law. [*See, e.g.*, Byrd v. BT Foods, Inc., 948 So. 2d 921 (Fla. Ct. App. 2007); Ramirez v. New York State Div. of Human Rights, 5 A.D.3d 235, 773 N.Y.S.2d 400, 2004 N.Y. Slip Op. 01825 (2004).]

Q 7:178   How is a person tested for HIV infection?

Blood tests that screen for the presence of AIDS (HIV-1) antibodies are available. One common test, the Enzyme-Linked Immunosorbent Assay (ELISA), produces a relatively large number of false-positive results, but is recognized as a good initial screen. When a positive result is obtained by using the ELISA, it should be followed up with a more sensitive, confirming test, such as the Western Blot Analysis, to corroborate the presence of the HIV antibodies in the person's bloodstream. Note that these tests detect the presence of antibodies (or HIV seropositivity), meaning that the victim's body has produced a product intended to combat HIV; by implication, the presence of the virus is assumed, although a small body of scientific evidence has arisen recently suggesting the possibility of the AIDS syndrome in the absence of HIV. (Regarding whether and when an employer might be entitled to require that an applicant or employee be tested for HIV, see Q 3:9.)

Q 7:179   Which health care workers are covered by OSHA's AIDS enforcement procedures?

The AIDS enforcement procedures apply to virtually all employees of health care facilities, including physicians, nurses, dentists, dental workers, optometrists, podiatrists, chiropractors, laboratory and blood bank technologists and technicians, research laboratory scientists, phlebotomists, dialysis personnel, paramedics, emergency medical technicians, medical examiners, morticians, housekeepers, laundry workers, and others whose work may involve direct contact with body fluids from living individuals or corpses.

Despite this seemingly sweeping definition, the procedures state, just one page later, that "ward clerks and administrators have virtually no increased risk of contact with body fluids [and] are thus at no greater risk of contracting blood-borne diseases than other members of the general population."

Q 7:180   Can health care professionals transmit AIDS to their patients?

Very rarely, a health care professional can transmit AIDS to a patient. A series of somewhat sensational cases highlighted this rare, but nonetheless frightening, possibility of transmittal during the early days of the AIDS crisis. [*See*

Karassik and Kayser, "AIDS and the Health Care Provider," *The Health Lawyer* (1992).] More common is the danger of transmittal of AIDS by a patient to a worker. This most commonly occurs because of needles, other sharp instruments or bites that break the worker's skin. The proper techniques for protecting both workers and patients are now well known and widely publicized. [*See, e.g.*, http://www.avert.org/needlestick.htm.]

Q 7:181   Are health care institutions required to know if their employees have AIDS?

Neither the CDC nor OSHA mandates AIDS testing. "On the contrary, mandatory testing of health care workers for HIV antibody is specifically not recommended for reasons relating to cost, delay in seroconversion, privacy and consent." [Krebs-Markrich, "The HIV-Infected Health Care Worker in the Hospital," *1993 Health Law Handbook* (Gosfield, ed.) at 196] Health care institutions are required to inquire into the health of physicians seeking clinical privileges [*see* Joint Commission on Accreditation of Healthcare Organizations, Accreditation Manual for Hospitals, 1992, medical staff standard 2.4.1.3], and the CDC does require such workers who perform invasive procedures to know their own HIV status. [*See* Centers for Disease Control, "Recommendations for Preventing Transmission of Human Immunodeficiency Virus and Hepatitis B Virus to Patients During Exposure-Prone Invasive Procedures," *Morbidity and Mortality Weekly Report* 40, No. RR8 (1991).] Nonetheless, when hospitals become aware of a worker's HIV-positive status in a manner that the employee considers an invasion of privacy or breach of confidentiality, or acts on such knowledge to terminate or restrict the activities of that employee, litigation can result. Some early examples are:

1. *In re Milton S. Hershey Medical Center* [595 A.2d 1290 (Pa. Super. Ct. 1991)], where a resident physician was accidentally cut by the attending physician during an invasive procedure. He later voluntarily submitted to HIV testing, informed the hospital of the positive result, and took a voluntary leave of absence.

2. *In re Westchester County Medical Center* [Docket No. 915042, Decision No. CR 191, Appeals Board, Department of Health and Human Services (Apr. 20, 1992)], concerned the decision of a major New York hospital to prohibit an HIV-positive pharmacist from preparing medications that were intended to be injected into patients. The pharmacist brought an administrative action under the Rehabilitation Act of 1973 (see chapters 1 and 4), pleading disability discrimination. The administrative law judge ruled against the hospital's argument that these preparations constituted exposure-prone, invasive procedures, and stated:

> None of Westchester County Medical Center's witnesses . . . could do more than speculate as to the theoretical chain of events by which [the pharmacist] might communicate the virus. None of these witnesses could point to a study or studies which verified that [the hospital's] infection scenario represented anything more

than a theoretical possibility. None of these witnesses could identify evidence that showed that there was a realistic probability that
[he] would ever contaminate a parenteral product with his own
blood.

In another case, the estate of a health care worker sued the former employer,
which had learned of the employee's HIV status while the employee was
actually a patient in the hospital, which had breached the employee's privacy
right as a patient. [Estate of Behringer v. Medical Ctr. at Princeton, 249 N.J.
Super. 597, 592 A.2d 1251 (1991)]

In 2008, a Texas case held that, while an HIV-positive patient could sue the
public hospital for invasion of privacy with relation to improper revelation of his
condition, the implicated employee was immune from a separate suit arising
from the same subject matter. [Burdett v. Doe, 2008 Tex. App. LEXIS 9502 (Tex.
App. Austin Dec. 17, 2008)]

Q 7:182   Should a health care institution reveal a health care professional's HIV-positive status to its patients who may be served by that professional?

The Guidelines issued by the CDC recommend that:

[P]rospective patients of HIV- or HBV (hepatitis B)-infected health care
workers should be notified of the HIV or HBV status of the infected
health care worker before undergoing invasive, exposure-prone
procedures.

This recommendation, which sets the rights of the patient directly against the
privacy rights of the worker, set off a firestorm of debate when it was announced
by the CDC. At least one influential commission soundly rejected the recommendation, stating:

The Commission believes that a blanket policy of disclosure of the
health care provider's HIV status to patients would not only fail to make
the health care workplace safer, it would also have a deleterious impact
on access to health care. ["Preventing HIV Transmission in Health Care
Settings," Report of the National Commission on AIDS, July 1992, at 28]

Federal law requires the states to certify to the Secretary of Health and
Human Services that they have adopted the CDC Guidelines or substantially
equivalent guidelines of their own. [42 U.S.C. §§ 300ee(2)] Some states have
adopted the CDC Guidelines almost verbatim. [See, e.g., Iowa SB 2323 (1992).]
Other states have elected to go their own way on the issue of patient
information. New York is a good example:

[R]equiring health care workers to inform patients or employers that
they are HIV or HBV positive would only serve as a deterrent to workers
seeking voluntary testing and medical evaluation. It would also endanger the professional careers of competent and needed health personnel
who pose no risk to patients.

[New York State Department of Health, Policy Statement and Guidelines, Aug. 1992]

With regard to the impact of revelation of HIV-positive status upon the professional's career, the case of *Estate of Behringer v. The Medical Center at Princeton* [249 N.J. Super. 597, 592 A.2d 1251 (1991)] is telling. In this case, the patient was diagnosed as being HIV-positive when he was an inpatient at the hospital where he was employed. After a brief absence from his practice, Dr. Behringer returned to discover that numerous colleagues and patients had learned of the laboratory test results. As time went on, his practice diminished substantially. Meanwhile the hospital's trustees voted to adopt an "informed consent" form that would be presented to patients before undergoing surgery by an HIV-positive surgeon. As a consequence, no patients agreed to undergo a surgical procedure performed by any such physician and therefore, in the words of the New Jersey appellate court, the special consent form became a "de facto prohibition" of doctors such as Behringer from the practice of surgery in the defendant hospital. Nevertheless, the court decided to uphold the hospital's decisions to: (1) adopt the special "informed consent" form; and (2) suspend the plaintiff's surgical privileges. In so holding, the superior court stated that while the requirement the consent form imposed upon the doctor:

> may not be surmountable absent further education of both the public and the medical community about the realities of HIV and AIDS . . . the difficulties created by the public reaction to AIDS cannot deprive the patient of making the ultimate decision where the ultimate risk is so significant. . . . Where the ultimate harm is death, even the presence of a low risk of transmission justifies the adoption of a policy which precludes invasive procedures when there is "any" risk of transmission. . . . The ultimate risk to the patient is so absolute, so devastating, that it is untenable to argue against informed consent combined with a restriction on procedures which present "any risk" to the patient. [*Behringer*, at 1283]

Q 7:183 Are there any precautions involving health care workers on which all governmental agencies and policy-making groups agree?

In the words of one knowledgeable commentator, "Despite the considerable variability in their respective guidelines, the CDC, the commission, published state guidelines, and professional associations appear to speak with one voice concerning the need for universal precautions and enforcement of vigorous infection control procedures in health care institutions." [Krebs-Markrich, "The HIV-Infected Health Care Worker in the Hospital," *1993 Health Law Handbook* (Gosfield, ed.) at 294] According to this commentator, these various agencies and commissions agree on at least the following standards:

1. Hospitals and other health care institutions should have appropriate infection control (IC) procedures in effect.

2. These institutions should also monitor compliance with these procedures.

3. They should likewise enforce the procedures, including by means of all necessary and appropriate disciplinary action (necessary and appropriate disciplinary action could include restriction or denial of clinical privileges and reporting of violations to the proper state or professional enforcement bodies).

Q 7:184   What types of inspections do OSHA's AIDS procedures call for?

The procedures modify OSHA's usual inspection practices in a number of ways. First, all health service providers [Standard Industry Code (SIC) 80] and funeral homes and crematories [SIC 7261] from a list, such as Dun's Marketing Service, are placed in a pool by each OSHA regional administrator. (Establishments with fewer than 11 employees are excluded.) A list of inspection targets will be randomly drawn from the pool. This list will be narrowed by some additional bureaucratic procedures.

When one of these targeting facilities is visited, the inspector will locate the administrator, medical director, or other person in charge and present his or her appropriate credentials. If the inspector is refused admission, the next step will be to get a search warrant. The inspection will then focus on areas of "primary concern" (e.g., emergency rooms, operating rooms, direct patient care areas, laboratories, and X-ray facilities). "Secondary areas" are laundry and housekeeping facilities.

Q 7:185   What documents will an OSHA inspector want to see during an AIDS inspection?

The OSHA inspector will be particularly interested in the establishment's infection control program and its injury records. An infection control (IC) program normally will be a written policy "relating to the control of infectious disease hazards where employees may be exposed to direct contact with body fluids." As to recordkeeping, the new OSHA procedure makes the following observation:

> Needle sticks, like any other puncture wound, are considered injuries for record keeping purposes due to the instantaneous nature of the event. Only those work-related injuries that involve loss of consciousness, transfer to another job, restriction of work or motion, or medical treatment are required to be put on the OSHA 200 form. Use of prescription medication (beyond a single dose for minor injury or discomfort) is considered medical treatment. Therefore, any needle stick requiring medical treatment, e.g., gamma globulin, hepatitis B immune globulin, hepatitis B vaccine, etc., shall be recorded. In addition, since this type of treatment is considered absolutely necessary, and must be administered by a physician or licensed medical personnel, such an injury cannot be considered minor.

Q 7:186   What if a facility does not have a formal IC program for hepatitis and AIDS?

If there is no written IC program, the inspector will determine the effectiveness of the facility's program by interviewing employees and inspecting the premises. Even with a formal, written IC program, it is likely that the inspector will conduct a walk-through examination of the facility and informally interview employees.

Q 7:187   What will the OSHA inspector's walk-through inspection be like?

During the walk-through examination, the inspector will spot check various areas of the facility to ensure that the IC program is: actually in place; operating as documented; and effective.

Q 7:188   Where can an employer get information on the requirements for an acceptable IC program?

OSHA's instructions are found in the Code of Federal Regulations. [29 C.F.R. §§ 1910.132(a), 1910.132(c), 1910.22(a)(1), 1910.22(a)(2), 1910.141(a)(4)(i), 1910.141(a)(4)(ii), and 1910.145(F)]

Depending on the level of in-house expertise, employers may want to consult legal counsel or an OSHA-oriented consulting firm for additional information on acceptable IC programs.

Q 7:189   What is OSHA's citation policy with respect to AIDS and hepatitis inspections?

Citations normally will be issued for violations found in the following areas: PPE; housekeeping; sanitation and waste disposal; and accident prevention signs and tags.

In addition, health care facilities, like all employers, come under OSHA's general duty to maintain a safe workplace. In fact, a 2003 OSHA initiative involved solicitation of public comment on new guidelines for nursing homes. [BNA *Occupational Safety & Health Daily*, Sept. 27, 2002]

Q 7:190   Is AIDS transmittable in the workplace?

In most workplace situations AIDS cannot be transmitted. This conclusion is based on evidence that the AIDS virus can be passed from one person to another only by means of certain bodily fluids such as semen and blood. The likelihood of exchanging these kinds of fluids in the work environment is minimal, so the conclusion is that AIDS cannot readily be transmitted in the workplace and therefore does not pose a hazard therein. The prevalent theory is that such acts as shaking hands, sneezing, or coming into contact with a victim's saliva are insufficient to transmit the disease.

Q 7:191   What are the recommendations of the Centers for Disease Control of the U.S. Public Health Service?

First, it is important to note that the CDC does not impose mandatory obligations on employers. The CDC's recommendations emphasize that AIDS is a blood-borne and sexually transmitted disease and is not spread by casual contact, such as a handshake or a kiss. The CDC does not recommend routine testing of employees for the AIDS virus, and such testing could lead to legal liability for employers. The CDC recommendations concentrate on health care facilities, where it is felt that employees are at a much greater risk of exposure to the AIDS virus. The CDC also has examined the risk of exposure to AIDS for food-service and personal-service workers.

Q 7:192   What does the CDC recommend with respect to health care professionals?

The CDC recommends "universal precautions" for health care workers who have contact with patients, patients' blood or other bodily fluids, and corpses. Nurses, doctors, dentists, laboratory and blood bank technologists, and dialysis personnel are the primary groups considered; paramedics, emergency medical technicians, morticians, and other workers in a health care setting are also taken into account. *Universal precautions* mean that certain precautions should be taken whether or not the particular patient is known to be or suspected of being an AIDS carrier. All bodily fluids and blood should be treated as if potentially infective (and indeed there are other diseases, such as hepatitis B, that can be transmitted in much the same way). The CDC recommends that health care workers avoid injuries from needles, scalpels, and other sharp instruments during procedures as well as during the cleaning and disposal of such instruments. Needles should not be recapped, bent, broken by hand, or otherwise handled in a way that might result in a cut or abrasion. Syringes, needles, scalpel blades, and other disposable sharp instruments should be put in puncture-resistant containers for disposal. Health care workers should use "barrier precautions" such as gloves when touching blood, body fluids, and mucous membranes. The gloves should be changed and discarded after each contact with a patient. Masks, protective eyewear, face shields, gowns, and aprons should be worn in any procedure that might generate droplets of blood or bodily fluids. Hands and other skin surfaces should be washed immediately and thoroughly after contamination with blood or bodily fluids. Direct mouth-to-mouth resuscitation should be avoided by using mouthpieces, resuscitation bags, and similar types of ventilation devices. Pregnant workers are advised by the CDC to pay particular attention to these kinds of precautions.

Q 7:193   What do OSHA's blood-borne diseases rules require?

OSHA's blood-borne diseases rules include:

1. Provide the hepatitis B vaccine and vaccination series free of charge to all employees who risk occupational exposure to blood-borne pathogens.

2. Develop written exposure control plans that are designed to minimize or eliminate risk of exposure.

3. Provide engineering controls such as puncture-resistant containers, work practices such as hand washing, and appropriate PPE.

4. Initiate post-exposure evaluation and follow-up for all employees who are exposed on the job, plus preventive treatment and counseling.

5. Post, where appropriate, hazard communications such as warning labels and signs identifying containers and work areas that may contain potentially infectious materials.

6. Maintain records of medical information on employees who have been exposed to potentially infectious materials for the duration of each employee's job plus 30 years.

Q 7:194   What rules establish blood-borne pathogen procedures?

In November 2001, OSHA released a compliance directive intended to update the blood-borne pathogen standards and rules. It provides:

- For incorporation of the requirements of the Needlestick Safety and Prevention Act, enacted by Congress a year earlier;

- That employers select safer needle devices as they are developed and improved upon and that they involve their employees in making such selections;

- That employers' annual exposure-control plans evaluate needle devices that enter the marketplace each year;

- That employers actually document how they have involved their employees in these activities;

- That employers establish and maintain a sharps injury log for recording injuries caused by contaminated sharps;

- That compliance officers bear in mind, when conducting inspections, that no one safer medical device is appropriate in all health care situations; that the standard to impose on employers is to "consider and implement devices that are appropriate, commercially available and effective";

- Detailed instructions for the inspection of multi-employer work sites, including home health services, physicians, and other health professionals in independent practices.

The complete directive plus relevant forms is accessible at www.osha.gov/ pls/oshaweb/owadisp.show_document?p_table = DIRECTIVES&p_id = 2570. [See OSHA Trade News Release, Nov. 28, 2001, at http://www.osha.gov/pls/ oshaweb/owadisp.show_document?p_table = NEWS_RELEASES&p_id = 1260.]

In 2005, the U.S. Public Health Service issued its updated guidelines for occupational exposures to such pathogens. [See http://www.cdc.gov/mmwr/ preview/mmwrhtml/rr5409a1.htm.] Comprehensive coverage of both OSHA and USPHS rules and guidelines is available at: http://www.osha.gov/SLTC/ bloodbornepathogens/index.html.

Q 7:195   What are the penalties for violating OSHA's blood-borne disease rule?

OSHA permits the Secretary of Labor to impose a fine as high as $70,000 for each willful or repeated violation, and as high as $7,000 for every non-serious violation of its provisions. [29 U.S.C. § 666(a)(c)] Where a willful violation results in the death of an employee, an additional $10,000 fine plus—and, more significantly—a six-month prison term for responsible company officials are among potential penalties. [29 U.S.C. § 666(e)]

Q 7:196   What are OSHA's needlestick regulations?

OSHA's needlestick regulations were promulgated pursuant to the Needlestick Safety and Prevention Act. They require employers who use needles in the workplace to do the following:

1. Identify and select safer needlesticks;
2. Provide employees who administer needlesticks with input into purchase decisions;
3. Conduct annual reviews of their exposure plan;
4. Maintain a needlestick log; and
5. Maintain employee privacy.

Q 7:197   What precautions should morticians take?

The precautions outlined in Q 7:192 with respect to health care workers should be practiced by morticians as well.

Q 7:198   Which personal-service workers must be mindful of AIDS contamination?

The workers whom the CDC has identified in this category include hairdressers, barbers, masseurs and masseuses, cosmetologists, and a variety of other occupational groups whose work involves close contact with the skin and other parts of clients' bodies. Although the risk of contamination in these occupations is considered by the CDC to be much smaller than with health care employees, the possibility of transmitting the disease exists if either the worker or the client has an open lesion or cut that could leave blood on an instrument. Sterilization appears to be the answer, especially in a case of tattooing, ear piercing, or acupuncture. When possible, disposable instruments should be used on only one customer and then discarded in an appropriate manner.

Q 7:199   What precaution does the CDC advise with respect to food-service workers?

The CDC does not recommend that persons infected with the AIDS virus be routinely restricted from working in the food and beverage industries.

Appropriate standards for the preparation of food and sanitation of the work areas should, of course, be followed. Any food contaminated with blood (e.g., as the result of an employee cutting himself or herself while preparing the food) should be discarded under any circumstances.

Q 7:200   Are restaurant workers and their customers at risk from employees who have tested HIV-positive?

The CDC does not recommend any special precautions concerning HIV in the food service industry. It sees no danger of spreading the infection in that environment. When the ADA was being debated in Congress, an effort was mounted by certain factions of the restaurant industry to carve out of the Act an exemption with regard to HIV-positive employees attempting to continue working in that line of business. Resisting this lobbying effort, Congress made it clear that AIDS is a protected disability under the ADA, and made no exception to this general principle with regard to restaurants and other food services. [H.R. Rep. No. 485, 101st Cong., 2d Sess., pt. 2 at 5152 (1990)] Thus, while under the Act the Secretary of Health and Human Services is mandated to develop a list of communicable diseases that will disqualify food handlers from employment, this list will not include HIV. [*See* 29 C.F.R. § 1630.16(e)(1); 56 Fed. Reg. 22726 (May 16, 1991); Research Institute of America, *Analysis of the Americans with Disabilities Act and the EEOC Regulations* (Aug. 1991) § 403.]

Q 7:201   What should a supervisor do if an employee discloses he or she is HIV-positive?

The supervisor whose employee discloses he or she is HIV-positive should:

1. Begin with a supportive response.
2. Find out why he or she is being told.
3. Ask if he or she is the only one being told.
4. Ask if he or she has permission to share the disclosure.
5. Advise the employee that no further disclosure is required and that confidentiality will be respected.
6. If the employee asks the supervisor to share the information with co-workers, the supervisor should have the employee put the request in writing.

Q 7:202   What should a supervisor do to protect medical information's confidentiality?

Relevant state and federal laws and regulations may impose specific requirements, as may the rules of some professional and industry organizations. But in general:

1. Require confidentiality with regard to all medical conditions, not just life-threatening ones.

2. Protect files from unauthorized access; this may require maintaining separate personnel and medical files on employees.

3. Pre-plan how to respond to inappropriate inquiries, such as "He has AIDS, doesn't he?"

4. Explain to affected employees the circumstances under which disclosure to others may be required by law or business necessity.

Note: Employers also will want to confer with legal counsel concerning whether federal HIPAA regulations concerning confidentiality of medical information apply to some or all of their in-house health care related activities/functions. [See the Department of Health and Human Service's Office of Civil Rights for addition information; http://www.hhs.gov/ocr/hipaa.]

Q 7:203   What should supervisors do to prevent HIV/AIDS discrimination?

To prevent HIV/AIDS discrimination, supervisors should:

1. Make sure that employees are aware of how to report incidents of HIV/AIDS discrimination.

2. Maintain contact with HIV/AIDS-affected employees; do not assume that, if no complaints are received, then no discrimination or harassment is occurring.

3. Treat any incident as a disciplinary issue.

4. Enforce a "zero tolerance" policy with regard to jokes about HIV/AIDS.

Q 7:204   What should supervisors do to manage co-worker fears of HIV/AIDS?

To manage co-worker fears of HIV/AIDS, supervisors should:

1. Provide competent training on HIV transmission and prevention.

2. Provide first aid training that includes universal precautions.

3. Provide counseling to employees concerned about HIV-positive co-workers.

4. Reply to workers demanding information about HIV co-workers that almost any answer given would violate state or federal laws.

5. Bear in mind that irrational co-worker fears may be a disabling situation in the workplace but is not a protected disability under the ADA or analogous state law.

Q 7:205   Should an employee with the AIDS virus be restricted in the use of any of the facilities in the workplace?

The CDC takes the position that there is no reason to prevent AIDS carriers from using telephones, toilets, cafeterias, or other common facilities. Certainly any common area that is contaminated with blood (such as a sink used in the administration of first aid) should be cleaned and sterilized immediately in all cases, not merely in a case in which an employee is suspected of being an AIDS carrier.

Q 7:206 Should the confidentiality of an AIDS carrier be maintained by the employer?

Unquestionably, if an employee voluntarily informs someone at the company of a positive antibody test or an active AIDS condition, or if the employer gets this information from an insurance form, the information should be maintained in strictest confidence. State law may require confidentiality for medical information. Furthermore, legal liability for invasion of privacy and defamation provides additional legal impetus for the employer to respect the privacy and confidentiality of someone who has AIDS or who is HIV-positive. [*See also* the U.S. Department of Health and Human Services Office of Civil Rights Web site for information on HIPAA regulations, which may apply to your organization: http://www.hhs.gov/ocr/hipaa; *see also*, U.S. Department of Health and Human Services Fact Sheet, "Your Rights as a Person with HIV Infection or AIDS," http://www.hhs.gov/ocr/civilrights/resources/factsheets/hivaids.pdf.]

Q 7:207 What should a policy regarding AIDS in the workplace cover?

AIDS in the workplace policies should cover:

1. The facts about AIDS and the limited ways that it can be transmitted in the workplace;
2. The company's position on testing (which should be that testing will not be conducted except in unusual circumstances);
3. A notice that reasonable accommodation will be made to enable a person with AIDS to perform his or her job, if possible; and
4. A description of the company's educational program on AIDS.

Q 7:208 What educational program should a company have?

The kind of time and money a company decides to invest in an AIDS education program will depend on the company's size and resources, and the likelihood that AIDS will become an issue in the workplace. Many larger companies have quite sophisticated and extremely effective AIDS education programs. These companies have taken the view that in order to reach all employees effectively, several communication methods should be used. For instance, a Philadelphia pharmaceuticals company developed a policy stating that it would not test for AIDS, nor would it discriminate against employees who have AIDS. The company then proceeded to announce this policy and the facts about AIDS in a newsletter, in a personal letter to employees (with a brochure) sent to the employees' homes, with a videotape, in face-to-face seminars, and, finally, in the employee handbook.

Q 7:209   What rights do employees have with respect to co-workers who have AIDS?

The employer has a general duty to furnish a workplace free from recognized hazards, and employees have the right to refuse to work in the face of uncorrected hazards. Furthermore, under the NLRA, employees (whether unionized or not) have the right to engage in concerted activity to protect themselves. With respect to AIDS, both of these laws would require that employees have at least some reasonable basis for their refusal to work with someone who has AIDS. Arguably, if the employer has properly attempted to educate employees and there is no factual basis to believe that a hazard exists, the OSH Act and NLRA would not seem to protect from employer discipline those employees who refuse to work; however, the employer should handle employees' concerns with care. For instance, an arbitrator in Minnesota reinstated a prison guard who had been fired for refusing to perform pat-down searches of prisoners because of his fear of AIDS. The arbitrator found that this fear was partially generated by a memorandum distributed in the prison by its warden. Also, the arbitrator took into account that the warden changed his policy and began permitting other guards to wear gloves during pat-down searches after the guard had been fired. Thus, if the company has not taken appropriate steps to allay the unreasonable fears of employees, these fears may rise to the level of reasonableness, and NLRA and the Act may provide some protection to employees under such circumstances.

Q 7:210   Do employees have the right to know that co-workers have AIDS?

There is no legal right, either under right-to-know regulations or other laws, for employees to know that a co-worker has AIDS. To the contrary, statutes involving confidentiality of medical information, plus the common law of privacy and defamation, may create a right for the employee with AIDS to keep this information confidential.

Q 7:211   Where can employers turn for information and advice concerning dealing with HIV/AIDS in the workplace?

Some good sources of support include:

- American Red Cross National Headquarters, AIDS Education Division, http://www.healthfinder.gov/orgs/HR0128.htm
- National AIDS Housing Coalition, http://nationalaidshousing.org/nahcresources/
- National CDC AIDS Hotline, http://www.cdc.gov/hiv/
- San Francisco AIDS Foundation, http://www.sfaf.org/aboutsfaf/releases/bush_report.html

Drug Abuse

Q 7:212   What is the Drug-Free Workplace Act of 1988?

The Drug-Free Workplace Act of 1988 [Pub. L. No. 100-690] is a federal law that requires federal contractors and federal grant recipients to provide a drug-free workplace or, if they are individuals, to refrain from engaging in unlawful drug-related activities when performing the contract or conducting the grant activity. Federal contractors and federal grant recipients must certify to the contracting or granting agency that they will abide by the requirements of the Act, which became effective on March 16, 1989. Any entity, other than an individual, that desires to be considered a responsible source of government contract supplies, for purposes of being awarded a contract for goods or services in the amount of $25,000 or more, must certify to the contracting agency that it will provide a drug-free workplace.

Q 7:213   What actions must an employer take to provide a drug-free workplace within the meaning of the Act?

To provide a drug-free workplace within the meaning of the Act, an employer must meet seven requirements:

1. Publish a statement notifying employees that engaging in unlawful drug-related activity is prohibited in the workplace—the statement must also specify what actions will be taken if employees violate the prohibition.

2. Establish a drug-free awareness program for employees.

3. Provide each employee engaged in the performance of a government contract or grant with a copy of the published prohibition statement.

4. Include in the published prohibition statement notice that employment on the government contract or grant is conditioned on the employee abiding by the terms of the statement and notifying the employer within five days of any criminal drug statute conviction for a workplace violation.

5. Notify the contracting or granting agency within 10 days of receiving notice, from an employee or otherwise, of such a conviction.

6. Either impose sanctions up to and including termination on any employee who has been convicted for the workplace violation of a criminal drug statute or require that the convicted employee participate in a federal, state, or agency-approved drug abuse assistance or rehabilitation program.

7. Make a good faith effort to maintain a drug-free workplace.

These requirements apply both to federal contractors and federal grant recipients.

Q 7:214   What constitutes unlawful drug-related activity within the meaning of the Act?

The unlawful manufacture, distribution, dispensing, possession, or use of a controlled substance constitutes unlawful drug-related activity within the meaning of the Act.

Q 7:215   Must employers make reasonable efforts to provide employees with a drug-free workplace?

The Drug-Free Workplace Act of 1988 requires all federal contractors and federal grant recipients to make a good-faith effort to maintain a drug-free workplace. In so doing, employers must prohibit unlawful drug-related activities on their premises. Employers must also notify employees of the prohibition and the penalty for violating it, require employees to notify the employer within five days of their criminal conviction for a drug violation occurring in the workplace, and discipline any such employees or require that they attend a drug rehabilitation program. Furthermore, federal contractors and federal grant recipients must certify that they will not unlawfully manufacture, distribute, dispense, possess, or use a controlled substance in the performance of a contract or during the conduct of any activity funded by the grant.

Q 7:216   What information must a drug-free awareness program provide to employees?

A drug-free awareness program must inform employees about: the dangers of workplace drug abuse; the employer's policy of maintaining a drug-free workplace; drug counseling, rehabilitation, and assistance programs available to employees; and penalties that may be imposed for drug abuse violations.

Q 7:217   What actions may be taken against a federal contractor or federal grant recipient failing to abide by the drug-free workplace requirement?

Failure to abide by the drug-free workplace requirement may result in the suspension of payments under the contract or grant, termination of the contract or grant, or suspension or debarment of the contractor or grant recipient. These actions are not mutually exclusive; any combination may be taken in response to a single incident. These measures, or any combination thereof, may also be imposed if a contractor or grant recipient provides the contracting or granting agency a false certification, or if the contractor or grant recipient fails to make a good-faith effort to provide a drug-free workplace.

Q 7:218   What is the effect of debarment?

A federal contractor or grant recipient that has been debarred will be ineligible for the award of any federal agency contract or grant and for participation in any future federal agency contract or grant for a period of up to five years. (See chapter 9.)

Q 7:219   What will indicate that a federal contractor or grant recipient has failed to make a good-faith effort to provide a drug-free workplace?

If a number of employees of a government contractor or grant recipient are convicted for workplace violations of criminal drug statutes, this may indicate that the contractor or grant recipient has not made the required good-faith effort to provide a drug-free workplace.

Q 7:220   What special procedures must be followed before measures can be taken against a federal contractor that violates the Drug-Free Workplace Act?

Before measures can be taken against a federal contractor, a contracting officer must make a written determination that cause for action exists. A contracting officer must initiate an appropriate proceeding to determine what, if any, measures should be taken. The contracting agency must conduct the proceeding in accordance with its own procedural rules and those of the federal acquisition regulation. The procedural rules of the federal acquisition regulation are designed to provide a full and fair proceeding. Requirements include the provision of notice and the opportunity to respond in writing or in person.

Q 7:221   Is there a time limit within which an employer must respond to an employee who has been convicted of a workplace violation of a criminal drug abuse statute?

Yes. An employer must either impose sanctions or require participation in a drug abuse assistance or rehabilitation program within 30 days after receiving notice from an employee of a conviction.

Q 7:222   Will action always be taken against a federal contractor or grant recipient that has failed to abide by the drug-free workplace requirement, failed to make a good-faith effort, or made a false certification?

No. Action may be waived if the head of the contracting agency determines that taking action would result in severe disruption of the agency to the detriment of the federal government or the public. The head of the granting agency may also waive action if he or she determines that taking action would not be in the public interest.

Q 7:223   Does the Drug-Free Workplace Act mandate employee drug testing?

No. The Drug-Free Workplace Act does not generally require drug testing of government contractor employees; however, the Department of Defense (DoD) has issued interim regulations that require contractors to establish workplace drug testing programs or appropriate alternatives. Any drug testing an employer institutes should be done only to uncover illegal drug use by employees in sensitive positions (e.g., an employee who has been granted access to classified information or whose job the contractor believes to involve national security, health, or safety or that demands a high level of trust and confidence). The contractor may also institute drug testing when it has a reasonable suspicion that an employee uses illegal drugs, when an employee has been involved in an accident or unsafe practice, as part of a follow-up to rehabilitation for past drug use, or as part of a voluntary employee drug-testing program. A contractor is required to follow the DoD regulations if the contract involves access to classified information, the contracting officer determines that the regulations are necessary for protecting national security, health, and so forth, and the contract obligations (or the pertinent part thereof) are to be performed in the United States.

Q 7:224   Do the provisions of the Drug-Free Workplace Act or the DoD rules provide for mandatory penalties for employees who refuse to participate in a drug testing program?

Neither the Act nor the DoD rules require that a contractor penalize an employee for failure to participate in a drug testing program the contractor institutes. However, a contractor runs the risk of making a false certification if it does not make a good-faith effort to maintain a drug-free workplace; this effort may include a notation that certain employees refuse to participate in an otherwise valid drug-testing program.

Q 7:225   Will mandatory testing of employees or penalties for refusing to participate in a test subject a contractor to a possible lawsuit by an employee?

Several courts have held that mandatory drug testing is a violation of an employee's right of privacy. Some courts also find that random or mandatory drug testing is an unreasonable search and seizure under the Fourth Amendment. Other courts have held that testing and other searches based on a reasonable, individual, and particularized suspicion are valid and constitutional. Still other courts have found that an employer was liable for a tortious invasion of employee's privacy, among other things, for firing an employee who refused to participate in a drug test. [See National Treas. Emps. Union v. Von Raab, 489 U.S. 656 (1989) (mandatory drug testing impacts on federal employees' Fourth Amendment rights, but under at least some circumstances the government-employer's interest in testing outweighs the employee's constitutional rights); Skinner v. Railway Labor Executives' Ass'n, 489 U.S. 602

(1989) (Fourth Amendment applies to railroad administration regulations but tests following train accidents were reasonable under the circumstances); *see also* Luedtke v. Nabors Alaska Drilling, Inc., 768 P.2d 1123 (Alaska 1989) (random drug tests by private employer unsuccessfully challenged as violations of employee's privacy rights under Alaska constitution; Jennings v. Mince Tech. Labs., Inc., 765 S.W.2d 497 (Tex. Civ. App. 1989) (random drug test not tortious invasion of employees' privacy); *but see* Hennessey v. Coastal Eagle Point Oil Co., 589 A.2d 170 (N.J. Super. 1991) (urine testing may implicate employees' privacy rights); Luck v. Southern Pac. Transp., 218 Cal. App. 3d 1 (1990) (where employee was not involved in dangerous or safety-related work, unwilling participation in random urinalysis was invasion of privacy); Borse v. Piece Goods Shop Inc., 963 F.2d 611 (3d Cir. 1991) (employee fired for refusing to sign waiver permitting urinalysis drug test and/or search of personal property at workplace may have wrongful discharge claim under Pennsylvania's exception to at-will employment doctrine).]

Q 7:226   What are the most serious drugs with which employers should be concerned?

The federal Drug Enforcement Agency identifies the following on its Schedule I as the most dangerous and addicting drugs:

- Opiates
- Opium derivatives
- Marijuana
- Hallucinogenic substances
- Depressants

Q 7:227   Which states have enacted medical marijuana laws and how do they fit into the Drug-Free Workplace Act?

Medical marijuana is legal in one-third of jurisdictions. At the time of this writing, 19 states and the District of Columbia have enacted medical marijuana laws:

1. Alaska (1998)
2. Arizona (2010)
3. California (1996)
4. Colorado (2000)
5. Connecticut (2012)
6. District of Columbia (2010)
7. Delaware (2011)
8. Hawaii (2000)
9. Maine (1999)
10. Massachusetts (2012)

11. Michigan (2008)
12. Montana (2004)
13. Nevada (2000)
14. New Jersey (2010)
15. New Mexico (2007)
16. Oregon (1998)
17. Rhode Island (2006)
18. Vermont (2004)
19. Washington (1998)

The bottom line is that there is still much left to be decided regarding medical marijuana use and the Drug-Free Workplace Act, so employers should proceed with caution. As courts rule on the many challenges before them, employers will receive more guidance on how to approach the laws in their own workplaces. For now, it is wise to consult legal counsel before taking any action.

Q 7:228   What is the federal policy on medical marijuana use?

In October 2009, the U.S. Department of Justice announced its policy on medical marijuana use under color of state law. The new guidelines explain, "The Department of Justice is committed to the enforcement of the Controlled Substances Act in all States. Congress has determined that marijuana is a dangerous drug, and the illegal distribution and sale of marijuana is a serious crime and provides a significant source of revenue to large-scale criminal enterprises, gangs, and cartels. One timely example underscores the importance of our efforts to prosecute significant marijuana traffickers: marijuana distribution in the United States remains the single largest source of revenue for the Mexican cartels." However, said Attorney General Eric Holder, "It will not be a priority to use federal resources to prosecute patients with serious illnesses or their caregivers who are complying with state laws on medical marijuana, but we will not tolerate drug traffickers who hide behind claims of compliance with state law to mask activities that are clearly illegal." Holder said,"This balanced policy formalizes a sensible approach that the Department has been following since January: effectively focus our resources on serious drug traffickers while taking into account state and local laws." [http://www.justice.gov/opa/pr/2009/October/09-ag-1119.html; The DEA Position on Marijuana, Jan. 2011, accessed at http://www.justice.gov/dea/docs/marijuana_position_2011.pdf]

Q 7:229   When will the federal government take an interest in marijuana commerce in a medical marijuana state?

Any of the following characteristics could indicate that a state is not in clear compliance with federal law and might potentially attract the attention of the federal government:

• unlawful possession or unlawful use of firearms;

- violence;
- sales to minors;
- financial and marketing activities inconsistent with the terms, conditions, or purposes of state law, including evidence of money laundering activity and/or financial gains or excessive amounts of cash inconsistent with purported compliance with state or local law;
- amounts of marijuana inconsistent with purported compliance with state or local law;
- illegal possession or sale of other controlled substances; or
- ties to other criminal enterprises.

While the guidelines are encouraging to those involved in aspects of medical marijuana use (i.e., patients, caregivers, doctors, and providers), they contain a caveat that leaves the door open for discretionary enforcement of federal law:

> Of course, no state can authorize violations of federal law, and the list of factors above is not intended to describe exhaustively when a federal prosecution may be warranted. Accordingly, in prosecutions under the Controlled Substances Act, federal prosecutors are not expected to charge, prove, or otherwise establish any state law violations. Indeed, this memorandum does not alter in any way the Department's authority to enforce federal law, including laws prohibiting the manufacture, production, distribution, possession, or use of marijuana on federal property. This guidance regarding resource allocation does not "legalize" marijuana or provide a legal defense to a violation of federal law, nor is it intended to create any privileges, benefits, or rights, substantive or procedural, enforceable by any individual, party or witness in any administrative, civil, or criminal matter. Nor does clear and unambiguous compliance with state law or the absence of one or all of the above factors create a legal defense to a violation of the Controlled Substances Act. Rather, this memorandum is intended solely as a guide to the exercise of investigative and prosecutorial discretion.

[http://blogs.justice.gov/main/archives/192]

Q 7:230   What is the U.S. Supreme Court's position on marijuana use?

Californians were the first to carry their case to the nation's highest judicial forum. Marijuana users and growers under the California Compassionate Use Act launched their attack on the federal Controlled Substances Act (CSA) on the theory that the latter violated the Constitution's Commerce Clause. [Gonzales v. Raich, 545 U.S. 1 (2005)]

California's Compassionate Use Act authorizes limited marijuana use for medicinal purposes. Plaintiffs Raich and Monson were California residents who both used doctor-recommended marijuana for serious medical conditions. After federal Drug Enforcement Administration agents seized and destroyed all six of Monson's cannabis plants, they brought this action seeking injunctive and declaratory relief prohibiting the enforcement of the CSA to the extent it prevented them from possessing, obtaining, or manufacturing cannabis for their personal medical use. They claimed that enforcing the CSA against them violated the Commerce Clause and other constitutional provisions. The district court denied their motion for a preliminary injunction, but the Ninth Circuit reversed, finding that they had demonstrated a strong likelihood of success on the claim that the CSA is an unconstitutional exercise of Congress's Commerce Clause authority as applied to the intrastate, non-commercial cultivation and possession of cannabis for personal medical purposes as recommended by a patient's physician pursuant to valid California state law.

The Supreme Court, however, reversed the decision. Six Justices reached all the way back to a 1942 precedent to hold that the plaintiffs' strictly local activity affected interstate commerce sufficiently to permit federal intrusion. The Court said, "In assessing the scope of Congress' Commerce Clause authority, the Court need not determine whether respondents' activities, taken in the aggregate, substantially affect interstate commerce in fact, but only whether a 'rational basis' exists for so concluding. Given the enforcement difficulties that attend distinguishing between marijuana cultivated locally and marijuana grown elsewhere, and concerns about diversion into illicit channels, the Court has no difficulty concluding that Congress had a rational basis for believing that failure to regulate the intrastate manufacture and possession of marijuana would leave a gaping hole in the CSA."

Q 7:231 Do the new medical marijuana laws require employers to accommodate an employee's medical marijuana use?

Most likely, no. The new laws specifically state that companies can still have certain drug-use policies for their employees, and federal law still prohibits any possession of marijuana. The highest courts in California, Montana, Oregon, and Washington have ruled that employers do not have to accommodate medical marijuana use. In 2008, the California Supreme Court held that the state's Fair Employment and Housing Act does not require an employer to accommodate an employee's medical marijuana use. Nor did the Compassionate Use Act provide a clear mandate of public policy, preventing an employee's termination for failing to pass a drug test. The court concluded, that the Compassionate Use Act provides a defense in state criminal prosecutions, but was not intended to eliminate employer's legitimate interest in whether employees used drugs banned by federal law or to otherwise extend to employment law. [Ross v. RagingWire Telecomms., Inc., 42 Cal. 4th 920, 174 P.3d 200 (2008)] In 2012, the Ninth Circuit held that physician-supervised marijuana use was, in fact, federally prohibited drug use and, as such, was not protected by the ADA. [James v. City of Costa Mesa, 684 F.3d 825 (9th Cir. 2012), *amended*, 700 F.3d 394 (9th Cir. 2012)]

However, the federal government has yet to provide a dispositive policy pronouncement. An executive order could clear up the apparent conflict between the Drug Free Workplace Act, and the ADA and state marijuana statutes, at least as government contractors' drug-testing obligations are concerned. But until that happens, terminations of employment grounded upon marijuana use by disabled employees who are under their doctors' care pursuant to state medical marijuana laws will continue to be challenged in court.

Q 7:232   Are there any statutory protections for employees for medical marijuana use?

Yes. Some states have written protections for medical marijuana users directly into their statutes. Here are two examples:

- Arizona's statute state, "Unless failure to do so would cause an employer to lose a monetary or licensing related benefit under federal law or regulations, an employer may not discriminate against a person in hiring, termination or imposing any term or condition of employment or otherwise penalize a person based upon either: (1) the person's status as a cardholder [or] (2) a registered qualifying patient's positive test for marijuana components or metabolites, unless the patient used, possessed or was impaired by marijuana on the premises of the place of employment or during the hours of employment." [Ariz. Rev. Stat. § 36-2813 (2011)]

- Rhode Island's statute states, "No school, employer or landlord may refuse to enroll, employ or lease to or otherwise penalize a person solely for his or her status as a cardholder." [R.I. Gen. Laws § 21-28.6-4 (2011)] However, the chapter shall not permit "[a]ny person to undertake any task under the influence of marijuana, when doing so would constitute negligence or professional malpractice" or require "[a]n employer to accommodate the medical use of marijuana in any workplace." [R.I. Gen. Laws § 21-28.6-7]

However, whether state courts determine that these types of provisions provide a private right of action for employees or require employers to make accommodations remains to be seen. The issues have yet to be addressed in court, and employers have plenty of other defenses for maintaining drug-free workplace policies.

Q 7:233   Can an employer still fire or refuse to hire an employee for testing positive for THC in a drug test?

Yes. For example, Colorado law states in regard to the legalization of marijuana, "Nothing in this Section is intended to require an employer to permit or to accommodate the use, consumption, possession, transfer, display, transportation, sale or growing of marijuana in the workplace or to affect the ability of employers to have policies restricting the use of marijuana by employees." In other words, if a company has a zero tolerance drug policy, it can refuse to hire an applicant or fire an employee for using marijuana. That does not mean, of course, that employees would not continue to challenge such laws.

Employers cannot, however, discriminate against employees or applicants simply for obtaining a state registration card allowing them to use marijuana legally.

Q 7:234 How do "off-duty" laws impact the Act?

For the most part, companies do not need to accommodate employees' off-duty use of marijuana. However, currently seven medical marijuana states have implicit employee protections in place, where the law mentions only on-the-job consumption or impairment as grounds for termination—Colorado, Hawaii, Michigan, Montana, New Jersey, New Mexico, and Vermont. Two others, Rhode Island and Maine, have explicit protections for medical marijuana patients written into their legislation.

In the private sector, companies that are inclined to do so may choose to change their drug testing policies, but those that receive federal contracts are required to prohibit the use of marijuana as a condition of participation under the Drug-Free Workplace Act of 1988.

Colorado's Lawful Off-Duty Activities Law became a focus of courtroom controversy when plaintiff Brandon Coats, a telephone operator for defendant Dish Network, was fired for failing a company drug test back in 2010. Paralyzed as a teen and a medical-marijuana patient since 2009, Coats lost before the trial court in 2011, even though the employer admitted he had never been impaired on the job. [Kristen Wyatt & Gene Johnson, "Legal Pot and Drug Free Workplaces: A Bad Combination," *The Huffington Post*, Dec. 7, 2012, accessed at http://www.huffingtonpost.com/2012/12/07/legal-pot-workplace_n_2259589.html] The case remains pending before the state court of appeals. The case apparently will turn on whether state or federal law trumps.

Q 7:235 Can an employer still be held liable for accidents that occur because an employee was under the influence of marijuana?

Yes. Employers who allow off-duty marijuana use must consider the issue of liability. Should an employee come to work under the influence and pose a safety hazard? The employer could be found liable for any accidents that subsequently occur. The federal Department of Transportation, for example, issued new guidelines that prohibit the use of medical marijuana for transportation workers in safety-sensitive jobs including pilots, school bus drivers, truck drivers, subway operators, ship captains, and transit fire-armed security, even in states where it is legal.

Even if an employer is inclined to allow an employee to use medical marijuana outside the workplace, the employer must always remember that it is under a duty imposed by the OSH Act to provide a safe work place for all its employees. Some studies have shown that marijuana-using employees are more prone to accidents, injuries, and absenteeism. If the worker is in a safety-sensitive position, marijuana use is likely not a reasonable option.

Q 7:236 What are the minimum components of any workplace drug policy?

Any such policy, whether mandated by law or voluntarily adopted, should forbid:

- The use of illicit drugs;
- Impairment by drugs; and
- Possession of illicit drugs.

Workplace Violence

Q 7:237   What are the categories of workplace violence?

Workplace violence can be classified as follows:

1. Violence by emotionally enraged persons;
2. Violence by an angry spouse or relative of an employee;
3. Random violence;
4. Violence against law enforcement or security; or
5. Terrorism and hate crimes.

Q 7:238   What are some common characteristics of persons who commit workplace violence?

Persons who commit workplace violence can share the following characteristics:

- A history of violence
- Psychosis
- Romantic obsession
- Chemical dependence
- Depression
- Paranoia or being a pathological blamer
- Impaired neurological functioning
- Elevated frustration with work environment
- Interest in or obsession with weapons
- Personality disorder

Q 7:239   What possible indicia of potential workplace violence should supervisors look for?

Supervisors should look for:

- Alcohol abuse
- Drug abuse
- Impaired judgment
- Emotional difficulties
- Financial problems

- Legal problems
- Strained family relations
- Occupational failure
- Threats
- Absenteeism
- Deterioration of personal appearance, attitude, and behavior
- Deterioration of interpersonal relations
- Inefficiency

Q 7:240 What should supervisors and HR personnel do to document incidents of workplace violence or behavior indicative of potential workplace violence?

Incidents of workplace violence or possible violent behavior should be documented as follows:

1. Record incidents promptly;
2. Indicate date, time, and location;
3. Detail the behavior;
4. List all persons and work products involved;
5. Identify the performance standards and disciplinary rules violated;
6. Record the consequences of the action;
7. Record management's response; and
8. Record the employee's reaction to management's response.

Q 7:241 What are some do's and don'ts of supervisory response to indicia of potential workplace violence?

Supervisors should respond as follows to indicia of potential workplace violence:

1. Don't try to diagnose the behavior personally.
2. Don't discuss drinking unless it occurs on the job.
3. Don't moralize.
4. Don't be misled by sympathy-evoking tactics.
5. Don't cover up for a friend.
6. Don't put the individual into an isolated work area.
7. Don't ignore the problem or the signs of trouble.
8. Do remember that chemical dependence is progressive and likely will only get worse over time.
9. Do bring to the attention of suspected employees the company's employee assistance program.

10. Do make it clear that your organization is concerned with job performance, and that if performance does not improve, the job is in jeopardy.

11. Do explain that the employee must make the personal decision to seek help.

12. Do emphasize that the employee assistance program is confidential.

Q 7:242 What are some things do to prevent workplace violence?

To prevent workplace violence, an employer should:

1. Develop a written policy.
2. Form a crisis management team.
3. Develop policies on counseling, suspension, and termination.
4. Immediately investigate all incidents, such as threats.
5. Contact specialists for assistance.
6. Revise plans, policies, and procedures as information develops—be flexible.

Q 7:243 What guidance does OSHA provide for retail establishment workplace violence?

On January 27, 2010, OSHA released new recommendations on retail establishment workplace violence prevention. The new recommendations updated OSHA's guidance document "Recommendations for Workplace Violence Prevention Programs in Late-Night Retail Establishments" that addresses issues causing late-night retail workers to be killed on the job. The agency proffered the following facts:

- According to Bureau of Labor Statistics' data, 167 retail trade workers were killed in 2007. Nearly half of these were employed in late-night establishments such as gasoline stations, liquor, and convenience stores.

- Of these worker deaths, 39 killed were convenience store employees, 32 worked at gasoline stations, and 7 worked at liquor stores.

- The number of retail workers who died as a result of workplace violence has declined over the course of 10 years—from 286 in 1998 to 167 in 2007.

Another source provides more recent data:

- 405 workplace shootings were recorded in the United States in 2010.
- 24 percent of these shootings occurred in the retail industry.
- Only 17 of the 405 shootings occurred in the manufacturing industry, the lowest among all industrial sectors.
- In 2010, the United States recorded 270 workplace suicides. In 2011, the total was 227.

[http://content.yudu.com/Library/A1zcgk/2013WorkplaceViolenc/resources/10.htm]

The updated recommendations identify risk factors and describe feasible solutions. Although not exhaustive, these workplace violence guidelines include policy recommendations and practical corrective methods to help prevent and mitigate the effects of workplace violence in late-night retail establishments.

The complete recommendations are available at: http://www.osha.gov/Publications/osha3153.pdf.

On September 8, 2011, OSHA issued a directive on Enforcement Procedures for Investigating or Inspecting Incidents of Workplace Violence. The directive established uniform procedures for OSHA field staff for responding to incidents and complaints of workplace violence and conducting inspections in industries considered vulnerable to workplace violence, such as healthcare and social service settings, and late-night retail establishments. The agency provided these facts:

- Workplace violence is a serious recognized occupational hazard, ranking among the top four causes of death in workplaces during the past 15 years.
- More than 3,000 people died from workplace homicide between 2006 and 2010, according to BLS.
- Additional BLS data indicate that an average of more than 15,000 nonfatal workplace injury cases was reported annually during this time.
- One OSHA inspection of a Maine psychiatric hospital found more than 90 instances in which workers were assaulted on the job by patients from 2008 through 2010. The hospital was cited for not providing its workers with adequate safeguards against workplace violence and a fine of more than $6,000 was proposed. OSHA has also recently cited facilities in New York and Massachusetts where employees have been killed as a result of assaults.

OSHA launched a new Web page [http://www.osha.gov/SLTC/workplace violence/index.html] on Preventing Workplace Violence and published several workplace violence guidance documents including Recommendations for Workplace Violence Prevention Programs in Late-Night Retail Establishments and Guidelines for Preventing Workplace Violence for Health Care and Social Service Workers.

[http://www.osha.gov/pls/oshaweb/owadisp.show_document?p_table = NEWS_RELEASES&p_id = 20637]

Q 7:244 In our post-9/11 world, should an employer have an evacuation plan?

In the words of Labor Lawyer Louis Lessig, who practices with a firm in southern New Jersey, "Employers of all sizes are now drafting and revising emergency evacuation procedures. But, in order to adequately prepare, it is necessary to know in advance which employees, if any, will need assistance." In line with Mr. Lessig's observation, the EEOC released guidelines concerning the creation of emergency plans that comply with the ADA. The guide lists three ways in which employers can obtain the information Mr. Lessig says they need:

- The employer can ask about a new hire's needs in this regard after making an offer of employment and prior to the commencement of work;
- The employer is allowed to send out periodic surveys of all employees to ascertain such special needs; however, self-identification must be strictly voluntary and be used only in conjunction with construction of the emergency plan;
- The employer may ask all employees with declared disabilities if they will require such special assistance in the event of an evacuation of the work site.

Also worth noting is the ADA provision that, while in general, medical information must be maintained in confidentiality, relevant information can be provided by the employer to:

- Health care workers;
- Emergency coordinators;
- Floor captains; or
- A colleague designated to provide the special assistance required.

Particularly regarding small businesses, OSHA has posted an "eTool" on the Internet. This resource is intended to assist such small employers to wrestle with relevant OSH Act standards such as:

- Means of egress (29 C.F.R. § 1910.37);
- Emergency action and fire prevention plans (29 C.F.R. § 1910.38);
- Portable fire extinguishers (29 C.F.R. § 1910.157);
- Fixed extinguishing systems (29 C.F.R. § 1910.160);
- Fire detection systems (29 C.F.R. § 1910.164); and
- Employee alarm systems (29 C.F.R. § 1910.165).

The Web site covers:

- Evacuation procedures;
- Emergency escape route assignments;
- Procedures for employees who remain behind to handle critical systems;
- Procedures to account for all employees;
- Rescue and medical duties of designated employees;
- Means of reporting fires and other emergencies;
- Names and titles of persons to be contacted for explanation of procedures and duties; and
- Tips on evaluating your workplace.

[*BNA Occupation Safety & Health Daily*, Sept. 16, 2002; http://www.bna. com/occupational-safety--p4899/. *See also* the National Safety Council's Emergencies and Disasters Web site at http://www.nsc.org/Pages/ MedicalandNaturalDisasters.aspx]

Q 7:245 Does the ADA permit an employer to take action against a violent employee even when the violence is the result of a disability?

A 1996 case suggests that the answer to this question is yes. In *Poff v. Prudential Insurance Co.* [911 F. Supp. 856 (E.D. Pa. 1996)], the employee suffered health problems which caused him great pain. He fell one day at work, reinjuring the hip that was the focal point of his pain and suffering. Reacting to the recurrence of severe pain, the plaintiff punched a hole in the wall. This action caused the halon fire fighting system to discharge, forcing an evacuation of the entire facility. On these facts, the federal judge ruled that the company was entitled to terminate the plaintiff's employment, based upon the violent act.

Post-9/11 we can anticipate more courts (and arbitrators in unionized environments) to look favorably on fast action by employers in the face of violent employee behavior. On the other hand, adverse employment actions against employees or applicants who merely manifest the traits of potentially violent behavior are unlikely to be accorded court protection in the face of ADA challenges.

Note: In 2009, Congress enacted major amendments to the ADA. (See chapter 4 for a thorough discussion of these amendments.)

Q 7:246 Should there be another anthrax or other biological terrorism attack via the U.S. mail, what are appropriate procedures?

OSHA offers the following guidelines:

GENERAL MAIL HANDLING

- Be observant for suspicious envelopes and packages;
- Open all mail with a letter opener or by the method least likely to disturb the contents;
- Do not blow into envelopes;
- Do not shake or pour out the contents;
- Keep hands away from nose and mouth; and
- Wash hands after handling the mail.

THINGS THAT SHOULD TRIGGER SUSPICION

- Discoloration, crystallization, strange odor, or oil stains;
- Powder or residue;
- Protruding wires or aluminum foil;

- Excessive tape or string;
- Unusual size or unusual weight for its size;
- Lopsided or oddly shaped envelope;
- Postmark that does not match return address;
- Restrictive endorsement such as "Personal" or "Confidential";
- Excessive postage;
- Handwritten, block printed, or poorly typed addresses;
- Incorrect titles;
- Misspelling of common words;
- Lack of return address; and
- Addressed to someone no longer at your organization.

HANDLING A SUSPECT PACKAGE OR LETTER

- Stay calm;
- Do not shake or empty contents;
- Keep hands away from nose and mouth;
- Isolate the item;
- Cover it with anything available, such as an inverted trash can;
- Do not clean up any of the substance that spills;
- Avoid creating air currents;
- Wash hands with soap and water;
- Do not remove any potentially contaminated items from the area;
- Do not step on any substance that spills on the floor and try not to disturb it;
- If you are contaminated, keep your movements in your work site to a minimum; and remove heavily contaminated clothing, preferably in a shower, if one is available.

Contact your supervisor or designated responder; this person will determine what further action is called for, preferably with reference to a preexisting emergency and evacuation plan.

The CDC has issued guidelines for cleanup workers exposed to anthrax. These are based in part upon OSH Act regulations for hazardous waste cleanup operations. [29 C.F.R. § 1910.120] These CDC guidelines are available at: http://www.cdc.gov/mmwr.

Yet another resource for employers concerned about developing disaster plans post-9/11 is a federal report entitled "Learning from Disasters: Weapons of Mass Destruction Preparedness Through Worker Training." The report is the result of a Worker Education and Training Program Conference held in Raleigh, NC on April 25–26, 2002. It was funded out of EPA's Superfund coffers and is available from the Government Printing Office.

Q 7:247   What are the dimensions of workplace violence?

Homicide is the number two cause of death in the American workplace, and the number one cause of female deaths. Throughout the last decade of the twentieth century about 1,000 U.S. workers were murdered and another 1.5 million assaulted annually. The assaults included almost 400,000 aggravated assaults; 50,000 rapes and other sexual assaults; and 84,000 robberies. By 2000, however, the homicide rate had declined to a little under 700, thanks largely to improved security measures in American workplaces. Since then the annual rate has remained below 700, if one does not count the World Trade Center attack in 2001. More than 3,000 people died from workplace homicide between 2006 and 2010, and an average of more than 15,000 nonfatal workplace injury cases was reported annually during this time.

Three quarters of all worksite homicides involve firearms. The next most popular weapon of choice—blades—trails at a mere eight percent of all such deaths.

Some 330,000 retail workers are workplace crime victims annually, with convenience store clerks (61,000) and bartenders (26,000) leading the pack.

Nurses (70,000), doctors (10,000), and medical technicians (24,000) are also among the most frequently victimized workers in our nation.

But the leaders in workplace victimization are our teachers, who account for nearly half of all victims of workplace violence. The highest incidence is in junior/middle schools (47,000) with elementary and high schools each running around 30,000 violent incidents annually.

About 40 percent of all victims of workplace violence know their attackers.

[See http://www.osha.gov/SLTC/workplaceviolence/index.html#alliances and http://www.bls.gov/iif/oshwc/cfoi/cfoi_revised05.htm.]

In recent years, there has been an increase in school shootings, mainly perpetrated by mentally ill and/or disgruntled students, who shot fellow students, as well as employees (such as professors) before killing themselves. These events resulted in increased scrutiny on school safety, security programs, and devising and implementing preventative measures. According to one source, employers must, "creat[e] a culture in your workplace to deter violence, or spot potential violence, before it can happen." Employers can take the following measures:

- Treat employees with respect—while they work for you, during a termination, and even after they are no longer your employees.
- Flag at-risk employees for assistance.
- Offer employee assistance programs for those who need them.
- Involve security personnel and local law enforcement at the first hint that an employee might turn violent.

[http://www.ohioemployerlawblog.com/2012/08/do-you-know-what-to-do-when-violence.html]

Q 7:248 Are employers liable under state workers' compensation statutes for injuries sustained by employees due to workplace violence?

The majority of U.S. jurisdictions that have considered this question have held that employees' exclusive remedy is under the state's workers' compensation law. The test is generally stated as follows:

- The risk of assault was increased due to the nature or the location of the work; or
- The motive for the assault originated in the workplace.

[Larson, *The Law of Workmen's Compensation*, Volume 1, § 11.00 at 3-178]

Sometimes this can result in the employee being denied a meaningful remedy. An example is *Mack v. Strategic Materials, Inc.* [270 F. Supp. 2d 934 (E.D. Mich. 2003)], where the plaintiff was brutally beaten on his employer's premises. The state agency initially denied Mack workers' compensation benefits because the attack did not arise out of the employment relationship. He then sued his employer, Strategic Materials, on a negligence theory. He lost in a mandatory arbitration hearing and appealed to the federal district judge. The judge ruled that, even though the state agency denied Mack workers' compensation benefits, this did not determine that his claim failed to fall under the workers' compensation statute. To the contrary, said the district judge, Mack's exclusive remedy was an appeal of the benefits denial to the Workers' Compensation Bureau.

Q 7:249 Are there any exceptions to workers' compensation coverage of workplace violence liability?

The most common exception to workers' compensation coverage of workplace violence is the "intentional tort" distinction. For example:

- Pennsylvania common law has carved out an exception to workers' compensation coverage where "personal animus" has motivated an intentional injury of the employee. But an attack by a co-worker, even if motivated by the attacker's personal animosity for the victim, is still a workplace injury covered by the Pennsylvania compensation statute. [Tsaris v. Salkind Painting Co., 111 A.2d 176 (Pa. Super. 1955)]
- New Jersey law has created an exception to compensation coverage where: (1) the injury is caused either by an intentional attack or by horseplay; or (2) the claimant was the aggressor. [N.J. Stat. Ann. § 34:15-1 (West 2001)] In seeking to interpret this provision where aggressor and victim are co-workers, the Garden State's courts have considered whether the combatants also had a relationship outside the workplace, in which case it becomes less likely that workers' compensation exclusivity will apply. [Crenman v. Harrah's Marina Hotel Casino, 680 F. Supp. 150 (D. N.J. 1988)]

A second exception to workers' compensation coverage has developed in the common law with regard to an injured fetus being carried by an employee at the time of her workplace mishap. For example, the California Supreme Court unanimously ruled in 1997 that a child born with cerebral palsy, due to an outside contractor's operation of machinery without properly ventilating the workplace, enjoyed a negligence claim against the mother's employer. [*Cal-OSHA Reporter*, Vol. 24, p. 46 (Nov. 17, 1997)] This principle clearly carries over to situations in which a pregnant employee is assaulted or raped while on the job.

Q 7:250   What liability does an employer have to a third-party victim of workplace violence?

The national law firm of Morgan, Lewis & Bockius has identified three theories of employer liability to third-party victims. [Morikawa, Boles, Nugent & Cox, "Workplace Violence: Practical and Lawful Guidance from the Front Line," Morgan Lewis Labor & Employment Law Seminar, Oct. 1, 2003 at 1–8 *et seq.*]

- *Premises Liability.* Under the Restatement Second of Torts, § 344, owners and lessees of commercial premises are obliged to exercise reasonable care for the protection of invitees to the premises. This can include a·duty to warn visitors of possible dangers, as well as the more fundamental duty to take reasonable precautions to abate such threats.

- *Respondeat Superior.* This Latin term from the English common law implies that the master should respond for the torts of its servants, if committed in the course of performing their duties on the master's behalf. The principle has been applied to permit victimized plaintiffs to reach employers' deeper pockets, even where the malfeasing employees had clearly exceeded the behavior anticipated by their bosses. For example, in one early case, a driver-delivery man was charged with collecting payments from the retail grocery stores where he delivered his employer's ice cream products. In one instance, he actually assaulted a storekeeper who was behind in his payments. Although the ice cream manufacturer in no way ordered or condoned such violent behavior, the manufacturer was made to respond in money damages to the storekeeper for the injuries the driver had caused. More recently, a Pennsylvania sheriff's department was held liable for the extracurricular mayhem caused by a deputy in the line of duty. [D'Errico v. Defazio, 763 A.2d 424 (Pa. Super. 2000)]

- *Negligent Hiring, Retention and Supervision.* Section 317 of the Restatement Second of Torts states:

  A master is under a duty to exercise reasonable care to control his servant while acting outside the scope of his employment so as to prevent him from intentionally harming others or from so conducting himself as to create an unreasonable risk of bodily harm to them, if (a) the servant is upon the premises in possession of the master or upon which the servant is privileged to enter . . . or is using the chattel of the master, and (b) the master knows or has reason to know that he has the ability to control the servant. And knows or should know of the necessity and opportunity for exercising such control.

Q 7:251　Does a collective bargaining relationship affect issues of workplace violence?

Labor unions are taking an active interest in workplace safety. Workplace violence is no exception. For example, the United Autoworkers' agenda for workplace safety includes the following:

- Workplaces should be secure from outside intruders, including family members seeking to bring domestic disputes into the job site.

- Employers should establish "workplace assistant programs" to help out employees suffering from exceptional stress.

- Medical benefits should include mental health coverage.

- Counselors should be entitled and even obligated to convey threats to the targets of such employee threats.

- Employers should have anti-violence policies and unions should have input into these rules and regulations.

[61 BNA *Daily Labor Report* at E-1 (1999)]

The Association of Flight Attendants (AFA), representing some 47,000 airline workers, takes a "zero tolerance" position with regard to onboard violence. [83 BNA *Daily Labor Report* at A-5 (2000)] The AFA has teamed up with the International Association of machinists and the International Transport Workers' Federation to pursue a collective bargaining and legislative agenda to eliminate threats of in-flight acts of violence. [130 BNA *Daily Labor Report* at A-2 (2001)]

Such union initiatives clearly implicate the duty to bargain collectively about them, since such work rules directly impact terms and conditions of employment and therefore are mandatory subjects of collective bargaining. Thus, unionized employers should anticipate encountering such proposals at the bargaining table, if they have not already done so.

Q 7:252　How are arbitrators responding to acts of workplace violence?

In our experience, labor arbitrators are reluctant to reinstate employees that are terminated for perpetrating workplace violence, where the grievant guilt is proven. In the twenty-first century, where fisticuffs increasingly have given way to gunplay, this arbitral trend is predictably stronger than ever. Nonetheless, arbitrators often do take their lead from constitutional principles of due process, viewing termination of employment as "workplace capital punishment." Consequently, the following guidelines, outlined in one recent arbitration award, are probably considered by most experienced labor arbitrators in workplace-violence hearings:

- Did the employer give the grievant forewarning of the consequences of the workplace violence at issue in the grievance?

- Was the relevant work rule reasonably related to the efficient and safe running of the workplace?

- Did the employer, prior to administering discipline, conduct a reasonable investigation to ascertain the facts of the case?
- Was the investigation fair and objective?
- Did the investigation ascertain substantial evidence of the grievant's guilt?
- Has the relevant work rule been applied evenhandedly in the past?
- Was the discipline reasonably related to the seriousness of the offense?

[Meridian Medical Technologies, 115 BNA Labor Arbitrations 799 (2001)]

In one reported award, the arbitrator reinstated an employee fired for allegedly pointing a gun at a co-worker. The arbitrator based the award of reinstatement on the ground that the grievant denied doing the dirty deed and the employer could produce no corroborating witnesses. It seems that the arbitrator was influenced by testimony that two witnesses had been present at the alleged incident but were not produced at the hearing. [Georgia Pacific Corp., 115 BNA Labor Arbitrations 799 (2001)]

In another reported decision, an angry employee stormed out of the employer's plant and spent the next day at home cleaning his guns. The employer made a preemptive decision to terminate the worker and bar him from the workplace. Reinstating the grievant, the arbitrator noted that he was required to rule on "just cause" in light of the proven facts, and not upon the employer's speculations about possible future behavior. [Eaton Corp., 114 BNA Labor Arbitrations 1114 (2000)]

Q 7:253 What are the trends in federal common law regarding workplace violence?

The clear trend in the federal common law is supportive of employers who strive to prevent and punish workplace violence. For example:

- *Owens v. City of Durham.* [2002 U.S. Dist. LEXIS 19540 (MDNC)] The plaintiff, a white man, was fired for threatening and shoving a black co-worker who had taunted the plaintiff. The African American employee was disciplined, but not discharged. The court granted summary judgment in the plaintiff's subsequent reverse discrimination case, since the proof of his violent behavior was overwhelming and undisputed.
- *Taffe v. Illinois Dep't of Security.* [229 F. Supp. 2d 858 (N.D. Ill. 2002)] When the plaintiff, an African American, was terminated for statements that could reasonably be interpreted as threats of bodily harm to her manager (e.g., "Now I understand why postal workers shoot their managers"), she sued claiming that her termination actually was motivated by the employer's anticipation of her filing of a workers' compensation claim. The court granted the defendant's motion for summary judgment, noting that the injury on which she based her belated claim had occurred several years earlier and that the possibility of a compensation claim had been around long enough for the defendant to have acted on it long before the undisputed incidents of threatening statements.

- *White v. Henderson.* [33 Fed. App. 808 (6th Cir. 2002)] The appeals panel affirmed the district judge's summary disposition of the plaintiff's assorted discrimination claims, finding that the defendant had a "zero tolerance" policy regarding workplace violence and that the plaintiff's shouting and physical abuse, directed toward his co-worker/wife in the workplace, was undisputed.

- *Kirkland-Zuck v. Department of HUD.* [48 Fed. App. 749 (Fed. Cir. 2002)] The plaintiff fired for "disrespectful conduct" toward co-workers and clients, belatedly challenged on appeal the agency's failure to take into consideration her distress over the recent demise of her spouse. Since the related stress was not placed in evidence in the district court down below, the appeals panel affirmed the trial court's summary disposition of her claims.

- *Rivera-Aponte v. Restaurant Metropol.* [338 F.3d 9 (1st Cir. 2003)] The plaintiff tossed a tray of glasses at a co-worker, who required stitches at the emergency room and was deemed by the manager to have been the aggressor in light of interviews of co-workers who witnessed the altercation. The plaintiff challenged his termination under the Age Discrimination in Employment Act and a number of Puerto Rican laws. Affirming summary judgment against the plaintiff, who argued he had never been asked for his side of the story, the appeals panel held that, whether or not the termination was hasty, it clearly was not pre-textual.

- *Pineda v. United Parcel Service.* [360 F.3d 483 (5th Cir. 2004)] The plaintiff, fired for making threatening statements to co-workers, sued under Texas law alleging retaliatory discharge for giving a deposition in a co-worker's discrimination case. After removal of the case from state to federal court, the case reached a jury, which rendered a verdict in the plaintiff's favor. On appeal, the Fifth Circuit looked to Texas common law for guidance. The court found that guidance in *Wal-Mart Stores, Inc. v. Canchola*, [121 S.W.3d 735, 740 (Tex. 2003)], in which the Texas Supreme Court held that it was "not sufficient [for the plaintiff] to present evidence that the . . . investigation was imperfect, incomplete, or arrived at a possibly incorrect conclusion. He must show that the reason proffered by [the defendant] is 'false, and discrimination was the real reason.'" Finding the facts of *Pineda's* case strikingly similar to those in Wal-Mart's appeal, the federal appeals court vacated the jury's verdict.

- *McCoy v. City of Shreveport.* [492 F.3d 551 (5th Cir. 2007)] City did not take discriminatory or retaliatory adverse action against black female police lieutenant, despite contention that it created hostile work environment that caused her "constructive discharge," The court concluded that: (1) a reasonable person would not have felt compelled to resign; (2) she was not demoted and suffered no reduction in salary; (3) she was relieved of her responsibilities only at her own request; (4) city never indicated that she would not be reinstated; (5) she was not reassigned to menial work and never received offer of early retirement; (6) city's conduct of counseling her against workplace horseplay, retrieving her badge and gun, and placing her on administrative leave were not calculated to encourage her resignation; (7) a male sergeant's occasional boorish remarks and horse-play were not severe or pervasive, and he had already left police department when lieutenant chose to retire. Furthermore, a black police lieutenant's comment about workplace violence and taking care of the problem herself was legitimate, non-discriminatory reason for city to retrieve her gun and badge and place her on administrative leave. She failed to show that any of this was a pretext for retaliation, even though decision makers were aware of her complaint about treatment of black officers and placed her on leave shortly afterward. There was no evidence that they had ever engaged in discriminatory conduct or that white officers were treated differently.

Ergonomics

Q 7:254 What action did the Bush administration take with regard to ergonomics in 2001?

On March 20, 2001, President Bush signed a joint resolution of the two houses of Congress disapproving OSHA's ergonomics standard and, at the same time, pledged to find a solution to ergonomic-related problems affecting the nation's workforce.

On April 30, 2002, Assistant Secretary of Labor, John Henshaw, announced the formation of a National Advisory Committee on Ergonomics as part of OSHA's comprehensive approach to reducing ergonomic-related injuries. The comprehensive approach also includes:

- Guidelines;
- Research;
- Outreach and assistance; and
- Enforcement.

The committee will advise on:

- Industry and task-specific guidelines;
- Gaps in existing research;
- Methods of providing outreach; and
- Ways to improve communication among stakeholders in the ergonomic effort.

Q 7:255 What was OSHA's ergonomics standard?

OSHA's ergonomics standard was issued on November 14, 2000, and was intended to take effect on January 16, 2001. Acting under the authority of the Congressional Review Act of 1996, Congress and the President acted to abrogate the standard within two months of its promulgation to employers. The standards were harshly criticized by employers and their lobbyists as onerous and unreasonably costly. The Bush administration agreed.

Q 7:256 What remains of OSHA's ergonomics program?

Then-Labor Secretary Elaine L. Chau announced, in the wake of the Bush administration's abrogation of the ergonomics standards, that OSHA maintains the following principles with regard to ergonomics issues:

1. *Prevention:* OSHA urges employers to place a greater emphasis on preventing ergonomic injuries before they occur.

2. *Sound Science:* OSHA will approach—and urges employers to approach—ergonomics from the perspective of the best available research.

3. *Incentive-Driven:* OSHA will seek ways to cooperate with employers on this issue.

4. *Flexibility:* OSHA and employers should avoid a one-size-fits-all approach.

5. *Clarity:* Any approach should include short, simple, and common sense instructions and training.

In 2002, OSHA announced its first concrete applications of this fallback position to actual industrial settings. Early in 2003, an announcement came from Orlando, FL that OSHA would issue draft ergonomic guidelines for retail grocery stores and the poultry processing industry. In 2002, guidelines were issued for nursing homes, an industry that has become a particular target of OSHA during the last two years. In 2012, OSHA continues to pursue ergonomic issues when possible under the Act's general duty clause, while also continuing to advocate for its four-pronged approach to the problem. [*See* http://www.osha.gov/SLTC /ergonomics/four-pronged_factsheet.html.]

Q 7:257 Does OSHA have any enforcement power left with respect to ergonomics?

Yes. OSHA still may investigate and cite employers for ergonomics hazards under the OSH Act's general duty clause. In fact, with regard to the guidelines issued for the poultry, grocery, and nursing home industries in 2002, Administrator Henshaw expressly pointed to the general duty clause as the stick that will be used, should the carrot of improved employee health and wellness not prove to be a sufficient incentive for adoption of the guidelines. In 2009, OSHA notes the following enforcement activities:

- OSHA has issued 19 General Duty Clause violations for ergonomic hazards, 18 of which have been settled and one remains open. OSHA continues to evaluate workplace ergonomics.

- From January 1, 2002 through December 31, 2007 OSHA conducted 4,138 ergonomics inspections encompassing a variety of industries. Of these,

1,225 inspections were conducted in nursing and personal care facilities under a National Emphasis Program from July 2002 through the end of September 2003.

- A cross-cutting OSHA ergonomics response team evaluates and screens all inspection cases prior to issuing a citation.

- OSHA sent 593 hazard alert letters to notify employers of ergonomic problems in their facilities. Follow-up inspections at a sample of these facilities are being conducted to evaluate the progress of response to the hazard alert letters.

- Four Regional Emphasis Programs and four LEPs are underway across the country, focusing on ergonomic hazards in meat processing, health care, garment factories, and warehousing industries.

- OSHA named ergonomic coordinators for each of its 10 regional offices to assist staff, employers, employees, and other stakeholders with ergonomic issues.

- OSHA currently has five ergonomists throughout the country—in regional offices, the national office, the OSHA Training Institute and the Salt Lake Technical Center.

- The OSHA Training Institute has added a class to teach field personnel policies and procedures for ergonomics enforcement under the OSHA's four-pronged approach.

[http://www.osha.gov/SLTC/ergonomics/four-pronged_factsheet.html]

Additionally, in mid-2007, OSHA made another run at promulgating a rule requiring employers to drastically reduce ergonometric injuries. Suits filed by the U.S. Chamber of Commerce, the National Association of Manufacturers, and other business groups have been consolidated in the U.S. Court of Appeals for the District of Columbia Circuit.

Pandemic Flu

Q 7:258 Has OSHA issued any guidelines with regard to a potential influenza pandemic?

Yes. In February 2007, OSHA issued a new set of guidelines for coping with a potential influenza pandemic in the workplace. The main features of these guidelines include how a severe influenza pandemic will affect the workplace, how to prepare for a pandemic, how influenza spreads, and how to maintain operations in the midst of a pandemic. The entire publication containing these guidelines is accessible at http://www.osha.gov/Publications/influenza_pandemic.html.

Q 7:259   What are the differences among seasonal, pandemic, H1N1 (swine), and avian influenza?

Seasonal influenza refers to the periodic outbreaks of respiratory illness in the fall and winter in the United States. Outbreaks are typically limited; most people have some immunity to the circulating strain of the virus. A vaccine is prepared in advance of the seasonal influenza; it is designed to match the influenza viruses most likely to be circulating in the community. Employees living abroad and international business travelers should note that other geographic areas (e.g., the Southern Hemisphere) have different influenza seasons which may require different vaccines.

Pandemic influenza refers to a worldwide outbreak of influenza among people when a new strain of the virus emerges that has the ability to infect humans and to spread from person to person. During the early phases of an influenza pandemic, people might not have any natural immunity to the new strain, so the disease would spread rapidly among the population. A vaccine to protect people against illness from a pandemic influenza virus may not be widely available until many months after an influenza pandemic begins. It is important to emphasize that there currently is no influenza pandemic. However, pandemics have occurred throughout history, and many scientists believe that it is only a matter of time before another one occurs. Pandemics can vary in severity from something that seems simply like a bad flu season to an especially severe influenza pandemic that could lead to high levels of illness, death, social disruption, and economic loss. Swine flu (H1N1) appeared in the United States in spring 2009, and by mid-March of 2010 about 59 million Americans had contracted the virus.

Avian influenza, also known as the bird flu, is caused by the virus that infects wild birds and domestic poultry. Some forms of the avian influenza are worse than others. Avian influenza viruses are generally divided into two groups: low pathogenic avian influenza and highly pathogenic avian influenza. Low pathogenic avian influenza naturally occurs in wild birds and can spread to domestic birds. In most cases, it causes no signs of infection or only minor symptoms in birds. In general, these low pathogenic strains of the virus pose little threat to human health. Low pathogenic avian influenza virus H5 and H7 strains have the potential to mutate into highly pathogenic avian influenza and are, therefore, closely monitored. Highly pathogenic avian influenza spreads rapidly and has a high death rate in birds. Highly pathogenic avian influenza of the H5N1 strain is rapidly spreading in birds in some parts of the world.

Q 7:260   What guidance is OSHA offering with regard to avian and H1N1 (swine) flu?

Principal aspects of OSHA's guidance are:

- Good hygiene;
- Gloves;
- Frequent hand washing; and

- Respiratory equipment for anyone handling infected or suspect birds.

OSHA's Web site [http://www.osha.gov/dsg/guidance/avian-flu.html] provides specific, detailed sets of guidelines for:

- Farm workers and animal handlers;
- Lab workers;
- Medical personnel;
- Food handlers;
- Airline flight attendants; and
- Travelers to danger zones.

OSHA's H1N1 site is http://www.osha.gov/dsg/topics/pandemicflu/index. html.

Q 7:261   How can a severe influenza pandemic affect the workplace?

Unlike natural disasters or terrorist events, an influenza pandemic will be widespread, affecting multiple areas of the United States and other countries at the same time. A pandemic will also be an extended event, with multiple waves of outbreaks in the same geographic area; each outbreak could last from six to eight weeks. Waves of outbreaks may occur over a year or more. The workplace will likely experience:

- Absenteeism. A pandemic could affect as many as 40 percent of the workforce during periods of peak influenza illness. Employees could be absent because they are sick, must care for sick family members or for children if schools or day care centers are closed, are afraid to come to work, or the employer might not be notified that the employee has died.
- Change in patterns of commerce. During a pandemic, consumer demand for items related to infection control is likely to increase dramatically, while consumer interest in other goods may decline. Consumers may also change the ways in which they shop as a result of the pandemic. Consumers may try to shop at off-peak hours to reduce contact with other people, show increased interest in home delivery services, or prefer other options, such as drive-through service, to reduce person-to-person contact.
- Interrupted supply/delivery. Shipments of items from those geographic areas severely affected by the pandemic may be delayed or cancelled.

Q 7:262   Should an employer plan for a possible pandemic?

To reduce the impact of a pandemic on your operations, employees, customers, and the general public, OSHA states in its new pamphlet that it is important for all businesses and organizations to begin continuity planning for a pandemic now. Lack of continuity planning can result in a cascade of failures as employers attempt to address challenges of a pandemic with insufficient resources and employees who might not be adequately trained in the jobs they will be asked to perform. Proper planning will allow employers to better protect their employees and prepare for changing patterns of commerce and potential disruptions in supplies or services. Important tools for pandemic planning for employers are located at: http://www.pandemicflu.gov.

The U.S. government has placed a special emphasis on supporting pandemic influenza planning for public and private sector businesses deemed to be critical industries and key resources (CI/KR). Critical infrastructure are the 13 sectors that provide the production of essential goods and services, interconnectedness and operability, public safety, and security that contribute to a strong national defense and thriving economy. Key resources are facilities, sites, and groups of organized people whose destruction could cause large-scale injury, death, or destruction of property and/or profoundly damage our national prestige and confidence. With 85 percent of the nation's critical infrastructure in the hands of the private sector, the business community plays a vital role in ensuring national pandemic preparedness and response. Additional guidance for CI/KR business is available at: http://www.flu.gov/planning-preparedness/business/cikrpandemicinfluenzaguide.pdf.

Critical facilities and economic sectors identified by OSHA are:

- Government facilities
- Dams
- Commercial facilities
- Nuclear power plants
- Critical infrastructure
- Food and agriculture
- Public health and health care
- Banking and finance
- Chemical and hazardous materials
- Defense industrial base
- Water
- Energy
- Emergency services
- Information technology
- Telecommunications
- Postal and shipping
- Transportation
- National monuments and icons

Q 7:263   What steps should employers take to prepare for a potential pandemic?

OSHA recommends that every employer should do at least the following:

- Encourage sick employees to stay at home.

- Encourage your employees to wash their hands frequently with soap and water or with hand sanitizer if there is no soap and water available. Also, encourage your employees to avoid touching their noses, mouths, and eyes.

- Encourage your employees to cover their coughs and sneezes with a tissue, or to cough and sneeze into their upper sleeves if tissues are not available. All employees should wash their hands or use a hand sanitizer after they cough, sneeze, or blow their noses.

- Employees should avoid close contact with their coworkers and customers (maintain a separation of at least six feet). They should avoid shaking hands and always wash their hands after contact with others. Even if employees wear gloves, they should wash their hands upon removal of the gloves in case their hand(s) became contaminated during the removal process.

- Provide customers and the public with tissues and trash receptacles, and with a place to wash or disinfect their hands.

- Keep work surfaces, telephones, computer equipment, and other frequently touched surfaces and office equipment clean. Be sure that any cleaner used is safe and will not harm your employees or your office equipment. Use only disinfectants registered by the EPA, and follow all directions and safety precautions indicated on the label.

- Discourage your employees from using other employees' phones, desks, offices, or other work tools and equipment.

- Minimize situations where groups of people are crowded together, such as in a meeting. Use e-mail, phones, and text messages to communicate with each other. When meetings are necessary, avoid close contact by keeping a separation of at least six feet, where possible, and assure that the meeting room is properly ventilated.

- Reducing or eliminating unnecessary social interactions can be very effective in controlling the spread of infectious diseases. Reconsider all situations that permit or require employees, customers, and visitors (including family members) to enter the workplace. Workplaces that permit family visitors on site should consider restricting/eliminating that option during an influenza pandemic. Work sites with on-site day care should consider in advance whether these facilities will remain open or will be closed, and the impact of such decisions on employees and the business.

- Promote healthy lifestyles, including good nutrition, exercise, and smoking cessation. A person's overall health impacts their body's immune system and can affect their ability to fight off, or recover from, an infectious disease.

Q 7:264   How is influenza spread among workers?

According to OSHA, influenza is thought to be primarily spread through large droplets (droplet transmission) that directly contact the nose, mouth, or eyes. These droplets are produced when infected people cough, sneeze, or talk, sending the relatively large infectious droplets and very small sprays (aerosols) into the nearby air and into contact with other people. Large droplets can only travel a limited range; therefore, people should limit close contact (within six feet) with others when possible. To a lesser degree, human influenza is spread by touching objects contaminated with influenza viruses and then transferring the infected material from the hands to the nose, mouth, or eyes. Influenza may also be spread by very small infectious particles (aerosols) traveling in the air. The contribution of each route of exposure to influenza transmission is uncertain at this time and may vary based upon the characteristics of the influenza strain.

Q 7:265   How can employers maintain their operations in the midst of a pandemic?

OSHA new guidelines offer the following advice to employers:

- Develop a Disaster Plan
    - Develop a disaster plan that includes pandemic preparedness (*see* http://www.pandemicflu.gov/plan/businesschecklist.html), and review it and conduct drills regularly.
    - Be aware of and review federal, state, and local health department pandemic influenza plans. Incorporate appropriate actions from these plans into workplace disaster plans.
    - Prepare and plan for operations with a reduced workforce.
    - Work with your suppliers to ensure that you can continue to operate and provide services.
    - Develop a sick leave policy that does not penalize sick employees, thereby encouraging employees who have influenza-related symptoms (e.g., fever, headache, cough, sore throat, runny or stuffy nose, muscle aches, or upset stomach) to stay home so that they do not infect other employees. Recognize that employees with ill family members may need to stay home to care for them.
    - Identify possible exposure and health risks to your employees. Are employees potentially in contact with people with influenza such as in a hospital or clinic? Are your employees expected to have a lot of contact with the general public?
    - Minimize exposure to fellow employees or the public. For example, will more of your employees work from home? This may require enhancement of technology and communications equipment.
    - Identify business-essential positions and people required to sustain business-necessary functions and operations. Prepare to cross-train or develop ways to function in the absence of these positions. It is

recommended that employers train three or more employees to be able to sustain business-necessary functions and operations, and communicate the expectation for available employees to perform these functions if needed during a pandemic.

— Plan for downsizing services, but also anticipate any scenario that may require a surge in your services.

— Recognize that, in the course of normal daily life, all employees will have non-occupational risk factors at home and in community settings that should be reduced to the extent possible. Some employees will also have individual risk factors that should be considered by employers as they plan how the organization will respond to a potential pandemic (e.g., immuno-compromised individuals and pregnant women).

— Stockpile items such as soap, tissue, hand sanitizer, cleaning supplies, and recommended PPE. When stockpiling items, be aware of each product's shelf life and storage conditions (e.g., avoid areas that are damp or have temperature extremes) and incorporate product rotation (e.g., consume oldest supplies first) into your stockpile management program.

— Make sure that your disaster plan protects and supports your employees, customers, and the general public. Be aware of your employees' concerns about pay, leave, safety, and health. Informed employees who feel safe at work are less likely to be absent.

— Develop policies and practices that distance employees from each other, customers, and the general public. Consider practices to minimize face-to-face contact between employees, such as e-mail, Web sites, and teleconferences. Policies and practices that allow employees to work from home or to stagger their work shifts may be important as absenteeism rises.

— Organize and identify a central team of people or focal point to serve as a communication source, so that your employees and customers can have accurate information during the crisis.

— Work with your employees and their union(s) to address leave, pay, transportation, travel, childcare, absence, and other human resource issues.

— Provide your employees and customers in your workplace with easy access to infection control supplies, such as soap, hand sanitizers, PPE (such as gloves or surgical masks), tissues, and office cleaning supplies.

— Provide training, education, and informational material about business-essential job functions and employee health and safety, including proper hygiene practices and the use of any PPE to be used in the workplace. Be sure that informational material is available in a usable format for individuals with sensory disabilities and/or limited English proficiency. Encourage employees to take care of their health by eating right, getting plenty of rest, and getting a seasonal flu vaccination.

— Work with your insurance companies and state and local health agencies to provide information to employees and customers about medical care in the event of a pandemic.

— Assist employees in managing additional stressors related to the pandemic. These are likely to include distress related to personal or family illness; life disruption; grief related to loss of family, friends, or coworkers; loss of routine support systems; and similar challenges. Assuring timely and accurate communication will also be important throughout the duration of the pandemic in decreasing fear or worry. Employers should provide opportunities for support, counseling, and mental health assessment and referral should these be necessary. If present, Employee Assistance Programs can offer training and provide resources and other guidance on mental health and resiliency before and during a pandemic.

• Protect Employees and Customers

Educate and train employees in proper hand hygiene, cough etiquette, and social distancing techniques. Understand and develop work practice and engineering controls that could provide additional protection to your employees and customers, such as: drive-through service windows, clear plastic sneeze barriers, ventilation, and the proper selection, use, and disposal of PPE.

These are not comprehensive recommendations. The most important part of pandemic planning is to work with your employees, local and state agencies, and other employers to develop cooperative pandemic plans to maintain your operations and keep your employees and the public safe. Share what you know, be open to ideas from your employees, then identify and share effective health practices with other employers in your community and with your local chamber of commerce.

For most employers, protecting their employees will depend on emphasizing proper hygiene (disinfecting hands and surfaces) and practicing social distancing. Social distancing means reducing the frequency, proximity, and duration of contact between people (both employees and customers) to reduce the chances of spreading pandemic influenza from person-to-person. All employers should implement good hygiene and infection control practices.

Occupational safety and health professionals use a framework called the "hierarchy of controls" to select ways of dealing with workplace hazards. The hierarchy of controls prioritizes intervention strategies based on the premise that the best way to control a hazard is to systematically remove it from the workplace, rather than relying on employees to reduce their exposure. In the setting of a pandemic, this hierarchy should be used in concert with current public health recommendations. The types of measures that may be used to protect yourself, your employees, and your customers (listed from most effective to least effective) are: engineering controls, administrative controls, work practices, and PPE. Most employers will use a combination of control methods.

There are advantages and disadvantages to each type of control measure when considering the ease of implementation, effectiveness, and cost. For example, hygiene and social distancing can be implemented relatively easily and with little expense, but this control method requires employees to modify and maintain their behavior, which may be difficult to sustain. On the other hand, installing clear plastic barriers or a drive-through window will be more expensive and take a longer time to implement, although in the long run may be more effective at preventing transmission during a pandemic. Employers must evaluate their particular workplace to develop a plan for protecting their employees that may combine both immediate actions as well as longer-term solutions.

- Initiate Work Practice and Engineering Controls

Historically, infection control professionals have relied on PPE (e.g., surgical masks and gloves) to serve as a physical barrier to prevent the transmission of an infectious disease from one person to another. This reflects the fact that close interactions with infectious patients is an unavoidable part of many health care occupations. The principles of industrial hygiene demonstrate that work practice controls and engineering controls can also serve as barriers to transmission, and are less reliant on employee behavior to provide protection. Work practice controls are procedures for safe and proper work that are used to reduce the duration, frequency, or intensity of exposure to a hazard. When defining safe work practice controls, it is a good idea to ask your employees for their suggestions, because they have firsthand experience with the tasks. These controls should be understood and followed by managers, supervisors, and employees. When work practice controls are insufficient to protect employees, some employers may also need engineering controls.

Engineering controls involve making changes to the work environment to reduce work-related hazards. These types of controls are preferred over all others because they make permanent changes that reduce exposure to hazards and do not rely on employee or customer behavior. By reducing a hazard in the workplace, engineering controls can be the most cost-effective solutions for employers to implement.

During a pandemic, engineering controls may be effective in reducing exposure to some sources of pandemic influenza and not others. For example, installing sneeze guards between customers and employees would provide a barrier to transmission. The use of barrier protections, such as sneeze guards, is common practice for both infection control and industrial hygiene. However, while the installation of sneeze guards may reduce or prevent transmission between customers and employees, transmission may still occur between coworkers. Therefore, administrative controls and public health measures should be implemented along with engineering controls.

[http://www.osha.gov/Publications/influenza_pandemic.html]

Q 7:266   Are there OSHA guidelines for health care workers with regard to flu pandemics?

Yes. OSHA has released guidelines especially aimed at health care workers and their employers with regard to dealing with flu pandemics. The guidelines, "Pandemic Influenza Preparedness and Response Guidance for Healthcare Employers," can be found at: http://www.osha.gov/Publications/3328-05-2007-English.html. The topics covered include:

- Influenza:
  - Clinical presentation of seasonal influenza, prior influenza pandemics, and highly pathogenic avian influenza in humans
  - Clinical diagnosis of seasonal influenza and pandemic influenza
  - Laboratory diagnosis of seasonal influenza, avian, and pandemic influenza
  - Modes of transmission of seasonal and pandemic influenza
  - Treatment and prevention of seasonal and pandemic influenza
- Infection control
  - Standard precautions and transmission-based precautions
    - Standard precautions
    - Contact precautions
    - Droplet precautions
    - Airborne precautions
  - Compliance with infection control
    - Hand hygiene compliance
    - Respiratory protection compliance
- Organizational factors that affect adherence to infection control
  - Facility design, engineering, and environmental controls
    - Facility capacity
    - Engineering controls in improvised settings
    - Airborne infection isolation rooms
    - Engineering controls for aerosol-generating procedures for patients with pandemic influenza
    - Cohorting
    - Engineering controls in diagnostic and research laboratories
    - Autopsy rooms for cases of pandemic influenza
  - Administrative controls
    - Respiratory hygiene/cough etiquette
    - Pandemic influenza specimen collection and transport
    - Patient transport within health care facilities
    - Pre-hospital care and patient transport outside health care facilities
    - Staff education and training

- Care of the deceased
- Patient discharge
- Visitor policies
— Health care worker vaccination
— Antiviral medication for prophylaxis and treatment in health care workers
— Occupational medicine services
  - Worker protection
  - Recommendations for occupational health administrators
  - Occupational medical surveillance and staffing decisions
— PPE
  - Gloves
  - Gowns
  - Goggles/face shields
  - Respiratory protection for pandemic influenza
  - PPE for aerosol-generating procedures
  - Order for putting on and removing PPE
— Work practices
  - Hand hygiene
  - Other hygienic measures
  - Facility hygiene-practices and polices
  - Laboratory practices
- Pandemic influenza preparedness
  — Health care facility responsibilities during pandemic alert periods (HSC stages 0, 1)
  — Health care facility responsibilities during the pandemic (HSC stages 2-5)
  — Health care facility recovery and preparation for subsequent pandemic waves (HSC stage 6)
  — Incorporating pandemic plans into disaster plans
    - Pandemic planning for support of health care worker staff
    - Define essential staff and hospital services
    - Human resources
    - Information technology
    - Public health communications
    - Surveillance and protocols
    - Psychological support
    - Occupational health services

- Developing and providing employee screening for influenza-like illness
- Developing and providing immunization and treatment strategies
- Continuing baseline occupational health services
- Training
- Security
— Stockpiles of essential resources
  - Pandemic influenza vaccine
  - Antiviral medication
  - PPE
  - Outpatient services and clinics
  - Alternate care sites
- OSHA Standards of Special Importance
  — Respiratory Protection Standard (29 C.F.R. § 1910.134)
  — Personal Protective Equipment Standard (29 C.F.R. § 1910.132)
  — Bloodborne Pathogens Standard (29 C.F.R. § 1910.1030)

Green Job Hazards

Q 7:267 What are "green jobs"?

The Green Jobs Act of 2007 (H.R. 2847) allocated $125 million per year to create an energy efficiency and renewable energy worker training program, a pilot program to identify the skills and training programs, and subsequently the actual training of workers, for jobs in a wide range of environmentally friendly industries. However, the Act does not outline specifically what does or does not constitute a green job.

The Department of Energy considers "green" occupations those within the energy efficiency and renewable energy sectors; solar panel manufacturing, for example. The Occupational Information Network interprets "green" more broadly, including such work as energy efficient building, energy efficient vehicles, biofuels, renewable electric power, construction and retrofits, and manufacturing that uses sustainable materials and processes to produce sustainable products, as well as agriculture and education. The Bureau of Labor Statistics (BLS) currently classifies green jobs as those that produce green goods or services, or those whose employees help minimize businesses' environmental impact.

In short, the most accurate definition is simply those jobs that help to improve the environment. Green jobs also have the secondary goal of creating new jobs and revitalizing the economy by providing more stable, local jobs. Although a job may be environmentally friendly, it is not inherently worker friendly or safe, which is why employers must keep abreast of the new and often unexpected hazards facing green job workers.

BLS has approached the challenge of identifying green jobs from two perspectives: the output approach (which identifies establishments that produce green goods and services and counts the associated jobs) and the process approach (which identifies establishments that use environmentally friendly production processes and practices and counts the associated jobs).

Data from these efforts provide information on "green" employment and wages by industry and occupation. Although there may be interest in the prevalence and types of workplace injuries, illnesses, and fatalities of workers with green jobs, the two BLS surveys that identify green jobs do not directly collect these details, and the BLS survey on workplace safety and health does not currently identify green jobs. However, BLS workplace safety and health data use the same industry and occupation classification systems used in the green jobs studies.

The survey identified about 854,700 workers employed in GTP jobs in 2011, approximately 0.7 percent of total U.S. wage and salary employment. More than one-quarter of all green technologies and practices (GTP) jobs were in the building and grounds cleaning and maintenance occupational group, or in the installation, maintenance, and repair occupational group. The transportation and material moving; production; and construction and extraction occupational groups made up an additional 23 percent of GTP employment. Detailed occupations with the largest number of GTP jobs included janitors and cleaners, except maids and housekeeping cleaners, with 56,700 GTP jobs; heating, air conditioning, and refrigeration mechanics and installers (37,300); and general maintenance and repair workers (26,000). [http://www.bls.gov/opub/mlr/2013/01/art5full.pdf]

Q 7:268   What are some of the major hazards facing green job workers?

Many of the hazards facing green job workers are the same hazards that have long faced workers in more established industries, such as falls, electrical fires, and confined spaces. Other hazards are specific to the line of work, and were previously unidentified. For example, the creation of the Hanford Nuclear Reservation provided 4,000 new jobs in the area, but those jobs come with a litany of possible hazards, such as radiation and other contamination risks, as well as chronic beryllium disease, an incurable condition caused by exposure to beryllium dust. Following is an overview of many of the risks associated with common green job industries.

Biofuels. Because of a demand for low-carbon impact, the use of domestically sourced fuels has increased. The two major types of biofuels produced in the United States are ethanol, a highly flammable liquid used in up to 10 percent of automotive fuel sold in the United States and biodiesel, a combustible liquid. Biofuels are created using renewable resources like grains, vegetable oil, and treated industrial waste. Their manufacture can involve potentially dangerous chemical reactions. Potential hazards in biofuels production and handling include:

- Fire and explosion hazards
- Chemical reactivity hazards (including the rupture of equipment and piping, explosions, fires, and exposure to hazardous chemicals)
- Toxicity hazards (including exposure to methanol, caustic, sulfuric acid, ethanol, and biodiesel)

Wind Energy. Wind turbines are being manufactured and installed across the United States in order to generate electricity from wind. The hazards associated with this industry are not new, but employers should be well aware of them nonetheless.

- Falls
- Confined spaces (including risk of asphyxiation, exposure to a hazardous atmosphere, or the risk of engulfing a person who enters the space)
- Fires
- Lockout/tagout (procedures set in place to safeguard employees from the unexpected startup of equipment, or the release of hazardous energy during maintenance of equipment)
- Cranes, derricks, and hoists
- Electrical injuries (including arc flash burn hazards, electric shock, and thermal burn hazards)
- Machine guarding (including risk of severe injury such as crushed fingers or hands, amputations, burns or blindness)
- Respiratory protection (including risk of exposure to gases, vapors, and dusts)

Waste management and recycling. The percentage of waste recycled in the United States has doubled since 1985, and the industry—and its job opportunities—is only growing. Each aspect of the recycling industry has its own associated risks.

- Collection
  - Traffic safety (including crushing hazards associated with dumpsters and rear-loading trash trucks)
  - Ergonomics (including musculoskeletal disorders from lifting items that are too heavy or lifting too often)
- Scrap Metal Recycling
  - Lead overexposure
  - Moving parts injuries
  - Unexpected machine startup injuries
- Cardboard Baling
  - Moving parts injuries
  - Unexpected machine startup injuries

• Young workers (minors under the age of 18 may not load, operate, or unload certain machines, according to the Hazardous Occupations Act Order No. 12)

Green roofs. Growing in popularity throughout the United States, green roofs can be installed by companies that specialize in green roof technology, or an amalgamation of more traditional trades such as landscapers and roofing contractors. Some hazards are new while others are more familiar.

• Falls
• Personal protective equipment related hazards
• Exposure to silica dust (including risk of Silicosis or death from breathing in silica dust particles)
• Cranes, derricks, and hoists
• Powered industrial truck injuries
• Electrical injuries
• Heat/cold stress (including risk of heat stroke or heat exhaustion from exposure to the elements)

Solar energy. Solar energy is a growing sector for green jobs (two commercially viable solar energy sectors are solar electric and solar thermal heating), but various hazards are associated with the manufacture, installation, and maintenance of solar energy.

• Falls
• Lockout/tagout
• Crane and hoist injuries
• Electrical injuries
• Heat/cold stress
• Personal protective equipment related injuries

Geo-thermal energy. Geo-thermal energy uses the heat from the earth to create electricity, and to heat and cool buildings. Some systems use the earth's natural geothermal reservoirs to heat and cool buildings, while others pump water underground through piping and allow the earth to heat that water. Some geo-thermal systems use a brine or saltwater solution while others use glycol.

• Trenching and excavation related injuries (including risk of collapse and smothering)
• Silica dust exposure
• Personal protective equipment related injuries
• Welding and cutting injuries
• Falls

Weather insulating/sealing. Weatherizing, insulating, and sealing are important aspects of energy efficiency, but many types of weatherizing products (such as fiberglass, cellulose, spray polyurethane foam, spray polystyrene, and spray latex sealant) include blow-in and spray-on applications that can be hazardous to the health of workers. Extra training may be required to learn how to safely and accurately apply these products.

- Confined spaces
- Falls
- Electrical injuries
- Respiratory protection
- Personal protective equipment related injuries
- Ventilation
- Fires

Hydrogen fuel cells. Hydrogen fuel cells produce electricity without combustion (though hydrogen is a very flammable, potentially dangerous gas). The fuel cell industry is rapidly growing, as hydrogen fuel cells can be used to power vehicles, provide electricity for remote locations like remote weather stations, and serve as power plants. Hazards associated with the fuel cell industry include:

- Fire and explosion
- Freeze burns (from liquid hydrogen)
- Electrical injuries

Oil cleanup operations. Another aspect of green jobs are those jobs that work solely to help the environment, such as oil cleanup. These, however, come with many dangerous and unexpected hazards.

- Heat stress
- Boat and vessel related injuries
- Crude oil injuries (including risk of dermatitis and inhalation of toxic components)
- Dispersants (including risk of skin contamination, ocular exposure, ingestion exposure, and inhalation exposure)
- Drowning
- Emergency response and shoreline cleanup related injuries
- Ergonomics
- Fatigue
- Personal protective equipment related injuries
- Poisonous plants (including risk of bruises, burns, or damaged skin)
- Respiratory protection
- Severe weather and oil (including risk of rash caused by weathered oil)
- Slips, trips, and falls
- Snakes, insects, and rodents

Stress (including risk of emotional distress caused by a traumatic incident, such as witnessing the untimely death or injury of oil-covered wildlife, or the impact on fishing communities and the environment) [http://www.osha.gov/dep/greenjobs/index.html]

Q 7:269   What must employers do to protect workers from green job hazards?

OSH Act requires employers to comply with certain safety and health regulations and standards outlined by OSHA or by a state with an OSHA-approved plan. These regulations cover many of the hazards those working in green industries face, and outline standards for implementing safety controls and protocols. Further, the OSH Act's General Duty Clause, Section 5(a)(1), demands that employers provide all employees with a workplace "free from recognized hazards likely to cause death or serious physical harm." [http://www.osha.gov/dep/greenjobs/index.html] This clause can be enforced in the absence of an OSHA standard. The full list of standards and regulations can be read at: http://www.osha.gov/law-regs.html.

Q 7:270   What else can be done to protect green job workers?

The National Institute for Occupational Safety is leading an initiative called Prevention through Design (PtD) in order to "design out" hazards and risks to green job workers while green jobs are still in the early stages of being created and developed—before the risks are considered inherent to the jobs. Many companies and business leaders in the United States support PtD and see it as a cost-effective way to enhance occupational safety and health. Other countries are following suit. The United Kingdom, for example, requires construction companies, project owners, and architects to address safety and health issues, and companies have responded by altering their practices to comply with the new regulations. Similarly, Australia created the Australian National OHS Strategy 2002-2012 to eliminate hazards at the design stage, making it a national priority. [http://www.cdc.gov/niosh/topics/PTD/]

The National Institute for Occupational Safety and Health (NIOSH) has also outlined several ways in which green jobs could be better monitored for safety. The first is to define, categorize, and track green jobs in order to identify and better understand exactly what new hazards green job workers face and how those hazards affect worker safety and health. Then all products and processes associated with green jobs must be evaluated for safety and health, presently and over greater lengths of time. For example, 1-Bromopropane was introduced as an environmentally friendly alternative to ozone-depleting chlorofluorocarbons. Over time, however, studies began to show nervous system, reproductive, and other effects in workers and lab animals after prolonged exposure, illustrating the need for careful evaluation of all new products, even environmentally beneficial ones.

NIOSH also suggests making safety and health an integral part of green jobs training, as well as adding safety and health to green benchmarks. Although benchmarks exist to evaluate which jobs are green and sustainable, there are almost no guidelines for measuring the occupational safety of performing green jobs.

[http://blogs.cdc.gov/niosh-science-blog/2010/01/green-2/]

Chapter 8

Employee Compensation and Fringe Benefits

Employee compensation is a highly complex aspect of employment law involving legal wage restrictions that apply to a wide variety of occupations and compensation methods. This chapter provides updates concerning the Fair Labor Standards Act (FLSA) and Department of Labor (DOL) regulations that were effective August 2004.

Although employers generally are not required by law to provide fringe benefits to employees, there are many reasons for doing so. Fringe benefit plans give employers a competitive edge in attracting and retaining qualified employees. Once plans are established, employers must comply with legislative provisions that apply to their maintenance and the distribution of benefits.

Some fringe benefits are mandatory under federal law. The Family and Medical Leave Act (FMLA) requires covered employers to provide eligible employees as many as 12 weeks of job-protected unpaid leave during any 12-month period. This chapter discusses further developments involving the FMLA, including the DOL's final rules, and provides information to assist employers in complying with its requirements. In March 2010, President Barack Obama signed health care reform into law (the Patient Protection and Affordability Act and the Health Care and Education Reconciliation Act). This chapter discusses the laws' impact on employers.

Fair Labor Standards Act

Wages

Q 8:1 Must employers follow certain guidelines when compensating employees?

Yes. Wages paid to employees are largely regulated by federal and state wage laws. These laws typically set minimum wage rates and overtime compensation that must be paid to those employees who fall under their protection. Independent contractors are not employees under the Fair Labor Standards Act (FLSA). Whether a worker is an employee or independent contractor depends on numerous factors, most importantly whether the company exerts sufficient control over the worker. At issue in *Thibault v. Bellsouth Telecommunications, Inc.* [612 F.3d 843 (5th Cir. 2010)], was whether a splicer hired by a telecommunications company to repair telecommunication grids after a hurricane was an employee or independent contractor of the telephone company for purposes of the FLSA. Utilizing the "economic realities test," the court concluded that the splicer was in fact an independent contractor because, among other things, the telecommunication company did not control how the splicer did his work, the splicer supplied much of his own tools and equipment, and did not work exclusively for the telecommunications company.

Q 8:2 What federal law covers wages?

The FLSA, enacted in 1938, is the leading federal law regulating minimum wage and overtime compensation. The Act also regulates child labor and equal pay for equal work.

Q 8:3 What employees are covered by the FLSA?

The FLSA is very broad in its coverage. In general, it encompasses employees that are:

- Engaged in interstate commerce, including import and export;
- Engaged in the production of goods for interstate commerce; or
- In an enterprise engaged in interstate commerce.

The *production of goods*, according to FLSA regulations, includes "any closely related process or occupation directly essential" to the production of goods for interstate commerce. With respect to the third group, the so-called enterprise test has been broadly interpreted by the courts; thus, few employers today have employees that are not covered by the Act.

Q 8:4   Are students who are required to perform chores as part of their curriculum at a boarding school required to receive wages under the FLSA?

In *Blair v. Wills* [420 F.3d 823 (8th Cir. 2005)], the court was asked to determine whether students at a private boarding school who are required, as a condition of their enrollment, to perform chores are in fact employees for which they should be paid FLSA wages. This was a unique situation in that the students who performed chores were not "volunteers" in the true sense because they were compelled to perform these duties in conjunction with their education. It was uncontested that the students were not paid for their work and that the work that was performed would typically be performed by janitors or other maintenance personnel who would typically be paid for their services. Nonetheless, the school argued that the chores at this private boarding school were an integral part of the educational curriculum and that the chores primarily benefited the students, not the school. Although the court found that by having students perform these chores, the school certainly defrayed costs that it would have incurred had it hired employees to perform these tasks; the court nonetheless concluded that the activities of the students did not make them employees under the FLSA. Thus, FLSA wages were not required to be paid.

Q 8:5   Are prisoners that work employees under the FLSA?

Prisoners who work for the prison inside the prison are not the prison's employees for the purposes of the FLSA. [Loving v. Johnson, 455 F.3d 562, 563 (5th Cir. 2006)] The same is generally true for prisoners working inside a prison for private employers and prisoners on work release working outside the prison for a private employer. [*See* Alexander v. Sara, Inc., 721 F.2d 149, 150 (5th Cir. 1983) and Reimonenq v. Foti, 72 F.3d 472, 475–76 (5th Cir. 1996).] However, certain prisoners working for private firms on work release have been held to be employees of the private employer. [*See* Watson v. Graves, 909 F.2d 1549 (5th Cir. 1990).] However, a prisoner on sporadic work release that performs sporadic duties for an outside employer will not be considered an employee for FLSA purposes. [*See* Williams v. Henagan, 595 F.3d 610 (5th Cir. 2010).]

Q 8:6   Do unpaid internships violate the FLSA?

Over the last few years, the DOL has more rigorously scrutinized unpaid internships to determine if they violate the FLSA. "The Labor Department says it is cracking down on firms that fail to pay interns properly and expanding efforts to educate companies, colleges and students on the law regarding internships." [Steven Greenhouse, *The Unpaid Intern, Legal or Not*, N.Y. Times, Apr. 3, 2010, at B1] In the article, the head of the Wage and Hour Division at the DOL was quoted as saying, "If you're a for-profit employer or you want to pursue an internship with a for-profit employer, there aren't going to be many circumstances where you can have an internship and not be paid and still be in compliance with the law[.]" [Steven Greenhouse, *The Unpaid Intern, Legal or Not*, N.Y. Times, Apr. 3, 2010, at B1]

The DOL has derived a six-factor test to determine whether an intern is an "employee" within the meaning of the FLSA. The internship must meet all six factors, otherwise it is likely the program will be considered "employment" within the meaning of the FLSA, thus subjecting it to minimum wage requirements. The six factors are:

1. The training, even though it includes actual operation of the facilities of the employer, is similar to that which would be given in a vocational school;

2. The training is for the benefit of the trainee;

3. The trainees do not displace regular employees, but work under close observation;

4. The employer that provides the training derives no immediate advantage from the activities of the trainees and on occasion the employer's operations may actually be impeded;

5. The trainees are not necessarily entitled to a job at the completion of the training period; and

6. The employer and the trainee understand that the trainees are not entitled to wages for the time spent in training.

[Field Operations Handbook, § 10b11]

Q 8:7   Do illegal aliens have FLSA rights?

In *Zavala v. Wal-Mart Stores, Inc.* [393 F. Supp. 295 (D.N.J. 2005)], the court was asked to determine whether, in light of the U.S. Supreme Court decision in *Hoffman Plastic Compounds v. NLRB* [535 U.S. 137 (2002)], which held that illegal aliens did not have remedial rights under the NLRA, illegal aliens were afforded rights under the FLSA. Although Wal-Mart argued that *Hoffman* required the court to conclude that the individuals did not have rights under the FLSA, the court concluded that, unlike the Immigration Reform and Control Act, a growing number of courts have found that illegal aliens are to be paid FLSA wages for work performed.

The FLSA by its own terms broadly applies to all "employees" (i.e., any "individual employed by an employer"). [29 U.S.C. § 203(e)] Courts have held that an individual's status as a citizen or alien is irrelevant as to whether the FLSA applies, and undocumented aliens have long been afforded protection under the FLSA. [*See In re* Reyes, 814 F.2d 168, 170 (5th Cir. 1987).] In *Villareal v. El Chile, Inc.* [266 F.R.D., 207 (N.D. Ill. Mar. 1, 2010)], the court held that an employee's immigration status is not relevant to an FLSA claim for unpaid wages for work previously performed. In *Widjaja v. Kang Yue USA Corp.* [2010 WL 2132068 (E.D.N.Y. May 20, 2010)], the court denied the employer's motion to gain access to the plaintiffs' immigration status that sued their employer for wage claims under the FLSA.

Although the FLSA has long been applicable to agricultural workers entering the United States under the H-2A Visa Guest Worker Program, an employer challenged the FLSA's applicability to guest workers in the country on non-agricultural H-2B visas. Based upon the expansive definition of *employee* under the FLSA, the court in *Costellanos-Contreras v. Decatur Hotels, LLC* [488 F. Supp. 2d 565 (E.D. La. 2007)] held that the FLSA was applicable to guest workers entering this country on a non-agricultural H-2B visa.

Q 8:8 Are non-profit organizations covered under the FLSA?

Non-profit organizations may be covered under the FLSA, depending upon the facts of each particular case. In *Jacobs v. New York Foundling Hospital* [483 F. Supp. 2d 251 (E.D.N.Y. 2007)], the court held as a matter of first impression that a non-profit organization providing foster care, family, and adoption services was not covered under the FLSA.

Q 8:9 Does the FLSA apply to employees of a U.S. company who work in a foreign country?

Under Section 213(f) of the FLSA, the minimum wage and maximum hour provisions of the FLSA do not apply to an employee who performs work during the workweek within a foreign country or within a territory under the jurisdiction of the United States other than specifically enumerated jurisdictions. In *Kaluom v. Stolt Offshore, Inc.* [474 F. Supp. 2d 866 (S.D. Tex. 2007)], an offshore dredging company that maintained vessels in the Gulf of Mexico claimed that this exception applied to seamen on its vessels. However, reviewing the applicable section of the FLSA and its regulations, the court concluded that the foreign workplace exception applied to specific geographical locations, and the sections of the FLSA that specifically applied to seamen was applicable to the instant case.

Q 8:10 Are any categories of employees exempt from FLSA coverage?

Despite the broad categories of employees covered by the FLSA and comparable state laws, certain types of employees are generally exempt from these laws. These exemptions are based on the nature of the work performed. Employees employed in a bona fide executive, administrative, or professional capacity and outside salespersons (and a few other types of employees) are excluded from minimum wage and overtime compensation requirements, provided they meet certain standards set forth in the implementing regulations.

Q 8:11   Are domestic workers providing companionship services exempt from the FLSA?

The FLSA has regulations specifically exempting from the minimum wage and maximum hours rules of the FLSA persons employed in the domestic service to provide companionship services for individuals unable to care for themselves. [29 U.S.C. § 213(a)(15)] DOL regulations provide that the exception includes companionship workers employed by an agency other than the family or household using their services. [29 C.F.R. § 552.109(a)] These regulations have unsuccessfully been challenged in a variety of courts in 2007 [*see* Hanley v. Hand 'N Heart, LLC, 2007 WL 201088 (E.D. Va. Jan. 22, 2007) and Buckner v. Florida Habilitation Network, Inc., 489 F.3d 1151 (11th Cir. 2007)], culminating in a 2007 U.S. Supreme Court Decision in *Long Island Care at Home, LDT v. Coke* [127 S. Ct. 2339 (June 11, 2007)], wherein the Supreme Court held that the regulation providing for the application of FLSA's "companionship services exemption" to services rendered by persons employed by third parties is valid and binding.

Q 8:12   Are any employment practices not covered by the FLSA?

Although the FLSA sets minimum wage and overtime pay standards and regulates the employment of minors, it does not regulate a number of employment practices, including:

- Vacation, holiday, severance, or sick pay;
- Meal or rest periods, holidays off, or vacations;
- Premium pay for weekend or holiday work;
- Pay raises or fringe benefits;
- A discharge notice, reason for discharge, or immediate payment of final wages to terminated employees; and
- Any limit on the number of hours of work for persons 16 years of age and over.

These matters may be determined by employer policies, employee contracts, collective bargaining agreements, or other federal or state law.

Q 8:13   Is retaliation prohibited under the FLSA?

The FLSA provides that, "It shall be unlawful for any person to discharge or in any other discriminate against any employee because such employee has filed any complaint or caused to be instituted any proceeding under or related to this chapter." [29 U.S.C. § 215(a)(3)] The Sixth Circuit has held that informal complaints by employees to management regarding working conditions and pay are sufficient to constitute a "filed complaint" under this section. As such, any discrimination against an employee that lodges informal complaints to management concerning working conditions or pay may form the basis of a retaliation claim under the FLSA if there is evidence of a causal connection.

In *Montano-Perez v. Durrett Cheese Sales, Inc.* [2009 WL 3295021 (M.D. Tenn. Oct. 13, 2009)], employees who were immigrants were engaged in a labor dispute concerning their working conditions and pay with management that escalated to the point that police officers were called to the scene. The police officers arrested many of the immigrant employees and reported the arrested employees to ICE, the immigration authorities. The employees, among other things, filed a retaliation claim against the police officers for reporting them to ICE alleging that such activity amounted to discrimination against them for exercising their right under the FLSA to lodge complaints with management concerning working conditions and pay. The court, noting that the evidence disclosed facts in support of the employee's assertion that racial and ethnic animus toward the employees was a driving factor behind their arrest, detention, and reporting to ICE, concluded that a retaliation claim could be maintained. In *Mullins v. City of New York* [2010 WL 4609208 (2d Cir. Nov. 16, 2010)], police sergeants who filed an FLSA lawsuit for overtime, and were then subjected to investigations following deposition testimony, were able to establish a causal connection between the department's action and the employees' participation in the lawsuit, such that they could demonstrate a likelihood of success on merits for their claims of retaliation, supporting the imposition of a preliminary injunction against defendants.

The Supreme Court, in *Kasten v. Saint-Gobain Performance Plastics Corp.* [131 S. Ct. 1325 (2011)], held that the anti-retaliation provisions contained under the FLSA apply to oral as well as written complaints of a violation of the Act. In *Dellinger v. Science Applications International Corp.* [649 F.3d 226 (4th Cir. 2011)], in a matter of first impression, the court held that the retaliation provisions under the FLSA apply only to "employees" and not applicants, and as such an applicant cannot maintain a claim for retaliation under the FLSA. In *Kasten v. Saint-Gobain Performance Plastics Corp.* [703 F.3d 966 (7th Cir. 2012)], on remand from the Supreme Court, the court held that an employee's numerous complaints claiming that the location of the company's time clock was causing violations of the FLSA under its donning and doffing rules was protected activity under the FLSA, but remanded the matter to the trial court because of factual issues as to whether the employee's termination was due to the protected activity in violation of the retaliation provisions under the FLSA.

Minimum Wage

Q 8:14 What are *minimum wages*?

Minimum wages are the gross minimum hourly rates employers may pay protected workers, as set by federal wage and hour laws. In 1938, when the FLSA was passed, the minimum wage was set at $0.25 per hour. On July 24, 2008, the federal minimum wage was $6.55 per hour, and rose to $7.25 per hour effective July 24, 2009.

Q 8:15   Could a company be required to pay more than the minimum wage set by the FLSA?

A provision of the FLSA says that a state legislature may require a higher minimum compensation than that demanded by the federal law. A company that employs workers in one of those states must pay the higher minimum wage to them.

A growing number of large cities have adopted ordinances requiring city contractors to pay a "living wage," a minimum wage significantly greater than that required by the FLSA. For example, Detroit adopted the "Detroit Living Wage Ordinance," which requires city contractors to pay their employees an hourly wage that, on an annual basis (based on 40 hours per week, 50 weeks per year), is either 100 percent of the federal poverty level for a family of four according to federal guidelines if the employer provides health benefits, or 125 percent of the federal poverty level if no health benefits are provided. [*See* City of Detroit Ordinance No. 45-98.]

Q 8:16   How are employees' earnings computed for purposes of determining minimum wage compensation?

The concept of a minimum wage is relatively simple; however, payment of the minimum wage can be complicated, depending on the method of compensation an employer uses (e.g., hourly, weekly, or monthly). Some employees, such as machinists, are paid a piece-rate wage, earning a set amount for each piece completed. Others rely largely on tips from customers or on sales commissions as a percentage of their compensation.

The FLSA provides employers enough flexibility to allow for these different methods of compensation, as long as the overall compensation of each employee complies with the minimum wage standards. If an employee receives tips from customers, for example, an employer may reduce the minimum wage paid to that worker by as much as 40 percent, with the understanding that the difference will be made up by tips received by that employee. Similarly, the earnings of employees compensated on a piece-rate basis must average out to at least the minimum wage, provided that the time period over which the earnings are averaged is no longer than a single, seven-day, 40-hour work week. Thus, the earnings of an employee paid on a piece-rate basis may be less than the minimum wage for any single hour, provided that the total earnings for the week average out to the minimum wage. Similarly, an employer may reduce the minimum wage paid to a salesperson and make up the difference with commissions.

Q 8:17   Can monetary equivalents be included in wages for purposes of complying with minimum wage requirements?

The FLSA treats as compensation the reasonable costs an employer incurs furnishing an employee with board, lodging or other facilities, if such board, lodging, or other facilities are customarily furnished by the employer to its employees. The employee must not only receive these benefits but must also accept them voluntarily. If they are provided by an employer but are not used by an employee or are accepted under coercion, their cost cannot be added to the employee's earnings. In *Newsom v. Carolina Logistic Services, Inc.* [2012 WL 4320809 (N.D. Miss. 2012)], workers made a rather novel arrangement with their supervisor to clean the warehouse after they punched out for the day in exchange for a "banana-box" of food. At some point, the employees became dissatisfied with this arrangement and sued claiming they should be paid minimum wage and overtime under the FLSA. The company maintained, on the other hand, that the arrangement was one as an independent contractor such that the FLSA did not apply. Although the maintenance services were performed after hours, the court found that the workers were employees under the FLSA, and for which payment by a "banana-box" of food was clearly in violation of the FLSA.

Hours Worked

Q 8:18   What are *hours worked* under the FLSA?

As described under the implementing regulations of the FLSA, the term *employ* means "to suffer or permit to work." *Hours worked* apply to all hours that an employee is required to give the employer, even if no physical or mental exertion is necessary. [*See* 29 C.F.R. Ch. V, §§ 785.1, *et seq.*] In *Chao v. Gotham Registry, Inc.* [514 F.3d 280 (2d Cir. 2008)], at issue was whether the employer, a nurse referral agency, who had assigned nurses to work at hospitals was responsible for overtime performed by the nurses at the hospitals. It was undisputed that the overtime was not authorized by the employer referral agency and that the employer had a formal rule requiring its nurses to seek pre-approval of additional hours in order to secure payment for overtime, and that to the extent that overtime was worked, it was at the request of the hospital-client and not at the request or approved of the employer. Nonetheless, because the court found that the employer had sufficient knowledge that its employees were working overtime shifts, the court held that the employer had "permitted" the employee to work overtime, such that it was responsible for FLSA overtime violations. The employer had a duty to prevent the nurses from working additional hours, through discipline or other means, if it wished to not pay overtime. However, in *Alozie v. United States* [106 Fed. Cl. 765 (2012)], the court held that police officers that voluntarily worked through their 30-minute lunch break without any order or direction to do so from their supervisor, were not entitled to be paid for that time voluntarily worked. Importantly, the court noted that there was no evidence that the employer was aware that employees worked through their 30-minute lunch breaks, which were taken irregularly.

Q 8:19   Must employees be paid during rest periods?

As a general rule, rest periods of short duration—usually less than 20 minutes—must be counted and paid as hours worked. [*See* 29 C.F.R. Chap. IV, § 785.18.]

Q 8:20   Must meal breaks be treated as hours worked?

Bona fide meal breaks of 30 minutes or longer are not treated as hours worked and need not be paid; however, if the employee is required to remain at the work station to perform tasks (e.g., to answer the phone or wait on customers), this time must be treated as work time. [*See* 29 C.F.R. Ch. V, § 785.19.] However, in *Alozie v. United States* [106 Fed. Cl. 765 (2012)], the court held that police officers that voluntarily worked through their 30-minute lunch break without any order or direction to do so from their supervisor, were not entitled to be paid for that time voluntarily worked. Importantly, the court noted that there was no evidence that the employer was aware that employees worked through their 30-minute lunch breaks, which were taken irregularly.

Q 8:21   Must time spent on call be treated as hours worked?

The answer generally depends on whether the employee is free to use the time on call to personal advantage or must remain in one location (e.g., at the hospital, firehouse, or home) and await calls. If the employee can go out to a restaurant, the movies, and so forth (wearing a beeper, for instance), the time usually need not be compensated unless an actual call occurs; however, like most questions in wage and hour law, this rule can vary on a case-by-case basis.

The issue of what constitutes on-call time, such that the time is compensable under the FLSA, was addressed in *Adair v. Charter County of Wayne.* [452 F.3d 482 (6th Cir. 2006)] The claim was brought by a group of airport officers who complained that because they were required to carry pagers and, following the terrorist attacks of September 11, required to remain at home, that they were on call under the FLSA for which they were entitled to be paid FLSA wages. The court in analyzing the facts concluded that despite such restrictions, their activities at home were not restricted and they were in fact rarely called in during this time period, such that it was not sufficiently restrictive to be compensable under the FLSA.

Q 8:22   Are preliminary and post-work activities considered hours worked?

Activities that an employee performs in connection with work that are integral to the principal work activities are generally considered "hours worked" under the FLSA. If an activity is indispensable to the performance of work, such as changing in or out or closing down an operation, it is certainly considered hours worked. In addition, if an activity (e.g., wash-up) is customary in the industry, it is also usually considered work time.

Q 8:23   Are there any developments involving preliminary and post-work activities under the FLSA?

In *IBP, Inc. v. Alvarez* [126 S. Ct. 514 (2005)], the U.S. Supreme Court decided issues involving preliminary and post-work activities. At issue were the following: (1) whether time spent donning and doffing unique safety gear was compensable time worked under the FLSA, (2) whether the time spent by employees walking to their work stations after donning the special safety gear was compensable under the FLSA, and (3) whether the time spent waiting to don the special safety gear was compensable under the FLSA. Similar to the Tenth Circuit, the court held that because the safety gear was unique and necessary for these workers to engage in their work, donning and doffing the special protective gear was an "integral and indispensable part of their principal activities," such that donning and doffing the special safety gear constituted working time compensable by the FLSA. Because it was integral and indispensable to the employee's work, any time spent walking to and from the production floor after donning and before doffing the special safety gear, as well as time spent waiting to don the gear, would also be covered by the FLSA. However, the court concluded that time spent waiting to don protective gear would not be covered under the FLSA. In *Chao v. Akron Insulation and Supply, Inc.* [2006 WL 1675070 (6th Cir. 2006)], the court held that the shop time employees spent at the beginning of the day to receive assignments and supplies prior to traveling to a job site was indispensable to the employee's activities, and as such, was compensable time under the FLSA, as well as the employee's travel time from the shop to the employee's worksite.

However, if the work is not indispensable to the employee's work but is instead only incidental, the FLSA will not apply to that time spent. In *Buzek v. Pepsi Bottling Group, Inc.* [501 F. Supp. 876 (S.D. Tex. 2007)], at issue was whether time spent by an employee driving home from his last service call was compensable time under the FLSA. In his support, the employee claimed that transporting company tools in his company vehicle to his house and submitting end-of-the-day reports from his home were integral and indispensable to his job, such that his drive home each day should be compensable FLSA time. However, reviewing the work at issue, the court held that the activities were merely incidental and not integral to his activities, such that the time is not compensable FLSA time.

In *Andrako v. United States Steel Corp.* [632 F. Supp. 3d 398 (W.D. Pa. 2009)], at issue was whether time spent donning and doffing protective gear by employees at a coke manufacturing plant were "clothes" within the meaning of the FLSA exclusion, such that the time spent is not compensable working time under the FLSA. Although the court noted that the U.S. Supreme Court, in *IBP, Inc. v. Alvarez* [126 S. Ct. 514 (2005)], held that donning and doffing unique protective clothing which was integral and indispensible to their work, and is time worked under the FLSA, the court found that the issue of whether such protective gear fit within the clothing exclusion under the FLSA was not before the Supreme Court and concluded that the protective clothing in this case, such as flame retardant jackets and pants, glasses, boots, and hard hats unquestion-ably fell within the definition of the word "clothes" such that time spent was not compensable under the FLSA. On the other hand, the Court reasoned that even though the time spent donning and doffing protective gear is not compensable, post-donning and pre-doffing walking time was part of the work day itself such that the time is compensable under the FLSA. In a case of first impression, the Ninth Circuit held that, although police officers are required to wear uniforms in conjunction with their work, because the donning and doffing process is not required to be done on the employer's premises by any city law or rule, that those officers that choose to change at the workplace are not entitled to be compensated under the FLSA. [Bamonte v. City of Mesa, 598 F.3d 1217 (9th Cir. 2010)]

In *Perez v. Mountaire Farms, Inc.* [650 F.3d 350 (4th Cir. 2011)], the court held that donning and doffing of protective gear by employees at a chicken processing plant were integral and indispensible to chicken processing, thereby requiring compensation for time spent performing these activities at work, in accordance with the FLSA.

Q 8:24   Is travel time considered hours worked under the FLSA?

Regular travel to and from work is generally not considered work time under the FLSA; however, there are numerous instances in which other travel may be work time. For example, travel away from home that cuts into the employee's workday is work time.

Overtime

Q 8:25   Who is entitled to overtime compensation?

Employees who are covered by the FLSA or comparable state laws and are not otherwise exempt from these provisions are entitled to overtime pay at one-and-a-half times their regular pay for hours they worked in excess of 40 hours per workweek.

Q 8:26   What hours should be counted toward overtime eligibility?

Hours worked in excess of 40 hours per workweek should be counted as overtime. Generally, preliminary or post-work activities, such as employee travel to or from work, are not included in compensable time, subject to exception. If an employee is assigned duties while commuting to and from work (e.g., pickups and deliveries), this time may have to be included in the workweek total. For on-call employees, compensable overtime should be evaluated on the same basis as regular compensation. If on-call employees are not required to be present at their workplace at all times and are free to attend to personal business when not actually working, the non-working hours prob-ably need not be included as compensable overtime; however, this may not be the case if on-call employees must remain at their workplace when they are on call or are otherwise prevented from engaging in personal pursuits (see Qs 8:21 and 8:24). In addition, lunch hours are not considered hours worked. For this reason, many employers establish policies that employees are not permitted to work during their lunch hours to prevent an employee from inadvertently working over 40 hours in a workweek.

Q 8:27   What is an employee's regular rate of pay for purposes of computing overtime?

The FLSA requires that all remuneration for employment paid to the employee must be included in the employee's regular rate of pay for purposes of determining overtime computation. In *Acton v. City of Columbia, Missouri* [436 F.3d 969 (8th Cir. 2006)], the court held that sums paid to firefighters in accordance with a sick leave buy-back provision under the collective bargaining agreement constituted remuneration for employment under the FLSA, such that those sums must be taken into consideration for purposes of determining the firefighters' regular rate of pay, which in turn is used in determining overtime compensation.

Q 8:28   Can salaried employees be entitled to overtime compensation?

Yes, but only if the salaried employee is non-exempt. If the company pays the non-exempt employee a salary, the employee is nonetheless entitled to one-and-one-half times his or her regular rate of pay (i.e., time-and-a-half) for the number of hours that exceeds the 40-hour workweek. To compute this, the company must determine the employee's hourly rate (usually by dividing the number of hours worked into the salary); however, if the employee is exempt (see Q 8:37), no overtime compensation is required under the FLSA.

Q 8:29   What is a *fluctuating workweek plan*?

As indicated in Q 8:28, the usual method of calculating overtime entitlement for salaried employees is to divide the hours worked into the salary and to pay time-and-a-half for hours in excess of 40; however, other options are available under the wage and hour regulations. One of these is called the *fluctuating workweek plan*. Under this plan, an employer can agree that the employee will receive a salary for all straight-time hours worked in any given week. Thus, the employee's hourly rate varies from week to week.

Example. An employee is paid $400 per week. Under the normal situation described in Q 8:28, the employee's salary covers 40 hours of work, and the rate is $10 per hour. For each additional hour of work, the employee would be entitled to an additional $15 of pay. Under a fluctuating workweek plan, if the employee worked 50 hours, that employee's straight-time wage rate for that week would be $8 per hour (i.e., $400/50 hours); therefore, that employee would be entitled to only $12 per hour for each hour in excess of 40.

Q 8:30   What is a *Belo agreement*?

The *Belo agreement* derives its name from an important U.S. Supreme Court decision that defined the instances in which an employee need not be paid overtime. [Walling v. A. H. Belo Corp., 316 U.S. 624 (1942)] The Court held that an employer may pay an employee a straight salary for all hours worked, whether this includes more or less than 40 hours in a given workweek, if:

- The employee works fluctuating hours that vary above and below 40 hours;
- A written agreement exists between the employer and employee; and
- The fluctuations are irregular and cannot be predicted.

Q 8:31   Must a company pay employees overtime if they are paid by a rate other than hourly or salary (e.g., tips or piece rate)?

Yes, if the employee is not otherwise exempted from coverage under the FLSA, the employee is entitled to time-and-a-half for hours worked in excess of 40, regardless of the method of compensation. The DOL provides detailed regulations and guidelines for calculating overtime under atypical situations, and employers should contact the DOL's Wage and Hour Administration when questions arise concerning overtime to employees compensated by piece rate, tips, or some other method.

Q 8:32   If an employee works two different jobs at the same company, and his or her workweek totals more than 40 hours for the two jobs, must the employee be paid overtime?

Generally speaking, such an employee must be paid time-and-a-half for all hours in excess of 40, notwithstanding the fact that the employee may have worked the two different jobs at two different wage rates. The DOL provides formulas for melding two different rates to determine an appropriate overtime rate. These formulas are fairly complex, and the Wage and Hour Administration should be contacted if questions arise regarding them.

Q 8:33   If an employee works two different jobs at two different companies, and his or her workweek totals more than 40 hours for the two jobs, must the employee be paid overtime?

Provided that the two companies are truly two separate and unrelated companies, overtime will not be due. However, if the two employers stand in relation to each other such that a joint employment situation exists, as defined under the FLSA, then the hours worked for both employers will be used for purposes of determining whether or not overtime is owed. Under the FLSA, two or more employers may be treated as joint employers if any one of the following is determined to have existed:

- Where there is an arrangement between the employers to share the employee's services, as, for example, to interchange employees; or

- Where one employer is acting directly or indirectly in the interest of the other employer in relation to the employee; or

- Where the employers are not completely disassociated with respect to the employment of a particular employee and may be deemed to share control of the employee, directly or indirectly, by reason of the fact that one employer controls, is controlled by, or is under common control with the other employer.

Q 8:34 What is *comp time* and can private employers use comp time to avoid paying overtime?

The term *comp time* is typically referred to as a policy whereby an employee, who regularly works 40 hours in a workweek, takes a few hours off in week 1 and makes up those hours in week 2 but does not receive overtime in week 2. Although many private employers continue to utilize this practice, and there are regular attempts by both the executive branch and the legislature to consider such proposals for private employers, to date, comp time for private employers is not a safe harbor from overtime obligations under the FLSA.

Exemptions

Q 8:35 Are there any exemptions to minimum wage and overtime standards under the FLSA?

Yes. Generally, four categories of employees are exempt: executives; administrators; professionals; and outside salespersons.

The FLSA also contains a potpourri of other total and partial exemptions. In many cases, they reflect political issues that were important to certain congressional leaders at one time or another. Thus, special rules apply to various industries and activities—such as fire and police forces, retail and service establishments, hospitals, domestic service, the tobacco industry, and interurban transportation. The rules are also somewhat different for companies operating in Puerto Rico, the Virgin Islands, and American Samoa.

Q 8:36 What is meant by a *bona fide salary*?

Receipt of a *bona fide salary* is the threshold requirement for exemption from eligibility for overtime pay. No matter how well an employee's job fits into one of the exemptions for overtime compensation under the FLSA (i.e., executive, professional, administrator, or outside salesperson), the exemption does not apply if the employee is paid by the hour.

Rather, the employee must receive a salary on a weekly or less frequent (e.g., biweekly or monthly) schedule. Subject to limited exceptions, the salary must not be reduced because of absences from the job. The essence of the salary basis requirement is that, subject to limited exceptions, employees must receive their full salary for any week they perform work, regardless of the number of days or hours worked. [*See* 29 C.F.R. § 541.118.]

Q 8:37　If an employer pays an employee a salary, is the employee exempt from the FLSA minimum wage and overtime provisions?

Not necessarily. In the first place, only specific employees are exempt from the FLSA. The major exceptions are: employees employed in a bona fide executive capacity [29 C.F.R. § 541.100]; employees employed in a bona fide administrative capacity [29 C.F.R. § 541.200]; employees employed in a bona fide professional capacity [29 C.F.R. § 541.300]; and outside salespersons [29 C.F.R. § 541.500]. Although it is true that, to maintain an exemption, an otherwise exempt employee must be paid on a salary basis, just paying an employee a salary will not work to make an employee exempt, if he or she does not meet one of the recognized exemptions under the FLSA. For example, if a clerical employee does not meet the administrative criteria, paying the clerical employee a salary will not make his or her position a bona fide administrative position. As a result, this clerical employee, although paid a salary, is subject to the overtime provisions to the extent the employee works more than 40 hours in a workweek.

Moreover, even if an employee fits within an exemption, if the employee is not paid on a salary basis, as defined under FLSA regulations, the exemption is lost. Under FLSA regulations, even if an employee receives a salary, the salary basis requirement can be violated, and the exemptions lost, if an employer makes impermissible deductions from an exempt employee's paycheck.

Q 8:38　Under the DOL's regulations, can companies deduct from an exempt employee's salary without destroying the employee's exempt status under the FLSA?

The DOL's regulations, which took effect August 23, 2004, expand the number of permissible deductions from an exempt employee's salary without affecting the employee's exempt status from four to seven. The seven exceptions from the "no pay-docking" rule are as follows:

- Absences from work for one or more full days for personal reasons, other than sickness or disability;
- Absences from work for one or more full days due to sickness or disability if deductions are made under a bona fide plan, policy, or practice of providing wage replacement benefits for these types of absences;
- To off-set any amounts received as payment for jury fees, witness fees, or military pay;
- Penalties imposed in good faith for violating safety rules for "major significance";
- Unpaid disciplinary suspension of one or more full days imposed in good faith for violations of workplace conduct rules;

- Proportionate part of employee's full salary may be paid for time actually worked in the first and last weeks of employment; and
- Unpaid leave taken pursuant to the FMLA.

The most significant addition is the ability of employers now to suspend exempt employees, without pay, for violations of written workplace conduct rules. Historically, this has not been an option for an employer, but the regulations now provide the employer with the ability to impose harsh discipline for such violations against exempt employees, short of termination.

Q 8:39   What happens if the employer has a practice of making improper deductions from salaried exempt employees?

Under the new regulations, if an employer has an actual practice of making improper deductions from salaried exempt employees, the exemption is lost during the time period in which the improper deductions were made for all employees, in the same job classification, who were working for the same managers responsible for the actual improper deductions. [29 C.F.R. § 541.603(b)] However, if the deductions are isolated or inadvertent, it will not result in a loss of the exemption if the employer reimburses the employee for the improper deductions. In addition, the new regulations contain a "safe harbor," which provides that if the employer maintains a clearly communicated policy that prohibits improper pay deductions, and includes a complaint mechanism for employees to report improper deductions and reimburses employees for improper deductions, the employer will not lose the exemption for any employees unless the employer willfully violates the policy. [29 C.F.R. § 541.603(d)]

Q 8:40   Which employer policies can run afoul of the salary basis requirement for exempt employees?

Certainly, any policy that would provide for unpaid leaves for jury duty, witness attendance, military leave, and the like would run afoul of the salary basis requirement, if the exempt employee performed any work in a workweek. Moreover, seemingly innocent and innocuous policies, like vacation or personal day policies, can be implemented in ways that would violate the salary basis requirement.

Example. An employer permits earned paid personal days to be used in half-day segments. An exempt employee with a half-day paid personal day takes three-quarters of a day off during a workweek. If the employer pays the exempt employee three-quarters of a day's pay ($\frac{1}{4}$ day worked + $\frac{1}{2}$ paid personal day), in essence, the employee is being docked $\frac{1}{4}$ day for personal reasons. The regulations only permit deductions for one day or more for personal reasons. [29 C.F.R. § 541.602]

Q 8:41   Are threats to dock pay sufficient to run afoul of the salary basis requirement for exempt employees?

Under both the old regulations, 29 C.F.R. § 541.118, and the new regulations, 29 C.F.R. § 541.602, in order to maintain a salary basis, the salary must not be "subject to reduction because of variations in the quality or quantity of the work performed." The issue of whether an employee's salary is "subject to reduction" was addressed by the Sixth Circuit in *Whisman v. Ford Motor Co.* [157 Fed. Appx. 792 (6th Cir. 2005)] In that case, exempt employees for Ford Motor Company claimed that Ford had violated the salary basis requirement by adopting a policy requiring its salaried employees to swipe their electronic identification badges to record their ingress and egress from the plant, and threatened that failure to do so could lead to possible "pay adjustments." Although no evidence existed that any salaried employee's base pay had ever been docked as a result of this policy, the employees argued that because the policy threatened pay adjustments, their salary was "subject to" reductions based on the quality or quantity of work performed. Citing the Supreme Court case of *Auer v. Robbins* [519 U.S. 452 (1997)], the court concluded that employees are subject to a reduction in pay when they are covered by a policy that permits disciplinary or other deductions in pay as a practical matter. That standard, the court held, would be met if either an actual practice of making the deductions had occurred, or if the employment policy created a "significant likelihood" of such deductions. In this case, the court concluded that the threat did not amount to subjecting the salaried exempt employees to deductions as a practical matter, and held that the policy and threatened pay adjustment did not defeat the salary basis test under the FLSA. However, in *McBride v. Peak Wellness Center, Inc.* [688 F.3d 698 (10th Cir. 2012)], the court held that docking time from accrued leave for attendance issues is not an impermissible docking of pay in violation of the salary basis requirements for exempt employees.

Q 8:42   How is an exempt employee to be paid if he or she begins or terminates employment during the workweek?

Although the salary basis requirement may not permit such deductions during the exempt employee's tenure, the regulations specifically authorize the payment of a proportionate week for days actually worked upon commencement and termination of employment. [29 C.F.R. § 541.602]

Q 8:43   What is the definition for *exempt executive employees* under the DOL's regulations?

DOL regulations provide a more expansive test for determining whether an employee satisfies the requirements of an *exempt executive employee*. Generally, to be considered an executive the employee must satisfy the following criteria.

- The employee's primary duty is the management of the enterprise or of a customarily recognized department or subdivision;

- Customarily and regularly directs the work of two or more other employees; and
- Has the authority to hire and fire other employees or whose suggestions and recommendations as to hiring, firing, advancement, promotion, or other change of status of other employees are given particular weight.

To be the employee's primary duty, it must be the principal, main, major, or most important duty that the employee performs. Factors to consider under the new regulations include:

- Relative importance of the exempt duties;
- Amount of time spent performing exempt work;
- Relative freedom from direct supervision; and
- Relationship between the employee's salary and the wages paid to other employees for the same kind of non-exempt work.

Generally, employees who spend more than 50 percent of their time performing exempt work will generally satisfy the primary duty requirement. However, importantly the regulations do not require that exempt employees spend more than 50 percent of their time performing exempt work. Recent case law suggests that the "executive" exemption may apply to workers that one may not typically consider an executive. In *Ramos v. Valdor Specialty Foods, Inc.* [687 F.3d 554 (2d Cir. 2012)], at issue was whether a group of so-called "captains" in an employer's wholesale food warehouse were "executives" under the FLSA. Each captain was assigned a number of workers that would pull inventory from the warehouse to be loaded on trucks for delivery. Importantly, each captain, and the so-called pickers were assigned a distinct work area in the warehouse, and each captain supervised the pickers' work and had significant influence in such issues as hiring, termination, discipline, and the like. Although some might argue that management of an assigned work area for this purpose does not meet the requirement of management of an "enterprise or customarily recognized department or subdivision," the court, in reviewing the regulations, determined that the assigned work areas within the warehouse were a customarily recognized department, such that the captains fell within the executive exemption under the FLSA.

Q 8:44 What do the DOL's regulations provide relative to the administrative exemption?

For purposes of the FLSA, the definition of an *administrative exemption* has been expanded by the DOL. Under the new regulations, an employee will be considered exempt under the administrative exemption if:

- The employee's primary duty is the performance of office or non-manual work directly related to the management or general business operations of the employer or the employer's customers; and
- The employee's primary duty includes the exercise of discretion and independent judgment with respect to matters of significance.

As with the executive exemption, the primary duty requirement will be satisfied if it is the employee's principal, main, major, or most important duty that the employee performs. Factors to consider include, but are not limited to the following:

- Relative importance of the exempt duties;
- Amount of time spent performing exempt work;
- Relative freedom from direct supervision; and
- Relationship between the employee's salary and the wages paid to other employees for the same kind of non-exempt work.

Generally, although not required, employees who spend more than 50 percent of their time performing exempt work will satisfy the primary duty requirement.

Work directly related to management or general business operations refers to work that must be directly related to assisting with the running or servicing of the business and does not include working on a manufacturing production line or selling a product in a retail or service establishment. Work related to the employer's customers includes employees acting as advisors or consultants to clients or customers such as tax experts or financial consultants. A number of factors will be considered to determine whether or not the employee exercises discretion and independent judgment, such as:

- The comparison and evaluation of possible courses of conduct, and acting or making a decision after the various possibilities have been considered;
- Whether the employee has the authority to formulate, affect, interpret, or implement management policies or operating practices; and
- Whether the employee carries out major assignments in conducting the operations of the business.

The employee will still satisfy the discretion and independent judgment requirement even if his or her decisions and recommendations are reviewed at a higher level and, upon occasion, revised or reversed. Discretion and independent judgment does not include:

- Applying well-established techniques, procedures, or specific standards described in manuals or other sources;
- Clerical or secretarial work;
- Recording or tabulating data; or
- Performing mechanical, repetitive, recurrent, or routine work.

At issue in *Robinson-Smith v. Government Employees Ins. Co.* [590 F.3d 886 (D.C. Cir. 2010)], was whether automobile damage adjustors satisfied the administrative exemption under the DOL's regulations effective August 23, 2004. Because the adjustors exercised discretion and independent judgment in damage assessment, and made independent choices for claims free from their immediate direction or supervision, the court held that the adjusters, having met other requirements for the administrative exemption, exercised enough discretion and independent judgment to satisfy the requirements of the administrative exemption. At issue in *Reiseck v. Universal Communications of Miami, Inc.* [591 F.3d 101 (2d Cir. 2010)], was whether a salesperson satisfied the administrative exemption. Although the employee claimed, because she was engaged in sales, that her primary duty was related to the "management or business operations of the employer or the employer's customers," the court found that the salesperson's primary duty did not involve management or business operations of the customer base, but rather, selling specific advertising space to specific clients and as such, could not be considered an administrative employee under the DOL exemptions. In *Dewalt v. Greencroft Goshen, Inc.* [2012 WL 5362889 (N.D. Ind. Oct. 30, 2012)], the court held that a marketing associate of a continuing care retirement community had sufficient discretion and independent judgment in the recruitment of residents such that she fit within the administrative exemption under the FLSA.

Q 8:45   Are working foremen bona fide executives under the FLSA?

The DOL's regulations identify two types of working foremen who ordinarily are not exempt from the overtime provisions of the FLSA:

* Straw bosses or gang leaders who work beside their co-workers performing the same tasks as they perform; and
* Working foremen who, although they do not work alongside their subordinates, perform routine, non-exempt tasks of their own.

If the non-exempt work consumes most of the employee's time, he or she does not qualify for the executive exemption from the FLSA, regardless of how well the employee is compensated in salary.

Q 8:46   Is a job title a sufficient yardstick of whether or not an employee is a bona fide administrator under the FLSA?

No. To the contrary, the DOL's regulations are replete with warnings that job titles alone are not sufficient to establish an employee's administrative status. "It should be particularly noted that this is a field which is rife with honorific titles that do not adequately portray the nature of the employee's duties." [29 C.F.R. § 541.201(3)(i)]

The employees for whom exemption is sought under the term *administrative* have extremely diverse functions and a wide variety of titles. A title alone is of little or no assistance in determining the true importance of an employee to the employer or his or her exempt or non-exempt status under the regulations. Titles can be had cheaply and are of no determinative value. [29 C.F.R. § 541.201(b)(1)]

Q 8:47   What are the DOL's regulations for exempt professionals?

Under the DOL's regulations, an employee will be considered exempt under the Learned Professional Exemption if:

- The employee's primary duty must be the performance of work requiring advance knowledge;
- In a field of science or learning;
- Customarily acquired by a prolonged course of specialized intellectual instruction.

The determination of primary duty is consistent with that for executive and administrative exemptions under the regulations. (See Qs 8:43 and 8:44.) Fields of science or learning must be occupations with recognized professional status as distinguished from the mechanical arts or skilled trades, such as:

- Law;
- Theology;
- Medicine;
- Pharmacy;
- Accounting;
- Teaching;
- Architecture;
- Engineering;
- Actuarial computation;
- Physical sciences;
- Chemical sciences; and
- Biological sciences.

In *Pignataro v. Port Authority of New York and New Jersey* [593 F.3d 265 (3d Cir. 2010)], the court held that helicopter pilots were not engaged in the performance of work requiring "advanced knowledge in a field of science or learning customarily required by a prolonged course of specialized intellectual instruction" and hence were not exempt under the learned professional exemption. Although the pilots were required to be certified, have requisite hours of flying time, and earn commercial pilot certificates, none of the certifications required that the helicopter pilots have academic degrees and did not require a prolonged course of specialized intellectual instruction and study. At issue in *Solis v. Washington* [656 F.3d 1079 (9th Cir. 2011)] was whether social workers working for Washington's Department of Social and Health Services fell within the "Learned Professional" exemption under the DOL regulations, which took effect in August 2004. Reviewing the training, education, and experience needed to qualify as a social worker, the court concluded that the position did not require a "prolonged course of specialized intellectual instruction" as required under the DOL regulations and, as such, held that the social workers did not qualify for the exemption.

Q 8:48   What are the DOL's regulations with respect to exemptions for creative professionals?

Under the DOL's regulations, creative professionals are exempt under the FLSA. To be a creative professional, the employee's primary duty must be the performance of work requiring invention, imagination, originality, or talent in a recognized field of creative endeavor. Recognized creative endeavors include:

- Music;
- Writing;
- Acting; and
- Graphic arts.

In *Wang v. Chinese Daily News, Inc.* [623 F.3d 743 (9th Cir. 2010)], a case of first impression, the court held that, although certain journalists may satisfy the criteria for creative professionals, the journalists of the community publication at issue were primarily engaged in providing news relating to public information by gathering facts of routine community activities, as opposed to more sophisticated analysis and investigative reporting, which might be found in more sophisticated national-level papers, and as such, did not satisfy the criteria for the creative professional's exemption.

Q 8:49   Are computer programmers exempt as professionals under the FLSA?

One area of expansion (recognized by the DOL through amendments to 29 C.F.R. § 541) becoming more prevalent in our increasingly technologically sophisticated society is the recognition of computer programmers and related occupations as eligible for exemptions as professionals under the FLSA. Specifically, the regulations provide that:

> Computer systems analysts, computer programmers, software engineers, or other similarly skilled workers in the computer software field are eligible for exemption as professionals.

Employees that qualify for this exemption are "highly skilled" computer systems analysts, programmers, or individuals who perform related software functions. In order to be considered for the exemption, the employee's primary duty must consist of one or more of the following:

- The application of systems analyst techniques and procedures, including consulting with users to determine hardware, software, or a system's functional specifications;
- The design, development, documentation, analysis, creation, testing, or modification of computer systems or programs, including prototypes, based on and related to system design specifications;
- The design, documentation, testing, creation, or modification of computer programs related to machine operating systems;
- A combination of the aforementioned duties.

This exemption specifically does not include employees engaged in the operation or the manufacture, repair, or maintenance of computer hardware and related equipment. Similarly, employees whose work is dependent upon, or facilitated by, the use of computers and computer software programs, but who are not in computer systems analysis and programming occupations, are not within the exemption. [See 29 C.F.R. § 541.400.] For example, machine operators who perform machining functions with CAD/CAM computerized machining systems are not performing the level of programming and analyst functions necessary for this exemption.

Q 8:50   Are there minimum salary levels that executive, administrative, and professional employees must meet to enable them to be considered exempt under the FLSA?

Under DOL regulations, these employees must be paid a minimum salary level of $455 per week. The DOL regulations create a hybrid exemption for highly compensated employees that customarily and regularly perform any one or more of the exempt duties identified under the standard test for executive, administrative, or professional exemptions. To be considered a highly compensated employee, the employee's total annual compensation must be at least $100,000 and must receive at least $455 per week paid on a salary or fee basis.

Q 8:51   What are the DOL regulations concerning outside sales employee exemptions?

Under the regulations, an employee falls under the exempt position of outside sales employee if the employee's primary duty is making sales or obtaining orders or contracts for services or for use of facilities for which a consideration will be paid by the client or customer and who is customarily engaged away from the employer's place or places of business in performing such primary duties.

The primary duty requirement is determined consistent with that used for executive or administrative exemptions. (See Qs 8:43 and 8:44.) In determining the primary duty of an outside sales employee, work performed incidental to and in conjunction with the employee's outside sales or solicitation—including incidental deliveries and collections—will be regarded as exempt outside sales work.

The issue of whether the outside sales representative must actually be involved in making sales or obtaining orders and contracts is unsettled. In *Palacios v. Boehringer Ingelheim Pharmaceuticals, Inc.* [2011 WL 2837464 (S.D. Fla. July 12, 2011)], the court held that although pharmaceutical sales representatives were engaged in promotion activity related to their employer's pharmaceutical products, because no sales contracts or orders were obtained by the representatives in connection with their promotional activities, they could not fit within the outside sales exemption. On the other hand, in *Christopher v. Smithkline Beecham Corp., DBA* [635 F.3d 383 (9th Cir. 2010)], the Ninth Circuit concluded that pharmaceutical sales representatives, although not directly involved in sales, were clearly involved in outside sales activities for which they were paid commissions attributable to sales of their employer's products, did fall within the exemption despite the fact that these representatives were not directly involved in any sales. Unlike conventional industries, the court noted that the pharmaceutical industry is heavily regulated and the purchaser in this case is not the patient but rather the physician that prescribes the drug and who the representatives solicit and promote pharmaceutical products. For these reasons, the court concluded that the representatives fell within the exemption. The Supreme Court in a 5-4 decision affirmed the decision of the Ninth Circuit, holding that obtaining non-binding commitments from physicians to prescribe prescription drugs, qualifies as an outside salesman exemption under the FLSA. [Christopher v. Smithkline Beecham Corp., 132 S. Ct. 2156 (2012)]

Q 8:52 Are public employees treated differently from private-sector employees under the DOL's approach to the so-called white collar exemptions to the FLSA?

Recognizing that many public-sector employers are obligated by statutory or constitutional provisions to deduct salary from state and local government employees for missed hours of work, the DOL in 1992 issued its "Final Rule on FLSA Exemptions for Public Employees" [57 Fed. Reg. 37,677 (1992)], which preserves the exempt status of public executives, administrators, and professionals who are paid a salary that is subject to hourly deductions because of statute, ordinance, regulation, policy, or practice.

Why did the DOL revise the salary test applicable to public employees, but not private employees? The DOL feared that judicial applications of the regulations' salary test created a potential for enormous, unforeseen liability against public employers that could threaten their fiscal integrity. [56 Fed. Reg. 45,825 (1991)]

Q 8:53 What is the DOL's new "safe harbor" for impermissible deductions from an exempt employee's salary?

Under the DOL's regulations [29 C.F.R. § 541.603], an employer who makes an impermissible deduction from an exempt employee's salary, which could destroy the exemption for all employees in the same classification during the time period that the improper deduction was made, can still maintain the exemption if:

- The employer has a clearly communicated policy prohibiting improper pay deductions (preferably in writing);
- The policy contains a complaint mechanism and reimburses employees for improper deductions; and
- The employer makes a good-faith commitment to comply in the future.

[29 C.F.R. § 541.603]

A sample "safe harbor" policy is contained at the DOL's Web site at http://www.dol.gov.

Q 8:54   What are the most common mistakes that employers make with regard to the FLSA exemptions from minimum wage and overtime pay requirements?

The most common mistake of employers operating in white collar environments is to treat all employees as if they were exempt. Employers often erroneously assume that overtime obligations may be ignored because secretaries and office personnel are paid on a salary basis. Employers must pay exempt employees on a salary basis to maintain the exemption; however, paying someone a salary does not make him or her exempt. For example, suppose that an employee at a physician's office, with the title "Office Administrator" performs numerous functions at the office, including answering phones, filing medical records, and billing. He supervises no one, and although some of this work may fit within the category of an administrator (one of the exemptions under the FLSA), he does not do enough "exempt" work to satisfy the requirements of the FLSA. Nonetheless, the physician, who is tired of the headaches associated with having the employee keep time records and computing overtime (the employee regularly works 50 hours a week), decides to average out the employee's usual weekly pay and just pay a flat salary, regardless of hours worked. If this employee continues to work 50 hours per week, the physician would violate the FLSA to the extent the employee is not paid overtime for hours worked in excess of 40 hours weekly.

In addition, some employers maintain policies that undermine the exempt status of exempt employees. They include docking the salary of exempt employees for less than one day for such matters as absences and sickness. The result can be to destroy the salary status on which an executive, administrative, or professional exemption must be based. Employers are better advised to use their disciplinary system to control such problems.

Lastly, many employers determine whether an employee is exempt from the title for the position, rather than analyzing the duties and responsibilities of the position to determine if the position fits within the exemption as outlined in the DOL regulations. This is a mistake. Just as paying someone a salary does not make that person exempt, likewise, giving someone a title (e.g., administrator) does not make him or her exempt. The fact that titles alone are inadequate for purposes of properly characterizing employees as exempt or non-exempt can be demonstrated by the comparison of two cases involving whether fire service paramedics qualify for an exemption under the FLSA that provides an employer with a so-called Section 7(k) workweek exception that allows the employer to extend beyond the 40 hour workweek for purposes of overtime computation. [29 U.S.C. § 207(k)] Since 1999, the FLSA has adopted a new definition of employees "engaged in fire protection activities" that qualify for the Section 207(k) exemption and define an employee engaged in "fire protection activities" as one who, among other things, is trained in fire suppression and has the legal authority and responsibility to engage in fire suppression. [29 U.S.C. § 203(y)] In *Huff v. Dekalb County, Georgia* [516 F.3d 1273 (11th Cir. 2008)], the paramedics at issue were clearly trained in fire suppression, but at issue was whether they had the responsibility to engage in fire suppression, one of the requirements to fall within the exemption. Although, as a matter of policy, commanders did not actually order the paramedics to engage in fire suppression, the court found that the paramedics had advanced fire fighting training, were equipped with "turn-out" gear, were regularly sent to fire scenes and policy required them to be available to assist with fire suppression if they are needed. As such, the court held that they did have the responsibility to engage in fire suppression, such that the FLSA exemption applied. On the other hand, in *Yates v. The City of Pennsylvania* [527 F.3d 299 (3d Cir. 2008)], the court came to the opposite conclusion holding that fire service paramedics did not fall within the exemption. Specifically, these paramedics, as opposed to the paramedics in the *Huff* case discussed above, were not fully cross-trained as fire fighters, were not permitted to staff fire apparatuses, were not provided turn-out gear, and were called to a fire scene only for the purposes of providing medical care. As such, these paramedics did not qualify for the FLSA exemption.

Violations and Penalties

Q 8:55   What remedies are available to an employee if an employer fails to comply with minimum wage and overtime provisions?

An employer that fails to comply with federal or state minimum wage and overtime compensation laws may be ordered to change its compensation practices to conform to legal standards. In addition, the employer may be required to pay, as damages, the amount of minimum wages and overtime compensation wrongfully withheld. An employer may also be required to pay additional damages (e.g., liquidated damages) as a penalty for non-compliance. In addition, if the employer has policies that have violated the salary basis requirement for an exempt employee, the employer must pay overtime compensation for the employee as if he or she were non-exempt. Although back pay, overtime pay, liquidated damages and penalties are all provided for under varying circumstances under the FLSA, punitive damages are not specifically referenced in the statute and as such, are not awardable under the FLSA. [Allen v. Garden City Co-Op., Inc., 2009 WL 2777246 (D. Kan. Aug. 27, 2009)]

Q 8:56   Who is the "employer" for purposes of FLSA liability?

An employer is broadly defined under the FLSA as "any person acting as directly or indirectly in the interest of an employer in relation to an employee and includes a public agency but does not include any labor organization (other than when acting as an employer) or anyone acting in a capacity of officer or agent of such labor organization." [29 U.S.C. § 203(d)]

As it relates to individual liability, courts have interpreted the statutory language to mean that individuals who have sufficient operational control of significant aspects of the corporation's day-to-day functions may fall within the definition of an employer under the FLSA such that they are individually liable for violations, including payment of unpaid overtime, minimum wages, and the like.

At issue in *Alvarez Perez v. Sanford-Orlando Kennel Club, Inc.* [515 F.3d 1150 (11th Cir. 2008)] was whether the majority shareholder and officer of a race track could be held individually liable for violations of the FLSA. Recognizing that corporate officers with operational control of a corporation are employers, jointly and severally liable with the company under the FLSA for unpaid wages, the court concluded that in the case at hand, the owner had not been involved in the day-to-day operations of the race track for years and was not directly responsible for the supervision of the employees during the relevant years. As such, the court affirmed the trial court's dismissal of individual liability.

In certain instances, more than one employer may be deemed to be an employer of an employee under the FLSA. The determination of whether an employer-employee relationship exists for the purposes of the FLSA on grounded in the "economic realities" as opposed to technical concepts and relationships. Analyzing the economic realities of the circumstances as a whole, as opposed to isolated factors, four factors have been identified as helpful in determining whether a putative employer-employee relationship exist: whether the employer (1) had the right to hire and fire the employees, (2) supervised and controlled work schedules or conditions of employment, (3) determined the method and rate of payment, and (4) maintained employment records. [Herman v. RSR Sec. Servs. LTD, 172 F.3d 132, 139 (2d Cir. 1999)]

In *Barfield v. New York City Health and Hospitals Corporation* [537 F.3d 132 (2d Cir. 2008)], one of the issues was whether a hospital was liable for overtime pay due a nurse who was employed by an independent nursing referral agency and assigned to the hospital to perform services. Reviewing the economic realities of the situation, the court concluded that the hospital, although not formally the nurse's employer, exercised sufficient functional and formal control over the nurse to qualify the hospital as her joint employer.

Q 8:57   What are *liquidated damages*?

Liquidated damages are assessed at an amount equal to the minimum wage and overtime compensation wrongfully withheld; thus, if an employer, in violation of federal or state wage laws, failed to pay an employee $5,000 in minimum wages and overtime, it may be liable for $10,000 in damages—comprising $5,000 in withheld compensation and $5,000 in liquidated damages. An employer may also be required to pay the legal fees incurred by an employee seeking minimum wage and overtime compensation.

An employer may avoid assessment of liquidated damages if it demonstrates that it acted in good faith when failing to pay minimum wages or overtime and had a reasonable basis for believing that it was not violating any federal or state regulation. The employer must show that it honestly intended to ascertain and follow the applicable wage laws. A plea of ignorance usually does not suffice.

Q 8:58 Who can sue an employer for minimum wages and overtime?

The FLSA provides a cause of action both to the wronged employee and to the Secretary of Labor. If the Secretary of Labor brings a legal action against the employer, the employee's right of action is automatically terminated by the filing of the secretary's lawsuit. Subsequently, the employee must depend on the secretary's attorneys to collect the wages due.

Q 8:59 What is the statute of limitations for the employee or the Secretary of Labor in collecting back pay?

The FLSA has a two-year statute of limitations for collecting back wages for non-willful violations of the law; it goes back three years for willful violations.

Q 8:60 What is a *willful violation* of the FLSA?

In *McLaughlin v. Richland Shoe Co.* [486 U.S. 128 (1988)], the U.S. Supreme Court adopted a definition of a *willful violation* of the FLSA. Under *McLaughlin,* an employer is guilty of a willful violation, triggering a three-year statute of limitations, only when it acts with actual knowledge or reckless disregard of whether its compensation scheme violates the FLSA. The Court rejected the DOL's suggestion that willfulness is present when the employer knows that the FLSA may apply but proceeds without a reasonable basis for believing its procedures are in compliance with the law. The Supreme Court felt that this sanction was punitive in nature and therefore should be triggered only when a company has a fairly high level of culpability.

Q 8:61 When is an employer required to pay an employee double damages under the FLSA?

Section 216 of the FLSA [29 U.S.C. § 216], states that any employer that violates the overtime or minimum wage provision of the Act "shall be liable to the employee or employees affected in the amount of their unpaid minimum wages, or their unpaid overtime compensation . . . , and in an additional equal amount as liquidated damages." Read in a vacuum, this provision would permit the successful employee-plaintiff to receive double damages in every successful lawsuit for back wages.

In 1947, to clarify and amend the FLSA, Congress passed the Portal-to-Portal Act, [29 U.S.C. § 260], which provides employers with some relief from FLSA Section 216's liquidated damage provision. Although double damages are intended to compensate the successful employee-litigant for the wait and difficulty in collecting the back wages, Section 260 states:

> If the employer shows to the satisfaction of the court that the act or omission giving rise to such action was in good faith and that he had reasonable grounds for believing that his act or omission was not a violation of the Fair Labor Standards Act of 1938 . . . , the court may, in its sound discretion, award no liquidated damages.

The court also is accorded discretion to award liquidated damages of less than 100 percent of the back wages won by the successful employee-plaintiff.

Child Labor

Q 8:62   What laws restrict the use of child labor?

Besides the FLSA, virtually every state has laws controlling the use of child labor. Child-labor legislation focuses chiefly on two issues—the number of hours that children are employed and the type of work that they perform.

Q 8:63   How do the various state laws on child labor interact with provisions of the FLSA?

The child-labor provisions of the FLSA apply in every state; however, when a state's law offers greater protection to its children, the state law supersedes any lesser protections afforded by the FLSA.

Q 8:64   Are there any other federal laws that deal with child labor?

In addition to the FLSA, three important federal laws deal with child labor:

- The Walsh-Healey Act sets wage and hour standards under federal supply contracts;
- The Mineral Land Leasing Act applies to mines that are operated on lands leased from the federal government; and
- The Interstate Commerce Act has regulations limiting the employment of children as drivers in interstate commerce.

Q 8:65   How do the federal child-labor laws regulate the labor of children?

Federal laws deal with the problem of child labor on an occupational, rather than an industrial, basis. This means that, in general, children are not forbidden to work in any particular industry. Rather, the kinds of jobs that they may do are limited by the law. Generally, dangerous jobs cannot be performed by children. Other jobs are acceptable but must be performed only outside of regular school hours and only for a limited number of hours per day.

Q 8:66   What are the penalties for violating child-labor laws?

Violation of child-labor laws can result in fines and, in very serious cases, imprisonment.

Compensation and Withholding

Q 8:67 What are merit-pay procedures, and are they legal?

Merit pay, as the name suggests, is tied to performance, as compared to the across-the-board increases typically mandated by collective bargaining agreements. Merit increases are almost never entirely open-ended. Rather, supervisors are usually allowed to recommend raises within the parameters of a company-wide policy. First, such a policy must prescribe when such raises can be given (typically with an annual or semi-annual performance review). Reviews may be staggered according to employees' anniversary dates of hire or at the fulfillment of a probationary period. Alternatively, some companies conduct all annual reviews at a particular point in the calendar or fiscal year.

From accounting and cash-flow standpoints, each alternative offers advantages and disadvantages; the same is true from the human resources perspective. Conducting all reviews during approximately the same time frame allows easier oversight and helps the human resources staff monitor the relative uniformity of standards and results across departments. Staggering reviews according to anniversaries permits each supervisor to give each subordinate greater personal attention but probably gives the human resources staff a bit more difficulty in both tracking anniversary dates and monitoring the relative uniformity of standards within and across departments.

The relative uniformity of standards is legally significant because the disparate treatment of minority or female employees can result in discrimination charges. Worth noting in this regard is that merit-pay programs do not automatically violate the federal Equal Pay Act. Although that law requires that women and men who do essentially the same work receive the same pay, the Act expressly permits discrepancies in compensation reflecting such differences as seniority, skill, and productivity. Nonetheless, discrepancies in increases between, for example, blacks and whites or females and males that cannot be explained by productivity or other performance records may violate Title VII of the Civil Rights Act of 1964. Similarly, a divergence of merit increases that is unfavorable to older workers may be prima facie evidence of age discrimination in violation of the Age Discrimination in Employment Act (ADEA); however, if a job category has a salary ceiling that older employees have already attained (or nearly attained), this may constitute a business justification for such a discrepancy.

Q 8:68 What is the difference between a merit increase and a promotion increase?

Merit increases are made within the salary range of the employee's present job. A *promotion increase*, as the term suggests, occurs with a job promotion. Typically, the newly promoted employee moves to the bottom rung of the range for the new position.

Q 8:69   To what compensation and benefits are part-time employees entitled?

Like full-time workers, part-timers are entitled to the minimum hourly wage set by federal law or any higher minimum hourly rate set by an individual state's minimum wage law. Federal law also requires companies to make Social Security contributions on behalf of part-time employees. Under the requirements of the Employee Retirement Income Security Act (ERISA), part-time employees who work at least 20 hours per week, or 1,000 hours per year, must be allowed to participate in the company's retirement plan, if any. Part-timers can be, and frequently are, excluded from such non-mandatory fringe benefits as health insurance, life insurance, and dental insurance.

The FMLA may be applicable to workers who are considered part-time. Under the FMLA, an employee who has worked as few as 1,250 hours during the preceding 12-month period may be eligible for FMLA leave, provided he or she meets two additional requirements—provided services for at least 12 months and worked at a work site where there are at least 50 employees within a 75-mile radius.

Q 8:70   What deductions does the law commonly require from an employee's paycheck?

Federal law requires both employers and employees to contribute into the Social Security system. The Internal Revenue Code requires employers to withhold from their employees' paychecks income tax deductions based on reasonable estimates of what the employee's annual tax obligations are likely to be. Many states and municipalities also impose income taxes for which deductions must be taken. Federal labor law permits employers to withhold union dues, pursuant to an appropriate clause in a collective bargaining agreement, with each member's written authorization. It also allows pretax deductions for employee pension plan contributions and employee contributions into other welfare benefit plans, such as health insurance in so-called cafeteria plans.

Q 8:71   How can an employee affect payroll withholding?

Upon initial employment, every employee completes a W-4 form, reflecting the number of deductions he or she claims (for example, the employee plus a dependent spouse and children). The number of deductions determines the percentage of pay the employer withholds from each paycheck. The employee is permitted to fill out and sign a new W-4 form at any time. An employee who, for example, anticipates extraordinary deductions from income for the given year may increase the number of claimed dependents so as to decrease income tax withholding from his or her paycheck.

Employees can also determine, up to specified legal limits, their percentage of contributions to employer-sponsored 401(k), cafeteria, and savings plans.

Q 8:72   What can an employer do if the employee refuses to provide information required by the IRS for religious reasons?

In *Seaworthy v. Pearson* [203 F.3d 1056 (8th Cir. 2000)], a terminated employee claimed religious discrimination when he was fired for refusal to provide a Social Security number to the employer as required by the Internal Revenue Service (IRS). The terminated employee cited religious reasons, claiming that the number is a "mark of the beast." The court rejected the claim, holding that accommodation for religious belief does not include requiring the employer to violate the IRS laws. This holding in *Seaworth* was followed in *Baltgalvis v. Newport News Shipbuilding, Inc.* [132 F. Supp. 2d 414 (E.D. Va. 2001), reported in 16 *Employment Discrimination Report (EDR)* (BNA) 381 (Mar. 14, 2001); *see also* Sutton v. Providence St. Joseph Med. Ctr., 192 F.3d 826 (9th Cir. 1999) (requested accommodation by employee to not provide employer with Social Security number for religious reasons poses an undue hardship on employer—requiring employer to violate federal law which requires employers to provide employees' Social Security numbers).]

Q 8:73   What are the legal penalties for improper withholding?

Employers who fail to withhold income and Social Security taxes (for example, because they have incorrectly categorized their employees as independent contractors) may be held liable to the IRS for such deductions, together with employer Federal Unemployment Tax Act and Federal Income Contributions Act (FICA) contributions, penalties, and interest. With respect to an employer's own obligation to pay payroll taxes, failure to do so is an offense not dischargeable even in bankruptcy. Corporate officers may be held personally liable for such taxes, if they are responsible for the company's failure to set aside and turn over such taxes.

Q 8:74   Must an employer take tax deductions from employees' bonuses and severance payments?

Yes. Bonuses and severance payments to terminated employees constitute income realized by these employees; therefore, all appropriate payroll deductions are generally demanded by law.

Fringe Benefits

Q 8:75   What are *fringe benefits*?

Fringe benefits can mean virtually any emolument of employment that an employee receives beyond a basic salary—including pensions, various types of insurance (e.g., health, life, or disability), paid vacation, company cars, paid sick leave, and expense accounts.

Q 8:76 What types of fringe benefits can be offered to employees?

The term *fringe benefits* applies to a wide range of policies and benefits, other than wages, that employers provide for employees, including:

- Cash bonus and incentive awards;
- Employee stock ownership plans (ESOPs);
- Profit-sharing plans (i.e., defined contribution plans);
- Pension and retirement plans (i.e., defined benefit plans);
- Cash or deferral plans, such as 401(k) plans;
- Life insurance;
- Medical benefits (i.e., health, dental, and optical);
- Disability plans (short- and long-term);
- Dependent care assistance plans;
- Cafeteria plans;
- Vacation benefits and holiday pay;
- Sick-day policies;
- Policies for medical leaves of absence;
- Personal days; and
- Severance plans.

Q 8:77 Is a company legally required to provide its employees with fringe benefits?

No. With limited exceptions, no laws require an employer to give employees any specific fringe benefits. There are, however, a few exceptions to this general rule. For instance, under the FMLA, covered employers must provide eligible employees as many as 12 weeks at job-protected, unpaid leave during any 12-month period. In addition, at least three states currently require employers to provide pregnant employees unpaid maternity leave with guaranteed job rights thereafter. [California Fair Employment and Housing Act §§ 12945, 12945.2 (Family Rights Act of 1991); New Jersey Family Leave Act, 34 N.J. Stats. §§ 11B-1-11B-16 (1990); Montana Human Rights Act, 49-2-310] Some states mandate severance pay in the case of plant closings. [*See, e.g.,* 26 Maine Stats §§ 625-B(1)–625-B(6).] Generally, however, the decision to provide fringe benefits is left to the individual employer or to collective bargaining between the employer and the employees. Once such a bargain is made, however, federal and state law can come dramatically into play; therefore, the decision to provide fringe benefits, and the nature of the fringe benefits to be provided, should be considered carefully.

Employee Retirement Income Security Act

Q 8:78 Does a federal law cover pensions and employee welfare benefit plans?

Yes. In 1974, Congress enacted ERISA. [29 U.S.C. §§ 1001 *et seq.*] This comprehensive federal legislation covers pension plans and almost all other forms of employee welfare benefits plans.

Q 8:79 Why was ERISA enacted?

ERISA was passed in response to numerous instances of pension fund mismanagement and abuse. In some cases, the pension benefits of retired employees were reduced or terminated because their pension plan had not been adequately funded or had been depleted through mismanagement. In other instances, employees retiring after 20 years of service were ineligible for pensions because of complex and strict eligibility requirements. ERISA was intended to prevent such abuses and to protect the interests of employees and their beneficiaries.

Q 8:80 What types of plans are covered by ERISA?

ERISA is a broad comprehensive federal statute that provides rights to participants and beneficiaries relating to employee benefit plans as defined under ERISA. There are generally two types of plans covered by ERISA—employee welfare benefit plans and pension plans.

Employee welfare benefit plans provide beneficiaries or participants with benefits for medical, sickness, hospital, disability, death, unemployment, or vacation benefits, or apprenticeship or other training programs, daycare centers, scholarship funds, pre-paid legal services, or severance benefits. [29 U.S.C. § 1002 (1)] Payroll practices, including sick days and paid vacation days, that are paid out of an employer's general operating assets are generally not considered part of employee welfare benefit plans. [*See* Shea v. Wells Fargo Armored Serv. Corp., 810 F.2d 372 (2d Cir. 1987).]

Pension benefit plans provide retirement income or deferred compensation to employees. [29 U.S.C. § 1002 (1)(A)] Typical pension plans include defined benefit plans and defined contribution plans, which include profit sharing plans and 401(k) plans.

Q 8:81 How does ERISA protect employee pension plans?

ERISA imposes standards of conduct and responsibility on applicable plan fiduciaries (i.e., persons having authority or control over the management of pension fund assets). The law also requires that plan administrators disclose relevant financial information to employees and the government. It sets certain minimum standards that pension plans must meet in order to qualify for preferential tax treatment, and it provides legal remedies to employees and their beneficiaries for violations.

Q 8:82   To whom do the ERISA provisions apply?

ERISA generally applies to private employers that maintain employee benefit plans. It covers: almost all employers except federal, state, and local government entities and tax-exempt churches; plans maintained solely to comply with a state workers' compensation, unemployment, or disability insurance law; and plans that are maintained by multinational corporations primarily for the benefit of non-resident aliens.

Q 8:83   What are the main features of ERISA?

The two main features are the imposition of standards for fiduciary responsibility and the setting of minimum standards for pension plan requirements.

Q 8:84   Are employee benefits covered by ERISA?

Many fringe benefits are referred to as employee welfare benefit plans under the Act. Some ERISA provisions apply to such plans; others do not. For example, fringe benefits normally do not vest (as pension benefits do). On the other hand, employers are required to develop, maintain, and administer welfare benefit plans with the same high level of responsibility with which they maintain pension plans.

Q 8:85   What sort of fringe benefits make up employee welfare benefit plans?

Such diverse fringe benefits as severance pay and the continuation of health insurance for retirees have been held by various courts to come under the provisions of ERISA. Thus, at the very least, these benefits cannot be administered in an arbitrary and capricious fashion by the employer, even if the employer has made no contractual commitment to the employees about them.

Q 8:86   Can a creditor garnish an employee's welfare plan benefits?

Although ERISA regulations prevent creditors from garnishing or attaching an employee's pension benefits, the U.S. Supreme Court has held that the same protection does not extend to other welfare benefit plans. [Mackey v. Lanier Collections Agency & Serv. Inc., 486 U.S. 825 (1988)] In other words, if a creditor can garnish the money under a state garnishment statute, ERISA does not pre-empt such garnishment. For example, an employee's vacation or holiday pay is not protected from a garnishment order, even though the Act clearly covers this benefit for other purposes.

Q 8:87   Can an employee execute a binding release of vested pension rights under ERISA?

ERISA's anti-alienation provision [29 U.S.C. § 1056(d)], prevents most creditors from attaching or garnishing an employee's pension benefits. This is so even if the employee attempts to assign or alienate them. Logic suggests that an employee likewise cannot execute a binding release to relinquish a vested right in a pension plan; however, the U.S. Court of Appeals for the Third Circuit in 1993 reached a contrary conclusion in a case in which the employee released his ERISA rights as part of a broad release in a severance agreement. The appeals court overturned the trial judge's order that Philadelphia National Bank pay the plaintiff, William McVeigh, some $51,000 from the estate of John T. Dorrance, who had employed McVeigh to fly Dorrance's personal aircraft for nine years. When Dorrance died in April 1989, he had 25 employees. The bank offered each a lump-sum severance payment, using the formula of a month's pay for each year of service to the decedent. The release in the severance agreement was a broad one that expressly included claims under "any retirement plan." The court found nothing in ERISA to make such a provision in a termination agreement invalid. [1993 *BNA Daily Labor Report* 63, Apr. 6, 1993, at 1]

Q 8:88   Who is a fiduciary under ERISA?

A fiduciary can be any person exercising discretionary authority or control over the management of the benefit plan or the disposition of the plan's assets. It can also be anyone who renders or has the authority or responsibility to render investment advice (for which he or she is compensated) about the plan's money or other property. Anyone who has any discretionary authority or responsibility in the administration of the plan is also a fiduciary. Consultants and advisors are not normally considered fiduciaries but may be found to be fiduciaries if their expertise is used in a managerial, administrative, or advisory capacity. ERISA requires that all pension plans designate at least one fiduciary to manage and control the plan's operation.

Q 8:89   What liability does a non-fiduciary advisor have under ERISA?

Under ERISA, non-fiduciary advisors to pension plans-usually referred to as "service providers"—can conceivably include attorneys, accountants, actuaries, money managers and consultants; this latter term being a catch-all for advisors who may not fit into any of the foregoing standard categories. The liability of non-fiduciary service providers has never been explicitly covered in ERISA or its amendments.

Q 8:90   What are the fiduciary responsibilities under ERISA?

They are as follows:

- All pension plans must be written and must provide a procedure for establishing and administering funding policy that is consistent with the plan's objectives and the law's requirements.

- The plan must specify the manner in which contributions to the fund and payments from the fund will be made.

- The plan must describe the procedure for allocating responsibility for plan administration and operation.

- The plan's assets must be held in trust.

- There must be a procedure for handling claims made by participants and beneficiaries.

Q 8:91 To what standards are fiduciaries held under ERISA?

Fiduciaries are held to the common law of the "prudent man rule." The fiduciary must act "with the care, skill, prudence, and diligence that a prudent man acting in a like capacity and familiar with such matters would use in the conduct of an enterprise of like character." For instance, fiduciaries must discharge their duties solely in the interest of the participants and their beneficiaries for the exclusive purpose of providing benefits to them and defraying the reasonable expenses of the plan. A fiduciary must diversify the plan's investments to minimize the risk of large losses, unless under particular circumstances it would be more prudent not to diversify.

Q 8:92 What behavior must a fiduciary avoid under ERISA?

A fiduciary or other person with an interest in a plan normally cannot: sell or lease property to or from the plan; extend credit to the plan; or furnish goods, services, or facilities to the plan. ERISA also prohibits the transfer of plan assets to, or for the use of, a person with an interest in the plan. Indeed, fiduciaries cannot use or deal with the assets of the plan for their own interests. Fiduciaries are also forbidden to receive any consideration or to benefit personally from persons involved with any transaction that involves the plan's assets. The plan cannot invest more than 10 percent of its assets in the securities or property of an employer of the participating employees, and such investments must still meet the prudent man rule, as outlined in Q 8:91. However, unintentional or innocent mistakes generally do not result in a breach of fiduciary duty. In *Bell v. Pfizer, Inc.* [2010 WL 3385949 (2d Cir. Aug. 30, 2010)], the court held that it was not a breach of fiduciary duty for unintentional misstatements regarding non-ERISA plan consequences of a retirement decision. Similarly, in *Shook v. Avaya, Inc.* [2010 WL 4292065 (3d Cir. Nov. 2, 2010)], the court held that no ERISA claim could be maintained by a participant for an alleged miscalculation made by the employer as to the expected pension benefits for his wife's retirement, when the participant could provide no evidence that he detrimentally relied on the alleged misrepresentation.

Q 8:93   Who constitutes a person with an interest in a plan under ERISA rules?

ERISA defines a *person with an interest in the plan* to include a fiduciary, a person providing services to the plan, an employer whose employees are covered by the plan or an owner having 50 percent or more interest in such an employer.

Q 8:94   What liability does a fiduciary face for breaching a fiduciary duty?

A fiduciary is liable for any losses resulting from the breach of any duties, responsibilities, or obligations to the plan. The fiduciary must refund any profits made through personal use of the plan's assets. The fiduciary may be subject to any other equitable or remedial measures that a court may deem appropriate, including removal of the fiduciary.

Q 8:95   Can a fiduciary be liable for the breach of duty by a co-fiduciary?

There are three circumstances under which a fiduciary can be liable for the wrongful acts of a co-fiduciary:

- Knowingly participating in, or trying to conceal, a wrongful act or omission of another fiduciary;
- Enabling another fiduciary to commit a breach by failing to comply with his or her own fiduciary responsibilities; and
- Failing to make reasonable efforts to remedy a breach by another fiduciary after becoming aware of it.

Q 8:96   Can a fiduciary avoid liability through an exculpatory clause in a plan?

No. Exculpatory clauses, which seek to protect fiduciaries from liability for breaches of their duties, are generally held to be void because they contravene public policy. A fiduciary can procure insurance against liability for breach of duty; however, if the plan provides such insurance for the fiduciary, the insurance company must be allowed to recover from the fiduciary any amounts paid out under the policy.

Q 8:97   Are fiduciaries responsible for events occurring before and after their tenure?

No. Fiduciaries are not responsible for other people's breaches of fiduciary duties that occur either before or after they are fiduciaries of the plan.

Q 8:98   Who enforces ERISA's requirements on fiduciary duty?

Fiduciary duties under ERISA are enforced by the DOL. Plan participants and beneficiaries also have the right to attempt to enforce their own rights through plan grievance procedures, and, once those are exhausted, through court actions. The DOL can bring a lawsuit against a fiduciary who breaches any duties, obligations, or responsibilities under the Act. Plan participants or beneficiaries bringing such a lawsuit, if successful, can also recover legal fees and costs. The IRS can impose an excise tax against a plan receiving preferential tax treatment if the plan engages in prohibited transactions. Alternatively, the Secretary of Labor can level a civil penalty against the plan for the same types of violations.

Q 8:99   What types of pension plans does ERISA recognize?

ERISA recognizes defined benefit plans and defined contribution plans.

Q 8:100   What is a *defined benefit plan*?

It is a pension plan that ensures that eligible employees or their beneficiaries receive a specified monthly income for life.

Q 8:101   How does ERISA ensure that eligible employees or their beneficiaries receive a guaranteed benefit under a defined benefit pension plan?

ERISA provides an insurance plan to guarantee the benefits. That insurance plan is administered by the Pension Benefit Guaranty Corporation (PBGC), which is a quasi-independent governmental entity created by ERISA and financed by a premium levied against employers. The PBGC was created to insure employees against the loss of their benefits when a defined benefit plan is terminated. The PBGC collects a premium toward an insurance fund from employers offering pensions with defined benefits. If an employer cannot meet the payment requirements of a defined benefit plan, the PBGC pays monthly benefits to the participating employees, up to a maximum monthly amount.

Q 8:102   What is a *defined contribution pension plan*?

It is a plan under which an employer makes a fixed-share contribution to a retirement account for each employee. These funds are invested on behalf of the participating employees, who receive the proceeds on retirement.

Q 8:103   Are defined contribution plans insured by the PBGC?

No. The pension benefits under a defined contribution plan are not insured against failure of the company and are not covered by the PBGC.

Q 8:104   Do pension plans receive preferential tax treatment under ERISA?

Pension plans can receive preferential tax treatment if they are "qualified plans"—that is, if they meet certain minimum requirements set forth by ERISA.

Q 8:105   What is *vesting*?

Vesting is the legal event that makes an employee's entitlement to plan benefits non-forfeitable. Vesting applies only to pension plans, not to other employee benefit plans; however, an employer can commit to continuing other kinds of benefit plans. For example, it can contractually promise employees that their health insurance benefits will continue after retirement. Once such a promise is made and the employee retires, the employer may find it difficult to renege on it legally. But vesting affects retirees' ability to renege as well. In *Wood v. Detroit Diesel Corp.* [607 F.3d 427 (6th Cir. 2010)], the court held that collectively bargained agreements capping an employer's contribution for retiree health benefits continued to apply to retirees who retired during the time period the caps were in place, despite non-renewal of the caps in later collectively bargained agreements. Essentially, the retirees' health benefits vested at the point of retirement while those caps were in place.

Q 8:106   What are ERISA vesting requirements?

Pension benefits are vested when an employee has a non-forfeitable right to those benefits, even if the employee, at the present time, has no legal right to collect them or is not employed by that particular employer at the time of retirement. When language in a collective bargaining agreement that applies to retired workers clearly provides for company paid medical insurance until age 65, the right becomes vested, and cannot be overcome by general reservation of rights language contained in the plan documents. [Alday v. Raytheon Co., 693 F.3d 772 (9th Cir. 2012)] However, when the plan documents clearly provide that retiree benefits are not vested, and the collective bargaining agreement is silent on the issue, no vesting will occur. [Maytag Corp. v. Int'l Union, United Auto., Aerospace & Agric. Implement Workers of Am., 687 F.3d 1076 (8th Cir. 2012)]

Q 8:107   Can a company ever reduce an employee's pension benefits on account of other benefits received by the employee on retirement?

Yes. Even though an employee has the vested right to enjoy pension plan benefits after the required amount of time, under some circumstances the amount of these benefits may be reduced on a dollar-for-dollar basis as a result of benefits the employee receives from some other program. For instance, some pension plans take into account Social Security payments received by employees. Under ERISA, a qualified plan can be offset by Social Security payments received by the employee. This right to offset benefits against money paid from other sources is known as integration of benefits. The employer should consult legal counsel to determine which benefits from other sources may or may not be integrated with the company's pension plan benefits.

Q 8:108   Can benefit plans covered by ERISA be modified orally?

Oral modification of benefit plans has been rejected under ERISA rules. Under pre-empted state law, an employer used to be able to argue that if it made oral representations to an employee about benefits, the employee could not later deny or contradict those representations. Now, when ERISA applies, changes to a written plan must likewise be in writing.

Q 8:109   Does ERISA create minimum funding requirements for pension plans?

Companies with tax-qualified pension plans must set aside enough money each year to cover the benefit liabilities that accrue under the plan during a particular year. These monies are maintained in a funding standard account (i.e., an account that is charged annually with amounts that must be paid to meet minimum funding standards). ERISA also requires payment of pay-service costs—that is, the costs of earned benefits that had been unfunded prior to passage of the law. These must be paid according to a formula on a year-by-year basis as well. Liability resulting from experienced gains and deficiencies of the plan must be amortized in equal installments over no more than 15 years.

Q 8:110   Does discrimination law apply to pension plans?

Qualified pension plans are not allowed to discriminate in favor of the officers, shareholders, or highly compensated employees of the company. Discrimination is prohibited with respect to benefits, contributions, and coverage of employee classifications. A plan can, however, be limited to salaried or clerical workers—that is, wage-earning (hourly) employees can be excluded. Contributions and benefits of employees must bear a uniform relationship to their total compensation.

Q 8:111   Does ERISA create any reporting and disclosure requirements?

Pension plan administrators have a number of reporting and disclosure obligations under ERISA. They must provide the government and the plan participants with the information necessary to enforce and protect participant rights, ensure non-discriminatory operation of the plan, discover prohibited transactions, and give advance warning of a possible plan failure.

Q 8:112   What information must a pension plan provide to its participants?

A pension plan must provide participants and beneficiaries with a summary plan description. It must contain the name and address of the plan and its administrator and trustee, requirements for participation, vesting and disqualification rules, procedures for presenting claims, and procedures for appealing the denial of a claim. The plan must also provide participants and beneficiaries with a summary of any significant modifications to the plan and an annual report.

Q 8:113   What information must the pension plan provide to the DOL?

A pension plan must file a summary plan description similar to the one that it gives to participants and beneficiaries, and a summary of any material modifications made to the plan. In addition, the PBGC requires a detailed annual premium filing form and notice of any "reportable event"—that is, changes reducing payable benefits, inability to pay the benefits that are due, failure to meet a minimum funding standard, or a transaction with an owner. If a plan intends to terminate, a notice of that intent must be filed with the PBGC at least 10 days before the termination is effective. Very detailed financial disclosure forms must be filed with the IRS each year.

Q 8:114   Can a company terminate a pension plan?

Yes, ERISA allows for the termination of virtually any pension plan, provided the company follows the laws that protect the beneficiaries of the plan and those with vested rights in the plan.

Q 8:115   What steps are required to terminate a pension plan?

First, the notice of intention to terminate the plan must be filed with the PBGC not less than 10 days before the termination takes effect. The PBGC will then step in to ensure that all rights are protected in the wake of the plan's termination.

Q 8:116   What does the PBGC do when a plan is terminated?

The PBGC pays minimum monthly benefits to those receiving payments under the plan.

Q 8:117   Upon termination of a pension plan, how are the plan's assets allocated?

ERISA outlines a list of priorities for the allocation of a terminated plan's assets:

- Voluntary employee contributions;
- Required employee contributions;
- Benefits to participants who have been receiving benefits for at least three years;
- All other insured benefits;
- All other non-forfeitable benefits;
- All other benefits.

If the assets are insufficient to handle all of the claims within any one of the classes, assets are allocated on a pro rata basis within the last subclass that receives benefits under the allocation.

Q 8:118 If a pension plan has insufficient assets to satisfy claims, is the employer liable?

The employer is liable to the PBGC for 100 percent of the underfunding; however, this liability is limited to 30 percent of the employer's net worth. This liability constitutes a government lien against the employer's property and is treated as a federal tax lien.

Q 8:119 Is the owner of a corporation personally liable for an underfunded pension plan?

In 1989, one U.S. appeals court ruled that the president and sole shareholder of a company in default on its pension funds was not personally liable to make up the deficiencies. Four multi-employer pension plans had sued the company for claimed arrears. The corporation declared bankruptcy, and a federal judge ruled that the president, its sole shareholder, had to pay arrears. The appellate court overruled the judge, finding that neither the plain meaning nor the legislative history of ERISA calls for an alter-ego interpretation. [Scarbrough v. Perez, 870 F.2d 1079 (6th Cir. 1989)]

Similarly, the Seventh Circuit Court of Appeals held that former corporate officers of a defunct corporation could not be held personally liable, absent circumstances calling for "piercing the corporate veil," for delinquent contributions to plumbers' union pension and welfare funds. [Plumbers' Pensions Fund v. Niedrich, 891 F.2d 1297 (7th Cir. 1989)] This same court concluded differently, however, in a case in which the non-union half of a "double-breasted" trucking and excavating operation was found to be the alter ego of the unionized firm. The excavator's labor contract with the Teamsters Union required weekly pension contributions for three drivers. The owner first tried to talk the Teamsters into canceling the contract out of business necessity. When the union refused, the owners started up the on-union firm, took over the hauling operations, and stopped the pension contributions. Even though the new firm's trucking operations were later diversified, the court found it was started up only to avoid the pension obligations; therefore, the court found one company to be the alter ego of the other and ordered it to make the contributions current. [Cent States Pension Fund v. Sloan, 902 F.2d 593 (7th Cir. 1990)]

Q 8:120   Can a company that terminates a plan recover surplus funds in it?

If there are surplus funds in a pension plan after it has been terminated and the appropriate allocations have been made, the employer can recover that surplus under certain circumstances:

- All liabilities to participating employees and beneficiaries under the plan must have been satisfied;
- The recovery of surplus assets does not violate any section of the law; and
- The pension plan must provide that the employer may recover surplus funds.

Q 8:121   Can an employer withdraw from a multi-employer pension plan?

When ERISA was first enacted, multi-employer pension plans were not covered; however, the Multiemployer Pension Plan Amendments Act of 1980 extended the PBGC's authority to these kinds of plans. Under these amendments, an employer wishing to withdraw from a multi-employer plan must pay its proportionate share of any unfunded vested benefits in the plan. The calculations of unfunded vested benefits and the employer's individual share are very complex, involving a rolling five-year experience period. Some employers have been unpleasantly surprised to discover just how large their withdrawal liability had grown over time. For instance, a client who was trying to sell his business for $500,000 learned that his withdrawal liability from the Teamster's Pension Plan Fund for Philadelphia and vicinity was almost half the asking price.

Q 8:122   Who enforces ERISA?

Responsibility for enforcing ERISA is spread among several governmental entities. Fiduciary duties and reporting requirements are enforced by the DOL. The IRS enforces minimum vesting and participation requirements and imposes tax penalties for funding violations and prohibited transactions. The PBGC steps in when a plan is terminated, ensuring that the beneficiaries do not lose their benefits. Finally, individual participants and beneficiaries may act as "private attorney generals" by bringing lawsuits to enforce their rights.

Q 8:123   Are there criminal penalties for violating ERISA?

Yes. ERISA provides criminal penalties for willful violations of reporting and disclosure requirements. A person who willfully violates one of these requirements may be subject to a fine of up to $5,000, a prison term of up to one year, or both. Corporate and union fiduciaries may be subject to a fine of up to $100,000.

Q 8:124   What civil actions can be brought against a pension plan under ERISA rules?

A participant or beneficiary in a plan can sue if the plan administrator fails to furnish information to which that person is entitled. A civil suit can also be brought to recover benefits that are due under a plan. A participant may collect up to $100 a day in penalties from an administrator who fails to provide, on request, the information to which the participant is entitled. Participants, beneficiaries, and the Secretary of Labor may bring lawsuits to clarify rights to future benefits, to enjoin a violation of ERISA or the terms of a pension plan, and to obtain relief from a breach of fiduciary duties.

Q 8:125   What types of claims can be brought by participants and beneficiaries under ERISA?

The various claims provided for participants and beneficiaries under ERISA generally can be categorized as follows:

- Claims for benefits;
- Failure to comply with technical disclosure and notification requirements;
- Breach of fiduciary duty; and
- Discrimination.

A claim for benefits under an employee benefit plan is provided under ERISA Section 502(a)(1)(B). This section provides a civil cause of action by a participant or beneficiary to recover benefits under a plan or to enforce rights under the term of the plan. Before such a claim can be brought to court, aggrieved beneficiaries or participants are generally required to exhaust the administrative remedies of appeal that must be contained within a plan, unless it can be demonstrated that resort to administrative remedies would be futile. [Miller v. Metropolitan Life Ins. Co., 925 F.2d 979 (6th Cir. 1991)]

The standard of review by a court is limited with respect to benefit claims. Assuming that the language of the plan at issue provides the plan administrator with discretion to determine benefits due under a plan (which most do), a de novo review of the denial is generally not permitted. Instead, the sole determination is whether the plan administrator abused its discretion based upon the information available to the plan administrator before it made its decision. In essence, by this standard, the plan administrator does not necessarily have to make the right decision. The decision needs to be reasonable, based upon information reasonably available to the administrator at the time the decision is made.

Violations of ERISA technical reporting, disclosure, and notification requirements are penalized. In addition, there is a penalty of up to $100 per day for the failure or refusal of a plan to provide information requested by a participant or beneficiary within 30 days of the request. [ERISA § 502(a)(1)(A)]

The fiduciary obligations contained within ERISA are broad, but essentially regulate the creation and administration of plans, as well as investment of plan assets. Fiduciaries are held to the "prudent man rule," which means that the fiduciary must act "with the care, skill, prudence, and diligence that a prudent man acting in a like capacity and familiar with such matters would use in the conduct of an enterprise of like nature." In essence, fiduciaries are required to exercise their duties solely in the interest of participants and beneficiaries, and to diversify the plan's investments to minimize the risk of large losses. [ERISA § 404(a)(1)] As the court held in *Guyan International, Inc. v. Professional Benefits Administrators, Inc.* [689 F.3d 793 (6th Cir. 2012)], plan administrators who engage in self-dealing with fund assets, leaving hundreds of thousands of dollars of unpaid claims for plan participants, clearly breached their fiduciary duties. However, merely showing lack of diversity does not result in fiduciary liability, unless the participants can establish that the failure to diversify resulted in losses to the plan. [Plasterer's Local Union No. 96 Pension Plan v. Pepper, 2011 WL 6000580 (4th Cir. Dec. 1, 2011)] In *Guididas v. Community National Bank Corp.* [2012 WL 3025162 (M.D. Fla. July 24, 2012)], the court held that a fiduciary, who was aware of a bank's improper business and banking practices, breached its fiduciary duty when it continued to offer the bank's stock as an investment option despite this knowledge. Sections 409 and 502 of the statute provide that a fiduciary breaching fiduciary duties may be liable to "make good" any losses to the plan resulting from the breach, restore any unlawful profits made by the fiduciary as a result of an impermissible use of plan assets, and award such other equitable relief as the court deems appropriate. It is important to note that breach of fiduciary duty does not result in monetary relief to the individual participants or beneficiaries; instead, the plan receives any benefits due. A widow who claimed breach of fiduciary duty resulting in cancellation of her deceased husband's life insurance policy was not entitled to recover individualized benefits equal to the lost value of the insurance policy for breach of fiduciary duty under ERISA. [*Walker v. Federal Exp. Corp.*, 492 Fed. Appx. 559 (6th Cir. 2012)] However, when there is no wrongful affirmative action or misrepresentation that interferes with benefits, breach of fiduciary duty will be much more difficult to demonstrate. Such was the case in *Green v. ExxonMobil Corp.* [470 F.3d 415 (1st Cir. 2006)] In the case, various life insurance benefit applications were not sent to a newly hired employee until after he died, about one week after he started to work. Although the applications, it would seem, should have been available for the employee to fill out on his first day of employment, such was not the case and this failure may have resulted in a significant loss of benefits for his beneficiaries. Nonetheless, the court concluded a fiduciary's duty of care is that of reasonable diligence, and sending out application forms within a week or so after employment commences, with no promise or plan deadline to the contrary, did not violate this standard and left the beneficiaries with no claims for breach of fiduciary duty. In *Stark v. Mars, Inc.* [2012 WL 2918410 (S.D. Ohio, July 17, 2012)], the court did not find breach of fiduciary duty in connection with erroneous values provided to an employee regarding an employee's pension benefits. In *Loomis v. Exelon Corp.* [658 F.3d 667 (7th Cir. 2011)], the participants in a defined contribution plan claimed that the administrators had violated their fiduciary duty by offering so-called "retail" mutual funds as opposed to "wholesale" funds that did not have the expenses of the retail mutual funds. Even though the employer had the ability to offer wholesale or institutional funds, the court held that it was not a breach of fiduciary duty to offer the retail funds in which the participants received the same terms and bore the same expenses as the general public.

Under Section 510 of ERISA, participants or beneficiaries can bring claims against employers who discriminate against them for exercising any right to which they are entitled under the employee benefit plan or for interfering with the attainment of any right for which they may become eligible under the plan. To establish a prima facie case, generally the plaintiff must demonstrate through direct or circumstantial evidence that he or she was discharged, fined, suspended, expelled, disciplined, or discriminated against for exercising rights under the plan or to interfere with the attainment of benefits under the plan. (See Q 8:130.)

Q 8:126   How do courts determine whether there is an abuse of discretion by a plan administrator with discretion under the plan documents?

In *Belluardo v. Cox Enterprises, Inc.* [2005 WL 3078632 (6th Cir.) (unpublished decision)], newspaper carriers claimed that they were entitled to pension benefits under the newspaper's pension plan. At issue was language in the plan that defined covered employees as "any employee of the company except any employee . . . who is classified as a commissioned newspaper carrier under the company's personnel policy." Although newspapers historically have treated newspaper carriers as independent contractors and not employees, the newspaper carriers claimed that they did not fit within the exemption under the plan documents because there was no written personnel policy that classified them as commissioned newspaper carriers, in accordance with the terms of the plan documents. After determining that the plan documents provided the plan administrators with discretion, the court concluded that its review was limited to whether the plan administrators abused their discretion in interpreting the plan documents and concluded that the administrator's interpretation of the term personnel policy in the plan documents to include past practices in addition to written documents was reasonable and not an abuse of discretion. As such, the court found the newspaper carriers were properly excluded under the exemption contained in the plan as commissioned newspaper carriers who would not qualify for pension benefits.

In *Sherwood v. United Parcel Flexible Benefits Plan Short-Term Disability Plan* [156 Fed. Appx. 941 (9th Cir. 2005)], an employee who was denied short-term disability benefits challenged the decision under ERISA Section 502. When the employee made claim for benefits, she submitted detailed information concerning her reaction to various medications due to her chronic hepatitis, but the plan administrator was confused and sought further medical evidence to substantiate her report. When further information was not provided, the plan administrator denied the claim. Although the employee claimed that the administrator cherry-picked which information to consider and/or failed to request pertinent information, the court, finding that the plan administrator had discretion under the plan documents, concluded that the administrator's insistence on additional evidence may not have been the best or only way in which the administrator might have exercised its discretion. The court found that exercise of discretion by the administrator was reasonable and that an abuse of discretion had not occurred. Similarly, in matters where plan documents provide administrators with discretion, this deference that courts provide to the decisions of plan administrators includes issues concerning the interpretation of plan documents. In *Colucci v. AGFA Corporation Severance Pay Plan* [431 F.3d 170 (4th Cir. 2005)], at issue was whether an employee's first day of employment with an employer, under the plan documents for purposes of determining seniority and benefit payments, was the employee's original hire date or the date the employee was rehired after resigning from the position previously. Although the plan itself did not contain an explanation, the court concluded that, in view of the discretion given to the plan administrator under the plan documents, the decision that the "first day" related to the date that the employee was rehired after resigning was not an abuse of discretion. Similarly, in *Johnson v. Burt Bell/Pete Rozelle NFL* [468 F.3d 1082 (8th Cir. 2006)], in determining whether a board decision under the plan as to Johnson's date of disability was appropriate, the court only reviewed the matter under a deferential standard that provided discretion to the board and limited the court's consideration as to whether an abuse of discretion by the board had occurred, despite claims of conflict of interest.

In *Kovach v. Zurich American Insurance Co.* [587 F.3d 323 (6th Cir. 2009)], a beneficiary of an accidental death and dismemberment policy sued a plan administrator challenging the denial of benefits in connection with a motorcycle accident. The plan administrator denied the benefits on the basis that the beneficiary was intoxicated at the time of the motorcycle accident. Because of the intoxication, the plan administrator claimed that the incident was not "accidental" within the terms of the policy and, in any event, was a "self-inflicted" wound, an exception from coverage. Although the court acknowledged that the beneficiary intentionally drank in excess and then rode his motorcycle, the court found that he did not do so with the mind toward harming himself and therefore could not be considered "self-inflicted" and could not view the accident as "highly likely" to occur as the result of the drinking which would be necessary to find that the incident was not "accidental." As a result, the court found the plan administrator's decision to be arbitrary and capricious.

In *Manning v. American Republic Insurance Co.* [604 F.3d 1030 (8th Cir. 2010)], the court held that a plan administrator with discretionary authority to determine eligibility for benefits did not abuse its discretion in denying a claim for short-term disability benefits when it declined to consider certifications offered by a physician's assistant, and the employee failed to document the allegedly disabling medical condition by objective disabling signs and systems.

In *Khoury v. Group Health Plan, Inc.* [615 F.3d 946 (8th Cir. 2010)], the court held that a plan administrator, having discretionary authority, did not abuse its discretion when, in determining "basic monthly earnings" from which long-term disability payments would be determined, did not take into consideration wages paid for on-call work performed by the physician during his employment. The court found that the on-call services were essentially extra work and akin to overtime, which the plan did not provide to be taken into consideration for determining the "basic monthly earnings" from which long-term disability payments would be determined.

In *Weitzenkamp v. Unum Life Insurance Co. of America* [2011 WL 4375637 (7th Cir. Oct. 25, 2011)], the court held that a 24-month limitation in a disability policy for conditions primarily based on self-reported symptoms did not apply to a condition that was diagnosed and objectively verifiable, even though the primary symptom, pain, involved self-reporting. The court concluded that the plan administrator's interpretation and application of the limitation was arbitrary and capricious. In *Riley v. Sun Life and Health Insurance Co.* [657 F.3d 739 (8th Cir. 2011)], at issue was the decision of the plan administrator to offset disability benefits against benefits the employee was receiving under the Veteran's Benefits Act. Although the plan provided the plan administrator with discretion to determine benefits, for which an abuse of discretion standard would apply, the court held that the administrator's decision to apply the offset was not a decision that was based on the administrator's construction of existing law and as such, the determination was reviewed *de novo*. The court held that the offset was an improper interpretation of law.

Q 8:127   Is it a conflict of interest to be both the plan administrator and the payer of benefits?

In the U.S. Supreme Court case of *Metropolitan Life Insurance Company v. Glenn* [128 S. Ct. 2343 (2008)], the Court held that a conflict of interest arising from the dual role of an entity as both the ERISA plan administrator and the payer of plan benefits may be taken into consideration in determining whether the plan administrator has abused its discretion in denying benefits, although the Court allowed that the significance of the dual role necessarily depended on the facts of each particular case. Having established that the conflict of interest could be taken into consideration, the Court then affirmed a court of appeals decision to set aside the insurance company's denial of benefits in light of the facts that demonstrated that the insurance company, which was both the plan administrator and payer of benefits, failed to reconcile its conclusion that the plaintiff could not work with the Social Security Administration's conclusion that plaintiff could, failed to provide all of the treating physician reports to its own hired experts, failed to take into account evidence indicating that the plaintiff's condition was aggravated, and the insurance company's focus on one report suggesting that plaintiff could work, as opposed to other more detailed reports indicating that plaintiff could not.

Q 8:128   Does ERISA require companies to extend coverage for domestic partners?

No. Although a number of companies have adopted policies that extend coverage to domestic partners, there is no federal law requiring such an extension at this time.

Q 8:129   Can beneficiaries or participants maintain claims under state law for damages caused by a misrepresentation by a plan administrator in connection with an ERISA benefit plan?

Section 514(a) of ERISA [29 U.S.C. § 1144(a)] pre-empts "[a]ny and all state laws insofar as they may now or hereafter relate to any employee benefit plan." The U.S. Supreme Court, in *Shaw v. Delta Airlines, Inc.* [463 U.S. 85 (1983)], held that Congress used the words "relate to" in the above section in their "broadest sense." As such, with few exceptions, state law claims, including those founded under state common law, are generally considered to be pre-empted by ERISA legislation, and recourse for beneficiaries and plan participants exists only under the prescribed bases for relief under ERISA. As such, common-law state claims of fraud, misrepresentation, and the like against plan administrators for damages allegedly caused by misrepresentations were held to be pre-empted by federal law in *Juntunen v. Blue Cross Blue Shield of Michigan.* [2003 Mich. App. LEXIS 1308 (Mich. Ct. App. May 29, 2003)] In addition, state law claims that are inconsistent with or impact on fiduciary rights under ERISA are pre-empted. In *Hutchison v. Fifth Third Bank Corp.* [2006 WL 3436040 (6th Cir. 2006)], participants in an ESOP brought a state court action against their employer, claiming that amendments to the ESOP were a breach of contract. The court, finding that the amendments were consistent with the plan documents, held that such a claim could not be maintained and was pre-empted by federal law. Similarly, in *Helfrich v. Exxon Mobile Corp.* [465 F.3d 566 (3d Cir. 2006)], the court refused to analyze an employee's claim for severance benefits under extra-ERISA rules such as "unilateral contract principals" under common law, but rather, found the employees were not entitled to severance benefits by utilization of analysis under the ERISA framework.

However, the Fifth Circuit joined a growing number of circuits that recognize the common-law doctrine of equitable estoppel as a cognizable legal theory under ERISA for misrepresentations. In a case of first impression, the court in *Mello v. Sara Lee Corp.* [431 F.3d 440 (5th Cir. 2005)] concluded that equitable estoppel is available to an employee if the employee can establish (1) material misrepresentation, (2) reasonable and detrimental reliance upon the representation, and (3) extraordinary circumstances. In *Mello*, the employee demonstrated that she had been continuously told for some time that although she had been working with the defendant company for only a few years, her employer would credit her service date from the date she started with the prior employer that the company purchased. This representation was made continually, and the employee also received various illustrations informing her that her pension benefits would be based on the credited service date. However, the actual plan documents were explicit that such crediting of her prior service would not be made, and as such, the court concluded that the plaintiff could not have reasonably relied upon the misrepresentations because the plan terms clearly provided that her prior service would not be credited in connection with determining her pension benefits.

State laws that apply broadly to health care institutions and health benefit providers but do not "relate" to an employee benefit plan are not pre-empted by ERISA. For example, in *Pharmaceutical Care Management Ass'n v. Rowe* [429 F.3d 294 (1st Cir. 2005)], a national trade association of pharmacy benefit managers brought an action seeking to enjoin enforcement of Maine's Unfair Prescription Drug Practices Act. The Act, among other things, made pharmacy benefit managers fiduciaries in relation to their role as middlemen in providing prescription drugs from manufacturers to pharmacies, and established a number of requirements that must be met by the pharmacy benefit managers. Although much of the work performed by pharmacy benefit managers clearly would have had some effect on drugs that may have been covered under a variety of employee welfare benefit plans, the court concluded that the pharmacy benefit managers were not fiduciaries, under ERISA, and that the law had no "connection to" or "reference to" an employee welfare benefit plan, such that pre-emption was not warranted. [*See* California Div. of Labor Standards Enforcement v. Dillingham Constr., NA, Inc., 519 U.S. 316, 324 (1997).] In *Stevenson v. Bank of New York Co.*, Inc. [609 F.3d 56 (2d Cir. 2010)], an employee brought an action against his former employer and various executives for state common law claims of breach of contract, misrepresentation, and fraud based on the defendants' alleged failure to honor their promise to maintain various benefits and pension during the tenure of a manager. Because the claims, in and of themselves, did not actually relate to the welfare benefit plans themselves, but rather, formed the alleged considerations for the continuation of benefits, the court held that the claims were separate and distinct from the plans themselves, and as such, were not preempted under ERISA.

Q 8:130   How are discrimination claims handled under ERISA?

Under Section 501 of ERISA, participants or beneficiaries can bring claims against employers who discriminate against them for exercising any right to which they are entitled under the employee benefit plan or for interfering with the attainment of any right for which they may become eligible under the plan. To establish a prima facie case, generally the plaintiff must demonstrate through direct or circumstantial evidence that he or she was discharged, fined, suspended, expelled, disciplined, or discriminated against for exercising rights under the plan or someone interfered with the attainment of benefits under the plan. A common scenario is an employee who is fired just prior to attaining benefits under a plan, such as a pension plan, who believes the firing was intended to avoid providing plan benefits. It is important to note that Section 510 discrimination claims are specific intent claims that require the plaintiff to provide evidence showing "specific intent" to discriminate. To constitute specific intent, the employment action at issue must be motivated by prohibited discrimination and interference under Section 510. Both direct and circumstantial evidence can be utilized for purposes of demonstrating specific intent, much in the same way that direct or circumstantial evidence is utilized for purposes of inferring discriminatory conduct in connection with Title VII. Aside from egregious instances of willful misconduct, relief is generally limited to equitable relief and monitory damages equal to the benefits denied. Such damages as mental distress and money losses in excess of contractual rights are generally not accorded.

Despite ERISA's broad pre-emption provisions, ERISA does not pre-empt federal law, and federal discrimination claims outside ERISA are actionable if the termination runs afoul of other federal civil rights statutes. For example, the ADEA prohibits discharge because of age. [29 U.S.C. § 623(a)] It is not unusual that a claim based on the allegations that an employer terminated an employee to avoid pension benefits under ERISA is supplemented by an ADEA claim, claiming that age was a determining factor in the decision, because most voluntary retirement systems are age-based, at least in part.

Q 8:131   What courts have jurisdiction over ERISA lawsuits?

The federal courts have exclusive jurisdiction over all lawsuits brought under ERISA, except for actions to recover benefits or to clarify the right to future benefits, which can be brought in state or federal court. A qualified pension plan must provide a method for claim resolution. Participants and beneficiaries must usually exhaust these plan procedures and remedies for resolving claims before going to court.

Q 8:132   Can an employer terminate or modify welfare benefits being paid to its retirees?

ERISA does not mandate the vesting of welfare, as opposed to pension, benefits; the issue of lifetime entitlement and modification depends on contract principles. Whether or not the employer formed a binding and enforceable contract with the employee to continue a welfare benefit for life after retirement may depend on statute or the common law of contract. In *Johnson v. Lend Lease Real Estate Investment* [467 F.3d 1131 (8th Cir. 2006)], an employer had sent letters to former employees, advising them that the employer would continue, at its cost, to provide health and medical benefits through its welfare benefit plans and did in fact continue such benefits for many years. However, when the employer terminated its operations in the United States, it also terminated its prior arrangement for the continuation of benefits for former employees. The employees sued under ERISA, claiming that the termination letters constituted free-standing plans under ERISA for which they were entitled to benefits for life. The court, in reviewing the letters, concluded the letters in and of themselves did not constitute an ERISA plan, but rather was a gratuitous arrangement referencing benefits through the company's ERISA-based plans, which all provided for amendments and/or terminations. As such, the former employee's ERISA claim was dismissed in the district court and was upheld by the Eighth Circuit.

When a collective bargaining agreement is involved, Section 301 of the Labor Management Relations (Taft-Hartley) Act is relevant to the lawsuit. [*See, e.g.,* UAW v. Yard-Man Inc., 716 F.2d 1476 (6th Cir. 1983).] Beyond ERISA and this Act, principles of common-law contract interpretation are relevant.

Some of the factors that can give rise to an inference of lifetime coverage include:

- Oral or written statements to retirees;
- Statements and proposals made during contract negotiations;
- Continuation of insurance during strikes;
- A cost-analysis completed in preparation for a plant shutdown;
- Changes or the lack of changes in the benefits of former retirees, and whether or not any such changes were contested; and
- Failure by the employer to disclose a limitation on the benefit in a summary plan description.

In determining whether the plan provides for vested benefits, courts review the plan documents to determine what promises and representations have been made by the employer. In *Halbach v. Great-West Life & Annuity Insurance Company* [522 F. Supp. 2d 1154 (E.D. Mo. 2007)], at issue was whether benefits for disabled individuals who obtained long-term disability coverage had vested. Although the plan documents specifically provided for amendment or termination of plan benefits, the amending language also provided that such amendment or termination "shall not divest a participant of benefits under the plan to which he has become entitled." [*Halbach* at 1170.] Moreover, the plan specifically stated that all long-term disability recipients' benefits would continue "throughout the term of the participants' long-term disability or until age 65." [*Halbach* at 1170.] As such, the court concluded that the benefits became vested upon a determination of disability, and, therefore, the employer could not amend or terminate the benefits as they related to those participants whose benefits had become vested.

Q 8:133 Have there been any U.S. Supreme Court decisions involving ERISA?

In U.S. Supreme Court case *Raymond B. Yates, M.D., P.C. Profit Sharing Plan v. Hendon* [541 U.S. 1 (2004)], at issue was whether a sole shareholder and president of a professional corporation, in his capacity as a working owner, could qualify as a "participant" in an ERISA plan. The action was brought against the background of a bankruptcy, wherein the owner made a loan repayment to the plan just prior to the filing of his bankruptcy petition. If, as a sole shareholder and president of the professional corporation, he was not deemed to be a participant in an ERISA plan, a loan payment would be a voidable preference that would have to be returned to the trustee. On the other hand, if he was found to be a participant in an ERISA plan, the loan repayment to his plan would be shielded from the trustee under ERISA law. Although the court recognized there were prior circuit court decisions that, in related matters, held that self-employed owners of a pension plan's corporate sponsor are not "employees" under ERISA, the court nonetheless concluded that Congress intended working owners to qualify as plan participants, provided that the plan covers not only working owners but also their non-owner employees. Because from the plan's inception at least one person other than the shareholder and owner and his wife was a plan participant, the court concluded that the plan was covered by ERISA and the loan repayment to the plan prior to filing bankruptcy could not be obtained by the bankruptcy trustee as a voidable preference.

The Supreme Court reversed a Fifth Circuit decision holding that state law claims against a health maintenance organization (HMO) were not pre-empted by ERISA. [Aetna Health, Inc. v. Davila, 542 U.S. 200 (2004)] In the case, participants in an ERISA plan sued the plan administrators under a Texas statute alleging that they had suffered injuries due to the HMO administrators' decision not to provide coverage for treatment recommended by their physicians. Although the Fifth Circuit found that the alleged refusal to cover certain medical services was not pre-empted, the Supreme Court held that the claim fit squarely within remedies available under ERISA for alleged wrongful denial of benefits, and was therefore fully pre-empted by federal law.

ERISA contains a provision that prohibits any pension plan amendment that would reduce a participant's "accrued benefit." [29 U.S.C. § 1054(g)(1)] In situations where amendments are not reserved under plan documents, the anti-cutback rule works to protect employees' legitimate expectations to receive the benefits they were promised. In a case before the Supreme Court, an individual had retired under a plan that contained certain "disqualifying employment" which, if obtained after retirement, would suspend monthly payments until the disqualifying employment was stopped. After the employee at issue retired, the plan expanded the definition of "disqualifying employment," which specifically included the position that the employee took after retirement. The retired employee claimed that the expansion of the disqualifying employment clause violated ERISA's anti-cutback rules in that the accrued benefit to which he had been promised was being cutback, due to the expansion of the disqualifying employment section of the plan. The Supreme Court agreed, holding that an amendment placing materially greater restrictions on the receipt of a benefit reduces the benefit just as surely as a decrease in the size of the monthly benefit amount. [See Central Laborers' Pension Fund v. Heinz, 541 U.S. 739 (2004).]

At issue before the U.S. Supreme Court in LaRue v. DeWolff, Boberg & Associates, Inc. [128 S. Ct. 1020 (2008)] was whether an individual, who claimed that his 401(k) plan employer/administrator breached its fiduciary duties by failing to follow the participant's directions for making changes to investments in a plan account could pursue a claim to have the losses recovered under ERISA. Although the court noted that in general, remedies exist under ERISA for entire plans and not individuals, the court reasoned that ERISA also provides for "make whole" relief such that restoring benefits that would have existed in the plan, but for alleged breach of fiduciary duties, is proper under ERISA. As such, when a breach of fiduciary duty impairs the value of plan assets in a participant's individual account, ERISA allows a remedy for the lost value of plan assets resulting from the breach of fiduciary duty. Similarly, the Eleventh Circuit, in *Lanfear v. Home Depot, Inc.* [536 F.3d 1217 (11th Cir. 2008)], held that an employee's claim against an employer alleging a decrease in the value of a defined contribution account due to alleged breach of fiduciary duty was a claim for restoration of plan benefits, and as such was a proper ERISA claim.

The U.S. Supreme Court in *Kennedy v. Plan Administrator for DuPont Savings and Investment Plan* [129 S. Ct. 865 (2009)], held it was the plan administrator's duty under ERISA to follow the participant's beneficiary designation of his ex-wife despite claims of a common law waiver of benefits by the ex-spouse in connection with the divorce.

Workers' Compensation Insurance

Q 8:134   What is *workers' compensation insurance?*

Workers' compensation insurance was developed at the beginning of this century and is intended to compensate an employee for on-the-job injuries and provide income when such injuries prevent the employee from working either temporarily or permanently. It is the only insurance required by federal and most state laws. Workers' compensation laws have been enacted by the states, and although there are differences in the laws and their administration, there are also many similarities. It is essential that an employer check the compensation law for the state in which the business is located.

Q 8:135   How does an employee qualify for workers' compensation benefits?

To collect workers' compensation benefits, an employee must be injured in the course of employment. If the employee is injured at home, over the weekend or while on vacation, the employee cannot collect benefits under the workers' compensation system. Under most state workers' compensation laws, the injury must have occurred by accident. If the employee is injured by the intentional act of the employer or some other person, many state systems do not provide compensation benefits, although the injured employee can usually obtain relief under tort law, outside of workers' compensation.

Q 8:136   Is an employee entitled to workers' compensation benefits if the on-the-job injury is the result of negligence?

Yes. A worker who is injured because of either his or her own or someone else's negligence can still collect workers' compensation benefits. Only intentional injuries, either self-inflicted or caused by another, are excluded.

Q 8:137   Is workers' compensation more beneficial to the employee than a common-law personal injury lawsuit?

One of the main reasons that the states have adopted the workers' compensation concept is that, before this type of law, employees found it expensive, time-consuming, and difficult to sue their employers successfully. Employers defended such lawsuits by arguing that the employee had assumed the risk of his or her job, that the employee had been negligent, or that the employee had been injured by the negligence of a co-worker and therefore the company was not responsible. All of these traditional defenses have been eliminated by the workers' compensation laws, and thus an employee is entitled to benefits even if he or she is injured because of personal negligence or that of a co-worker. In addition, workers' compensation benefits are usually paid promptly by the insurance carrier or the employer and cannot be arbitrarily terminated by the insurer without appropriate legal process.

Q 8:138   Does the employer receive any advantages from participating in a workers' compensation plan?

The workers' compensation laws provide that participating employers have limited liability—that is, their damages are limited to the payment schedules provided under the law. This is generally preferable to personal injury law, under which a jury can award vast sums of money to injured plaintiffs.

Q 8:139   Can an employee waive his or her rights to receive workers' compensation benefits within a private agreement with the employer, such as a severance agreement?

Generally, workers' compensation plans are program created by state legislatures, grounded in public policy, to provide benefits for employees who are injured on the job, regardless of fault. As such, as a general rule, employees cannot waive their rights to workers' compensation benefits, except in connection with the legislative scheme created by statute. As is the case in Michigan, individuals cannot waive their rights to receive benefits under the state created workers' compensation statutes, except as may otherwise be approved during the claims process in redemptions of claims, as specifically provided by statute. [Mich. Comp. Laws Ann. § 418.815]

Q 8:140   What benefits can an employee receive under a typical workers' compensation law?

As a general rule, state workers' compensation laws provide for two types of benefits. First, weekly or biweekly salary supplements are payable to employees who are permanently or temporarily disabled, whether the disability is total or partial. These benefits may have some time limitation but generally continue for the duration of the disability. By contrast, workers who suffer the loss of a body part may receive, under some state laws, a scheduled lump-sum payment to compensate for the loss or a specified number of weeks of compensation, irrespective of the time period during which the injury actually disables the employee. The law also provides for the payment of medical expenses and often covers therapy and retraining costs for an employee who can no longer perform his or her previous job.

Q 8:141   What if the company disagrees with the worker about the compensability of an on-the-job injury?

State systems vary with respect to how disputes under their workers' compensation laws are handled. Many states have a workers' compensation bureau or board with referees to hear disputes over such issues as whether the injury really occurred in the course of employment and whether the employee is still disabled or has recovered enough to return to work. Other states stipulate that such disputes should be settled within the state court system.

Q 8:142   How can an employer prevent workers' compensation "scamming"?

With the cost of workers' compensation claims climbing (even more than group health insurance premiums by most estimates), preventing workers' compensation scams and malingering is an essential part of most companies' loss control programs. Many experts suggest the following as essential to a successful loss-prevention program:

* Employee safety training to prevent legitimate workplace injuries;
* Creation of light-duty programs for workers who are either recovering from or particularly susceptible to certain injuries;
* Insistence upon early reporting of all job-related injuries, with severe disciplinary penalties (such as termination of employment) for failure to make an early and accurate report of any injury sustained; and
* Consistent, regular contact with off-work employees who are collecting workers' compensation benefits, such as through hand delivery of their benefit checks, and even, when appropriate, video surveillance.

Q 8:143   Is an injury sustained while commuting to work covered by workers' compensation insurance?

Generally, commuting time is not work time; however, if an employee is injured while working out of the home as a salesperson, taking work home on the instructions of the boss, or traveling directly from home to a remote job site, the travel may be considered work time, rendering the employee eligible for workers' compensation benefits. Many state courts have held that injuries occurring while driving a car on the employer's property, such as in an employee parking lot, are on-the-job injuries eligible for workers' compensation benefits.

Q 8:144   Is an injury sustained during a lunch hour or other free period covered by workers' compensation insurance?

In general, injuries occurring during lunch or other break times on the employer's premises are covered by workers' compensation insurance. This could include a twisted ankle suffered while playing basketball in a court provided in the employee parking lot. This rule also extends to workers who are injured while eating their lunches at a remote job site. For instance, if a truck driver stops by the side of the road, gets out to eat lunch at a roadside picnic table, and is hit by another motorist, that injury probably is covered.

Q 8:145   What happens if an employee is injured by a piece of equipment manufactured by a third party?

The employer must still provide the employee workers' compensation benefits; however, the employer's liability is limited to the remedies under the workers' compensation law. The manufacturer of the equipment is subject to a third-party lawsuit under personal injury and product liability law in a state or federal court.

Q 8:146   If the employee sues a third party for his or her injuries, can the employer recover any of the workers' compensation benefits paid to that employee?

The employer or its insurance carrier has a subrogation right to money that is recovered by the employee in a third-party action against the manufacturer of the machinery or other product that was directly responsible for the employee's injury. In many states, the insurance carrier or the employer can confront the third-party manufacturer directly to exercise this subrogation interest.

Q 8:147   How does the Americans with Disabilities Act (ADA) affect workers' compensation?

Just as the Act affects which benefits an employer must provide under group health insurance plans, it also affects workers' compensation. First, workers' compensation provisions cannot pre-empt an employee's right to be free from disability discrimination under the provisions of the ADA. Second, the employer may not inquire into an applicant's workers' compensation history before making a conditional job offer. An employer may, however, make such an inquiry, if it does so of all applicants, after the conditional offer of employment has been made and accepted. One reason that an employer might want to have a regular program of post-employment inquiries concerning workers' compensation claims is to be able to substantiate when post-employment injuries are in fact second injuries (i.e., prior on-the-job injuries only aggravated by the new employment experience) subject to a state workers' compensation second injury fund.

Unemployment and Health Insurance

Q 8:148   What is *unemployment insurance*?

Unemployment insurance is a publicly funded insurance plan that provides compensation to people who are out of work through no fault of their own but who are available and willing to take a job. Almost all employers must pay unemployment tax to the state(s) in which they do business. The rate of this tax is usually determined by the amount of money needed by the state to pay benefits to unemployed workers, as well as the amount of benefits the laid-off employees of the particular employer have collected in the recent past. Often employees are taxed to support this fund as well.

Q 8:149   What is a *health maintenance organization*?

A *health maintenance organization* (HMO) is a type of health insurance plan. Under a typical health insurance plan, a patient goes to a doctor of his or her choice, and the insurance company pays some or all of the medical or hospital bills. Under an HMO plan, a member's medical care is reimbursed only if it is obtained from participating healthcare providers. Under some HMO plans, members must go to a clinic or hospital designated by the HMO to provide services under the plan. Generally, all medical expenses are covered by the plan; usually, there are no deductibles or upper limits. HMOs sometimes charge lower or more stable employer-paid premiums than do conventional health insurers; however, employees lose some discretion in choosing health care providers.

Q 8:150   Must an employer that offers traditional health insurance provide employees the option of joining an HMO?

A company must offer an HMO option if all of the following factors apply:

- The company offers a traditional health insurance plan;
- The company comes under the minimum-wage requirements of the Federal Labor Standards Act;
- During the previous calendar quarter, the company employed at least 25 workers; and
- The company receives a written request from a qualified HMO that covers a service area in which at least 25 of the company's employees live.

These requirements are set by the Health Maintenance Organization Act; however, the employer is not required to pay more for health benefits as a result of offering a qualified HMO option than it would otherwise pay for health benefits under a collective bargaining agreement or other employer-employee contract in effect at the time the HMO is included in the health benefit plan.

Q 8:151   May an employer alter its health care coverage to save money?

Subject to analysis under discrimination and contract law, employers are free to alter health care coverage.

In 1991, the U.S. Court of Appeals for the Fifth Circuit held in *McGann v. H&H Music Co.* [946 F.2d 401 (5th Cir. 1991)] that an employer is permitted by ERISA to exclude AIDS from the conditions covered by its $1 million major medical plan, relegating HIV/AIDS to a far more modest amount ($5,000) of major medical insurance. The U.S. Court of Appeals for the Eleventh Circuit held, however, that Section 510 of ERISA "prohibits employers from discharging employees to avoid paying benefits but permits employers to reduce or terminate nonvested benefits simply by changing the terms of the plan." [1993 *BNA Daily Labor Report* 51, Mar. 18, 1993, at 1]

Employers retain the right under ERISA to alter non-vested employee benefit plans for non-discriminatory reasons, when the change is aimed at a category of coverage or services rather than at particular individual(s) in the company's workforce. Indeed, the Eleventh Circuit in another 1993 decision permitted a Georgia-based chain of furniture stores to set a $25,000 cap on AIDS-related claims. [1993 *BNA Daily Labor Report* 51, Mar. 18, 1993, at 1] The issue is whether the employer can articulate a legitimate non-discriminatory reason for its action, which does not have a disparate impact on a protected group or suspect class. (See chapter 4 for a more detailed examination of discrimination.)

An employer may find itself in violation of contractual obligations if it elects to reduce benefits. The issue is whether the employer has made an enforceable promise regarding the nature, extent, and duration of health insurance.

Q 8:152   What are the health care reform laws recently signed into law and how do they affect employers?

On March 23, 2010, President Barack Obama signed the Patient Protection and Affordable Care Act [H.R. 3590, Pub. L. No. 111-148] into law. Then on March 30, 2010, the President signed the related Health Care and Education Reconciliation Act [H.R. 4872, Pub. L. No. 111-152] into law. Below is a summary of the provisions of these Acts that may impact the employers as they relate to health care. Most of the requirements are expected to take effect in 2014.

Amendments to FLSA

The Acts amend the FLSA to require certain employers to automatically enroll new full-time employees and continue the enrollment of current employees in one of the health benefit plans offered through the employer. [H.R. 3590, § 1511] Employers subject to this requirement are those that (1) employ more than 200 full-time employees, and (2) offer employees enrollment in one or more health benefit plans. The automatic enrollment program must include adequate notice and the opportunity for an employee to opt out of any such coverage.

Employers also have the duty to inform employees of their coverage options, including any options that may be available through an "Exchange" established by each state to help individuals and small businesses to obtain coverage. [H.R. 3590, § 1512] The notice must inform the employees of the existence of the Exchange and potential tax credits that may be available through the Exchange.

In addition, employers with 50 or more employees must provide employees who are nursing mothers with a reasonable break time during the child's first year to express milk. [H.R. 3590, § 4207] Such employers must also provide a private place, other than a bathroom, where the mother may express milk shielded from view and free from intrusion from coworkers and the public. The employer will not be required to compensate an employee receiving the break time. Employers with less than 50 employees are not subject to this requirement if the requirements would pose an undue hardship.

Amendments to the Code

The Acts make several amendments to the Code, generally in order to incentivize employers to provide health care to employees.

Large Employers. Large employers (generally those with 50 or more employees) must pay an assessment of $2,000 per full-time employee (not including the first 30 employees) if the employer (1) does not offer coverage, and (2) has at least one full-time employee who receives a premium assistance tax credit through the Exchange or cost-sharing reduction under the Acts. [H.R. 3590, § 1513; H.R. 4872, § 1003] In addition, employers that offer coverage that is not affordable or coverage that does not cover at least 60 percent of allowable costs must pay $3,000 for any employee that receives a tax credit through the Exchange up to a cap of $2,000 for every full-time employee.

The Act requires large employers to either offer health insurance to their full-time employees or pay a penalty through the IRS. A full-time employee is defined as an employee who averages 30 or more hours per week. A large employer is one that averages 50 or more full-time employees and full-time equivalent employees (FTEs).

To determine if an employer is a large employer necessitates finding out the number of employees who average at least 30 hours a week in 2013 and adding to that figure the number of FTEs. The number of FTEs an employer has is based upon taking the aggregate monthly hours worked by part-time employees (those who work fewer than 30 hours per week) counted on a monthly basis during calendar year 2013, divided by 120. Consequently, whether an employer has 50 or more employees triggering compliance in 2014 not only includes employees who work more than 30 hours per week but an equivalency based on hours worked by part-time employees during 2013.

If an employer is a large employer resulting from the formula that is outlined above, it must provide minimum essential health care coverage going forward to all employees who average at least 30 hours a week during a previous period, which can vary between 3 and 12 months during 2013. Minimum essential coverage is subject to a number of criteria. The amount an employee may pay as a share of the premium is based upon the employee's Form W-2 income.

Small Businesses. The Acts provide tax credits for small businesses that contribute at least 50 percent of an employee's health insurance premium costs. [H.R. 3590, § 1421] The small business must employ no more than 25 full-time employees and the average annual wage of such employees must not exceed a given threshold. For the years 2011 through 2013, an eligible employer may receive a credit in the amount of 35 percent of the employer's contributions; in 2014, the credit increases to 50 percent of such contributions.

All Employers. Employers must disclose the value of the benefit provided by the employer for each employee's health insurance coverage on the employee's annual Form W-2. [H.R. 3590, § 9002]

Q 8:153   What policies can employers incorporate to enhance their ability to modify their health care plans without liability?

To allow employers flexibility in amending or terminating employee health plans, without having to face potential liability under contract law, employers should take great care to ensure that they provide, in their policies and agreements, provisions that disavow any contractual obligations to continue the benefit and notify employees of the employer's right to alter, amend, or discontinue of any of the plans at the employer's sole discretion. An example of such language follows:

INSURANCE BENEFITS

Subject to various eligibility requirements and waiting periods, Full-Time employees that have completed 90 days of continuous service with the Company may enroll themselves, their spouse, and eligible dependents (per the plan) in medical group health insurance plan maintained by the Company.

The cost of the group health insurance benefits are borne by the Company and our employees. Please refer to the applicable group health benefit plan booklet for further information regarding eligibility, waiting periods, employee contribution to premium cost, and coverage. Booklets can be obtained by contacting Human Resources.

Note: THE COMPANY RESERVES THE RIGHT TO ALTER, AMEND, OR DISCONTINUE ANY OR ALL INSURANCE BENEFITS OR AMOUNT OF EMPLOYEE CONTRIBUTION AT ANY TIME AND FOR ANY REASON. PLEASE NOTE THAT THE TERMS AND CONDITIONS OF THE INSURANCE POLICIES THEMSELVES ARE CONTROLLING, NOTWITHSTANDING ANY REPRESENTATION OR STATEMENT IN THIS MANUAL OR ANY OTHER PUBLICATION OR COMMUNICATION.

Q 8:154   Will HIPAA Privacy Rules affect an employer's ability to receive protected health information concerning its employees?

The HIPAA Privacy Rules require covered entities to refrain from disclosing protected health information (PHI) they possess concerning individuals, except as expressly provided in the regulations. Although covered entities do not generally include employers and plan sponsors of health care plans, a health care plan, which is a covered entity, would not be permitted to disclose PHI concerning the individuals to the employer or plan sponsor unless the employer and plan sponsor agree to comply with the privacy schemes required to be adopted by covered entities. (See chapter 5 for more information concerning HIPAA Privacy Rules.)

Disability Insurance

Q 8:155　Are employees entitled to disability insurance?

Employees generally are not entitled as a matter of law to disability insurance; however, a number of states tax employers and employees to provide disability insurance under programs analogous to unemployment compensation plans.

Q 8:156　Are pregnant employees entitled to disability insurance?

Under the Pregnancy Discrimination Act, if employees who are injured or ill are eligible for short- and long-term disability benefits, employees disabled by pregnancy must be accorded the same benefit. Similarly, if the employer provides unpaid or paid leaves of absence to employees for any reason, that employer is well-advised to offer maternity leave as well.

The Family and Medical Leave Act

Q 8:157　What is the *Family and Medical Leave Act*?

The FMLA allows eligible employees as many as 12 weeks of unpaid job-protected leave in any 12-month period for: absences attributable to a serious health condition of the employee; absences needed to care for an employee's spouse, child, or parent with a serious health condition; absences to care for an employee's child after birth, or placement for adoption for foster care. The federal statute joins 12 state statutes that provide some form of unpaid leave to workers employed by private corporations.

Q 8:158　What are the highlights of the FMLA?

They are as follows:

- The statute applies only to private employers with 50 or more employees.
- Federal civil service employees, state and local government workers, and employees of Congress also are covered.
- To be eligible under the Act, an employee must have worked for the company at least 12 months before the leave, must have logged at least 1,250 hours on the job during the previous 12-month period, and must work at a work site where the employer employs 50 or more employees within a 75-mile radius.

- Eligible employees are entitled to 12 weeks of unpaid leave during a 12-month period.
- The company can require the eligible employee to use first any paid sick leave or accrued vacation time as part of the 12-week unpaid absence from work.
- An employee on leave under the law can continue receiving health benefits under the same terms and conditions as if he or she was not on leave.
- Such an unpaid leave must be granted for an employee's own serious illness, the care of a seriously ill parent, spouse or child, or in connection with the birth or adoption of a child.
- Intermittent periods of leave are available when medically necessary or by mutual agreement of employer and employee.
- Upon return from the leave of absence, the employee must be given the same or an equivalent position as that held before the unpaid absence.

Although the Eleventh Amendment provides the states with immunity from suit in federal court, Congress may abrogate this immunity if it makes its intention to abrogate unmistakably clear in the statutory language. The state of Nevada challenged the constitutionality of the application of the FMLA to states in *The Nevada Department of Human Resources v. Hibbs.* [538 U.S. 721 (May 27, 2003)] The Supreme Court stated, after review of the FMLA, that the statutory language clearly intended to abrogate the state's Eleventh Amendment immunity from suit in federal court for violations of the FMLA and, as a result, held that the FMLA is applicable to state employees.

Q 8:159   How does an employer determine whether it employs enough people to come under the mandate of the FMLA?

Employers often believe that they do not meet the requirement of 50 or more employees. On closer examination, they may be surprised to discover that FMLA applies. This confusion occurs for many reasons.

The first reason is that an employer need not have 50 or more employees throughout the calendar year. The employer only needs 50 or more employees "for each working day during each of twenty (20) or more calendar workweeks in the current or preceding calendar year." In other words, if during at least 20 workweeks in the current or preceding calendar year an employer employed 50 or more employees, the FMLA applies to it. The 20 workweeks need not be consecutive. This is particularly important for seasonal businesses in which, at times, the number of employees exceeds 50 temporarily.

Another reason is that the employees who are counted toward the 50-employee threshold comprise a larger population than that typically presumed by the employer. Not only are full-time employees counted, but also are part-time and temporary employees. Even employees on temporary leaves of absence are counted, provided the employer has a reasonable expectation that those employees will return to active employment. Employees who have been laid off indefinitely are not counted. As long as an employee is maintained on the payroll during any workweek, he or she must be counted.

In addition, the regulations adopt an expansive definition of the employment relationship. Individuals considered independent contractors by the employer may well be determined to be employees. The courts consider many factors in determining whether an independent contractor is an employee for purposes of the Act. Of all the factors, the most pivotal is control. The extent to which an employer controls working conditions and the manner in which work is accomplished and retains the authority to hire, supervise, and fire, indicates whether an employment or independent-contractor relationship exists. Regardless of written documents and agreements to the contrary, if the former is found to exist, so-called independent contractors will be counted toward the 50-employee threshold.

Lastly, under joint employment and/or integrated employer rules, for purposes of determining whether the 50-employee threshold is met in leased employee situations, employees who are treated as employees of the leasing company are also treated as employees of the company that leases the employees.

Q 8:160   If an employer leases its employees, does it still have obligations under the FMLA?

Possibly. Under the FMLA, an employee judged to be employed by two or more separate and distinct entities is counted as an employee of both entities, even if he or she is not maintained on the payroll of one of them. Joint employment is typically determined by reviewing the relationship of the employee with the entities. To the extent that they share the employee's services or the control of his or her work, directly or indirectly, the employee is employed by both entities for purposes of the Act. Typically, this situation arises when a company leases employees from a temporary service or leasing agency. In those instances, leased employees are counted by both the leasing company and the company that leases its employees in determining whether either company meets the 50-employee threshold. (For example, if XYZ maintains 15 employees on its payroll but leases 40 employees from a leasing company for 20 or more weeks during the current or preceding calendar year, it meets the 50-or-more-employee threshold.)

Q 8:161   If two companies are related, may all their employees be counted to determine whether the company meets the 50-or-more-employee threshold?

Yes. In addition to joint employment, the FMLA provides that two or more separate entities may be deemed a single employer if they meet the integrated-employer test. Once that test is met, all employees of all integrated employers are counted. Determining whether separate entities should be treated as an integrated employer involves examining the total circumstances of their relationship. Factors include but are not limited to:

- The existence of common management;
- The inter-relatedness of operations;
- Whether the control of labor relations is centralized; and
- The degree of common ownership and financial control.

Q 8:162   Can an employer have successor liability under the FMLA?

Under the FMLA, an employer can be deemed to be a "successor in interest" to a covered employer, such that it has FMLA obligations to its employees, even if the employees would be ineligible for FMLA leave by virtue of time worked for the successor employer. [29 C.F.R. § 825.107] The factors to consider in determining whether successor liability can be imposed include the substantial continuity of the same business operations; use of the same plant; continuity of the work force; similarity of jobs and working conditions; similarity of supervisory personnel; similarity in machinery, equipment, and production methods; similarity of products and services; and the ability of the predecessor to provide relief. [29 C.F.R. § 825.107]

In *Sullivan v. Dollar Tree Stores, Inc.* [623 F.3d 770 (9th Cir. 2010)], an employee who did not have sufficient time worked to be eligible for FMLA leave with her employer, claimed that her employer was in actuality a successor in interest of her prior employer for which the successor would then be liable under the FMLA. Based on the fact that the new employer merely bought the lease of the prior employer from bankruptcy, engaged in retail operations much different from that of the prior employer, and hired only a small number of the former bankrupt employer's employees demonstrated that the new employer was not a successor in interest.

Q 8:163   If an employer has 50 or more employees as determined by the FMLA's regulations, are all the employees entitled to FMLA leave?

Not necessarily. This question raises one of the biggest misconceptions employers have about the Act. An employer can have thousands of employees but not one who is eligible to take a leave under the Act. Employees must meet the following three criteria to qualify for leave:

- The employee must have been employed by the employer for at least 12 months. The regulations provide that the months need not be consecutive, that any part of any week an employee is maintained on a payroll is counted as a week of employment, and 52 weeks of employment satisfies the 12-month requirement. [29 C.F.R. § 825.110(b)]
- The employee must have worked at least 1,250 hours during the 12 months immediately preceding the commencement of the leave. The employer must utilize principles under the FLSA for determining compensable hours of work, with pivotal standards for determining "actual hours worked." [29 C.F.R. § 825.110(c)]

- The employee must work at a site where 50 or more employees of the same employer work at a work site within a 75-mile radius. The 75-mile radius is determined by utilizing the shortest route possible using surface roads on public streets, or, if surface roads are not available, the most commonly employed mode of transportation in the area. [29 C.F.R. § 825.111]

With the exception of returning military personnel under the Uniformed Services Employment and Reemployment Rights Act (USERRA), hours worked means hours worked. For example, in *Plumley v. Southern Container, Inc.* [303 F.3d 364 (1st Cir. 2002)], the court would not count hours attributable to an award of back pay received by an employee in a grievance decision as hours worked towards the 1,250 hour threshold. [*See* 19 *Employment Discrimination Report (EDR)* (BNA) 333 (Sept. 25, 2002).]

Q 8:164   How do you determine whether an employee has worked the minimum 1,250 hours?

Under the regulations, hours worked is determined under the FLSA. [29 C.F.R. § 825.110(c)] Under the FLSA, any accurate accounting of actual hours worked under FLSA's principles may be used. In the event the employer does not maintain accurate records, the regulations provide that the employer has the burden to demonstrate that the requisite hours have not been worked.

However, in *Erdman v. Nationwide Insurance Co.* [510 F. Supp. 2d 363 (M.D. Pa. 2007)], the employee, according to her time records, worked a total of 1,179.75 hours in a 12-month period immediately preceding the commencement of her leave, less than the requisite 1,250 hours worked for FMLA eligibility, but claimed to have worked additional hours from her home, which, if counted, would make her eligible for FMLA leave. Although she claimed her employer was aware of her time spent at home working, given that she did not submit time sheets for this additional time, was not compensated for this time, and could not demonstrate that her employer was aware of such work, hours worked at home under these circumstances would not be counted toward FMLA eligibility.

The issue of whether an employee had the requisite number of hours worked was also at issue in *Maples v. Illinois Bell Telephone Co.* [594 F. Supp. 2d 937 (N.D. Ill. 2009)] The employee, a union steward, wanted credit for time spent on internal union business in addition to his other hours worked to satisfy the 1,250 hours of service required under the FMLA during the previous 12-month period. Although the FMLA does not define "hours of service," the statute specifies that the legal standards established under the FLSA shall apply to determine whether an employee meets the requisite hours of service. Under the FLSA, time spent adjusting grievances by union employees on the employer's premises is considered hours worked and in addition, the FLSA will count other union time as hours worked as provided in the relevant collective bargaining agreement or as treated as a matter of custom and practice between the union and employer. Although the time spent by the employee on internal union business far exceeded time spent in adjusting grievances on the employer's premises, historically, the employer had treated all internal union business time worked as hours worked for the union steward under the FMLA, and as such, time spent on internal union business for the employee was creditable toward FMLA eligibility.

In *Bailey v. Pregis Innovative Packaging, Inc.* [600 F.3d 748 (7th Cir. 2010)], an employee claimed her employer had violated the FMLA when her employment was terminated. As to eligibility however, the employee had not worked 1,250 hours in the prior 12 months, but claimed eligibility because her failure to work 1,250 hours was due to prior FMLA leave taken. The court, in rejecting the claim, said that the requirement that the employee work 1,250 hours in the prior 12 months cannot be "tolled" due to the fact that the employee was unable to achieve 1,250 hours due to previous FMLA leave.

Q 8:165   Can time spent on military leave be used to satisfy the eligibility requirements under the FMLA?

Although the eligibility requirements of 1,250 hours generally equates to hours worked, in July 2002, the DOL issued a memorandum clarifying the interplay between the eligibility requirements of the FMLA and the provisions of USERRA, which provide that service members returning from military leave are entitled to all the benefits of employment they would have received if they had been continuously employed. In its memorandum, the DOL concluded that USERRA requires that the hours that the military personnel would have worked if they had not been called to duty should be counted as actual hours worked for purposes of determining eligibility. [*See* discussion in 19 *Employment Discrimination Report (EDR)* (BNA) 129 (July 31, 2002).]

Q 8:166   Do military personnel and their families have expanded coverage under the FMLA?

In January 2008, the National Defense Authorization Act (NDAA) [Pub. L. No. 110-181] was enacted which, among other things, amended the FMLA to provide two new leave entitlements for military personnel and their families as follows:

Military Care Giver Leave. Also known as Covered Service Member Leave, this new entitlement allows eligible employees who are family members of a covered service member to take up to 26 work weeks of leave in a single 12-month period to care for a covered service member with a serious illness or injury incurred in the line of duty. This provision also extends FMLA protection to additional family members (i.e., next of kin) beyond those who may take FMLA leave for other qualifying reasons.

Qualifying Exigency Leave. The second new leave entitlement enacted by the NDAA provides that the normal 12 weeks of FMLA job protected leave available to eligible employees with a covered military member serving in the National Guard or Reserves may use FMLA leave for "any qualifying exigency" which arises from the fact that the military member is on active duty or called to active duty status in support of military operations. "Qualifying exigency" according to the DOL's final rules effective January 16, 2009 refers to a broad number of activities including short notice deployment, military events and related activities, child care and school activities, counseling, financial and legal arrangements, rest and recuperation, and post-deployment activities.

Q 8:167 Are there any specific rules for teachers as they relate to the 1,250 hours worked within the previous 12-month requirement for eligibility under the FMLA?

Teachers present a unique situation. With summers off and various breaks throughout the school year, teachers may or may not meet this threshold, depending on how much time they spend working throughout the school day. Under the FLSA, hours worked include time that the employee "suffered" or was "permitted" to work. Therefore, time spent preparing lessons or checking schoolwork after the school bell rings at the end of the day would be hours worked. As exempt employees, however, time records may not be maintained and so a certain determination cannot be made [29 C.F.R. § 541.3(a)(3)]. Given this situation, FMLA regulations provide that a full-time teacher is "deemed" to meet the 1,250 hour test unless the employer can clearly demonstrate that the teacher did not work 1,250 hours in the previous 12 months.

Q 8:168 If an employer does not have 50 employees but, nonetheless, includes an FMLA policy in its handbook, are the employees entitled to FMLA leave under federal law?

This question was squarely faced by the Sixth Circuit in *Douglas v. EG Baldwin & Associates, Inc.* [150 F.3d 604 (6th Cir. 1998)] Although the employer did not have the requisite 50 employees for 20 or more calendar weeks in the current or preceding year to be considered an "employer covered by the Act," nonetheless it included an FMLA policy in its handbook. Although the employee argued that the employer was subject to the FMLA, the court concluded that because the employer did not meet the statutory requirement of "employer"—because it did not employ the requisite number of employees—the court lacked jurisdiction to consider the claim.

However, the *Douglas* decision may be questioned in light of a 2006 U.S. Supreme Court precedent. In *Minard v. ITC Deltacom Communications, Inc.* [447 F.3d 352 (5th Cir. 2006)], an employer had mistakenly told an employee that she was eligible for FMLA leave. In fact, this employee did not work at a work site where there were 50 or more employees within a 50-mile radius. However, in light of the February 2006 U.S. Supreme Court decision of *Arbaugh v. Y & H Corp.* [546 U.S. 500 (2006)], which held that Title VII's requirement for employers to have 15 or more employees was not jurisdictional, but rather an essential ingredient in a Title VII claim, the court held that the eligibility criteria for employees under the FMLA was also not jurisdictional, such that there existed triable issues as to whether the employee relied, to her detriment, on the employer's misrepresentation and remanded the matter for further proceedings.

Q 8:169   How can an employer determine whether two sites are within 75 miles of one another?

Generally, "work site" refers to the location that the employee reports to or, if none, from which the employee's work is assigned. Having established the work site of the employee, the employer determines whether 50 or more employees are employed within 75 miles of it.

It is important to understand how 75 miles is computed under the FMLA. Is it 75 miles via the common roadways or as the crow flies? The distance is measured by surface miles over public streets, roads, highways and waterways, by the shortest route. If surface transportation is not available, the distance is measured by using the most frequently employed mode of transportation in the area. If travel by bush pilot is the only means of transportation available, air miles by regular air routes would be used.

Q 8:170   Under what circumstances are employers required to grant FMLA leave?

Employers covered by the Act are required to grant leaves to eligible employees for:

- The birth and care of a newborn;
- Placement with the employee of a son or daughter for adoption or foster care;
- Care of the employee's spouse, son, daughter, or parent with a serious health condition; or
- A serious health condition that makes the employee unable to perform the functions of his or her job.

In January, 2008, the FMLA was expanded to provide leave entitlement for military personnel and their families to provide care to covered service members and to attend to personal matters arising from being called to active duty. (See Q 8:166.)

Q 8:171   Does the FMLA pre-empt state leave laws?

In many respects, the FMLA is patterned after the Federal Labor Standards Act, which for more than half a century has governed minimum wage and overtime pay. Neither Act pre-empts any state statute that provides more generous provisions.

Q 8:172   How is the FMLA enforced?

As is the FLSA, the FMLA is administered and enforced by the DOL. Employees who believe the FMLA has been violated can file claims with the DOL. In addition, employees can institute private litigation to seek redress for violations. A private lawsuit must be filed within two years after the violation or within three years if the employer acted willfully.

Q 8:173   How does the act define *parent* and *son* or *daughter*?

Congress defined these terms broadly. The terms *son* or *daughter* include "biological, adopted, or foster child, legal ward, or a child of a person standing in loco parentis." The relevant congressional committee report explains that "the terms 'parent' and 'son or daughter' [should] be broadly construed to ensure that an employee who actually has day-to-day responsibility for caring for a child is entitled to leave even if the employee does not have a biological or legal relationship to that child." Children include dependents under 18 years of age and older offspring who cannot care for themselves because of a mental or physical disability.

Q 8:174   What does *spouse* mean under the FMLA?

A person who is considered the spouse of an employee is essentially determined by state marriage laws. The state law to be considered is not, according to the FMLA, the state where the employee's work site is located, but the state where the employee resides. If that state, for example, recognizes common-law marriages, a spouse in a common-law marriage is covered by the Act. Unless recognized by state law, domestic partners are not considered "spouses" under the Act.

Q 8:175   Has the DOL issued regulations and rules implementing the FMLA?

The DOL published its final regulations in the Federal Register on January 6, 1995. These regulations took effect on April 6, 1995. Under the statute, employees of covered employers (those with 50 or more employees) enjoy three fundamental rights:

- Eligible employees are entitled to unpaid leave for as long as 12 weeks in any 12-month period for the birth or care of a child, adoption or receipt of a child for foster care, the serious health condition of a family member (such as child, spouse, or parent), or the employee's own serious health condition preventing job performance.
- While on leave, the employee is entitled to continuation of health insurance on the same terms as before the leave.
- The employee must be reinstated to the same or an equivalent job as the one held before taking the leave of absence.

Under the regulations, the designation of absences as FMLA leaves is a burden shared by employers and employees. The employee must merely provide the employer sufficient, timely information to enable it to determine how to designate the leave. The employer may require that this information include certification from a health care provider. On receiving sufficient information, the employer must designate the absence as an FMLA leave within two days and notify the employee accordingly.

On-the-job injuries that result in absences from work may be counted concurrently as FMLA leave, provided the injury is a serious health condition; however, if the employer fails to tell the worker that the compensable absence is being counted as a leave under the Act, the employer may lose the right to later credit the time off toward FMLA leave time.

The regulations contain a model notice of FMLA rights that covered employers should post prominently at each work site. The regulations may be found in Title 29 of the Code of Federal Regulations.

In November 2008, the DOL adopted its final FMLA rules, effective January 16, 2009, which provide guidance regarding some open-ended issues posed by its prior rules. With respect to the definition of a serious health condition which involves more than three consecutive full days of incapacity plus two visits to a health care provider, the two visits must occur within 30 days of the beginning of the period of incapacity and the first visit must take place within seven days of the first day of incapacity. Under prior regulations, a serious health condition was also determined to have occurred if the incapacity is more than three consecutive full calendar days plus a regimen of continuing treatment. The new rules clarify that the first visit to a health care provider in connection with this definition must take place within seven days of the first day of incapacity. With respect to the definition of serious health condition involving "periodic visits" for chronic health conditions, the final rules provide guidance by providing that "periodic visits" means that the employee must have at least two visits to a health care provider per year.

The final FMLA rules adopted by the DOL have been revised to reflect current law following the Supreme Court's decision in *Ragsdale*. Specifically, the final rules remove the categorical penalty provisions and clarify that when an employee suffers individualized harm because the employer failed to follow the notification rules, the employer may be liable.

The DOL's final rules clarify an employee's obligation with respect to providing notice to the employer for unforeseeable leave. The final rules provide that the employee must follow the employer's usual and customary call-in procedures for reporting an absence (e.g., before the employee's shift starts), absent unusual circumstances. Many employers hope that this change will result in employees providing more timely notice of FMLA leave, which was noted by the DOL to have been stated to have been an issue with many employers.

Under the DOL's final rules, the DOL added a requirement that when engaged in the medical certification process, any contact by the employer with the health care provider of the employee must be through the employer's health care provider, the employer's human resource professional, leave administrator or other management official, but in no case may the contact be made by the employee's direct supervisor. Moreover, employers may not ask the employee's health care provider for additional information beyond that required by the certification form itself. In addition, if the employer deems the medical certification to be incomplete or insufficient, the employer must specify in writing what information is lacking and give the employee seven calendar days to cure the deficiency.

Clarifying an open-ended issue under the prior regulations, the new rules adopted by the DOL effective January 16, 2009 provide that for illness of long duration, or intermittent reoccurring conditions, under the final rules employers can request recertification of an ongoing condition every six months in conjunction with an absence.

Q 8:176   What is a *serious health condition* allowing for unpaid leave under the FMLA?

The regulations define a *serious health condition* as any one of the following:

Hospital care. Inpatient care (i.e., an overnight stay) in a hospital, hospice, or residential medical care facility, including any period of incapacity or subsequent treatment in connection with or consequent to such impatient care.

Absence plus treatment. A period of incapacity of more than three consecutive calendar days (including any subsequent treatment or period of incapacity relating to the same condition), that also involves:

- Treatment two or more times by a health care provider, by a nurse or physician's assistant under direct supervision of a health care provider, or by a provider of health care services (e.g., physical therapist) under orders of, or on referral by, a health care provider; or
- Treatment by a health care provider on at least one occasion that results in a regiment of continuing treatment under the supervision of the health care provider.

The fact that Christian Science practitioners are specifically included as health care providers in the regulations does not, however, mean that other spiritual healing practitioners fall within the FMLA. In *Tayag v. Lahey Clinic Hospital* [632 F.3d 788 (1st Cir. 2011)], the court held that a spiritual healing pilgrimage that the employee made for multiple weeks during her employment did not amount to medical care under the FMLA and, as such, was not permitted under the FMLA. In *Jones v. C&D Technologies, Inc.* [684 F.3d 673 (7th Cir. 2012)], the court held that an employee did not have a serious health condition when he missed work one morning attributable to back pain and anxiety and visited his physician's clinic to obtain a prescription refill, but was never physically examined by his physician.

The final rules adopted by the DOL provide additional guidance. Specifically, with respect to the definition of a *serious health condition*, which involves more than three consecutive full days of incapacity plus two visits to a health care provider, the two visits must occur within 30 days of the beginning of the period of incapacity and the first visit must take place within seven days of the first day of incapacity. Under prior regulations, a serious health condition was also determined to have occurred if the incapacity is more than three consecutive full calendar days plus a regimen of continuing treatment. The new rules clarify that the first visit to a health care provider in connection with this definition must take place within seven days of the first day of incapacity. With respect to the definition of *serious health condition* involving "periodic visits" for chronic health conditions, the final rules provide guidance by providing that "periodic visits" means that the employee must have at least two visits to a health care provider per year.

Pregnancy. Any period of incapacity resulting from pregnancy or for prenatal care.

Chronic conditions requiring treatments. A chronic condition that:

* Requires periodic visits for treatment by a health care provider or by a nurse or physician's assistant under direct supervision of a health care provider;

* Continues over an extended period of time (including recurring episodes of a single underlying condition); and

* May cause episodic rather than a continuing period of incapacity (e.g., asthma, diabetes, or epilepsy).

Permanent/long-term conditions requiring supervision. A period of incapacity that is permanent or long-term because of a condition for which treatment may not be effective. The employee or family member must be under the continuing supervision of, but need not be receiving active treatment by, a health care provider. Examples include Alzheimer's, a severe stroke, or the terminal stages of a disease.

Multiple treatments (non-chronic condition). Any period of absence to receive multiple treatments (including any period of recovery therefrom) by a health care provider or by a provider of health care services under orders of, or on referral by, a health care provider, either for restorative surgery after an accident or other injury or for a condition that would likely result in a period of incapacity of more than three consecutive calendar days in the absence of medical intervention or treatment, such as cancer (chemotherapy, radiation, etc.), severe arthritis (physical therapy), or kidney disease (dialysis).

Q 8:177   When is the employee unable to perform the functions of his or her position?

Under the FMLA, an employee is considered unable to perform his or her functions if the employee is unable to work at all or to perform any one of the essential functions of the employee's position. *Essential functions* are defined under the ADA. If an employee must be absent for medical treatment for a serious health condition, he or she is determined to be unable to perform the functions of his or her position.

Q 8:178   What does it mean that an employee is needed to care for a spouse, child, or parent?

The phrase "needed to care for" is defined broadly under the FMLA. The phrase encompasses not only physical care, but psychological care as well. Providing psychological comfort and reassurance for a family member with a serious health condition is sufficient. In addition, the phrase covers a situation where the employee is needed to fill in for others who are caring for a family member.

Q 8:179 If an employee's spouse, child, or parent dies, can FMLA leave be taken?

FMLA leave is only applicable to situations where the employee is needed to care for a child, spouse or partner with a serious health condition. Once the child, spouse or partner dies, FMLA would no longer be applicable. If the death results in a serious health condition for a living spouse, parent or child, FMLA leave would apply if the employee was needed to care for them.

Q 8:180 Can an employee be "needed to care for" a family member if the family member is in inpatient care at a medical facility providing 24-hour care?

Under the FMLA regulations, the term *needed to care for* means physically caring for one's needs but also includes providing psychological comfort and reassurance that is beneficial to the family member. As a result, providing beneficial comfort bedside to an inpatient family member at a medical facility would qualify under the regulations. [29 C.F.R. § 825.116]

Q 8:181 How much leave may an employee take?

The FMLA provides that an eligible employee is entitled to a total of 12 workweeks of leave during any 12-month period; it does not, however, dictate how the 12-month period is to be determined. Rather, the employer may select among different methods. For instance, an employer may select a calendar year, any other fixed 12-month leave year (for example, a fiscal year or employee's anniversary date), a 12-month period measured forward from the date any employee's FMLA leave begins, or a rolling 12-month period measured backward from the date the employee started his or her leave. Once an employer has chosen one of the alternatives, it must apply it consistently and uniformly to all employees.

Each of the choices has its benefits and disadvantages. The calendar year is, from an administrative standpoint, probably the easiest selection; however, with this approach, an employee can stack back-to-back 12-week FMLA leaves. Likewise, electing any fixed 12-month period (e.g., benefit year, fiscal year, or anniversary year), incurs the same stacking problem. A rolling 12-month period measured backward from any use of an FMLA leave prevents stacking, but this alternative requires more administrative effort to account for leave taken.

Q 8:182   If a husband and wife are employed by the same employer, are they each eligible for 12 weeks of leave under the FMLA?

It depends. If attributable to their own serious health condition, each employee qualifies for 12 weeks of leave during any 12-month period; however, for the birth, adoption, foster care, or care for an employee's parent, the Act provides that the husband and wife's combined leave may not exceed 12 weeks during any 12-month period.

Q 8:183   Can an employer prevent a husband and wife employed by the same employer from using FMLA on the same day?

In *Werner v. Ford Motor Co.* [2007 WL 1114946 (S.D. Ohio Apr. 13, 2007)], at issue was a policy adopted by Ford that did not allow FMLA leave to both parents employed by Ford to care for the same family member on the same day. Although the regulations do not specifically deal with the issue, the court held that, in this matter of first impression, and although not directly on point, sufficient direction was given in the regulations concerning spouses who work for the same company and uses of FMLA leave to demonstrate that Ford's policy was in violation of the FMLA.

Q 8:184   Does FMLA leave have to be taken all at once, or may it be taken intermittently?

If the leave is taken for the birth of a child or placement of a child for adoption or foster care, the employee must take the leave in one block. On the other hand, if the leave is the result of an employee's serious health condition or the serious health condition of an employee's spouse, parent or child, the leave may be taken intermittently or on a reduced leave schedule, provided it is medically necessary. The term *medically necessary* is loosely defined under the Act and would certainly include any time off needed for medical treatment or to care for a family member undergoing medical treatment. The regulations provide that an employee needing intermittent leave, or leave on a reduced schedule, must attempt to schedule the leave in a way so as not to disrupt the employer's employment operations.

There is no minimum for a reduced leave schedule. The amount of leave time that is taken depends on the needs of the employee. Generally, an employee may not be required to take more leave than necessary to address the circumstances that precipitated the need for the leave. An employer may not allocate an entire day to FMLA leave when only 30 minutes were taken, even if the employer handles all other absences this way. If the employer's payroll system cannot account for less than one hour away from work, then a 30-minute absence from work may be counted as one hour of leave under the Act.

Q 8:185   Can an employer assign an employee who needs intermittent or reduced FMLA leave to another position that better accommodates the intermittent or reduced leave schedule?

Yes. The regulations specifically provide that an employer may transfer the employee on an intermittent or reduced leave schedule to another position that better accommodates the intermittent or reduced leave. [29 C.F.R. §§ 825.117 and 825.204] The transfer must only last as long as the need for reduced or intermittent leave exists, and the employee must receive equivalent pay and benefits with the alternate position. This may require an employer to increase the pay and benefits typically associated with the alternate position for the employee. If the need for reduced or intermittent leave is such that a part-time position is warranted, the regulations allow the transfer as long as the part-time position does not result in the use of more FMLA than necessary. Although equivalent pay is required, this does not mean someone who works 20 hours a week would receive the same payroll check he or she earned at 40 hours a week. Paying the employee the same rate of pay, $10 per hour for both positions, is acceptable. Benefits may not be reduced, even if unavailable for other part-time employees. Reducing benefits where the benefit is earned based on the number of hours worked, like vacation time, is allowed.

Q 8:186   If an employee takes a reduced FMLA leave, how does the employer calculate this time off against the employee's entitlement of 12 weeks?

Generally, an employee's time off on a reduced-leave schedule is allocated against his or her total leave on a pro rata basis. Employees are entitled to 12 weeks of leave during any 12-month period. If an employee who typically works 40 hours per week is away from work for 20 hours during a workweek for FMLA purposes, one-half of a week may be used. If an employee typically works part-time at 20 hours a week, 20 hours away during a workweek for leave constitutes one week.

Q 8:187   Is FMLA leave paid or unpaid?

Leave is specifically unpaid. Nonetheless, many employers have written policies that provide paid time off benefits for various circumstances. Most employers offer paid vacations, sick time, and (under certain circumstances) leave. These employers may require that paid time-off benefits be used in connection with an FMLA leave when such a leave is demanded. As a result, an employee on FMLA leave may be paid, in full or in part, for some of that time, under his or her employer's policies. If an employer wants its employees to coordinate leaves under the FMLA with their paid time-off benefits, it must make this policy clear to them in its employee handbooks, manuals, policy statements, or other written information explaining employee benefits.

Q 8:188   Under what circumstances may an employer designate leave, paid or unpaid, as FMLA leave?

Employers may designate a paid or unpaid leave as an FMLA leave promptly after finding out that the leave is being taken for a FMLA-sanctioned reason. Generally, *promptly* is defined as two business days, absent extenuating circumstances. If the employer fails to designate a leave promptly, the regulations provide that it may lose the right to do so at a later time. For instance, the regulations provide that an employer that knew a leave qualified under the FMLA cannot retroactively designate it later as FMLA leave after the employee has returned to work. [29 C.F.R. § 825.208] However, a U.S. Supreme Court decision suggests that this type of a "penalty" for an employer may not be warranted in all occasions. In *Ragsdale v. Wolverine World Wide, Inc.* [535 U.S. 81 (2002)], the Court held that analogous regulations were not enforceable. The Court held that the Secretary of Labor's regulations [29 C.F.R. § 825.700(a)], which provide that an employer cannot count paid or unpaid leaves under its own policies toward FMLA leave unless it designates it as such, was beyond the scope of the secretary's authority. Essentially, the Court likened the rule to a categorical penalty that was not supported by law. [*Ragsdale*, 535 U.S. at 88–89] However, the Court explicitly stated that its decision did not address the validity of the notice and designation requirements themselves, suggesting that these rules may be valid in circumstances where prejudice may be shown, but the per se penalty against the employer for a violation of the rules is not. [*Ragsdale*, 535 U.S. at 96] The court allowed that a different result could occur if the employee could show prejudice. [*Ragsdale*, 535 U.S. at 96] The *Ragsdale* ruling was followed by the Third Circuit in *Fogleman v. Greater Hazelton Health Alliance* [122 Fed. Appx. 581 (3d Cir. 2004)] In the case, an employee who had not been advised of her FMLA rights had been on a leave that extended beyond 12 weeks. Following *Ragsdale*, the court found that in order to show prejudice the employee was required to demonstrate that had she been advised of her FMLA rights, she could have returned to work after the 12-week period. However, the testimony in the case indicated that the employee was not able to return to her position at the expiration of the 12-week period, and as such, there was no prejudice for the employer having failed to provide notice to the employee of her FMLA rights. The DOL's final rules follow *Ragsdale*, and remove the categorical penalty provisions under prior regulations.

Q 8:189   Must an employer maintain all benefits for an employee during an FMLA leave?

No. Employers must only continue the employee's group health plan benefits for the duration of the leave. Group health benefits include medical, surgical, hospital, dental and eye care, mental health counseling, and substance-abuse treatment. Group health plan benefits do not include such items as life insurance, holiday pay, and vacation benefits.

Q 8:190   If there is a co-payment, must an employer pay 100 percent of an employee's premiums for a group health plan while he or she is on FMLA leave?

No. Employers are obligated only to continue group health benefits in the same manner and nature as if the employee had continued working. Employees on leave have no greater rights in connection with those benefits than do employees actively working for the employer. When a co-payment is required, the employer must notify the employee of that fact and the date by which the employee must pay it. Generally, requiring the employee to make the payment when the employer used to deduct it from his or her paycheck is a suitable arrangement. Due dates based on the employer's deadlines for paying the premium are also permissible.

Q 8:191   If an employee fails to pay his or her co-payments, is the employer obligated to pay 100 percent of the premium?

Technically, no. If an employee fails to make co-payments and the employer has complied with the regulations on notifying the employee about payment due dates, the employer is not obligated to pick up the difference; however, the FMLA also provides that after the employee returns, the employer must restore the employee's benefits, including group health benefits, to the previous level. This means that the group health benefit must be restored with no waiting period, preexisting illness limitation, or other limitations commonly found when a person leaves and then reenters a plan. As a result, many employers, if they cannot make the necessary arrangements with their insurance companies, voluntarily pay 100 percent of the premium, with the understanding that they will seek the co-payment contribution from the employee at the end of the leave.

Q 8:192   Can an employer recover its costs for maintaining group health coverage from an employee who does not return from a leave?

Yes, under very limited circumstances. To the extent that the employee's failure to return to work is not because of the employee's or employee's family member's serious health condition or is otherwise beyond the employee's control, the employer can demand its costs for maintaining group health care coverage and may institute legal action, if necessary. The opportunity to recover costs is limited, for the instances in which costs cannot be recovered are broadly drawn in the statute.

Q 8:193   What obligations does an employer have to restore an employee to his or her position and benefits at the end of a leave?

The FMLA requires that an employee be restored to the same or equivalent position he or she had before taking leave. *Equivalent* is defined to mean a virtually identical position, including pay, benefits, working conditions, perquisites, privileges, and status. This definition is unique and should be considered before any decision is made about restoring an employee to a position that is not the same he or she held previously. *Equivalent* does not mean "comparable" for purposes of the Act. Although, in a 2011 case, an employee claimed that her employer violated the FMLA when she returned from maternity leave by not reassigning her to the project that she directed before going on maternity leave, the court found that the position was nonetheless equivalent under the FMLA because it was the same position, with the same rates of pay and benefits. [Duchateau v. Camp Dresser & McKee, Inc., 2011 WL 4599837 (S.D. Fla. Oct. 4, 2011)]

Although employees must be restored, they are subject to any changes in benefit levels that occurred during the employee's leave that affected the entire work force. The employee cannot be required to requalify for any benefits he or she enjoyed before the leave began. This applies not only to health benefits but to all other employee benefits, including life and disability insurance.

Q 8:194   Do any circumstances relieve an employer from its obligation to reinstate an employee after an FMLA leave?

Yes. The FMLA provides that an employee on a leave has no greater right to employment than if the employee had been continuously working. Thus, if an employer can demonstrate that an employee would otherwise have been terminated or laid off because of downsizing, restructuring or a similar occurrence, the employer is not obligated to reinstate the employee. The burden is on the employer to demonstrate the legitimacy of its decision, and, to the extent that the employer's decision is a pretext merely to rid itself of an employee with a serious health condition, the employer will face liability under the FMLA.

Employers also are not obligated to reinstate key employees if doing so would cause "substantial and grievous economic injury" to the employer. A *key employee* is defined as a salaried employee who is among the highest paid 10 percent of the employer's workers within 75 miles of the employee's work site. Although frequently touted as a significant limitation designed to prevent hardship for employers, the FMLA clearly limits this exception, making it available only under extreme and unique circumstances. The "standard of substantial and grievous economic injury" is much more stringent than the "undue hardship" test under the ADA. The economic injury must essentially threaten the very economic viability of the company. Although the inevitability of bankruptcy in the event of reinstatement is not a requirement, a consequence of nearly this magnitude is clearly intended by the FMLA. Merely costing much is not sufficient.

Q 8:195   What notice is an employee required to provide in connection with FMLA leave?

If a leave is foreseeable, the FMLA requires that an employee provide at least 30 days' notice. If the need for leave is not foreseeable, the employee need only provide notice as soon as "practicable." This is not as soon as possible, or as soon as practical, but somewhere in between. But failure to provide the required notice does not mean that FMLA leave can be denied entirely. All an employer can do is to refuse FMLA time off until 30 days after notice is given. To the extent the employee can take time off under an employer's policies (e.g., vacation and sick days), the employee may obtain time-off benefits before 30 days expire. The DOL's final rules on the FMLA, published November 17, 2008 and effective January 16, 2009, clarify an employee's obligation with respect to providing notice to the employer for unforeseeable leave. The final rules provide that the employee must follow the employer's usual and customary call-in procedures for reporting an absence (e.g., before the employee's shift starts), absent unusual circumstances. Many employers hope that this change will result in employees providing more timely notice of FMLA leave, which was noted by the DOL to have been stated to have been an issue with many employers.

Notice by an employee is broadly construed under the FMLA. An employee need not provide written notice to an employer to receive an FMLA leave, despite an employer's written policies to the contrary. In addition, the employee need not designate the request for leave as a request for FMLA leave. All the employee needs to do is verbally inform management of a need for leave for a condition that qualifies under the FMLA. At that point, the employer must verify the reasons for the request if it wishes to do so, and notify the employee promptly whether he or she may take the leave under the FMLA.

Various factual scenarios can produce seemingly inconsistent results when an employer is trying to determine whether an employee has fulfilled his or her obligations to provide sufficient notice of need for FMLA leave. For example, in *Stevenson v. Hyre Electric Co.* [505 F.3d 720 (7th Cir. 2007)], it was undisputed that the employee did not provide either written or verbal notice to her employer of a need for FMLA leave. However, the facts showed that the employee at issue had an extreme and physical response to a stray dog entering her work space at the company. The response was so extreme that the employee left work, stayed home for several days, and when she attempted to return to work, she was unable to function and demonstrated "erratic" and "emotional" behavior. Her co-workers were apparently very concerned about her behavior and actually locked her out of the building as a result. Based on this unique set of facts, the court concluded that it was an issue of fact whether the company, which was aware of her erratic and bizarre behavior, should have been on notice of her need for leave, which was attributable to a serious health condition under the FMLA. On the other hand, in *Rask v. Fresenius Medical Care North America* [509 F.3d 466 (8th Cir. 2007)], the court found that an employee, who merely told her supervisor that she was "diagnosed with depression" when asked to explain various absences from work was not sufficient notice of a need for leave in connection with a serious health condition under the FMLA. In *Kobus v. College of St. Scholastica, Inc.,* [608 F.3d 1034 (8th Cir. 2010)], the court held that a former employee who merely notified his employer that he had head and neck pain caused by stress and anxiety, and did not provide medical information to the employer when requested, did not provide sufficient information to provide the employer notice that he was requesting to take leave under the FMLA. In *Saenz v. Harlingen Medical Center, LP* [613 F.3d 576 (5th Cir. 2010)], the employee did not provide notice to the employer of a need for leave for a condition that qualified with the FMLA, resulting in her termination. However, the court found that information provided by the former employee's mother to the employer that her daughter was suffering from a medical condition and was hospitalized, raised an issue of fact as to whether sufficient notice had been given, reversing a decision dismissing the FMLA case. In *Lichtenstein v. University of Pittsburgh Medical Center* [691 F.3d 294 (3d Cir. 2012)], the court held that an employee that called her supervisor stating that she was in the emergency room with her mother who had been taken there via ambulance and that she would not be able to work that day, provided sufficient notice to the employer that her absence may be covered under the FMLA.

Even if sufficient notification for a need for time off attributable to a condition that qualifies under the FMLA is made, employees have continuing obligations to keep their employers reasonably informed as to their need for continued time off and projected return date. In *Righi v. SMC Corp.* [632 F.3d 404 (7th Cir. 2011)], the court held that the employee had no rights under the FMLA because the employee failed to respond to the employer's repeated attempts to contact him as it related to his stated need for time off to care for his mother. The court noted that the employee did not respond to 15 phone calls that the employer made to him over a six-day period which the court found "dooms" his FMLA claim.

Q 8:196 What should an employer do once it receives verbal notice of an employee's need to take a leave that may fall under the FMLA?

Once an employee informs an employer of the need for a leave that may qualify under the FMLA, the employer should ask the employee to certify the reasons for the leave and its qualifications under the FMLA by filling out the DOL's forms WH 380 or WH 381, available from the U.S. Printing Office, government bookstores in many federal buildings, or the DOL itself. Upon receipt of a completed form (or a similar substitute) from the employee or the employee's health care provider, the employer should determine whether the time off qualifies under the Act. If it does, the employee should be promptly notified of the determination and advised about his or her rights and obligations under the FMLA. However, if the medical certification information is insufficient or incomplete, such that it does not support a condition that falls under the FMLA, the Sixth Circuit has held that the employer was entitled to deny medical leave and terminate the employee for excessive absenteeism with no liability under the FMLA. [Nawrocki v. United Methodist Ret. Communities, Inc., 2006 WL 890685 (6th Cir. 2006)] Similarly, the court in *Miedema v. Facility Concession Services, Inc.* [2012 WL 3868887 (5th Cir. Sept. 6, 2012)], the court held that an employee's physician's response to a request for certification that was incomplete and not rectified, despite the employer's request for additional information, permitted the employer to terminate the employee for his continued absence.

Q 8:197 What may an employer do if it questions the medical certification that it receives from the employee or the employee's health care provider?

If an employer receives a completed certification signed by a health care provider, it may not request additional information from that provider. A health care provider representing the employer may, however, contact the employee's provider to clarify and authenticate the medical certification. In addition, if the employer has reason to doubt the validity of the medical certification, it may require the employee to obtain a second opinion from another provider at the employer's expense. With the exception of rural areas where the availability of physicians is limited, the employer must generally use a provider with whom it does not regularly deal for this second opinion.

The FMLA also provides a mechanism for obtaining a third opinion in the event of a conflict between the first and second. Again, the third opinion is at the employer's expense. If the employee and the employer both approve the selection of the medical professional providing it, the third opinion is final and binding. If no agreement between the employer and employee can be reached, the good faith of each party is analyzed to determine whose opinion is controlling. If the employer does not attempt, in good faith, to reach an agreement with the employee as to the third medical professional, the employer is automatically bound by the first certification provided by the employee. Similarly, if the employee does not attempt, in good faith, to reach an agreement as to the third medical professional, the employee will be bound by the second certification obtained at the request of the employer. The issue of good faith is resolved when claims are presented in state court or the DOL.

Employees may engage in behavior during an FMLA leave, which is entirely inconsistent with the professed need for leave itself, and cause the employer to question the employee's need for leave. For example, in *Jaszczyszyn v. Advantage Health Physician Network* [2012 WL 5416616 (6th Cir. Nov. 7, 2012)], an employee, while on FMLA leave purportedly due to a total disability, posted information on her Facebook page showing her engaging in social activities at a local festival, which on their face, belied the purported total disability that the employee had claimed. Not surprisingly, the employee's claim of retaliation was rejected by the Sixth Circuit, holding that her FMLA leave was fraudulent.

Q 8:198 Can an employer obtain medical re-certifications after the commencement of FMLA leave?

Yes, if it does so for reasonable and legitimate reasons. Generally, seeking recertification more often than every 30 days is impermissible unless there are changed circumstances or the employer receives information that leads it to question the veracity of the employee's stated reasons for absence. Under the DOL's final rules, recertification for illnesses of long duration can occur every six months.

Q 8:199   Must an employee report to his or her employer during FMLA leave?

An employer may require an employee on FMLA leave to report periodically on his or her status and intent to return to work. This requirement should be communicated, preferably in writing, to the employee at the commencement of the FMLA leave, and this policy must be consistent with the employer's requirements with respect to all other employees on any sort of leave. In other words, this requirement must not discriminate against individuals on FMLA leave. In addition, it cannot be used to harass an employee on FMLA leave. For example, requiring employees to call in every day and speak with their supervisors would be considered onerous, particularly for an employee with a chronic condition who may be absent for many weeks.

Q 8:200   May an employer require an employee to provide a fitness-for-duty report before returning to work?

Yes. Employers may adopt uniformly applied policies or practices that require all employees similarly situated who take time off for medical conditions to get certification from their health care providers that they can resume work. Any related examination must, however, be limited to job-related inquiries in accordance with the ADA. Furthermore, the certification may refer only to the health condition that necessitated FMLA leave.

Q 8:201   If an employee cannot return to work after all FMLA time has elapsed, what further obligations might an employer have?

Assuming that the employee cannot return to work and has been so certified by a medical professional, and the employee has used all his or her FMLA leave, the employer has no further obligations under the FMLA at this time. This does not necessarily end the inquiry. The employee may have rights under the ADA. If the employee's serious health condition qualifies as a disability and he or she is otherwise qualified under the ADA, the employee may have rights under the Act for an accommodation that the employer must provide. The Equal Employment Opportunity Commission considers flexible leave policies as possible accommodations. In *Garcia-Ayala v. Lederle Parenterals, Inc.* [212 F.3d 638 (1st Cir. 2000)], the U.S. Court of Appeals for the First Circuit held that a two-month extension for an employee who had been on leave for at least one year was a reasonable accommodation under the ADA. [*See* 14 *Employment Discrimination Report (EDR)* (BNA) 22 (May 31, 2000).] However, if the medical evidence is undisputed that the employee could not have been able to return to work within a 12-week period, no FMLA violation can occur. In *Edgar v. Jac Products, Inc.* [443 F.3d 501 (6th Cir. 2006)], all the medical evidence available demonstrated that the former employee was not capable of returning to work within the 12-month FMLA period. As such, the court concluded that the plaintiff could not sustain a FMLA claim predicated upon her discharge, despite the fact that the company was unaware of this medical information until after it made its decision to terminate the employee's employment.

Q 8:202   What general problems have emerged since the FMLA has been in effect?

Although there are a myriad of specific technical issues involving the FMLA, the most general problems experienced by employees involve the practical administration of the FMLA.

Under the regulations, the employer bears the burden, once sufficient notice is provided by the employee for the need for time off for a FMLA qualifying event, to notify the employee that the time off is being allotted to FMLA leave. The regulations require this notice to be made by the employer within two business days, confirmed in writing by the next following pay day. [29 C.F.R. § 825.208(b)(1)] The FMLA regulations envision a level of communication among the employer, employee, and health care provider that, quite frankly, does not actually exist in many circumstances. It is the employee's obligation to provide notice of a request for FMLA leave; however, under the regulations, the employee need not mention the words FMLA but need only communicate to the employer the need for time off for a condition or situation the employee or supervisor is supposed to determine fits within the FMLA. With most employers providing vacation days, sick days, personal days and the like, employees do not often articulate sufficient information from which an employer can determine whether the situation fits within the FMLA. Even when sufficient information is provided verbally, the supervisor that receives the information may not understand the FMLA or circumstances that enable an individual to receive FMLA time and therefore may never communicate to the office manager or human resource department that the requested time off is allocable to FMLA time. It is the employer's obligation to designate whether time off will be allocated to available FMLA time, and the employer who wants to ensure that all eligible FMLA time off is allocated to each employee's allotted FMLA leave time will have difficulty obtaining suitable information to administer this federal benefit properly.

Even assuming that sufficient information is given and recognized so that FMLA time could be allocated, the certification requirements, which seem logical and sound on paper, do not actually work in all circumstances. Under the FMLA, an employer who receives information suggesting that the FMLA may be applicable but is not sure can send the employee a medical certification form, to be filled out by the health care provider, certifying whether the time off is attributable to FMLA leave; however, by the time the form is sent out, the employee is often already back to work and has no interest or need to go to the doctor. Even if the employee is still under the care of the physician, the physician is often reluctant to fill out these forms absent an appointment for which the employee may be charged. Furthermore, even if the certification forms are filled out, they often fail to include the information required for the employer to make a cogent decision as to whether or not FMLA time has been used.

Although it is true that the regulations permit an employer to deny FMLA time when the employee does not provide the required certification, or sufficient information to determine if FMLA is applicable, in many circumstances this means nothing. If the employee has already returned to work, denying FMLA leave for days the employee may have missed in the past means little as a practical matter. As employers become more familiar with their rights and obligations, and health care providers become more familiar with the certification requirements, this process may become less problematic; however, proper administration of the FMLA today is a cumbersome task that takes great patience and diligence.

Q 8:203   Is retaliation prohibited under the FMLA?

There are three provisions under the FMLA that courts apply to establish retaliation claims. Section 2615(a) of the FMLA provides that, "It shall be unlawful for any employer to interfere with, restrain, or deny the exercise of or the attempt to exercise, any right provided under this subchapter" [29 U.S.C. § 2615(a)(1)] Subsection 2 from this provision provides, "It shall be unlawful for any employer to discharge or in any other manner discriminate against any individual for opposing any practice made unlawful by this subchapter." [29 U.S.C. § 2615(a)(2)] In addition, 29 C.F.R. § 825.220(c), prohibits employers from "discriminating against employees or prospective employees who had used FMLA leave." There are many recent cases demonstrating the employer's potential for liability when employees suffer adverse employment actions following the exercise or attempted exercise of their rights under the FMLA.

In *Erdman v. Nationwide Insurance Co.* [582 F.3d 500 (3d Cir. 2009)], an employee claimed that he had been terminated as a result of his request to take FMLA leave. The employer claimed that a retaliation claim could not be maintained because the employee had merely requested the right to take the leave, as opposed to having taking the leave itself. The court, reviewing both the statutory provisions of Section 2615(a) and its regulations concluded that retaliation claims extended not only to those that have taken leave, but those that requested as well. However, if a clear request for time off in connection with an FMLA qualifying event has not occurred, a retaliation claim cannot be maintained. In *Fischer v. NYC Department of Education* [2009 WL 3213082 (E.D.N.Y. Sept. 30, 2009)], an employee had not requested time off for an FMLA qualifying condition, but had merely requested a medical leave form. The employee claimed that he had suffered adverse employment action as a result of having requested the leave form, but the court concluded that merely requesting the medical leave form, without more, was insufficient to show that he had exercised rights protected by the FMLA, such that a retaliation claim could not be maintained.

In *Pellegrino v. Communication Workers of America, AFL-CIO, CLC* [2011 WL 1930607 (W.D. Pa. May 19, 2011)], the court held that an employee terminated for violating company policy by engaging in unapproved travel during a time period that she was accepting sick leave pay served as a legitimate reason for termination and not retaliation under the FMLA. An employee who was terminated soon after she returned from FMLA leave for showing lewd pictures to patients prior to commencement of her leave could not maintain a retaliation claim under the FMLA as a result of her termination. [Adams v. Fayette Home Care & Hospice, 452 Fed. Appx. 137 (3d Cir. Pa. 2011)] As with most retaliation claims, timing is an issue, and the close proximity in time of the adverse employment action with the exercise of FMLA rights typically sets the stage for possible retaliation claims. Although courts generally hold that timing is usually insufficient, in and of itself, to support a claim, any additional relevant evidence together with close proximity in timing, will generally allow employees to maintain a retaliation claim.

In *Follis v. Memorial Medical Center* [2009 WL 2972342 (C.D. Ill. Sept. 11, 2009)], an employee who was terminated soon after requesting intermittent leave under the FMLA filed a retaliation claim against her employer. Although the court acknowledged that timing alone was insufficient to support the claim, the employee testified that her supervisor expressed opposition to the intermittent leave request when it was requested and the court held this information, together with the proximity in timing, was sufficient to survive the employer's motion for summary disposition. In *Schaff v. Smithkline Beecham Corp.* [602 F.3d 1236 (11th Cir. 2010)], an employee who was demoted following maternity leave under the FMLA claimed retaliation, but the court affirmed the dismissal of the case because, although the plaintiff claimed that timing showed causation and retaliation, the court found that the professional deficiencies that the employer discovered in the employee's work while the employee was on leave provided legitimate reasons for the demotion. Similarly, in *Estrada v. Cypress Semiconductor (Minnesota), Inc.* [616 F.3d 866 (8th Cir. 2010)], the court rejected a claim that termination was an interference with the former employee's rights under the FMLA, finding that the employer's termination of her employment for poor attendance was well-documented and justified and that the employer would have made the same termination decision regardless of whether the employee had exercised her alleged FMLA rights. In *Krutzig v. Pulte Home Corp.* [602 F.3d 1231 (11th Cir. 2010)], the court held that the failure of the employer to have knowledge of an employee's request for FMLA leave precluded any claim for retaliation under the FMLA. An employee who claimed that she could not return to work upon conclusion of her FMLA leave because the employer's discriminatory and retaliatory conduct did not state a claim under the FMLA. The court held that, as a matter of first impression, the employee's claim that the employer exacerbated her condition such that she was incapable of returning to work at the end of her 12-week FMLA allotment was not a viable theory of liability under the FMLA. [Breneisein v. Motorola, Inc., 656 F.3d 701 (7th Cir. 2011)]

Although employees must be "eligible" to obtain an FMLA leave, there may be circumstances when an ineligible employee can nonetheless maintain a retaliation claim under the FMLA.

In *Reynolds v. Inter-Industry Conference on Auto Collision Repair* [594 F. Supp. 2d 925 (N.D. Ill. 2009)], an employee who, at the time, was ineligible for FMLA leave, requested time off under the FMLA after the period that he would have been eligible under the FMLA. Even though the employee was terminated prior to becoming eligible under the FMLA, the court nonetheless concluded that this employee could maintain a retaliation claim because he would have been eligible by the time the requested time off occurred.

Q 8:204　What specific areas pose the most difficulties for employers in the administration of the FMLA?

Although the FMLA is challenging, and many areas pose difficulties in its administration, the following appear to be the most prevalent:

Interaction between the FMLA and other company policies for paid leave or time off. The FMLA is only applicable to relatively large employers (50 or more employees), and many of these employers have company policies for paid time off for sickness, personal days, vacation or disability, in addition to FMLA time. It is permissible for an employer to count FMLA concurrent with other time-off benefits, provided the employee is advised of the allocation to FMLA time. This decision must be made and communicated promptly (typically within two business days) after the employer has knowledge that the time off qualifies for FMLA leave, and cannot be made retroactively. [29 C.F.R. § 825.208(b) and (c)]

Intermittent or reduced leave schedules. Although in some situations (e.g., birth, foster care, or adoption) leave must be taken in blocks of time, intermittent or reduced leave is permissible if medically necessary because of the employee's own serious health condition, or in circumstances where the employee is needed to care for a spouse, child, or parent suffering from a serious health condition. This type of leave poses unique administrative burdens. In the first place, the employer may only allocate time off to FMLA leave that actually qualifies for FMLA leave. If an employee, taking intermittent leave to care for a spouse, takes a half-day of personal leave for personal reasons other than to care for the spouse (e.g., to go to the beach) that half-day could not be allocated to FMLA leave. In addition, FMLA leave allocations are not made by the hour, but by the week using the employee's regular work hours within the week as a basis. As a result, an employee who regularly works 30 hours per week and uses 10 hours for FMLA purposes during one week will have one-third of a week allocated to FMLA time.

Recognizing when FMLA applies. An employer cannot allocate time to an employee's FMLA leave bank unless it first recognizes that the time off qualifies as FMLA leave. This is particularly difficult, given that the regulations do not require the employee to ask specifically for FMLA leave. Rather, the employee need only verbally indicate a need for time off and articulate a reason that qualifies for FMLA leave.

Q 8:205　What can employers do to attempt to ease difficulties with respect to the administration of the FMLA?

First and foremost, employers need to educate employees and supervisors regarding the circumstances under which FMLA time is applicable. Even though a company may have trained human resource professionals, if that department does not receive sufficient information to recognize that leave can be allocated to FMLA, it will not make the proper allocation. As a result, the people in the field, employees and supervisors, must be cognizant of the FMLA and the circumstances under which it is available, so that they can properly provide information to human resources regarding time off that can be attributed to

FMLA time. In addition, the company should funnel all FMLA issues to one person or a group of people who understand the FMLA to facilitate the extremely technical administration process and ensure diligence on behalf of the employer.

Once information is received that indicates FMLA time may be allocable, if certification is reasonably necessary then certification forms should be sent out and their return monitored. The FMLA allows employers to deny FMLA time if an employee does not respond to certification requests. Again, this should be diligently monitored by the employer. The DOL has prepared two different forms for use with the certification process, both a prototype notice to the employee in response to an FMLA request and a physician's certification form. Those companies lacking the ability to create forms that are consistent with FMLA regulations are highly recommended to use the DOL forms.

In addition, those people responsible for administering the FMLA should obtain a copy of the current FMLA regulations. They can be received by contacting the DOL, Wage and Hour Division. They can also be found in the Code of Federal Regulations, 29 C.F.R. Part 825, the FMLA of 1993; Final Rule. Although the regulations are weighty, they are written in plain English, in question and answer format, and are not terribly difficult to understand. Undoubtedly, an employment attorney may need to be consulted from time to time regarding interpretation of the regulations; however, the regulations themselves provide answers to many simple questions in a straightforward and understandable manner.

Lastly, employers need to adopt procedures to track the use of FMLA time accurately and efficiently. Many of the procedures employers now implement do not work. These employers have attendance cards, with FMLA as one of many other different designations for time off, including vacation, personal day, and short-term disability. The FMLA bank is often used concurrently with other time-off benefits, and forms that do not permit the dual tracking of company-provided benefits and FMLA use will not be adequate. In addition, every time FMLA is used, someone needs to review the applicable time period during which the leave is provided to ascertain the availability of leave. For example, if a rolling 12-month period is usual, measuring back 12 months from the use of leave, the administrator needs to look back constantly within a 12-month period to assess the continued availability of FMLA leave.

Q 8:206   Are there any court decisions interpreting the FMLA and its regulations?

Sufficient time has passed since the enactment of the FMLA for court decisions to be reported involving the interpretation of the FMLA and its regulations as promulgated by the DOL. In January 1998, a federal judge ruled that language contained within the DOL regulations is unconstitutional. [See Seaman v. Downtown P'ship of Baltimore, Inc., 991 F. Supp. 751 (D. Md. 1998).] Specifically, the FMLA provides that to be eligible for family medical leave, the employee must have worked for the employer for 12 months, performed at least 1,250 hours of service for the employer, and work at a work site where there are 50 or more employees within a 75-mile radius. In *Seaman*, the employer had granted an FMLA leave to an employee who was not eligible under the literal language of the FMLA because she had not worked for the employer for 12 months. During the leave, the employee was terminated and sued the employer, claiming rights under the FMLA. The DOL regulations provide that once an employer declares an employee to be eligible, whether he or she is or not, the employer is stuck with that decision and cannot "subsequently challenge the employee's eligibility." [29 C.F.R. § 825.110(d)] In addressing this situation, the court found that the employee was not eligible for FMLA leave and that the DOL did not have authority to extend eligibility, as envisioned, under the preceding regulation. ["Federal Judge Finds That Department of Labor Regulation Is At Odds With Plain Language of FMLA," 10(4) *Employment Discrimination Report (EDR)* (BNA) 107–08 (Jan. 28, 1998)]

The U.S. Supreme Court ruled that an FMLA regulation exceeded the authority of the Secretary of Labor by providing a categorical penalty against employees who fail to designate leave time as FMLA leave time. [Ragsdale v. Wolverine World Wide, Inc., 535 U.S. 81 (2002)] The regulation at issue [29 C.F.R. § 825.700(a)] provides that if an employee takes a paid or unpaid leave, and if the employer fails to designate the leave as counting toward FMLA leave, the leave does not count against the FMLA entitlement. In this case, the employee had taken 30 weeks of leave, clearly qualified for FMLA leave, but no designation by the employer had been made. Although the regulation section would require a different result, the Court held the regulation to be beyond the scope of the secretary's authority, rendering it unenforceable. The *Ragsdale* ruling was also followed by the Third Circuit in *Fogleman v. Greater Hazelton Health Alliance*. [122 Fed. Appx. 581 (3d Cir. 2004)] In that case, an employee who had not been advised of her FMLA rights had been on a leave that extended beyond 12 weeks. Following *Ragsdale*, the court found that in order to show prejudice, the employee was required to demonstrate that had she been advised of her FMLA rights, she could have returned to work after the 12-week period. However, the testimony in the case indicated that the employee was not able to return to her position at the expiration of the 12-week period, and as such, there was no prejudice for the employer having failed to provide notice to the employee of her FMLA rights. However, if an employee can demonstrate prejudice by failure of an employer to provide notice of application of leave toward the FMLA, such failure may result in the time off not being counted toward FMLA leave. Such was the case in *Downey v. Rodney J. Strain Jr.* [510 F.3d 534 (5th Cir. 2007)] In the case, the employee had time off for which the employer had never notified her that the time off would be attributable to FMLA leave. When time off for a subsequent surgery, when added to the prior leave, was determined by the Company to exceed 12 weeks, it then transferred the claimant to a different job upon her return, claiming that she had exhausted her FMLA leave rights before the end of her leave in connection with her surgery. The issue was whether the prior time off could be counted toward her FMLA allotment, despite the fact that she had never received notice from the company in connection with her prior leave. Based upon the claimant's claims that if she been aware of the allocation to FMLA for her prior leave, she could have rescheduled her surgery to a later time period to take advantage of additional FMLA accruals, the court held that the claimant was prejudiced by the company's failure to notify her of its allocation to FMLA leave for her prior leave and as such, upheld the determination that the prior leave could not be counted against the claimant's FMLA allotment.

In addition, numerous decisions emphasize the need for the employee to give adequate notice in order to receive protection under the FMLA. Generally, these cases involve situations where employers fire employees for absenteeism problems, and the employees claim that the absences were properly attributed to FMLA leave time, for which firing would be a violation of the FMLA. Although the regulations do not require the employee to articulate the words "Family and Medical Leave Act," it is incumbent upon the employee to provide sufficient information to the employer of a need for time off for a condition that qualifies for FMLA treatment. As such, if the employee does not undertake reasonable notice, no protection will be afforded, as seen in *Satterfield v. Wal-Mart Stores, Inc.* [135 F.3d 973 (5th Cir. 1998)] In *Satterfield*, the employee was discharged for excessive absences over a three-week period. According to the facts of the case, the cashier provided little information about the reason for her absences, indicating on just one occasion that she would not be in on just "that [one] day" because she was sick. In reviewing the facts, the court found the information provided by the employee was insufficient for purposes of invoking protection under the FMLA. [*See* "5th Cir. Reverses $50,000 Award to Worker Who Gave Incomplete FMLA Notice," 10 *Employment Discrimination Report (EDR)* (BNA) 285 (Mar. 4, 1998).]

If adequate notice is provided, courts are willing to award damages and penalties against employers who violate the FMLA, even if they are completely ignorant of the law. For example, in *Hayes v. Larry Klein Wholesale Meats & Provisions, Inc.* [No. 96 1592 CIV (D.C. Fla. Feb. 9, 1998)], a federal judge ordered a company to pay over $140,000, together with attorneys' fees and costs to an employee who had been fired after he notified the company that he would not be able to come in, so that he could care for his wife following surgery. [*See* "Man Awarded $140,000 After Being Fired from Missing Work to Care for Ailing Wife," 10(8) *Employment Discrimination Report (EDR)* (BNA) 251 (Feb. 25, 1998).] Similarly, in *Knussman v. Maryland* [65 F. Supp. 2d 353 (D. Md. 1999)], a state trooper was awarded $375,000 by a jury for his employer's refusal to grant him leave to care for his spouse and newborn. [*See* 12 *Employment Discrimination Report (EDR)* (BNA) 196 (Feb. 10, 1999).] In *Armstead v. Caesars Atlantic Hotel/Casino* [(D.N.J. No. 98-CV-4563)], a blackjack dealer was reported to have obtained a $500,000 judgment as a result of a termination in violation of the FMLA. [*See* 16 *Employment Discrimination Report (EDR)* (BNA) 23 (Jan. 3, 2001).]

In joint employment situations, the determination of the appropriate work site to use for purposes of determining whether the employer has 50 or more employees within 75 miles of the employer's work site can pose difficulties. Under the regulations promulgated by the Secretary of Labor, two entities may be considered joint employers when they both exercise some control over the work or working conditions of the employee. [29 C.F.R. § 825.106(a)] Typically, joint employment will be found to exist when a temporary agency supplies employees to another employer. Under the regulations in joint employment situations, the primary employer—the employer with the authority to hire, fire, make payroll, and provide benefits—is responsible for providing FMLA leave, and the regulations further provide that it is the primary employer's work site that is used for purposes of determining whether or not the employee works at a work site with 50 or more employees within 75 miles. [29 C.F.R. § 825.111(a)(3)] However, this regulation posed difficulty for the Tenth Circuit in *Harbert v. Healthcare Services Group, Inc.* [391 F.3d 1140 (10th Cir. 2004)] In that case, a housekeeping service employee who regularly worked at a work site where there were fewer than 50 employees within 75 miles claimed that she was denied eligibility for FMLA leave in violation of the Act because her primary employer had more than 50 employees at its work site in another town. Her primary employer countered that it had no obligations under the FMLA because the work site where the plaintiff regularly worked was the appropriate work site to determine whether or not the 50/75 threshold was met. Although the regulations, if followed, clearly would have made the primary employer's work site the appropriate work site for purposes of determining whether or not the threshold was met, the court concluded that the regulations were invalid and constituted an arbitrary and capricious use of the Secretary of Labor's authority to promulgate regulations. The court reasoned that the 50/75 test was in place so as not to impose an undue burden on employers in providing leave and that to arbitrarily pick a work site other than the work site where the employee regularly worked, merely because joint employment was determined to have occurred, was inconsistent with the statute.

In addition to satisfying the criterion above (i.e., having worked 1,250 hours during the previous 12 months), to be eligible, an employee must also have been employed for 12 months. The question of when an employer is to make the determination as to whether the employee has satisfied the 12 months requirement was faced by the Third Circuit in *Renart v. Chartwells.* [122 Fed. Appx. 559 (3d Cir. 2004)] In that case, the employee commenced employment on November 4, 1998, commenced her leave on October 26, 1999, and was terminated on November 5, 1999. Although she did not have 12 months of employment when her leave commenced on October 26, 1999, she satisfied the 12-month criterion as of November 4, 1999, the day before her termination. The employee argued that, because she was employed more than 12 months before her termination, her leave under both the FMLA and companion state law should have commenced as of November 4, 1998. However, the court, in reviewing the regulations, determined that the decision of eligibility for FMLA shall be determined "as of the date the leave commences." [29 C.F.R. § 825.110(d)] As such, because the employee had not been employed for 12 months at the time her leave commenced, October 26, 1999, she was ineligible for FMLA leave and leave under a similar state statute.

In *Brumbalough v. Camelot Care Center, Inc.* [427 F.3d 996 (6th Cir. 2005)], the court held in this case of first impression that, in light of specific damages listed in the FMLA and its regulations for violations—which do not specifically provide for emotional damages—emotional damages are not recoverable under the FMLA. In *Pagan-Colon v. Walgreen's of San Patricio, Inc.* [697 F.3d 1 (1st Cir. 2012)], the court held, in a case of first impression, that overtime pay that the employee regularly received for overtime work was properly included within an FMLA back pay award. With respect to money damages, the Supreme Court, in 2012, held that the FMLA did not abrogate the state's sovereign immunity from money damages for violations of the FMLA. [Coleman v. Court of Appeals of Md., 132 S. Ct. 1327 (2012)]

Q 8:207   What common mistakes do employers make with regard to the FMLA?

The following problems are representative of the types of mistakes employers consistently make in the administration of FMLA.

- *Failure to review eligibility criteria.* Covered employers under the FMLA must have 50 or more employees during 20 or more calendar workweeks in the current or preceding calendar year. Most employers are able to determine whether they are FMLA-covered employers without much difficulty; however, if they determine they are covered, they often do not recognize that employees also must meet eligibility criteria before the FMLA will apply. Specifically, to be eligible an employee must:
  — Have worked for the employer for 12 months (not necessarily consecutive),
  — Have performed 1,250 hours of service for the employer, and
  — Work at a work site where there are 50 employees or more within a 75-mile radius.

Many employers, once they recognize they are covered, assume improperly that all of their employees are covered by FMLA and routinely provide FMLA leave to people who are not eligible. This practice can pose numerous problems.

Example. An individual, prior to a leave, has performed 1,250 hours of service but has not been employed by the employer for 12 months. This employee is ineligible for leave, but the employer mistakenly tells the employee she is on an FMLA leave and starts counting time toward the 12-week allotment. Later, before the 12-week allotment is utilized, the employee returns to work and then meets the criterion of 12 months of employment with the employer, and then goes back on leave. At this point, the employee is eligible for FMLA leave, and if the employer denies leave for the full 12-week period, relying on mistaken FMLA leave in the past, the employer violates the FMLA regulations as they are written.

- As a result, employers need to make certain that before they attribute time to FMLA the employee must meet the eligibility criteria for purposes of utilizing FMLA time.
- *Failure to recognize time off as FMLA qualifying.* It is not unusual for employers to fail to allocate FMLA time to an employee's FMLA bank for many reasons. Generally, the situations involve an employee who does not

specifically request FMLA time, but indicates to the supervisor the need for time off work as a vacation, personal day, or the like for circumstances that qualify as FMLA time. For example, an employee may be undergoing inpatient surgery the next week and would like to take vacation days to cover the surgery and recuperation. Although paid time-off benefits may be available, the time off would be allocated to FMLA leave for the period of absence necessitated by the surgery.

- *Failure to notify the employee of FMLA time.* Once an employer receives sufficient information to determine an individual is eligible for FMLA leave, it must notify the employee that the time off is being allocated to FMLA time. If an employer fails to notify the employee properly, the regulations provide that an employer may not retroactively allocate the time to FMLA time, even if the time off would be properly allocated to the employee's 12-week entitlement. [29 C.F.R. § 825.208] However, in cases where the employee cannot claim any prejudice as a result of such failure on behalf of the employer, the U.S. Supreme Court has held that the employee has no recourse under the FMLA. [Ragsdale v. Wolverine World Wide, Inc. 535 U.S. 81 (2002)]

- *Lack of diligence during certification process.* The regulations allow the employer to have a certification filled out by the relevant health care provider to determine whether the situation falls within the criteria established under the FMLA; however, simply sending a certification form is not adequate. The employer must monitor the situation to make sure that the information comes back, and if it does, that it is adequate for purposes of the FMLA. Employers are not permitted, once the health care provider has certified the condition as qualifying, to circumvent the certification by contacting the health care provider for more information. The employer is required to take it at face value unless it has reason to believe it is inaccurate. If it does, its only recourse is to have the employee examined by another health care provider, not affiliated with the employer, and at the employer's expense for purposes of certification. If the health care provider selected by the employer confirms the designation, the employer must abide by that designation. If confirmation is not made, the regulations provide that both the employer and the employee will select a third physician, in good faith, whose decision will be binding. If the parties cannot agree on a suitable physician and the employee fails to act in good faith, the decision of the health care provider selected by the employer will control. On the other hand, if the employer acts in bad faith with regard to the selection of a third health care provider, the determination by the employee's health care provider will control. In addition, the regulations prevent the employer from unduly harassing employees through the certification process when they are on FMLA leave and generally prohibits, absent extenuating circumstances, recertifications occurring more than once every 30 days. The certification provisions are technical and rigorous, and employers must understand them to ensure that they properly follow the regulations issued by the DOL.

- *Lack of training.* The FMLA is difficult to administer, and many of the problems that develop are a result of a supervisor's lack of understanding of FMLA policies and procedures. It is generally advisable that, in addition to office or HR staff, supervisors be trained to assist in identifying situations involving an employee's time off that may be allocable to FMLA. Training will make supervisors more knowledgeable of the FMLA allocation scheme and provide them the tools needed to assist in the implementation of an FMLA policy. Particularly in relation to allocating time off to FMLA, the supervisors in the field often obtain the notification and, if they are untrained, they will not spot vacation days, personal days, or other paid time off as FMLA-qualifying occurrences that can be allocated to each employee's FMLA bank under the regulations. As the regulations provide, employees need not request FMLA leave but merely communicate a need for time off for an FMLA-qualifying occurrence. The term "FMLA" does not need to be communicated.

Q 8:208   For what damages can an employer be liable if a violation of the FMLA is found?

An employer can be liable for the following damages if a violation of the FMLA is determined to have occurred:

- Lost wages/benefits;
- Interest on damages;
- Liquidated damages equal to lost wages/benefits; and/or
- Employment, reinstatement, or other equitable relief.

In *Pagan-Colon v. Walgreen's of San Patricio, Inc.* [697 F.3d 1 (1st Cir. 2012)], the court held, in a case of first impression, that overtime pay that the employee regularly received for overtime work was properly included within an FMLA back pay award. With respect to money damages, the Supreme Court, in 2012, held that the FMLA did not abrogate the state's sovereign immunity from money damages for violations of the FMLA. [Coleman v. Court of Appeals of Md., 132 S. Ct. 1327 (2012)]

Q 8:209   Are emotional distress damages awardable under the FMLA?

The Sixth Circuit in *Brumbalough v. Camelot Care Center, Inc.* [427 F.3d 996 (6th Cir. 2005)] addressed the issue of whether emotional distress damages are recoverable under the FMLA. In what the Sixth Circuit determined was a case of first impression before the circuit, the court held that because the FMLA specifically lists the type of damages for which the employer may be liable and includes damages only insofar as they are monetary losses of the employee, such as salary and benefits and certain liquidated damages, the FMLA does not permit recovery for emotional distress.

Q 8:210   Is it a violation of the FMLA to deny bonuses for employees who use sick pay in conjunction with an FMLA leave?

In *Chubb v. City of Omaha, Nebraska* [424 F.3d 831 (8th Cir. 2005)], the court held that a city's policy of denying an annual leave bonus for an employee who used sick pay is not a violation of FMLA. The court reasoned that it was the employee's election to take the sick pay in conjunction with an FMLA leave, and as such, having elected sick pay, which is not required under the FMLA, the city could then deny the employee an annual leave bonus that is available only for employees who do not use sick pay during the year.

Sick Leave

Q 8:211   Are employees entitled to paid sick leave?

No state or federal law requires paid sick leave; however, most employers provide this benefit to maintain employee morale and to keep valued employees from changing jobs.

COBRA

Q 8:212   Which employers are subject to COBRA?

An employer that employs 20 or more persons and maintains a group health plan must offer continuation coverage to qualified beneficiaries at their expense. [I.R.C. § 4980B(d)] Under Consolidated Omnibus Budget Reconciliation Act (COBRA) legislation, the definition of *employee* can include an independent contractor.

Q 8:213   Are there any other exceptions to the application of COBRA other than the small employer exception?

Plans adopted by churches and governmental plans are excepted from COBRA, although rules similar to COBRA apply to governmental plans. With respect to church plans, it is insufficient for the employer to merely have some affiliation or relationship with a church. In *Polk v. Dubuis Health Systems, d/b/a Dubuis Hospital of Alexandria* [2007 WL 2890262 (W.D. La. Sept. 28, 2007)], a hospital, which was a non-profit corporation where the sole corporate member was a non-profit corporation established and operated by religious groups, was nonetheless not a "church plan" because the governing board, through which its executives autonomously conducted the daily operations of its health facility, including primarily lay people, and no evidence was found that any denominational requirement existed for any employee or customer of the health care institution. As such, the court concluded that the benefit plan at issue was not a "church plan" and, therefore, had to comply with the requirements of COBRA.

Q 8:214   What is a *qualifying event* under COBRA?

It is any event that would normally result in a loss of coverage for the covered employee or qualified beneficiary, were it not for the application of COBRA. These events are:

- The death of the covered employee;
- The termination (other than by reason of gross misconduct) or reduction of hours of the covered employee's employment;
- Divorce or legal separation;
- The covered employee's becoming entitled to Medicare benefits;
- A dependent child ceasing to meet dependency requirements; or
- A proceeding in a case under federal bankruptcy law with respect to the employer from whose employment the covered employee retired at any time.

[I.R.C. § 4980B(f)(3)]

Q 8:215   Is legal separation a qualifying event under COBRA?

Although divorce as a qualifying event is self-evident and needs little definition, the issue of what constitutes a legal separation such that a qualifying event has occurred under COBRA can be more problematic. For example, in *Simpson v. TD Williamson, Inc.* [414 F.3d 1203 (10th Cir. 2005)], the issue was whether protective orders entered by a court in a pending divorce action requiring the husband to "stay away from his wife" during their divorce action was tantamount to a "legal separation," thereby triggering COBRA notice requirements and the wife's corresponding obligation to pay premiums for continued coverage. In the case, the plan administrator considered the protective order a qualifying event, sent a COBRA notice to the wife, and, when the wife failed to pay COBRA premiums, terminated her coverage. Although not defined under the regulations or statute, the court noted that other courts that had reviewed the requirements of "legal separation" concluded that the term is uniformly understood to mean a formal, judicial alteration of the marital relationship. [*See Simpson* at 1205, citing Nehme v. INS, 252 F.3d 415 (5th Cir. 2001).] The court held that to constitute a legal separation, the separation must result from a judicial declaration of legal separation cognizant under state domestic laws. As such, the court concluded that the protective order was insufficient to create a legal separation under state law and, therefore, the COBRA notice sent by the plan administrator was sent in error because a qualifying event had not occurred, and the wife's failure to make premium payments could not be used as a basis to terminate her coverage.

Q 8:216   Who must be offered continuation coverage when a qualifying event occurs?

Continuation coverage must be offered to any covered employee to whom a qualifying event occurs. A *covered employee* is any individual who is (or was) covered under a group health plan by virtue of that individual's employment or previous employment with the employer.

Continuation coverage must also be offered to any qualified beneficiary. A *qualified beneficiary* is any individual who is (or was) a beneficiary under the plan as the spouse or dependent child of the covered employee. In addition, with the passage of the Health Insurance Portability and Accountability Act of 1996 (HIPAA), effective January 1, 1997, a child born to or placed for adoption with a covered employee during COBRA coverage is also a qualified beneficiary. In addition, when the qualifying event is the termination of employment or reduction of hours, a covered employee is considered a qualified beneficiary. [I.R.C. §§ 4980B(f), 4980B(g)]

Although an employer need not pay health insurance costs for employees while they are on strike, strikers do not forfeit their COBRA rights. They are entitled to notice and opportunity to continue their group health insurance at their own expense. Indeed, New York Telephone found it could not shorten the 45-day grace period for making the initial premium payment in the case of its striking workers. [Communications Workers of Am. v. NYNEX Corp., 12 E.B.C. Cas. 1049 (2d Cir. 1990)]

Q 8:217   After notice, how long do qualified beneficiaries have to elect COBRA continuation coverage?

COBRA provides that the election period must end no earlier than 60 days after the date the qualified beneficiary was notified of the right to continued coverage. [I.R.C. § 4980B(f)(5)(A)] However, it is important to note that the 60-day election period is not a maximum 60-day period set by statute, but rather is the minimum election period required by COBRA. This point was addressed squarely in *LifeCare Hospitals, Inc. v. Health Plus of Louisiana, Inc.* [418 F.3d 436 (5th Cir. 2005)] In that case, the employer terminated the employment of a gravely ill employee and informed the employee's spouse of COBRA continuation coverage rights in or about July 2001, but coverage was not elected by the participants until December 2001, well after the expiration of 60 days. However, the court found that there was nothing in the plan documents that limited the election period to 60 days, but rather referenced COBRA, which provides only that the election period be at least 60 days in duration after notice of COBRA continuation rights. As such, the court concluded that the December 2001 election was timely and required the provider to pay the employee's medical expenses.

Q 8:218   How long must the COBRA coverage last?

Generally, a qualified beneficiary is entitled to COBRA coverage for as many as 18 months after a qualifying event. If a second qualifying event occurs before expiration of this 18-month period, coverage may be extended to 36 months. For qualified beneficiaries who are disabled on or before a qualifying event, COBRA provides 11 months beyond the initial 18. HIPAA amended COBRA eligibility to include qualified beneficiaries disabled within 60 days of COBRA coverage;

however, COBRA coverage may be terminated, subject to requirements, when the qualified beneficiary becomes covered by another group health plan or becomes eligible for Medicare benefits.

Before HIPAA, COBRA continuation did not end when a beneficiary became covered by a new employer's plan if the new plan excluded preexisting medical conditions. HIPAA limits the circumstances under which a group health plan can impose limitations on preexisting conditions. If the limitation is not applicable under HIPAA, COBRA coverage may be terminated. In addition, if an employee becomes eligible for Medicare during the 18-month COBRA eligibility period, any beneficiary under that COBRA coverage can continue the coverage for 36 months from the date of the employee's entitlement for Medicare benefits.

Q 8:219   What are the notices required under COBRA?

When an employee begins coverage under a group health plan, written notice of COBRA rights must be given to the employee and his or her spouse. If a qualifying event occurs (other than a change in dependency status of a child, a divorce, or a legal separation), the employer must give notice to the plan administrator within 30 days of the qualifying event. In the event of divorce or legal separation or when a child ceases to be a dependent, the covered employee or qualified beneficiary must notify the plan administrator within 60 days of such event. Within 14 days of receipt of that notice, the plan administrator must notify the covered employee and any qualified beneficiary of his or her COBRA rights. [I.R.C. § 4980B(f)(6)] It is not sufficient merely to notify the employee on behalf of other qualified beneficiaries. Employers are at risk if they do not undertake adequate procedures and/or policies to demonstrate that proper notice has been sent. In *Tufano v. Riegel Transportation Co., Inc.* [2006 WL 335693 (E.D.N.Y. Feb. 11, 2006)], a former employee who underwent a surgical operation claimed that he had never received COBRA notification and in fact thought his coverage had been continued. Although it is the burden of the former employee to demonstrate that he did not receive his COBRA notification, the company was its own administrator and had no proof of the notice having been sent out other than an unsigned "file copy" of the COBRA notification letter with no indication of it having been mailed, and the person responsible for the notice could not remember mailing the letter or typing the plaintiff's COBRA notice. Although an employer or plan administrator who sends proper notice to the covered employee's last known address is deemed to be in good-faith compliance with the COBRA notification requirements and, in such instances, it is presumed that the notice was properly addressed and mailed is received, this presumption can only arise if the office practice is organized in such a way so as to ensure the likelihood that notice is always properly addressed and mailed. The court found the procedures that the company followed were shoddy, and therefore not entitled to the presumption that the notice was mailed. This, together with the apparent fact that the employee thought his insurance had continued, as he contacted the insurance company for preapproval for his surgical procedure prior to the surgical operation, the court concluded that the former employee proved by the preponderance of the evidence that he did not receive the COBRA notice and the employer was then obligated to pay this former employee's medical bill. COBRA does not require that the beneficiary or dependents actually receive the required notice, but rather notice sent by the employer by first-class mail to the covered employee or beneficiary's last known address is generally deemed to be sufficient under COBRA. As such, when an administrator mailed notice to the employee and beneficiary to the same address that appeared on the health insurance enrollment form filled out by the employee, such notice was deemed good faith compliance with COBRA despite the fact that it did not contain the employee and beneficiary's apartment number, such that the notice was not actually received. [Robinson-Reeder v. American Council on Educ., 674 F. Supp. 2d 49 (D.D.C. 2009)] In *Gomez v. St. Vincent Health, Inc.* [649 F.3d 583 (7th Cir. 2011)], the court held that when employees did not receive proper notice of their COBRA continuation rights after a qualifying event occurred, it was not error for the lower court to award damages equal to the employee's out-of-pocket costs expended for medical treatment that would have been covered by insurance had COBRA notices been properly sent to the employee, minus whatever premium cost the employee would have incurred for COBRA continuation of the medical insurance at issue.

In addition, HIPAA required that all health care plans subject to COBRA notify qualified beneficiaries on or before November 1, 1996, of HIPAA changes to COBRA. HIPAA also required that, beginning June 1, 1997, group health plans furnish certificates of coverage related to events occurring after October 1, 1996, to COBRA participants to help establish creditable coverage.

Q 8:220   What are the sanctions for failing to comply with COBRA?

An employer is assessed a tax of $100 per day for each failure to properly notify a qualified beneficiary of his or her COBRA rights. (The tax for failure with respect to family coverage is $200 per day per family.) The non-compliance period may extend six months after the date on which the continuation coverage could be terminated. For example, if an employee is terminated and the employer fails to provide the COBRA notice, the non-compliance period is 24 months (18 months continuation for terminated employees plus six months). Under certain circumstances, a third party that administers the health plan for the employer may be held liable for this tax.

No excise tax is assessed if the failure is not the result of willful neglect and is corrected within 30 days. In addition, there is an aggregate dollar limit on the tax when the failure has a reasonable cause. This limit is equal to the lesser of 10 percent of aggregate cost the employer pays or incurs in providing for health coverage or $500,000. Finally, if it is shown that the failure would not have been discovered by an employer exercising reasonable diligence, no tax is imposed. [I.R.C. §§ 4980B(c) and 4980B(f)]

Q 8:221   Have there been any recent changes in COBRA?

The Health Insurance and Accountability Act of 1996 made many changes in health care law, including to COBRA. The more significant changes to COBRA require that group health plans and health insurance issuers furnish a certificate of "creditable coverage" to an individual (1) who loses coverage, (2) who becomes eligible for COBRA, and (3) whose COBRA coverage ceases. Creditable coverage, utilizing the "standard method," is a day-for-day credit for previous continuous health care coverage (including COBRA coverage) that occurs without a break in coverage of 63 days or more. The number of creditable coverage days is used, under HIPAA, to reduce the amount of any preexisting illness limitation (already limited by HIPAA to 12 months for regular enrollees or 18 months for late enrollees) in the employee's next health care plan (seemingly a rather bizarre method to reduce preexisting illness limitations).

The American Recovery and Reinvestment Act of 2009 (ARRA) [Pub. L. No. 111-5] temporarily changed the employer's duties under COBRA. Under the ARRA, as amended, a covered employee who is "involuntarily terminated" between September 1, 2008 and May 31, 2010 may be considered an "assistance eligible individual" (AEI) and receive a 65 percent subsidy of the COBRA premium he or she pays. An AEI may receive such subsidy for a maximum of nine months. According to the ARRA, the employee's COBRA premiums will be deemed to be paid in full as long as the employee pays 35 percent of the premium.

In the case of an underwritten group plan, the employer must first advance 65 percent of the subsidy. Then the employer will be entitled to be repaid by the federal government in the form of an offset credit against the federal quarterly payroll taxes that are paid to the federal government. This can be offset against employee income-tax withholdings and both the employee's and the employer's FICA tax.

Where an employer does not have the assets to pay the 65 percent subsidy, it appears that there is no authority as of yet regarding the required actions of such employer or how the employer may receive a tax credit. If the employer no longer provides any group health policy for any of its employees, the rule that it need not offer COBRA coverage to its former employees still applies.

The ARRA was made effective as of February 17, 2009, but the premium subsidies begin as of the first premium period after the bill was signed. Thus, the ARRA applies for a premium billing as of March 1, 2009 and an eligible employee may begin to receive a subsidy beginning March 1, 2009.

The bill is not retroactive. Therefore, even where an employee was terminated between September 1, 2008 and March 1, 2009, an employer need not pay any subsidies for premiums owed by the employee prior to March 1, 2009.

A one-time notice must be sent to all possible current and former COBRA beneficiaries who may qualify for a subsidy (not just the covered employee), regarding (a) the subsidy, (b) the one-time special extended election period, and (c) other information about ARRA rights. These notices must be provided by April 18, 2009.

Those already on COBRA then have 90 days after the notice to elect the subsidy. Those who rejected or were discontinued from COBRA but are now eligible for the premium subsidy have 60 days following the notice to elect COBRA with a the premium subsidy.

People newly eligible for COBRA coverage (i.e., terminated on or after February 17, 2009, when the ARRA was enacted) will be informed about the ARRA subsidy through the general COBRA notice that they receive within 45 days of being laid off.

Q 8:222   What are the HIPAA Privacy Rules and do they apply to employers?

The HIPAA Privacy Rules adopted by Department of Health & Human Services (HHS) apply to health care plans, health care providers, and clearinghouses. The Privacy Rules work in conjunction with Security Rules, Breach Notification Rules, and Enforcement Rules to prevent the use and disclosure of PHI. Although non-health care provider employers are not covered, their health care plans are covered, such that employers that sponsor health care plans are required to adopt policies and procedures to prevent the use and disclosure of the PHI of plan participants. (See chapter 5 for additional information regarding HIPAA.)

Chapter 9

Government Contractors

This chapter describes the security clearance procedures government contractors must follow to protect classified information. This chapter also discusses the Office of Federal Contract Compliance Programs' (OFCCP) affirmative action obligations for government contractors, as well as the wages and benefits contractors must provide. The chapter concludes with a discussion of the Sarbanes-Oxley Act and whistleblowers in government contracting.

Security Clearances

Q 9:1 What steps must a contractor take to protect classified information that it obtains pursuant to bidding for a contract or in performing a contract for the U.S. Department of Defense?

A contractor is required to follow numerous steps to protect classified information, including appointing a U.S. citizen to direct and supervise appropriate security measures, limiting the disclosure of information to authorized persons only, providing suitable methods for safeguarding classified information, performing security checks within its facility, and providing limited access to restricted areas. The extensive list of duties the contractor is required to perform is set forth in the Industrial Security Manual for Safeguarding Classified Information, published by the U.S. Department of Defense. Non-citizen employees are generally restricted from access to classified information.

Q 9:2   What are the purposes of security clearances?

Personal security investigations and security clearances are intended to protect military intelligence and technology from threats posed by:

1. Foreign intelligence services;

2. Subversive organizations, such as terrorist groups; and

3. Individuals susceptible to improper influences or who have records of dishonest conduct.

Q 9:3   What are the levels of classified information?

There are three levels, or categories, of classified information:

*   *Confidential*: Applies to information, the unauthorized disclosure of which can reasonably be expected to damage the national security.

*   *Secret*: Disclosure can reasonably be expected to seriously damage the national security.

*   *Top Secret*: Disclosure poses an exceptionally grave threat to the national security.

Other less well-known categories of sensitive information include:

*   *Sensitive Compartmented Information*: This is information so sensitive that even top secret designation is not deemed sufficient.

*   *For Official Use Only*: On the opposite end of the spectrum, this type of data is not deemed to merit even a confidential classification but is subject to the federal Privacy Act.

Q 9:4   What is the National Industrial Security Program?

The National Industrial Security Program (NISP) is the U.S. authority for managing the needs of private industry to access classified information. The NISP was established in 1993 by Executive Order 12829. The National Security Council sets policy for the NISP, while the Director of the Information Security Oversight Office (ISOO) is the implementing authority. Under the ISOO, the Secretary of Defense is designated as the Executive Agent; the NISP also recognizes four different Cognizant Security Agencies, all of which have equal authority: the Department of Defense, the Department of Energy, the Central Intelligence Agency, and the Nuclear Regulatory Commission.

The NISP Operating Manual is available at http://www.fas.org/sgp/library/nispom/nispom2006.pdf. Chapter 2 of the Manual discusses security clearances. There are two types of clearances depending on who or what is cleared:

1. A facility clearance (FCL) is an administrative determination that a company is eligible for access to classified information or award of a classified contract. A contract award may be made prior to the issuance of an FCL. In those cases, the contractor will be processed for an FCL at the

appropriate level and must meet eligibility requirements for access to classified information. However, the contractor will not be afforded access to classified information until the FCL has been granted.

2. A personal security clearance (PSC) is one that is issued to an individual employee designated by the contractor.

There are six essential rules that determine whether a contractor can apply for, and expect to obtain, a PSC for a particular employee or category of employees:

1. An employee may be processed for a Personal Clearance (PCL) when the contractor determines that access is essential in the performance of tasks or services related to the fulfillment of a classified contract. A PCL is valid for access to classified information at the same or lower level of classification as the level of the clearance granted.

2. The Cognizant Security Agency (CSA) will determine eligibility for access to classified information in accordance with the national standards and notify the contractor that eligibility has been granted. The CSA will notify the contractor when an employee's PCL has been denied, suspended, or revoked. The contractor shall immediately deny access to classified information to any employee when notified of a denial, revocation or suspension. When the CSA has designated a database as the system of record for contractor eligibility and access, the contractor shall be responsible for annotating and maintaining the accuracy of their employees' access records. Specific procedures will be provided by the CSA.

3. Within a Multiple Facility Organization (MFO) or within the same corporate family, contractors may centrally manage eligibility and access records.

4. The contractor shall limit requests for PCLs to the minimal number of employees necessary for operational efficiency, consistent with contractual obligations and other requirements of the NISP Operating Manual. Requests for PCLs shall not be made to establish "pools" of cleared employees.

5. The contractor shall not submit a request for a PCL to one agency if the employee applicant is cleared or is in process for a PCL by another agency. In such cases, to permit clearance verification, the contractor should provide the new agency with the full name, date and place of birth, Social Security number, clearing agency and type of investigation.

6. Access to Sensitive Compartmented Information (SCI) and Special Access Programs (SAP) information is a determination made by the granting authority.

Q 9:5   What are the basic requirements for security clearance for a contractor's employees?

Generally, only U.S. citizens can be granted a standard security clearance. A naturalized U.S. citizen whose country of origin is determined to have interests adverse to the United States must have been a U.S. citizen for five years or have resided in the United States for the past 10 years. To be cleared for confidential information, an individual must be at least 16 years old; to be cleared for secret or top-secret information, an individual must be at least 18 years old; and any non-U.S. citizens must be at least 21 years old to be cleared for secret or top secret information.

Q 9:6   What is the process for obtaining a security clearance?

For confidential and secret clearances, the steps are:

- National agency check: This is a computerized search of investigative files and other records in the custody of such federal agencies as the FBI and Office of Personnel Management;
- Local agency check: This is a review of criminal history records in the hands of local law enforcement agencies, including local police departments and county sheriffs in those jurisdictions where the subject lived, attended schools, and worked.

For top secret clearances:

- Single scope background investigation: This includes field interviews with references, co-workers, employers, friends, educators, neighbors, and others who know or knew the subject; examination of employment, court, and other available records; and, an interview with the subject him/herself.

Q 9:7   What factors determine approval or disapproval of the subject of a security clearance procedure?

So-called "Adjudicator Guidelines" are used by the federal government to evaluate the information gathered in a security clearance investigation. Factors that will absolutely result in denial of a clearance under the current, post-9/11 guidelines are:

- Conviction of a crime in any court of the United States, resulting in a prison term in excess of one year;
- Current illegal use of or addiction to a controlled substance as defined by the Controlled Substances Act [21 U.S.C. § 802];
- Mental incompetence as determined by a Department of Defense–approved mental health professional;
- Dishonorable discharge from the U.S. military.

Other factors that commonly will be considered in whether or not to grant a clearance will include:

- Citizenship status of the subject and his/her immediate family members;
- History of drug and alcohol use;
- Honesty and trustworthiness;

- General character;
- Foreign travel history; and
- Financial responsibility.

Q 9:8   How long does it take to get a security clearance?

The Transition Assistance Online Web site states,

> It depends on several factors, and the type of investigation. In the past three years, DoD has had a significant backlog of security clearances and reinvestigations pending, most especially for top secret level access. In general, expect a confidential or secret clearance to take between 1 and 3 months. A top secret will probably take between 4 and 8 months. However, some individuals have been waiting for the results of their top secret investigation for more than one year. In general, the more there is to investigate, the longer the investigation will take. Expect the investigation to take longer if you have:
>
> - Lived or worked in several geographic locations or overseas.
> - Traveled outside of the United States.
> - Relatives who have lived outside of the United States.
> - Background information that is difficult to obtain or involves issues that require an expansion of your case.
>
> [http://www.taonline.com/securityclearances/]

Q 9:9   Who grants security clearances?

Clearances for top-secret, secret, or sensitive information or restricted data are granted solely by the U.S. Department of Defense. A contractor may grant a clearance for confidential information only.

Q 9:10   Can a negative decision on an employee's clearance be appealed?

Yes. A denial will be accompanied by a statement of the reason(s). This information can be clarified or supplemented by the employee. The Department of Defense maintains a Web site for appeal of security clearance denials. This site will walk the employee through the appellate process. (See Qs 9:17 and 9:18.)

Q 9:11   For how long is a security clearance valid?

Periodic reinvestigation is required:

- Every 5 years for top secret;
- Every 10 years for secret; and
- Every 15 years for confidential.

Q 9:12   Are polygraph tests required as part of the security clearance investigation?

Under relevant regulations and directives [DOD Directive 5210.48 and DOD Reg. 5320.48R], a polygraph examination may be requested by the investigators to help them resolve "serious credible derogatory information." The subject must consent and neither refusal to consent nor failure to pass the polygraph exam can be the sole basis for denial of a clearance; there must be at least some independent, corroborative evidence as well.

As a point of information, polygraph exams are mandatory for all applicants for employment with, or assignment or loan (for example, of an employee of a government contractor) to, the National Security Agency and the Central Intelligence Agency.

Q 9:13   Who conducts security clearance investigations?

The Defense Security Service (DSS) conducts investigations. The DSS does not make any security clearance determinations or recommendations. It gathers information. Once the information has been gathered and verified, and all its investigations completed, the DSS presents the information to the relevant military service's adjudicator authority (each military service has its own), which determines whether or not to grant the security clearance, using standards set by that particular authority.

Q 9:14   May immigrants be granted security clearances?

An immigrant alien may be granted a limited access authorization if:

1. His or her access is limited to a specific government contract;
2. He or she possesses a rare or unusual expertise;
3. A qualified U.S. citizen cannot be hired in sufficient time to meet the contractual requirement the individual will fulfill; and
4. He or she resides permanently in the United States, has a green card, and certifies his or her intent to become a U.S. citizen as soon as possible.

Q 9:15   Are employers required to verify the citizenship of immigrant employees?

It varies from state to state. Alabama Governor Robert Bentley recently signed into law an immigration enforcement bill similar to Arizona SB 1070, known as HB 56. The employment provisions require that all employers enroll in E-Verify, and that all employers that are state/public contractors, grant recipients, and others that receive state incentives register with and use E-Verify. The contractor provision took effect on January 1, 2012, and the E-Verify rule took effect on April 1, 2012. [http://articles.latimes.com/2011/jun/10/nation/la-na-alabama-immigration-20110610]

In Georgia SB 529, a law made effective on July 1, 2007, called the Georgia Security & Immigration Compliance Act, requires certain public employers and any contractors and subcontractors of a public employee to register with E-Verify. Employers must withhold state income tax at a rate of six percent of payments to any individual who has failed to provide a valid taxpayer identification number. The law also provides an additional adjustment to taxable income corporations with respect to certain disallowances and disallows as a business expense compensation paid by a taxpayer to an unauthorized employee. [Society for Human Resource Management]

At the federal level, the newest version of Form I-9 took effect in early 2013.

- Form I-9 is used for verifying the identity and employment authorization of individuals hired for employment in the United States. All U.S. employers must ensure proper completion of Form I-9 for each individual they hire for employment in the United States. This includes citizens and non-citizens. Both employees and employers (or authorized representatives of the employer) must complete the form. On the form, an employee must attest to his or her employment authorization. The employee must also present his or her employer with acceptable documents evidencing identity and employment authorization. The employer must examine the employment eligibility and identity document(s) an employee presents to determine whether the document(s) reasonably appear to be genuine and to relate to the employee and record the document information on the Form I-9. The list of acceptable documents can be found on the last page of the form. Employers must retain Form I-9 for a designated period and make it available for inspection by authorized government officers. Note: State agencies may use Form I-9. Also, some agricultural recruiters and referrers for a fee may be required to use Form I-9.

- Edition Date: Although employers should begin using the 03/08/13 dated form right away, older forms dated 02/02/09 and 08/07/09 will be accepted until May 7, 2013. Beginning May 7, 2013, only the 03/08/13 will be accepted. The revision date is on the lower left corner of the form.

- Do not file Form I-9 with USCIS or U.S. Immigrations and Customs Enforcement (ICE). Employers must have a completed Form I-9 on file for each person on their payroll who is required to complete the form. Form I-9 must be retained and stored by the employer either for three years after the date of hire or for one year after employment is terminated, whichever is later. The form must be available for inspection by authorized U.S. Government officials from the Department of Homeland Security, Department of Labor, or Department of Justice.

- The Spanish version of Form I-9 may be filled out by employers and employees in Puerto Rico ONLY. Spanish-speaking employers and employees in the 50 states and other U.S. territories may print this for their reference, but may only complete the form in English to meet employment eligibility verification requirements.

[http://www.uscis.gov/portal/site/uscis/menuitem.5af9bb95919f35e66f6141
76543f6d1a/?vgnextoid = 31b3ab0a43b5d010VgnVCM10000048f3d6a1RCRD&
vgnextchannel = db029c7755cb9010VgnVCM10000045f3d6a1RCRD]

Q 9:16　Are resources available to help employers get security clearances for their employees or to locate employees who hold security clearances?

Some organizations ready and willing to provide this service include the following:

- Military.com—Military.com, a Monster company, helps employers find and reach qualified candidates with military experience. [http://www.military.com/Careers/EmployerPage/0,14544,,00.html?ESRC = msn_vethiring.kw&np = 1]
- TAOnline.com—A comprehensive resource for government job seekers that contains job listings plus guidance on everything from resume preparation to security clearances. [http://taonline.com]
- About.com—This site covers a wide range of topics from home repair to military careers. Its military/government career pages include comprehensive information on security clearances. [http://usmilitary.about.com/cs/generalinfo/a/security.htm]

Q 9:17　Can a government agency be sued for blocking a security clearance?

A 2008 case presents the possibility of government liability for denying or blocking a security clearance, when that results in the employee's inability to continue in his job. The plaintiff, Tilghman C. Perry Jr., became a permanent employee of the United States Postal Service in 1984, working in Detroit, Michigan. The Postal Service terminated the plaintiff's employment in 1997, allegedly because he had threatened his supervisor. After the plaintiff filed a Title VII employment discrimination lawsuit in federal court, the Postal Service agreed to a settlement in 1999, which included, among other things, a promise "not to disclose facts related to Plaintiff's termination from employment in response to an inquiry from any source outside the United States Postal Service." The Postal Service had not since employed the plaintiff.

According to the plaintiff, he was not technically terminated; instead, he remained employed by the Postal Service during the course of his wrongful termination lawsuit. When the parties settled, he was then allowed to resign.

After 1997, the plaintiff held a number of truck-driving jobs, including temporary positions with the United Parcel Service (UPS). Sometime between February and April 2005, the plaintiff applied for a permanent position with UPS in its West Chester, Pennsylvania, facility in suburban Philadelphia. UPS offered him a position in April, subject to a 30-day trial period. The plaintiff began this trial period on June 13, 2005. On or around July 18, 2005, UPS terminated the plaintiff's employment. According to the plaintiff, this decision came with no warning and in response to no incident; he performed his job adequately and to his supervisor's complete satisfaction. The plaintiff further alleged that, in response to his inquiries, the UPS supervisor who delivered the termination notice failed to specify the reasons for the decision, vaguely referencing "work history," the plaintiff's "character," the fact that the plaintiff wanted to be home with his son, and that another more qualified candidate was available.

Deeply disappointed, the plaintiff went on to apply for other truck-driving positions. Beginning in mid-September 2005, the plaintiff worked for Kemcorp. Kemcorp was a Highway Contract Route (HCR) contractor for the U.S. Postal Service, meaning it carried mail on behalf of the Postal Service between Postal Service facilities. The plaintiff was hired to drive the transport trucks. As a transport truck driver, the plaintiff was told that he would have to undergo a security clearance check with the Postal Service. Kemcorp's contract with the Postal Service mandated this kind of clearance for anyone coming into contact with the mail. (To perform the clearance, the HCR contractor would send an employee's information to a regional office of the Postal Service. The regional office, in turn, would send the information to the U.S. Postal Inspection Service, which is the arm of the Postal Service that performs security clearances. According to the Postal Service's guidelines on screening employees, when clearance is denied to an applicant, the Inspection Service sends a letter to the regional office "denying the clearance and indicating the reason for denial.")

Before the plaintiff's security clearance was completed, he received a temporary clearance. About a month later, in October 2005, the U.S. Postal Service denied the plaintiff's clearance because it learned of his firing and the surrounding circumstances. According to the plaintiff, a manager at Kemcorp delivered the news that his security clearance had been rejected. The Kemcorp supervisor explained that a Postal Service employee had told him "that you threatened your boss in Detroit and you have to turn in your badge and you're not allowed on . . . postal or government property." As a result of the denial of the security clearance and the disclosure, Kemcorp terminated the plaintiff's employment.

The plaintiff, proceeding *pro se*, brought an action against John E. Potter, Postmaster General, alleging that the Postal Service violated the 1999 settlement agreement by disclosing facts related to his termination to (1) UPS and (2) Kemcorp. On these facts, the federal judge ruled concerning the terms of the settlement agreement "that these terms are not ambiguous." First, the "source" of the inquiry was Kemcorp, not the Postal Service's regional office. The plaintiff filled out a work history form given to him by Kemcorp employees. Kemcorp then submitted the form to the Postal Service. By funneling the clearance request through multiple offices within the Postal Service, the Postal Service did not change the inquiry's source. The inquiry clearly had only one source—Kemcorp. Second, the intended meaning of the word "outside" in this context is also clear. Kemcorp was not a part of the Postal Service. It was an independent company that had a contract with the U.S. Postal Service. If the parties meant to exempt disclosures within the Postal Service and those made to any company with which the Postal Service contracted, it should have included such terms.

The Court was mindful that, to some extent, the Postal Service was required to disclose this information by the legal obligations set forth in its contract with Kemcorp and, more generally, by the need to ensure that the people who are handling the mail are trustworthy. However, this did not excuse the Postal Service for breach for at least two reasons. First, the Postal Service could have simply denied the security clearance without disclosing the underlying reasons to Kemcorp. Second, it could have included in the settlement agreement a clause that allowed disclosure "in the event that it had a legal obligation to do so."

Furthermore, the court declined the defendant's invitation to find that the plaintiff had suffered no damage as a result of the breach of the settlement agreement. To the contrary, "On the basis of the present record, the Court cannot agree. It is unclear what would have occurred had the Postal Service not disclosed the underlying reasons for Plaintiff's termination. Therefore, an issue of fact exists as to what, if any, damages Plaintiff suffered as a result of the alleged breach of the settlement agreement." [Perry v. Potter, 2008 WL 200272 (E.D. Pa. 2008)]

Q 9:18 Can a government agency be sued for revoking a security clearance?

Revocation—like denial—of a clearance is a serious matter. Thus, it is no surprise that denials generate litigation. A case on point is *El-Ganayni v. U.S. Department of Energy*. [2010 WL 961855 (U.S. Ct. App. 3d Cir. Jan. 11, 2010)] The plaintiff, Dr. Abdel El-Ganayni, filed a three-count complaint against the Department of Energy. The plaintiff claimed that the revocation of his security clearance and his subsequent termination was based on his political criticisms, a violation of First Amendment rights; violation of his Fifth Amendment "equal protection" rights as a Muslim and an Egyptian; and violation of his rights under the federal Administrative Procedure Act alleging the DOE did not follow its own regulations in revoking his clearance.

The federal district judge in western Pennsylvania granted the government's motion to dismiss, and the plaintiff appealed. On appeal, the Third Circuit, sitting in Philadelphia, affirmed the trial court, holding that the plaintiff's Constitutional allegations fell short of supporting a claim and that the DOE had sufficiently followed its own rules in revoking the clearance.

The appeals panel noted,

> To state a prima facie case of First Amendment retaliation, the plaintiff must show that: (1) his conduct was constitutionally protected, and (2) his protected activity was a substantial or motivating factor in the alleged retaliatory action. The judges held that it would be impossible for the plaintiff to make his in light of the rule laid down by the U.S. Supreme Court more than 20 years ago in *Department of the Navy v. Egan*, 484 U.S. 518, 108 S.Ct. 818, 98 L.Ed.2d 918 (1988). In *Egan*, the Court acknowledged the general rule that agency action is presumptively reviewable, but noted that this presumption has its limits, and that it "runs aground when it encounters concerns of national security."

Applying this rule here, the Third Circuit held that, even if El-Ganayni could bear the heavy burden of making out his Constitutional claims, the DOE could not be required to explain its reasons for revoking the clearance. Consequently, not only plaintiff's First Amendment, but also his Fifth Amendment, claims were dead on arrival.

With regard to his APA-based claim that the DOE failed to follow its own published procedures, the judges found that,

> the Secretary need only state that a "procedure set forth in this section" cannot be made available. As the District Court correctly noted, this certification does not require any particular degree of specificity. Here, Secretary Bodman certified that the procedures set forth in Executive Order 10865, Section 5.2(a) of Executive Order 12968, and the regulations at 10 C.F.R. § 710.26–710.30 could not be made available to El-Ganayni in a manner consistent with national security. While Bodman did not list each and every procedure available under each of those provisions, we are satisfied that his identification of the procedures that could not be used was sufficient to satisfy Section 5.2(d). Essentially, the Secretary construed a singular term in Section 5.2(d)-'the particular procedure'-as also encompassing the plural, *i.e.,* all of the procedures enumerated in Section 5.2(a). We cannot say that this interpretation of Section 5.2(d) was "plainly erroneous."

What we can conclude from this January 2010 decision from a highly influential court of appeals is that a revocation of a security clearance by one of the so-called Cognizant Security Agencies (see Q 9:4) will be difficult, if not impossible, to successfully challenge in federal court.

In another case, an employee of the National Geospatial-Intelligence Agency, Mahmoud Hegab, sued the agency for allegedly revoking his security clearance because his wife attended an Islamic school and worked for a Muslim charity. NGA employs 16,000 workers who supply data and other imagery to the military, and a top security clearance is necessary for all employees due to the nature of the agency's work. Hegab was a budget analyst with a top security clearance at NGA, but his clearance was revoked immediately after he got married.

According to the lawsuit, NGA officials informed Hegab that they were concerned about his wife's schooling at the Islamic Saudi Academy, which has been criticized by groups such as the U.S. Commission on International Religious Freedom for use of a curriculum that, similar to that in Saudi Arabia, some claim promotes intolerance against other religions, particularly Judaism and Christianity. NGA cited that, along with her charity work with Islamic Relief USA, as reason for revoking the security clearance. Furthermore, NGA cited his wife's participation in a 2003 anti-war rally sponsored by the ANSWER coalition, a left-wing group that has, at times, worked with Palestinian activists, and her time serving as president of the student group Students for Justice in Palestine at George Mason University. NGA eventually withdrew its concerns regarding Hegab's wife's attendance at the Saudi Academy, but said its other concerns remained.

Hegab's lawyer, Sheldon Cohen, wrote in the lawsuit that "the revocation of plaintiff's security clearance . . . was based solely on plaintiff's wife's religion,

Islam, her constitutionally protected speech, and her association with . . . an Islamic faith-based organization." [http://lubbockonline.com/filed-online/2011-10-06/former-worker-sues-secretive-us-security-agency-alleging-bias-against-wife#.T3xVM79WovI]

Judge James C. Cacheris of the Eastern District of Virginia dismissed the lawsuit on the grounds that, regardless of whether or not Hegab's allegations were true, the court lacked the authority to review the underlying basis of the dispute. The judge stated:

> A determination of whether Hegab's security clearance was revoked due to legitimate national security concerns or, as Hegab alleges, constitutionally impermissible bases would necessarily require a review of the merits of NGA's decision. Absent clear congressional directive, which Hegab fails to identify, such a review is flatly prohibited by Egan and Fourth Circuit precedent.

[Hegab v. Long, 2012 WL 162117 (E.D. Va. Jan. 19, 2012)]

In this case, *Egan* refers to the 1988 Supreme Court decision in *Department of the Navy v. Egan*, which supports broad and unreviewable executive branch authority in regard to national security policy. [http://www.fas.org/blog/secrecy/2012/01/hegab_dismissal.html]

Q 9:19   What privacy rights do the employees of government contractors have?

In *National Aeronautics and Space Administration v. Nelson* [131 S. Ct. 746 (2011)], the U.S. Supreme Court ruled NASA's standard background checks, as applied to contract employees, do not violate a constitutional right to informational privacy. In this case, government-contractor employees at NASA's Jet Propulsion Laboratory (JPL), which is operated by the California Institute of Technology (Cal Tech), were not subject to government background checks at the time they were hired, but that changed when the President ordered the adoption of uniform identification standards for both federal civil servants and contractor employees. The Department of Commerce mandated that contract employees with long-term access to federal facilities complete a standard background check, typically the National Agency Check with Inquiries (NACI), by October 2007. NASA modified its contract with Cal Tech to reflect the new requirement, and JPL announced that employees who did not complete the NACI process in time would be denied access to JPL and face termination by Cal Tech. The NACI process, long used for prospective civil servants, begins with the employee filling out a standard form, SF-85. SF-85 asks whether an employee has "used, possessed, supplied, or manufactured illegal drugs" in the last year. If so, the employee must provide details, including information about "treatment or counseling received." The employee must also sign a release authorizing the government to obtain personal information from schools, employers, and others during its investigation. Once SF-85 is completed, the government sends the employee's references a questionnaire (Form 42) that asks open-ended questions about whether they have "any reason to question" the employee's "honesty or trustworthiness," or have "adverse information" concerning a variety of other matters. All SF-85 and Form 42 responses are subject to the protections of the Privacy Act.

With the deadline for completing the NACI process drawing near, respondents brought suit, claiming, as relevant here, that the background check process violates a constitutional right to informational privacy. The District Court declined to issue a preliminary injunction, but the Ninth Circuit reversed. It held that SF-85's inquiries into recent drug involvement furthered the government's interest in combating illegal drug use, but that the drug "treatment or counseling" question furthered no legitimate interest and was thus likely to be held unconstitutional. It also held that Form 42's open-ended questions were not narrowly tailored to meet the government's interests in verifying contractors' identities and ensuring JPL's security, and thus also likely violated respondents' informational privacy rights.

Reversing, the High Court held that "[t]he challenged questions on SF-85 and Form 42 are reasonable, employment-related inquiries that further the Government's interests in managing its internal operations," and "reject[ed] the argument that the Government has a constitutional burden to demonstrate that its employment background questions are 'necessary' or the least restrictive means of furthering its interests."

Significance for government contractors. The bottom line for government contractors is that their employees have no constitutional privacy interest shielding them from inquiries by the government. Under the majority view, while some privacy right protecting personal information may abide in the U.S. Constitution, that right does not reach the kinds of questions NASA was asking the plaintiffs in this case. Under Scalia's concurring opinion, no such right exists within the Constitution. The difference is that the majority view leaves the door open, if only a crack, for a later challenge to a still-more-intrusive inquiry by this or some other government entity, while under Scalia's view, the door would be slammed firmly and permanently shut. For practical purposes, contract employees must answer inquiries posed by federal agencies.

Affirmative Action

Q 9:20   Is a government contractor required to provide affirmative action programs?

Procuring agencies must include in all contracts a clause requiring the contractor to certify whether it has established an affirmative action program at its facilities. Exemptions to the requirement may be made for contracts that the contracting agency determines to be essential to national security, contracts for goods or services totaling less than $10,000 in value, contracts for work outside of the United States, contracts with state or local governments, or other contracts that the director of the Office of Federal Contract Compliance Programs (OFCCP) determines to be subject to special circumstances that justify exemption.

Q 9:21   Does the government contractor's affirmative action obligation place it in a dilemma?

Many federal contractors, as well as universities receiving federal funds, feel hooked on the horns of the affirmative action dilemma. The dilemma is posed by the mixed signals from Washington, as well as some state governments, concerning what contractors can and cannot do. Loss managers on many college campuses are deliberating over it.

In 2003, the U.S. Supreme Court decided in *Grutter v. Bollinger* [539 U.S. 982 (2003)] that a diverse student body is a legitimate consideration when making admissions decisions. This news led not only to admissions policies according weight to race and ethnicity, but also to speculation about—and some implementation of—faculty search policies that embodied an analogous principle with regard to race and ethnicity of the faculty.

A backlash against *Grutter* has quietly gained momentum. In November 2006, Michigan passed a constitutional amendment essentially intended to neutralize *Grutter* on the state's public university campuses. On December 4, 2006, the Supreme Court revisited its 2003 ruling, hearing oral arguments in two cases in which the plaintiffs are challenging their states' attempts to inject *Grutter*'s principles in the K-12 environment. Louisville and Seattle parents are asking the Supreme Court to revisit their landmark affirmative action decision and declare that school district schemes to consider race in making school assignments are unconstitutional.

> **Note:** "In the November 2006 election, 58 percent of Michigan's voters approved a proposal that amended the state Constitution. The amendment banned discrimination, or the granting of preferential treatment, in public education, government contracting and public employment based on race, sex, ethnicity or national origin." [http://www.upi.com/Top_News/US/2013/03/31/Under-the-US-Supreme-Court-Do-cases-sound-death-knell-for-affirmative-action/UPI-84731364715000/#ixzz2Ra7PV3Eq] In March 2013 the U.S. Supreme Court agreed to hear a challenge to the legality under the U.S. Constitution of this state constitution amendment. And, on June 24, 2013, the Court ruled 7-1 in a case involving the University of Texas admissions policies, that the school's preferential admissions policy could stand, if on remand UT could prove a need. The Michigan case will be argued in the Fall 2013 term.

In light of these developments, what is the hapless human resources director to do? Abandoning affirmative action seems unwise. The OFCCP continues to compel annual updating and filing of affirmative action plans. More important, from a practical standpoint, abandoning a commitment to diversity not only opens an institution to a possible adverse impact discrimination suit, but also places it at a disadvantage in competing for the some of the fastest growing segments of the American workforce, such as Hispanics.

Some solutions are sure to survive whatever the Supreme Court next decides. States such as Texas, responding to earlier anti–affirmative action appeal court decisions with regard to high school admissions standards, report significant success from percentage-based high school admissions policies (Texas state universities admit the top 10 percent from all Texas high schools); partnering programs with urban high schools; and other race-neutral initiatives of this type. Meanwhile, many schools regularly reach out to minority faculty applicants by expressing their interest in professors who can relate to diverse student bodies. Such strategies can help schools resolve the affirmative action dilemma.

In the hiring arena, similar strategies can work. However, it must be noted at the outset that at least some circuit courts are out in front of the Supreme Court in its consideration of the applicability of *Grutter* in other arenas. What some of these mid-level federal forums have concluded does not bode well for employers. In *Lomack v. City of Newark* [463 F.3d 303 (3d Cir. 2006)], the appeals panel rejected an effort of the city-defendant to transfer firefighters in order to create racial balance among its fire stations. Furthermore, the U.S. Supreme Court decisions pending in June 2013, as this publication went to press, could further erode the leeway afforded to "creative" affirmative action schemes by *Grutter*.

Q 9:22 What is the OFCCP's final rule on affirmative action for government contractors?

The OFCCP's final rule on affirmative action for government contractors is the lengthy regulation that took effect on December 13, 2000. It is the new set of implementing regulations for Executive Order 11246. It can be found at 41 C.F.R. Parts 60-1 and 60-2. A sample affirmative action program that comports with this rule is accessible at http://www.dol.gov/ofccp/regs/compliance/pdf/ sampleaap.pdf . Also see Q 9:91 for the OFCCP's new proposed regulations that would implement Section 503 of the Rehabilitation Act of 1973, as well as revise the nondiscrimination provisions to conform to changes made by the ADA Amendments Act of 2008.

Q 9:23 What does the OFCCP's final rule on affirmative action for government contractors do?

In general, the rule refocuses the regulatory emphasis from the development of a document that complies with highly prescriptive standards to a performance-based standard that effectively implements an affirmative action program into the overall management plan of the contractor. The rule also introduces a new tool—the Equal Opportunity Survey—intended to aid contractors in assessing their pay and other personnel practices, while increasing the efficiency and effectiveness of program monitoring.

Q 9:24 What is OFCCP's Directive 306?

Directive 306, entitled "Complying with Nondiscrimination Provisions: Criminal Record Restrictions and Discrimination Based on Race and National Origin," became effective in January 2013. The purpose of the Directive is to provide information to federal contractors and subcontractors and federally-assisted construction contractors and subcontractors about: (1) the circumstances in which exclusions of applicants or employees based on their criminal records may violate existing nondiscrimination obligations; (2) the Training and Employment Guidance Letter (TEGL) 31-11 issued on May 25, 2012 to the American Job Center network and other covered entities in the public workforce system by the DOL's Employment and Training Administration (ETA) and Civil Rights Center (CRC); and (3) the Enforcement Guidance issued by the Equal Employment Opportunity Commission (EEOC) on April 25, 2012.

The agency explained that in recent decades, the number of Americans who have had contact with the criminal justice system has increased exponentially. OFCCP estimates that about one in three adults now has a criminal-history record, "which often consists of an arrest that did not lead to conviction, a conviction for which the person was not sentenced to a term of incarceration, or a conviction for a non-violent crime." The directive adds, "On any given day, about 2.3 million people are incarcerated and each year 700,000 people are released from prison and almost 13 million are admitted to—and released from local jails."

The agency correctly notes what is common knowledge, i.e., racial and ethnic disparities are reflected in incarceration rates. According to the Pew Center on the States, one in 106 white men, one in 36 Hispanic men, and one in 15 African American men are incarcerated. Additionally, on average, one in 31 adults is under correctional control (i.e., probation, parole, or incarceration), including one in 45 white adults, one in 27 Hispanic adults and one in 11 African American adults.

OFCCP speculates, "Racial and ethnic disparities may also be reflected in other criminal history records. For example, although African Americans constitute approximately 13 percent of the overall population, they account for 28 percent of those arrested and almost 40 percent of the incarcerated population."

The directive goes on to caution, "In light of these racial and ethnic disparities, contractors should be mindful of federal antidiscrimination laws if they choose to rely on job applicants' criminal history records for purposes of employment decisions. Hiring policies and practices that exclude workers with criminal records may run afoul of such laws, which prohibit intentional discrimination on the basis of race, national origin, or other protected bases, and policies or practices that have a disparate impact on these protected groups and cannot be justified as job related and consistent with business necessity. Policies that exclude people from employment based on the mere existence of a criminal history record and that do not take into account the age and nature of an offense, for example, are likely to unjustifiably restrict the employment opportunities of individuals with conviction histories. Due to racial and ethnic disparities in the criminal justice system, such policies are likely to violate federal antidiscrimination law. Accordingly, contractors should carefully consider their legal obligations before adopting such policies." [http://www.dol.gov/ofccp/regs/compliance/directives/dir306.htm]

Q 9:25   What must a contractor do if his/her criminal record policy has a disparate impact on a protected class?

First, the employer must be prepared to prove that the policy is job related and driven by a business necessity.

Second, an arrest, viewed alone, does not prove guilt. Thus, at a minimum, the employer must give the applicant an opportunity to explain what happened leading up to the arrest.

Third, the policy provides a three-factor test of whether or not a criminal-conduct exclusion is "job related and consistent with business necessity." [http://www.dol.gov/ofccp/regs/compliance/directives/dir306.htm]

Q 9:26   What are best practices regarding Directive 306?

OFCCP suggests the following best practices:

- Criminal record screening practices should be applied on a case-by-case basis and involving an individualized assessment in every instance.
- Policies should be narrowly tailored to track essential job requirements and the actual circumstances under which jobs are performed.
- Policies should consider and spell out the duration of specific exclusions for specific crimes; not every crime should be subject to the same exclusionary span of time, i.e., the less the offense and/or the more remote in time, the less likely that it ought to prohibit hiring.
- More broadly, the agency suggests that contractors consider not making criminal-records inquiries at all; if a contractor feels it must do so, then the inquiry should be limited to convictions, with all the foregoing best practices in place.
- And, finally, confidentiality should be carefully observed and enforced.

[http://www.dol.gov/ofccp/regs/compliance/directives/dir306.htm]

Q 9:27   What is the posting requirement dictated by Directive 306?

Contractors that post job announcements with American Job Centers must follow the following rules under Directive 306:

- *When an employer (including contractors) registers with an American Job Center (or other covered entity) to use the Job Bank, the TEGL requires the covered entity to send the employer a prescribed notice ("Notice #1 for Employers Regarding Job Bank Nondiscrimination and Criminal Record Exclusions") explaining that the covered entity must comply with federal civil rights laws which, due to the likely adverse impact of criminal record exclusions on protected groups, generally prohibit categorical exclusions of individuals based solely on an arrest or conviction history.*
- *Covered entities will be required to use a system (automated or otherwise) for identifying vacancy announcements that include hiring restrictions based on arrest and/or conviction records.*

- *When covered entities identify job postings that exclude individuals based on arrest and/or conviction history, they must provide employers that have posted these vacancy announcements a notice ("Notice #2 for Employers Regarding Job Postings Containing Criminal Record Exclusions"19) that gives the employer the opportunity to remove or edit the vacancy announcement.*

The Directive goes on to state:

"Covered entities may continue to post vacancy announcements containing language excluding candidates based on criminal history only when accompanied by a notice to job seekers ("Notice #3 for Job Seekers to be Attached to Job Postings with Criminal Record Exclusions") explaining that the exclusions in the posting may have an adverse impact on protected groups and informing them that individuals with criminal history records are not prohibited from applying for the posted position."

[http://www.dol.gov/ofccp/regs/compliance/directives/dir306.htm]

Q 9:28   What about screening and referrals based on criminal record?

The Directive states, "Covered entity staff should refrain from screening and refusing to make referrals because an applicant has a criminal history record. Job seekers who are referred for positions where the job posting takes criminal history into account are to be given a copy of Notice #3 For Job Seekers along with the job announcement." [http://www.dol.gov/ofccp/regs/compliance/directives/dir306.htm]

Q 9:29   What other laws are implicated in hiring decisions revolving around criminal record checks?

OFCCP adds that other laws are implicated in hiring decisions revolving around criminal record checks:

- The Fair Credit Reporting Act (FCRA) imposes a number of obligations on employers that wish to use criminal background checks to screen applicants. This law requires the employer to obtain the applicant's permission before asking a background screening company for a criminal history report, and requires the employer to provide the applicant with a copy of the report and a summary of the applicant's rights before the employer takes an adverse action (such as denying an application for employment) based on information in the criminal history report. For more information: http://www.ftc.gov/bcp/edu/pubs/consumer/credit/cre36.shtm.
- The Work Opportunity Tax Credit (WOTC) and the Federal Bonding Program (FBP) are two incentives to support employers' hiring of individuals with conviction histories. The WOTC provides a credit of 25-40 percent of first-year wages, or $1,500–$2,400, for employers that hire qualified individuals with felony convictions. For more information:

http://www.doleta.gov/wotc. Through the FBP, funded and administered by the U.S. Department of Labor, fidelity insurance bonds are available to reimburse the employer for any loss due to employee theft of money or property, with no employer deductible. For more information: http://www.bonds4jobs.com/index.html.

Attorney Susan K. Lessak of the international law firm Pepper Hamilton adds, "The Directive also references a May 2012 Guidance Letter issued by the U.S. Department of Labor's Employment and Training Administration, which advises public workforce system entities (and other entities that receive federal financial assistance to operate job banks, to provide assistance to job seekers in locating and obtaining employment, and to assist employers by screening and referring qualified applicants) to adopt safeguards to prevent discrimination and promote employment opportunities for individuals with criminal records. Government contractors subject to the Vietnam Era Veterans' Readjustment Assistance Act are required to list employment openings with an employment service office, which are entities covered by the Guidance Letter, and should be aware of the procedures outlined in the Guidance Letter."

She adds, "It is possible that the OFCCP will ask to review a contractor's criminal records policy and practices during an affirmative action audit. In light of the OFCCP's Directive, federal government contractors and subcontractors should review carefully their policies and practices governing the hiring of applicants with criminal records to make sure that they incorporate the *Green* factors and contemplate an individual assessment of the particular circumstances of the job and the applicant's criminal history." [http://www.pepperlaw.com/publications_update.aspx?ArticleKey = 2558]

Her reference is to *Green v. Missouri Pacific Railroad* [549 F.2d 1158 (8th Cir. 1977)], a decision that early on announced the standards incorporated in OFCCP's best practices.

In *Green,* the court found that the plaintiff and all other African Americans were automatically disqualified from employment, if they had criminal convictions. It required the trial judge to determine on remand if Green had the qualifications for the job he had sought and, if so, award him back-pay and attorney fees. The trial judge subsequently ordered "that defendants, its agents, servants and employees shall be and are enjoined from disqualifying and denying employment to an applicant solely and automatically for the reason that the applicant has been convicted of a criminal offense; provided, however, that nothing herein shall prevent defendant . . . from considering an applicants' prior criminal record as a factor in making individual hiring decisions so long as defendant takes into account the nature and gravity of the offense or offenses, the time that has passed since the conviction and/or completion of sentence, and the nature of the job for which the applicant has applied."

Q 9:30   What does the OFCCP's final rule provide regarding record retention?

Personnel and employment records are required under 41 C.F.R. Section 60-1.12 to be retained for at least two years, except for government contractors with fewer than 150 employees or no government contract greater than $150,000. Such contractors need to retain such records for a minimum of only one year. Such records include, but are not necessarily limited to, records involving:

- Hiring;
- Assignment;
- Promotion;
- Demotion;
- Transfer;
- Layoff;
- Termination;
- Rates of pay;
- Other compensation terms;
- Apprenticeship and training selections;
- Requests for reasonable accommodation;
- Results of physical exams;
- Applications and resumes;
- Tests and test results; and
- Interview notes.

However, in 2011 the OFCCP proposed new regulations that would revise the rules that implement Section 503 of the Rehabilitation Act of 1973, as well as revise the nondiscrimination provisions to conform to changes made by the ADA Amendments Act of 2008. With regard to recordkeeping requirements, contractors would be required to collect and maintain significantly more data, including (according to the Associated General Contractors of America Web site, http://news.agc.org/2012/01/11/ofccp-proposes-changes-to-affirmative-action-obligations-related-to-individuals-with-disabilities-2/):

- Total number of referrals from approved employment delivery organizations such as One-Stop Career Centers as well as organizations with which the contractor has a linkage agreement;
- Total number of applicants for employment;
- Number of applicants who are known to be individuals with disabilities;
- Ratio of known applicants with disabilities to total applicants;
- Total number of job openings;
- Total number of jobs filled;
- Number of known individuals with disabilities hired;
- Ratio of hires with known disabilities to total hires; and

- Ratio of job openings to job openings filled.

As this publication went to press, OFFCP was promising imminent Release of the Final Regulations.

(See Q 9:91 for more information on these proposed changes.)

Q 9:31 What should a contractor do with records if the contractor is aware of a pending discrimination claim?

If the contractor has received a notice that a discrimination complaint has been filed against it, that a compliance evaluation has been initiated, or that an enforcement action has been commenced, the contractor must preserve all relevant personnel records until the complaint or action has been finally resolved. *Relevant personnel records* in this context may predictably include:

- All personnel and employment records relating to the complainant;
- Records relating to all employees holding similar positions as the one sought after or held by the complainant; and
- Applications, resumes, and test papers submitted by all successful and unsuccessful applicants for the position for which the complainant unsuccessfully applied.

Q 9:32 What else must government contractors do in maintaining records under the new final rule?

Contractors must still maintain an affirmative action plan and a record of their good faith efforts to fulfill the goals contained in its affirmative action plan. They must also be able to identify in the records they maintain under 41 C.F.R. Section 6-1.12 the gender, race, and ethnicity of all employees and, where reasonably possible, the same information on each job applicant. Contractors must be ready, willing, and able to supply this information to the OFCCP upon request.

Q 9:33 Who must have an affirmative action plan under the OFCCP's final rule?

The OFCCP's final rule requires the following government contractors to maintain affirmative action plans:

1. Non-construction (supply and service) contractors with 50 or more employees and at least one contract valued at $50,000 or more (or government bills of lading expected to attain a total value of $50,000 or more over a 12-month time frame);
2. Depositories for government funds; and
3. Financial institutions serving as issuing and paying agents for U.S. savings bonds and notes.

A sample affirmative action program that comports with the rule is accessible at http://www.dol.gov/ofccp/regs/compliance/pdf/sampleaap.pdf.

Q 9:34   Under the OFCCP's affirmative action plan requirements, which groups of employees must be covered?

Three groups of employees must be covered by affirmative action plans:

1. Women and minorities [*See* Executive Order 11246; 41 C.F.R. Parts 60-1 and 60-2.]

2. Individuals with disabilities [*See* Section 503 of the Rehabilitation Act of 1973; 41 C.F.R. Part 60-741.]

3. Veterans [*See* Vietnam Era Veterans Readjustment Assistance Act of 1974; Veterans Employment Opportunities Act of 1998; Veterans Benefits and Health Care Improvement Act of 2000; Jobs for Veterans Act of 2002; 41 C.F.R. Parts 60-25 and 61-250.]

A sample affirmative action program that comports with the rule is accessible at http://www.dol.gov/ofccp/regs/compliance/pdf/sampleaap.pdf.

Q 9:35   What must the affirmative action plan cover with regard to each of the identified employee groups?

The affirmative action plan for women and minorities must be both retrospective and prospective. In other words, it should look back at the last year's data and inquire, "How well did we do?" and it should look forward and ask, "What should our firm do differently in the year ahead to improve the representation of women and minorities in those job groups where we have placement goals?" The women and minorities affirmative action plans must contain the firm's analysis of its confidential and proprietary data relevant to answering these questions. In contrast, the affirmative action plans for disabled individuals and veterans need not include data analysis.

Q 9:36   How many plans must a multi-location contractor prepare?

Each individual establishment employing 50 or more employees must have its own affirmative action plan. Smaller, stand-alone sites may either have their own affirmative action plans or be a part of the plan prepared by the larger human resources unit responsible for that site or the plan prepared by the corporate official to which the site reports. So-called "corporate initiative employees" who are managed out of corporate headquarters can be counted either in the corporate headquarters affirmative action plan or the affirmative action plan of the separate location where the employee is based.

Q 9:37   Who are the employees for the purposes of the affirmative action plan?

Every employee to whom a corporation issued a W-2 is an employee for purposes of the data in an affirmative action plan. Expatriate employees are included and should be counted in the corporate headquarters' affirmative action plan. Aliens employed by the company overseas are not included.

Temporary workers employed for three years or less or who are paid by a leasing agency or other third party may or may not be included in affirmative action plan data at the employer's discretion, even if there are a large number of them. Interns and co-op students, again, may or may not be counted at the employer's discretion.

Q 9:38   What must contractors that have affirmative action plans do with regard to their subcontractors?

If any such subcontractor meets one or more of the criteria listed in Q 9:33 the contractor must require that subcontractor to have an affirmative action plan, too.

Q 9:39   Must a government contractor have an affirmative action program?

Government contractors and subcontractors subject to the affirmative action plan requirement under the categories set forth in Q 9:33 must also have an affirmative action program.

Q 9:40   What is the purpose of an affirmative action program?

An *affirmative action program* is defined by the new final rule as a management tool designed to ensure equal employment opportunity (EEO). The central premise, according to 41 C.F.R. Section 60-2.10, is that, absent discrimination, over time a contractor's workforce in general will reflect the gender, racial, and ethnic profile of the labor pools from which the contractor recruits and hires.

Q 9:41   What quantitative analyses should a contractor use in its affirmative action program?

The affirmative action program of a government contractor should include the following quantitative analyses:

1. An organizational profile;
2. A job group analysis;
3. The identities of the incumbents in the various job groups;
4. A determination of availability of various categories of employees by race, gender, and ethnicity within the labor pool for each of the job groups;
5. A comparison of availability to incumbency;
6. Placement goals;
7. Designation of responsibility for implementation of the program;
8. Identification of problem areas;
9. Action-oriented programs; and
10. Provision for periodic internal audits.

Q 9:42 What should the organizational profile contain?

The organizational profile in the contractor's affirmative action program should include the following components:

1. A detailed graph, chart, or spreadsheet reflecting the contractor's organizational structure;

2. The name of each unit in the contractor's organization;

3. The job title, gender, race, and ethnicity of each unit supervisor;

4. The total number of male and female incumbents in each unit;

5. The total numbers of males and females of African American, Hispanic, Asian/Pacific Islander, Native American/Alaskan Native backgrounds; and

6. A workforce analysis consisting of the job titles in each unit or under each collective bargaining agreement.

Q 9:43 Of whom should the contractor be taking a data snapshot for reporting purposes?

Contractors should take a data snapshot for employees in the following categories:

*   Applicants
*   Hires
*   Promotions and Transfers
*   Terminations

Q 9:44 What information should be gathered on people in each of these data snapshot categories?

The following information should be collected for the data snapshot categories listed above:

*   Race
*   Gender
*   EEO-1 classification category
*   Hire date (if applicable)
*   Annual salary (if applicable)
*   Birth date (usually used as a proxy for experience)
*   Job title (if applicable)
*   Physical location (if applicable)

Q 9:45   Are there any coding tips for compiling these data snapshots?

The following coding tips can assist in compiling the data snapshots:

- The snapshot can be taken at the close of the calendar or the fiscal year.
- Coding should be internally accurate and consistent across the corporation.
- Microsoft Excel's "Unmatched Query Wizard" (Microsoft Access) can help with a discrepancy check.

Q 9:46   What is a *job group analysis*?

A *job group analysis* is a method of combining job titles within an establishment according to similar:

- Content (duties and responsibilities);
- Wage rates; and
- Opportunities (for training, transfers, promotions, pay, mobility, and other enhancements).

Q 9:47   How can a contractor develop its job group analysis?

Job groups are the centerpiece of any affirmative action plan. OFCCP and the EEOC currently recognize ten broad groups. [*See* "EEO-1 Job Classification Guide," http://www.eeoc.gov/eeo1survey/jobclassguide.html.] Job titles can be obtained from the 2000 census codes. Smaller contractors may formulate their job groups according to the EEO-1 report. [*See* http://www.eeoc.gov/index.cfm.]

A typical organization profile for purposes of job group analysis will use an organization chart and go department by department. Next, the contractor may do a salary sort, from lowest to highest, by department. In assigning each of these employees to 1 of the 10 EEO job categories (groups), contractors should keep in mind that similarly titled employees may in fact fall into different job groups. Contractors should be particularly careful about employees with the generic title "project manager," which may mean more than one thing, even within a single organization.

Q 9:48   How can a contractor cross-check its job group analysis data?

When compiling job group analysis data, contractors should cross-check to ensure that the following conditions are met:

- All new employees hired during the last AAP reporting year and whose employment was not subsequently terminated during that year should appear in the year-end snapshot.
- All employees whose employment was terminated during the last AAP year, and who were not subsequently rehired by the company, should be excluded from the year-end snapshot.

- All new hires for the reported year should also appear as applicants for that year.
- All employees with hire dates in the reported year should appear on the hire list for that year.
- All employees with the same job title should appear in the same EEO category (currently 10) (except that such generic government-contractor titles as "project manager" may require more precise parsing out of individual employees with that common title).
- All internal and external applicants should appear on the appropriate worksheets.
- No employee should appear more than once in a snapshot.
- Each employee should have a unique identifier (e.g., Social Security number, employee ID number).
- Particular care should be taken in correctly and consistently coding job title and race.

Q 9:49   How can a contractor use Microsoft Access to cross-check the company's job group analysis data?

When using Microsoft Access to cross-check its job group analysis data, a contractor can import relevant Excel files, including employees' unique identifiers (e.g., Social Security number, employee ID number). Contractors also should use the "Unmatched Query Wizard" function.

Q 9:50   What is meant by *placement goals*?

Placement goals are objectives or targets deemed by the contractor to be reasonably attainable by good faith efforts to make the affirmative action program work.

Q 9:51   How does a contractor set its placement goals?

The contractor can conduct the following analysis to set its placement goals:

- An external availability analysis will answer the threshold question: "What percentage of the labor pool, from which we draw applicants for the job titles we have included in each job group, consists of (1) women and (2) minorities?" The labor pool is the geographic region from which the company recruits for each job group. For executives and top professionals, this may be a national or even an international region; for blue-collar and clerical employees, the pool may be a single city or metropolitan region.
- Next, an internal availability analysis answers the concomitant question: "What percentage of the workforce consists of women and minorities who are available to us to potentially move into job groups by means of transfers and promotions?" This analysis will look at the feeder pools from which such transfers and promotions have historically occurred.

- Next, a two-factor analysis should answer the question: "Combining the internal and external categories of available women and minorities, what is the overall availability of these two groups in the overall labor pool?" An employer may want to give one factor or the other higher weight based upon a closer look at the prior year's employment transactions as compared with a longer historical perspective, which might indicate anomalies that occurred in the "snapshot" of the past year.

Q 9:52   Are there any tips about setting placement goals?

After the job group analysis, placement goals are the most important part of the AAP. The contractor should keep the following in mind when setting placement goals:

- Placement goals cannot be quotas—quotas are illegal.
- Legal counsel recommend using the so-called "80 percent rule," seeking to utilize in the composition of each job group the number of women and minorities that equals 80 percent of the percentage of women and minorities in the labor pool for that job group.
- Some companies use the "standard deviation" method, asking whether the percentage difference between the number of women and minorities in each of the company's job groups is significantly different from the percentage of women and minorities in the relevant labor pool.
- Labor counsel caution that almost any other method starts to look a lot like a quota.

Q 9:53   How does the OFCCP use 2010 Census data?

The OFCCP requires covered federal contractors and subcontractors to prepare and maintain affirmative action programs. [See 41 C.F.R. § 60-2.1.] The OFCCP regulations also specify the details of the requirements for these affirmative action programs. [See 41 C.F.R. §§ 60-2.10 through 60-2.17.]

One of the requirements of an affirmative action program is determining the availability of qualified minorities or women for job openings. *Availability* is defined as "an estimate of the number of qualified minorities or women available for employment in a given job group, expressed as a percentage of all qualified persons available for employment in the job group." [41 C.F.R. § 60-2.14(a)] "The purpose of the availability determination is to establish a benchmark against which the demographic composition of the contractor's incumbent workforce can be compared in order to determine whether barriers to EEO may exist within particular job groups." [41 C.F.R. § 60-2.14(a)] Job groups are groupings of "jobs at the establishment with similar content, wage rates, and opportunities." [41 C.F.R. § 60-2.12(b)] "Similarity of content refers to the duties and responsibilities of the job titles which make up the job group. Similarity of opportunities refers to training, transfers, promotions, pay, mobility, and other career enhancement opportunities offered by the jobs within the job group." [41 C.F.R. § 60-2.12(b)] The OFCCP regulations further require that "[t]he contractor must use the most current and discrete statistical information available to derive availability figures." [41 C.F.R. § 60-2.14(d)] "Examples of such information include census data, data from local job service offices, and data from colleges or other training institutions." [41 C.F.R. § 60-2.14(d)]

The American Community Survey (ACS) 2010 Special EEO File (Tabulation) from the Census Bureau was released in the fall of 2012. According to the Census Bureau:

> Just as the Special EEO File has been the primary benchmark in civil rights monitoring and enforcement for determining the racial, ethnic and gender composition of labor markets, within specified geographies and job categories, it was hoped that the next EEO File would have the same status for determining benchmarks by disability and citizenship. This will definitely not be the case for disability statistics, as they cannot be included for technical reasons. Citizenship data, which was specifically added to the EEO File to address federal employment issues, will be included in the next Special EEO File. However, the size for the smallest geographic levels (i.e., counties, aggregated counties, or places) will probably be 100,000 or more—rather than the 50,000 or more for other variables. The citizenship data should not affect the availability of tables or cross-tabulations by larger geographic areas, i.e., Combined Statistical Areas (CBA's); Core Based Statistical Areas (CBSA's); states; and the United States. Again, irrespective of the variable, only tables and cross-tabulations that are permitted by the Census Bureau's Disclosure Review Board will be produced, which might mean that some desired tabulations and cross-tabulations may not be possible due to confidentiality concerns.

[Affirmative Action News, Feb. 4, 2011, accessible at http://affirmative actionnews.blogspot.com/2011/02/2010-eeo-census-file-update-3.html]

Q 9:54   What is a *designation of responsibility*?

The contractor must designate a responsible employee—often with the title of affirmative action officer or equal opportunity officer—to take primary responsibility for the affirmative action plan and program. This official can have these duties on a part-time basis in a smaller organization. For instance, the affirmative action officer may primarily be the human resources director for the firm.

Q 9:55   What sorts of problem areas might the contractor's plan and program identify?

By comparing the composition of the incumbent workforce with the available categories of employees in the labor pool and by reviewing its goals, the contractor might identify such problem areas as:

1. The under-utilization of minorities or females in particular units or job categories of the organization in comparison with these groups' availability in the designated labor pool;

2. Selection disparities in application flows, hirings, promotions, or terminations; and

3. Disparities in compensation.

Q 9:56　What is the OFCCP's Functional Affirmative Action Program (FAAP)?

FAAP refers to the development and preparation of an affirmative action plan based on functional or business units within a corporate structure rather than an affirmative action plan based solely on an establishment's location. Factors that may be considered when determining whether an FAAP is appropriate for a particular contractor are:

1. Whether a functional or business unit operates somewhat autonomously;

2. Whether a functional or business unit has its own managing official; and

3. Whether a functional or business unit operates as a separate cost center.

[*See* http://www.dol.gov/.]

Q 9:57　What sanctions may a contractor suffer for failure to comply with affirmative action requirements?

The contract may be canceled, terminated, or suspended for failure to comply with the government's affirmative action requirements. Further, the contractor's name may appear in a public list of "nonawardable prospective contractors," which is tantamount to a suspension or debarment from performing government contracts.

Q 9:58　Which government agency enforces affirmative action programs with government contractors?

Like most U.S. employers, government contractors are subject to the EEOC's jurisdiction. But in addition to the EEOC, the OFCCP is charged with ensuring that contractors comply with their affirmative action requirements. A disappointed employee or job applicant not only can file a discrimination charge with the EEOC, but also can file a complaint with the OFCCP, which may then review the contractor's entire affirmative action program.

Q 9:59　What is the OFCCP's mission?

OFCCP administers and enforces three legal authorities that require EEO: Executive Order 11246, as amended; Section 503 of the Rehabilitation Act of 1973, as amended; and the Vietnam Veterans' Readjustment Assistance Act of 1974, as amended, [38 U.S.C. 4212]. Taken together, these laws ban discrimination and require Federal contractors and subcontractors to take affirmative action to ensure that all individuals have an equal opportunity for employment, without regard to race, color, religion, sex, national origin, disability or status as a Vietnam era or special disabled veteran.

Q 9:60   Are there recordkeeping rules of which contractors need to be aware?

The Internet Applicant final rule, issued by the OFCCP, addresses recordkeeping by federal contractors and subcontractors about the Internet hiring process and the solicitation of race, gender, and ethnicity of Internet applicants. The rule is the product of a lengthy deliberative process, including public input, to develop a definition of *Internet applicant* that is relevant in the Internet age (added to 41 C.F.R. § 60-1.3). The recordkeeping requirements of the rule (amending 41 C.F.R. § 60-1.12) are meant to provide meaningful data that the OFCCP says it will use to enhance its enforcement of the nondiscrimination laws.

(*See* http://www.dol.gov/ofccp/regs/compliance/faqs/iappfaqs.htm for guidance on electronic-recordkeeping procedures and resources.)

Q 9:61   What other obligations does a contractor have vis-à-vis the OFCCP?

Contractors have the following obligations in relation to OFCCP:

- Filing of EEO-1 and VETS-100 forms
- Posting requisite EEO posters, the company's EEO and anti-harassment policies, and notice of the availability of the non-confidential parts of its AAPs (usually made available in the human resources offices)

Q 9:62   Where can a government contractor get more information and necessary forms?

The following on-line resources are available:

- OFCCP's Web site—http://www.dol.gov/ofccp/
- EEO-1 Forms—http://www.eeoc.gov/eeo1survey/
- VETS-100 Forms—http://www.dol.gov/vets/vets-100.html

Q 9:63   How are contractors chosen for OFCCP audits?

According to the OFCCP, a combination of some 17 separate factors determines its selection of targets for audits. The most significant exercise conducted by the agency seems to be a comparison of the contractor's workforce profile from its EEO-1 form to the profiles of similar establishments in the same industry in the same region and with the labor market data from the 2000 census for that region. Companies with profiles dramatically different from their competitors and/or from the local labor pool are deemed most likely to present systemic discrimination issues.

Q 9:64   How will a contractor find out if the firm is the target of an OFCCP audit?

Companies targeted for an audit will get a Corporate Scheduling Announcement Letter (CSAL). The CSAL is notification to a corporation that two or more of its establishments are on the list of contractor establishments selected to undergo a compliance evaluation during the scheduling cycle. The list is generated from OFCCP's Federal Contractor Selection System (FCSS). It is not a letter scheduling a compliance evaluation. The purposes of the CSAL are to:

- Provide the contractor's internal EEO staff notice to obtain management support for EEO and self-audit efforts;

- Encourage contractors to take advantage of OFCCP compliance assistance offerings;

- Encourage contractors to focus on self-audit efforts that, if problems are adequately analyzed and corrected, saves OFCCP time/resources when we do an evaluation; and

- Help contractors manage/budget the amount of time required for evaluation activity.

Q 9:65   Can the company avoid an OFCCP audit after receiving a notice?

If the company believes that it is not a covered government contractor, or that certain facilities—such as those owned by a subsidiary—are not covered, it can challenge the OFCCP's jurisdiction. The government provides an on-line aid to making this determination at http://www.dol.gov/elaws/esa/ofccp/determine.asp.

This site contains some simple tests that will help you determine whether the targeted company and/or facility is covered.

Q 9:66   What is the OFCCP's focus in its enforcement agenda if the company is audited?

The OFCCP focuses on the following:

- Adverse impact of the company's hiring rules and practices and, to a lesser degree, its rules and practices for promotion and employment termination.

- The company's compensation practices; however, the agency's new standards on compensation are not yet final, so this aspect probably would not be pushed as hard as the hiring practices piece. All the same, almost all of the agency's regional offices currently use a rule-of-thumb approach toward triggering close scrutiny of a company's compensation practices. The relevant questions are as follows:

  — Is the average difference in compensation between women and men two percent or higher?

— Is the average difference in compensation between minorities and non-minorities two percent or higher?

— Are 30 percent or more of women or minorities adversely affected by this difference?

— Is the number of women or minorities who are adversely affected by the compensation difference at least three times larger than the number of men or non-minorities adversely affected by the disparity?

Q 9:67   What should the company have ready for an OFCCP on-site visit?

In the event of an OFCCP on-site visit, the company should be prepared with the following documents and postings:

- I-9 Forms.
- Beck notices.
- Company's EEO policy.
- Company's anti-harassment policy.
- Federal six-in-one poster (must now include the Uniformed Services Employment and Reemployment Rights Act). Two sources of these posters are: http://www.ontimesupplies.com/Labor_Law_Posters_Human_Resources_subsection_224_page_1.html; http:www.shoplet.com/office/cgi-bin/categories.cgi?catid = 5&sid = 36&ssid = 224
- Relevant state EEO posters, if any (*see* http://www.laborlawposter.us/)
- Notice of availability of AAP for viewing

Last but not least, managers should be prepared for interviews with OFCCP auditors.

Q 9:68   What is *Executive Order 11246?*

President Kennedy is credited with the initial conception of both the 1964 Civil Rights Act and Executive Order 11246. Both were adopted after his assassination under his successor, Lyndon B. Johnson, who signed the Executive Order in 1965, thereby requiring all government contractors to agree to refrain from job discrimination.

Executive Order 11246 states at Section 202(d) that:

> [T]he contracting agency or the Secretary of Labor may direct that any bidder or prospective contractor or subcontractor shall submit . . . a statement in writing . . . to the effect that the signer's practices and policies do not discriminate on the grounds of race, color, religion, sex or national origin, and that the signer either will affirmatively cooperate in the implementation of the policy and provisions of this order or that it consents and agrees that recruitment, employment, and the terms and conditions of employment under the proposed contract shall be in accordance with the purposes and provisions of the order.

Section 201 empowers the Secretary of Labor to adopt rules and regulations deemed "necessary and appropriate to achieve the purposes" of the order. Among the rules and regulations adopted and promulgated by the U.S. Department of Labor (DOL) are those requiring contractors and subcontractors to develop and implement affirmative action plans. [*See* 29 C.F.R. § 1608 and 41 C.F.R. § 60-2.]

Q 9:69   What happens if a contractor violates Executive Order 11246?

An employee or applicant wishing to charge a government contractor with a violation of Executive Order 11246 can file a complaint with the OFCCP within 180 days of the alleged violation. The OFCCP either can investigate the complaint itself or refer it to the EEOC. If the OFCCP investigates, the inquiry must be completed within 60 days.

If, as a result of the OFCCP investigation, the agency finds reason to believe that the executive order was violated, the contractor is served with a "show cause" notice, directing the company to provide a response as to why enforcement proceedings should not be instituted against it. The contracting firm is afforded 30 days in which to proffer any such evidence. During this same 30-day period, the OFCCP has the obligation to try to resolve the case through mediation and conciliation efforts between the parties.

If neither the company's show-cause response nor the agency's conciliation efforts brings the case to a conclusion, the director of the OFCCP may refer the complaint to the office of the Secretary of Labor for the initiation of administrative enforcement proceedings, or alternatively to the U.S. Department of Justice for judicial enforcement proceedings. The complaining employee or applicant cannot initiate a private lawsuit against the government contractor, but can sue the OFCCP to force the agency to elect one of these two enforcement alternatives in the event that the agency fails to act of its own volition. [Legal Aid Soc'y v. Brennan, 608 F.2d 1319 (9th Cir. 1979)]

Administrative enforcement proceedings include a hearing before an administrative law judge (ALJ), whose decision is open to review by the Secretary of Labor. The Secretary's disposition of the ALJ's decision in turn is subject to review in an appropriate federal district court. [Firestone Co v. Marshall, 507 F. Supp. 1330 (E.D. Tex. 1981)]

Among the available remedies are: injunctions against further violations by the employer; hiring or reinstatement (with or without back pay); or the awarding of retroactive seniority or promotion to the complaining employee or applicant, as deemed by the ALJ or court as necessary to make the aggrieved person whole. Additionally, the offending firm may have its government contract suspended or canceled and may be declared ineligible to compete for future contracts.

Q 9:70   What are examples of an employee charging a government contractor with a violation of Executive Order 11246?

In *Roncallo v. Sikorsky Aircraft Corp.* [2010 WL 4365764 (D. Conn. Oct. 22, 2010)], the plaintiff sued his employer for employment discrimination. The plaintiff claimed, among other things, that Sikorsky failed to promote him on the basis of his race and sex, in violation of Title VII of the Civil Rights Act of 1964, and that Sikorsky retaliated against him following his filing of a complaint and his federal lawsuit, also in violation of Title VII.

Judge Kravitz granted defendant Sikorsky's motion for summary judgment at the close of discovery in the case. According to Judge Kravitz:

> Mr. Roncallo can offer no direct evidence that Sikorsky acted with a discriminatory motive, and he has not given the Court a reason to conclude that Sikorsky's proffered explanation for its decision to close Job Requisition No. 68047 should not be given credence. [citation omitted] Although the fact that the company decided to close the position following Mr. Mascola's recommendation of four white male candidates may be sufficient to give rise to "speculation and conjecture," it is not sufficient to defeat Sikorsky's lawful explanation for its action or to support an ultimate inference of unlawful discrimination.

Regarding the plaintiff's related retaliation claim, the judge concluded that the "petty slights" of which Roncallo complained, the company's relocating him from an office to a cubicle, and his "pure speculation" that the firm provided some "damaging references to prospective employers," even taken together, did not rise to the level of a violation of the law.

In 2011 FedEx agreed to a settlement of $3 million in order to resolve charges of hiring discrimination from the federal contractors FedEx Ground Package System, Inc. and FedEx SmartPost, Inc. OFCCP compliance officers found evidence that FedEx's processes for hiring employers, including discrimination based on race, sex, and national origin against specific groups at 23 facilities in 15 states, were in direct violation of Executive Order 11246.

The OFCCP conducted compliance reviews over a period of seven years at FedEx facilities across the country, and also found "extensive violations" of the Order's recordkeeping requirements.

The terms of the settlement include $3 million in back pay and interest to be paid by the contractors to 21,635 persons who were not hired for entry-level positions at FedEx, as well as offering jobs to 1,703 of the applicants when jobs become available. FedEx must also remedy any discriminatory hiring practices, create an equal employment opportunity training program, and maintain records as required by the Order. [http://www.humanresourcesjournal.com/2012/03/fedex-to-pay-3-million-for-discriminating-against-21635-applicants/]

In another 2011 case, AstraZeneca, one of the largest pharmaceutical companies in the world, was charged with pay discrimination for allegedly discriminating against female sales specialists by paying them salaries that averaged $1,700 less than those of male specialists. The OFCCP found that the company failed to meet the standards set forth by Executive Order 11246 when it failed to ensure that workers were paid fairly, regardless of national origin, color, race, religion, and sex.

AstraZeneca agreed to a settlement of $250,000, and also had to radically update its affirmative action plan and recordkeeping practices. [http://www. dol.gov/opa/media/press/ofccp/OFCCP20110829.htm]

Q 9:71   What is the *Adarand Constructors* case and how does it affect the OFCCP's affirmative action mission?

A bare majority of five U.S. Supreme Court justices, led by Justice Sandra Day O'Connor, announced in June 1995 that from now on federal affirmative action programs must be reviewed by the courts under the "strict scrutiny" standard, which had been announced by the high court five years earlier. The case concerned a guardrail subcontractor that was the low bidder but lost a highway contract in Colorado to a Hispanic competitor as a result of a federal program that gave a bonus to a prime contractor for hiring a minority-owned firm as a subcontractor. In reinstating the disappointed subcontractor's claim, Justice O'Connor wrote for the majority that the Fifth and Fourteenth Amendments to the U.S. Constitution "protect persons, not groups." [Adarand Constructors, Inc. v. Pena, 515 U.S. 200 (1995)]

Writing for the four dissenters, Justice John Paul Stevens decried what he termed the majority's deviation from established precedent. He disparaged Justice O'Connor's opinion as a "disconcerting lecture about the evils of governmental racial classifications." Calling the majority's demand for equal treatment for all "the difference between the 'No Trespassing' sign and a welcome mat," he warned that the opinion in essence "would treat a Dixiecrat Senator's decision to vote against Thurgood Marshall's confirmation in order to keep African Americans off the Supreme Court as on a par with President Johnson's evaluation of his nominee's race as a positive factor."

The Court's sole African American, Justice Clarence Thomas, voted with the majority, casting the fifth and deciding vote. Justice Thomas wrote a separate opinion in which he called affirmative action "racial paternalism" that "can be as poisonous and pernicious as any other form of discrimination." In his own concurring opinion, Justice Antonin Scalia opined that the government "can never have a 'compelling interest' in discriminating on the basis of race in order to 'make up for' past discrimination."

Justice O'Connor noted that strict scrutiny, while a difficult evidentiary standard for a governmental entity touting a preference to overcome, is not intended by the Court to be an impossible constitutional hurdle. Nonetheless, liberals and minority groups criticized the decision as a step backward in American race relations and minority-group progress.

While the opinion does not come from an employment case, it has implications for affirmative action decisions affecting hiring, promotion, and firing. Employers, such as government contractors and universities, long distinguished for their vigorous affirmative action initiatives, may have to reexamine their policies in light of the new tougher standard enunciated by the Supreme Court.

> In testimony before the Senate Labor Committee following the *Adarand Constructors* decision, the OFCCP head, Shirley J. Wilcher, insisted that the ruling would not affect the agency's affirmative action mandate. Stating that the OFCCP's "goals and timetables" program for hiring minorities, veterans, women, and the disabled are not a subterfuge for quotas.

["Shirley J. Wilcher's Statement to Senate Labor Committee," 1995 *BNA Daily Labor Report* 116, June 16, 1995, at d31]

Q 9:72　Is there such a thing as affirmative action in favor of unions with regard to federal government contracts?

One of the first acts of George W. Bush upon becoming President of the United States was the issuance of an Executive Order, which in effect rescinded a contrary decree by President Bill Clinton. Bush's February 2001 Executive Order mandated absolute neutrality with regard to unionized versus non-unionized government contractors with regard to their contract relationships with the federal government.

> One of President Barack Obama's earliest acts in 2009 was to countermand Bush's order, issuing Executive Order 13502. The Executive Order was signed on February 6, 2009 and stated it should be the government's policy to encourage the use of labor agreements to avoid misunderstandings about the cost of labor, and to ensure that one contractor's workforce problems during a project not delay other teams involved in the contract. [74 Fed. Reg. 6985 (Feb. 11, 2009)]

Q 9:73　Does the federal government engage in affirmative action by means of the contracts it awards?

The federal government is capable of engaging in affirmative action not only by requiring its myriad agencies, contractors, and subcontractors to act affirmatively to engage minority group members as employees and subcontractors, but also by the content of the contracts that are let out for bids. The U.S. Supreme Court's decision in *Adarand Constructors Inc. v. Pena* [515 U.S. 200 (1995)], has curbed Uncle Sam's ability to mandate set-asides for minority- and female-owned enterprises during the past decade. Furthermore, the Supreme Court's rulings in two affirmative action cases involving the University of Michigan reaffirmed its historic *Bakke* decision to the effect that affirmative action programs which mandate quotas are illegal. [*See* Gratz v. Bollinger, 539 U.S. 244, (2003).]

Q 9:74   What is the current status of affirmative action?

While court cases have continued to chip away at affirmative action across the country, government contractors and nonprofits receiving federal funding must assume that in the area of affirmative action, the OFCCP, the DOL, and the Department of Education, and other responsible federal agencies will continue to require compliance with existing obligations.

In spring 2003 the U.S. Supreme Court revisited the issue of affirmative action in college admissions for the first time in a quarter century. These decisions were announced in April 2003. [Gratz v. Bollinger, 539 U.S. 244 (2003) and Grutter v. Bollinger 539 U.S. 306 (2003)] In these two cases involving the University of Michigan, a divided Court concluded that the university's undergraduate admission program, which automatically awarded 20 points toward admission to applicants of color was an illegal quota system. But on the other hand, accepting the contention of *amicus curiae* from both higher education and the corporate sector that diverse student bodies on our college campuses is a compelling state interest, the Court majority led by Justice Sandra Day O'Connor condoned the law school's practice of taking race into consideration as one significant factor in its admissions decisions.

In 2006, Michigan voters passed a state constitution amendment that in essence overruled the Supreme Court's decisions by outlawing all favoritism based on race. This amendment was challenged and the U.S. Court of Appeals for the Sixth Circuit held by a vote of 8-7, sitting as a whole, that the amendment violated the Equal Protection Clause of the Fourteenth Amendment to the U.S. Constitution. In March 2013, the U.S. Supreme Court agreed to the hear case. The Court will hear arguments in Fall 2013 and announce its decision in Spring 2014.

[Coalition to Defend Affirmative Action v. Regents of Univ. of Mich., 701 F.3d 466 (6th Cir. 2012), *cert. granted*, Schuette v. Coalition to Defend Affirmative Action, 133 S. Ct. 1633 (2013)]

Q 9:75   What is the significance of the *Piscataway* case?

In *Piscataway*, Taxman and an African American teacher were hired on the same day to teach the same subject in the Piscataway School. During the years of their employment there they received substantially comparable performance evaluations. When a layoff necessitated letting go one or the other of them, as the least senior teachers in their department, the school board let go Taxman and never denied that the African American teacher was retained purely because of her race in order to fulfill perceived affirmative action obligations by maintaining diversity in her department. Taxman sued for reverse discrimination and won in both the trial and mid-level appellate courts. The U.S. Court of Appeals for the Third Circuit held that Piscataway's affirmative action policy was unlawful under the antidiscrimination mandate of Title VII.

The case made national news when the National Association for the Advancement of Colored People (NAACP) joined with the city's school board in settling the case, paying $433,500 in compensatory damages to Taxman.

The announcement of the settlement, after the U.S. Supreme Court agreed to hear the school district's appeal of the case, shocked many advocates of affirmative action while disappointing many of affirmative action's opponents, who believed that this would be the case under which the Supreme Court would eliminate affirmative action once and for all.

Officials of the NAACP subsequently explained that the case was a bad one to send to the high court because school board officials had blatantly laid off Taxman in favor of her African American colleague purely for racial considerations. Thus, the likelihood of a devastating loss for affirmative action proponents in the Supreme Court seemed inevitable. [Taxman v. Board of Educ. of Piscataway, 91 F.3d 1547 (3d Cir. 1996)]

Q 9:76 What does *Piscataway* mean for government contractors?

Because the NAACP settled the case before the Supreme Court could review it, the *Piscataway* case is binding legal precedent only for the three states (New Jersey, Pennsylvania, Delaware, plus the Commonwealth of Puerto Rico) under the Third Circuit's jurisdiction. Officials of the NAACP and other expert observers have no doubt, however, that in a case with facts similar to *Piscataway*'s, the Supreme Court will agree with the Third Circuit and declare any such affirmative action policy to be illegal discrimination. Consequently, government contractors should assume that employment decisions (hiring, firing, layoff, promotion, raises, etc.) based solely on an employee's race, color, gender, or national origin will be found by the federal courts to be illegal discrimination. However, the Supreme Court took a fresh look at affirmative action in college admissions during its spring 2003 term and the ruling in that case was being closely watched, as it seemed bound to have an impact upon the hiring and firing practices of government contractors too. [*See* Gratz v. Bollinger, 539 U.S. 244 (2003)] However, in reaction to the decision, in 2006 Michigan voters passed a state constitution amendment that in essence overruled the Supreme Court's decision by outlawing all favoritism based on race. This amendment was challenged and the U.S. Court of Appeals for the Sixth Circuit held by a vote of 8-7, sitting as a whole, that the amendment violated the Equal Protection Clause of the Fourteenth Amendment to the U.S. Constitution. In March 2013, the U.S. Supreme Court heard oral arguments on the case. The Court's decision was still pending as this publication goes to press. [Coalition to Defend Affirmative Action v. Regents of Univ. of Mich., 701 F.3d 466 (6th Cir. 2012), *cert. granted*, Schuette v. Coalition to Defend Affirmative Action, 133 S. Ct. 1633 (2013)]

Additionally, in its spring 2013 term, the Court heard arguments in another affirmative action case, this one a challenge to the Texas "Top Ten Percent Plan," under which the top 10 percent of graduating seniors from each of the Lone Star State's high schools is guaranteed admission into the premier state university. On June 24, 2013, the Court by a vote of 7-1 remanded the case to the Fifth Circuit, saying UT's program might pass muster, if the school can demonstrate a need to promote diversity. [Fisher v. University of Tex. at Austin, 644 F.3d 301 (5th Cir. 2011) *cert. granted*, 132 S. Ct. 1536 (2012)]

Q 9:77   In light of current federal case law, what should government contractors do with regard to affirmative action?

Government contractors should seek to set a balance between their affirmative action obligations, mandated by the OFCCP, and the restrictions and cautionary guidance laid down in the recent federal decisions. The Supreme Court in its two spring 2003 University of Michigan decisions stated clearly that racial quotas are no more acceptable now than they were 25 years ago when the Court announced its famous *Bakke* decision. On the other hand, the Court has not outlawed efforts aimed at insuring that racial minorities are represented in hiring pools; nor does the Court appear to object to considering race as one factor in hiring decisions. If, as the Court concedes, racial diversity on college campuses is a compelling state interest, racial diversity in a corporation's workforce would appear to be equally compelling given the diverse make-up of the American workforce itself. The balance the authors are suggesting might best be set by following these guidelines:

1. Ensure that all of the organization's affirmative action initiatives are undertaken in connection to an affirmative action plan.
2. Demonstrate that the affirmative action plan is remedial.
3. Indicate that the plan is voluntary.
4. The plan must not trample the rights of non-minority employees unnecessarily.
5. The plan must be temporary and must be updated periodically (ideally on an annual basis).

Q 9:78   How can a government contractor show that its affirmative action plan is remedial?

The company must conduct a self-analysis to determine if and where racial imbalances exist. The self-analysis is conducted in the following order:

1. Identify the various categories of employees in the workforce.
2. Determine the appropriate labor pool from which these employees may be drawn (e.g., international, national, regional, statewide, or purely local).
3. Ascertain the percentage of relevant minority groups represented in the appropriate labor pool.
4. Ascertain the percentage of these same minority groups represented in the company's workforce in each of the broad job categories.

If the percentage of minorities represented in any of the identified job categories within the organization is below the percentage in the appropriate labor pool, then the organization has identified a need to undertake remedial efforts.

Q 9:79   What is the appropriate labor pool for a particular job category?

To make this determination, follow these guidelines:

1. Job categories should be broadly defined (e.g., clericals, maintenance, production, supervisory).

2. Ascertain how broadly the organization has advertised for candidates in each of these categories.

3. Typically, the higher the levels of status, responsibility, and compensation entailed in the job category, the larger the geographic spread of the appropriate labor pool; for example, a corporation may engage in a worldwide search for a new CEO, conduct national searches for other top executives, confine its search to its home state or region with respect to professional employees such as engineers and lawyers, and look only locally for secretaries, production workers, and janitorial staff.

4. This same geographic region, then, should be used to define the appropriate labor pool in each identified category.

Q 9:80   What should a contractor's affirmative action policy state?

The basic, boilerplate affirmative action policy will be about two typed pages in length and should contain the following statements [41 C.F.R. § 60-2.20]:

1. At _____, we are committed to maintaining an environment of nondiscrimination in compliance with the provisions of state and federal equal opportunity laws as they apply to our employees. Specifically, _____'s activities will be administered without regard to race, color, religion, national origin, sex [sexual orientation, if mandated by state or local law], handicap/disability, age, or Vietnam-era disabled veteran status.

2. In an effort to achieve more than just minimal compliance with the law, _____ seeks to create an environment that understands, fosters, and embraces the value of diversity among its employees. To that end, various diversity-related programs are routinely sponsored by _____ and employees are encouraged to participate in these activities.

3. _____ is committed to both equal employment opportunity (EEO) and to affirmative action (AA). Equal employment opportunity refers to the right of individuals to be judged upon the basis of relevant skills, experience, and previous performance and not on criteria irrelevant to the performance of their jobs. Affirmative action requires that special efforts be used to search for qualified female, minority, disabled, and Vietnam-veteran-era candidates and to insure that they are considered for available positions along with other qualified applicants. Affirmative action does not require that "quotas" or "set asides" be established for minorities or women; however, where minorities or women are underutilized in a particular job group, hiring and promotional goals will be established, per the requirements of Executive Order 11246.

4. In keeping with _____'s official EEO policy, _____ will continue to recruit, hire, train, and promote into all job levels the most qualified persons

without regard to race, color, sex [sexual orientation, if appropriate in your jurisdiction], religion, national origin, handicap, disability, or Vietnam-era veteran status. This policy shall apply to all employment actions, including but not limited to recruitment, hiring, upgrading, promotion, transfer, demotion, layoff, recall, termination, rates of pay or other forms of compensation, and selection for training.

5. As [Chairman, CEO, or President] of _____, I am committed to principles of equal employment opportunity and affirmative action. In order to ensure this policy's dissemination and implementation throughout all levels of the organization, I have selected _____ [director of human resources or other job title, as appropriate] as Affirmative Action Officer for _____.

6. In furtherance of its policy of equal employment opportunity and affirmative action, _____ has developed a written affirmative action plan that contains specific and results-oriented procedures to which _____ is committed to apply every good faith effort. Procedures without efforts to make them work are meaningless, and effort without the guidance of specific meaningful procedures is ineffective.

7. _____'s complete affirmative action plan is available for review by applicants and employees upon request during normal business hours at various company locations. For details, please contact Human Resources at extension _____.

8. Administrators and supervisors are responsible for assuring that equal employment opportunity and, where applicable, affirmative action are practiced in all personnel activities and decisions throughout their areas of responsibility.

9. Signature and date.

Q 9:81 What components should the government contractor's affirmative action program contain?

The typical affirmative action program, implementing the broad goals of the boilerplate affirmative action program, usually contains the following components:

1. *Statement of purpose.* This section states that the affirmative action program is submitted to the OFCCP and adopted by the organization as a set of specific and results-oriented procedures and that the organization is committed to all good-faith efforts to correct deficiencies in full utilization of minorities and women.

2. *Responsibility for program implementation.* This section reiterates the identity of the affirmative action officer and lists his or her main duties and responsibilities.

3. *Dissemination.* This portion indicates exactly how the organization will insure that the plan is communicated to its relevant audiences. Some

examples are: employee handbook, company policy manual, new-employee orientations, employee training programs, written and verbal communications to recruiting sources outside the organization, and incorporation of a statement in standard company contract forms.

4. *Internal audit and reporting system.* Mandated by the OFCCP regulations, this section explains how the organization will monitor its own compliance and progress under the program.

5. *Development and execution of programs.* The OFCCP regulations suggest the following: distribution to recruitment sources of accurate position descriptions and worker specifications; implementation of "action-oriented" programs; an anti-nepotism policy; and due process policies for the appeal of discrimination-based grievances.

6. *Human resources policies and procedures.* This section should contain the human resources policies and procedures that help assure and implement the organization's compliance with its affirmative action policy. Policies and procedures to be included concern: recruitment, employment, administrative and management development and training, committee participation, and job posting.

7. *Support of action programs.* The regulations call for the organization to engage in "active support of local and national community action programs designed to improve the employment opportunities of minorities and women."

8. *Religion and national origin guidelines.* Not specifically required by the regulations, but many contractors voluntarily include them.

9. *Adherence to sex discrimination guidelines.* This is a mandatory section stating that the organization has in the past and will continue to prohibit sex discrimination.

10. *Affirmative action program for disabled persons.* This section contains the organization's policies and procedures with regard to providing reasonable accommodation to individuals with known disabilities in the absence of undue hardship to the organization.

11. *Identification of specific activities.* Some examples are: targeting recruitment publications with a high percentage of minority and female readers; circulating job postings to organizations serving minority and female job seekers; and improving the corporate climate for minorities and females.

12. *Identification of problem areas.* This section lists, usually as an attachment in the form of tables, the under-utilized job groups for minorities and women.

13. *Consideration of minorities and women not currently in the workforce.* This might include: apprenticeship programs, internship programs, and cooperative work/study programs.

14. *Workforce analysis.* Also an attachment to the program document.

15. *Identification of job groups.* Also an attachment to the program document.

16. *Establishment of goals and timetables.* Not to be confused with "quotas" or "set asides," this emphasizes good faith efforts to remedy the under-utilization identified in the immediately preceding sections.

Q 9:82   What types of community involvement efforts might the government contractor undertake to assist in achieving affirmative action program goals?

The OFCCP regulations [41 C.F.R. §§ 60-2.13(I) and 60-2.26] suggest the following:

1. Service on the boards of trustees of universities, colleges, and private high schools with substantial minority student populations;
2. Programs that bring community leaders or students from minority groups into the organization and familiarize them with it;
3. Attendance at college fairs and high school career days at institutions with large minority student populations;
4. Service on the boards of relevant nonprofits, such as statewide affirmative action officers associations, NOW, and similar organizations;
5. Attendance at training and diversity programs sponsored by any of the foregoing institutions; or
6. Sponsor corporate programs open to women and/or minority groups at corporate facilities, such as programs on women's health or minority career advancement.

Q 9:83   What are the typical duties of the affirmative action officer?

Affirmative action officers generally have the following responsibilities:

1. Coordinating the development of the contractor's affirmative action policy and program;
2. Assisting senior management and human resources in the development of hiring and promotional goals for each EEO job group;
3. Monitoring personnel procedures, policies, and practices to insure implementation of EEO and affirmative action policies;
4. Developing EEO and affirmative action policies and procedures;
5. Developing and maintaining internal and external communication sources to distribute information on EEO and affirmative action;
6. Responding to actual or potential discrimination charges;
7. Reviewing and monitoring personnel transactions (e.g., applications, hires, promotions, or terminations) to measure the program's effectiveness recommending changes; identifying specific goals and objectives attained during the affirmative action program year, informing management of current EEO developments and deficiencies;
8. Assisting supervisors and administrators in the development of training programs;

9. Assisting supervisors and administrators in counseling minority and female employees regarding career development and promotion potential;

10. Assisting supervisors and administrators in the identification of problem areas and establishing related solutions, goals, and objectives;

11. Conducting periodic audits of applicant flow, hiring, transfers, promotions, and training activities;

12. Ensuring that EEO posters are properly displayed according to the law; and

13. Communicating with senior management and supervisors on their responsibilities, such as remediating sexual harassment and preventing discrimination.

Q 9:84   How might a government contractor disseminate affirmative action and EEO policies internally?

The OFCCP and related regulations require or suggest:

1. Make the affirmative action plan available to individuals in the human resources office and elsewhere in the company.

2. Make human resources the central location for advising employees and applicants on affirmative action and EEO aspects of application, hiring, promotion, training, and disciplinary matters.

3. Discuss affirmative action and EEO policies as part of new-employee orientation.

4. Highlight and discuss affirmative action and EEO policies at annual performance reviews and on other occasions that present themselves throughout the plan year.

5. Publish articles and notices periodically in company newsletters and magazines.

6. Reflect diversity in illustrations used in company publications.

7. Send re-affirmation notices to all employees annually.

[*See, e.g.*, 41 C.F.R. § 60-2.13(B).]

Q 9:85   How might a government contractor disseminate affirmative action and EEO policies externally?

The OFCCP and related regulations suggest the following:

1. Inform recruiting sources, community leaders, schools, and other businesses of the company's affirmative action program and request that they actively recruit and refer minority and female candidates to the company.

2. Notify in writing minority and women's organizations, community agencies, community leaders, schools, and colleges periodically of the company's affirmative action program and its specific recruitment needs.

3. Include affirmative action and non-discrimination clauses in contracts, recruiting announcements, and advertisements.

4. Inform applicants of the company's affirmative action program.

5. Post federal and state affirmative action and EEO posters in prominent places where visitors to the company are likely to notice them.

6. Send written notice to subcontractors and vendors (for government contracts this is a legal requirement and not just a suggestion).

7. Include an affirmative action/EEO statement on applications for employment and on any employment/human resources Web site the company may maintain.

8. Train all personnel who are engaged in recruitment activities.

9. Make company personnel available through the public relations speakers bureau or otherwise for talks to minority and women's organizations.

Q 9:86   What affirmative action/EEO policies ought to be put in place within the government contractor's organization?

Policies on the following subjects are highly recommended:

1. Routine announcements of vacancies to diverse agencies, organizations, and individuals;

2. Written procedures to facilitate employee claims of discrimination;

3. Due process procedures for employee grievances and discrimination complaints;

4. Equitable and nondiscriminatory benefits, such as disability leaves;

5. Reasonable accommodation for the permanently and temporarily disabled in the workforce;

6. Anti-nepotism;

7. No retirement age limit.

Q 9:87   What should be the affirmative action content of major human resource policies of government contractors?

Recruitment:

1. All job openings are posted so that everyone who might be qualified has an opportunity to apply.

2. Listings of job openings are sent on a regular (weekly) basis to minority and women's organizations, employment agencies, and community leaders.

3. A page on the company's Web site is devoted to job openings.

4. Recruitment ads are placed in minority and women's publications in the appropriate job categories and job markets.

5. Recruitment brochures reflect diversity in their illustrations and language.

Employment:

1. Human resources staff validate position requirements using job performance criteria.
2. Approved position descriptions and worker specifications are available to all personnel involved in recruiting, screening, and hiring.
3. Human resources complies with office of federal contract compliance programs requirements for the validation of any employment tests and other selection procedures.
4. Policies, programs, and procedures are given periodic human resources department review.

Q 9:88 What effect will the existence of a consent decree have on a government contractor's affirmative action obligations?

The existence of a consent decree—under which a government contractor settled a lawsuit by agreeing to a court order requiring affirmative action—may be sufficient to overcome the limitations on affirmative action imposed by the Supreme Court and other federal courts in their recent decisions cutting back on affirmative action activities. The major legal rules regarding consent decrees as they pertain to affirmative action are as follows:

- In *Sheet Metal Workers' Local* 28 v. *EEOC* [106 S. Ct. 3019 (1986)], the Supreme Court held that consent decrees could give favorable treatment not only to identifiable victims of a company's discriminatory practices, but also to unharmed members of the relevant minority group.
- In *Martin v. Wilks* [490 U.S. 755 (1989)], the Supreme Court ruled that persons who had prior notice of a discrimination suit and the pending consent decree, and who failed to intervene in the action, cannot later bring a reverse discrimination case to try and overturn the consent decree and eliminate the affirmative action mandated under it.

Taken together, these cases mean that if a court makes appropriate findings of prior discriminatory behavior by a corporation, the court can enter a consent decree. If opponents of the decree fail to challenge the court's findings of fact in the decree prior to its entry, they cannot later complain of the affirmative action that properly results from that decree.

Q 9:89 Must a government contractor make light-duty work available to disabled employees in order to comply with Section 503 of the Rehabilitation Act?

In *OFCCP v. Cissell Manufacturing Co.* [Case No. 87-OFC-26 (Feb. 14, 1994)], the Assistant Secretary of Labor, sitting as a sort of appellate court judge, couched the issue and answer as follows:

> The central issue in this case is whether a government contractor may refuse to comply with the obligation to make reasonable accommodation to the physical limitations of an employee under Section 503 of the

> Rehabilitation Act of 1973 . . . because it has a company policy of no "light duty" jobs. . . . I find that such a refusal violates Section 503.

In this case, complainant Larry Brown suffered an on-the-job injury in 1983, when he was a production welder assembling parts for commercial clothes dryers. Three doctors independently diagnosed a condition that constituted a form of arthritis. The company's doctor suggested that the complainant "try to avoid jobs with excessive bending and lifting at the knees." An independent orthopedist recommended that Brown "avoid kneeling, deep knee bending, and stairs as much as possible."

When Brown reported to work with a doctor's note containing such recommendations in October 1984, his foreman told him to "hit the clock." His union steward was told by Cissell's personnel office that no light-duty work was available for Brown. Brown next took 26 weeks of paid sick leave and two successive 90-day leaves of absence without pay. Finally, on July 11, 1985, the director of corporate relations wrote a letter to the complainant, advising him that "if you are not released to perform regular duties with no restrictions by 10/10/85 your employment status will become termination." Brown then filed his OFCCP complaint.

Following a hearing, an ALJ held that Brown was disabled under the Rehabilitation Act, because Cissell had treated him as unable to hold any job at the plant, that he was actually qualified to hold several welder jobs, and that Cissell's failure to accommodate him violated Section 503. Consequently, the ALJ proposed reinstatement with back pay, but no debarment for Cissell provided the contractor complied.

Reviewing the ALJ's ruling, the Assistant Secretary of Labor found that "given the actual functioning and circumstances of Cissell's business, Cissell did not show that making reasonable accommodation to Mr. Brown's handicap by assigning him to jobs that did not require excessive stooping and bending would impose an undue burden." [*Id.*] *Cissell*, in some ways, is not an ideal case from which to draw conclusions about the OFCCP's attitude toward light-duty jobs, as reasonable accommodations, going forward. The decision mildly chides the complainant for failing to consult his union about its attitude concerning the status of light duty in light of the labor contract and for failing avidly to seek jobs outside the welding trade with his employer. The company, too, was criticized for creating confusion concerning Brown's employment status between 1984 and 1988.

The decision makes it clear that government contractors must at least explore light-duty accommodations of disabled employees or risk back pay exposure under the Rehabilitation Act.

Q 9:90   Who qualifies as a person with a disability?

Under the amended Americans with Disabilities Act (ADA), the definition of *disabled* is so very broad that many employees qualify for its protections and may not even realize it. According to the ADA (patterned after the Rehabilitation Act, and nearly identical to its definition), it defines *disabled* in three parts:

> An individual with a disability is a person who: (1) has a physical or mental impairment that substantially limits one or more major life activities; OR (2) has a record of such an impairment; OR (3) is regarded as having such an impairment.
>
> A *physical impairment* is defined by ADA as "any physiological disorder or condition, cosmetic disfigurement, or anatomical loss affecting one or more of the following body systems: neurological, musculoskeletal, special sense organs, respiratory (including speech organs), cardiovascular, reproductive, digestive, genitourinary, hemic and lymphatic, skin, and endocrine."
>
> Neither ADA nor the regulations that implement it list all the diseases or conditions that are covered, because it would be impossible to provide a comprehensive list, given the variety of possible impairments.

[http://www.dhs.wisconsin.gov/disabilities/physical/definition.htm]

Because many disabilities are not visible, however, employers may face the additional obstacle of applicants and employees who do not voluntarily self-identify as disabled. Thus, employers may have a difficult time meeting, or providing proof of meeting, the OFCCP's hiring goal.

In order to combat this predicted issue, the new regulations also require that contractors allow all applicants to self-identify as individuals with disabilities, using "the language and manner prescribed by the Director and published on the OFCCP Web site," when the applicant applies for or is considered for employment, as well as post-offer. Furthermore, contractors would also be required to survey employees annually, as well as anonymously, regarding whether he or she believes his or herself to be an individual with a disability.

Q 9:91   What changes have recently been made regarding the affirmative action requirements for disabled workers?

The current affirmative action requirements of E.O. 11246 and Section 503 of the Rehabilitation Act of 1973 do not have set hiring goals like they do for the hiring of minorities and women. For the past 40 years, a "good faith" effort to hire people with disabilities was all that was required of contractors. As it stands, the unemployment rate for the disabled is one and a half times that of people without disabilities, and the Bureau of Labor Statistics (BLS) found that 79.2 percent of all persons with disabilities are not in the workforce.

[http://www.dickinsonlaw.com/2011/12/sweeping-changes-in-affirmative-action-requirements-for-disabled-workers-proposed-today/]

In 2011, the OFCCP proposed new regulations that would revise the rules that implement Section 503 of the Rehabilitation Act of 1973, as well as revise the nondiscrimination provisions to conform to changes made by the ADA Amendments Act of 2008. The proposed regulations would set a goal that seven percent of federal contractors' (and federal subcontractors') workforce be people with disabilities, along with a sub-goal of two percent for individuals with particularly severe disabilities. The proposed regulations would also create new requirements regarding data collection, recordkeeping, training, and policy dissemination. According to Patricia Shue, the director of the OFCCP, the proposal would also "define specific goals, require real accountability and provide the clearest possible guidance for employers seeking to comply with the law."

[http://gtpac.org/2011/12/labor-sets-disabled-worker-hiring-goal-for-contractors/]

Specifically, the proposal seeks to alter the way in which contractors communicate affirmative action requirements by requiring that contractors:

1. Disseminate affirmative action policies in internal policy manuals and discuss those policies at employee orientation and/or training programs;

2. Issue notices of worker rights under Section 503 in accessible formats for employees working offsite (such as electronic postings) and for employees with visual impairments;

3. Conduct an annual review of personnel processes annually (rather than the loosely termed "periodically" from the previous regulations), and outlining the specific steps a contractor must take in said review. The contractor must also document personnel actions taken with regard to individuals with disabilities "to provide greater transparency between the contractor, its applicants/employees, and OFCCP as to the reasons for their personnel actions"; and

4. Meet with and/or send notification of AAP obligations to third parties with whom the contractors do business, such as union officials and subcontractors.

[http://www.dcemploymentlawupdate.com/2011/12/articles/agency-rule making/ofccp-proposes-changes-to-rules-governing-contractor-nondiscrimination-and-affirmative-action-requirements-for-individuals-with-disabilities/]

With regard to recordkeeping requirements, contractors would be required to collect and maintain significantly more data, including (according to the Associated General Contractors of America Web site, http://news.agc.org/2012/01/11/ofccp-proposes-changes-to-affirmative-action-obligations-related-to-individuals-with-disabilities-2/):

1. Total number of referrals from approved employment delivery organizations such as One-Stop Career Centers as well as organizations with which the contractor has a linkage agreement;

2. Total number of applicants for employment;

3. Number of applicants who are known to be individuals with disabilities;

4. Ratio of known applicants with disabilities to total applicants;

5. Total number of job openings;

6. Total number of jobs filled;

11. Number of known individuals with disabilities hired;

12. Ratio of hires with known disabilities to total hires; and

13. Ratio of job openings to job openings filled.

The proposal would also require that contractors enter into linkage agreements and take part in community outreach programs. These additional responsibilities include the obligation to:

1. Review outreach and recruitment activities annually to evaluate their effectiveness in identifying and recruiting qualified individuals with disabilities;

2. Incorporate affirmative action plans into policy manuals and discuss the program in orientation and management training programs;

3. Develop internal procedures to further inform employees about the affirmative action plan;

4. Develop extensive specified written procedures for processing requests for reasonable accommodation;

5. Annually review and revise physical and mental job qualification standards; and

6. Annually evaluate compliance with utilization goals.

Note: The most recent regulatory changes under the ADA are always readily accessible at http://www.ada.gov/.

Q 9:92   What guidance has OFCCP promulgated regarding the ADAAA?

The ADA Amendments Act (ADAAA) [Pub. L. No. 110-325] overturned a series of Supreme Court decisions that interpreted the Americans with Disabilities Act of 1990 (ADA) in a way that made it difficult to prove that an impairment is a "disability." The ADAAA makes significant changes to the ADA's definition of *disability* that broadens the scope of coverage under both the ADA and Section 503 of the Rehabilitation Act.

The OFCCP has provided a set of Frequently Asked Questions to assist government contractors with compliance issues involving the ADAAA: http://www.dol.gov/ofccp/TAguides/new_contractors_guide.htm

The agency has also posted guidance for contractors who wish to implement online application systems in order to help insure equal application opportunity to potential employees. This guidance is available at: http://www.dol.gov/ofccp/regs/compliance/faqs/dir281faqs.htm

Last, but not least, the OFCCP has posted guidance on its FY 2011 compliance-evaluation schedule at: http://webapps.dol.gov/FederalRegister/HtmlDisplay.aspx?DocId=24536&AgencyId=15.

Wages and Benefits

Q 9:93   What laws govern wages and benefits of government contractors?

One law is the Walsh-Healey Public Contracts Act (PCA), which applies to manufacturers and so-called "regular dealers" who sell goods to the U.S. government. In recent years, the DOL has limited enforcement of wage and hour issues under this law to minimum wages, overtime pay, and essentially the same fundamental issues covered by the Fair Labor Standards Act (FLSA), which applies to almost all employers. (See Q 9:137 for PCA contract exemptions.)

The Davis-Bacon Act controls wages, benefits, and working conditions of "laborers and mechanics" employed by contractors in the construction, alteration, or repair of public buildings and public works. The Act requires contracts in excess of $2,000 to set forth the minimum wages to be paid to all classes of laborers that a contractor employs under the contract. Contractors and subcontractors may not pay less than the federal minimum wage. Davis-Bacon's rules and regulations generally also apply to construction contracts under a group of more narrow federal statutes, and are supplemented by other laws aimed at preventing cheating in the payment of construction contract workers.

In 1965, a gap in this federal scheme was filled by the enactment of the Service Contract Act. Apparently anticipating the post-industrial transition to a service economy, the Act applies to the wide range of services, from janitorial to sophisticated consulting, which the federal government contracts for.

Q 9:94   How does the DOL enforce proper payment of wages and fringe benefits by government contractors?

There is no private right of action for employees under either Davis-Bacon or the Service Contract Act, the legal rationale being that privity of contract runs between the contractor and the government, and therefore it is to the government that any such right accrues.

Administrative enforcement of Davis-Bacon and Service Contract Act is entrusted to various administrative boards, such as the Wage Appeals Board and the Armed Services Board of Contract Appeals. Such boards, and their ALJs who hear cases, are empowered to adjudicate challenges by government contractors and would-be contractors of the DOL's wage determinations when the procurement process is initiated. While the decisions of these boards can often be taken to the appropriate U.S. Court of Appeals, federal courts have limited jurisdiction (at best) to interfere with this administrative process.

In auditing contractors and their reports, the DOL is concerned primarily with ensuring that contributions were made at least quarterly, irrevocably to the employee or the benefit plan, and following an accurate computation. Relevant records include payroll records and contractor statements of compliance.

When a violation is found to be minor (e.g., less than $1,000) and non-willful, and future compliance is not in doubt, restitution alone (to the eligible employees) may be acceptable to the DOL.

When larger amounts or more egregious circumstances are detected, the DOL may:

1. Withhold unpaid funds under the contract pending resolution of the claim;

2. Terminate the contract;

3. Seek liquidated (double) damages;

4. Seek debarment from further federal contract work against the offending contractor for as much as three years; or

5. In some instances, seek criminal penalties.

Q 9:95   What are wage determinations?

Before the DOL can prescribe minimum wages and fringe benefits for employees doing work under Davis-Bacon and Service Contract Act contracts, it must have a way to determine the appropriate wages and benefits for a particular part of the country.

Like other government agencies, the DOL has divided the nation into 10 geographic regions and established regional headquarters in 10 major cities. Regional staff in each of these offices use mail and telephone surveys of contractors subject to Davis-Bacon in their particular region to learn what these contractors are paying in wages and benefits. Under the guidance of a manual developed for this purpose, government wage specialists may select "any rate that is paid more than the majority of the time," according to a top DOL wage administrator in Philadelphia.

Under the Service Contract Act, the DOL's Bureau of Labor Statistics in Washington conducts such surveys under an inter-agency contract with the DOL's Wage and Hour Division. The explanation for this dichotomy between Davis-Bacon and the Service Contract Act regarding survey techniques apparently relates to the DOL's perception of the trades and professions involved. Experience has taught the government's wage experts that in the building trades, there is a great deal of variance depending on geography.

Under the Service Contract Act, there is an ongoing effort to extend wage determinations geographically and temporally both for uniformity and cost efficiency of the Bureau of Labor Statistics' surveys. Thus, a current pilot program is testing the efficacy of "blanket wage determinations" that will stay in place at a major facility, such as a military post or federal building in a major city, for an extended period (e.g., one year) rather than preparing a Standard Form 98 wage determination for every procurement of a new contract.

Q 9:96   Where can a government contractor get wage determinations?

Wage determinations are available from the Wage Determinations OnLine Web site (http://www.wdol.gov).

This Web site provides a single location for federal contracting officers to use in obtaining appropriate Service Contract Act and Davis-Bacon Act wage determinations for each official contract action. The Web site is available to the general public as well. Guidance in selecting wage determinations from this Web site is provided in the WDOL.gov User's Guide.

Q 9:97   Are wage determinations ever unnecessary?

In the event of a national emergency, the President is empowered to suspend Davis-Bacon wage determinations and allow government contractors to pay lower than comparable regional wages. This occurred in September 2005 for the region hit hardest by Hurricane Katrina. In a letter notifying Congress of his decision, President Bush wrote, "I have found that the conditions caused by Hurricane Katrina constitute a 'national emergency.'"

Q 9:98   Can a government contractor substitute one fringe benefit for another?

Yes. The DOL recognizes that it is not always practical, or even possible, for a particular contractor to provide precisely the type and mix of benefits found to be prevalent in the relevant geographic area. For example, the current legal limit on the portability of pension plans means that contributions to an employer plan, especially in construction, in which workers move from project to project and employer to employer, would benefit the employer's long-term employees only. Thus, the DOL permits substitution of one benefit for another, and even the substitution of the cash equivalent applied as a supplement to the hourly rate. The most striking example can be found in Service Contract Act wage determinations that permit fringe benefit obligations to be discharged by paying to the employee on his regular payday, in addition to the monetary wage required, a cash amount per hour in lieu of the specified fringe benefits, provided such amount is equivalent to the cost of the fringe benefits required. Records are kept separately showing the amounts to be paid for fringe benefits. However, under a 1970 amendment to the Service Contract Act, if an incumbent contractor has provided certain fringe benefits under a collective bargaining agreement, the successor contractor must match the wages and fringe benefits under the agreement. [http://www.dol.gov/whd/regs/compliance/web/SCA_FAQ.htm] In general, the Service Contract Act requires more precise identification, communication to employees, and recordkeeping as to fringe benefits and substitution than does Davis-Bacon.

Q 9:99   How should government contractors determine which benefits to provide or which substitutions to make?

In determining which benefits to provide and which substitutions to make, contractors must calculate the values of both prevailing benefits and the benefits (if any) that they propose to offer in substitution. Strategically, they must consider not only the dollars and cents issue, but also such broader corporate concerns as: the effect of a given mix of pay and benefits on recruitment, morale, work incentive, and retention of the workforce; the value of a given compensation package in preventing unionization; and the long-term effect on the company of the introduction of certain benefits that may outlive the particular contract.

Contractors do not have absolute discretion in making these tactical and strategic determinations. Fringe benefits on the DOL's "menu" include the following:

- Medical and hospital care;
- Pension plans;
- Compensation for work-related injuries;
- Life and accident insurance;
- Disability benefits;
- Vacation and holiday pay; and
- Apprenticeship programs.

The DOL also accepts substitution of other bona fide fringe benefits not otherwise required by federal, state, or local law to be provided.

The "not otherwise required" phrase has been interpreted by the DOL's Wage and Hour Administrator to exclude credit for such mandatory payments as the contractor's contributions to Social Security. Furthermore, an employer's own contributions (such as co-payments to a group health insurance plan) and fringe benefit payments by the employer itself that are tied to non-government contract work by the particular employee cannot be counted toward equating the prevailing fringe benefit package. And these substitution decisions, once made, must be maintained throughout the term of the particular contract.

Q 9:100   How does a government contractor calculate cash equivalency?

Sometimes the wage determination itself sets the cash equivalent. When the DOL states the value of a fringe benefit as a specific dollar amount per week or month, the contractor paying the cash equivalent will do so on an hourly basis. This is done by multiplying (for example) the monthly amount by 12, dividing that amount by 52 (the weeks), and dividing it again by 40 to obtain the hourly amount. This amount is then added into the employee's hourly wage rate.

Calculating the cash equivalent of a paid vacation is a bit more complex. Assume the DOL's determination calls for a week of paid vacation after a year of service with the contractor or any successor corporation. Work performed by the employee before and after the wage determination is issued must be counted in calculating that employee's eligibility for the vacation benefit.

Next, if the contractor prefers to pay the employee the cash value of the week's vacation, it multiplies that worker's hourly wage rate by the number of hours of vacation time. If the vacation benefit is not specified in hours by the wage determination, the contractor should assume a standard 8-hour day and a 40-hour workweek. Again, the contractor is permitted to pay this cash equivalent to the employee on an hourly basis, spread across the whole year. To make this calculation, the contractor divides the dollar value of a week's vacation by 2,080 (the standard number of working hours in 52 weeks), and the quotient of this calculation is added into the employee's hourly wage rate.

One more example may be helpful. If the DOL's applicable wage determination includes holidays, the contractor can give days off with pay of its choosing; it need not adhere strictly to the list of holidays in the determination. Alternatively, the contractor can require an employee to work the designated holiday and pay double-time. Or, the contractor can multiply the number of holidays on the list by eight (the hours in the workday), divide by 2,080, and add the result of this calculation to the employee's hourly wage rate.

There may be a distinct cash flow (and, therefore, competitive) advantage in spreading some or all of these fringe benefit costs across 2,080 work hours because any savings for the contractor would be enhanced by employee absenteeism; however, labor unions, competition with other companies for skilled employees, and workforce morale combine to restrict a contractor's ability to replace such popular benefits as vacations and holidays with cash equivalents.

Q 9:101   How should a government contractor treat temporary and part-time employees with respect to fringe benefits?

Whenever a wage determination fails to distinguish between full-time, part-time and temporary employees, these latter two categories are entitled to their pro-rata share of the contractor's benefit package. Of course, if a requirement for a paid vacation is a full year of employment, a temporary employee of lesser tenure would not qualify for paid vacation; however, if the contractor chooses not to provide paid holidays to temporary and part-time employees, then these workers must be proportionately compensated with the cash equivalent or some substitute fringe benefit.

As with the FLSA and virtually all the other federal contract laws, the fringe benefit requirements of the Service Contract Act are based on the central concept of the "workweek." Thus, the concept affects the contractor's obligation to pay part-timers pro-rated holiday pay, which is covered in the regulations as follows:

> All employees, including part-time and temporary employees, are entitled to a proportionate share of the required holiday fringe benefits to which full-time employees are entitled under a determination, if they perform any work in the workweek in which the holiday occurs.

[Wage & Hour Admin. Op., Jan. 28, 1970]

Note: Like all employers, government contractors should be mindful of the definition of "full-time employee", i.e., 30 or more hours per week, in the Patient Protection And Affordable Care Act.

Q 9:102　What are bona fide benefits and prohibited offsets?

For an employee fringe benefit to be bona fide—(in other words, to count toward the employer's fringe benefit obligations under the DOL's applicable wage determination)—the benefit must be provided at the employer's expense. A timely illustration of this principle involves employee health insurance. With increasing frequency in the 1990s, employers require their employees to contribute to the insurance premiums for their group health plans. These employee contributions cannot be counted toward the employer's overall fringe benefit obligation.

Additionally, most employer payments that are already required by some other federal, state, or local law cannot be counted toward the employer's obligation under the wage determination. This prohibition covers Social Security (FICA) contributions by the employer, as well as the company's share of such payments as state unemployment taxes. In New Jersey, for example, this requirement would include payments for unemployment taxes and for a state disability fund.

Some employees may spend a part of their workday on a government contract, while devoting other working hours to non-government work. In such circumstances, fringe benefit payments attributable to non-government contract work cannot be counted toward setting off the government contractor's obligations under the wage determination attached to the government contract.

Q 9:103　What are *sunshine funds* and does the DOL view them as fringe benefits?

The term *sunshine funds* has broad application in the United States. Almost any fund set aside for miscellaneous charitable work or good deeds can be labeled "sunshine funds." In the context of government contracting, the term typically refers to any of the following:

1. Funds expended by an employer for such events as company picnics, Christmas parties, and other social functions;
2. Money spent for flowers for hospitalized employees, magazine subscriptions, professional association and club dues, incentive awards, bonuses for recruiting new employees; or
3. Provision of employee lounges and recreation rooms.

All of these expenditures are considered the contractor-employer's business expenses. [*See* Wage & Hour Admin. Op. No. WH-358 of Nov. 7, 1975.]

Sunshine funds are not considered fringe benefits under the DOL wage determination.

Of course, the contractor's provision of tools, uniforms or safety gear, such as respirators and ear plugs, cannot qualify as a bona fide fringe benefit.

Q 9:104   What are the restrictions on wage deductions?

The skyrocketing cost of health insurance has led many employers in recent years to press for or raise employee contributions. Other traditional deductions from wages include union dues pursuant to a collective bargaining agreement, U.S. savings bond purchases, credit union contributions, and repayment of employee loans such as vacation pay advances. The Copeland Anti-Kickback Act makes it essential that government contractors performing public works comprehend which deductions they can and cannot make legally, whether for employee benefits or otherwise. This Act covers virtually all construction projects, whether financed in whole or only in part by federal funds.

Q 9:105   Why has the federal government enacted the Copeland Anti-Kickback Act for the construction industry in particular?

Attorneys and human resources professionals familiar with the federal labor laws, notably the National Labor Relations Act (NLRA) and the closely connected Labor Management Relations Act (LMRA), know that the construction industry has received special treatment in several significant respects regarding the Copeland Anti-Kickback Act. For example, the LMRA permits employers and unions in the construction trades to enter pre-hire agreements under which such a union is automatically recognized as the bargaining representative of the contractor's employees, without the formalities of an organizing drive and a National Labor Relations Board (NLRB) election. The rationale behind this unique exception to the formalities normally imposed by the NLRB upon both unions and employers is not unrelated to the Copeland Anti-Kickback Act's reason for existence.

The pre-hire provisions of the LMRA recognize that construction projects, in contrast to factories and other places of business, are of relatively short duration. Consequently, in many instances a project would be completed, and the contractor and its subcontractors long gone, before a trade union could organize the employees and the NLRB could hold an election.

A similar appreciation of this unique aspect of the construction industry—its mobility and the concurrent mobility of its workforce—were among the rationales underlying enactment of the Copeland Anti-Kickback Act. Today kickbacks are infrequent. Typically, in a blatant instance, a foreman or other supervisor simply tells the employees something like, "I have to pay you $15 per hour under this contract. But you normally get $13 per hour from us so we expect you to turn back $2 per hour after you cash your paycheck."

Q 9:106   Are there types of kickbacks other than cash?

Yes. Fringe benefit kickback schemes exist, but are believed to be rarer than cash kickbacks. They are also more difficult for the DOL to detect, as they usually involve deposits to an employee welfare benefit plan on paper and siphoning of the funds into operating capital in reality. Such siphoning is possible because DOL regulations requiring all trustees to be unaffiliated with the employer-contractor have been superseded by the Employee Retirement Income Security Act of 1974 (ERISA), which allows a company, its officers, or managers to be trustees without invalidating the plan. Thus, the DOL no longer enforces contrary regulations under Davis-Bacon, even though they remain on the books. This situation may be partially responsible for the reported increased interest within the DOL in revitalizing the Copeland Anti-Kickback Act criminal enforcement program.

Q 9:107   What sorts of payroll deductions are excluded from the Copeland Anti-Kickback Act?

Bona fide payroll deductions for employee contributions into benefit plans are permissible under the Copeland Anti-Kickback Act. Likewise, employee-authorized deductions for U.S. savings bonds and United Way contributions are allowed under the Act and relevant DOL regulations.

Union dues and initiation fees constitute legal deductions under the Act, if made in connection with a check-off clause in the collective bargaining agreement, but union fines and special assessments are not.

Repayment of bona fide short-term loans by the employer to certain employees may be legally acceptable, but a notarized statement of each employee's freely given consent should be obtained before the deductions are taken. Deductions connected with long-term loans, such as a mortgage loan, are less likely to be countered by the DOL; therefore, if made to accommodate a relocating new-hire, for example, such loans should be transferred to an arm's-length commercial lender as soon as possible.

Q 9:108   May a government contractor recover the costs of recruiting and training employees?

Pursuant to restrictions set forth in the federal acquisition regulations [BNA Wage & Hour Manual, 99:1551], a contractor may charge recruitment costs against a contract, including educational testing programs and travel and relocation costs connected with recruiting new employees. Also subject to restrictions, the contractor may charge the government for the costs of training and educating employees, including those incurred for materials, textbooks, tuition, and fees.

Q 9:109   What does the Davis-Bacon Act cover?

The Davis-Bacon Act is found at 40 U.S.C. Section 276a and its implementing regulations at 29 C.F.R. Parts 1, 3, 5, 6, and 7. The Act and its related regulations apply to contractors and subcontractors performing federally funded or assisted contracts exceeding $2,000 in the construction, alteration, or repair (including painting and redecorating) of public buildings and other public works.

Q 9:110   What are the basic provisions of the Davis-Bacon Act?

The Davis-Bacon Act generally provides the following:

1. Laborers and mechanics must be paid not less than the wage rates and fringe benefits determined by the Secretary of Labor to be the prevailing rates in the area where the work takes place.
2. Apprentices and trainees may be employed at less than the prevailing rates, but must be employed pursuant to a program registered with the DOL or a state apprenticeship agency recognized by the DOL. Similarly, trainees must be in a certified training program under department auspices.
3. Employees must be paid one and one-half times their basic hourly rate for all hours worked in excess of 40 in the workweek.
   Note: This is the same rule as pertains to most other wage workers under the FLSA (see chapter 8).
4. Employees must be paid weekly.
5. Contractors and subcontractors must submit weekly certified payroll records to the contracting federal agency.

Q 9:111   What penalties are imposed by the Davis-Bacon Act?

Davis-Bacon Act violations are penalized in the following manner:

- Contract termination
- Debarment for a maximum of three years
- Withholding of periodic or final payments

Q 9:112   What are the government contractor's appellate rights under the Davis-Bacon Act?

Appeals of violations and debarments are filed with the Administrative Review Board and are heard by an ALJ. The ALJ's decision is subject to further possible appeals in the federal courts.

Q 9:113   What is the Davis-Bacon Act's effect on state contracts?

Since 1931, the Act has been extended to control the prevailing wage requirements in some 60 related statutes that cumulatively provide federal assistance for construction projects via grants, loans, insurance, and loan guarantees. Some examples of such federal statutes, which serve as conduits of these funds to the states, are:

- Federal-Aid Highway Acts
- Housing and Community Development Act of 1974
- Federal Water Pollution Control Act

For more information on related state laws and issues, see the Web site of the National Association of Government Officials (NAGLO).

Q 9:114   What are the coverage provisions of the Contract Work Hours and Safety Standards Act?

The Contract Work Hours and Safety Standards Act can be found at 40 U.S.C. Sections 327 *et seq.* Its implementing regulations are located at 29 C.F.R. Part 5.

The Act is applicable to contractors and subcontractors with federal service contracts, construction contracts, and supply contracts in excess of $100,000, contracts entered into by the U.S. government, any of its agencies or instrumentalities, the federal territories, the District of Columbia, and states conducting construction under any federal funding statute relating back to Davis-Bacon Act standards (see Q 9:113).

Contracts exempted from the Act's coverage include:

- Transportation, whether by land or water;
- Transmission of intelligence information;
- Purchases of supplies on the open market; and
- Walsh-Healey Act work (see Q 9:93).

Q 9:115   What are the basic provisions of the Contract Work Hours and Safety Standards Act?

The Contract Work Hours and Safety Standards Act basically provides:

1. Payment of wages at one and one-half times the basic wage rate for hours in excess of 40 in any workweek [**Note:** This requirement is also contained in the FLSA (see chapter 8) and in the Service Contract, Walsh-Healey, and Davis-Bacon Acts (see Q 9:93)]

2. Prohibition of unsanitary, hazardous, and dangerous working conditions. [**Note:** These conditions also are prohibited by the Occupational Safety and Health Act (see chapter 7)]

Q 9:116   What are the penalties under the Contract Work Hours and Safety Standards Act?

Penalties under the Act include:

- Fines;
- Imprisonment;
- Liquidated damages;
- Withholding of periodic and final payments;
- Damages in private actions by wronged employees;
- Contract termination; and
- Debarment for a maximum of three years.

Q 9:117   What is the appeals process under the Contract Work Hours and Safety Standards Act?

Appeals are heard by ALJs of the Administrative Review Board. Those decisions are appealable to the federal courts.

Withholding of periodic or final payments as liquidated damages for unpaid wages is appealed to the head of the contracting agency. Further appeal to the U.S. Claims Court is available.

Q 9:118   What is the Contract Work Hours and Safety Standards Act's effect on state contracts?

The Act applies to state contracts financed in whole or in part by federal grants or loans, as well as loans of public funds insured or guaranteed by the federal government.

Q 9:119   What are the coverage provisions of the McNamara-O'Hara Service Contract Act?

This Act is found at 41 U.S.C. Sections 351 *et seq.* Its implementing regulations are located at 29 C.F.R. Parts 4, 6, and 8.

The Act covers U.S. and District of Columbia contracts for services using "service employees." Such employees are defined as all those who perform services, except bona fide executives, administrators, and professionals.

Note: The tests for these exemptions under the FLSA were modified, effective August 23, 2005. Notably the minimum salary necessary to support such exemptions was substantially raised for the first time in decades. The substantive definitions of each exemption category, while not dramatically altered, were "tweaked" in ways that might have legal significance to readers, depending upon the industry in which they are engaged. Readers should be aware that for the first time under these new regulations, computer workers are treated as a separate category for exemption purposes. (See chapter 8 for detailed treatment)

The Act does not apply to:

1. Construction contracts;
2. Walsh-Healey Act contracts;
3. Transportation of people and freight where a published tariff pertains;
4. Furnishing of telephone, telegraph, radio, or cable services;
5. Public utility services;
6. Employee leasing to federal agencies;
7. Postal contract services with the U.S. Postal Service;
8. Services performed outside the United States; or
9. Exemptions promulgated by the Secretary of Labor from time to time in the public interest.

Q 9:120   What are the basic provisions of the Service Contract Act?

The Act requires payment of prevailing wages and benefits as set by the DOL, or the wages and benefits specified in predecessor collective bargaining agreements with bona fide labor organizations. If the particular service contract is for less than $2,500, the contractor may pay the minimum wage and overtime pay as specified by the Fair Labor Standards Act (see chapter 8) and the Contract Work Hours and Safety Standards Act.

Q 9:121   Does the Service Contract Act apply to all government contract work?

No, the Act does not apply to:

1. Construction contracts (see the Davis-Bacon Act, Qs 9:109–9:113);
2. Manufacturing of products for the government (see the Walsh-Healey Act, Qs 9:137–9:141);
3. Contracts for cartage by plane, train, bus, truck, ship, or pipeline;
4. Services provided by telecommunications technology;
5. Public utilities; and
6. Postal services.

The Act covers all other services performed under federal contracts for the U.S. government inside the United States, including Puerto Rico, the U.S. Virgin Islands, the outer continental shelf, American Samoa, Guam, Wake Island, and America's other Pacific possessions.

Q 9:122   How can one obtain a Service Contract Act directory?

The Service Contract Act directory can be viewed at: http://www.dol.gov/whd/regs/compliance/wage/.

Q 9:123   What health and safety standards apply to Service Contract Act contracts?

OSHA rules and regulations apply to all job sites where Service Contract Act contracts are performed (see chapter 7). OSHA administers health and safety matters for Service Contract Act contracts.

Q 9:124   Does the Secretary of Labor have a statutory obligation to file suit on behalf of an employee who accuses a government contractor of retaliation under the OSH Act?

In this post-9/11 environment, a court decision indicates that the DOL enjoys significant discretion, even when the employee's retaliation claim appears to have merit, if national security is implicated. The case upon which we base this conclusion involved some of the most dangerous government contracting work in the world—the operation of chemical weapons incinerators at the Johnston Atoll Chemical Agent Disposal System. The plaintiff clearly was an expert in this unusual activity. And his safety complaints were found by an OSHA investigator to have merit despite employer claims that he was just using scare tactics about management's safety practices to stir up his co-workers. Notwithstanding this finding, the DOL refused to initiate a court action on the plaintiff's behalf because the agency perceived a jurisdictional conflict with the U.S. Army. Instead, the case was turned over to the Army, which investigated but took no action on behalf of the plaintiff, who had been terminated by the contractor. The plaintiff then challenged the DOL's initial decision to defer to the military.

Affirming the Secretary of Labor's right to make such a deferral, the U.S. Court of Appeals for the District of Columbia held that, even though the DOL found that the plaintiff's activity was not protected by OSHA because the Army's jurisdiction trumped that of the agency, the Secretary was within her rights not to take the case any further in the judicial system. [Wood v. Department of Labor, 275 F.3d 107, 348 U.S. App. D.C. 328, 19 BNA OSH Cases 1727, 2001 CCH OSH Decisions 32,517 (D.C. Cir. Dec 28, 2001)]

For our readers, the significance of this decision lies in its holding that—at least where defense contracts are concerned—national defense and security interests may trump disgruntled employees' challenges to contractors' human resources decisions, such as where whistleblower retaliation becomes an issue.

Q 9:125   How are prevailing wage determinations developed?

Wage determinations are based on available data for wages in a specific locality. Where a specific rate is paid to more than 50 percent of workers in a job category within the locality, that rate becomes the prevailing wage rate for that job in that locality. Where no such rate can be identified, the median rate, as calculated by the Bureau of Labor Statistics, will prevail.

Q 9:126   How often should government contractors update their prevailing wage determinations?

Prevailing wage determinations should be reviewed and updated annually.

Q 9:127   How can a contractor get a wage determination, if no published determination is readily available?

The contractor should download a Standard Form 98 from the DOL Web site [http://www.dol.gov/dol/contact/index.htm], or request the form from its contracting officer. Return the completed form to the contracting officer, who typically will get an answer from DOL's Wage & Hour Division within 20 days. The status of the request can be checked in the interim by calling 1-202-219-7096.

Q 9:128   Is the prevailing wage determination a minimum hourly rate?

Yes. It becomes the minimum hourly rate for that job classification under that government contract, while it is performed in the specified locality.

Q 9:129   How are wage rates determined when particular jobs have not been surveyed in a given locality?

The DOL then slots such jobs between or into categories of similar jobs that have known rates in that particular locality.

Q 9:130   Do prevailing wage rates ever go down?

Yes. The Bureau of Labor Standards is charged with continually surveying wage rates, so that in times of economic downturn or high labor availability, if it finds that the average wage in a job category has declined, the prevailing rate will be reduced accordingly.

Q 9:131   How will a rise or fall in the prevailing rate affect current contracts?

In general, if the agency with which a contract is held is aware of a revision in the prevailing rate after the contract was signed, the agency is obliged to substitute that revision for the relevant rates previously inserted into the contract. The contractor or its attorney should check 29 C.F.R. Section 4.5(a)(2) to ascertain exactly when new rates must or must not be substituted in existing contracts.

Q 9:132   Under the Service Contract Act, do tips count toward the prevailing wage rates?

Employees who regularly receive at least $30 per month in tips can have those tips counted toward prevailing wage rate compliance by the contractor if:

1. The contractor notifies the relevant employees in advance of the contractor's intent to take a tip credit;
2. The employees get to retain all their tips, no matter the total amount;
3. The contractor maintains records that demonstrate that wages plus tips equal the prevailing wage rate; and
4. Any relevant collective bargaining agreement allows for the tip credit.

Q 9:133   What if an employee works in two different jobs with two different prevailing wage rates during a single workweek?

The employee must receive the higher of the two prevailing hourly rates for all work performed during that workweek.

Q 9:134   How do service employees know the rates they are supposed to be paid under the Service Contract Act wage determinations?

The contractor must deliver a written notice of the appropriate wage rate to the employee on the date he or she commences work under the contract.

Q 9:135   What are the penalties under the Service Contract Act?

Service Contract Act penalties include:

1. Contract termination;
2. Liability for the government's consequential damages;
3. Withholding of periodic and final payments; or
4. Debarment for a maximum of three years.

Q 9:136   What is the appeals process under the Service Contract Act?

Appeals are taken to an ALJ of the Administrative Review Board. Further appeal is possible in the federal courts.

Q 9:137   What are the coverage provisions of the Walsh-Healey Public Contracts Act?

The Act is found at 41 U.S.C. Sections 35 *et seq.* Its implementing regulations are located at 41 C.F.R. Parts 50-201, 202, and 206, and it covers the manufacture and furnishing of materials, supplies, articles, and equipment valued in excess of $10,000 in a single public contract.

Exemptions are recognized both by employee classification and by type of contract. Employee exemptions include:

1. Executives;
2. Administrators;
3. Professionals; and
4. Outside sales personnel.

All of the above are also exempted by the Fair Labor Standards Act (see chapter 8). Note that the regulations defining these exemptions, and in particular the minimum salaries required to support them, were amended by regulations that took effect on August 23, 2005.

Contract exemptions include:

1. Certain "open market" purchases;
2. Purchases of perishables;
3. Certain agricultural products from original producers;
4. Contracts for public utility services and certain transportation and communication services;
5. Supplies manufactured or furnished outside the United States (including Puerto Rico) or the Virgin Islands;
6. Contracts administratively exempted by the Secretary of Labor in special circumstances.

Enforcement is essentially the same as under the FLSA (see chapter 8).

Q 9:138   What are the basic provisions of the Walsh-Healey Act?

Contractors must pay the federal minimum wage, except with respect to apprentices, students in vocational education programs and disabled workers, provided the contractor has obtained DOL certification for such exemptions. Overtime for hours in excess of 40 in a workweek must be paid, as is required by the Fair Labor Standards Act (see chapter 8) and other federal statutes covered previously.

Contractors may not employ:

1. Children under age 16;
2. Convicts; or
3. Workers in unsanitary and unsafe conditions. (The Occupational Safety and Health Act [chapter 7] and the Mine Safety and Health Administration may also be implicated here.)

Q 9:139   What are the penalties under the Walsh-Healey Act?

Penalties for Walsh-Healey Act violations include:

1. Fines;

2. Withholding of periodic and final payments;

3. Contract cancellation; or

4. Debarment for a maximum of three years.

Q 9:140   What is the appeals process under the Walsh-Healey Act?

Appeals are heard by ALJs within the Administrative Review Board. Those decisions may be appealed in the federal courts.

Q 9:141   What is the Walsh-Healey Act's effect on state contracts?

Like the Fair Labor Standards Act (see chapter 8), the Walsh-Healey Act allows states to set higher minimum wage and tougher child labor standards for contractors performing in those states. Thus, a contractor may have to look to three different statutes and related regulations in a particular state:

1. Walsh-Healey Act;

2. Fair Labor Standards Act; and

3. Related state statutes.

Q 9:142   What are the coverage provisions of the Copeland Anti-Kickback Act?

The Act can be found at 18 U.S.C. Section 874 and 40 U.S.C. Section 276c. Its implementing regulations are located at 29 C.F.R. Part 3.

The Act covers all federal contracts in excess of $2,000, except where the federal government's only involvement is as a loan guarantor.

Q 9:143   What are the basic provisions of the Copeland Anti-Kickback Act?

The Act forbids:

1. In any manner inducing an employee to give back any part of her or his compensation; or

2. Making impermissible payroll deductions.

The Act requires weekly statements of wages and benefits for all employees under the contract.

Q 9:144   What are the penalties under the Copeland Anti-Kickback Act?

Penalties for violating the Act's provisions include:

- Fines;

- Imprisonment;

- Contract cancellation; and
- Debarment.

Q 9:145　What is the appeals process under the Copeland Anti-Kickback Act?

While some minor violations may be heard by ALJs under the aegis of the Administrative Review Board, most civil and criminal sanctions are pursued by the federal government within the federal court system in the first instance.

Q 9:146　May a contractor charge the government for employee wage rates that are beyond those charged to commercial customers?

No. Discriminatory pricing against the government is forbidden, and costs that include greater compensation payments to employees than they would be paid for non-government work are prohibited. Further, fringe benefits such as insurance premiums and holiday pay are not direct costs of a particular contract; they are overhead costs that are negotiated separately under the contract. Overhead may include the cost of providing employee health and welfare activities, such as first-aid classes or income tax information.

Q 9:147　Are contractors required to inform the government if they have used consultants to aid in obtaining government contracts?

Yes. The federal acquisition regulations require a contractor to report to the government any arrangement it makes with a non-employee individual or entity whereby the individual obtains or solicits a contract and is paid contingent on success. When the contractor provides a guarantee that it has not employed any such individual or entity, a breach of the guarantee may result in contract annulment or deduction from the contract price of any contingent fee paid.

Q 9:148　What restrictions are placed on the hiring of former government employees by government contractors?

A former government employee employed by a contractor is forbidden by federal criminal law to represent the contractor with regard to any judicial proceeding or to attempt to obtain a contract or pursue another particular matter in which he or she participated personally while a government employee. Further, a former government employee will commit a criminal act if, within two years after being employed by the government, he or she represents a government contractor before the U.S. government to obtain a contract, ruling, or determination if such a determination pertains to a matter that was actually pending under his or her official responsibility as a government employee within one year prior to his or her termination or in which he or she participated personally as a government officer or employee. The prohibition also extends to partners of the former government employee and carries with it substantial criminal penalties. The law does not prohibit a former government employee from performing certain acts on behalf of the contractor, such as giving testimony or furnishing scientific or technological information under procedures that the particular government agency considers acceptable. In addition, a recent regulation requires that the contractor certify that it has not offered employment or inducement to a government employee in return for a contract or otherwise sought selection or proprietary information.

Q 9:149 Are conflicts of interest involving current and former government employees a concern for government contractors?

The federal government can enter into contracts with its own employees or business organizations controlled by such employees only when it can demonstrate a compelling reason for doing so, such as no alternative reasonable method of getting the job done. [Federal Acquisition Regulations (FAR) 3.602; Keyes, *Government Contracts in a Nutshell*, at 41 (West Group 1990)] In other words, in a typical situation, a government contracting officer is prohibited from "knowingly making an award of a contract to a government employee or to a business concern or other organization owned or substantially owned or controlled by one or more government employees." [FAR 3.601]

Government employees themselves are prohibited by statute and are subject to serious penalties from representing the federal government in any matter in which they have a personal financial interest. Obvious examples of such conflicts of interest include those in which a federal employee participates in letting a government contract under which the employee will ultimately receive a share of the government contractor's profits. [*See, e.g.*, K&R Eng'g Co., Inc. v. United States, 222 Ct. Claims. 340, 616 F.2d 469 (1980).]

In contrast to such a blatant example, the involvement of former government employees is often not so clear-cut. While federal law restricts former employees' involvement in contracts that were actually pending when they were employed by the federal government, the use by government contractors of retired military officers and other such former government workers as consultants has not always resulted in disqualification for a given contract or punishment of the retired or resigned federal employee. [*See, e.g.*, NKF Eng'g, Inc. v. United States, 9 Ct. Claims. 585 (1986), *vacated*, 805 F.2d 372 (Fed. Cir. 1986) (use of retired deputy director of Naval Sea Systems Command as consultant on contract for which he had done the evaluation of contractors' initial proposals before retiring did not disqualify contractor, according to U.S. appellate court, which vacated the Claims Court's contrary holding).]

Q 9:150 What other labor restrictions apply to government contractors?

Under the Walsh-Healey Act, contractors may not employ children or convicts when fulfilling government contracts. *Children* are defined in the federal acquisition regulations as persons under 16 years of age. Convicts do not include those persons convicted but on parole or otherwise discharged from prison. A contractor must also maintain and make available for inspection employment records listing the name, address, sex, and occupation of each employee, as well as wage and employment records for each. A contractor must stipulate that the performance of the contract for the government does not entail working conditions that are unsanitary or hazardous to the health and safety of employees. Contractors may satisfy this requirement by showing compliance with the health and safety laws of the state in which the contract is performed.

Q 9:151   Do the federal acquisition regulations place any restrictions on collective bargaining agreements between government contractors and labor unions?

Government contractors are typically subject to an assortment of requirements and restrictions with respect to the subcontracting of portions of their prime contracts with the U.S. government. For example, government contracts in excess of $500,000 typically contain a provision requiring the prime contractor to carry out its subcontracting activities in a way calculated to ensure that small businesses are afforded a fair opportunity to compete for their share of the subcontracted work. [Keyes, *Government Contracts in a Nutshell*, at 454 (West Group 1990)] Furthermore, subcontracts cannot result in labor compensation costs "to the extent they result from provisions of labor-management agreements that, as they apply to work in performing government contracts, are determined to be unreasonable because they are either unwarranted by the character and circumstances of the work or discriminatory against the government." [FAR 31.206(b)(4)(c)] Additionally, where a union forces a prime contractor to enter into subcontracts only with unionized subcontractors, such subcontracts may result not only in a violation of the foregoing federal acquisition regulations, but also of the federal antitrust laws as well. [Connell Constr. Co. v. Plumbers Local 100, 421 U.S. 616 (1973)]

Consequently, although the NLRA requires employers to bargain in good faith with unions representing their employees, a government contractor or subcontractor cannot avoid the restrictions placed on it by the federal acquisition regulations. [Keyes, at 453] Thus, the federal courts have held that union proposals that would violate such federal regulations are not subject to collective bargaining.

Q 9:152   What are the OFCCP's best compensation practices for government contractors?

The OFCCP recommends:

1. Periodic self-audits of wages and benefits;
2. Immediate correction of any problems identified in the self-audit;
3. Creation of procedures and practices aimed at ensuring that wage and benefit decisions are based on job-related criteria;
4. Where pay is tied to performance, the use of measurable criteria that clearly distinguish between levels of performance;

5. Clear definitions of subjective requirements such as "shows initiative";

6. Management training in evaluating their subordinates; and

7. Periodic reviews of the impact of changes in wages, benefits, performance reviews, and personnel policies upon minority and female employees.

Q 9:153   What recent reforms did the Obama Administration and Congress enact for government contractors?

On January 3, 2013, House Small Business Committee Chairman Sam Graves (R-MO) released the following statement on the President signing into law the National Defense Authorization Act of 2013 (NDAA), which includes contracting reform legislation reported by the House Small Business Committee:

> Today marks the culmination of a comprehensive effort to reform contracting policy so that small businesses can better compete in the federal procurement marketplace. In the beginning of the 112th Congress, our Committee made it a priority to listen to the concerns of small contractors who want to seek business opportunities with the federal government. The process uncovered various barriers that made it harder for small businesses to succeed, so we introduced and reported out legislation to address the problems. The small business provisions in the NDAA will help make sure existing small business goals are actually met, empower small business advocates, and crack down on fraud. I'm very proud of the Committee's bipartisan work. These reforms will help small businesses compete in the federal marketplace, bring efficiency and cost-savings to the taxpayer, and create jobs while doing it.

In early 2012, the Small Business Committee introduced a series of contracting reform bills. The legislation was the result of the findings of 10 contracting hearings during 2011. On May 10, 2012, the House Armed Services Committee voted to include the Committee's contracting reform legislation into the NDAA, which the House passed on Friday, May 18, 2012. On December 20, 2012, the House passed the National Defense Authorization Act Conference Report. The President signed the legislation into law in early 2013.

Some notable contracting provisions include:

- Enforcing existing small business contracting goals by requiring that meeting the goals be a part of senior agency employee reviews and bonus discussions. The federal government has missed the 23 percent small business goal for six consecutive years.

- Changing limitations on subcontracting from cost to price, which will make it easier for small businesses to comply with procurement rules, while also allowing them to team together to pursue larger contracts.

- Preventing contracting fraud by placing penalties on violating limitations on subcontracting, and making it easier to suspend and debar companies intentionally defrauding the government.

- Helping woman-owned small contractors by removing the set-aside caps on the women's contracting program.

- Requiring the SBA to develop size standards that accurately define what is a small business for each of the over 1,100 industries where small firms operate, instead of allowing SBA to continue taking short cuts for its own administrative convenience.

- Giving small business a "safe harbor" if they acted on a written advisory opinion from either a Small Business Development Center or Procurement Technical Assistance Center and violated a rule by mistake.

- Bringing transparency to insourcing decisions by requiring OMB and agencies to publish procedures, methodologies, and guidance documents associated with the decisions.

- Fighting contract bundling, the practice of grouping several contracts together for bidding, thereby making it difficult for small businesses to compete. The law requires additional oversight and a report that will analyze whether contract bundlings are justified.

[http://smallbusiness.house.gov/news/documentsingle.aspx?DocumentID = 316226]

Q 9:154　Do "living wage laws" as applied to government contractors pass Constitutional muster?

The most authoritative decision to date on this controversy can be found in *RUI One Corporation v. City of Berkeley.* [371 F.3d 1137 (9th Cir. 2004), *cert. denied*, 543 U.S. 1081 (2005)] In this case, the City of Berkeley (CA) enacted its living wage ordinance on June 27, 2000. [*See* Berkeley Ordinance No. 6548-N.S. (2000)] The ordinance mandated minimum hourly wages and employee benefits for employers that received some form of financial benefit from the city (e.g., city contract awardees, lessees of city property, and city financial aid recipients), and that met specified criteria (i.e., number of employees, annual revenues).

Accompanying the ordinance were the City Council's findings explaining the reasoning behind the ordinance. The council expressed its concern that "far too many people working in Berkeley . . . live below or near the poverty line" and that, therefore, "the privilege of using public property to operate a business enterprise should not be granted to parties that will exacerbate the problems associated with inadequate compensation of workers." It also found that the absence of employer-sponsored health insurance plans ultimately resulted in higher healthcare costs for the city, state, and federal governments. Therefore, the city mandated that employers meeting the relevant criteria be required to pay their employees a minimum of $9.75 per hour, unless they did not provide their employees with health benefits, in which case they had to pay them a minimum of $11.37 per hour.

The minimum wages exceeded then and at the time the Ninth Circuit issued its decision both the federal and state minimum wage requirements. At the time of the ordinance's enactment, federal law required a minimum wage of $5.15 per hour [29 U.S.C. § 206(a)(1)] and California law required a minimum wage of $5.75 per hour. California had raised its minimum wage to $6.25 per hour in

2001, and most recently to $8.00 per hour, effective January 1, 2008. [Cal. Code Regs. tit. 8, § 11000(2)]

The ordinance required employers to provide their employees a minimum of 22 days off per year for vacation, sick leave, or personal necessity, of which at least 12 days were to be paid. It also required that a provision mandating compliance with its terms be included in every new or amended city contract or lease. It included a mechanism for receiving employee complaints and a private right of action for employees in county and state courts.

Before enacting the living wage ordinance, the city commissioned a feasibility and cost study. The study concluded that the cost of the ordinance on city lessees could be borne in three ways, by: (1) the City, in the form of lower lease revenue upon renegotiation of the leases; (2) the affected employers, in the form of reduced profits; and/or (3) consumers who purchase products or services from the affected businesses, in the form of higher prices. Although all three of these cost-bearing mechanisms would likely be implicated, it was impossible to conclude what the "split" among them would be. The study's authors apparently assumed that the living wage ordinance would be implemented for city lessees only upon the renegotiation of their lease contracts.

On March 23, 1968, RUI's predecessor in interest, Manning's, Inc., entered into a 50-year lease (expiring in 2018) with the city for land located on the public-trust tidelands in the Berkeley Marina. The lease agreement required the lessee to "construct, maintain and operate thereon a major first-class restaurant and cocktail lounge for the convenience and promotion of commerce, navigation and fishery in the Berkeley Marina and for no other purpose." The annual rent due the city was the greater of $11,400 or 2.5 percent of the restaurant's gross receipts (i.e., before the restaurant deducts operating expenses and labor costs). The lease also contained a number of specific provisions, including provisions requiring the lessee to charge its customers reasonable rates consistent with similar establishments in the San Francisco Bay area (the "reasonable rate requirement") and to "employ its best judgment, efforts and abilities" to maximize profits and enhance the reputation of the Berkeley Marina.

On October 19, 2000, RUI filed a complaint for declaratory and injunctive relief against the city in the U.S. District Court for the Northern District of California, alleging that the Living Wage Ordinance violated the Contract Clause, Equal Protection Clause, and Due Process Clause of the U.S. Constitution. About one year later, the district court permitted the Hotel Employees & Restaurant Employees Union, Local 2850, to intervene on behalf of the City. RUI subsequently moved for summary judgment, alleging *inter alia* that the Marina Amendment was unconstitutional. The district court *sua sponte* granted summary judgment to the City and Local 2850, holding that the ordinance was not unconstitutional. The parties stipulated to judgment, and this appeal followed.

Affirming the federal trial judge, the Ninth Circuit panel reviewing the case did not offend any of the three Constitutional provisions relied upon by RUI. Two of the three judges held,

We . . . uphold the City's judgment on the basis of the findings it provided. It is more than reasonable that the City should expect Marina businesses, which receive so many benefits from the City in the form of improvements and lack of competition due to the development moratorium, and which operate on land held in the public trust, to contribute to the welfare of the surrounding community and not to exacerbate its problems. Although RUI claims that any benefit it receives is offset by the rent it pays the City, it is certainly "plausible" for the City legislators to believe that rent alone does not adequately discharge Marina businesses' responsibilities to the public and City. Furthermore, it is certainly "plausible" that certain members of the public might be deterred from patronizing the Berkeley Marina if they knew that the businesses there paid their employees less than a living wage.

However, one of the three members of the appeals panel, Circuit Judge Bybee, wrote a long and well-reasoned dissent, which clearly lays out the game plan for government contractors intent upon challenging similar statutes or ordinances, whether federal, state, or local in their origin. Other decisions implicating the issue of living-wage laws include:

- *Godlewska v. Human Development Association, Inc.* [2013 WL 25649 (E.D.N.Y. 2013)] Home healthcare attendants employed by not-for-profit contractor brought action against City of New York, New York City Human Resources Administration (HRA), and HRA commissioner seeking unpaid prevailing, minimum and overtime wages, and attorney fees for retaliation under the Fair Labor Standards Act (FLSA) and New York common law, and alleging violations of Racketeer Influenced and Corrupt Organizations Act (RICO) and various state law claims, including New York City's Living-Wage Law, N.Y.C. Code Section 6-109. The case was dismissed on the ground that the defendants did not exercise formal control over the plaintiff-employees.

- *Urresta v. MBJ Cafeteria Corp.* [2011 WL 4962969 (S.D.N.Y. 2011)] Plaintiff's living-wage law claim dismissed for failure to exhaust prefatory administrative processes.

- *Pellon v. Business Representation International, Inc.* [528 F. Supp. 2d 1306 (S.D. Fla. 2007)] Court declined to exercise pendant jurisdiction over claim under Florida's Living-Wage Law in this FLSA action.

Q 9:155   Do states have analogous prevailing wage laws, and if so, do they always pass Constitutional scrutiny?

The answer to the first half of this question is an unequivocal "yes." As with the federal FLSA (see chapter 8), the federal prevailing wage acts have their counterparts in almost every state, where these "baby" acts regulate wages and benefits under state, and often also local, government contracts.

As for the second half of the question, our answer is a qualified "yes." These state statutes usually pass muster under the federal Constitution. However, there are cases where they have not. *Tri-M Group, LLC v. Sharp* [705 F. Supp. 2d 335 (D. Del. 2010)], is a case where it did not. In this case, the plaintiff, Tri-M

Group, LLC, brought this action for declaratory and injunctive relief against defendant Thomas B. Sharp, at the time the Secretary of the State of Delaware Department of Labor ("DDOL"), alleging that the DDOL had discriminated against the plaintiff and other out-of-state contractors by refusing to recognize their out-of-state registered apprentices for purposes of the Delaware Prevailing Wage Law, consequently burdening interstate commerce without justification in violation of the Commerce Clause of the U.S. Constitution. In lieu of a response, the defendant moved to dismiss for lack of subject matter jurisdiction and for failure to state a claim under Federal Rule of Civil Procedure 12(b)(1) and 12(b)(6). Following oral argument on the motion, the court allowed the defendant to supplement the record with evidence of legislative history and states with regulations similar to the prevailing wage regulations at issue. The court subsequently denied defendant's motion. Discovery proceeded and finally closed, at which time both sides moved for a summary judgment in their favor. U.S. District Judge Sue L. Robinson ruled, "Economic protectionism in this form results in discrimination to out-of-state businesses and subjects the regulation to strict scrutiny, in this case, rendering the scheme invalid under the . . . commerce clause."

Whistleblowers

Q 9:156   How often have whistleblowers suffered retaliation?

Academic studies indicate that retaliation has been documented in 90 percent of all whistleblower cases.

Q 9:157   Given that nine out of ten whistleblowers will suffer retaliation, how much protection does the law accord them?

Whistleblowers, in theory, enjoy the protection of the federal Office of Special Counsel and the Whistleblower Protection Act of 1989, as amended in 1994. However, the Government Accountability Project (GAP), established in 1977 to help protect whistleblowers, admits that despite its efforts and the proliferation of federal and state laws in the ensuing 25 years, "[all] too often . . . federal workers who try to defend their whistleblowing rights before administrative judges find that these rights exist on paper only. Whistleblowers in the private sector face an even weaker patchwork of legal defenses." In addition to "inadequate legal protection," GAP lists among the likely costs of whistleblowing:

1. Emotional and mental pain and suffering;
2. Loss of the support of friends and colleagues; and
3. Job loss.

Q 9:158   What are some of the legal helps and hurdles relevant to whistleblowers in government contracting?

The helps and hindrances include:

1. Especially with regard to defense contractors, overlapping national security and defense considerations that can deprive agencies like OSHA of jurisdiction to prevent and remedy illegal retaliation.

2. The contractor's negative behavior toward the whistleblower is not actionable unless it is sufficiently severe to constitute "adverse employment action" under Title VII of the 1964 Civil Rights Act. [Moore v. California Institute of Tech. Jet Propulsion Lab., 275 F.3d 838, 160 Ed. Law. Rep. 304, 2 Cal. Daily Op. Serv. 82, 2002 DAR Daily Journal 103 (9th Cir. Jan 4, 2002)] (The cited case concerns retaliation charges following whistleblower activities of the plaintiff, pursuant to anti-retaliation provisions of the False Claims Act, 31 U.S.C. § 3730(h) and the Major Fraud Act, 18 U.S.C. § 1031.)

3. The federal Whistleblower Protection Act shields federal employees. Employees of government contractors must look to one of the 28 whistleblower protection provisions tucked into an assortment of federal statutes. The best known is the OSH Act. About 50 percent of the others involve some segment of environmental protection. The usual forum is a DOL administrative hearing, although the False Claims Act opens the federal courts to whistleblowers alleging contractor fraud under federal contracts. While this appears at first blush as comprehensive protection—overkill in the eyes of some contractors—GAP criticizes these protections as "piecemeal" and often obscure.

4. Some 42 states and the District of Columbia have gotten into the game by enacting their own dizzying variety of whistleblower protection statutes. Additionally, the common law of wrongful discharge in many states recognizes a public policy exception to employment at will for at least some types of retaliatory discharge that can implicate whistleblowing. Again, while these laws and decisions comprise a substantial body of whistleblower protection, the shear variety of approaches and standards makes dealing with whistleblowing a potential nightmare for contractors and employees alike.

Q 9:159   What are a whistleblower's odds of winning a retaliation claim?

The success rate of whistleblower actions is estimated at 33 percent at this writing. While on one hand, this rate is up from 10 percent 25 years ago, the statistic is derived from reported decisions. The success rate of unreported decisions such as those dismissed without a published opinion or withdrawn on threat of dismissal at the lowest level of the relevant judicial process is believed to be much lower. However, that success rate is likely to experience a marked increase thanks to the Sarbanes-Oxley Act, discussed in Q 9:163.

Q 9:160   What advice does an advocacy group such as the Government Accountability Project give to would-be whistleblowers?

Typical advice usually includes the following:

1. Contact a support or advocacy group for an attorney referral. Other sources of attorneys include the American Bar Association and the Martindale-Hubbell Lawyers Locator.
2. Summarize the story in writing before contacting any attorney;
3. Seek to build an attorney's confidence in the initial interview while also asking the appropriate questions of the selected lawyer;
4. Confirm that attorney-client privilege applies to the initial interview as well as to any subsequent conferences and conversations with any involved attorney(s);
5. Research the attorney's track record in these specific kinds of cases;
6. Formulate and communicate to legal counsel clear goals and objectives;
7. Clarify financial burdens and options at the outset of retaining legal representation and embarking of whistleblowing and/or retaliation-claim activities;
8. Clarify respective time commitments between whistleblower/plaintiff and legal counsel; and
9. Clarify the whistleblower/plaintiff's and the attorney's respective roles in settlement negotiations and other actions that may occur in what may be a very dynamic situation both within and outside of the litigation.

Q 9:161   What is a *qui tam action*?

A special kind of whistleblowing, where allegations of fraud against the federal government are concerned, is a so-called *qui tam action*. "Qui tam" is short for a long Latin phrase dating from the enactment of anti-fraud laws, aimed at dishonest government contractors, during the Civil War. Under the terms of the relevant federal statutes, a private citizen—who can be, and often is, a government contractor's own employee—becomes a "relator" when he or she brings allegations of contract fraud to the U.S. Attorney's attention. If the government goes to court and is successful in collecting on the qui tam claim, the relator actually shares in the government's monetary recovery against the contractor. [*See, e.g.*, United States v. Rockwell Int'l Corp., 282 F.3d 787 (10th Cir. 2002).]

Q 9:162   Can a qui tam action be accompanied by a retaliation claim?

Yes. In fact, as is the case with many federal causes of action, notably in the employment discrimination arena, a retaliation claim may survive dismissal of the underlying substantive cause of action. An example in the qui tam arena is *U.S. ex rel. Sanchez v. Lymphatx, Inc.* [2010 WL 547499 (11th Cir. Feb. 18, 2010)]

In this case, Plaintiff Laika Sanchez appealed from the district court's order dismissing her *qui tam* complaint on behalf of the United States against Lymphatx and its owners for violations of the False Claims Act. [31 U.S.C. §§ 3729-30] The district court concluded that Sanchez had failed to plead her allegations of fraud with the particularity required by Federal Rule of Civil Procedure 9(b) and that she had failed to state a claim for retaliation under 31 U.S.C. § 3730(h). Sanchez argues that the district court erred in dismissing her complaint for failure to state a claim, and in closing her case without granting her leave to amend. [*See* Fed. R. Civ. P. 12(b)(6).]

To state a claim premised on fraud, Sanchez needed to "state with particularity the circumstances constituting [the] fraud." [Fed. R. Civ. P. 9(b); *see also* United States *ex rel.* Clausen v. Lab. Corp. of Am., 290 F.3d 1301, 1308 (11th Cir. 2002) ("Rule 9(b) does apply to actions under the False Claims Act.")] In her complaint, Sanchez alleged that the defendants had knowingly submitted false claims to Medicare for lymphedema treatments performed by massage therapists. She further alleged that the defendants had intentionally billed Medicare for services they did not provide and that she had gained personal knowledge of these billing practices through her employment as Lymphatx's office manager.

The appellate court explained that,

> in addition to her general accusations of false billing, Sanchez needed to plead "facts as to time, place, and substance of the defendants' alleged fraud, specifically, the details of the defendants' allegedly fraudulent acts, when they occurred, and who engaged in them." Despite her assertion that she had direct knowledge of the defendants' billing and patient records, Sanchez failed to provide any specific details regarding either the dates on or the frequency with which the defendants submitted false claims, the amounts of those claims, or the patients whose treatment served as the basis for the claims. Without these or similar details, Sanchez's complaint lacks the "indicia of reliability" necessary under Rule 9(b) to support her conclusory allegations of wrongdoing. In other words, because she failed "to allege at least some examples of actual false claims," Sanchez could not "lay a complete foundation for the rest of [her] allegations." The district court therefore appropriately dismissed the four claims alleging fraudulent billing.

The appeals panel went on to examine the plaintiff's claim that she had been punished by her employer for raising the red flag. As to this count of her complaint, the judges said,

> Sanchez's allegations that she complained about the defendants' "unlawful actions" and warned them that they were "incurring significant criminal and civil liability" would have been sufficient, if proven, to support a reasonable conclusion that the defendants were aware of the possibility of litigation under the False Claims Act. Because her retaliation claim did not depend on allegations of fraud, Sanchez's complaint only needed "a short and plain statement of the claim showing that [she was] entitled to relief." [Fed. R. Civ. P. 8(a)] We conclude that she

satisfied this requirement and that the district court therefore erred in dismissing her claim for retaliatory discharge.

Although this decision throws the company back into the federal trial court's clutches, it is likely that the exposure now is substantially less than if the underlying qui tam action itself had survived. Had that ugly eventuality materialized, the defendant would potentially face an obligation to return all the government funds it had obtained through its fraudulent behavior, if proven. With this specter put aside, the firm probably only faces the possibility of paying back pay and other damages to the plaintiff. Of course, if the company was never guilty of the illegal behavior of which Sanchez complained, then it has bought itself a retaliation claim where it never ought to have been hauled into court in the first place.

Q 9:163   What is the *Sarbanes-Oxley Act*?

On July 30, 2002, Congress passed and the President signed the Sarbanes-Oxley Act. The Act is thus far the single most significant piece of legislation to come out of the Enron/Worldcom/Arthur Anderson accounting scandals, which helped deepen the post-9/11 market decline and related economic recession. The Act amends the Securities and Exchange Acts of 1933 and 1934, as well as ERISA, plus the Investment Advisers Act of 1940 and the U.S. Criminal Code. Most significantly for those concerned with termination of employment, the Sarbanes-Oxley Act includes two provisions, one criminal and the other civil, for the protection of employees who report improper conduct by corporate officials concerning securities fraud and corruption. [*See* 18 U.S.C. §§ 1513(e), 1514A.]

Q 9:164   How does the Sarbanes-Oxley Act change the existing landscape of whistleblower laws and rules?

Human resources professionals are used to dealing with whistleblowers. Literally dozens of federal laws, such as OSHA and Title VII, protect employees who blow the whistle on illegal practices or who cooperate in investigations and testify at hearings from employer retaliation, such as employment termination. Literally dozens of states have jumped on the whistleblower bandwagon, adding a dizzying variety of whistleblower laws to the panoply of rules and regulations that human resources managers and employment lawyers must consider before initiating "industrial capital punishment" (i.e., firing a miscreant worker). In those increasingly rare jurisdictions or circumstances in which no federal or state anti-retaliation rule is implicated, the courts have shown themselves more than willing to carve out a public policy exception to employment at will, where the plaintiff provides proof that he or she was fired for reporting or restricting illegal supervisory activity.

The Sarbanes-Oxley Act is unique in making whistleblower retaliation a federal crime that can result in officer/director defendants going to prison. Perhaps the scariest aspect of the Act's criminal provision [18 U.S.C. § 1513(e)], is that it can be used to punish retaliation against persons who provide information to law enforcement officials relating to the possible commission of any federal offense, not just securities fraud, albeit securities fraud was the catalyst for the legislation. The provision makes it a crime to "knowingly, with the intent to retaliate, take . . . any action harmful to any person, including interference with lawful employment or livelihood of any person, for providing a law enforcement officer any truthful information relating to the commission or possible commission of any Federal offense." Individuals found guilty under this proviso may be fined up to $250,000 and imprisoned up to 10 years. Corporate defendants can face up to $500,000 fine, if convicted.

Q 9:165   What are the Sarbanes-Oxley Act's civil penalties?

A child of corporate greed and accounting scandals, the Act's legislative history indicates that its whistleblower provisions are intended primarily to protect employees of publicly-traded companies acting in the public interest to try to prevent officer/director wrongdoing and "to encourage and protect those who report fraudulent activity that can damage innocent investors in publicly traded companies." [148 Cong. Record § 7418-01] To the extent that Congress evinced its intent to uniformly regulate whistleblowing from within large national and multinational firms, the Act can be expected to preempt the myriad state statutes referred to above.

The civil liability whistleblower language reads as follows:

> No [publicly traded] company . . . or officer, employee, contractor, subcontractor or agent of such company, may discharge, demote, suspend, threaten, harass, or in any other manner discriminate against an employee in the terms and conditions of employment because of any lawful act done by the employee—
>
> (1) to provide information, cause information to be provided, or otherwise assist in an investigation regarding conduct that the employee reasonably believes constitutes a violation of: (a) any rule or regulation of the SEC; (b) any provision of federal law relating to fraud against shareholders; or (c) federal criminal law provisions prohibiting mail fraud, bank fraud, or fraud by wire, radio, or television, when the information or assistance is provided to or the investigation is conducted by—
>
> a federal regulatory or law enforcement agency;
>
> any member of Congress or any committee of Congress; or
>
> a person with supervisory authority over the employee; [or]
>
> [a] person working for the employer who has the authority to investigate, discover, or terminate misconduct; or
>
> (2) to file, cause to be filed, testify, participate in, or otherwise assist in a proceeding filed or about to be filed . . . relating to [any of the rules, regulations and statutes referenced in (1) above].

This provision applies to the following employers:

1. All U.S. domestic publicly traded corporations;

2. All nonpublic companies whose debt instruments are publicly traded; and

3. All foreign companies registered to do business in the United States.

Q 9:166   Who are covered employees under the Sarbanes-Oxley Act?

With regard to covered employees, cases decided under other federal whistleblower laws may provide some guidance. For example, cases decided under the analogous provisions of the Energy Reorganization Act of 1974 lead to the conclusion that former, as well as current, employees will be accorded protection. [*See, e.g.*, Connecticut Light & Power v. Secretary of Labor, 85 F.3d 89, 94 (2d Cir. 1996) ("Despite Delcore's status as a former employee, he fell within the scope of employee because the alleged discrimination arose out of the employment relationship.").] Title VII cases tend to come out the same way. [*See, e.g.*, Robinson v. Shell Oil Co., 519 U.S. 337 (1997).]

Q 9:167   What are the Sarbanes-Oxley Act's enforcement procedures?

The Act adopts the procedures set forth in the Aviation Investment and Reform Act for the 21st Century, known colloquially as AIR21. [49 U.S.C. § 42121] Specifically, whistleblowers should "[s]eek relief . . . by (A) filing a complaint with the Secretary of Labor . . . [which complaint] shall be governed under the rules and procedures set forth in" [AIR21]. While the threshold, then, is a complaint to the DOL, if the agency has not issued a final decision within 180 days of the filing, the complainant can initiate a claim in federal district court.

Concerning the DOL procedures:

1. The aggrieved employee must file within 90 days of the retaliation.
2. DOL will then notify the party(ies) named in the complaint, who must be afforded an opportunity to respond and to proffer witness statements on its/their own behalf.
3. Within 60 days from the filing of the initial complaint, the DOL must conduct its own investigation in an effort to ascertain whether there is reasonable cause to believe that the charges of retaliation are meritorious; the trigger for this investigation is the complainant's prima facie showing that the protected activity was a contributing factor in the negative personnel action that followed. This trigger can only be disarmed by a clear and convincing showing by the charged parties that the complainant's allegations are untrue. [*See, e.g.*, Trimmer v. United States Dep't of Labor, 174 F.3d 1098, 1101 (10th Cir. 1999) ("only if the employee establishes a prima facie case and the employer fails to disprove the allegation by clear and convincing evidence may the Secretary even investigate the complaint"); Stone & Webster Eng'g Corp. v. Herman, 115 F.3d 1568, 1572 (11th Cir. 1997) ("Under this framework, a complainant must first pass a gatekeeper test before an inquiry may commence."); *see also* Dysert v. Secretary of Labor, 105 F.3d 607 (11th Cir. 1997); Marano v. Dep't of Justice, 2 F.3d 1137 (Fed. Cir. 1993) (interpreting the Whistleblower Protection Act, 5 U.S.C. § 1221(e)(1)).]

4. Important to note is the relaxed standard of liability, adopted from the federal Whistleblower Protection Act:

> the words "a contributing factor" . . . mean any factor which, alone or in connection with other factors, tends to affect in any way the outcome of the decision. This test is specifically intended to overrule existing case law, which requires a whistleblower to prove that his protected conduct was a "significant," "motivating," "substantial," or "predominant," factor in a personnel action in order to overturn the action.

Q 9:168   What are the remedies under the Sarbanes-Oxley Act?

If the employer is unable to satisfy the DOL by clear and convincing evidence that exactly the same personnel action would have occurred in the absence of the complainant's protected activities—and who can show clearly and convincingly that the complainant's protected behavior in no way affected the personnel action?—the agency "shall issue" a preliminary order reinstating the complainant with back pay. Such an order is effective immediately and cannot be stayed pending adjudication of objections. Thus, the stakes at this early stage of the litigation are exceptionally high, analogous to a preliminary hearing in an injunction proceeding wherein the plaintiff typically needs to satisfy the judge or chancellor that irreversible harm will result if the preliminary court order does not issue.

Within 30 days of the DOL's preliminary decision, the losing party may file a challenge that will be heard in front of an ALJ. This will be a full-fledged evidentiary hearing resulting in a recommendation from the ALJ to the DOL. Employment attorneys at the prestigious national law firm Morgan, Lewis & Bockius, headquartered in Philadelphia, have stated, "We believe that the plaintiffs' bar will contend that the [investigatory] 'clear and convincing' standard will apply to a hearing conducted by an ALJ" as well. In this hearing pre-Sarbanes-Oxley Act conduct by the parties will be fully admissible.

The loser at the ALJ-level may take an appeal to the U.S. Court of Appeals for the jurisdiction in which the alleged violation occurred or the circuit in which the complainant resided on the date of the violation. The Administrative Procedures Act [5 U.S.C. § 706(2)(A)], allows reversal of the agency determination only when the department's "findings and conclusion [are] found to be . . . arbitrary, capricious, an abuse of discretion, or otherwise not in accordance with law."

Q 9:169   What about settlements and private actions under the Sarbanes-Oxley Act?

Once the DOL is in the picture, it has the authority to approve or disapprove any subsequent settlement reached between or among the parties to the complaint. On top of the relaxed standard for proving up illegal retaliation and the onerous preliminary remedies, this third-party approval process poses yet another hurdle to resolving such complaints favorably to the employer.

And, finally, the failure of the DOL to issue a final decision within 180 days opens the doors of the federal courthouse to the complainant's private action. The case can be filed in any appropriate U.S. district court under normal federal rules of civil procedure involving jurisdiction and venue, but without regard to the amount of money in controversy. While the Sarbanes-Oxley Act is silent on the allocation of burdens of proof and the like, Morgan Lewis attorneys caution that "we expect complainants and the plaintiffs' bar to argue that the burdens discussed above regarding the pre-investigatory stage at the DOL would apply to the investigatory stage at the ALJ hearing, the findings of the Secretary of Labor, and a case filed in federal court" (i.e., that once the plaintiff has put forward a prima facie case of retaliation, the defendants must show by clear and convincing evidence that the same adverse personnel action would have occurred in the absence of the alleged protected conduct, which is an extremely difficult burden, if district judges impose it, in light of the relaxed "affected in any way" test borrowed from the federal Whistleblower Protection Act).

Q 9:170   Can an employer's employment contract compel its employees to submit their Sarbanes-Oxley claims to arbitration?

Most commentators have concluded that an arbitration clause in an employment contract will not be an effective bar to subsequent filing of a Sarbanes-Oxley claim with the DOL. However, at least one federal court came to the contrary conclusion. [*See* Boss v. Salomon Smith Barney, Inc., 263 F. Supp. 2d 684, 19 IER Cases 1796 (S.D.N.Y. 2003) (Employee, a research analyst for investment bank, filed action claiming he was ordered to share draft research report with investment bankers contrary to established rules, policies and procedures, and was terminated in retaliation for failing to change his recommendations despite being pressured to do so, and seeking damages and reinstatement. Employer moved to stay litigation and compel arbitration before NASD. The District Court, Owen, J., held that employee's whistleblowing claims, brought pursuant to Sarbanes-Oxley Corporate Reform Act of 2002, were not exempt from mandatory industry arbitration.).]

Q 9:171   What are the available final remedies under the Sarbanes-Oxley Act?

If the complainant/plaintiff ultimately prevails, the Act allows for:

1. Reinstatement;
2. Back pay;
3. Special damages including, potentially, litigation costs, witness fees, attorneys' fees; and
4. "All relief necessary to make the employee whole," which may include damages for pain, suffering, humiliation, and emotional distress.

Q 9:172   What are some recent pronouncements under the Sarbanes-Oxley Act?

Robinson v. U.S. Department of Labor [2010 WL 5394869 (7th Cir. Dec.27, 2010)]: Discover Financial Services, a wholly owned subsidiary of Morgan Stanley, fired the plaintiff six months after she had submitted a memo to the firm's president and its chief financial officer, purportedly reporting improper business practices. Robinson filed a complaint with the DOL, contending that she was a victim of retaliation in violation of the Sarbanes-Oxley Act. Following a 10-day hearing, an administrative law judge ruled that Robinson was fired for her poor job performance. The DOL's Administrative Review Board affirmed the ALJ's ruling and Robinson appealed to the Seventh Circuit. The appeals panel affirmed, holding that, although Robinson was a senior auditor, whistleblowing was not the basis of her job termination. Rather, the record reflected a history of complaints about her abrasiveness, her inability to accept constructive criticism, and the need for her to improve her communication skills.

Free Enterprise Fund v. Public Co. Accounting Oversight Board [130 S. Ct. 3138 (2010)]: In 2010, an accounting firm brought action challenging the constitutionality of the Sarbanes-Oxley Act on the grounds that because the Public Company Accounting Oversight Board (PCAOB), which supervises compliance with the Act, has regulatory powers over the accounting industry, PCAOB officers should be appointed by the President, rather than by the Securities and Exchange Commission. Further, because the law lacks a "severability clause," if part of the law is judged unconstitutional, so is the remainder. The Supreme Court ended up separating that portion of the Act, but kept the remaining laws associated with the Act intact.

Dronsejko v. Thornton [2011 WL 167245 (10th Cir. Jan. 20, 2011)]: In this case, the Tenth Circuit affirmed the dismissal of a shareholders' securities-fraud class action suit, holding among other things that sanctions imposed on the defendant-auditors by the Sarbanes-Oxley Public Company Accounting Oversight Board could not be used to fix liability on the defendants by the shareholders. The plaintiffs needed their own evidence that the auditors acted recklessly in order for the class to prevail. The First Circuit heard two separate cases in February 2012 and found that whistleblower protection under the Sarbanes-Oxley Act was not available to former employees of privately held firms in the mutual fund business. Within the meaning of the whistleblower protection provision of the Sarbanes-Oxley Act (SOA), the term employee referred to only employees of defined public companies, not employees of a public company's officers, employees, contractors, subcontractors, or agents. [Lawson v. FMR LLC, 2012 WL 335647 (1st Cir. Feb. 3, 2012)] In both cases, the plaintiffs sued their employers, private companies that advise managers of mutual funds, pursuant to the Investment Company Act of 1940. Both employees alleged retaliation for being whistleblowers.

The court stated that:

- Only the employees of the defined public companies are covered by whistleblower provisions; the clause "officer, employee, contractor, subcontractor, or agent of such company" goes to who is prohibited from retaliating or discriminating, not to who is a covered employee and so does not violate the rule against rendering superfluous any statutory language;

- The text of § 1514A(a) first identifies covered employers: those with a class of securities registered under Section 12 of the 1934 Act or those that file reports with the SEC pursuant to Section 15(d) of the 1934 Act. Such public companies may not retaliate against their own employees who engage in protected activity;

- Next, Section 1514A(a) enumerates a list of representatives of such employers, including those who are contractors or subcontractors, and they are also barred from retaliating against employees of the covered public-company employer who engage in protected activity;

- Although there is a close relationship between the private investment adviser defendants and their client mutual funds, as pointed out by the plaintiffs and the SEC as amicus curiae, the two entities were purposely separated by Congress.

Q 9:173 Why should government contractors care about Sarbanes Oxley and subsequent whistleblower statutes?

Regarding the first part of this question, according to the Philadelphia-based international law firm of Pepper Hamilton:

> Why should [even] privately held government contractors be concerned about SOX provisions that do not apply specifically to them? . . .
>
> Investors, lenders, vendors and business partners are insisting on some level of compliance, even from privately held companies
>
> Potential buyers (particularly public companies) are demanding compliance from potential targets and are using a lack of compliance as a negotiating tool to justify reduced price
>
> IPO market expects full compliance, and pre-IPO companies that have implemented changes may be viewed as more attractive IPO candidates [and]
>
> Courts and regulators probably will judge corporate conduct and develop new rules and regulations assuming SOX compliance—in other words, separate standards for private and public companies are unlikely.

["Government Contracts Update: The Effects of Sarbanes-Oxley on Privately Held Government Contractors," Pepper Hamilton LLP, Apr. 8, 2005, accessed at http://www.atssa.com/galleries/default-file/Effects_of_Sarbanes_Oxley.pdf]

On July 21, 2010, President Obama signed into law the Dodd-Frank Wall Street Reform and Consumer Protection Act (H.R. 4173). [Pub. L. No. 111-203] Among the Act's many provisions, the one of greatest interest to government contractors extends the concept of a *qui tam* (see Q 9:161) to Wall Street. The Act amended the Commodity Exchange Act to say that, if an employee's disclosure of wrongdoing to the federal Commodities Futures Trading Commission results in a sanction exceeding $1 million, the whistleblowing worker will get anywhere from 10 to 30 percent of the sanction actually collected by the agency. The new law also created a three-year statute of limitations under the False Claims Act. [*See* Riddle v. DynCorp Int'l, Inc., 733 F. Supp. 2d 743 (N.D. Tex. 2010).]

However, New York Rep. Michael Grimm introduced the Whistleblower Improvement Act of 2011 (H.R. 2483), a bill that seeks to eradicate many of the protections for whistleblowers created by the Dodd-Frank Act. Grimm's bill would force whistleblowers to report information relating to internal misconduct first to his or her employer, and only afterwards to a regulatory agency. Such a requirement would give law-breaking companies far too much time to dodge law enforcement and to intimidate whistleblowers from coming forward. The bill would also legalize retaliation against whistleblowers if a company has any policy or document barring employees from communicating with the government, and it would remove any incentives or rewards for would-be whistleblowers by eliminating the minimum reward requirement. H.R. 2483 has already passed through the House Subcommittee on Capital Markets and Government Sponsored Enterprises and may be considered by the House Financial Services Committee. The U.S. Chamber of Commerce is also lobbying for the bill.

[http://www.truth-out.org/new-bill-weaken-protections-incentives-whistle blowers-sneaks-through-committee/1329337939]

On November 30, 2010, the FDA Food Safety Modernization Act (S. 510) passed the Senate and provides, among other things, the "most comprehensive whistleblower protections for food service workers in history. It includes sweeping protections for corporate employees who report any food violations enforced by the FDA (see Section 402: Employee Protections)." [Government Accountability Project, "Recent Legislative Victories," http://www.whistle blower.org/program-areas/legislation]

Sarbanes-Oxley, Dodd-Frank, and the FDA Acts are all progeny of the False Claims Act [31 U.S.C. §§ 3729–3733], which was enacted shortly after the American Civil War. The False Claims Act reflected the government's concern about perceived government-contractor fraud during the war between the states. Under this complex web of federal whistleblower statutes, government contractors are now particularly, but certainly not uniquely, vulnerable to *qui tam*-type whistleblower actions.

Given this particular vulnerability, government contractors may wish to join the alarm being raised against this marked enhancement of the federal whistleblower regime. According to writer Thomas Brom in the *California Lawyer*, "In December (2010), the Washington, D.C., based Association of Corporate Counsel (ACC) sent the SEC a letter signed by 270 chief legal officers of U.S. corporations, demanding that the commission require whistleblowers to use existing internal compliance and reporting systems before they report any suspected wrongdoing." [Thomas Brom, "Whistle While You Work," *California*

Lawyer, Feb. 2011, accessed at http://www.callawyer.com/clstory. cfm?pubdt = 201102&eid = 913848&evid = 1]

Seeking to have such a requirement enshrined in the federal statutory scheme, including the False Claims Act, would go a long way toward shielding government contractors from the most devastating potentials of *qui tam* liability.

Q 9:174   Has the use of arbitration in disputes between government contractors and their employees been curtailed by the federal law?

Yes. The so-called Franken Amendment to the 2010 Department of Defense Appropriations Act prohibits government contractors from enforcing arbitration clauses in employment contracts, when the employee's claim involves sexual assault or sexual harassment. In championing the amendment, Minnesota's Senator Al Franken said, "Arbitration is conducted behind closed doors, doesn't allow you a jury of your peers, and fails to establish precedent. Many of our nation's most cherished civil rights were established by individuals bringing claims in court. Arbitration has its place in our system, but handling claims of sexual assault and egregious violations of civil rights is not its place."

Businesses entering contracts with the United States that are valued at more than $1 million must agree up front to refrain from imposing arbitration clauses upon employees and subcontractors that extend the ADR requirement to Title VII and/or sexual-assault tort claims. Contractors also must promise not to try to enforce any such existing arbitration agreements. The Department of Defense is authorized to waive this provision in situations where national security interests are allegedly at stake.

Senator Franken's amendment was inspired by a highly publicized case coming out of Iraq. In this case, Plaintiff Jamie Leigh Jones began working for Halliburton/KBR in 2004 as an administrative assistant in Houston, Texas. She alleged that while initially employed, she was sexually harassed by her supervisor, and, because of this, she demanded to be moved to another department.

On July 21, 2005, Jones signed a contract with Defendant Overseas Administrative Services (OAS), a foreign, wholly owned subsidiary of Halliburton/KBR, to be employed as clerical worker for the company in Baghdad. Paragraph 26 of this contract provided, in pertinent part:

> You . . . agree that you will be bound by and accept as a condition of your employment the terms of the Halliburton Dispute Resolution Program which are herein incorporated by reference. You understand that the Dispute Resolution Program requires, as its last step, that any and all claims that you might have against Employer related to your employment, including your termination, and any and all personal injury claim[s] arising in the workplace, you have against other parent or affiliate of Employer, must be submitted to binding arbitration instead of to the court system.

The incorporated DRP, in turn, provided:

> "Dispute" means all legal and equitable claims, demands, and contro-
> versies, of whatever nature or kind, whether in contract, tort, under
> statute or regulation, or some other law, between persons bound by the
> Plan or by an agreement to resolve Disputes under the Plan . . .
> including, but not limited to, any matters with respect to . . . any
> personal injury allegedly incurred in or about a Company workplace.

Jones' job assignment placed her in the U.S. Army's Central Command Area
of Operations, located in the so-called "Green Zone" of Baghdad. The Green
Zone is a ten-square-kilometer area that was initially the center of the Coalition
Provisional Authority after the Iraqi invasion, and continues to be the center of
the international presence in the city. Not long after her arrival, claimed Jones,
she was raped. Further, she claimed that she was treated more like a perpetrator
than a victim.

Initially, Jones filed a complaint with the Equal Employment Opportunity
Commission. It conducted an investigation and determined: (1) she had been
sexually assaulted by one or more employees; (2) physical trauma was apparent; and (3) Halliburton/KBR's investigation had been inadequate. Jones then
more or less simultaneously requested arbitration under her employment
contract and initiated a federal law suit. The defendant moved to stay the suit
pending the arbitration.

The district court granted in part and denied in part Halliburton/KBR's
motion. The district judge compelled arbitration of all her claims, except: (1)
assault and battery; (2) intentional infliction of emotional distress arising out of
the alleged assault; (3) negligent hiring, retention, and supervision of employees
involved in the alleged assault; and (4) false imprisonment. The district court
concluded there was a valid agreement to arbitrate, rejecting Jones' contentions
that there was no meeting of the minds; the arbitration clause was fraudulently
induced; the provision was contrary to public policy, and enforcing the agreement would be unconscionable. It also rejected Jones' alternative contention
that, pursuant to the equitable doctrine of unclean hands, the arbitration
agreement should not be enforced.

The district court ordered litigation of the four non-arbitrable claims stayed
until arbitration was completed on the other claims. The remaining claims were
ordered to be arbitrated. Jones' counsel filed an interlocutory appeal in June
2008.

In September 2009, the Fifth Circuit affirmed, holding:

1. The question of whether an employee's personal injury claims are within
   scope of the arbitration clause is governed by Federal Arbitration Act
   (FAA), not the Texas Arbitration Act;

2. The employee's claims for assault and battery, intentional infliction of
   emotional distress, negligent hiring, retention, and supervision, and false
   imprisonment were not "related to" her employment within meaning of
   arbitration provision, so as to be arbitrable; and

3. Such claims did not arise "in or about the workplace" within meaning of employer's dispute resolution program (DRP), so as to be arbitrable.

[Jones v. Halliburton, 583 F.3d 228 (5th Cir. 2009)]

Despite the appellate panel's ruling that a significant portion of Jones' claims were not subject to arbitration, Senator Franken's office asserted, "The amendment seeks to narrowly target the most egregious violations and applies to defense contracts, many of which are administered abroad, where women are the most vulnerable and least likely to have support resources. The amendment will apply to many contractors that have already demonstrated their incompetence in efficiently carrying out defense contracts, and have further demonstrated their unwillingness and their inability to protect women from sexual assault." Given the extensive litigation demanded of Jones in order to establish her right to proceed in federal court with those claims, and the stay of her court claims pending the arbitration of what remained for private ADR, the senator's critique may be well taken.

The Franken Amendment may be only the tip of an iceberg intended to scuttle the replacement of federal agency and court remedies for discrimination claims with private ADR agreements. The Arbitration Fairness Act of 2009 was introduced in late 2009 in the House by Congressman Johnson of Georgia and in the Senate by Senator Feingold of Wisconsin. If ultimately enacted, the bill most likely will prohibit nearly all mandatory ADR agreements involving employment discrimination and other civil rights-related matters.

The bill's official summary states that it:

> declares that no predispute arbitration agreement shall be valid or enforceable if it requires arbitration of:
>
> (1) an employment, consumer, or franchise dispute, or
>
> (2) a dispute arising under any statute intended to protect civil rights. [It also] declares . . . that the validity or enforceability of an agreement to arbitrate shall be determined by a court, under federal law, rather than an arbitrator, irrespective of whether the party resisting arbitration challenges the arbitration agreement specifically or in conjunction with other terms of the contract containing such agreement. [And it] exempts from this Act arbitration provisions in collective bargaining agreements.

[http://www.opencongress.org/bill/111-h1020/show]

NOTE: The Arbitration Fairness Act has been reintroduced in each subsequent session of Congress but as of April 2013, as this publication goes to press, the Act has yet to even reach the floor for a vote.

Chapter 10

Public Employees

The Federal Service Labor-Management Relations Act of 1978 (FSLMRA) established a permanent structure for labor relations in the federal public sector. It created the Federal Labor Relations Authority (FLRA) responsible for administering the Act, and granted federal employees (with some exemptions) the right to organize and bargain collectively. It also prohibited strikes and other specific practices. Public sector labor relations statutes vary among the states. Some states and municipalities have laws providing employees with a limited right to strike and collective bargaining powers. These as well as public employee constitutional and civil rights, compensation, whistleblower protections, and ethical issues are discussed in this chapter.

Collective Bargaining

Federal Employees

Q 10:1 Do public employees have the right to join unions, bargain collectively, and strike?

The rights of public sector employees to organize and bargain collectively are relatively recent legal developments, as compared to the federal National Labor Relations Act (NLRA), which was effective in 1935. The NLRA, which structures labor relations in the private sector, excludes employees of federal, state, and local governments from its coverage. (See chapter 11.) Only in the last few decades of the twentieth century did Congress, the executive branch, and the states adopt legal provisions allowing public employees some rights to organize and bargain collectively.

Although many labor relations issues in the public sector are similar to those in the private sector, the following are significant differences:

1. *Constitutional issues.* Actions taken by government employers with regard to their employees may raise issues of the constitutional rights of those employees. Both the U.S. Constitution and the various state constitutions regulate and limit governmental action affecting citizens. Because public sector workers are citizens and employees, their constitutional rights must be respected by their employers; therefore, the public sector employer may be limited by constitutional provisions in its attempts to discipline or regulate its employees. The private sector employer faces no similar constitutional problems.

2. *Right to strike.* The right to strike is protected by Section 7 of the NLRA for private sector workers. Public sector workers, in general, do not have the right to strike. The activities of the government employer are generally vital to the public interest; disruptions of those activities because of labor disputes could imperil the welfare of the public. For that reason, the right to strike by public sector workers may be prohibited (as in the federal government and most states) or limited to certain employees whose refusal to work would not endanger the public safety or welfare.

3. *Scope of issues for collective bargaining.* In the private sector, the duty to bargain encompasses the broadly defined matters of "wages, hours, and other terms and conditions of employment." In the public sector, matters relating to terms and conditions of employment also may affect the legally required activities or duties of the public sector employer. To bargain over such issues could, in effect, involve delegating to the union the determination of functions and the exercise of authority legally given to the government; therefore, the scope of collective bargaining must be limited on such issues so that the governmental employer does not abdicate its authority. For this reason, the scope of collective bargaining is more restrictive than in the private sector. The various federal and state provisions narrowly define *terms and conditions* of employment. Indeed, some state legislation does not provide for bargaining at all, but rather for consultation or "meeting and conferring" on such issues.

Q 10:2 Do federal employees have the right to join unions, bargain collectively, and strike?

Federal employees have the right to join unions and bargain collectively; however, Section 7116(b)(7) of the Federal Service Labor-Management Relations Act of 1978 (FSLMRA) makes it an unfair labor practice to call, participate in, or condone a strike or slowdown against a federal agency. Thus, in August 1981, President Ronald Reagan fired and permanently replaced 11,000 striking air traffic controllers and busted their union. These actions were subsequently sanctioned by the U.S. Court of Appeals for the District of Columbia. [*See* PATCO v. FLRA, 110 BNA L.R.R.M. 2676 (D.C. Cir. 1982).]

Q 10:3   When did federal employees receive the right to unionize?

It is not known precisely when federal employees began negotiating over the terms of their employment, but informal bargaining began as early as 1883. In that year, the Pendelton Act, known as the Civil Services Act, was passed. It granted Congress the sole authority to set wages, hours, and other terms and conditions of federal employment. This Act led to informal bargaining and congressional lobbying by federal employees seeking higher wages and better conditions.

In 1906, President Theodore Roosevelt halted informal bargaining by issuing an executive order forbidding federal employees, or their associations, from soliciting increases in pay, either before Congress, its committees, or before the heads of the executive agencies. Employees violating the order faced dismissal.

In the years following the executive order, Congress passed several laws that gave limited rights of organization to some federal workers. The Lloyd-La Follette Act of 1912 gave postal workers the right to join unions. In 1920, the federal government negotiated the terms of a contract with the union representing construction workers building the government-sponsored Alaskan Railroad.

It was not until 1962, with the issuing of Executive Order 10988 by President John Kennedy, that large numbers of federal employees were given the right to organize and to present their views on terms and conditions of employment to the agencies for which they worked.

Executive Order 10988 was supplemented by Executive Order 11491, which was issued in 1969 by President Richard Nixon. That order placed the entire program of employee-management relations under the supervision and control of the Federal Labor Relations Council.

The FSLMRA, which was enacted as part of the Civil Service Reform Act of 1978 and took effect in January 1979, was the first comprehensive enactment covering labor relations in the federal government.

Q 10:4   What is the *FSLMRA*?

The *FSLMRA*, which was modeled after the NLRA, established a permanent structure for labor relations in the federal public sector. It created the Federal Labor Relations Authority (FLRA) to administer the Act, and it granted federal employees the right to organize and bargain collectively. It also prohibited strikes and other specific practices.

The FSLMRA covers federal workers employed by a federal agency or who have ceased to work for the agency because of an unfair labor practice. Most federal agencies are covered, but some are specifically exempted—e.g., the FBI, the CIA, the National Security Agency, the General Accounting Office, the

Tennessee Valley Authority, the FLRA, and the Federal Service Impasse Panel. Furthermore, any agency that the President determines is investigative in nature, or has a primary function of intelligence and thus would not be amenable to FSLMRA coverage because of national security, may be excluded. The FSLMRA also excludes certain employees from coverage. Non-citizens working outside of the United States for federal agencies, supervisory and management employees, and certain foreign-service officers are exempted. In addition, the Act excludes any federal employee from participating in an illegal strike.

The Thurmond Act of 1969 prohibits military personnel from belonging to a union. That Act makes it a felony for enlisted personnel to join a union or for military officers or their representatives to recognize or to bargain with a union. The Thurmond Act does not apply to civilian employees of the military.

Those employees covered by the FSLMRA are granted the right to form, join, or assist any labor organization, or to refrain from such activity, freely and without reprisal. Employees may act as representatives of a labor organization and present views of the organization, or refrain from such activity. Employees may also present views of the organization to the heads of agencies, the executive branch, and Congress.

Q 10:5   How is the FSLMRA administered?

The FSLMRA created the FLRA, which assumed the duties of the Federal Labor Relations Council created by Executive Order 11491. The FLRA is the central authority responsible for the administration of the FSLMRA.

The FLRA is composed of three members nominated by the President and confirmed by the Senate. The members serve five-year terms. The FLRA is empowered to: (a) determine the appropriateness of units for representation; (b) supervise or conduct elections to determine if a labor organization has been selected as the exclusive representative by a majority of the employees in the appropriate unit; (c) resolve issues relating to the duty to bargain in good faith; and (d) resolve complaints of unfair labor practices.

The FLRA has the authority to hold hearings and issue subpoenas. It may order any agency or union to cease and desist from violating the provisions of the FSLMRA, and it can enlist the federal courts in proceedings against unions that strike illegally. The FLRA may take any remedial actions it deems appropriate in carrying out the policies of the Act. [See http://www.flra.gov, for more information.]

Q 10:6   How are bargaining units determined for federal employees?

Under the FSLMRA, a union becomes the exclusive representative of an appropriate unit of employees when it has been selected by a majority of votes cast in a representation election. When selected, the union becomes the sole representative of the employees in the unit and is authorized to negotiate the terms and conditions of employment of the employees in the unit. The union must fairly represent all employees in the unit, without discrimination or regard to union membership.

The FLRA is authorized to settle issues involving representation, such as the determination of the appropriate unit and the holding of representation elections. The FLRA ensures employees the fullest possible freedom in exercising their rights under the FSLMRA in determining the unit and ensures a clear and identifiable community of interest among the employees in the unit to promote effective dealing with the agency involved. The FLRA may determine the appropriateness of a unit on an agency, plant, installation, functional, or other basis.

Units may not include any management or supervisory employees, confidential employees, employees engaged in personnel work (except those in a purely clerical capacity), employees doing investigative work that directly affects national security, employees administering the FSLMRA, or employees primarily engaged in investigation or audit functions relating to the work of individuals whose duties affect the internal security of an agency.

Any employees engaged in administering any provision of law relating to labor-management relations may not be represented by a labor organization that is affiliated with an organization representing other individuals under the Act. An appropriate unit may include professional and non-professional employees only if the professional employees, by majority vote, approve including non-professional employees.

Q 10:7 How are representation elections conducted in the federal sector?

The procedures for representation elections under the FSLMRA closely resemble those for elections under the NLRA:

1. The Act allows for holding consent elections to determine the exclusive representative of a bargaining unit.

2. The FLRA may investigate the question of representation, including holding an election, if a petition is filed by any person alleging that 30 percent of the employees in a unit wish to be represented by a union for the purpose of collective bargaining. When a petition is filed alleging that 30 percent of the members of a bargaining unit no longer wish to be represented by their exclusive representative union, the FLRA will investigate the representation question.

3. If the FLRA finds reasonable cause to believe that a representation question exists, it will provide, upon reasonable notice, an opportunity for a hearing.

4. If, on the basis of the hearing, the FLRA finds that a question of representation does exist, it will conduct a representation election by secret ballot. An election will not be held if the unit has held a valid election within the preceding 12 months.

5. When an election is scheduled, a union may intervene and be placed on the ballot if it can show that it is already the unit's exclusive representative or that it has the support of at least 10 percent of the employees in the unit.

6. The election is by secret ballot, and the employees choose between the union or unions and "no representation."

7. If no choice receives a majority of votes cast, a runoff election is held between the two choices receiving the higher number of votes. The results of the election are certified; if a union receives a majority of votes cast, it becomes the exclusive representative of the employees of the unit.

Q 10:8   What rights does the successful union enjoy as bargaining representative of federal employees under the FSLMRA?

A union that has obtained exclusive representation status can be present at any formal discussions between the agency and unit employees concerning grievances, personnel policies and practices, or other conditions of employment.

The exclusive representative also must be given the opportunity to be present at any examination of an employer in the unit in connection with an agency investigation that the employee reasonably believes may result in disciplinary action against him or her, provided that the employee involved has requested such representation. (This right is the equivalent of the Weingarten rights established by the National Labor Relations Board (NLRB) for organized employees in the private sector.)

Q 10:9   What are union consultation rights in the federal sector?

If the employees of an agency have not designated a union as their exclusive representative on an agency-wide basis, a union that represents a substantial number of agency employees may be granted consultation rights. Consultation rights entitle the union to be informed of any substantive change in employment conditions the agency proposes. The union is to be permitted reasonable time to present its views and recommendations regarding the proposed changes. The agency must consider the union's recommendations before taking final action, and it must provide the union with written reasons for taking the final action.

Q 10:10   How is collective bargaining conducted with federal employees?

The FSLMRA requires that agencies and the exclusive representative of agency employees meet and negotiate in good faith. *Good faith* is defined as approaching the negotiations with a sincere resolve to reach a collective bargaining agreement, meeting at reasonable times and convenient places as frequently as may be necessary, and being represented at negotiations by duly authorized representatives prepared to discuss and negotiate on any condition of employment.

The Act defines *conditions of employment* as including personnel policies, practices and other matters, whether established by rule, regulation or otherwise, that affect working conditions. However, the Act excludes the following from being defined as conditions of employment: (a) policies relating to prohibited political activity; (b) matters relating to the classification of any position; and (c) policies or matters that are provided for by federal statute.

Wages are not subject to collective bargaining. Federal "blue-collar" employees are paid under the coordinated Federal Wage System, which provides for pay comparable to pay for similar jobs in the private sector. Federal "white-collar" employees are paid under the General Schedule (GS) and increases and changes in GS pay scales are made by presidential order.

The FSLMRA contains a strong management's rights clause, which also restricts the scope of collective bargaining. According to that clause, collective bargaining is not to affect the authority of any management official or any agency to determine the mission, budget, organization, number of employees, or the internal security practices of the agency. Furthermore, management's right to hire, assign, direct, lay off, retain or suspend, reduce in grade or pay, or to take disciplinary action against any employee is not subject to negotiation. Decisions to assign work, to contract out work, or to select candidates to fill positions are not subject to negotiation. The Act also precludes bargaining over any actions necessary to carry out the mission of the agency during emergencies.

The duty to bargain extends to matters that are the subject of any rule or regulation, as long as the particular rule or regulation is not government-wide; however, if the agency determines that there is a compelling need for such a regulation, it can refuse to bargain over that regulation. The exclusive representative must be given an opportunity to show the FLRA that no compelling need exists.

Q 10:11   Does a federal agency's duty to bargain in good faith include a duty to provide the union with information?

The agency's duty to bargain includes the obligation to furnish, upon request by the exclusive representative, data and information normally maintained by the agency. Such data must be reasonably available and necessary for full and proper discussion of subjects within the scope of bargaining. Data related to the guidance, training, advice, or counsel of management or supervisors relating to collective bargaining are excluded from the obligation to provide information. The duty to bargain in good faith also includes the duty to execute a written document embodying the terms of agreement, if either party so requests.

Q 10:12   Can federal employees be disciplined for improper behavior, amounting to sexual harassment, during collective bargaining activities?

In *American Federation of Government Employees Local 3254 and Grissom Air Force Base* [F.M.C.S. Arb. No. 93-19558 (Jan. 17, 1994)], Federal Mediation and Conciliation Service (FMCS) arbitrator B.J. Speroff ruled that, while rough language may be a legitimate part of the give-and-take across the negotiating table, a continuation of such language outside the negotiating sessions was inappropriate and subject to disciplinary action by the employer-agency. The arbitrator therefore denied a union grievance filed on behalf of a union representative who was given a 14-day suspension from work for his crude language directed at a female agency representative outside the building at the conclusion of a negotiating session.

Speroff noted that "robust debate" around the bargaining table justifies some rough language, and the presence of more women on both sides of the table does not alter negotiators' free speech right to express themselves in terms that might be viewed as inappropriate or offensive to females in some other context.

Although the federal chief negotiator may have been offended by the local union president's remarks at the bargaining session, Speroff said that she had no sexual harassment claim based upon hostile environment, because the remarks were made spontaneously in the heat of collective bargaining. But once the parties had left the building, the president's lewd remarks, "spoken in public and away from the negotiating table, being uttered sans provocation, can in no way constitute a privileged or protected activity, and, indeed, become a form of sexual harassment."

Q 10:13   How are bargaining impasses resolved under the FSLMRA?

The FSLMRA created the Federal Service Impasses Panel, which is authorized to take any action necessary to resolve an impasse in negotiations.

The FMCS, created by the Taft-Hartley Act, also assists in the resolution of impasses by providing mediation service for the parties. If the mediation efforts fail to lead to an agreement, either party may request that the Federal Service Impasses Panel consider the dispute. The Panel may recommend procedures for resolving the impasse or assist the parties in any other way it deems appropriate. The formal impasse resolution procedures may include hearings, fact finding, recommendations for settlement, or directed settlement. With the approval of the Panel, the Parties also may seek binding arbitration of the impasse.

The Federal Service Impasses Panel has seven Presidential appointees who serve on a part-time basis, one of whom serves as Chairman. The Panel resolves impasses between federal agencies and unions representing federal employees arising from negotiations over conditions of employment under the Federal Service Labor-Management Relations Statute, the Federal Employees Flexible and Compressed Work Schedules Act, and the Panama Canal Act of 1979. If bargaining between the parties, followed by mediation assistance, proves unsuccessful, the Panel has the authority to recommend procedures and to take whatever action it deems necessary to resolve the impasse. The Panel's staff also supports the Foreign Service Impasse Disputes Panel in resolving impasses arising under the Foreign Service Act of 1980.

Q 10:14   How broad are the powers of the Federal Service Impasses Panel?

The Federal Service Impasses Panel has broad statutory authority to resolve negotiation impasses over conditions of employment in the federal sector. Once it determines to assert jurisdiction in a dispute, the Panel may recommend or direct the use of procedures for resolving an impasse through any method it deems appropriate. If the procedure selected does not result in a settlement, the Panel may then take whatever final action is necessary to resolve the dispute, including the issuance of a Decision and Order. It is binding during the term of the parties' collective bargaining agreement unless the parties agree otherwise. Because the Panel believes that the voluntary resolution of impasses are superior to those imposed by a third party, after considering the parties' preferences, where circumstances warrant the Panel will select the procedure most likely to lead to a voluntary settlement. Consistent with this belief, the Panel encourages the parties to continue efforts to resolve the issues voluntarily at any stage of case processing. [*See* http://www.flra.gov/fsip/fsip_drp.html.]

Q 10:15   Is grievance arbitration allowed under the FSLMRA?

The FSLMRA provides that all collective agreements under it must contain a grievance procedure that provides for binding arbitration as the final step in resolving grievances. If arbitration is invoked, either party may appeal the arbitrator's decision to the FLRA for review within 30 days of the granting of the award. Upon review, the FLRA may overturn the arbitrator's award only if it is contrary to a law, rule, or regulation, or is inconsistent with the standards for review of private sector awards by the federal courts. If no appeal is taken from the arbitrator's award within 30 days of the award, the arbitrator's award is final and binding.

When a grievance involves matters subject to a statutory review procedure, the employee may choose to pursue the complaint through the statutory procedure or through the negotiated grievance procedure. Grievances alleging discrimination in violation of Title VII of the Civil Rights Act of 1964 provide the grievant such a choice. The grievant can pursue the complaint through the grievance process or through the Title VII procedure.

Performance ratings, demotions, and suspensions or removals that are subject to Civil Service review procedures may be pursued either through the Civil Service procedures or a grievance.

Q 10:16   Are unfair labor practices covered by the FSLMRA?

The FSLMRA prohibits unfair labor practices by agencies and unions. The unfair labor practices defined in the Act are similar to those defined by Section 8(a) and (b) of the NRLA.

Unfair labor practices by agencies prohibited under the FSLMRA include:

1. Interference or restraint of the exercise of employees' rights under the Act;

2. Encouraging or discouraging union membership by discrimination in conditions of employment;

3. Sponsoring or controlling a union;

4. Disciplining or discriminating against an employee for filing a complaint under the Act;

5. Refusing to negotiate in good faith; and

6. Refusing to cooperate in impasse procedures.

It is also an unfair labor practice for an agency to enforce any rule or regulation that conflicts with a preexisting collective bargaining agreement.

Union unfair labor practices prohibited under the FSLMRA include:

1. Interfering with or restraining the exercise of employees' rights under the Act;

2. Coercing or fining a member for the purpose of impeding job performance;

3. Discriminating against an employee on the basis of race, color, creed, national origin, sex, age, civil service status, political affiliation, marital status, or handicap; and

4. Refusing to negotiate in good faith; and

5. Refusing to cooperate in impasse procedures.

It is also an unfair labor practice for a union to call or condone a strike, work slowdown or stoppage, or to picket the agency if the picketing interferes with the agency's operations. (Informational picketing that does not interfere with agency operations is allowed.)

Q 10:17   What unfair labor practice procedures are there under the FSLMRA?

Upon the filing of a complaint alleging unfair labor practices with the FLRA, the General Counsel's Office of the FLRA investigates the complaint and attempts to reach a voluntary settlement. If no settlement is reached and the investigation uncovers evidence that the Act has been violated, a complaint will be issued. The complaint contains a notice of the charge and sets a date for a hearing before the FLRA. The party against whom the complaint is filed has the opportunity to file an answer to the complaint and to appear at the hearing to contest the charges.

If the FLRA finds, by a preponderance of the evidence that a violation has occurred, it will issue written findings and an appropriate remedial order. FLRA decisions are subject to judicial review by the federal courts of appeals.

Q 10:18   What are the remedies for unfair labor practices under the FSLMRA?

The FLRA has broad authority for fashioning remedial orders for unfair labor practices. Remedial orders may include:

1. Cease and desist orders;

2. Reinstatement with back pay;

3. Renegotiation of the agreement between the parties with retroactive effect; or

4. Any other action deemed necessary to carry out the purposes of the Act.

When a union has been found by the FLRA to have intentionally engaged in a strike or work stoppage in violation of the Act, the FLRA may:

1. Revoke the exclusive representation status of the union; or

2. Take any other disciplinary action deemed appropriate (employees engaging in illegal strikes are subject to dismissal); or

3. Seek injunctions, restraining orders, or contempt citations in federal courts against striking unions.

The FLRA's Office of the General Counsel plays a key role in enforcing these rules. Like the Federal Service Impasses Panel (described above), this Office enjoys broad powers. In its own words:

> The Office of the General Counsel (OGC) is the FLRA's independent investigator and prosecutor. The General Counsel, who is appointed by the President with the advice and consent of the Senate for a five-year term, is responsible for the management of the OGC, including the management of the FLRA's seven Regional Offices. Under the provisions of the Federal Vacancies Reform Act of 1998, the Deputy General Counsel serves as the Acting General Counsel when this position is vacant. The General Counsel, through the seven Regional Offices, is initially responsible for processing unfair labor practice (ULP) allegations and representation matters filed with the FLRA. As to ULP matters, the Regional Offices investigate, settle, and determine whether to dismiss or prosecute ULP charges. The General Counsel also decides appeals of a Regional Director's decision not to issue a ULP complaint. The Regional Offices also ensure compliance with all ULP orders issued by the Authority. The resolution of representation matters includes, among other things, conducting elections and making appropriate unit determinations. The OGC encourages the use of various alternative dispute resolution techniques in striving to help parties in the Federal sector achieve a stable and productive labor-management relationship. This is accomplished through the use of facilitation, intervention, training and education programs. [*See* http://www.flra.gov/gc/message.html.]

Q 10:19   Can the courts review FLRA decisions?

Final orders, other than bargaining unit determinations and arbitration awards, are subject to review in the U.S. courts of appeals. The party seeking review has 10 days from the issuance of the FLRA decision to file a petition for review with the court of appeals for the appropriate circuit. Unless specifically authorized by the appeals court, the filing of a petition for review does not stay an FLRA order.

Upon review, the court may affirm, enforce, modify, or set aside an FLRA order. Findings of fact by the FLRA are deemed conclusive if supported by substantial evidence. The order of the court of appeals is subject to discretionary review by the U.S. Supreme Court.

Q 10:20 What impact does the Homeland Security Act have on the structure of the federal bureaucracy?

Congress, in late November 2002, overwhelmingly voted to enact the Homeland Security Act. [Pub. L. No. 107-296, 116 Stat. 2135 (Nov. 25, 2002)] The Act created a new cabinet-level agency for preventing and responding to terrorist attacks. Former Pennsylvania Governor Tom Ridge was named the new department's first secretary. Wasting no time, President Bush signed the new law on November 25th.

The new Department of Homeland Security (DHS) combined 22 agencies, employing 170,000 federal workers and controlling a combined initial budget of $37.4 billion. The key pieces of the homeland security puzzle are:

- *U.S. Coast Guard*: The 225-year-old, quasi-military organization, first founded as an arm of the U.S. Treasury tasked with interdicting smugglers following the founding of the new nation—and later combined with the U.S. Lifesaving Service, giving it a humanitarian flavor—is mandated to reorganize to make its main mission protection of America's 361 ports and 95,000 miles of coastline. Maritime Safety and Security Teams will be at the heart of fulfilling this mission.

- *Customs Service*: This agency is tasked principally with tightening security along America's porous 5,500-mile Canadian border (including the 1,500 mile boundary Canada shares with Alaska) and the 2,200-mile line that divides the United States from Mexico. Some 5,000 new agents, added since 9/11, supplemented by more vehicles, will help. But commentators say that more and better technology, if made available, will be the key to success.

- *Federal Emergency Management Agency (FEMA)*: FEMA's task is to coordinate the initial responses of emergency workers in the wake of any terrorist attack. Firefighters, police, paramedic, and other first-responders must be made to communicate and coordinate more effectively.

- *Immigration and Naturalization Service (INS)*: The INS implemented SEVIS, a computerized system for tracking foreign students. In 2009, SEVIS is a robust system with an excellent "Help Desk" function and other features, such as batch-processing of large universities' foreign-student populations. Meanwhile, the INS was divided into two agencies: (1) Citizenship and Immigration Services (USCIS), which deals with the rules and regulations involved in a foreigner's transition from alien immigrant to U.S. citizen; and (2) Immigration and Customs Enforcement (ICE), which is the quasi-military enforcement arm of the old agency. ICE is responsible for SEVIS.

- *Secret Service*: Famed for its role in protecting Presidents, investigating financial crimes and combating cyber-attacks on the country's financial and telecommunications infrastructures are the less glamorous, less visible, but critical anti-terrorist missions of this agency.

- *Transportation Security Administration (TSA)*: The TSA includes the federal screeners, whom readers well know if they have had a recent close encounter of the search kind at an airport while engaged in business or vacation travel.

Q 10:21   What is the current status of labor relations in the Department of Homeland Security?

Following lengthy bureaucratic and legal battles over what, if any, organizing and collective bargaining rights employees of the Department of Homeland Security (DHS) would have, the new cabinet-level department capitulated in 2008. After losing its courtroom bid to shed itself of the unions that came as excess baggage with the agencies that comprise DHS, the department agreed to abide by regular civil-serve and labor-management procedures.

[Stephen Barr, "DHS Withdraws Bid to Curb Union Rights," *Washington Post*, Feb. 20, 2008, accessed at http://articles.washingtonpost.com/2008-02-20/opinions/36904870_1_personnel-system-larry-orluskie-homeland-security]

In response to President Obama's 2009 Executive Order 13522, which created a National Council on Federal Labor-Management Relations, the DHS developed a formal plan on how the Department would implement the Executive Order and received certification and approval for this plan by the National Council on April 7, 2010. In this plan, Secretary Napolitano established the DHS Labor-Management Forum, which is chaired by Deputy Secretary Lute with membership from components with bargaining unit employees, the national presidents, and Department of Homeland Security union representatives of the American Federation of Government Employees, National Treasury Employees Union, National Border Patrol Council and the Chief Human Capital Officer.

The Forum began meeting in June 2010. Additional information may be accessed at http://www.dhs.gov/dhs-labor-management-forum.

Meanwhile, in May 2013, DHS unions threw their weight against the immigration reform bill proposed in the U.S. Senate by the so-called "Gang of Eight." Two unions, representing a total of 20,000 DHS employees—12,000 of whom are responsible for issuing immigration documents and 8,000 of whom are charged with deportation of illegals—contended that the bill, if enacted, would jeopardize public safety. This posture by USCIS and USICE employees is bound to strain labor management relations in the forum and in the department at large.

[Ruben Navarette, "'Rogue' DHS unions follow Obama's lead on deportation," CNN, May 22, 2013, accessed at http://www.cnn.com/2013/05/22/opinion/navarrette-immigration-dhs-unions]

Q 10:22   What was the National Security Personnel System?

The National Security Personnel System was a "pay for performance" compensation system by Congress in 2004-2005 for the U.S. Department of Defense (DOD). It was intended to reward "the best and the brightest." Not surprisingly, it was enormously unpopular with rank-and-file workers. Highly controversial from its inception, it was never fully implemented. On October 29, 2009, President Obama signed new legislation that repealed the NSPS. With its repeal, the predecessor (traditional) pay DOD pay systems were reinstated. However, this reversion to the old "reliable" pay structures caused its own set of issues, as some DOD employees complained that the reversion resulted in downgrades. The 2009 legislation gave DOD two years to revert nearly a quarter million employees to the old system (the "General Schedule"). The sheer volume of the task allegedly resulted in numerous errors and some lawsuits, before the transition was complete.

[Stephen Losey, "In NSPS' wake: confusion and lawsuits," Federal Times, Mar. 4, 2012, accessed at http://www.federaltimes.com/article/20120304/ DEPARTMENTS01/203040307/In-NSPS-wake-confusion-lawsuits]

State Employees

Q 10:23   Are state and municipal employees allowed to strike?

Most state public sector labor relations statutes prohibit strikes by public employees. Statutes in other states, such as Hawaii, Michigan, Pennsylvania, and Vermont, allow strikes by employees whose jobs do not immediately affect the public health, safety, and welfare. Still other states' statutes allow for strikes in situations in which the public employer refuses to negotiate or to abide by an arbitration award.

State and municipal employees in the following states are accorded a limited right to strike:

- Alaska
- Hawaii
- Idaho
- Illinois
- Minnesota
- Montana
- Oregon
- Pennsylvania
- Vermont
- Wisconsin

Limitations on the right to strike in these jurisdictions may include:

1. The strike must not endanger public safety.

2. Impasse-resolution procedures must be exhausted.

3. The strike may be enjoined after a specified duration.

Q 10:24   What happens if state or municipal employees illegally strike?

Penalties for illegal strikes vary from state to state. New York's Taylor Law, which prohibits all strikes by public employees, is typical in allowing fines or loss of dues and check-off provisions against the offending union. Employees who participate in illegal strikes in New York may face probation, loss of job, or loss of pay. Courts may issue injunctions or restraining orders against illegal strikes.

Disciplining public sector employees, even those who have taken part in illegal strikes, may pose constitutional problems for public-sector employers. The employer must ensure that any disciplinary procedure ensures the employee's "due process," including adequate notice of and an opportunity to participate in a hearing on the proposed penalty.

Q 10:25   Have any state or municipal employees been awarded the right to strike by judicial fiat?

The California Supreme Court has held that public employees have the right to strike under state common law, provided the strike is not a "substantial and imminent" threat to public health and safety. [County Sanitation Dist. No. 2 of Los Angeles Local 660, Serv. Emps. Intl. Union, 38 Cal. 564 (1985)]

Q 10:26   How does a typical state statute balance public safety against the right of its employees to strike?

The Alaskan law is fairly typical of laws in the minority of states according state and municipal employees a limited right to strike:

1. It denies the right to "protective services" (i.e., police, fire, and paramedics);

2. It gives a limited right to utility, sanitation, and school employees;

3. It gives an unlimited right to other (i.e., non-essential) public employees.

An example of list item 1 is Pennsylvania's so-called Act 111, which denies police officers and firefighters the right to strike. To counterbalance this denial, Pennsylvania provides for binding interest arbitration regarding collective bargaining impasses. In order to accommodate this compromise, Article III, Section 31 of the Pennsylvania Constitution was amended in 1968, when the act was passed, to eliminate an express constitutional prohibition of such arbitration. Binding arbitration under Act 111 is conducted in front of a panel of arbitrators. Refusal by the loser to abide by the panel's award is subject to enforcement and appeal proceedings before the Pennsylvania Labor Relations Board (PLRB). The process is exemplified by a case in which, "[f]ollowing the certification of the Teamsters union as the exclusive representative of a bargaining unit of county detectives the parties bargained to impasse for a CBA and eventually submitted the dispute to interest arbitration under Act 111. An arbitration panel subsequently issued an award that included increases in wages and benefits in excess of what the county unilaterally budgeted to pay the unit members. The county commissioners ratified the non-economic terms of the agreement, but rejected the economic improvements and unilaterally imposed a countywide wage and benefit package. A PLRB hearing examiner concluded the county's refusal to fund the award's financial portion for 2005 constituted an unfair practice in violation of Section 6(1)(a) and (c) of the Pennsylvania Labor Relations Act (PLRA)." On appeal from the hearing examiner to the full board, the PLRB explained the differences between Act 111 and the Public Employee Relations Act of 1970, which applies to all other public employees in the Commonwealth.

> The County's arguments fundamentally fail to account for differences between interest arbitration under Act 111 and interest arbitration for . . . employees under the Public Employee Relations Act of 1970 (PERA). The legislative and constitutional history of Act 111 compared to that of PERA is instructive. In 1968 the General Assembly enacted Act 111 providing for "binding" interest arbitration for police and fire employees who otherwise were denied a right to strike in support of bargaining proposals. Because the Pennsylvania Constitution did not allow for binding arbitration, Article III, Section 31 of the Constitution was amended thirty-eight years ago to provide for "binding" interest arbitration for policemen, such as the County's detectives. In response to this well-established constitutional and legislative history, the County argues that it may, prior to the arbitration process, budget for wages for these employees and then refuse to comply with a binding award under the Constitutional and legislative scheme.
>
> In its exceptions the County makes no justification for its refusal to comply with the Constitution, legislative, and Supreme Court mandates to implement the Act 111 interest arbitration award. Instead, it argues the unfounded and self-imposed claim that legislative action is required to fund the award, and therefore it need not comply. First, this claim is not even viable for purposes of Act 111, Washington Arbitration Case, supra; City of Farrell v. Fraternal Order of Police Lodge No. 34, 538 Pa. 75, 645 A.2d 1294 (1994), and therefore, the County's refusal to fund the Act 111 interest arbitration award for the County Detectives is, as a matter of law, an unfair labor practice in violation of Section 6(1)(a) and (e) of the PLRA, and the County's exceptions challenging the hearing examiner's conclusions in that regard are dismissed.

[Teamsters Local No. 764 v. Lycoming Cnty., 37 Pennsylvania Pub. Emp. Rept. 15 (PLRB 2006)]

Q 10:27   Do the states have public sector labor laws?

In 1954, Wisconsin adopted a public employee labor relations law covering state, county, and municipal employees. Since that first legal provision for state public sector labor relations, approximately 40 states have adopted provisions relating to public sector labor relations [See http://www.afscme.org/members/1 1075.cfm for a complete listing.] The various state laws differ widely in their treatment of issues such as employee coverage, impasse-resolution procedures, and restrictions on the scope of bargaining. Because of the diversity of the statutes, it is not possible to discuss them in detail. The remaining portion of this chapter therefore discusses certain general features of state public sector labor relations statutes.

Q 10:28   What is the coverage of state public sector labor laws?

As noted, some 40 states have provisions for some labor relations activity by state or local employees. Most of those states have adopted statutes that provide for organizing rights and for collective bargaining by public employees. Some states that have no statutes dealing with public sector labor relations allow voluntary collective bargaining by public employees based on court decisions. Other states, while not restricting the rights of public employees to join unions, prohibit collective bargaining by public employees based on statutory prohibitions or court decisions.

In those states having public sector labor relations statutes, the pattern of coverage of those statutes varies. Some statutes cover all state and local employees; others cover only local or only state employees. Some states have several statutes, including separate laws covering teachers, police, and firefighters. Some states also allow for the enactment of municipal labor relations legislation. New York City, for example, has established an Office of Collective Bargaining by means of a city ordinance.

Q 10:29   Do state and municipal employees have a constitutional right to bargain collectively?

The courts generally have held that there is no constitutionally protected right to bargain collectively. For that reason, the courts have upheld restrictions or prohibitions on the right to bargain. However, the right to join unions or to organize has been held to be protected by the constitutional freedom of association under the First and Fourteenth Amendments. Because the right to organize is constitutionally protected, restrictions on that right of public employees have consistently been struck down by the courts.

A small minority of state constitutions specifically accord employees the right to organize and bargain collectively. [See, e.g., New Jersey Const., Art. I, Para. 19, which reads as to public employees, "Persons in public employment shall have the right to organize, present to and make known to the State, or any of its political subdivisions or agencies, their grievances and proposals through representatives of their own choosing." For a comprehensive discussion of this provision, see South Jersey Catholic Sch. Teachers Org. v. St. Theresa of the Infant Jesus Church Elementary Sch., 150 N.J. 575, 696 A.2d 709 (1997).]

But while public employees in general may have the right to organize, many states exclude supervisors and managerial or confidential employees from unionizing. Other states may allow those employees to organize, but provide for bargaining units separate from other employees. The courts generally have upheld exclusions of managerial, supervisory, and confidential employees from organizing and bargaining.

Q 10:30   Are state and municipal employees permitted to unionize?

Most of the state statutes authorizing public sector labor relations provide for exclusive bargaining representatives of the employees. The statutes generally create a Public Employee Relations Board (PERB) to administer the Act and to determine representation issues and unfair labor practice complaints.

Q 10:31   How are appropriate bargaining units determined in the majority of states that permit public employees to unionize?

The determination of appropriate bargaining units is generally the function of the PERB agency created by the particular statute. Some statutes provide for bargaining by all categories of public employees, while other statutes may specifically define appropriate units, such as teachers within a particular school district. When the PERB is entrusted with determining the appropriate unit, it generally considers community interest factors such as:

1. The nature of work;
2. Similarity of working conditions;
3. Efficiency of administration; and
4. The desires of the employees.

Police and law enforcement officers and firefighters generally are in separate district-wide units (or state-wide units for state law enforcement officers). Faculty at public universities may be organized in state-wide units or may bargain on an institutional unit basis.

In general, PERB agencies seek to avoid a proliferation of small units.

Q 10:32   What are the typical procedures for conducting representation elections at the state and local levels?

The procedures for holding representation elections for units of public employees generally resemble those under the FSLMRA and the NLRA:

1. The union seeking representation rights petitions the PERB requesting an election.
2. The union must demonstrate some minimum level of employee support within the unit.
3. If the parties fail to reach agreement on the bargaining unit definition, the eligibility of employees to vote and the date and other details of the election, the PERB settles such issues after holding hearings on them.
4. The elections are by secret ballot, and the results are certified by the PERB.
5. Either party may file objections to the election.
6. The PERB will review the challenges and could order a new election if the challenges are upheld.

Q 10:33 Are some state and municipal employees not entitled to unionize?

One federal appellate court decision has held that some countervailing governmental interests are so significant that they outweigh public employees' First Amendment rights of speech and assembly, which form the basis of a constitutional right to organize. [Gregorich v. Lund, 54 F.3d 410 (7th Cir. 1995)] The plaintiff in this case was a research attorney for the Illinois Fourth District Court of Appeals. The defendant was the presiding judge of that court. When attorney Gregorich attempted to unionize his fellow attorneys, Judge Lund fired him. Gregorich sued in federal district court, contending that the termination violated his First Amendment rights. The federal trial judge agreed, but on appeal, the Seventh Circuit, which sits in Chicago, said that the staff attorneys' privity "not only to internal memoranda and draft opinions, but also to the judges' very thought processes," justified Judge Lund's decision to dismiss the plaintiff and squelch the unionization effort. [*See also* "Court Attorney's Attempt to Unionize Justifies Firing, Seventh Circuit Says," 1995 *BNA Daily Labor Report*, 101, May 25, 1995, at d10.]

Q 10:34 How is collective bargaining handled at the state and local levels?

A majority of states have provisions requiring, or at least permitting, some form of collective bargaining. Some statutes may use the term *meet and confer* rather than collective bargaining, but in actual operation the process is not substantially different from collective bargaining.

The scope of bargaining subjects may be restricted to protect the statutory authority of, or to ensure the provision of essential functions by, the public employer. Additionally, the public employer may be legally prohibited from agreeing with the union on particular subjects. For example, if state law requires a minimum number of evaluations of employees annually, the employer may not agree to a lesser number of evaluations.

Public sector labor relations statutes generally have broad management-rights clauses. As a result, the subjects of "wages, hours and other terms and conditions" of employment may be defined more narrowly than in the private sector under the NLRA.

The state PERBs generally classify subjects for bargaining into mandatory, permissive, and illegal subjects. *Mandatory topics* involve the narrowly defined matters relating to wages, hours, and other terms and conditions of employment. *Permissive subjects* generally are those related to government policy, the employer's function, or matters of management rights. *Illegal subjects* may include those matters to which the employer is precluded by law from agreeing. Some states may prohibit bargaining over certain terms that may be classified as permissive in other states.

Most states that allow public-employee collective bargaining mirror the federal scheme, as represented by the NLRA and enforced by the NLRB (see chapter 11), in the way they handle collective bargaining. Where one of the parties has negotiated in bad faith, or refuses to negotiate at all, the concept of "unfair labor practice" is a common remedy. For example, in a California case, the Public Employee Relations Board's

> ALJ found that the employer-community college district violated [the Educational Employment Relations Act] provisions by unilaterally contracting out its police services to a municipality without providing the union with notice and opportunity to negotiate that decision. The ALJ rejected the employer's argument that the charge was untimely and/or that the union waived its right to bargain on the issue in question. The ALJ issued a cease and desist order and directed the employer, upon demand from the union, to restore positions in its independent police services unit, to reinstate bargaining unit employees, and to rescind the contract with the municipality. The ALJ also directed the employer to make all affected employees whole for losses suffered as a result of its unlawful action. The employer's conduct denied the union its statutory right to represent bargaining unit members and interfered with bargaining unit members' right to be represented by the union, the ALJ reasoned. The ALJ overruled PERB's holding in Barstow Unified School District, 28 PERC 28068 [PERB 1997] (holding that union waived its right to demand bargaining of subcontracting of transportation services through contract language), to the extent it conflicted with his determination that the employer didn't establish a clear and unmistakable waiver as a matter of law.

[Long Beach Cmty. Coll. Dist. Police Officers Ass'n v. Long Beach Cmty. Coll. Dist., 30 Public Employee Report for California 16 (Dec. 13, 2005)]

Because most state laws restrict or prohibit strikes by public employees, they must provide some alternative means for resolving bargaining impasses. Most statutes provide for a process that includes fact-finding, mediation, and ultimately, interest arbitration. Mediation is generally the first step in the impasse resolution process; the mediator may be appointed by the PERB at the request of either party. The mediator attempts to offer suggestions and to reduce the number of issues in dispute. If the mediation is unsuccessful, fact-finding is the second step. Each party presents its case to the fact finder, who will issue a report defining the issues in dispute and establishing the reasonableness of each side's position. The fact-finder's report may be released to the public in an attempt to bring the pressure of public opinion upon the parties to force a settlement. If no resolution is reached after mediation and fact-finding, the statutes generally provide for interest arbitration. The arbitration may be either voluntary or compulsory, and it may be binding or non-binding. Compulsory, binding arbitration is generally found in statutes dealing with employees who provide essential services, such as firefighters and police. Non-binding arbitration awards may be disregarded by the public employer if it so chooses; binding arbitration awards bind both parties to the arbitrator's settlement of the dispute.

In several states, the arbitration of bargaining disputes has been challenged as being an illegal delegation of the public employer's legal authority to the arbitrator. Most state courts have upheld the legality of arbitration; examples are Maine, Michigan, Minnesota, New York, Pennsylvania, and Washington. In some states, however, courts have held compulsory arbitration to be illegal. Such was the case in Colorado, South Dakota, Texas, and Utah. Some statutes allow for judicial review of arbitration awards, generally on grounds of whether the award is unreasonable, arbitrary, or capricious.

Q 10:35   Which states have statutes governing school teachers' collective bargaining rights?

The following states have statutes that govern the collective bargaining rights of school teachers:

- Alaska
- California
- Delaware
- Idaho
- Illinois
- Indiana
- Kansas
- Maryland
- Nebraska
- North Dakota
- Oklahoma
- Rhode Island
- Tennessee
- Vermont
- Washington

The following states give teachers a limited right to strike:

- Hawaii
- Montana
- Oregon
- Pennsylvania

Q 10:36   What changes have occurred on the public employee collective bargaining landscape from 2011 to present ?

After the November 2010 mid-term elections, the switch from liberal Democrats to conservative Republicans in many governors' mansions saw several states move toward ending collective bargaining by public employees. The developments are discussed below.

The Wisconsin Case. On March 11, 2011, Wisconsin's Governor Scott Walker signed the 2011 Wisconsin Act 10, a controversial bill that limits the collective bargaining power for the state's public employees (except for firefighters, police, and state patrol troopers), and require state employees to pay more for their health care and pensions. The new law is labeled "An Act relating to: state finances, collective bargaining for public employees, compensation and fringe benefits of public employees, the state civil service system, the Medical Assistance program."

[Accessed at http://www.foxnews.com/politics/2011/03/11/walker-signs-stripping-unions-collective-bargaining-rights/#ixzz1GUAXo0rB; the actual statute can be accessed at http://www.jsonline.com/news/statepolitics/118677754 .html, by clicking the link to the pdf version.]

On March 18, 2011, Dane County Circuit Judge Maryann Sumi granted a restraining order, temporarily preventing the Wisconsin Secretary of State from publishing the law. [http://www.nytimes.com/2011/03/19/us/19wisconsin. html] Less than a week after the judge issued the TRO, the governor defied the court and permitted the publication of the new law in the Wisconsin code. [http://www.outsidethebeltway.com/wisconsin-defies-court-order-publishes-collective-bargaining-law/]

On June 14, 2011, the state supreme court ordered the reinstatement of Governor Walker's bill. The court overruled the restraining order granted by Sumi, finding that the Legislature did not violate the Wisconsin Constitution, the committee of lawmakers was not subject to the state's open meetings law, and therefore did not violate that law when it approved the governor's bill and allowed the Senate to take it up. The court ruled that Sumi's ruling exceeded her jurisdiction and was in the *void ab initio*, or "invalid from the outset."

However, Chief Justice Shirley Abrahamson dissented, writing that the majority ruling "reached a predetermined conclusion not based on the facts and the law, which undermines the majority's ultimate decision . . . make their own findings of fact, mischaracterize the parties' arguments, misinterpret statutes, minimize (if not eliminate) Wisconsin constitutional guarantees, and misstate case law, appearing to silently overrule case law dating back to at least 1891."

While Republicans praised the court's decision, Democrats decried it for the court's finding that lawmakers do not have the follow the open meetings law, as the committee did not give the required 24 hours notice prior to the meeting, essentially saying that the Legislature is above the law. [http://www.jsonline. com/news/statepolitics/123859034.html]

As a result of the new bill, the city projected savings of at least $25 million a year—and as much as $36 million in 2012—from healthcare benefit changes it didn't have to negotiate with unions. Still, in March 2012 union supporters from around the world gathered in Wisconsin to rally for the governor's recall, and a record number of educators retired after the bill was signed into law. The Wisconsin state pension fund received 18,780 retirement applications from state and local governments and school districts in 2011, representing a 79 percent increase from the average in each of the previous seven years. [http://www. weeklystandard.com/blogs/scott-walkers-collective-bargaining-bill-working_ 582151.html and http://www.huffingtonpost.com/2012/03/09/scott-walker-anti-union-law_n_1335658.html]

On March 30, 2012, the state's election commission ruled that the governor's adversaries had met the requirements for the recall vote, which was scheduled for June 2012. The governor subsequently survived that recall election.

Meanwhile, the legal challenge to the law continued. On April 25, 2013, a Wisconsin appellate court urged the state's supreme court to review the case. [Madison Teachers, Inc. v. Walker, 2013 WL 1760805 (Wis. App. Apr. 25, 2013)]

The Ohio Case. On March 3, 2011, the Ohio legislature passed a massive revision of the state's public sector collective bargaining act. The chief changes are described as follows:

1. S.B. 5 places significant restrictions on the subjects that can be brought to the bargaining table for public employees. Specifically, bargaining will not be permitted about health insurance benefits, employer assistance towards the employee share of pension contributions, privatization of public services, staffing levels, and certain other management rights.

2. S.B. 5 prohibits strikes by all public employees. Previously, Ohio collective bargaining law prohibited strikes only by police officers, firefighters, and other specified employees whose jobs have a direct impact on public safety. S.B. 5 makes it illegal for all public employees to strike and imposes extraordinary penalties if public employees do strike. Striking employees can be terminated, and can be subjected to substantial financial penalties.

3. S.B. 5 establishes a new procedure for dispute resolution in bargaining. Under existing law, if contract negotiations reach a stalemate, the parties typically first have a hearing before a neutral "fact-finder." The fact-finder issues recommendations for resolving the dispute, but either the union or the employer can reject those recommendations. In the case of police, firefighters, and other specified safety employees who are prohibited from striking, the dispute then goes to a hearing before another neutral person whose decision is binding. The theory is that since those employees do not have the leverage of the threat of a strike, there has to be a neutral person to break the deadlock in the bargaining. S.B. 5 eliminates the binding arbitration step and prohibits all employees from striking. In cases where bargaining reaches a stalemate, the fact-finding proceeding will be followed first. If either party rejects the fact-finder's report, the employer's last best offer and the union's last best offer will be presented to the legislative body (i.e., City Council in the case of a municipality) which will conduct a public hearing and then vote to accept either the last best offer of the union or the last best offer of the employer.

[Mike Underwood, "Ohio Senate Passes Massive Reform to Public Sector Collective Bargaining Law," *Employer Law Report* (Mar. 3, 2011)]

On November 8, 2011, Ohioans voted to repeal the law, with 63 percent of voters against the bill, and a union-backed committee that formed to repeal the law raised approximately $30 million for the effort. This marked a major setback for Ohio Governor John Kasich and those with similar initiatives. [http://www.latimes.com/news/politics/la-pn-ohio-issue-2-20111108,0,63215.story]

The New Jersey Case.

In September 2010, Governor Chris Christie proposed a broad package of reform measures aimed at making "the state and local employee pension system sustainable for current and future retirees and to bring fairness and affordability to the public employee health benefits system." A January 11, 2011, press release from the governor's office asserted, "The cost of these already expensive systems continues to grow and threatens to collapse the pension system and force state and local governments to expend limited resources on overgenerous pension and health benefits." The release added, "The current pension system is underfunded by $54 billion and, unless reforms are enacted, that number will grow to $183 billion by 2041, even if the taxpayers make all statutorily required pension fund contributions".

The governor proposed to reduce anticipated 2041 underfunding from $183 Billion to $23 billion, and increase the aggregate funded ratio from the 2011 level of 66 percent to 90 percent over the next three decades.

A reform statute passed in June 2011 eliminated retiree cost-of-living adjustments, even for current retirees. This is expected by some commentators to save New Jersey taxpayers an estimated $120 billion over the next 30 years. The Christie Administration is claiming savings closer to $130 billion.

In April 2013, the state treasurer announced anticipated savings of $540 million for the year ahead. In a press release, the governor commented, "The tough decisions we made in 2011 to get our pension and benefit costs under control are paying dividends every year for New Jersey's overburdened property taxpayers. The combination of pension and benefit reform and other bipartisan reforms such as the 2 percent cap on annual increases in local property taxes, the reform of interest arbitration and promoting shared services are all bringing well-deserved relief to middle-class taxpayers."

"The total amount that local governments and school districts will have to contribute to the two major pension funds in the budget for the new fiscal year beginning July 1 will be $1.57 billion, compared to the $2.11 billion without the reforms, according to Treasury."

[Jarrett Renshaw, "N.J. Pension reform spurs savings, Treasury Department says," *Newark Star-Ledger*, Apr. 12, 2013, available at http://www.nj.com/politics/index.ssf/2013/04/pension_reform_spurs_savings.html]

Other states. Other states' legislators have introduced bills that would limit or even abolish collective bargaining rights for public employees, including in Tennessee, Iowa, Michigan, Kansas, Illinois, and Arizona. On the other hand, three Missouri Democrats recently submitted a bill that would make it illegal for state legislators to do so much as suggest laws that would limit unions' collective bargaining rights.

Several states, such as Kansas and Maine, have passed bills that would restrict political fundraising by public employee unions and teachers. The (mostly Republican) proponents of such bills claim that they remove any government influence from payroll deductions, while opponents of such bills claim that they are an unlawful effort to keep employees from participating in the political process, or even an effort to eliminate public employee unions altogether.

Finally, in most cases, public employees must fund the applicable union—usually in the form of "fair share" payments—even if they decline to become members of the union themselves. However, some states are attempting to pass bills that would change that. In Oregon, for example, Initiative Petition 9 aims to allow employees to withhold both their membership and their money.

[http://voteoregonllc.org/ePetitions.php]

Q 10:37   What are *sunshine* laws?

Some states have adopted open-meeting, or *sunshine*, laws that require meetings of public bodies to be open to the public. Such laws may present a problem for collective bargaining by public employers because they may allow members of the general public to take part in the bargaining process. In some states, such as Ohio, collective bargaining is exempted from the open-meeting or sunshine law. In other states, the right of the public to participate in the bargaining process is legally protected.

Q 10:38   How are bargaining impasses handled at the state and local levels?

Because most state laws restrict or prohibit strikes by public employees, they must provide some alternative means for resolving bargaining impasses. Most statutes provide for a process that includes fact-finding, mediation, and ultimately, interest arbitration.

Mediation is generally the first step in the impasse resolution process; the mediator may be appointed by the PERB at the request of either party. The mediator attempts to offer suggestions and to reduce the number of issues in dispute.

If mediation is unsuccessful, fact-finding is the second step. Each party presents its case to the fact-finder, who issues a report defining the issues in dispute and establishing the reasonableness of the positions of each side. The fact-finder's report may be released to the public in an attempt to bring the pressure of public opinion on the parties to force a settlement.

If no resolution is reached after mediation and fact-finding, the statutes generally provide for interest arbitration. The arbitration may be either voluntary or compulsory and may be binding or non-binding. Compulsory, binding arbitration is generally found in statutes dealing with employees who provide essential services, such as firefighters and police. Non-binding arbitration awards may be disregarded by the public employer if it so chooses; binding arbitration awards bind both parties to the arbitrator's settlement of the dispute.

In several states, the arbitration of bargaining disputes has been challenged as being an illegal delegation of the public employer's legal authority to the arbitrator. Most state courts have upheld the legality of arbitration, including

New York, Michigan, Minnesota, Maine, Washington, and Pennsylvania. In some states, such as Texas, South Dakota, Colorado, and Utah, however, courts have held compulsory arbitration to be illegal.

Some statutes allow for judicial review of arbitration awards, generally to determine if the award is unreasonable, arbitrary, or capricious.

Q 10:39   What are the major trends affecting public employee collective bargaining at the state and local levels?

Some major trends continue to affect state and local public employee collective bargaining:

- Privatization;
- Restricting or stripping altogether collective bargaining rights;
- Attacks on union dues; and
- Attacks on teacher tenure.

Q 10:40   What is *privatization*?

Privatization is the shifting of a public function to total or partial private control. Partial privatization is achieved by contracting out traditionally public services (such as police, prisons, or schools) to private corporations that remain under the control of a public body (such as a city council). Total privatization places such a private contractor under the control of private citizens rather than a public entity.

Q 10:41   What is meant by *contracting out*?

Some observers argue that all public employment is essentially a form of contracting out—the contract is, simply, with the individual police officer, teacher, or prison guard, or with their labor organization. But contracting out's modern meaning is to turn over the function of operating a prison, a school, or a police force to a private corporation. (The material in this section should be read in conjunction with chapter 9, Government Contractors.)

Q 10:42   What problems do the proponents of contracting out/privatization believe these practices can solve?

Proponents of contracting out and privatization believe these practices will have the following benefits:

1. Private entities have a strong motive for reducing costs, thus benefiting the municipality and its taxpayers.
2. Contracting out will increase innovation.

Q 10:43   What problems do the critics of contracting out/privatization see in the practice?

According to AFSCME, privatization is

> Driven by wrong-minded public officials and corporate greed, contracts for public services are doled out without regard to cost effectiveness or quality. Time and time again, the public pays more and gets lower quality of services while public workers are laid off and corruption scandals make the news. AFSCME is fighting hard to preserve quality public services, ensure that public service employees are treated fairly and hold elected officials accountable to the public. [http://www.afsc me.org/issues/76.cfm]

AFSCME's critique of privatization includes the following alleged shortfalls:

- Contracting out costs more than advocates claim because indirect and hidden costs of service delivery are often ignored. Such costs include expenditures for contract monitoring and administration, conversion costs, charges for "extra" work, and the contractor's use of public equipment and facilities. The Government Finance Officers Association estimates that such costs can add up to 25 percent to the price of a contract.

- The quality of service can deteriorate when profit is the prime motivation in service delivery. As many examples show, the profit motive can be an incentive to "cut corners," especially when contract specifications are vague or poorly defined. Public employees routinely perform tasks outside their official job descriptions. Those duties usually are not included in contract specifications, and public managers no longer have the flexibility to get them done.

- There is an adverse economic impact on communities when state or local governments contract out, particularly with companies located in other parts of the country or overseas. The local employment base is eroded when good jobs are replaced with low-wage jobs. Resources are drained from the local economy as profits flow out of the community.

- Dependence on contractors increases as in-house expertise and capacity is reduced or eliminated. This loss of leverage can lead to price gouging by contractors in future contract negotiations. When contractors "low ball" their bids (offer an attractive price on the first bid to win the contract and then raise prices in subsequent renewals), governments are especially vulnerable.

- Public accountability is diminished because complaints from citizens cannot be directly and quickly addressed by the state or local government. In addition, private companies are not subject to the same public scrutiny as government entities, which are required to operate in an open arena. These conditions create opportunities for corruption, such as bid rigging, bribery, and kickbacks.

[*See* http://www.afscme.org/.]

Q 10:44   What are some recent examples of privatization in the public sector?

Some examples of recent developments in privatization include:

- *Alabama.* Republicans in the Alabama Legislature are currently pushing a bill that would take funding from already cash-strapped public schools in an attempt to privatize public schools. The reason? A recent report from a task force led by former Secretary of State Condoleezza Rice and Joel Klein, the former chancellor of New York City's school system, stated that the nation's security and economic prosperity are at risk if America's schools don't improve. However, the Alabama AFL-CIO stated, "Research has continually shown that charter schools are a detriment to public education." Most experts agree. [http://blog.locustfork.net/2012/03/republican-legislators-push-charter-schools-to-privatize-public-education/] The Alabama Accountability Act (HB84) was approved in 2012. HB84 says parents of students zoned for public schools designated as failing will receive tax credits to help pay the cost of attending a private school or a non-failing public school.

- *California.* In April 2009, Oakland joined a growing list of cities turning to private security forces to supplement public police officers in the face of tight budgets. Faced with an $85 million deficit, the city was spending 65 percent of its total budget on police and fire services. In March 2010, the city of San Carlos announced that it would outsource police and fire protection services to save the city an estimated $3 million to $5.5 million. [http://www.mercurynews.com/peninsula/ci_14636884?nclick_check = 1]

- *Florida.* Floridians introduced SB 2036 and SB 2038 in an effort to privatize the Florida prison system—in secret. The measures would allow the state government to privatize any government function in secret, allow the government to secretly outsource work, and give agencies the option of not reporting the privatization of a program until after it has already been implemented, effectively denying citizens of the right to object. The bills were eventually rejected, however. [http://www.addictinginfo.org/2012/01/18/florida-republicans-introduce-bill-that-would-keep-privatization-a-secret-from-the-people/]

- *Maryland.* On March 15, 2010, a union representing many state workers released a report stating the state has cut 3,500 positions over the past three years while increasing spending on contracts by 30 percent. A spokesman for Maryland Gov. Martin O'Malley said the cuts were necessary to get Maryland through the recession with a balanced budget. He added that increased contract spending is likely due to spending federal stimulus dollars on construction projects. [http://www.afscmeinfocenter.org/cgi-bin/mt/mt-search.cgi?blog_id = 7&tag = Maryland&limit = 20]

- *Illinois.* In 2011, Mayor Daley of Chicago chose to privatize its entire parking system, with mixed results (and not a little controversy and anger over meter rate increases). "Dumb" parking meters were replaced with new "smart," solar-powered boxes at a cost of more than $40 million, and meter rates were raised for the first time in two decades. The changes were made in order to establish a long-term reserve fund to replace revenue, retire debt, and shift risk, as well as to improve efficiency and quality of service.

David Zavattero, deputy director of the Chicago Department of Transportation, said that the city "lacked the resources" to manage its parking facilities effectively on its own. By privatizing, the city gave up revenues from parking, but gained the investment of new technology and all its included rewards. [http://www.minnpost.com/cityscape/2011/12/what-happened-when-chicago-privatized-its-parking-system]

- *Indiana.* On March 8, 2010, dozens of school custodians of Fort Wayne Community Schools protested the proposal to outsource custodial work to reduce costs. [http://www.wane.com/dpp/news/wane-ftwayne-FWCS-custodians-oppose-outsourcing-idea]

- *Minnesota.* A bill to privatize the state's fish hatcheries and tree nurseries was introduced in the state legislation in March 2009 and remains pending. [*See* http://www.afscmeinfocenter.org/cgi-bin/mt/mt-search.cgi?blog_id = 7&tag = Minnesota&limit = 20.]

- *New Jersey.* A law enacted by the state legislature in early 2009 gives private clean-up firms increased authority in dealing with toxic-waste spills.

  Also in New Jersey, Governor Chris Christie announced in early 2012 a pilot program that will allow private companies to run public schools in some of the state's persistently underperforming school districts. Interestingly, only months earlier the state's highest court found Christie's education cuts of $1 billion unconstitutional, and ordered the state to spend $500 million on its poorest schools in the following year. Christie signed the bill giving private firms the authority to run failing public schools in three inner-city districts in 2012. [http://www.huffingtonpost.com/2011/06/11/chris-christie-schools_n_875262.html]

- *Texas.* On March 13, 2010, the Dallas News reported that: "A former state official who played a major role in the state's biggest privatization fiasco is now making money trying to help Texas fix the problems that resulted. Gregg Phillips was the state's No. 2 social services official several years ago, and he led a push to hire a private company to evaluate applications for public assistance. Now his Austin-based company, AutoGov Inc., has received $207,500 since November to help the state eliminate errors in deciding whether an applicant gets food stamps or other aid and how much recipients get. AutoGov was hired without other companies having a chance to bid for the work." [http://www.dallasnews.com/shared content/dws/news/texassouthwest/stories/031410dntexprivatization. 42c97d3.html]

- *New York.* A scandal erupted in 2011 regarding the CityTime project, an effort to modernize New York's payroll system, streamline employee timekeeping, and discipline public workers who were padding their paychecks with undeserved overtime. The project was supposed to save the city millions of dollars, but the administration had trouble keeping tabs on the goings-on of the outside contract.

The project was contracted out to Gerard Denault, a former executive with Science Applications International Corporation, who worked as the project's senior manager. Denault was charged with receiving over $5 million in kickbacks, as well as wire fraud conspiracy and money laundering, and several other CityTime consultants were accused of manipulating the city into paying out expensive contracts to business that they controlled, and then redirecting portions of that money to enrich themselves. [http://topics.nytimes.com/top/reference/timestopics/organizations/o/office_of_payroll_administration_nyc/citytime/index.html?inline = nyt-classifier#]

The city paid $652 million for the CityTime project (though it originally expected to pay $73 million, a price that ballooned over a period of seven years), as well as a $41 million bill that it withheld payment on when the scandal came to light. In March of 2012, federal authorities announced that Science Applications Internal Corporation would pay over $500 million in restitution to the city and waive the $41 million bill—making it the largest amount ever to be paid to resolve an accusation of contract fraud involving a state or local government. [http://www.nytimes.com/2012/03/15/nyregion/contractor-in-citytime-payroll-scandal-to-pay-record-500-million.html?pagewanted = all]

There is also much controversy in Utica, New York, over a proposal to privatize school custodians—a decision that could result in over 100 employees, many with over 20 years of service under their belts, losing their jobs. The measures could save the district about $2.2 million annually, which would put a sizeable dent in the estimated $10 million shortfall predicted for 2012-2013 school year. The union was invited to submit a bid proposal to compete with private firms, but the district said that it would not bargain as it had in previous years. [http://www.macombdaily.com/articles/2012/03/16/news/doc4f63507690bb8254545774.txt]

- *Worldwide.* The threat of water privatization. According to the United Nations, 31 countries are facing water scarcity and 1 billion people lack access to clean drinking water. The demand for water is increasing as water sources are rapidly decreasing. According to Public Citizen, a non-profit consumer advocacy organization, "Rather than taking the dramatic action necessary to protect precious water resources, governments around the world are retreating from their responsibilities. Instead of acting decisively, they are bending to the will of giant transnational corporations that are poised to profit from the shortage of water. Fortune magazine has predicted that 'water is the oil of the 21st century' and corporations are rushing to invest in the water business." [http://www.citizen.org/cmep/Water/general/]

Most recently in 2013, there have been considerations for privatizing the U.S. Postal Service. Some conservatives would prefer to go even further and shift the Postal Service to a "public-private hybrid delivery model." In that case, private companies would handle the large majority of mail operations. [http://reason.org/news/show/apr-2013-postal-service.html]

Q 10:45 What is meant by *takeovers* in the public sector?

Closely related to privatization is the trend toward takeovers. For example, in the 1990s, Congress took control over many of the municipal services previously provided by the fiscally depleted and poorly managed District of Columbia. In 2000–2001, many of the functions and powers of the city government of Camden, New Jersey, were placed under state control while the incumbent mayor was tried and imprisoned for corruption.

Many school districts also experienced takeovers, when state legislators found that students were not receiving even minimally acceptable educations. This occurred in the final two decades of the twentieth century in Newark and Paterson, New Jersey; Hartford, Connecticut; and Detroit, Michigan.

In some instances, as in the Philadelphia school district, the schools have moved to a combination of publicly run and privatized schools, creating a competitive environment for a performance/price experiment in public education.

Q 10:46 What is meant by *reconstitution* in the public sector?

Similar to takeovers, reconstitution is a means of trying to improve the quality of public education, typically by negotiations among the state, school district officials and teachers' unions, which, if successful, result in the redesign of curricula, teacher work rules and qualifications, and other key components of the educational process. Some places where reconstitution has been attempted in recent years with mixed levels of success are New York City, San Francisco, and Cleveland.

Q 10:47 Are public employees' rights under collective bargaining agreements protected in situations of privatization, takeover, and reconstitution?

When privatization is the issue, the ability of a public employee union to block the effort may depend upon the existence of anti-subcontracting protections in the union's collective bargaining agreement. When the motivation is fiscal in nature, public employers sometimes enjoy the ability to abrogate collectively bargained obligations when appropriations are unavailable to fund those obligations (just as private-sector employers may be able to turn to the bankruptcy courts for legal relief from collectively negotiated obligations to their workers. (See "Bankruptcies, Mergers, and Acquisitions" in chapter 11.)

In takeover and reconstitution efforts, the courts have been disinclined to take union concerns into consideration. For example, in the major school takeover and reconstitution cases, court desegregation orders and new legislation have been effective in circumventing collectively bargained obligations, while denying unions standing to challenge the state actions. [*See, e.g.*, San Francisco NAACP v. San Francisco Unified Sch. Dist., No. 78-1445 (N.D. Cal. 1982); Reed v. Rhodes, 869 F. Supp. 1265 (N.D. Ohio 1994); Ohio Rev. Code Ann. §§ 3311.71–3311.73, 3302.01, *et seq.*; Shegog v. Board of Educ. of Chicago, 194 F.3d 836 (7th Cir. 1999);

Maryland Code Ann., Educ. Reform § 4-309; Maryland Regs. Code tit. 13A; Baltimore Teachers Union v. Maryland State Bd. of Educ., Civil Action No. 4-C-00-001937 (Circuit Ct. of Baltimore City, filed Apr. 21, 2000).]

Q 10:48   What are some examples of efforts to limit the scope of collective bargaining in the public sector?

Hand-in-hand with the rise of trends such as privatization, takeovers, and reconstitutions of public institutions, such as schools and prisons, a number of state legislatures have moved to restrict the scope of collective bargaining for public employee unions more broadly than merely seeking to circumvent them:

1. In 1993, Wisconsin enacted a law that capped "qualified economic offers" of wages and fringe benefits and required that an increase in one column be accompanied by a decrease in the other. [1993 Wisconsin Act 16]

2. In 1994, Michigan enacted legislation that:

   a. Expanded the prohibition against strikes in the education sector;

   b. Prohibited bargaining over subcontracting of non-instructional support services in the education sector;

   c. Prohibited bargaining over the length of the school year and day;

   d. Prohibited bargaining over the use of volunteers in schools; and

   e. Prohibited bargaining over experimental and pilot programs. [*See* Michigan AFL-CIO v. Michigan Empt. Relations Comm'n, 453 Mich. 362 (1995).]

3. In 1995, Illinois amended the state's collective bargaining law to prohibit bargaining in K-12 and community colleges concerning class size, layoffs, privatization, class schedules, and school calendars. Additionally, non-certificated employees lost tenure.

4. In 1998, when the school superintendent shut down the Philadelphia schools for lack of money, the Pennsylvania legislature passed a new law limiting school employee collective bargaining rights in financially distressed school districts. [1998 Pa. Legislative Service Act 1998-46] In August 2000, the Philadelphia Federation of Teachers (PFT) requested the Philadelphia School District to maintain the terms and conditions of the collective agreement set to expire August 31; the school district declined, citing the new state statute. The PFT sued and the action was later dismissed. [Kirsch v. School Dist. of Philadelphia, No. 563 Pa. 345 (Pa. 2000)]

5. More recently, in an oblique attack on a public union's collective bargaining rights, the State of Washington and a class of non-union public school employees brought two separate lawsuits against the public education employees' union, alleging that the union had violated a state statute by using non-member employees' agency-shop fees to make political expenditures without their affirmative authorization. In the state's case, the state Superior Court granted partial summary judgment for the state and, after trial, found that union had violated the statute. In the non-members'

case, the Superior Court denied the union's motion for dismissal and stayed the proceedings pending an interlocutory appeal. Union appealed both cases. The state Court of Appeals reversed the judgment for the state, and reversed the trial court's order in the non-members' case in an unpublished opinion, holding in each case that the statute was unconstitutional. Review was granted and the two cases were consolidated. The Supreme Court of Washington affirmed, agreeing that the statute's affirmative-consent requirement violated the First Amendment and certiorari was granted. The U.S. Supreme Court unanimously held that it does not violate the First Amendment for a state to require that its public-sector labor unions receive affirmative authorization from a non-member before spending that non-member's agency-shop fees for election-related purposes. [Davenport v. Washington Educ. Ass'n, 551 U.S. 177 (2007)] (See Q 10:59 for further discussion of limits on union-dues requirements in the public sector.)

6. In 2011, Republican senators of Wisconsin adopted a bill that will greatly curtail collective bargaining rights for workers in the public sector in an effort to balance its budget and allow the private sector to create new jobs. Despite a months-long stalemate between Democrats and Republicans, the bill was eventually pushed through on a technicality: Republicans removed the elements of Governor Scott Walker's original bill that related to appropriating funds, thus lifting a requirement that 20 senators be present for the vote. Only 19 senators were present at the time of voting, as Senate Democrats had left the state in order to prevent a quorum. In the end, Republicans approved the measure 18 to 1.

Democrats condemned the Republicans' actions, saying that it was a violation of open meetings requirements. [http://www.nytimes.com/2011/03/10/us/10wisconsin.html?pagewanted = all] (See Q 10:36 for more information on this bill.)

Q 10:49 What are some recent efforts made to restrict organized labor?

Several states and legislators have introduced bills that would limit or even deny collective bargaining rights. Some of these bills include:

- *Federal: Senate Bill 5811*. Democratic Senator Rodney Tom introduced a bill that would mandate that wellness programs be a part of state employees' health plans starting on January 1, 2014. Senate Bill 5811 also would remove health care from the issues that are subject to collective bargaining. [http://www.theolympian.com/2013/02/18/2428487/no-collective-bargaining-for-state.html]

- *Tennessee*. A bill was introduced that would deny teachers the right to negotiate through collective bargaining with boards of education about working conditions.

- *Wisconsin*. Governor Scott Walker's law, 2011 Wisconsin Act 10 that essentially eliminates collective bargaining for public employees, also requires employees to pay half of their pension costs and at least 12 percent of health care costs. It repeals most bargaining rights currently held by public employees, makes it legal for public employees to refuse to make payments to unions, and requires unions to hold annual elections just to remain in existence. As this publication goes to press, a challenge to the law was on the Wisconsin Supreme Court's doorstep.

- *Ohio.* Senate Bill 5, which would have abolished most collective bargaining rights for public workers, was enacted but later repealed by voter referendum.

- *Iowa.* House Study Bill 117 would take health insurance and layoff procedures from the items that must be negotiated under the state's collective bargaining laws for public employees. The bill is expected to pass.

- *Michigan.* Several bills are in the works, including:

  - House Bill 4205: This bill would repeal the state's prevailing wage law that requires union-scale pay for all public construction projects, and which establishes rates of pay based on collective bargaining.

  - SB 120: This bill would allow counties and local governments to create "right-to-work" zones, in which employers would be prohibited from requiring workers to be union members as a condition of employment.

  - House Bill 4205: This bill would repeal binding arbitration for police and firefighters. [http://www.csg.org/pubs/capitolideas/enews/issue66_2.aspx]

- *Illinois.* Governor Pat Quinn signed SB 1556, a bill that allows the governor to deny collective bargaining rights for up to 3,580 managers and supervisors. The law applies to "managerial or supervisory positions under the governor and other statewide offices—such as the secretary of state and attorney general—that are not currently represented by a union or those who have gained representation since December 2008." [http://www.myfoxtampabay.com/story/21895248/quinn-signs-state-employee-union-restrictions#ixzz2QZT29p2s]

- *Kansas.* House Bill 2027 would drastically reduce teachers' collective bargaining rights: "The measure would reduce from 30 to five the number of issues that teachers could negotiate with local school boards. For example, teachers could still negotiate for pay and sick leave but not performance evaluations. And opponents of the bill said even pay negotiations would be undermined because the legislation would allow an alternative pay plan for some teachers." [http://www2.ljworld.com/news/2013/mar/06/bill-limiting-collective-bargaining-teachers-draws/]

- *Arizona.* There are four bills recently passed that restrict organized labor in the state:

  - SB1348: Prohibits public employers from paying a public employee for any union activity, although employees are still able to receive compensated leave for personal reasons.

  - SB1349: Public employers are prohibited from deducting any payments to a third party from an employee's paycheck unless the employee provides annual written or electronic permission.

- SB1350: Prohibits those providing contracted labor or services to the state or a political subdivision, such as a city or town, from striking or stopping work in any other way. [http://www.azcentral.com/news/politics/articles/20130218bills-target-public-sector-unions.html?nclick_check = 1]

On the other hand, three Missouri Democrats recently signed a bill that would make it illegal for state legislators to do so much as suggest laws that would limit unions' collective bargaining rights. The bill would prevent (ever-popular) suggestions of right-to-work laws, as the text states, "Any member of the general assembly who proposes a piece of legislation that further restricts the right of an individual to bargain collectively, as set forth under section 29, article I of the Missouri Constitution, shall be guilty of a class D felony." [http://patdollard.com/2013/02/missouri-dems-propose-bill-to-make-it-a-felony-to-limit-union-power/]

Q 10:50   Can employee unions deduct money from members' paychecks in order to fund political activities?

Several states have passed bills that would restrict political fundraising by public employee unions and teachers. The (mostly Republican) proponents of such bills claims that they remove any government influence from payroll deductions, while opponents of such bills claim that they are an unlawful effort to keep employees from participating in the political process, or even an effort to eliminate public employee unions altogether. Some examples of current such bills include:

- *Kansas.* In 2013, the Kansas Senate approved a bill prohibiting public employee unions from deducting money from members' paychecks to pay for political activities. The bill was approved 24-16, with only Republicans voting for it. The House later approved the bill as well. [http://www2.ljworld.com/news/2013/mar/14/senate-approves-chamber-backed-bill-opposed-unions/; http://news.yahoo.com/kan-house-passes-bill-public-151648380.html]
- *Maine.* Rep. Peter Johnson, R-Greenville, submitted a bill that would prevent a conflict of interest by prohibiting public employee unions from contributing to campaigns of candidates for state office.

[http://bangordailynews.com/2013/01/24/news/state/gop-lawmakers-bill-would-bar-public-employee-unions-from-giving-to-political-campaigns/]

Q 10:51   Can public employees opt out of funding public employee unions?

In most cases, public employees must fund the applicable union—usually in the form of "fair share" payments—even if they decline to become members of the union themselves. However, some states are attempting to pass bills that would change that. In Oregon, for example, Initiative Petition 9 aims to allow employees to withhold both their membership and their money. In Wisconsin,

Governor Scott Walker has proposed a bill that would essentially eliminate collective bargaining for public employees, make it legal for public employees to refuse to make payments to unions, and require unions to hold annual elections just to remain in existence. Such measures would, of course, erode funding overall for public employee unions, but proponents of such bills claim it is a civil rights issue, and not anti-union. [http://www.oregonlive.com/opinion/index. ssf/2013/03/a_timely_debate_about_union_fu.html]

Q 10:52   What efforts have been made to limit teacher tenure?

A number of states have placed restrictions on teacher tenure:

1. Colorado, Florida, Massachusetts, New Mexico, and South Dakota have replaced the term *tenure* with terms such as *non-renewal contract* and *continuing contract*, but have retained many of the guarantees of continued employment on good behavior. [*See* Colorado Rev. Stat. Ann. § 22-63-203; Fla. Stat. Ann. § 231.61; Mass. Gen. Laws Ann. ch. 71, § 22-10-1.]

2. Connecticut, Michigan, and New York have streamlined the process by which tenure can be rescinded and a teacher's employment terminated. [Conn. Gen. Stat. Ann. § 5-242; Mich. Comp. Laws Ann. § 3.91; N.Y. Educ. Law § 3012]

3. Wisconsin has eliminated statutory tenure but permits collective bargaining of tenure-like protections. [Wis. Stat. Ann. § 118.22]

4. Nebraska has eliminated K-12 teacher tenures. [http://www.nsea.org/policy/salaries/teacher_tenure.htm]

5. In Michigan, Bills 4625, 4626, 4627, and 4628, now Public Acts 100-103 were signed into law in 2011. The laws create standardized evaluation methods to measure instructor effectiveness and increase the requirements for achieving and maintaining tenure. Teachers must complete five probationary years of teaching, rather than four, during which time a local controlling board evaluate and rate the teacher's effectiveness. If the teacher receives three "effective" ratings consecutively, and after completing four years at the same school, he or she will receive tenure. The laws also eliminate the "last in, first out" seniority policy that traditionally protected teachers with the most experience. [http://news.heartland.org/newspaper-article/2011/08/03/mi-legislature-limits-teacher-tenure]

6. In Illinois, education reform measure, SB 7, was approved 112-1. SB 7 seeks to create new restrictions on job-protecting tenure, make layoff decisions based on ability and credentials rather than seniority, and to make it easier to fire tenured teachers. The initiative aims to "improve learning by improving instruction" and was overwhelmingly approved. [http://www.rrstar.com/carousel/x447609020/Illinois-House-sends-school-reform-bill-to-Pat-Quinn]

7. In Idaho, Governor C.L. Otter signed a bill to eliminate tenure for new teachers and teachers who have yet to attain it, as part of an effort to reform the state's K-12 system. Supporters of the legislation claim that it will give more power to locally elected school board officials in regard to

labor relations. However, the Idaho Education Association claims that the plan will only take rights away from teachers and unions. Under the new proposal, teachers with seniority would not be automatically safe from school district workforce cuts. [http://www.stateline.org/live/details/story?contentId = 560323 and http://www.foxnews.com/politics/2011/03/09/idaho-votes-phase-teacher-tenure-restrict-collective-bargaining/]

8. Several other states have signed bills that end the "last-in, first-out" layoff policy that has ruled for so long. These bills prohibit using seniority as the main factor in deciding whether or not to fire a teacher.

9. On March 13, 2009, the Kentucky Community and Technical College System Board of Regents followed through on its December 2008 proposal to end tenure at the 14 two-year colleges in the system. Beginning July 1, 2009, all new faculty were offered either one- to four-year contracts or at-will employee status. The 168 faculty members eligible for tenure at the time were grandfathered in under the old policy. [http://www.thefreelibrary.com/Kentucky + colleges + tenures + for + new + faculty.–a0198472061]

In higher education, the clear trend, some three decades in the making, has reduced tenured faculty from 65 percent of the total professorate to a mere 35 percent today.

A similar trend is visible in the K-12. For example, in November 2009, the *New York Times* reported that New York City public schools would immediately begin to use student test scores as a factor in deciding which teachers earn tenure, a proposal that has been bitterly opposed by the teachers' union and criticized as putting too much weight on standardized exams. [http://www.nytimes.com/2009/11/26/education/26teachers.html?_r = 1] This marks a significant shift from the typical American approach: a teacher who keeps her nose clean and earns her master's degree is more or less automatically tenured upon completion of a specified number of years . . . usually five or fewer.

Higher education administrators also are looking for creative ways to avoid the lifetime commitment that the award of tenure can include. For example, reported *Inside Higher Ed* on March 10, 2010 [http://www.insidehighered.com/news/2010/03/10/webster], the majority of junior faculty of Webster University, headquartered in St. Louis and with satellite campuses across the globe, are choosing term contracts that require performance review every five years. The carrot is a guaranteed paid-sabbatical leave, also every fifth year. ["In Lieu of Tenure," *Inside Higher Ed*, Mar. 10, 2010]

It may even be a mistake to think that tenure is an effective shield against termination. Consider the case of Clark Atlanta University. In February 2009, the school laid off 100 employees, including 70 full-time faculty members, some with tenure. [http://www.insidehighered.com/news/2009/02/09/cau]

The AAUP has subsequently issued a report in which the profession/labor organization "concludes that the university's administration declared a nonexistent 'enrollment emergency' last February as a pretext for firing about

55 full-time faculty members without due process." [http://chronicle.com/article/AAUP-Report-Slams-Clark/63515/] The affected professors were paid four weeks of unconditional severance salary. The report concluded that they were denied academic due process to which they were entitled under the university's regulations as well as AAUP-supported standards and that the administration's alleged "enrollment emergency" was a pretext for avoiding affordance of due process. The report also concluded that the administration, in selecting faculty members for release based mainly on its assessment of their relative lack of merit, effectively dismissed them for cause. Finally, the committee concluded that the one month of severance salary offered by the administration unconditionally to all dismissed faculty members was sorely deficient and that the modest additional amount of severance subsequently offered was a deplorable means of pressuring vulnerable faculty members to forfeit avenues of appeal otherwise open to them and to release the university from any further claims. [http://www.aaup.org/AAUP/pubsres/academe/2010/JF/nb/nb7.htm]

Similar reports are emerging from the K-12 public school arena. Most dramatic of these is the February decision of the Central Falls, Rhode Island, school board to fire all its teachers at the end of this academic year. [Jennifer D. Jordan, "Every Central Falls Teacher Fired, Labor Outrage," *Providence Journal*, February 24, 2010]

The news story goes on to note that the U.S. Education Secretary Arne Duncan "applauded" the board members for "showing courage and doing the right thing for kids." By contrast, President George Nee of the Rhode Island AFL-CIO called the mass firing, "immoral, illegal, unjust, irresponsible, disgraceful and disrespectful," according to the newspaper's account.

"Duncan is requiring states, for the first time, to identify their lowest 5 percent of schools—those that have chronically poor performance and low graduation rates—and fix them using one of four methods: school closure; takeover by a charter or school-management organization; transformation which requires a longer school day, among other changes; and 'turnaround' which requires the entire teaching staff be fired and no more than 50 percent rehired in the fall." [http://www.projo.com/news/content/central_falls_trustees_vote_02-24-10_EOHI83C_v59.3c21342.html]

In 2013, North Carolina state Senate leader Phil Berger proposed Senate Bill 361, which would end teacher tenure and allow school boards to use their financial resources as they see fit. Berger said he thought there were only a small number of ineffective teachers in North Carolina, "but if it's one teacher and it's a teacher that's teaching your child, it's a huge problem."

After June 30, 2014, tenure would no longer be awarded, and teachers could be offered employment contracts of between one and three years. Multiyear contracts would only be offered if teachers met specific requirements under a state program for assessing teacher performance.

Berger also said he did not anticipate lowering the amount of money teachers make, but those details have yet to be ironed out. [http://www.newsobserver.com/2013/03/19/2763319/berger-announces-major-education.html#storylink = cpy]

Similarly in Missouri, education reformers are proposing a bill that would eliminate teacher tenure and require performance-based evaluations of teachers. Public teachers would be at-will employees rather than tenured after five years of service, employment contracts would be limited to three years at most, and schools would be forced to perform teacher evaluations "based upon quantifiable student performance data as measured by objective criteria" (i.e., standardized test scores). The proposal also details the reasons a teacher could be fired, including "immoral conduct." [http://eagnews.org/missouri-citizens-seek-end-to-tenure-tougher-teacher-evaluations/]

Q 10:53   Is progressive discipline of tenured employees used?

Yes. Progressive discipline requires that employers impose progressively more severe penalties for successive violations of employment rules and regulations. Such a disciplinary system of progressively more serious punishments for repeated misconduct provides important protection for faculty because it builds in additional safeguards of due process. The system is also helpful to administrators because it provides the opportunity to deal with improper behavior before it worsens. In an academic setting, the least severe is a written reprimand to the professor's or the K-12 teacher's personnel file. While this may seem a small step for an administrator, it can be a giant step on the road to reforming a recalcitrant senior faculty member. More severe steps can include denial of a scheduled pay increase; a reduction in salary, either temporary or permanent; and suspension without pay. All have been upheld by various courts in a variety of jurisdictions.

The issue of faculty discipline is problematic for many reasons. Serious misconduct, such as falsification of credentials, sexual harassment of students or colleagues, or plagiarism, may justify dismissal of a tenured faculty member. Misconduct that is less serious, but still falls short of expected standards, will probably require some form of discipline. Few colleges and universities have policies specific to the discipline of faculty short of termination. However, many institutions address only the termination of a tenured appointment. It is necessary to examine the function of discipline in the academic environment and to develop standards of professional conduct for faculty.

Typically, in business situations, systems of progressive discipline begin with an oral warning to the employee after the first violation, a written warning after the second violation, a suspension without pay for the third, and termination for the fourth violation. In this model, a decision maker will review the employee's discipline history. This history is taken into consideration when deciding if the present discipline is appropriate.

Employees are protected by this model because they are made aware of problematic behavior and have the opportunity to change behavior before sanctions are applied. In the academic setting, administrators and faculty members may be better off with sanctions that are less severe than dismissal, which would enable them to respond early to inappropriate faculty behavior. This would also result in the ultimate imposition of dismissal for only the most serious misconduct.

Using discipline short of dismissal can be effective when dealing with a faculty member who exhibits a history of mild but repeated inappropriate behavior with students or staff, or neglect of teaching or research. This is a way of establishing a record of the misconduct and the institution's response in the event that the behavior persists and there is a movement for dismissal. Therefore, prompt attention to misconduct followed by progressive discipline, carries the possibility of "rehabilitating" a questionable faculty member while it also lays the groundwork for eventual dismissal. Common sense tells us that intervention before the behavior becomes a serious problem for the institution is the best plan.

Q 10:54   What is an example of a court upholding progressive discipline culminating in termination of a tenured employee?

In *Trimble v. West Virginia Board of Directors* [209 W. Va. 420 (2001)], the Supreme Court of Appeals of West Virginia ruled that the administration "should not have fired a tenured professor for insubordination before resorting to other progressive disciplinary measures" under West Virginia's constitution. The court stated that the tenured professor, who had an unblemished record, had a protected property interest in his position. Under the circumstances of the case, the court found that due process requires the educational institution to use progressive discipline to attempt the correct insubordinate behavior before it may resort to termination.

Majority and dissenting opinions. The appeals court majority held, "The prior employment termination decisions of this Court and decisions in other jurisdictions, lead us to our conclusion and result and holding that constitutional due process is denied when a tenured public higher education teacher, who has a previously unblemished record, is immediately terminated for an incident of insubordination that is minor in its consequences. Under such circumstances, due process requires the educational institution to impose progressive disciplinary sanctions in an attempt to correct the teacher's insubordinate conduct before it may resort to termination." The dissenting panelist complained,

> In addition, the majority sends an unmistakable message to State college and university administrations that even the most recalcitrant, inflexible, and uncooperative tenured teachers cannot be fired absent a protracted, and most likely futile, effort to bring them into line. The undisputed facts indicate that the appellant missed at least four instructional meetings, adamantly refused to complete a syllabus in the required format, and, when advised of the College's intention to terminate his employment for insubordination, declined an opportunity to meet with administrators to rebut the charges and discuss the matter. It was only *after* his termination that he filed the grievance that has ended up in this Court. Despite these facts, the majority finds that the appellant's termination was improper. The majority opinion unreasonably burdens college administrators with the extra expense, in both time and money, of additional hearings and delays prior to the termination of ineffective or insubordinate employees. It thus robs administrators of the ability to take quick and decisive action. One casualty of this unnecessary extra expense may be the ability to dispense a quality education at a reasonable cost.

While the dissenting justice had a point, the case nevertheless stood for the proposition that progressive discipline, ending if necessary in termination of employment, was sanctioned by the court.

Q 10:55   Are there any standards for disciplining tenured employees?

The American Association of University Professors (AAUP) has developed a *Statement on Professional Ethics*, which states:

- Professors, guided by a deep conviction of the worth and dignity of the advancement of knowledge, recognize the special responsibilities placed upon them. Their primary responsibility to their subject is to seek and to state the truth as they see it. To this end professors devote their energies to developing and improving their scholarly competence. They accept the obligation to exercise critical self-discipline and judgment in using, extending, and transmitting knowledge. They practice intellectual honesty. Although professors may follow subsidiary interests, these interests must never seriously hamper or compromise their freedom of inquiry.

- As teachers, professors encourage the free pursuit of learning in their students. They hold before them the best scholarly and ethical standards of their discipline. Professors demonstrate respect for students as individuals and adhere to their proper roles as intellectual guides and counselors. Professors make every reasonable effort to foster honest academic conduct and to ensure that their evaluations of students reflect each student's true merit. They respect the confidential nature of the relationship between professor and student. They avoid any exploitation, harassment, or discriminatory treatment of students. They acknowledge significant academic or scholarly assistance from them. They protect their academic freedom.

- As colleagues, professors have obligations that derive from common membership in the community of scholars. Professors do not discriminate against or harass colleagues. They respect and defend the free inquiry of associates. In the exchange of criticism and ideas, professors show due respect for the opinions of others. Professors acknowledge academic debt and strive to be objective in their professional judgment of colleagues. Professors accept their share of faculty responsibilities for the governance of their institution.

- As members of an academic institution, professors seek above all to be effective teachers and scholars. Although professors observe the stated regulations of the institution, provided the regulations do not contravene academic freedom, they maintain their right to criticize and seek revision. Professors give due regard to their paramount responsibilities within their institution in determining the amount and character of work done outside it. When considering the interruption or termination of their service, professors recognize the effect of their decision upon the program of the institution and give due notice of their intentions.

- As members of their community, professors have the rights and obligations of other citizens. Professors measure the urgency of these obligations in the light of their responsibilities to their subject, to their students, to their profession, and to their institution. When they speak or act as private persons, they avoid creating the impression of speaking or acting for their college or university. As citizens engaged in a profession that depends upon freedom for its health and integrity, professors have a particular obligation to promote conditions of free inquiry and to further public understanding of academic freedom.

The *Statement on Professional Ethics* has been incorporated into faculty handbooks and collective bargaining agreements at hundreds of colleges and universities.

Sanctions short of termination of employment. Since 1973, an AAUP Commission on Academic Tenure recommended "that each institution develop and adopt an enumeration of sanctions short of dismissal that may be applied in cases of demonstrated irresponsibility or professional misconduct for which some penalty short of dismissal should be imposed. These sanctions and the due-process procedures for complaint, hearing, judgment, and appeal should be developed initially by joint faculty-administrative action." The following sanctions short of dismissal were identified:

- Oral reprimand;
- Written reprimand;
- A recorded reprimand;
- Restitution (for instance, payment for damage done to individuals or to the institution);
- Loss of prospective benefits for a stated period (for instance, suspension of "regular" or "merit" increase in salary or suspension of promotion eligibility);
- A fine;
- Reduction in salary for a stated period;
- Suspension from service for a stated period, without other prejudice.

Q 10:56   What is the applicability of these standards to K-12 public school employees?

In *Kirkland v. St. Vrain Valley School District* [464 F.3d 1182 (10th Cir. 2006)], the District hired Kirkland in 1999 to be the assistant superintendent in charge of the District's auxiliary services. In that position, Kirkland supervised 10 District departments, including the financial services department. Kirkland was employed pursuant to a series of one-year contracts, the last of which ran from July 1, 2002, through June 30, 2003.

In November 2002, Kirkland informed Superintendent Randy Zila that one of Kirkland's employees in the finance department had made several accounting errors that had resulted in an unexpected and dramatic shortfall in the District's budget. Due to these accounting errors, the District had been operating under the mistaken belief that it had a slight budget surplus; in fact, the District had between a $9 and $13 million deficit, and would not be able to meet its next payroll. The District could only continue operating if it received "substantial loans from the State of Colorado and [implemented] significant spending cuts."

After this budget shortfall came to light, Superintendent Randy Zila and Assistant Superintendent Tom Garcia met with Kirkland, on November 13, 2002, and informed Kirkland that the School Board (the Board) had lost confidence in his ability to provide the Board with accurate budget information. They requested that Kirkland resign. By the end of this meeting, Kirkland had agreed to resign in return for the District's continuing to pay him his salary and benefits through the remainder of his one-year employment contract. Garcia "accepted" Kirkland's handwritten resignation. Several days later, however, at the November 16 school board meeting, the Board rejected Kirkland's resignation and the resignation agreement. The Board instead placed Kirkland on unpaid administrative leave.

In April 2003, Kirkland and the District reached a termination agreement. That written agreement, dated April 15, 2003, provided that Kirkland would "not request a hearing by the Board of Education regarding the termination," and in return, the Board would terminate Kirkland's employment without public comment. The Board did so on April 23, 2003.

Unpaid leave as valid disciplinary action. The appeals panel observed that in *Gilbert v. Homar* [520 U.S. 924 (1997)], the U.S. Supreme Court noted, "We have not had occasion to decide whether the protections of the Due Process Clause extend to discipline of tenured public employees short of termination." The panel then defined the issue before them as whether the plaintiff had received all the process due to him, when he was suspended without pay in lieu of outright termination. The judges, referencing *Gilbert*, stated, "in determining what process is due, account must be taken of the length and finality of the deprivation. [Distinguishing] the employee in *Loudermill*, who faced termination, [from the employee in *Gilbert*, who] faced only a temporary suspension without pay [, the Court noted that] [s]o long as the suspended employee receives a sufficiently prompt post-suspension hearing, the lost income is relatively insubstantial (compared with termination), and fringe benefits such as health and life insurance are often not affected at all."

Applying this standard, the Tenth Circuit held, "In this case, Kirkland had the right to pursue a post-suspension grievance immediately following his suspension. And this grievance procedure provided for expedited review. So, although Kirkland has a private interest that will be affected by a suspension, that effect is attenuated by the relatively prompt post-suspension hearing that is provided." In other words, the appeals panel was satisfied that the plaintiff had received all the process he deserved. This suggests that, if accorded appropriate, prompt procedural rights, tenured employees in the K-12 environment can be subjected to progressive discipline, potentially leading to termination of employment, under similar standards as those outlined above for tenured employees in higher education and research organizations.

In fact, the court went on to suggest that no notice is demanded before the imposition of progressive discipline upon a K-12 tenured employee.

> After weighing these factors, we conclude Kirkland was not constitutionally entitled to notice and an opportunity to respond *before* the District suspended him without pay. In particular, the District's strong interest in suspending Kirkland, under circumstances requiring quick action to address the budget shortfall, outweigh Kirkland's temporary loss of pay. This is particularly true in light of the post-suspension grievance procedure that Kirkland could have promptly invoked upon his suspension without pay. In light of our conclusion that Kirkland was not entitled to pre-suspension due process, he has failed to allege a constitutional violation resulting from the District suspending him without pay before providing notice and an opportunity for Kirkland to respond. Therefore, the individual Defendants are entitled to qualified immunity on this claim as well.

Q 10:57   How do social media figure in disciplinary issues involving full-time faculty at public universities?

Indiscreet postings by faculty on social networking sites, notably Facebook, have led to disciplinary actions, up to and including termination:

1. In February 2010, Sociology Professor Gloria Y. Gadsen was escorted off the campus of Pennsylvania's East Stroudsburg University, a part of the Commonwealth's 14-campus state university system, and subsequently terminated, after she posted on her Facebook page, "Had a good day today, didn't want to kill even one student," and "Does anyone know where I can find a very discrete hitman, it's been that kind of a day." Facebook then became the scene of a "save Professor Gadsen" campaign. She was eventually reinstated.

   [Castagnera, James Ottavio & John Lanza, "Social Networking and Faculty Discipline: A Pennsylvania Case Points Toward Confrontational Times, Requiring Collective Bargaining Attention," *Journal of Collective Bargaining in the Academy*, V.1, No. 1 (Dec. 2010), accessible at http://thekeep.eiu.edu/jcba/vol2/iss1/5/]

2. In May 2011, Arkansas State University's Mountain Home campus fired the director of its funeral science program, after he wrote on his Facebook wall that he "hopes this teaching gig works out. Guess I shouldn't have cheated through mortuary school and faked people out. Crap!" The professor, who was there on a two-year contract subsequently sued the school, alleging that the real reason for his firing was an inquiry he made to a school official about the possible misdirection of student fees. [http://findarticles.com/p/articles/mi_hb5248/is_18_28/ai_n57526938/].

   As a general proposition, it can be stated that the issue of what faculty at public universities may and may not say remains a highly controversial one, implicating the First Amendment free-speech and academic freedom, as well as privacy/search-and-seizure concerns.

Q 10:58   Have faculty at public universities been required to reveal what they said in their e-mail accounts?

In several states, conservative think tanks and GOP party members have sought to obtain the e-mail accounts of public university professors, using the particular state's freedom of information act as the pry bar to break open the accounts:

- In March 2011, the Wisconsin Republican Party filed a motion in court seeking access to the personal e-mails of three University of Wisconsin professors. The request demanded copies of "all emails in and out of [Prof. Cronon's] state email account from January 1, 2011 to present which reference any of the following terms: Republican, Scott Walker, recall, collective bargaining, AFSCME [American Federation of State, County, and Municipal Employees], WEAC [Wisconsin Education Association Council], rally, union, Alberta Darling, Randy Hopper, Dan Kapanke, Rob Cowles, Scott Fitzgerald [Senate majority leader], Sheila Harsdorf, Luther Olsen, Glenn Grothman, Mary Lazich, Jeff Fitzgerald [speaker of the assembly], Marty Beil [executive director of the Wisconsin State Employees Union], or Mary Bell [president of WEAC]." The legislators referenced in the request were fending off recall campaigns. [http://hnn.us/roundup/entries/137911.html]

- In Michigan, a conservative think tank, the Mackinac Center for Public Policy, similarly sought access through a public-records request to the e-mail accounts of faculty in the labor studies programs at Wayne State, the University of Michigan and Michigan State. [http://www.aft.org/new spubs/news/2011/041311email.cfm]

- In November 2011, a Prince William County Circuit Court Judge in Virginia issued a ruling in a controversy involving the University of Virginia and a former faculty member, whose area of expertise was climate change. A Freedom of Information Act request brought by the American Tradition Institute sought extensive records, many of which the University of Virginia and Professor Michael Mann contended were protected by privilege. The judge allowed Mann, who by then was a professor at Penn State, to intervene in the case, and further ordered that the documents the University of Virginia deemed to be exempt from the FOIA request be reviewed in camera at the institute's expense. [http://www.virginia.edu/uvatoday/newsRelease.php?id = 16541]

  Bottom line, these assaults on public employees' e-mail accounts are only one aspect of the struggle being played out in the public education environment, both at the K-12 as well as the university levels, and this struggle in turn is only an aspect of the larger ideological and political struggle between conservative state governors and legislators, on the one hand, and the more liberal teachers, public employee unions and the like, in such states as Michigan, New Jersey, Pennsylvania, and Wisconsin. (See Qs 10:44 and 10:48.)

Q 10:59   What initiatives have states taken to limit union dues requirements?

The following are examples of actions taken by the states to attempt to limit union dues requirements:

1. California State Proposition 226 would have forbidden public employee unions from using dues for political contributions without their members' express permission. The proposition was rejected by California voters in 1998.

2. In 1998, Nevada tried to enact a law that would have required union members to request in writing that their employers earmark a portion of their union dues deductions for political purposes. The bill was declared unconstitutional before it was ever enacted. [Nevadans for Fairness v. Heller, 1998 WL 357316 (D. Nev. June 10, 1998)]

3. Ohio's 1995 law, aimed at prohibiting deductions from public employer payrolls for political purposes, also prohibited solicitation of public employees for political contributions. It was successfully challenged by public employee unions on First Amendment grounds. [Toledo Area AFL-CIO Council v. Pizza, 154 F.3d 307 (6th Cir. 1998); United Auto Workers, Local 1112 v. Philonena, 700 N.E.2d 936 (Ohio App. 1998)]

4. Michigan's statute, requiring both employers and unions to get permission at least annually for payroll/dues deductions for political purposes, passed constitutional muster. [Michigan State AFL-CIO v. Miller, 103 F.3d 1240 (6th Cir. 1997)]

5. Voters in Washington State enacted an initiative restricting the use of dues paid by agency-dues members of the bargaining unit from use for political purposes. The new law was challenged by the Washington Education Association. The case reached the U.S. Supreme Court, which held that the law does not violate the First Amendment. [*See* Davenport v. Washington Educ. Ass'n, 551 U.S. 177 (2007).]

6. In Oregon, Initiative Petition 9 aims to allow employees to withhold both their membership and their money.

7. In Wisconsin, Governor Scott Walker's law, which essentially ends collective bargaining in the state, survived Supreme Court review. [State ex. rel. Ozanne. V. Fitzgerald, 334 wis. 2d 70, 798 N.W.2d 436 (2011).] However, the appeal was dismissed on a legal technicality. By early 2013, a similar case had worked its way back to the Court of Appeals, which urged the Supreme Court to reach the merits of the plaintiffs' constitutionality claims. [Madison Teachers, Inc. V. Walker, 2013 wh1760805 (Wis. App., Apr. 25, 2013).]

Q 10:60   Can a public employer abrogate collective bargaining agreement provisions in times of fiscal emergency?

In the leading decision of the 1990s, the court approved Baltimore's abrogation of its collective agreements with its municipal employees by enacting forced layoffs and furloughs for all public employees except firefighters. [Baltimore Teachers Union v. Mayor and City Council of Baltimore, 6 F.3d 1012 (4th Cir. 1993), *cert. denied*, 510 U.S. 1141 (1994)]

In 2001, a group of unions brought an action, challenging a District of Columbia Financial Responsibility and Management Authority order abrogating provisions of existing collective bargaining agreements regarding calculation of overtime pay. After the District Court ruled that the Control Board had exceeded its statutory authority, Congress retroactively ratified the order. On the Control Board's motion to dismiss the suit, the District Court held that: (1) Congress did not improperly delegate its power to impose overtime wage standards by ratifying the Control Board's order, and (2) Congress was not constitutionally precluded from ratifying the order. [American Fed'n of Gov't Emps. v. District of Columbia, 133 F. Supp. 2d 35 (D.D.C. 2001)]

In 2011, the governors and legislators of a number of financially strapped states chose to radically amend their public sector labor laws rather than seeking relief from extant collective agreements in their courts. (See Q 10:36.)

Q 10:61   Can a public employer sever relations with its unions on the basis of the unions' organized crime affiliations?

Characterizing a memorandum of understanding between certain unions that provided labor at the Javits Convention Center and New York Convention Center Operating Corporation (NYCCOC) as being "a far cry" from the kind of contract that creates a constitutionally protected property interest in employment, the Second Circuit ruled that the Governor of New York was free to deal with other unions and to hire other workers if and when he wanted. [Abramson v. Pataki, 169 BNA L.R.R.M. 2336 (2d Cir. 2002)]

Under the memorandum of understanding between three labor unions and the New York Trade Show Contractors' Association and the NYCCOC, workers employed to move and set up exhibits in the Javits Center were drawn from the unions' hiring halls. In the wake of mid-1990s allegations of organized crime influence on the unions and the center, the governor denounced the memorandum of understanding (MOU) and had the state agency enter into direct relations with two unions from which it drew a largely new contingent of workers. Disappointed employees, who had enjoyed regular work under the old arrangement, sued the governor and the state.

The appeals court held that for a range of reasons the plaintiffs could not make out, as a matter of law, a cognizable constitutional claim to any property or liberty interests that had been violated by the public employer:

- The MOU did not require the NYCCOC to employ any specific workers at the Javits Center;

- The MOU did not involve the NYCCOC in the hiring of contractors;
- The MOU therefore did not create an employment relationship between the state agency and the plaintiffs/union members; and
- Even if an employment relationship could have been made out, nothing in the MOU prevented the agency from terminating that relationship at will.

Q 10:62   Does a state legislature violate public employees' equal protection rights if a new law limits their collective bargaining rights while allowing other employees in the same state to enjoy such rights?

No. Clearly, states are entitled to limit the unionization, collective bargaining, and work stoppage rights of employees with special responsibilities, such as police, firefighters, and teachers.

But what if some police, firefighters, or teachers are singled out for special limitations on these rights? This was the issue that confronted the U.S. Supreme Court in a case in which the Ohio legislature enacted a law denying university professors the right to bargain about their teaching workloads, while allowing teachers and professors at all other levels of public education to continue bargaining on this issue.

Holding that the Fourteenth Amendment is not offended by a state's action if there is a "rational relationship between the disparity of treatment and some legitimate governmental interest," the Court recognized the state's desire to have university faculty spend more time teaching students at state institutions to be such a legitimate interest. Significantly, the Court rejected the union's contention that there existed no evidence in the record to indicate that denying the professors collective bargaining rights enjoyed by all other public teachers had in fact increased their classroom time. The Court countered that this was not the crux of the issue; instead, the fact that a state legislature could rationally believe that its law would result in increased teaching time was sufficient to enable the statute to pass constitutional scrutiny. [Central State Univ. v. American Ass'n of Univ. Professors, Cent. State Univ. Chapter, 526 U.S. 124 (1999)]

Constitutional and Civil Rights

Q 10:63   Do public employees enjoy workplace rights under federal and state constitutions?

Federal, state, and local government agencies must conform their actions to the Bill of Rights and later U.S. constitutional amendments. State constitutions also contain constraints on government activities. Courts have long held that such constitutional rules as due process of law apply to government agencies in their roles as employers. For example, when the U.S. Supreme Court renders a decision restricting police officers' powers of search and seizure respecting crime suspects, courts will likely require supervisors of government employees to observe the same restrictions when investigations lead them into employees' desks or lockers. Perhaps most significant in recent years has been the legal battle revolving around mandatory drug tests for government workers. Additionally, First Amendment rights of speech and assembly have been used to support public employee unionization efforts.

Q 10:64   What are the limits imposed upon public employees' free-speech rights?

The employment practices of public employers may be matters of public concern—citizens and taxpayers may want to express their views on matters such as benefits for domestic partners, family leave, pension benefits, and even workforces. Public employees have a dual role: They are employees who are affected by such practices or policies, and they are also citizens (and taxpayers). Do the public employees, as citizens, have the right to speak out on matters relating to their employer's practices? Can a public employer prohibit its employees from speaking out on such issues? Does the First Amendment freedom of speech protect those employees from disciplinary action by the employer? How far does the First Amendment protection extend—does it cover all work-related speech of public employees? That is the question addressed by the Justice Kennedy and the Supreme Court in *Garcetti v. Ceballos*. [547 U.S. 410 (2006)]

Richard Ceballos was employed since 1989 as a deputy district attorney for the Los Angeles County District Attorney's Office. During the period relevant to this case, Ceballos was a calendar deputy in the office's Pomona branch, and in this capacity he exercised certain supervisory responsibilities over other lawyers. In February 2000, a defense attorney contacted Ceballos about a pending criminal case. The defense attorney said there were inaccuracies in an affidavit used to obtain a critical search warrant. The attorney informed Ceballos that he had filed a motion to challenge the warrant, but he also wanted Ceballos to review the case. After examining the affidavit and visiting the location it described, Ceballos determined the affidavit contained serious misrepresentations. Ceballos spoke with the warrant affiant, a deputy sheriff from the Los Angeles County Sheriff's Department, but he did not receive a satisfactory explanation for the perceived inaccuracies. He relayed his findings to his supervisors, Najera and Sundstedt, and followed up by preparing a disposition memorandum. The memo explained Ceballos' concerns and recommended dismissal of the case. Ceballos submitted the memo to Sundstedt for his review. A few days later, Ceballos presented Sundstedt with another memo, this one describing a second telephone conversation between Ceballos and the warrant affiant. Based on Ceballos' statements, a meeting was held to discuss the affidavit. Attendees included Ceballos, Sundstedt, and Najera, as well as the warrant affiant and other employees from the sheriff's department. The meeting allegedly became heated, with one lieutenant sharply criticizing Ceballos for his handling of the case. Despite Ceballos' concerns, Sundstedt decided to proceed with the prosecution, pending disposition of the defense motion to challenge.

The trial court held a hearing on the motion. Ceballos was called by the defense and recounted his observations about the affidavit, but the trial court rejected the challenge to the warrant.

Ceballos claimed that, in the aftermath of these events, he was subjected to a series of retaliatory employment actions. The actions included reassignment from his calendar deputy position to a trial deputy position, transfer to another courthouse, and denial of a promotion. Ceballos initiated an employment grievance, but the grievance was denied based on a finding that he had not suffered any retaliation. Unsatisfied, Ceballos sued in the United States District Court for the Central District of California, asserting that the petitioners violated the First and Fourteenth Amendments by retaliating against him based on his memo.

The petitioners responded that Ceballos' memo was not protected speech under the First Amendment. The petitioners moved for summary judgment, and the District Court granted their motion. Noting that Ceballos wrote his memo pursuant to his employment duties, the court concluded he was not entitled to First Amendment protection for the memo's contents. The Court of Appeals for the Ninth Circuit reversed, holding that "Ceballos's allegations of wrongdoing in the memorandum constitute protected speech under the First Amendment." In reaching its conclusion, the court looked to the First Amendment analysis set forth in two other Supreme Court cases. [Pickering v. Board of Educ. of Twp. High Sch. Dist. 205, Will Cnty., 391 U.S. 563 (1968); Connick v. Myers, 461 U.S. 138 (1983)] *Connick* instructs courts to begin by considering whether the expressions in question were made by the speaker "as a citizen upon matters of public concern." The Court of Appeals determined that Ceballos' memo, which recited what he thought to be governmental misconduct, was "inherently a matter of public concern." The court did not, however, consider whether the speech was made in Ceballos' capacity as a citizen. Instead, it relied on Circuit precedent, rejecting the idea that "a public employee's speech is deprived of First Amendment protection whenever those views are expressed, to government workers or others, pursuant to an employment responsibility." Having concluded that Ceballos' memo satisfied the public-concern requirement, the Court of Appeals proceeded to balance Ceballos' interest in his speech against his supervisors' interest in responding to it. The court struck the balance in Ceballos' favor, noting that petitioners "failed even to suggest disruption or inefficiency in the workings of the District Attorney's Office" as a result of the memo. The court further concluded that Ceballos' First Amendment rights were clearly established and that petitioners' actions were not objectively reasonable.

The Court made clear that public employees do not surrender all their First Amendment rights by reason of their employment. Instead, the First Amendment protects a public employee's right, in certain circumstances, to speak as a citizen addressing matters of public concern. *Pickering* provides a useful starting point in explaining the Court's doctrine. In that case, the relevant speech was a teacher's letter to a local newspaper, addressing issues including the funding policies of his school board. "The problem in any case," the Court stated, "is to arrive at a balance between the interests of the teacher, as a citizen, in commenting upon matters of public concern and the interest of the State, as an employer, in promoting the efficiency of the public services it performs through its employees." The Court found the teacher's speech "neither [was] shown nor can be presumed to have in any way either impeded the teacher's proper performance of his daily duties in the classroom or to have interfered with the regular operation of the schools generally." Thus, the Court concluded that "the interest of the school administration in limiting teachers' opportunities to contribute to public debate is not significantly greater than its interest in limiting a similar contribution by any member of the general public."

In *Garcetti*, Richard Ceballos believed the affidavit used to obtain a search warrant contained serious misrepresentations. He conveyed his opinion and recommendation in a memo to his supervisor. The fact that Ceballos expressed his views inside his office, instead of publicly, was not dispositive. Employees, in some cases, may receive First Amendment protection for expressions made at work. The controlling factor in *Garcetti* was that Ceballos' expressions were made pursuant to his duties as a calendar deputy. That consideration—the fact that Ceballos spoke as a prosecutor fulfilling a responsibility to advise his supervisor about how best to proceed with a pending case—distinguished Ceballos' case from those in which the First Amendment provides protection against discipline. The Supreme Court held that when public employees make statements pursuant to their official duties, the employees are not speaking as citizens for First Amendment purposes, and the Constitution does not insulate their communications from employer discipline.

The Supreme Court concluded that the First Amendment does not prohibit managerial discipline based on an employee's expressions made pursuant to official responsibilities. Because Ceballos' memo fell into this category, his allegation of unconstitutional retaliation was rejected because the First Amendment does not shield from discipline the expressions employees make pursuant to their professional duties. Therefore, a constitutional cause of action does not exist behind every statement a public employee makes in the course of doing his or her job.

The judgment of the Court of Appeals was reversed, and the case was remanded for proceedings consistent with the opinion.

(See also Qs 10:57 and 10:58, which deal with disciplinary issues arising from public employees—in these cases, faculty members at public universities—social-network and e-mail accounts.)

Playing out in Delaware as this publication went to press was the case of a public employee, represented by AFSCME, who was suspended after a co-worker complained that he felt harassed by the Confederate flag license plate that the former employee displayed on his personal automobile, which he drove to work. The Delaware Chapter of the American Civil Liberties Union took the employee's case, and advised the state's Department of Transportation that its action was unconstitutional.

In a published statement, the ACLU asserted, "Several federal courts have addressed this precise issue. They have repeatedly found that flags and other symbols, including Confederate Flag license plates, are entitled to First Amendment protection because they are variants of free speech. In a 2001 fourth circuit opinion, they went so far as to say: 'Flags, especially flags of a political sort, enjoy an honored position in the First Amendment hierarchy.'"

[http://www.aclu-de.org/news/aclu-de-intervenes-in-deldot-disciplinary-action/2012/03/29/]

Q 10:65   Do public employees have Fourth Amendment search-and-seizure rights where text messaging is involved?

In the spring of 2010, the nation's high court granted a writ of certiorari in *City of Ontario, Cal. v. Quon*, a case in which police officers' sexually explicit text messages resulted in disciplinary action.

On October 24, 2001, Arch Wireless contracted to provide text-messaging services for the City of Ontario, California. The city received 20 two-way alphanumeric pagers, which it distributed to its employees, including Ontario Police Department Sergeants Quon and Trujillo, in late 2001 or early 2002. Although the police sergeants were told that pager communications were not private, a supervisor allowed Quon to use the pager for personal use as long as he reimbursed the department for the overages. Quon reimbursed the department for overages but after some time, it was concluded that this payment system was not efficient. An investigation was launched and transcripts were requested to determine whether the messages were business related. According to the Memorandum, the transcripts revealed that Quon "had exceeded his monthly allotted characters by 15,158 characters," and that many of these messages were personal in nature and were often sexually explicit. These messages were directed to and received from, among others, the other plaintiffs in the case. Quon and his fellow officers, as well as one spouse, sued Arch Wireless, asserting Section 1983 claims grounded in Fourth Amendment unreasonable search-and-seizure. The U.S. District Court granted summary judgment for the defendant. The plaintiffs appealed.

On appeal, the court held:

1. The wireless provider was an "electronic communication service" (ECS) under federal Stored Communications Act (SCA), and had violated the SCA by releasing archived transcripts to the city. (Note: The SCA was enacted in 1986. It does not stand-alone, but rather it forms a part of the Electronic Communications Privacy Act and is codified at 18 U.S.C. §§ 2701 through 2712. The statute regulates voluntary and compelled disclosures of "stored wire and electronic communications and transactional records" held by third-party Internet service providers (ISPs));

2. The police officers had a reasonable expectation of privacy in the content of their text messages, given the informal policy of no auditing of messages upon payment for usage overages;

3. The scope of the department's search of text messages was unreasonable and violative of the Fourth Amendment, given less intrusive alternatives;

4. The police chief enjoyed a qualified immunity as to the Fourth Amendment claim; however,

5. The city and the police department were not protected by statutory immunity against invasion of the plaintiffs' privacy claim under California Constitution.

[Quon v. Arch Wireless Operating Co., Inc., 529 F.3d 892 (9th Cir. 2008), *cert. granted*, City of Ontario, Cal. v. Quon, 2009 WL 1146443, 77 U.S.L.W. 3619 (2009)]

On June 17, 2010, the Supreme Court unanimously reversed the Ninth Circuit, holding that review of an employee's text messages on an employer-issued electronic device does not violate the Fourth Amendment on the facts of this case. [Case No. 08-1332]

In *United States v. Ahrndt* [2010 WL 373994 (Or. 2010)], the judge quoted the *Quon* case:

> In January, Judge King of the federal district court in Oregon quoted *Quon* to the effect that, "The extent to which the Fourth Amendment provides protection for the contents of electronic communications in the Internet age is an open question. The recently minted standard of electronic communication via e-mails, text messages, and other means opens a new frontier in Fourth Amendment jurisprudence that has been little explored." In the case before His Honor, on February 21, 2007, a woman referred to as JH in the court papers was using her personal computer at her home in Aloha, Oregon. She was connected to the Internet via her own wireless network, but when her wireless network malfunctioned, her computer automatically picked up another nearby network that broadcasted wireless internet in a roughly 400 foot radius.
>
> JH began using her iTunes software. When JH opened her iTunes, she noticed another user's library was available for sharing. JH opened the shared library and found a subfolder called "Dad's Limewire Tunes." JH opened Dad's Limewire Tunes and observed files with names such as "11-yr old masturbating" and numerous obscene words. She reported what she saw to the sheriff's office, which obtained search warrants and tracked down the offending computer.
>
> When its own was prosecuted and attempted to suppress the evidence obtained via the warrants, Judge King held on these facts, "Having failed to demonstrate either a reasonable objective or subjective expectation of privacy, defendant cannot invoke the protections of the Fourth Amendment. When JH and Officer McCullough accessed the child pornography in defendant's iTunes library, no search occurred. The affidavits for the search warrants, therefore, were not tainted. I need not reach whether probable cause existed to issue the warrants without Officer McCullough's statement about initially viewing the files."

[United States v. Ahrndt, 2010 WL 373994 (Or. Jan. 28, 2010)]

In an article in the *Federal Criminal Defense Journal*, Juan A. Albino argues,

> The SCA is at odds with the Fourth Amendment requirement of prob-
> able cause to search constitutionally protected information. If a govern-
> ment agent wants to search text messages stored in an individual's cell
> phone, he needs a search warrant based on probable cause to comply
> with the Fourth Amendment. The agent may avoid the warrant require-
> ment, however, by presenting the electronic information service pro-
> vider with a subpoena, which does not require judicial oversight,
> obtaining access to all text messages that are 180 days or older. This
> undermines the Fourth Amendment's constitutional protection.

Albino adds,

> Privately kept information should not be left unprotected pursuant to a
> time limit. The SCA should be revised to reflect the expectations of
> individuals using electronic information. Electronic communication
> (text messages or e-mails), have replaced traditional ways of commu-
> nicating (letters and public telephones). New technological innovations
> in communication should be afforded the same constitutional protec-
> tions that were provided for the older mediums of communication.

[Juan A. Albino, "Do Defendants Have a Privacy Interest in Their Cell Phone's
Text Messages and E-Mails?" *Federal Criminal Defense Journal,* II (2009) at 47-
48.]

It seems unlikely that the Court's conservative majority will take it upon
themselves to rewrite the statute. However, the current Court does enjoy a
reasonably solid record in the area of civil liberties and may find a way to
enhance text-messagers' constitutional security from searches and seizures of
their message context.

Regardless of how the Supreme Court comes out on the *Quon* case, private
employers may find that at least for the time being they are relatively unaffected.
In the words of the Privacy Rights Clearinghouse, "New technologies make it possible for employers to monitor many aspects of their employees' jobs, especially
on telephones, computer terminals, through electronic and voice mail, and when
employees are using the Internet. Such monitoring is virtually unregulated.
Therefore, unless company policy specifically states otherwise (and even this is
not assured), your employer may listen, watch and read most of your workplace
communications." [http://www.privacyrights.org/fs/fs7-work.htm]

Note, too, that the Connecticut Supreme Court wrestled with a similar issue
involving GPS tracking devices and the subsequent disciplining of city police
officers on the basis of the information gathered. [Gerardi v. City of Bridgeport,
294 Conn. 461, 985 A.2d 328 (2010)]

Q 10:66   What is meant by *due process of law?*

The Fifth and Fourteenth Amendments to the U.S. Constitution forbid
government entities, such as the police and the courts, to deprive people of their
liberty or property without following appropriate legal procedures. The Fifth

Amendment, which is part of the original Bill of Rights, applies to the federal government. The Fourteenth Amendment, adopted shortly after the Civil War, places similar restraints upon state and local government.

When, for instance, a government agency proposes to discipline, or perhaps even to discharge, an employee, the agency typically must advise the employee of the accusations against her and afford her the opportunity to respond, possibly in the context of a formal disciplinary proceeding. Often there are appeal rights or recourse to an adversarial hearing before a forum such as the Merit System Protection Board in the federal civil service.

Q 10:67   What does *equal protection of the law* mean?

Closely related to the Due Process clause of the Fourteenth Amendment to the U.S. Constitution is the Equal Protection clause. This provision requires state and local governments to apply their laws evenly to all citizens.

For purposes of public employment, the clause can be used to restrict the government's use of affirmative action programs. For instance, in *Krupa v. New Castle County* [732 F. Supp. 497, 506 (D. Del. 1990)], a group of white police officers challenged the promotion of black counterparts under the county's affirmative action plan. Holding that absent evidence of past discrimination the county could not favor the black police, the federal judge observed that the Equal Protection clause of the Fourteenth Amendment provides that "[N]o State shall make or enforce any law which shall . . . deny to any person within its jurisdiction the equal protection of the laws." Judicial review of racially preferential state employment actions under this clause requires an equal application of its provisions regardless of whether the allegedly aggrieved individual is a member of a minority or majority class.

Q 10:68   Does drug testing violate the Due Process and Equal Protection clauses of the Constitution?

On March 21, 1989, just five days after the effective date of the Drug-Free Workplace Act, the Supreme Court announced two closely related decisions that together seek to limit drug testing by the federal government, both within the bureaucracy and the regulated private sector. By implication, these two cases give important clues as to what government contractors and grantees can or cannot do, bearing in mind that private employers are not directly subject to the restrictions in the Bill of Rights (for drug testing purposes, the Fourth, Fifth, and Fourteenth Amendments).

National Treasury Employees Union v. Von Raab [489 U.S. 656 (1989)], concerns the constitutionality of a drug-testing program announced by the Commissioner of the U.S. Customs Service in 1986. The program called for urinalysis, designed to detect marijuana, cocaine, opiates, amphetamines, and phencyclidine. Any employee seeking promotion or transfer to any one of the following three job categories had to submit to the test:

1. Jobs directly involving interdiction of illegal drugs;

2. Positions requiring the carrying of a firearm; or

3. Assignments involving classified materials.

The courts disagreed on the program's constitutionality. The federal district court enjoined its operation, but a divided panel of the Court of Appeals for the Fifth Circuit reversed. The case then went to the U.S. Supreme Court.

The U.S. Supreme Court affirmed in part and reversed in part. First, the Court found that the collection and analysis of employees' urine samples was a search, which therefore had to meet the reasonableness requirement of the Fourth Amendment. Consequently:

> [T]he public interest in the Customs Service program had to be balanced against the privacy concerns implicated by the tests, without reference to the usual presumption in favor of the warrant and probable cause procedures specified in the Fourth Amendment, because the program was not designed to serve the ordinary needs of law enforcement.

Next, in applying the reasonableness test, the Court held that the U.S. Customs Service needed no search warrants to collect the samples, and with regard to jobs involving firearms or drug interdiction, the policy was reasonable even absent probable cause or individualized suspicion. On the other hand, regarding jobs requiring access to classified documents, the drug-testing program struck the Court's majority as an overly broad response to the Commissioner's concerns. Therefore, on remand, the Fifth Circuit was instructed to ascertain what Customs Service materials were considered "classified" and which employees might be tested under this category.

Skinner v. Railway Labor Executives' Association [489 U.S. 602 (1989)], involved the imposition of federal drug rules on the employees of private, but heavily regulated, corporations, specifically railroads.

The Federal Railroad Administration (FRA), responding to evidence (notably a much-publicized Amtrak wreck involving fatalities) indicating that railroad employees' drug and alcohol abuse posed a threat to public safety, promulgated drug and alcohol testing regulations. Subpart C of these regulations required railroads to test employees involved in train accidents.

Subpart D allowed, but did not require, testing when supervisors had "a reasonable suspicion" that an employee was "under the influence" or had contributed to an accident or dangerous incident. The federal district court that first judged the regulations decided that the regulations were reasonable intrusions of employees' privacy interests. The Court of Appeals for the Ninth Circuit reversed the trial court, finding that, because the regulations did not require a showing of individualized suspicion, they were constitutionally invalid.

The U.S. Supreme Court held that:

1. The Fourth Amendment applied to FRA regulations, even though it was left to private employers to apply them;

2. The tests were reasonable under the circumstances, reflecting the government's interest in public safety; and

3. A search warrant was not essential for the regulations to pass constitutional muster, because this procedure would delay necessarily prompt testing.

Q 10:69   What are some tips for conducting constitutional drug tests?

Times to consider testing:

1. Pre-employment;
2. Pre-promotion;
3. Annual physical;
4. Reasonable suspicion;
5. For cause;
6. Post-accident; and
7. Treatment follow-up.

Things a drug policy should include:

1. Drugs being tested for;
2. Who will be tested;
3. Under what conditions an employee may/will be tested;
4. Consequences of a positive test result;
5. Consequences of refusing test; and
6. Who pays.

Drug testing procedures:

1. Chain of custody;
2. Confirmation testing; and
3. Cut-off levels.

Pre-testing checklist:

1. Identify all relevant federal and state laws;
2. Talk to relevant union officials;
3. Identify and visit a DHHS-certified lab;
4. Identify and visit the specimen collection site;
5. Contract with a medical review officer;
6. Develop a system to insure confidentiality;
7. Designate the person to receive test results;
8. Write a clear and concise policy;
9. Have the policy reviewed by legal counsel;
10. Notify employees 30 to 60 days before the program goes into effect; and
11. Communicate the policy and the intent to adhere to it.

Q 10:70   What are the Department of Transportation guidelines on drug testing?

The Omnibus Transportation Employee Testing Act of 1991 requires drug and alcohol testing of safety-sensitive transportation employees in aviation, trucking, railroads, mass transit, pipelines, and other transportation industries. DOT publishes rules on who must conduct drug and alcohol tests, how to conduct those tests, and what procedures to use when testing. These regulations cover all transportation employers, safety-sensitive transportation employees, and service agents—roughly 12.1 million people. Encompassed in 49 C.F.R. Part 40, the Office of Drug & Alcohol Policy & Compliance publishes, implements, and provides authoritative interpretations of these rules.

Q 10:71   Which alcohol screening devices are approved by the DOT guidelines?

1. AK Solutions, Inc., Palisades Park, NJ: Alcoscan AL-2500, AlcoChecker, AlcoKey, AlcoMate, AlcoMate Pro, Alcoscan AL-5000, Alcoscan AL-6000.

2. Alco Check International, Hudsonville, MI: Alco Check 3000 D.O.T., Alco Check 9000.

3. Akers Biosciences, Inc., Thorofare, NJ: Breath Alcohol .02 Detection System.

4. BAC Solutions, Inc., Birmingham, MI: BACmaster.

5. B.E.S.T. Labs., Boardman, OH: PB9000e.

6. Chematics, Inc., North Webster, IN: ALCO-SCREEN 02TM 2

7. CMI , Inc., Owensboro, KY: Intoxilyzer 500 (aka: Alcometer 500—Lion Laboratories).

8. First Innovative Technology Group, Ltd., Hong Kong: AAT198—Pro.

9. Guth Laboratories, Inc., Harrisburg, PA: Alco Tector Mark X, Mark X Alcohol Checker, Alcotector WAT89EC-1.

10. Han International Co., Ltd., Seoul, Korea 3: A.B.I. (Alcohol Breath Indicator).

11. KHN Solutions, LLC, San Francisco, CA: BACTRACK Select S50 10, BACTRACK Select S80.1.

12. Lion Laboratories, Ltd., Wales, United Kingdom: Alcometer 500 (aka: Intoxilyzer 500—CMI, Inc.).

13. OraSure Technologies, Inc., Bethlehem, PA: Q.E.D. A150 Saliva Alcohol Test.

14. PAS Systems International, Inc., Fredericksburg, VA: PAS Vr.

15. Q3 Innovations, Inc., Independence, IA: AlcoHAWK Precision, Alco-HAWK Slim, AlcoHAWK Slim 2, AlcoHAWK Elite, AlcoHAWK ABI (aka: A.B.I. (Alcohol Breath Indicator) by Han Intl.), AlcoHAWK Micro, AlcoHAWK PRO (aka: AlcoMate by AK Solutions), AlcoHAWK PT 500.

16. Repco Marketing, Inc., Raleigh, NC: Alco Tec III.

17. Seju Co. of Taejeon, Korea: Safe-Slim.

18. Sound Off, Inc., Hudsonville, MI: Digitox D.O.T.

19. Varian, Inc., Lake Forest, CA: On-Site Alcohol 5

Q 10:72 Which companies sell breath-testing devices that are approved by the DOT guidelines?

- Alcohol Countermeasure Systems Corp. Mississauga, Ontario, Canada: Alcolab, Alert J4X.ec, Drivesafe, Elan, Ensure, and Snap
- BAC Systems, Inc., Ontario, Canada: Breath Analysis Compute
- CAMEC Ltd., North Shields, Tyne and Ware, England: IR Breath Analyzer
- CMI, Inc., Owensboro, KY: Intoxilyzer (numerous models)
- Draeger Safety, Inc., Durango, CO: Alcotest (numerous models)
- Gall's Inc., Lexington, KY: Alcohol Detection System—A.D.S. 500 and others
- Intoximeters, Inc., St. Louis, MO: Photo Electric Intoximeter; GC Intoximeter MK II; and others
- Komyo Kitagawa, Kogyo, K.K.: Alcolyzer DPA-2; Breath Alcohol Meter PAM 101B
- Lifeloc Technologies, Inc. (formerly Lifeloc, Inc.), Wheat Ridge, CO: PBA 3000B and others
- Lion Laboratories, Ltd., Cardiff, Wales, UK: Alcolmeter (various models)
- Luckey Laboratories, San Bernadino, CA: Alco-Analyzer Model 1000
- National Draeger, Inc., Durango, CO: Alcotest (various models)
- National Patent Analytical Systems, Inc., Mansfield, OH: BAC DataMaster (with or without the Delta-1 accessory)
- Omicron Systems, Palo Alto, CA: Intoxilyzer (various models)
- Plus 4 Engineering, Minturn, CO: 5000 Plus4*
- Seres, Paris, France: Alco Master
- Siemans-Allis, Cherry Hill, NJ: Alcomat
- Smith and Wesson Electronics, Springfield, MA: Breathalyzer (various models)
- Sound-Off, Inc., Hudsonville, MI: AlcoData
- Stephenson Corp.: Breathalyzer 900
- U.S. Alcohol Testing, Inc./Protection Devices, Inc., Rancho Cucamonga, CA: Alco-Analyzer 1000 Alco-Analyzer 2000
- Verax Systems, Inc., Fairport, NY: BAC Verifier (various models)

Q 10:73   Have due process of law and equal protection under the law become statutory?

After the Civil War and the adoption of the Thirteenth, Fourteenth, and Fifteenth Amendments to the Constitution, Congress passed a series of civil rights statutes, today codified at Title 42, Sections 1981–1985, of the U.S. Code. Among these laws, 42 U.S.C. § 1983 forbids state action that deprives citizens of due process and equal protection of the law. A Section 1983 lawsuit is among the most common means for a public employee to challenge a governmental employer's alleged deprivation of that employee's constitutional rights. Successful employee-litigants can obtain compensatory, and even punitive damages, plus attorneys' fees in some circumstances.

Q 10:74   Can 42 U.S.C. Section 1983 be the basis of a lawsuit by an employee against a private employer?

Like the Bill of Rights itself, Section 1983 is directed only at wrongdoing by state actors—meaning governmental entities. Therefore, this section is not usually available to private-sector employees. Among highly regulated industries and certain classes of government contractors, the nexus between the private employee and the regulating or contracting agency of federal or state government may be so close that the employer's deeds amount to state action. For instance, in *Skinner v. Railway Labor Executive's Association* [489 U.S. 602 (1989)], the U.S. Supreme Court held that the FRA's drug-testing rules for railroad workers were subject to Fourth Amendment search and seizure limits, even though the FRA's rules were enforced by privately run railroads. By contrast, private colleges and universities usually have been held not to be state actors, even when substantially supported by state funding.

Q 10:75   How much "due process of law" is enough?

Finding that a charge of "lack of candor" does not require a showing of intent on the part of the accused public employee, the Federal Circuit affirmed the decision of the Merit Systems Protection Board that FBI Agent Andrew Ludlum should have his dismissal from employment reduced to a 120-day suspension. [Ludlum v. Department of Justice, 278 F.3d 1280 (Fed. Cir. 2002)]

This case arose from a complaint filed by a suspect stopped by Agent Ludlum while he had his daughter in his bureau car. Upon inquiry from his supervisor, Ludlum admitted that he had picked up his daughter from day care on at least three occasions when his wife was unable to do so. He subsequently signed a sworn affidavit to that effect. Following up on the affidavit, the agency discovered other occasions when Ludlum had logged his daughter out of the day care center. The plaintiff then executed a second sworn statement in which he admitted the truth of these additional instances of misusing his government vehicle. However, he equivocated, claiming that his failure to mention them was due to faulty memory, since these occasions were not the result of emergency calls from his wife and therefore did not stick out in his mind at the time of the first affidavit, albeit there were 14 such documented violations in the space of a year. Faced with this falsification of records, plus other time and attendance violations in the plaintiff's record, an agency official fired him. Appealing to the Merit Systems Protection Board, the plaintiff contended that his misstatement was a lapse of memory and not an instance of fraud. Characterizing the case as extremely close, the Board agreed with Ludlum and ordered his reinstatement with a 120-day unpaid suspension as the proper penalty. Ludlum appealed to the circuit court. The appeals panel held that, unlike fraud, lack of candor is an offense that does not require the accusing agency to prove actual intent on the part of its transgressing employee. Disagreeing with the majority, dissenting Judge Gajarsa contended that Merit System Protection precedents suggest that a *mens rea* component must be proven to support disciplinary action for alleged lack of candor as well. [*See* Boyd v. Department of Justice, 13 M.S.P.B. 97, 14 M.S.P.R. 427 (1983); Frederick v. Department of Justice, 52 M.S.P.R. 126 (1991).]

Q 10:76   Is a public employee entitled to a pre-suspension hearing?

In *Gilbert v. Homar* [520 U.S. 924 Ct. 1473 (1997)], the U.S. Supreme Court held that a public employee accused of committing a felony could be suspended, pending resolution of the criminal charges, without being accorded a pre-suspension hearing.

In general, this case established a three-prong test of when such a hearing might be required. The test, which has broader application, balances:

1. The nature of the private interest affected by the official action;
2. The risk of an erroneous deprivation of due process; and
3. The governmental interest implicated in the personnel action.

In 2009, the U.S. Court of Appeals for the Third Circuit considered the case of a computer technician employed by a Delaware school district, who in a Section 1983 action contended his termination violated Constitutional due process. Quoting *Gilbert v. Homar* [520 U.S. 924 (1997)] for the proposition, "Due process is flexible and calls for such procedural protections as the particular situation demands," the appeals panel held:

> Even if school board employee had a property interest in his job as a computer technician, board did not violate his right to procedural due process in terminating his employment; employee was issued five disciplinary memos prior to termination, each memo specifically out-lined instances of poor performance or inappropriate behavior and warned that failure to improve could result in disciplinary action, supervisors gave employee memos at face-to-face meetings and orally explained them, employee submitted letter to board after his termination date responding to the charges against him, and board considered this letter in a meeting.

[Biliski v. Red Clay Consol. Sch. Dist. Bd. of Educ., 574 F.3d 214 (3d Cir. 2009)]

Q 10:77   To how much due process is a probationary employee entitled?

In *Montes-Rodriguez v. Merit Systems Protection Board* [65 Fed. Appx. 306 (Fed. Cir. 2003), *cert. denied*, 124 S. Ct. 335 (2003)], a probationary animal-caretaker in the U.S. Department of Agriculture claimed she had been unfairly fired for disagreeing with co-workers who contended that the people behind the 9/11 terrorist attacks should be identified and "nuked." She alleged that her supervisor overheard her take issue with these views and terminated her in retaliation. The agency retorted that she had been terminated for her repeated tardy arrivals, impermissibly lengthy lunch breaks, and failure to perform some of the specified duties of her job.

After the Merit Systems Protection Board dismissed her case for want of jurisdiction over a probationary employee, she appealed to the U.S. Court of Appeals for the Federal Circuit. The appellate panel hearing the arguments ruled that the federal regulation that forbids firing a worker "based on affiliation with any party or candidate" [*see* Mastriano v. FAA, 714 F.2d 1152 (Fed. Cir. 1983)] cannot be stretched to protect the expression of an unpopular opinion where party affiliation forms no part of the case. Furthermore—and of broader implication—since "a probationary employee in an initial appointment . . . does not have the right to appeal her termination on other then narrow grounds set by statute and regulation," the termination must be upheld regardless of which motive was the true reason for her being fired.

Q 10:78   Does sovereign immunity affect the public employee's right to sue a government employer?

State legislatures have the right to accord sovereign immunity to state and local government agencies. During the second half of this century many states have elected, however, to abrogate sovereign immunity that is to permit citizens to sue, at least for some causes of action. More significantly, state sovereign immunity statutes cannot affect federally created legal rights, such as the right to sue under 42 U.S.C. § 1983.

The U.S. Supreme Court has held that employees seeking to sue the state itself may be prohibited by the Eleventh Amendment to the Constitution. [*See* Quern v. Jordan, 440 U.S. 332 (1979).] Thus, while public employees enjoy constitutional rights of due process and equal protection of law with respect to their jobs, their right to sue presents complex procedural questions relating to the separation of powers between the state and federal governments. Some court decisions seem to have eroded this Eleventh Amendment immunity from suit:

1. In *Garrett v. University of Alabama at Birmingham Bd. of Trustees* [344 F.3d 1288 (11th Cir. 2003)], the court held that the state's acceptance of federal funds under the 1972 Rehabilitation Act worked a waiver of Eleventh Amendment immunity from suit by a state employee suing under the federal statute.

2. In *Nevada Department of Human Resources v. Hibbs* [538 U.S. 721 (2003)], the Supreme Court held that state employees may recover money damages in federal court in the event of the state's failure to comply with the family-care provision of the Family and Medical Leave Act. The majority view, written by Chief Justice Rehnquist, reasoned that "Congress may abrogate Eleventh Amendment immunity in federal court if it makes its intention to abrogate unmistakably clear in the language of the statute and acts pursuant to a valid exercise of its power under the enforcement section of the Fourteenth Amendment."

3. Another Supreme Court case, *Tennessee v. Lane* [541 U.S. 509 (2004)], held that "Title II of the ADA, as applied to cases implicating the fundamental right of access to the courts, constitutes a valid exercise of Congress' enforcement power under the Fourteenth Amendment." The majority opinion, penned by Justice Stevens, went on to hold that:

> As it applies to the class of cases implicating the fundamental right of access to the courts, Title II constitutes a valid exercise of Congress' authority under § 5 of the Fourteenth Amendment to enforce that Amendment's substantive guarantees. (pp. 1984–1994).
>
> (a) Determining whether Congress has constitutionally abrogated a State's Eleventh Amendment immunity requires resolution of two predicate questions: (1) whether Congress unequivocally expressed its intent to abrogate; and (2) if so, whether it acted pursuant to a valid grant of constitutional authority. *Kimel v. Florida Board of Regents*, [528 U.S. 62, 73, 120 S. Ct. 631, 145 L. Ed. 2d 522 (2000)]. The first question is easily answered here, since the ADA specifically provides for abrogation. [*See* ADA § 12202] With regard to the second question, Congress can abrogate state sovereign immunity pursuant to a valid exercise of its power under § 5 of the Fourteenth Amendment. [*See, e.g.*, Fitzpatrick v. Bitzer, 427 U.S. 445, 456, 96 S. Ct. 2666, 49 L. Ed. 2d 614 (1976)] That power is not, however, unlimited. While Congress must have a wide berth in devising appropriate remedial and preventative measures for unconstitutional actions, those measures may not work a "substantive change in the governing law." [City of Boerne v. Flores, 521 U.S. 507, 519, 117 S. Ct. 2157, 138 L. Ed. 2d 624 (1997)] In *Boerne*, the Court set forth the test for distinguishing between permissible remedial legislation and unconstitutional substantive redefinition: Section 5 legislation is valid if it exhibits "a congruence and proportionality" between an injury and the means adopted to prevent or remedy it. [City of Boerne v. Flores, 521 U.S. 507 at 520] Applying the *Boerne* test in *Board of Trustees v. Garrett* [531 U.S. 356 (2001)], the Court concluded that ADA Title I was not a valid exercise of Congress' § 5 power because the historical record and the statute's broad sweep suggested that Title I's true aim was not so much enforcement, but an attempt to "rewrite" this Court's Fourteenth Amendment jurisprudence. [531 U.S., at

372–374, 121 S. Ct. 955] In view of significant differences between Titles I and II, however, *Garrett* left open the question whether Title II is a valid exercise of Congress' § 5 power. . . . " [531 U.S., at 372–374, 121 S. Ct. 955]

Q 10:79　Does the Federal Tort Claims Act protect federal employees from malpractice suits?

In a unanimous decision, penned by Justice Ginsburg, the high court held that a veteran's battery claim against the United States for damage done during eye surgery is authorized under amendments to the Federal Tort Claims Act. [Levin v. United States, __S. Ct.__, 2013 WL 776447 (Mar. 4, 2013)]

The veteran, Steven Levin, suffered injuries as a result of cataract surgery performed at a U.S. Naval Hospital. He filed suit, naming the United States and the surgeon as defendants and asserting, *inter alia*, a claim of battery, based on his alleged withdrawal of consent to operate shortly before the surgery took place. Finding that the surgeon had acted within the scope of his employment, the district court released him and substituted the United States as sole defendant. The government moved to dismiss, based on the FTCA's "intentional tort" exception. The district judge granted the motion and the Ninth Circuit agreed.

The Justices, however, had a different opinion. In the words of one group of experts, "The Gonzalez Act (10 U.S.C. § 1089), which protects medical personnel in the armed forces from individual malpractice liability for conduct within the scope of their employment, provides that the FTCA's damages remedy against the United States is the *exclusive means of recovery* for plaintiffs alleging malpractice by covered employees. In particular, the Gonzalez Act provides with regard to defense of certain suits arising out of medical malpractice that (a) The remedy against the United States provided by section[ ] 1346 (b) . . . of title 28 for damages for personal injury . . . caused by the negligent or wrongful act or omission of any physician . . . or . . . other supporting personnel . . . of the armed forces . . . while acting within the scope of his duties or employment therein or therefore shall hereafter be exclusive of any other civil action or proceeding by reason of the same subject matter against such physician . . . or other supporting personnel (or the estate of such person) whose act or omission gave rise to such action or proceeding. . . . but the Gonzalez Act also provides, *(e) For purposes of this section, the provisions of section 2680 (h) of title 28 shall not apply to any cause of action arising out of a negligent or wrongful act or omission in the performance of medical . . . functions. . . .* " [Medical Malpractice Lawyers.com, Jan. 14, 2013, accessed at http://medicalmalpracticelawyers. com/blog/tag/gonzalez-act/]

The Supreme Court held in this case that the Gonzalez Act abrogates the FTCA's intentional-tort exception and allows Levin's malpractice case to proceed. In so holding, the Court paid special attention to 10 U.S.C. § 1089(a), which reads, "For purposes of this section, the provisions of section 2680(h) of title 28 [the FTCA's intentional tort exception] shall not apply to any cause of action arising out of a negligent or wrongful act or omission in the performance of medical, dental, or related health care functions (including clinical studies and investigations)."

Q 10:80   Are government employees protected by anti-discrimination laws?

Some might say they are overly protected. The following case is on point.

This case began with race discrimination complaints in 1991 and 1992; the litigation outlived three successive Treasury Department Secretaries and came to the Court of Appeals in Chicago carrying three case captions, the most current being *Jordan v. O'Neill* [28 Fed. Appx. 548 (7th Cir. 2002)]. In January 1991, the plaintiff made an informal complaint to an Equal Employment Opportunity (EEO) Counselor at the National Finance Center of Customs in Indianapolis, Indiana. The Customs Equal Employment Office functions much like the Equal Employment Opportunity Commission (EEOC) in policing employment discrimination in the private sector. At the counselor's suggestion, the plaintiff upgraded her complaint to the formal level but it was never processed beyond the informal stage.

In 1994, Jordan filed her second complaint, this time alleging a continuing pattern of discrimination plus, now, retaliation. Customs EEO this time split the complaint into two parts and began its processing. The continuing violation subsequently was dismissed with the agency issuing the plaintiff a "right to sue" letter. She in turn filed a complaint in U.S. District Court. Responding to a motion for partial summary judgment, the district judge ruled that Customs had come forward with legitimate business reasons, which Jordan failed to refute, for failing to promote her to the rank of accountant. Next, conducting a bench trial on the plaintiff's remaining claims, the court found that she had missed the 45-day time limit imposed upon federal employees for filing their federal suits. Thus, the remaining counts were dismissed as well.

Meanwhile, Customs EEO dismissed the retaliation piece of the plaintiff's second complaint, alluding to a regulation requiring all parts of a complaint to be dismissed when any one part winds up in federal court. This put the plaintiff back in federal district court, which again agreed with Customs that this part of her claim should likewise be dismissed. A 1995 formal complaint also failed to pass muster with the trial court, which was affirmed by the Seventh Circuit. [*See* Jordan v. Summers, 205 F.3d 337 (7th Cir. 2000).]

In the final act of this long drama, the plaintiff pinned her hopes on the agency's failure to process her earliest (1991) complaint. The appeals court, perhaps revealing its frustration, stated that "we reiterate that failure to process a complaint does not state a discrimination claim against the agency." Furthermore, the court found that all of the plaintiff's complaints revolved around the same core concern—failure of the agency to ever promote her. Consequently, while the facts before the court in this most recent appeal were not precisely the same as those that had come up to the court half a dozen years earlier, they were "essentially the same," such that the rule of *res judicata* provided a separate but equal ground for denying this second bite of the apple.

In a related case, an employee of the National Geospatial-Intelligence Agency, Mahmoud Hegab, sued the agency for discrimination for allegedly revoking his security clearance because his wife attended an Islamic school and worked for a Muslim charity. NGA employs 16,00 workers who supply data and other imagery to the military, and a top security clearance is necessary for all employees due to the nature of the agency's work. Hegab was a budget analyst with a top security clearance at NGA, but his clearance was revoked immediately after he got married.

According to the lawsuit, NGA officials informed Hegab that they were concerned about his wife's schooling at the Islamic Saudi Academy, which has been criticized by groups such as the U.S. Commission on International Religious Freedom for use of a curriculum that, similar to that in Saudi Arabia, some claim promotes intolerance against other religions, particularly Judaism and Christianity. NGA cited that, along with her charity work with Islamic Relief USA, as reason for revoking the security clearance. Furthermore, NGA cited his wife's participation in a 2003 anti-war rally sponsored by the ANSWER coalition, a left-wing group that has, at times, worked with Palestinian activists, and her time serving as president of the student group Students for Justice in Palestine at George Mason University. NGA eventually withdrew its concerns regarding Hegab's wife's attendance at the Saudi Academy, but said its other concerns remained.

Hegab's lawyer, Sheldon Cohen, wrote in the lawsuit that "the revocation of plaintiff's security clearance . . . was based solely on plaintiff's wife's religion, Islam, her constitutionally protected speech, and her association with . . . an Islamic faith-based organization." [http://lubbockonline.com/filed-online/2011-10-06/former-worker-sues-secretive-us-security-agency-alleging-bias-against-wife#.T3xVM79WovI]

Judge James C. Cacheris of the Eastern District of Virginia dismissed the lawsuit on the grounds that, regardless of whether or not Hegab's allegations were true, the court lacked the authority to review the underlying basis of the dispute. The judge stated:

> A determination of whether Hegab's security clearance was revoked due to legitimate national security concerns or, as Hegab alleges, constitutionally impermissible bases would necessarily require a review of the merits of NGA's decision. Absent clear congressional directive, which Hegab fails to identify, such a review is flatly prohibited by *Egan* and Fourth Circuit precedent.

In this case, *Egan* refers to the 1988 Supreme Court decision in *Department of the Navy v. Egan*, which supports broad and unreviewable executive branch authority in regard to national security policy. [http://www.fas.org/blog/secrecy/2012/01/hegab_dismissal.html]

Q 10:81   Has the use of alternative dispute resolution (ADR) of discrimination claims increased in the federal sector?

In 1991, the EEOC began a pilot mediation program in four of its field offices (Philadelphia, New Orleans, Houston, and the Washington field office), and later on, similar pilot programs were established in all district offices. Based on the success of the pilots and the recommendations of the agency's ADR Task Force, the EEOC concluded that mediation was a viable, and perhaps a preferable alternative to the traditional investigatory methods used to resolve charges of employment discrimination, and that a full-fledged ADR program should be implemented. In 1995, the EEOC adopted its policy statement on ADR setting forth core principles for an ADR program. Following the development of the program's operational framework in 1998, and receipt of start-up funding in federal FY 1999, the EEOC's ADR mediation program was fully implemented in April 1999.

The EEOC's program uses a combination of internal mediators employed by EEOC and external contract mediators. Field offices sometimes also use pro bono, or volunteer, mediators. All mediators are trained in both mediation and the laws enforced by EEOC. As neutrals, the mediators apply their knowledge and experience as facilitators to explore the underlying dispute and to try to achieve resolutions which are mutually satisfactory to both parties. While more traditional remedies may be explored in mediation, many mediations involve creative approaches to resolving the dispute which are designed to meet the specific, sometimes unique, needs and interests of the parties. In many cases a non-monetary benefit is the only benefit that changes hands, according to the agency.

The EEOC typically offers mediation soon after the charge has been filed and prior to further investigation. The agency evaluates each charge to see if it is appropriate for mediation. Charges which the EEOC has determined to be without merit are not eligible for mediation. In most instances, charges which require additional investigation on the merits are eligible. The parties may request mediation, however, at any stage of the administrative process. In 2002, the EEOC expanded its use of mediation to attempt resolution at the conciliation stage, after a finding of discrimination had been issued, in appropriate cases.

The EEOC has also implemented an additional initiative to further expand and promote the use of mediation and ADR. The agency encourages employers to enter into Universal Agreements to Mediate (UAMs) at the local, regional, or national levels. These UAMs facilitate an employer's agreement to mediate and expedite the mediation process by providing identified points of contact for the EEOC and the employer for scheduling the mediation. As of September 2010, there were 1,573 UAMs with local employees and 214 UAMs with national or regional employers, according to the agency. [See http://www.eeoc.gov/eeoc/mediation/history.cfm.]

Q 10:82   Are federal employees treated any differently than other workers under federal anti-discrimination laws?

When the Civil Rights Act of 1964 was enacted, Title VII excluded the federal government from its definition of employer. The statute also stated, however, that all employment decisions in the United States should be discrimination-free and it authorized the President to issue executive orders. In fact, a series of executive orders was issued over the years. Additionally, the U.S. Constitution arguably prohibits job discrimination, as does the Code of Federal Regulations. Yet, as late as the early 1970s, federal courts disagreed over whether or not sovereign immunity denied federal workers a private cause of action for employment discrimination. In 1972, congressional hearings and reports revealed under-representation of minorities and females in the federal bureaucracy, and poor administrative procedures for addressing the problem. In the 1972 amendments to the Civil Rights Act of 1964 and the Civil Service Reform Act of 1978, Congress placed the federal government under Title VII's jurisdiction and transferred enforcement jurisdiction from the Civil Service Commission to the EEOC.

Q 10:83   Does the EEOC enforce the federal anti-discrimination laws in the federal sector in the same manner as in private employment?

Even after Congress extended Title VII's coverage to the federal bureaucracy and gave jurisdiction to the EEOC the federal government continued to enjoy significant advantages over other employers covered by federal anti-discrimination laws. Enforcement also was burdened by some unique complications. On one hand, federal workers were required to initiate the administrative process within 30 days of the discriminatory employment action or lose the right to do so. Many federal workers lost legitimate discrimination claims as a consequence of this brief limitation period. On the other hand, depending on the facts and circumstances of the case, the federal worker would have been able, up to a point, to pursue parallel remedies under EEO and civil service procedures. Consequently, treatment of federal employees under federal anti-discrimination acts came under substantial criticism by civil rights advocates, federal workers and their unions, and the advocates who represented them. Congress finally reacted to this criticism in 1991.

Before November 1991, Congress was itself exempt from the very civil rights acts it has passed. But part of the Civil Rights Act of 1991 (CRA '91) extends significant protection to federal employees. Sections 301–320 of CRA '91 are entitled to the Government Employment Rights Act of 1991 (GERA). GERA establishes a fair employment office for congressional employees. This office will handle discrimination complaints, initiated by congressional employees within 180 days, under a four-part procedure, consisting of:

1. Counseling;
2. Mediation;
3. Formal complaint and hearing before a board; and
4. Review by the select committee on ethics.

Q 10:84   How did the Civil Rights Act of 1991 alter the way federal job discrimination cases are administered?

Section 114 of CRA '91 extends the period for federal employees to initiate a charge of job discrimination from 30 days to 90 days. This is still only half the time accorded (180 days) private employees to institute discrimination complaints with the EEOC. (Private sector employees may have up to 300 days in the majority of states, referred to as "deferral states" because they offer a state law alternative.) Likewise, federal workers now have 90 days to initiate a lawsuit after termination of EEOC proceedings, instead of the mere 30 days they previously had; this is the same 90 days given private employees after they receive an EEOC "letter to sue." Most complainants come before the EEOC without representation, and legal representation is often hard to obtain in contingent-fee job discrimination cases, so 30 days could be too short a time even for a meritorious plaintiff to obtain competent legal counsel. Furthermore, a new study indicates that minority employees of the federal government are fired at three times the rate of firing for white employees, perhaps suggesting the need for still more reform of the process of federal discrimination cases.

Q 10:85   Did the Civil Rights Act of 1991 extend rights to any state employees?

Members of an elected state official's personal staff and key policy makers, previously exempt from the protections of the federal anti-discrimination acts, will now be permitted to pursue a remedy before the EEOC with limited judicial review in lieu of a full-blown right to a federal lawsuit.

Q 10:86   Does the Age Discrimination Act extend to state and municipal employees?

Yes, even where safety forces and the state's policy powers are implicated. [*See, e.g.*, Doane v. City of Omaha, 115 F.3d 624 (8th Cir. 1997); Francis v. City of Meridian, 129 F.3d 281 (2d Cir 1997).]

Note, too, that in *Tennessee v. Lane* [541 U.S. 509 (2004)], the court held that, "Title II of the ADA, as applied to cases implicating the fundamental right of access to the courts, constitutes a valid exercise of Congress' enforcement power under the Fourteenth Amendment."

Q 10:87   How do state anti-discrimination acts protect state workers?

Almost every state has enacted its own civil rights or human relations act. By and large, state and municipal employees enjoy the same rights and procedures as their private-sector counterparts. These rights and procedures vary widely from state to state. Most states have established commissions that, through work-sharing agreements and interlocking regulations, cooperate closely with the EEOC. Beyond the investigation stage, the multitude of state statutes may require conciliation efforts, administrative hearings, or recourse to state courts. The remedies and damages can range from back wages, through reinstatement, to compensatory and punitive damages, these latter remedies having become available under Title VII only with passage of the Civil Rights Act of 1991.

Q 10:88   What are the legal standards for adjudicating claims of religious discrimination made by public employees?

Holding that the sincerity of the employee's alleged religious beliefs is a quintessential question for the fact-finder at trial, the Court of Appeals for the First Circuit reversed the trial judge and reinstated a case in which the public employer fired a Seventh Day Adventist at the behest of the union he refused to join in compliance with the terms of the collective bargaining agreement. [Equal Employment Opportunity Comm'n v. Union Independiente de la Autoridad de Acueductos y Alcantarillados de Puerto Rico, 279 F.3d 49 (1st Cir. 2002)]

In this case, the employee, when hired, did not state that he objected to joining a union. Only when his probationary period was up did he reveal this religious prohibition, which likewise required the accommodation of not being available to do Saturday work. At the union's behest, the Commonwealth of Puerto Rico fired him. The EEOC filed suit on his behalf and won a partial summary judgment. The union appealed.

On appeal, the panel agreed that Seventh Day Adventism is a recognized faith and that aversion to union affiliation is a well-established and successfully litigated tenet of the faith. However, the court also ruled that the individual adherent must be shown to sincerely subscribe to the tenets of the faith. In this case, the defendant had adduced evidence that undermined the honesty of the employee's asserted beliefs. "For example, there is record evidence that Cruz lied on an employment application; that he is divorced; that he took an oath before a notary upon becoming a public employee; and that he works five days a week (instead of the six required by the faith)." Such evidence, tending to show behavior contrary to the tenets of a faith, is "relevant to the fact finder's evaluation of sincerity." Consequently, the appeals panel said the case must be remanded for trial on this disputed issue of fact.

In *Holmes v. Marion County Office of Family and Children* [349 F.3d 914, 92 Fair Empl. Prac. Cas. (BNA) 1678, 7th Cir. (Ind.), Nov. 19, 2003], the Seventh Circuit controversially ruled that "(1) [the] fact that child-welfare employee's disparate treatment claim could be litigated in federal court did not preclude employer's interlocutory appeal of denial of Eleventh Amendment immunity with respect to religious accommodation claim; (2) county's Office of Family and Children was part of state of Indiana for purposes of Eleventh Amendment; (3) and Eleventh Amendment barred religious accommodation claim."

Compensation

Q 10:89 Can public employees whose pay is subject to disciplinary deductions still be exempt from wage and hour laws?

The U.S. Supreme Court has held that public employees whose pay is subject to deductions, as penalties for disciplinary infractions, may still be *bona fide* executives, administrators, or professionals. In a case involving police sergeants and lieutenants in of St. Louis, the Supreme Court held that the "salary basis" requirement for exemption from the overtime provisions of the Fair Labor Standards Act was not defeated by the occasional penalties imposed by the city's police commissioners against errant officers who otherwise met the executive exemption. [Auer v. Robbins, 519 U.S. 452 (1997)]

In fact, the plaintiff police officers, who sought back pay in the nature of overtime compensation on the theory that the threat of disciplinary deductions in the police manual destroyed the salary basis of their compensation, lost every step of the way. The trial judge's ruling against them was affirmed by the Court of Appeals for the Eighth Circuit [65 F.3d 702 (8th Cir. 1995)], before advancing to the Supreme Court. The Board of Police Commissioners cited the nation's highest federal forum Labor Department regulations, which seem to condone the occasional debits against a salary that are not deemed by the agency's Wage and Hour Division as undermining the sanctity of the salary itself. These regulations say that *bona fide* executives, administrators, and professionals must earn a minimum amount of money on a "salaried basis" [29 C.F.R. §§ 541.1(f), 541.2(e), and 541(e) (1996)], which amount is not "subject to reduction because of variations in the quality or quantity of work performed." [29 C.F.R. § 541.118(a)] All of the federal courts from bottom to top found that the disciplinary deductions were so rare as not to constitute a regular practice of impinging upon the police officers' salaries in violation of the spirit and intent of the regulations.

Q 10:90 Are federal employees covered by the federal Fair Labor Standards Act?

Most federal employees have been covered by the FLSA since 1966. The Congressional Accountability Act of 1995 [Pub. L. No. 104-1, 109 Stat. 3 (Jan. 23, 1995)], extended FLSA coverage to employees of:

1. The Senate;
2. The House of Representatives;
3. The Capitol Guide Service;
4. The Capitol Police;
5. The Congressional Budget Office;
6. The Office of the Architect of the Capitol;
7. The Office of the Attending Physician; and
8. The Office of Technology Assessment.

Q 10:91   Are state and local governments subject to the FLSA?

The Supreme Court, in *National League of Cities v. Usery* [426 U.S. 833 (1976)], held the extension to cover state and local government employees unconstitutional. *Garcia v. San Antonio Metropolitan Transit Authority* [469 U.S. 528 (1985)], revisited the issue of whether a state or local government, in this case a municipally owned transit system, is subject to the minimum wage and overtime regulation of FLSA. *National League of Cities* had held that the FLSA could not be applied to cover state and local government employees engaged in what it called "traditional government functions."

That case spawned so much litigation over what was included in "traditional government functions" that in *Garcia* the Supreme Court overruled *National League of Cities*, rejecting the "traditional functions" test as "unworkable." The Court held that the FLSA applies to state and municipal employees.

After *Garcia*, Congress amended the FLSA to permit states and municipalities to grant employees compensatory time off in lieu of overtime pay.

Q 10:92   Can state and local governments force their employees to use up their compensatory time?

An issue left open by the *Garcia* decision and the amending of the FLSA to permit the award of compensatory time in lieu of premium pay was whether public employers could then force their workers to use up that compensatory time. The U.S. Supreme Court answered this question in *Christensen v. Harris County* [120 U.S. 1655 (2000)]. Like *Garcia*, the case came to the high court from Texas.

The plaintiffs were 127 deputy sheriffs who opposed the county's policy of requiring the use of accumulated compensatory time in lieu of "banking" it for a later cash payment, as the post-*Garcia* FLSA amendments contemplate as a possible alternative. In an opinion written by Justice Clarence Thomas, the Court concluded that nothing in either the FLSA or its implementing regulations prevented the county from making compensatory time compulsory. In other words, the Court approved mandatory paid layoffs to enable the public entity to clear compensatory time from the books and avoid making premium payments out of the public coffers.

Q 10:93   Are state and municipal workers eligible for unemployment compensation?

In most states most public employees are eligible for unemployment compensation when out of work through no fault of their own. Typical exceptions to eligibility are:

1. Elected officials who are voted out of office;
2. Upper-level political appointees who serve at the whim of the governor or the mayor of a city;

3. State legislators and city council members with respect to their roles as such (if these elected posts are part-time, they remain eligible with regard to their regular, private sector jobs);

4. Students employed by state and local government during the summer, part-time during the school year, and during holiday seasons; or

5. Temporary employees hired for emergency situations such as storms, floods, or forest fires.

Q 10:94   What are the employee benefits most commonly provided by public employers to their employees?

Full-time state and municipal employees enjoy the following employee benefits nationally:

Type of Benefit	Percentage of Full-Time Employees
Paid holidays	89
Paid vacations	87
Paid personal days	39
Paid lunch break	11
Paid funeral leave	63
Paid military leave	83
Paid sick leave	93
Sickness and accident insurance	23
Long-term disability	26
Medical insurance	93
Dental insurance	62
Life insurance	88
Pension plan	95
Transportation subsidy (e.g., parking)	79
Bonuses	38
Legal services	8
Wellness program	64

Q 10:95   What are some recent developments regarding pension plans and other public employee benefits?

As a result of strained budgets and even bankruptcy, 45 states have either cut pension benefits or increased mandatory employee retirement plan contributions, or both, since 2009. Some cutbacks affect current workers and retirees by changing how pensions are calculated, but the majority will affect new hires, most of which will receive significantly fewer benefits than their predecessors.

Some examples of these new types of bills include:

- *House Bill 1165.* This measure would cap the amount of salary on which retirees could earn the compounded 3 percent cost of living adjustment [COLA] at $25,000. Anyone earning more pension income would receive a flat COLA of $750 annually. Under the bill, retirees would not be eligible for a COLA until they have been retired for five years or they reach age 67, whichever comes first. The bill also would apply to current retirees who are now receiving COLAs.

- *House Bill 1154.* This bill would "cap pensionable salary at the Social Security wage base, which is $113,700 in 2013, or the employee's current salary, whichever is greater."

- *HB 1166.* This would "increase the retirement age for employees younger than 46. Employees from 40 to 45 would see a one-year increase, employees 35 to 39 would see a three-year increase and employees 34 and younger would see a five-year increase." [http://illinoisissuesblog. blogspot.com/2013/03/house-passes-bill-to-cut-colas-on.html]

- *Oregon.* A proposed bill that "would limit cost of living increases to retired public employees, including teachers, city and state workers. The Democrats who crafted the plan say they tried to shield those earning the smallest pensions. They say the money it saves would be used to prevent cuts to education, healthcare and other public services." [http://www. opb.org/news/article/npr-oregon-senate-passes-pension-cutting-plan/]

- *California.* Governor Jerry Brown signed into law "sweeping pension changes that will save California taxpayers billions of dollars in the future and aims to reform a system that is woefully underfunded." The new law increases the retirement age for new employees depending on their job, caps the annual payout at $132,120, and requires workers who are not contributing half of their retirement costs to pay more. [http://www. huffingtonpost.com/2012/09/12/california-pension-reform-bill_n_1878662. html]

- *New York.* "Gov. Andrew Cuomo signed legislation giving some future public employees a chance to choose between a 401(k) plan and a defined benefit plan, increasing their employee DB contributions and raising their DB plan retirement age." [http://www.pionline.com/article/20120316/ DAILYREG/120319908]

However, some unions are suing in an attempt to reverse the cuts, particularly in regard to workers who were already in service before the cuts took effect. Thus, many of these laws are on hold until a decision can be reached.

Ethical Issues

Q 10:96   What are examples of public employee misuse of government property?

Misuse of government property by public employees includes the following actions:

1. Using government stationery, envelopes, and postage for personal mail (likewise personal use of overnight delivery service accounts);
2. Using government photocopy and fax equipment for personal use;
3. Using government-owned or leased vehicles or aircraft for personal business or pleasure;
4. Using government telephones and e-mail accounts for personal communications; or
5. Selling commercial products in a government building.

Q 10:97   What is the typical government policy on public employees accepting gifts from third parties?

Public employees usually are forbidden to solicit or accept anything of monetary value from any person who:

1. Has sought or currently is seeking a contractual, financial, or other business relationship with the employee's agency;
2. Conducts operations or activities that are regulated by the employee's agency; or
3. Has interests that could be substantially affected by the employee's performance (or non-performance) of her/his duties.

Things of monetary value subject to these restrictions include gifts, gratuities, favors, entertainment, and loans.

Q 10:98   Can a law enforcement officer accept a gift from a confidential informant or make a gift of contraband to such a confidential informant?

No. In a termination case, where a police officer claimed he had been fired for union activity, the municipality was able to prove that he was fired for allowing his confidential informant to keep an amount of crack cocaine. The Florida Public Employees Relations Committee sustained the challenged discharge, ruling that his action amounted to a level of misconduct deserving of termination of employment. [Palm Beach Cnty. Police Benevolent Ass'n v. City of Greenacres, 26 Florida Pub. Emp. Reporter 31207 (July 25, 2000)]

Additionally, the Committee concurred in the hearing officer's finding that the officer's acceptance of a gift from that same informant was also misconduct, adding weight to the rightness of the termination decision. The Committee did not go so far as to find that the taking of property—which may have been stolen—from the informant, standing alone, would have been sufficient to warrant a firing of the much-decorated officer.

This case puts the legal spotlight on a gray issue of ethical conduct. Police commonly use informants (or "snitches") in their investigations. These informants often are criminals or closely allied with criminals. The ethical standards of such police officers are necessarily severely tested at times as they seek to be effective in this shadowland.

Q 10:99   Do federal regulations prohibit the acceptance of lunch by federal officials attending a conference co-sponsored by a private-sector firm and the agency employing those officials?

If the agency previously accepted the private contractor's contribution to the cost of the lunches under appropriate statutory authority [see 5 C.F.R. § 2635.203(b)(8)], then the federal employees were entitled to eat the lunches. If the federal employees subsequently paid to the contractor the value of the lunches, then they were entitled to eat them. Under any other circumstances, federal law considers the free lunches an inappropriate gift. [Office of Government Ethics Letter to an Agency Inspector General's Office dated Oct. 15, 1998 (1998 WL 1229121)]

Q 10:100   Do federal regulations prohibit a government contractor from absorbing the costs of a conference co-sponsored by a federal agency?

The answer to this question depends on the federal agency's authority under its organic (enabling) statute. It is not an issue of individual federal employee conduct or ethics. The federal Standards of Conduct, enforced by the Office of Government Ethics, do not apply to these situations. The individual agency's legal counsel must instead make a determination of whether the agency's enabling act allows it to accept this cost deferment from a private firm. [Office of Government Ethics Letter to an Agency Inspector General's Office dated Oct. 15, 1998 (1998 WL 1229121)]

Q 10:101   Can federal employees use government vehicles to attend a conference paid for by a private contractor?

Federal employees may use government vehicles only for "authorized purposes." [41 C.F.R. subpart 101-38.3] The federal Standards of Conduct define *authorized purposes* as "those purposes for which Government property is made available to members of the public or those purposes authorized in accordance with law or regulation." [Standards of Conduct § 2635.704(a)]

Under these rules, the answer to the question is probably "yes," if the conference is "widely attended"—meaning that a large number of persons are expected to attend and that persons with a diversity of views and/or interests will be present, so that the appearance of possible collusion or *ex parte* communication is dissipated. [5 C.F.R. § 2635.204(g)(2)]

Q 10:102 Can federal employees accept ground transportation from private contractors while conducting site visits to the contractors' job sites?

Yes. Such ground transportation is accepted by the government agency as a defrayal of the agency's expenses. Consequently, provided the agency's own enabling statute does not forbid the acceptance by the agency of such assistance, the agency's employees may avail themselves of this service. [Office of Government Ethic Letter to a Private Organization dated Jun. 25, 1998 (1998 WL 1181841 (OGE))]

This circumstance must be contrasted with a situation in which the same federal employees accept such transportation for their personal benefit or recreation. Such transportation services clearly constitute an illegal gift. [5 U.S.C. § 7352; 5 C.F.R. §§ 2635.203(d) and 7353(a)]

Q 10:103 Is it legal for a federal employee to accept gifts from his/her spouse's employer, even though the employer is a government contractor who may have dealings with the federal employee's agency?

If the private firm who employs the federal worker's spouse would not have given the gifts but for the federal employee's official position with the government, then the gifts are illegal. [5 C.F.R. § 2635.203(e)] On the other hand, if the gifts are given to the federal employee purely in his/her capacity as spouse, and are the same sorts of gifts that are given simultaneously to other spouses of the contractor's employees (e.g., Christmas gifts, spouse-accompanied holidays) then the gifts most likely are legal. [Office of Government Ethics Letter to the General Counsel of a Federal Agency dated Jan. 14, 1998 (1998 WL 1181112 (OGE))] Such gifts, while they may be ethical and legal, must be reported by the federal employee/spouse on a financial disclosure report form (SF 278). [5 C.F.R. § 2634.202(c)]

Q 10:104 Can federal employees accept an invitation to attend an anniversary party thrown by a government contractor, where the employees are viewed by the contractor as having played an integral part in the company's growth?

No. Under these facts, the contractor clearly is a "prohibited source" from whom the federal workers are barred from accepting gifts. [5 C.F.R. § 2635.203(d)] Because attendance at the party will involve consumption of things of monetary value [5 C.F.R. § 2635.203(b)], such attendance is generally not permissible. [Office of Government Ethics Letter to an Organization dated Sept. 11, 1998 (1998 WL 1181848)]

Q 10:105   Who is forbidden from achieving personal gain from a public employee's official position?

The following people and entities are forbidden to achieve personal gain from a public employee's official position:

1. The employee;

2. The spouse;

3. The minor children;

4. Any organization served by the employee as an officer, director, trustee, partner, or employee; or

5. Any organization with which the employee is negotiating a future employment relationship.

Q 10:106   Do public employees enjoy whistleblower protection?

An ever-increasing number of public employees enjoy whistleblower protection. This is also true of government contractors' employees. (See chapter 9.) The following applies to public employee whistleblower protection:

1. The federal Whistleblower Protection Act protects federal employees. Additionally some 28 other federal statutes contain whistleblower protection provisions;

2. Forty-two states and the District of Columbia have enacted whistleblower protection statutes;

3. The success rate of reported whistleblower protection actions is approximately 33 percent nationwide;

4. Ninety percent of whistleblowers report subsequent retaliation;

5. The primary channel of investigation of whistleblower complaints at the federal level is the Office of the Inspector General (each federal agency has such an office, though names and titles will vary across the federal bureaucracy);

6. Accusations of retaliation against whistleblowers are investigated by the Office of Special Counsel, established by Congress and better known for its investigations of presidential misconduct in recent years;

7. The False Claims Act is an alternative route for whistleblowers, where alleged fraud in a federal contract situation is involved.

Public employers and employees wishing to ascertain specific whistleblower rights under a given federal statute or under a particular state's laws should consult legal counsel. No assumptions should be made with regard to the reach or remedies under such laws. Some statutes protect only public employees while others also protect workers in the private sector, such as employees of government contractors. Some provide private rights of action to employees while others are limited to agency investigations of alleged public employer wrongdoing. Some provide remedies for alleged retaliation while others leave it to the courts to provide relief (e.g., under the common law of wrongful discharge).

A recent U.S. Appeals for the First Circuit case held that the whistleblower protections afforded by the Sarbanes-Oxley Act of 2002 (SOX) cover only employees of public companies, and do not extend to the employees of a public company's contractors or subcontractors, which individually comprised private companies. The judge stated: "Although there is a close relationship between the private investment adviser defendants and their client mutual funds, as pointed out by the plaintiffs and the SEC as amicus curiae, the two entities are separate because Congress wanted it that way. Had Congress intended to ignore that separation and cover the employees of private investment advisers for whistleblower protections, it would have done so explicitly in § 1514A(a). However, it did not." [Lawson v. Fidelity Mgmt. & Research LLC, No. 10-2240 (1st Cir. 2012)]

For the time being, this holding provides private company employers a strong defense against claims of retaliation from employees. However, Congress may well revisit the issue in light of this case and decide to extend the scope of protections.

A loophole regarding the Whistleblower Protection Act recently came to light: Public Health Service (PHS) employees of the U.S. Food and Drug Administration do not enjoy whistleblower protections. Because they are part of a uniformed service, PHS employees are excluded from the whistleblower protections afforded to federal civilians, and because they are not members of the armed services, they are excluded from the protections provided to members of the military. FDA employee Paul Hardy, a PHS biomedical engineer, blew the whistle on safety issues with a breast cancer detection device by contacting members of Congress, and was subsequently investigated and fired. Hardy was found ineligible for the protections afforded under the Whistleblower Protection Act. [http://www.washingtonpost.com/politics/for-public-health-service-officers-no-protection-for-whistleblowing/2012/03/13/gIQAQVXaAS_story.html?wprss = rss_homepage]

Some relatively recent developments at the state level include:

1. *Minnesota*. High Court Clarifies Whistleblower Rules: In this case, employees of a county-owned print shop claimed their firing violated the state's Whistleblower Act and the Minnesota Occupational Safety and Health Act (MOSHA). Reversing a summary judgment, the high court reinstated their case, holding that: (1) the plaintiffs' whistleblower and MOSHA claims could be pursued simultaneously in court; (2) the plaintiffs had a constitutional right to a jury trial on both counts; (3) an employee's report can bring that worker under the Whistleblower Act's protection even if it doesn't implicate a clear public policy; and (4) the pleadings need not specify which laws were allegedly violated by the employer. [Abraham v. County of Hennepin, 693 N.W.2d 342 (Minn. 2002)]

2. *New Jersey.* Cops' Complaint Not Covered by Conscientious Employee Protection Act: Under the Garden State's Conscientious Employee Protection Act (CEPA), the plaintiff must prove that: (1) he reasonably believed illegal conduct was occurring; (2) he disclosed or threatened to disclose the conduct to a supervisor or a public body; (3) the employer retaliated; and (4) there was a causal nexus between the whistleblowing and the retaliatory action. In this case, the police officers claimed they were suspended for reporting overtime abuse by a fellow officer. Noting that no officer was either fired or demoted, the court found that the officers were punished for violating the chain of command by going around their superiors on the force and talking directly to the city's mayor about the alleged overtime violations. This was against the rules, especially during an ongoing investigation of the allegations. Finding that the actions taken against the officers were relatively minor, and that only discharge and demotion are covered by the Act, the case's dismissal was affirmed. [Hancock v. Borough of Oaklyn, 347 N.J. Super. 350, 790 A.2d 186 (App. Div. 2002) (**Note:** On Aug. 11, 2003, the N.J. Supreme Court allowed punitive damages under CEPA)]

3. *California.* In March 2010, in a reverse-whistleblower incident, the California Department of Industrial Relations asked Cal-OSHA employees in essence to blow the whistle on themselves. The employees were asked to answer questions under penalty of perjury about volunteer and private activity completely unrelated to work. Workers were also ordered to surrender all relevant records from their "home computers or other personal electronic devices." Following protest, the agency modified their inquiry to limit questions to use of state resources in preparing outside presentations. [http://www.peer.org/news/news_id.php?row_id = 1319]

4. *Ohio.* In 2012, the Ohio House and Senate passed a bill, sponsored by State Representative Ross McGregor, which will set up a fraud tracking system for fraud reported to the Ohio Auditor and provide whistleblowing protections to those who report fraud. The bill will create a toll-free hotline, Web site, and mailbox where anyone can report suspected fraud by any public office or official. Public workers will also be protected from retaliation or disciplinary action for such reporting. [http://www.empl oymentlawattorneyoh.com/2012/01/whistleblowing-protection-increas ing-for-public-employees.shtml]

Q 10:107   What are significant developments on the public employee whistleblower front?

In *Carson v. United States Office of Special Counsel* [633 F.3d 487 (6th Cir. 2011)], a pro se litigant, Joseph P. Carson, had sought a writ of mandamus to compel the Office of Special Counsel to investigate complaints that he had filed and to make reports to the Department of Energy. The district court dismissed his action and denied his motion to amend his complaint. In late February 2011, on appeal, the Sixth Circuit affirmed. The decision preserves the discretion accorded to the Office of Special Counsel under the statute, to determine whether or not a would-be whistleblower's charges have merit.

Merit System Protection Board. Turning to Westlaw, one finds 13 reported decisions of the forum, intended to protect the rights of federal employees, all titled *Carson v. Department of Energy*, dating from 1998 to 2008. Virtually all of these cases grew out of Carson's procedural complaints concerning the Energy Department's execution of a predecessor settlement agreement he had reached with the agency. The facts underlying the settlement, as summed up succinctly in the most recent of these reported MSPB decisions are:

> In January 1990, the appellant began his employment with the agency as a GS-14 General Engineer in the Site Resident Program of the agency's Office of Environment, Safety and Health (EH) at Oak Ridge Laboratory in Oak Ridge, Tennessee. [Compliance File (CF), Tab 1, Exhibit 4 at 3.] Between 1991 and 1997, the appellant made numerous disclosures involving safety issues. [*Id.* at 4.] From 1996 to 1998, the appellant filed three IRA appeals against the agency alleging that the agency had retaliated against him for his whistleblowing activity by: rating his performance in 1995 as "exceeds fully successful" rather than "outstanding"; removing surveillance duties from his work responsibilities in 1997; issuing a letter of admonishment to him on December 19, 1997; and directing his reassignment from Oak Ridge to EH Headquarters in Germantown, Maryland, in December 1997.

[109 M.S.P.B. 213 (2008)]

Westlaw also reveals 25 reported U.S. district, appellate, and Supreme Court decisions involving Carson, the most recent being the Sixth Circuit ruling discussed above. Notable is *Carson v. Merit Systems Protection Board*. [257 Fed. Appx. 268 (Fed. Cir. 2007), *reh'g en banc denied* (2009), *cert. denied,* 130 S. Ct. 3313 (2010)]. In the *amici curiae* May 5, 2010, brief filed in support of Carson's motion for certiorari by OSC Watch, we find:

> This case should be very **good news** for America—Joseph Carson, PE, has uncovered a previously unidentified significant contributing factor for much of which has befallen America since 1979 and besets it now—a near complete breakdown in the nondiscretionary statutory framework to protect, adequately, federal employees from PPP's—and it is something that can be readily fixed.
>
> This breakdown centers on OSC's 31-year long interpretation of (what is now) 5 U.S.C. § 1214(e), that its reporting requirements do not apply to OSC's determinations about PPP's and other violations within its enforcement jurisdiction and MSPB's 31-year long interpretation of (what is now) 5 U.S.C. § 1204(a)(3), that its "special studies" do not ever need to consider OSC's interpretation of and compliance with its nondiscretionary statutory duties to protect federal employees from PPP's nor agency heads interpretation of and compliance with their nondiscretionary statutory duty to "prevent PPP's," per 5 U.S.C. § 2302(c). As a predictable result, agency heads are unable to comply with this vital duty, because OSC's interpretation of § 1214(e) and MSPB's interpretation of > § 1204(a)(3) keep them "in the dark" as to whether their employees are adequately protected from PPP's.

All parties to this brief desire "justice for all" where "all" are the 25,000 or more federal employees who have filed about 50,000 PPP complaints with OSC since 1979, alleging about 100,000 specific PPP's. Almost all of these individuals did not obtain the tangible nondiscretionary statutory protection OSC owed them—a written determination whether "there is reasonable grounds/cause to believe" the alleged PPP occurred and, if positive, an OSC report of that determination to the involved agency head, per 5 U.S.C. § 1214(e). [2010 WL 1848206]

On OSC Watch's "Whistleblower Support Blog," [http://gflorencescott.word press.com/tag/osc-watch/] Carson identifies himself as "'dean' of the current federal whistleblowers" and chair of the organization's steering committee. Thus, the Carson case discussed here must be read in the context of a decades-long crusade by Carson and compatriots against what they perceive to be a failure by the government to appropriately enforce the whistleblower laws of the United States. It seems highly unlikely that this will be his final foray into litigation land.

Occupational Health and Safety

Q 10:108   Are state employees protected by occupational health and safety laws?

As pointed out in chapter 7, state and local employees are not covered by the federal OSH Act. However, as further noted in that chapter, Congress did empower the states to enact their own occupational safety and health acts to protect their public employees. The list below provides status of the 50 states and contact information for those states with health and safety statutes:

State	Status	Agency	Comments
Alabama	Not Applicable		
Alaska	Federally Approved State Plan	Department of Labor Labor Standards and Safety Division 1111 W. 8th Street, Room 306 Juneau, AK 99801-1149 (907) 465-4855 Fax: (907) 465-6012 http://labor.alaska.gov/lss/home.htm	
Arizona	Federally Approved State Plan	Industrial Commission 800 W. Washington Phoenix, AZ 85007 (602) 542-5795 Fax: (602) 542-1614	

State	Status	Agency	Comments
Arkansas	Right-to-Know Law: A.S. Title 8, Chapter 7, 8-1-1001 to 1016, 11-2-110 covers public employees	Department of Labor Public Employees Right to Know 10421 West Markham Little Rock, AR 72205 (501) 682-4500 http://www.labor.ar.gov/ Pages/default.aspx	
California	Federally Approved State Plan	CalOSHA http://www.dir.ca.gov/ occupational_safety.html	CalOSHA has developed its own standards beyond federal OSHA.
Colorado	Executive Order DO138-89 July 28, 1989 covers State employees.	Colorado Department of Personnel General Support Services, Division of Risk Management 1313 Sherman, Room 114 Denver, CO 80203 (303) 866-2439 http://www.colorado.gov/ dpa/dhr/temp/riskover.htm	Not federally approved; the state "will attempt" to provide a safe and healthful workplace. It does not adopt federal OSHA standards.
Connecticut	Federally Approved State Plan for Public Employees	Department of Labor Connecticut Department of Labor 200 Folly Brook Boulevard Wethersfield, CT 06109 Phone: (860) 263-6000 E-mail: dol.webhelp@ct.gov http://www.ctdol.state.ct. us/osha/osha.htm	State law covers public employees. Private-sector employees are covered by federal OSHA.

State	Status	Agency	Comments
Delaware	Delaware Hazardous Chemical Information Act	Department of Labor Division of Industrial Affairs 4425 North Market Street Wilmington, DE 19802 (302) 761-8176 http://www. delawareworks.com/ industrialaffairs/welcome. shtml	
District of Columbia	Public Employee OSHA Plan	Office of Occupational Safety and Health 200 Constitution Avenue Northwest Washington, DC 20210-0001 (202) 693-1999	Non-federally approved public employee OSHA plan.
Florida	SB 230 repealed F.S. 442 "Occupational Safety and Health" effective June 30, 2000. As a result, the 17 offices of the Division of Safety were closed.		
Georgia	Not Applicable		
Hawaii	Federally Approved State Plan	Department of Labor and Industrial Relations 830 Punchbowl Street Honolulu, HI 96813 (808) 586-9100 Fax: (808) 586-9104 http://hawaii.gov/labor/	
Idaho	Not Applicable		

State	Status	Agency	Comments
Illinois	Safety Inspection and Education Act & The Health and Safety Act	Department of Labor 900 S. Spring Street Springfield, IL 62704 (217) 782-6206 Fax: (217) 782-0596 http://www.state.il.us/ agency/idol/index.htm	Non-federally approved public employee OSHA plan.
Indiana	Federally Approved State Plan	Department of Labor 402 West Washington Street, Room W-195 Indianapolis, IN 46204 (317) 232-2655 Fax: (317) 233-3790 http://www.ai.org/labor/ iosha/	
Iowa	Federally Approved State Plan	Division of Labor Services Iowa Workforce Development 1000 E. Grand Avenue Des Moines, IA 50319-0209 (515) 281-5387 Fax: (515) 281-7995 http://www.iowaworkforce. org/labor/	
Kansas State	OSHA Law KSA 44-636 and State Right-to-Know Law	Department of Human Resources Division of Workers Compensation Industrial Safety and Health Section 800 SW Jackson, Suite 600 Topeka, KS 66612 (785) 296-4386 http://www.dol.ks.gov/ Default.aspx	Non-federally approved public employee OSHA plan.

State	Status	Agency	Comments
Kentucky	Federally Approved State Plan	Labor Cabinet Kentucky OSHA Program 1047 U.S. Highway 127 South, Suite 4 Frankfort, KY 40601 (502) 564-3070 Fax: (502) 564-5387 http://www.labor.ky.gov/	
Louisiana	Hazardous Material Information, Development, Preparedness	Department of Labor 1001 N. 23rd Street Baton Rouge, LA 70804 (225) 342-9601 http://www.ldol.state.la.us/	
Maine	MRSA Title 26, Chapter 6, Occupational Safety Rules and Regulations Board	Department of Labor Bureau of Labor Standards 54 Statehouse Station Augusta, ME 04333 (207) 623-7900 http://www.maine.gov/labor/	Non-federally approved public employee OSHA plan.
Maryland	Federally Approved State Plan	Department of Labor, Licensing and Regulation Division of Labor and Industry, MOSH 10946 Golden West Drive, Suite 160 Hunt Valley, MD 21031 (410) 527-4447 Fax: (410) 527-4495 http://www.dllr.state.md.us/labor/mosh.html	
Massachusetts	Hazardous Substances Disclosure by Employers Act	Department of Labor and Workforce Development One Ashburton Place, Suite 2112 Boston, MA 02108 (617) 626-7122	

State	Status	Agency	Comments
Michigan	Federally Approved State Plan	Department of Consumer and Industry Services Bureau of Safety and Regulation (MIOSHA) 7150 Harris Drive Lansing, MI 48909-813 (517) 322-1814 Fax: (517) 322-1775 MIOSHA Complaint Hotline 800-866-4674 (TO-MIOSHA) http://www.michigan.gov/lara/0,1607,7-154-11407---,00.html	
Minnesota	Federally Approved State Plan	Department of Labor and Industry MNOSHA 443 Lafayette Road St. Paul, MN 55155-4307 (651) 284-5005 Fax: (651) 284-5741 http://www.dli.mn.gov/main.asp	MNOSHA has a standard to protect against exposure to heat and the right-to-know standard includes infectious diseases.
Mississippi	Not Applicable		
Missouri	Right-to-Know Law	Department of Labor and Industrial Relations Division of Labor Standards P.O. Box 504 Jefferson City, MD 65102 (573) 751-9691 http://labor.mo.gov/	
Montana	Employee and Community Hazardous Chemical Information	Department of Labor Safety Bureau P.O. Box 1728 Helena, MT 59624 (406) 444-2840 http://dli.mt.gov/	

State	Status	Agency	Comments
Nebraska	Workplace Safety Consultation Program	Safety & Labor Standards Division 550 South 16th Street, Box 94600 Lincoln, NE 68509 (402) 471-3405 http://dol.nebraska.gov/center. cfm?PRICAT=2&SUBCAT =5Z0	Employers must have safety committees with equal representation between the employer and workers. Employers must have an Effective Written Injury Prevention Program.
Nevada	Federally Approved State Plan	Division of Industrial Relations Occupational Safety and Health Enforcement Section 1301 North Green Valley Parkway, Suite 200 Henderson, NV 89074 (702) 486-9020 Fax: (702) 990-0365 http://dirweb.state.nv.us/	
New Hampshire	Public Employee OSHA Law Workers Right-to-Know Act, RSA 277-A	Department of Labor Safety and Training Division 95 Pleasant Street Concord, NH 03301 (603) 271-3171 http://www.nh.gov/labor/	Non-federally approved public employee OSHA plan.
New Jersey	Federally Approved State Plan for Public Employees	Department of Labor Public Employees Occupational Safety and Health (PEOSH) P.O. Box 369 135 East State Street Trenton, NJ 08625-0369 (609) 984-1863 health hazards (609) 633-3896 safety hazards Fax: (609) 292-3749 http://www.state.nj.us/ health/peosh/index.shtml	State law covers public employees. Private-sector employees are covered by federal OSHA.

State	Status	Agency	Comments
New Mexico	Federally Approved State Plan	Environment Department Occupational Health and Safety Bureau 525 Camino de los Marquez, Suite 3 Santa Fe, NM 87505 (505) 827-4230 http://www.nmenv.state.nm.us/	
New York	Federally Approved State Plan for Public Employees	Department of Labor Public Employee Safety and Health (PESH) W. Averell Harriman State Building #12 Albany, NY 12240 (518) 457-9000 Fax: (518) 457-5545 http://www.labor.ny.gov/home	State law covers public employees. Private-sector employees are covered by federal OSHA.
North Carolina	Federally Approved State Plan	Division of Occupational Safety and Health 4 West Edenton Street Raleigh, NC 27601-1092 (919) 733-0359 or 1-800-LABOR-NC Complaints: (919) 733-3322 http://www.nclabor.com/osha/osh.htm	
North Dakota	North Dakota State Worker Right-to-Know Act	Workers' Compensation Bureau 1600 E Century Ave #1 Bismarck, ND 58503 (701) 328-3800 or 1-800-777-5033	

State	Status	Agency	Comments
Ohio	Public Employment Risk Reduction Program	Ohio Department of Commerce Division of Labor & Worker Safety 50 West Broad Street, 28th Floor Columbus, Ohio 43215 (614) 644-2239 or 1-800-671-6858 http://www.com.ohio.gov/	Non-federally approved public employee OSHA plan.
Oklahoma	OSHA Law and OK Hazard Communication Standard (40 OK 401)	OK Department of Labor PEOSH Division 4001 N. Lincoln Boulevard Oklahoma City, OK 73105-5212 (405) 528-1500 ext. 273 1-888-269-5353 outside Oklahoma City http://www.ok.gov/	Non-federally approved public employee OSHA plan.
Oregon	Federally Approved State Plan	Department of Consumer and Business Services Occupational Safety and Health Division 350 Winter Street, NE, Room 430 Salem, OR 97310 (503) 378-3272 Fax: (503) 947-7461 http://www.cbs.state.or.us/external/osha/index.html	
Pennsylvania	Worker and Community Right-to-Know Act	Department of Labor Bureau of Pennsafe Room 1503 7th and Forester Streets Harrisburg, PA 17108 (717) 783-2071 http://www.dli.state.pa.us/portal/server.pt/community/l_i_home/5278	

State	Status	Agency	Comments
Puerto Rico	Federally Approved Program	Puerto Rico Department of Labor and Human Resources Edificio Prudencio Rivera Martinez Building 505 Munoz Rivera Avenue G.P.O. Box 3088 Hato Rey, PR 00918 (809) 754-2119 Fax: (787) 753-9550	
Rhode Island	Hazardous Substance Right-to-Know Act	Department of Labor Division of Occupational Safety and Health 1511 Pontiac Avenue Cranston, RI 02920 (401) 462-8870 http://www.dlt.state.ri.us/	
South Carolina	Federally Approved State Plan	Department of Labor, Licensing & Regulation Office of OSHA 110 Centerview Drive P.O. Box 11329 Columbia, SC 29210-1329 (803) 896-7665 Fax: (803) 896-7670 http://www.llr.state.sc.us/	
South Dakota	Not Applicable		
Tennessee	Federally Approved State Plan	Department of Labor 220 Fench Landing Drive Nashville, TN 37243-1002 (615) 741-2793 Fax: (615) 741-5078 http://www.state.tn.us/labor-wfd/tosha.html	

State	Status	Agency	Comments
Texas	State Right-to-Know Law	Toxic Substances Control Division 209 West 14th Street Austin, TX 78701 (512) 225-1300 http://www.sos.state.tx.us/	
Utah	Federally Approved State Plan	Utah Labor Commission Utah Occupational Safety and Health 160 East 300 South, 3rd Floor P.O. Box 146650 Salt Lake City, UT 84114-6650 (801) 530-6901 Fax: (801) 530-7606 http://laborcommission.utah.gov/divisions/UOSH/index.html	
Vermont	Federally Approved State Plan	Department of Labor and Industry VOSHA 5 Green Mountain Drive P.O. Box 488 Montpelier, VT 05601-0488 (802) 828-4000 Fax: (802) 888-4022 http://www.labor.vermont.gov/VDOLHomePage/ContactUs/tabid/377/Default.aspx	
Virgin Islands		Division of Occupational Safety and Health (VIDOSH) 21-23 Hospital Street Christiansted, St. Croix VI 00802 (340) 776-3700 Fax: (340) 773-0094	

State	Status	Agency	Comments
Virginia	Federally Approved State Plan	Department of Labor and Industry VOSH 13 South 13th Street Richmond, VA 23219 (804) 371-2327 http://www.doli.virginia.gov/	
Washington	Federally Approved State Plan	Department of Labor and Industries WISHA P.O. Box 44000 Olympia, WA 98504-4000 (360) 902-4200 Fax: (360) 902-5619 http://www.lni.wa.gov/Safety/default.asp	
West Virginia	Hazardous Substances Law	Department of Labor Capitol Complex Building 6, Room B749 Charleston, WV 25305 (304) 558-7890	
Wisconsin	Public Employee Only Law	Department of Commerce Safety and Buildings Division 201 West Washington Avenue Madison, WI 53701 (608) 266-3151 http://www.commerce.state.wi.us/SB/SB-HomePage.html	Non-federally approved public employee OSHA plan.
Wyoming		Federally Approved State Plan Wyoming Workers' Safety (OSHA) 1510 E. Pershing Blvd., West Wing Cheyenne, WY 82002 (307) 777-7261 http://www.wyomingworkforce.org/Pages/default.aspx	

[Courtesy of AFSCME, http://www.afscme.org/health/safe14.htm, and re-printed with permission. Updated on Apr. 24, 2013, using http://www.osha.gov/dcsp/osp/index.html]

Chapter 11

Labor Unions

The rights conferred upon labor unions and union employees are generally derived from the authority of the National Labor Relations Act (NLRA), which followed closely on the heels of the Norris-LaGuardia Act during the New Deal era of the 1930s. The NLRA is the "rule book" that labor organizations must follow when attempting to unionize companies that are covered by it. Likewise, an employer confronted with efforts to organize a union must be aware of the statutory mandates and prohibitions that apply to it as well as to the labor organization. The statute also governs the collective bargaining relationship after a group of employees has selected a union to represent it. This chapter provides information on developments in evolving areas concerning the NLRA.

Union Organizing

Q 11:1   What is a *labor union*?

A *labor union* is an organization that may be incorporated, but usually is not, that is formed under the authority of the federal labor laws (notably the NLRA or the Railway Labor Act for railroads and airlines) or under an analogous state law covering public employees. Its purpose is to represent eligible and interested employees in negotiating the terms and conditions of their employment. The largest combination of labor unions in the United States is the American Federation of Labor-Congress of Industrial Unions (AFL-CIO).

Q 11:2 Do employees have the right to belong to a labor union?

Yes. The NLRA, as amended by the Taft-Hartley Act in 1947, gives most private-sector employees the right to join a labor union and to authorize that union to negotiate with their employers on their behalf; however, the NLRA also affords employees the right to refrain from joining and participating in a labor union. This right has been strengthened in states that have passed right-to-work laws pursuant to a provision in the Taft-Hartley Act.

Q 11:3 Why does a labor union target a particular company for unionization?

A labor union may try to organize the employees of a company for several reasons. First, the company may be particularly large and visible with many employees. Second, the company may be involved in a heavily organized industry in which the employees traditionally have been represented by a particular union (e.g., steel, automobiles, and coal mining). Third, the company may have a large percentage of dissatisfied employees, rendering it susceptible to unionization.

Q 11:4 How can a company avoid being unionized?

One of the best ways to avoid unionization is to provide employees with some or all of the things that a union can provide. Many studies have shown that job security and compensation are the two main concerns of most employees. Many companies therefore give non-union employees competitive compensation packages and a workplace due-process program that provides them a sense of job security. Open communication, fair and evenhanded treatment, and predictable behavior by the employer all help to increase employee security. Secure, well-paid employees will not pay dues to put a union between themselves and their companies.

Q 11:5 What should a company do if it becomes the target of a union organizing drive?

A company should:

- Conduct a meeting of supervisors and managers to explain what actions to avoid;
- Determine the grievances or problems that led employees to seek a union's help or that may lead employees to join the union; and

- Plan a campaign to defuse the organizing drive, preferably before an election petition has been filed with the National Labor Relations Board (NLRB).

A company should not:

- Interrogate employees about their interest in the union or union activities;
- Discharge or otherwise punish employees who are trying to organize for the union;
- Make threats or promises to employees; or
- Conduct surveillance of employees at organizing meetings or other union activities.

Q 11:6   How does a union organize a company's employees?

Disgruntled employees often ask the union to organize them and their co-workers. The union then asks these employees to be inside organizers. The union may call organizing meetings or a business agent may visit the job site to distribute union authorization cards and other union literature.

Organized labor revealed that:

> In analyzing the reasons for winning or losing an election, generally we can track the outcome back to the early days of the campaign. Although organizers sometimes claim "we lost the election in the last two days," this is rarely the case. Since we know that companies will unleash major issues in the last days or weeks of the campaign . . . it is incumbent upon the organizers to build a foundation that will withstand this inevitable assault. This means building a strong committee, made up of a representative group of key leaders, who can prepare their co-workers for the management campaign.

[The Blitz, *A Manual for Organizers on How to Run Fast-paced Pre-petition Campaigns*, AFL-CIO]

The book quoted above is published by the AFL-CIO as a handbook on a union organizing technique known as the blitz. Credit for development of the blitz technique is given to organizer Richard Bensinger of the Amalgamated Clothing and Textile Workers Union. ["Labor's Newest Strategy for Winning Elections," *Labor Relations Ink* 4, Feb. 1993, at 3] Although the handbook does not contain anything truly revolutionary, it is described as a blueprint for doing what unions have always done during organizing drives, but doing it faster and more efficiently.

Blitz campaigns are divided into two phases—preparation and action. The preparation phase involves building a list of employees and recruiting volunteers to help in the organization effort. This phase can take weeks or months. Regardless of the time involved, the key to success is secrecy. When the corporate hierarchy becomes aware of this phase of the organizing, the blitz is probably doomed to failure. The union uses a small, but ever-growing committee to build a list of eligible voters.

The action phase is divided into steps. The first step involves training as many volunteers as available to make house calls on all eligible voters. Because these calls are made two or three times, the volunteer committee may be supplemented by union staffers or paid workers, generally union members from other corporations within the general geographic area. The second step ideally occurs during a blitz week. Monday and Tuesday of such a week are typically devoted to training the house callers (during an organizing drive or election campaign, union representatives, but not employer representatives, are permitted by the NLRA to make house calls). Wednesday, Thursday, and Friday are usually devoted to house calls. The goal is to make contact with at least 60 percent of all eligible voters. By the following Monday, a representation petition is filed with the NLRB. In a well-executed blitz, management does not know the drive is underway until the first day of home visits, at the earliest. Labor claims that using the blitz has increased its success rate from 45 percent to 65 percent or better.

Q 11:7   May a union representative enter company premises?

No. The general rule is that a union organizer who is not an employee of the company cannot enter company premises, but the NLRB has carved out some exceptions. For example, if a job site is remote or if safety considerations discourage or prevent the union from contacting employees anywhere but on the job site, an organizer may enter company premises. At times, union organizers have been permitted to enter a lumber camp or to board a ship, but this right was carefully circumscribed by the NLRB, especially the board members appointed by Ronald Reagan and George Bush. The NLRB has also permitted union organizers to distribute literature in company parking lots when street traffic outside the company's gates would endanger the organizers.

In a 1992 decision involving an organizing drive by the United Food and Commercial Workers, the U.S. Supreme Court upheld the right of a Connecticut company to keep union organizers from passing out leaflets and placing fliers on the windshields of cars at a parking lot it owned. By a six to three vote, the Court found that the NLRB erred in granting union organizers the right to trespass on private property to get their message to employees. The case involved a department store owned by Lechmere, Inc. located in a shopping mall in Newington, Connecticut.

In his first opinion for the Court, Justice Clarence Thomas said that federal labor law, by its plain terms, confers rights only on employees, not on unions or organizers; therefore, as a rule, an employer cannot be forced to allow the distribution of literature by labor organizers on its property. "Access to employees, not success in winning them over, is the critical issue—although success, or lack thereof, may be relevant in determining whether reasonable access exists," he wrote. [Lechmere, Inc. v. NLRB, 502 U.S. 527 (1992); *see also* James O. Castagnera & Thomas J Bender, Jr., "Justice Thomas and NLRB Refine Unions' Rights to Organize and Picket," *Employment Law Update* (Philadelphia: Saul, Ewing, Remick & Saul, Apr. 1992 at 1).]

Q 11:8 May employees engage in organizing efforts and hand out literature on company property?

Yes. Employees may discuss unionism and solicit their co-workers, provided that these activities occur before and after their shifts or during lunch and break times; employees are not entitled to engage in these activities when they should be working. It may also be permissible for an employee to give co-workers union flyers or authorization cards in a lunchroom, locker room, or parking lot; however, they may not distribute literature on the work floor, where the paper could create a hazard.

Q 11:9 How can an employer ensure that employees do not abuse their rights to discuss the union and to solicit one another at the workplace?

An employer should adopt a no-solicitation rule. A valid, legal no-solicitation rule might read as follows:

> Persons not employed by this company will not be permitted to solicit on behalf of any cause or organization at any time on company property. No person employed by this company will be permitted to solicit on behalf of any cause or organization during working time or in work areas during work time. Working time is defined as all hours of work exclusive of authorized break or rest periods, meal periods, and other authorized nonworking periods. Any non-employee found violating this rule will be removed from company property. Any employee found violating this rule will be subject to discipline up to and including discharge.

Q 11:10 Are there any reasons that an employer cannot enforce a no-solicitation rule?

Although companies can establish "across-the-board" prohibitions on non-employee solicitation on company premises, if a company establishes a policy to prohibit non-employee union solicitation, but allows other non-employees access to company premises for purposes of solicitation, the policy will be considered facially discriminatory. [See the seminal decision NLRB v. Babcock & Wilcox, Co., 351 U.S. 105 (1956).] This principle was addressed in *American Postal Workers Union, AFL-CIO v. NLRB* [370 F.3d 25 (D.C. Cir. 2004)]. In the case, the company had a published policy of prohibiting non-employee union solicitation on company property. Although the union claimed that this policy on its face was facially discriminatory, the court found that the policy was part of an overall one prohibiting any type of non-employee solicitation on company premises. As such, the court concluded that the company's policy was not discriminatory and therefore valid.

Q 11:11   Does an employer have the right to communicate its views about unions to employees?

Yes. An employer can do so in employee meetings and through letters and other literature distributed to employees; however, an employer may not threaten employees with discipline, discharge, or plant closure if they support a union. An employer cannot make promises incumbent on employees avoiding the union. The information disseminated about the union and unionism, as well as information about the company, must be truthful. A statement claiming that a union is dominated by a particular racial group, even if true, may constitute an unfair labor practice. Allegations that a union is dominated by organized crime or is inclined to lead its members into long and bitter strikes may be permissible but must be handled carefully to ensure its accuracy.

Q 11:12   Do employers have obligations to inform employees of their rights under the NLRA?

In August 2011, the NLRB issued a final rule entitled "Notification of Employee Rights under the National Relations Act." The rule (1) required that the employer post notices informing employees of their rights under the NLRA, and (2) provided that failure to post such notice was an unfair labor practice for which the statute of limitations would be tolled against employers who failed to post. Not surprisingly, the rule was challenged and the first court to address the issue, the District Court of the District of Columbia, held that the broad rule-making authority of the NLRB under the NLRA provided authority to require employers to post the required notice, but held that that portion of the rule that provides that failure to post was an unfair labor practice for which the statute of limitations would be tolled exceeded the authority of the NLRB. [*National Ass'n of Manufacturers v. NLRB*, 846 F. Supp. 2d 34 (D.D.C. 2012)] This decision was enjoined pending appeal. [*National Ass'n of Manufacturers v. NLRB*, 2012 WL 4328371 (D.C. Cir. Apr. 17, 2012)] While the appeal of the District of Columbia case was pending, a district court in South Carolina found the rule in its totality overstepped the authority of the NLRB. [*Chamber of Commerce v. NLRB*, 856 F. Supp 2d 778 (D.S.C. 2012) (NLRB lacked authority to require employers to post notices informing employees of their rights under the NLRA)]

The National Labor Relations Board

Q 11:13   How does the NLRB fit into the organizing process?

The NLRA, which was passed in the 1930s, prohibited unfair labor practices—most notably, employers' interference with their employees' right to engage in union activity. In 1947, the Taft-Hartley Act was passed to prohibit unfair union practices. The NLRB is the independent governmental agency empowered by Congress to enforce these laws. Among its many duties, the NLRB must accept representation petitions filed by labor unions and employees, investigate the validity of those petitions, and conduct elections by secret ballot. If a union wins an election by secret ballot, the NLRB can certify that union as the bargaining representative for the group (or bargaining unit) of the employees that chose it. In 2012, the NLRB purportedly amended its procedures for determining whether the majority of employees wanted to be represented by a union—amendments that some viewed as favorable for union representation and unfavorable to employers. The rule was purportedly adopted by a vote of two NLRB members, but without the attendance of the third board member. The purported rule was challenged and in 2012, a district court found that the required quorum of three members for rule making purposes was not met and, therefore, the two board members did not have authority to pass a rule amending the procedures for determining whether the employees wanted union representation. [*Chamber of Commerce v. NLRB*, 2012 WL 1664028 (D.D.C. May 14, 2012)]

Q 11:14   Is an arbitration award enforceable when it contradicts an NLRB decision?

No. An arbitration award that contradicts an earlier NLRB ruling is unenforceable according to a case decided by the Court of Appeals for the Ninth Circuit. The union claimed that two related corporations under a double-breasting arrangement (whereby separate union and non-union operations are run by a common owner) were alter egos—that is, the arrangement was created to avoid the employer's obligations under the National Labor Relations Act. The NLRB agreed. Later, during a grievance arbitration, the arbitrator ruled that the two firms did not meet the test of common or joint control. According to the federal court, the NLRB holding was binding. [A. Dariano & Sons Inc. v. District Council of Painters, 869 F.2d 514 (9th Cir. 1989)]

Q 11:15   When does the NLRB defer an unfair labor practice charge to arbitration?

When an employee files an unfair labor practice charge, but the employer demands an arbitration under the labor contract, the current NLRB practice is to defer the matter to the arbitrator if the unfair labor practice claim implicates a parallel provision in the collective bargaining agreement; however, some federal courts of appeals, which are charged with reviewing and enforcing labor board orders, have demonstrated their disagreement with this standard of deferral. [*See, e.g.*, NLRB v. Motor Convoy, Inc., 673 F.2d 734 (4th Cir. 1982); Richmond Tank Car Co. v. NLRB, 721 F.2d 499 (5th Cir. 1983); American Freight Sys. Inc. v. NLRB, 722 F.2d 828 (D.C. Cir. 1983).] In other words, just because some clause in the labor contract is parallel to language in the Taft-Hartley Act (e.g., a clause forbidding discrimination by the employer based on employees' union affiliation—a common clause), that clause does not necessarily free the board to defer its obligation to the private-party grievance procedure.

Representation Elections

Q 11:16   What must a union do to get an NLRB election?

The union must show that at least 30 percent of the employees in the appropriate bargaining unit want representation. In practice, a union rarely files a representation petition with the NLRB until a substantial majority of the employees have signed authorization cards.

Q 11:17   Can a union offer enticements to workers before a representation election to curry their votes?

No. In 1989, the NLRB held that a union that offered free medical testing two days before an election so tainted the vote that its victory had to be set aside. The union offered screenings for high blood pressure, lung functions, cholesterol level, and diabetes. The tests were given in two vans bearing the union logo. The NLRB concluded that workers who took the tests believed they had gotten a gift from the union and that it was a benefit they would lose if they did not retain the union. This, the NLRB felt, was no different than an employer giving gifts during the campaign period. [Mailing Servs., Inc., 293 N.L.R.B. 58 (1989)]

Q 11:18   What is an *authorization card*?

A union *authorization card* usually states that an employee seeks union representation in collective bargaining with the employer. Although union organizers often tell employees that these cards merely indicate their desire for a representation election, generally the card actually signifies that the employee wants that union to be the group's representative.

Q 11:19   Can a union become the collective bargaining representative of employees on the basis of authorization cards alone?

Yes. A union can become the collective bargaining representative of a company's employees without a secret ballot election if the union presents authorization cards signed by a majority of the employees and the employer or one of the company's managers reviews those cards and perceives that the union has obtained a majority. Supervisors should therefore be instructed at the start of a union organizing effort to refuse to touch, take possession of, or review authorization cards that might be offered by a union representative, because doing so might be construed as a review by the employer.

Q 11:20   Can an employer interfere with a union's ability to communicate with its employees?

Section 8 of the NLRA makes it an unfair labor practice to "interfere with, restrain or coerce employees in the exercise of the rights guaranteed" in Section 7 of the NLRA [29 U.S.C. § 158(a)(1)]. Section 7 of the NLRA in turn provides employees the "right to self-organization, to form, join or assist labor organizations . . . and to engage in other concerted activities for the purpose of collective bargaining or other mutual aid or protection." [29 U.S.C. § 157] As such, an employer violates the NLRA when it interferes with its employees' right to communicate with their union, their statutory representative. This principle was reiterated in *ATC Vancom of California, LP v. NLRB*. [370 F.3d 692 (7th Cir. 2004)] At issue in the case was whether the employer could limit the union's ability to communicate with its members via a designated space on bulletin boards for the union's use. At the time, the employees were being asked to decertify their existing union and elect another union in its place. The employer claimed, that in the midst of this contest, it could prevent the union in power from utilizing the union designated bulletin board space for its benefit, citing a new California statute, the so-called California Neutrality Statute which placed limits on the expenditures of state funds and the conduct of state contractors from preventing, promoting, or deterring union organizing. Citing the NLRA, and the dubious applicability of the California statute, the court concluded that the employer's action was an unfair labor practice violating federal law.

Q 11:21 Can a union picket a business when trying to organize its employees?

Yes. As a general rule, a union can picket an employer for as many as 30 days before filing an election petition with the NLRB. A union may also be entitled to picket for a longer period to protest the employer's poor wages or benefits; this is called area-standards picketing.

Q 11:22 What happens after a union files a petition with the NLRB?

The NLRB first determines whether the union is supported (e.g., through signed authorization cards) by at least 30 percent of the workers that the union seeks to represent. If it is, a board agent starts laying the groundwork for an election by secret ballot. Then the appropriate bargaining unit, list of eligible voters, date and place of the election, and other details are outlined. They are determined either by mutual agreement of the company and the union or by the board's decision following a hearing.

Q 11:23 Is there an election campaign?

Yes. The length of the campaign is generally about 30 days. During this campaign the company can defend itself and attempt to persuade the employee voters to vote against the union.

Q 11:24 Can a company win an election?

Yes. Unions lose more elections than they win. The chances of winning are probably high enough for an employer to invest the time and money necessary to conduct an effective campaign. This generally means hiring a professional consultant or labor lawyer.

Q 11:25 Can a company's efforts defeat a union organizing drive?

Yes. A company that vigorously opposes unionization enjoys a substantially better chance of defeating a union than a company that does not address the issue of organizing. First, companies that practice effective employment policies tend to have satisfied employees with no desire to unionize. Second, although labor unions have long held that (as in Canada) companies in the United States should remain neutral during union organizing efforts, the NLRB under Ronald Reagan's administration expanded employers' rights to question employees about union interest and to communicate the company's views to the workers. This expansion has not been revised significantly.

Bargaining Units and Related Employment Practices

Q 11:26 What constitutes an appropriate bargaining unit of employees?

All employees in a bargaining unit should share common work interests, such as similar pay, status, and benefits. The NLRB tends to prefer bargaining units defined by location, especially if the company's several facilities are distant from one another.

Supervisors, confidential secretaries, and security guards are generally excluded from units representing other categories of employees. Supervisors and managers are not covered by the protection and organizing rights of the NLRA. Professional employees may be allowed, if they choose, to form their own separate unit, though they may be represented by the same union.

Q 11:27 Are registered nurses at a medical facility "supervisors" such that they are not covered by the protection and organizing rights under the NLRA?

Under the NLRA, supervisors are excluded from the rights and protections under the NLRA. One criterion for determining whether an employer is a supervisor is if he or she exercises "independent judgement" in "responsibly . . . direct[ing] other employees in the employer's interest." [29 U.S.C. § 152 (11)] In *NLRB v. Kentucky River Community Care, Inc.*, the U.S. Supreme Court was asked to consider whether registered nurses at a medical facility were supervisors, such that the employer had no obligation to bargain with the union representing their bargaining unit. The Court found that although they may have lacked independent judgment in exercising their authority over others, they nonetheless exercised "ordinary professional or technical judgment in directing less-skilled employees to deliver services in accordance with employer specified standards," which was sufficient to make them supervisors and therefore outside of the protections and rights under the NLRA. [532 U.S. 706, 707 (2001)]

In *Lakeland Health Care Assocs., LLC v. NLRB* [696 F.3d 1332 (11th Cir. 2012)], at issue was whether licensed practical nurses (LPNs) were "supervisors" under the NLRA. Finding that the LPNs had authority to discipline and influence in hiring/firing certified nursing assistants (CNAs), exercised independent judgments in scheduling CNAs, and that LPN's interests were aligned with management, the court found the LPNs were supervisors such that they were not protected by the NLRA.

Q 11:28   Are independent contractors covered by the NLRA?

No. Independent contractors are not employees covered by the protection of the NLRA. The tough question is defining the difference between independent contractors and actual employees. Generally, the definition depends on whether the company has the right to control how such workers perform their jobs.

Some of the factors that indicate that a person is an employee include:

- Working for only one employer;
- Being provided work space, tools, and materials by the employer; and
- Being required to be on the job at certain times on specified work days.

Factors suggesting an independent contractor status include:

- Being allowed to come and go at will;
- Being allowed to decide how to accomplish the general goals set; and
- Receiving no fringe benefits.

If most of these factors suggest that a worker is an independent contractor, the NLRA does not protect him or her with respect to labor organizing activities.

In 1989, a group of rabbis who performed "kosher kills" for a Chicago meat packer were determined to be independent contractors after they sought to be represented by Local 100-A of the United Food and Commercial Workers Union. The rabbis, known as schoctim, were compensated according to the number of kills they performed in accordance with Orthodox Jewish principles, received no fringe benefits from the company, were not subject to the firm's disciplinary policy, and were accorded complete discretion on how they handled their task.

Another interesting case was decided by the NLRB early in 1991. The board found that the Coca-Cola Company had violated the Taft-Hartley Act by forbidding a janitorial worker at its Atlanta headquarters from distributing literature about an organizing drive by the Service Employees Union. Coca-Cola had contracted with Southern Services, Inc. to perform its janitorial work, and Southern Services actually employed the janitor. Because the janitor was distributing information at her normal place of employment and was not a trespasser, the NLRB held that the Act protected the janitor's right to distribute the information. [1991 *BNA Daily Labor Report* 15, Jan. 23, 1991, at 2]

Q 11:29   If a union is certified by the NLRB to represent some of a company's employees, what legal obligation does the company have?

The company has the legal duty to bargain in good faith with the union.

Q 11:30   What does bargaining in good faith mean?

Briefly, bargaining in good faith involves listening to the other side, keeping an open mind, and trying to reach an agreement. It involves being available to meet and confer at reasonable times and places. It does not mean that a company has a legal obligation to make a concession. A company has the legal right to bargain to an impasse, if good-faith negotiating does not bring the two sides together.

Q 11:31   Is collective bargaining necessarily an adversarial exercise?

Typically in contract negotiations, both sides (or at least the union representatives) come to the bargaining table with a list of demands. The posture on both sides ranges from mildly to stridently adversarial, but this stance is not necessarily inevitable. For example, in 1996–1997 the Ford Motor Company surprised other American auto manufacturers by the success of its revolutionary approach to achieving cooperation between labor and management in its bargaining relationship with the United Auto Workers.

Q 11:32   What is a *collective bargaining agreement*?

Commonly called a labor contract, a *collective bargaining agreement* is a pact between a union and company that covers the terms and conditions of employment of the unionized employees.

Q 11:33   Is an employer's refusal to execute a collective bargaining agreement a continuing violation of the NLRA?

No. If an employer refuses to sign, the clock starts ticking on a six-month statute of limitations. The aggrieved union must file its charge of unfair labor practice within that six-month period or risk losing the opportunity for a remedy thereafter.

Q 11:34   Does the NLRA preempt a claim made on the basis of state law?

Not always. State common law recognizes a tort action for injurious interference with a contractual relationship. For example, a tort action occasionally has been invoked by one college or professional sports team against another for stealing away a coach. A member of the Teamsters Union sued the Seaboard Railroad System for allegedly getting his employer, a subcontractor of Seaboard's, to fire him in retaliation for filing OSH Act charges against Seaboard.

Even though the union had grieved the discharge and an arbitrator had ruled against the employee, a federal court allowed the employee to proceed with his action against Seaboard, which was not a party to the Teamster labor contract under which the arbitration was brought. The plaintiff's tort theory was that Seaboard wrongfully interfered with his employment relationship with the subcontractor. [Dougherty v. Parsec, Inc., 872 F.2d 766 (6th Cir. 1989)]

In contrast, another federal court refused to allow a coal miner to pursue a state law action against the United Mine Workers of America for alleged negligence in carrying out a mine inspection. According to the court, the union's duty came from the collective bargaining agreement. Consequently, the miner-member had to sue for breach of that agreement under Section 301 of the Taft-Hartley Act, if he sued at all. [Sluder v. UMW Int'l & Dist. 12, 892 F.2d 549 (7th Cir. 1989)]

It is well settled under several Supreme Court decisions that employment discrimination suits are not preempted by the grievance arbitration procedures in labor contracts. Beyond that, whether or when a disgruntled unionized employee can sue an employer or union—outside the umbrella of the labor acts, the NLRA, and the collective bargaining agreement—continues to evolve on a case-by-case basis.

For example, the Court of Appeals for the Fourth Circuit held that a West Virginia statute, which sought to prevent local police from enforcing the state's criminal trespass law in the context of a labor dispute, was preempted by federal labor law. In an appeal that grew out of a 1989 United Mine Workers strike, the court ruled that a motion for preliminary injunction by Rum Creek Coal Sales, ordering the state police to enforce the trespass act, should have been granted. [Rum Creek Coal Sales, Inc. v. Caperton, 926 F.2d 353 (4th Cir. 1991)]

A U.S. District Court in Pennsylvania ruled that an employee's state law claims against a union for allegedly aiding and abetting a racially hostile work environment were pre-empted by federal law. Because the claim arose from the union's activities in investigating grievances, obligations proscribed under federal law, the state law claims were pre-empted. [15 *Employment Discrimination Report (EDR)* (BNA) 14 (Oct. 11, 2000)]

Q 11:35 What is a *union shop*?

A *union shop* is a company or company facility in which employees who come under a labor contract between the employer and a union must join that union and begin paying dues sometime (typically 30 days) after being hired.

Q 11:36 Is a union shop legal?

In most states, union shops are legal. Closed shops, which hire only those who already belong to the union, are illegal. In addition, states are allowed by the Taft-Hartley Act to pass right-to-work laws. In a right-to-work state, union shops are illegal. Sometimes these laws make agency shops illegal as well. In 2013, Michigan passed right-to-work laws that took effect on March 28, 2013.

Q 11:37   What is an *agency shop*?

In an *agency shop*, employees covered by a collective bargaining agreement can choose whether or not to join the union; however, if an employee decides not to become a union member, he or she must still pay an agency fee to the union in return for the services (e.g., negotiation and grievance representation) performed by the union. However, employees who choose not to participate in union activities may, in certain circumstances, validly refuse to wear uniforms that contain union logos, even when both the company and the union require the wearing of union logos for all employees. In *Lee v. NLRB* [393 F.3d 491 (4th Cir. 2005)], a telecommunications company and the representative union required, as part of its collective bargaining agreement, that all employees within certain job categories wear uniforms containing logos of the company and the union regardless of whether they were members of the union or not. The petitioners, non-union members, claimed that this violated their Section 7 rights under the NLRA, which protects those employees who choose not to participate in union activities. Although the court found in certain cases "special circumstances" when the employer can demonstrate legitimate reasons for the requirement, it concluded that "special circumstances" did not exist here merely because the requirement was contained in the collective bargaining agreement. The court also found that forcing non-union members to wear the union logo was an impermissible intrusion upon those employees' right to not participate in union activities as provided under the NLRA.

Q 11:38   Can a union at an "agency shop" require an opt-out as opposed to opt-in procedure for employees who are not required to pay a portion of their union dues attributable to non-bargaining matters?

The U.S. Supreme Court held, in the seminal decision *Communication Workers of America v. Beck* [487 U.S. 735 (1998)], that in an agency shop, as opposed to a union shop situation, union employees are not required to pay dues that may be attributable to things other than use for negotiating with management. In order to comply with *Beck*, in *White v. Communications Workers of America, AFL-CIO, Local 13000* [370 F.3d 346 (3d Cir. 2004)], the union had adopted an opt-out procedure, which required employees to notify unions during a limited period of time each year that they intended to refrain from paying the portion of their compulsory dues that the union did not need to use for labor-management negotiations. The union notified employees of the opt-out procedure in one of its newsletters each year. The employee in *White* felt that the restrictive and limited nature of the opt-out procedure effectively violated his First Amendment rights, and sought to have the opt-out procedure declared unconstitutional. The Third Circuit, recognizing that there is some split among courts, concluded that although unions were created by a federal law, it did not afford the requisite state action involvement such that the Constitution was inapplicable. The Third Circuit affirmed the trial court's dismissal of the employee's claim.

Q 11:39 Can the union that represents a company's employees force the company to collect fees and dues from the employees?

A union check-off clause, requiring the employer to deduct dues directly from paychecks, is a subject for collective bargaining. In states where such a clause is legal, unions usually bargain hard to include it in their labor contracts.

Q 11:40 Do unionized employees have a right to union representation in disciplinary matters?

Yes. Union employees have Weingarten rights (named for a famous NLRB case discussed below) that allow a union representative (e.g., a steward or an officer) to be present whenever an employee interview could lead to disciplinary action by the employer.

These so-called Weingarten rights have their genesis in the U.S. Supreme Court decision of *NLRB v. J. Weingarten, Inc.* [420 U.S. 251 (1975)] In interpreting the NLRA, the Court held in *Weingarten* that a private sector employee has a statutory right under the NLRA to refuse to submit, without union representation, to an investigatory interview that the employee reasonably believes might result in discipline. However, Weingarten rights do not extend to all circumstances where issues of an employee's performance are discussed with management.

In *In re Grievance of Vermont State Employees' Ass'n, Inc. and Dargie* [893 A.2d 333 (Vt. 2005)], the issue was whether a union employee was entitled to have a union representative present during two meetings she had with management where her performance deficiencies were discussed. Specifically, one meeting involved discussions concerning the employee's absences, and the other concerned the employee's lack of performance. Although performance issues were discussed, the Court concluded that discipline was not meted out at any of the meetings, and in light of Vermont precedent—which prohibits the imposition of discipline if the employer fails to give the employee notice of Weingarten rights—held that lack of such notice from the employer necessarily made the employee's subjective belief that discipline might result from the meetings unreasonable. As such, no Weingarten rights were violated.

Q 11:41 What is the union's duty to the employees it represents?

The union must represent all of its members fairly and without discrimination.

Q 11:42 What is the union's *duty of fair representation*?

The union must treat all members equally. It must also investigate employee grievances and represent all aggrieved members in a responsible and reasonable manner in relation to the employer. This duty does not prevent the union from settling grievances, even if the settlement does not please every concerned member. The union also has no obligation to conduct every employee grievance or disciplinary matter through arbitration.

Q 11:43   How far is a union entitled to go to protect employees' health and safety?

In 1989, the NLRB ruled that Glass Workers Local 193 had the right to enter a glass container plant and take heat measurements. [American Nat'l Can Co., Foster-Forbes Glass Div., 293 N.L.R.B. 110 (Apr. 28, 1989)] The NLRB derived its decision from a close analysis of the labor contract. One provision granted the union's international representative the right to visit plants to investigate grievances arising out of the interpretation or application of the contract. Another provision called for "additional relief . . . where heat or cold conditions warrant." Yet another clause required the company to "provide adequate heat, light, and ventilation to employees" and to "continue its best effort to devise systems to control drafts, noise, fumes, dust, grease, and job hazards." Putting all these provisions together, the NLRB concluded that the union had the right to collect the heat data.

Two observations, one practical and the other legal, may be appropriate here: First, heat levels constitute a very serious health concern in the glass-making industry. Second, the NLRB looked to the collective bargaining agreement for guidance, not to OSHA or anywhere else outside its area of expertise.

Q 11:44   Can the provisions of a collective bargaining agreement supersede the requirements of the federal discrimination statutes?

Yes, under some limited circumstances. The federal discrimination statutes—Title VII, the Age Discrimination in Employment Act (ADEA), the Americans with Disabilities Act (ADA), and some lesser enactments—appear to permit labor contracts to supersede federal discrimination statutes in two general situations.

When a collective bargaining agreement contains, as almost all do, a grievance arbitration procedure, the federal courts require an aggrieved employee to submit the grievance, even one based on employment discrimination, to the arbitrator. Historically, such union members were also permitted to pursue remedies concurrently or subsequently under Title VII or the ADEA. However, in *14 Penn Plaza LLC v. Pyett* [129 S. Ct. 1456 (2009)], the U.S. Supreme Court held that when a mandatory grievance arbitration provision in a CBA clearly and unmistakably contains a waiver of a union member's right to pursue a civil rights claim in court, the union member must proceed in accordance with grievance arbitration. In the case, the CBA contained specific language requiring union members to submit all claims of employment discrimination, including the ADEA claims at issue, to grievance arbitrators. As such, the Court concluded that the instant case could not be maintained outside the arbitration process. However, when mandatory arbitration language is not contained within a CBA, state law discrimination claims that do not involve the CBA and are not related to prior claims of violations of the NLRA filed in federal court, are not preempted by the NLRA. [*See* Domnister v. Exclusive Ambulette, Inc., 607 F.3d 84 (2d Cir. 2010).] In the area of seniority, the terms of a labor contract may prevail over the requirements of federal discrimination statutes.

Two major discrimination Acts expressly recognize the historic importance of seniority in labor-management relations. Title VII of the 1964 Civil Rights Act states in pertinent part:

> Notwithstanding any other provision of this subchapter, it shall not be an unlawful employment practice for an employer to apply different standards of compensation, or different terms, conditions, or privileges of employment pursuant to a bona fide seniority or merit system . . . provided that such differences are not the result of an intention to discriminate because of race, color, religion, sex, or national origin. [42 U.S.C. § 2000e-2(h) (1981)]

Similarly, the ADEA reads as follows:

> It shall not be unlawful for an employer, employment agency, or labor organization . . . to observe the terms of a bona fide seniority system or any bona fide employee benefit plan such as retirement, pension, or insurance plan, which is not a subterfuge to evade the purposes of this chapter, except that no such employee benefit plan shall excuse the failure to hire any individual. [29 U.S.C. § 623(f)(2) (1978)]

In other instances, federal law supersedes provisions under collective bargaining agreements. For example, the regulations under the Family and Medical Leave Act (FMLA) specifically provide that its reinstatement obligations to an equivalent position cannot be violated on the basis of a collective bargaining agreement that would require otherwise. As the regulation states: "For example, a provision of a CBA which provides for reinstatement to a position that is not equivalent because of seniority (e.g., provides lesser pay) is superseded by the FMLA." [29 C.F.R. § 825.700]

Q 11:45 Can the NLRB award back pay to an undocumented alien who is not legally authorized to work in the United States for an unfair labor practice committed by the employer?

In *Hoffman Plastic Compounds, Inc. v. NLRB* [535 U.S. 137 (2002)], the U.S. Supreme Court reviewed whether the NLRB had the authority to award remedial back pay relief for an unfair labor practice of the employer to an undocumented alien who utilized fraudulent documentation in connection with the Immigration Reform and Control Act (IRCA) mandated I-9 process during hiring. After reviewing the requirements of IRCA and the I-9 process, and given that there was no dispute that the employee had used fraudulent documents to gain employment, the Court held that an illegal alien could not be given back pay remedies under the NLRA for an unfair labor practice. [Hoffman Plastic Compounds, Inc. v. NLRB, 535 U.S. 137, 150 (2002)] IRCA contains both civil and criminal liability for an employee who uses fraudulent documents in the I-9 process and provides similar liability to an employer that knowingly allows an undocumented alien to continue to work at its facility. [IRCA, 8 U.S.C. § 1324a(a)(2)] The Court held that allowing the NLRB to award back pay to an illegal alien would "unduly trench" upon the clear mandates of IRCA. However, in what some may view as a direct affront to *Hoffman,* in *Agri Processor Co., Inc. v. NLRB* [514 F.3d 1 (9th Cir. 2008)], the Ninth Circuit held that illegal aliens were "employees" as the term is defined under the NLRA, and as such, are entitled to protection by the NLRA. The court distinguished *Hoffman,* by saying that it only applied to the issue of what remedies could be awarded to undocumented workers upon a finding of an unfair labor practice by the NLRB. In *Sandoval v. Rizzuti Farms, Ltd.*, [2009 WL 959478 (E.D. Wash. Apr. 7, 2009)] the court was faced with the issue of whether to allow the employer to obtain information regarding the plaintiffs' immigration status in connection with a class action complaint alleging violation of several federal and state laws protecting workers. The court held that the potential harm in providing immigration information to the employer outweighed any benefit in connection with these proceedings and granted the issuance of a protective order to prevent the employer from obtaining such information.

Q 11:46   What happens when the employer's obligations to an individual under the ADA conflict with the employer's obligations to the workforce under a collective bargaining agreement?

The ADA contains reasonable accommodation obligations that may occasionally conflict with rights and obligations contained under a collective bargaining agreement negotiated between a union and the employer. As one commentator wrote:

> While the ADA fosters equal employment opportunities for all Americans without regard to disability, its drafters ignored a very serious problem. The ADA, while promoting the rights of individual Americans in the workplace, conflicts dramatically with the [NLRA], an act designed to promote the collective rights in the workplace. The ADA, the regulations, and the Interpretive Guidance all fail to address the issue of how to reasonably accommodate an individual with a disability under the ADA in a union setting where such rights are typically received as part of a collective bargaining agreement. As a result of this oversight, conflicts between the NLRA and the ADA have arisen. [Pritchard, "Avoiding the Inevitable: Resolving the Conflicts Between the ADA and the NLRA," [11 *The Labor Lawyer* 375 (1995)]

Typically, these conflicts involve accommodations required under the ADA but in conflict with the obligations contained under the collective bargaining agreement. For example, assume a worker cannot perform the essential functions of his or her position, but a vacant position in another department matches the individual's qualifications and would accommodate the individual's disability; however, under the collective bargaining agreement, this vacant position requires job posting, with seniority determining which individual applicant will receive the position. Assume, under this hypothetical, that the disabled individual can only be awarded the position by overstepping the seniority rights of other applicants for the position in violation of the collective bargaining agreement. With regard to seniority, courts have generally held that the collective bargaining agreement essentially "trumps" the ADA, and that requiring an employer to violate the collective bargaining agreement is an unreasonable accommodation that is not required under the ADA. For example, the Third Circuit in *Kralik v. Durbin* [130 F.3d 76 (3d Cir. 1997)], adopted the reasoning of *Eckles v. Consolidated Rail Corp.*, which held, "[t]he ADA does not require disabled individuals to be accommodated by sacrificing the collectively bargained bona fide seniority rights of other employees." [94 F.3d 1041, 1051 (7th Cir 1996); *see also* 9 *Employment Discrimination Report (EDR)* (BNA) 823 (Dec. 24, 1997).]

The Equal Employment Opportunity Commission (EEOC) has taken the position that the "per se" approach reflected by the court in *Kralik* and *Eckles* is inappropriate, and the analysis should proceed under the undue hardship analysis provided under the ADA. However, the court in *Kralik* stated that "the requested accommodation is unreasonable because it would require the employer to violate its collective bargaining agreement and run the risks that violation entails." [9 *Employment Discrimination Report (EDR)* (BNA) 848–53 (Dec. 24, 1997)]

Similarly, in the companion cases of *Willis v. Pacific Maritime Ass'n* [162 F.3d 561 (9th Cir. 1998)] and *Gomez v. Pacific Maritime Ass'n* [No. 97-16779 (9th Cir. Dec. 11, 1998)], the Ninth Circuit ruled that an employer was not required under the ADA to transfer disabled employees to light-duty positions for which they were qualified, if to do so would violate the seniority requirements for the light-duty positions in accordance with the *bona fide* seniority provisions under the collective bargaining agreement. In essence, a reasonable accommodation does not include a requirement that the employer violate a collective bargaining agreement in order to accommodate a qualified person with a disability. [11 *Employment Discrimination Report (EDR)* (BNA) 803 (Dec. 16, 1998)]

If the seniority system is not pursuant to a collective bargaining agreement, but rather a system unilaterally imposed by the employer, it was thought that a different result may occur. In the Ninth Circuit case *Barnett v. U.S. Air, Inc.* [228 F.3d 1105 (9th Cir. 2000)], the U.S. Court of Appeals held that it was not an unreasonable accommodation to reassign an employee with a disability to a position for which he was qualified, despite the fact that to do so would run afoul of a company-imposed seniority system. [15 *Employment Discrimination Report (EDR)* (BNA) 498 (Oct. 11, 2000)] However, the U.S. Supreme Court, on appeal, vacated the Ninth Circuit's opinion, holding that absent special circumstances, it is unreasonable for an employer to have to violate its seniority system to accommodate an employee under the ADA. [U.S. Airways v. Barnett, 535 U.S. 391 (2002)] The *Barnett* decision has been criticized by some as a further indication of the Supreme Court's attempts to limit ADA claims. [*See* 19 *Employment Discrimination Report (EDR)* (BNA) 197 (Aug. 14, 2002).] However, in *Dilley v. Super Valu, Inc.* [296 F.3d 958 (10th Cir. Colo. 2002)], the court held that *Barnett* did not make an accommodation unreasonable merely because it may potentially violate a seniority system, noting that *Barnett* was based on an actual violation. [19 *Employment Discrimination Report (EDR)* (BNA) 136 (July 31, 2002)]

Q 11:47   What happens when the employer's obligation to an individual under the FMLA conflicts with the employer's obligations to the workforce under a collective bargaining agreement?

One would assume that issues involving a collective bargaining agreement and the FMLA would be treated consistently with issues involving a collective bargaining agreement and the ADA; and that, essentially, FMLA obligations such as reinstatement would not require an employer to violate a collective bargaining agreement. However, according to the regulations issued by the Department of Labor, this is not the case. As to reinstatement obligations, the FMLA regulations specifically provide that "a provision of a collective bargaining agreement which provides for reinstatement to a position that is not equivalent because of seniority (e.g., provides lesser pay) is superseded by the FMLA." [29 C.F.R. § 825.700]

The ADA requires reasonable accommodation, and courts have consistently held that it is unreasonable for an employer to be required to violate seniority rules under a collective bargaining agreement to accommodate a disabled employee. On the other hand, the FMLA's requirement of leave and reinstatement is not qualified by reasonableness; therefore, in accordance with Department of Labor regulations, the FMLA obligations must be followed even if this means a violation of the collective bargaining agreement.

Even the "special rules" that apply to employees of schools, although allowing the determination of an equivalent position for restoration to be in accordance with established written policies and collective bargaining agreements nonetheless require that the restoration obligations to an equivalent position be substantially the same as that required under the FMLA for other employees. [29 C.F.R. § 825.604]

The more difficult issue is whether an employer that has a right under the FMLA to transfer an employee to an alternate position to better accommodate an intermittent or reduced leave schedule can violate the seniority or pay provisions in a collective bargaining agreement. Under the FMLA, if such a transfer occurs, the employee must maintain equivalent pay and benefits in the new position, and most likely this would run afoul of the collective bargaining agreement.

Although, under the FMLA, the employer has the right to seek a transfer if the employer has entered into a collective bargaining agreement that impinges on that right, it would appear that the collective bargaining agreement should control, and that the employer could not seek a transfer that would not clearly violate the collective bargaining agreement, unless authorized and agreed to by the employee and union. The regulations themselves suggest this result, as they provide that "[t]ransfer to an alternate provision may require compliance with any applicable collective bargaining agreement, federal law (such as the Americans with Disabilities Act), and state law." [29 C.F.R. § 825.204]

To attempt to alleviate issues involving compliance under the FMLA, commentators suggest that potential problems be addressed during the collective bargaining process to avoid these issues. [*See* "Unionized Employers May Want to Negotiate ADA and FMLA Compliance, Attorney Advises," 14 *Employment Discrimination Report (EDR)* (BNA) 796 (June 7, 2000).]

Q 11:48   Can a *bona fide* seniority system supersede the requirements of Title VII of the 1964 Civil Rights Act?

Yes. Section 703(h) of Title VII says, "it shall not be an unlawful employment practice for an employer to apply different standards of compensation, or different terms, conditions, or privileges of employment pursuant to a bona fide seniority . . . system. . . ." [42 U.S.C. § 2000e-2(h) (1981)] The U.S. Supreme Court has twice rendered significant interpretations of this exception to Title VII's general prohibition against job discrimination. In a 1977 decision, the Court heard a case brought by a Trans World Airlines (TWA) employee, who belonged to the Worldwide Church of God, which forbade working from sundown Friday to sundown Saturday. Under the applicable collective bargaining agreement, the plaintiff was subject to a seniority system that gave more senior employees first choice of job and shift assignments. When the plaintiff was assigned a Saturday shift and refused to work it, the airline agreed to allow the union to switch shifts, but the union refused to go against the seniority system. The plaintiff complained that a reasonable accommodation by the airline was to buck the terms of the labor contract and make the shift change. Seven justices disagreed with the plaintiff's position, saying in their majority opinion:

> Both the union and TWA had agreed to the seniority system; the union was unwilling to entertain a variance over the objections of men senior to Hardison; and for TWA to have arranged unilaterally for a swap would have amounted to a breach of the collective bargaining agreement. . . . Hardison and the EEOC insist that the statutory obligation to accommodate religious needs takes precedence over both the collective bargaining contract and the rights of TWA's other employees . . . but we do not believe that the duty to accommodate requires TWA to take steps inconsistent with the otherwise valid agreement. [Trans World Airlines v. Hardison, 432 U.S. 63 (1977)]

Next came *Lorance v. AT&T Technologies Inc.* [490 U.S. 900 (1989)], in which the Supreme Court held that employees must mount a legal challenge immediately against any seniority rules, even though the provisions might only directly affect them in the future, or the employees run the risk of having their later lawsuit or discrimination charge held to be untimely. *Lorance* was expressly overruled by a provision of the 1991 Civil Rights Act, which states in Section 205(a)(2) that the statute of limitations for filing Title VII charges of discrimination (usually 300 days) begins to run with regard to an unlawful employment practice, such as a discriminatory seniority system, on the date the illegal practice is initiated or "has been applied to affect adversely the person aggrieved, whichever is later." Section 205(b) then says that if a seniority system is included in a collective bargaining agreement with the intent by the bargaining parties to discriminate, either its adoption or its application to particular persons can constitute a discriminatory act, triggering a cause for action and starting the running of the statutory time limitation.

Although *Lorance* is clearly overruled by the provisions of the 1991 Civil Rights Act, *Trans World Airlines v. Hardison* remains good law under Title VII, apparently allowing employers and unions to rely on *bona fide* seniority provisions in their labor contracts as a sound basis for denying reasonable accommodations that go against such contract clauses.

In *Virts v. Consolidated Freightways Corp.* [No. 00-5501 (6th Cir. Apr. 4, 2002)], the court followed the *Hardison* decision, holding that a company was not required to violate a collective bargaining agreement in order to accommodate an employee's religious beliefs. In this case, the male truck driver claimed that his religious beliefs would not allow him to drive on so-called "sleeper runs" with a female co-worker. Although the court reportedly did not question the sincerity of the trucker's beliefs, it nonetheless held that an accommodation for the trucker would contravene the collective bargaining agreement and therefore was unreasonable. [18 *Employment Discrimination Report (EDR)* (BNA) 433 (Apr. 10, 2002)]

Q 11:49   Can a *bona fide* seniority system supersede the prohibition of age discrimination contained in the Age Discrimination in Employment Act?

Yes. Like Title VII, the Age Discrimination in Employment Act contains a clause that provides limited protection to *bona fide* seniority systems against the Act's otherwise sweeping prohibition of age discrimination. [*See* 29 U.S.C. § 623(f)(2) (1982).] In *United States v. McMann* [434 U.S. 192 (1977)], the Supreme Court held that a *bona fide* seniority system could lawfully mandate involuntary retirement of union members. This case was overruled a year later, when the Act was amended to forbid mandates of involuntary retirement in seniority clauses and retirement plans. Because the concept of reasonable accommodation is not a legal consideration in age discrimination cases, the only thing this provision does is clarify the fact that seniority systems in collective bargaining agreements remain a legal part of the labor-management landscape.

Q 11:50 Does a collective bargaining agreement that requires arbitration of employment disputes take precedence over judicial redress under federal civil rights laws?

Most collective bargaining agreements provide for the arbitration of all disputes relating to employment; however, the Supreme Court in a 1974 decision held that union employees may resort to federal court to seek redress under federal civil rights laws, without exhaustion of arbitration required under a collective bargaining agreement. [*See* Alexander v. Gardner-Denver, 7 F.E.P. Cases 81 (1974).] In *Gilmer v. Interstate/Johnson Lane Corp.* [500 U.S. 20 (1991)], the Supreme Court condoned the enforceability of binding arbitration agreements under limited circumstances. Although most courts since *Gilmer* have continued to follow the *Gardner-Denver* decision, the Fourth Circuit, in *Wright v. Universal Maritime Service Corp.* [1997 WL 422869 (4th Cir. July 29, 1997)], held that the failure of a union employee to seek arbitration as required by an arbitration clause contained within a collective bargaining agreement precluded the employee's ability to maintain a federal civil rights claim in federal court. The Supreme Court agreed in March 1998 to review the *Wright* decision. [*See* Wright v. Maritime Serv. Corp., 522 U.S. 1146 (1998).]

In November 1998, the Supreme Court issued its long-awaited decision in *Wright*. [Wright v. Universal Maritime Serv. Corp. 525 U.S. 70 (1998)] The petitioner, Wright, was a longshoreman subject to a collective bargaining agreement and Longshore Seniority Plan that contained fairly standard arbitration clauses. The collective bargaining agreement arbitration clause was general and contained requirements that matters under dispute be submitted to arbitration. The seniority plan was similarly general and required the arbitration of any dispute concerning or arising out of the terms or conditions of the agreement. The petitioner had filed suit under the ADA, claiming discrimination for the respondent's refusal to employ him following his settlement of a claim for disability benefits for injuries he sustained on the job.

Although, noting the apparent collision between the principles enunciated in *Gilmer* and *Gardener-Davis*, the Supreme Court in *Wright* side-stepped the issue altogether, holding that the general language contained in the arbitration clauses was not sufficient under *Gilmer* to amount to a waiver of the right to pursue an ADA claim in a court of law. As the court stated:

> We hold that the collective bargaining agreement in this case does not contain a clear and unmistakable waiver of the covered employees' rights to a judicial forum for federal claims of employment discrimination. We do not reach the question whether such a waiver would be enforceable. The judgment of the Fourth Circuit is vacated, and the case is remanded for further proceedings consisted with this opinion. [*Wright*, 525 U.S. at 82]

The language in *Gilmer* did not specifically mention the waiver of statutory rights, but merely required the arbitration of any dispute, claim, or controversy the court determined to be sufficient to encompass statutory claims. Nonetheless, the Court reconciled its holding in *Wright* with *Gilmer* by differentiating between an agreement signed by an individual waiving personal rights and a collective bargaining agreement that, if effective in the case at hand, would involve a union's waiver of the statutory rights of its represented employees. In the latter case, a clear and unmistakable waiver would be necessary under *Gilmer*; however, if there was such a clear and unmistakable waiver within a collective bargaining agreement arbitration clause, would it be enforceable and require the arbitration of federal statutory claims? This question was answered by the U.S. Supreme Court in *14 Penn Plaza, LLC v. Pyett* [129 S. Ct. 1456 (2009)] The case involved a collective bargaining agreement that contained a provision barring discrimination under the ADEA, and specifically provided that all covered claims were subject to the collective bargaining agreement's grievance and arbitration procedures as an exclusive and sole remedy. As such, the Court concluded that arbitration of an ADEA claim of one of the union members was required.

Illegal Activities

Q 11:51   What happens to a labor union when its leadership is guilty of racketeering?

The union falls into receivership, and a trustee is appointed to run it. For example, in 1990, Roofers Union Local 30-30B was placed under a federal court decreeship in Philadelphia after 14 officers were found guilty of violating the Racketeer Influenced and Corrupt Organizations Act for bribing local judges and threatening non-union roofing contractors within the union's jurisdiction. [United States v. Local 30, United Slate, Tile & Composition Roofers, Damp & Waterproof Workers Ass'n, 1989 WL 69483, 135 L.R.R.M. 3113 (E.D. Pa. June 19, 1989)] As a result, a court liaison officer was appointed by the federal judge to oversee the local union's affairs. Other requirements were imposed as well:

- The union had to adopt a grievance and arbitration procedure;
- All collective bargaining agreements had to be countersigned by the liaison officer;
- The convicted former officers were barred from having any further contact with the union or any roofing job; and
- The court took control of all union expenditures.

The court could have gone even further by imposing a trusteeship and ousting the local's newly elected officers. Other unions that have been under Department of Justice scrutiny involving allegations of corruption include the Teamsters and Laborers; however, the Philadelphia Roofers Union posed a particularly egregious example of corruption, because its activities included providing judges with union favors and bribes.

Q 11:52   What happens to a labor union when it directs or condones a violent strike?

The union can be held liable for the employer's losses, including lost profits. It can be ordered to stop the strike, and if it defies the order, it can be severely fined for contempt of court.

For example, in 1989, the United Mine Workers of America struck the Clinchfield Company in southwest Virginia. When the company attempted to mine coal with replacement workers, the strikers, acting under union direction, conducted sit-ins to block traffic in and out of the mines, occupied a coal breaker (i.e., a processing plant), assembled convoys across state highways to block the transport of coal, threw rocks and shot at coal trucks, and threatened and assaulted replacement workers.

The company obtained a labor injunction from the circuit court for Russell County, but the union and its members defied it, incurring $52 million in fines for contempt of the court. When the strike was finally settled, the union insisted that the court vacate the huge contempt fines. The court, however, refused.

The court appointed a special commissioner with authority to collect the fines on behalf of the commonwealth and the relevant counties. In a benchmark decision, *John L. Bagwell, Special Commissioner v. United Mine Workers of America* [244 Va. 463 (1992)], the Virginia Supreme Court, in late 1992, upheld the enormous penalties against the union, finding that they were neither excessive nor a violation of its due process of law rights or the federal labor laws and policies. [Morse, "Virginia Supreme Court Affirms Fines Against UMWA," 1 *Labor Relations Ink* 3, Jan. 1993, at 1]

In 1994, the U.S. Supreme Court unanimously vacated the $52 million fine. Had the high court failed to do so, the union would have had to declare bankruptcy. ["Year in Review: Board Appointments, Court Rulings Brought Changes in Labor Field in '94," 1995 *BNA Daily Labor Report* 17, Jan. 26, 1995, at d17] The Court's decision does not mean that such fines will not be upheld in future cases of union violence and defiance of court orders.

Q 11:53   Can union members sue their union for leading them to commit illegal activities?

Yes. For example, a group of former employees of Royal Harvest Foods, a poultry processing plant in Springfield, Massachusetts, sued the United Food and Commercial Workers Union because a business agent induced them to conduct a wildcat strike that cost them their jobs. According to the evidence at trial, the business agent encouraged non-strikers to join in once the wildcat was underway, saying that more participants were needed for the strike to succeed. The hapless members sued the union for breach of its duty of fair representation under Taft-Hartley.

Q 11:54   Can a union member sue the union for unfair operation of its hiring hall?

Yes. In *Breininger v. Sheet Metal Workers, Local 6* [493 U.S. 67 (1989)], the Supreme Court held that a union member who claimed to be a victim of hiring-hall discrimination could file either an unfair labor practice charge with the NLRB or a lawsuit in federal court under Section 301 of the Labor-Management Relations (i.e., Taft-Hartley) Act.

On March 18, 1991, the Court of Appeals for the Third Circuit took the *Breininger* holding a step farther. The appeals court ruled that, when union members sue their local union for discriminatory hiring-hall practices in breach of its duty of fair representation, the most appropriate state statute of limitations (and not the six-month limitation for unfair labor practice charges before the NLRB) should be applied by the federal court. [Brenner v. Local 514, United Bhd. of Carpenters & Joiners of Am., 927 F.2d 1283 (3d Cir. 1991)]

Grievance Arbitration

Q 11:55   What is *grievance arbitration*?

Almost all collective bargaining agreements (i.e., labor contracts) contain a grievance procedure. It may call for several steps to resolve a problem:

- An employee subject to disciplinary action who has a grievance (e.g., denial of a vacation request) usually must start the procedure within a specified time (e.g., within three days of the event) by bringing the matter, either orally or in writing, to the attention of his or her immediate supervisor.
- If the issue is not settled at this stage, the grievance moves to the next step, a meeting between the shop steward and the department manager.
- If the grievance is still unresolved, a third meeting may occur, perhaps between the union business agent and the company's personnel director.
- If these steps do not lead to a resolution, the union may submit the grievance to the American Arbitration Association to obtain a list of professional arbitrators from which the union and the company can choose.
- The arbitrator will hold a hearing and reach a decision that, with few exceptions, will be final and binding on the parties.

Q 11:56   What is *interest arbitration*?

Interest arbitration signifies the arbitrator's role in breaking a deadlock between a company and a union in negotiating one or more issues of a collective bargaining agreement. Interest arbitration is rare in the private sector but is much more common in public employment, especially when safety forces (e.g., police and firefighters) are involved. Interest arbitration is often used then to break deadlocks on wages and other contract terms in lieu of the right to strike or lock out.

Disputes and Decertification

Q 11:57 What is a *lockout*?

A *lockout* occurs when an employer refuses to allow employees to work without a signed contract. A lockout is used to pressure the union into agreeing to the company's position on a new labor agreement.

Q 11:58 When can a union call a strike?

The vast majority of labor contracts contain no-strike clauses, which prohibit a union from calling for a work stoppage during the term of the agreement; however, once the collective bargaining agreement has expired, the union can call a strike if a new contract has not been made. The strike is the union's principal economic weapon.

Q 11:59 Can the company continue to operate during a strike?

Yes. From a legal standpoint, the employer can keep operating during a strike, even if this means hiring replacement workers. As a practical matter, the company may find it unrealistic to do so, perhaps because of a lack of available replacement employees or a desire not to antagonize the union or strikers.

Q 11:60 Once unionized, can a company ever get rid of the union?

Yes. It is not easy to get rid of a labor union, but it is legally possible. This is generally accomplished by demonstrating to the NLRB's satisfaction that the union no longer enjoys the loyalty of a majority of the employees it claims to represent. The most common method of proving this is by circulating a decertification petition and holding a decertification election.

Q 11:61 What is a *decertification petition*?

A *decertification petition* is a request for a representation election, filed by employees who are currently represented by a labor union but who desire to decertify the union as their representative for collective bargaining. As with the representation petition that initially elected the union as bargaining representative, the decertification petition must be supported by at least 30 percent of the represented (i.e., unionized) employees.

Q 11:62   When can a company's unionized employees file a decertification petition?

Employees covered by a current collective bargaining agreement can file a decertification petition at two times—between the 90th and 60th day before the expiration of the current collective bargaining agreement (i.e., the so-called window period) or after the collective bargaining agreement expires, provided that no new agreement has been negotiated between the employer and the union.

Q 11:63   Can an employer encourage its unionized employees to file a decertification petition?

No. It is illegal for an employer to encourage unionized employees to eliminate their union; however, if one or more employees questions management about the procedure for eliminating the union, management can advise them to visit the NLRB to learn about a decertification election.

Q 11:64   Can a company ever withdraw recognition from the union?

Yes. If the employer has a good-faith belief, based on objective evidence, that the union no longer enjoys the support of a majority of the unionized employees, the employer may be able to withdraw recognition from the union. This rarely happens during the term of a collective bargaining agreement, unless the union has virtually abandoned the enforcement and maintenance of the agreement (e.g., ceased to investigate and negotiate grievances, collect dues, or perform other basic functions under the collective bargaining agreement). During the period between the 90th and 60th day before the expiration of the collective bargaining agreement, an employer with objective evidence that the union has lost a majority of support may file a petition for a new election with the NLRB. Following expiration and before negotiation of a new collective bargaining agreement, the employer may likewise seek a representation election or withdraw recognition from the union, based on objective evidence of the union's loss of majority support.

Q 11:65   What objective evidence supports an employer's good-faith belief that a union has lost majority support among the employees?

Factors and events that the NLRB may consider in determining whether the employer has legally withdrawn recognition from the union are:

- Extensive, rapid turnover of employees in the bargaining unit, especially as the result of hiring permanent replacements for striking workers;
- Withdrawal of authorization for dues check-off by a majority of the employees in the bargaining unit;
- A petition presented to the employer by a majority of the employees, requesting the company to withdraw recognition of the union; and

- Failure of the union to enforce the union contract, investigate grievances, hold meetings, or otherwise function normally.

As a general rule, no single factor supports withdrawal of recognition. Rather, the board decides whether the employer had sufficient grounds for harboring a good-faith belief in the union's loss of majority support.

Q 11:66   Can the hiring of replacement workers during a strike give rise to a good-faith doubt about the union's continuing majority support?

Possibly. It is well established in labor law that a struck employer can hire replacement workers, assuming it can find new employees willing to cross the picket line. The company can even hire replacement workers on a permanent basis. Whether such permanent replacements can be considered pro- or anti-union has been a subject of substantial controversy for many years. The NLRB's view has shifted back and forth, as its makeup has been altered by expiring terms and new presidential appointments. Currently, the NLRB and the Supreme Court agree that replacement workers should not be presumed to be either for or against the union. Consequently, an employer that has permanently replaced a majority of the striking workforce cannot withdraw recognition from the union, claiming a good-faith doubt about the union's continued majority support solely on that basis.

Good-faith doubt has, in fact, become a difficult position for a company to maintain. It cannot be based on a nose count of replacement employees, nor can it be based on a secret-ballot poll, because such a poll can itself be justified only by a good-faith doubt.

Q 11:67   Can employers hire permanent replacements for striking employees?

Yes. Organized labor has not yet succeeded in lobbying Congress to overrule the Supreme Court's historic decision in *Mackay Radio & Tel. Co. v. NLRB* [304 U.S. 333 (1938)], holding that a company can legally replace economic strikers. Under *Mackay's* long-standing "rules of the game" an employer can hire permanent replacements for striking employees if the strike is over wages and other economic aspects of employment, but it must reinstate strikers who protest their employer's unfair labor practices. Unions have long argued that, because most strikes are strictly economic, the *Mackay* rule gives companies an unfair advantage. When unions claimed a third of all U.S. workers and nearly 100 percent of blue-collar employees in some key U.S. industries (e.g., steel and autos), *Mackay* was rather academic, because organized labor could compel reinstatement without loss of seniority at the end of a strike; however, as the Greyhound strike demonstrated, the waning of union power has made the 15 percent of unionized U.S. workers vulnerable to permanent replacement whenever they take to their picket lines.

Congress has resisted organized labor's efforts to pass a law that overrules *Mackay*, although related bills have been introduced in virtually every session in recent years. Consequently, organized labor has turned to the state legislatures for relief. For instance, in 1991, the Delaware legislature passed a striker replacement bill that ensured the rights of strikers to reinstatement for six months from the inception of a work stoppage; however, the bill was vetoed by Governor Castle, who thought it was pre-empted by federal labor law. President Clinton's attempt to forbid government contractors from hiring permanent replacements was overturned in federal court in 1996.

Almost an entire workforce was permanently replaced during the course of a lengthy (i.e., two-year) strike. The Detroit News/Detroit Free Press strike ended early in 1997 with the strikers offering to return to work. The strikers found themselves on a waiting list for preferential rehiring as suitable positions opened in the future.

The issue of whether, in an economic strike, employers have legitimately hired permanent replacements to the striking workers turns on the totality of the circumstances and whether, in fact, the employer had a legitimate reason in having to hire so-called permanent replacements. However, as many know, most employees who are hired today typically sign at-will disclaimers indicating that their employment may be terminated at any time, with or without cause. The issue of whether an at-will disclaimer does away with the "permanent" nature of employment was addressed in *United Steel, Paper, and Forestry, Rubber, Manufacturing, Energy, Allied Industrial and Service Workers International Union, AFL-CIO v. NLRB.* [544 F.3d 841 (7th Cir. 2008)] Reviewing the totality of the circumstances and the decision of the NLRB, the court held that the at-will disclaimer did not, under these facts, do away with the "permanent" nature of the replacements hired by the company during the economic strike.

Bankruptcies, Mergers, and Acquisitions

Q 11:68 During the term of a labor contract, what company business decisions must be negotiated with the union?

A company that has a collective bargaining relationship with a union must bargain about decisions that affect wages, hours, and conditions of employment. Some of the company's business decisions that are closely related to these categories must be negotiated also, unless the union clearly and unequivocally waives its right to negotiate (for instance, in an unambiguous provision in the collective bargaining agreement). The decision to subcontract work normally performed by the unionized employees is an example of a business decision that must be negotiated. On the other hand, the company's decision to close a plant or department is fundamental to entrepreneurial control and usually need not be negotiated with the union, although the company is probably obligated to discuss the effects that a closing or similar decision may have on the unionized workers.

Q 11:69   When must a company open its financial books to a union during labor negotiations?

The general rule is that when a company claims during labor negotiations that it is financially unable to pay the wages and benefits being demanded by the union, the union has a right to demand disclosure of financial information to support the company's contention. This is a long-established doctrine in labor law. [See NLRB v. Truitt Mfg. Co., 351 U.S. 149 (1956) ("[I]t is settled law that when an employer seeks to justify the refusal of a wage increase upon an economic basis . . . , good faith bargaining under the act requires that upon request the employer attempt to substantiate its economic position by reasonable proof.").]

The NLRA states, however, that neither party to labor negotiations must make a particular concession to be viewed as bargaining in good faith. [29 U.S.C. § 158(d)] Consequently, a company can always contend that it is unwilling to agree to the union's wage demands, without going so far as to say that the firm is unable to agree to those increases.

During the 1980s, walking the line between claiming unwillingness, as opposed to inability, to pay became a part of the fine art of concession bargaining as firms demanded rollbacks in wages and benefits from their unionized employees. During the 1990s, a new approach was used with increasing frequency. Employers argued that by acceding to union wage and benefits demands, they would place themselves in an uncompetitive position in the marketplace, where the higher wage would adversely affect sales.

The NLRB confronted such an argument in a case involving Nielson Lithographing Co. [305 N.L.R.B. 90, 138 L.R.R.M. 1441 (1991)] The case has a long and tortured history. [See 279 N.L.R.B. 877 (1986), enforcement denied, 854 F.2d 1063 (7th Cir. 1988), on remand, 305 N.L.R.B. 90.]

The company and the union, which had a collective bargaining history dating back three decades, entered contract negotiations in 1985. The company confronted the union with 76 proposals—including lengthening the workday; reducing wages and health insurance benefits, shift premiums, and holiday pay; and reducing job retraining programs. In making these proposals, the company never claimed that it could not pay more than what was proposed. Rather, it contended that "the costs in our contract were prohibitive, and [we] needed to have concessions . . . to compete with the competitors. . . . The trends showed [us] that [we] would have a worse problem in the future." The labor board said, "[Nielson went] beyond the expression of a mere unwillingness to continue paying the costs of its collective-bargaining agreement; by its words and conduct [Nielson] conveyed to the union an inability to pay . . . and thus triggered a duty to disclose financial information."

On appeal, the federal court disagreed, citing one of its own precedents on the issue:

> Nielson . . . never claimed that it was unable to pay the existing scale of wages and benefits. It admitted to being profitable but said it wanted to

bring its wage bill into line with the wages paid by competitors to whom it was losing sales. A company can survive, certainly in the short run and often in the long run, even though it is paying higher wages than its competitors. The company may have some other cost advantage; its competitors may price above their costs; the market may be expanding rapidly. The company will grow less rapidly than if its costs were lower and may stagnate and decline, but it need not die. There is thus no contradiction in a company's stating on the one hand that it is profitable and on the other hand that its costs are higher than its competitors' and it wants to reduce them. The board concedes that if this is all Nielson said, Nielson had no duty to open its books to the union. [129 BNA L.R.R.M. 2367, 2368 (1992)]

The court remanded the case for the board's further consideration, and the board ruled that a claim "of competitive disadvantage is not the same as a claim of financial inability to pay . . . and does not raise any obligation . . . to turn over the requested information."

The *Nielson* case began in the mid-1980s, when leveraged buyouts, mergers, and union busting were the order of the day. The board brought the case to a close in the 1990s, when its significance to corporations, struggling to compete in an increasingly competitive marketplace, made *Nielson* an important decision. *Nielson* frees companies to focus employees' and their unions' attention on hard international and national realities without having to bare confidential financial information that might be leaked to the competition. Even in light of the current economic expansion, the core remains significant. In 2012, *KLB Industries, Inc. v. NLRB* [2012 WL 6013449 (D.C. Cir. Dec. 4, 2012)], the court held that when an employer uses claims of competitive disadvantage to support its position seeking wage concessions, it is incumbent upon the employer to provide the union information in response to targeted requests relating the employer's lack of competitiveness claim.

Q 11:70   Must a company negotiate with a union over its decision to close its doors?

No. The NLRB has held that a company is not required to bargain over management decisions that affect the basic nature or direction of the business; however, when labor costs are the basis for a decision to close, the employer must bargain over its decision to do so. [Otis Elevator Co. (Otis II), 269 N.L.R.B. 891 (1984)]

When an employer decides to close a plant entirely, as opposed to subcontracting or transferring work, the law permits the employer to make such a decision without bargaining with the union.

Q 11:71   Must an employer closing its doors bargain over the effects of the closing?

Yes. Once an employer decides to close a plant, it must bargain with the union over the effects of the closure on bargaining unit employees. Such employees' rights to job security, severance pay, pensions, and other accrued benefits may be addressed. As with any other negotiation with a union, an employer is not required to grant any benefits or make any concessions. Its only requirement is to bargain in good faith. [NLRA § 8(d); *see also* JD Lunsford Plumbing, Heating & Air Conditioning, 254 N.L.R.B. 1360 (1981).]

Q 11:72   Can a union's right to negotiate survive the termination of the collective bargaining agreement?

Yes. The union's right to bargain on behalf of the employees it represents is a right separate and distinct from rights contained in the collective bargaining agreement. Unless the employees vote to decertify the union or the employer legally withdraws recognition, the right to negotiate survives not only the expiration of the labor contract but also the closing of a part of the employer's business, such as a particular plant.

Q 11:73   What happens to the bargaining duty if the company goes out of business?

A complete discontinuation of the business terminates the employer's duty to bargain; however, a sham discontinuation, such as a mere change of name and location, is not sufficient. The NLRB brands a company that tries this a "runaway shop." It treats the new firm and the old company and location as a single employer, imposing the union's labor contract on the "new" enterprise.

Q 11:74   What happens to the collective bargaining agreement when a unionized company goes into bankruptcy?

A bankrupt company can ask the U.S. bankruptcy judge handling its case to allow it to reject or modify its collective bargaining agreement(s). Under the Bankruptcy Amendments and Federal Judgeship Act of 1984 [11 U.S.C. § 1113], the bankruptcy judge can grant the debtor-company's request only after the company shows that:

- The company first made a proposal to the union for modification of the labor agreement.
- The proposal to the union was based on the best available information at the time it was made.
- The proposed modifications are necessary for the company's successful reorganization.
- All parties will be treated fairly under the proposal.
- The union has received all the information it needs to evaluate the proposal.
- The company has met with the union to discuss the proposal.
- At such meetings, the company conferred in good faith with the union.
- The union rejected the proposal without good cause.

The circumstances, on balance, favor unilateral implementation of the proposed rejection or modification of the collective bargaining agreement by the company.

Q 11:75   Do the Bankruptcy Code's provisions for an automatic stay apply to arbitrations under a collective bargaining agreement?

Probably not. The Bankruptcy Code's stay provisions say that as soon as a voluntary or involuntary bankruptcy petition is filed, all other lawsuits (whether in state or federal court) must be placed on hold, pending the resolution of the bankruptcy case. Usually litigants with claims against the debtor-company file proofs of claim with the bankruptcy court and pursue their claims in that arena; those who fail to do so risk losing their claims through the debtor's discharge by the bankruptcy court. Although the judicial trend is to apply the Code's stay provisions to lawsuits by unions against debtor-companies, the courts appear willing to permit arbitrations under collective bargaining agreements to proceed, at least up to the point where the bankruptcy court permits a debtor to reject the labor contract itself.

Q 11:76   What happens to the labor contracts in a unionized company if it is purchased by another company?

If the acquiring company buys the stock of the unionized firm, the buyer steps into the shoes of the former shareholders. The buyer gets all of the seller's assets and liabilities, including its labor agreements and union relationships. If the buyer purchases a unionized company's assets only and not the common stock, liabilities do not automatically follow. In this case, the buyer does not automatically assume the seller's labor contracts, nor must the buyer necessarily recognize and bargain with the seller's unions.

Q 11:77   When must the buyer of a unionized company's assets recognize and negotiate with the seller's union?

The asset purchaser becomes the seller's successor and must recognize and bargain with the seller's union(s) if a majority of the buyer's relevant bargaining unit consists of unionized employees of the former owner.

Q 11:78   Can the asset buyer that hires a majority of the workforce from among the asset seller's employees avoid being a successor?

Yes. If the purchaser buys and reopens the facility long after the seller closes it, the buyer may avoid successorship status. Similarly, if the asset purchaser uses the assets, such as a plant or warehouse facility, to engage in a completely different line of business from the seller's or integrates the assets and employees into a much larger organization, the buyer may escape successorship status because of the drastic operational change.

Picketing

Q 11:79   Can a union picket a non-union company?

Yes. A union can set up a picket line to organize the employees of a non-union company. The picket line may remain for 30 days, after which a union must either file an election petition with the NLRB or cease picketing. A union can also picket a non-union company to protest low wages that are inconsistent with union standards for the geographic area, or it can picket a company that has allied itself with a primary employer with which the union has a legitimate labor dispute.

Q 11:80   Are there limits to what is considered lawful picketing at a non-union company?

Although unions have the right to picket and it is a violation of the NLRA for an employer to interfere with, restrain, or coerce employees in the exercise of these rights, there are limits to what is considered lawful picketing. In *CSX Hotels, Inc. v. NLRB* [377 F.3d 394 (4th Cir. 2004)], the union had claimed that the company unlawfully infringed on its picketing rights by contacting the police. At issue was picketing that was occurring adjacent to a major thoroughfare through the county that was particularly congested during morning and afternoon commutes. The evidence demonstrated that the picketers were stationed just inches off the roadway and mere feet from a construction entrance. Viewing pictures of the picketing and testimony from police as to the dangerous nature of the roadway, even without the picketers close presence, the court concluded that the company did not violate the law by calling local law enforcement officials and asking them to assess the situation and take appropriate action due to the dangers caused by the picketing that was taking place in close proximity to the road in question.

Q 11:81   Can labor unions picket employers' homes?

Yes. In 1988, the Supreme Court ruled that a Milwaukee municipality's law that banned picketing in front of a private home was unconstitutional. [Frisby v. Schultz, 487 U.S. 474 (1988)] The case arose from the picketing of a doctor's home by anti-abortion activists. Although it was not a labor law case per se, the same principles seem to apply to union picketing of an employer's home in the course of a labor dispute or organization drive.

Q 11:82   How does a company become an ally that may be picketed?

An ally is a company that agrees to do work and fill orders on behalf of a company being struck by its employees.

Q 11:83   What is a *secondary employer?*

The *primary employer* is a company with which the union has a legitimate labor dispute; a *secondary employer* is any other company with which the union has no dispute but that the union may picket to force the primary employer to meet the union's demands. For instance, a union on strike against a steel manufacturer might picket the car producer that buys the sheet metal for the car bodies, thus attempting to convince the car maker to pressure the steel manufacturer to settle the strike. This is a secondary boycott. It is usually illegal unless the secondary employer is the primary employer's ally. So-called "secondary boycotts" typically involve picketing a secondary employer that conducts business with the primary employer in an effort to exert pressure against the primary employer. Although § 8 (b)(4)(ii)(B) of the NLRA makes it illegal per se to "induce or encourage" employees of a secondary employer to strike, not every effort to exert pressure against the secondary employer is illegal. In the U.S. Supreme Court case of *Edward J. DeBartolo Corp. v. Florida Gulf Coast Building & Construction Trades Council* [108 S. Ct. 1392 (1988)], the Court held that hand-billing directed at the customers of a secondary employer may not be coercive such that it runs afoul of the NLRA. There have been far more intrusive conduct held to not run afoul of the NLRA's secondary boycott rules.

In *Sheet Metal Workers International Association Local 15 AFL-CIO v. NLRB* [491 F.3d 429 (D.C. Cir. 2007)], the union had engaged in picketing at a hospital that did business with the primary employer involving, among other things, a dramatic "mock funeral" in an effort to persuade customers not to patronize the hospital that was a secondary employer to the primary employer. The "mock funeral" procession was comprised of a person costumed as the "grim reaper" and other people portraying pallbearers carrying a coffin and handing out leaflets stating, "Going to Brandon Hospital Should Not Be a Grave Decision," and detailing several malpractice suits against the hospital. The procession walked back and forth over a distance of about 400 feet on a sidewalk, which was located across the street from the hospital and parallel to the front of the hospital. Following *DeBartolo*, the court concluded that the mock funeral was not coercive in violation of the NLRA but was consistent with the union's rights under the First Amendment.

Q 11:84   How can a company protect itself if it gets caught up in a labor dispute that does not directly concern it?

Under the NLRA, both companies and unions can file unfair labor practice charges with the NLRB. If the NLRB issues a complaint after promptly investigating a charge, it usually refers the case to an administrative law judge for trial and resolution. In the case of secondary boycotts and similar illegal picketing and work stoppages, the NLRB may have both a right and a duty to ask a federal judge for an injunction against the illegal union activity.

Unfair Labor Practices

Q 11:85   What is an *unfair labor practice*?

An *unfair labor practice* is a violation of one or more of the restrictions listed in Section 8 of the NLRA. Typical ones include:

- Failure to negotiate in good faith;
- Interfering with a worker's exercise of rights guaranteed by the NLRA; or
- Punishing workers for engaging in concerted activities.

Q 11:86   Who can commit an unfair labor practice?

Both employers and labor unions can commit unfair labor practices by engaging in activities proscribed by the NLRA.

Q 11:87   Who can complain about an unfair labor practice?

Anyone can file an unfair labor practice charge with the NLRB.

Q 11:88   What happens when someone files an unfair labor practice charge?

When a person files an unfair labor practice charge with the NLRB, a board agent investigates the merits of the charge.

Q 11:89   What happens if the board agent finds that the charge has merit?

The NLRB general counsel issues a complaint against the employer or labor organization against which the charge was filed.

Q 11:90   What happens after the NLRB general counsel issues a complaint?

The case is heard by an administrative law judge. An attorney in the general counsel's office of the NLRB represents the charging party. The judge's decision may be appealed to the NLRB's Washington office and appealed still farther to an appropriate U.S. Court of Appeals. In rare instances the U.S. Supreme Court hears such cases.

Q 11:91   What happens if the NLRB agent finds no merit in an unfair labor practice charge?

The charge is dismissed. The dismissal may be appealed by the charging party to the general counsel's office in Washington. The general counsel can either reinstate the case or affirm its dismissal.

Q 11:92   Can the decision of the NLRB's general counsel to dismiss an unfair labor practice complaint be reviewed?

No. The general counsel's withdrawal of a complaint, even after the hearing before an administrative law judge had started but before any evidence on the complaint's merits had been introduced, was determined by the Court of Appeals for the Ninth Circuit to be an unreviewable, unappealable decision. This ruling expands the historically well-settled proposition that the general counsel's decision not to issue a complaint on an unfair labor practice charge is without appeal. [International Bhd. of Boilermakers v. NLRB, 872 F.2d 331 (9th Cir. 1989)]

Q 11:93   Do employees have the right to engage in concerted activities in the workplace?

Yes. Section 7 of the NLRA gives employees the right to engage in concerted activity, whether or not they are unionized; therefore, it is an unfair labor practice to fire employees engaged in such activities. For instance, if a group of employees walk out of their shop to protest cold temperatures in the shop during winter months, the employer cannot retaliate by firing them. In one case, the NLRB filed a complaint against a company for discharging one of its employees for violation of the company's social media policy. The employee posted comments regarding her supervisor on Facebook, to which co-workers added their comments. This, claimed the NLRB, was "concerted activity" protected under the NLRA. Although the case was settled, and the issue was not decided, this case represents a cautionary tale for employers that mete out discipline to employees for violations of their social media policies. In *Medco Health Solutions of Las Vegas, Inc. v. NLRB* [701 F.3d 710 (D.C. Cir. 2012)], a worker represented by a union wore a T-shirt to work that was critical of a program designed by the employer to reward employee achievement. Specifically, the company had adopted a "WOW" program to provide non-compensatory awards to employees for achievement. The shirt, bearing the union logo contained the message "I don't need a WOW to do my job." The company found the shirt offensive and believed it could detrimentally impact their customer relationships, as their customers were routinely brought to the work area for tours and other purposes, and ordered the employee to remove the T-shirt. The employees challenged the employer's actions and the NLRB found that the employer had engaged in an unfair labor practice by, among other things, ordering the employee to remove his shirt. On appeal, the court held that although the shirt constituted "concerted protected activity," they did not feel the NLRB properly considered the employer's position that the T-shirt would negatively affect customer relations and remanded the matter for further proceedings.

However, in the U.S. Supreme Court decision *BE&K Construction Co. v. NLRB* [536 U.S. 516 (2002)], the Court held that an employer that filed unsuccessful litigation against a union in order to allegedly retaliate against the union for engaging in protected activity is not liable for an unfair labor practice so long as the litigation is reasonably based.

Q 11:94 Can employees be engaged in protected concerted activity when using social media?

Over the last few years, the NLRB has reviewed disciplinary actions associated with employees' use of social media to determine whether the employees were engaged in protected activity under the NLRA. For example, the NLRB filed a case against a company for discharging one of its employees for a violation of the company's social media policy, which prohibited, among other things, posting disparaging comments about the company and its management on social media sites. [NLRB v. American Med. Response of Conn., Case No. 34-CA-12 567, Region 34] The employee posted comments (some were disparaging) regarding her supervisor on Facebook, to which co-workers added their comments. This, claimed the NLRB, was "concerted activity" protected under the NLRA. Although the case was settled, and no decision rendered, employers should be cautious when discharging employees for violations of social media policies because, if the employee was engaged in "concerted activity" with co-workers, the NLRB may maintain that such discharge is a violation under the NLRA.

The NLRB, through the Office of the General Counsel, Division of Operations-Management, issued a memorandum in August, 2011 concerning social media cases over the prior year. [Memorandum OM 11-74 (Aug. 18, 2011)] The release was supplemented by an additional memorandum in January 2012. [Memorandum OM 12-31 (Jan. 24, 2012)] Although there remain many issues to be resolved or clarified as to what the NLRB considers to be Section 7 protected concerted activity as it relates to employees' use of social media, some general guidelines emerge:

- Involvement of co-workers on social media site to discuss terms and conditions of employment is probably protected concerted activity;
- Offensive posts that do not relate to terms or conditions of employment or seek to involve co-workers are probably not protected.

Q 11:95 Can social media policies violate the NLRA?

Social media policies are all-the-rage now as employers seek to limit employees' use of social media in a way that could negatively impact the company. However, as the NLRB has indicated (see Q 11:94) employees may be engaged in Section 7 protected concerted activity when using social media, such that enforcement of social media policies may be an unfair labor practice. As such, the NLRB considers blanket prohibitions from displaying a company logo or uniform, as well as blanket non-disparagement policies, in violation of Section 7, because such conduct may occur in connection with concerted protected activity. [Memorandum OM 11-74 and OM 12-31, issued through the office of the General Counsel, Division of Operations-Mgmt., Aug. 18, 2011 and Jan. 24, 2012, respectively]

Q 11:96   Does an employer commit an unfair labor practice by refusing to hire applicants who are being paid by a union to help organize the employer?

Yes. In 1995, the U.S. Supreme Court ruled that an employer who turned away electricians being paid by their union to help organize the employer had violated the NLRA by illegally discriminating against these union adherents. The fact that the applicants were in the paid service of their union did not alter their status as potential employees of the employer, thus subject to the NLRA's protection from discriminatory hiring decisions. [NLRB v. Town & Country Elec. Inc., 516 U.S. 85 (1995)]

Q 11:97   Can related corporations be drawn into a labor dispute?

No. Parent, subsidiary, and brother and sister corporations generally cannot be picketed by a union that has a dispute with a related corporate entity, nor can such a separate but related company be forced to share legal liability for an unfair labor practice brought to the attention of the NLRB by a union. Only by becoming involved in the related, unionized company's labor relations and corporate affairs can the parent or sister company be made to share labor law liability under the same labor contract as a single employer. Otherwise, such picketing is a secondary activity and therefore an unfair labor practice.

Q 11:98   Can one owner, shareholder, or holding company acquire and operate unionized and non-unionized companies simultaneously?

Yes. The unionized firms' labor contracts and bargaining duties do not hold for the non-unionized entities, provided that day-to-day labor relations, corporate labor policies, and the normal indicia of corporate integrity and separateness are carefully maintained and the non-unionized entity was not created merely to avoid or circumvent the unionized company's labor contract commitments. If these provisions are satisfied, then there is no unfair labor practice.

Q 11:99   Can a labor union have an ownership interest in a company in which it represents employees?

Yes. Employee Stock Ownership Plans (ESOPs) are offered with increasing frequency to unionized employees in return for wage and fringe benefit concessions or in lieu of a pension plan. Indeed, sometimes the sale, merger, acquisition, or continued operation of a plant or company depends on a union's willingness to agree to the use of ESOPs in the transactions. ESOPs cause a conflict for the unions, which find their members represented on both sides of the bargaining table. If care is taken to separate the interests of the employee-shareholders as owners from their interests as unionized employees, such arrangements can be legal and functional and can include union participation. There is no unfair labor practice.

Q 11:100   Is the team approach to production legal under the NLRA?

Yes. An employer may implement participatory management systems and involve its employees fully in the firm's work processes without committing the unfair labor practice of creating an employer-dominated labor organization. This is true whether the company is unionized or not. [Vons Grocery Co., 320 N.L.R.B. 5 (1995)]

Q 11:101   May an employer disavow a collective bargaining agreement on the basis of a good-faith doubt that the union continues to enjoy the majority support of the employees it purports to represent?

Usually not. An employer harboring a good-faith doubt about a union's continuing majority support among the employer's relevant workforce may withdraw recognition and refuse to bargain any more with the union. If the employer's good-faith doubt is confirmed, no unfair labor practice has occurred; however, if the employer and the union have entered into a binding collective bargaining agreement, the employer must abide by that contract.

Between these two extremes is the situation in which the good-faith doubt is expressed after the parties have agreed to a new collective agreement but the contract has not yet been signed. Under these circumstances, the U.S. Supreme Court held that Auciello Iron Works was aware of the facts supporting its good-faith doubt before it made a complete contract offer, which the union accepted. Therefore, the employer could not subsequently disavow the new labor contract and withdraw its recognition of the union. That was an unfair labor practice. [Auciello Iron Works, Inc. v. NLRB, 517 U.S. 781 (1996)]

Q 11:102   Can a single employee engage in protected concerted activity?

Yes. An employee who acts on behalf of a group of co-workers may be engaging in protected concerted activity. Punishing that employee may consequently be an unfair labor practice. [NLRB v. City Disposal Sys., 465 U.S. 822 (1984)] In *Alton H. Piester, LLC v. NLRB* [591 F.3d 332 (4th Cir. 2010)], the court held that continued protests by a truck driver concerning a fuel surcharge being imposed by the company amounted to concerted activity protected by the NLRA because the protests, although presented individually, were a continuation of protests that involved concerted activity.

Q 11:103   Do an employer's anti-union comments to employees constitute an unfair labor practice?

No. Such remarks are protected by the First Amendment and express provisions of the NLRA. So long as such remarks do not contain a threat of retaliation for union activities, they are not an unfair labor practice.

However, in certain situations, expressed anti-union animus can rise to the level of an unfair labor practice by being an interference with, a restraint or coercion of employees in the exercise of their rights under Section 8(a)(1) of the NLRA. In *Progressive Electric, Inc. v. NLRB* [453 F.3d 538 (D.C. Cir. 2006)], a contractor who discovered that paid union organizers were attempting to obtain jobs at his non-union shop, a practice known as "salting," organized a meeting of his employees and stated that the union's attempts at organizing would cost "all you guys your jobs," and the company had to put a "stop to it." The owner then went on in "colorful" language to describe his dislike of unions. Under these facts, the court held that the employer had engaged in interference and coercion, and upheld a determination of an unfair labor practice by the NLRB.

Q 11:104   Is an employer's limitation of soliciting on company property an unfair labor practice?

Generally, no. An employer may deny outside union organizers access to the employer's private property and require its own employees to engage in union activities only during non-working times, provided such rules are uniformly applied to all organizations and solicitations and not just to unions and organizing activities. [*See* Lechmere, Inc. v. NLRB, 502 U.S. 527 (1992).]

Q 11:105   Can an employer interrogate its employees about their union affiliations or interests?

Generally, no. Under the following carefully controlled circumstances, an employer may poll its employees about union adherence:

- The employer must poll in response to a union claim of majority support.
- The employees must be informed of the poll's purpose.
- The employees must be assured that no reprisals will result.
- The poll must be taken by secret ballot.

Q 11:106   Does a union commit an unfair labor practice by coercing employees or employers to recognize it?

Yes. A union is no more entitled to try to force employees to support it than an employer is entitled to try to force its employees to reject a union and organizing activities. Furthermore, a union is guilty of an unfair labor practice (and possibly racketeering, too) if it tries to coerce an employer into recognizing it without demonstrating that it enjoys the support of a majority of the employees (in the appropriate bargaining unit). In *Laborers' International Union of North America, Local 578 v. NLRB* [594 F.3d 732 (10th Cir. 2010)], the court held that a union commits an unfair labor practice when it persuades an employer to fire an employee for failing to pay his union dues.

Q 11:107   May an employer promise its employees rewards for rejecting a union?

No. Although promises of benefits may seem to be just the opposite of illegal coercion, the NLRB considers such promises to be a fist inside a velvet glove. Because employees understand that the hand that gives can also take away, such promises and benefits are considered illegally coercive and therefore an unfair labor practice.

Q 11:108   May an employer dominate its employees' labor union?

No. An employer may neither establish a company union nor seek to dominate an independent union, for example by paying its officers or otherwise financially supporting the union.

Q 11:109   May an employer encourage or discourage union membership?

Yes. An employer can take a position for or against a union, so long as it does not apply coercion or rewards to enforce this view. Similarly, a labor union may seek to persuade employees to join up and vote for it, but it may coerce them to do so.

Q 11:110   What is *featherbedding*?

Featherbedding is the practice of coercing an employer to pay union members for work that is never really performed. It is an unfair labor practice.

Q 11:111   Does a company commit an unfair labor practice if it provides a gift to its employees without first bargaining with the union?

Section 8(d) of the NLRA requires bargaining between the employer and the union with respect to "wages, hours and other terms and conditions of employment." In *Unite Here v. National Labor Relations Board* [546 F.3d 239 (2d Cir. 2008)], an employer issued a one-time stock award in equal amounts to all employees after an initial public proffering, in recognition of the employees' contribution to the company. Each employee in the company received a one-time transfer of 100 shares of the company's stock. The union filed a charge with the NLRB claiming that the company's conduct was an unfair labor practice in that the company had a duty to bargain with reference to the stock issuance. The court upheld the NLRB, which concluded that this one-time issuance of stock was a gift for which no bargaining was required under federal law.

Chapter 12

Immigration and Naturalization

The Immigration and Nationality Act is the fundamental immigration statute and it has evolved over the years. The Immigration Reform and Control Act of 1986 (IRCA) and the Immigration Act of 1990 are two of the important changes to the statute. IRCA has helped control illegal immigration primarily by creating civil and criminal penalties for employers who hire illegal immigrants. The Immigration Act of 1990 was landmark legislation that increased the annual maximum of employment-based visas allowed. The rise in illegal immigration has pushed immigration reform to the forefront once more. Many states have enacted legislation affecting employment of illegal immigrants. In addition to these topics, this chapter also covers discrimination on the basis of an individual's national origin or citizenship status with respect to hiring, recruitment, or referral for employment.

Basics

Q 12:1   What is the fundamental U.S. immigration law?

The fundamental U.S. immigration statute is the Immigration and Nationality Act (INA) of 1952. Prior to its passage, U.S. immigration was governed by a variety of federal statutes that were not collected under a single title of the U.S. Code.

Q 12:2 What laws have amended the INA of 1952?

The INA has been amended many times. When Congress enacts a law, it generally does not rewrite the entire body of law, or even entire sections of a law, but instead adds to or changes specific words within a section. These changes are then reflected within the larger body of law.

The language changing the larger body of law is generally referred to as the "amendatory" language. Following is a list of laws "amending" both the INA and the U.S. Code:

1. Pub. L. No. 99-603—Immigration Reform and Control Act of 1986
2. Pub. L. No. 100-102—In part, as amended by Pub. L. No. 101-167, Pub. L. No. 101-513, and Pub. L. No. 101-649—Amerasian Immigration
3. Pub. L. No. 101-649—Immigration Act of 1990
4. Pub. L. No. 102-232—Miscellaneous and Technical Immigration and Naturalization Amendments of 1991
5. Pub. L. No. 102-395—The Judiciary Appropriations Act, 1993
6. Pub. L. No. 103-236—To authorize appropriations for the Department of State, the U.S. Information Agency and related agencies, and for other purposes
7. Pub. L. No. 103-415—Technical and Conforming Amendments
8. Pub. L. No. 103-416—Immigration and Nationality Technical Corrections Act of 1994
9. Pub. L. No. 104-51—Immigration and Nationality Act; Amendment
10. Pub. L. No. 104-114—To seek international sanctions against the Castro government in Cuba, to plan for support of a transition government leading to a democratically elected government in Cuba, and for other purposes
11. Pub. L. No. 104-132—Antiterrorism and Effective Death Penalty Act of 1996
12. Pub. L. No. 104-208—Illegal Immigration Reform and Immigrant Responsibility Act of 1996
13. Pub. L. No. 104-302—To extend the authorized period of stay within the United States for certain nurses
14. Pub. L. No. 105-38—Amends the Immigration and Nationality Technical Corrections Act of 1994 (Pub. L. No. 103-416)
15. Pub. L. No. 105-46—Continuing Appropriations, 1998
16. Pub. L. No. 105-54—Extension of deadlines for religious workers and for paperwork changes in employer sanctions; and to require the Secretary of State to waive or reduce fee for charitable service workers
17. Pub. L. No. 105-65—Departments of Veterans Affairs and Housing and Urban Development, and Independent Agencies Appropriations Act, 1998

18. Pub. L. No. 105-73—To amend the INA to exempt internationally adopted children 10 years of age or younger from the immunization requirement in Section 212(a)(1)(A)(ii) of such Act

19. Pub. L. No. 105-78—Departments of Labor, Health and Human Services, and Education Appropriations Act, 1998

20. Pub. L. No. 105-85—National Defense Authorization Act, 1998

21. Pub. L. No. 105-100—Nicaraguan Adjustment and Central American Relief Act

22. Pub. L. No. 105-119—Departments of Commerce, Justice, and State, the Judiciary, and Related Agencies Appropriations Act, 1998

23. Pub. L. No. 105-139—Technical corrections to the Nicaraguan Adjustment and Central American Relief Act

24. Pub. L. No. 105-141—To establish a program in local prisons to identify, prior to arraignment, criminal aliens and aliens who are unlawfully present in the United States, and for other purposes

25. Pub. L. No. 105-173—Immigration and Nationality—Visa Waiver Pilot Program—Data Regarding Nonimmigrant Overstay Rates

26. Pub. L. No. 105-259—Extension of Date of Development of Automated Entry-Exit Control System

27. Pub. L. 105-277—Omnibus Consolidated Appropriations

28. Pub. L. No. 105-292—International Religious Freedom Act of 1998

29. Pub. L. No. 105-306—Non-citizen Benefit Clarification and Other Technical Amendments Act of 1998

30. Pub. L. No. 105-319—Irish Peace Process Cultural and Training Act of 1998

31. Pub. L. No. 105-320—Torture Victims Relief Act of 1998

32. Pub. L. No. 105-332—Carl D. Perkins Vocational and Applied Technology Education Amendments of 1998

33. Pub. L. No. 105-360—Extension into Fiscal Year 1999 of visa processing period for diversity applicants whose visa processing was suspended during Fiscal Year 1998 due to embassy bombings

34. Pub. L. No. 106-78—Making appropriations for Agriculture, Rural Development, Food and Drug Administration, and Related Agencies programs for the Fiscal Year ending September 30, 2000, and for other purposes

35. Pub. L. No. 106-95—Nursing Relief for Disadvantaged Areas Act of 1999

36. Pub. L. No. 106-104—To extend the "S" nonimmigrant visa category for two additional years, and to authorize appropriations for the refugee assistance program

37. Pub. L. No. 106-113—Consolidated appropriations for the Fiscal Year ending September 30, 2000, and for other purposes

38. Pub. L. No. 106-120—Intelligence Authorization Act for Fiscal Year 2000

39. Pub. L. No. 106-139—Adopted alien who is less than 18 years of age may be considered a child if adopted with or after a sibling who is considered a child under the Act

40. Pub. L. No. 106-185—Civil Asset Forfeiture Reform Act of 2000

41. Pub. L. No. 106-207—Hmong Veteran's Naturalization Act of 2000

42. Pub. L. No. 106-215—Immigration and Naturalization Service Data Management Improvement Act of 2000

43. Pub. L. No. 106-246—Aiding Colombian Terrorists

44. Pub. L. No. 106-279—Inter-country Adoption Act of 2000

45. Pub. L. No. 106-311—Fee Increase for the Employees of H-1B Non-immigrant Workers Act of 2000

46. Pub. L. No. 106-313—American Competitiveness in the Twenty-first Century Act of 2000

47. Pub. L. No. 106-378—Adjustment of Status of Certain Syrian Nationals

48. Pub. L. No. 106-386—Victims of Trafficking and Violence Protection Act of 2000

49. Pub. L. No. 106-395—Child Citizenship Act of 2000

50. Pub. L. No. 106-396—Visa Waiver Permanent Program Act

51. Pub. L. No. 106-406—International Patient Act of 2000

52. Pub. L. No. 106-409—Religious Workers Act of 2000

53. Pub. L. No. 106-415—Extension of Hmong Veterans' Naturalization Act of 2000

54. Pub. L. No. 106-429—Making appropriations for foreign operations, export financing, and related programs for the Fiscal Year ending September 30, 2001, and for other purposes

55. Pub. L. No. 106-448—Waiver of Oath of Renunciation and Allegiance for Naturalization of Aliens Having Certain Disabilities Act of 2000

56. Pub. L. No. 106-451—Wartime Violation of Italian Americans Civil Liberties Act

57. Pub. L. No. 106-484—Bring Them Home Alive Act of 2000

58. Pub. L. No. 106-536—Special immigrant status for certain United States international broadcasting employees

59. Pub. L. No. 106-553—Making appropriations for the government of the District of Columbia and other activities chargeable in whole or in part against the revenues of said District of Columbia for the Fiscal Year ending September 30, 2001 and for other purposes

60. Pub. L. No. 106-554—Consolidated Appropriations Act of 2001

61. Pub. L. No. 106-570—Assistance for International Malaria Control Act

62. Pub. L. No. 107-43—United States-Jordan Free Trade Area Implementation Act

63. Pub. L. No. 107-45—To provide permanent authority for the admission of "S" visa non-immigrants

64. Pub. L. No. 107-56—Uniting and Strengthening America by Providing Appropriate Tools Required to Intercept and Obstruct Terrorism (USA Patriot Act) Act of 2001

65. Pub. L. No. 107-77—Departments of Commerce, Justice, and State, the Judiciary, and Related Agencies Appropriations Act, 2002

66. Pub. L. No. 107-108—Intelligence Authorization Act for Fiscal Year 2002

67. Pub. L. No. 107-124—Provide work authorization for nonimmigrant spouses of treaty traders and treaty investors

68. Pub. L. No. 107-125—Provide work authorization for nonimmigrant spouses of intracompany transferees

69. Pub. L. No. 107-128—Extend pilot program for employment eligibility verification

70. Pub. L. No. 107-150—Family Sponsor Immigration Act of 2002

71. Pub. L. No. 107-173—Enhanced Security and Visa Entry Reform Act of 2002

72. Pub. L. No. 107-206—2002 Supplemental Appropriations Act for Further Recovery from and Response to Terrorist Attacks on the United States

73. Pub. L. No. 107-208—Child Status Protection Act

74. Pub. L. No. 107-234—Extension of Irish Peace Process Cultural and Training Program

75. Pub. L. No. 107-258—Persian Gulf War POW/MIA Accountability Act of 2002

76. Pub. L. No. 107-273—21st Century Department of Justice Appropriations Authorization Act

77. Pub. L. No. 107-274—Border Commuter Student Act of 2002

78. Pub. L. No. 107-296—Homeland Security Act of 2002

79. Pub. L. No. 108-7—Consolidated Appropriations Resolution, 2003

80. Pub. L. No. 108-77—United States-Chile Free Trade Agreement Implementation Act

81. Pub. L. No. 108-78—United States-Singapore Free Trade Agreement Implementation Act

82. Pub. L. No. 108-90—Department of Homeland Security Appropriations Act, 2004

83. Pub. L. No. 108-99—Extension of the Special Immigrant Religious Worker Program

84. Pub. L. No. 108-136—National Defense Authorization Act for Fiscal Year 2004

85. Pub. L. No. 108-156—Basic Pilot Program Extension and Expansion Act of 2003

86. Pub. L. No. 108-177—Intelligence Authorization Act for Fiscal Year 2004

87. Pub. L. No. 108-193—Trafficking Victims Protection Reauthorization Act of 2003

88. Pub. L. No. 108-199—Consolidated Appropriations Act, 20

89. Pub. L. No. 108-390—To improve the process for verifying an individual's eligibility for employment

90. Pub. L. No. 108-441—To improve access to physicians in medically underserved areas

91. Pub. L. No. 108-447—Consolidated Appropriations Act, 2005 (Includes L-1 Visa and H-1B Visa Reform Act, and the H-1B Visa Reform Act of 2004)

92. Pub. L. No. 108-449—To amend and extend the Irish Peace Process Cultural and Training Program Act of 1998

93. Pub. L. No. 108-458—Intelligence Reform and Terrorism Prevention Act of 2004

Q 12:3 Where can these laws be accessed?

These federal laws can be accessed on the U.S. Citizenship and Immigration Services (USCIS) Web site at: http://www.uscis.gov/portal/site/uscis.

Federal government information and guidance include:

1. U.S. Citizenship and Immigration Services [http://www.uscis.gov/portal/site/uscis]

2. U.S. Immigration and Customs Enforcement (ICE) [http://www.ice.gov/about/index.htm]

3. U.S. Department of Justice [http://www.justice.gov/crt/about/osc/htm/WebOverview2005.php/]

4. U.S. Social Security Administration (SSA) [http://www.ssa.gov/aboutus/]

5. Federal Bureau of Investigation [http://www.fbi.gov/aboutus.htm]

6. U.S. Department of Labor [http://www.dol.gov/opa/aboutdol/mission.htm]

7. U.S. Department of State [http://travel.state.gov/visa/visa_1750.html]

Immigrant-advocacy organizations include:

1. Catholic Legal Immigration Network, Inc. [http://www.cliniclegal.org/Aboutus.html]

2. National Network for Immigrant and Refugee Rights
   [http://www.nnirr.org/drupal/]

3. American Immigration Lawyers Association
   [http://www.aila.org]

Other immigration-policy resources include:

1. Federation for American Immigration Reform
   [http://www.fairus.org]

2. American Immigration Network.

   [http://www.usavisanow.com/]

3. BNA Web Watch [http://www.bna.com].

Q 12:4   What proposals have been made regarding immigration reform?

In early 2013, President Obama introduced a single, comprehensive plan for immigration reform. The president's plan shifts the focus in determining who can come to the United States from family ties to U.S. citizens to putting a much bigger emphasis on work skills and employment opportunities. The plan is based on the following four ideas:

- *Strengthen borders.* The president has doubled the number of border patrol agents since 2004, but the new draft of the bill would increase border security (exactly how much is currently unspecified), allow the DHS to expand technological improvements along the border and add 140 new immigration judges to process the heavy flow of people who violate immigration laws. The bill would also increase the inspection fees that border-crossers already pay.

- *Crack down on companies that hire undocumented workers.* The bill would hold companies that exploit illegal workers accountable for their actions, as well as provide companies that use documented workers a way to verify that their employees are in the country legally. The bill would expand the E-Verify system, which checks the immigration status of workers seeking jobs.

- *Allow/require undocumented workers to earn citizenship.* The proposal would provide undocumented immigrants a legal way to earn citizenship. Immigrants living in the United States illegally would have to pass national security and criminal background checks, pay taxes and a penalty, and learn English before they can earn their citizenship. In return, there would be no uncertainty about their ability to become U.S. citizens if they meet the eligibility criteria. The proposal would also allow innocent young people brought to the country by their parents a chance to earn their citizenship more quickly if they serve in the military or pursue higher education.

- *Streamline the legal immigration system.* This streamlining would not only make it easier for vulnerable immigrants—victims of violence or abuse—to gain citizenship, but it would also encourage job-creating entrepreneurs, skilled workers, and STEM graduates to stay in the United States by making it easier for them to obtain citizenship.

[http://www.washingtonpost.com/blogs/wonkblog/wp/2013/01/29/read-president-obamas-immigration-proposal/]

On June 11, 2013, the Senate voted 82-15 to commence debate on the immigration-reform bill proposed by the so-called "gang of eight," a bi-partisan group of Senators, whose proposal would:

- Allow the nation's estimated 11 million illegal aliens to achieve citizenship within 13 years;
- Require aspiring illegals to pass a criminal record check, learn English, pay taxes, and a minimum fine of $2,000, following a decade-long waiting period;
- Add $6.5 billion to the budget for securing the border with Mexico;
- Retool the immigration system to admit more high-tech and lower-skilled workers on short-term work visas.

President Obama signaled his support for the legislation.

[http://www.usatoday.com/story/news/politics/2013/06/11/senate-begins-immigration-debate/2411509/]

Q 12:5　What effect would immigration reform have on the economy, employers, and employees?

A new study by the Center for American Progress suggests that immigration reform would actually be a boon to the U.S. economy, as well as the economic standing of all Americans. In one scenario, granting full citizenship and full legal rights to undocumented immigrants would increase the country's gross domestic product, create more jobs, increase American salaries, and increase tax revenue. [http://www.triplepundit.com/2013/04/immigration-reform/]

More specifically for employers and employees, immigration reform would have an effect on the workplace in several ways:

- **Streamline of the legal immigration system will attract more skilled workers in valued fields**. Authorities will reduce the backlogs for those workers who are eligible to immigrate to the United States and grant green cards to those people who graduate from U.S. universities with a master's or doctoral degree in science, technology, engineering, or mathematics (STEM degrees).
- **Increased employment verification.** There will most likely be an enhanced, mandatory E-Verify system. The system will help employers avoid hiring employees using false documents and will increase the penalties for those employers who choose to hire illegal immigrants anyway. The enhanced system will hopefully be faster and more reliable in preventing identity theft than the current one.
- **Admit new workers and protect the rights of current employees**. Employers will be allowed to hire non-citizen immigrant workers if they can show they were unable to find an American to fill the position, without displacing or exploiting either American or immigrant workers. Immigration laws will also tend to the needs of lower sectors of the economy, such as agriculture (sectors, which rely on immigrants to work). The laws will admit more or less lower-skilled workers depending on the need.

Q 12:6 Of all the many laws amending INA 1952, which are the most important?

- The Immigration Reform and Control Act of 1986 (IRCA)
- The Immigration Act of 1990

Q 12:7 What was the purpose of IRCA?

The purpose of IRCA was to:

1. Provide a solution for controlling illegal immigration to the United States;
2. Make some changes in the U.S. system of legal immigration; and
3. Provide a controlled legalization program for undocumented aliens who entered the United States before 1982.

Q 12:8 How has IRCA helped control illegal immigration?

Primarily by the creation of civil and criminal penalties for employers who hire undocumented (illegal) aliens.

Q 12:9 How did IRCA change the way predecessor laws classified immigrants?

IRCA altered several immigration provisions of the INA of 1952. First, a new immigrant category for dependents of employees of international organizations was created. IRCA recognized the unique position of children and spouses of long-term international organization employees when those employees die, transfer, or retire. It is often difficult for children and spouses to become reoriented to their original society and culture. For all purposes, these individuals are "Americanized." The special immigrant category recognizes their Americanization and allows the individuals to remain in this country if they meet certain residence requirements.

Second, IRCA restricted the ability of many foreign students to adjust their status to that of lawful permanent resident aliens. This modification was aimed at reducing the number of foreign students who remain in the United States. IRCA also altered the allocation of visas and created a visa waiver program.

Finally, IRCA modified the former H-2 program for temporary workers by adding the H-2A program for temporary agricultural workers. It also established a mechanism by which "special agricultural workers" are admitted to perform field work in perishable crops. Under this mechanism, agricultural workers move freely between employers without penalty and are fully protected under all federal, state, and local labor laws. This mechanism creates a legal workforce without decreasing the number of workers available to harvest perishable crops.

Q 12:10   Did IRCA legalize undocumented aliens already in the United States?

IRCA provided a one-shot amnesty program under which illegal aliens who entered the United States before January 1, 1982, could become legalized. Applications for the amnesty program were accepted for an 18-month period that ended in April 1988.

Q 12:11   Did employers have to fire undocumented employees hired prior to the effective date of IRCA?

No. IRCA "grandfathered" workers hired prior to November 6, 1986; however, although the employers were not subject to sanctions, the grandfather provisions of IRCA did not make it lawful for an unauthorized alien to accept employment. Consequently, the alien was (and is) still subject to deportation for accepting employment.

Q 12:12   Which employees are affected by IRCA?

IRCA applies only to unauthorized aliens hired after November 6, 1986. It does not apply to employees hired before that time.

Q 12:13   Who are unauthorized aliens?

Unauthorized aliens are aliens who enter the United States illegally or whose immigration status does not permit employment in the United States.

Q 12:14   What happens to an unauthorized alien employee?

A worker who is not authorized to be in the United States can be arrested and deported.

Q 12:15   Is there trafficking in illegal aliens?

Unquestionably, human trafficking occurs around the globe, including the trafficking in illegal aliens in the United States. However, because this activity is illegal, and therefore covert, authoritative sources vary widely in their estimates of the extent of this activity. The UNESCO Trafficking Statistics Project has stated,

> When it comes to statistics, trafficking of girls and women is one of several highly emotive issues which seem to overwhelm critical faculties. Numbers take on a life of their own, gaining acceptance through repetition, often with little inquiry into their derivations. Journalists, bowing to the pressures of editors, demand numbers, any number. Organizations feel compelled to supply them, lending false precisions and spurious authority to many reports. The UNESCO TRAFFICKING STATISTICS PROJECT is a first step toward clarifying what we

know, what we think we know, and what we don't know about trafficking.

According to a Public Broadcasting System program, "The most cited statistics on trafficking come from the U.S. State Department's annual reports on trafficking in persons. According to the 2005 report, 600,000 to 800,000 people are trafficked across international borders each year, with 14,500 to 17,500 trafficked into the United States. The report does not provide data on sexual exploitation specifically; the numbers include people trafficked for any sort of forced labor." This is consistent with earlier FBI estimates.

[http://www.pbs.org/wgbh/pages/frontline/slaves/etc/stats.html]

A January 2013 ICE Fact Sheet, while agreeing that thousands of people are victims of human trafficking annually, differentiated "human trafficking" from "human smuggling" as follows:

> Human trafficking and human smuggling are distinct criminal activities, and the terms are not interchangeable. Human trafficking centers on exploitation and is generally defined as:
>
> - Sex trafficking in which a commercial sex act is induced by force, fraud or coercion, or in which the person induced to perform such act has not attained 18 years of age; or
>
> - Recruitment, harboring, transportation, provision or obtaining of a person for labor or services, through the use of force, fraud or coercion for the purpose of subjection to involuntary servitude, peonage, debt bondage or slavery.
>
> Human smuggling centers on transportation and is generally defined as:
>
> - Importation of people into the United States involving deliberate evasion of immigration laws. This offense includes bringing illegal aliens into the country, as well as the unlawful transportation and harboring of aliens already in the United States.

[http://www.ice.gov/news/library/factsheets/human-trafficking.htm]

Q 12:16   What is the U.S. government doing about human trafficking?

Recent FBI initiatives include:

- Working with other local, state, and federal law enforcement agencies and national victim-based advocacy groups in joint task forces that combine resources and expertise on the issue.

- Victim specialists (along with victims specialists from the U.S. Attorney Offices and/or other non-government victim assistance service providers) work with human trafficking victims to not only advise them of their rights as victims but also to assure they get the help they need to address their short-term and long-term needs—like legal and repatriation services, immigration relief, housing, employment, education, job training, and child care.

- Participating in the Human Smuggling Trafficking Center (HSTC) created in July 2004 by the Secretary of State, the Secretary of Homeland Security, and the Attorney General. The HSTC serves as a fusion center for information on human smuggling and trafficking, bringing together analysts, officers, and investigators from such agencies as the CIA, the FBI, the Department of State, and the DHS.

- Supporting the Southeast European Cooperative Initiative (SECI), which works to combat human trafficking and other cross-border crime issues in the region (and ultimately stop their spread around the world).

[http://www.fbi.gov/hq/cid/civilrights/trafficking_initiatives.htm]

The U.S. Department of Human Services Administration for Children and Families runs the Rescue & Restore campaign, the purpose of which is to increase the number of identified trafficking victims and to help those victims receive the benefits and services needed to live safely in the United States. The first phase of the campaign focuses on outreach to those individuals who most likely encounter victims on a daily basis, but may not recognize them as victims of human trafficking. By initially educating health care providers, social service organizations and the law enforcement community about the issue of human trafficking, the agency says it hopes to encourage these intermediaries to look beneath the surface by recognizing clues and asking the right questions because they may be the only outsiders with the chance to reach out and help victims.

The agency lists as a critical component of the Rescue & Restore campaign, the creation of the National Human Trafficking Resource Center, 1-888-3737-888, which connects victims of trafficking to Non-Government Organizations (NGOs) who can help victims in their local area. The resource center helps intermediaries determine whether they have encountered a victim of human trafficking, helps connect victims to resources and coordinates with local social service organizations to protect and serve victims of trafficking.

[http://www.acf.hhs.gov/trafficking/rescue_restore/index.html]

On April 22, 2013, Kansas Governor Sam Brownback signed into law a new statute designed to combat human trafficking and the sexual exploitation of young women. [House Bill No. 2034] The law:

- Creates the crime of commercial sexual exploitation of a child, which applies to children ages 14–17;

- Makes commercial exploitation a felony punishable by a minimum 25-year term if the victim is under 14;

- Fines of up to $5,000 per incident will fund victim treatment centers.

The law's text is accessible at

http://www.kslegislature.org/li/b2013_14/measures/documents/hb2034_enrolled.pdf.

Q 12:17   Is there any way to "legalize" an alien employee?

Yes, through a process called "labor certification." This process usually requires a lawyer. Many attorneys, especially in urban areas, hold themselves out as immigration lawyers. Immigration is a complicated specialty. Furthermore, fees vary widely. To shop for a competent immigration lawyer, check the Internet, where many competent immigration lawyers have posted their credentials; contact your local bar association's referral service, which is typically posted on the Internet; or contact a local immigration-aid society (many nationalities have one).

The DOL made significant changes in the Labor Certification Process, effective in 2005. The "Program Electronic Review Management Regulations" initiated a new electronic method for application filing and processing.

If any of the immigration reform plans in the works come to bear fruit, a new plan would most likely allow undocumented workers to earn citizenship. Immigrants living here illegally would have to pass national security and criminal background checks, pay taxes and a penalty, and learn English before they can earn their citizenship. In return, there would be no uncertainty about their ability to become U.S. citizens if they meet the eligibility criteria.

Q 12:18   How does IRCA affect employers?

Employers cannot expect to hire illegal aliens with impunity. Any employer that recruits or hires unauthorized aliens and/or continues to employ unauthorized aliens is subject to civil and possibly criminal penalties.

Q 12:19   What must employers do to comply with IRCA?

Employers must verify the employment eligibility of any employee hired.

Q 12:20   What pre-employment question must be asked?

The pre-employment question that must be asked is: Is the employee a U.S. citizen or lawfully authorized to work in the United States?

Q 12:21   How does an employer verify an employee's employment eligibility?

To comply with verification requirements, an employer must show that it has examined documents that establish both: (1) the employment authorization; and (2) the identity of the employee. A U.S. passport, certificate of U.S. citizenship, certificate of naturalization, or certain resident alien cards establish both. Employment authorization documents include a Social Security card or a birth certificate. Identity documents include a driver's license, other state-issued card, or under certain circumstances, other documentation approved by the Attorney General.

Q 12:22   Which documents are acceptable for identification and employment authorization?

For identity:

- Driver's license
- Other state-issued I.D. card (e.g., a Pennsylvania Liquor Control Board I.D. card)

For employment authorization:

- Social Security card
- Birth certificate

For satisfaction of both categories:

- U.S. passport
- Certificate of U.S. citizenship
- Certificate of naturalization
- Certain resident-alien cards
- Unexpired foreign passport with attached visa authorizing U.S. employment
- Alien registration card with photo

Note: A new I-9 form was released by the government in March 2013 for use beginning in May 2013. No predecessor versions of the form are acceptable. The latest version of the form is available online at http://www.uscis.gov/files/form/i-9.pdf.

The I-9 Handbook for Employers is available at: http://www.uscis.gov/files/form/m-274.pdf.

A number of organizations offer I-9 electronic compilation and storage services to corporate clients. These include:

- I-9 Advantage [http://www.i9advantage.com/]
- I-9 Express [http://www.newi9.com/]
- HireRight [http://www.hireright.com/Electronic-I-9-Solution.aspx]

Q 12:23   What is the employer's responsibility for the authenticity of documents?

The employer is expected to examine the proffered documents. If they appear reasonably on their face to be genuine and to relate to the person presenting them, they are to be accepted. To refuse to accept such documents, in fact, may be viewed by the INS as an unfair immigration-related employment practice. On the other hand, if the document does not appear reasonably on its face to be genuine or to relate to the person presenting it, the employer is expected to refuse to accept it. Instead, that employer should contact the local INS office closest to the employer's facility and request assistance.

Q 12:24   What happens if the employer accepts the documentation and completes the I-9 and then later it turns out that the employee was not legally authorized to work after all?

Under these circumstances, if the employer has followed the advice in Q 12:23 with regard to the documents listed in Q 12:22, that employer will not be guilty of a verification violation and, all else being equal, should not be charged. If charged, the employer can raise the "good faith" defense, since the employer did not knowingly hire an illegal alien.

An employee, in a case of alleged national-origin discrimination, was permitted to obtain through discovery and enter into evidence in her case a letter proving that she had produced her passport during her I-9 processing. The federal judge ruled with regard to her motion to compel discovery, "The October 25, 2004 letter is relevant. It tends to make it more probable that plaintiff brought her passport—a document which reveals her national origin—as opposed to another valid form of identification which would not reveal her national origin because defendant's letter requested that she bring 'proof of citizenship.' Defendant's motion to exclude all evidence related to plaintiff's hiring by defendant in November 2004, including the letter, will accordingly be denied in part."

However, in so holding, the judge cut off the plaintiff's attempt to expand her case including an accusation of document abuse against her employer. Although the plaintiff argued that the request in this letter was inconsistent with IRCA, the plaintiff didn't dispute that in practice the defendant accepted all documentation deemed acceptable by form I-9. She also didn't argue that she or other employees were in fact required to show more or different documents than what the law allows. The letter was declared irrelevant with respect to showing that the defendant's proffered legitimate, non-discriminatory reason for terminating her was pretext. This letter was issued two years prior to the incident involving the plaintiff. Additionally, the letter was written by one Vincent J. Fenerty, Jr. who was not involved in the decision to terminate her. Even if the letter were circumstantial evidence that in October/November of 2004 Fenerty and others who may have been involved in the issuing of the letter had an intent to discriminate against non-citizens, that didn't make it more or less probable that in September/October of 2006 defendant William Raymond and others involved in the decision to terminate plaintiff had an intent to discriminate against Haitians, the court stated.

[Cange v. Philadelphia Parking Auth., 2010 WL 365468 (E.D. Pa. Feb. 1, 2010)]

Q 12:25   May an employer accept a photocopy of a document if one is presented by the applicant/new employee?

No. Only original documents are acceptable. The one exception to this hard-and-fast rule is a certified copy of a birth certificate.

Q 12:26   May an employer fire an employee who fails to produce the required documentation?

An employee who fails to provide required documentation within three business days of being hired may be terminated from employment. If the employee claims the documents were lost or stolen, a receipt for a request for replacement documents will suffice for the time being. In that case, the employee has an additional 90 days in which to present those replacement documents to the employer, whose human resources department should make sure that there is a follow-up request should the employee fail to proffer the replacement documents within the time allotted by law. Remember, these policies must be applied uniformly to all employees in order to avoid a charge of immigrant-related discrimination.

Q 12:27   Can an alien be employed prior to work-authorized visa status?

No, an individual who has not yet obtained a work-authorized visa status cannot be employed pending receipt of that status.

Q 12:28   Can an alien serve as an unpaid volunteer while awaiting the award of work-authorized visa status?

No, the DOL takes the position that, if the work would normally be subject to monetary compensation, then it is not volunteer work.

Q 12:29   Can an alien work while an extension of work-authorized visa status is pending?

Yes, if the extension involves the same employee and the same employer, and if it was timely filed, the alien worker can continue working for that same employer for up to 240 days while the application is being processed.

Q 12:30   What records must be kept following verification?

The employer and employee must fill out an INS form called an I-9. The I-9 form must be kept for: (1) three years after the person is hired; or (2) one year after the person is terminated, whichever is later. The I-9 form contains a document checklist showing the evidence used to verify the employee's legal right to work. The I-9 form does not require that copies of the documentation be retained, but the employer may make copies and keep them on record; however, if copies of the inspected documents are retained, it may be possible for the INS to second-guess the good faith of the employer in accepting such documents if they are later found to be forgeries.

The employer must also sign a sworn statement, under penalty of perjury, that to its knowledge, the employee's documents are genuine.

Because IRCA limits the uses to which the I-9 forms and backup documents can be used, employers may have to keep such information in a file separate from employee personnel files to avoid any claim of their improper use by law-enforcement agencies or the employer.

Note: A new I-9 form was released by the government in March 2013 for use beginning in May 2013. No predecessor versions of the form are acceptable. The new version is available online at http://www.uscis.gov/files/form/i-9 .pdf.

Q 12:31 Must an employer verify every employee?

Yes. If only foreign-looking employees are checked, the employer is guilty of discrimination. The Act contains an anti-discrimination provision stating that it is an unfair employment practice for an employer to discriminate on the basis of citizenship status or national origin. This provision applies only to employers with four or more employees.

The employer must make a verification check at the time of hiring. Only agricultural employers get a 24-hour grace period; agricultural employees must be verified within 24 hours of hiring.

If an employer hires an unauthorized alien or continues employment of an unauthorized alien hired after November 26, 1986, that employer will be fined and may be imprisoned. IRCA provides both civil and criminal penalties. Beginning in 1988, fines for all offenses were imposed without first-offense warnings. An employer who failed to obey the preceding regulation was subject to penalties. The following is a listing of civil penalties that may be imposed:

1. First offense: $372 to $3,200 for each unauthorized alien hired;

2. Second offense: $3,200 to $6,500 for each unauthorized alien hired; and

3. More than one prior offense: $4,300 to $16,000 for each unauthorized alien hired.

4. Failure to verify employees subjects the employer to a fine of $100 to $1,000 for each unverified employee.

5. Any employer that engages in "pattern or practice" violations is subject to a maximum fine of $3,000 for each unauthorized alien, six-months imprisonment, or both. Pattern or practice violations are regular, repeated, and intentional activities. They do not include isolated or accidental acts. The criminal penalties cited apply only to employers who have employed, recruited, or referred undocumented aliens. The penalties do not apply to verification violations.

Q 12:32 What must an employer do upon learning that an illegal alien has been hired?

In *Mester Manufacturing Co. v. Immigration and Naturalization Service* [879 F.2d 561 (9th Cir. 1989)], the court held that where the employer had notice from the INS that the alien identification numbers provided by the employees on their I-9 forms could not be verified by the agency as authentic, that employer in effect had constructive knowledge of the employees' illegal status (See Q 12:30 for a definition of the I-9 form). The constructive notice triggered the employer's duty to suspend or terminate the employees or risk legal sanctions.

Q 12:33 How can an employer verify an alien's right to work in the United States?

Since August 3, 1993, all permanent resident aliens must possess the newest version of the Alien Registration Card (Form I-551). Employers have received some additional assistance from the federal Social Security Administration (SSA), which now affixes the notice "VALID FOR WORK ONLY WITH INS AUTHORIZATION" on Social Security cards issued to aliens with temporary work authorization only. This type of limited-use Social Security card should be accepted by employers only in conjunction with appropriate INS-issued work authorization documents. This should prevent an alien whose work authorization has expired from trying to get new employment by using the Social Security card as one form of identification, thereby misleading the prospective employer. [*See* 57 Fed. Reg. 28,700 and 28,872 (June 29, 1992).]

Q 12:34 What happens when a company makes a "good faith" mistake in verifying eligibility for employment?

The ICE should explain the problem and allow the employer 10 days to make the correction without penalty.

With regard to the employee who uses such fraudulent documentation to obtain employment, subsequent discovery of the fraud may disqualify the illegal alien from pursuing a claim for lost wages. Furthermore, if he or she "knowingly" presented such documentation, an IRCA violation will also be considered by ICE to have occurred. The illegal alien cannot escape such liability by claiming lack of knowledge of invalidity of a piece of documentation, such as a fraudulent Social Security card. [*See* Ambrosi v. 1085 Park Avenue LLC, 2008 WL 4386751 (S.D.N.Y. 2008).]

Q 12:35 Upon what documentation may an employer belonging to a multi-employer bargaining unit affiliated with a labor organization rely in verifying work eligibility for a prospective employer?

An I-9 form completed by a prior employer that is a member of the same multi-employer collective bargaining organization is acceptable, provided the I-9 is no more than three years old.

Q 12:36 Which specific documents constitute acceptable verification of an applicant's eligibility for employment?

Two types of documentation are required by the INS: (1) Form I-9 proof of employment authorization; and (2) proof of identity (see the general categories listed in Q 12:22). Without exception, the documents must be originals, not photocopies or other facsimiles.

Certain specific INS forms can be used to help establish both identification and employment eligibility:

1. An unexpired reentry permit (Form I-327);
2. A temporary I-551 printed notation on certain machine-readable immigrant visas;
3. Valid passports for citizens of the Federated States of Micronesia (FSM) and the Republic of the Marshall Islands (RMI);
4. Form I-94 or Form I-94A indicating nonimmigrant admission under the Compact of Free Association Between the United States and the FSM or RMI; and
5. An unexpired Refugee Travel form (Form I-571).

Under the INS regulations, the following documents help establish identity, but not employment eligibility:

1. State-issued driver's license with photo affixed;
2. School ID card with photo affixed;
3. Voter registration card;
4. Dependent's ID card with respect to a member of the U.S. armed forces;
5. Merchant mariner card issued by the U.S. Coast Guard;
6. American Indian tribal documents;
7. Canadian driver's license; and
8. Any other ID card issued by a federal, state, or local governmental entity that either has a photo affixed to it or gives physical information about the holder (such as name, date of birth, address, height, weight, and eye color).

The following documents, according to the regulations, establish employment eligibility, but do not verify the applicant's identity:

1. Citizenship Identification Card (Form I-197);
2. Certificate of Birth Abroad (Form FS-545); and
3. Resident Citizen Card (I-179).

In the "Chinese menu" approach adopted by the INS regulations, the employer must have from the applicant one item from the first list or one each from the second two lists. Finally, note that in using documents from the first list (those that are acceptable for both identity and right-to-work purposes), if the applicant presents two documents attached to one another (e.g., foreign passport plus employment authorization form), the employer must record the ID numbers and expiration dates of both. [*See* 56 Fed. Reg. 41,767 (Aug. 23, 1991).]

Q 12:37   Can an employer specify which documents are acceptable to verify applicant identification and right to work?

Under USCIS regulations, applicants can submit the documents of their choice to meet the identification and right-to-work requirements of the Immigration Act; however, if the employer finds the initial documents submitted to be inadequate, the company has the right to request additional documentation. [28 C.F.R. § 44.200(a)(3)] Furthermore, no person representing an employer should sign the certification at the bottom of the I-9 form unless and until any doubts have been resolved concerning the authenticity of the proffered documentation. The ICE and Justice Department have attempted to prosecute employer representatives for allegedly making false certifications, which is illegal under 8 U.S.C. Section 1546.

Q 12:38   Are there any "paper-free" record keeping options?

Under the relevant law:

1. An electronic signature may be used by both the employee and the employer to attest to an electronic Form I-9;
2. Employers are allowed to maintain I-9s in PDF or other electronic formats; and
3. Employers are allowed to convert and maintain existing paper I-9s into electronic formats.

Some companies which provide this service are:

- I-9 Advantage [http://www.i9advantage.com/]
- I-9 Express [http://www.newi9.com/]
- HireRight [http://www.hireright.com/Electronic-I-9-Solution.aspx]

Employers, however, are still required to personally verify original employment eligibility documents (or certified copies, in the case of birth certificates) in "hard" versus electronic form.

Q 12:39   Must an employer verify an employee referred by a state employment agency?

No, this is unnecessary as long as the employer has documentation of the agency's referral that specifically certifies that the agency has satisfied such requirements. If this documentation is not available, the employer must get independent verification.

Q 12:40 Must employment agencies and other persons or entities recruiting for a fee verify a prospect's employment eligibility?

Yes. Prior to recruiting for a fee or referring for employment for a fee, the entity must complete an I-9 form even though the entity is not an employer per se.

Performing this function does not in itself make the employment agency a joint employer for purposes of imposing, for example, liability for national origin discrimination committed by the employer to whom the plaintiff was sent. [*See* Lima v. Addeco, 634 F. Supp. 2d 394 (S.D.N.Y. 2009).]

Q 12:41 How is ICE organized?

With the establishment of the DHS, the functions, expertise, resources, and jurisdictions of several once-fragmented border and security agencies were merged and reconstituted into ICE, the DHS's largest investigative bureau. The agencies that were either moved entirely or merged in part, based upon law enforcement functions, included the investigative and intelligence resources of the U.S. Customs Service, the INS, the Federal Protective Service and, as of November 2003, the Federal Air Marshals Service.

ICE is the investigative arm of the Border and Transportation Security Directorate (BTS), the operational directorate within the DHS tasked with securing the nation's borders and safeguarding its transportation infrastructure. The largest component within the DHS, BTS employs more than 100,000 men and women. ICE brings together more than 20,000 employees who focus on the enforcement of immigration and customs laws within the United States, the protection of specified federal buildings, and air and marine enforcement. By unifying previously fragmented investigative functions, ICE will deliver effective and comprehensive enforcement. ICE is led by an Assistant Secretary who reports directly to the Under Secretary for BTS.

ICE is composed of the following operational Divisions:

1. *Office of Investigations*—responsible for investigating a range of issues, including human smuggling; narcotics, weapons and all other contraband smuggling; export enforcement, such as investigating illegal arms exports and exports of dual-use equipment that may threaten national security; financial crimes, such as money laundering, commercial fraud, and intellectual property rights (including commercial counterfeiting) violations; cybercrime; immigration crime; and human rights violations.

2. *Office of Detention and Removal*—responsible for promoting public safety and national security by ensuring the departure from the United States of all removable aliens through the fair enforcement of the nation's immigration laws.

3. *Office of Federal Air Marshal Service (FAMS)*—responsible for promoting confidence in our nations' civil aviation system through the effective deployment of Federal Air Marshals to detect, deter, and defeat hostile acts targeting U.S. air carriers, airports, passengers, and crews.

4. *Office of Federal Protective Service*—responsible for policing, securing, and ensuring a safe environment in which federal agencies can conduct their business by reducing threats posed against the more than 8,800 federal facilities nationwide.

5. *Office of Intelligence*—responsible for the collection, analysis, and dissemination of strategic and tactical intelligence data for use by the operational elements of ICE and the DHS.

Q 12:42   Can ICE enter a business to look for I-9s?

Yes. ICE may enter a place of business without a subpoena or a search warrant, if it provides three days' warning. If the INS has probable cause to believe an employer is violating the law, it can enter the workplace without warning after obtaining a subpoena or search warrant.

In *United States v. Cheung* [2009 WL 3415980 (6th Cir. Oct. 22, 2009)], the defendant stood on trial for charges of conspiring to harbor illegal aliens for commercial advantage or private financial gain. Local police and officials from ICE began an investigation after a neighbor reported a suspiciously large number of people living in a single-family home owned by Shi and Wang. At about 10:00 each morning, a white van licensed to the Empire Buffet would appear at the house, and a large number of individuals would enter the van to go to the Empire Buffet. Every night the van would return at about 10:00 or 10:30. Agent Roger Werner of ICE observed the same pattern at another restaurant Defendant Cheung owned in Florence, Kentucky: A white van would take workers from a house to the restaurant and back at roughly the same times as the Empire Buffet van would.

On October 16, 2007, local police and Agent Werner stopped the Empire Buffet van en route to the restaurant, then searched the house where the workers had been living. Four of the passengers, as well as another person the police found in the house, were illegal immigrants from Mexico.

Agent Werner went to the restaurant and asked to speak to the manager. Wang directed him to Cheung. When Agent Werner asked for the workers' I-9 forms, Cheung had none. Although he later produced some I-9 forms, Cheung never produced any forms for the five individuals in question. The Empire Buffet, it also turned out, had not paid unemployment taxes on the wages of any of these individuals.

The jury convicted him of conspiring to harbor illegal aliens. On appeal, the Sixth Circuit found no violations of Cheung's Constitutional rights with regard to any of ICE's actions in building the case against him.

Q 12:43   What is a good example of ICE enforcement actions?

An example of ICE enforcement took place during the first week of March 2007. ICE agents raided a leather factory in New Bedford, Massachusetts. Supported by local law enforcement, ICE arrested 361 workers. Most were female sewing-machine operators. Most hailed from Guatemala or El Salvador. The Michael Bianco Inc. plant employed a total of 500 workers, who made backpacks and vests for the U.S. military under an $83 million federal contract.

The arrests were hardly completed before the public relations war commenced. The U.S. Attorney, in a public statement, characterized the illegals as "exploited workers with low-paying jobs and horrible working conditions."

Ultimately, the war of words made its way into a federal courthouse. By November 2007, the detainees' main case had climbed all the way to the U.S. Court of Appeals for the Second Circuit. [Aguilar v. U.S. Immigration and Customs Enforcement Div. of the Dep't of Homeland Security, 510 F.3d 1 (1st Cir. 2007)] According to the appeals panel:

> With respect to the detainees themselves, the petitioners aver that ICE inhibited their exercise of the right to counsel. According to the petitioners, a squad of volunteer lawyers who had offered to provide the detainees with guidance was turned away from Fort Devens on March 7. The next day, the lawyers were allowed to meet with those detainees (some thirty in number) who had expressly requested legal advice. The petitioners allege that, notwithstanding this largesse, some detainees were denied access to counsel after they arrived in Texas.
>
> On the afternoon of March 8, the Guatemalan consul, acting as next friend of the detainees (many of whom were Guatemalan nationals), filed a petition for a writ of habeas corpus and a complaint for declaratory and injunctive relief in the United States District Court for the District of Massachusetts. The action sought the detainees' immediate release or, in the alternative, a temporary restraining order halting further transfers. The district court enjoined ICE from moving any of the remaining detainees out of Massachusetts pending further order of the court.

The Second Circuit noted that the lower court had been faced with a plethora of Constitutional claims and legal issues, and that "the district court patiently sorted through them and, in a thoughtful rescript, eventually dismissed the action for want of subject matter jurisdiction." Adding that "no simple, one-size-fits-all answer to the questions presented by the parties," the court went on to conclude:

> We have scoured the case law for any authority suggesting that claims similar to those asserted here are actionable under the substantive component of the Due Process Clause, and we have found none. That chasm is important because, given the scarcity of "guideposts for responsible decisionmaking in this unchartered area," courts must be "reluctant to expand the concept of substantive due process." [Washington v. Glucksberg, 521 U.S. 702, 720 (1997) (quoting Collins v. Harker Heights, 503 U.S. 115, 125 (1992)]
>
> This unfortunate case is a paradigmatic example of an instance in which the prudential principle announced by the Collins Court should be heeded. Accordingly, we dismiss the petitioners' substantive due process claims for failure to satisfy the prerequisites of Federal Rule of Civil Procedure 12(b)(6).

Not content with that conclusion, the court went on to castigate ICE for some of its actions.

> We are sensitive to the concerns raised by the petitioners and are conscious that undocumented workers, like all persons who are on American soil, have certain inalienable rights. But in the first instance, it is Congress—not the judiciary—that has the responsibility of prescribing a framework for the vindication of those rights. When Congress speaks clearly and formulates a regime that satisfies constitutional imperatives, the courts must follow Congress's lead. In that sense, it does not matter whether a court approves or disapproves of an agency's *modus operandi.*
>
> We add only two comments. First, we applaud the able district judge for the skill and sensitivity with which he handled this highly charged case. Second, we express our hope that ICE, though it has prevailed, nonetheless will treat this chiaroscuro series of events as a learning experience in order to devise better, less ham-handed ways of carrying out its important responsibilities.

Even more recently, ICE deported from the United States:

- A Salvadoran murder suspect wanted in El Salvador for double homicide;
- A Nicaraguan national known as the "DC Groper," who was convicted of sexually assaulting women in the DuPont Circle area of northwest D.C.;
- A Korean national wanted in her native country for operating a Los Angeles-based prostitution ring;
- A Mexican criminal alien wanted in his native country for firearms-related charges;
- A Mexican drug lord who was responsible for multi-ton shipments of cocaine to associates in the United States, and was also wanted for a murder in his home country.

[http://www.ice.gov/news/releases/]

Q 12:44 How is ICE handling cases involving hiring aliens with false I-9 papers?

IRCA empowers ICE to fine an employer $1,000 for each documentation-violation related to the I-9 requirements. Egregious violators can also be indicted for conspiracy to violate the immigration laws which is a much more serious offense (i.e., a felony under federal law).

In July 2009, ICE launched an I-9 audit initiative, by issuing Notices of Inspection (NOIs) to 652 businesses nationwide—which was more than ICE had issued throughout all of prior fiscal years. The notices alerted business owners that ICE would be inspecting their hiring records to determine whether or not they were complying with employment eligibility verification laws and regulations. According to an ICE spokesperson, "Inspections are one of the most powerful tools the federal government has to enforce employment and immigration laws. This new initiative illustrates ICE's increased focus on holding employers accountable for their hiring practices and efforts to ensure a legal workforce." [http://www.ice.gov/news/releases/0907/090701washington .htm]

If an employer receives an audit notice from ICE, this advice from the law firm of Jackson Lewis is worth keeping in mind: "Employers that receive audit notices should make careful note of the date by which a response must be submitted to ICE and contact their immigration counsel as soon as possible to review the subpoena and coordinate their responses. Employers should avoid any detailed discussion of their I-9 processes with the ICE representative." [http://www.jacksonlewis.com/legalupdates/article.cfm?aid = 1914]

In June 2011, the Obama administration notified 1,000 companies in all 50 states that the government would soon inspect their hiring records. This represents a surge in I-9 inspections in the past year. The audits result in the firing of every illegal immigrant discovered on a company's payroll, and sometimes result in managerial personnel being criminally charged. [Miriam Jordan, "More 'Silent Raids' Over Immigration," *Wall Street Journal*, June 16, 2011, accessed at http://online.wsj.com/article/SB10001424052702304186404 576387843087137216.html] For example, Edward Schlacht, a supervisor at Grigg Box Company in Detroit, was arrested by ICE agents on criminal charges of knowingly accepting false documentation in the course of hiring undocu-mented workers. [http://www.ice.gov/news/releases/1111/111129detroit .htm]

In *United States v. Mejia-Flores* [2012 WL 525485 (D. Neb. Feb. 16, 2012)], it was found that illegal workers suspected of using stolen identities were entitled to Miranda warnings from ICE agents. They were entitled to the protections afforded by the Fourth and Fifth Amendments, because the investigation was criminal in nature and the workers rightly considered themselves to be "in custody."

Discrimination Against Aliens

Q 12:45   What do the anti-discrimination provisions of IRCA do that Title VII has not already done?

The anti-discrimination provisions of IRCA supplement those of Title VII in three important ways:

1. They extend civil rights protections to aliens, a group not covered by Title VII;
2. They expand the number of employers covered by anti-discrimination provisions from those with 15 or more employees (Title VII) to employers with three or more employees; and
3. They create an Office of Special Counsel and provide an alternative to an Equal Employment Opportunity Commission (EEOC) determination of the presence or absence of discrimination in the workplace.

Q 12:46   What is the legal definition of an *alien*?

An *alien* is an individual who is in the United States and is not a U.S. citizen. [8 U.S.C. § 1101(a)(3)]

In a class action suit, the Ninth Circuit held that all aliens detained for more than six months without a bond hearing constituted a class for litigation purposes. No further definition was demanded in order for the class action to proceed. [Rodriguez v. Hayes, 578 F.3d 1032 (9th Cir. 2009)]

Q 12:47   What are the types of aliens in the United States?

There are three general types of aliens in the United States:

1. *Legal immigrants*: individuals who are legally in the United States with the intent to reside there permanently.
2. *Non-immigrants*: individuals who enter the United States for a temporary stay and for a specific purpose, which might be work, study, or tourism.
3. *Illegal immigrants*: individuals who intend to remain permanently in the United States but who lack an appropriate visa status.

Q 12:48   What conduct is prohibited by the anti-discrimination provisions of IRCA?

IRCA prohibits discrimination on the basis of an individual's national origin or citizenship status with respect to hiring, recruitment, or referral for employment; however, the anti-discrimination provisions do not apply when an employer's employees must be U.S. citizens for the employer to comply with federal or state law or regulations.

Q 12:49   What pre-employment questions cannot be asked?

Pre-employment questions that cannot be asked are as follows:

1. Where was the employee or the employee's parents born?
2. What is the employee's nationality, parentage, or ancestry?
3. What language is spoken in the employee's home or what is the employee's first language?
4. What are the names and addresses of any relative other than a spouse or children who are dependents of the applicant?

Q 12:50   As currently interpreted, are employers liable for unintentional acts of discrimination against illegal aliens under the anti-discrimination provisions of IRCA?

The Special Counsel charged with enforcement of IRCA's anti-discrimination provisions has said that employers would be liable only if they intended to discriminate on the basis of a person's national origin or "alienage." Employers are not liable for unintentional acts that nevertheless have a harmful effect on aliens.

Q 12:51   How can an employer successfully defend itself against a discrimination claim?

In *Turner v. University of Washington* [2007 WL 4365789 (W.D. Wash. 2007)], the plaintiff, an Ethiopian immigrant, claimed that a variety of adverse employment actions were motivated by her employer's animosity toward her race and nationality. In ruling against the plaintiff on all her federal and state discrimination claims, however, the judge clearly regretted what he concluded was a tragic inter-personal situation, caused primarily by the plaintiff's own abrasive personality. Some of the specific incidents that took place included:

1. As early as 1999, the plaintiff exhibited unprofessional behavior at UWEB. In September of 1999, Cyndi Long, an E & O coordinator supervised by the plaintiff, ultimately left UWEB because of adverse interactions with the plaintiff. Before Ms. Long's departure, the plaintiff asked Ruth Johnston, a UW employee with a doctorate in organizational development and known within the UW community as someone willing to help resolve interpersonal conflicts, to report on the cause of the difficulties between Ms. Long and the plaintiff. As part of this report, Dr. Johnston commented generally on the UWEB staff's general impression of the plaintiff, stating that "[Plaintiff] is . . . seen generally as difficult to work with. She is perceived to be condescending, directive, demanding and picky, and unwilling to share credit with others. She is seen as working particularly well with those senior to her and particularly poorly with those junior to her. Some have talked with her about their issues with her, and others are fearful to do so. Staff sometimes avoid her or accommodate immediately to her needs in order to keep surface harmony."

2. By April 2002, the plaintiff's unprofessional, confrontational behavior elevated to aggressive conduct during a meeting with Kahreen Tebeau, an African American UWEB E & O program coordinator under the plaintiff's supervision. At trial, Caren Tidwell and Sheri Ireton credibly testified that Ms. Tebeau stepped out of her meeting with the plaintiff with disheveled clothing exclaiming that the plaintiff had just physically grabbed Ms. Tebeau to keep her from leaving the meeting. Although the plaintiff and Ms. Tebeau were the only people present in the room during this meeting, the Court found that the version of this event reported by Ms. Tebeau to others more credible than the plaintiff's story based on the factors identified in 9th Circuit Jury Instruction 1.11. The Court found that given Ms. Tebeau's circumstance and position at UWEB, there was no reason for her to distort the truth of her interaction with the plaintiff. The plaintiff was clearly minimizing the encounter and its impact on Ms. Tebeau.

3. Later, Nina Hanlon, Ms. Tebeau's replacement as E & O program coordinator, was involved in an incident in March of 2003 with the plaintiff while working on the NSF annual report. During a meeting with the plaintiff, Ms. Hanlon was frightened by the plaintiff's aggressive finger-pointing "bullying" behavior. On cross-examination, Ms. Hanlon testified that the plaintiff's

emotional control at this meeting was not appropriate. As a result of her negative interactions with the plaintiff, Ms. Hanlon requested to be reassigned out of UWEB.

4. In April of 2003, Lorease Kendrick, a UW Senior Human Resources Consultant who is also African American, investigated the verbal complaint Ms. Hanlon lodged against the plaintiff as a result of the March 2003 incident. At some point in April, the plaintiff called Ms. Kendrick to ask whether she had found that the accusations against the plaintiff were the product of racial discrimination. When the plaintiff was informed by Ms. Kendrick that the findings did not support discrimination, the plaintiff became very angry that Ms. Kendrick could not "see" that the complaint about the incident was the result of discrimination. On cross-examination Ms. Kendrick credibly testified that she felt very uncomfortable and surprised by the plaintiff's reaction because Ms. Kendrick believed that they had previously enjoyed a cordial relationship at UW.

5. Also in 2003, Mike Keller was assigned the UW University Complaint Investigation and Resolution Office (UCIRO) investigator for the plaintiff's discrimination and retaliation complaint lodged with UCIRO in April 2003. In November of 2003, Mr. Keller met with the plaintiff, in part, to provide the plaintiff with his preliminary findings. After delivering information to the plaintiff that she found unfavorable to her claim, as reported in Mr. Keller's contemporaneous notes from the meeting, the plaintiff became aggressive and offensive toward Mr. Keller. Mr. Keller credibly testified that at this meeting the plaintiff insulted him, clenching her fist, and that Mr. Keller informed the plaintiff that the very type of aggressive behavior that she was exhibiting in the meeting with him was the reason why others reacted negatively to her.

The judge in this case was something of a poet and a philosopher. His opinion is a great example of the law as literature. The decision concludes:

> Ms. Turner's life story is a compelling one. The Court will never forget her testimony about her love of her native country's star-filled sky or how much her mother's confidence that she would be the first one in her family to be a college graduate inspired her to achieve great things. Her joy at dancing again at her daughter's wedding shows that Ms. Turner is capable of experiencing joy again. As Ms. Turner's able counsel pointed out in closing argument, the process of coming forward and telling your story can help a person repair the damage caused by negative events. While the Court has not found that the plaintiff proved her legal claims against the defendants, there is no denying that Ms. Turner clearly had a profoundly positive effect on the lives of young women such as Mariana Loya, who credited much of her success to Ms. Turner. And of course her daughter, Dr. Diana Turner, is such an impressive woman who attributes much of her success to the support and encouragement she received from her mother.

The defendants were fortunate in having defense counsel capable of presenting the interpersonal nuances that led the parties to trial and a judge who was sufficiently perceptive to distinguish between such interpersonal and managerial failures and illegal discrimination.

Q 12:52   What constitutes a prima facie case of discrimination against an alien under IRCA?

The same general legal standard applies to alien discrimination cases under IRCA as has historically been applied by the federal courts in Title VII and ADEA cases. This test was enunciated by the Supreme Court in two major cases, *McDonnell Douglas Corp. v. Green* [411 U.S. 792 (1973)] and *Texas Department of Community Affairs v. Burdine* [450 U.S. 248 (1981)]. [*See also* 28 C.F.R. § 44.200(a).] The *prima facie* case consists of the plaintiff showing:

1. Membership in one of the groups protected from discrimination by IRCA (i.e., U.S. naturalized citizen, permanent resident alien, refugee, person granted asylum, or otherwise legalized alien);
2. Application for position;
3. Rejection by the employer; and
4. A continued search by the employer followed by the filling of the job with someone having similar qualifications as the rejected plaintiff, but not in the protected class.

Q 12:53   Are other groups protected by anti-discrimination legislation?

Yes, under the terms of IRCA, U.S. naturalized citizens, permanent resident aliens, refugees, individuals who have been granted asylum, and newly legalized aliens are covered.

Q 12:54   Are all employers covered by the anti-discrimination provisions of IRCA?

No. Employers with three or fewer employees are exempt from IRCA's anti-discrimination provisions. Those employers with more than three but fewer than 15 employees are covered exclusively by the anti-discrimination provisions of IRCA. Employers with 15 or more employees are prohibited from discriminating on the basis of national origin and citizenship status by Title VII of the Civil Rights Act of 1964 and are subject to the new provisions of IRCA only with respect to citizenship status claims filed with the Office of Special Counsel.

Q 12:55   Are aliens with AIDS protected from extradition?

No. In 2001, the Court of Appeals for the Ninth Circuit ruled that a deported alien who went back into the United States seeking medical assistance for AIDS was not entitled to use the "necessity defense" to avoid a second deportation. [United States v. Arellano-Rivera, 244 F.3d 1119 (9th Cir. 2001)]

Q 12:56   Are aliens with HIV/AIDS admissible into the United States?

In November 2009, the Centers for Disease Control removed HIV infection from the list of "communicable diseases of public health significance," effective January 4, 2010. "The rule means that HIV-positive foreign nationals will no longer be inadmissible to the United States or require waivers in order to be approved for nonimmigrant or immigrant visas. It also means HIV testing will no longer be part of immigration medical exams." [http://www.huntonimmigration lawblog.com/2009/11/articles/immigrant-visas/hivpositive-aliens-no-longer-inadmissible-to-us/; *see also* 74 Fed. Reg. 56547 (Nov. 2, 2009).] The CDC made its decision based on current medical and scientific knowledge, and public health practice, that "HIV infection is not spread by casual contact, through the air, or from food or water."

As discussed in Qs 7:175 through 7:177, the CDC seems to be on sound ground in asserting that "HIV infection is not spread by casual contact, through the air, or from food or water." However, this relaxation of the rules should not be interpreted as a signal that ICE is also relaxing its enforcement activities with regard to the requirement that aliens entering the United States must pass a medical examination. For example, at about the same time that the revision was announced in November 2009 by the CDC, ICE announced the arrest of a Los Angeles physician for allegedly falsifying medical examination records, including records implicating HIV infection. Among the allegations against the doctor was an affidavit stating that he told an ICE undercover agent who went to the defendant's office posing as an alien patient that he was not going to "disturb his blood" and that he "did not look like he had AIDS." The physician faces up to 80 years in prison for his alleged execution of fraudulent I-693 Forms, falsely attesting to immigrants' medical fitness to enter the United States. [http://www.ice.gov/pi/nr/0911/091103losangeles.htm]

All the same, employers cannot refuse to hire non-citizens, who are otherwise qualified to accept employment in the United States on the basis of HIV/AIDS.

Q 12:57   What are the possible sanctions for violation of the anti-discrimination provisions of IRCA?

For the first violation, an employer can be ordered to provide back pay for up to two years and to pay civil fines of up to $1,000 for each individual discriminated against. For subsequent violations, the fine can increase to $3,000 for each individual discriminated against. In addition, if the employer is found to have been "unreasonable in law and in fact," attorneys' fees may be awarded to successful claimants.

Q 12:58   Did the Immigration Act of 1990 add anything to IRCA's protection of aliens against discrimination?

The Immigration Act of 1990 expanded the protection of aliens against discrimination in two new ways:

1. It is an unfair employment practice for a company to require an alien to produce different or more documentation than is required by IRCA [*see* 28 C.F.R. § 44.200(a)(3)]; and

2. Coercion, intimidation, or retaliation against a person who seeks to exercise rights under IRCA, files a charge under IRCA, or assists in an investigation or testifies at an INS hearing is also an unfair employment practice. [28 C.F.R. § 44.200(a)(2)]

Q 12:59   Which government agencies share jurisdiction in cases involving charges of national origin discrimination?

Under Title VII of the 1964 Civil Rights Act [42 U.S.C. § 2000e-17], the EEOC has jurisdiction over employers of 15 or more employees and, therefore, can investigate charges of national origin discrimination involving such entities.

A victim of national origin discrimination can file a charge with the Office of Special Counsel of the DOL. The Office of Special Counsel for Immigration-Related Unfair Employment Practices in the Department's Civil Rights Division protects immigrants and other workers from employment discrimination based upon citizenship status, national origin, language, accent, or similar factors.

Persons who believe they have been discriminated against because they are immigrants have both places to file a complaint. They may call the Office of the Special Counsel—the enforcement agency for employers with four to 14 employees—toll-free at 1-800-255-7688. Those working for a larger firm may file a complaint with the nearest EEOC office or by calling 1-800-669-4000.

Q 12:60   What has the Supreme Court said about English-only rules in the workplace?

In 2001, the U.S. Supreme Court by a vote of 5-4 ruled that there is no private right of action to challenge English-only rules under Title VI of the 1964 Civil Rights Act. The plaintiffs challenged the Alabama Department of Public Safety's policy of requiring that all parts of the state's driver license examination be in English—and only in English.

The department's policy was enacted in fulfillment of an amendment to the Alabama Constitution, which designates English as the "official language of the state of Alabama" and expressly requires that Alabama officials take "all steps necessary to ensure that the role of English as the common language of the state of Alabama is preserved and enhanced."

Although the department previously had administered the test in several foreign languages, the new approach approved by the Supreme Court also bans interpreters, translation dictionaries, and other aids. [*See* Alexander v. Sandoval, 532 U.S. 275 (2001).]

In June 2009, the U.S. District Court in Western New York ruled that a Hispanic employee's challenge of his employer's English-only rule, as a form of employment discrimination under Title VII, was subject to the arbitration provision of the worker's employment contract. The arbitration agreement, executed by the plaintiff in conjunction with his employment application, stated:

> If there should be any disagreement arising out of this application for employment, it is important for both of us to be able to address that disagreement expeditiously and fairly. Therefore, this arbitration agreement requires you and us, Coca-Cola Enterprises Inc. and its subsidiaries and affiliated companies ("CCE"), to arbitrate any legal claim related to your application for employment, the hiring decision, or your subsequent employment with CCE . . .

> CCE and I agree that any claims that arise between us will be resolved in accordance with this arbitration agreement unless CCE, upon notice, adopts a different alternative dispute resolution program (such as "Solutions:," which applies only to Employees, as defined therein) in which case that program (including its rules), to the extent of its terms, shall supersede and replace this arbitration agreement, and I agree to be bound by said program.

According to the complaint, the plaintiff and some Hispanic co-workers were admonished by the production manager and told to stop speaking Spanish in the workplace, throughout the facility and on the walkie-talkies under the direct threat of disciplinary action including termination. He claimed that he complained that the rule was unfair but the production manager replied that it was rude to speak Spanish and he felt that Hispanic employees, including the plaintiff were making innuendos about the non-Hispanics behind managers' backs.

The plaintiff went to HR and complained, but allegedly got no action. He subsequently complained to the EEOC alleging discrimination and retaliation. He later sued. In granting the defendant-employer's motion to stay the proceedings and compel arbitration, the district judge rejected the plaintiff's contentions that he was unable to read the arbitration agreement and therefore shouldn't be held to it. His Honor found to the contrary that the plaintiff was able to read English and furthermore "even if the employee could not read or understand English it was his responsibility to make a reasonable effort to have the agreement made clear to him." [Molina v. Coca-Cola Enters., Inc., 2009 WL 1606433 (W.D.N.Y. June 8, 2009)]

On a related note, there is a bill in the 112th Congress called the English Language Unity Act (S. 503), which seeks to require that all official government functions be conducted in English, and only English, in order to "promote the English language within the respective States." Some consider the proposed bill mean-spirited and discriminatory. The bill was assigned to a congressional committee on March 6, 2013, which will consider it before possibly sending it on to the House or Senate as a whole. [http://thomas.loc.gov/cgi-bin/query/z?c1 12:S.503.IS:]

Q 12:61   What are the federal rules involving DNA testing of children born abroad seeking citizenship?

To establish that a child born abroad acquired derivative U.S. citizenship, the INA requires that a blood and a legal relationship exist between the child and the U.S. citizen parent. Volume 22 of C.F.R Section 51.40 provides that the burden of proof is upon the applicant to establish a claim to U.S. citizenship. When primary and secondary documentary evidence are deemed insufficient to establish such a claim, parentage blood testing is an option available to applicants. The Department of State appreciates that this situation may be troubling to some parents in light of religious and cultural issues, but under the circumstances, it often appears that there is no other way to establish the child's claim to U.S. citizenship. If such tests establish the blood relationship, the Department of State expedites issuance of a consular Report of Birth of a U.S. Citizen Abroad and a U.S. passport, provided applicable requirements of the INA concerning birth out of wedlock and establishment of a legal relationship (acknowledgment of paternity and legitimization prior to the child's 18th birthday) have been met. Additional information regarding arranging the blood test, locations for testing, and types of samples collected can be found at http://travel.state.gov/visa/immigrants/info/info_1337.html.

Q 12:62   Are the children of illegal immigrants entitled to attend public schools?

Yes. As early as 1982, the U.S. Supreme Court held that:

- Illegal aliens are included under the protections provided by the equal protection clause of the 14th Amendment to the U.S. Constitution.
- The discrimination inherent in a Texas statute, which withheld state education funding from school districts for illegal immigrants, and which allowed school districts to deny enrollment to such "illegals," was not "rational," unless it furthered a substantial state goal.
- The "illegal" status of the children in question, standing alone, was an insubstantial reason for denying them the same educational opportunities as other children in their communities.
- No national policy exists for denying such children an elementary education.
- The state's rationale—preservation of finite funding—was insufficient to sustain the statute against constitutional challenge.

[Plyler v. Doe, 457 U.S. 202 (U.S. 1982), *accord* Toll v. Moreno, 458 U.S. 1 (1982) (University of Maryland's policy of denying treaty organization aliens the opportunity to pay reduced, in-state tuition constituted a violation of the Supremacy Clause)]

While the right to attend public K-12 schools remains intact, in reaction to these decisions, the Congress passed statutes aimed at preventing these same students from advancing to public institutions of higher education. Meanwhile some seven states passed statutes of their own, permitting in-state tuition advantages for their illegal-alien residents. Out-of-state students, subject to much higher rates for attending the same state schools, have been challenging these statutes ever since. One example of such a challenge is *Day v. Sebelius.* [376 F. Supp. 2d 1022 (D. Kan., 2005)] This case is discussed in detail in Q 12:66.

Q 12:63   Has Congress enacted any laws in response to the Supreme Court's decisions regarding illegal aliens' rights to enjoy the same educational benefits as states afford their own citizens?

In *Toll v. Moreno* [458 U.S. 1 (1982)], the Supreme Court declared that a Maryland statute, which denied residency status to non-immigrant aliens, thus also denying them the opportunity to pay the reduced rate at the University of Maryland, violated the supremacy clause of the Constitution.

Two statutes enacted within weeks of one another in 1996 are widely viewed as being, among other things, responses to the Supreme Court's 1982 rulings, which afforded the children of illegal aliens the right to attend public schools and required states to provide non-immigrant alien residents the same reduced in-state tuition rates available to resident citizens. These two statutes are:

1. The Personal Responsibility and Work Opportunity Reconciliation Act of 1996 [H.R. 3734], and

2. The Illegal Immigration Reform and Immigrant Responsibility Act of 1996 (IIRIRA) [Pub. L. No. 104-208]. Specifically, this statute states, "Notwithstanding any other provision of law, an alien who is not lawfully present in the United States shall not be eligible on the basis of residence within a State (or a political subdivision) for any postsecondary education benefit unless a citizen or national of the United States is eligible for such a benefit (in no less an amount, duration, and scope) without regard to whether the citizen or national is such a resident." [8 U.S.C. § 1623] Note that this provision did not entirely overrule the Supreme Court's *Toll* decision, which in fact dealt with an alien presenting the United States under a non-immigrant visa, but the statute does limit the reach of *Toll* to the extent that it has been interpreted to afford the same benefits to illegal aliens.

Q 12:64   What does the IIRIRA say about illegal aliens' access to state-sponsored benefits?

The IIRIRA contains the following relevant provisions:

1. In general, illegal aliens are "not eligible for any State or local public benefit."

2. Exceptions to the general rule are made for (a) emergency medical care; (b) short-term, in-kind emergency disaster relief; (c) public health immunization and treatment of the symptoms of communicable diseases; (d) soup kitchens and similar fundamental services for the protection of life and safety.

3. "State or local public benefit" is defined as "any grant, contract, loan, professional license, or commercial license provided by an agency of a State or local government" or by their appropriated funds.

[8 U.S.C. § 1621]

Q 12:65 Do any states allow illegal immigrants to attend their public universities at reduced, in-state tuition rates?

Yes, currently the following states have statutes permitting illegal aliens to attend their public universities at the reduced, in-state tuition rates:

1. California
2. Illinois
3. Kansas
4. New York
5. Oklahoma
6. Texas
7. Utah
8. Washington

By contrast, two states, Alaska and Mississippi, have statutes that specifically prevent illegal aliens from attending their higher education institutions at reduced, in-state rates.

In Georgia, SB 458 is moving quickly through state legislature, and contains provisions that would ban undocumented students from all public universities and colleges in Georgia, even though they are already paying out-of-state tuition. However, a similar provision in an Alabama law was blocked by the courts in 2012. [http://www.huffingtonpost.com/azadeh-shahshahani/georgia-immigration-law_b_1374333.html]

Q 12:66 Have state statutes that allow illegal aliens to attend public universities at reduced, in-state tuition rates been challenged?

Yes. In the leading case, *Day v. Sebelius* [376 F. Supp. 2d 1022 (D. Kan. 2005), *affirmed*, Day v. Bond, 500 F.3d 1127 (10th Cir. 2007), *rehearing en banc denied*, 511 F.3d 1030 (10th Cir. 2007)], the Kansas legislature had passed such a statute in 2004. The seven other states that had passed legislation to provide in-state tuition rates to illegal aliens are: California, Illinois, New York, Oklahoma, Texas, Utah, and Washington. The legislature of Maryland had passed legislation to allow in-state tuition to illegal aliens, but the legislation was vetoed by the governor. At least two states had specifically passed statutes that do not allow illegal aliens to gain resident tuition status: Alaska and Mississippi. The legislature of Virginia had passed legislation prohibiting illegal aliens from receiving resident tuition, but the legislation was vetoed by the governor. The court stated that it believed this was the first case to challenge the type of legislation passed by Kansas.

The plaintiffs' complaint consisted of seven claims for relief:

In Count 1, which was entitled "Violation of 8 U.S.C. § 1621," plaintiffs contended that K.S.A. 76-731a violated 8 U.S.C. § 1621. According to the plaintiffs, § 1621 prohibited any state from offering any post-secondary educational benefit, including instate tuition, to illegal aliens. The plaintiffs further alleged that K.S.A. 76-731a didn't meet the statutory loophole set forth in 8 U.S.C. § 1621(d), which allowed states under certain circumstances to provide eligibility for illegal aliens to state benefits, because it didn't contain the express statutory language required by federal law.

In Count 2, which was entitled "Violation of 8 U.S.C. § 1623," the plaintiffs asserted that K.S.A. 76-731a violates 8 U.S.C. § 1623(a). According to the plaintiffs, § 1623 prohibited any state from providing any postsecondary education benefit, including in-state tuition, to an illegal alien unless a United States citizen was eligible for the same benefit. The plaintiffs further asserted that § 1623 eliminated the application of 8 U.S.C. § 1621(d).

In Count 3, which was entitled "Violation of Regulations Governing Alien Students," plaintiffs contended that K.S.A. 76-731a violated the comprehensive regulatory scheme enacted by the federal government to govern the admission of nonimmigrant aliens to the United States for the purpose of enrolling them as students at postsecondary educational institutions. They specifically pointed to the Student and Exchange Visitor Information System (SEVIS), a comprehensive computerized system designed to track international students and exchange students. (See Qs 12:129 through 12:143.) The plaintiffs contended that K.S.A. 76-731a frustrated this federal purpose by allowing aliens to illegally pose as students at Kansas institutions of higher education while remaining outside the SEVIS registration system.

In Count 4, which was entitled "Preemption," The plaintiffs claimed that K.S.A. 76-731a is preempted by the federal regulation of immigration. They suggested that Congress clearly intended to "occupy the field" in the area of regulating the provision of public benefits to aliens without a lawful immigration status. They asserted: "The power to regulate immigration is unquestionably an exclusively federal power, and any state statute that regulates immigration is unconstitutional and therefore proscribed. . . . States can neither add to nor take from conditions lawfully imposed upon the admission or residence of aliens in the United States. . . . [K.S.A. 76-731a] is preempted because it is impossible for a person who is an illegal alien or otherwise present in the United States to both receive postsecondary education under [K.S.A. 76-731a], and to comply with federal immigration law."

In Count 5, which was entitled "Creation of Residence Status Contrary to Federal Law," they alleged that K.S.A. 76-731a created residence status for illegal aliens contrary to federal law. They asserted: "Congress has created a legal disability under federal law that renders illegal aliens incapable of claiming bona fide legal domicile in Kansas, notwithstanding the fact of physical presence or a subjective 'intent' to remain indefinitely in the jurisdiction." They further alleged: "None of the members of the class of alien beneficiaries of [K.S.A.

76-731a] who are illegal aliens possesses federal authorization to remain in the United States for even the shortest period of time, and therefore cannot, as a matter of law, acquire or possess the requisite intent to be a legal resident or domiciliary of Kansas. Kansas may not deem such non-citizens to possess such intent, nor alternatively waive such intent by exercise of its legislative powers." By doing so, they in effect argued that K.S.A. 76-731a violated the comprehensive scheme established by federal law for aliens.

In Count 6, which was entitled "Infringement Upon Exclusive Federal Powers," the plaintiffs asserted that K.S.A. 76-731a impermissibly infringed on Constitutional powers reserved to the federal government. They contended that the challenged Kansas law violates Congress' power over the regulation of interstate commerce and foreign affairs.

Finally, in Count 7, which was entitled "Violation of Equal Protection Clause of U.S. Constitution," the plaintiffs contended that K.S.A. 76-731a violated the Equal Protection Clause of the United States Constitution. They asserted that equal protection was denied to them based upon the following argument: "Illegal aliens have been deemed by Defendants to be Kansas residents for the express purpose of affording such aliens state postsecondary education benefits to which they are not entitled under federal law. Defendants have further denied nonresident U.S. citizens Plaintiffs the identical postsecondary education benefits to which they are expressly entitled by federal law."

The district judge held:

1. Interveners were not required to show standing;

2. The Governor did not meet *Ex parte Young* exception to Eleventh Amendment immunity; but;

3. The plaintiffs, students and parents, lacked standing under federal statute prohibiting states from offering in-state tuition to illegal aliens; and

4. No private right of action was created by the statute in limiting illegal aliens' eligibility for higher education benefits based on residence; and, finally,

5. The plaintiffs lacked standing under Equal Protection Clause.

The net effect of this decision is to leave the underlying substantive issues for other battles on other days. These battles continue down to the present in a number of states.

In December 2005, another group of plaintiffs commenced a similar action against the regents of the University of California system, likewise challenging a statute that enables illegal aliens resident in the state to pay reduced tuition rates, while the plaintiffs and similarly situated, out-of-state students pay greater, often substantially greater, tuition bills. The California Court of Appeal held the statute was preempted by the federal law, although the court agreed with the federal district court in the foregoing Kansas case, it concluded that the plaintiffs in this case did indeed suffer a violation of their Equal Protection rights under the "Privileges and Immunities" clause of the Fourteenth Amendment of the Constitution, The court held, "We conclude that, on remand, the trial court shall give plaintiffs the opportunity to amend their complaint as to the equal protection claim." [Martinez v. Regents of Univ. of California, 83 Cal. Rptr. 3d 518 (App. 2008), *petition to review granted*, 198 P.3d 1, 87 Cal. Rptr. 3d 198 (2008)] The petition was later denied and the case dismissed. [Martinez v. Regents of the Univ. of California, 131 S. Ct. 2961 (2011)]

Q 12:67 What was the Hazleton, Pennsylvania, Illegal Immigration Relief Act Ordinance?

The controversial ordinance stated:

A. It is unlawful for any business entity to recruit, hire for employment, or continue to employ, or to permit, dispatch, or instruct any person who is an unlawful worker to perform work in whole or part within the City. Every business entity that applies for a business permit to engage in any type of work in the City shall sign an affidavit, prepared by the City Solicitor, affirming that they do not knowingly utilize the services or hire any person who is an unlawful worker.

B. Enforcement: The Hazleton Code Enforcement Office shall enforce the requirements of this section.

1. An enforcement action shall be initiated by means of a written signed complaint to the Hazleton Code Enforcement Office submitted by any City official, business entity, or City resident. A valid complaint shall include an allegation which describes the alleged violator(s) as well as the actions constituting the violation, and the date and location where such actions occurred.

2. A complaint which alleges a violation solely or primarily on the basis of national origin, ethnicity, or race shall be deemed invalid and shall not be enforced.

3. Upon receipt of a valid complaint, the Hazleton Code Enforcement Office shall, within three business days, request identity information from the business entity regarding any persons alleged to be unlawful workers. The Hazleton Code Enforcement Office shall suspend the business permit of any business entity which fails, within three business days after receipt of the request, to provide such information. In instances where an unlawful worker is alleged to be an unauthorized alien, as defined in United States Code Title 8, subsection 1324a(h)(3), the Hazleton Code Enforcement Office shall submit identity data required by the federal government to verify, pursuant to United States Code Title 8, section 1373, the immigration status of such person(s), and shall provide the business entity with written confirmation of that verification.

4. The Hazleton Code Enforcement Office shall suspend the business permit of any business entity which fails correct a violation of this section within three business days after notification of the violation by the Hazleton Code Enforcement Office.

5. The Hazleton Code Enforcement Office shall not suspend the business permit of a business entity if, prior to the date of the violation, the business entity had verified the work authorization of the alleged unlawful worker(s) using the Basic Pilot Program.

6. The suspension shall terminate one business day after a legal representative of the business entity submits, at a City office designated by the City Solicitor, a sworn affidavit stating that the violation has ended.

a. The affidavit shall include a description of the specific measures and actions taken by the business entity to end the violation, and shall include the name, address and other adequate identifying information of the unlawful workers related to the complaint.

b. Where two or more of the unlawful workers were verified by the federal government to be unauthorized aliens, the legal representative of the business entity shall submit to the Hazleton Code Enforcement Office, in addition to the prescribed affidavit, documentation acceptable to the City Solicitor which confirms that the business entity has enrolled in and will participate in the Basic Pilot Program for the duration of the validity of the business permit granted to the business entity.

7. For a second or subsequent violation, the Hazleton Code Enforcement Office shall suspend the business permit of a business entity for a period of twenty days. After the end of the suspension period, and upon receipt of the prescribed affidavit, the Hazleton Code Enforcement Office shall reinstate the business permit. The Hazleton Code Enforcement Office shall forward the affidavit, complaint, and associated documents to the appropriate federal enforcement agency, pursuant to United States Code Title 8, section 1373. In the case of an unlawful worker disqualified by state law not related to immigration, the Hazleton Code Enforcement Office shall forward the affidavit, complaint, and associated documents to the appropriate state enforcement agency.

Concerning renting to undocumented aliens, Hazleton's ordinance says,

A. It is unlawful for any person or business entity that owns a dwelling unit in the City to harbor an illegal alien in the dwelling unit, knowing or in reckless disregard of the fact that an alien has come to, entered, or remains in the United States in violation of law, unless such harboring is otherwise expressly permitted by federal law.

1. For the purposes of this section, to let, lease, or rent a dwelling unit to an illegal alien, knowing or in reckless disregard of the fact that an alien has come to, entered, or remains in the United States in violation of law, shall be deemed to constitute harboring. To suffer or permit the occupancy of the dwelling unit by an illegal alien, knowing or in reckless disregard of the fact that an alien has come to, entered, or remains in

the United States in violation of law, shall also be deemed to constitute harboring.

2. A separate violation shall be deemed to have been committed on each day that such harboring occurs, and for each adult illegal alien harbored in the dwelling unit, beginning one business day after receipt of a notice of violation from the Hazleton Code Enforcement Office.

3. A separate violation of this section shall be deemed to have been committed for each business day on which the owner fails to provide the Hazleton Code Enforcement Office with identity data needed to obtain a federal verification of immigration status, beginning three days after the owner receives written notice from the Hazleton Code Enforcement Office.

The enforcement provisions of the ordinance include the following:

The Hazleton Code Enforcement Office shall enforce the requirements of this section.

1. An enforcement action shall be initiated by means of a written signed complaint to the Hazleton Code Enforcement Office submitted by any official, business entity, or resident of the City. A valid complaint shall include an allegation which describes the alleged violator(s) as well as the actions constituting the violation, and the date and location where such actions occurred.

2. A complaint which alleges a violation solely or primarily on the basis of national origin, ethnicity, or race shall be deemed invalid and shall not be enforced.

3. Upon receipt of a valid written complaint, the Hazleton Code Enforcement Office shall, pursuant to United States Code Title 8, section 1373(c), verify with the federal government the immigration status of a person seeking to use, occupy, lease, or rent a dwelling unit in the City. The Hazleton Code Enforcement Office shall submit identity data required by the federal government to verify immigration status. The City shall forward identity data provided by the owner to the federal government, and shall provide the property owner with written confirmation of that verification.

4. If after five business days following receipt of written notice from the City that a violation has occurred and that the immigration status of any alleged illegal alien has been verified, pursuant to United States Code Title 8, section 1373(c), the owner of the dwelling unit fails to correct a violation of this section, the Hazleton Code Enforcement Office shall deny or suspend the rental license of the dwelling unit.

5. For the period of suspension, the owner of the dwelling unit shall not be permitted to collect any rent, payment, fee, or any other form of compensation from, or on behalf of, any tenant or occupant in the dwelling unit.

6. The denial or suspension shall terminate one business day after a legal representative of the dwelling unit owner submits to the Hazleton Code Enforcement Office a sworn affidavit stating that each and every violation has ended. The affidavit shall include a description of the specific measures and actions taken by the business entity to end the violation, and shall include the name, address and other adequate identifying information for the illegal aliens who were the subject of the complaint.

7. The Hazleton Code Enforcement Office shall forward the affidavit, complaint, and associated documents to the appropriate federal enforcement agency, pursuant to United States Code Title 8, section 1373.

8. Any dwelling unit owner who commits a second or subsequent violation of this section shall be subject to a fine of two hundred and fifty dollars ($250) for each separate violation. The suspension provisions of this section applicable to a first violation shall also apply.

9. Upon the request of a dwelling unit owner, the Hazleton Code Enforcement Office shall, pursuant to United States Code Title 8, section 1373(c), verify with the federal government the lawful immigration status of a person seeking to use, occupy, lease, or rent a dwelling unit in the City. The penalties in this section shall not apply in the case of dwelling unit occupants whose status as an alien lawfully present in the United States has been verified.

Q 12:68 Did other U.S. municipalities copy Hazleton, Pennsylvania's Illegal Immigration Relief Act Ordinance?

Taking their lead from Hazleton, Pennsylvania, more than 100 U.S. municipalities in 27 states have taken up consideration of ordinances aimed at dealing with illegal aliens. Some examples include:

California. On October 4, 2006, the city of Escondido passed an ordinance by a city council vote of 3-2. According to the *San Diego Union Tribune*:

> Under the ordinance, residents, businesses and city officials can file written complaints with the city if they suspect a landlord is renting to illegal immigrants. Complaints based "solely or primarily on the basis of national origin, ethnicity, or race shall be deemed invalid," the ordinance says. After complaints are filed, landlords would have to provide documentation to the city of their tenants' immigration status. The city would then ask the federal government to verify the documents. If tenants are found to be illegal immigrants, landlords would be given 10 days to evict them or face suspension of their business licenses. Repeat offenders could face misdemeanor charges and fines.

Missouri. During the summer of 2006, the aldermen (town council) of Valley Park passed an ordinance, which said that landlords could be fined for renting to illegal immigrants, and businesses could lose their licenses for five years for hiring them. In March 2007, the ordinance was declared illegal by a state court. According to the *St. Louis Post-Dispatch*, the judge:

> ruled that the ordinances conflicted with state landlord-tenant laws—which spell out precise rules for how tenants can be evicted—and that a city of Valley Park's size cannot levy such damaging penalties against businesses.

> The Board of Aldermen has tinkered with the ordinances. Instead of fining landlords, the new version says landlords can lose their occupancy permits if they are found renting to illegals. Another change: businesses caught employing illegals can lose their licenses for up to 20 days, instead of five years.

Texas. In November 2006, the city council of Farmers Branch unanimously passed an ordinance authorizing fines for landlords who rent to illegal aliens and also declared English to be the official language of the community. The council indicated at time of passage its expectation of litigation challenging the law.

Indeed, virtually all such ordinances, after enactment, have been challenged by the ACLU and/or pro-immigration interest groups. As this supplement goes to press, none of the ordinances have been actively enforced,and in 2010 the Hazleton ordinance was ruled unconstitutional by federal appeals court.

Q 12:69   What are some of the legal grounds upon which local anti-illegal-alien ordinances were being challenged in court?

The successful challenge of Valley Park, Missouri's ordinance in state court on the basis of conflict with state-wide landlord-tenant laws is the exception. In most cases, challenges are grounded upon conflicts with the U.S. Constitution and/or federal statutory law.

More typically, courtroom challenges revolve around the Fourteenth Amendment to the U.S. Constitution, which requires among other things that all persons be accorded due process of law. For instance, in the Hazleton, Pennsylvania case, U.S. District Judge James M. Munley reportedly ruminated on the record about due process, where the ordinance refers appeals to a local District Justice, an official deemed by the Plaintiff ACLU to be too lowly and uninformed on immigration law to determine such appeals.

In *Lozano v. City of Hazleton* [496 F. Supp. 2d 477 (M.D. Pa. 2007)], the federal judge ruled that:

1. Other than owners of businesses that had closed, plaintiffs had standing to challenge ordinances.

2. Immigrants who had an uncertain immigration status were entitled to proceed anonymously.

3. Ordinances that regulated employment of undocumented aliens was pre-empted.

4. Landlord/tenant provisions of ordinance, which required proof of legal citizenship and/or residency in order to obtain the required occupancy permit, violated the due process rights of tenants and owners/landlords.

5. Ordinances that provided penalties for those who employed or provided rental housing for undocumented persons in the city did not violate equal protection.

6. Section 1981 forbade the city from prohibiting undocumented aliens from entering into leases.

Other challenges are grounded upon notions of federal preemption. These cases contend that the Congress has co-opted the field of immigration law, as is appropriate for an issue which affects all areas of the United States and implicates our national borders.

Q 12:70   Have any states taken independent action to curb illegal immigration?

Alabama. On May 18, 2012, Alabama Governor Robert Bentley signed into law House Bill 658, an immigration enforcement bill that made changes to the state's immigration law, HB 56, and which is similar to Arizona SB 1070. The employment provisions require that all employers enroll in E-Verify, and that all employers that are state/public contractors, grant recipients, and others that receive state incentives register with and use E-Verify. The contractor provision took effect on January 1, 2012, and the E-Verify rule took effect on April 1, 2012. There is no apparent sanction for failure to follow these provisions, but complying with the law will ensure employers safety from liability under Alabama law for knowingly employing an unauthorized worker.

The Obama administration soon challenged the Alabama Act. A group of private parties, led by the Hispanic Interest Coalition of Alabama, also sued to enjoin implementation of the act. The consolidated cases reached the U.S. Court of Appeals for the Eleventh Circuit late in 2010, where the law received mixed reviews. The Court of Appeals held that the plaintiffs demonstrated substantial likelihood of prevailing on the merits, and were entitled to an injunction pending appeal, but only as to some of challenged provisions, such as that making it a criminal misdemeanor for an alien unlawfully present in the United States to willfully fail to complete or carry an alien registration document. Specifically, the appellate panel held:

• Enforcement of the provision making it a criminal misdemeanor for an alien unlawfully present in the United States to willfully fail to complete or carry an alien registration document would be enjoined pending the federal government's and private parties' appeal from district court order denying their motion for a preliminary injunction with respect to this statute as allegedly preempted by provisions of the Immigration and Nationality Act (INA); the plaintiffs had demonstrated substantial likelihood of prevailing on the merits, as well as substantial risk of irreparable injury if the statute were enforced.

- Enforcement of the provision requiring (1) law enforcement officers, upon making any lawful stop, detention, or arrest, and upon reasonable suspicion that the person stopped, detained, or arrested is unlawfully present in the United States, to make a reasonable attempt, when practicable, to determine his or her citizenship and immigration status; (2) forbidding law enforcement from considering race, color, or national origin in implementing this statute; and (3) creating a presumption of lawful presence if the person stopped, detained, or arrested produces certain enumerated forms of identification, would not be enjoined pending the federal government's and private parties' appeal from the district court order denying their motion for preliminary injunction with respect to this statute as allegedly preempted by provisions of the INA; the plaintiffs failed to satisfy their burden of proof on all four requirements for injunction pending appeal.

- Enforcement of the provision that makes it a felony for an alien not lawfully present in the United States to enter into or attempt to enter into a "business transaction" with State of Alabama or any political subdivision, including applying for or renewing a driver's license (but not applying for marriage license), would not be enjoined pending the federal government's and private parties' appeal from the district court order denying their motion for preliminary injunction with respect to this statute as allegedly preempted by provisions of the INA.

As for the E-Verify provisions, the ruling of the U.S. District judge in one of the two consolidated cases stands. [Hispanic Interest Coalition of Alabama v. Bentley, 5:11-CV-2484-SLB, 2011 WL 5516953 (N.D. Ala. Sept. 28, 2011)]

Arizona. A law aimed at penalizing employment of illegal immigrants was intended to take effect January 1, 2008. In December 2007, a federal judge dismissed a challenge to the statutes, holding that the suing "organizations lacked standing to challenge enforcement provisions of Legal Arizona Workers Act on basis of threat of prosecution or loss of Fourth Amendment rights." [Arizona Contractors Ass'n, Inc. v. Napolitano, 2007 WL 4293641 (D. Ariz. Dec. 7, 2007)] The judge also held that because county prosecutors were charged with enforcing the law, they were the proper defendants in the suit. Undeterred, the plaintiffs returned to court in mid-December, seeking to cure the standing issue and obtain a TRO. [Arizona Contractors Ass'n, Inc. v. Candelaria, 2007 WL 4404445 (D. Ariz. Dec. 13, 2007)] The court at that time ordered a hearing on the motion for a TRO. On December 21, 2007, the federal judge declined to issue the TRO. As this litigation dragged on, the Arizona legislature amended the act, effective May 1, 2008. The Legal Arizona Workers Act [A.R.S. §§ 23-211–214] as amended effective May 1, 2008 to meet the then-pending legal challenges, states in pertinent part:

> **A.** An employer shall not intentionally employ an unauthorized alien or knowingly employ an unauthorized alien.
>
> **B.** On receipt of a complaint that an employer allegedly intentionally employs an unauthorized alien or knowingly employs an unauthorized alien, the attorney general or county attorney shall investigate whether

the employer has violated subsection A. When investigating a complaint, the attorney general or county attorney shall verify the work authorization of the alleged unauthorized alien with the federal government pursuant to 8 United States Code § 1373(c). A state, county or local official shall not attempt to independently make a final determination on whether an alien is authorized to work in the United States. An alien's immigration status or work authorization status shall be verified with the federal government pursuant to 8 United States Code § 1373(c). A person who knowingly files a false and frivolous complaint under this subsection is guilty of a class 3 misdemeanor.

C. If, after an investigation, the attorney general or county attorney determines that the complaint is not frivolous:

1. The attorney general or county attorney shall notify the United States immigration and customs enforcement of the unauthorized alien.

2. The attorney general or county attorney shall notify the local law enforcement agency of the unauthorized alien.

3. The attorney general shall notify the appropriate county attorney to bring an action pursuant to subsection D if the complaint was originally filed with the attorney general.

D. An action for a violation of subsection A shall be brought against the employer by the county attorney in the county where the unauthorized alien employee is employed. The county attorney shall not bring an action against any employer for any violation of subsection A that occurs before January 1, 2008. A second violation of this section shall be based only on an unauthorized alien who is employed by the employer after an action has been brought for a violation of subsection A.

E. For any action in superior court under this section, the court shall expedite the action, including assigning the hearing at the earliest practicable date.

F. On a finding of a violation of subsection A:

1. For a first violation during a three-year period that is a knowing violation of subsection A, the court:

(a) Shall order the employer to terminate the employment of all unauthorized aliens.

(b) Shall order the employer to be subject to a three-year probationary period. During the probationary period the employer shall file quarterly reports with the county attorney of each new employee who is hired by the employer at the specific location where the unauthorized alien performed work.

(c) Shall order the employer to file a signed sworn affidavit with the county attorney within three business days after the order is issued. The affidavit shall state that the employer has terminated the employment of all unauthorized aliens and that the employer will not intentionally or knowingly employ an unauthorized alien. The court shall order the appropriate agencies to suspend all licenses subject to this subdivision that are held by the employer if the employer fails to file a signed sworn affidavit with the county attorney within three business days after the order is issued. All licenses that are suspended under this subdivision shall remain suspended until the employer files a signed sworn affidavit with the county attorney. Notwithstanding any other law, on filing of the affidavit the suspended licenses shall be reinstated immediately by the appropriate agencies. For the purposes of this subdivision, the licenses that are subject to suspension under this subdivision are all licenses that are held by the employer and that are necessary to operate the employer's business at the employer's business location where the unauthorized alien performed work. If a license is not necessary to operate the employer's business at the specific location where the unauthorized alien performed work, but a license is necessary to operate the employer's business in general, the licenses that are subject to suspension under this subdivision are all licenses that are held by the employer at the employer's primary place of business. On receipt of the court's order and notwithstanding any other law, the appropriate agencies shall suspend the licenses according to the court's order. The court shall send a copy of the court's order to the attorney general and the attorney general shall maintain the copy pursuant to subsection G.

(d) May order the appropriate agencies to suspend all licenses described in subdivision (c) of this paragraph that are held by the employer for not to exceed ten business days. The court shall base its decision to suspend under this subdivision on any evidence or information submitted to it during the action for a violation of this subsection and shall consider the following factors, if relevant:

(i) The number of unauthorized aliens employed by the employer.

(ii) Any prior misconduct by the employer.

(iii) The degree of harm resulting from the violation.

(iv) Whether the employer made good-faith efforts to comply with any applicable requirements.

(v) The duration of the violation.

(vi) The role of the directors, officers or principals of the employer in the violation.

(vii) Any other factors the court deems appropriate.

2. For a first violation during a five-year period that is an intentional violation of subsection A, the court shall:

(a) Order the employer to terminate the employment of all unauthorized aliens.

(b) Order the employer to be subject to a five-year probationary period. During the probationary period the employer shall file quarterly reports with the county attorney of each new employee who is hired by the employer at the specific location where the unauthorized alien performed work.

(c) Order the appropriate agencies to suspend all licenses, described in subdivision (d) of this paragraph that are held by the employer for a minimum of ten days. The court shall base its decision on the length of the suspension under this subdivision on any evidence or information submitted to it during the action for a violation of this subsection and shall consider the following factors, if relevant:

(i) The number of unauthorized aliens employed by the employer.

(ii) Any prior misconduct by the employer.

(iii) The degree of harm resulting from the violation.

(iv) Whether the employer made good-faith efforts to comply with any applicable requirements.

(v) The duration of the violation.

(vi) The role of the directors, officers or principals of the employer in the violation.

(vii) Any other factors the court deems appropriate.

(d) Order the employer to file a signed sworn affidavit with the county attorney. The affidavit shall state that the employer has terminated the employment of all unauthorized aliens and that the employer will not intentionally or knowingly employ an unauthorized alien. All licenses that are suspended under this subdivision shall remain suspended until the employer files a signed sworn affidavit with the county attorney. For the purposes of this subdivision, the licenses that are subject to suspension under this subdivision are all licenses that are held by the employer and that are necessary to operate the employer's business at the employer's business location where the unauthorized alien performed work. If a license is not necessary to operate the employer's business at the specific location where the unauthorized alien performed work, but a license is necessary to operate the employer's business in general, the licenses that are subject to suspension under this subdivision are all licenses that are held by the employer at the employer's primary place of business. On receipt of the court's order and notwithstanding any other law, the appropriate agencies shall suspend the licenses according to the court's order. The court shall send a copy of the court's order to the attorney general and the attorney general shall maintain the copy pursuant to subsection G.

3. For a second violation of subsection A during the period of probation, the court shall order the appropriate agencies to permanently revoke all licenses that are held by the employer and that are necessary to operate the employer's business at the employer's business location where the unauthorized alien

performed work. If a license is not necessary to operate the employer's business at the specific location where the unauthorized alien performed work, but a license is necessary to operate the employer's business in general, the court shall order the appropriate agencies to permanently revoke all licenses that are held by the employer at the employer's primary place of business. On receipt of the order and notwithstanding any other law, the appropriate agencies shall immediately revoke the licenses.

G. The attorney general shall maintain copies of court orders that are received pursuant to subsection F and shall maintain a database of the employers who have a first violation of subsection A and make the court orders available on the attorney general's website.

H. On determining whether an employee is an unauthorized alien, the court shall consider only the federal government's determination pursuant to 8 United States Code § 1373(c). The federal government's determination creates a rebuttable presumption of the employee's lawful status. The court may take judicial notice of the federal government's determination and may request the federal government to provide automated or testimonial verification pursuant to 8 United States Code § 1373(c).

I. For the purposes of this section, proof of verifying the employment authorization of an employee through the basic pilot program creates a rebuttable presumption that an employer did not intentionally employ an unauthorized alien or knowingly employ an unauthorized alien.

J. For the purposes of this section, an employer who establishes that it has complied in good faith with the requirements of 8 United States Code § 1324b establishes an affirmative defense that the employer did not intentionally or knowingly employ an unauthorized alien.

[Ariz. Rev. Statutes 23–212 (Jan. 1, 2008, as amended May 1, 2008)]

In 2011, the U.S. Supreme Court held that the law was not preempted by federal immigration laws, such as the Immigration Reform and Control Act, and that its requirements were not in conflict with federal rules and regulations.

[Chamber of Commerce of the United States v. Whiting, 131 S. Ct. 1968 (2011)]

Meanwhile, in April 2010, a new statute was signed by Governor Jan Brewer requiring immigrants to carry their alien registration documents whenever they are in public and authorizes police to question persons whom they suspect of being in the United States illegally. Less than a month later, the law was amended. The original language required the police to ascertain a person's legal status during any "lawful contact." Critics pointed out that this would require an inquiry even if the contact was nothing more than someone asking driving directions. Under the revised legislation, police are obliged to check documents only in instances involving those who are detained and arrested. Additionally, the law was clarified to make clear that racial profiling is absolutely forbidden. [S.B. 1070; http://azgovernor.gov/dms/upload/SB_1070_Signed.pdf; *see also* http://articles.latimes.com/2010/may/01/nation/la-na-arizona-immigration-

20100501.] Needless to say, this statute, too, was challenged in the federal courts and worked its way up to the nation's highest court.

In June 2012, the U.S. Supreme Court held that three of the four major provisions of the statute were unconstitutional, and were preempted by federal law. Those three provisions would have:

1. Required legal immigrant to carry their registration documents at all times;

2. Allowed the state police to arrest any individual on suspicion of being an illegal immigrant;

3. Make it a crime for an illegal immigrant to seek or hold a job in the state.

The Justices unanimously upheld the provision that allows the state police to investigate the immigration status of an individual who is stopped, detained, or arrested, if the arresting officers have a reasonable suspicion that the individual is an illegal alien.

[Arizona v. United States, 132 S. Ct. 2492 (2012)]

Missouri. In October 2007, Governor Matt Blunt of Missouri stepped into the front ranks of state-based efforts to deal with illegal immigrants. At that time, his office issued a press release, which highlighted Governor Blunt's new directive in the fight against illegal immigration in Missouri, offering his support to local prosecutors in their efforts to fight against illegal immigration. The Governor also called on his administration to work with ICE for authority under Section 287g of the Immigration and Nationality Act, which would deputize state law enforcement officers to enforce federal laws and protect Missourians against illegal immigration. The governor also directed state law enforcement agencies to verify the immigration status of every criminal presented for incarceration.

In addition, he took significant steps to shield taxpayers' money from supporting building projects that employ illegal workers, such as conducting random on-site inspections of all projects accompanied by the tax credit recipient to monitor and retrieve documentation regarding the legal status of all workers,and performing a Compliance by Written Demand action for all tax credit recipients.

Finally the governor issued a letter to the Missouri Housing Development Commission that outlined principles for the Commission to consider regarding illegal immigration, which included possible sanctions of up to a lifetime ban of contractors and developers that knowingly employ illegal immigrants in violation of federal law.

As described in the summary of the press release, the state of Missouri cancelled a contract with Sam's Janitorial, which was owned by an African-born U.S. citizen named Asamoah-Boadu. Twenty-five of Sam's employees were arrested in a sting operation in March 2007, after the state's manager of custodial operations detected inconsistencies in work documents. The Capitol Police and federal ICE agency cooperated in the subsequent investigation. In October 2007, Sam's sued the state. The case, *Asamoah-Boadu v. Missouri* [No.

07AC-CC00983 (Mo. Cir. Ct., 2007)] alleged breach of contract, violation of the federal Civil Rights Act of 1866 [*see* 42 U.S.C. 1981], the federal Civil Rights Act of 1871 [*see* 42 U.S.C. 1983], and the Fifth and Fourteenth Amendments of the U.S. Constitution, as well as a claim that Governor Blunt's Executive Order 07-13—under which the contract to clean nine state buildings was cancelled—exceeds the chief executive's authority under the Missouri constitution. The suit remained pending when this edition went to press.

Kansas. Kansas legislature recently fought to repeal a statute, House Bill 2192, allowing in-state tuition for illegal immigrant students. [http://cjonline.com/news/2013-03-20/emotions-flow-during-immigrant-tuition-hearing]

Georgia. In 2013, Georgia passed Senate Bill 160, which expands the state's 2011 crackdown on illegal immigration and stops illegal immigrants from getting state driver's licenses, grants, public housing and retirement benefits. [http://www.ajc.com/news/news/state-regional-govt-politics/illegal-immigration-crackdown-expansion-okd/nW683/]

More recently, though, states have been moving in a more positive direction for immigrants overall, such as in the following states.

Colorado. In 2013, Colorado passed bill, SB 13-033, which allows illegal immigrants to obtain in-state tuition fees. Under SB 33, also known as ASSET or "Advancing Students For a Stronger Economy Tomorrow," illegal immigrants are eligible for the College Opportunity Stipend, a taxpayer-funded voucher that goes toward paying for college. The stipend in the 2012-13 year is $31 per credit hour, with a maximum of $930 for 30 credit hours per academic year. Most of the Republican House caucus is opposed to the bill. [http://www.journal-advocate.com/ci_22764960/state-tuition-illegals-passes]

Oregon. In 2013, House Bill 2787 was passed, and will allow in-state tuition for immigrant students who graduate from high school or its equivalent in Oregon, who attend Oregon schools for three previous years and are in the United States for five years, and who intend to seek legal status or citizenship in the United States. These students would not qualify for state or federal financial aid. [http://www.statesmanjournal.com/article/20130321/UPDATE/13032 1024/Oregon-Senate-passes-state-tuition-immigrant-students?nclick_check = 1]

Maryland. If passed, a new Maryland bill will allow immigrants who are unable to prove legal residency to obtain and renew valid driver's licenses. The stated reasoning is that allowing illegal immigrants to have valid driver's licenses will also make them able to purchase car insurance and make the streets safer for everyone.The Maryland Senate approved the bill on March 24, 2013. On April 14, 2013, the lower house followed suit with Governor Martin O' Malley poised to sign it.

Q 12:71 Have any of these state initiatives survived courtroom challenges?

One state statute that stands out from the crowd by virtue of having so far survived all legal challenges is the Legal Arizona Workers Act. In December

2007, a federal judge considered whether or not the new law could withstand a typical constitutional challenge. [*See* Arizona Contractors Association v. Napolitano, 2007 U.S. Dist. LEXIS 96194 (D. Ariz. Dec. 21, 2007).] When the plaintiffs initiated their challenge to the statute, the judge initially held that, since county prosecutors were charged with enforcing the law, they were the proper defendants in the suit. The plaintiffs, therefore, were dismissed for lacking standing. Undeterred, they returned to court, seeking to cure the standing issue and obtain a temporary restraining order (TRO). The court this time ordered a hearing on the motion for a TRO, which would prevent enforcement of the law pending a final resolution of their constitutional challenge. The federal judge declined to issue the TRO.

During the subsequent 12 months, the matter proceeded to hearing, and the district court dismissed the Arizona Attorney General for lack of subject matter jurisdiction, because he lacked the authority to bring enforcement actions. The court ruled in favor of the remaining defendants on the merits. It held that the act is not expressly pre-empted by IRCA because the act is a licensing law within the meaning of the federal statute's savings clause. It held that neither the act's sanction provisions nor the provision mandating use of the federal government's E-Verify identification system was inconsistent with federal policy, and thus they were not impliedly preempted. Finally, the court held that the act did not, on its face, violate due process because employers' due process rights were adequately protected.

In November 2009, the Maricopa County Attorney filed the first employer-sanctions suit under the act. The civil action alleged the Scottsdale Art Factory's manager, Michelle Hardas, allegedly hired illegal labor by using a "subcontractor" which was in reality an employee who was not authorized to work in the United States. The complaint stated, "Hardas has used the provision of limited liability companies, designed to protect legitimate businesses, as a way of gaining an unfair economic advantage over legitimate businesses by continuing to hire employees who are not authorized to be employed in the United States."

The suit asks the court to order the defendant to fire all illegal aliens and comply with the law. It also prays for the penalty of a ten-day suspension of the company's license to do business. County Attorney Andrew Thomas stated, "This first employer-sanctions case is the capstone on our office's efforts to stop illegal immigration. The idea that state and local law enforcement can successfully and legally combat illegal immigration has moved from a provocative theory a few years ago to reality today." [http://www.mcaodocuments.com/press/20091118_a.pdf]

Immigration Act of 1990

Q 12:72   What is the *Immigration Act of 1990*?

Primarily, the *Immigration Act of 1990* constituted a restructuring of this nation's priorities in admitting skilled immigrants. This landmark legislation increased the annual maximum of employment-based visas from 54,000 to 140,000. Also, the Act replaced the 20,000-visas-per-country standard with new calculations that were intended to benefit citizens from countries considered by Congress to have been affected adversely by prior legislation. Additionally, total family based visas were annually increased to 465,000 for each of the next three federal Fiscal Years, then to 480,000 thereafter.

Q 12:73 What categories of skilled immigrants did the Immigration Act of 1990 favor?

The law authorized the annual increase in permanent resident visas from 54,000 to 140,000 in 5 categories:

1. *Priority workers.* These are defined as immigrants with "extraordinary ability" in the arts, athletics, business, education, or the sciences. The application must reflect a national or international reputation, extensively documented achievements, and the stated intention to continue working in the field of high accomplishment plus the potential to "substantially benefit" the United States. Also included in this category are internationally recognized professors with substantial teaching or research experience, plus an offer of tenure or a tenure-track position at a U.S. institution. Executives sponsored and employed by multinational corporations are also included.

2. *Professionals with advanced degrees and aliens of exceptional ability.* In lieu of the "extraordinary ability" required of priority workers, "exceptional ability" plus labor certification, such as a job offer, is required. A bachelor's degree plus five years of experience is likely to be the bare minimum to meet this category's alternative criterion of an advanced degree.

3. *Other professionals and skilled workers.* Along with having labor certification, applicants must offer some special skill or a bachelor's degree.

4. *Special immigrants.* This category includes, for example, ministers and other religious workers.

5. *Investors.* The category consists of immigrants willing and able to invest at least $1 million in a business that will employ at least 10 Americans. The requisite investment can be more modest for as many as 3,000 of these applicants who intend to put their money in certain targeted areas, such as rural regions or locales with high unemployment.

Q 12:74 What does the Immigration Act of 1990 require with regard to family based immigration quotas?

The Act increases the number of available visas overall and, in particular, it increases visas allotted to the spouses and minor children of permanent resident aliens in the following preferential order:

1. Unmarried sons and daughters of U.S. citizens;

2. Spouses, minor children, and unmarried sons and daughters (regardless of age) of permanent resident aliens;

3. Married sons and daughters of U.S. citizens; and

4. Sisters and brothers of adult U.S. citizens.

Q 12:75 Are there any regulations interpreting and enforcing the Immigration Act of 1990?

Yes. The regulations are published at 8 C.F.R. Parts 1, 103, 214, 274a, and 299; 22 C.F.R. Part 44; 24 C.F.R. Part 49; and 29 C.F.R. Part 501.

Q 12:76 How can an employee who is a foreign national change status to permanent resident?

The employee can achieve permanent resident status by:

1. Being sponsored by a close family member who is a U.S. citizen or permanent resident;

2. Having an employer who meets one of the employment or occupational categories that qualify, including hiring:

   a. Employees of extraordinary ability;

   b. Outstanding professors and scientists;

   c. Multinational executives;

   d. Professionals with advanced degrees.

This process is described in the instructions accompanying Form I-485, Applications for Status as Permanent Resident.

Q 12:77 How can a company help a visiting foreign national obtain a visa extension?

Visa extensions are issued by the USCIS visa office, which will reissue E, H, I, L, O, and P visas. The following must be provided to the visa office:

- Passport with E, H, I, L, O, or P visa stamp;
- Application Form DS-156;
- Valid, original Form I-94 (copies are unacceptable);
- Copy of current Form I-171 or I-797, if the visa is an H, L, O, or P type;
- Detailed letter from the employee regarding his or her position with the company and his or her travel itinerary; and
- Self-addressed envelope.

Send this application package to:

U.S. Department of State
Visa Services
Road 1500

2401 E Street NW
Washington, D.C. 20226

Q 12:78   How can a company help an alien employee avoid deportation?

Such an employee may be able to avoid deportation by:

1. Obtaining a waiver based upon hardship; an employee who has worked for the company in the United States for at least seven years is afforded a presumption of hardship when faced with deportation.

2. Obtaining a suspension of the deportation order pending permanent resident application by showing: (a) seven years of physical presence in the United States; (b) good moral character; (c) hardship.

3. Obtaining conditional permanent resident status by marrying a U.S. citizen or permanent resident.

4. Seeking asylum by alleging fear of persecution for: (a) political opinions; (b) religious beliefs; (c) nationality; (d) race; or (e) membership in any persecuted group.

Failing all of the preceding, the alien employee may be best off applying for a voluntary departure, which should make it a lot easier for him or her to apply for and obtain subsequent readmission.

Q 12:79   Does the Immigration Act of 1990 provide any protection against displacement of U.S. employees by immigrants?

The law requires the DOL to balance its increases in employment-based immigration with specific new protections for U.S. citizens. These protections include employer notification to employees in advance of hiring aliens. Such an employer will have to notify either the affected employees' union or post notices in the plant if the employees are not organized. A second protection mandated by the new law is "attestation-like processes" to protect the wages and working conditions of Americans when companies hire certain categories of nonimmigrant aliens, such as D-Visa crews to perform longshoremen's work, H-1B specialty occupations, and students with F-visas who accept off-campus employment. Employers hiring such temporary employees must file attestations with the DOL to the effect that they will pay prevailing wages and provide appropriate working conditions. Employees will have a grievance procedure through which to challenge these hiring practices.

A third mandate requires the DOL to develop a labor market information program to identify occupational shortages and surpluses of skilled workers for streamlining visa processing, while hopefully protecting Americans who might otherwise be displaced from overstocked occupations.

The law also calls for state grants to be used to educate and train U.S. workers to fill shortage categories that would otherwise be filled by alien employees. Underemployed Americans are to be the special targets for these grants.

Q 12:80   Where can I find compliance information regarding the Immigration Act of 1990?

See the DOL Web site at http://www.dol.gov/dol/compliance/comp-ina. htm. This site offers links to all relevant regulations, including the following:

1. The law;
2. The regulations;
3. Regulations on the Temporary Employment of Aliens in the United States; and
4. Regulations on Enforcement of Contractual Obligations for Temporary Alien/Agricultural Workers Admitted under Section 216 of the INA.

DOL Guidance Materials:

1. Employment Law Guide: Authorized Workers
2. Employment Law Guide: Crewmembers (D-1 Visas)
3. Employment Law Guide: Workers in Professional and Specialty Occupations (H-1B Visas)
4. H-1B (Professional and Specialty Occupation Visas) Interim Final Regulations Fact Sheet
5. Employment Law Guide: Nurses (H-1C Visas)
6. Employment Law Guide: Temporary Agricultural Workers (H-2A Visas)
7. H-2A (Temporary Agricultural Worker Visas) Fact Sheet
8. Employment Law Guide: Temporary Nonagricultural Workers (H-2B Visas)
9. Employment Law Guide: Permanent Employment of Workers Based on Immigration

Forms and Instructions:

1. Foreign Labor Certification (Employment & Training Administration)
2. Form I-9, Employment Eligibility Verification
3. Application of U.S. Labor Laws to Immigrant Workers Fact Sheet
4. Application of U.S. Labor Laws to Immigrant Worker Fact Sheet (Korean) (PDF)
5. Aplicación de las Leyes Laborales de los EE UU a Obreros Inmigrantes Hoja de Datos (Español)
6. Fair Labor Standards Act (FLSA) Application to Foreign Commercial Vehicle Operators Fact Sheet
7. Aplicación de la Ley de Normas Razonables de Trabajo a los Conductores Extranjeros de Vehículos Comerciales Hoja de Datos (Español)

Q 12:81   What is an *affidavit of support*?

Effective December 19, 1997, sponsoring family members of new immigrants to the United States must complete an affidavit of support in which they document a minimum annual income that is at or above 125 percent of the federal poverty benchmark and attest to their intent to support the new arrival.

Q 12:82 What is a *multinational executive green card petition*?

Section 203 of the Immigration Act of 1990 allows for a "multinational business executive" corporate transfer green card petition. Under this section of the statute, an alien who is an executive or manager with a foreign-based corporation may apply for a green card (alien registration card) once the company has established a U.S. branch office, affiliate, subsidiary, or joint venture that has been operating for at least a year. To qualify for the green card under this provision, both the foreign parent and the American operation must be actively engaged in business activities, and the U.S. operation must be able to demonstrate at least enough earnings to pay the applicant's salary, benefits, and payroll taxes.

Q 12:83 What is the estimated processing time for a multinational executive green card petition?

The estimated processing time for this type of petition is four months. USCIS has taken the following steps to aid applicants of employment-based petitions:

- Increasing the emphasis on processing employment-based petitions. The goal is to complete adjudication on the older I-140 petitions and to process newer petitions within the targeted processing time of four months. The agency claims to have met this goal.

- Issuing employment authorization documents valid for two years, as needed.

- Working with the State Department to make sure every available visa number gets used. In 2007, it had more visas available in the family based categories than were needed, so as permitted by law, it transferred those available family based visas for use in the employment-based application process.

[*See* https://egov.uscis.gov/cris/processingTimesDisplay.do?serviceCenter = 993&displaySCProcTimes = Service%20Center%20Processing%20Dates; http://www.uscis.gov/ilink/docView/AFM/HTML/AFM/0-0-0-1/0-0-0-6330/0-0-0-64 23.html.]

NOTE: For an additional fee of $1,225, premium processing is possible. USCIS guarantees 15-day premium processing.[http://www.uscis.gov/portal/site/ uscis/menuitem.5af9bb95919f35e66f614176543f6d1a/?vgnextoid = 971b60657 dd68210VgnVCM100000082ca60aRCRD&vgnextchannel = db029c7755cb9010V gnVCM10000045f3d6a1RCRD]

Q 12:84   What types of temporary workers' visas are allowed under the Immigration Act of 1990?

The general classification of most such visas is "H." These types of visas include:

1. H-1A: Registered nurses

2. H-1B: Specialty occupations requiring theoretical grounding and practical application of a body of highly specialized knowledge, demanding completion of a specific course of higher education. Labor attestation is issued by the U.S. Secretary of Labor, and includes government-to-government research and development activities and co-production projects of the U.S. Department of Defense.

3. H-2A: Temporary and seasonal agricultural workers

4. H-2B: Temporary and seasonal nonagricultural workers. A temporary labor certification is needed from the U.S. Secretary of Labor.

5. H-3: Trainees for other than the medical and academic professions. This does apply to training in the education of disabled children.

Other classifications include:

1. L: Intracompany transferees who, during the preceding three years, were employed abroad for at least an uninterrupted one-year stretch, and who will be employed by a branch, parent, subsidiary, or affiliate in the United States of the same employer, and finally, who will work in an executive, managerial, or "specialized knowledge" role at the U.S. operation.

2. O-1: Persons possessing "extraordinary ability" in the arts, athletics, business, the sciences, education, motion pictures, or television.

3. O-2: Persons accompanying an O-1 "extraordinary ability" alien.

4. P-1: Individual athletes and entertainers, as well as team members and members of performing groups.

5. P-3: Performers whose programs are culturally unique.

6. Q-1: Participants in cultural exchange programs.

Q 12:85   How does one apply for a temporary worker's visa?

For consideration as a non-immigrant entering the United States on a temporary worker's visa, the applicant must get her or his prospective employer to file a Labor Condition Application (LCA) with the DOL. The LCA must: (1) attest that the employer intends to pay prevailing wages for the position; and (2) list the working conditions in detail that are being offered. The employer also must file a Form I-129, "Petition for Non-immigrant Worker," with the INS. There is a filing fee of $320 and a sponsorship fee of $1,500. Once the INS approves, the employer is sent a Form I-797 "Notice of Approval." Once the employer has received this favorable response the alien worker may apply for the visa.

Q 12:86   What are the most important things to know about an H-1B visa?

1. The H-1B is the most common temporary-worker visa. It is initially issued for a three-year period and is subject to renewal for an additional three years. [*See* 8 C.F.R. § 215.2(h) and Pub. L. No. 107-273, American Competitiveness in the Twenty-First Century Act of 2002.]

2. In limited circumstances, the H-1B may extend in one-year increments beyond the usual six-year limit.

3. Processing an H-1B typically takes three to five months. However, premium processing (15 days) is available for an additional $1,000 fee, payable to CIS.

4. Transfer of H-1B status from one employer to another is permitted if: (a) the alien entered the U.S. lawfully; (b) the alien has not violated her or his status by working in the United States without authorization; and (c) the transfer request is filed before the expiration of the alien's current H-1B status. This is called "H-1B portability" and is done via a portability petition. The employee may work for the new employer while the position is pending; however, if the portability petition is denied, employment authorization ends immediately.

5. Prior to filing an H-1B petition, the employer must obtain an approved Form ETA-9035, LCA. This is obtained from the DOL, which will issue it if the employer attests that it will: (a) pay the alien worker the higher of the prevailing wage for the occupation or the wage paid to U.S. workers performing the same job; and (b) hiring the alien will not adversely affect wages and working conditions of U.S. workers. The application has been streamlined and can be electronically filed on the DOL Web site.

6. The employer also must post notices of the job opening at two locations on the work site for 10 working days before filling the position with the alien worker. Note that the position need not be otherwise advertised to U.S. workers.

7. Employers must maintain a "public access file" for each of their H-1B employees. The file should be created within 24 hours of filing the LCA with the DOL. This file must contain: proof of the prevailing wage; a copy of the LCA; verification of job posting; proof that the alien employee received a copy of the LCA; statement of the wage rate; an actual wage statement; and benefits documentation. The file must be maintained for at least a year beyond the length of employment.

Q 12:87   Who enforces labor standards involving H-1B workers?

The DOL's Wage & Hour Division is charged with enforcing H-1B employers' labor standards obligations and protecting the rights of H-1B workers. [*See* http://www.dol.gov/dol/topic/wages/index.htm.] The USCIS also plays a key role in the processing of petitions for H-1B visas and H-1B Visa extensions. [http://www.uscis.gov]

Q 12:88   What is a "specialty occupation" that qualifies for an H-1B visa?

A "specialty occupation" is defined by the USCIS as follows:

- Bachelor's or higher degree or its equivalent is normally the minimum entry requirement for the position
- The degree requirement for the job is common to the industry or the job is so complex or unique that it can be performed only by an individual with a degree
- The employer normally requires a degree or its equivalent for the position
- The nature of the specific duties is so specialized and complex that the knowledge required to perform the duties is usually associated with the attainment of a bachelor's or higher degree*
- Full state licensure, if the job requires a license to practice the specialty occupation in the state
- Completion of a U.S. bachelor's or higher degree (or its foreign equivalent) in the specific specialty or a related field
- Education, training, or experience in the specialty that is equivalent to the completion of such a degree.

[http://www.uscis.gov/]

Q 12:89   Does an amended H-1B need to be filed in the case of a merger or acquisition?

No. As long as the acquiring company is assuming all the obligations of the acquired firm, no amended forms need to be filed for non-immigrant aliens employed by the acquired firm at the time of the transaction. [78 No. 13 *Interpreter Releases* 609 (Apr. 2, 2001)]

Q 12:90   Can an H-1B alien worker travel to his or her home country on a visit in between jobs?

Yes. An H-1B alien worker who is changing U.S. jobs is permitted to travel outside the United States between jobs and will be readmitted during the period of the first visa's validity plus 10 days, provided the alien:

1. Is otherwise admissible;
2. Has a valid passport;
3. Has a prior Form I-94 or Form I-797; and
4. Has a filing receipt or other evidence that the new employer has filed for a new H-1B visa.

Q 12:91   Do foreign broadcasters now receive preferential immigration status to the United States?

Yes. The State Department's Bureau of Consular Affairs in March 2000 published an interim rule amending 22 C.F.R. Section 42.32 and according a special, employment-based immigrant classification to so-called "international broadcasters." The special classification applies to those broadcasters who enter the United States to work for the International Broadcasting Bureau of the Broadcasting Board of Governors. The rule provides for 100 such visas per year, including spouses and children. [78 No. 12 *Interpreter Releases* 569 (Mar. 26, 2001)]

Q 12:92   What is the U.S.A. Immigration Services green card program?

The USAIS makes available 50,000 green cards (permanent resident visas) annually through its Green Card Lottery Program. Green Card Lottery applications can be submitted online at http://www.usagreencardlottery.org, which gives the applicant instant access to the agency's database. [*See* http://www.us-immigration.com/ and http://www.usagcls.com/index.asp?Prom = google USA-GC.]

Details include:

1. Official U.S. government program, Congress approved;
2. A chance to legally live and work in the United States with a legal green card;
3. 50,000 winners and their families will win a U.S. green card every year;
4. Easy online registration;
5. Double chances for married people to win the green card lottery; and
6. Winners receive a FREE airline ticket from USAGCLS.

Q 12:93   What are the basic criteria for green card eligibility?

- Nativity in an eligible country; and
- Ability to meet the educational and/or training background for a U.S. worker requirement.

Q 12:94   What if a potential green card applicant fails to meet the basic requirement of nativity in an eligible country?

A potential green card applicant who lacks this basic qualification may still successfully apply for a green card if his or her spouse's country of nativity is on the eligibility list, or if at least one of the applicant's parents was born in a qualifying country.

Q 12:95   What are the educational and/or training criteria to participate in the annual green card lottery?

- The equivalent of a high school education and/or;
- At least two years of experience in a relevant trade or profession.

Q 12:96   What are the ways an alien can obtain permanent residence in the United States?

- Immigration through a resident family member;
- Immigration through employment (e.g., a green card, as outlined above);
- Immigration through investment in a U.S.-based business;
- Immigration through the Diversity Lottery [http://travel.state.gov/visa/immigrants/types/types_1318.html];
- Immigration through international adoption.

Q 12:97   What are the types of non-immigration/temporary residence visas?

- Business and pleasure visitors;
- Temporary workers;
- Students attending U.S. schools (see discussion of new legislation and proposed legislation, below);
- Foreign nationals entering as a fiancé of a U.S. citizen;
- Exchange visitors; and
- NAFTA professionals.

Q 12:98   How will an employer hiring an alien under the H-1B portability provisions comply with I-9 requirements?

The current regulations [8 C.F.R. § 274A.12(b)(20)] authorize employment after a request for extension of the visa has been filed. The I-9 form currently contains no provision for this authorization. Therefore, the INS recommends that the employer follow the documentation procedures currently in place. Typically, this will involve attaching a copy of the receipt for the filed petition, together with a copy of the alien's Form I-94, to the I-9.

Q 12:99   What documentation is required for a temporary worker's visa?

The applicant must submit to the INS the following documentation:

1. Application Form OF-156;
2. A valid passport;
3. One photo, 1.5 inches (37 mm) square, showing the applicant's full face without head covering against a light background;

4. The Form I-797 from the prospective employer; and

5. Proof of a binding-ties residence outside the United States (no exact specifications are given under the regulations for how this requirement may be met; INS and consular officials and/or immigration counsel should be consulted).

Q 12:100   Can family members accompany the recipient of a temporary worker's visa?

With the exception of the Q-1 "cultural exchange" visa, these visas allow the spouse and unmarried children of the visa recipient to accompany the worker as non-immigrants. Any such spouse or child receiving such a temporary visa that piggybacks onto the temporary worker's visa is forbidden to accept employment in the United States.

Q 12:101   Are there time limits on a temporary worker's visas?

All temporary workers' visas will be issued with time limits. If the task is not completed as the specific time limit approaches, the holder may apply for an extension in order to complete the job.

Q 12:102   What do the INS final regulations on H-1B visas do?

The final regulations implement statutory amendments to the H-1B program enacted earlier in 1998 by Congress. The H-1B program is the primary means by which U.S. employers can temporarily employ non-immigrant foreign nationals in specialized professional jobs. The rules implement changes to the federal statutory scheme affected by the American Competitiveness and Workforce Improvement Act of 1998 (ACWIA) (sometimes styled the American Competitiveness in the Twenty-First Century Act).

Q 12:103   How did the ACWIA change the H-1B program?

The ACWIA changed the H-1B program in five primary ways:

1. The current law limits the cap of H-1Bs to 65,000 as the number of aliens who may be issued an H-1B visa or otherwise provided H-1B status. (The numerical limitation was temporarily raised to 195,000 in FY2001, FY2002, and FY2003.) In addition, all H-1B non-immigrants who work at (but not necessarily for) universities and non-profit research facilities are excluded from the numerical cap. This means that contractors working at, but not directly employed by the institution may be exempt from the cap. New non-displacement (layoff) and recruitment attestations are temporarily required until October 1, 2003, by H-1B employers who are classified as "H-1B dependent" or have been adjudicated "willful violators" of H-1B rules in the past. These non-displacement provisions prohibit these employers from replacing U.S. workers with H-1B workers and from placing H-1B workers at other employers' work sites where U.S. workers are

being laid off. The recruitment provision requires these employers to first try to find U.S. workers to fill positions before hiring H-1B workers and to hire such U.S. workers as are at least equally well qualified for the positions.

2. U.S. employers must offer H-1B workers the same employee benefits they offer to their U.S. workers.

3. Employers must continue to pay H-1B workers while they are in "non-productive status" because of lack of work or lack of license.

4. Whistleblower protections are provided for employees, including both former employees and applicants, who disclose information to the INS about violations or who cooperate in an INS investigation.

5. The DOJ and the DOL are authorized to permit whistleblowing H-1B workers to remain in the United States for up to six years after blowing the whistle.

Q 12:104   Where and how does an employer apply for an H-1B visa?

The DOL's Employment and Training Administration is responsible for processing applications, which are called Labor Certification Applications (LCAs). Employer petitions are adjudicated by the INS, which also processes requests for adjustment of status if the worker is already present in the United States. Visas for actual entry into the United States are issued by the State Department.

For an additional $1,000 fee, the agency will expedite the application; as all such actions were taking longer than normal in 2003, employers are well-advised to spend this extra money if expeditious employment of foreign job applicants in the United States is a priority consideration.

A $500 fraud-prevention fee also took effect March 8, 2006.

Information on filing and processing LCAs can be obtained at http://www. foreignlaborcert.doleta.gov/. DOL press releases and announcements concerning H-1B applications can be found at http://www.dol.gov.

Q 12:105   What other fees may be involved in an H-1B petition?

For fy 2014, USCIS lists the following possible fees:

- Base filing fee:
  - $325
- American Competitiveness and Workforce Improvement Act of 1998 (ACWIA) fee:
- (see H-1B Data Collection and Filing Fee Exemption Supplement, Part B):
  - $750 for employers with 1 to 25 ful-time equivalent employees, unless exempt.
  - $1,500 for employers with 26 or more full-time equivalent employees, unless exempt.

Fraud Prevention and Detection fee:

• $500 to be submitted with a request for initial H-1B status or with a request for a beneficiary already in H-1B status to change employers (does not apply to Chile/Singapore H-1B1 petitions).

Public Law 111-230:

• $2,000 to be submitted by a petitioner which employs 50 or more employees in the United States where more than 50 percent of its employees in the united States are in H-1B or L-1 nonimmigrant status.

• Must be submitted with a request for initial H-1B status or a request for a beneficiary already in H-1B status to change employers.

Premium Processing fee:

• $1,225 for employers seeking Premium Processing Service.

Q 12:106   Is the H-1B visa portable?

Yes. H-1B alien workers are allowed to change jobs during the pendency of a new application filed by the new employer. This rule pertains, provided:

1. The worker has been lawfully admitted in the first instance;
2. The new petition is filed by the new employer before the expiration of the alien's current visa; and
3. The alien has not worked without authorization prior to the filing of the new petition.

Q 12:107   What is the *PERM Program*?

On March 28, 2005, the DOL's long-awaited Program Electronic Review Management (PERM) regulation went into effect. The regulation changes the procedures by which employers now file for labor certification of their alien employees. Reduction in Recruitment (RIR) and other traditional filings are no longer acceptable. PERM applies to all labor certifications now.

A new system for LCA and PERM applications was rolled out by the DOL in 2009 with the LCA system being introduced in early 2009 and the new PERM system in the spring of 2009. The DOL stated that all pre-PERM labor certification cases had been completed by the Backlog Reduction Centers and that the only remaining cases were on appeal at the Board of Alien Labor Certification Appeals (BALCA).

Processing times for appeals of cases filed in December 2006 were being adjudicated in early 2009; appeals predicated on government error were being reviewed immediately. The DOL indicated that it would continue to closely review applications for employees in sectors where the company and/or the industry was experiencing lay-offs.

[Thomas Espanza, "Department of Labor Provides Updates on PERM Program," Law Offices of Thomas Espanza Jr., http://www.tomesparza.com/department-of-labor-provides-updates-on-perm-program/]

Q 12:108   What are employers seeking labor certifications under PERM required to do?

1. Obtain a prevailing-wage determination from a State Workforce Agency; and

2. Submit its electronic ETA-9089.

The government claims that this procedure will reduce the processing time from two to four years down to a mere 45 days. For additional information on PERM call VISANOW at 1-888-484-7269.

Relationship of Other Laws to Aliens and Immigration

Q 12:109   Can illegal aliens sue employers for violations of the FLSA?

At least one U.S. appellate court has held that even though an illegal alien may be working in the United States in violation of federal law, he or she is still entitled to sue a company that improperly pays minimum wages or overtime under the FLSA. The rationale behind this ruling is that immigration laws and the FLSA have essentially the same purpose—preventing exploitation of employees. The court reasoned that bringing undocumented aliens within the scope of the FLSA would reduce the incentive to hire such workers at wage rates less than that demanded by law for documented aliens. [Patel v. Quality Inn South, 846 F.2d 700 (11th Cir. 1988)]

Additionally, the U.S. District Court for the Northern District of California held that an illegal alien's filing of a wage claim under the FLSA was a protected activity, and therefore, when the employer retaliated by reporting the illegal alien to the INS (now the ICE), the alien had the right to sue for illegal retaliation as well. [Singh v. Jutla & C.D. & R.'s Oil, Inc., 214 F. Supp. 2d 1056, 147 CCH Labor Cases P 34,609, 8 BNA W&H Cases 2d 165 (N.D. Cal. 2002)]

However, distinguishing *Singh*, the U.S. District Court for Kansas refused to permit illegal aliens who were injured while being transported in a truck that was in an auto accident to recover against the defendants for wages lost due to their injuries. "[T]he court finds that this argument is not applicable . . . as [the plaintiff] is seeking damages based on projected earnings rather than work already performed." [Hernandez-Cortez v. Hernandez, 2003 WL 22519678 (D. Kan. Nov. 4, 2003)]

More recently, former restaurant employees brought an action against a franchisee that owned and operated a restaurant, the individual who owned and operated the franchisee, and the parent company-franchisor, alleging that the defendants knowingly provided illegal aliens with names and Social Security numbers of American citizens to use for illegal employment, unlawfully took the illegal employees' tips, discriminated on the basis of race, and retaliated against employees who challenged those and other practices. In April 2010, the U.S. Court of Appeals for the Eleventh Circuit held, "One element of the section of the Immigration and Nationality Act (INA) criminalizing the hiring for employment of at least 10 aliens with actual knowledge that the individuals are unauthorized aliens is that the defendant had actual knowledge that the illegal aliens who were hired had been brought into the country in violation of the section of the INA governing the bringing in and harboring of certain aliens. Immigration and Nationality Act, § 274(a), (a)(3)(A), 8 U.S.C.A. § 1324(a), (a)(3)(A)."

The court went on to hold, "If an employer hires 10 or more illegal aliens with knowledge that they are unauthorized aliens who have been illegally brought into this country, the employer may be fined, sentenced to as much as five years in prison, or both, and such crime would be a Racketeer Influenced and Corrupt Organizations Act (RICO) predicate act. Immigration and Nationality Act, § 274(a)(3)(A), 8 U.S.C.A. § 1324(a)(3)(A); 18 U.S.C.A. § 1961(1)(F)."

And, finally, the court ruled, "Former restaurant employees' allegations that employers knowingly supplied aliens with jobs and with social security numbers to facilitate their employment amounted to allegations of 'encouraging or inducing' within meaning of statute criminalizing encouraging and inducing an alien to enter the United States illegally, and stated a predicate act of racketeering under the Racketeer Influenced and Corrupt Organizations Act (RICO). Immigration and Nationality Act, § 274(a)(1)(A)(iv), 8 U.S.C.A. § 1324(a)(1)(A)(iv); 18 U.S.C.A. § 1961(1)(F)."

The federal district judge was reversed on this count of the plaintiffs' complaint and the case was remanded. The significance is that this ruling takes illegal aliens' wage claims to a whole new level of legal liability. The taking of the illegal employees' tips, if true, constituted a viable FLSA claim. But, going far, far beyond such a claim, the plaintiffs in this case went not merely to the criminal provisions of the immigration law, but took another giant step, bringing RICO into the picture. This decision should stand as a warning to employers who contemplate exploiting illegal workers that criminal liability, as well as significant punitive damages, may be among the risks they are running. [Edwards v. Prime, Inc., 2010 WL 1404280 (11th Cir. Apr. 9, 2010.)]

Q 12:110   Do illegal aliens enjoy other rights under U.S. law?

In *King v. ZirMed, Inc.* [2007 WL 3306100 (W.D. Ky. 2007)], the plaintiff brought suit against the defendants, alleging they had deprived him of 6.25 million shares of ZirMed, Inc. stock, of which he was the legally valid owner. The defendants counterclaimed, alleging various statutory and common-law violations by the plaintiff that, among other things, foreclosed him from claiming entitlement to the 6.25 million shares.

In October 2000, plaintiff Russell King, a citizen of the United Kingdom, began work as an executive at ZirMed, Inc., in Louisville, Kentucky, pursuant to a three-year employment agreement that, among other things, allowed for his compensation to be accrued as an unpaid obligation of ZirMed instead of being paid out to him, in case the company's financial situation required it. Upon beginning employment, the plaintiff also entered into a stock option agreement, under which he would be granted three million options if certain profitability levels were reached. The stock option agreement expired in October 2003. In January 2001, the plaintiff was granted another one million options.

In May 2001, the plaintiff became president and CEO of ZirMed, at which point the prior CEO's four million options were transferred to the plaintiff, and any company-performance-based conditions were removed from the options, such that they vested immediately. All eight million of the plaintiff's options at that time expired in October 2003. The plaintiff ultimately returned five million of his options to ZirMed in April 2003, and allowed his remaining options to expire in October 2003.

In January 2004, the plaintiff and ZirMed entered into a new employment agreement as well as two new stock option agreements. In the first stock option agreement, the plaintiff received the right to purchase 250,000 shares of ZirMed stock. In the second stock option agreement, the plaintiff received the right to purchase six million shares of ZirMed stock. On January 27, 2004, the plaintiff attempted to exercise all 6.25 million of these options. As consideration, the plaintiff requested cancellation of $62,500 of accrued payments owed by ZirMed. On January 29, 2004, ZirMed issued a stock certificate to the plaintiff, evidencing his ownership of 6.25 million shares.

In June 2004, the plaintiff was denied reentry into the United States, following a personal trip abroad. It was determined that despite having first come to the United States in 1990, having been married for eight years to a United States citizen, having received a valid Social Security card, and having received conditional permanent resident status and an alien registration card, the plaintiff had failed to file the requisite documents to remove his "conditional" status. Therefore, the plaintiff effectively had been in the United States illegally prior to his departure on the trip from which he was returning, and was now ineligible to reenter the United States. The plaintiff endeavored to continue in his role as CEO of ZirMed, setting up operations in Toronto and continuing to participate in company management. He also applied for a visa that would allow him to return to Louisville.

On October 11, 2004, ZirMed's board of directors voted to terminate the plaintiff's employment with the company, invoking the "for cause" provision of his employment agreement. New management was retained, and in January 2004, that new management acted to confiscate the plaintiff's 6.25 million shares, canceling them on the company's books and noting that they were improperly granted.

When the plaintiff sued, challenging the company's right to fire him and confiscate his stock, the directors raised a number of defenses, notably for purposes of understanding the legal impact of illegal-alien status that the plaintiff's illegal-alien status worked to void his contracts with the company.

In response to the foregoing defense, the district judge commented, "This breathtakingly broad public-policy-based argument relies on the Immigration Control and Reform Act of 1986, 8 U.S.C. § 1324 ('IRCA'), which makes it illegal for an employer to employ an illegal immigrant, and for illegal immigrants to 'subvert the employer verification system by tendering fraudulent documents.'" [Hoffman Plastic Compounds, Inc. v. NLRB, 535 U.S. 137, 148 (2002)]. The defendants argued that *Hoffman,* which denied an administrative award of back pay for the period after an illegal alien (who had procured employment using fraudulent documents) had been fired on the grounds that such an award would violate IRCA, should be interpreted as promulgating a broad rule that illegal alien employees have no ability to enforce the terms of contracts into which they have entered with their employers. Such a rule would expand *Hoffman* beyond the remedies offered in specific federal statutes into the realm of contract-enforceability, which has U.S. Constitutional implications.

> This expansive reading of *Hoffman,* which would deprive illegal immigrant employees of such things as basic rights to contracts, has been rejected by courts considering circumstances not directly analogous to those in *Hoffman* [*see, e.g.,* Flores v. Amigon, 233 F. Supp. 2d 462 (E.D.N.Y. 2002)(rejecting application of Hoffman in the context of an illegal immigrant's action to recover unpaid wages)], and would effectively require this Court to wholly deprive illegal immigrants of the ability to enter any and all enforceable contracts, whether those contracts were directly related to their illegal immigration or not. This is a step the Court is unwilling to take, as it flies in the face of 42 U.S.C. § 1981, which grants 'all persons within the jurisdiction of the United States" the "same right . . . to make and enforce contracts." [*Cf.* Martinez v. Fox Valley Bus Lines, 17 F. Supp. 576, 577 (D. Ill. 1936)(rejecting the idea that "if an alien . . . is unlawfully in the United States he may be despoiled of his property, contracts with him may be breached . . . [and] he is without [civil] redress")].

> Unlike in *Hoffman,* here Plaintiff provided no fraudulent documents to ZirMed in order to procure employment. Indeed, there are at best significant factual ambiguities as to whether he himself was aware of his status as an illegal immigrant until he was denied reentry into the United States in June 2004, whether ZirMed ever inquired about Plaintiff's immigration status before or during his employment, and whether and how Plaintiff ever disclosed anything about his immigration status to ZirMed. The facts before the Supreme Court in *Hoffman* were simply not those presented here, and thus *Hoffman* does not dictate the sweeping conclusion urged upon the Court by Defendants.

> Furthermore, the options agreements can hardly be said to be "so connected with an illegal purpose as to be inseparable from it" [Zeitz v. Foley, 264 S.W.2d 267, 268 (Ky. 1954)], since where courts have found such inseparability, the violation of law is a "direct object" of the contract, and the argument of illegality is something more than a "pretext" invoked by a party to "escape [its] obligations." [*Zeitz* at 269] Though IRCA unquestionably makes illegal the employment of illegal immigrants and expresses a public policy against such employment, the logical leap between this proposition and the idea that no contract

entered into by an illegal immigrant is enforceable by that illegal immigrant is not dictated by *Hoffman,* is contradicted by the United States Code, and will not be accepted by this Court as a way of dispensing with this case.

In mid-December, not long after the *King* decision discussed above, ZirMed sued the law firm of Frost-Brown-Todd, alleging an undisclosed conflict of interest. According to an article in the Louisville Courier-Journal on December 13, 2007, "The suit says Frost Brown attorney William Strench, while engaged to provide legal services to ZirMed, also represented the company's former chief executive in contract negotiations in 2003 but didn't disclose that to ZirMed. The result, the suit says, was an employment agreement that was more favorable to the executive, Russell King, than was in the company's interest. Frost Brown hasn't responded to the suit. But an attorney for the law firm, Jim Milliman, said ZirMed was aware that Strench was representing King in the contract talks. He cited a December 2003 report from the stockholders' committee that negotiated the employment agreement. The report noted that Frost Brown had been granted 'a limited waiver of its conflict of interest in order to represent King in the negotiation.' ZirMed's suit, filed Nov. 30 in Jefferson Circuit Court, asks that Frost Brown Todd be required to return attorney fees received from ZirMed and pay punitive damages. The suit doesn't request a specific sum."

Meanwhile, the newspaper account continued, King and the company settled King's claims for an undisclosed amount.

Q 12:111   Does state law apply to defining aliens' rights?

In 1994, the Court of Appeals for the Ninth Circuit, sitting in San Francisco, said that the INS erred in ordering the deportation of a Canadian woman because of a drug conviction. While the woman was vulnerable to being deported because of the crime, family ties in the United States are grounds recognized by the INS as sufficient to counterbalance the conviction. The deportee's boyfriend testified that the couple had established the equivalent of a common-law marriage and would formalize the relationship, if given the opportunity.

The INS rejected the "family ties" argument because California, where the couple resided, does not recognize common-law marriage. Reversing the agency's decision, the Ninth Circuit, citing a Supreme Court decision, said that "in the absence of a plain indication to the contrary . . . Congress when it enacts a statute is not making the application of the federal act dependent on the state law." [Kahn v. Immigration and Naturalization Serv., 20 F.3d 960 (9th Cir. 1994) *citing* Jerome v. United States, 318 U.S. 101 (1943)]

Aliens (illegal or not) probably enjoy the right to prosecute tort claims where their state law rights are violated by private entities. This is one conclusion that reasonably can be drawn from a case in which the public's seemingly insatiable hunger for "real life" reporting led CBS into the apartment of a group of plaintiffs who are now suing CBS for invasion of privacy and infliction of emotional harm. The case concerns the search of the plaintiff's apartment by U.S. Treasury agents investigating a possible credit card fraud scheme. The agents were accompanied by a news crew from the CBS program "Street Stories." According to the court, "The CBS crew followed and taped the agents as they searched the apartment and [the plaintiffs'] belongings. They took close-up pictures of the interiors of closets, personal letters, family pictures, and even a homey maxim on the wall." [Ayeni v. CBS, Inc., 848 F. Supp. 362 (E.D.N.Y. 1994)]

Although the court does not say so specifically, the facts of the case imply that the plaintiffs may well have been recent arrivals to the United States. Clearly they were uncertain about their privacy rights under U.S. constitutional and state tort law. No evidence of credit card fraud was found. When the plaintiffs sued the federal agents and CBS, the latter contended that the suit must be dismissed because the TV crew was shielded behind the agents' qualified immunity from suit. Finding that the videotaping of the plaintiffs' apartment amounted to a search and seizure under the U.S. Constitution and that the agents' search warrant did not permit them to extend its authorization to a private entity to participate in the otherwise legal search, the court held that CBS was not entitled to use an affirmative immunity defense to defeat the plaintiffs' action. [848 F. Supp. 362]

The principles enunciated in the *Ayeni* case can be extended by analogy to a situation in which, for example, an employer attempts to ascertain the authenticity of an applicant's employment documentation by means of some sort of private investigation. The quasi-official nature of such a background investigation cannot be expected to immunize the employer from a state court privacy action should the investigation overstep its bounds. Thus, in 1996, the INS seemed to be increasing pressure to crack down on document fraud by illegal immigrants. [*See* "Administration's Immigration Effort More Likely to Succeed, Says INS Chief," *BNA Daily Report For Executives*, Apr. 13, 1995.] Employers would be ill-advised to respond to this pressure by taking steps that result in the invasion of even an illegal alien's privacy. [See chapters 5 and 6; *see also* Castagnera & Szvetitz, "The Search for a 'Hire' Authority," *Convenience Store Decisions*, Jan. 1995, at 38.]

In April 2010, the U.S. Court of Appeals for the Eleventh Circuit affirmed dismissal of a claim that the defendant-employer's taking of the illegal-alien employees' tips was conversion under Alabama state law. However, the decision seems to have turned on the narrow language of the Alabama statute, rather than on the court's jurisdiction to consider the pendant state claim or the viability of such a claim in the context of a case that was cognizable primarily under federal law.

The implication is that, under different facts, this pendant state claim was cognizable by the federal district judge. [Edwards v. Prime, Inc., 2010 WL 1404280 (11th Cir. Apr. 9, 2010)] (See Q 12:109 for additional discussion of this case.)

Q 12:112   What is *NAFTA*?

NAFTA is the North American Free Trade Agreement. For general information on the employment-related provisions of NAFTA, see chapter 15.

In early March 2010, a small group of American lawmakers introduced H.R.4759 to withdraw the United States from NAFTA. [*See* http://www.openc ongress.org/bill/111-h4759/show.] Led by Representative Gene Taylor, Democrat from Mississippi, the bill, if enacted, would require the President to give Mexico and Canada six-months' notice of the United States's exit from the 16-year-old treaty. Congressman Taylor told the news media, "At a time when 10 to 12 percent of the American people are unemployed, I think Congress has an obligation to put people back to work."

[http://www.reuters.com/article/idUSTRE6233MS20100304]

The bill arrived at a time when President Obama was calling for action on trade treaties with Columbia, Panama, and South Korea. It suggests that the President's own party may be a significant impediment to any plans he may have for extending free-trade agreements. Withdrawal from NAFTA, of course, would affect the ease with which Canadian nationals in particular are able to work on both sides of the border.

Q 12:113   Does NAFTA simplify the visa application process for Mexican and Canadian professionals seeking to enter the United States?

NAFTA simplifies the visa application procedure for professionals classified in the H-1 category. These professionals, coming from Canada or Mexico, may apply for a TN temporary work visa at any Class "A" port of entry. Such a TN visa will be valid for a full year and is renewable indefinitely. Furthermore, under NAFTA, there are no numerical limits on such visas either by nationality or by corporate employer.

Q 12:114   How are visa applications handled under NAFTA?

Under the NAFTA Handbook issued in July 31, 2011, applications are to be handled "on the spot," unless the inspector finds the application so deficient in information that he or she can neither grant nor deny it based on the available information. The handbook is available on various Web sites, including Apple iTunes and Amazon, for approximately $100.

In cases of application deficiency, the inspector will prepare a Form I-160A, "Notice of Refusal of Admission/Parole in the United States." The form will list the additional evidence needed for the final determination to be made.

Results of inspections will be posted on the Interagency Border Inspection System.

The inspector who rules that an alien is ineligible for admission under the NAFTA rules will:

1. Advise the alien of his or her inadmissibility;
2. Discuss with the alien other possible benefits available via the CIS;

3. Advise the alien of the right to a hearing on the determination before an Immigration Judge; and

4. Prepare the Form I-160A.

Q 12:115   Which professional workers qualify for the NAFTA TN-1 free trade professional work visa?

Professionals eligible for the TN-1 free trade professional work visa include:

- Accountants
- Architects
- Claims adjusters
- Computer systems analysts
- Economists
- Engineers
- Foresters
- Graphic designers
- Hotel managers
- Land surveyors
- Landscape architects
- Lawyers
- Librarians
- Management consultants
- Mathematicians
- Medical allied professionals
- Research assistants
- Scientific technologists and technicians
- Scientists
- Social workers
- Teachers and professors
- Technical writers
- Urban planners
- Vocational counselors

Q 12:116   To qualify for the TN-1 free trade professional work visa, what must the applicant do?

In order to apply at a Class "A" port of entry, the alien applicant must provide the INS office there with a letter from his or her U.S., Mexican, or Canadian employer as proof of his or her professional qualifications. With regard to most of these professions, proof of a bachelor's degree will suffice, unless (as with law) an advanced degree and license are also necessary to establish the right to practice. Computer systems analysts and medical technologists, at the opposite extreme of the professional spectrum, must show some sort of post-secondary diploma (such as the foreign equivalent of an associate's [two-year] degree from a U.S. community college) and evidence of at least three years of professional experience.

Q 12:117   Does NAFTA liberalize freedom of travel by Mexican and Canadian business visitors to the United States?

Under NAFTA, acceptable B-1 (business visitor) visa activities have been expanded to include cross-border visits by Mexican and Canadian nationals engaged in:

1. *Research*: Scientists and statisticians conducting independent research on behalf of Canadian and Mexican for-profit and nonprofit enterprises;

2. *Agriculture*: Managers supervising harvesting operations;

3. *Manufacturing*: Purchasing agents and production managers;

4. *Marketing*: Market researchers and analysts conducting independent market research studies;

5. *Sales*: Sales representatives, technical representatives, and agents negotiating deals and taking orders;

6. *Distribution*: Transportation operators delivering to or picking up from U.S. locations with no intermediate loading or unloading;

7. *After-sale servicing*: Installment, repair, and maintenance personnel with specialized knowledge of the foreign seller's contractual commitments, warranties, trade secrets, etc.; and

8. *General service*: Professionals qualified for entry into the United States on an H-1 Visa and receiving no remuneration within the United States. These commonly will include:

    • Management and supervisory personnel;
    • Computer specialists;
    • Financial services personnel;
    • Public relations and advertising professionals;
    • Tourism personnel; and
    • Translators and interpreters.

[For listings of the major provisions of Mexican and Canadian labor and employment laws, see chapter 15.]

Q 12:118   How is the DOL processing applications for temporary agricultural workers?

The DOL's Employment and Training Administration published a General Administration Letter (No. 2-01) on April 18, 2001, in which it established centralized processing locations in each state for its H-2A temporary agricultural labor program. [66 Fed. Reg. 19,984–19,986]

The H-2A regulations [20 C.F.R. § 655.101] require simultaneous submission of an H-2A application to the Employment and Training Administration's regional office and the state employment security agency for the relevant geographic region. Thereafter, most processing functions are performed by the responsible state agency, especially with respect to the recruitment portion of the employer's application.

Q 12:119   Do temporary agricultural worker visas apply to vegetation management jobs?

Yes. The H-2A visa program is intended to meet a shortage of American agricultural workers by permitting growers to import foreign labor temporarily. Some employers, who use sheep and goats to manage vegetation growth, have argued that the H-2A requirement did not affect them.

On April 16, 2001, the DOL's Employment and Training Administration announced that in fact the H-2A program does apply to such vegetation-management programs as well. [66 Fed. Reg. 19,525–19,526]

Q 12:120   What must an employer do if an employee working under an H-2A visa quits employment?

Any departure from employment must be reported to the state employment agency's relevant regional office, whether the termination or departure is voluntary or involuntary. Such notice must be given within 48 hours after the employer becomes aware of the job abandonment or conducts the termination. Furthermore, USCIS should be notified via e-mail: CSC-X.H-2AAbs@dhs.gov

Or by mail: California Service Center, Attn Div X/BCU ACD, P.O. Box 30050, Laguna Niguel, CA 92607-3004

Questions on this requirement can be directed to the e-mail address above.

Q 12:121   Must aliens working in the United States file federal income tax returns?

Yes. Both resident and nonresident aliens must file federal tax returns—IRS Form 1040-NR—for any tax years in which they engage in a business or are employed in the United States. [26 C.F.R. § 1.6012] This is true even if the alien's U.S. income tax obligation has been fully covered by the employer's payroll withholding or by tax treaty benefits.

Q 12:122   When is an alien employee's IRS Form 1040-NR due for filing?

It must be filed by the 15th day of the sixth month after the end of the tax year, or the 15th day of the fourth month after the end of the tax year if the income was wages subject to withholding. [26 C.F.R. § 1.6072-1(c)]

Q 12:123   Must an alien employee get IRS clearance before departing the United States?

Yes. Whether a resident or nonresident alien, the worker usually must get a Certificate of Tax Compliance—also called a "sailing permit"—before departing the United States. To obtain a sailing permit, the departing alien worker should file either a Form 1040C, if he or she has taxable income to report, or a Form 2063, if she or he has no taxable income to report prior to departure. [I.R.C. § 6851, 29 C.F.R. § 1.6851-2(a)(2)]

Q 12:124   Must a foreign partnership with partners working in the United States file a federal tax return?

Yes. If the foreign partnership has gross income from American sources or that is "effectively connected" to its U.S. trade or business activities, it must file a Form 1065. [I.R.C. § 6031(e)]

Q 12:125   Must a U.S. employer withhold payroll taxes from the wages and salaries of alien employees working in the United States?

Yes. The compensation, including pension payments from exempt (qualified) employer pension funds, is subject to the same withholding rules as are applied to employees who are American citizens.

Q 12:126   Are there any exceptions to the requirement that a U.S. employer withhold payroll taxes from compensation paid to alien employees working in the United States?

Yes. The exceptions are:

1. Income other than compensation for personal services (e.g., profits from a U.S. business) [I.R.C. §§ 1441(c)(1), 1442(a)]; or

2. Income exempted by an applicable tax treaty with the alien's home nation.

Q 12:127   What are *tax treaties*?

The U.S. government has entered into bilateral tax treaties with several dozen other nations. (For a complete listing, see chapter 15.) Each such treaty is somewhat unique. To ascertain whether an alien employee is covered by a tax treaty, first check chapter 15 of this book to see whether such a treaty exists between the United States and that employee's home nation. If such a treaty exists, a copy can be obtained from any of the following sources:

- The IRS;
- The U.S. Department of State;
- The embassy or consulate of the relevant foreign country;
- Any local library that is a U.S. government document depository; or
- Any local law school library.

Q 12:128   What must an alien working in the United States do to take advantage of a tax treaty?

In order to take advantage of a tax treaty, an alien employee must file a Form 8233 with the employer. The revised form, issued March 2009, is available at http://www.irs.gov/pub/irs-pdf/f8233.pdf.

Q 12:129   What is *SEVIS*?

This is a program, instituted in 2003, under which institutions of higher education are required to track international students arriving on their campuses under both F-1 and J-1 (exchange student) visas. The program, web based, imposes much more rigorous requirements on colleges and universities for keeping track of such students. The purpose is to prevent international students from using such visas to enter the United States and then vanishing into the general population or failing to return to their home countries at the conclusion of their courses of study. Since August 1, 2003, all F-1 and J-1 student visa holders are required to be on the SEVIS system.

Q 12:130   What is the *Patriot Act of 2001*?

This anti-terrorist law will reach into both public and private workplaces in many ways. Potential impact on employers' and workers' rights can be anticipated. The law's major features include:

- Roving wiretap authorizations for law enforcement officials;
- Increased penalties for terrorist acts, illegal possession of weapons grade biological materials, and harboring terrorists;
- Treasury Department powers to obtain foreign banking information and to prohibit U.S. bankers from dealing with such offshore entities;
- Subpoena powers for e-mail addresses;
- Inter-agency information sharing among law enforcement and spy agencies;
- Increased border security; and
- Detention of suspected aliens.

On the one hand, employers who cooperate with law enforcement or intelligence agency officials exercising these new powers may be shielded from liability to employees whose job rights suffer as a result. On the other hand, employees who cooperate with government officials may very well be accorded protection from employer retaliation by federal and state courts. Such protection may be accorded under federal and state common law rules regarding terminations that offend clear mandates of public policy. Alternatively, courts called upon to fashion remedies for employees that are terminated (e.g., because they report suspect company activities), may look to existing federal anti-retaliation laws. Likewise, while (as noted above) employers may be shielded from liability when cooperating with law enforcement officials under some form of federal common law privilege, it's equally possible that an overzealous employer may be found to have run afoul of existing federal statutes, such as preexisting wire-tap legislation.

The USA Patriot Act Sunset Extension Act of 2011 was pending before both houses of Congress, until May 26, 2011, when President Barack Obama signed the bill. The main provisions of the bill introduced in the House of Representatives are:

A Compromise with Broad Support. This bill is essentially identical to the compromise measure that recently passed the Senate Judiciary Committee with bipartisan support (Mike Lee of Utah voted in favor). It makes meaningful improvements to the Patriot Act and related authorities, yet has the support of the Administration and the intelligence community.

New Sunsets. Section 2 of the Bill reauthorizes the Business Records, Lone Wolf, and Roving Wiretaps provisions for two and a half years—until December 2013. For the first time, it puts a sunset in the use of National Security Letters. Finally, it moves the sunset on the FISA Amendments Act from the end of 2012 to 2013 so that all these inter-related surveillance authorities can be considered together in a non-election year.

Factual Basis Requirement for Business Records Orders. Section 3 modifies the standard for obtaining a FISA court order to obtain business records. It eliminates the overbroad presumption of relevance in these cases, and requires the Government to provide a written statement of the facts and circumstances that justify the applicant's belief that the tangible things sought are relevant. (DOJ says it already does this as a matter of practice so this would not be an operational burden.) The bill contains additional protections for bookseller or library records. These can be obtained only if the Government shows a direct connection between the records and a terrorist or other agent of a foreign power.

Improvements to National Security Letter Process. The bill makes a number of changes to NSL practices and procedures, in response to the numerous abuses of this tool.

Gag Orders. Section 5 clarifies the standards for including a gag order in a national security letter. Section 6 significantly improves the process for challenging these gag orders, eliminating the one-year waiting requirement in current law and removing the power of high level government officials to foreclose judicial review by "conclusively certifying" that the gag order is needed. This section also corrects the constitutional defects in NSL gag orders found by the Second Circuit Court of Appeals in Doe v. Mukasey, 549 F.3d 861 (2d Cir. 2008), and implements the court's suggestion for a constitutionally sound process.

Factual Basis Requirement. Section 7 requires the FBI to keep a written record of the facts and circumstances on which it relies to support certain NSLs.

Minimization Procedures. Requires DOJ to implement minimization procedures for NSL collected information, just as it does for FISA collected information, and requires periodic review and notice to Congress regarding changes to these procedures. (DOJ has already begun implementing such procedures, as an administrative matter.)

Roving Wiretaps. Section 15 tightens up the use of roving wiretaps by requiring a description "with particularity" of the target of such wiretaps in cases where the target's name and identity is not known. This will eliminate the possibility of so-called John Doe roving wiretaps.

Sneak and Peek Searches. Current law requires notification of a sneak and peek (or delayed notice) search within 30 days. Section 11 shortens this time to seven days, or a longer period if specifically justified.

Improved procedures for FISA Pen Registers and Trap and Trace Devices. Section 4 modifies the standard for Pen Register and Trap and Trace devices, which collect info on calls or e-mails to and from a particular communications facility. The bill requires the government to provide a written statement of the facts and circumstances showing that the information to be collected is relevant to a national security investigation and so strengthens judicial oversight. This section also requires minimization procedures for this type of collection, which are not required under current law, and makes those procedures subject to court review.

Enhanced Public Reporting on NSLs and FISA. Sections 8 and 9 require enhanced public reporting of the number of NSLs issued each year, and an annual unclassified report on how FISA authorities are used, including their impact on the privacy of United States persons. This report shall be readily accessible on the Internet.

Enhanced Audits. Section 10 requires the DOJ Office of Inspector General to conduct audits on the use during 2007–2011 of the Business Records provision, NSLs, and the use of pen registers/trap and trace devices, including both the effectiveness of these tools and any improper or illegal uses. This section also requires the Inspectors General of the Intelligence Community to submit separate reports that also review these three provisions. The audits covering the years 2007–2009 must be completed by March 31, 2012. The audits for the years 2010–2011 must be completed by March, 31, 2013. These due dates ensure that Congress will have time to fully consider the findings of the audits prior to the December 31, 2013 sunsets in the bill.

[http://democrats.judiciary.house.gov/press-release/conyers-introduces-patriot-compromise]

Q 12:131   What are the direct immigration impacts of the Patriot Act of 2001?

Under the authority of the Patriot Act, former Attorney General John Ashcroft moved quickly to establish a Foreign Terrorist Tracking Task Force. Its stated purpose was to identify and deport terrorists and to keep other such undesirables from gaining admission into the United States. A total of 46 groups and organizations were designated as terrorist in orientation. ICE played a key role in this effort, enjoying among other things a tripling of agents along the U.S.-Canada border, plus broad powers to detain non-citizens suspected of terrorist affiliations.

Q 12:132   What is the *REAL ID Act*?

After years of congressional debate and delays over the Real ID Act (H.B. 418), which originally passed back in 2005, but hung for five more years in a limbo state, the law is essentially in full force and effective as of May 2011, under the auspices of the Department of Homeland Security's (DHS) final regulations. [6 C.F.R. Part 37; *see* http://edocket.access.gpo.gov/2008/08-140.htm] The DHS has issued a final rule to establish minimum standards for state-issued driver's licenses and identification cards in accordance with the Act.

These regulations set standards for states to meet the requirements of the Act, including:

- information and security features that must be incorporated into each card;
- proof of identity and lawful status of an applicant;
- verification of the source documents provided by an applicant; and
- security standards for the offices that issue licenses and identification cards.

This final rule also provides a process for states to seek an additional extension of the compliance deadline to May 11, 2011, by demonstrating material compliance with the core requirements of the Act and this rule. [http://www.ncsl.org/issues-research/transport/real-id-act-of-2005.aspx]

Literally all 50 states had applied for extensions of the requirement to comply with the law, while Congress continued to debate the statute's future. But by Fall 2009, half of all the states had passed binding legislation or resolutions to participate in the program. Now, with the release of DHS's regulations the REAL ID Act will finally take effect. [http://www.judicialwatch.org/blog/2012/03/real-id-act-may-finally-be-enforced-in-2013/]

Q 12:133   What is the status of the L-1 "Business Visitor" Visa?

The L-1 Visa Reform Act amended previous legislation to address the "outsourcing" of L-1B temporary workers. An L-1B nonimmigrant is an alien who has been employed overseas by a firm with an affiliated entity in the United

States, who comes to the United States to perform services for the international entity that involve specialized knowledge. L-1B temporary workers can no longer work primarily at a worksite other than that of their petitioning employer if either: (a) the work is controlled and supervised by a different employer or (b) the offsite arrangement is essentially one to provide a non-petitioning party with local labor for hire, rather than a service related to the specialized knowledge of the petitioning employer.

USCIS interprets the "control and supervision" provisions of the law to require an L-1B petitioning employer to retain ultimate authority over the worker. The determination as to whether an alien is or will be employed primarily at a worksite other than that of the petitioner depends on the specific facts presented. In addition, the bar does not apply if the satisfactory performance of such off-site employment duties requires that the L-1B temporary worker must have specialized or advanced knowledge of the petitioning employer's product, service, or other interests, as defined under current USCIS regulations. General skills or duties that relate to ordinary business or work activities do not meet the test of whether specialized knowledge is required for the work.

The "outsourcing" provisions described above apply to all L-1B petitions filed with USCIS after June 6, 2005, and include extensions and amendments involving individuals currently in L-1 status.

The Act also requires that all L-1 temporary workers must have worked for a period of no less than one year outside the United States for an employer with a qualifying relationship to the petitioning employer. Previously, participants in the "blanket L-1" program could participate after as little as six months of qualifying employment. This change applies to petitions for initial L-1 classification filed with USCIS after June 6, 2005; extensions of status under the blanket program are not affected by this new provision.

[*See* http://www.uscis.gov/files/pressrelease/L1_VisaReformAct_062305. pdf.]

Q 12:134   What is the "U.S. Visit" Program?

The DHS's US-VISIT program provides visa-issuing posts and ports of entry with the biometric technology that enables the U.S. government to establish and verify a foreign visitor's identity when he/she visits the United States.

In many cases, this process begins overseas at a U.S. visa issuing post, where a traveler's biometrics—digital fingerprints and a photograph—are collected and checked against a watch list of known criminals and suspected terrorists. When the traveler arrives in the United States, immigration officials collect the same biometrics to verify that the person at the port is the same person who received the visa. Immigration officials use this information to help them make visa-issuance and admission decisions as part of the visa application process or entry inspection.

Unlike names and dates of birth, which can be changed, biometrics are unique and virtually impossible to forge. Collecting biometrics helps the U.S. government prevent people from using fraudulent documents to enter the country illegally. Collecting biometrics also helps protect aliens' identities in the event their travel documents are lost or stolen, according to the agency.

[See http://www.ice.gov/news/library/factsheets/us-visit.htm.]

Q 12:135   What types of non-immigrant student visas does the USCIS issue?

The USCIS issues three general types of non-immigrant student visas:

1. The F-1 visa is issued to international (alien) students who typically intend to study in the United States for several years and earn a degree.
2. The J-1 visa is issued to international students who are exchange visitors to the United States, studying at an American university for a semester or two and then returning to their home institutions to complete their studies.
3. The M-1 visa is similar to the F-1, but is issued to international students who are studying at post-secondary trade schools.

Q 12:136   How are international students tracked by ICE?

All post-secondary schools that admit international students must track these students on SEVIS, a computer database accessible only to designated school officials and responsible officers.

Q 12:137   What is the function of the ICE Compliance Enforcement Unit?

The Compliance Enforcement Unit (CEU) is charged with tracking and pursuing foreign students, exchange visitors, and other non-immigrant visitors who violate their immigration status. The CEU draws upon various government databases to gather and analyze leads on visitors to the United States, identify potential security or criminal threats, and ensure full compliance with immigration laws. The CEU develops leads on immigration violators by collecting and examining data from three key national databases:

- The U.S. Visitor and Immigrant Status Indicator Technology (US-VISIT) program, administered by DHS, verifies the identities of incoming visitors and ensures compliance with visa and immigration policies. US-VISIT collects travel information and biometric identifiers such as fingerprints to verify the identity of visitors to the United States upon their arrival and departure.
- The Student Exchange Visitor Information System (SEVIS) is an Internet-based program, administered by ICE, which maintains data on roughly one million non-immigrant foreign students and exchange visitors during their stay in the United States. SEVIS was developed in 2002 to improve

nationwide coordination and communication in monitoring student visa activity. (See Q 12:129.)

- The National Security Entry Exit Registration System (NSEERS) is a DHS-administered registry of selected foreign visitors who, based upon country of origin or other intelligence-based criteria, may present an elevated national security concern.

Since its creation in June 2003, the CEU has reportedly reviewed more than 550,000 leads compiled from these databases. Of these leads, nearly 16,000 revealed potential violations of U.S. visa or immigration law and were immediately referred to ICE field offices for investigation. To date, ICE claims that these investigations have resulted in approximately 3,190 arrests.

[*See* http://www.ice.gov/pi/news/factsheets/enforce070117.htm.]

Q 12:138　　Are international students holding F-1 visas allowed to work?

The answer is a qualified, and complicated, "yes." Some of the main circumstances under which such students may work are:

- They may work on campus at the institutions they are attending, provided they have Social Security numbers.
- After one academic year, F-1 students are allowed to apply for Optional Practical Training (OPT). OPT is available on a full- or part-time basis with third parties, including private corporations, provided the job relates to the course of study pursued by the student. Students typically reserve their period of OPT eligibility (one year full-time or two years part-time) for after graduation.
- F-1 students also may work for third parties off campus if they can establish an economic hardship that did not exist at the time that they were issued visas to attend school in the United States.
- After one academic year of university attendance in the United States, an F-1 student may be permitted to work for a third-party employer off campus under a university-sponsored program of Curricular Practical Training (CPT). Typically, a bona fide CPT program must be for college credit and be an integral part of the student's curricular requirements. Use of CPT typically does not prevent subsequent use of OPT.

Q 12:139　　How does an F-1 visa holder go about getting a Social Security number?

The SSA requires that an F-1 visa holder applying for a Social Security number present the following four documents:

1. A valid passport;
2. A valid INS Form I-20, issued by the university he or she is attending;
3. A valid F-1 visa; and

4. An offer letter from the prospective employer (which usually will be the university the student is attending).

The Administration is then required to provide the local office or sub-office of the U.S. ICE agency with an opportunity to review and approve the application. This requirement sometimes can result in a lengthy delay in the issuance of the Social Security number, although most applications are successfully processed within a couple of weeks. Delays can sometimes be overcome by employer recourse to the office of the local congressional representative, which typically has a staffer charged with assisting constituents in such matters.

Q 12:140 Can international students employed under one-year OPT authorizations become permanent employees of the company?

Yes. Most international students seeking OPT employment opportunities with American corporations have hopes of remaining in the United States and in the employ of these American companies. The one-year OPT commitment enables the employer to ascertain the alien worker's suitability for long-term employment with the firm. In instances where the relationship has proved promising, the company's human resources department can sponsor the alien worker for an H-1B visa. The H-1B visa, if obtained, is good for three years with the possibility of a single renewal period of like length. From there, the alien-employee typically will apply for permanent residency (i.e., a "green card").

Q 12:141 Are J-1 exchange students allowed to work while studying in the United States?

Like their F-1 counterparts, J-1 exchange students are allowed to work on campus if they have Social Security numbers. In order to obtain a Social Security number, a J-1 exchange student must apply at a local SSA office and present with his or her application the following four documents:

1. A valid passport;
2. A valid J-1 visa;
3. A valid DS (Department of State) Form 2019; and
4. A letter from the university's responsible office allowing employment.
5. J-1 exchange students also are allowed to work for third-party employers off campus for purposes of practical training, if the program is approved by the responsible officer. Such employment for training purposes can occur during or immediately after the studies pursued on the college campus.

Q 12:142   How does an F-1 international student qualify for OPT?

International students holding F-1 visas must meet the following requirements to qualify for OPT:

- The student can apply no sooner than one academic year after commencing his or her U.S. studies.
- The student must apply before completing those studies.
- The application is sent to the USCIS service center with jurisdiction over the university where the student is studying.
- The applicant need not have a specific job offer in hand at the time of application, but must express intent to pursue a job opportunity related to his or her course of study.
- The applicant must have maintained unbroken F-1 status while in the United States and must hold a valid passport and INS Form I-20.

Q 12:143   What is an M-1 visa?

The M-1 category includes students in vocational or other nonacademic programs, other than language training. Approval for the attendance of nonacademic students may be solicited by a community college or junior college that provides vocational or technical training and awards associate degrees; a vocational high school; a trade school; or a school of nonacademic training other than language training. Employment rules under this category are approximately the same as under the F-1 visa (see Q 12:142).

Q 12:144   What is ICE doing by way of workplace law enforcement?

ICE has dramatically enhanced its efforts to combat the unlawful employment of illegal aliens in the United States. ICE's comprehensive strategy for effective worksite enforcement is said by the agency to be "aimed at promoting national security, protecting critical infrastructure and ensuring fair labor standards."

Under this strategy, ICE reports that it is "targeting unscrupulous employers of illegal aliens, seeking to initiate criminal prosecutions and cause asset forfeitures. ICE believes that the serious nature of these actions on culpable individuals will be a more sufficient deterrence to those who may not share the goal of fostering a sound and legal workforce."

In the past, administrative fines often proved to hold little deterrence value for violators. Many employers came to view these fines as simply the "cost of doing business." Administrative fines were ignored, not paid in a timely matter, or mitigated down over several years. Under its tougher policy, in criminal cases, ICE is often pursuing charges of harboring illegal aliens, money laundering, and/or knowingly hiring illegal aliens. Harboring illegal aliens is a felony with a potential 10-year prison sentence. Money laundering is a felony with a potential 20-year prison sentence. ICE has found these criminal sanctions to be a far greater deterrent to illegal employment schemes than administrative sanctions.

ICE argues, "The best measure of this new strategy lies in the number of arrests ICE has made for criminal violations in worksite enforcement investigations."

Latest budgetary data, enforcement fact sheets, and policy statements are all available at http://www.ice.gov/news/library/factsheets/.

Q 12:145   What are some state laws that affect immigration in the United States?

Even prior to the 2007 immigration debate in Congress, many state legislatures had begun enacting laws intended to impact illegal, and sometimes also legal, immigrants present within their jurisdictions. With the failure of Congress to enact sweeping immigration reform, more states have since joined the trend toward state regulation of this important area of public policy, despite the fact that it has traditionally been deemed the exclusive province of federal law. According to a February 8, 2012 survey published and distributed by Morgan Lewis, "The ongoing failure to achieve federal immigration reform continues to inspire even more state government activity. As a result, the United States is creating a patchwork of immigration compliance obligations for employers operating in various jurisdictions." The ACLU and others have regularly challenged these state, and often also municipal, enactments. Challenges have met with mixed results. (See Qs 12:70 and Q 12:71.)

Morgan Lewis adds, "Readers should bear in mind that state immigration laws are largely untested in terms of their enforcement. In many instances there are unanswered questions, including (a) whether an E-Verify mandate applies only to employees within the state; (b) whether thresholds for numbers of employees refer only to employees within the state; (c) whether a law impacting state vendors applies to all vendors or only to a subset, e.g., service providers, government end-users; (d) the constitutionality of the statute or executive order; and (e) the sanction, if any, for violating the provision." [http://www. morganlewis.com/documents/50StateSurvey_StateImmigrationLaws_July 2012.pdf]

Below is a summary of relevant state laws as of May 2013. Readers are advised to keep a close watch on this mercurial aspect of immigration law and policy.

Alabama

In 2008, the legislature adopted two resolutions, the first stating that any person illegally voting or registering to vote can be charged with a "Class C" felony and the second establishing a Joint Interim Patriotic Immigration Commission. [National Conference of State Legislatures]

In 2005, the legislature adopted a resolution that urged private enterprises doing business in the state, with the assistance of the state Department of

Homeland Security, to become active participants in the state's Basic Pilot Program for controlling illegal immigration. [Bureau of National Affairs]

On May 18, 2012, Alabama Governor Robert Bentley signed into law House Bill 658, an immigration enforcement bill that made changes to the state's immigration law, HB 56, and which is similar to Arizona SB 1070. The employment provisions require that all employers enroll in E-Verify, and that all employers that are state or public contractors, grant recipients, and others that receive state incentives register with and use E-Verify. The contractor provision took effect on January 1, 2012, and the E-Verify rule took effect on April 1, 2012. There is no apparent sanction for failure to follow these provisions, but complying with the law will ensure employers safety from liability under Alabama law for knowingly employing an unauthorized worker.

Alaska

As of April 2013, there appears to be no current state immigration laws affecting employment eligibility verification.

Arizona

Arizona's E-Verify law (HB 2779) (see Q 12:70) became effective on January 1, 2008, with two key features. First, it authorizes the imposition of a business license penalty against any employer who knowingly or intentionally hires unauthorized employees after the effective date. For an employer's initial offense, its business license can be suspended. A further offense can result in permanent revocation of an employer's license to do business in Arizona. Second, the law requires all Arizona employers to enroll in the federal government's E-Verify program to confirm the work eligibility of all new hires. If the employer shows that it has verified the worker's status, a rebuttable presumption arises that the employer did not knowingly or intentionally employ an undocumented worker. Additional legislation, effective September 30, 2008, prohibits government entities from awarding a contract to any contractor or subcontractor that fails to use E-Verify.

The Arizona Legal Workers Act is the only act to have survived all legal challenges thus far. In December 2007, a federal judge considered whether or not the new law could withstand a typical constitutional challenge. [Arizona Contractors Ass'n v. Napolitano, 2007 WL 4570303 (D. Ariz. Dec. 21, 2007)] Since county prosecutors were charged with enforcing the law, the judge initially held that they were the proper defendants in the suit, and the plaintiffs were dismissed for lacking standing. The plaintiffs eventually returned to court, seeking to cure the standing issue and to obtain a temporary restraining order (TRO). The court ordered a hearing on the motion for a TRO, which would prevent enforcement of the law pending a final resolution of their constitutional challenge. The federal judge declined to issue the TRO.

In the following 12 months, the matter proceeded to hearing, and the district court dismissed the Arizona Attorney General for lack of subject matter jurisdiction, because he lacked the authority to bring enforcement actions. The court ruled in favor of the remaining defendants on the merits. It held that the act is not expressly preempted by federal immigration law because the act is a licensing law within the meaning of the federal statute's savings clause. It held that neither the act's sanction provisions nor the provision mandating use of the federal government's E-Verify identification system were inconsistent with federal policy, and thus they were not impliedly preempted. Finally, the court held that the act did not, on its face, violate due process because employers' due process rights were adequately protected.

In November 2009, the Maricopa County Attorney filed the first employer-sanctions suit under the act. The civil action alleged that the Scottsdale Art Factory's manager, Michelle Hardas, allegedly hired illegal labor by using a "subcontractor" which was in reality an employee who was not authorized to work in the United States. The complaint stated, "Hardas has used the provision of limited liability companies, designed to protect legitimate businesses, as a way of gaining an unfair economic advantage over legitimate businesses by continuing to hire employees who are not authorized to be employed in the United States."

The suit asked the court to order the defendant to fire all illegal aliens and comply with the law. It also prays for the penalty of a ten-day suspension of the company's license to do business. County Attorney Andrew Thomas stated, "This first employer-sanctions case is the capstone on our office's efforts to stop illegal immigration. The idea that state and local law enforcement can successfully and legally combat illegal immigration has moved from a provocative theory a few years ago to reality today." [http://www.mcaodocuments.com/press/20091118_a.pdf]

In May 2011, the Arizona statute achieved complete success, when the U.S. Supreme Court held that it affirmed the lower federal courts, which had held that the law was not preempted by the federal regulatory scheme. Writing for the majority, Chief Justice Roberts stated that federal immigration law

> expressly reserves to the States the authority to impose sanctions on employers hiring unauthorized workers, through licensing and similar laws. In exercising that authority, Arizona has taken the route least likely to cause tension with federal law. It uses the Federal Government's own definition of "unauthorized alien," it relies solely on the Federal Government's own determination of who is an unauthorized alien, and it requires Arizona employers to use the Federal Government's own system for checking employee status. If even this gives rise to impermissible conflicts with federal law, then there really is no way for the State to implement licensing sanctions, contrary to the express terms of the savings clause.
>
> Because Arizona's unauthorized alien employment law fits within the confines of IRCA's savings clause and does not conflict with federal immigration law, the judgment of the United States Court of Appeals for the Ninth Circuit is affirmed.

[Chamber of Commerce of the United States v. Whiting, 131 S. Ct. 1968 (2011)]

NOTE: However, as discussed in Q 12:70, above, Arizona's more recent law, involving police enforcement activities aimed at illegal aliens was, by and large, stricken down by the Supreme Court.

[*See* Arizona v. United States, 132 S. Ct. 2492 (2012).]

Arizona's SB 1070 (the Support Our Law and Safe Neighborhoods Act) was also reconsidered, and some portions of the law were upheld. Arguments were presented to the Supreme Court in April 2012, with many justices appearing to favor the law. SB 1070, one of the strictest and broadest anti-illegal immigration measures in recent history, contains several provisions that require police to check the immigration status of anyone stopped during a lawful stop when there is a reasonable suspicion that the person might be an illegal immigrant, and to detain those individuals who could not provide evidence of legal citizenship. Challenged soon after it became law, much of the law was blocked from taking effect. Former U.S. solicitor general Paul Clement argued that states have an "inherent police power" to enforce laws within their borders. The Supreme Court reached a decision in *Arizona v. U.S.* in June 2012. Three of four provisions were struck down: section 3, section 5(C), and section 6. In essence, this means that (1) illegals can still look for and work in Arizona without penalty and (2) Arizona cannot punish illegals with state penalties for breaking federal immigration laws and police cannot use "reasonable suspicion" to justify asking about legal status but can ask about legal status after a crime has been committed.   [http://articles.latimes.com/2011/dec/12/news/la-pn-arizona-immag-20111212]

Arkansas

A law (HB 1024), signed in February 2007, prohibits state agencies from entering into contracts with businesses that knowingly employ or contract with illegal immigrants. These certification requirements apply to all contractors seeking to enter into a contract with a state agency for professional services, technical services, or construction where the value of the contract is $25,000 or more.

California

As of April 2011, there appears to be no current state immigration laws affecting employment eligibility verification. There are, however, a growing number of county and municipal ordinances with respect to E-Verify. For example, Temecula, Lake Elsinore, and Menifee (in Riverside County) all have mandatory E-Verify rules, as does Lancaster in Los Angeles County.

In October 2010, Governor Jerry Brown signed a law that nullified local E-Verify ordinances, such as those previously in effect in several California counties. Under the statutes, E-Verify may be used only when required as a condition of receiving federal funds.

Colorado

A law (HB 1073), effective August 8, 2007, relates to the use of the Basic Pilot Program (now E-Verify) and prohibits a state agency or political subdivision from entering into a service contract with a contractor who knowingly employs an illegal alien to work on the contract or who knowingly contracts with a subcontractor who employs an illegal alien to perform work under the contract. [Society for Human Resource Management]

HB 1314 requires proof of lawful residence in the United States for receipt of public benefits.

HB 1343, signed in June 2006, prohibits state agencies from entering into contract agreements with contractors who knowingly employ illegal immigrants. Recent amendments require prospective contractors to verify legal work status of all new hires through either E-Verify or a new program administered by Colorado's Department of Labor and Employment (DOLE). If the contractor discovers an illegal alien is employed, the contractor must alert the state agency within three days. [National Conference of State Legislatures]

HB 1001, signed in July 2006, requires that contractors verify the work status of their employees before applying for economic development incentive awards. Contractors receiving awards and later found to employ unauthorized workers must repay the funds and will be ineligible for another award for five years. [National Conference of State Legislatures]

HB 1015, signed in July 2006, mandates that employers withhold 4.63 percent from the wages of an employee who lacks a valid Social Security number, a valid taxpayer ID number, or an IRS-issued taxpayer ID for nonresident aliens. [National Conference of State Legislatures]

HB 1017, also signed in July 2006, requires that all employers examine the work status of each new employee within 20 days of hire and retain proof that employees are in a legal work status. The state has the power to audit and verify the proof. Employers hiring unauthorized workers face a penalty of $5,000 for the first offense if found to be guilty of "reckless disregard" in submitting requested documents, or for submitting falsified documents. [National Conference of State Legislatures]

Connecticut

As of April 2013, there appear to be no state immigration laws affecting employment eligibility verification.

Delaware

A law (HB 147), signed in July 2007, limits the expiration date on a driver's license or identification card issued to a temporary foreign national to the period of time that he or she is authorized to remain in the United States.

SB 132 was signed in 2011. The bill provides that contractors receiving public funds shall comply with federal immigration law, specifically the Immigration Reform and Control Act, 1324a prohibiting the employment of illegal aliens. [Immigration Reform Law Institute]

District of Columbia

As of April 2013, there appear to be no state immigration laws affecting employment eligibility verification.

Florida

On February 5, 2010, Governor Rick Scott signed Executive Order 11-02, which requires that states agencies, contractors, and subcontractors use E-Verify. The Executive Order requires:

1. All agencies under the direction of the governor to verify the employment eligibility of all current and prospective agency employees through the U.S. Department of Homeland Security's E-Verify system.

2. All agencies under the direction of the governor to include, as a condition of all state contracts, an express requirement that contractors utilize the U.S. Department of Homeland Security's E-Verify system to confirm the employment eligibility of:

(a) All persons employed during the contract term by the contractor to perform employment duties within Florida; and

(b) All persons (including subcontractors) assigned by the contractor to perform work pursuant to the contract with the state agency.

3. Agencies not under the direction of the governor are encouraged to confirm the employment eligibility of their current and prospective employees using the E-Verify system, and to require contractors to use the E-Verify system to confirm the employment eligibility of their employees and subcontractors.

Aspects of the Executive Order are sure to draw a court challenge, in particular those provisions requiring the use of E-Verify for "current and prospective" state agency employees and those that suggest that contractors confirm the employment eligibility of "all persons and employers during the contract term." With the exception of certain federal contractors, E-Verify may only be used for new hires at this time. Soon, state agencies will most likely take steps to (a) amend existing contracts to include the new E-Verify requirement; and (b) ensure that the E-Verify requirement is part of future contracts.

Georgia

SB 529, a law made effective on July 1, 2007, called the Georgia Security & Immigration Compliance Act, requires certain public employers and any contractors and subcontractors of a public employee to register with E-Verify. Employers must withhold state income tax at a rate of 6 percent of payments to any individual who has failed to provide a valid taxpayer identification number. The law also provides an additional adjustment to taxable income corporations with respect to certain disallowances and disallows as a business expense compensation paid by a taxpayer to an unauthorized employee. [Society for Human Resource Management]

Furthermore, Georgia Governor Sonny Perdue signed into law an addendum to SB 529, HB 2, which went into effect on January 1, 2010. The new provisions included:

1. Public employers will be required to post their federally issued E-Verify user identification number and date of authorization to use E-Verify on their Web site.

2. Public officials will be required to verify that those who receive public benefits are in the United States legally, using the Systematic Alien Verification for Entitlements (SAVE) database; and

3. Georgia jails must make broader efforts to determine if a prisoner is legally present in the country. [http://www.ebiinc.com/everify-georgia.html#ixzz1JY alR2MJ]

SB 458 is moving quickly through state legislature, and contains provisions that would (1) ban undocumented students from all public universities and colleges in Georgia (even though they are already paying out-of-state tuition) and (2) prohibit state and local governments from accepting many foreign passports as proof of identification. However, provisions like these were blocked in regard to a similar Alabama law earlier this year. [http://www. huffingtonpost.com/azadeh-shahshahani/georgia-immigration-law_b_1374333. html]

Georgia HB 87, otherwise known as a "show me your papers" law, became effective in 2011. Many contended that the law's implementation ushered in discrimination, racial profiling, and anti-immigrant bigotry. [http://colorlines. com/archives/2012/03/alabama_and_georgias_anti-immigrant_laws_head_ back_to_court.html]

Hawaii

HB 1750, a law signed on May 2007, requires that all persons seeking employment with the government of the state must be citizens, nationals, or permanent resident aliens of the United States or eligible under federal law for unrestricted employment in the United States. [National Conference of State Legislatures]

Idaho

Governor Jim Risch issued an executive order on December 13, 2006, requiring that state agencies participate in the E-Verify system. Furthermore, all workers employed for the state through contractors must also be from companies that have been verified to have eligible employees. [National Conference of State Legislatures] Current law only applies to state government employees. [http://www.Stateline.org]

Illinois

On March 12, 2009, a federal court in Illinois struck down H 1744, signed in August 2007, a law that would have prohibited employers from enrolling in E-Verify until the SSA and DHS databases are able to make a determination within three days on 99 percent of the tentative non-confirmation notices issued to employers. [United States v. Illinois, C.D. Ill., No. 07-3261, Mar. 12, 2009] Because of this, Illinois enacted the Illinois Right to Privacy in the Workplace Act, which does not require the use of E-Verify, but does place additional statutory obligations on employers within the state that do use E-Verify. Effective January 1, 2010, employers must complete an attestation at the time of E-Verify enrollment (or by January 30, 2010, if already enrolled) verifying that responsible employees have completed the DHS E-Verify tutorial. Employers must also demonstrate that they have posted applicable E-Verify and Office of Special Counsel for Immigration-Related Unfair Employment Practices (OSC) notices at the workplace. In accordance with the DHS's Memorandum of Understanding (MOU) entered into by E-Verify participants, employers are prohibited from terminating employees prior to receiving a final non-confirmation of employment authorization from E-Verify and from using E-Verify to prescreen employment applicants. However, the Illinois law allows injured employees to file a claim against the employer in accordance with the Illinois Human Rights Act.

Indiana

As of April 2013, there appear to be no state immigration laws affecting employment eligibility verification.

Iowa

SF 562, a law effective as of July 1, 2007, provides that any business receiving economic development assistance from the state must be subject to contract provisions stating that all of its employees are either U.S. citizens who reside within the United States or are authorized to work in the United States pursuant to federal law, including legal resident aliens. [Immigration Business News]

Kansas

As of April 2013, there appear to be no state immigration laws affecting employment eligibility verification.

Kentucky

As of April 2013, there appear to be no state immigration laws affecting employment eligibility verification.

Louisiana

SB 753, a law signed in June 2006, allows any state agency or department to conduct an investigation of a contractor's hiring policies if the contractor is suspected of hiring unauthorized immigrants. The district attorney can issue an order to fire undocumented workers, and, if the contractor does not comply within 10 days of receiving notice, the contractor is subject to penalties of up to $10,000. This applies only to contractors employing more than 10 people. [National Conference of State Legislatures]

Maine

As of April 2013, there appear to be no state immigration laws affecting employment eligibility verification.

Maryland

As of April 2013, there appear to be no state immigration laws affecting employment eligibility verification.

Massachusetts

As of April 2013, there appear to be no state immigration laws affecting employment eligibility verification.

As of February 23, 2007, Massachusetts Executive Order (EO) 481 disallows the use of undocumented workers on state contracts and requires that executive branch contractors certify that they will not consciously use undocumented workers while working on the contract; will confirm the immigration status of all workers without engaging in unlawful discrimination; and will not knowingly or recklessly alter, falsify, or accept altered or falsified documents from any such worker. [Immigration Business News]

Michigan

SB 229, a law signed in October 2007, directs state agencies to consider the immigration and residency status of persons employed by a prospective contractor and whether the use of non-citizen workers would be detrimental to the state.

Minnesota

Governor Tim Pawlenty issued EO 08-01, an order that was published January 14, 2008 and took effect on January 29, 2008. The Minnesota Department of Administration is charged with enacting the executive order. Important provisions of EO 08-01 include a stipulation that all companies awarded state contracts in excess of $50,000 confirm the employment eligibility of newly hired employees through E-Verify; a stipulation that the Minnesota executive branch use E-Verify; and a requirement that all "recipients of business subsidies" validate that they are in compliance with federal immigration laws governing the rights of individuals to work in the United States. Exactly how the state plans to implement and enforce EO 08-01 is unclear; however, vendors and contractors of all tiers with state contracts in excess of $50,000 are required to execute a State of Minnesota—Immigration Status Certification, confirming the company's obligation to complete E-Verify employment verifications "for all newly hired employees in the United States who will perform work on behalf of the State of Minnesota."

Mississippi

On March 17, 2008, Governor Barbour signed Mississippi SB 2988 into law. The law requires E-Verify participation for Mississippi employers. State agencies and employers with at least 250 employees were required to be in compliance by July 1, 2008; employers with 100–249 employees were required to comply by

July 1, 2009; employers with 30–99 employees and all other employers must comply by July 1, 2010. Penalties include loss of public contracts for up to three years, loss of licenses for up to one year, or both. Furthermore, the law makes it a felony for unauthorized workers to consciously accept or perform work in the state and it creates a private cause of action for legal U.S. residents laid off and replaced by unauthorized workers. The statute's definition of *employee* limits the breadth of the law to those individuals hired to perform work within the state of Mississippi, and to limit applicability to those employers who report income paid to employed or contracted personnel in Mississippi.

Missouri

On July 7, 2008, Governor Matt Blunt signed into law the bill HB 1549, which makes it mandatory for all state agencies and local governments in Missouri, as well as private contractors with the state, to use E-Verify for newly hired workers. The bill was effective as of January 1, 2009. The law allows the state to terminate contracts with businesses that hire illegal workers, to withhold up to 25 percent of the value of contracts with these businesses, and to suspend them from further contracts with the state for up to three years. In the event of a second offense, a business can be permanently barred from doing business with the state. The law also requires suspension of local licenses, permits, and exemptions for employers who knowingly hire unlawful workers. Further provisions relate to limitations on public benefits, immigration training for state police, and prohibitions on misclassifying workers as independent contractors when the employer knew that the worker should be classified as an employee.

HB 2058, signed on June 11, 2008, requires that any applicant of a tax credit program who knowingly and directly employs unauthorized aliens has to forfeit any tax credits and must repay the amount of any tax credits claimed during the time when the applicant employed an unauthorized alien.

Montana

SB 214, a law signed in April 2007, revises laws relating to independent contractors and excludes from the definition of employment services performed by an alien having a residence in a foreign country coming temporarily to the United States to perform agricultural labor or services, or an alien who is a bona fide student and who seeks to enter the United States temporarily and solely for the purpose of pursuing a course of study. [National Conference of State Legislatures]

HB 111, a law signed in March 2007, revises unemployment insurance law and excludes from the definition of *employment* services performed by an alien having a residence in a foreign country coming temporarily to the United States to perform agricultural labor or services.

Nebraska

Nebraska Governor Dave Heineman signed into law LB 403 on April 8, 2009, a bill requiring public employers (i.e., state agencies and political subdivisions) and contractors to register with and use the E-Verify program to determine the employment eligibility of new hires starting October 1, 2009. Public contractors are defined as "any contractor or his or her subcontractor who is awarded a contract by a public employer for the physical performance of services within the state of Nebraska." The law also requires Nebraska's public employers to verify the legal status of all applicants trying to collect public benefits, prohibiting public employers from providing benefits to any person illegally present in the United States.

Nevada

In June 2007, Governor Gibbons signed the law AB 383 that dispenses administrative fines for those business licenses that are found to employ illegal aliens. This bill also requires the authentication of an employee's Social Security number. [Immigration Reform Law Institute]

New Hampshire

As of May 19, 2006, the bill HB 1278 increases the fine for violating certain labor laws that protect the jobs of citizens from $1,000 to $2,500 per day. Any person, partnership, agency, firm, or corporation violating any provision of RSA 275-A shall be subject to a civil penalty of up to $2,500 for each day of noncompliance, imposed by the labor commissioner in accordance with the procedures established in RSA 273:11-a. Any person aggrieved by the commissioner's assessment of such penalty may appeal in accordance with RSA 273:11-b. [http://www.lawlogix.com/i-9-and-e-verify-compliance/state-map]

New Jersey

As of April 2013, there appear to be no state immigration laws affecting employment eligibility verification.

New Mexico

As of April 2013, there appear to be no state immigration laws affecting employment eligibility verification.

New York

As of April 2013, there appear to be no state immigration laws affecting employment eligibility verification.

North Carolina

Enacted in 2006, SB 1523 requires all state agencies, offices, and universities to use E-Verify for employees hired on or after January 1, 2007, except for employees of local education agencies hired on or after March 1, 2007. As of May 2008, North Carolina had other pending bills related to employer-based and/or employee-based immigration law. [National Conference of State Legislatures]

Current law only applies to state government employees. [http://www.Stat eline.org]

North Dakota

As of April 2013, there appear to be no state immigration laws affecting employment eligibility verification.

Ohio

As of April 2013, there appear to be no state immigration laws affecting employment eligibility verification.

Oklahoma

The Oklahoma Taxpayer and Citizen Protection Act, signed in May 2007, requires state and local government agencies and private employers with government contracts to check the immigration status of applicants for employment by verifying Social Security numbers. A federal court in Oklahoma, which found that it is "substantially likely" that the law is preempted by federal immigration law, enjoined implementation of the law on June 4, 2008. The law originally required employers to withhold state income tax at a rate of 6 percent of the amount of compensation paid to an individual if the individual has failed to provide a valid Social Security number. It also required that public employers use the federal government's E-Verify system as of November 1, 2007 and that state contractors use E-Verify by July 1, 2008.

The injunction also stops implementation of a law that gives those American citizens fired from a job the right to sue their former employer if an illegal immigrant works for the company. The law would apply not only to those with government contracts, but to all companies in Oklahoma.

Oregon

SB 202, a law effective as of January 1, 2008, amends Oregon labor law to prohibit holders of farm labor contractor licenses from hiring "an alien not legally present or legally employable in the United States." It permits any person, including the Commissioner of the Bureau of Labor, to bring suit against any person to enjoin that person from using the services of a farm labor contractor who employs illegal aliens. The Commissioner may also impose civil fines against violators. [Immigration Business News]

Pennsylvania

On July 5, 2012, Governor Tom Corbett signed the Public Works Employment Verification Act (SB 637) into law. Under the act, effective January 1, 2013, all public works contractors and subcontractors are required to use E-Verify for all new hires. Subcontractors who are only suppliers are exempt from the law. A contractor must execute a certification of compliance as a prerequisite to being awarded a public works contract. The Department of General Services has the authority to investigate compliance based either on complaints or random inspections. Failure to comply can result in a sanction that ranges from a warning letter for an initial violation to debarment for egregious violations.

HB 2319, a law signed in May 2006 and known as the Prohibition of Illegal Alien Labor on Assisted Project Act, defines an "illegal alien" as one who violates federal immigration laws yet is a paid employee within the state. This bill bars the use of labor by illegal immigrants on projects financed by grants or loans from the state government. Appropriate federal authorities should be contacted if a contractor who intentionally employs illegal aliens accepts a state contract. [National Conference of State Legislatures]

Rhode Island

Governor Lincoln Chafee issued Executive Order 08-01 on November 5, 2011, reversing his predecessor's 2008 Executive Order regarding the mandatory use of E-Verify.

South Carolina

On June 4, 2008, Governor Sanford signed House Bill 4400, the South Carolina Illegal Immigration Reform Act. This legislation requires all South Carolina employers to use E-Verify. Large employers (more than 500 employees) were required to comply by January 2009; all other employers were required to comply by July 2010. For each employee not verified, employers could be fined between $100 and $1,000 and the violation would be reported to federal officials. Employers found to have knowingly hired illegal immigrants face suspension of their business license for 10–30 days for a first offense, and up to five years for a third offense. Licenses could be revoked in the most egregious cases. Further provisions include: creation of an information Web site and telephone call center for reporting suspected violations of immigration law, a prohibition on treating any wages paid to an undocumented worker as a deductible business expense, and the mandatory withholding of 7 percent of all compensation paid to an undocumented worker.

South Dakota

As of April 2013, there appear to be no state immigration laws affecting employment eligibility verification.

Tennessee

HB 111, a law enacted in June 2006, bars contractors from contracting with state agencies within one year of the discovery that the contractor employs illegal immigrants. [National Conference of State Legislatures]

SB 903, a law signed in May 2007, calls for the suspension of the business license of an employer for knowingly hiring an illegal alien. For a first violation, the company's license would be suspended until the illegal worker is terminated. For second and subsequent violations, the suspension would be for one year. As with the Arizona law, the employer's participation in the federal government's E-Verify program serves as a defense to a claim that the employer has violated the law. [Society for Human Resource Management]

HB 729, signed in January 2008, mandates that all Tennessee employers who knowingly hire illegal immigrants or fail to adequately check their status of illegal immigrants could have their business license suspended for one year. [http://www.lawlogix.com/i-9-and-e-verify-compliance/state-map]

The Tennessee Lawful Employment Act (SB 1669, HB 1378) was signed into law by Governor Bill Haslam on June 7, 2011. The law requires employers either to register with and use E-Verify or to request from an employee and retain a photocopy of one document from a list of acceptable documents in addition to fulfilling the federal Form I-9 requirements. The law is being phased in according to employer size:

- January 1, 2012: Employers with 500 + employees and government entities
- July 1, 2012: Employers with 200 to 499 employees
- January 1, 2013: Employers with 6 to 199 employees

The documents that might be accepted in lieu of E-Verify participation are extensive, but do not coincide completely with the federal Form I-9 list of acceptable documents. The documents should be copied prior to commencement of employment. The list includes:

- A valid Tennessee driver's license or photo identification license issued by the Department of Safety
- A valid driver's license or photo identification license issued by another state where the issuance requirements are at least as strict as those in Tennessee, as determined by the Department of Safety;
- An official birth certificate issued by a U.S. state, jurisdiction, or territory;
- A U.S. government–issued certified birth certificate;
- A valid, unexpired U.S. passport;
- A U.S. Certificate of Birth Abroad;
- A Consular Report of Birth Abroad of a citizen of the United States;
- A Certificate of Citizenship;
- A Certificate of Naturalization;
- A U.S. Citizen Identification Card; or
- Valid Alien Registration documentation or other proof of current immigration registration recognized by the DHS that contains the individual's complete legal name and current alien admission number or alien file number.

The law also requires that employers request and retain one of the documents listed above for any non-employee individual with whom it contracts for labor. Under federal law, employers are prohibited from contracting with individuals whom they know to be unauthorized to work, but there is no affirmative requirement that employment eligibility and identity be verified.

Texas

HB 1196, a law effective as of September 1, 2007, requires all Texas businesses that receive taxpayer-subsidized job creation grants and tax abatements to certify that they will not consciously employ undocumented workers. In the certified statement, businesses must declare that if convicted of engaging in a pattern or practice of violations of federal law governing unlawful employment of illegal workers, the business must repay the amount of the public subsidy with interest within 120 days of receiving notice of the violation, at a specified rate and term. The law also authorizes a public agency, local taxing jurisdiction, economic development corporation, or the Texas attorney general to bring a civil action to recover funds if a business hires workers not legally in the United States. The bill applies to a business's subsidiary, affiliate, or franchise, or any person with whom the business contracts. [Bureau of National Affairs]

Utah

Governor Herbert signed into law SB 251, "Verification of Employment Eligibility," on March 31, 2010. The law requires that private employers who employ 15 or more employees use a "status verification system" (either E-Verify or SSNVS) to verify the federal legal working status of every new hire. Foreign national employees in H-2A or H-2B nonimmigrant status are excluded. There is no sanction or liability for failure to comply with the law. Employers may register with the Utah Department of Commerce certifying their compliance with the law. The Department of Commerce is required to publish on the Internet a list of companies that have registered under the law.

Former Governor Huntsman signed into law Utah SB 81 on March 13, 2008, which was effective as of July 1, 2009. The law mandates that all public employers, as well as their contractors of any tier, use an electronic employment eligibility verification system (either E-Verify or SSNVS) to confirm employment eligibility. The requirement applies only to contracts entered into for the physical performance of services after July 1, 2009, and to employees hired after the law takes effect.

Vermont

As of April 2013, there appear to be no state immigration laws affecting employment eligibility verification.

Virginia

HB 1298 was signed into law and effective July 1, 2008. This law does not impose any additional employer obligations; however, it creates a state criminal offense for employers who fail to fulfill their existing employment eligibility verification obligations under existing federal immigration law. Furthermore, HB 926 was signed into law to authorize regulatory boards to revoke state licenses, registrations, certificates, or authorizations in the event of a state or federal conviction for knowingly employing an unlawful worker. Since July 1, 2008, all public contracts for goods and services have included a provision that the contractor does not and will not consciously employ an unauthorized worker during the performance of the contract. On April 11, 2010, Governor Bob McDonnell signed HB 737, a law that requires agencies of the Commonwealth to enroll in the E-Verify program by December 1, 2012, and to use the Program for each newly hired employee who will perform work within the Commonwealth.

Washington

As of April 2013, there appear to be no state immigration laws affecting employment eligibility verification.

West Virginia

SB 70, a law signed in April 2007, makes it unlawful for any employer to consciously employ an unauthorized worker. Employers are required to confirm a prospective employee's legal status or authorization to work. The law also calls for penalties for employing unauthorized workers, including fines, jail sentences, and the revocation of business licenses. [National Conference of State Legislatures]

Wisconsin

As of April 2013, there appear to be no state immigration laws affecting employment eligibility verification.

Wyoming

As of April 2013, there appear to be no state immigration laws affecting employment eligibility verification.

[Morgan Lewis, "50-State Survey of State Immigration Law Affecting Employers," January 2011, available at:http://www.morganlewis.com/documents/50StateSurvey_StateImmigrationLaws_July2012.pdf]

Chapter 13

Employment Termination

Employment termination is far and away the most likely source of employment litigation. No single action or procedure can prevent all wrongful discharge suits and employment discrimination charges, but the human resources professional or company executive who recognizes where the dangers lie can vastly increase the odds of preventing litigation or reducing exposure if litigation is filed. This chapter discusses recent cases addressing various issues involving the federal Worker Adjustment and Retraining Notification Act (WARN).

Termination Issues

Q 13:1   What is *termination for good cause*?

There is no single simple definition of what constitutes *good cause* for terminating an employee. Courts and arbitrators recognize that certain conduct is outside the realm of appropriate behavior and justifies discipline, sometimes including immediate termination or termination after prior discipline. Examples of good cause for immediate termination are intoxication on the job, fighting on the job, theft of employer property, and gross insubordination. Conduct that normally involves prior warning and discipline to constitute good cause for termination includes absenteeism and tardiness, repeated instances of negligent job performance, and repeated instances of inappropriate dress or language on the job.

Under collective bargaining agreements, arbitrators typically require the employer to prove that the employee violated a well-known and sensible rule. In the words of the leading commentators on labor arbitration, "Where suspension or discharge is a possible penalty for violation of a rule, the rule must be reasonable, consistently applied and enforced, and widely disseminated." [Elkouri & Elkouri, *How Arbitration Works*, 183 BNA (1991)] In the arbitration case, *Albertson's Inc. and UFCW Local 555* [115 L.R.R. L.A. 886], an arbitrator reinstated a woman who was fired for insubordination for refusing to stick out her tongue to show her manager that she was not wearing a tongue ring, which was a violation of company policy. [17 *Employment Discrimination Report (EDR)* (BNA) 28 (July 4, 2001)] Although the company adopted a no-tongue-ring rule after customer complaints, the arbitrator noted that the process of proving one's compliance with the process (sticking out one's tongue) was highly intrusive and previously unannounced. [17 *Employment Discrimination Report (EDR)* (BNA) 28 (July 4, 2001)] However, in the arbitration case, *Albertson's Inc. and IFCWU Local 324* [117 L.R.R. L.A. 39 (Apr. 29, 2002)], the company's fortunes changed, and the arbitrator upheld the discharge of an employee for repeated ethnic slurs, despite the lack of prior progressive discipline, reportedly holding that zero tolerance for violations of a harassment policy is justified. [19 *Employment Discrimination Report (EDR)* (BNA) 222 (Aug. 21, 2002)]

What is good cause depends on the circumstances. Some conduct is widely recognized as so wrong as to require termination of employment on the first offense. Even if the employer does not publicize rules against such conduct, an arbitrator or court will probably sustain a discharge based on egregious behavior. "Unless the conduct proscribed is so clearly wrong that it need not be specifically referenced, an arbitrator will usually refuse to sustain a discharge where management did not give an employee adequate notice." [Elkouri & Elkouri, at 183]

Even if the rules are thoroughly disseminated, many arbitrators and courts are reluctant to find a discharge to be based on good cause unless one of two factors are found: either the offense is so serious as to justify firing on the first occasion or the employee has received counseling on prior occasions but has nonetheless persisted in the inappropriate conduct. Some cases in which arbitrators have sustained a termination for just cause on the first offense are:

- *Burger Iron Co.* [92 B.N.A. L.A. 1100 (Arbitrator Dworkin 1987)]: Using and selling drugs on the company's premises.

- *OK Grocery Co.* [92 B.N.A. L.A. 441 (Arbitrator Stoltenberg 1989)]: Extortion of money from co-workers.

- *Eastern Air Lines* [90 B.N.A. L.A. 272 (Arbitrator Jedel 1987)]: Use of the company's e-mail system to send messages disparaging the company and its management (for further discussion of the e-mail issue, see Qs 5:26 and 6:29).

- *Safeway Stores* [89 B.N.A. L.A. 627 (Arbitrator Staudohar 1987)]: Negligent sale of alcoholic beverages to minors.

Q 13:2   Is good cause required for termination?

Under most collective bargaining agreements, cause is required for termination. In a non-union setting, at-will employees, by definition, can be terminated with or without cause. If its at-will status is successfully challenged, to avoid liability the employer must prove, however, that the employee was dismissed for good cause. Even if an employer's at-will status survives a challenge, the employer may still have to prove that it decided to terminate the employee for legitimate, non-discriminatory reasons. There are many theories under which employers may be liable to a discharged employee even if the employee was an at-will employee. These theories include the following:

1. *Discrimination.* The Americans with Disabilities Act, Age Discrimination in Employment Act (ADEA), Title VII, and companion state laws prohibit discharge on the basis of a protected category (i.e., age, race, color, sex, national origin, religion, pregnancy, and/or disability).

2. *Harassment.* It is a violation of Title VII for an employer to discharge an employer for refusal to submit to unwelcome sexual advances.

3. *Public Policy.* In what, in many states, are viewed as public policy exceptions to the at-will doctrines, it is a violation of law for an employer to discharge an employee for the employee's exercise of a right conferred by law (i.e., filing a workers' compensation claim), or to fire an employee for refusing to violate the law.

4. *Retaliation.* It is illegal under Title VII and many state laws for an employer to fire an employee for objecting to civil rights violations, or participating in a proceeding filed under Title VII.

To defend these cases, the employer typically tries to demonstrate that its decision was not based on illegal motive, but rather legitimate reasons. Therefore, to reduce risk and exposure to discrimination claims, employers—including employers at-will—should always be able to show good cause for termination.

Q 13:3   Do arbitrators consider an employee's prior work record in deciding whether there exists just cause for termination?

When an employer's work rules require progressive discipline, an arbitrator or court will almost always require that the procedure be faithfully followed, unless the employee's offense was so serious as to compel immediate termination on the first occurrence. Furthermore, if a collective bargaining agreement or a company's disciplinary policy states that prior discipline will be expunged from an employee's personnel file after a specified time period, an arbitrator will usually refuse to give any weight to infractions that should have been expunged when determining if the most recent infraction merited termination. [*See, e.g.,* Trailways Computer Transit, 92 B.N.A. L.A. 503 (Arbitrator Marcus 1989); Southern California Permanente Med. Group, 92 B.N.A. L.A. 41 (Arbitrator Richman 1989).]

On the other hand, an arbitrator might consider an employee's work record to determine if it merits mitigation of the punishment. [*See, e.g.*, Babcock & Wilcox Co., 90 B.N.A. L.A. 607 (Arbitrator Ruben 1987).] If a labor contract or employer work rules do not permit an arbitrator to do this, a decision reversing a termination based on past work history may be overturned in a court challenge. [*See, e.g.*, Georgia-Pacific Corp. v. Paperworkers Local 27, 864 F.2d 940 (1st Cir. 1988); Pennsylvania Liquor Control Bd. v. Independent State Stores Union, 553 A.2d 948 (Pa. 1989).]

By itself, an employee's length of service with the company usually will not save an employee who has committed a serious offense. For instance, in the case of an employee who was fired for engaging in sexual harassment, the arbitrator sustained the termination as just, despite the employee's 32 years with the company, because of the seriousness of the offense and the company's history of firing managers and non-supervisors for such conduct. [Schlage Lock Co., 88 B.N.A. L.A. 75 (Arbitrator Wyman 1986)]

Q 13:4   Can a single incident of inappropriate behavior be considered good cause for termination?

Certain serious violations of company policy or the law support immediate termination. Common examples include:

- Possession or use of alcohol or drugs on the job;
- Being under the influence of alcohol or drugs on the job;
- Fighting on the job;
- Stealing on the job;
- Committing a serious safety violation;
- Sexual harassment;
- Gross insubordination;
- Sabotage;
- Violence; and
- Theft of trade secrets.

Q 13:5   What is a *progressive disciplinary system*?

In a typical progressive disciplinary system, minor infractions of work rules (e.g., absenteeism, tardiness, and minor neglect of job duties) subject the employee to increasingly severe levels of discipline. Typical steps in a progressive discipline system are the following:

- Non-disciplinary counseling;
- First verbal warning;
- Second verbal warning;
- First written warning;
- Second written warning;

- Suspension of one to three days without pay; and
- Discharge from employment.

The number and types of these progressive disciplinary steps vary from company to company. Generally speaking, for an employee's disciplinary situation to move from one step to the next, the employee need not have violated the same work rule. On the other hand, corporations usually expunge employee work records after a certain period of time passes without incident (e.g., a rolling 12-month period).

Q 13:6   Should employers use progressive discipline?

The informal use of progressive discipline is typical when disciplining employees, particularly for minor infractions such as tardiness and absenteeism. Written disciplinary policies that mandate progressive levels of discipline, based on the type and number of infractions, have both benefits and detriments.

On the one hand, a written progressive discipline policy that mandates specific discipline for infractions provides certainty and also ensures that employees are treated in the same manner with respect to similar infractions. In that sense, such a policy is an effective defense to a discrimination claim arising from the discipline. The difficulty with a rigid, mandatory, progressive disciplinary policy is, however, that an employer must take disciplinary action against an employee even when it does not wish to do so. Progressive disciplinary systems are not flexible, and extenuating circumstances cannot be taken into account when meting out discipline.

In addition, if a progressive disciplinary system is mandatory and not written carefully, it may undermine the employer's at-will status. An employer cannot, for instance, maintain that it can terminate with or without cause, while its progressive disciplinary policy provides that employees will be disciplined or terminated only in accordance with a mandatory progressive disciplinary system. The advisability of such a system depends on whether the employer wants to maintain at-will status and whether it needs flexibility in meting out discipline. If an employer wants to maintain its at-will status, it should provide flexibility in its policy.

Moreover, rigid progressive discipline policies can, if not monitored, create compliance problems under federal law. For example, under the Family and Medical Leave Act (FMLA), employees are permitted 12 weeks of job-protected leave during any 12-month period, which leave can be taken intermittently if medically necessary. A no-fault progressive discipline attendance policy will often, if not carefully monitored, include occurrences that are protected time off under the FMLA. Any adverse employment action taken that depends on absences that qualify for FMLA protection would violate the FMLA.

Nonetheless, for a number of reasons utilization of progressive discipline is recommended as a general approach to disciplining employees. First, through a system of progressively more severe discipline for infractions, employees are made aware of their violations and provided with an opportunity to change this behavior. Second, if utilization of progressive discipline ultimately results in discharge, the personnel file should demonstrate the legitimate nature of the discharge, with copies of prior, less severe discipline noted in the file (i.e., written warnings, suspensions, and the like). Having this type of documentation goes a long way to defending claims of discrimination or other illegal motive in connection with the termination.

Q 13:7   What steps should be taken before discharging an employee?

An employer can take many practical steps to help guard against a lawsuit, including a critical review by the employer. Before termination, a company official other than the supervisor making the recommendation to terminate should critically review the situation with the supervisor and review the employee's personnel file, the relevant work rules, and any other pertinent information. This critical review should not be a "rubber-stamp" process, but rather, an objective analysis of the facts to evaluate the termination recommendation and spot and address potential problems. A critical review should address the following considerations:

- Look for a record of prior disciplinary action. If the recommendation for discharge is based on continuing problems, look for prior disciplinary measures that should have been documented in the personnel file. If not, find out why. A discharge based upon continuing problems for which there is no prior disciplinary record is risky and will be viewed with skepticism and suspicion if the decision is later challenged (e.g., has the employee recently complained of harassment by a co-worker or supervisor, been subjected to racial or sex-based slurs, or threatened to complain to the authorities about alleged illegal activity). Might any potential protected-class issue be involved (e.g., an older worker or replaced by a significantly younger worker or mass layoff breaking along race or sex lines)? If the answer to any of these is yes, the basis and rationale for the termination should be carefully scrutinized to ensure that legitimate non-discriminatory reasons can be demonstrated to defend against a potential future claim.

- Determine whether this employee is being treated consistently with other employees in similar circumstances. Is the discharge recommendation consistent with how the employer has treated other similarly situated employees for similar infractions? If not, defense in any future litigation based on wrongful discharge or discrimination will be difficult.

- Has the employee been confronted? There are always at least two sides to every story, and the employee must have the opportunity to explain his or her actions or conduct prior to termination.

- Look for specificity. The supervisor should be required to articulate specific reasons for the termination. Vague suggestions of poor attitude or failure to get along with co-workers or management should not be accepted.

- Consult with an employment lawyer before taking action. Most supervisors, once they have made a decision to recommend termination, like to move fast, fire the employee, and get the matter behind them. Discharging an employee is never pleasant, and the more time spent analyzing and brooding over the issue only works to extend this unpleasant situation in the eyes of management. Some supervisors even feel it is a mark of managerial competence and courage to mete out terminations quickly, once they have made their decisions, demonstrating their ability to handle difficult matters and make tough decisions.

The negative consequence attendant to poor discharge decisions can be astronomical. It goes without saying in our litigious society that a poor decision can saddle a company with tremendous liability as to attorneys' fees, costs, verdicts, and awards. Even if after a critical review by another company official the company agrees that discharge is appropriate, it is almost always advisable that the company take a deep breath and consult with an experienced employment lawyer before taking action. By having the matter analyzed by an attorney keenly focused on potential risks and exposure, the company will better understand the potential consequences of its actions. The attorney will be better suited to ask the right questions to spot potential problems and determine the relative risks and benefits involved.

Do not expect an answer from counsel during a short telephone conference conducted as the employee goes to the supervisor's office to be terminated. The attorney will undoubtedly want to review the personnel file, analyze the sufficiency of the evidence of infractions and the severity of the infractions, and see how the employer has disciplined other similarly situated employees for similar infractions. It may be that termination is premature, based on the existing records as reflected by the personnel file, and requires a written warning advising the employee that further infractions may lead to dismissal. It may be that the risks are too great (*i.e.*, the supervisor is complaining of vague attitude problems that have occurred for some time, the personnel file is void of discipline and the employee, just yesterday, threatened to call the local wage/hour board to report suspected violations of state wage/hour laws, which is a *prima facie* whistleblower's claim in most jurisdictions). Absent extremely unique circumstances, discharge decisions do not have to be made quickly. Even in situations that would prompt most to act quickly (i.e., fighting), the employer should suspend the employee, undertake an investigation of the incident, and arrive at a supportable decision after consulting with counsel. A useful checklist of these and other items to consider before discharge follows:

TERMINATION CHECK LIST

- Determine whether discharge is appropriate. Don't shoot from the hip. Is the employee salvageable or hard to replace? Has the employee been sufficiently warned?
- Determine the real reason for the discharge and say so. Poor performance is not the only acceptable reason.

- Review the documents in the employee's personnel file. Look for prior discipline. Look for employee evaluations inconsistent with termination. Reminder: There is no substitute for paper.

- Review protected classes. Look at race, color, age, sex, religion, national origin, and disability.

- Check how other similarly situated employees have been treated. Is the employee being replaced, and if so, by whom (review protected classes to spot issues regarding possible illegal motive)?

- Review recent events. Has the employee complained of anything lately?

- Be alert for evidence of retaliation, cover-up, or papering a file after the fact.

- Determine whether a severance agreement and release is appropriate.

- Plan the discharge and stick with it. Who will be there? What will be said? Do not let the departing employee bait you into an argument or put you on the defensive.

- Document your investigation and what was done and said at the time of termination.

- Determine how you want to handle a claim for unemployment compensation.

Q 13:8   What guidelines can employers follow to avoid employment-related suits?

The following list is a set of practical guidelines developed by Thomas L. Boyer, Esq., based on his experience as a labor-management attorney:

- There is no substitute for paper. With respect to prior discipline, if it isn't in writing, it doesn't exist. In most jurisdictions, absent extremely unique circumstances, terminating an employee without prior written discipline is almost never advisable.

- Treat them all alike—consistency is everything. Treating similar situations similarly is the basis for defending discrimination and wrongful-discharge claims.

- Never make promises. Employers can endeavor, attempt and hope, but they should never promise. Promises may lead to enforceable obligations that, if violated, lead to lawsuits.

- Employees are not expected to know anything that management did not tell them. Work rules should alert employees of what is expected of them, and discipline should always occur when warranted. Review your work rules to ensure they are up to date.

- No question or suggestion is so stupid that it does not deserve a response. Employers should demonstrate respect for their employees. Major litigation or union organizing efforts sometimes originate from the most minor of complaints (e.g., the condition of the restroom).

- Employees need to believe that what they do is important. Everybody needs to be needed; every job is deserving of respect.

- Management must show an interest in employees' jobs. Aloofness breeds dislike and distrust; taking a sincere interest in the work employees do helps combat the "we/them" attitude prevalent in many industries.

- If it does not cost much, do it. Employers should not be quick to say "no" to employee suggestions. Instead of responding to employee requests by asking "why," the company should ask "why not." If the benefit of a request seems nebulous (e.g., a company picnic) but the cost is relatively low, both from a liability and cost standpoint, the company should do it.

In most situations, probably the most important guideline involves proper documentation of discipline. Whether employers like it or not, the employee's personnel file will be the foundation against which the employer's actions will be judged if the termination is second guessed by a judge, arbitrator, or jury. A termination unsupported by a prior written warning in the personnel file is risky, except in extreme situations. Most terminations involve continual and repeated violations of company policies and procedures. Although no law requires it, most people will question the legitimacy of the termination if the employee was not previously informed in writing that his or her job was in jeopardy. Verbal warnings of this kind are insufficient and may unnecessarily expose the company to liability and expense. As discussed in chapters 2 and 4, even an at-will employer can still be found liable under federal or state discrimination law, whistleblower's protection laws, violations in public policy, and the like. The ability to articulate, with supporting documentation, the legitimacy of the decision goes a long way to reducing the risk of and exposure to employee litigation.

Q 13:9 What type of disciplinary documentation should an employer expect in a personnel file?

If a supervisor is complaining about repeated and continuous infractions, the employer should expect to see written discipline for the prior infractions. This discipline should take the form of written corroboration that the prior discipline has been effectuated, including an acknowledgment by the employee that the discipline occurred, even if the employee did not agree. Memos to the personnel file by a supervisor without the employee's acknowledgment are questionable, and allow the employee to claim at a later time that the discipline never occurred. In addition, if annual evaluations are conducted, the written evaluations should be reviewed to assess their consistency with any disciplinary documentation in the file.

Q 13:10 Should an employer consider using employment contracts with arbitration clauses to avoid employment-related lawsuits?

Since the U.S. Supreme Court's decision in *Circuit City Stores, Inc. v. Adams* [532 U.S. 105 (2001)], the prospect of permitting employers to rely on mandatory pre-dispute arbitration contracts to force arbitration and circumvent discrimination suits in court is now a reality. Whether to utilize arbitration as a vehicle to resolve disputes, as opposed to redress in court, is a decision that involves analysis of the many differences between arbitration and judicial proceedings. On one hand, arbitration is generally viewed as less formal, less time-consuming, less costly, and reduces the risk of runaway jury verdicts. On the other hand, the process may lend itself to more claims with individuals filing on their own, without benefit of counsel.

Q 13:11　Are all pre-dispute arbitration agreements enforceable?

The Federal Arbitration Act (FAA) provides that pre-dispute arbitration agreements, "shall be valid, irrevocable and enforceable save upon such grounds as exist at law or in equity for the revocation of any contract." [9 U.S.C. § 2] The U.S. Supreme Court has stated that the purpose of the FAA is, "to reverse the long-standing judicial hostility toward arbitration agreements . . . and to place [arbitration agreements] upon the same footing as other contracts." [Green Tree Financial Corp., Ala. v. Randolph, 531 U.S. 17, 89 (2000) (quoting Gilmer v. Interstate/Johnson Lane Corp., 500 U.S. 20, 24 (1991))] Accordingly, courts have adopted a presumption in favor of arbitration and a party seeking to invalidate an arbitration agreement generally bears the burden of establishing its invalidity. [*See* Gilmer, 500 U.S. at 26.]

In *Carter v. Countrywide Credit Industries, Inc.* [326 F.3d 294 (5th Cir. 2004)], employees seeking to pursue FLSA claims in court alleged that arbitration agreements executed in the application process were both procedurally and substantively unconscionable. Procedurally, the employees claimed that the agreement, which was offered to them by the company during the application phase, was essentially coerced from the employees lest they not obtain a job unless they signed the agreement. The employees also claimed that the agreement was substantively unconscionable in that it contained a forum selection provision clause and a requirement that the employees share the costs of the arbitration.

In reviewing the issues with respect to procedural unconscionability and forum selection, the court concluded that the agreements were not coerced and that the forum selection agreed to was reasonable and not unconscionably invalid. With respect to the fee-splitting issue, although there are many courts that have struck down similar agreements based on an individual's inability to pay his or her costs under the arbitration agreement [*see, e.g.,* Livingston v. Associates Fin., Inc., 339 F.3d 553, 557 (7th Cir. 2003)], the court concluded that the issue was rendered moot based upon the company's agreement to waive the fee-splitting portion of the arbitration agreement and bear all the costs of arbitration. Although a similar agreement was held unconscionable under California law in *Ferguson v. Countrywide Credit Industries, Inc.* [298 F.3d 778 (9th Cir. 2002)], the Fifth Circuit concluded that, based on its analysis and the company's agreement to pay the arbitration costs, that the arbitration agreement at issue was enforceable.

In *Baldeo v. Darden Restaurants, Inc.* [2005 WL 44703 (E.D.N.Y. Jan. 11, 2005)], the court found that an arbitration agreement that provided for arbitration of "claims under state and federal law relating to harassment or discrimination, as well as other employment-related claims" but did not apparently cover issues like performance reviews, benefit programs, pay rates and the like was not ambiguous, and required the arbitration of the plaintiff's discrimination case under New York law.

Although pre-dispute arbitration agreements have long been held to apply to Title VII and other employment statutes requiring that cases be brought in arbitration rather than courts, under the Employee Polygraph Protection Act (EPPA), the statute specifically provides that "the rights and procedures provided by [the EPPA] may not be waived by contract or otherwise . . . " [29 U.S.C. § 2005(d)], and as such, will not require an employee who claims violation of the EPPA to arbitrate those claims under a contract signed with the employer. [Harmon v. CB Squared Servs. Inc., 2009 WL 234982 (E.D. Va. Jan. 30, 2009)]

Q 13:12   What reasonable termination procedures should employers follow?

The following procedures applicable to both disciplinary and non-disciplinary terminations are generally acknowledged in the personnel management area:

- Termination should take place early in the week. This practice is considered preferable to the late Friday discharge, popular some time ago. It affords the employee time to seek professional and personal support, as opposed to brooding over the termination over a weekend.

- Termination should be discussed face-to-face and privately. Notification by mail or memorandum denies the employee a chance to raise questions regarding the termination. It may also add to the employee's stress, increase the employee's anger, and threaten his or her self-esteem.

- The employer should explain the reason for termination. Even an at-will employer should articulate the reasons for termination. Many grounds for litigation (e.g., discrimination) are applicable to the at-will employer, and failure to provide a reason suggests that the employer had something to hide, such as illegal discrimination.

- The reasons for termination should be properly documented in the employee's personnel file.

- The employer should allow the employee to remove personal items from a desk, locker, and work area without embarrassment. The employer concerned about theft should "assist" the employee in retrieving and removing personal items.

- Only appropriate co-workers or customers should be told of the termination, and they should hear it directly from the proper management source.

- The employer may consider providing discretionary severance benefits to help reduce the pressure and anxiety the employee will feel regarding finances; however, more than nominal severance should always be conditioned upon the employee signing a release or waiver of claims.

- Outplacement assistance may be appropriate, depending on the reasons for discharge and the size of the employer.

- An employer should generally provide only title held and dates of employment when giving references.

- Consider potential security issues. If the employer has a legitimate basis to believe that the discharge may involve issues of security, either as to violence or the stealing of property or confidential information, the employer should undertake reasonable and prudent steps to diminish the threat. Alerting security or the local police department in advance, ensuring the discharged employee has no access to confidential materials on his or her way out of the facility, and other measures may be reasonable under the circumstances; however, if these concerns are motivated by prejudice and paranoia, instituting such measures can be powerful evidence of bias or prejudice to support a later claim of discrimination or wrongful discharge. If the employer goes overboard, the actions, in and of themselves, may support claims of defamation, intentional infliction of emotional distress, or the like.

Q 13:13   How should the company handle a terminated employee who refuses to leave the premises?

Upon termination, the employee's emotions may take over, and out of anger or resentment, the employee may refuse to leave, or he or she may report the next morning as if nothing had happened. Such employees may be sincerely distraught, disoriented or confused, or they may be faking the whole thing. The first thing the employer should remember is that the roles of management and security are not that of amateur psychologist. If a lawsuit ensues from mistreatment or defamation of the discharged employee, a jury will hear only the objective manifestations of the employee's confusion or emotional distress and the objective responses of the company's representatives. Therefore, every such situation should be treated as if the employee's behavior is authentic.

The employee who refuses to vacate the workplace after being told of the termination and the requirement to leave should be given a written notice, which should be read aloud before being handed over to the fired worker. Then, unless the employer fears theft or sabotage of company property, it should give the employee a reasonable amount of time to gather up personal possessions, regain emotional control, and prepare to leave the premises in quiet dignity. Even if theft or sabotage are concerns, the employee can be accorded reasonable time, but in the presence of a security guard or manager.

The written notice that is read and handed to the employee should also state that no company property can be taken or used by the employee. In other words, not only must all handbooks, manuals, printouts, and other company property be left behind, but they cannot be duplicated on the company's copy machine. Company keys and credit cards must be turned over to the human resources department or to security. If the employee fills a carton or briefcase with personal items, either the process should be observed by a company representative or the containers should be examined before the employee leaves the premises.

Finally, the written notice that is read aloud to the employee should contain a warning that, if the employee fails to leave the premises by the required deadline, he or she will be forcibly escorted by the company's own security personnel or the local police, if the company does not have appropriately trained and qualified security professionals.

The employee who refuses to vacate the premises, stating, for example, "You have no right to fire me," should be isolated from other employees, except for security and management personnel assigned to accomplish an efficient but dignified removal of the employee from the premises. The recalcitrant dischargee may believe that the employment contract, labor agreement, or employee handbook prevents the termination of employment. The individual may also think that leaving the premises voluntarily somehow prejudices his or her legal right to challenge the removal later. This might occur if the employee has said, "I quit," then thought better of it, while management has taken the employee literally and proceeded with the termination process. Alternatively, the dischargee may want to put on a show for as many witnesses as possible to bolster a later claim of defamation or emotional distress. In either situation, removing the employee's secretary from the area, disconnecting the employee's extension from the phone system, and otherwise isolating the dischargee should make the dischargee feel his or her efforts are futile, even foolish.

At each step in the removal process, the employee should be advised verbally of exactly what the employer's representatives intend to do. Under no circumstances should any company representative touch the employee.

If the employee does not leave when the deadline arrives, the local police should be summoned to forcibly remove or arrest him or her. Even if the employer has first-rate security personnel and even though the police should be used only as a last resort, employers should almost always call them when physical contact seems to be necessary.

Once the recalcitrant employee is off the premises, the employer should alter all its access codes. It should also consider changing some locks, even though the employee has surrendered a set of company keys. Security personnel should be told that the employee is not welcome on the premises, and the dischargee should not be permitted to return, except by prior appointment with appropriate personnel, who should be summoned to meet the employee on arrival and be required to stay with him or her throughout the return visit. Meeting with employees who were particularly recalcitrant about vacating the premises should be held at an off-site, neutral location. This advice also applies to employees guilty of dishonest behavior that was discovered before or after the discharge.

Q 13:14   Does "I quit" really mean "I quit"?

One reason an employee may refuse to leave the company's premises after being terminated or may report to work the next day is that the employee said "I quit" but did not mean it or changed his or her mind later. The employee may even have stormed out of the building, cleaned out his or her locker, punched the time card, or otherwise indicated that the "quit" was voluntary and intended. The employee may even have meant it at the moment but reconsidered later, during a long night or on awaking to the harsh light of unemployment.

Consequently, the employee's behavior and the context of the resignation are important facts in many situations. Words spoken by the employee in anger or under duress are less likely to count as evidence of a genuine intent to quit than words spoken calmly in circumstances that are not charged with confrontation or emotion. Indicia of a genuine intent to quit include an employee:

- Following the procedure of the human resources department;
- Cleaning out his or her office, desk, or locker;
- Turning in keys and company property;
- Filling out forms to receive pension contributions; and
- Leaving the job before end of the shift.

Even if the employee clearly does quit, the employer may still be legally determined to have discharged the employee under the constructive discharge doctrine. Under the doctrine, if the circumstances are so intolerable that a reasonable person would be compelled to resign, the resignation amounts to a constructive discharge in most jurisdictions.

Q 13:15   Can an employee who quits still sue the employer?

Many employers believe that if a problem employee quits or resigns, they have somehow "dodged the bullet" and they have no risk of being sued. Although this is usually the case where resignation is truly voluntary, numerous situations exist under which an employee quits but can still pursue claims against the employer.

Constructive discharge is a common law theory under which courts will treat a quit as a discharge by the employer. If the employer has made working conditions so intolerable that an ordinary reasonable person would be compelled to quit employment, courts will treat the situation as a termination by the employer; however, the ability to demonstrate constructive discharge is not sufficient in and of itself to support a cause of action. Employees can be fired without liability under state or federal law, and treating a resignation as a constructive discharge is not a cause of action. If the constructive discharge connects up with claims of discrimination, retaliation, or wrongful discharge in violation of an express or implied contract, the employee can pursue the employer and seek damages for lost wages and benefits, together with emotional damages and other relief for non-contractual violations under state and federal law.

In addition, even if the quit is voluntary in a true sense, and not sufficient for purposes of demonstrating constructive discharge, other claims can still be maintained with regard to the employee's tenure. Claims for denial of promotion, wrongful demotion, harassment, and the like may relate to events prior to quitting and may form the basis for future claims. Although the wage loss component for damages will be limited in many circumstances because resignation was voluntary, the claim itself may still be viable. For example, assume an employee has been exposed to a hostile work environment and the company has failed to take action despite complaints to management. Even if the employee voluntarily quits for reasons having nothing to do with harassment (e.g., relocation because of marriage), the employee would still have the right to pursue the employer for harassment and claim emotional damages for the illegal activity, despite having no apparent wage loss damages.

Q 13:16   Can an employer lock a terminated employee's desk drawers, files, and office?

When the employee's office, desk, and file cabinets are all the property of the company, the company certainly has the legal right to secure this property at any time. When there exists a risk that the employee, having been informed of his or her termination, will remove company property (e.g., confidential information in the nature of trade secrets or customer information), the employer is well-advised to secure its property from the employee; however, several cautionary notes are in order:

- The employer must be careful that such actions, which may be viewed by the terminated employee's co-workers, do not constructively defame the terminated employee.
- The employee has the right to retrieve personal property that may be in the office, file cabinets, or desk drawers.
- To the extent that the termination can be carried out in a civil manner without unnecessarily destroying whatever goodwill may remain between the employer and employee, it should be. Subjecting the employee to the annoyance and humiliation of locking his or her office, desk drawers, and file cabinets does not further that end.

For all of these reasons, the best human resources practice is for the director of security, the terminated employee's immediate supervisor, or the human resources director to accompany the employee following the termination meeting to his or her office, where they can both examine the contents of the desk and file cabinets, sorting out company property from personal property. In this way, the employee can leave the premises with all personal possessions and a modicum of personal dignity as well.

With respect to public employees, the restrictions in the Bill of Rights (and perhaps the relevant state constitution) against unlawful searches and seizures may apply in these circumstances. Under present Supreme Court doctrine, an individual may not be subjected to unreasonable search and seizure; therefore, when an employee has a reasonable expectation of privacy, it is a violation of that employee's constitutional rights to engage in a search and seizure even on the employer's premises. What is reasonable varies from employer to employer and facility to facility. For example, depending upon the personnel practices of a particular public employer, a terminated employee may reasonably expect privacy with respect to his or her locked desk drawers or personal automobile but not with respect to file cabinets in or around the office.

Severance and Release Agreements

Q 13:17   Can an employee be required to sign an agreement not to sue as a condition of receiving severance benefits?

To be enforceable, any release of claims must be supported by valid consideration. This means, for example, that the employer cannot condition the receipt of benefits to which the employee is already legally entitled on the execution of a release. Thus, if an employee has vested pension rights protected by ERISA, a release conditioning receipt of those benefits on its execution would not only be unenforceable by law but might constitute a violation of the Act. In the case of severance payments, if they are given to all employees pursuant to a severance plan or policy or an employee handbook, then singling out some employees and conditioning their receipt of these benefits on their signing a release would not result in an enforceable waiver and release agreement. On the other hand, an employer with no severance policy can require the execution of a release as a condition of severance. To be enforceable, a release of claims and covenant not to sue must be knowingly and voluntarily signed. Generally, this would mean that the release should be understandable, written in plain English, should specify what rights the employee is waiving and releasing (specific discrimination status should be listed), and the employee should be given a reasonable opportunity to consider the agreement. For workers 40 or older, far more specific requirements are necessary under federal law in order to release claims under the ADEA (see Q 13:18).

Q 13:18   What is meant by a *knowing and voluntary release of claims*?

Although employers would prefer it to be otherwise, a release that is not knowingly and voluntarily entered into is usually not enforceable. Generally, a release is considered knowingly and voluntarily executed when the employee clearly understands that he or she is releasing certain specific causes of action that may otherwise be available to him or her after termination and when the employee signs this release without coercion or duress. Federal courts traditionally have tended to require that statutes such as Title VII be specifically identified in the language of the release. Indeed, the Older Workers Benefit Protection Act (OWBPA) makes this a statutory requirement with respect to the ADEA. It also requires that a valid release of rights under the ADEA provide the employee a period of time to consider the release, consult an attorney, and revoke the release after execution. (See Q 13:19 for the requirements of the

OWBPA.) In *Cole v. Gaming Entertainment, L.L.C.* [199 F. Supp. 2d 208 (D. Del. 2002)], the court held that a release that contained most of the language necessary to make for a knowing and voluntary waiver was nonetheless insufficient because the supervisors who presented the release to the employee told the employee that it must be signed and returned quickly or the severance would not be paid, despite the fact that the release provided otherwise. [18 *Employment Discrimination Report (EDR)* (BNA) 640 (May 29, 2002)] Nonetheless, if the release comports with the OWBPA, an employee will not be able to maintain that the release was not knowingly or voluntarily entered into merely because the employee felt pressured to sign a release. In *O'Neill v. The New York Times Co.* [2004 WL 1047941 (D. Mass. May 7, 2004)], a journalist claimed that a release that was signed in conjunction with his acceptance of an early retirement program was void because he felt that he had "no choice" but to accept it. Noting, however, that employees who did not accept the early retirement program nonetheless kept their jobs, the court concluded that there was no evidence that the employee's signature on the release was "involuntary." In *Ridinger v. Dow Jones & Co., Inc.* [651 F.3d 309 (2d Cir. 2011)], an individual who had signed a release with his prior employer claimed that it was written in a manner that could not be understood by the average employee because although, on the one hand, language in the release provided that the release was a waiver of any and all claims under the ADEA, language also provided that the waiver and release did not apply to claims under the ADEA after the date the employee signed the agreement. The court in interpreting the language found no inconsistency, as the release and waiver language related to claims through the date the agreement was signed, and as such, found that it was not void for lack of clarity.

Q 13:19 What are the general elements of an enforceable release of claims and the requirements of OWPBA to release federal age claims?

At a bare minimum, an enforceable release of claims should:

- Be written plainly, in understandable language;
- Identify the rights that the employee is waiving, with particular reference to federal and state civil rights statutes;
- Identify who is being released (e.g., the employer, its employees, officers, or stockholders);
- Identify the consideration for the release; and
- Allow the employee sufficient time to consider the release before signing.

Releases are legal documents and to be enforceable they must be supported by consideration. Although the amount of consideration required is not specified by law, adequate consideration in return for the release must be more than that to which the employee is otherwise entitled under the employer's policies. If an employer merely offers the employee paid vacation time, which is already required in accordance with employer policies and relevant law, the vacation pay will not be sufficient consideration for purposes of binding the release.

In addition, the OWBPA [29 U.S.C. § 626(f)] specifies certain requirements that the release must meet in order to be an enforceable release of age claims under the ADEA.

The following seven requirements are necessary for a valid waiver under the ADEA:

- The waiver of ADEA claims must be part of an overall agreement between the employer and the employee, written in plain, everyday English.

- The waiver section of the agreement must specifically refer to rights or claims arising under the ADEA, not just make a general reference to discrimination laws or federal laws or the like.

- The waiver cannot be prospective—that is, it cannot seek to waive rights or a cause of action that may arise because of the company's actions or behavior after the date the agreement is signed.

- The employee must receive good consideration (*i.e.*, a thing of value) for executing the waiver, and that consideration must be given by the company in addition to anything of value (*e.g.*, severance benefits under a pre-existing severance policy) that the employee would have been entitled to without signing the waiver.

- The employee must be told in writing that he or she should consult an attorney before executing the agreement.

- The employee must be given reasonable time in which to decide whether to execute the wavier. This reasonable time is 21 days, provided the release is only offered to one person.

- The employee must be notified that he or she is given seven days to revoke the agreement after it is signed by the employee.

If the release is offered to more than one person, the OWBPA contains additional requirements that should be reviewed carefully with counsel. Additional time—45 days as opposed to 21 days—must be allotted for reviewing the release, and the employer must provide information to the employees of the ages and job positions of those who have been provided releases, together with those who have not, within all units, groups, or classifications that were considered. This information enables the employee to determine whether age claims may arise in connection with the circumstances under which the release is offered by the employer. The information that must be provided is contained in section 7(f)(1)(H) of the ADEA [19 U.S.C. § 626(f)] and requires the following:

- Written information describing the class, unit, or group covered by the program, eligibility factors, and any time limits applicable to the program; and

- The job title and ages of all individuals selected or eligible for the program, and the same information regarding all individuals who were not selected or eligible for the program within the same classification or unit.

Determination of the "unit" for purposes of determining how much information needs to be provided has been clarified by the EEOC in its regulations. [29 C.F.R. § 1625] Essentially, the designation refers to those classes, units, job categories, plants, departments, or other groups that were considered by the employer. If the methodology was 10 percent reduction in X Division, Division X would be the unit for purposes of providing information. If it was 10 percent reduction in Y job classification, all employees in Y job classification would be the unit.

The EEOC regulations also describe how information regarding job classifications and the ages of the persons being terminated should be presented. The regulations specifically provide that "the use of age bands broader than one year (such as 'age 20–30') are not acceptable." [29 C.F.R. § 1625.22(f)(4)(ii)] The guidelines also provide that if an agreement does not meet all of the requirements of the federal age discrimination law it will not be valid. [*See* Waiver of Rights and Claims Under the Age Discrimination in Employment Act (ADEA), 29 C.F.R. § 1625.22.]

The requirements of the OWBPA must be diligently followed in order to release an age claim under the ADEA. In *Kaminski v. CoreStates Financial Corp.* [1998 U.S. Dist. LEXIS 18579 (E.D. Pa. Nov. 17, 1998)], an employee had signed a release that, according to the language, was a waiver of all claims under state and federal law and specifically identified certain federal and state laws, but not the ADEA. The court found that the release was not valid under the ADEA, because it did not list the ADEA specifically. Although the release stated it was a release of all state and federal claims, it was not. This was a material misrepresentation of fact upon which the employee claims she relied in not pursuing an ADEA claim after she signed the release, thereby equitably tolling the 300-day statute of limitations for ADEA claims. [*See* 11 *Employment Discrimination Report (EDR)* (BNA) 826 (Dec. 16, 1998).]

If the release complies with the OWBPA, it will be enforceable, even if the employee claims that the release was not knowingly or voluntarily entered into. In *Kendrick v. K-Mart Corp.* [238 F.3d 421 (6th Cir. 2000)], an employee was given a release that complied with the OWBPA, providing him, among other things, 45 days to consider and 7 days to revoke after he signed. The employee claimed that he never read it and that he was told by his manager to sign it the same day (which he did); nonetheless, the Sixth Circuit upheld the district court's ruling that the release was in compliance and therefore enforceable. [*See* discussion of the lower court's decision in 14 *Employment Discrimination Report (EDR)* (BNA) 354 (Mar. 15, 2000).] However, if the employer makes representations concerning the release which would pressure the employee into signing without adequate time for consideration, the court may determine that such conduct makes the release unenforceable because not knowingly or voluntarily entered into. (See discussion of *Cole* decision in Q 13:18.)

Q 13:20   What is an example of a severance/release agreement?

Although these agreements vary greatly depending upon state law and the facts in any one circumstance, below is a general format.

SEVERANCE AND RELEASE AGREEMENT

This Severance and Release Agreement (Agreement) is entered into between XYZ, Inc. (Employer) and _____ (Employee).

Employer is selling its business and operations and, as additional compensation to those employees permanently laid-off by Employer on or about _____ as a result of the sale of Employer's business and operations and to resolve any and all complaints or disputes between Employer and Employee related to Employee's employment or separation of employment from Employer, Employer and Employee enter into the following Agreement:

Payment. If Employee returns a signed copy of this Agreement to Employer, Employer will provide Employee a lump sum payment in the amount of $ _____ minus applicable federal, state, and/or local tax withholdings, after the expiration of the 7-day revocation period explained in Paragraph 9 of this Agreement referenced below.

Employee understands that the foregoing is all Employee is entitled to receive from Employer except for pension or 401(k) benefits to which Employee may be entitled. Employee will receive no further wage, vacation, commission, bonus, or other similar payments from Employer.

Employee further agrees that the payments and other benefits described above are more than Employer is required to provide under its regular policies and procedures.

Complete Release. Employee agrees to release Employer, any related companies, and the employees, officers, and directors of any of them from any and all claims or demands Employee may have based on Employee's employment with Employer or separation from that employment. This includes, without limitation, a release of any rights or claims Employee may have under the Age Discrimination in Employment Act, which prohibits age discrimination in employment; Title VII of the Civil Rights Act of 1964, as amended by the Civil Rights Act of 1991, which prohibits discrimination in employment based on race, color, national origin, religion, or sex; the Americans with Disabilities Act and Michigan's Persons With Disabilities Civil Rights Act, which prohibit discrimination against individuals with disabilities; the Elliott-Larsen Civil Rights Act, which prohibits discrimination based on race, color, religion, national origin, age, sex, marital status, height, and weight; and any other applicable federal, state, or local laws or regulations. The release also includes a release by Employee of any claims for wrongful discharge or any related tort or other actions. This Release covers both claims that Employee knows about and those he or she may not know about. Notwithstanding anything in this Agreement to the contrary, this Agreement is not intended to waive any right which, as a matter of public policy and/or law, cannot be waived by this Agreement.

No Future Lawsuits or Claims. Employee promises never to file a lawsuit or administrative claim or otherwise assert any claims that are released in Paragraph 2 of this Agreement.

Confidentiality. Employee agrees to keep the promises and agreements of this Agreement confidential. Specifically, Employee promises never to publicize, communicate, or otherwise make public the terms of this Agreement, except as necessary to seek professional advice concerning this Agreement.

Non-Admission of Liability. By entering into this Agreement, Employer does not admit that it has done anything wrong.

Consequences of Employee Violation of Promises. If Employee breaks his or her promise in Paragraph 3 of this Agreement and files a lawsuit or claim based on legal claims that Employee has released, Employee will pay for all costs incurred by Employer, any related companies, or the directors, officers, or employees of any of them, including reasonable attorneys' fees, in defending against Employee's claim.

Employee further recognizes that even if he or she violates the terms of Paragraph 3, this Agreement shall remain in full force and effect, including Employee's Complete Release in Paragraph 2.

Period for Review and Consideration Release. Employee understands that he or she has been given a period of 45 days to review and consider this Agreement before signing it. Employee further understands that he or she may use as much of this 45-day period as he or she wishes before signing. In order for this Agreement to be effective, it must be received by Employer no later than the close of the business day on the 45th day after Employee received this Agreement. If the signed Agreement is not received by then, this Agreement shall become null and void.

Encouragement to Consult with Attorney. Employee acknowledges that he or she was encouraged to consult with an attorney before signing this Agreement.

Employee's Right to Revoke Release. Employee may revoke this Agreement within seven (7) days of signing it. Revocation can be made by delivering a written notice of revocation to Employer, either by hand or by certified mail, return receipt requested. For any such revocation to be effective, written notice must be received no later than the close of the business day on the seventh day after Employee signs this Agreement. If Employee revokes this Agreement, it shall not be effective or enforceable, and Employee will not receive any of the compensation described in Paragraph 1 of this Agreement.

Information Acknowledgment. Employee acknowledges that, contemporaneously with receiving this Agreement, Employee received an informational packet which Employer stated contains the positions and ages of all employees who were considered to receive this Agreement but were not selected, and the position and ages of all employees that received this Agreement.

Entire Agreement. For the purpose of implementing a full and complete release and discharge of claims, Employee expressly acknowledges that this Agreement is intended to include in its effect, without limitation, all the claims described in the preceding paragraphs, whether known or unknown, suspected or unsuspected, and that this

Agreement contemplates the extinction of all claims related to Employee's employment and separation of employment with Employer including claims for attorneys' fees. Employee expressly waives any right to assert, after the execution of this Agreement, that any such claim, demand, obligation, or cause of action has, through ignorance or oversight, been omitted from the scope of the releases contained in the Agreement.

This is the entire agreement between Employee and Employer except any agreements related to Employee's pension or 401(k) benefits. Employer has made no promises to Employee other than those in this Agreement.

EMPLOYEE ACKNOWLEDGES THAT HE/SHE HAS READ THIS AGREEMENT, UNDERSTANDS IT, AND IS VOLUNTARILY ENTERING INTO IT.

PLEASE READ THIS AGREEMENT CAREFULLY. IT CONTAINS A RELEASE OF ALL KNOWN AND UNKNOWN CLAIMS.

XYZ, INC. _____ EMPLOYEE _____

By: _____ Social Security Number: _____

Its: President

Date: _____ Date: _____

Q 13:21 Can employers require an employee to sign a release on the spot?

A release is rarely considered voluntary if an employee has signed it only because the employer said he or she must during the termination meeting to receive benefits. The OWBPA expressly prohibits such on-the-spot executions of releases of claims under the ADEA, however, even in cases in which the OWBPA does not apply and a terminated employee is given an ultimatum to sign a release on the spot in return for severance benefits, the release could probably not be enforced. (See also *Cole* discussion in Q 13:18 above.) However, in a case involving similar facts before the Sixth Circuit, the court concluded that the release was knowingly and voluntarily entered into. In *Kendrick v. K-Mart Corporation Corp.* [238 F.3d 421 (6th Cir. 2000)], an employee was given a release that complied with the OWBPA providing him, among other things, 45 days to consider the release and 7 days to revoke it after he signed. Although the employee claimed that he never read the release and that he was told by his manager to sign it the same day, which he did, the court concluded that the release was in compliance with the OWBPA and therefore enforceable.

Q 13:22 If, after a release is provided, there are modifications to the document, does it restart the 21-day or 45-day time period for consideration of the release by the employee?

Under the EEOC regulations [29 C.F.R. § 1625(e)(4)], if the offer (release) is modified such that there are "material changes" to the offer, the clock is reset, and the 21- or 45-day period commences with the revised offer. On the other hand, if the changes are not "material," the clock does not reset. However, the parties can agree in writing that the clock does not reset, even for material changes.

Q 13:23 Can a former employee who later challenges a waiver and release of claims in court be required to tender back the consideration paid for the release?

Under the traditional rules of contract law, a plaintiff challenging the validity of an agreement is generally required to tender back the consideration that was paid under the agreement; however, in *Long v. Sears Roebuck & Co.* [1997 U.S. App. LEXIS 4989 (3d Cir. Mar. 11, 1997)], the Third Circuit, after reviewing the OWBPA and the so-called tender-back argument, concluded that tender back of consideration paid for a faulty release under the OWBPA was not a condition to maintaining an age claim under the ADEA. Although some courts have decided otherwise [*see* Hines v. ABB Veteo Gray, Inc., 8 *Employment Discrimination Report (EDR)* (BNA) 89 (Jan. 15, 1997)], the Supreme Court settled the issue in *Oubre v. Entergy Operations, Inc.* [522 U.S. 422 (1998)], holding that tender back is not required when the consideration was paid in connection with a release that did not comply with OWBPA requirements, which govern the release of federal age claims under the ADEA. Thus, an employee can maintain a claim against an employer, despite the fact that the employee has received or continues to receive compensation or benefits under a release that was previously signed, if the release does not comport with the requirements of the OWBPA. In December 2000, the EEOC issued its final regulations on the issue effective January 10, 2001, adopting the *Oubre* decision and further clarifying the Commission's position on the issue. In addition to other things, the EEOC regulations provide that a company cannot avoid the "no tender back" holding of *Oubre* through another provision in the release, like a covenant-not-to-use provision. [*See* "Final EEOC Regulations Set Boundaries on Legality of Waivers Under Age Bias Act," 15 *Employment Discrimination Report (EDR)* (BNA) 767 (Dec. 13, 2000).]

Q 13:24 Is it important for the employer to calculate promptly and carefully the money due and owing to a terminated employee?

For two reasons, an employer should calculate carefully and pay promptly all money due and owing to a discharged employee:

- Failure to make prompt and proper payment can constitute a violation of the relevant state's wage payment and collection act, a violation that, if without good excuse, can result in serious penalties and the award of attorneys' fees in the wake of a successful collection action. Some state statutes even include criminal penalties, although these tend to be rarely invoked.

- A release of claims is not enforceable unless the employee has received some meaningful consideration over and above what the employer already owes. Although no statute or case has set a minimum payment as constituting adequate consideration, when the employer and employee have made a mutual mistake about the actual amount of money being paid in excess of wages and benefits or severance pay under a pre-existing policy, a court is likely to allow the employee to rescind the release.

Q 13:25   Are severance arrangements subject to ERISA?

The Employee Retirement Income Security Act (ERISA) governs pensions and many other types of employee benefit plans. True severance plans adopted by the employer for the benefit of employees are employee-welfare benefit plans governed by the Act; however, limited use of severance arrangements as consideration for a release on a case-by-case basis are not generally considered subject to it. Consequently, employers must be sensitive to the interplay of the Act with the federal discrimination statutes and other state and federal laws.

Plant Closings, Mass Layoffs, and WARN

Q 13:26   Does any federal law require a company to notify employees of its decision to close its operations?

The WARN [29 U.S.C. §§ 2101, *et seq.*], which took effect in 1989, requires large employers that are planning a plant closing or mass layoff to give affected employees at least 60 days' notice of such employment actions. In addition, the Labor Management Relations Act requires unionized companies to provide "reasonable notice" to unions of a decision to close operations.

Q 13:27   Which employers are covered by WARN?

All companies with 100 or more employees (excluding part-time employees) or those with 100 or more employees (including all part-time employees who work, in the aggregate, at least 4,000 hours per year exclusive of overtime) are covered by WARN, whether or not their employees are represented by a union. Employees on temporary layoff or on leave who have a reasonable expectation of recall are included as employees for purposes of the Act. A worker has a reasonable expectation of recall when he or she is notified or understands through industry practice that his or her employment with the company has been only temporarily interrupted and that he or she will be recalled to the same or a similar job. In *Ellis v. DHL Express, Inc.* [633 F.3d 522 (7th Cir. 2011)], the court held that employees who had accepted negotiated severance agreements in anticipation of the closing of the defendant's facilities left voluntarily and thus were not counted for purposes of triggering notice requirements required under WARN.

Generally WARN does not apply to federal, state, or local governments. Rather, WARN applies to employers engaged in a "business enterprise." As such, a Chapter 11 SIPA trustee charged under law with the responsibility of liquidating a business was not operating a business as a going concern but, by law, liquidating the business such that WARN was not applicable to layoffs occurring during the liquidation process. [*In re MF Global Holdings, Ltd.*, 2012 WL 5211827 (Bankr. S.D.N.Y. Oct. 23, 2012)] However, there exists many "quasi" municipal corporations that may be engaged in a business enterprise such that WARN applies. Such was the case in *Castro v. Chicago Housing Authority* [360 F.3d. 721 (7th Cir. 2004)]. In *Castro*, police officers sued the Chicago Housing Authority (CHA) under the Act alleging that the CHA had failed to warn them in accordance with WARN before closing its police department. Its officers claimed that WARN applied to the CHA because it was a quasi-public entity that engaged in a business enterprise. The court, in reviewing the statute and regulations found that public and quasi-public entities that engage in business that are separately organized from the regular government and, have their own governing bodies, and have independent authorities to manage their personnel and assets are a covered employer under WARN. In reviewing the day-to-day operations of the CHA, the court concluded that the CHA was a covered employer, in that it regularly engaged in business by renting, leasing, purchasing and selling real estate and, moreover, independently managed its assets, raised its own revenue, and made its own investments. As such, the court concluded that the CHA had violated WARN by failing to follow its notification procedures prior to closing its police department.

Q 13:28   What constitutes a *plant closing* under WARN?

A *plant closing* is a permanent or temporary shutdown of a single site of employment, or one or more facilities or operating units within a single site of employment, resulting in 50 or more employees (excluding part-time employees) losing employment during any 30-day period. Any employment action resulting in the effective cessation of production or the work a unit performs, even if a few employees remain, is a shutdown.

Q 13:29   What is a *mass layoff* under WARN?

A *mass layoff* is a reduction in workforce that is not caused by a plant closing but results in an employment loss at a single site of employment during any 30-day period of at least 33 percent of the active employees (excluding part-time employees) or at least 50 employees (excluding part-time employees). If 500 or more full-time employees are affected, notice is required even if the affected number of employees is less than 33 percent of the workforce.

The difference between a plant closing and a mass layoff is that a plant closing involves an employment loss resulting from the shutdown of one or more distinct units within a single site or the entire site. A mass layoff occurs when there is an employment loss regardless of whether one or more units at the site are shut down.

Q 13:30   Who are *affected employees*?

Affected employees are those who may reasonably be expected to lose their jobs (through bumping, the exercise of seniority rights, or other means) because of proposed plant closings or mass layoffs. To the extent that the employer can reasonably be expected to identify these employees, it must give them notice. Unlike the National Labor Relations Act's definition of *employees*, WARN defines *affected employees* to include managers and supervisors. Business partners, consultants, contract employees who have a separate employment relationship with another employer and are paid by that other employer, or those who are self-employed are not affected employees under WARN.

Q 13:31   What is a *single site of employment*?

The term *single site of employment* can refer to either a single location or a group of contiguous locations. For example, buildings that form a campus or industrial park, or separate facilities across the street from one another, may be considered a single site of employment. Separate buildings or areas that are not directly connected or are not in immediate proximity to one another may be considered a single site of employment if they are in reasonable geographic proximity, are used for the same purpose, and share the same company equipment. An example is an employer that operates several warehouses within a geographic area and transfers or rotates the same employees from one facility to another. When two plants that are managed by a single employer are located on opposite sides of a town, each plant is a separate site if it employs different workers. Similarly, contiguous buildings that are owned by a single employer but that have separate management, produce different products, and employ separate workforces are separate single sites of employment. However, in at least one case, the court found a single job site to exist despite the fact that the site existed of multiple buildings in close proximity to one another. In *Gorini v. AMP, Inc.* [94 Fed. Appx. 913 (3d Cir. 2004)], AMP Inc., a successor to TYCO, maintained numerous facilities within an area but claimed that they did not comprise a single job site such that all employees could be counted together for purposes of determining whether there had previously been a mass layoff to which WARN would apply. The court, in reviewing the regulations, concluded that a single job site can be either a single location or a group of locations in reasonable geographic proximity under the same management with the same operational purpose, citing 20 C.F.R Section 639.3(I). In reviewing the sites, the court concluded that although the employment sites were not necessarily absolutely contiguous, it was sufficient under WARN that the sites were all "in the greater Harrisburg area in multiple contiguous connected TYCO facilities. The buildings were close together, and shared employees, job functions and services." [*Gorini*, 94 Fed. Appx. 913 at 920] In *In re Storehouse Inc.* [2010 WL 4453849 (E.D. Va. Nov. 3, 2010)], a laid-off manager who maintained an office at a small retail establishment in Richmond with less than 50 employees claimed his "worksite" included corporate headquarters in Atlanta, Georgia, as a "single site of employment" in order to meet the 50 employee threshold for a plant closing under WARN. Although the former manager periodically traveled to corporate headquarters and reported to his boss in Atlanta, the court found that the manager consistently reported to his small office in Richmond, which the court held was his "single site" of employment.

Q 13:32   Who must give 60 days' notice?

The employer is responsible for designating the most appropriate person within its organization to prepare and serve the required notice.

In the case of the sale of all or part of a business, the seller is responsible for providing notice of any plant closing or mass layoff that occurs up to and including the effective date of the sale. The buyer must provide notice of any plant closing or mass layoff that takes place after the date of sale. If the buyer plans on effecting a plant closing or mass layoff within 60 days of purchase, the seller may give notice to the affected employees as the buyer's agent. If the seller fails to give notice, the buyer is nevertheless responsible for giving notice. Under these circumstances, the buyer and seller should determine the impact of the sale on workers and arrange to give notice to affected employees if the parties to the transaction anticipate a mass layoff or plant closing.

Q 13:33   Who must receive notice?

If affected employees are represented by a union, written notice must be served on the union's chief elected officer. If there is no union, notice must be served on each affected employee individually. Notice must also be served on the state's dislocated-worker unit and the chief elected official of the local government within which a closing or layoff is to occur.

Q 13:34   What must the notice contain?

When the affected employees are represented by a union, the notice must contain:

- The name and address of the employment site at which the closing or layoff will occur;
- The name and telephone number of a company official to contact for further information;
- A statement indicating whether the closing or layoff is expected to be permanent or temporary;
- Confirmation of whether the entire plant is to be closed;
- The schedule for making separations from service, including the anticipated date of the first separation; and
- The names and titles of the individuals currently holding affected jobs.

When the affected employees are not represented by a union, the notice must be written in language employees can understand and must indicate:

- Whether the layoff will be permanent or temporary;
- Whether the entire plant will be closed;
- When the plant closing or mass layoff will commence;
- The date on which the individual employee will be separated;
- Whether or not employees have bumping rights; and
- The name and telephone number of a company official to contact for further information.

The notice that is provided to the state's dislocated-worker unit and the head of the local government must contain all of the information in the notice to the union or individual employee. If a union is involved, the notice must also contain the name of each union representing affected employees and the name and address of the chief elected officer of each union.

Q 13:35   How must the notice be served?

The notice may be served in any way that ensures receipt of the notice at least 60 days before the plant closing or mass layoff. For example, first-class mail or personal delivery with optional signed receipt are acceptable methods of delivery. Another viable option, when affected employees must be notified directly, is inserting the notice into pay envelopes.

Q 13:36   May notice be given less than 60 days in advance in certain circumstances?

WARN's notification period may be less than 60 days in three circumstances:

- A faltering company;
- An unforeseeable business circumstance; or
- A natural disaster.

Q 13:37   When is a company a *faltering company* for purposes of WARN?

The faltering-company exception permits a financially troubled business to avoid the 60-day advance warning if it is actively seeking financing through any commercially reasonable method, with a realistic opportunity of obtaining such financing, or is seeking new business at the time notice would have been required. This exception applies only to plant closings, not mass layoffs. The amount of capital or volume of new business sought, if obtained, must be sufficient to have enabled the company to avert or postpone the shutdown. In *In re FF Acquisition Corp.* [438 B.R. 886 (Bankr. N.D. Miss. 2010)], the court held that the bankrupt company satisfied the requirements of the faltering company exception when, without prior notice, its lender dramatically reduced its advance rate on the company's receivables and ultimately refused to provide the company with additional capital, resulting in the plant closing and bankruptcy filing. As such, the 60-day WARN Act notice did not apply.

Because of the fact-sensitive nature of the inquiry into what is reasonable or realistic, employers seeking to invoke the faltering-company exception under WARN are especially cautioned to consult an attorney to ensure that they are not running afoul of WARN. For example, in *In re APA Transport Corp Consolidated Litigation* [541 F.3d 233 (3d Cir. 2008)], a trucking company claimed it fell within the faltering company exception because it was in financial trouble, and had notified its lender that it intended to seek additional financing to alleviate its economic situation. However, reviewing the statute, the court concluded that this informal activity was not enough to fall within the faltering company exception because the company was not "actively seeking financing" at the time the 60-day notice should have been sent.

However, even under the faltering-company exception, some notice, albeit reduced notice, is required to be given prior to the shutdown. In *United Mine Workers of America International Union v. Lehigh Coal and Navigation Co.* [2006 WL 2623888 (M.D. Pa. Sept. 12, 2006)], the company attempted to use the "faltering company" defense to exempt its failure to provide notice. However, the court found that the defendant failed to present any evidence that prior reduced notice was given to the employee, and that after-the-fact notice does not cure the failure to give reduced notice prior to shutdown. As such, the court concluded that the company could not take advantage of the faltering business defense at trial.

Q 13:38   When does the exception for unforeseeable business circumstances apply?

Business circumstances that were not reasonably foreseeable when the 60-day notice would have had to have been sent excuse the employer in the case of plant closings and mass layoffs. An important indication of a business circumstance that is not reasonably foreseeable is a sudden, dramatic, and unexpected action or condition outside the employer's control. For example, a strike at the employer's major supplier, an important client's unexpected withdrawal from a major contract with the employer, an unexpected and severe economic downturn, and a government-ordered closing of an employment site without prior notice might be considered business circumstances that could not have been foreseen.

In *Roquet v. Arthur Andersen LLP* [398 F.3d 585 (7th Cir. 2005)], a class of former employees brought a WARN Act claim against Arthur Andersen for its failure to provide 60 days notice prior to laying them off in connection with Arthur Andersen's much publicized break-up in 2002. Arthur Andersen defended by saying that its need to lay off employees was sudden and dramatic and a result of the Department of Justice's (DOJ's) announcement on March 1, 2002, that it was going to seek an indictment against the company. The court, after reviewing the facts and the disastrous consequences this news had on its business, concluded that the mass layoffs and terminations that were determined to be necessary soon after the DOJ's notice clearly fell within the unforeseen business circumstances exception. As the court concluded, the reason for layoffs was not reasonably foreseeable 60 days before the decision to lay off employees was made. Although Arthur Andersen had known for some time it was under investigation, the news of the indictment was "sudden, dramatic and unexpected," with disastrous impact on the business such that no violation of WARN was found.

In *Weekes-Walker v. Macomb County Greyhound Park, Inc.* [2012 WL 2870705 (M.D. Ala. July 26, 2012)], the court held that a large gambling and entertainment complex that closed its doors on the eve of a raid by state officials could not utilize the unforeseen business circumstance defense because it never provided adequate notice as soon as practicable, as required for the defense.

In *Acevedo v. Heinemann's Bakeries, Inc.* [2008 WL 1702091 (N.D. Ill. Apr. 9, 2008)], the company claimed that the unforeseen circumstances exception was applicable because of the decision of its lending source to discontinue providing it a revolving line of credit to pay its operating costs. However, reviewing the facts, the court concluded it was unclear whether the lender's decision necessarily caused the permanent plant closing in that, including but not limited to, plaintiffs alleged that even after the funding was revoked, the defendant had the ability to continue the operations of the plant for 60 days prior to closing. As such, the court held that there were issues of fact as to whether the exception was applicable, and denied a motion for summary disposition with respect to this issue.

In *Grosse v. Hale-Halsell Co* [554 F.3d 870 (10th Cir. 2009)], all former employees of a company sued claiming WARN Act violations because the company did not provide at least 60 days notice in advance of the mass layoff. The company claimed that the unforeseen circumstance exception applied since the abrupt mass layoff was occasioned by the loss of its primary customer. In essence, the court found that the withdrawal of its customer was essentially the straw that broke the camel's back—a straw that was not foreseeable, and which caused the decision to layoff its workers. As such, the court found no WARN violation.

In *Pearce v. Faurecia Exhaust Systems, Inc.* [2012 WL 2884748 (S.D. Ohio July 13, 2012)], the court held that an auto supplier that was forced to close its doors as a result of Chrysler's bankruptcy filing fit within the unforeseen business circumstances exception because it did not learn of the filing until after the filing, despite rumors of the bankruptcy before the filing.

In *United Steel Workers of America Local 2660 v. United States Steel Corp.* [683 F.3d 882 (8th Cir. 2012)], the court found that the sudden economic crisis of late 2008 and resulting dramatic decline in customer orders fit within the exemption of an unforeseeable business circumstance in connection with a mass layoff at an iron ore plant.

Q 13:39 When does a natural disaster exempt an employer from the 60-day notice requirement?

Advance notice may be precluded when a plant closing or mass layoff is caused by a flood, earthquake, drought, storm, tidal wave, or similar natural disaster; however, the information in the notice must still be given as soon as practicable, whether before or after the employment loss.

The natural-disaster exception does not apply when a natural disaster indirectly causes a plant closing or mass layoff; however, the employer may be able to use the exception for unforeseeable business circumstances under such conditions.

Q 13:40   Is a WARN notice required when there is a government-ordered takeover of private businesses?

This novel issue presented itself in *Deveraturda v. Globe Aviation Security Services* [454 F.3d 1043 (9th Cir. 2006)], when, after September 11, 2001, the government federalized airport and security screeners throughout the country. In this case, the employers did not provide a WARN notice when the government took control and the employers ceased operations. The employees pursued a class action against their employers for WARN violations. Although novel, the court concluded that because this was not an employer-ordered closure, but rather was a unilateral and absolute order by the government to federalize airport security, WARN should have no application.

Q 13:41   What is an employer's liability if it fails to give the required notice under WARN?

An employer may be assessed back pay for each affected employee for each day of violation, up to 60 days. The employer is further liable for the cost of employee benefits for each day of violation. An employer that fails to provide the required notice to the local government is subject to a civil penalty of as much as $500 for each day of violation. Judges can, however, reduce damages if they find that the employer acted in good faith and had reasonable grounds to believe it complied with WARN. Liability may be further reduced by wages and voluntary payments paid by the employer to employees during the violation period and employer payments or service credits provided to employees under employee benefit plans during the violation period.

In *Long v. Dunlop Sports Group Americas, Inc.* [454 F. Supp. 2d 520 (D.S.C. 2007)], employees of a golf ball manufacturing plant claimed that WARN Act violations occurred in connection with the company's shutdown without prior notice as required by WARN. However, the facts demonstrated that although no notice was given prior to shutdown, the employer notified all employees on the date of the shutdown and continued to pay the full wages of the employees for the next 60 days, except for 22 employees who left during the 60-day period to begin employment with another employer. As to those 22 employees, because they left voluntarily to work for another employer, no employment loss occurred under WARN, such that a violation of the Act did not occur.

Q 13:42   Can lenders of companies who are in control of financial decisions be liable for back pay and benefits upon a finding of a WARN Act violation?

A few courts have been asked to determine whether liability for WARN violations can extend beyond the employer to lenders and secured creditors who are said to be in control of the employer's financial decisions during periods of delinquency. This issue arises because the WARN Act applies to mass plant closings and layoffs, many of which are defunct companies, and it is not unusual for creditors to become intimately involved with companies in trying to save their investment before the bottom falls out. Because the defunct companies may not have the wherewithal to pay for violations, plaintiffs are attempting to determine whether this liability can be extended to the company's lenders, who obviously are in a better position to pay any penalties. In *Smith v. Ajax Magnathermic Corp.* [144 Fed. Appx. 482 (6th Cir. 2005)], the plaintiff was attempting to hold a consortium of lenders liable for WARN Act violations, alleging that the consortium of lenders was in actual control of the business operations and had inserted a consulting firm to manage the employer's operations on a day-to-day basis. Although the court noted that previous cases had failed because the lender defendants typically do not have sufficient control over the operations to be held liable, nonetheless, it adopted the Ninth Circuit's analysis that if sufficient control of the business enterprise in a normal commercial sense can be demonstrated, lender liability under WARN may be appropriate. However, if the degree of control is no more than the creditor's seeking to protect its security interests and acting only to preserve the business assets for liquidation or sale, liability under WARN would not come into play. Because the plaintiff in *Smith* had alleged sufficient facts to establish the level of control required to maintain a claim under WARN against the lenders, the court reversed the dismissal of the WARN Act claim against the lenders and remanded the matter for further proceedings.

The issue of whether an employer's creditor can be held liable under WARN was considered by the Second Circuit in *Coppola v. Bear Stearns & Co., Inc.* [499 F.3d 144 (2d Cir. 2007)]. In the case, the employees of an employer that had shut down claimed that the creditor was an employer under WARN and, therefore, responsible for WARN Act violations. However, the court, in reviewing the facts, determined that the creditor was not responsible for operating the business as a going concern on a day-to-day basis, which would be necessary to attach WARN liability, but rather, merely acted to protect its security interest and preserve the business assets, such that no WARN Act liability was applicable to the creditor.

Termination Documentation and References

Q 13:43   Should a termination be documented?

All terminations should be properly documented, indicating both the effective date of the termination and the reason(s) for termination. Preferably, this information should be contained in a separation report that is shown to the employee during the termination interview and initialed by the employee to indicate that he or she has reviewed it. The document should then be placed in the employee's personnel file.

Q 13:44　How much detail should be contained in a separation report?

The level of detail needed varies from situation to situation, but the following guidelines should be remembered:

- Too much detail is a problem. If a separation report provides a list of reasons for discharge but fails to include an important item, the employer will have a hard time relying on that item in future litigation.

- No detail is a problem. If the employer provides no reasons for termination, it will have no documentation to corroborate its testimony in later litigation, or worse, the employee will maintain that no reason was given to hide illegal discrimination.

- The separation report should include a general reference to the categorical reasons for termination (e.g., attendance problems, insubordination, or violation of work rules), with a reference to a few examples, not intended to be exhaustive. This approach covers the reasons in broad terms and provides some, but not all, of the specifics. This serves to lend credibility to the document but does not box the employer in on the specifics in later litigation.

Q 13:45　Should employers provide references for former employees?

Since the U.S. Supreme Court decision in *Robinson v. Shell Oil Co.* [519 U.S. 337 (1997)], it is clear that former employees can sue their former employers for violations of Title VII that occur after termination of the employment relationship. In *Robinson*, the employee claimed that his former employer provided a negative reference in retaliation for his filing of a charge with the EEOC after he was fired. In addition, a whole host of additional claims can arise from an alleged "blackballing" or negative reference, including defamation and invasion of privacy.

If an employer provides only favorable references but says nothing in unfavorable situations, the company seeking a reference might infer a negative reference if no information is provided. On the other hand, if the employer gives a falsely favorable reference for someone who does not deserve it, the employer faces potential liability to the company seeking a reference.

Although the failure to disclose known facts regarding an applicant can expose an employer to liability (e.g., failing to warn an employer of a former employee's dangerous propensities), employers concerned about liability issues generally adopt a policy of not providing references, good or bad, for any employee. Instead, they merely confirm an employee's name, dates of employment, and positions held—except in the unavoidable case when the former employee may present a danger to others. This may be the employer's safest approach from a legal perspective. If all employers adopted this approach, attempting to obtain meaningful references would be futile. Undoubtedly in response to this dilemma, some states, like Michigan, have passed legislation to provide employers who provide references a safe harbor from civil liability, provided that the information given concerning the employee's job performance is: documented in the personnel file; provided in good faith; and not knowingly false, misleading, or provided in reckless disregard of the truth. [Mich. Comp. Laws Ann. § 423.452] Many employers will not respond to requests for references unless the former employee requests the information to be provided to the potential employer in writing and formally releases the employer from any liability associated with furnishing the requested information to the potential employer. In such cases, defamation claims will be difficult to maintain because of the release of claims and because the statements from the former employer to the potential employer would be subject to a qualified privilege. [*See* Taylor v. Amcor Flexibles, Inc., 2009 WL 3754195 (D.N.J. Nov. 4, 2009).]

Chapter 14

Managing Labor and Employment Litigation

The corporation that has not experienced some form of employment litigation is the exception. Despite all the advice that an employer gleans from attorneys, accountants, and other outside advisers—and despite all the best intentions of management—lawsuits and charges still occur. This chapter discusses the litigation process and provides practical advice on avoiding employee claims, managing cases, and controlling litigation costs and expenses.

The Litigation Process

Q 14:1 What is the first thing an employer should do if it receives a threat of an employment claim, such as a demand letter from an attorney?

Demand letters should not be ignored. The employer should forward any such letter immediately to its employment attorney for consideration. The first determination to be made is whether the employer should undertake an internal investigation of the matter. If this is an alleged harassment situation of first impression, under the principles enunciated in *Ellerth* and *Faragher*, the employer may need to investigate the matter to demonstrate its commitment to preventing and correcting harassment. [Burlington Indus., Inc. v. Ellerth, 524 U.S. 742 (1998); Faragher v. City of Boca Raton, 524 U.S. 775 (1998)] If, on the other hand, the matter does not require a formal harassment investigation, it is still good practice for the employer's attorney to review the personnel records at issue, discuss the matter with relevant employees and supervisors, and decide whether a written response is warranted. In addition, the attorney should review any relevant insurance policies to determine if coverage is available. If so, the notice requirements should be reviewed to determine if the carrier should be put on notice of the claim. This is particularly important with the advent of employment practices liability insurance (EPLI) policies. Most of these policies are claims-made policies and typically only apply to third-party claims first made during the applicable coverage time-period under the policy. As such, if the insurance company is not notified, and coverage under a policy lapses, a new policy period begins and the insured may have difficulty with coverage.

Q 14:2   What is the first thing an employer should do upon receiving pleadings or charges?

Upon service of a complaint or administrative charge, employers have a limited amount of time to file an answer or respond to the charge. They should, therefore, immediately secure appropriate legal counsel. In addition, potentially relevant insurance policies should be reviewed for possible coverage, and if any of the allegations fall within coverage, copies of the pleadings or charge should be promptly forwarded to the insurer, pursuant to the notice requirements of the policy. This is particularly important. Insurance products that provide for coverage of employment litigation are commonly referred to as EPLI. Most of these policies are claims-made policies, which means that they cover claims first made during the coverage period. A condition of coverage of most of their policies is that the insurance company receive notice of the claim after it is made within a relatively short time period. If notice is not provided, as required by the policy, an insurance company may have the ability to deny coverage, particularly if the lack of timely notice results in prejudice to the defense of the claim.

Q 14:3   Should a company turn all employment claims into its EPLI insurance company, even if it feels it may be able to resolve the matter within its deductible?

Particularly for what is perceived by the company to be marginal and weak claims which are not full fledged lawsuits (i.e., Equal Employment Opportunity Commission [EEOC] claims), some companies may consider not submitting the claims and possibly affecting their renewal premium. Rather, their own attorney may attempt to dispose of the matter or resolve it within the amount of the company's deductible. This can be a risky approach. If the claim is not disposed of as the company planned, the insurance company may have defenses to a tender of the claim at a later time, particularly if the delay has prejudiced the defense of the file.

Q 14:4   Is it necessary to secure private counsel if the claim involves an administrative charge?

Companies need not be represented by counsel in defending charges before the EEOC or most state civil rights commissions; however, counsel is advisable. Attorneys who are familiar with the law and process and have experience dealing with the administrative agency at issue are equipped to confront the necessary issues, assess potential risk and exposure, and communicate with the agency, both in providing the initial response and through the investigation. Moreover, even if the charge is dismissed, the matter is not necessarily concluded. The complainant still has a limited right to pursue the matter in court, and anything provided to the agency can be obtained by opposing counsel under a Freedom of Information Act request to be used against the employer in later litigation.

Q 14:5   Is it advisable to secure private counsel at the outset if the matter might be covered by insurance?

Securing an attorney at the outset is advisable for many reasons. After the pleadings or charge is sent to the insurer, it takes time for the insurer to respond as to coverage. Often, the insurer does not do so until after deadlines to respond to the complaint or charge have passed. The employer's counsel can, at a minimum, usually obtain an extension, pending resolution of the coverage issues. In addition, an attorney can assist in working out coverage issues that arise. Many times, an insurance company agrees to defend the matter under a "reservation of rights," only to later disavow defense or indemnity obligations. In such circumstances, independent counsel can monitor litigation for the company and step in if the insurer later disavows coverage in whole or in part.

Q 14:6   When faced with employment litigation, how should an employer select legal counsel?

If the corporation already enjoys a working relationship with an attorney, he or she is the first person outside the company who should be consulted. Corporate counsel may not be appropriate to handle the case, but they usually should be asked to recommend an attorney specializing in such work. The company's regular corporate counsel may not be an experienced litigator, and even if he or she is, the attorney may not be sufficiently conversant with labor and employment law to defend the corporation. The company should discuss the following issues before retaining an attorney:

- The number of similar cases the attorney has handled;
- Whether the attorney will handle the case personally or assign part or all of it to a subordinate—and if so, the difference in their billing rates;
- The attorney's hourly rate or other method of billing for services;
- The attorney's estimate of the cost of the litigation, preferably broken down as follows:

- — Preliminary work: investigation of the facts, preliminary legal research, answering the complaint, preliminary motions (if any)
- — Discovery stage: number and cost of oral depositions, interrogatories, requests for documents, and responses to the other side's requests for the same
- — Pre-trial motions: motion for summary disposition, motions in limine, pre-trial memorandum or order
- — Trial and post-trial motions

- • Whether settlement overtures might be advisable and, if so, the attorney's view as to what an appropriate settlement might be.

Q 14:7   What are the typical phases and procedures in a lawsuit brought by an employee or former employee against a corporation?

The phases and procedures in a lawsuit brought by an employee are described below.

Pre-litigation discussions. Rarely does an employee or former employee commence an action without his or her attorney first contacting the company's management or in-house counsel, usually by letter, stating the employee's claims, threatening a suit, and demanding damages. It is not unusual for a copy of the employee's personnel file to be requested in those jurisdictions where state laws allow the review of personnel files by current and former employees. This pre-litigation phase may be brief or may extend over several months of discussion, depending on the company's response, the applicability of any statute of limitations, and a host of other factors, including the employee's temperament.

Complaint. If the claim is not resolved during the pre-litigation phase, the plaintiff-employee's attorney may file a complaint with the federal or state court with jurisdiction over the alleged cause of action. The complaint must be filed before the statute of limitations on the employee's cause(s) of action expires.

The level of detail of the facts that must be pled in the complaint varies among jurisdictions. Under the Federal Rules of Civil Procedure, which have been adopted in large part by many state court systems, "A pleading which sets forth a claim for relief . . . shall contain (1) a short and plain statement of the grounds on which the court's jurisdiction depends . . . , (2) a short and plain statement of the claim showing that the pleader is entitled to relief, and (3) a demand for judgment for the relief the pleader seeks." [Fed. R. Civ. P. 8(a)] This is called *notice pleading*, because the plaintiff needs to plead only enough facts to notify the defendant of the nature of the action and permit that defendant to admit or to deny. By contrast, some states still hold to so-called *fact pleading*, which requires much more detailed statements of the underlying facts supporting the alleged cause of action.

Answer. Once the complaint has been served properly, the company and any individually named managerial defendants must file an answer within the time allowed by the court's procedural rules. In lieu of an answer, the company's attorney may file a motion, for example, to dismiss the action if the complaint does not state a cause that the court recognizes as a valid basis to recover damages.

As with the complaint, the answer must be as detailed or sketchy as the rules of civil procedure in the particular jurisdiction demand. The defendants also are permitted in the answer to:

- Make a counterclaim against the plaintiff, for instance, if a former sales-person owes unearned draw against commissions;
- Join other parties as additional defendants (e.g., the other companies in a joint-employer relationship, a labor union that shares responsibility for an alleged wrong, or an insurer that ought to be defending the company); and
- Make a cross-claim against one of the other defendants, as if to argue that if the company is liable to the plaintiff-employee, then a manager individually named ought to make the company whole for any damages it has to pay.

Affirmative defenses. With the answer, the defendant will raise any affirmative defenses it may have to the complaint, such as at-will employment in breach of implied contract cases, statute of frauds if the complaint seeks to enforce a promise which by its terms cannot be performed within a year, and failure to mitigate damages if the plaintiff is seeking lost wages that would have been mitigated by other employment.

Discovery. In general, discovery is the process through which the two sides in a lawsuit learn more about one another's case and the evidence that will be used to prove it. As with almost all aspects of litigation, the rules of discovery vary somewhat among states. The Federal Rules of Civil Procedure have become something of a standard across the nation, and almost all states have adopted or adapted them. The major tools attorneys use in conducting discovery are:

- *Interrogatories.* These are written questions demanded of the other party, which that party must answer under pain of perjury and within a specific time.
- *Requests for the production of documents and things.* In conjunction with, or separate from, interrogatories, an attorney can require his or her opponents to produce documents that relate to the lawsuit. Typical examples in employment litigation include the personnel file of the plaintiff and those of other employees of the defendant-corporation; payroll records; the company's employee handbook, other personnel policies, and employee benefits plans; disciplinary records; medical records; correspondence; and date books, telephone logs, and computer records (whether in hard copy or in electronic form). The inspection of premises also may be demanded. Other items that may be examined include tools, vehicles, computers, drugs, and lockers.
- *Admissions.* These are statements that one side can require the other side to admit or deny under pain of perjury or other possible court sanctions for

dishonesty. If a party admits to a particular statement, the other side can use this admission as evidence at trial.

- *Depositions.* Typically, when a party to the lawsuit or a third-party witness is summoned to an oral deposition, that individual is placed under oath by a court reporter who then makes a transcript of the questioning by opposing counsel. Counsel for the party being questioned as well as anyone who plans to call the witness at trial may also ask questions after opposing counsel has finished. Usually a deposition is taken only to discover what the party or witness contends are the facts of the case; however, a discovery deposition also can be used at trial to impugn the integrity of a party or other witness who tells a different version of the facts on the witness stand. Occasionally, when a third-party witness will be out of the country, is ill or otherwise is unavailable for trial, the deposition is taken in lieu of the testimony that the witness would normally have been expected to give in court. In this case, the deposition is read to the jury by the attorney whose witness was the deponent.

- *Automatic disclosure and mandatory discovery.* Available for adoption as of December 31, 1993, the Federal Rule of Civil Procedure 26 was amended to include a lengthy prefatory provision requiring early identification of discoverable materials and potential witnesses, plus a meeting among counsel to resolve potential discovery problems and to set a discovery schedule. The rule permits federal judicial districts to opt out of the new provisions or to adopt them in modified form.

Motion practice. Among the motions that may be filed by the parties during the course of the litigation are:

- *Motion for judgment on the pleadings.* When the complaint, answer, any counterclaims, and replies to those counterclaims have been filed, the pleadings are considered closed. If one party believes that the other party's pleadings are inadequate to sustain (or to deny) the cause at issue in the suit, that party may ask the court to grant judgment against the pleader on the basis of those early court filings. The court will grant this motion only if, on viewing all the pleaded facts in the light most favorable to the party against whom the motion is filed, it sees no way that party could win the case. Usually, when a party's pleadings are inadequate, the court will give the party 30 days to amend the pleadings and correct the errors or inadequacies.

- *Motion to compel discovery and motion for a protective order.* Sometimes the parties do not agree on which documents should be provided to the other side or which questions should be answered in interrogatories or oral depositions. At other times, one of the parties may simply be slow in responding to a request for documents or a set of interrogatories. In such circumstances, the court usually requires the parties to work out their discovery disputes amicably without bothering the judge. If an amicable resolution is impossible, the party seeking the discovery can move the court to order the recalcitrant party to cooperate with the discovery requests. On the other hand, the party refusing to respond to the discovery request, perhaps believing it to be unduly burdensome or that it violates the attorney-client privilege, may file a motion asking the judge in the case (or the motion court judge in some jurisdictions) to forbid the other side from demanding the documents or answers requested. This request is for a protective order.

- *Motion for summary judgment.* When the discovery process is complete or nearly complete, one of the parties may file a motion contending that, based on the facts that both sides admit to be true, a judgment should be entered in the moving party's favor without a trial. Although summary judgment motions are more often granted than motions for judgment on the pleadings, the burden on the moving party is great—if any facts remain in dispute on which a jury might find in favor of the other party, the moving party's summary judgment motion will be denied.

- *Motion in limine.* Before a case comes to trial, one or both litigants may request that the court forbid opposing counsel from presenting certain evidence, or evidence on certain issues, to the jury (e.g., because the evidence is irrelevant or prejudicial).

Alternative dispute resolution (ADR). Many states have some form of ADR process that cases may go through, typically following discovery but before trial. Some forms of ADR involve formal case evaluation or mediation by attorneys retained by the court to attempt to arrive at a figure that might settle the case, assuming all parties agree. Other forms of ADR involve more informal settlement conferences with an assigned judge who works with the parties and their attorneys to determine whether there is a basis to resolve the matter short of trial. Still others involve a newer process referred to as facilitation, where a trained facilitator works with the parties in an effort to facilitate a resolution.

Trial. Although in some jurisdictions as much as 90 percent of all litigation ends in settlement, some cases must be resolved in a courtroom. Trial may take place before a jury or a judge alone; the latter is called a bench trial. Since the passage of the Civil Rights Act of 1991, litigants in Title VII cases are no longer limited to bench trials but may demand trial by jury. The same right applies to age and disability discrimination suits under federal and many state laws. Actions for wrongful discharge and breach of employment contract actions also carry the right to jury trial in most instances. If neither party demands a jury, the right is not enforced automatically but instead may be deemed to have been waived. Whether a bench or jury trial, the major components of the proceeding are:

- Opening statements by the parties' legal counsels;
- Presentation of the plaintiff's case;
- Possible motion by defense counsel for a directed verdict at the close of the plaintiff's case;
- Presentation of the defendant's case;
- Counsel's closing arguments;
- If a jury trial, jury instructions by the judge followed by the jury's deliberations;

- If a bench trial, a verbal bench decision entered by the judge after hearing both sides' arguments or after deliberation upon receipt of a post-trial briefing by both sides, a written decision, and verdict.

Q 14:8   What happens after a judge or jury has rendered a verdict?

A disappointed party may file one of several motions following a verdict. If the trial was before a judge sitting without a jury, a party may file a motion for reconsideration or for a new trial. If it was a jury verdict, the loser may ask the judge to enter a contrary judgment notwithstanding the jury's verdict or request a new trial.

Whether post-trial motions are filed, the parties have the right to file an appeal to the next highest court in the state or federal court system. Ordinarily, an appeal must be based on a serious procedural error made by the trial judge or some misinterpretation of the law that the judge applied in deciding the case or in sending it to the jury for determination.

The federal and most state court systems include an intermediate and a supreme court of appeals. Although in most civil cases a dissatisfied party (because both parties may be dissatisfied with a portion of the judgment entered by the court, there may be cross appeals) has the right to appeal to the intermediate court (e.g., the appropriate U.S. Court of Appeals), most supreme courts are not required to take all cases appealed beyond the intermediate level. For instance, the U.S. Supreme Court grants *certiorari* (i.e., certification of the case from the appellate court to it for further consideration) to only a tiny percentage of the cases in which one or both parties request the court's consideration.

Q 14:9   Are attorneys willing to represent employee-plaintiffs on a contingent fee basis?

Employees sometimes found it hard to obtain competent counsel on a contingency fee basis when laws such as Title VII and the Age Discrimination in Employment Act permitted only back pay and reinstatement as remedies in a typical case; however, the 1991 Civil Rights Act permits juries to award compensatory and punitive damages, and as a result, contingent fee is the standard arrangement with plaintiff lawyers in employment litigation.

To encourage employees to act as private prosecutors with regard to the violation of federal and state employment laws, many of these statutes either mandate or permit the award of reasonable attorneys' fees to prevailing plaintiffs. When such statutes are involved in employment law litigation, contingency fee agreements normally are written to allow such court-awarded fees to be factored into the overall fee arrangement.

Q 14:10   Can attorneys' fees be awarded to successful plaintiffs or defendants?

In duty of fair representation cases involving claims by union members against unions, courts can award reasonable attorneys' fees to successful complainants; however, such awards are not mandatory. For example, in a case in which former employees of the John Morrell & Co. packing plant won $4.7 million in damages against the United Food & Commercial Workers Union, the Court of Appeals for the Tenth Circuit reversed the trial judge's additional award of $2.2 million in attorneys' fees. ["Court Finds UFCW Breached Duty, But Vacates Fee Award," 1993 *BNA Daily Labor Report* 101 May 27, 1993 at 1]

Attorney-fee provisions in federal labor and employment statutes vary from those that provide that the courts may award reasonable fees to prevailing parties [*see, e.g.,* Title VII, 42 U.S.C. § 2000e-5(k)] to those that mandate fees to a prevailing employee-plaintiff. [*See, e.g.,* 29 U.S.C. § 216(b), which applies to successfully prosecuted private actions under the Fair Labor Standards and Age Discrimination in Employment Acts.] Under some of these statutes, in rare instances of frivolous lawsuits, courts have awarded fees to the prevailing employer-defendant. [*See, e.g.,* Christiansburg Garment Co. v. EEOC, 434 U.S. 412 (1978); *see also* Fed. R. Civ. Pro. 11 ("The signature of an attorney or party constitutes a certification that . . . to the best of the signer's knowledge, information, and belief . . . it is well grounded in fact and is warranted by existing law, and that it is not interposed for an improper purpose. . . . If a pleading, motion, or other paper is signed in violation of this rule, the court, upon motion or upon its own initiative, shall impose upon the person who signed it . . . an appropriate sanction. . . . ").]

Q 14:11   What is a *class action suit?*

The Federal Rules of Civil Procedure permit one or more plaintiffs to commence a lawsuit on behalf of all persons who allegedly have the same claim against one or more defendants, even though not every such person has been contacted and agreed to join in the action, if the litigants meet the following criteria:

- The proposed class is so numerous that actual joinder of all members in the action is impracticable;
- There exist questions of law or fact common to all members of the proposed class; and
- The claims or defenses of the representative litigants are typical of the claims of all the class members.

The U.S. Department of Labor frequently prosecutes class actions on behalf of large groups of employees and former employees of companies, which the department contends failed to pay minimum wages or appropriate overtime premiums over a period of years. The EEOC has brought class actions against corporations that have discriminated against employees or applicants of a particular race or sex. Private litigants can sometimes do so as well.

Q 14:12   Are FLSA class action lawsuits gaining in popularity?

Back in 1999, a paper presented to a meeting of the ABA signaled a trend toward more FLSA class actions. [Walker & Chung, "Trends in Workplace Litigation: The Rising Popularity of FLSA Class Actions" (ABA Aug. 9, 1999)] As the paper points out, because companies usually have common payroll practices and policies, commonality of law and facts (a requirements for a class action, see Q 14:11) would be more common in FLSA claims, and as such, particularly suited for FLSA class actions. From an employer's perspective, what may seem like a rather benign FLSA claim from an individual for an alleged violation of federal wage laws becomes a tsunami when multiplied by the number of similarly affected workers in a class action. Articles posted over the last few years evidence this growing trend and the need for employers to ensure that their compensation policies do not run afoul of the FLSA. [See "FLSA Class Actions: The Bane of the Employer's Existence," http://www.wagehourlaw. foxrothschild.com (July 17, 2007); "FLSA Class Action Overtime Suits—Are You Next?" http://www.hrdailyadvisor.blr.com (Mar. 31, 2008); "FLSA Impacts 72 Percent Increase in Class Action Lawsuits," http://www.hrtools.com/legal; "Recent Trends in FLSA Hybrid Collective/Class Actions," Falcone, Elizabeth, http://www.ogletreedeakins.com/publications (June 16, 2011).]

In an effort to put the potential fire out, some defendants have attempted to forestall the certification of class status by responding to a FLSA complaint by an individual seeking to certify the claim as a class action with an offer of judgment for the full amount of the individual's claim, in an attempt to render the lawsuit moot and stop it in its tracks. However, such a ploy was rebuffed by the court in *Sandoz v. Cingular Wireless, LLC,* [553 F.3d 913 (5th Cir. 2008)] where, despite the offer of judgment, the court allowed the class certification attempt to continue.

Q 14:13   Can the courts penalize former employees who bring frivolous lawsuits?

Yes, but this rarely happens. In the federal courts, Federal Rule of Civil Procedure 11 permits the award of the other party's costs and attorneys' fees for frivolous and bad-faith actions. For example, in 1991, the Court of Appeals for the Fourth Circuit approved on appeal a $10,000 sanction imposed by the trial judge on a plaintiff who had filed employment claims against his former employer. The plaintiff was a pharmacist who happened to have some legal training. The district judge found that he had persisted in pursuing repetitive, spurious conduct throughout the action. After it won the suit, the defendant-hospital moved for $43,000 in fees and expenses accrued in the district court and an appeal. A U.S. magistrate considered the motion and recommended $10,000. In affirming this award against the plaintiff-pharmacist, the Fourth Circuit found that he was guilty of a "total failure . . . to do any investigation whatsoever into the relevant facts of law." The court also concluded that, as the plaintiff had become the owner of a pharmacy, he had the means to pay the sanction. In another 1991 decision, the Court of Appeals for the Sixth Circuit required the plaintiff's attorney to pay $36,000 to the other side for forcing the employer to defend two frivolous reverse-discrimination cases. [*See* 1991 *BNA Daily Labor Report* 63 Apr. 2, 1991.] An attorney was sanctioned by a federal district judge in New Jersey for failing reasonably to investigate the matter before filing a retaliation case under Title VII for her client. [*See* 16 *Employment Discrimination Report (EDR)* (BNA) 193 (Feb. 7, 2001).]

In *Jiminez v. Madison Area Technical College* [No. 00-6-424-C (W.D. Wis. Aug. 13, 2001)], it was reported that a federal judge issued Rule 11 sanctions against an attorney that failed to adequately question his client about documentary evidence of harassment which the court concluded were fraudulent. The court apparently felt that proper investigation would have revealed the lack of authenticity of the evidence. [*See* "Attorney Sanctioned; Did Not Question Client's 13 'Smoking Gun' Documents," 17 *Employment Discrimination Report (EDR)* (BNA) 384 (Sept. 26, 2001); *see also* "Plaintiff's Lawyer Must Pay $59,000 in Fees for Pursuing Reverse Discrimination Claims," 17 *Employment Discrimination Report (EDR)* (BNA) 323 (Sept. 12, 2001), wherein it was reported that a court sanctioned a plaintiff's attorney for pursuing litigation and engaging in settlement discussions which made it clear to the court that the attorney was more interested in obtaining an adequate attorneys' fee than the best interests of the client.]

Many states have enacted statutes or adopted procedural rules similar to Federal Rule of Civil Procedure 11. Some federal statutes, such as the Employee Retirement Income Security Act, permit the award of attorneys' fees to either side at the trial court's discretion. Such statutes as Title VII were meant to be remedial, and the award of fees to successful plaintiffs was expressly allowed by Congress to encourage wronged employees to act as private prosecutors, helping to eradicate job discrimination. Consequently, most courts, including the Supreme Court, have concluded that successful defendant-employers should not easily win their fees and expenses from employee-plaintiffs and their attorneys.

In *Larie v. Ferris State University Board of Trustees* [No. 98-012539-AZ (Mich. Ct. App. Jan. 24, 2003)], the Michigan Court of Appeals upheld sanctions against a law firm that filed a frivolous claim of retaliation. Under Michigan law, a case can be determined to be frivolous if any one of the following is demonstrated:

- The party's primary purpose in initiating the action or asserting the defense was to harass, embarrass, or injure the prevailing party;
- The party had no reasonable basis to believe that the facts underlying the party's legal position were in fact true; or
- The party's legal position was devoid of arguable legal merit. [Mich. Comp. Laws Ann. § 600.2591(3)(a)]

Case Management

Q 14:14   What factors should an employer consider in deciding whether a case should be settled?

Each case is unique, with specific factors to be considered. A competent labor attorney can assist the employer in identifying and evaluating the following factors:

The likelihood of success. Is the employee or the employer likely to succeed? This is a difficult issue. The company may be convinced that the former employee's cause of action is meritless or even frivolous; indeed, management may believe the case is grounded in perjured testimony. Nonetheless, unless counsel is certain that the court will dismiss the case, a potential for exposure exists. The real issue is the nature and extent of this exposure. Here, experienced employment law counsel is invaluable to advise the client of the risks.

Defense costs. It is not unusual for a victorious employer, brimming with glee after a successful verdict, to lose enthusiasm once it tallies the fees and expenses incurred in the matter. Litigation is extremely expensive, and consideration of the bottom line is always advisable. Even in weak cases, counsel may advise an early settlement, especially if it can be achieved for nuisance value. Nuisance value may be something less than the cost of defending the action to a resolution in court, possibly at an early stage in the proceedings. If so, that decision would be one made as a pure dollars-and-sense business judgment. In some cases, it may be wise to swallow one's pride and make the settlement overture to the plaintiff's attorney.

Company policies and morale. The company must also consider the following long-term issues that can transcend short-term financial reasons for settling the case:

- Is an important company policy at stake in the case that could be undermined by a settlement?
- Will a settlement, even for a small amount of money, send a message to workers that the corporation is an easy mark, encouraging others to bring similar suits?
- Will a settlement tell management that the company's top executives are not prepared to expend legal fees and mount a defense to back up front-line supervisors' personnel decisions? In other words, will management morale suffer from a settlement?

The company is always right. It is rare that a supervisor or company will ever believe that they have done anything wrong, and most claims are considered frivolous by company officials. Although some truly frivolous claims are filed, many claims that are considered frivolous may nonetheless result in real exposure to the company. Even if the company does not believe an illegal motive was involved, the circumstances and timing of a decision (i.e., discharge of an employee one day after the employee complains about harassment) may allow a jury to infer that illegal motive was behind the decision. Counsel needs to avoid the desire to tell the company what it wants to hear, and remember that counsel is paid to give advice, even if it is not likely to be well received by the company.

The best and worst case scenario. It can be very helpful, in analyzing settlement goals or options, to have an employment attorney chart the best and worst case scenarios, both in terms of result and cost associated with obtaining that result. In addition, the company should press its attorneys to provide it with an educated guess as to the likelihood of each of the outcomes. When faced with this information and the predictable uncertainties of either result as expressed by the attorney, even the most principled of clients will opt for the certainty of resolution, assuming it can be had at successful levels in light of the merits of the case.

Q 14:15   How much does it cost a company to litigate a lawsuit?

Because the cost of litigating a case varies greatly from one lawsuit to another, cost is difficult to predict. A lawsuit may settle early or drag on through trial and even appeal. A lawyer may require many depositions and lots of other discovery to prepare for trial, or only a few witnesses and documents may be necessary.

Nonetheless, after initial consultation or some investigation, experienced labor lawyers have an idea of how much it will cost to bring a particular employment case to conclusion. One attorney who has left the private practice of law to specialize in counseling corporations on buying legal services has suggested companies take the following steps in ascertaining legal fees, whether for litigation matters or otherwise:

- Obtain a layperson's understanding of the main legal issues involved in the case (e.g., by reviewing materials readily available from trade associations, government agencies, and other human resource professionals in the same industry, as well as publications written for non-lawyers).
- Gather the relevant documents and understand them thoroughly before taking them to the attorney to be consulted.
- Define the company's economic and non-economic goals in the case.
- Try to determine how much the company is willing, or can afford, to spend in defending or in settling the suit.
- Determine whether the company must resolve the dispute by a particular date because of a pending merger, for example, or other transaction in which pending litigation could be debilitating.
- Ask about the likely sequence of activities and events and explore areas in which corporate personnel might participate to keep legal fees and expenses down (e.g., by searching for additional relevant documents or investigating facts).
- Discuss the specifics of the law firm's billing practices—when and how often the matter will be billed and how the work of the various personnel (e.g., associate attorneys, paralegals, and private investigators) will be monitored.

- Tell the law firm that the company will not pay for time spent educating inexperienced associate attorneys who may be involved.

- Commit preparatory work and discussions with legal counsel to writing.

[Harwi, "Dealing Effectively with a Lawyer," *Legal Triage News*, Jan. 1993, at 2]

Only recently have some high-volume users of legal services begun treating the legal profession as they would any other group of vendors. A growing trend is to move away from hourly billing toward billing by case or other project, much as other independent contractors must bid and perform at their own risk of misapprehending the difficulties involved. In addition, organizations are discovering that data over a wide range of litigation can be collected and used to model the likely costs and liability exposures in future, similar lawsuits. The bottom line is that soon legal fees and other litigation costs may change, at least for such major users as insurers. These users will reduce their unit costs. Also helping to push prices down is the trend toward using ADR techniques.

Q 14:16   How can employers manage their legal fees?

In employment litigation, defense costs are of great concern to employers, sometimes a greater concern than liability. Defense attorneys generally bill by the hourly rate, and given the time and effort needed to mount a defense, attorneys' fees are significant. Managing those legal fees is essential. Some measures can help manage these fees. Companies are advised to:

- Require written retainer agreements specifying the attorney involved and his or her hourly rates;

- Consider alternatives to the hourly rate, such as flat billing and value billing for various stages of the litigation (e.g., initial pleadings, interrogatories and document discovery, depositions, mediation, preparation for trial, trial, and appeal);

- Consider hiring in-house legal counsel or paralegals to conduct or assist the litigation;

- Utilize in-house staff to assemble documents and initial responses to discovery requests, to be reviewed and revised by an attorney, as needed;

- Require outside attorneys to establish a budget for the various stages of litigation and only pay for charges in excess of any budget limitations if the work was previously authorized;

- Send a request for a quotation to a number of law firms (attorneys are increasingly required to respond to these requests, and the practice, common among municipalities, is becoming more prevalent in the private sector);

- Require detailed monthly billing and assign an employee to review the billing carefully before authorizing payment; and

- Require attorneys to provide regular reports (every 60 days), advising the company on the assessment of the claim as to liability, their strategies to defend the claim, the plaintiff's potential damages associated with the claim, and settlement recommendations, if any. This forces the attorney to address the "big picture" at an early state rather than mindlessly "working" the file until the matter matures for trial down the road.

Q 14:17   Can legal fees be budgeted, and does this benefit the employer?

The most common complaint of companies regarding defense costs is surprise. Legal fees vary widely from month to month, depending on the activities undertaken during the month, and employers are often shocked when a large bill hits their office. Budgeting is not a science, but it does serve to provide some information to companies with respect to anticipated legal fees in connection with the defense of litigation. It is difficult, if not close to impossible, for a defense lawyer to predict the defense cost accurately in a case. Cases evolve, and the defense lawyer cannot control how the plaintiff's lawyer pursues the case. Discovery is a right, not a privilege, and a tenacious and diligent plaintiff's lawyer can require defense counsel to spend an inordinate amount of time responding to discovery requests. This cannot be anticipated or projected in any real sense by defense counsel in a budget. Despite these factors, budgeting does have value for companies and defense counsel is strongly encouraged to provide an initial budget that spells out costs for the various phases of the standard litigation process, which can be supplemented and amended as the case proceeds. At least then companies will have the best information available as to how much their defense costs will be.

Q 14:18   How do attorneys prepare a budget for litigation?

Although budgets can take many forms, and necessarily will need to be revised as the litigation proceeds, below is a sample working budget prepared by the authors in connection with the defense of a discrimination claim. This sample was created for a case whose defense was covered by insurance under an EPLI policy, and as a result, the hourly "insurance defense" rates are significantly less than hourly rates typically charged in private practice.

Projected Budget

Phase of Budget/Details			Cost
Preliminary Proceedings			**$5,675.00**
Client meetings and factual investigation			**$2,600.00**
Attorney Information	Hours	Rate/Hr	
Partner Interview of Witnesses (approx. 8)	8.00	$175.00	$1,400.00
Associate Interview of Witnesses (approx. 8)	8.00	$150.00	$1,200.00

			$	0.00
			$	0.00
Total Fees:	16.00	–	$	2,600.00
Additional Costs			$	0.00
Case/legal analysis			**$ 2,900.00**	
Attorney Information	Hours	Rate/Hr		
Partner	8.00	$175.00	$	1,400.00
Associate	10.00	$150.00	$	1,500.00
			$	0.00
			$	0.00
Total Fees:		–	$	2,900.00
Development of litigation budget			**$ 175.00**	
Attorney Information	Hours	Rate/Hr		
Partner	1.00	$175.00	$	175.00
			$	0.00
			$	0.00
			$	0.00
Total Fees:	1.00	–	$	175.00
Preliminary Pleadings			**$ 4,975.00**	
Legal research			**$ 3,125.00**	
Attorney Information	Hours	Rate/Hr		
Partner	5.00	$175.00	$	875.00
Associate	15.00	$150.00	$	2,250.00
			$	0.00
			$	0.00
Total Fees:		–	$	3,125.00
Additional Costs			$	0.00
Preparation and filing of pleadings			**$ 1,850.00**	
Attorney Information	Hours	Rate/Hr		
Partner	2.00	$175.00	$	350.00
Associate	10.00	$150.00	$	1,500.00
			$	0.00
			$	0.00
Total Fees:		–	$	1,850.00
General Discovery			**$34,750.00**	
Interrogatories, document requests, & request for admissions			**$ 2,600.00**	

Attorney Information	Hours	Rate/Hr	
Partner	2.00	$175.00	$ 350.00
Associate	15.00	$150.00	$2,250.00
			$ 0.00
			$ 0.00
Total Fees:		–	$2,600.00
Additional Costs			$ 0.00

Review adversary's response to discovery requests   **$1,100.00**

Attorney Information	Hours	Rate/Hr	
Partner	2.00	$175.00	$ 350.00
Associate	5.00	$150.00	$ 750.00
			$ 0.00
			$ 0.00
Total Fees:		–	$1,100.00
Additional Costs			$ 0.00

Further request for interrogatories, documents, and admissions   **$ 800.00**

Attorney Information	Hours	Rate/Hr	
Partner	2.00	$175.00	$ 350.00
Associate	3.00	$150.00	$ 450.00
			$ 0.00
			$ 0.00
Total Fees:			$ 800.00
Additional Costs			$ 0.00

Review of relevant client files and documents   **$2,375.00**

Attorney Information	Hours	Rate/Hr	
Partner	5.00	$175.00	$ 875.00
Associate	10.00	$150.00	$1,500.00
			$ 0.00
			$ 0.00
Total Fees:		–	$2,375.00
Additional Costs			$ 0.00

Preparation of objections and responses to adversary's requests   **$3,125.00**

Attorney Information	Hours	Rate/Hr	
Partner	5.00	$175.00	$ 875.00
Associate	15.00	$150.00	$2,250.00

			$	0.00
			$	0.00
Total Fees:	20.00	–	$	3,125.00
Additional Costs			$	0.00
Further response to adversary's request for additional information			**$ 1.850.00**	
Attorney Information	Hours	Rate/Hr		
Partner	2.00	$175.00	$	350.00
Associate	10.00	$150.00	$	1,500.00
			$	0.00
Total Fees:	12.00	–	$	1.850.00
Additional Costs			$	0.00
Preparation for and taking depositions—fact witness			**$12,475.00**	
Attorney Information	Hours	Rate/Hr		
Plaintiff	7.00	$175.00	$	1,225.00
Plaintiff lay witnesses approx. 9 @ 3 hours each	27.00	$175.00	$	4,725.00
Travel to Depositions	3.00	$175.00	$	525.00
			$	0.00
Total Fees:	37.00	–	$	6,475.00
Additional Costs	6000.00		$	6,000.00
Preparation for and defending depositions—fact witness			**$ 8,575.00**	
Attorney Information	Hours	Rate/Hr		
8 @ 5 hours each	40.00	$175.00	$	7,000.00
Defendant	6.00	$175.00	$	1,050.00
Travel to Depositions	3.00	$175.00	$	525.00
			$	0.00
Total Fees:	49.00	–	$	8,575.00
Additional Costs				
Discovery motions—research and preparation			**$ 1,850.00**	
Attorney Information	Hours	Rate/Hr		
Partner	2.00	$175.00	$	350.00
Associate	10.00	$150.00	$	1,500.00
Total Fees:		–	$	1,850.00
Additional Costs				

	Hours	Rate/Hr		
Expert Witnesses			$	5,300.00
Identification, retention, and meetings with experts			$	700.00
Attorney Information	Hours	Rate/Hr		
Partner	4.00	$175.00	$	700.00
			$	0.00
			$	0.00
			$	0.00
Total Fees:	–		$	700.00
Additional Costs				
Prepare for and attend all expert depositions			$	4,600.00
Attorney Information	Hours	Rate/Hr		
Plaintiff: 1 Expert	6.00	$175.00	$	1,050.00
Defendant: 1 Expert	6.00	$175.00	$	1,050.00
			$	0.00
			$	0.00
			$	0.00
			$	0.00
			$	0.00
Total Fees:	12.00	–	$	2,100.00
Additional Costs	2500.00		$	2,500.00
Motions			**$14,000.00**	
Summary judgment			$	7,000.00
Attorney Information	Hours	Rate/Hr		
Partner	8.00	$175.00	$	1,400.00
Associate	20.00	$150.00	$	3,000.00
Travel to Hearing	12.00	$175.00	$	2,100.00
			$	0.00
Total Fees:	40.00	–	$	6,500.00
Additional Costs	500.00		$	500.00
Motions in limine			$	7,000.00
Attorney Information	Hours	Rate/Hr		
Partner	8.00	$175.00	$	1,400.00
Associate	20.00	$150.00	$	3,000.00
Travel to Hearing	12.00	$175.00	$	2,100.00
			$	0.00
Total Fees:	40.00	–	$	6,500.00
Additional Costs	500.00		$	500.00

	Hours	Rate/Hr		
Other substantive motions			$	0.00
Attorney Information	Hours	Rate/Hr		
			$	0.00
			$	0.00
			$	0.00
			$	0.00
Experts			$	0.00
Total Fees:		–	$	0.00
Additional Costs			$	0.00
Pretrial Appearances			**$**	**5,300.00**
Status and pretrial conferences			**$**	**1,200.00**
Attorney Information	Hours	Rate/Hr		
Partner	2.00	$175.00	$	350.00
Travel	2.00	$175.00	$	350.00
			$	0.00
			$	0.00
Total Fees:	4.00	–	$	700.00
Additional Costs	500.00		$	500.00
Settlement conferences/other ADR			**$**	**4,100.00**
Attorney Information	Hours	Rate/Hr		
Partner	8.00	$175.00	$	1,400.00
Associate	8.00	$150.00	$	1,200.00
			$	0.00
			$	0.00
Total Fees:	16.00	–	$	2,600.00
Additional Costs	1500.00		$	1,500.00
Trial			**$20,355.00**	
Preparation of trial documents/briefs/ motions			**$**	**3,875.00**
Attorney Information	Hours	Rate/Hr		
Partner	5.00	$175.00	$	875.00
Associate	20.00	$150.00	$	3,000.00
			$	0.00
			$	0.00
			$	0.00
Total Fees:	25.00	–	$	3,875.00
Additional Costs			$	0.00

Preparation for trial/other			$ 6,480.00
Attorney Information	Hours	Rate/Hr	
Partner	20.00	$175.00	$ 3,500.00
Associate	20.00	$150.00	$ 3,000.00
			$ 0.00
			$ 0.00
			$ 0.00
Total Fees:	40.00	–	$ 6,480.00
Additional Costs			$ 0.00
Trial			**$10,000.00**
Attorney Information	Hours	Rate/Hr	
Partner	40.00	$175.00	$ 7,000.00
Associate	20.00	$150.00	$ 3,000.00
			$ 0.00
			$ 0.00
			$ 0.00
Total Fees:	60.00	–	$10,000.00
Additional Costs			$ 0.00
Post Trial Motions			**$ 2,375.00**
Preparation and filing of motions			**$ 2,375.00**
Attorney Information	Hours	Rate/Hr	
Partner	5.00	$175.00	$ 875.00
Associate	10.00	$150.00	$ 1,500.00
			$ 0.00
			$ 0.00
Total Fees:	15.00	–	$ 2,375.00
Additional Costs			$ 0.00
Appeals			$ 0.00
Totals			$91,950.00

Q 14:19   What is *value billing*?

At some point in the past, the hourly rate became the measure for compensating attorneys. The idea of value billing, which is really an old concept, has been resurrected as an alternative. *Value billing*, in its strictest sense, is a specific price for a particular project or a piece of a project without regard to the number of hours spent on it. Although the hourly rate tends to be the benchmark for judging whether value billing is attractive to a client, value billing also provides certainty with respect to legal expenses. For many employers, particularly those that rely heavily on budgets in tracking their performance, value billing is a wise alternative to the somewhat unpredictable nature of the hourly fee system.

Q 14:20   What steps can an employer take to reduce legal fees, even if it retains its attorneys on an hourly basis?

An employer can follow these guidelines:

- There will be no payment for summarizing deposition transcripts, unless specifically authorized by the company. Most court reporters can provide comprehensive indexes and computer disks for transcripts, making the time-consuming process of drafting deposition summaries unnecessary.

- The attorney should prepare and initial a monthly, detailed billing statement that specifies the time spent for each entry.

- The employer should specify the attorneys in the firm who can perform work on the case. Although using several attorneys within a firm can benefit a client, increasing the number of attorneys involved in a matter necessarily increases the billing. Therefore, the employer should limit the attorneys to those needed and require the firm to get its authorization before involving other attorneys in the matter.

- Most law firms, when asked, will agree not to bill a client for internal copying charges, secretarial overtime, local telephone charges, and other incidental administrative charges.

- The company should require a comprehensive risk-and-exposure analysis of the case early on and have it updated every 60 days thereafter.

- The company should consider requiring the attorney to provide a budget of attorneys' fees.

- Pre-trial discovery motions can be time-consuming and costly. Usually, they are not required if the attorneys on both sides can agree among themselves to work out the inevitable scheduling difficulties for pre-trial discovery. The employer should discourage pre-trial discovery motions and require approval before they are filed.

- The employer should assign in-house staff the responsibility to assemble documents and information in response to discovery requests. The corporate attorney will do all of this work if required; however, it is tedious, time-consuming, and costly. It is better to utilize in-house staff for these seemingly mundane but important tasks, and have the attorney review the information for preparation and finalization of pleadings.

- Legal research is an essential part of practicing law. But research that is not managed can run on unnecessarily, driving up costs. The company should require the law firm to seek its approval for any single research project that extends beyond a certain limit (e.g., 10 hours).

- Although meetings are an important means of communication between a client and his or her attorney, meetings tend to be very time consuming and costly. If the meeting is held at the client's location and if more than one attorney is present, the cost of the meeting can be great in relationship to the benefits obtained. In addition, it is this author's experience that most meetings last at least one hour even if the business portion of the meeting could be conducted in half of that time. Consider conference phone calls, e-mail, or other means of communication when a meeting is not necessary.

To avoid uncertainty, the employer should put all guidelines in writing and clearly spell them out in any retainer agreement.

Q 14:21   What is *EPLI*, and is it a good idea?

EPLI is employment practices liability insurance that employers purchase to insure them against employment claims. Over the years, EPLI has spread like wildfire throughout the country. More and more carriers are offering this type of insurance, and more and more insurance agents are soliciting their clients to purchase it. Although many different such products exist, insurance is generally available to cover both liability and defense costs up to various limits. Liability typically covers a wide range of potential liability including federal and state discrimination claims and wrongful discharge. The benefit of EPLI is clear. Employment law is risky, and every company is concerned about defense costs and the horrific case that might result in great liability. Insurance is a means of stabilizing costs, through premiums, and providing legal defense and protection in the event of a large verdict or award.

As with any insurance product, the terms and conditions between polices vary, and the language should be reviewed carefully with an experienced employment attorney. Language that specifically defines covered occurrences and does not contain broad references to any and all claims under enumerated federal or state statutes needs to be reviewed carefully to ascertain whether there are any holes in the coverage. Recognize that the employment area is one of the most heavily regulated areas in the law, and policies that focus on the obvious federal or state civil rights statutes but fail to address other potential claims, such as claims under the Family Medical Leave Act (FMLA) or common law breach of contract claims, may not provide the level of coverage expected by the insured.

It is also important to understand that most EPLI policies are claims-made policies, which means they only cover claims first made during the insurance period. The product will typically disavow coverage for any claims made prior to the insurance period. Because there are many different types of claims that an employer can lodge against a company, such as an EEOC charge followed by a federal lawsuit, the company needs to ensure that the insurance company is notified each time a particular claim is made. Failure to notify an insurance company of an administrative charge may result in a denial of coverage if litigation is filed sometime thereafter.

Q 14:22   If a company purchases EPLI, will it be able to retain its own attorneys to defend it in employment litigation?

Probably not. Most EPLI insurers require the use of attorneys it has selected to provide a defense. These attorneys are maintained on a so-called "Panel List" and are selected on the basis of their experience in handling employment litigation and their agreement to abide by the insurance company's billing guidelines and procedures.

Q 14:23   Does a law firm hired and paid for by an insurance company really represent the employer's interests?

It had better. Although paid by the insurance company, the client is the employer, not the insurance company, and attorneys owe their clients various duties and responsibilities under the rules of professional conduct adopted in states throughout the country.

Alternative Dispute Resolution

Q 14:24   What is *alternative dispute resolution*?

Although many terms are used in connection with the ADR process (with facilitation, mediation, and arbitration being the most common) there are essentially two types of ADR—binding ADR and nonbinding ADR. Except for various types of ADR required in some states (e.g., nonbinding ADR is required for all civil actions in Michigan), the decision to undergo ADR is voluntary and may be contained in an agreement entered into prior to dispute, or agreed to in an attempt to resolve the dispute after the dispute arises. Nonbinding ADR is usually termed facilitation or mediation. In *facilitation*, typically the parties agree upon the selection of a facilitator, and the parties and their representatives meet with the facilitator to determine whether there is any basis for resolving the dispute at that time. This process is typically informal and the facilitator works with both sides in an effort to arrive at a realistic compromise of their varying positions. *Mediation*, although similar to facilitation, usually involves nonbinding case evaluation of a claim wherein the mediator(s) issue an award after presentation of the claims and defenses by the respective attorneys, which either side can accept or reject, often in accordance with local court rule. In case evaluation, the mediators attempt to issue an award to which they believe both sides should agree to resolve the case. Arbitration, on the other hand, is binding ADR, whereby the parties present their case, much in the same way that a case would be presented at trial, to the arbitrator. The arbitrator then makes a final decision in the case, typically referred to as an award. These awards are generally final and binding, absent evidence of bias, fraud, or the like. Most states have arbitration statutes that govern the process and provide for limited judicial review of an arbitrator's award under extreme circumstances.

Parties can voluntarily agree to submit employment disputes to any form of ADR as they see fit after the dispute arises. Whether an employee can agree to submit to binding ADR prior to dispute was the subject of great debate in the legal community, until *Circuit City Stores, Inc. v. Adams* [532 U.S. 105 (2001)], where the U.S. Supreme Court upheld use of a binding pre-dispute arbitration agreement to require the employment claim be submitted to arbitration.

Q 14:25   What are the advantages of binding arbitration?

Employment discrimination claims are costly and time-consuming. Binding arbitration is a relatively similar and more straightforward process that does not involve the time and expense associated with traditional judicial litigation. In addition, from an employer's perspective, binding arbitration may be viewed as a wise alternative because it does not involve a jury trial. There are three good reasons why employers should agree to binding arbitration: (1) no jury; (2) no jury; and (3) no jury. The absence of a risk of runaway jury verdicts, together with reduced defense costs, is sufficient to warrant consideration of binding arbitration by an employer in almost every case.

Q 14:26   What procedures are typically followed in the binding arbitration of employment disputes?

The Employment Arbitration Rules and Mediation Procedures, last amended November 1, 2009 (Arbitration Rules), as established by the American Arbitration Association (AAA), are a good example of the procedures involved in connection with the arbitration of employment disputes. The Arbitration Rules provide a process for the selection of arbitrator(s) (i.e., a single arbitrator or three or more arbitrators), establish schedules for the determination of administrative fees, and provide a process for the matter to proceed from initial filing to hearing. As a result of amendments to the Arbitration Rules, if arbitration is a result of an "employer-promulgated plan," the employer pays the fees in connection with the arbitration, which includes the arbitrator's fee and AAA administrative fees. However, if the arbitration agreement is contained within an "individually negotiated" employment agreement or contract, the arbitrator's fees are split between the parties, and the employee must pay, subject to hardship waivers and deferrals, the filing fees provided for under the rules. Because discovery is so critical to both the prosecution and defense of an employment dispute, the Arbitration Rules allow for reasonable discovery as determined by the arbitrator(s), in light of the expedited nature of arbitration proceedings but nonetheless allowing for a full and fair discovery of the issues at hand. The Arbitration Rules also provide for voluntary mediation, should the parties desire. Mediation involves informal meetings before the parties with a mediator to ascertain whether or not a mutually acceptable resolution of the matter can be obtained prior to binding arbitration. The Arbitration Rules provide that the award from a hearing must be in writing, provide written reasons for the award unless the parties provide otherwise, and provide that the award is final and binding subject to judicial review only as provided by law. A complete copy of the rules can be found at AAA's Web site at http://www.adr.org.

Q 14:27   What is *nonbinding facilitation*, how much does it cost, and is it beneficial?

The use of nonbinding facilitation is growing. The EEOC has established an ADR program in many locales, inviting participants in selected charges to submit to nonbinding facilitation. In Fiscal Year 2012, the EEOC reported that it successfully resolved 8,704 charges· through its nonbinding facilitation/mediation process out of 11,380 that took part in the process, resulting in a success rate of 76 percent. In Michigan, facilitation is available as an additional form of ADR in its court rules. In litigation, facilitation is best served after initial discovery but before finalization of all discovery and preparation necessary to present the case at trial. From a defense standpoint, one of the benefits of settlement, and therefore facilitation, early on is to avoid the inevitable expense and effort in connection with a trial. On the other hand, if facilitation is attempted too early, before initial discovery and depositions of critical witnesses, facilitation efforts can be hampered because the parties are not yet able to analyze the strengths or weaknesses of their positions objectively and, as a result, tend to overstate their positions and resulting offers and demands.

Assuming the timing is right, facilitation can be a successful vehicle for resolving disputes. The selection of a facilitator is critical. Generally, the parties should select an individual whom both parties respect and recognize as an objective professional who is experienced in the area of employment law. Undoubtedly, the need for a facilitator bespeaks the inability of the parties themselves to solve a dispute, and the facilitator must be able to sway the parties into ultimately agreeing to compromise their positions. In addition, the facilitator selected should be someone who will "roll up their sleeves" and do his or her best to try to effectuate resolution of the case. Calling references of other attorneys that have used the facilitator in the past can provide useful information on this point. There is nothing more frustrating than having a facilitator declare an impasse early on after initial posturing by each side. The key to a good facilitator is one who has the patience and diligence to allow the process to evolve and determine if settlement can be reached.

Facilitators typically charge an hourly fee, and the process of facilitation should be expected to last about a day. The facilitator will generally ask each party to provide a written summary of its position, together with any relevant documents or records (including the personnel file), and these documents and records will be reviewed prior to the facilitation meeting itself. During the facilitation meeting, although many different approaches might be taken, the facilitator will generally ask each party to state its respective position, the facilitator will ask questions, and initial offers and demands will be enunciated. After this, the parties will usually be asked to move to separate rooms with the facilitator jockeying between the groups working them slowly and diligently toward compromise.

Employment cases are emotional ones, and generally take time to work toward facilitation. It is recommended that the facilitator prepare a confidentiality agreement, which will assist facilitation. The confidentiality agreement typically provides that any statement made during the facilitation process is confidential and will only be used in connection with the facilitation. The facilitator agrees to keep confidential and not discuss with the other side any information provided to the facilitator in confidence by either side during the facilitation process, and the facilitator will not be called as a witness regarding statements made during the facilitation process other than in connection with the enforcement of an agreement reached as a result of the facilitation. Typically, the parties agree to split fees of the facilitator, and in light of current hourly rates nationally, parties should each expect to spend between $1,500 and $2,500 for the typical one-day facilitation.

Facilitation can be beneficial, and there is really no downside to the process. The process is relatively inexpensive and allows the parties to determine if the case can be resolved. Even if the case is not resolved, the facilitation process often serves as a springboard for further settlement discussions. Facilitation should not, however, be undertaken if either party shows no genuine interest in resolving the dispute. Most cases, strong or weak, have a number that either side would consider to resolve the issue. But if either party is not interested in settlement and, either through inexperience or principle, wants its "day in court," facilitation will likely be a waste of time.

Avoiding Employee Claims

Q 14:28   What can employers do to help reduce their risk of exposure to employee claims?

Although claims cannot be eliminated with a magic wand, reasonable procedures adopted by employers can minimize the risk of being sued and, if they are sued, reduce the exposure. Below is a set of guidelines geared toward this goal:

- *The hiring process.* There are numerous protected categories under both federal and state civil rights laws. Interviewers should be admonished not to treat applicants differently on the basis of protective categories, or make any inquiry into protected areas, lest the applicant think that such inquiry is an indication of bias. As to issues of disability, it is always advisable that no inquiry as to a medical condition be made, even if apparent and obvious, until after a bona fide offer of employment.

- *Harassment.* Employers should adopt and disseminate a written policy against harassment in all forms. The policy should both encourage complaints and provide for a prompt and thorough investigation of complaints. Employees and supervisors should be trained to identify illegal harassment, know their responsibilities for coming forward to complain of harassment, and be familiar with the investigation process.

- *Civil rights training.* Employees and supervisors should to be trained as to how discrimination claims can be maintained, both through direct evidence and circumstantial evidence, together with additional emphasis on retaliation and public policy claims.

- *Written discipline.* Supervisors need to mete out written discipline when needed and take the time to provide accurate performance evaluations.

- *Discharge of an employee.* Before discharging an employee, an employer should review the matter to ensure that a proper investigation for the infraction has been taken, that the discipline is even-handed and consistent with the individual's personnel file, and that similar infractions for similarly situated employees resulted in similar discipline. If the discharge is for poor performance over time, prior written discipline should alert the employee of the problem and notify the employee that his or her job is in jeopardy if poor performance continues.

- *Avoid bad timing.* Bad timing issues come into play in a number of different types of lawsuits, including pregnancy discrimination claims, retaliation claims, and whistleblower claims. If an employee suffers an adverse employment action soon after the employee declares her pregnancy, complains of harassment, or threatens to report the employer to a government agency, the tendency is to believe that the action was taken for an improper or illegal motive, absent clear proof to the contrary.

- *FMLA.* Supervisors should understand the employer's FMLA policies and procedures and be trained to spot time off that may be allocable to an employee's FMLA allotment.

Employers should give serious consideration to engaging experienced employment and labor counsel to assist in making decisions that may have an adverse impact on personnel. Unless you are a trained and experienced employment attorney, you will have a difficult time determining the "best practices" to reduce the risk and exposure to claims in any given situation. Each employment matter is different, and legal advice in this area is rarely black and white, but varies for each individual situation. By seeking legal advice in connection with employment decisions, employees can avoid the vast amounts of time and money spent defending decisions made without benefit of counsel.

Q 14:29   What is a *labor audit?*

The term *labor audit* refers to a process of review and analysis typically undertaken by an employment lawyer to determine what, if any, recommendations should be made to help reduce an employer's risk and exposure to employee claims.

Although no formal guidelines have been established for this process, it generally includes:

- Review of applications and the hiring process and procedures;
- Review of mandatory postings;
- Review of disciplinary forms and procedures;

- Review of handbook or other written policies and procedures;
- Consideration of necessary training of employees and/or supervisors;
- Review of employee contracts such as employment agreements, non-competition agreements, pre-dispute arbitration agreements, confidentiality agreements, and/or assignment of ideas and inventions agreements;
- Review of employee classifications (exempt or non-exempt) and wage/hour compliance under the FLSA and state law;
- Review of any collective bargaining agreements with management to identify problems and concerns;
- Review of sample personnel files to assess if "best practices" are in use; and
- Assessment of FMLA, COBRA, IRCA I-9, and HIPAA compliance.

After a review has taken place, recommendations are typically made as to what the employer can do to create and/or modify its policies and procedures toward reducing the employer's risk and exposure to employment claims.

Chapter 15

Employment Law in the Global Marketplace

Before 1964—when the federal Civil Rights Act, which includes Title VII's outlawing of employment discrimination—an American labor lawyer need only have known the National Labor Relations Act (NLRA) to practice competently. Now employment lawyers and human resources executives must be versed not only in multiple U.S. HR laws, but also in both international law and the employment laws and policies of the world's major nations. Additionally, a working knowledge of U.S. immigration law is virtually a "must," as new arrivals and employees of overseas subsidiaries increasingly figure into the workforces of American-based firms.

Americans do business in almost all of the approximately 200 sovereign nations of the world. The economies of these many countries span the spectrum from free markets to communist dictatorships (although these latter entities have declined dramatically in number and influence). Political systems and governmental attitudes toward unions and workers' rights vary just as widely around the world. Labor and tax laws and practices necessarily vary just as dramatically. This chapter covers international employment law issues.

International Labor Relations

Q 15:1   What is the *North American Free Trade Agreement*?

The *North American Free Trade Agreement (NAFTA)* was ratified by the U.S. Senate and the enabling legislation enacted by the U.S. Congress as a whole in 1993. It creates an enormous free trade zone consisting of Mexico, the United States, and Canada—essentially all of the North American continent. The main purpose of NAFTA is to meet the preserved economic threat of the European Union (EU) on the other side of the Atlantic.

NAFTA is supplemented by two significant side agreements:

1. The North American Agreement on Labor Cooperation;

2. The North American Agreement on Environmental Cooperation.

(For more on the North American Agreement on Labor Cooperation, see chapter 1. For immigration aspects of NAFTA, see chapter 12.)

Q 15:2   Which other laws and treaties have an effect on international labor relations?

U.S.-based companies and business people doing, or seeking to do, business globally must be mindful of the following legal rules:

1. Treaties made by the executive branch of the U.S. government and ratified by the U.S. Senate have the same force and effect as U.S. statutes. In other words, they are federal laws.

2. Among the most important treaties that are a part of U.S. labor and employment law are the tax treaties that have been enacted between and among all of America's major trading partners. Awareness and knowledge of these tax treaties is critical to American workers dispatched overseas by their multinational corporate employers.

Q 15:3   Which other international labor laws may be relevant to Americans doing business globally?

The International Labor Organization (ILO) is a branch of the United Nations. Based in Geneva, the ILO has promulgated a vast scheme of labor and employment laws, regulations, and guidelines. ILO "laws" cannot supersede an individual nation's sovereignty unless that nation affirmatively adopts any such laws. The United States is not a signatory to many ILO enactments or pronouncements; however, U.S. labor and employment in many instances is equal or superior to the ILO scheme in according rights and remedies to workers within our borders (exceptions involved labor organization rights and employment security versus employment at will). All the same, Americans doing business globally must be mindful of ILO legal principles possibly adopted by the nations in which they are doing business and possibly employing personnel. United States' embassies and consulates should be consulted not only about the labor and employment laws of the host nation but also about any such relevant ILO rules and regulations.

International conventions to which the United States is a signatory that should be noted when doing business abroad, and that can affect international labor relations and employment litigation, include:

1. *Convention on the Service Abroad of Judicial and Extrajudicial Documents in Civil or Commercial Matters*: facilitates and standardizes the service of legal processes, such as complaints, summons, and subpoenas, in pursuit of litigation, including labor and employment litigation.

2. *Convention on the Recognition and Enforcement of Foreign Arbitral Awards*: assures that signatory states will enforce arbitral awards, including labor and employment arbitration awards, against parties found within their jurisdictions.

3. *Convention on the Taking of Evidence Abroad in Civil or Commercial Matters*: a judicial authority (e.g., a court) in one contracting state may request its counterpart in another contracting state to facilitate such discovery activities as the taking of depositions or sworn statements in support of litigation, including labor and employment litigation.

4. *Convention on the Civil Aspects of International Child Abduction*: bears a close relationship to efforts to control and eliminate exploitation of child labor.

5. *Domestic Workers Convention:* a 2011 convention that recognizes the significant contribution of domestic workers to the global economy, including substantial income transfers within and between countries, by guaranteeing domestic workers labor protections equivalent to those of other workers.

The major conventions on labor and employment, adopted under the auspices of the United Nations and the ILO, most of which have not been signed by the United States (primarily because they may conflict with existing U.S. labor and employment laws), are as follows:

Title of Convention	*Date of Adoption*
Convention Concerning Abolition of Forced Labour	June 25, 1957 (The United States is a signatory)
Abolition of Forced Labour Convention	January 17, 1958
Discrimination (Employment and Occupation)	June 25, 1958
Employment Policy Convention	July 9, 1964
Convention Concerning the Promotion of Collective Bargaining	June 19, 1981
Convention Concerning Employment Promotion and Protection	June 21, 1988

Q 15:4 What role does the concept of corporate social responsibility play in the global marketplace?

According to Senior Fellow and Director of Globalization Studies Susan Aaronson of the Kenan Institute, Washington Center, global corporate social responsibility is:

- A foreign policy issue in that corporations are ambassadors of their nation's values;

- An economic issue in that America's future markets are overseas; and

- A moral issue on which the reputation of the corporation, its management, and shareholders depends on doing business abroad.

Whether corporate social responsibility extends to treatment of foreign employees may depend upon the policies and laws of the host nation. For example, in a vigorous effort to eradicate child labor and slavery, Brazil has enacted a "National Pact" which includes placing firms profiting from child and slave workers on a so-called "Dirty List."

In the United Kingdom, a nation characterized in the recent past by protection and encouragement of labor (see Q 15:14), a Minister of Corporate Social Responsibility was appointed for the first time in 2000. The United Kingdom, Germany, and Belgium require private pension funds to report on the social responsibility performances of the companies in which they have invested their members' contributions. Because of their historically protective attitudes toward their labor forces, it must be noted that private pensions constitute only small fractions of the overall retirement schemes in these nations. Since 2001, the Dutch government has required all firms seeking taxpayer-funded export credits to attest to their adherence to specified social responsibility guidelines. In 2002, France for the first time mandated disclosure of corporate social and environmental performance.

In the United States, the mission of promoting "labor and corporate social responsibility falls to a unit of the Department of State" (DOS). Strengthening respect for worker rights and promoting corporate social responsibility around the world contributes to the U.S. foreign policy goals of democracy promotion, free trade, international development, and human rights.

The State Department's Office of International Labor and Corporate Social Responsibility, part of the Bureau of Democracy, Human Rights and Labor, promotes these issues in partnership with the private sector, organized labor, non-governmental organizations (NGOs), intergovernmental organizations, international organizations, and other U.S. federal agencies.

Key priority areas include:

- Promoting organized labor and their role as reformers in developing countries;

- Partnering with the private sector to protect human rights, including workers' rights, and to promote good governance, transparency, and the rule of law;

- Promoting labor rights through free trade agreements and other international negotiations; and

- Combating child labor, forced labor, and trafficking in persons.

The State Department supports projects that promote these goals, including an anti-sweatshop initiative to fund the development of approaches to combat sweatshop labor in overseas factories. Since 2000, nearly $18 million in projects have been funded through this initiative. [*See* http://2001-2009.state.gov/g/drl/lbr/.]

Q 15:5   What are the characteristics of a socially responsible corporation in the global marketplace?

Unilever is frequently cited as an exemplar of corporate social responsibility. The firm's own vision statement is: "As a multi-local multinational we aim to play our part in addressing global environmental and social concerns through local actions and in partnership with local governments and organizations." [http://www.unilever.com/ourvalues/] It expands upon that vision statement in its corporate history, saying:

> In the late 19th century the businesses that would later become Unilever were among the most philanthropic of their time. They set up projects to improve the lot of their workers and created products with a positive social impact, making hygiene and personal care commonplace and improving nutrition through adding vitamins to foods that were already daily staples. Today, Unilever still believes that success means acting with "the highest standards of corporate behavior towards our employees, consumers and the societies and world in which we live." Over the years we've launched or participated in an ever-growing range of initiatives to source sustainable supplies of raw materials, protect environments, support local communities and much more.

> Through this timeline you'll see how our brand portfolio has evolved. At the beginning of the 21st century, our Path to Growth strategy focused us on global high-potential brands and our Vitality mission is taking us into a new phase of development. More than ever, our brands are helping people "feel good, look good and get more out of life"—a sentiment close to Lord Leverhulme's heart over a hundred years ago.

[http://www.unilever.com/ourcompany/aboutunilever/history/default.asp]

Now one of the largest global corporations, Unilever's published policy on employees is as follows:

> Unilever is committed to diversity in a working environment where there is mutual trust and respect and where everyone feels responsible for the performance and reputation of our company. We will recruit, employ and promote employees on the sole basis of the qualifications and abilities needed for the work to be performed. We are committed to safe and healthy working conditions for all employees. We will not use any form of forced, compulsory or child labor. We are committed to working with employees to develop and enhance each individual's skills and capabilities. We respect the dignity of the individual and the

right of employees to freedom of association. We will maintain good communications with employees through company based information and consultation procedures.

[http://www.unilever.com/aboutus/purposeandprinciples/ourprinciples/]

These values are far from alien to U.S. society and corporations. The difference is that Unilever, a company with its genesis in the Lever Brothers firm of the 1890s, has reportedly put these policies into action in the global labor arena.

Q 15:6   What is the NetFreedom Task Force?

Former Secretary of State Condoleezza Rice established the Global Internet Freedom Task Force (GIFT, currently known as the NetFreedom Task Force) on February 14, 2006, as an internal State Department coordination group to address challenges to freedom of expression and the free flow of information on the Internet. The core aims of the GIFT are to maximize freedom of expression and the free flow of information and ideas, to minimize the success of repressive regimes in censoring and silencing legitimate debate, and to promote access to information and ideas over the Internet. We refer to such freedom of expression on the Internet as "Internet freedom." Since its launch in February 2006, the Task Force has developed a robust global Internet strategy that aims to monitor and respond to threats to Internet freedom and to advance the frontiers of Internet freedom by expanding access to the Internet. In executing this strategy, the State Department is coordinating its efforts with other U.S. government agencies and the National Security and National Economic Councils.

The GIFT strategy is organized around three priorities:

- Monitoring Internet freedom in countries around the world.
  - U.S. embassies around the globe are tasked with monitoring the Internet in their respective nations and including instances of censorship in their annual human-rights reports.
- Responding to challenges to Internet freedom.
  - When State Department officials detect serious incidents of Internet repression, they are instructed to express concern promptly and directly to the foreign government involved. The DOS claims to be committed to pressing the message on Internet freedom in official dialogues with other countries, especially those in which Internet freedom is threatened. The DOS also says it will work with like-minded governments to promote Internet freedom and to press other governments to live up to their existing international commitments regarding freedom of expression and the free flow of information and ideas. The department adds that it will work to ensure existing international commitments to the free flow of information and freedom of expression are upheld and replicated in appropriate international forums. DOS says it also stands ready to engage appropriately with the technology industry, NGOs, and other stakeholders in a process aimed at developing shared principles to guide private sector activities in restrictive economies.

- Advancing Internet freedom by expanding access to the Internet.
  - Through multiple U.S. government programs (including USAID projects and The Telecommunications Leadership Program) and public-private partnerships (The Digital Freedom Initiative), the U.S. government promotes expanded Internet access and the availability of information and communication technologies (ICTs) in developing countries. Since 2004, the U.S. government has spent more than $250 million on projects that include providing telecommunications infrastructure, Internet access, computer hardware, and support for regulatory reform in order to ensure sustainable infrastructure development. These projects also include the design of Web sites and databases and training on ICTs.
  - Where appropriate, the government supports the provision of unfiltered information to people living under conditions of censorship.

[See http://www.america.gov/st/democracyhrenglish/2008/July/20080715 094516xjsnommis0.3989832.html and http://www.state.gov/e/eb/cip/net Freedom/index.htm]

Q 15:7 Can a U.S. state's whistleblower law trump an international treaty?

In a case of first impression, the U.S. Court of Appeals for the Ninth Circuit held that a treaty between the U.S. and Japan does not trump California's whistleblower statute in a claim pursued by American employees of a Japanese airline. [Ventress v. Japan Airlines, 486 F.3d 1111 (9th Cir. 2007)]

Facts. JAL is a Japanese commercial air carrier based in Tokyo. HACS, a Hawaii corporation with its principal place of business in Honolulu, provides contract flight crews to JAL. Plaintiffs Ventress and Crawford were employed by HACS to perform services for JAL flights. The plaintiffs' employment agreements with HACS contained mandatory arbitration provisions.

In December 2002, Ventress and Crawford jointly filed a complaint against JAL and HACS in the U.S. District Court for the Central District of California. The complaint alleged that JAL required a seriously ill pilot to fly in June 2001, in violation of American and Japanese aviation laws as well as JAL's own operations manual. Crawford expressed his concern to a JAL official in Honolulu in July 2001. Afterward, he experienced harassment from his superiors, including repeated performance checks, questions, and homework assignments. In December 2001, HACS informed Crawford that his assignment to JAL was cancelled because of unsatisfactory performance. That same month, Ventress submitted reports on the June incidents to JAL, HACS, and aviation regulators. Ventress claimed repeated harassment from JAL thereafter, including demands to undergo psychiatric evaluations. Ventress was not allowed to fly after September 2001. The complaint sought recovery for violation of California's whistleblower statute, wrongful termination in violation of the public policy protecting whistleblowers, and emotional distress. All claims were brought under California law.

The California whistleblower law states in pertinent part: "An employer may not retaliate against an employee for disclosing information to a government or law enforcement agency, where the employee has reasonable cause to believe that the information discloses a violation of state or federal statute, or a violation or noncompliance with a state or federal regulation." [Cal. Labor Code § 1102.5(b)]

Additionally, the litigants alleged that their terminations violated the public policy expressed in 49 U.S.C. § 42121(a)(1), which prohibits air carriers from discriminating against any employee because the employee "provided, caused to be provided, or is about to provide (with any knowledge of the employer) or cause to be provided to the employer or Federal Government information relating to any violation or alleged violation of any order, regulation, or standard of the Federal Aviation Administration."

In July 2003, the California district court granted the defendants' motion to transfer the case to the District of Hawaii. The district court explained that nearly all the events giving rise to the complaint occurred in international air space or in Hawaii, and that Hawaii was the more convenient forum for potential witnesses and for accessing HACS' personnel records. After the venue change, plaintiffs moved to amend the complaint to replace their California law claims with Hawaii law claims. A magistrate judge denied that motion, and plaintiffs appealed to the Hawaii district court.

In October 2004, the Hawaii district court granted judgment on the pleadings for JAL on the ground that all the plaintiffs' claims were preempted by the Friendship, Commerce, and Navigation Treaty, U.S.-Japan, April 2, 1953 [4 U.S.T.2063] (Japan FCN Treaty). The court further held that the emotional distress claims failed as a matter of California law, even if they were not preempted. The court declined to rule on the plaintiffs' appeal of the denial of leave to amend, saying that the issue was mooted by its decision on treaty preemption. The court then severed the claims against HACS and entered a stipulation and order staying further proceedings pending arbitration. After Ventress and Crawford disputed the applicable arbitration rules, the court entered an order compelling arbitration under the commercial rules of the American Arbitration Association (AAA).

Ventress and Crawford filed separate appeals from the judgment for JAL. Although Ventress and Crawford were represented by the same lawyer when they filed the complaint, Ventress then proceeded *pro se*. Ventress alone appealed the change of venue and the order placing arbitration under AAA commercial rules.

Issues. The consolidated appeals present three questions: (1) whether the Hawaii district court erred in ruling that the Japan FCN Treaty preempted the plaintiffs' claims under California's whistleblower protection laws, (2) whether the California district court abused its discretion in transferring the case to Hawaii, and (3) whether the interlocutory order compelling arbitration is appealable. The district court held that the emotional distress claims failed as a matter of California law, and neither of the plaintiffs appealed that decision.

Regarding the preemption issue, the appeals panel noted, "The post-World War II Friendship, Commerce and Navigation treaties were negotiated in a period characterized by so-called 'percentile' restrictions which required American companies operating abroad to hire a certain percentage of citizens of the host country. These restrictions were thought to have the effect of inhibiting American companies operating abroad from hiring the people in whom they had the greatest confidence. Similarly, a number of states had laws restricting or banning the employment of aliens by foreign companies doing business within the state. The legislative history of the post-war treaties suggests that both parties deemed the right to utilize the services of their own nationals in managerial, technical, and confidential capacities to be critical."

Therefore, continued the court,

> Given the purpose and history of the FCN treaties, our sister circuits have consistently held that foreign employers do not enjoy immunity from domestic employment laws that do not interfere with the employers' ability to hire their fellow citizens. In *MacNamra v. Korean Air Lines,* 863 F.2d 1135 (3d. Cir. Pa 1988) the Third Circuit considered a provision in the Korea FCN treaty that is identical in language to article VIII(1). The plaintiff, having been terminated by his Korean employer and replaced by a Korean citizen, sought recovery for race, national origin and age discrimination. The employer argued that it enjoyed treaty conferred immunity from federal anti-discrimination statutes. The court disagreed. The court explained that the treaty's negotiating history "[wa]s barren of any suggestion that Article VIII(1) was intended to achieve anything other than the right to utilize one's own citizens in the capacities specified." *Id.* at 1145. Rather, the provision "was intended to confer no greater right than an employer's freedom to choose the nationality of its executive labor pool." *Id.* at 1146. If the provision conferred broad immunity from domestic employment laws, the drafters would not have specifically guaranteed the right to hire technical experts regardless of professional qualification requirements under local law. Such language would have been superfluous. *Id.* at 1145. Although the Korean employer had a treaty right to discriminate in favor of Korean citizens, the treaty afforded no immunity from liability for race, age and national origin discrimination.

Consequently, the court concluded,

> We hold that the district court erred by construing article VIII(1) to confer on Japanese employers blanket immunity from state employment law. In the district court's view, JAL's immunity was sufficiently broad that judgment was appropriate even though the pleadings were silent on whether the plaintiffs were replaced by Japanese citizens. In other words, the district court believed that JAL has a treaty right to ignore domestic employment law even for personnel decisions that involved only non-Japanese citizens. Taken to its logical conclusion, such an expansive construction of article VIII(1) would lead to absurd results, such as exempting foreign employers from collective bargaining laws. [citation omitted] As the circuits that have addressed the question have uniformly found, the main purpose of article VIII(1) is to guarantee

the ability of each signatory's companies the ability to staff critical managerial and technical positions overseas with their fellow citizens. California's whistleblower protection laws merely prevent JAL from retaliating against employees for reporting and resisting the employer's domestic law violations; the laws in no way conflict with JAL's limited treaty right to discriminate in favor of Japanese citizens. In the absence of conflict, there can be no preemption.

Q 15:8   Do other regions of the world have the equivalent of the American Worker Adjustment and Retraining Notification (WARN) Act?

Yes, examples of WARN-type acts, aimed at mitigating the impact of mass layoffs and plant closings are outlined next.

European Union

Collective redundancies. This Directive requires employers to consult staff representatives in the case of collective redundancies. It specifies the points which these consultations must cover and the useful information which the employer is required to provide during the consultations. In addition, the Directive establishes the procedure and practical arrangements for collective redundancies.

Council Directive 98/59/EC of July 20, 1998, on the approximation of the laws of the Member States relating to collective redundancies

The Directive does not apply to:

- Collective redundancies effected under contracts of employment concluded for limited periods of time or for specific tasks except where such redundancies take place prior to the date of expiry or the completion of such contracts;
- Workers employed by public administrative bodies or by establishments governed by public law; and
- The crews of seagoing vessels.

Consultations. Any employer contemplating collective redundancies must hold consultations with the workers' representatives with a view to reaching an agreement. These consultations shall, at least, cover ways and means of avoiding collective redundancies or reducing the number of workers affected, and of mitigating the consequences by recourse to accompanying social measures aimed at redeploying or retraining those workers made redundant.

Information to be provided by the employer. The Directive specifies that Member States may make provision for workers' representatives to call on the services of experts in accordance with measures in force at national level. The employer is to provide workers' representatives with all relevant information during the course of the consultations and, in any event, is to notify them of the following in writing:

- The reasons;
- The period during which redundancies are to be effected;

- The number and category of workers normally employed;
- The number to be made redundant;
- The criteria used to select those workers to be made redundant; and
- The method used to calculate compensation (where applicable).

Procedure for collective redundancies. The Directive outlines the following procedure:

- The employer notifies the competent public authority in writing of any projected collective redundancies. This notification must contain all the relevant information concerning the projected redundancies and consultations held, except for the method used to calculate compensation. However, where the cessation of activity is the result of a judicial decision, notification is only necessary at the express request of the authority.
- The employer forwards a copy of the notification to the workers' representatives, who may send comments to the competent public authority.
- Collective redundancies take effect at the earliest 30 days after the notification; the competent public authority uses this period to seek solutions. Member States may grant the public authority the power to reduce this period or to extend it to 60 days following notification in cases where the problems cannot be resolved. This is not compulsory for collective redundancies following a cessation of activity resulting from a judicial decision. Wider powers of extension may be granted. The employer must be informed of any extension and the grounds for it before expiry of the initial period.

[http://europa.eu/]

Canada

British Columbia. For the period ending December 31, 2005, a collective agreement must not contain a provision that

(a) Restricts or limits a health sector employer from laying off an employee;

(b) Subject to paragraph (c), requires a health sector employer to meet conditions before giving layoff notice;

(c) Requires a health sector employer to provide more than 60 days' notice of layoff to an employee directly or indirectly affected and to the trade union representing the employee; or

(d) Provides an employee with bumping options other than the bumping options set out in the regulations.

[S.B.C. 2002, c. 2, s. 9]

New Brunswick

30(1). Except where cause for dismissal exists, and subject to subsection (3) and to sections 31 and 32, an employer shall not terminate or lay off an employee without having given at least

(a) Two weeks' notice in writing, where the employee has been employed by the employer for a continuous period of employment of six months or more but less than five years; and

(b) Four weeks' notice in writing, where the employee has been employed by the employer for a continuous period of employment of five years or more.

30(2). Where an employer dismisses an employee for cause he shall do so in writing, setting out the reasons for such action, and, subject to section 31, unless this section is complied with no dismissal without notice is valid notwithstanding that cause for such action exists.

30(3). Where an employee is given notice of termination or layoff by the employer but continues to work for the employer for a period of one month or more beyond the end of the notice period, the notice is extinguished and the employer shall only terminate or lay off the employee after giving a new notice in accordance with subsection (1).

[S.N.B. 1982, c. E-7.2, s. 30]

31(1). Notwithstanding section 30, an employer may lay off an employee without notice

(a) Where a lack of work exists, due to any reason unforeseen by the employer at the time notice would otherwise have been given, for such period as the lack of work continues due to that reason; or

(b) For any reason, for a period of up to six days.

31(2). Notwithstanding § 30, an employer may terminate or lay off, without notice, an employee who has refused reasonable alternate employment offered by the employer as an alternative to being terminated or laid off.

31(3). Section 30 does not apply where

(a) The termination of the employment relationship is due to the completion by the employee of a definite assignment that the employee was hired to perform over a period not exceeding 12 months, whether or not the exact period was stated in the employment contract;

(b) An employee has completed a term of employment that was fixed in the employment contract, unless the employee is employed for a period of three months beyond that period;

(c) An employee retires under a bona fide retirement plan;

(d) The employee is doing construction work in the construction industry;

(e) The termination or layoff results from the normal seasonal reduction, closure or suspension of an operation; or

(f) The termination of the employment relationship arises under such other circumstances as are prescribed by regulation.

[S.N.B. 1982, c. E-7.2, s. 31]

India

1. Do you have a plant closing law in your jurisdiction and if so, what does it require?

Yes. The Industrial Disputes Act, 1947 ("IDA") prescribes the procedure for closing down of an undertaking.

1.2 Closure of an undertaking employing 50 to 100 persons

An undertaking is defined as an undertaking in which an industry i.e. means of any business, trade, undertaking, manufacturing or calling of employers including any calling, service, employment, handicraft, or industrial occupation or a vocation or workmen, is carried on.

If the undertaking proposed to be closed down employs more than 50 (fifty) but less than 100 (one hundred) persons, the employer intending to close down the undertaking is required to serve 60 (sixty) days prior notice on the appropriate government (which may be state or the central/federal government depending on the nature of the undertaking) in a prescribed format specifying the reasons for the intended closure. Every employee who has been in continuous employment of the employer for more than an year is entitled to receive one months prior written notice indicating the reasons for retrenchment or wages in lieu of such notice and is also entitled to received compensation equal to 15 (fifteen) days average pay for every completed year of continuous service or part thereof in excess of 6 (six) months.

The aforesaid procedures are subject to certain exceptions contained in the Industrial Disputes Act, 1947.

1.3 Closure of an undertaking employing more than 100 persons

Undertakings of industrial establishments such as factories (defined in the Factories Act, 1948, to mean a place where manufacturing activity is carried on), mines or plantations employing more than 100 persons are required to obtain prior permission of the appropriate government at least 90 days before the date of intended closure. The application for grant of permission must clearly state the reasons for the intended closure and a copy of the said application should be served on the appropriate government and the representatives of the workmen simultaneously. Based on several prescribed factors, the appropriate government is required to either permit or refuse to grant permission for closure. If no communication from the appropriate government is received within 60 (sixty) days from the date on which application for permission for closure was made, the permission applied for is deemed to have been granted. If the permission for closure is granted or is deemed to have been granted, subject to review powers of the appropriate government, every employee who is employed in the undertaking immediately before the date of application for permission to close was made, is entitled to receive compensation equal to 15 (fifteen) days average pay for every completed year of continuous service or part thereof in excess of 6 (six) months.

[*Lex Mundi Labor and Employment Desk Book*, available at http://www.lexmundi.com/images/lexmundi/PDF/LaborEmployment/Labor_Employment_DeskBook/LaborEmployment_India.pdf]

Q 15:9   What are the three common patterns of labor and employment laws around the globe?

American business people, human resources professionals, and labor lawyers conducting business globally can anticipate encountering general types of labor and employment law patterns, depending upon the countries and regions in which they do business. These patterns usually are labeled:

* Suppression;
* Toleration; and
* Protection and encouragement.

Q 15:10   What are the characteristics of a labor and employment law scheme that emphasizes suppression?

Legal schemes that emphasize suppression typically outlaw labor unions and accord few, if any, legal rights to workers in nations that adopt such schemes. Labor unions often are labeled illegal conspiracies or restraints of trade. Workplace safety laws often are either non-existent or not enforced. Anti-discrimination provisions also are usually absent from such legal systems.

Globally, legal systems aimed at suppressing labor unions and workers' rights tend to emulate the eighteenth and nineteenth century British and American experiences—that is, developing nations with emerging economies, struggling to achieve their own belated industrial revolutions have tended to deny legitimacy to organized labor and to accord workers limited, if any, legal rights. For example, in the wake of the U.S. Senate's ratification of NAFTA, the International Brotherhood of Teamsters and other American labor unions attempting to organize Mexican workers filed unfair labor practice charges against multinational corporations, notably Honeywell and GE, operating factories south of the border. The charges accused these companies in complicity with the Mexican government of thwarting union organizing in their Mexican operations.

Other multinational corporations, notably Nike, have been sharply criticized for operating manufacturing plants in Asian and other developing labor markets where wage rates are mere fractions of American minimums and safety concerns allegedly are largely ignored. On the other hand, North Korea—the last genuine Marxist dictatorship in the world—has announced a 2,000 percent wage increase for most workers and a series of new initiatives intended to foster capitalism within its borders, most likely emulating the Chinese model. Thus, it seems that Western capitalism and Asian socialism are converging toward what will be a new economic order in the Far East.

Q 15:11   What are the characteristics of a labor law scheme that emphasizes tolerance?

Nations practicing a policy of tolerance to labor unions and workers' rights tend neither to support nor repress organized labor. The United States between 1900 and 1932, when Franklin Roosevelt inaugurated the New Deal, is an example of this public policy approach. Certain people might add that this is unofficial U.S.

policy toward organized labor today. The federal and state scheme of anti-discrimination, workplace safety, wrongful discharge, and other employment laws in the United States, however, belie such a criticism. In other words, while organized labor has steadily declined in all but public employment in the United States and has been the target of criticism and even hostility, notably under the Reagan administration in the 1980s, individual employee's rights have steadily increased under federal and state legislation from the 1960s into the new century.

Q 15:12   What is an example of a modern nation that emphasizes tolerance in its labor and employment law scheme?

Thailand is a significant player in America's global business picture. Companies such as Jockey and Nike are among the major manufacturers of shoes and other clothing that have opened factories in Thailand to ship cheaply made goods to the United States and Europe by the shipload. Thailand also is a good current example of the "tolerance" model. Labor organizations such as the Garment Industry Workers Union are tolerated in Thailand. Labor issues are governed by three statutes: the Social Security Act, the Labor Relations Act, and the Labor Protection Act. Additionally, the government sets public employee wage rates under the authority of the State Enterprise Labor Relations Act. Major provisions of these laws include:

- *Termination of employment.* Employees dismissed without cause are entitled to severance pay, pegged to length of service. No severance is required, where the worker has been dismissed for dishonesty; a criminal act against the employer; intentional causing of loss to the employer; gross negligence; neglect of duties for three consecutive days without a good excuse; conviction and incarceration; or violation of a work rule following a prior warning.

- *Pensions.* Covered employees can retire at 55. Workers who contribute into the fund for at least 180 months get at least 20 percent of their salary, averaged across 60 months. The Social Security fund applies to private sector employees, while the government pension fund covers public employees.

- *Labor relations.* The Labor Relations Act deals with agreements on mandatory terms of employment in workplaces with 20 or more employees; labor dispute resolution mechanisms; employer and employee organizations established under the act; and unfair labor practices. Four sorts, or levels, of labor organizations are recognized under the act: employee committees; labor unions; labor federations; and labor counsels and congresses.

- *Public employees.* The State Enterprise Labor Relations Act provides the framework for public employee unions. At least 10 employees are needed to form a union and at least 10 percent of the workforce must petition for the union. Civil servants, including teachers, are prohibited from forming unions, but can form associations, which do not bargain collectively.

- *Foreign workers.* The Alien Employment Act is administered by the Department of Employment of the Ministry of Labor. The department sets minimum wage rates and issues visas.

[Deloitte, *Taxation and Investment in Thailand 2013*, accessed at http://www
.deloitte.com/assets/Dcom-Global/Local%20Assets/Documents/Tax/Taxation
%20and%20Investment%20Guides/2013/dttl_tax_guide_2013_Thailand.pdf]

Q 15:13   What are the characteristics of an employment law scheme that emphasizes protection and encouragement?

Such a legal system includes statutes or common law rules that not only
allow but also provide incentives to workers to join labor unions and enforce
their rights in front of government agencies and in its courts.

Q 15:14   What are some examples of countries or regions that emphasize protection and encouragement in their labor and employment law schemes?

From 1936, when the NLRA was passed, until about 1980, the United States
encouraged organized labor. Great Britain encouraged the joining of labor
unions from 1940 to about 1980. Japan briefly encouraged labor unions during
the U.S. occupation following World War II. Canada and Germany remain
nations that today encourage labor organizations.

The United States may still be characterized as a nation that encourages and
protects workers' rights by means of its complicated and pervasive scheme of
employment laws such as Title VII, the Americans with Disabilities Act (ADA),
the Age Discrimination in Employment Act (ADEA), the Employee Retirement
Income Security Act, and the Occupational Safety and Health Act. The EU
likewise affords workers in its member nations substantial employment rights,
although migrant labor from outside the EU may find that it enjoys fewer *de jure*,
or at least *de facto*, rights and protections.

Table 15.1 Comparison of Labor and Employment Laws

Country	Labor Law	Employment Discrimination
United States	NLRA (1935, 1947, 1958)	Equal Pay Act (1963) Title VII (1964) ADEA (1967) ADA (1990)
Canada	Provincially based; generally "yes" in both categories, but does vary from province to province.	

Table 15.1 Comparison of Labor and Employment Laws (*cont'd*)

Country	Labor Law	Employment Discrimination
United Kingdom	Trade Unions & Labour Relations Act (1974–76) Employment Protection Act (1975) Employment Acts (1980, 1982)	Equal Pay Act (1970) Sex Discrimination Act (1975) Race Relations Act (1976)
Germany	Works Council Act (1972)	Law of Jan. 24, 1952

Q 15:15 Can corporations doing business in foreign nations rely upon consistent, even-handed application of employment and labor laws?

No, not necessarily. To the contrary, while the brief outlines offered in this section provide a general sense of the labor and employment public-policy schemes of the major regions of the world, informal and illegal practices frequently play an important role, and sometimes even dominate, how business gets done. Employment laws, along with environmental rules and regulations, while expressing high ideals and aspirations, are often ignored, unenforced, or circumvented. Consequently, American companies sending workers into foreign venues or employing foreign workers in their homelands should master the nuances—both cultural and extra-legal—by means of such resources as:

- Local agents and business managers;
- Joint ventures with local enterprises and entrepreneurs;
- Acquisition or establishment of local subsidiaries or sister corporations; and
- Retention of local lawyers or local offices of major American firms with international practices.

Q 15:16 How does the United States compare with some of its international rivals in terms of labor organization?

According to data released by the Bureau of Labor Statistics on January 23, 2013 [http://www.bls.gov/news.release/union2.nr0.htm], in 2012, 11.3 percent of the workforce belonged to labor unions. It is down from 2011, falling from 11.8 percent. Union membership has decreased similarly in other countries such as Australia, Japan, and much of Europe. [http://www.hrpolicy.org/downloads/2012/BEERG/No_5_2012.pdf]

By comparison, some of America's major competitors in the developed world reported the following union adherence figures:

Canada	4.5 million	30.4%
Japan	10 million	18.7%
Germany	11.3 million	26%
Britain	9 million	29%

[http://www.nationmaster.com/graph/lab_tra_uni_mem-labor-trade-union-membership]

The following is a list of international labor organizations:

- International Labor Rights Fund (ILRF) (a non profit organization dedicated to preserving the rights of workers around the world with a particular emphasis on sweatshops and child labor)
- Fair Labor Association (FLA) (a non-profit organization designed to complement existing international and national labor laws)
- International Centre for Trade Union Rights (an organizing and campaigning body for trade unions and trade unionists)
- International Labor Organization (ILO) (an agency of the United Nations to deal with labor issues)
- Socialist International (a worldwide organization of social democratic, labor, and democratic socialist political parties)

Q 15:17   What changes are occurring in labor relations and labor unions in the debt-strapped, economically stagnant European Union?

As EU nations struggle to control their budgets and reduce deficits by any means possible, and the European debt crisis seemingly far from over, unions and employee rights are at risk. Since 2009, the EU has struggled with a slow-moving but unrelenting crisis over the debts faced by its weakest economies, such as Greece and Portugal, and those most affected by the global recession, such as Ireland, creating some of the deepest tensions to affect the union in recent memory. A string of negotiations, bailouts, and austerity packages have failed to ease the minds of investors or provide the growth that is so desperately needed in order to allow struggling countries to pay off debt. [http://topics.nytimes.com/top/reference/timestopics/subjects/e/european_sovereign_debt_crisis/index.html]

The economic crisis has become a political one as well. Political turmoil, instability, and union protests and strikes are sweeping through Europe, with mixed outcomes. Working conditions are also deteriorating, broadening and reinforcing social inequalities between workers, especially in terms of health, as a result of harsh austerity programs. These austerity programs have been used throughout Europe to apply strong pressure for change in labor relations, social protection, and pension schemes, often to the detriment of unions and individual workers. Workers' rights have been curtailed to different extents depending on the country. Changes in the legal framework aim at primarily "making certain temporary concessions permanent; introducing further flexibility in contractual relations in an already uncertain and precarious working environment (particularly in relation to working hours, hiring and firing procedures, fixed-term contracts); decentralizing existing and working collective bargaining mechanisms at different levels; leaving social partners without clear definitions of their status and scope of activity; and complicating rules and procedures for collective actions and conflict resolution." [http://survey.ituc-csi.org/Europe-Global.html?lang = en]

In Belgium, much of the country came to a standstill when a national strike, the first in Belgium since 1993, coincided with a one-day summit of European Union leaders in Brussels. The rail network was shut down, flights were disrupted, and public transportation services were suspended. As one of many EU nations searching for means to curb its budget, Belgium recently pledged to bring its public sector deficit below the EU limit of 3 percent of gross domestic product in 2012 in order to avoid an EU fine and to reassure investors that it has its finances under control. The plan to raise the effective retirement age, raise taxes, and cut spending—amounting to more than €12 billion ($15 million) for the year 2012—has angered unions. [http://www.eubusiness.com/news-eu/belgium-social.eld] However, a likely stagnation of growth will further force the government to seek savings when it revises its budget, causing union leaders to fear it may suspend its system of wage indexation, as it is criticized by the European Commission and international economic organizations for driving up prices and undermining Belgium's competitive position.

Union leaders said, "the rich should shoulder more of the austerity burden," and urged the EU to issue joint Eurobonds in order to cut interest rates for weaker nations. Rudy De Leeuw, president of the ABVV union group, said: "Europe must hand out eurobonds, it must help the strikers who have bailed out banks and it must take steps for long-term growth." [http://www.hrpolicy.org/downloads/2012/BEERG/No_5_2012.pdf]

Spanish workers also declared a nationwide strike in March 2012 over labor reforms that workers saw as too pro-business. The government claimed that the purpose of the labor reforms was to bring flexibility to the workplace and to simplify the rules for employers, but unions pointed out that the reforms also make it easier and cheaper to fire workers and to cut wages unilaterally. Austerity measures designed to lower the national deficit to within EU limits will most likely result in tens of billions of euros worth of cuts and steep tax hikes. Although the strike claimed an average of 77 percent participation, the government called the strike a mere nuisance for the country. [http://www.bbc.co.uk/news/world-europe-17545174]

Whether labor reforms are helping Spain's employment problem is still up for debate. Prime Minister Mariano Rajoy followed the same policies Germany put in place a decade ago to reinvigorate its economy, easing firing laws and cutting back the country's jobless benefits, putting pressure on those unemployed to seek work. Spain's labor costs have begun to fall, in part due to employers' newfound ability to hire and fire at lower cost, resulting in increased foreign investment and car industry exports. According to Alberto Nadal, deputy energy minister, "Spain is adjusting its current account deficit without devaluing its currency for the first time in its economic history." [http://www.businessweek.com/articles/2013-01-03/spains-labor-reforms-start-to-yield-results]

Others, however, are less optimistic. Spain's unemployment rate remains at 26 percent and is not falling at any remarkable speed. And as one article says, "Labour market reforms of this sort do not do much more than redistribute the (possibly fewer) available jobs. For every job in the 'competitive' Spanish car industry, read one job gone in the French, Italian, Belgian, Swedish or German car industry." [http://www.guardian.co.uk/commentisfree/2013/feb/17/spain-labour-reforms-wont-bring-growth]

A union merger occurred between the European trade union federations of metalworkers (EMF), chemical workers (EMCEF), and textile workers (ETUF:TCL) in June 2012. Executives of the three federations held a joint meeting earlier in order to designate senior officials for the new federation. They agreed upon the following positions: Michael Vassiliadis, current EMCEF President, as the new federation's chairman; EMF general secretary, Ulrich Eckelmann, as the new general secretary; and Bart Samyn (EMF), Sylvain Lefebvre (EMCEF), and Luc Triangle (ETUF:TCL), as deputy general secretaries.

This pooling of resources and expertise is just one example of the ways in which unions are searching for new ways to rebuild declining membership, and it is likely that similar campaigns will follow in the future.

The federation also adopted a resolution that criticized an upcoming proposal from the European Commission, which will most likely aim to place restrictions on the right to strike in certain circumstances. The resolution says:

1. The single market is not an end to itself, but is established in order to achieve social progress for the peoples of the European Union.

2. Economic freedoms and competition rules cannot have priority over fundamental social rights and social progress. In the event of conflict, social rights shall take precedence.

3. Economic freedoms cannot be interpreted as giving undertakings the right to exercise them in order to evade or circumvent national, social, and employment laws and practices, or for the purposes of unfair competition with regard to wages and working conditions.

4. The rights to bargain collectively and to take industrial action are fundamental and nonnegotiable. [http://www.hrpolicy.org/downloads/2012/BEERG/No_5_2012.pdf]

In Germany, the Federal Ministry of Economics and Technology (BMWi), the Federal Ministry of Labour and Social Affairs (BMAS) and the Federal Employment Agency (BA) jointly launched the Qualified Professionals Initiative in early 2013, a program that seeks to raise awareness of the effects of a skilled labor shortage, help companies attract or retain qualified workers, and stimulate the participation of domestic and foreign skilled workers in the labor force. Only 25,000 skilled laborers come to Germany annually, a figure that is considered low compared to other countries.

One big change is the introduction of the EU Blue Card. Since the beginning of 2013, non-EU university graduates or similarly highly qualified persons may enter the German labor market if they meet the following qualifications: they must already have signed an employment contract with an employer based in Germany where they will earn a minimum annual gross salary of €46,400. For urgently needed professionals, such as doctors and engineers, the minimum annual gross salary required is only €36,200.

The results of this program have been promising, at least at first glance. On February 18, 2013, the Federal Minister of the Interior, Hans-Peter Friedrich, presented preliminary figures on the usage of the EU Blue Card. During the six months after the first revision of the wage thresholds, which took effect in August 2012, 4,126 qualified experts received a Blue Card enabling them to live and work in Germany. More than two thirds of those individuals, however, were already living in Germany, with the remainder coming mainly from China, India, Russia, and the United States.

An analysis by the Organization for Economic Cooperation and Development (OECD) of the program stated that the EU Blue Card program alone would not be enough to make Germany attractive to foreign skilled workers and graduates. The OECD has suggested lowering immigration barriers for highly skilled professionals to further alleviate the issue. [http://www.eurofound.europa.eu/eiro/2013/02/articles/de1302029i.htm]

In early 2013, French unions agreed to "pro-corporate labor reforms." The French employers' federation Medef and the trade unions agreed upon greater flexibility for corporations in regard to job security. Under the new provisions, employers' will be allowed to introduce unlimited short-time working for a period of up to two years, resulting in a reduction in workers' income. Employers will be able to use the threat of layoffs to impose the short-time working regime where unions covering a majority of workers accept such a proposal. Further, employers will be allowed to shift workers from task to task, as they wish. In return, unions claim that the companies will share the benefits they gain upon returning to profitability.

The main negotiator for Medef, Patrick Bernasconi declared in regard to the agreement, "We have reason to be happy after three months of work." [http://www.wsws.org/en/articles/2013/01/16/fran-j16.html]

In 2013, France passed a labor bill through the lower house of parliament that will overhaul the labor system in France and loosen hiring and firing rules. The bill "aims to inject more flexibility into a system the IMF, OECD, and ratings agencies say is to blame for chronically high unemployment because it gives some workers too much job security and others too little." Its reception has been mixed, but 62 percent of respondents to a survey claimed to support the bill. Members of France's second-largest union, CGT, called the bill "traitorous." Protesters lined the streets when the bill was being passed. [http://news.yahoo.com/frances-lower-house-passes-labor-bill-amid-protests-171607933--business.html]

Greece, a country experiencing its sixth year in a recession, will be sticking with its tough austerity measures, holding out hope for a debt relief deal with emergency creditors. Greece struck a deal with rescue creditors expected to secure it €8.8 billion ($11.55 billion) in further loan payouts, following weeks of negotiations that will result in an unheard of 15,000 layoffs in the public sector. The austerity measures, which are viewed with bitterness by most, include slashing incomes, hiking taxes, and overhauling an inflated, largely inefficient public sector. The cuts brought unemployment to a record 27 percent, with almost 1,000 jobs lost every day over the past three years in the private sector. On April 16, 2013, the seamen's union called for a 24-hour, nationwide strike to protest reforms that they claim will undermine their ability to collectively bargain. [http://bigstory.ap.org/article/greek-ferry-seamen-launch-24-hour-strike]

Q 15:18   What is meant by *European corporatism*?

Between the end of World War II and about 1980, many European countries pursued a policy of insuring labor unions the right to represent their workers on a national basis. Such monopolies on labor relations in key industries resulted in collective bargaining on a nationwide scale. Since about 1980, this system of corporatism has been evolving into more cooperative relationships between these large, powerful, officially recognized unions and major companies.

For example, Americans doing business in Germany or with German companies should be aware that under German law:

1. Fundamental labor regulations are found in the Civil and Commercial Code.
2. Employees—notably juveniles, the disabled, and pregnant and nursing mothers—are provided substantial safety and health protection.
3. All employees are protected from arbitrary dismissal.
4. Discharge without notice is not allowed except for cause.
5. Collective bargaining agreements are between employers' associations and trade unions.
6. The government can, and does, impose the terms of collective bargaining agreements upon unorganized employers in the same industries.
7. Unions are represented on the boards of directors of major corporations.
8. Co-determination of working conditions is mandated by the Works Council Act of 1972.
9. Co-determination is created by four separate statutory frameworks and applies to: (a) the mining and steel industries; (b) all corporations carrying the designation "AG" or "GmbH" and having at least 2,000 employees; and (c) subsidiaries of foreign corporations if they carry one of the aforesaid designations.
10. Co-determination means having a supervisory board, half the members of which are elected by the shareholders, and half of whom are chosen by the employees; the supervisory board then appoints the board of management of the firm by a two-thirds vote.

Q 15:19   What is the Japanese approach to labor and employee relations?

The Japanese now are famous for pioneering quality control, quality circles, and the team approach to workplace relations. Underlying this approach is the cultural concept called *gaman*, meaning perseverance and self-denial in pursuit of the organization's and the group's larger good.

Q 15:20   What are the "golden rules" of Japanese employee relations?

The Japanese golden rules are:

1. The team approach to work;
2. The forbidding of craft unions, which tend to break down integrated teams;
3. Company-wide unions include both labor and management in their ranks;
4. Collective bargaining is conducted in an environment of shared knowledge of the company's real financial condition;
5. Seniority rules are absent;
6. Labor markets are created within corporate "families" so that employees are able to spend their entire careers within one such family;
7. Ongoing, significant in-house training and employee development;
8. An absence of mid-career recruiting among corporations;
9. The *ringi* system, under which suggestions for change are encouraged and accepted from all levels within the corporate hierarchy;
10. An exceptional level of employment security;
11. Few extraneous indicia of status differentials among the various levels of labor and management;
12. Layoffs are used only as an absolute last resort;
13. Job rotations are frequently practiced;
14. Peer group competition within single corporations for top management positions;
15. Large bonuses supplement salaries and wages in good times; and
16. Group responsibility and accountability are emphasized over individual accountability and responsibility.

Q 15:21   How is collective bargaining done in Japan?

Instead of adversarial labor negotiations, which characterize labor relations in the United States, Japanese intra-corporate "joint consultation committees" are comprised of the rank-and-file and executives who discuss problems and seek mutually acceptable solutions. The search for consensus within strict rules of decorum is the hallmark of Japanese labor and employee relations.

Q 15:22 How does the Japanese legal system differ from its U.S. counterpart?

In the United States there are more than 300 lawyers for every 100,000 people. In Japan there are only about 12 lawyers per 100,000 Japanese citizens. Lawsuits of any kind are rare, discouraged, and difficult to pursue. Although Japan's democracy, including its labor laws, owes much to the American post-World War II occupation, the distinctive cultural characteristics noted in the preceding questions and answers have molded Japanese labor and employment relations into a pattern quite distinctive from that in the United States.

Some of the main tenets of Japanese labor law are the following:

1. Rules of employment must be established by every employer of 10 or more workers, and the rules must be in compliance with minimum standards set by the Labor Standards Law.
2. Establishing of rules requires: (a) presentation of them to the representative employee; and (b) filing with the Prefectural Labor Standards Supervising Office.
3. Rules cover:
   - Wages;
   - Hours;
   - Time off;
   - Holidays;
   - Paid vacations;
   - Dismissal;
   - Retirement allowances, if customary in the industry;
   - Safety;
   - Sanitation; and
   - Workers' compensation.
4. Collective bargaining agreements are made between employers and unions pursuant to the Labor Union Law.
5. When three-fourths of all workers potentially covered by a collective agreement join the union, the agreement becomes applicable to all workers in that unit.
6. Collective bargaining agreements do not require government approval.
7. Injunctions and damages are available in actions for breaches of collective bargaining agreements.
8. Collective bargaining agreements may be for three years or less, and if no term is specified, may be terminated upon 90 days' notice.

Q 15:23 What are typical benefits afforded employees under rules of employment and collective bargaining agreements in Japan?

Typical employee benefits under rules of employment and collective bargaining agreements include:

1. Pensions;

2. Bonuses;

3. Medical benefits;

4. Housing facilities or allowances; and

5. Discharges are rare, and at a minimum require 30 days' notice or pay in lieu of notice; in the largest corporations, lifetime employment has been the general rule.

Q 15:24 What is an example of a Japanese company that has faced gender discrimination charges in the workplace?

In *Cyphers v. Toshiba America* [2011 WL 1302983 (S.D.N.Y. Feb. 25, 2011)], a senior HR executive initiated a $100 million class action lawsuit against Toshiba America, her former employer. The plaintiff asserted that Toshiba America pays female employees lower salaries and bonuses than men who perform similar work and steers women toward lower-grade positions and favors men in promotions.

According to the labor law firm Robertson & Lum LLP:

> [T]his lawsuit seems to have some reflections of the broader gender disparity and workplace discrimination issues that can be seen in Toshiba's home country, Japan. In that country, labor discrepancies between the genders are much broader than in the US. In the US, for instance, women's wages constitute about 80% of male wages, according to statistics for 2008. In Japan, women's wages are just 68% of the wages of men in the same year. The Japanese Ministry of Health Labor and Welfare blames these disparities on the fact that there are far fewer women employees in executive/middle manager positions in Japan. According to a 2009 survey, just 1.2% of executives at listed Japanese firms are female, compared to 13.5% at American Fortune 500 firms.

[http://www.rlemploymentlaw.com/_blog/Civil_Litigation_Blog/calendar/2011/3/]

Q 15:25 Have the Chinese allowed any labor law reforms?

On December 31, 2007, the *Hong Kong Standard* reported, "Tomorrow, Chinese workers enter a new era. The introduction of much-heralded labor laws will offer increased protection to employees, many of whom have suffered greatly to manufacture the greatest economic miracle in human history." The *Standard* goes on to observe, "The new laws have been remarkable in that they have been more open to public comment and debate than is generally accepted in China. Nearly 200,000 submissions were received, many from workers themselves, in an almost unique nod to democratic lawmaking." [James Rose, "Hard Labor on Worker Protection," *Hong Kong Standard*, Dec 31, 2007 http://www.thehongkon gstandard.com/Openads-2.0.11-pr1/adclick.php?n = af4]

The new legislation focuses on five major areas:

• Employment contracts are made both legally binding and mandatory;

• Employee probation periods must be monitored;

• Collective bargaining negotiated by the government-affiliated All-China Federation of Trade Unions are encouraged (similar to the mid-1930s, when the U.S. Congress enacted the NLRA and other laws to stimulate unionization of U.S. workers);

• Health and safety standards are enhanced; and

• Various notorious schemes and shady practices in the hiring sector are outlawed.

Although this looks promising on its face, the *Standard's* James Rose opined, "All well and good, but already loopholes are appearing." He explained, "The giant technology firm Huawei has sought to twist the laws to oblige workers to renegotiate employment contracts in a way that works in part to circumvent long-term employment provisions in the company's interests. The private sector, both foreign and domestic, cadged at the laws. But the political reality is that Beijing had to act on worker standards, and the private sector knows it. During the 1990s and into the 2000s, tens of millions of workers have been laid off and some hundreds of millions, mostly rural Chinese, are part of the floating country within a country, looking for jobs and a means of existence."

Rose added, "The Maoist-era worker culture—of life-long employment, stable wages set by the government, government-run companies providing housing, education, health care and social security—is long gone. Now the post-Deng era means growing unemployment, less job security and wage rip-offs everywhere. Such numbers have the ability to focus even the minds of Beijing's cosseted mandarins. Workers are becoming aware of their clout and are mobilizing. In recent years, their jostling power has been noted around the country's industrial and urban centers. These political imperatives give a hint of the depth of politics behind the new labor laws."

Additionally, Rose pointed to world opinion as another pressure point upon the Chinese government to enact and enforce better labor and employment laws and policies:

"China's lawmakers are aware that the world is looking more harshly on the country and its shoddy working standards. The search for sustainable supply chains, often undertaken by firms trying to rebound from reputation-tarnishing supply chain exposés [sweatshops, bad environmental practices] is by now fervent."

Rose's points are well placed. During 2007, Chinese manufacturers and food producers were plagued by discoveries of such dangerous pollutants as lead paint in certain products, resulting many times in significant recalls. The quality control issues would seem to be inseparable from the qualifications and overall quality of the workforce.

Dispute resolution reform. The package of Chinese labor legislation includes a new statute governing the mediation and arbitration of labor disputes. China's leading legislative body adopted the law on labor dispute mediation and arbitration on December 29, 2007. It claims to be aimed at "fair and timely" settlement of disputes and lowering the costs for workers seeking to establish their rights. This new law takes effect on May 1, 2008. Following the requisite three readings, the law was approved by lawmakers attending the weeklong 31st session of the Standing Committee of the National People's Congress (NPC).

"To solve labor disputes fairly and in a timely way, the law has strengthened the role of grassroots mediation institutions, improved the arbitration system, and clearly stated that labor dispute arbitration is free of charge," said Wu Bangguo, the NPC Standing Committee chairman, who presided over the closing session. "It will shorten the cycle of labor dispute settlement, lower the cost for laborers to safeguard their lawful rights, and is conducive to the development of a harmonious relations between employees and employers."

According to China View, the online news service of Xinhua News Agency, "The new law has four chapters and 54 clauses, and it follows the labor contract law and the law on employment promotion in being approved this year to improve China's labor systems. It stipulates that when workers file a complaint, authorities in charge of labor affairs should deal with employers that underpay or fail to pay wages, other compensation or medical fees for job-related injuries." [http://www.chinaview.cn/index.htm]

Data released by the NPC Law Committee show that about 30 percent of labor disputes concern pay, with wage payment and collection, especially at year's end, playing a prominent role in many such confrontations. NPC Standing Committee members contended that many labor disputes could be avoided if responsible authorities intensify supervision of companies and deal with major violations in a timely manner. Under the new law, a business organization is entitled to establish its own labor mediation committee to solve internal disputes at its own level. Such a committee should include employees and management representatives. When disputes occur, litigants can either turn to the committee or one of a number of grassroots people's labor dispute mediation organizations.

Disputes concerning pay, medical fees, and work-related-injury compensation can be settled by arbitration if the amount in dispute is less than the equivalent one year's pay at local minimum monthly wage. The arbitration award is intended to have the effect of law. Working time, holidays, and social insurance also are covered by the statute.

"The law is intended to help solve labor disputes fairly without going to court," Li Yuan, an official with the NPC Law Committee, told a press conference held at the conclusion of the legislative session.

NPC statistics indicate that labor disputes have risen continuously since predecessor ADR procedures were adopted back in 1987. Between 1987 and 2005, labor dispute organizations at all levels dealt with a total of 1.72 million cases involving 5.32 million employees. The rate of increase is currently 27.3 percent annually.

Echoing concerns frequently voiced in the United States, China View comments, "However, there are problems with the arbitration system. For instance, arbitrators are rarely professionally trained and thus lack credibility. Further, although arbitration is supposed to be cheaper than going to court, the actual process is often long and therefore expensive."

On a related note, the China Labour Bulletin published case studies on "how the country's embryonic collective bargaining process is beginning to develop," based on two recent disputes. The first dispute, at the Citizen Watch Factory in Shenzhen, was resolved through formal collective bargaining between labor and management. The second dispute, which took place during a protest at a Tesco supermarket in the Zhejiang city of Jinhua, was resolved through tripartite talks between local government, employees, and the supermarket employer. The Chinese Labour Bulletin said the two disputes "showed that while collective bargaining is still in its infancy in China, and participants from labor, management and the government still have much to learn about getting the best out of the negotiation process, nonetheless there are some very encouraging signs." [http://www.hrpolicy.org/downloads/2012/BEERG/No_5_2012.pdf]

[The case studies can be viewed in their entirety at: http://www.clb.org.hk/en/files/share/File/general/Collective_Bargaining_at_Shenzhen.pdf/.]

Q 15:26   What are the main characteristics of labor relations and employment law in the People's Republic of China?

Labor and employment laws generally accord Chinese workers the following rights:

1. Prohibition of child labor by children under age 16;
2. An eight-hour workday;
3. A 44-hour workweek;
4. Prohibition of employment discrimination based on gender, religion, race, or nationality;
5. Ninety days of maternity leave;
6. Minimum wages to be set at the province level;
7. A national unemployment insurance scheme;
8. A national job retraining scheme; and
9. A requirement that foreign corporations doing business on the mainland establish company labor unions for their Chinese workers.

The Chinese took control of Hong Kong from Great Britain in 1999 and have largely let the island continue as a bastion of capitalism and finance in the Far

East. Concurrently, China has developed another enclave of entrepreneurship in Shanghai, now the Mainland China headquarters of numerous multinational corporations and one of China's first private institutions of higher learning, the Shanghai Sanda Institute.

Under the People's Republic of China's (PRC) Labor Contract Law, a non-competition agreement must be supported by sufficient severance pay, if it is to be enforceable. The current PRC Labor Contract Law went into effect on January 1, 2008. The non-compete and trade secret provisions read as follows:

> **Article 23.** Employers and workers may stipulate such issues as keeping confidential the business secrets and intellectual property rights of the employers in the labor contract.
>
> With respect to a worker who has the obligation of keeping secrets, the employer may stipulate non-competition clauses with the worker in the labor contract or in the confidentiality agreement and stipulate that economic compensations shall be given to the worker by month within the non-competition period after the labor contract is cancelled or terminated. Where the worker is in violation of the stipulation on non-competition, he shall pay a penalty for breach of contract to the employer.
>
> **Article 24.** The personnel under non-competition shall be limited to senior managers, senior technicians and other personnel who have the obligation to keep secrets in the entity. The range, geographical scope and time limit for non-competition shall be stipulated by the employer and the worker. The stipulation relating to non-competition shall not violate any law or regulation.
>
> After the cancellation or termination of a labor contract, the period of non-competition for any of the persons referred to in the preceding paragraph to work for any other employer producing or engaging in products of the same category or conducting business of the same category as this employer shall not be more than two years.
>
> **Article 25.** Except for the circumstances as prescribed in Articles 22 and 23 of this Law, the employer shall not stipulate in the labor contract that the worker shall pay the penalty for breach of contract.

The entire statute can be accessed at http://www.bjreview.com.cn/document/txt/2007-10/16/content_80896.htm.

In two Chinese courts, the Beijing Dongcheng and Nanjing Gulou District People's Courts, two cases were heard that paid particular attention to an employment contract containing a non-competition agreement. In the Beijing case, Liu was formerly employed by a high-tech medical company, where he had signed a two-year labor contract. The contract included a non-competition agreement. Under the terms of the non-competition agreement, Liu was not allowed, while employed by the company, to engage in any part-time work of in a similar or competitive enterprises. He was also prohibited from founding or investing in another company which engaged in the same business as his employer. The agreement also prohibited Liu, during his employment or after his employment, from soliciting his employer's clients or employees for a competitor.

Liu's non-competition agreement did not specify any rights or benefits that would flow to him, if he fully complied.

In January 2007, Liu tendered his resignation and requested compensation for complying with the non-competition agreement. The company refused to pay Liu anything for his proffered compliance. To the contrary, the company, believing that Liu already had violated the non-competition agreement, filed a claim with the Beijing Labor Dispute Arbitration committee, claiming RMB 300,000 (note: also known as the Yuan) in alleged damages. The arbitration committee denied the company's claim, finding a lack of evidence. The company then filed an appeal with the Beijing People's Court.

The court ruled that since the non-competition agreement only stipulated the employee's responsibilities, without granting the supporting compensation, the agreement was patently unfair, violated the Labor Contract law, and therefore was invalid. [http://www.legalnetlink.net/announcements/2009/China_Labor _Insights_July%2017.pdf]

In the Nanjing case, the parties had entered a non-competition agreement and trade secrets accord which in fact did provide for post-employment compensation in support of the agreed-upon restraints. However, the court once again invalidated the compact, this time because the compensation was deemed to be "too low." In reaching this determination, the judges referenced a Jiangsu Province local labor rule, which apparently provided that the annualized compensation for a non-competition agreement should be no less than one-third of what the former employee earned during the last 12 months of employment. In this case, only a mere month's salary was to be paid for a full year of restraint. The employer's contention that it had actually paid three-months' worth of salary did not dissuade the court, since that was still less than the third required by the local law.

Worth noting here is that, unlike many American jurisdictions, the Nanjing court appears not to have considered reforming—blue-penciling, as it is sometimes called—the agreement. The court could have raised the compensation to the third called for, thus fulfilling the apparent intent of the parties when they entered the contract. Instead, it voided the agreement outright.

Chinalawblog.com offers this January 20, 2010, summary by Steve Dickson of Chinese non-compete rules:

> An employment agreement may include provisions intended to protect the trade secrets of the employer. A non-competition agreement may be included in support of such protections.
>
> The employer must pay reasonable compensation on a monthly basis to the employee during the term of the non-competition period. There is no definition of "reasonable compensation." Commentaries suggest employees should be compensated in a manner equivalent to their salary with the company. Others suggest that compensation is only required at the level of the current minimum wage in the relevant jurisdiction.

Non-competition agreements are limited to executives, technical personnel and other personnel who have access to trade secrets. Cases have held that senior sales staff are included in this category. On the other hand, blanket agreements that apply to all employees are invalid.

The terms of the restriction must be "reasonable" in length of restriction, business scope and geographic area. A term in excess of two years is prohibited. The scope requirement is strictly interpreted. It is not sufficient that the employee is working in the same general area as the former employer. Competition must be specific and direct.

If the employee violates the terms of the non-compete agreement, the employee can be held liable for a payment of contract damages to the employer. The amount of contract damages must be reasonable. Excessive damages that are clearly punitive will be rejected.

[http://www.chinalawblog.com/2010/01/employee_noncompete_agreements.html]

The international law firm of Winston & Strawn LLP observed in a newsletter,

Lessons learned from these cases are that, although the confidentiality obligations would not be affected if so agreed in the relevant labor contract or confidentiality agreement, the noncompetition obligation must be supported by a corresponding economic compensation to make it effective and enforceable. . . . It is advisable for the employer to check the local labor rules applicable to the employment with its employee, in addition to the national laws and regulations to ensure full compliance. . . . We understand that PRC courts and arbitration tribunals have taken a similar position on this issue.

Q 15:27   Have any significant reforms occurred affecting Chinese employers and employees?

On April 3, 2011, a new social insurance law took effect in the People's Republic of China. According to the law firm Picozzi & Morigi, "Generally speaking, the Social Insurance Law primarily aims to prevent the improper use of social security funds and give general rights for all citizens, including city residents, flexible employment, migrant workers and foreigners working in China to access and enjoy five categories of insurance. Considering Social Insurance Law is the first law covering social security issues in China (in the past, only regulations were issued by Chinese government regarding social security issues), it shall be considered as a great signal that China is making his effort to strengthen the social insurance system on a national wide basis to improve welfare and working condition." [http://www.picozzimorigi.cn/main/reports.php?id = 69]

The new law provides for the following five basic social security insurances: pension, medical, unemployment, work-related injury, and maternity. Significant aspects of the new law include:

- Basic pension, basic medical, and unemployment insurance are portable for individuals in cases when an individual changes a job or moves to another province or city.

- When an individual reaches the statutory retirement age, the basic pension insurance is calculated on a segmented basis and is paid uniformly.

- A unified national social insurance number for each citizen will be established, of which the identification card number will be the social insurance number.

In a move that could improve working conditions across China, the manufacturing giant Foxconn (who manufactures electronics for Apple, which joined the Fair Labor Association (FLA)) has vowed to implement reforms in its plants, including curtailing working hours and significantly increasing hourly wages. During a recent inspection, the FLA discovered Foxconn in violation of over 40 Chinese regulations. Plants often forced workers to work for over 60 hours per week and sometimes more than 11 days in a row. In interviews with Foxconn workers, the FLA found that 43 percent of workers had witnessed or fallen victim to accidents, and almost two-thirds of workers said compensation did not meet their basic needs, nor did unions adequately represent them. Often wages were too low to pay for health care or education. Apple's decision to join the FLA came after widespread criticism of the labor practices of its manufacturers and suppliers. [http://www.nytimes.com/2012/03/30/business/apple-supplier-in-china-pledges-changes-in-working-conditions.html?pagewanted = all]

On December 28, 2012, the Standing Committee of the National People's Congress issued a decision regarding amending the Labor Contract Law of the People's Republic of China, which is effective July 1, 2013. These are the first amendments to the Labor Contract Law (LCL) since it was issued on January 1, 2008.

In China, "dispatch agencies," third-party labor suppliers that recruit and hire employees on behalf of other companies, are common. The dispatch agency is in fact the direct employer of the dispatched employee, even if the employee does work for another company. Dispatched workers are meant to be temporary, but they sometimes end up as long-term employees, and their status makes them particularly in danger of receiving lower pay for doing work equal to that of direct hires. Many companies in China abuse this labor system in order to minimize the impact of some of the employee-friendly provisions of the LCL. The new amendments seek to rectify the situation and avoid further abuses of the law with the following modifications:

- *Stricter limitations on labor outsourcing arrangements.* Current rules generally permit long-term labor outsourcing for many positions. The Amendments underline the fact that labor outsourcing was originally intended, and should only be used, as supplemental to directly hired employees.

  The Amendments restrict and clarify the circumstances in which labor outsourcing can be used. Effective from July 1, 2013, employers can only use outsourced workers to fill temporary, ancillary, or substitute positions. According to the amendments:

- *a "temporary" position is one which lasts no longer than six months*
- *an "ancillary" position is one that is meant to provide a supporting role to the employer's core business functions*
- *a "substitute" position is one which provides temporary replacement cover for another employee who is away on vacation or on study leave, etc.*

These definitions, despite still being somewhat hazy, are intended to narrow the acceptable uses of labor outsourcing and close loopholes left in the LCL that gave the impression that other categories of outsourced workers might be permitted. Further, employers will be strictly limited in the percentage of outsourced workers they may have; however, the exact percentage to be stipulated in the new rules has not yet be released.

- *Equal pay for equal work.* Article 63 of the LCL already requires employers to pay outsourced workers equal pay for equal work. The Amendments simply reiterate that after July 1, 2013, all compensation (including basic salary, bonuses, subsidies, and allowances, etc.) received by outsourced workers must be on par with the employer's directly hired employees in comparable positions.

- *Stricter requirements for labor outsourcing agencies.* Article 57 of the LCL has been amended to make it more difficult for labor outsourcing agencies to enter the industry and continue operating. Beginning on July 1, 2013, all labor outsourcing agencies must have the following:
  - *registered capital of not less than RMB 2 million (currently it is only RMB 500,000);*
  - *must operate from fixed office premises;*
  - *must have facilities suitable for the conduct of the business; and*
  - *must be managed responsibly.*

All agencies established after July 1, 2013 will need to meet the new local labor bureau requirements before they can be licensed. Existing agencies that are already licensed have until July 1, 2014 to meet local labor bureau requirements before renewing their business registration. Any agency that fails to meet the outlined local labor bureau requirements will be unable to register and thus be prohibited from providing labor outsourcing services.

- *More severe penalties.* Changes to Article 92 of the LCL give the authorities power to impose substantial penalties for those agencies that violate the LCL, including the following:
  - *Local labor bureaus can order employers to cure violations of the new hiring provisions, and failure to comply could result in fines ranging from RMB 5,000 to RMB 10,000 per worker.*
  - *Labor outsourcing agencies operating without a proper license can be fined up to RMB 50,000 and will also be liable to receive a fine of between one and five times the amount of any income they receive while operating without a license.*

Any labor contracts or labor dispatch agreements that were entered into before the Amendments went into effect may be carried out until their expiration, but they must be revised according to the stipulation in the Amendments that regular employees and dispatched employees receive identical compensation. Labor dispatch businesses that are already running must obtain an administrative license and complete company alteration registration within a year from the date of the implementation of the Amendments if they wish to continue conducting business.

The Amendments are bound, even designed, to make labor outsourcing a less appealing source of employees and will ultimately limit flexibility in hiring practices in China. Companies will have to make plans to replace any outsourced workers with directly hired staff, or, at least, make sure they comply with the "equal pay" rule, and will most likely find themselves reevaluating growth plans and looking for other ways to save costs. [http://www.lexology. com/library/detail.aspx?g = 8ea0018a-4fa5-4ee6-8c8f-d12fe90ff4db]

Q 15:28   Has India experienced any significant economic changes that could impact international labor and employment law issues?

In early January 2008, an Indian conglomerate called TATA proposed to purchase Land Rover and Jaguar from the Ford Motor Company. The proposal marked a watershed in globalization. Britain's largest colony, which until its independence in 1947 was known as "the jewel in the crown," is now a sufficiently powerful economy if it is contemplating the purchase of two automotive brands that historically have been as much a part of the British national identity as fish and chips. Immediately, on the heels of this stunning announcement came demands from English workers who were concerned about termination of their employment.

According to the *Daily Mail* on January 4, 2008, "Unions last night demanded assurances that up to 20,000 British car jobs were safe as motor giant Ford announced formally that it was poised to sell Jaguar and Land Rover to India." [http://www.dailymail.co.uk/pages/live/articles/news/news.html?in_article_ id = 506064&in_page_id = 1770]

The British union's general secretary, Tony Woodley, contended, "We need further and more detailed meetings and discussions with Ford and TATA which will focus on the job security of our members in the Jaguar, Land Rover and Ford plants in the UK. There are also crucial issues around wages, terms and conditions and pensions to address before any final decision is considered."

Changing approaches to labor and employment. British union leaders are probably right to worry about the impact of the pending TATA acquisition on their members' employment security. Britain is a member of the EU. On November 22, 2006, the European Commission inaugurated a public debate on adapting European labor laws to what it called "the modern world of work." Issues identified in the so-called "green paper" issue by the commission included:

- Adoption by the EU and member nations of new types of employment contracts outside the traditional practice of permanent, full-time positions historically characteristic of most West European nations;

- Enactment of uniform labor and employment rules across member nations to help insure a level playing field for both workers and businesses throughout the EU;

- Improved labor-market information gathering and dissemination to workers across national borders; and

- Measures to close the gap between permanent employees and freelance workers.

[See http://ec.europa.eu/employment_social/emplweb/news/news_en.cfm?id = 189.]

One goal of the EU and many of its member nations is to break out of the straitjacket of guaranteed, lifetime jobs for workers. This effort has met with stiff resistance at the national level. Notably, the French government's attempt to enforce a law that allowed employers to provide "young workers" with two-year "trial contracts" resulted in workers and students protesting in the streets.

The European Commission's attempt to tackle this thorny issue at the trans-national level has made for some strange bedfellows. Organizations representing freelance workers, especially in the IT sector, were calling on members to oppose proposals put forward in the so-called "green paper." These opponents seem to suspect that those freelancers and contingent workers at the top of the food chain will find their activities and opportunities curtailed or narrowed by bureaucratic restraints. While temporary workers at the bottom of the EU economy may gain wages, benefits, and job security under the commission's proposals, if enacted into law, IT professionals and others in high-demand occupations seem to see themselves as probable losers under current reforms. Other losers are likely to be unionized workers, such as those at Jaguar and Land Rover, who previously could expect "cradle to grave" security.

Q 15:29 What are the main characteristics of labor relations and employment law in Australia and New Zealand?

Until about 1990, the lands down under based their labor law scheme on arbitration awards, rather than collective bargaining between unions and corporations. Unions tended to be organized along craft lines, like the AFL, as opposed to industry lines, such as the member unions of the CIO. Increased competition from the Asian Tigers of the Pacific Rim forced labor law reform in New Zealand and Australia around the start of the present decade.

In New Zealand, a 1987 law established a wage-setting process composed of:

1. "Awards" mandated between a single union and multiple employers;

2. "Composite awards" mandated between multiple unions on one side and multiple employers on the other; and

3. "Agreements" and "composite agreements" voluntarily agreed between and among unions and employers.

The 1991 Employment Contract Bill abolished the practice of settling disputes by binding arbitration and mandates negotiated collective bargaining agreements. Since this shift from compulsory arbitration to voluntary agreements, the number of New Zealand workers covered by collective bargaining agreements has declined from 721,000 to 610,000—a 15 percent decrease.

In Australia, the Industrial Relations Reform Act of 1993 worked a similar shift from compulsory, binding arbitration of wage and other labor disputes to one of collective bargaining of voluntary agreements. According to the U.S. Department of Labor's Bureau of International Labor Affairs:

> Australian Law provides workers, including public servants, the right of association free from government or political control. However, most local unions belong to state branches of the Australian Labor Party (ALP). Unions may form and join federations freely, and they actively participate in international bodies. Federal, state and territories' law provides workers with the right to organize and bargain collectively, protecting them from anti-union discrimination.

In 1994, the implicit right to strike was legalized, confined to the period of bargaining. Although there are no federal laws prohibiting it, forced labor, including forced and bonded labor by children, is generally not practiced. The enforcement of state compulsory educational requirements effectively prevents most children from joining the workforce until they are 15 or 16 years of age. In 2001, the New South Wales State Government enacted regulations to strengthen protections of children in the workplace.

The minimum standards of wages, working hours, and conditions are set by a series of "awards" (basic contracts for individual industries). Differing wage rates are awarded for individual trades and professions, covering 80 percent of all workers, enough to provide a decent standard of living for a worker and family. In the past two decades, there have been substantial increases in the percentage of temporary workers, not entitled to full employment benefits. Federal or state occupational health and safety laws apply to every workplace.

Australia is believed to be a destination country for a small number of trafficked women in the sex industry. In the past, these women have worked in sweatshops in textiles, clothing and footwear industries, service industries, and prostitution. Some NGOs assist trafficking victims.

Most notably, effective January 2013, the Australian Fair Work Act of 2009 was amended to permit fathers and partners to enjoy two weeks of paid parental leave.

Federal Workplace Relations Minister Bill Shorten announced in May 2013 an additional amendment to the act, which will place workplace bullying under the purview of the Fair Work Commission. That revision took effect on July 1, 2013. [http://www.mondaq.com/australia/x/239194/employee + rights + labour + relations/Workplace + Bullying + A + Message + for + all + Employers]

Also in 2013, an Australian court recognized a retaliation claim, where the plaintiff alleged that she had been fired for exercising a workplace right.

[Devonshire v. Magellan Powertronics Pty Ltd, FMCA 2007 (2013)]

However, in another case, an employee, who claimed he was fired in retaliation for making complaints and inquiries about his employment, the court rejected the claim, finding that the plaintiff had merely been griping rather than challenging a breach of his employment rights.

[Harrison v. In Control Pty Ltd, FMCA 149 (2013)]

Q 15:30   What are the main characteristics of labor relations and employment law on the African continent?

Africa is a vast, diverse, and tumultuous continent where colonization has been replaced in many regions by dictatorships, some of which are extremely repressive. Poverty remains endemic to many parts of the continent.

Some generalizations about labor relations and employment law worth noting are:

1. In the former British colonies, the "mother country" established the African Mineworkers Union before granting independence.

2. In a number of African nations, such as Zambia, it was the central government that took the initiative in creating workers' councils rather than allowing or promoting free trade unions.

3. Additionally, tribal chiefs and councils continue to exert substantial control over work rules and the terms and conditions of employment on the local level.

But, even more so than in some of the other nations discussed above, businesses seeking to operate in Africa need to be aware of cultural, political, economic, and health conditions that drive (or more often defeat) free enterprise activities. These include:

- HIV/AIDS: No firm can do business in equatorial or southern Africa without taking into account the pervasiveness of HIV/AIDS in the workforce and the general population. An estimated 16 million people have died from AIDS since its first detection and identification as a distinct disease, and 25 million more are believed to be infected with HIV. In South Africa the estimate is 20 percent of all adults—one in five. In Botswana the estimate is 36 percent. While the countries of the African continent in general do not have the highly developed legal/social systems of the West (e.g., workers' compensation, health insurance, tort law, etc.), a workforce that reflects this kind of epidemic promises to be a managerial nightmare. The human resources professional must be prepared to encounter taboos against discussion of sex, a lack of education on the modalities of HIV/AIDS transmission, second-class legal and social status of women, and high treatment costs compared to wages and salaries—all identified as factors fostering the continued spread of the disease.

• In west and central Africa, as remarkable as it may seem in the year 2005, an estimated 200,000 children are sold into slavery annually, according to UNICEF. An example is the ongoing enslavement of the Dinkas, animist tribes of the southern Sudan, where Arab militias, following an age-old tradition encountered by the mid-19th century explorers like Stanley and Livingston, invade the tribal villages, kill the men, and enslave the women and children. The sales price for a child may be as low as $15. [*See* http://www.infoplease.com/spot/slavery1.html.]

• War and terrorism continue to be constant concerns on the African continent. The litany of continual crises—ranging from tribal genocide to Muslim extremist terrorist attacks—does not require recitation here.

In sum, the four horsemen of the apocalypse ride high in Africa, overshadowing most legal considerations that drive investment decisions elsewhere in the world. Uganda is a rare bright spot in sub-Saharan Africa, where an intensive education program at the grassroots level has resulted in the widely publicized stemming of the AIDS epidemic.

Detailed information on current labor and employment laws and issues on the African continent can be found at http://www-sul.stanford.edu/depts/ssr g/africa/labor.html.

Q 15:31 What are the main characteristics of labor relations and employment law in Canada?

Our northern neighbor historically has shared many common characteristics with the United States. Both countries continue to maintain their heritage of common law inherited from Great Britain. Under the common law system, many legal rules are created by court precedents, recorded in legal opinions published in law reports; however, both countries now rely increasingly on statutory enactments of their main labor and employment laws.

In the 1960s, just about the same percentage of workers was unionized in each nation. But today, while the unionized workforce in the United States has declined, fully a third of Canada's workers remain in labor unions.

Canadian labor boards are empowered to:

1. Certify unions as collective bargaining representatives in the absence of representation elections;

2. Make final and binding decisions on unfair labor practice charges expeditiously; and

3. Impose a first contract as a remedy for an employer's failure to negotiate in good faith.

These three powers stand in stark contrast to the powers enjoyed by the U.S. National Labor Relations Board (NLRB) and probably go a long way toward explaining the sustained membership levels in Canadian, as contrasted to U.S., labor organizations.

Additionally, Canadian workers enjoy most of the same employment law rights that currently are enjoyed by their U.S. counterparts.

The following court and agency decisions are worth noting:

- In Regina v. Cole [2011 ONCA 218], the Ontario Court of Appeal considered the privacy rights of a school teacher, accused of viewing child pornography, with regard to his workplace computer. The court held, "[T]he appellant had a reasonable expectation of privacy from state intrusion in the personal use of his work computer and in the contents of his personal files on its hard drive. However, his expectation of privacy was modified. He had no expectation of privacy with respect to access to his hard drive by his employer's technician for the limited purpose of maintaining the technical integrity of the school's information network and the laptop."

- In *Saltsov v. Rolnick* [2010 ONSC 914 (CanLII)], the Ontario Divisional Court held that, when an employer unilaterally introduces a fundamental change to the employment contract, such that the employee is entitled to treat it as a constructive discharge, the limitation period begins to run when the employee elects to reject the change.

- In *Bennett v. Cunningham* [2011 ONSC 28 (CanLII)], the Ontario Divisional Court held in the case of a young attorney fired by her firm that a finding of just case for dismissal must be supported by the judge's consideration of the "contextual factors" surrounding the alleged improper behavior.

- In *4137566 Canada Ltd. And Clements* [2011 HRTO 106 (CanLII)], the Ontario Human Rights Tribunal ruled that the confidentiality provision in a severance agreement requires only that the terms of the settlement, but not the existence of the settlement, be kept secret by the departing employee.

- In *Tutty v. Attorney General* [2011 FC 57 (CanLII)], the Human Rights Commission ruled that the duty to accommodate a disabled employee does not insulate that employee from unrelated, adverse business decisions, such as the elimination of positions in the workplace.

- In *Disotell v. Kraft Canada, Inc.* [2010 ONSC 3793 (CanLII)], the court held that a constructive dismissal occurred when the company refused to take any steps to end the prolonged and aggressive teasing, which amounted to sex harassment by the plaintiff's supervisor.

- In 2012, the federal government passed legislation that will repeal part of the Canadian Human Rights Act and a section of the Canada Labor Code, making mandatory retirement illegal (except in cases where an employer can prove that mandatory retirement is an occupational requirement) as of December 15, 2012. [http://www.millerthomson.com/en/blog/canadian-labour-employment-law-blog/2012-archives/feds-do-away-with-mandatory-retirement]

- In *Vey v. Keeprite Refrigeration (National Refrigeration Air Conditioning Canada Crop)* [2012 Carswell Ont 663 (Ont. Lab. Rel. Bd.)], the Ontario Labor Relations Board found that a single argument between two employees, including shouting and a derogatory comment, was not enough to constitute harassment. [http://www.employmentlawtoday. com/ArticleView.aspx?l = 1&articleid = 2691]

- In *Dominguez v. Northland Properties Corp,* [2012 Carswell BC 518 (B.C. S.C.)] and for the first time in Canada, the British Columbia Supreme Court has certified a foreign workers' claim for damages as a class action. Northland Properties, a company operating Denny's restaurants that employ a large number of foreign workers, faces allegations of repeated breaches of an employment contract, such as failing to pay for overtime and employment-related expenses. Herminia Dominguez, a temporary foreign worker of Northland, will serve as the representative plaintiff in the class action, representing approximately 75 current and former employees. The employer faces financial liability and the possibility of a large monetary award against it, and could also face a two-year suspension from the Temporary Foreign Worker Program. [http://www. employmentlawtoday.com/ArticleView.aspx?l = 1&articleid = 2700]

Q 15:32   What are some of the main tenets of Mexico's labor laws?

While Mexico is often cited as having a suppressive labor law system, the problem lies more with lack of enforcement than an absence of reasonably progressive laws. Mexico's Federal Constitution, Title VI, covers labor and social security. Pursuant to its mandate, Congress has passed laws on:

- "Permanent" employees, day laborers, domestics, and artisans;
- Almost all labor contracts;
- Maximum duration of work (eight-hour days, seven-hour night shifts);
- Prohibition of unhealthful and dangerous conditions for women and minors;
- Prohibition of child labor under age 14;
- Six-hour days for minors aged 14 to 16;
- Maximum six-day workweeks;
- Twelve weeks of maternity leave;
- Minimum wages sufficient for subsistence and education of children;
- Equal pay for equal work;
- Protection from garnishment and attachment of wages;
- Employer responsibility for job-related injuries and illnesses;
- Employees' right to organize unions; and
- Overtime pay.

Q 15:33   What are the main characteristics of Mexican employment law?

Mexican law rejects employment at will and gives to each Mexican worker the right to hold a job for a specified period of time unless earlier terminated for cause. Of course on the shifting sands of Mexican economic fortunes, this legal distinction does nothing to insure full employment of Mexican workers.

Nevertheless, the Federal Labor Law of 1970 does contain the following key provisions:

1. Mandatory employment contracts for individual workers
2. Legally implied individual contracts if no actual contracts are executed
3. "For cause" termination includes:
   - Obtaining the job with false documents
   - Dishonesty on the job
   - Fighting or other violence on the job
   - Damaging company property, whether negligently or on purpose
   - Immoral behavior on the job
   - Three unexcused absences
4. Remedies for unjust termination:
   - Reinstatement or three months' severance pay
   - Back pay
5. Mandated benefits:
   - Year-end bonus
   - Paid vacation
   - Paid holidays
   - Profit sharing

Collective agreements are legal but cannot impinge on or diminish individual rights. Most collective agreements are national in scope. Strikes are legal but can be greatly restricted by action of the Mexican Conciliation and Arbitration Board.

NAFTA was followed by the signing of the North American Agreement on Labor Cooperation, aimed at creating relative parity among labor law and standards among the U.S., Canada, and Mexico. The details of this agreement can be found on the U.S. Department of Labor's Web site at http://www.dol.gov/ILAB/regs/naalc/naalc.htm.

On January 10, 2011, the NAFTA Free Trade Commission issued the following statement in the wake of its meeting in Mexico City: "We have recently marked seventeen years since the entry into force of the North American Free Trade Agreement (NAFTA). Since 1994, trade has blossomed, investment has increased, and all three countries have become more competitive. From 1993 to 2009, trade among the NAFTA countries has more than doubled, from $288 billion to $701 billion. Each day the NAFTA countries conduct nearly $1.9 billion in trilateral trade. The benefits of expanding trade have flowed to businesses, farmers, workers, and consumers." The manifesto went on to assert:

- NAFTA was instrumental in North America's recovery from the Great Recession;
- NAFTA has created jobs in all three signatory nations;
- Cooperation in the regulatory arena has reduced unnecessary governmental restrictions on the flow of commerce;
- A new bilateral agreement will now permit a manufacturer of telecommunications equipment in any of the three nations to test it only once, in the country of manufacture;
- New "Rules of Origin" will make more manufactured goods eligible for duty-free transit across national boundaries;
- "Green" products will now get particularly favorable treatment with regard to transnational tariffs;
- The nations' commerce and trade ministries have been committed to cooperating more closely;
- In particular, labor secretaries have been instructed to cooperate more closely with the North American Commission for Labor Cooperation;
- The North American Steel Trade Committee was commended for its efforts to resolve international disputes in this particularly sensitive area of commercial and labor relations.

[http://www.ustr.gov/about-us/press-office/press-releases/2011/january/ joint-statement-january-10-2011-meeting-nafta-free]

Reading between the lines, what the Commission is claiming is that progress is being made in those sore spots that attract the most criticism, including the disparities in labor costs and environmental and safety standards between our neighbor to the south and the rest of North America. Meanwhile, with the borderland drug war raging in such "sister" cities as Juarez, one must wonder just how real the alleged progress toward a more progressive socio-economic and political Mexico really is.

Q 15:34   What issues are high on Great Britain's labor and employment agenda?

At the State Opening of Parliament in mid-November 2009, Queen Elizabeth II gave her traditional annual speech, written by the Government, in which she outlined the bills that would be presented for enactment in the year ahead. Highlights that affected U.S. employers conducting business and employing people in Great Britain, included:

- Financial Services Bill: Not unlike similar legislation that worked its way through the labyrinth of the U.S. Congress (i.e., the Dodd-Frank Act); this piece of British legislation aims at beefing up the regulatory arm of the national government. If enacted it will increase the power of the Financial Services Authority (FSA) to regulate institutions in the financial services sector. The FSA also will receive the right to step in and void "overly risky" employment contracts and compensation schemes. The bill also aims for the creation of a new Council for Financial Stability, replacing the current Standing Committee. The Chancellor of the Exchequer (Britain's equivalent to the American Treasury Secretary) will chair the new entity, which will be staffed by representatives of the Bank of England, the Treasury, and the FSA. The Council will analyze risks to the financial services sector, hopefully to avoid any repetition of the turmoil of the past two years. This bill came into force in April 2013.

- Fiscal Responsibility Act 2010: This law forces the halving of Britain's national debt (now about £825 billion) over the next four years. The law lays out the following "initial duties":

  1. The Treasury must ensure that, for each of the financial years ending in 2011 to 2016, public sector net borrowing expressed as a percentage of gross domestic product is less than it was for the preceding financial year.

  2. The Treasury must ensure that, for the financial year ending in 2014, public sector net borrowing expressed as a percentage of gross domestic product is no more than half of what it was for the financial year ending in 2010.

  3. The Treasury must ensure that—

     (a) public sector net debt as at the end of the financial year ending in 2016 expressed as a percentage of gross domestic product (centered on 31 March 2016), is less than

     (b) public sector net debt as at the end of the previous financial year expressed as a percentage of gross domestic product (centered on 31 March 2015). [http://www.legislation.gov.uk/ukpga/2010/3/contents]

  This Act was granted Royal Assent on February 10, 2010, but was repealed by section 10(c) of the Budget Responsibility and National Audit Act 2011 on March 23, 2011.

- Equality Act 2010: The most apt analogy is to Title VII of the American 1964 Civil Rights Act. This anti-discrimination legislation had been knocking around Parliament for a while. It was granted Royal Assent on April 8, 2010 and became effective in October 2010.

  The primary purpose of the Act is to consolidate the complicated and numerous array of acts and regulations that formed the basis of anti-discrimination law in Great Britain. These include the Equal Pay Act 1970, the Sex Discrimination Act 1975, the Race Relations Act 1976, the Disability Discrimination Act 1995, and three major statutory instruments protecting discrimination in employment on grounds of religion or belief, sexual orientation, and age. This legislation has the same goals as the four major EU Equal Treatment Directives, whose provisions it mirrors and implements. The provisions include the following:

1. It requires equal treatment in access to employment as well as private and public services, regardless of the protected characteristics of age, disability, gender reassignment, marriage and civil partnership, race, religion or belief, sex, and sexual orientation. In the case of gender, there are special protections for pregnant women. However the Act allows transsexual people to be barred from gender-specific services if that is "a proportionate means of achieving a legitimate aim."

2. In the case of disability, employers and service providers are under a duty to make reasonable adjustments to their workplaces to overcome barriers experienced by disabled people. In this regard, the Equality Act 2010 did not change the law. Under Section 217, with limited exceptions the Act does not apply to Northern Ireland.

    [http://en.wikipedia.org/wiki/Equality_Act_2010]

- Temporary and Agency Workers Bill: This bill was intended to incorporate into British law Agency Workers Directive 2008/104/EC. Under its terms, temporary works—so-called agency workers—would achieve parity in their terms and conditions of employment after 12 weeks on the job. Wages, working hours, holidays, and other benefits will be encompassed. Among those miscellaneous benefits might be childcare and transportation services, as well as the right to learn of and apply for permanent appointments. Instead of enacting the bill, Parliament chose to implement the EC directive itself in December 2011.

Other noteworthy labor-related items of interest to readers doing business in Britain:

- Starting in April 2010, the income tax rate for Brits earning more than £150,000 became 50 percent.

- The National Insurance Contribution Rate (NIC) increased by 1 percent, effective April 2011, with the top rate for employers climbing to 13.8 percent and that of employees to 2 percent.

- Also effective in April 2010, skilled migrant workers' right to work in Britain is being determined on a point system with two tiers. Tier One is highly skilled workers, while Tier Two applies to skilled workers with actual job offers.

- New "Additional Paternity Leave" regulations allow the new mom to transfer the second half of her 12-month maternity leave entitlement to dad, provided the mother returns to work.

- Another employee-leave innovation is the right to take unpaid time off to train. The right applies only to employees of organizations with 250 or more workers and extends to all employees in April 2011.

- Extension of workers' right to a flexible schedule. On September 30, 2010, the UK government announced that the right to request a flexible working arrangement would be extended beyond its original April 2011 sunset provision, as part of an ostensible effort to create a more fair and family-friendly England. Such a request can now include:

— A change in the number of hours an employee works;

— A change in the employee's work schedule; or

— A change of workplace location, including working at home.

Additionally, where the original regulations reached only workers with young or disabled children, now parents of children under 17, or 17 and disabled, and employees caring for disabled adults, are eligible to ask. As of April 2012, the parent of any dependent, younger than 18 will be eligible for the benefit.

It is important for readers with UK workers to note that this is a right to make a request. Once you receive such a request, you are obliged to give it your good-faith consideration. However, you are entitled to turn it down if there is a "clear business reason" for saying "no." What this British rule is not is a right to shift to flextime or part-time employment. All it does is create a process for employees to make the request.

On the other hand, some pundits predict there will eventually be mandatory flextime rights for all employees in the United Kingdom.

• Appellate court interprets UK's "WARN" Act. The Transfer of Undertakings (Protection of Employment) Regulations 2006—commonly called the TUPE—provides protection for British employees when the employer engages in a sale of its assets or the entire business. As such, TUPE is the UK's functional equivalent of the American WARN Act and similar state statutes. TUPE defines affected employees as "any employees of the transferor or transferee who may be affected by the transfer or by measures taken in connection with it." In a 2010 case, the court found the vendor of a rest home did not adequately inform employees of the sale of the business. [Todd v. M.J. Strain and Care Concern, 2010 WL 2976710 (Employment Appeal Tribunal—Scotland)]

In 2013, the government initiated changes to TUPE affecting collective redundancy consultation and the applicability of collective agreements post transfer. Under revised rules, effective April 6, firms proposing to layoff 100 or more employees must undertake a 45-day consultancy period to discuss the proposed furloughs with the relevant unions. This change cut the 90-day consultancy period in half.

This revision is just one piece of the government's wide-ranging review of UK employment law, which also has doubled the number of years an employee must hold a job before enjoying the right to pursue an unfair-dismissal claim.

[Hilary Osborne, "Cut to redundancy consultation period 'could be counter-productive,'" *The Guardian*, Apr. 5, 2013, accessed at http://www.guardian.co.uk/money/2013/apr/05/cut-redundancy-consultation-counter-productive]

Q 15:35   What issues are high on France's labor and employment agenda?

In May 2012, the French Constitutional Council repealed the country's sexual-harassment law, Section 222-33 of the Penal Code. The law had defined sex harassment as the "act of harassing others to gain sexual favors." The statute carried a potential fine in excess of $18,000 (US) and a possible one-year prison term. The council considered the definition to be far too vague for fair enforcement. France was then without a sex-harassment law for only three months. National outrage at repeal resulted in the Parliament passing a new statute in July 2012. The new law defines sex harassment as "imposing on someone, in a repeated way, words or actions that have a sexual connotation and either affecting the person's dignity because of their degrading or humiliating nature or putting him or her in an intimidating, hostile or offensive situation." The law, which extends into the workplace, carries a possible two-year incarceration and a maximum fine of €30,000. Harassing a disabled person can result in an enhanced sentence of three years.

[http://www.crossborderemployer.com/post/2013/01/22/Employment-Law-in-France-The-Basics.aspx]

In early 2013, several French employer associations and three major labor unions agreed to the enactment of major labor law reforms. Heralded as potentially the most significant changes in decades they promise to liberalize for employers their ability to release workers for economic reasons; lower the costs of layoffs; and allow the lowering of wages temporarily in the face of an economic downturn.

[http://www.crossborderemployer.com/post/2013/01/22/Employment-Law-in-France-The-Basics.aspx]

Employment Law and Multinational Corporations

Q 15:36   What is the legal status of the multinational corporation?

In the United States, a multinational corporation will be deemed a "citizen" of the state where it is incorporated and the state where its major operations are located. The corporation will be amenable to suit in any state where it is doing business, although a state may decline to exercise jurisdiction over a claim arising elsewhere and not involving any of its own citizens.

Some countries consider multinational corporations to be stateless, a condition that may influence the company's ability to enforce its contracts and other legal rights in such jurisdictions.

Typically, American employees of U.S. multinational corporations outnumber the employees of any other host country, although collectively foreign employees in all foreign locations may outnumber their American counterparts.

Q 15:37   What labor and employment laws apply to employees of U.S. multinational corporations?

As a general proposition, U.S. federal labor and employment laws apply to:

1. American employees, whether located in the United States or overseas; and

2. Foreign employees working on U.S. soil.

Q 15:38   Can U.S. employees of U.S. multinational corporations ever be covered by foreign laws?

Yes, U.S. employees of U.S. multinational corporations can be subject to foreign law under at least the following circumstances:

1. Americans working abroad are subject to local civil and criminal laws and the jurisdiction of local courts and tribunals, especially with regard to their activities off company property and with local foreign nationals, such as when traveling or shopping.

2. By means of an individual employment contract, an American worker employed by a U.S. multinational company can agree that the labor and employment laws of the host nation shall govern the employment relationship or that the host country's courts or labor tribunals will have venue and jurisdiction over any such disputes.

3. The U.S. multinational corporation, such as companies operating maciodoro plants in Mexico under NAFTA, may be required by U.S. treaty to submit to the jurisdiction of foreign labor and employment laws and foreign tribunals.

4. Employees traveling to England on U.S. employer's behalf are advised that they might expect some close questioning upon arrival at a British port of entry. Employees normally based outside the United Kingdom and flying in to visit the firm's England offices will be required to satisfy immigration officers that:

   - They are not selling goods or services directly to the UK public
   - Are based abroad and have no intention of transferring their base of operations to Britain . . . not even temporarily
   - Will not be paid their salaries from a UK source

Note: This compensation restriction does not go so far as to prevent the British-based operation from providing such business travelers with reasonable reimbursement for expenses incurred during the visit.

Permissible business activities U.S. employees may perform in Britain include:

- One-off training in techniques and work practices
- Attending meetings and conferences, including appearing as a conference speaker

- Negotiating deals and signing of contracts
- Fact finding
- Site visits
- Delivery of goods
- Delivery of passengers, e.g., by piloting a corporate jet
- Installation, debugging, and enhancing of software products
- Assessment customer requirements on a consultancy basis
- Service or repair of machinery previously sold and subject to an initial warranty or guarantee
- Assembly and installation of machinery too heavy to ship in one piece
- Interpreting services for other legitimate business visitors
- Board-level director visits

Q 15:39 Are foreign multinational corporations subject to U.S. labor and employment laws?

Foreign multinational corporations, such as Japanese car companies doing business in the United States, are subject to U.S. and local labor and employment laws. Americans employed by these companies overseas do not, however, enjoy the protection of U.S. labor and employment laws.

Q 15:40 How have U.S. workers fared in suing foreign multinational corporations doing business in the United States?

The leading decision in this area of U.S. labor and employment law is *Fortino v. Quasar Co.* [950 F.2d 389 (7th Cir. 1991)] In this case, the Japanese executive in charge of the U.S. subsidiary of a Japanese parent corporation reorganized the U.S. operation, adding 10 Japanese executives on loan from the parent and discharging a number of U.S. counterparts. The U.S. executives sued, alleging national origin discrimination in violation of Title VII of the 1964 Civil Rights Act. The federal district court agreed and after a trial awarded the plaintiffs $3 million in damages. On appeal, the Seventh Circuit reversed, noting that the discharged Americans included some Japanese-Americans whose national origin apparently had failed to protect them from being fired. It held that the Japanese who replaced the Americans were given the jobs on the basis of citizenship, a category not protected by Title VII, rather than national origin, which is the protected category.

In other cases involving sexual harassment and assorted labor relations claims, Americans employed in the United States by foreign multinational corporations have fared better. But the *Quasar* case aptly illustrates how tricky such transnational actions can be.

Q 15:41   How have foreign workers fared in suing U.S.-based corporations in American courts?

The Alien Tort Claims Act was enacted in 1789 as part of the original Judiciary Act. [28 U.S.C. § 1350] In its original form, it simply said that "[t]he district courts shall have original jurisdiction of any civil action by an alien for a tort only, committed in violation of the law of nations or a treaty of the United States." For almost two centuries, the statute lay relatively dormant, supporting jurisdiction in only a handful of cases. In recent years, however, the statute has been rediscovered by attorneys seeking to vindicate the rights of foreign workers allegedly oppressed by U.S. multi-national corporations.

For example, two U.S. Courts of Appeals decisions were announced in December, 2008, interpreting the Alien Tort Claims Act as it may or may not apply to labor-related claims. The decisions in *Sarei v. Rio Tinto, PLC* [550 F.3d 822 (9th Cir. Cal. 2008)] and *Romero v. Drummond Company* [552 F.3d 1303 (11th Cir. Ala. 2008)] offer mixed messages but, by and large, bode well for multi-national corporate-defendants. In *Sarei*, plaintiffs filed an Alien Tort Statute suit against Rio Tinto, PLC alleging that they were the victims of numerous violations of international law as the result of Rio Tinto's mining operations on the island of Bougainville, Papua New Guinea. Initially, the court remanded the case to the district court for the Central District of California, stating that certain claims brought under the ATS "are appropriately considered for exhaustion under both domestic prudential standards and core principles of international law." In July 2009, however, the district court declined to find that a prudential exhaustion requirement was appropriate given the nature of the plaintiffs' claims.

In *Romero*, a Columbian labor union sued executives of Drummond, Ltd., the Colombian subsidiary of an American coal mining company located principally in Alabama, paid paramilitary operatives to torture and assassinate leaders of the union, SINTRAMIENERGETICA. In 2002 and 2003, the union and several of its leaders and relatives of deceased leaders sued Drummond and its parent company and executives under the Alien Tort Statute, and the Torture Victim Protection Act of 1991. On these complex facts and complicated legal issues, the appellate court held:

1. Torture Victim Protection Act allows suits against corporate defendants;

2. Alien Tort Statute contains no express exception for corporations, and the statute grants jurisdiction over complaints of torture against corporate defendants;

3. Plaintiffs failed to satisfy "state action" requirement of the Torture Victim Protection Act;

4. District court did not abuse its discretion in refusing to exercise supplemental jurisdiction over plaintiffs' wrongful death claim under Colombian law;

5. District court did not abuse its discretion in denying plaintiffs' motion for additional continuance when they were not able to complete letter rogatory process to secure witness' testimony for rescheduled trial date;

6. District court did not abuse its discretion in excluding testimony of late-disclosed witnesses; and

7. District court did not abuse its discretion in refusing to allow plaintiffs' proffered experts to testify.

In sum, the panel affirmed the district judge, essentially defeating the plaintiffs' claims.

Q 15:42   Should multinational corporations consider using binding arbitration to settle employment disputes?

Arbitration has become the dispute resolution method of choice for U.S. companies for many reasons:

1. Employment litigation has mushroomed in the past two decades—to wit, employment cases are the most numerous suits on most federal judges' overburdened dockets.

2. The cost of defending an action can make fighting a claim through to a jury verdict prohibitively expensive, even if the company ultimately prevails.

3. Juries in some jurisdictions are all too ready to award substantial compensatory and even punitive damages, whereas an arbitrator might predictably be more conservative in assessing damages.

4. Added to these general concerns are issues of obtaining fairness in a foreign court, identifying and retaining competent local counsel, travel expenses and executive time commitments during the course of the suit and the trial, and widely varying notions of due process, burden of proof, etc. across national boundaries and major cultures.

Q 15:43   Where can a multinational corporation interested in handling employment disputes by binding arbitration look for expertise?

Organizations that provide international arbitration support include the International Chamber of Commerce (ICC) and the AAA. The questions that follow summarize the international arbitration rules of the AAA without in any way endorsing or recommending the AAA. These rules are summarized here for illustrative purposes only.

Q 15:44   What language should a corporate employer use to include binding arbitration in an employment contract?

The AAA recommends the following contract language: *"Any controversy or claim arising out of or relating to this contract shall be determined by arbitration in accordance with the International Arbitration Rules of the American Arbitration Association.*" The parties may wish to consider adding: (1) "The number of arbitrators will be (one or three)"; (2) "The place of arbitration will be (city/country)"; or (3) "The language(s) of the arbitration will be." AAA adds that parties are encouraged when writing their contracts or when a dispute arises to request a conference, in person or by telephone, with the AAA to discuss an appropriate method for selection of arbitrators or any other matter that might facilitate efficient arbitration of the dispute.

Q 15:45   What procedures will the parties follow in an international arbitration?

Under AAA rules, the parties are free to adopt any mutually agreeable procedure for appointing arbitrators or may designate arbitrators upon whom they agree. Parties can reach agreements concerning appointing arbitrators either when writing their contracts or after a dispute has arisen. This flexible procedure permits parties to utilize whatever method best suits their needs.

For example, parties may choose to have a sole arbitrator or a tribunal of three or more arbitrators. They may agree that arbitrators shall be appointed by the AAA or that each side shall designate one arbitrator and those two will name a third, with the AAA making appointments if the tribunal is not promptly formed by that procedure. Parties may mutually request the AAA to submit to them a list of arbitrators from which each can delete names that are not acceptable or the parties may instruct the AAA to appoint arbitrators without the submission of lists, or may leave that matter to the sole discretion of the AAA. Parties also may agree on a variety of other methods for establishing the tribunal. In any event, if parties are unable to agree on a procedure for appointing arbitrators or on the designation of arbitrators, the AAA, after inviting consultation by the parties, will appoint the arbitrators. The rules therefore provide for the fullest exercise of party autonomy, while assuring that the AAA is available to act if the parties cannot reach mutual agreement.

Q 15:46   Are there any alternatives to binding arbitration?

Parties may wish to consider the possibility of mediation or conciliation. This too can be discussed with the AAA, either when the contract is being written or after a dispute arises. The AAA is prepared to arrange for mediation or conciliation anywhere in the world.

Q 15:47   How is a binding arbitration case commenced?

Parties filing an international case with the AAA can do so by contacting any one of the regional offices or the Association's International Center for Dispute Resolution. The contact information can be found at http://www.adr.org/aaa/faces/home/.

Q 15:48   How will AAA provide services once an arbitration has been commenced?

The AAA administrator can provide services through its International Center, located in New York City, or through the facilities of arbitral institutions with which it has agreements of cooperation.

Q 15:49   Who is the claimant in arbitration?

Usually, the claimant will be the employee. Unless the parties have specified to the contrary, the corporation may also decide to commence arbitration.

Q 15:50   How does a party initiate an arbitration?

Arbitration is initiated via the following procedures:

1. The party initiating arbitration ("claimant") will give written notice of arbitration to the administrator and at the same time to the party against whom a claim is being made ("respondent").

2. Arbitral proceedings will be deemed to commence on the date on which the administrator receives the notice of arbitration.

3. The notice of arbitration will contain a statement of claim including the following: (a) a demand that the dispute be referred to arbitration; (b) the names and addresses of the parties; (c) a reference to the arbitration clause or agreement that is invoked; (d) a reference to any contract out of or in relation to which the dispute arises; (e) a description of the claim and an indication of the facts supporting it; and (f) the relief or remedy sought and the amount claimed. The notice may also include proposals as to the means of designating and the number of arbitrators, the place of arbitration, and the language(s) of the arbitration.

Q 15:51   What will the AAA administrator do upon receiving notice of the intent to arbitrate a dispute?

Upon receipt of the notice of arbitration, the administrator will communicate with all parties with respect to the arbitration and will acknowledge the commencement of the arbitration.

Q 15:52   What must the respondent do upon receiving notice of the other party's intent to arbitrate a dispute?

Upon receiving notice of intent to arbitrate, the respondent shall do the following:

1. Within 30 days after the commencement of the arbitration, a respondent will submit a written statement of defense, responding to the issues raised in the notice of arbitration, to the claimant and any other parties, and to the administrator.

2. At the time a respondent submits its statement of defense, a respondent may make counterclaims or assert setoffs as to any claim covered by the agreement to arbitrate, as to which the claimant will within 30 days submit a written statement of defense to the respondent and any other parties and to the administrator.

3. A respondent will respond to the administrator, the claimant, and other parties within 30 days after the commencement of the arbitration as to any proposals the claimant may have made as to the number of arbitrators, the place of the arbitration or the language(s) of the arbitration, except to the extent that the parties have previously agreed as to these matters.

4. The arbitral tribunal, or the administrator if the arbitral tribunal has not yet been formed, may extend any of the time limits established here if it considers such an extension justified.

Q 15:53   Can the parties to arbitration ever amend their claims or defenses?

Yes. During the arbitral proceedings, any party may amend or supplement its claim, counterclaim or defense, unless the tribunal considers it inappropriate to allow such amendment or supplement because of the party's delay in making it, prejudice to the other parties, or any other circumstances. A party may not amend or supplement a claim or counterclaim if the amendment or supplement would fall outside the scope of the agreement to arbitrate.

Q 15:54   Who will serve as the arbitrator(s)?

If the parties have not agreed on the number of arbitrators, one arbitrator will be appointed unless the administrator determines in its discretion that three arbitrators are appropriate because of the large size, complexity, or other circumstances of the case.

1. The parties may mutually agree upon any procedure for appointing arbitrators and will inform the administrator as to such procedure.

2. The parties may mutually designate arbitrators, with or without the assistance of the administrator. When such designations are made, the parties will notify the administrator so that notice of the appointment can be communicated to the arbitrators, together with a copy of these rules.

3. If within 45 days after the commencement of the arbitration, all of the parties have not mutually agreed on a procedure for appointing the arbitrator(s) or have not mutually agreed on the designation of the arbitrator(s), the administrator will, at the written request of any party, appoint the arbitrator(s) and designate the presiding arbitrator. If all the parties have mutually agreed upon a procedure for appointing the arbitrator(s), but all appointments have not been made within the time limits provided in that procedure, the administrator will, at the written request of any party, perform all functions provided for in that procedure that remain to be performed.

4. In making such appointments, the administrator, after inviting consultation with the parties, will endeavor to select suitable arbitrators. At the request of any party or on its own initiative, the administrator may appoint nationals of a country other than that of any of the parties.

5. Unless the parties have agreed otherwise no later than 45 days after the commencement of the arbitration, if the notice of arbitration names two or more claimants or two or more respondents, the administrator will appoint all the arbitrators.

Q 15:55　What qualifications must the arbitrator(s) have?

1. Arbitrators acting under these rules will be impartial and independent. Prior to accepting appointment, a prospective arbitrator must disclose to the administrator any circumstance likely to give rise to justifiable doubts as to the arbitrator's impartiality or independence. If, at any stage during the arbitration, new circumstances arise that may give rise to such doubts, an arbitrator must promptly disclose such circumstances to the parties and to the administrator. Upon receipt of such information from an arbitrator or a party, the administrator will communicate it to the other parties and to the tribunal.

2. No party or anyone acting on its behalf will have any *ex parte* communication relating to the case with any arbitrator, or with any candidate for appointment as a party-appointed arbitrator, except to advise the candidate of the general nature of the controversy and of the anticipated proceedings, and to discuss the candidate's qualifications, availability, or independence in relation to the parties, or to discuss the suitability of candidates for selection as a third arbitrator where the parties or party-designated arbitrators are to participate in that selection. No party or anyone acting on its behalf will have any *ex parte* communication relating to the case with any candidate for presiding arbitrator.

Q 15:56　Can the parties challenge the appointment of an arbitrator?

Following are the conditions for challenging the appointment of an arbitrator:

1. A party may challenge any arbitrator whenever circumstances exist that give rise to justifiable doubts as to the arbitrator's impartiality or independence. A party wishing to challenge an arbitrator must send notice of the challenge to the administrator within 15 days after being notified of the appointment of the arbitrator, or within 15 days after the circumstances giving rise to the challenge become known to that party.

2. The challenge must state in writing the reasons for the challenge.

3. Upon receipt of such a challenge, the administrator will notify the other parties of the challenge. When an arbitrator has been challenged by one party, the other party or parties may agree to the acceptance of the challenge and, if they agree, the arbitrator will withdraw. The challenged

arbitrator may also withdraw from office in the absence of such an agreement. In neither case does withdrawal imply acceptance of the validity of the grounds for the challenge. If the other party or parties do not agree to the challenge or the challenged arbitrator does not withdraw, the administrator in its sole discretion will make the decision on the challenge.

Q 15:57   Can counsel represent the parties to an international arbitration?

Yes. Any party may be represented in the arbitration. The names, addresses, and telephone numbers of representatives must be communicated in writing to the other parties and to the administrator. Once the tribunal has been established, the parties or their representatives may communicate in writing directly with the tribunal.

Q 15:58   Where will the international arbitration be held?

The location for the international arbitration will be determined as follows:

1. If the parties disagree as to the place of arbitration, the administrator may initially determine the place of arbitration, subject to the power of the tribunal to determine finally the place of arbitration within 60 days after its constitution. All such determinations will be made with regard for the contentions of the parties and the circumstances of the arbitration.
2. The tribunal may hold conferences or hear witnesses or inspect property or documents at any place it deems appropriate. The parties will be given sufficient written notice to enable them to be present at any such proceedings.

Q 15:59   In what language(s) will the arbitration be held?

If the parties have not agreed otherwise, the language(s) of the arbitration will be that of the documents containing the arbitration agreement, subject to the power of the tribunal to determine otherwise based upon the contentions of the parties and the circumstances of the arbitration. The tribunal may order that any documents delivered in another language be accompanied by a translation into the language(s) of the arbitration.

Q 15:60   How will challenges to the arbitrator's jurisdiction be handled?

Challenges to the arbitrator's jurisdiction will be handled as follows:

1. The tribunal will have the power to rule on its own jurisdiction, including any objections with respect to the existence, scope, or validity of the arbitration agreement.
2. The tribunal will have the power to determine the existence or validity of a contract of which an arbitration clause forms a part. Such an

arbitration clause will be treated as an agreement independent of the other terms of the contract. A decision by the tribunal that the contract is null and void will not for that reason alone render the arbitration clause invalid.

3. A party must object to the jurisdiction of the tribunal or to the arbitrability of a claim or counterclaim no later than the filing of the statement of defense, as provided in Article 3, to the claim or counterclaim that gives rise to the objection. The tribunal may rule on such objections as a preliminary matter or as part of the final award.

Q 15:61   What procedures will the arbitrator(s) follow in conducting the arbitration hearing?

The arbitration hearing will be conducted as follows:

1. Subject to these rules, the tribunal may conduct the arbitration in whatever manner it considers appropriate, provided that the parties are treated with equality and that each party has the right to be heard and is given a fair opportunity to present its case.

2. The tribunal, exercising its discretion, will conduct the proceedings with a view to expediting the resolution of the dispute. It may conduct a preparatory conference with the parties for the purpose of organizing, scheduling, and agreeing to procedures to expedite the subsequent proceedings.

3. The tribunal may in its discretion direct the order of proof, bifurcate proceedings, exclude cumulative or irrelevant testimony or other evidence, and direct the parties to focus their presentations on the decision of issues that could dispose of all or part of the case.

4. Documents or information supplied to the tribunal by one party will at the same time be communicated by that party to the other party or parties.

Q 15:62   What written submissions may the parties make to the arbitrator(s)?

Written submissions to the arbitrator(s) will be handled as follows:

1. The tribunal may decide whether the parties can present any written statements in addition to statements of claims and counterclaims and statements of defense, and it will fix the periods of time for submitting any such statements.

2. The periods of time fixed by the tribunal for the communication of such written statements should not exceed 45 days. The tribunal may extend such time limits if it considers such an extension justified.

Q 15:63   How are written communications conducted during the pendency of the international arbitration?

Unless otherwise agreed by the parties or ordered by the tribunal, all notices, statements, and written communications may be served on a party by air mail, air courier, facsimile transmission, telex, telegram, or other written forms of electronic communication addressed to the party or its representative at its last known address or by personal service.

For the purposes of calculating any time limit specified in these rules in connection with required communications, that period will begin to run on the day following the day when a notice, statement, or written communication is received. If the last day of that period is an official holiday at the place received, the period is extended until the first business day that follows. Official holidays occurring during the running of the period of time are included in calculating the period.

Q 15:64   Who has the burden of proof and what evidence is admissible at the hearing?

Each party has the burden of proving the facts relied on to support its claim or defense. The tribunal may order a party to deliver to the tribunal and to the other parties a summary of the documents and other evidence the party intends to present in support of its claim, counterclaim, or defense. At any time during the proceedings, the tribunal may order the parties to produce other documents, exhibits, or other evidence it deems necessary or appropriate.

Q 15:65   When and how is the hearing conducted?

Following are the rules regarding how the arbitration hearing will be conducted:

1. The tribunal will give the parties at least 30 days' advance notice of the date, time, and place of the initial oral hearing. The tribunal will give reasonable notice of subsequent hearings.

2. At least 15 days before the hearings, each party will give the tribunal and the other parties the names and addresses of any witnesses it intends to present, the subject of their testimony, and the languages in which such witnesses will give their testimony.

3. At the request of the tribunal or pursuant to mutual agreement of the parties, the administrator will make arrangements for the interpretation of oral testimony or for a record of the hearing.

4. Hearings are private unless the parties agree otherwise or the law provides to the contrary. The tribunal may require any witness or witnesses to retire during the testimony of other witnesses. The tribunal may determine the manner in which witnesses are examined.

5. Evidence of witnesses may also be presented in the form of written statements signed by them.

6. The tribunal will determine the admissibility, relevance, materiality, and weight of the evidence offered by any party. The tribunal will take into account applicable principles of legal privilege, such as those involving the confidentiality of communications between a lawyer and client.

Q 15:66   Can the arbitrator(s) issue any interim orders while the arbitration hearing/award are pending?

At the request of any party, the tribunal may take whatever interim measures it deems necessary, including injunctive relief and measures for the protection or conservation of property. Such interim measures may take the form of an interim award and the tribunal may require security for the costs of such measures. A request for interim measures addressed by a party to a judicial authority will not be deemed incompatible with the agreement to arbitrate or a waiver of the right to arbitrate. The tribunal may in its discretion apportion costs associated with applications for interim relief in any interim award or in the final award.

Q 15:67   Are expert witnesses allowed in international arbitrations?

The tribunal may appoint one or more independent experts to report to it, in writing, on specific issues designated by the tribunal and communicated to the parties. The parties must provide such an expert with any relevant information or produce for inspection any relevant documents or goods that the expert may need for this report. Any dispute between a party and the expert as to the relevance of the requested information or goods will be referred to the tribunal for a decision.

Upon receipt of an expert's report, the tribunal will send a copy of the report to all parties and give the parties an opportunity to express, in writing, their opinions about the report. A party may examine any document on which the expert has relied in such a report. At the request of any party, the tribunal will give the parties an opportunity to question the expert at a hearing. At this hearing, the parties may present expert witnesses to testify on the points at issue.

Q 15:68   What happens if a party fails to participate in the arbitration process?

The tribunal may proceed with the arbitration if it determines that:

1. A party failed to file a statement of defense within the time established by the tribunal without showing sufficient cause for that failure.

2. A party, duly notified under these rules, failed to appear at a hearing without showing sufficient cause for that failure.

If a party, duly invited to produce evidence or take any other steps in the proceedings, fails to do so within the time established by the tribunal without showing sufficient cause for such failure, as determined by the tribunal, the tribunal may make the award on the evidence before it.

Q 15:69   How are the hearings closed?

After asking the parties if they have any further testimony or evidentiary submissions, and upon receiving negative replies or if satisfied that the record is complete, the tribunal may declare the hearings closed.

The tribunal in its discretion, on its own motion or upon application of a party, may reopen the hearings at any time before the award is made.

Q 15:70   How is a decision rendered in an international arbitration?

A decision in an international arbitration is rendered as follows:

1. When there is more than one arbitrator, any award, decision, or ruling of the arbitral tribunal will be made by a majority of the arbitrators. If any arbitrator fails to sign the award, the reason for the absence of that arbitrator's signature will be given with the award.

2. When the parties or the tribunal so authorize, the presiding arbitrator may make decisions or rulings on questions of procedure, subject to revision by the tribunal.

3. Awards will be made in writing, promptly by the tribunal, and will be final and binding on the parties. The parties undertake to carry out any such award without delay.

4. The tribunal will state the reasons upon which the award is based, unless the parties have agreed that no reasons need be given.

5. The award will contain the date and the place where the award was made. An award may be made public only with the consent of all parties or as required by law. The administrator will communicate copies of the award to the parties.

6. If the arbitration law of the country where the award is made requires the award to be filed or registered, the tribunal will comply with that requirement.

7. In addition to making a final award, the tribunal may make interim, interlocutory, or partial orders and awards.

Q 15:71   What laws apply in an international arbitration?

The following laws apply in an international arbitration:

1. The tribunal will apply the substantive law(s) or rules of law designated by the parties as applicable to the dispute. Failing such a designation by

    the parties, the tribunal will apply the law(s) or rules of law it determines to be appropriate.

2. In arbitrations involving the application of contracts, the tribunal will make its decision in accordance with the terms of the contract and will take into account usages of the trade applicable to the contract.

3. The tribunal will not decide as amiable compositeur or ex aequo et bono unless the parties have expressly authorized it to do so.

4. A monetary award will be in the currency or currencies of the contract unless the tribunal considers another currency more appropriate, and the tribunal may award such pre-award and post-award interest, simple or compound, as it considers appropriate, taking into consideration the contract and applicable law.

5. Unless the parties agree otherwise, the parties expressly waive and forego any right to punitive, exemplary, or similar damages unless a statute requires that compensatory damages be increased in a specified manner. This provision will not apply to any award of arbitration costs to a party to compensate for dilatory or bad faith conduct in the arbitration.

Q 15:72   What if the parties settle their dispute before the arbitrator renders an award?

If the parties settle the dispute before an award is made, the tribunal will terminate the arbitration and, if requested by all parties, may record the settlement in the form of an award on agreed terms. The tribunal is not obliged to give reasons for such an award.

If the continuation of the proceedings becomes unnecessary or impossible for any other reason, the tribunal will inform the parties of its intention to terminate the proceedings. The tribunal will, thereafter, issue an order terminating the arbitration, unless a party raises justifiable grounds for objection.

Q 15:73   How are costs apportioned in an international arbitration?

The tribunal will fix the costs of arbitration in its award. The tribunal may apportion such costs among the parties if it determines that such apportionment is reasonable, taking into account the circumstances of the case. Such costs may include: (1) the fees and expenses of the arbitrators; (2) the costs of assistance required by the tribunal, including its experts; (3) the fees and expenses of the administrator; (4) the reasonable costs for legal representation of a successful party; and (5) any such costs incurred in connection with an application for interim or emergency relief pursuant to Article 21.

Arbitrators will be compensated based upon their amounts of service, taking into account their stated rate of compensation and the size and complexity of the case. The administrator will arrange an appropriate daily or hourly rate, based on such considerations, with the parties and with each of the arbitrators as soon as practicable after the commencement of the arbitration. If the parties fail to agree on the terms of compensation, the administrator will establish an appropriate rate and communicate it in writing to the parties.

When a party files claims, the administrator may request the filing party to deposit appropriate amounts as an advance for the anticipated costs. During the course of the arbitral proceedings, the tribunal may request supplementary deposits from the parties. If the deposits requested are not paid in full within 30 days after the receipt of the request, the administrator will inform the parties, in order that one or the other of them may make the required payment. If such payments are not made, the tribunal may order the suspension or termination of the proceedings. After the award has been made, the administrator will render an accounting to the parties of the deposits received and return any unexpended balance to the parties.

Q 15:74   How is confidential information handled in an international arbitration?

Confidential information disclosed during the proceedings by the parties or by witnesses will not be divulged by an arbitrator or by the administrator. Unless otherwise agreed by the parties or required by applicable law, the members of the tribunal and the administrator will keep confidential all matters relating to the arbitration or the award.

Q 15:75   How are the arbitrators compensated in an international arbitration?

Under AAA rules of international arbitration, unless the parties agree otherwise, arbitrator compensation and administrative fees are subject to allocation by the arbitrator in the award. A nonrefundable initial filing fee is payable in full by a filing party when a claim, counterclaim, or additional claim is filed. A case service fee will be incurred for all cases that proceed to their first hearing. This fee will be payable in advance at the time that the first hearing is scheduled. This fee will be refunded at the conclusion of the case if no hearings have occurred.

If the AAA is not notified at least 24 hours before the time of the scheduled hearing, the case service fee will remain due and will not be refunded. These fees will be billed according to the following schedule:

- A non-refundable initial filing fee is payable in full by a filing party when a claim, counterclaim or additional claim is filed.

- A case service fee will be incurred for all cases that proceed to their first hearing. This fee will be payable in advance at the time that the first hearing is scheduled. This fee will be refunded at the conclusion of the case if no hearings have occurred. However, if the Association is not notified at least 24 hours before the time of the scheduled hearing, the case service fee will remain due and will not be refunded.

These fees will be billed in accordance with the following schedule:

Amount of Claim	Initial Filing Fee	Case Service Fee
Above $0 to $10,000	$ 750	$ 200
Above $10,000 to $75,000	$ 950	$ 300
Above $75,000 to $150,000	$ 1,800	$ 750
Above $150,000 to $300,000	$ 2,750	$1,250
Above $300,000 to $500,000	$ 4,250	$1,750
Above $500,000 to $1,000,000	$ 6,000	$2,500
Above $1,000,000 to $5,000,000	$ 8,000	$3,250
Above $5,000,000 to $10,000,000	$10,000	$4,000
Above $10,000,000	$12,500 plus. 01% of amount of claim above $10 million	$6,000
No Amount Stated	$ 3,250	$1,250

Fees are subject to increase if the amount of a claim or counterclaim is modified after the initial filing date. Fees are subject to decrease if the amount of a claim or counterclaim is modified before the first hearing.

The minimum fees for any case having three or more arbitrators are $2,750 for the filing fee, plus a $1,250 case service fee. Expedited Procedures are applied in any case where no disclosed claim or counterclaim exceeds $75,000, exclusive of interest and arbitration costs.

Parties on cases held in abeyance for one year by agreement, will be assessed an annual abeyance fee of $300. If a party refuses to pay the assessed fee, the other party or parties may pay the entire fee on behalf of all parties; otherwise the matter will be closed.

[*See* http://www.adr.org/aaa/ShowPDF?doc = ADRSTG_012009.]

Q 15:76 Does the NLRB have jurisdiction over foreign multinational corporations operating in the United States?

In general, the answer is yes; however, in one leading case a U.S. appeals court ruled that the Foreign Sovereign Immunities Act protected a bank that was wholly owned by a foreign government from liability for its unfair labor practices under the National Labor Relations Act. [State Bank of India v. NLRB, 808 F.2d 526 (2d Cir. 1987)]

Q 15:77   Does the NLRB have jurisdiction over U.S. multinational corporations' overseas operations?

The Board has jurisdiction over U.S. workers and U.S. flag vessels located overseas, but cannot exercise jurisdiction over foreign nationals employed by U.S. multinational corporations other than U.S. flag vessels at overseas facilities. [*See* NLRB v. Dredge Operators, 146 L.R.R.M. 2217 (5th Cir. 1994).]

International Taxation

Q 15:78   Are U.S. citizens and corporations taxed by the United States on their foreign income?

American citizens, other residents of the United States, and domestic corporations usually find that the income they earn outside the United States is taxable; however, some forms and sources of income, as well as some taxpayers, are exempted. With regard to foreign corporations doing business in the United States and nonresident aliens working here, usually only the money they make in connection with a U.S. job, trade, or business gets taxed by the federal government. [26 C.F.R. § 1.1-1(b)]

Q 15:79   Who is a U.S. citizen for tax purposes?

For U.S. tax purposes, the following individuals are considered U.S. citizens:

1. Every person born in America; and

2. Immigrants who have successfully completed the immigration process.

[26 C.F.R. § 1.1-1(c)]

Q 15:80   Who is defined as an *alien* for tax purposes?

A foreign person who has filed a "declaration of intent" to become a U.S. citizen, but who as yet has not been formally admitted to U.S. citizenship—which requires the final order of a naturalization court—is deemed to be an *alien* under applicable IRS regulations. [26 C.F.R. § 1.1-1(c)]

Q 15:81   What is meant by an individual worker's *foreign earned income*?

Foreign earned income is income earned from foreign sources that can be attributed to services performed outside the United States. The calculation includes wages and other compensation paid for personal services rendered. Compensation can include:

1. Cash (wages, salaries, professional fees);

2. Reimbursements and allowances (e.g., taxable moving expense reimbursements);

3. Chattel and real property (at fair market value); and

4. Sometimes, the worker's share of net profits of the enterprise (up to 30 percent), if the profits result from a mix of personal services and capital investment.

The calculation of foreign earned income does not include:

- Annuities; and
- Pensions.

[I.R.C. § 911; 26 C.F.R. § 1.911-3(c)(2)]

Q 15:82   Are there any exclusions from taxation of a U.S. worker's foreign earned income?

The Internal Revenue Code recognizes foreign earned income and foreign housing cost exclusions if the U.S. worker takes either of the following actions:

1. Establishes residency in the foreign country or countries where the services producing the earned income are being performed [26 C.F.R. § 911-1(a)];

2. Meets the "foreign presence" test, which means that for 12 consecutive months the worker has been performing services in one or more foreign countries for a total of no fewer than 330 days. [26 C.F.R. § 911-1(b)] Note: Paid vacation time spent abroad can be counted in this 330-day/ 12-month calculation.

Q 15:83   How does a U.S. worker establish foreign residency for purposes of qualifying for an exclusion from taxation of foreign earned income?

The IRS generally determines foreign residency by looking at the worker's "tax home." A tax home may be either of the following:

1. The principal place of business; or

2. The employment posting or station.

One of these two places can be the worker's tax home, notwithstanding that the worker's family lives somewhere else.

If the worker performs services on a regular basis in more than one location, the IRS makes the "tax home" determination by a "bundle of sticks" approach. Significant factors considered include:

1. How much time is actually spent in each of the locations;

2. The nature of the activity performed in each location; or

3. How much money is made in or from each location.

Q 15:84   When can a U.S. worker living abroad deduct housing expenses from foreign earned income?

If the worker's employer is not paying the housing expenses, then the worker is allowed to deduct them from foreign earned income. [I.R.C. § 911(c)(3)(A)] But the worker cannot take a deduction greater than the amount of that foreign earned income [I.R.C. § 911(c)(3)(B)], nor can a double deduction be taken against foreign earned income that already is excluded from taxation on some other basis. [I.R.C. §§ 911(c)(3)(C), 911(d)(6)]

Q 15:85   What are some examples of U.S. workers who meet the foreign presence test for exclusion of foreign earned income from taxation?

The IRS regulations provide the following examples:

- B, a U.S. citizen arrives in Venezuela from New York at 12:00 noon on April 24, 1982. B remains in Venezuela until 2:00 p.m. on March 21, 2000, at which time B departs for the United States. Among other possible 12-month periods, B is present in the foreign country for an aggregate of 330 full days during each of the following 12-month periods: March 21, 1982 through March 20, 1983; and April 25, 1982 through April 24, 1983.

- C, a U.S. citizen travels extensively from the time C leaves the United States on March 5, 1982, until the time C departs the United Kingdom on January 1, 1984 to return to the United States permanently. The schedule of C's travel and the number of full days at each location are:

Country	Arrival	Departure	Full Days in Country
United States		10 p.m., March 5, 1982	
United Kingdom	9 a.m., March 6, 1982	10 p.m., June 25, 1982	110
United States	11 a.m., June 30, 1982	1 p.m., July 19, 1999	0
France	3 p.m., July 24, 1982	11 a.m., Aug. 22, 1983	393
United States	4 p.m., Aug. 22, 1983	9 a.m., Sept. 4, 1983	0
United Kingdom	9 a.m., Sept. 5, 1983	9 a.m., Jan. 1, 1984	117
United States	1 p.m., Jan. 1, 1984		

Among other possible 12-month periods, C is present in a foreign country or countries for an aggregate of 330 full days during the following 12-month periods: March 2, 1999 through March 1, 2000; and January 21, 2000 through January 20, 2001. [26 C.F.R. § 1.911-2]

Q 15:86   Is there any limit on the overall exclusion that a U.S. worker can make from foreign earned income?

First, the total of earned income exclusion plus housing exclusion cannot be greater than total foreign earned income in the relevant tax year. [I.R.C. § 911(d)(7)] Second, the exclusion cannot exceed the percentage of foreign earned income that equals the number of qualifying days in the tax year divided by the total number of days in the tax year. [26 C.F.R. § 911-3(d)(2)] For example, if the worker minimally meets the "foreign presence" test by having spent 330 days working abroad, and the tax year contains 365 days, the formula is 330/365 or 90 percent. Third, the ceiling for 2008 is $87,600. [I.R.C. § 911(b)(2)(A)]

Q 15:87   In which tax year must the U.S. worker realize foreign earned income?

Generally, the IRS requires the U.S. worker to realize foreign earned income in the year the services were performed. [26 C.F.R. § 1.911-3(e)(1)] Foreign earned income may, however, be realized in the year received, instead of the year earned, if:

1. The period in which the payment is made is a normal payroll period of the employer and the particular employee;
2. The payroll period includes the last day of the employee's taxable year;
3. The payroll period does not exceed 16 days; and
4. The payment is part of a normal payroll and not a payment made particularly or exclusively to this particular employee.

[26 C.F.R. § 1.911-3(e)(3)]

Q 15:88   How does the IRS define *foreign country* for purposes of the foregoing rules, and are there any exceptions to the definition?

A *foreign country* includes:

1. Any territory under the sovereignty of a government other than the United States;
2. The territorial waters of a foreign country (as defined by U.S., not foreign, law);
3. The air space of the foreign country; or
4. The seabeds adjacent to the territorial waters of the foreign country (in accord with international law).

[26 C.F.R. § 1.911-2(h)]

Q 15:89   Are U.S. workers in U.S. possessions subject to U.S. income taxation?

U.S. workers who are *bona fide* residents of the following territories normally are not subject to U.S. income taxation (unless employed by the U.S. government):

- Guam;
- Northern Mariana Islands;
- American Samoa; and
- Puerto Rico.

[I.R.C. §§ 931(a), 931(d)(1), 933(1)]

Q 15:90   How should a U.S. worker seeking an exclusion from taxation of foreign earned income go about obtaining this exclusion?

In order to receive either a foreign earned income or a foreign housing exclusion, the worker/taxpayer must:

1. Make separate elections for each such sought-after exclusion on Form(s) 2555.
2. File each such election with the taxpayer's income tax return or with an amended return.
3. Include in each such election information sufficient to determine eligibility for the sought-after exclusion, including: name, address, and Social Security number; name of employer; whether or not the taxpayer has claimed such an exclusion in any of the previous five tax years; whether the individual has revoked any such exclusion in any prior tax year; the specific exclusion being elected; the foreign country or countries in which the taxpayer makes his or her home and the date on which each such home was established; the status claimed (either residence or physical presence); the qualifying period of residence or presence; the total foreign earned income, including the fair market value of any chattel or real property received as compensation; and housing expenses, if a housing exclusion is being elected.
4. Not owe any federal income tax net of the exclusion, or must pay the net taxes with the filing.

[26 C.F.R. § 1.911-7]

Q 15:91   Are U.S. workers double taxed by the United States and the foreign country where they earn their foreign earned income?

In addition to the exclusions of foreign earned income from U.S. income taxation discussed previously, the United States has entered into tax treaties with numerous foreign countries: Australia, Austria, Barbados, Belgium, Canada, China (except Hong Kong), Cyprus, Czech Republic, Denmark, Egypt, Finland, France, Germany, Greece, Hungary, Iceland, India, Indonesia, Ireland,

Israel, Italy, Jamaica, Japan, Luxembourg, Mexico, Morocco, Netherlands, New Zealand, Norway, Pakistan, Philippines, Poland, Portugal, Romania, Russia, Slovak Republic, South Korea, Spain, Sweden, Switzerland, Trinidad, Tunisia, United Kingdom, and numerous of the former components of the USSR.

While each of these treaties is somewhat unique, typically they provide for each country to credit its own citizens for taxes paid to the foreign host. [*See* I.R.C. § 894(a).]

A U.S. worker who gets the benefit of such a tax treaty cannot also elect a foreign residence or housing exclusion for the same income on top of the tax treaty protection from double taxation. Thus in high-tax countries such workers generally get no benefit from the available exclusions, because their U.S. tax obligations are often fully offset by the taxes they already have paid to their host countries.

Employee Safety Concerns in the Global Marketplace

Q 15:92   What are some of the bio-terror threats multinational employers should be aware of?

The Centers for Disease Control (CDC) lists the most likely threats:

- Tularemia
- Viral hemorrhagic fevers
- Anthrax
- Botulism
- Pneumonic plague
- Smallpox

Q 15:93   What should a multinational employer know about tularemia?

Tularemia is a serious, sometimes fatal disease caused by a bacterium, *Francisella tularensis*, which is found in animals (particularly rodents and rabbits). A person may contract tularemia in a variety of ways, including:

- Being bitten by an infected insect, such as a tick or deerfly;
- Handling the carcass of an infected animal;
- Eating or drinking contaminated food or water; and
- Breathing in the bacteria, *F. tularensis*

Since tularemia is not known to spread from person to person, an infected person does not need to be isolated. However, they should be treated as quickly as possible, as death can result if they are not administered the necessary antibiotics. Symptoms usually occur three to five days after exposure to the bacteria, but may not occur until as long as 14 days later. Symptoms include:

- Sudden fever;
- Chills;
- Muscle aches;
- Diarrhea;
- Headaches;
- Joint pain;
- Dry cough; and
- Progressive weakness.

However, other symptoms may occur depending on how the person contracted the virus. Inhalation is the most dangerous type of exposure, resulting in severe respiratory illness, life-threatening pneumonia, and systemic infection if left untreated.

To avoid tularemia, one should avoid contact with insects by using insect repellent that contains DEET or treating clothes with repellent that contains permethrin, wash hands often, cook food thoroughly, and make sure water comes from a safe and reliable source.

Q 15:94   What should a multinational employer know about viral hemorrhagic fevers?

The term *viral hemorrhagic fevers* (VHFs) refers to a group of illnesses that are caused by several different families of viruses. A viral hemorrhagic fever is a severe multisystem (in that it affects several organs) syndrome that usually damages the vascular system and impairs the body's ability to regulate itself, and is often accompanied by hemorrhage. Although the bleeding itself is rarely life threatening, many of these viruses are the cause of life-threatening diseases.

VHFs are caused by viruses in four families: arenaviruses, filoviruses, bunyaviruses, and flaviviruses. Transmission of the virus may occur in a variety of ways:

- Contact with the urine, feces, or other bodily secretions of rodents;
- Being bitten by or crushing an infected insect such as a tick;
- Caring for or slaughtering infected livestock; and
- Close contact with an infected person or his/her bodily fluids (such as through the use of an infected syringe or needle).

Symptoms vary for each specific virus, but the most common symptoms include:

- Pronounced fever;
- Fatigue;
- Dizziness;
- Muscle aches;

- Declining strength; and
- Exhaustion.

Severely ill patients may also experience bleeding under the skin, in internal organs, or from orifices such as mouth, eyes, or ears. They may also experience shock, nervous system malfunction, coma, delirium, seizures, and, occasionally, renal failure. There is no established cure for VHFs, and no vaccination to prevent them.

One may combat VHFs by avoiding contact with host species like rodents and insects by using insect repellent, bed nets, window screens, and protective clothing. Infected persons should be isolated as they may spread the disease to other people.

Q 15:95   What should a multinational employer know about anthrax?

Anthrax is an acute infectious disease caused by a spore-forming bacterium. It is most common in hoofed mammals but, as Americans learned in the autumn of 2001, it can infect and sometimes kill humans. Symptoms vary depending upon how it is contracted but generally appear about seven days after exposure. The forms of human anthrax are:

- Inhalation anthrax;
- Cutaneous anthrax; and
- Intestinal anthrax.

Initial symptoms of inhalation anthrax resemble a common cold. But after several days, breathing difficulties and shock ensue. It can be fatal.

Intestinal anthrax, caused by eating contaminated food, causes inflammation of the intestinal tract, nausea, appetite loss, vomiting (eventually blood), and acute diarrhea.

The CDC doubts that anthrax can be spread from person to person. Consequently, co-workers who have not themselves been infected with the disease need not be treated or immunized merely because they have had contact with a victim. For the victims themselves, early treatment with appropriate antibiotics is essential. Vaccination is also possible.

Q 15:96   What should a multinational employer know about botulism?

Botulism produces a toxin that paralyzes muscles. The disease appears in three forms:

- Foodborne botulism;
- Infant botulism; and
- Wound botulism.

With the foodborne variety, symptoms start anywhere from six hours to two weeks, but most commonly within 12 to 36 hours. They can include:

- Double vision;
- Blurred vision;
- Drooping eyelids;
- Slurred speech;
- Difficulty swallowing;
- Dry mouth; and
- Muscle weakness beginning at the shoulders and descending down through the body.

Paralysis of the breathing muscles can ultimately result in death unless the victim is aided by mechanical ventilation.

Like anthrax, botulism cannot be spread from one worker to another.

The CDC maintains a supply of the antitoxin, which can reduce the severity of the symptoms, greatly increasing the likelihood of complete recovery, which can take weeks to months.

Q 15:97   What should a multinational employer know about pneumonic plague?

Plague is a bacterium carried by rodents and their fleas. It can infect humans and other animals. Pneumonic plague attacks the lungs. Symptoms are:

- Fever;
- Headache;
- Weakness;
- Bloody sputum; and
- Pneumonia.

Septic shock results in death without early treatment. Worker-to-worker transmission occurs via respiratory droplets resulting from face-to-face exposure. Effective antibiotics are:

- Streptomycin;
- Tetracycline; and
- Chloramphenicol.

Although there is no vaccine, seven days of prophylactic antibiotics will protect persons exposed to the disease.

Q 15:98   What should a multinational employer know about smallpox?

The last reported case of smallpox occurred decades ago (1977), leading to a declaration by world health organizations that the disease had been eradicated. However, samples of the virus have been preserved in laboratories, making a terrorist attempt at starting a twenty-first century epidemic more than a theoretical possibility. Since humans are no longer vaccinated against the disease, the threat cannot be ignored.

Incubation takes 7 to 17 days (the average being 12) following infection. The characteristic rash appears on the face, followed by the arms and legs two to three days later. Pus-filled lesions leave the horrible scarring suffered by those who survive. Death occurs in 30 percent of cases.

The disease is spread from person to person by saliva. Victims are most infectious during the first week of the illness, but transmission is possible until all the lesions have lost their scabs.

Routine vaccination ended in 1962 and persons vaccinated up to that time are still assumed to be susceptible, along with the unvaccinated portion of the world population. The vaccine is not available although it can prevent or greatly lessen the severity of the disease, even within four days of exposure. The United States has an emergency supply of vaccine as there is no other known treatment.

Q 15:99   What is *Ebola* and what should a multinational employer know about it?

While not on the CDC's list of most likely bio-terror threats, Ebola is a severe, nasty, and often-fatal virus that attacks primates, including humans. Ebola is of greatest concern to employers doing business in Africa. Varieties are named for their places of origin:

- Ebola-Zaire;
- Ebola-Sudan; and
- Ebola-Ivory Coast.

Research firms importing primates from these regions must also be aware of Ebola. There is an Ebola-Reston, named for an outbreak at a research facility in Reston, Virginia, as chronicled in *The Hot Zone.*

The reservoir of the virus is unknown. Researchers have hypothesized that outbreaks begin with contact between an infected animal and the first human victim. After infection of the so-called "index case," the disease can be transmitted to co-workers and health care providers by direct contact with the victim's blood and other bodily fluids. Needle sticks are particularly dangerous, as with AIDS, which is believed to be Ebola's close relative. Symptoms progress as follows:

- Within a few days of infection, fever, headache, muscle ache, stomach pain, fatigue, and diarrhea; and
- Within about a week, chest pain, shock, blindness, bleeding, and finally death.

There is no standard treatment, but treatment usually includes:

- Balancing the patient's fluids and electrolytes;

- Maintaining oxygen status;
- Maintaining blood pressure; and
- Treatment for complicating infections.

Some physicians have tried transfusions of blood from Ebola survivors. The results, while not 100 percent effective, were promising.

The CDC, together with the World Health Organization, has developed a set of protocols for dealing with outbreaks. Multinational employers operating facilities in Africa may want to obtain *Infection Control for Viral Haemorrhagic Fevers in the African Health Care Setting* from the CDC or the World Health Organization.

Other viruses of lesser concern but still disruptive of employee travel in 2003 were SARS and West Nile virus.

Q 15:100   What is *terrorism*?

The federal government defines *terrorism* as "the use of force or violence against persons or property in violation of the criminal laws of the United States for purposes of intimidation, coercion or ransom."

Q 15:101   What is the definition of a *biological weapon*?

Biological weapons are infectious microbes or toxins, such as those discussed above, used to produce illness or death in people, animals, or plants. Aerosols or airborne particles can disperse them. Terrorists can use them to contaminate food or water. They may have immediate or delayed effect, and they can be extremely difficult to detect.

Q 15:102   What do terrorists target?

Favorite terrorist targets have been:

- International airports
- Large cities
- Major international events
- Resorts
- High-profile landmarks

Q 15:103   What should a multinational employer instruct its employees to do about the threat of terrorism?

- Be alert of the surrounding area;
- Take precautions when traveling;
- Be aware of conspicuous or unusual behavior;
- Do not accept packages from strangers;

- Do not leave luggage unattended;
- Know the host city's public transportation system and have a work site evacuation plan;
- Don't waste the company's or your own money on fancy emergency equipment;
- Stockpile the basics—food, water, first aid kits, flashlights;
- Know how to contact and get to the nearest U.S. embassy, consulate, or military installation;
- Keep on top of local news and political developments;
- Get to know the host country's local police and other safety forces and maintain good relations with them;
- Know the relevant local laws and have local legal counsel on retainer;
- Know the location and identities of local health care facilities and providers; and
- Know the procedures for medicating a stricken co-worker.

Q 15:104 What legal duty does a multinational employer have to protect its employees abroad from terrorism?

As with the Occupational Safety and Health Act's "general duty" clause, U.S. laws, the laws of many foreign states, and the conventions of the United Nations and the ILO place health and safety obligations on employers—including multinational corporations—which are broad enough to create or encompass a duty to take reasonable steps to guard against terrorism. Employees victimized by terrorism may enjoy a private right of action against the employer for failure to maintain a safe workplace, by either an appropriate U.S. district court or a local court of the host country.

Q 15:105 What steps might a multinational employer take to insulate itself against employee liability in the event of a terrorist attack on a foreign work site?

A multinational employer might try to extend workers' compensation immunity from suit by specifying its home state's workers' compensation law in the choice-of-law provision of its standard employment contracts, while seeking to negotiate an appropriate rider to its workers' compensation insurance policy to conform the coverage to the contract provision.

The employer's standard employment contracts might contain an arbitration clause specifying that all claims must be dealt with before an arbitrator under the rules and auspices of the ICC or the AAA.

Q 15:106   Should a multinational employer carry kidnap insurance for its employees working abroad?

Such coverage is certainly worth considering, particularly in those nations where kidnapping of executives has become fairly common. In making this decision, multinational employers should take into consideration the U.S. State Department's Counterterrorism Office policies on American hostages:

- The U.S. government will make no concessions to individuals or groups holding U.S. officials or private citizens hostage;
- The government will "use every appropriate resource to gain the safe return of American citizens held hostage;" and
- The government will deny hostage takers the benefits of ransoms, prisoner releases, policy changes, and other concessions.

Q 15:107   What dangers of arrest and incarceration do Americans working for multinational employers face when working abroad?

U.S. citizens are subject to local laws and regulations. Even ignorant violations by Americans working abroad can result in:

- Expulsion;
- Fines;
- Imprisonment; or
- In rare cases, such as for drug trafficking in some nations, capital punishment.

Q 15:108   What assistance can a multinational employer expect from the U.S. government if one of its American employees working abroad is arrested?

Article 36(a) of the Vienna Convention on Consular Relations of 1963 [21 U.S.T. 77, T.I.A.S. 6820, 596 U.N.S.T. 261] provides that consular officers shall have the rights of access and communication with arrested nationals. The U.S. State Department policy is to provide the following assistance in nations that have signed onboard this convention (i.e., most nations):

Upon initial notification of arrest:

- Visit the prisoner as soon as possible;
- Provide a listing of local attorneys;
- Provide information on local judicial procedures;
- Notify family and friends and relay requests for money and aid; and
- Obtain a Privacy Act consent form signature.

Ongoing support:

- Regular visits and regular reports to the State Department;
- Loans to qualified destitute prisoners under the Emergency Medical/ Dietary Assistance program [22 C.F.R. § 71.10];
- Dietary supplements;
- Medical and dental care [22 C.F.R. § 71.10], including examination by an independent physician, if appropriate;
- Family visits;
- Protesting abuse;
- Attending trial; and
- Information about application procedures for pardons and prisoner transfer treaties (if applicable).

Discretionary support:

- Reading materials, if allowed by local laws;
- Arranging with the local American community for special support, including meals and visits;
- Providing personal amenities if permitted by authorities and funded by the prisoner/the family;
- Expediting mail; and
- Inquiring about prisoner employment, correspondence courses, and the like during periods of lengthy incarceration.

What a consular officer cannot do:

- Demand the American prisoner's immediate release;
- Represent the American at trial;
- Give legal advice; or
- Pay legal fees or fines from U.S. government funds.

International Organizations

Q 15:109 What is the *International Labor Organization*?

The *ILO* is a specialized agency of the United Nations. Headquartered in Geneva, Switzerland, the ILO was founded in 1919 and was originally affiliated with the League of Nations. The United States was not a member of the League but did join the ILO in 1934. The ILO's mission, as outlined in its constitution, includes:

- Improvement of global labor conditions;
- Promotion of higher living standards; and
- Furtherance of social justice.

Q 15:110   How does the ILO seek to fulfill its mission?

The ILO strives to achieve international accords on subjects such as:

- Hours of work;
- Adequate wages;
- Protection of workers against occupational injuries and diseases;
- Protection of women and children from workplace exploitation; and
- Protection of expatriate workers.

Q 15:111   What is the structure of the ILO?

The ILO consists of:

- A general conference of four representatives from each member nation;
- A governing body of 56 representatives (28 of whom represent governments, 14 representing employers, and 14 representing labor unions);
- An International Labor Office under the supervision of the governing body.
- One hundred seventy-five nations currently belong to the ILO.

Q 15:112   What are the ILO's international labor standards?

The ILO's labor standards take the form of:

- Conventions that are subject to ratification by the member states. A convention does not bind a member state until that state's government ratifies it. The United States has refused to ratify a number of major ILO conventions.
- Recommendations are nonbinding instruments, which typically deal with subjects similar to those covered by the conventions, thus offering guidelines to ratifying nations for the implementation of the conventions once they are ratified.

Thus far, the ILO has adopted about 180 conventions and 185 recommendations.

Q 15:113   How are the ILO's international labor standards enforced?

The ILO seeks to enforce its labor standards by means of:

- Regular periodic reporting by member states;
- Specific allegations against member states; and
- Ad hoc ILO supervision in specific cases.

Q 15:114   What are *Global Unions*?

Recently the international trade union movement has begun to use the term *Global Unions* as an umbrella designation. These dozen affiliated labor organizations define themselves as follows: "Global Unions are international trade union organisations working together with a shared commitment to the ideals and principles of the trade union movement. They share a common determination to organize, to defend human rights and labour standards everywhere, and to promote the growth of trade unions for the benefit of all working men and women and their families." A list of affiliates may be found at http://www.global-unions.org/about-us.html.

Q 15:115   What are the other members of Global Unions?

Other members of Global Unions include:

- Education International [http://www.ei-ie.org/]
- International Federation of Building and Wood Workers [http://www .bwint.org/]
- International Federation of Chemical, Energy, Mine, and General Workers' Union [http://www.icem.org/]
- International Federation of Journalists [http://www.ifj.org]
- International Metalworkers' Federation [http://www.imfmetal.org]
- International Textile, Garment and Leatherworkers' Federation [http:// www.itglwf.org]
- International Transport Workers' Federation [http://www.itf.org.uk]
- International Union of Food, Agricultural, Hotel, Restaurant, Catering, Tobacco, and Allied Workers' Association [http://www.iuf.org]
- Public Services International [http://www.world-psi.org]
- Trade Union Advisory Committee [http://www.tuac.org]
- Union Network International [http://www.union-network.org]

Q 15:116   What is *UNI*?

UNI is an organization aimed at meeting the globalization of corporations, trade, and manufacturing head on. Reasoning that the global labor market no longer recognizes or is confined within the borders of traditional nation-states, UNI seeks to organize workers on an international scale. The organization targets multinational corporations, seeking to apply global pressure in order to organize local and regional corporate facilities. "When companies are local, unions can be local; when companies are national, unions must be national; when companies are global, unions must be global. Our aim is to build more effective alliances in multinationals," UNI explains. [http://www.uniglobalunion.org]

In 2012, UNI indicated sympathy with the Occupy Movement, which has been described as "an international protest movement directed towards social and economic inequality, its primary goal being to make the economic structure and power relations in society fairer. Different local groups have different foci, but among the prime concerns is the claim that big corporations and the global financial system control the world in an unstable way that disproportionately benefits a minority and is undermining democracy." [http://en.wikipedia.org/wiki/Occupy_movement]

The Occupy Movement is perhaps best known for its "Occupy Wall Street" campaign at the tail-end of the Great Recession in the United States. However, Occupy Movement protests and other actions have occurred in Australia, Belgium, Canada, Columbia, Cyprus, Denmark, France, Germany, Hong Kong, Israel, Italy, Malaysia, Mexico, Mongolia, New Zealand, Nigeria, Norway, Republic of Ireland, South Africa, South Korea, Switzerland, and the United Kingdom.

In an October 2011 press release, UNI announced that it "is giving its support to the massive popular protest 'Occupy Wall Street,' a movement for economic justice that is spreading across the United States and the world." It added, "The movement, which is support by UNI US affiliates, is a call for justice in the American economic and political system, including greater financial regulation, higher taxes for the richest Americans and the return of the social safety net. Members of the Occupy Wall Street movement have linked their fight to the revolutions in Tunisia and Egypt and to the massive protests against cuts to public spending and increase in taxes in Greece."

"We can clearly see the revolutionary spirit flowing around the world from North Africa and the Middle East to Spain, Greece and the US. It is now spreading to northern Europe, including the financial capital of London" said UNI General Secretary Philip Jennings. "Workers from every corner of the globe, whether they are young or old, man or woman, want a fair future where they can earn a decent living and support a family. Governments are failing to tackle the economic crisis and now people are taking to the streets demanding change. We expect to see these protests spread all over the world."

[http://www.uniglobalunion.org/__C1257537004AB759.nsf/0/7F0B36C86391 BBEBC1257922003AD747?Open&Highlight = 2,occupy]

Q 15:117   Who belongs to UNI?

UNI claims to hold the allegiance of approximately 15 million workers in 900 unions in 150 countries, representing employees in the following economic sectors:

- Commerce
- Electricity
- Finance
- Gaming
- Graphical
- Hair and beauty
- IBITS (industry, business services, information and computer technology)

- Media, entertainment, and the arts
- Postal
- Property services (cleaning and security)
- Social insurance
- Telecom
- Tourism

[http://www.uniglobalunion.org]

Q 15:118 On which employers has UNI focused?

UNI has targeted a list of 100 multinational employers. UNI has achieved labor contracts with the following targeted corporations:

- Carrefour (a Paris-based food retailer)
- Hennes & Mauritz of Sweden (trading as H&M stores in the United States)
- Falck (a Danish rescue, healthcare, and safety-training organization)
- Internet Security Systems (based in Atlanta, GA)
- Metro AG of Germany
- OTE (Greek telecommunications company)
- Telefónica (the Spanish telecom provider)
- Kimberly-Clark (headquartered in the U.S.)

Q 15:119 How can UNI be contacted?

UNI's contact information is as follows:

UNI Head Office—Switzerland
8-10 Avenue Reverdil
1260 Nyon
Fax: +41 22 365 21 21
E-mail: contact@uniglobalunion.org
Web site: http://www.uniglobalunion.org/

Q 15:120 How is it possible for an international union to organize U.S. companies?

A good example of how this can happen—offered by President Andy Stern of the Service Employees International Union (SEIU)—was the acquisition of three well-known U.S. security firms by Sweden-based Securitas. The American companies were Pinkerton, Burns International Services, and Loomis Fargo. At about the same time, Group 4 Securicor, a British-Danish outfit, picked up Wackenhut. "All of a sudden," commented Stern, "we found ourselves needing to talk more to CEOs in Europe than in America."

Attorney Gerald Hathaway of the New York firm Littler Mendelson noted that labor organizations are woven into the socioeconomic fabric of continental nations such as Germany, where union leaders commonly serve on boards of directors. Unions such as the SEIU are finding that they can deal with these parent corporations, imposing terms and conditions upon their U.S. subsidiaries.

[http://www.workforce.com/archive/feature/24/26/53/index.php?ht5labor%20unions%20labor%20unions]

Q 15:121 How do international unions such as UNI seek to bind multinational corporations?

UNI and similar international labor organizations seek to sign so-called "global framework agreements" capable of following the corporation to wherever it establishes operations around the world. The concept of a global agreement is well known in American labor relations, with unions hoping to represent a single employer's employees at multiple locations negotiating for an umbrella agreement that will apply wherever the union later achieves majority support from a location's workforce. [*See, e.g.*, Raley's and United Food and Commercial Workers, 336 NLRB 374 (2001) (The parties attempted to negotiate a global agreement that would cover any future demands for recognition by Local 588. They subsequently signed two separate agreements under which the Respondent recognized Local 588, pursuant to a card check, as the representative of its employees at the Yreka store and at one of the Redding stores.).]

Q 15:122 What is the *International Chamber of Commerce*?

The *ICC* describes itself as "the voice of world business championing the global economy as a force for economic growth, job creation and prosperity."

Q 15:123 What does the ICC do?

The ICC sets rules and standards for international business via:

- The ICC International Court of Arbitration, which handles about 500 cases a year;
- The ICC's Uniform Customs and Practice for Documentary Credits, used by banks to finance billions of dollars worth of world trade each year;
- ICC Incoterms, which have become the standard terms for thousands of international contracts annually; and
- ICC codes for self-regulation of e-commerce, advertising, and marketing.

Q 15:124 What were the ICC's origins?

The ICC was founded in 1919, concurrent with and as a counterweight to the International Labor Organization. Its stated purposes were (and are):

- Promotion of global trade and investment;
- Opening markets for goods and services; and
- Promoting the free flow of capital.

Q 15:125   How does the ICC fulfill its missions?

The ICC fulfills its missions by:

- Lobbying national governments in such public policy areas as intellectual property rights, transportation policies, trade laws and environmental regulations, as well as employment and labor regulation;
- Speaking for the international business community in news media;
- Partnering with the U.N. Conference on Trade and Development to assist the poorest member nations in attracting direct foreign investment;
- Mobilizing international business support for the New Partnership for Africa's Development;
- Sponsoring the World Chambers Congress as a biennial global forum for business;
- Holding regular regional conferences for business in Africa, Asia, Latin America, and the Arab world;
- Advocating for the interests of its thousands of member corporations and trade associations;
- Supporting government efforts to make the Doha trade round a success and providing business recommendations to the World Trade Organization;
- Providing input to the G8 summit;
- Spearheading the business contribution at UN summits on sustainable development, financing for development and the information society;
- Setting up an Investment Advisory Council in partnership with UNCTAD for the least-developed countries;
- Lobbying the United Nations as well as member nations; and
- Forging international rules that corporations can voluntarily incorporate into contracts, including employment contracts.

Q 15:126   How can one join the ICC?

The ICC provides information on its Web site at http://www.iccwbo.org/.

There are two ways to become a member of ICC:

1. Through affiliation with an ICC national committee or group; or
2. By direct membership with the ICC International Secretariat when a national committee/group has not yet been established in your country/territory.

Q 15:127 What is the cost of ICC membership?

National committees pay an annual subscription to ICC's International Secretariat in Paris to meet the organization's administrative expenses. The rate is proportionate to the economic importance of the country they represent. National committees are financially independent of the central body and are free to establish the level of their own membership subscriptions.

Direct members fall into two categories with their annual dues as follows:

- 1500 EUR (approximately US $3,000) per year for "local" members (i.e. local/us chambers of commerce, local companies, or professional individuals);
- 3000 EUR (approximately US $6,000) per year for "national" members (i.e. national chambers of commerce, national trade associations, national business organizations, as well as companies with a predominant international activity, and occupying a leading position in the country).

Additional information can be found at http://www.iccwbo.org.

Q 15:128 Who can establish a national committee?

Business and trade associations as well as individual companies and firms can apply for approval from ICC's World Council to establish an ICC national committee.

The ICC World Council considers the following criteria before giving its approval:

- Members of the proposed national committee must represent the main economic forces in the country concerned, which in turn should adhere to market economy principles; and
- The national committee must be able to participate regularly and effectively in ICC's work.

Note: Like the AAA, whose rules on international arbitration are discussed in detail above, the ICC offers international arbitration services, too. [*See* http://www.iccwbo.org/.]

The ICC's Commission on Arbitration claims to be a forum for experts to pool ideas and impact new policy on practical issues relating to international arbitration, the settlement of international business disputes and the legal and procedural aspects of arbitration. The commission also aims at examining ICC dispute settlement services in view of current developments, including new technologies. The commission task forces and groups count more than 500 members from 90 countries, including partners in international law firms, in-house counsel, law professors, experts in different dispute resolution services, and trade executives in member companies and international organizations.

ICC arbitration-related publications available on its Web site include:

- Amiable Composition and ex aequo et bono
- Guidelines for ICC Expertise Proceedings
- Trust and Arbitration
- National Rules of Procedure for Recognition and Enforcement of Foreign Arbitral Awards pursuant to the New York Convention of 1958
- Production of Electronic Documents in Arbitration
- Revision of the ICC Rules of Arbitration
- Arbitration involving States or State Entities

United States Code (U.S.C.)

[References are to question numbers.]

Statutory Authority in United States Code Sections:

Statutory Authority in United States Code Sections:

Code of Federal Regulations (C.F.R.)

[References are to question numbers.]

Table of Cases

[References are to question numbers.]

B

C

D

E

F

G

H

I

J

K

L

M

N

National Aeronautics and Space Administration v. Nelson, 131 S. Ct. 746 (2011) 9:19

O

P

Table of Cases

T

U

Table of Cases

Index

[References are to question numbers.]

A

Abortion
PDA, protection by, 4:77

Accents and national origin discrimination, 4:52

Accommodation. *See* Americans with Disabilities Act (ADA); Religious discrimination

ADA. *See* Americans with Disabilities Act

ADA Amendments Act (ADAAA), 1:50–1:58, 4:121, 7:245, 9:92. *See also* Americans with Disabilities Act
disability, expanded definition of, 1:50, 1:55, 4:121, 9:92
episodic impairments as disabilities, 1:55, 1:56, 4:147, 4:150
major life activity, defined, 1:55, 4:147
mitigating measures, prohibition against consideration of, in determination of disability, 1:56, 4:124, 4:147
periodic impairments as disabilities, 1:55, 1:56, 4:147, 4:150
"regarded as" disabled, qualifying as being, 4:124
transitory impairments, exclusion from protection, 4:124
remission, impairment in, 1:56
transitory impairment, defined, 4:124

ADEA. *See* Age Discrimination in Employment Act

ADR. *See* Alternative dispute resolution

Advertising and recruiting. *See* Hiring

Affirmative action
Adarand Constructors decision, 9:71
audits, 9:63–9:66
community involvement efforts, 9:82
consent decree, 9:88
contractors' criminal record policy, 9:25
laws implicating in hiring decisions, 9:29
screening and referrals, 9:28
contractors' obligations, 9:61
covered employees, 9:34–9:37
current status, 9:74
"designation of responsibility" defined, 9:54
Directive 306, 9:24
best practices, 9:26
posting requirement, 9:27
duties of affirmative action officer, 9:83
enforcement by EEOC and OFCCP, 9:58
entities required to have plan, 9:33–9:39
Executive Order 11246, 1:42, 4:38, 9:22, 9:59–9:70
federal government compliance, 9:73
final rule, 9:22–9:23, 9:30
forms, 9:62
Functional Affirmative Action Program (FAAP), 9:56
job group analysis
defined, 9:46
development of, 9:47–9:49
labor pool, determining appropriate, 9:79
multi-location employers, 9:36
OFCCP role, 9:20–9:23, 9:59
OFCCP guidance, 9:92
on-site OFCCP visits, 9:67
organizational profile, 9:42
data snapshot for reporting purposes, 9:43–9:45
pending discrimination claims, 9:31
Piscataway decision, significance of, 9:75–9:77
placement goals
defined, 9:50
setting of, 9:51, 9:52
policy
dissemination, 9:84, 9:85

G

P